THE OXFORD HANDBOOK OF

PHILOSOPHY AND DISABILITY

THE OXFORD HANDBOOK OF

PHILOSOPHY

AND

DISABILITY

Edited by

ADAM CURETON

and

DAVID WASSERMAN

OXFORD

UNIVERSITY PRESS

OXFORD
UNIVERSITY PRESS

Oxford University Press is a department of the University of Oxford. It furthers
the University's objective of excellence in research, scholarship, and education
by publishing worldwide. Oxford is a registered trade mark of Oxford University
Press in the UK and certain other countries.

Published in the United States of America by Oxford University Press
198 Madison Avenue, New York, NY 10016, United States of America.

Library of Congress Control Number: 2019920881

ISBN 978-0-19-062287-9

1 3 5 7 9 8 6 4 2

Printed by Sheridan Books, Inc., United States of America

For Julie and Susan, and in memory of Anita and Larry

Acknowledgments

Many people helped to make this volume possible. We are grateful to our institutions, departments, and colleagues at the University of Tennessee (Cureton) and the University of Maryland and the National Institutes of Health (Wasserman). Special thanks are due to the University of Tennessee for providing funds to Cureton that enabled us to organize a conference on the philosophy of disability in October 2017.

We appreciate the patience of our contributors as well as the significant time and effort they devoted to exploring important disability topics in novel, informative, and insightful ways.

We should also acknowledge the many wise scholars who have enhanced our collective understanding of disability. Many of them are listed in the bibliographies, but their influence on us and the contributors goes far beyond what can be adequately expressed in this volume. In particular, we want to mention two of our contributors, Anita Silvers and Lawrence C. Becker, to whom the volume is dedicated, as well as Adrienne Asch who has deeply influenced the ways that disability scholars approach issues of reproduction and parenting.

Oxford University Press editors and staff, particularly Lucy Randall, Hannah Doyle, and Arul Mozhi Kulothungan, have been very supportive, encouraging, and efficient throughout the process of putting this collection together.

Finally, we are especially grateful to our families for their love and support.

TABLE OF CONTENTS

PART THREE JUSTICE, EQUALITY, AND INCLUSION

PART FOUR KNOWLEDGE AND EMBODIMENT

PART FIVE RESPECT, APPRECIATION, AND CARE

PART SIX MORAL STATUS AND SIGNIFICANT MENTAL DISABILITIES

PART SEVEN INTELLECTUAL AND PSYCHIATRIC DISABILITY

LIST OF CONTRIBUTORS

Sean Aas is Assistant Professor of Philosophy and Senior Research Scholar at the Kennedy Institute of Philosophy at Georgetown University. He works primarily in political philosophy, as applied to issues around embodiment, opportunity, and public reason.

Linda Barclay, Senior Lecturer at Monash University, works in political philosophy, primarily in the areas of disability and egalitarianism. Her papers have appeared in journals such as *Journal of Applied Philosophy, Journal of Social Philosophy, Hypatia*, and *Journal of Moral Philosophy*, as well as in numerous anthologies.

Jonas-Sébastien Beaudry is an Assistant Professor of Law at McGill University (joint appointment with the Institute for Health and Social Policy) and a member of the Quebec Bar. His publications include a book on freedom of expression in Latin America and articles in the areas of legal history, human rights, ethics and disability law. He collaborates with disability organizations on public policy issues and is an advisor to the Vulnerable Persons Standard.

Lawrence C. Becker was Fellow of Hollins University, and Kenan Professor of Philosophy Emeritus at the College of William & Mary. He was the author of monographs and articles on the justification of moral judgments, the philosophical foundations of property rights, the virtue of reciprocity, the extent to which Stoic ethics is plausible today, and the way in which the human necessity for habilitation provides a framework for basic justice. He was an associate editor of the journal *Ethics* from 1985 to 2000, and the coeditor, with Charlotte B. Becker, of two editions of the *Encyclopedia of Ethics*.

Jessica Begon is an Assistant Professor in Political Theory at the University of Durham. Her research focuses on issues of distributive justice, paternalism, well-being, autonomy, public policy, and disability.

Jerome Bickenbach is Professor of Health Sciences and Health Policy, University of Lucerne, Switzerland and Professor Emeritus, Queen's University, Canada, Philosophy, Law, Medicine. He worked at the World Health Organization 1993 to 2005 on disability conceptualization, epidemiological and comparative international disability law and policy. He is author, co-author and editor of eleven books on disability policy and related areas and two hundred academic articles spanning disability policy, philosophy of disability, rehabilitation systems, health information system, health and disability epidemiology, and international, comparative human rights law.

Greg Bognar is Senior Lecturer in Practical Philosophy at Stockholm University and Senior Researcher at the Stockholm Centre for Healthcare Ethics (CHE). His research is in normative and applied ethics, especially bioethics and politics, philosophy, and economics (PPE). He is the author, with Iwao Hirose, of *The Ethics of Health Care Rationing: An Introduction* (Routledge, 2014).

Stephen M. Campbell, Assistant Professor of Philosophy at Bentley University, works primarily on conceptual and ethical issues related to well-being, death, enhancement, and disability. His work has appeared in Journal of the American Philosophical Association, *American Journal of Bioethics, Kennedy Institute of Ethics Journal, Ethical Theory and Moral Practice*, and *Journal of Applied Philosophy.*

Havi Carel is Professor of Philosophy at the University of Bristol. She is a Wellcome Trust Senior Investigator, leading the Life of Breath project (2014 to 2020; www.lifeofbreath.org). She is the author of *Phenomenology of Illness* (2016), *Illness* (2008, 2013, 2018 shortlisted for the Wellcome Trust Book Prize), and of *Life and Death in Freud and Heidegger* (2006). She was voted by students as a 'Best of Bristol' lecturer in 2016. She previously held grants from the AHRC, British Academy and Leverhulme Trust (http://www.bristol.ac.uk/school-of-arts/people/havi-h-carel/index.html).

Licia Carlson, Professor of Philosophy at Providence College, has focused much of her research on philosophy and intellectual disability. Her interests include bioethics, feminist philosophy, 20th century French philosophy, and the philosophy of music. She is the author of *The Faces of Intellectual Disability: Philosophical Reflections* (2009), and co-edited *Cognitive Disability and Its Challenge to Moral Philosophy* with Eva Feder Kittay (2010) and *Phenomenology and the Arts* with Peter Costello (2016).

Andy Clark is Professor of Cognitive Philosophy at the University of Sussex. He is the author of *Being There* (1997), *Mindware* (2001), *Natural-Born Cyborgs* (2003), *Supersizing the Mind* (2008) and *Surfing Uncertainty* (2015).

Jordan A. Conrad, MPhil., MSW., is a doctoral candidate at the Institute of Philosophy at Katholiek Universiteit Leuven, Visiting Scholar at the Center for Bioethics, NYU, Academic Associate at the Baltimore Washington Center for Psychoanalysis and Psychotherapy, and is currently practicing psychotherapy in New York City. He writes on issues related to disability, philosophy of psychiatry, and Nietzsche.

Alice Crary is University Distinguished Professor at the New School for Social Research and Visiting Fellow, Regent's Park College, Oxford. Crary's book *Inside Ethics* (Harvard, 2016) discusses the representation of human beings and animals in ethics. She has written widely about ethics and cognitive disability. She is currently completing a book, *Radical Animal,* that argues that the dehumanization of human beings and the hatred of animals are intertwined and that movements for human liberation need to challenge normative hierarchies that subjugate animals.

Mary Crossley is a Professor of Law and former Dean at the University of Pittsburgh School of Law. Her scholarship addresses issues of inequality in health care financing and delivery, focusing particularly on how people with disability experience the health care system.

Adam Cureton, Associate Professor of Philosophy at the University of Tennessee, works primarily in ethics, Kant and disability. He co-edited (with Kimberley Brownlee) *Disability and Disadvantage* (2009) and (with Thomas E. Hill) *Disability in Practice: Attitudes Policies and Relationships* (2018). He is the President of the Society for Philosophy and Disability.

Josh Dohmen is an Assistant Professor of Philosophy at Mississippi University for Women. His research interests include twentieth-century continental philosophy, philosophy of disability, and feminist epistemology. His article "'A Little of Her Language': Epistemic Injustice and Mental Disability" was awarded *Res Philosophica*'s 2016 essay prize.

Zoe Drayson is Assistant Professor of Philosophy at the University of California, Davis. Her research focuses on metaphysical and epistemological implications of cognitive science, and she has published on perception, consciousness, mental representation, and the nature of psychological explanation.

Leslie Francis is Distinguished Professor of Philosophy, Distinguished Alfred C. Emery Professor of Law, and Director of the Center for Law & Biomedical Sciences at the University of Utah. She recently published *Privacy: What Everyone Needs to Know* (with John Francis, Oxford 2017) and edited *The Oxford Handbook of Reproductive Ethics* (2017). She is the author of many articles about disability in philosophy and in law and frequently provides pro bono legal representation for people who are the subject of petitions for guardianship.

Rosemarie Garland-Thomson is Professor of English and bioethics at Emory University. Her work in critical disability studies and health humanities brings disability culture, ethics, and justice to a broad range of institutions and communities. She is co-editor of *About Us: Essays from the New York Times about Disability by People with Disabilities* and the author of *Staring: How We Look* and several other books.

Sara Goering is Associate Professor of Philosophy at the University of Washington, core faculty for the Program on Ethics, affiliate of the Disability Studies Program, and ethics thrust co-leader at the UW Center for Neurotechnology. Her work focuses on feminist philosophy, disability studies, and neuroethics.

Melinda C. Hall (PhD, Vanderbilt University) is an Associate Professor of Philosophy at Stetson University. She specializes in bioethics, Continental philosophy, and the philosophy of disability. In *The Bioethics of Enhancement: Transhumanism, Disability, and Biopolitics* (Lexington Books, 2016), Hall draws from Michel Foucault to demonstrate that disability is central to debates over enhancement. Hall's work also appears in *Disability Studies Quarterly, International Journal of Feminist Approaches to Bioethics*, and *Philosophy Compass*, among other venues.

Christie Hartley is Associate Professor of Philosophy at Georgia State University. Her publications include articles and book chapters on disability and justice and, with Lori

Watson, on political liberalism and sex equality. Hartley and Watson's book, *Equal Citizenship and Public Reason: A Feminist Political Liberalism*, was published in 2018 by Oxford University Press.

Thomas E. Hill, Jr., Professor Emeritus at the University of North Carolina at Chapel Hill, is author of essays in moral and political philosophy collected in *Autonomy and Self-Respect* (1991), *Dignity and Practical Reason in Kant's Moral Theory* (1992), *Respect, Pluralism, and Justice* (2000), *Human Welfare and Moral Worth* (2002), and *Virtue Rules and Justice (2012)*. He co-edited (with Arnulf Zweig) *Kant's Groundwork for the Metaphysics of Morals* (2002) and edited *A Blackwell Guide to Kant's Ethics* (2009).

Dana Howard is a philosopher at The Ohio State University Center for Bioethics, which is housed in the OSU Wexner Medical Center and the College of Medicine. She is also a member of the OSU Philosophy Department. She was a post-doctoral fellow in the Clinical Center Department of Bioethics at the National Institutes of Health and completed her PhD in Philosophy at Brown University.

Richard Hull is a Lecturer in Philosophy at the National University of Ireland, Galway. He is the author of *Deprivation and Freedom* (2007) and has published on a number of topics including disability, genetic technologies, parental responsibility and agent intention. He served two terms on the Irish Council for Bioethics and is a member of the Irish Government's National Advisory Committee on Bioethics. He teaches in the areas of ethics, political theory and applied philosophy.

Chris Kaposy is an Associate Professor of Bioethics in the Faculty of Medicine at Memorial University in St. John's, Newfoundland. He has research interests in cognitive disability and bioethics, and is author of *Choosing Down Syndrome: Ethics and New Prenatal Testing Technologies* (MIT Press).

Alexander Kaufman is Professor of Political Theory at the University of Georgia. His research explores the relation of central values of the democratic political tradition to issues and controversies in contemporary politics, including the justification of the welfare state; the nature of egalitarian justice; and the basis of democratic legitimacy. Kaufman's most recent book, *Rawls's Egalitarianism*, provides a new interpretation and analysis of John Rawls's theory of distributive justice.

Samuel J. Kerstein, Professor of Philosophy at the University of Maryland, works in bioethics, ethical theory, and Kant. He is the author of *Kant's Search for the Supreme Principle of Morality* (2002) and *How to Treat Persons* (2013), as well as articles on treating people merely as means, markets in organs, and the just distribution of scarce, life-saving resources.

Suzy Killmister is Lecturer in Philosophy at Monash University, Australia. Suzy works primarily in moral and political philosophy. Her first book *Taking the Measure of Autonomy: A Four-Dimensional Theory of Self-Governance* was recently published with Routledge, and her second book, *Contours of Dignity*, is forthcoming with Oxford University Press in 2020.

Eva Feder Kittay is Distinguished Professor Emeritus of Philosophy, Stony Brook University and a mother of a multiple disabled woman. Kittay has authored and edited books, as well as written numerous articles, on feminist philosophy, care ethics and disability theory. She has been awarded the APA and Phi Beta Kappa Leibowitz Award, a Guggenheim and an NEH Fellowship. She was President of the Eastern American Philosophical Association. Her latest book is *Learning From My Daughter: Valuing Disabled Minds and Matters of Care* (OUP 2019).

Eran Klein is a neurologist specializing in dementia at the Portland Veterans Administration Health Care System in Portland, Oregon, and holds appointments in the Department of Neurology at the Oregon Health and Science University (OHSU) and the Department of Philosophy at the University of Washington. He co-leads the ethics thrust at the UW Center for Neurotechnology (CNT). His current areas of interest in ethics include brain-computer interface technology and deep brain stimulation for neurologic and psychiatric illness.

Jason Marsh is an Associate Professor of Philosophy at St. Olaf College in Northfield, Minnesota, where he spends time thinking about healthcare ethics, population ethics, wellbeing, and the philosophy of religion. His articles have appeared in such journals as *Bioethics, Philosophy and Phenomenological Research*, and *The Monist*.

Coreen McGuire is a Postdoctoral Research Fellow on 'The Life of Breath Project' at the University of Bristol. Her research focuses on the historical use of spirometry technology in scaling and defining levels of respiratory disability. The role of measurement and standardization in creating categories of disability was a key component of her PhD research on telephony and hearing loss.

Julia Mosquera is a post-doc researcher in Philosophy at the Institute for Futures Studies (IF) in Stockholm. Julia's researcher focuses on egalitarianism, future generations, and disability. She also works on topics such as population ethics and climate change. Julia is the author of "An Egalitarian Argument Against Reducing Deprivation" (2017) and "Population Ethics and Disability" (forthcoming).

Christian Munthe is professor of practical philosophy at the Department of Philosophy, Linguistics and Theory of Science, as well as fellow of the Centre for Antibiotic Research (CARe) and the Centre for Ethics, Law and Mental Health (CELAM), all at the University of Gothenburg, Sweden. He has conducted extensive research on the ethics of genetic and reproductive technology, especially prenatal screening and preimplantation genetic testing.

Tom O'Shea is Senior Lecturer in Philosophy at the University of Roehampton. He is a moral and political philosopher whose research focuses on freedom in history, theory, and practice. His recent work develops civic republican accounts of medical ethics, mental capacity law, and the philosophy of work.

Christopher A. Riddle is Associate Professor of Philosophy at Utica College, where he also directs the Applied Ethics Institute. His work has been published in journals such as *The Journal of Social Philosophy, Bioethics, The American Journal of Bioethics, Essays in Philosophy, Medicine, Healthcare, & Philosophy*, and *Topoi*. He is the author of *Disability & Justice* (2014), *Human Rights, Disability, and Capabilities* (2016), and the editor of *From Disability Theory to Practice* (2018).

Julian Savulescu holds the Uehiro Chair in Practical Ethics at the University of Oxford. He directs the Oxford Martin Programme for Collective Responsibility for Infectious Disease and the Wellcome Centre for Ethics and Humanities. He is a Visiting Professorial Fellow in Biomedical Ethics at the Murdoch Children's Research Institute, and Distinguished International Visiting Professor in Law at the University of Melbourne. He is editor of the *Journal of Practical Ethics*.

Danny Scoccia, Professor Emeritus of New Mexico State University, writes on various topics related to liberal political morality, including free speech, paternalism, and legal moralism.

Jackie Leach Scully is Professor of Bioethics, and Director of the Disability Innovation Institute, at the University of New South Wales, Australia. Initially trained in the life sciences, her research interests include disability bioethics, feminist approaches to bioethics, and the socioethical consequences of selective reproductive technologies and genomics. She is the author of *Disability Bioethics: Moral Bodies, Moral Difference* (2008), and was a member of the Nuffield Council of Bioethics working group on human genome editing.

Tom Shakespeare is Professor of Disability Research at London School of Hygiene and Tropical Medicine, and was formerly with the World Health Organization. He is the author of *Disability Rights and Wrongs* (2006), and *Genetic Politics: From Eugenics to Genome* (2002), among others, and has published on various aspects of disability and bioethics. He was formerly a member of the (UK) Nuffield Council on Bioethics, and chair of the working group on Non-Invasive Prenatal Testing.

Joshua Shepherd is an Assistant Professor in Philosophy at Carleton University, and a Research Professor at the University of Barcelona. He works in the philosophy of mind, action, and practical ethics. His book *Consciousness and Moral Status* was published by Routledge in 2018.

Anita Silvers was Professor of Philosophy at San Francisco State University, where she began in 1967. She was a pioneer in writing philosophy about disability and a leader in achieving access to higher education for students with disabilities. For a quarter-century, Silvers was APA Pacific Division Secretary-Treasurer and a member of the APA Board. Her awards and honors include the Wang Family Excellence Award for extraordinary achievements in the California State University system, the Phi Beta Kappa/APA Lebowitz Prize, the APA Quinn Prize, and U.S. presidential appointment to the NEH National Council on the Humanities.

Joseph A. Stramondo is an Assistant Professor of Philosophy at San Diego State University, where he works in bioethics, philosophy of disability, and philosophy of technology. His writing appears in *The Hastings Center Report*, *Kennedy Institute of Ethics Journal*, *Science and Engineering Ethics*, *International Journal of Feminist Approaches to Bioethics*, and *Social Philosophy Today*.

Lorella Terzi is Professor of Philosophy of Education at the University of Roehampton, London. She is the author of '*Justice and Equality in Education*' (2008), which won the 2011 Nasen 'The Special Educational Needs Academic Book Award', and the editor of '*Special Educational Needs: A New Look*' by Mary Warnock and Brahm Norwich (2010). Her publications include numerous articles and book chapters about questions of disability, justice, and the capability approach.

Dr. Shelley L. Tremain holds a Ph.D. in Philosophy and has authored many books and articles on (among other topics) feminist philosophy of disability, ableism in philosophy, Foucault and disability, and disability and bioethics, including *Foucault and Feminist Philosophy of Disability*, the manuscript of which was awarded the 2016 Tobin Siebers Prize for Disability Studies in the Humanities Tremain is also the editor of two editions of *Foucault and the Government of Disability* and was the 2016 recipient of the Tanis Doe Award for Disability Study and Culture in Canada. Tremain blogs at BIOPOLITICAL PHILOSOPHY where she posts Dialogues on Disability, a series of interviews that, since April 2015, she has conducted with disabled philosophers.

John Vorhaus, Professor of Moral and Educational Philosophy at University of London, Institute of Education, works in applied ethics and disability. He is the author of *Giving Voice to Profound Disability* (2016) and *Valuing Profoundly Disabled People* (2018).

Jerome C. Wakefield, PhD., DSW, is University Professor, Professor of Social Work, Professor of Psychiatry, and Associate Faculty in the Center for Bioethics at NYU. He writes on philosophy of psychiatry. His coauthored book, The Loss of Sadness: How Psychiatry Transformed Normal Sorrow into Depressive Disorder (Oxford 2007), was named best psychology book of 2007 by the Association of Professional and Scholarly Publishers. His most recent book is *Freud and Philosophy of Mind, Volume 1: Reconstructing the Argument for Unconscious Mental States* (Palgrave-Macmillan 2018).

David Wasserman is a Visiting Research Scholar in the University of Maryland, College Park, Department of Philosophy and has been a consultant for the Clinical Center Department of Bioethics at the National Institutes of Health. He works primarily on ethical and policy issues in disability, genetics, reproduction, and neuroscience. He is co-author of *Debating Procreation* (with David Benatar, 2015).

David Wendler is a senior investigator and Head of the Section on Research Ethics in the Department of Bioethics at the NIH Clinical Center. He is a philosopher trained in the philosophy of science, and metaphysics and epistemology. Dr. Wendler is an attending on the Bioethics Consultation service and has served as a consultant to numerous organizations, including the Institute of Medicine, the World Health Organization, and the World Medical Association.

Dominic JC Wilkinson is Director of Medical Ethics and Professor of Medical Ethics at the Oxford Uehiro Centre for Practical Ethics, University of Oxford. He is also a consultant in newborn intensive care at the John Radcliffe Hospital, Oxford. Dominic is the author of *Death or Disability? The 'Carmentis Machine' and Decision-Making for Critically Ill Children* (OUP 2013). His co-authored books include *Medical Ethics and Law*, third edition (Elsevier 2019) and *Ethics, Conflict and Medical Treatment for Children, from Disagreement to Dissensus* (Elsevier, 2018).

INTRODUCTION

ADAM CURETON AND DAVID WASSERMAN

OVER the past three decades, philosophers have become increasingly interested in disability because it raises fundamental issues about the significance of variations in physical and mental functioning for human performance and well-being, for personal and social identity, for intimate relationships, for self-respect and respect for others, and for justice in the allocation of resources and the design of the physical and social environment. Previously, philosophers made only passing reference to disabilities when, for example, presenting challenges to theories of justice or well-being, discussing the allocation of scarce health-care resources, or debating the withdrawal of life support for severely impaired neonates. In contrast, scholars in other disciplines had written extensively about disability, often making ethical claims about the status or treatment of people with disabilities. Articles focusing mainly on disability did not begin to appear in philosophy journals until the mid 1980s and it was another decade before disability became a frequent topic of philosophical debate. This growth in interest among philosophers was informed in part by the field of Disability Studies, which emerged in the 1980s. Since 2000, there has been a striking increase in the number of philosophical and interdisciplinary articles, monographs, and anthologies on various aspects of disability.

Given this burgeoning philosophical activity, there is a need for a wide-ranging collection that 1) introduces philosophers and other scholars to the main conceptual and normative issues in disability and 2) advances the discussion of those issues in ways that help to set the terms of the philosophical agenda for disability. For these purposes, we have sought out some of the best philosophers writing on disability, while also recruiting philosophers whose work in other areas has great relevance for disability. We aim not only to present an overview of existing work but also to contribute to the growth and direction of the field. We seek to do so at a time when the philosophy of disability has established itself as an important area of inquiry, one that has drawn together many talented philosophers while continuing to expand its scope and audience.

Historical Overview

Philosophical thinking about disability has been informed by, and informed, the historical treatment of people with disabilities.[1] A general category of "disability," encompassing such diverse conditions as blindness, paralysis, intellectual impairment, and mental disorder, was apparently not recognized before the late nineteenth century, when the emerging concepts of normality yielded complementary notions of deviation. And even well into the next century, what is now called "disability" was lumped with "moral degeneracy" and criminality as falling on the lower tail of a normal distribution of valued social traits. Although the category may be fairly recent, people who would now be regarded as disabled have been subject to a far longer history of hostile, often brutal treatment.

For all of recorded history, individuals seen as deformed, deficient, or otherwise deviant have faced sustained abuse, neglect, exclusion, segregation, harassment, and exploitation; more recently, they have faced institutionalization, euthanasia, and sterilization. Disabled infants have been left to die from exposure or denied life-saving treatment; people with mental illness were killed as witches or euthanized for the "betterment" of the species; intellectually disabled children were given food containing highly radioactive elements as part of medical experiments; people with various kinds of disabilities were auctioned off to the lowest bidder for their care; people of unusual stature, morphology, or behavior were displayed in "freak shows" for popular entertainment; and people with many kinds of disabilities were confined to overcrowded and unsanitary asylums, workhouses, and other institutions where they were beaten, chained, locked in cages, neglected, shocked with electricity, and lobotomized, often under the guise of medical treatment.

These practices and actions, along with underlying social attitudes about disabled people as monstrous, deficient, deviant, pitiful, and burdensome, often interacted with the denigration of other groups, such as women, racial minorities, and immigrants. Husbands in nineteenth-century Britain, for example, could institutionalize their wives, who could face the removal of their reproductive organs to "treat" their "hysteria" or "nymphomania." African Americans were automatically labeled as "insane" in some towns on the 1840 US Census; many immigrants were denied entry to the United States for looking "mentally deficient"; and poor disabled people have often resorted to begging in order to sustain themselves.

There is, however, a brighter side to the history of disabled people that includes compensation for disabled soldiers and workers; reforms of charitable and institutional practices to help ensure more respectful care and support for disabled people; effective educational and treatment facilities; legal mechanisms for disabled people or their families to secure certain rights; government support for communities and families to care for disabled people; legal rights to treatment and to refuse treatment for those involuntarily committed to nursing homes and other facilities; technological advances in mobility devices and prosthetics; and organizations advocating for the interests of disabled people and for deinstitutionalization and supported community integration. Finally, and most importantly, there has been collective political action by disabled people themselves, culminating in the Disability Rights Movement.

Philosophers have contributed to both sides of this history. Aristotle, for example, regarded certain people with intellectual disabilities as "natural slaves"; Francis Bacon rejected the view of disability as an expression of God's wrath and argued for social and environmental modifications to treat impairments; John Locke proposed an influential distinction between mental illness and intellectual disability; and Jean Jacques Rousseau developed pedagogical ideas that helped improve education for disabled children.

The "first wave" of sustained and focused writing in disability and philosophy, from the mid-1980s to the late 1990s, was shaped by the introduction and widespread adoption of the social model of disability. This way of thinking about disability, which emphasizes the social contributions to the disadvantages that disabled people often face, was formulated by disability rights activists in the early 1970s and incorporated into disability legislation, most notably the Americans with Disabilities Act of 1990. Early philosophers of disability were also engaged by developments in their own, and other, disciplines. These included debates about extending civil-rights and antidiscrimination models beyond women and racial minorities to other disadvantaged groups; the meaning and significance of health and disease; the strength and priority of claims to alleviate or compensate for "natural disadvantage"; and the appropriate role of quality-of-life judgments in measuring the value of health-care interventions and in assessing the justifications for physician assisted death, prenatal testing for disability, and other controversial interventions. Early philosophers of disability were also drawn into broader societal debates about abortion and animal rights, which often relied on controversial comparisons to individuals with profound intellectual disabilities.

From the outset, philosophers writing about disability argued that civil rights and antidiscrimination models were appropriately applied to people with disabilities, although they disagreed about the need to qualify or limit their application. They took pointed exception to the offhand use of disability by mainstream philosophers as a paradigm of natural disadvantage, but they disagreed about whether it was useful to distinguish natural from social advantage at all and whether justice should be seen primarily as fair distribution or respectful treatment. They argued for greater attention to disability in debates about the meaning of health and disease but disagreed about how sharply disability needed to be distinguished from disease and illness. They challenged the ways in which quality-of-life judgments were made in assessing health-care interventions but disagreed about whether such judgments should play any significant role in distributing medical resources. They worried that much of the enthusiasm for physician assisted dying and prenatal testing was based on mistaken judgments about the quality of life enjoyed by people with disabilities but disagreed about the basic acceptability of those practices. And these philosophers were deeply skeptical of simplistic comparisons of individuals with intellectual disabilities to non-human animals but disagreed about whether the very idea of moral status should be reconceptualized or abandoned altogether.

These remain central areas of debate in disability and philosophy. Perhaps the most significant change in this area over the past two decades is that, instead of reacting mainly to developments in public policy and technology and to misconceptions in mainstream philosophy, philosophers of disability have formed their own vibrant community, developing, building on, criticizing, and refining theories and arguments about the conceptualization, valuation, and appropriate social responses to disability. This is hardly to suggest that no new topics or issues have emerged. A volume of this sort published twenty years ago would likely have contained no discussion of epistemic injustice or neurotechnology, for example, and little discussion of the complex dimensions of respect and care. But there has clearly been a strong continuity between the disability philosophy of the late twentieth and the early twenty-first centuries.

THE CONTENTS OF THIS VOLUME

To a large extent, our point of departure has been the existing literature on philosophy of disability—what has been written by those who regard themselves as philosophers of disability or who focus explicitly on disability. One of our objectives in selecting contributors and topics was to continue the vigorous conversations that has been going on over the past twenty years in philosophy journals and books about disability-related issues. We have also sought out philosophers who have not previously written about disability but who address issues with interesting affinities to topics discussed in the disability literature.

This modest and incremental approach has enabled our contributors to freely confront difficult boundary questions about what the philosophy of disability is fundamentally *about*: does "disability" refer in the first instance to a family of traits or conditions possessed by individuals; a kind of interaction between an individual's traits or conditions and her environment; a social group subject to exclusion and subordination; or a particular way of treating people for purposes of social control or political governance? Like some of our contributors, we regard disability as irreducibly "polysemic" and so have tried to avoid organizing this volume around any particular definition, model, or theory of disability.

By taking guidance mainly from the existing philosophical literature on disability and the community of philosophers that has evolved around it, we admittedly have risked bypassing relevant and important areas of inquiry not well represented in philosophy journals and books. In part through a vigilant review process and discussions with our contributors and other prominent scholars in the field, we sought to represent a wide and diverse array of perspectives. We have included contributors from other disciplines, from different philosophical approaches, from several countries, and from a variety of life experiences. We also afforded significant freedom to our contributors to approach their assigned topics in whatever ways they thought best. Although our aim was not to produce a fully comprehensive collection of philosophical work on issues of disability, we hope that the breadth of topics and contributors is great enough to engage philosophers from a variety of backgrounds and traditions, philosophers who have not previously written, or even thought much about, disability, and scholars from other disciplines.

One of the most fascinating features of philosophy of disability is that it engages with and reaches across various divides between the personal and the philosophical. Philosophy of disability often relies on, incorporates, and helps to make sense of living with a disability and interacting with disabled people in everyday life. Philosophy of disability can also be a tool for social progress by clarifying and theorizing ideas that shape public policy and social goals. And the discipline of philosophy itself is not immune from the same kinds of biases, prejudices, disrespect, and injustice that disadvantage disabled people in other areas of life. For these reasons, we have sought to include philosophers who are themselves disabled as well as those who have extensive first-hand experience with disabled family members, friends, or students. We have drawn on our own experiences of disability in framing the volume—one of us is legally blind while the other is a lifelong stutterer—while several of our contributors have done the same in writing their chapters.

A note on usage: our contributors differ in their preference for "person first" or "disability first" language. The former is preferred by those who regard disabilities as contingent features of individuals, however central to their personal or social identities. The latter preference is shared by two very different groups of contributors: those who regard disability as something imposed on people to control or exclude them and those who see disabilities, or certain disabilities, as essential rather than contingent features of personal identity. Proponents of "person first" language often see "disability first" language as a kind of synecdoche, ignoring the complex person behind the disability; proponents of "disability first" language often see "person first" language as mistakenly reifying disability, treating it as a thing rather than a social or political process. Along with several other contributors, we employ the terms interchangeably without thereby intending to express a substantive position in this debate.

Finally, we have dedicated this volume to two of our contributors, Anita Silvers and Lawrence C. Becker, who both passed away during its preparation. Anita and Larry were towering figures in the philosophy of disability who showed in word and deed that the life of the mind and the life of the advocate can be inextricably linked and mutually reinforcing. Through their scholarship, political engagement, mentoring, and advocacy, Anita and Larry laid the groundwork that in many ways made this volume possible.

Summaries of Chapters

1. Concepts, Models, and Perspectives of Disability

The point of departure for this section is the dichotomy between medical and social models of disability. The former understand disabilities as individual biomedical impairments whose adverse effects are mediated by the social environment; the latter understand disability as a relationship or interaction between a biomedical impairment and an adverse social environment. The medical model is usually not defended so much as assumed. It serves as a foil for social model theorists, for whom biomedical differences are not primarily sources of limitation but markers for discrimination and exclusion. Social models, in turn, have been criticized both for ignoring the pain and disruption caused by many impairments and for downplaying the extent to which impairments are themselves socially constructed, reflecting social, economic, political, and biomedical considerations. Although these criticisms are not necessarily incompatible, they emphasize different aspects of, and approaches to, disability. The essays in this section explore these and other approaches to thinking about the nature of disability.

In "Theoretical Strategies to Define Disability," Jonas-Sébastien Beaudry explores several philosophical strategies for unifying the many different and apparently inconsistent ways that the notion of disability is used in public policy, law, medicine, philosophy, and other contexts. These strategies vary in how determinate and systematic they are. Beaudry assesses them in terms of how well they match our considered judgments about the nature of disability and how well they meet the needs and interests of people commonly regarded as disabled. He then turns to a more radical approach, which is to abandon the search for a unified concept of disability. Embracing the multi-faceted nature of disability, Beaudry argues, is compatible with the more circumscribed aim of clarifying the notion of disability in different domains.

In "In Pursuit of Justice for Disability: Model Neutrality Revisited," Anita Silvers argues that models of disability should be evaluated, in part, by how well they serve their intended purposes. Some models of disability are used to determine, for example, who is eligible for certain forms of government assistance while others are also used to explain why people deserve those benefits. The models of disability employed by public health agencies, insurance programs, census bureaus, social security programs, medical professionals, and disability activists may differ from one another without necessarily conflicting, since they serve different classificatory and explanatory purposes. Such models become troublesome when they incorporate inappropriate evaluative elements or are used outside of their intended domains in ways that undermine justice and respect for disabled people.

In "Disability, Health, and Difference," Jerome Bickenbach describes an "interactional" model of disability: a detriment of performance in an area of life as a result of interactions between bodily capacities and environmental factors. He raises several objections to claims made by proponents of "minority group" models of disability, which regard disability as akin to gender and race. He then argues that his definition of disability correctly entails that disabled people cannot be perfectly healthy and that there is little or no point to arguing about whether disability makes an intrinsically negative difference to wellbeing (which is the topic of the next section). A significant advantage of an interactional model of disability, according to Bickenbach, is its emphasis on health interventions as well as modifications of the social environment.

In "Habilitative Health and Difference," Lawrence C. Becker develops a conception of disability as compromised "habilitative health." This conception avoids the dichotomy between medical and social models by drawing on a positive, non-medicalized notion of habilitative health, understood as a set of abilities to give and receive functional support to and from others; to preserve or improve one's own functioning; and to shape or modify the physical and social environment in ways that support one's functioning—with functioning assessed in terms of norms that are relativized to species and age. On his account, the myriad inabilities of all humans become disabilities only when the individual's habilitative skills are severely impaired, whether by disease, injury, or a hostile environment. Individuals with a variety of conditions conventionally labelled "disabilities," according to Becker, need not be disabled if they can comfortably perform necessary habilitative tasks; conversely, an individual with no conventionally labeled disabilities may be disabled if he cannot, because of his disposition or situation, perform those tasks.

In "Philosophy and the Apparatus of Disability," Shelley L. Tremain describes and defends a model of disability as a mechanism that is constructed and maintained by laws, informal norms, cultural understandings, and other exercises of "biopower." Impairments and disabilities do not exist apart from this culturally and historically contingent apparatus that, according to Tremain, arose in part as a means for people who saw themselves as "normal" to regulate those they labeled as "deviants." The discipline of philosophy itself, Tremain argues, is part of, and is maintained by, a social system that disables people. She argues, in particular, that the persistent marginalizing of disabled philosophers is based in part on the false and misleading assumption that impairment or disability are inherent and objective features of persons, when, according to Tremain, they are instead constructs that arise in power relations governing a wide array of practices, including professional accreditation.

Rosemarie Garland-Thomson also regards disability as a social construction, and in "Disability Liberation Theology," she emphasizes the ways in which the civil and human rights movements of the mid-twentieth century provided disabled people with the material and conceptual resources they needed to coalesce as a minority group united by political aims for justice and liberation from oppression. Such oppression, disabled people came to see, does not arise from their bodies but instead from environmental barriers, stigma, and other social factors. Yet this realization, according to Garland-Thomson, continues to be challenged by pervasive cultural influences, including theological images or narratives of, for example, Jesus suffering on the cross or healing the sick. Combatting these cultural trends, according to Garland-Thomson, requires symbolic action by disabled people that emphasizes their solidarity and pride, along with theological ideas, narratives and images that emphasize embodiment, relationships, and care.

2. Well-Being, Adaptation, and Causing Disability

The papers in this section explore the complex relationships of disability to well-being. Those relationships depend on how disability is understood, the subject of the previous section. Several of the contributors to this section begin with definitional work, sometimes referring to models, definitions, and approaches discussed in the first section. All agree that disability does not have the consistently negative impact on well-being assumed by many policymakers and philosophers. But they diverge in how they conceptualize or identify "disability," in how they explain its connection to well-being, and in what implications they think that relationship has for private decisions and public policy. Some accounts of disability posit a close connection between disability and diminished well-being. Others find that connection tenuous or highly complex. Those who regard "disability" as polysemic might question whether it even makes sense to argue about the relationship of disability to well-being, which may also be a polysemic concept.

In "Disabilities and Well-being: The Bad and the Neutral," Joshua Shepherd argues that the decisive consideration in whether a disability is a neutral or bad difference is whether it permits or precludes "control over one's situation." Shepherd illustrates this notion, which has interesting affinities with Becker's three kinds of habilitative abilities, by contrasting conditions in which such control is largely or entirely preserved, such as blindness, deafness, and other sensory disabilities, with those in which it is largely or completely absent, such as Locked-In Syndrome and Minimally Conscious States. He then applies the distinction to a wider range of familiar disabilities to assess whether, or the extent to which, they permit such control. Shepherd's account highlights both the striking heterogeneity of conditions regarded as disabilities and the possibility of assessing their impact on well-being in terms of a single feature.

The next two papers address, in distinctive ways, the challenge to claims of disability neutrality from the "causation objection" raised by several philosophers. According to this objection, if disability is just a neutral characteristic or mere difference that itself does not diminish well-being then it is no more objectionable to cause than to eliminate disability. Yet, defenders of the objection argue, causing disability is usually more objectionable than eliminating disability, so disability is not always a neutral characteristic with respect to well-being.

In "Causing Disability, Causing Non-Disability: What's the Moral Difference?" Joseph A. Stramondo and Stephen M. Campbell examine the alleged moral asymmetry between causing disability and eliminating disability. They resist the conclusion that this asymmetry supports the "Standard View" of disability as always or almost always bad for the individual. And they resist the conclusion, associated with Elizabeth Barnes, that there is no moral asymmetry here once interference and transition costs are accounted for. Stramondo and Campbell examine seven considerations that might fully or partially support the asymmetry without vindicating the Standard View, including the mere possibility that causing a disability will make a person worse off, the less reversible consequences in causing than in removing or preventing disability, and the substantial risk of stigma and discrimination. They conclude that these considerations cannot ground a general moral asymmetry between causing and eliminating disability but that they each might provide reasons not to cause disability in specific cases.

In "Why Inflicting Disability is Wrong: The Mere Difference View and The Causation Based Objection," Julia Mosquera focuses on Barnes's argument that causing disability is wrong only when it involves significant transition costs or nonconsensual interference with identity-determining traits. Mosquera counters that even when transition costs are eliminated, causing disability may be highly objectionable. And she finds several problems with the notion of "identity-determining traits," including vagueness and variability in what determines identity; the fact that many disabled people do not regard their disabilities as central to their identity; and the fact that it is often unobjectionable to attempt to modify, without consent, significant traits in children and even adults that are at least as identity-affecting as disability without obtaining their consent. She concludes by rejecting Barnes charge that proponents of the causation objection place an "epistemically precarious" reliance on the intuitions of a pervasively ableist society.

And in "Evaluative Diversity and the (Ir)Relevance of Well-Being," Sean Aas argues that the well-being of individuals with disabilities is of limited relevance to policy questions about the prevention and treatment of disability. The demands for equal respect and equal citizenship made by the disability community do not rest on claims that disabilities are neutral with respect to well-being. The strongest "expressivist" objections made to policies designed to prevent or eliminate disability focus on failures of respect rather than underestimations of well-being. And, in light of the variety of reasonable conceptions of the good life, it is unlikely that the best-argued claims of neutrality can win broad consensus. Disability advocates, according to Aas, should join with "public reason" liberals in adopting or developing outcome metrics for public policy that do not require comprehensive or controversial assessments of well-being.

3. Justice, Equality, and Inclusion

The chapters in this section illustrate how issues of disability inform and advance our understanding of the nature of justice for all people, not just those with disabilities. Ensuring justice for people with disabilities requires us to consider such issues as who is owed justice, the aims and metrics of justice, and the role of ideals in a theory of justice. Many of the essays, in one way or another, criticize aspects of John Rawls's influential theory of justice as fairness; several of them explore the importance of caring relationships for justice; and a few of them attempt to characterize an ideal kind of respectful and equal relationship among citizens. All of the essays are concerned with assessing and improving prominent theories of justice in ways that secure the fundamental interests of disabled people.

In "Contractualism, Disability, and Inclusion," Christie Hartley addresses the long-standing problem that social contract theories of justice exclude or marginalize people with significant disabilities who lack the capacity to cooperate in a social system. Hartley accepts that the role of justice is to fairly regulate social cooperation, but she argues that social cooperation includes any features or actions of persons that further or partially constitute an ideal of equal and mutually respectful relationships among all members of society. People with certain kinds of disabilities, who may not be able to contribute economically or politically, are nonetheless owed justice because they have the ability to promote or live out the ideal of equal and respectful social relations through emotional engagement and communication with other people.

In "Civic Republican Disability Justice," Tom O'Shea explores the relationship of equal citizenship by highlighting its incompatibility with relationships of domination. Drawing on the Civic Republican political tradition, O'Shea characterizes dominating relationships as those in which someone has arbitrary power over someone else who is dependent on their relationship, such as a wheelchair user who relies on a social worker to meet her basic needs. Challenging relationships of domination for disabled people, according to O'Shea, is a fundamental concern of justice that favors deinstitutionalization, anti-discrimination, reasonable accommodations, measures designed to help disabled people think for themselves, a universal basic income and mechanisms for complaint. A significant virtue of this framework, according to O'Shea, is that it helps us to understand and combat injustices in which disabled people depend on social workers, employers, and family members who can, even if they never do, exercise arbitrary power over them.

In "Disability and Disadvantage in the Capabilities Approach," Christopher A. Riddle begins by tracing the role of disability in assessing and developing several prominent theories of justice. He then argues that justice should be seen as a matter of eliminating or mitigating disadvantage and that the best way to assess disadvantage is in terms of a person's freedom and opportunity to be or do what she has reason to be or do. Someone is disadvantaged in this sense when she lacks the capability, for example, to be healthy or to engage in leisure activities as a result of such factors as coercion, limited resources, social stigma, or physical impairment. When a society cannot provide everyone the capabilities they need, Riddle suggests that it should prioritize capabilities that enhance other capabilities, such as by ensuring that everyone is healthy in ways that tend to promote capabilities of life, bodily integrity, and affiliation.

In "Disability and Partial Compliance Theory," Leslie Francis explores and criticizes some of the ways that disability figures into theories of justice that focus on ideal conditions. If such theories assume that disabled people of various types would not exist in such conditions then, according to Francis, their resulting principles will not secure justice for actual people of those kinds. And if ideal theories simply assume that principles of justice will be strictly complied with then, Francis argues, they are not suitable guides for addressing some of the most pressing problems that disabled people face, which involve widespread failures to comply with just legislation or questionable claims about the prohibitive costs involved in doing so. Francis goes on to sketch an alternative approach that focuses instead on making incremental improvements to securing the civil rights of people with disabilities in our non-ideal circumstances.

In "Fair Difference of Opportunity," Adam Cureton and Alexander Kaufman examine how a society should justly distribute opportunities to take up privileged occupations, careers, political offices, and other positions in society. Working within a Rawlsian framework, Cureton and Kaufman propose and defend a principle of differential access to offices and positions that, they argue, is more amenable to the interests of disabled people than Rawls's principle of fair equality of opportunity, which only corrects for the arbitrary influence of social circumstances and relies on a dubious distinction between natural and social endowments. Their alternative principle holds that if the opportunities of all can be improved by allowing more and better opportunities to some, then if certain other conditions are satisfied, such arrangements would be just. Cureton and Kaufman argue that disabled people and others would fare better under this principle than under Rawls's, both in terms of their opportunities to take up favorable offices and positions and in terms of their self-confidence and sense of self-worth.

And in "The Disability Case against Assisted Dying," Danny Scoccia describes and assesses three arguments that disability rights advocates have given against legally permitting only terminally ill people or others with significant disabilities to end their lives on their own, perhaps with the assistance of others, such as physicians. The first argument is that typically such choices are not autonomous or in the best interests of the person because of stigma and discrimination against disabled people, so assisted dying should be outlawed for the sake of these disabled people themselves. Second, laws that allow assisted dying diminish social support for people with disabilities and so should not be enacted or maintained. And, third, such laws express disparaging messages about disabled people, including that their lives are not worth living. Scoccia finds significant limitations in each of the three arguments and argues that all three are needed to reject disability-specific assisted dying laws while respecting the general legal right to refuse treatment.

4. Knowledge and Embodiment

The chapters in this section explore issues made pressing by the last two. The claims about well-being and justice examined in those sections often rely in part on testimony of people with disabilities about their own lives. That reliance raises questions addressed by the first two papers of this section: Has their testimony been unjustly discounted or devalued by the same assumptions about the apparent badness of disability challenged in the section "Well-Being, Adaptation, and Causing Disability"? Has the well-being of people with disabilities been reduced by the lack of "epistemic resources" available for understanding and interpreting their embodiment and experiences? What kind of authority should we accord the testimony of people with disabilities, or people without them, about how well they are doing in various contexts? And does the "adaptation" of people with disabilities to their conditions in any way reduce the credibility of their testimony?

The chapters by Jackie Leach Scully and Jason Marsh offer different, though compatible, perspectives on the epistemic authority of people with disabilities. They agree that disabled and nondisabled people have the same authority with respect to assessing their own well-being and that discounting the self-reports of people with disabilities can be a serious epistemic injustice.

In "Epistemic Exclusion, Injustice, and Disability," Scully argues that disability presents both a paradigm and a distinctive case of epistemic injustice. People with disabilities suffer *testimonial injustice*—their generally positive self-reports are given little credibility because of widespread prejudice, doubts about their competence, and the assumption that life with a major disability must be bad. They suffer *hermeneutic injustice* in being denied the epistemic resources to interpret their own experiences, as well as *contributory injustice* by the refusal to incorporate their experiences into the community's knowledge base. These forms of epistemic injustice, according to Scully, reinforce each other. And the injustice faced by people with disabilities is distinctive and especially severe. The heterogeneity of disabilities and the physical integration of disabled people into the larger society both hamper the acquisition of shared epistemic resources, while the epistemic exclusion of people with disabilities is reinforced by the biased assumptions of the health-care and social welfare systems.

Marsh would not disagree with this grim assessment. But he is concerned to point out the epistemic complexities and limitations in self-reports of well-being from both disabled and nondisabled people. In "What's Wrong With 'You Say You're Happy, But…' Reasoning?," Marsh observes that many such self-reports, including some that figure prominently in disability discourse, have a comparative aspect, and that people in general have more epistemic authority in reporting their own experiences than in comparing them to those of other people. It is thus generally unjust and disrespectful to second-guess people's judgments about how well they are doing. But people lack the same authority, and warrant less deference, in comparing their level of well-being to those of other people, particularly others with very different backgrounds or traits. We have good reason to discount the confident assertions of nondisabled people that their lives are much better than those of people with disabilities, or much better than they would be if they became disabled. But we should also be skeptical of corresponding judgments made by people with disabilities. In particular, we must not place too much weight on such comparative judgments in deciding if disabilities are mere- or bad-differences.

In "Interactions with Delusional Others: Reflections on Epistemic Failures and Virtues," Josh Dohmen considers a group of people with disabilities for whom the epistemic equality demanded by Scully and Marsh is more doubtful—people with significant delusions. While Dohmen recognizes that there are obvious reasons to discount the testimony of delusional individuals, he argues that the discounting should be far less radical, and far more nuanced, than commonly assumed. First, delusions should be seen as "extreme epistemic failures" that differ largely in degree from other epistemic failures. Second and relatedly, we must be cautious in attributing delusional rather than merely mistaken belief to people, especially people from marginalized groups. Third, people with delusions can still suffer significant epistemic injustice in having their testimony too readily dismissed. Finally, responsibility for delusions must be attributed not only to individual mental dysfunctions but to a social and political environment that actively encourages, or fails to adequately respond to, delusional beliefs. Dohmen ends with an appeal for epistemic humility, a virtue that promotes respectful interactions with delusional others.

And in "Disability, Rationality, and Justice: Disambiguating Adaptive Preferences," Jessica Begon explores a deep tension between, on the one hand, treating the preferences of people who adapt in various ways to adverse conditions as grounding claims of justice and, on the other hand, regarding some of those preferences as unreliable in ways that do not merit such concern. Begon develops separate accounts of what makes someone's preferences unreliable in the context of assessing her wellbeing and in the context of determining her claims of justice. In assessing well-being, an individual's preferences should not be discounted unless they are irrational. In assessing justice claims, even fully rational preferences can be discounted or set aside if they are a response to autonomy-limiting circumstances, for example, the preference of a disabled person not to engage in meaningful work because she has been excluded from such work or has internalized ableist judgments that she is not fit for it. The distinction between well-being and justice assessments enables us to respect the preferences of disabled people without letting rational adaptive preferences rule out legitimate justice claims.

5. Respect, Appreciation, and Care

The chapters in this section discuss the kinds of attitudes that we should have or aspire to have toward people with disabilities. We not only bring these attitudes to our assessments of many political and ethical issues, but they are also part of our relationships with disabled family members, friends, and even strangers. A common theme in this section is the importance of respect for persons and the need to develop a deeper understanding of respect by examining its role in relationships involving disabled people. Other attitudes, such as appreciation and care, are important as necessary complements to respect, but they also seem to conflict with respect in ways that are especially vivid to some disabled people. These chapters also attempt to address apparent conflicts in ways that enhance our understanding of the attitudes of respect, appreciation, and care.

The chapters by Thomas E. Hill and Adam Cureton are companion pieces that share a common conception of human dignity as a cluster of potentially competing values, including well-being, justice, appreciation, and respect, that should guide and constrain how we regard and treat ourselves and others. In "Ideals of Appreciation and Expressions of Respect," Hill explores two of these values, namely appreciation and expressions of "positive" respect, as ideal ways of responding to human dignity. The ideal of appreciation, according to Hill, involves being open to recognize and consider the many good features of people and their experiences. And the ideal of "positive" respect, Hill suggests, involves acknowledging and esteeming the worth of people as human beings and as the particular individuals that they are, as well as expressing that they matter in these ways through, for example, good manners and attentive listening. Hill applies these two components of human dignity to contexts in which we stand in close personal relationships with disabled people.

In "The Limiting Role of Respect," Cureton explores another aspect of human dignity, namely a "negative" kind of respect that involves resistance and limitation. He examines how this kind of respect can conflict with Hill's ideals of appreciation and positive respect. Negative respect, according to Cureton, includes tendencies not to make assumptions about other people without sufficient evidence, infringe on their privacy, or intrude on their responsibilities. Cureton argues that failures of negative respect underlie a legitimate concern that many disabled people have, which is that even well-meaning people sometimes overstep bounds of respect in the otherwise good and virtuous ways that they regard and treat us.

In "Respect, Identification, and Profound Cognitive Impairment," John Vorhaus considers whether a kind of respect for persons, namely one that involves attempting to take up someone's point of view, is an appropriate or required moral attitude for us to have toward people who lack a point of view because of profound cognitive impairment. Vorhaus explores what it takes to have a way of seeing the world, what is involved in identifying with the point of view of others, and why such identification respect is morally appropriate in various contexts. He argues that at the very least, we have moral reasons to try and identify with people who lack a point of view, even if doing so cannot succeed, because such efforts are likely to result in better treatment of such people than if we did not attempt to respect them in this way.

In "Care and Disability: Friends or Foes," Eva Feder Kittay develops a normative conception of care and applies her sophisticated moral framework to the idea of independence, which has been a dominant theme in the Disability Rights Movement. Kittay criticizes some of the supposed reasons for wanting to be self-reliant, but she admits that neglect and paternalism are real dangers to being dependent on other people in certain ways. Properly caring for someone, Kittay argues, forbids such disrespectful treatment by requiring us both to care about the needs of others and to ensure that those we care for recognize and accept our care as improving their situations.

And in "A Dignitarian Approach to Disability: From Moral Status to Social Status," Linda Barclay describes and defends a conception of dignity as the status a person has when she is regularly treated in accordance with formal and informal norms of social equality. Norms of social equality include not just laws but also informally created and enforced social rules. Although such norms vary among cultures, they share certain critical features. They forbid, for example, shunning other people and being condescending toward them; and they require, for example, politeness, good manners, and other forms of behavior that communicate our recognition of others as our social equals. Dignity of this kind is a relation between a person and the ways she is routinely treated by other people, who can give and take away her dignity by conforming to or violating existing norms of social equality. According to Barclay, we should confer dignity in this sense on all people, including those with cognitive disabilities, in order to avoid harming them or other disabled people directly or indirectly.

6. Moral Status and Significant Mental Disabilities

The chapters in this section examine the common moral belief that people with significant mental disabilities have the same moral status as people who are not disabled in these ways. One common explanation for why someone possesses moral interests, or claims that matter morally for her own sake, is that she possesses intrinsic features that give her this moral standing, such as a capacity to experience oneself as a being who is extended through time, capacities for rational, autonomous thought and choice, capacities to care and be cared for, or capacities to form morally valuable relationships. Views of this kind face the challenge of, on the one hand, explaining why a set of properties justifies the particular moral interests or claims that constitute moral status and, on the other, ensuring that people with significant mental disabilities have moral status. Some philosophers endorse criteria that are tied closely to these moral interests, even though some human beings are thereby excluded, while others endorse criteria that include all human beings and attempt to explain why those criteria ground the moral interests and claims that, on reflection, we think people have.

The first two chapters in this section take the second approach by proposing conceptions of what it is to be human and explaining why humans in this sense, including those with significant mental disabilities, have the same basic moral interests and claims.

In "Cognitive Disability and Moral Status," Alice Crary argues that all humans with cognitive disabilities deserve basic moral consideration simply because they are human. Drawing on our ordinary moral beliefs and practices, she develops a conception of "human" that includes moral, and not just empirical or scientific, content. Anyone who is human, in this sense, deserves attention and respect because part of being human is to have basic moral standing. Thinking about human beings in this morally laden way, Crary argues, avoids a significant mistake in discussions of moral status, namely a reliance on what she sees as a dubious dualism between purely natural and purely moral concepts.

In "Dignity, Respect, and Cognitive Disability," Suzy Killmister proposes a criterion for one kind of moral status that, she claims, explains why we owe people with significant mental disabilities several kinds of respect, such as not humiliating them, not treating them as mere objects, and (in appropriate circumstances) grieving over their deaths. Being human, according to Killmister, is ambiguous between, on the one hand, having certain natural properties of the sort that biologists study, and on the other, occupying the social position of "human," which is defined by various rights, powers, entitlements, and prerogatives. The two notions of "human" need not be coextensive (there can be biological humans who are not social humans), but in some societies, according to Killmister, people who are human in the first sense thereby occupy the social position "human" in the second sense, which entitles them to the kinds of respect she describes. Creating, maintaining, and treating others in accordance with this social position of dignity is morally appropriate, according to Killmister, because its existence in a society tends to produce better overall consequences than if the society did not generally endorse it.

Many disability advocates think that treating the moral status of disabled people as open for debate is deeply disrespectful. In "On Moral Status and Intellectual Disability: Challenging and Expanding the Debates," Licia Carlson considers how philosophical discussions about the moral status of people with intellectual disabilities should be conducted. The ways we speak about such people, Carlson argues, can express disrespectful messages and cause significant harm, particularly when we compare them to non-human animals for purposes of assessing whether they have moral status. We should try to avoid or counteract these messages and their adverse consequences by acknowledging how people with intellectual disabilities have historically been treated, learning about their capacities and experiences, engaging with them, reflecting on and correcting our own biases, and expressing philosophical humility.

7. Intellectual and Psychiatric Disability

The chapters in this section look beyond moral status to explore other important issues that arise in conceptualizing intellectual and psychiatric disabilities and in responding to people with those disabilities. Many intellectual and psychiatric disabilities are notoriously difficult to classify and diagnose, while others raise deep questions about the competence of people with those conditions to make important decisions about their own lives. The education of people with intellectual and psychiatric conditions is also an important concern of justice, which may require substantial revisions to current educational policy.

In "Neurodiversity, Autism, and Psychiatric Disability: The Harmful Dysfunction Perspective," Jerome C. Wakefield, David Wasserman, and Jordan A. Conrad assess neurodiversity claims as challenges to the diagnosis and classification of psychiatric disorders. Focusing on autism, they apply a leading account of disorder as harmful dysfunction to argue that, according to our best available evidence, the type of severe autism that was first diagnosed by Leo Kanner is a disorder because it arises from a biological dysfunction causing significant harm. They also conclude, however, that some conditions now classified as autistic, including what was once called Asperger's Syndrome, are not disorders but normal mental variations. Some neurodiversity advocates reject this sort of differential analysis by arguing that all conditions on the autism spectrum share a common core that is not a disorder. The authors explore several accounts of what this essence might be and argue that each of them either fails to define a common feature in autism or fails to explain why that feature is not in some cases caused by a harmful dysfunction. Other neurodiversity advocates claim that most conditions on the autism spectrum are not disorders because they do not cause harm or because the harm that typically accompanies them is socially mediated. The authors agree that much of the harm associated with autism arises from unreasonable or unjust social norms and practices, but they argue that some forms of autism directly cause harm, including socially mediated harm, in ways that do not disqualify them as disorders.

In "Beyond Instrumental Value: Respecting the Will of Others and Deciding on Their Behalf," Dana Howard and David Wendler argue that trustees who make decisions on behalf of people with certain kinds of intellectual disabilities should do so in ways that respect their agential capacities, including ones that are impaired. Respecting a person's capacities to make decisions for herself, according to Howard and Wendler, requires both taking her choices as, in themselves, providing reasons to fulfill them as well as not ignoring or acting as if the person lacks such capacities. Trustees for people with impaired agential capacities, they argue, thus have reasons to listen to, engage with, and adhere to the choices of those they represent as well as reasons to promote their welfare interests.

And in "Educational Justice for Students with Intellectual Disabilities," Lorella Terzi argues that educational resources should be distributed in ways that provide everyone with equal opportunity to develop talents, skills, and whatever else they need to participate as equals in society. Above this threshold, a just distribution would provide greater opportunities of this sort for some people as part of a scheme that improves such opportunities for people who are least advantaged. Terzi argues that this framework, which has deep roots in the capabilities approach to justice, is especially well suited to specify, explain, and secure the educational interests of people with intellectual disabilities. Equal participation in society, Terzi argues, includes not just economic or political engagement but also affective and social engagement. For this reason, people with intellectual disabilities are often entitled to additional educational resources so that they have the same opportunities as others to take part in valuable aspects of social life that are available to them.

8. Technology and Enhancement

The chapters in this section explore the complex relationship of disability to technology and the often conflicting and ambivalent views of philosophers of disability toward technological enhancement. The authors question several conventional views: that the mind, or the mental, is bounded by the skull; that there is a sharp opposition between disability and enhancement; and that the development of assistive and enhancing technologies for people with disabilities is driven by a medical model that treats disabilities as personal defects to be concealed, corrected, or circumvented. To varying extents, the authors challenge these conventional views as oversimplified. Mental abilities are a function not only of the mind but the body and the environment; even if we understand disability and enhancement as opposing notions, their relationship is highly complex; the use of assistive technology involves difficult tradeoffs (e.g., between physical functioning and social acceptance); and people with disabilities vary greatly in their attitudes toward technological assistance and enhancement, reflecting their diversity of perspectives and the heterogeneity of their conditions.

While challenging conventional views, the authors also raise significant concerns about the embrace of technology and enhancement. People with disabilities must participate in all stages of the development of technologies intended for them, and they must be wary of the promise that radical enhancement will virtually eliminate the functional and social disadvantages of disability and create an equal, if highly elevated, playing field. Even if technology can often be liberating for people with disabilities, it cannot replace the hard work of social and political reform.

In "A Symmetrical View of Disability and Enhancement," Stephen M. Campbell and David Wasserman canvass accounts of enhancement to see which best captures and explains the intuitive opposition between enhancement and disability. The best account, they argue, is one that defines a disability in highly relativized terms, as a capacity for achieving a given outcome through a given mode of action or function in a given environment significantly below what is typical for one's kind and that defines an enhancement as a capacity significantly above that level. Although this view may seem to support a medical model of disability as an internal defect, it incorporates several core features of a social model: It treats capacity as environmentally relative and recognizes the variety of modes through which an agent can achieve a given outcome. This view, according to Campbell and Wasserman, also has the welcome implications that almost all people are disabled, normal, and enhanced in different respects, that technological and medical interventions are often enhancing in some respects and disabling in others, and that there is no simple way to assess the impact of disability and enhancement on well-being.

In "Cognitive Disability and Embodied, Extended Minds," Zoe Drayson and Andy Clark argue that our cognitive capacity and performance are a function not only of our internal hardware and software but also of our bodies, relationships, and environments. Our computational and reasoning abilities depend to a surprising extent on our somatic activity; our memory and interaction with others depend on a variety of mnemonic tools and props. Understanding our minds as embodied and extended in these ways has important implications both for assessing and for responding to cognitive impairment. An individual's cognitive strengths and weaknesses should be assessed with reference to her somatic condition and her physical and social environment, while rehabilitation must go beyond a narrow biological and psychological focus to encompass changes in social interactions and physical surroundings.

In "The Visible and the Invisible: Disability, Assistive Technology, and Stigma," Coreen McGuire and Havi Carel offer a critical historical perspective on the development and adoption of assistive technologies by disabled people. They examine two cases of "invisible" illnesses/disabilities: Hearing loss and breathlessness. In both cases, technologies emerged in the first half of the twentieth century to mitigate the functional impact of the underlying impairments: telephonic voice amplification and assisted respiratory devices. These technologies were initially developed without consulting those expected to use them, who could best make difficult tradeoffs between improved function and increased visibility. As well as illustrating the importance of involving users in product development, these cases highlight the inadequacy of the medical/social model dichotomy in explaining the difficult choices involved in the development and use of technology: between improving function and concealing the impairment, and between different aspects of functional improvement. Assistive technologies that connect the individual with her environment often blur the boundaries between them, on which the medical/social model dichotomy rests.

In "Neurotechnologies and Justice by, with, and for Disabled People," Sara Goering and Eran Klein find many of the same issues as those identified by McGuire and Carel, now arising in the development and marketing of cutting-edge neurotechnologies. In one respect, these newer technologies are strikingly dissimilar from previous assistive technologies, since their assistive applications are often a secondary use or afterthought. Goering and Klein point out the injustice in testing these devices on people with disabilities who are not guaranteed access to any resulting benefits or only "trickle-down" benefits once the products have been marketed for their primary uses. They recognize, however, the potential value in products that are not developed exclusively for people with disabilities. If neurotechnologies are incorporated into a shared environment, they can enhance the participation of, and reduce the stigma faced by, people with disabilities. But that will only happen if a significant upfront investment is made and if, as McGuire and Carel emphasize, people with disabilities are involved in every stage of the development process.

In "Second Thoughts on Enhancement and Disability," Melinda C. Hall argues against proposals to radically enhance human physical and mental capacities. She critically examines the claim made by transhumanists—the most enthusiastic proponents of radical enhancement—that the rejection of species norms minimizes the significance of disabilities and supports people with disabilities as first adopters of many enhancement technologies. Hall considers two dominant transhumanist enhancement strategies: to transcend the confines of human embodiment (Nick Bostrom) and to genetically select the children expected to have the best lives (Julian Savulescu). She finds both strategies inimical to people with disabilities, epitomizing the fear of vulnerability and risk that pathologize disability. Hall analyzes these proposals in terms of Foucault's notion of "biopower" as a modern form of governance seeking to control population characteristics by shaping individual behavior. She concludes with a "counter-narrative" that emphasizes the ways that technology can be employed to make societies more inclusive for the people who inhabit them, rather than to alter the kinds of people who do.

9. Health-care Allocation

A considerable literature in health economics and applied ethics has debated whether or how disease and disability are relevant to the allocation of medical resources. Standard measures of benefit in cost-effectiveness analysis (CEA) reduce the value of a year of life saved by any shortfall in its expected quality, while standard techniques for assessing quality of life assign substantial "adjustments" for diseases and disabilities. A year of life with paraplegia, for example, may be assigned only 55 percent of the value of a year of life in full health.

This way of setting priorities in the allocation of scarce lifesaving resources has been met with two objections, one concerned with how quality of life is assessed and the other with its relevance for allocating those resources. The first objection concerns the reliance on nondisabled people, particularly health-care professionals, to assess the quality of life of people with diseases and disabilities. As the contributors to sections "Well-Being, Adaptation, and Causing Disability" and "Knowledge and Embodiment" also emphasize, nondisabled people generally judge the quality of life with various disabilities as much worse than do people with those disabilities. The second objection concerns the morally appropriate role of differences in quality of life, however assessed, in allocating lifesaving resources. Many ethicists, with or without a disability orientation, deny that the sole objective in allocating scarce lifesaving resources should be to maximize quality-adjusted life years. Some argue that this goal must be constrained by priority for the worse off; others that allocation schemes that favor those with better health prospects may discriminate against people with disabilities.

In "Cost-Effectiveness Analysis and Disability Discrimination," Greg Bognar argues that standard uses of CEA to allocate medical resources within health-care systems do not unjustly discriminate against disabled people. Such policies are normally evaluated by their average costs and benefits for a large group of patients, so if this ratio is low enough for typical patients then the interventions will not be denied to disabled patients, regardless of whether they will receive fewer benefits from it as a result of their disability. But policies that forgo costly and moderately beneficial interventions that are tailored to particular impairments will discriminate against disabled people if no other interventions are available to address the impairment. Bognar argues, however, that such policies do not involve *unjust* discrimination, although they may result in distributive injustice.

And in "Prioritization and Parity. Which Disabled Newborn Infants Should be Candidates for Scarce Life-Saving Treatment?," Dominic JC Wilkinson and Julian Savulescu argue that clinics should combine the values of fairness and benefit when allocating scarce medical resources to patients with conflicting claims on them. They suggest one way of doing so: First, in cases in which the allocation of a treatment among patients will affect the treatment of other patients, such as by taking up a machine that will be needed by others, the claims of the former patients are on a par only when they are above the threshold of cost-effectiveness. Second, in cases in which the allocation of a treatment will not have such indirect effects on others, the claims of the patients are equally valid when they are above a different threshold, namely one that affords equal weight to fairness and benefit. Under this proposal, Wilkinson and Savulescu maintain, people with disabilities are treated in ways that appropriately combine the values of fairness and benefit.

10. Reproduction and Parenting

The chapters in this section make it clear that decisions about creating and parenting children with disabilities raise issues distinct from those discussed in the previous sections of the volume. All the authors would agree, for example, that the impact of disability on well-being is only one of the morally relevant considerations that should guide individual and collective decision making in these areas. Four of the chapters in this section examine the use of reproductive technologies to select against future children with disabilities; the fifth examines parental decisions to prevent, correct, or mitigate disabilities.

In "Why People with Cognitive Disabilities are Justified in Feeling Disquieted by Prenatal Testing and Selective Termination," Chris Kaposy argues that people with cognitive disabilities are justifiably concerned about the use of prenatal testing to prevent the birth of embryos and fetuses diagnosed with those disabilities. He rejects three reassurances offered by bioethicists who defend the practice: that it is not people living with those disabilities who are targeted; that the decision to terminate an "affected" pregnancy need not be motivated by bias toward people with cognitive disabilities; and that termination decisions are rarely motivated by bias. Concerning the first, Kaposy maintains that the bias claimed to motivate termination decisions goes to the value and quality of the lives of actual as well as potential people with cognitive disabilities; concerning the second, he recognizes that termination decisions need not be motivated by bias, but insists that this is hardly reassuring to critics worried that many or most such decisions in fact are; third, he marshals evidence for the pervasiveness of bias against people with cognitive disabilities and for the influence of that bias on termination decisions. Kaposy emphasizes that false or exaggerated beliefs about the low quality of life with a cognitive disability are themselves likely to reflect bias rather than to offer an alternative explanation for termination decisions.

In "Reproductive Choice, in Context: Avoiding Excess and Deficiency?," Richard Hull and Tom Shakespeare examine the morality of prenatal testing for an increasingly wide range of conditions and traits. They argue that the complexity of the decisions facing prospective parents about the use of early and comprehensive prenatal genetic testing favors an Aristotelian approach, which emphasizes the importance of the specific circumstances in which these decisions are made and regards the virtuous prospective parent as one who seeks a mean between too much and too little selectivity. They begin by rejecting the views on opposing extremes: that selecting against disability is protecting the welfare of the child, and that such selection reflects the view that disability is worse than death. They then consider the multiplicity of personal, social, and economic considerations that prospective parents may reasonably take into account in deciding about testing and termination. Identifying, evaluating, and balancing these factors requires the practical wisdom, or *phronesis*, that is central to Aristotelian virtue. Such virtue also requires the ability to find a mean between the excess of overly fastidious or perfectionist standards for children and the deficiency of wholesale indifference to the expected quality of the future child's life, both of which ill-serve the ends of parenting.

In "Bioethics, Disability, and Selective Reproductive Technology: Taking Intersectionality Seriously," Christian Munthe introduces a different kind of complexity in the appraisal of disability objections to reproductive selection: the fact that individuals have multiple identities, some of which powerfully mediate the impact of social attitudes and practices on disability. Munthe draws on feminist analyses of intersectionality that point out the extent to which the disadvantages faced by an individual with a particular identity depend on her other identities. In the case of disability in postindustrial societies, for example, socioeconomic status may heavily mediate the impact of social biases and practical burdens in having a disabled child. In light of this mediation, it is oversimplified to regard selective reproductive technologies as directed only against disabled people. It is directed at least as much against, and discriminatory toward, people on the basis of poverty and gender. Munthe sees this intersectional analysis not as diminishing but expanding disability-based criticisms by placing them in a broader social context. In some circumstances, such an analysis might support, as a temporary measure, selection against medically costly disabilities to conserve truly scare resources for social justice—in particular, justice for people with disabilities. Although its opposition to selective termination might be qualified in such ways, an intersectional approach would avoid the demeaning competition among multiple identities for distributional and recognitional priority.

In "Procreation and Intellectual Disability: A Kantian Approach," Samuel J. Kerstein applies his Kantian-inspired account of dignity (KID) to assess reproductive decisions concerning children with intellectual disability. KID sets a negative and positive condition for respecting human dignity, which are, very roughly, not to use another person merely as a means and to treat other persons as having unconditional, preeminent worth. For Kerstein, a person's worth is conditioned only on having capacities to set, pursue, and coordinate ends and to be motivated by moral demands. On this account, individuals with Down syndrome are persons, but embryos and early fetuses are not. Terminating a fetus with Trisomy 21 would not violate either condition of KID, since the affected fetus is not a person and the individual decision to terminate does not intentionally do anything, let alone anything disrespectful, to existing people with Down syndrome. Kerstein contrasts a policy that banned state funding for implanting Trisomy-21 fetuses—such a policy might well be expected to undermine the personhood of existing people with Down and thereby offend their dignity. He argues further that parents do not violate KID if, for selfish reasons, they have a child with a severe but personhood-preserving intellectual disability instead of having a different, nondisabled child by waiting several months. Contra Paul Hurley and Rivka Weinberg, they do not use the child that they have merely as a means by subordinating her interests to theirs, since they could not have served the child's interests better by waiting. And contra David Wasserman, Kerstein denies that prospective parents must have a future child's good as one of their reasons for bringing her into existence.

And in "Parental Autonomy, Children with Disabilities, and Horizontal Identities," Mary Crossley draws on some of the same evidence of pervasive bias as Kaposy to oppose an uncritical deference to parental decisions about the prevention, correction, or mitigation of their children's disabilities. While the parents of children with disabilities are almost always deeply committed to their child's interests, they are not immune to mistaken or exaggerated views about the harmfulness of disability embraced and propagated by the wider society. The distorting impact of this bias may weaken the presumption that they will be acting in the best interests of their disabled child in making difficult decisions about risky or burdensome medical interventions. While Crossley is reluctant to have judges or other third parties second-guess such decisions she urges that non-disabled parents making them be given the same kind of information that the U.S. government is required to collect about the lives of children with prenatal disabilities. The provision of such information would help strike a balance between respecting parental autonomy and correcting harmful bias toward people with disabilities.

REFERENCES

Braddock, David L., and Susan L. Parish. 2001. "An Institutional History of Disability." In *Handbook of Disability Studies*, edited by Gary L. Albrecht, Katherine Seelman, and Michael Bury, 11–68. Thousand Oaks, CA: SAGE.

Davis, Lennard J. 2010. "Constructing Normalcy. " In *The Disability Studies Reader*, edited by Lennard J. Davis, 3–19. New York: Routledge.

NOTE

1. This and the next two paragraphs draw on Davis 2010 and on Braddock and Parish 2001.

PART ONE

CONCEPTS, MODELS, AND PERSPECTIVES OF DISABILITY

CHAPTER 1

THEORETICAL STRATEGIES TO DEFINE DISABILITY

JONAS-SÉBASTIEN BEAUDRY

"So utterly has he surpassed the whole human race in impudence that he tries with his single voice to persuade you all that I am not classed as disabled."

Lysias, *On the Refusal of a Pension to the Invalid*, §13 (403 BC)

HOW SHOULD WE MANAGE THE POLYSEMY OF A HIGHLY CONTESTED CONCEPT?

THE central case of disability seems deceptively obvious in popular culture: a severe, permanent impairment, such as tetraplegia or blindness. It is nonetheless impossible for policymakers and philosophers to agree on a single definition. Tom Shakespeare and Nicholas Watson (2001, 22) write that disability "is a complex dialectic of biological, psychological, cultural and sociopolitical factors, which cannot be extricated except with imprecision." Many researchers and institutions, like the World Health Organization (2002, 2), understand disability as an "umbrella" term in order to do justice (or surrender?) to its conceptual breadth. However, which phenomena and values are centrally denoted by or peripherally connected to the concept of disability remains a highly controversial question.

"[W]e all know what a disabled person is," Shakespeare (1999, 25) writes, "it is a common sense category, much as 'woman' or 'black person' or 'homosexual.' These are all words we use with confidence." Yet a closer inspection reveals that those categories (disability, race, gender, sexual orientation) taken to be natural features of certain individuals are at least partially socially constructed and may refer to *relations* between people or *expectations* imposed on people, rather than to a *kind* of people. For example, "disabled people" may denote nonworkers within specific settings or understandings of labor (Oliver 1990). They may be a necessary category of "outliers" for certain theories of the social contract to make sense, just as they may be described as those who cannot meaningfully participate in social institutions (Silvers and Francis 2005). Rather than denoting the "ab-normals" and the "dis-abled," the concept of disability can reveal questionable, hidden assumptions about "normal abilities." Thus, the recently blooming attention of philosophers to disability may pull at the thread of a greater fabric. Scrutinizing the ideologies and social imaginaries underlying disability discourses opens the door to revolutionary explorations of what justice, beauty, and morality could involve if we did not treat "different bodies" as outliers. Those cultural and philosophical critiques are not merely theoretical: they can lead to concrete, circumscribed policy changes urgently needed by "disabled people." As Lysias's speech on a disabled, aging tradesman pleading before the Council of Athens to keep his disability pension suggests, how we define disability has long had concrete repercussions on people's lives.

Descriptively speaking, the concept of "disability" can help us to explain some phenomena due to its close relationship with other concepts such as normality, abnormality, capacity, and incapacity. But, perhaps more importantly, how we understand disability has substantive normative implications. Concepts and models of disability can serve to attribute a certain value to the phenomena we call "disability" so that we can decide, individually or collectively, how we ought to react to them. Once a definition of disability is used in legal contexts and social movements or embedded in a policy, it can do both harm and good. For instance, it can contribute to marginalizing people with disabilities (PWD) or it can empower them to make claims through their right to equality. How we define disability in policies and laws will typically create assumptions—either implicitly or explicitly—about (1) its causes, whose problem it is, or where it is located; (2) how to properly respond to it; and (3) which actor(s) should shoulder this duty.

The concept of disability can be used to accomplish so much practical, political, legal, cultural, psychological, and theoretical (harmful or beneficial) "work" that cataloging that work with any kind of historical survey is impossible. To maintain a degree of generality while asking a specific question, I retreat to the realm of meta-philosophy and select some theoretical treatments of the concept of disability by categorizing them as answers to the issue of the concept's *polysemy*, that is, as philosophical strategies to handle the fact that "disability" has various meanings that cannot be reduced to one another.

Doubtless, the notion of "disability" poses problems other than polysemy, but the polysemic nature of disability is a feature worth reflecting on as a challenge faced by philosophers of this "highly indeterminate" (Boorse 2009, 55), if not "essentially contested," (Silvers 2003, 473) concept.

Philosophers must, one way or another, confront the range of phenomena that are called "disability" in their culture, as found in a variety of contexts (medical, social, activist, legal, artistic, biographical, popular, religious, etc.).

The polysemy of disability is an issue with important, long-standing, practical consequences. Jerome Bickenbach (2012) reports that countless definitions identifying different people and different needs govern differently purposed disability policies. He asks if
this plurality of meaning "is a sign of incoherence that should be remedied, inevitable
and something we just have to live with, or, finally, appropriate and perfectly acceptable"
(20). Barbara Altman (2001, 98) also points out that the polysemy of the concept of disability can have lamentable repercussions on the welfare of disabled people.[1]

I suggest that polysemy is a philosophically interesting feature of disability. This
claim, and the further claim that it may also be an ineliminable feature of disability,
should not be surprising given that disability is a multifaceted, evolving cultural object
that is commonly understood to have heterogenous referents. What is surprising is that
philosophers would assume that this polysemy is only a contingent, philosophically
uninteresting feature of disability: a cultural mess that they must clean up. Many philosophical disagreements about disability simply overlook the fact that the disputants are
talking about different phenomena (impairment vs. oppression, care vs. justice, legal vs.
extra-legal obligations, etc.). Some of those disagreements are more productively articulated as disagreements on how to handle the polysemy of disability (Beaudry 2016).

The five philosophical strategies I examine in this chapter define disability in ways
that deny, transcend, or embrace its polysemy. They include:

Determinate accounts that are

(1) reductionist or
(2) mixed.

Second-order accounts that are *open-ended* with regard to

(3) referents and/or
(4) value

and

(5) radically open-ended accounts.

The first two strategies aim at proposing a clear definition of disability by offering
determinate criteria to decide what counts as a disability. For instance, a reductionist
model might hold that disability is nothing other than a socially imposed obstacle to
reach opportunities available to others, such as the absence of a ramp preventing a
wheelchair user from accessing the grocery store. Another might equate disability with
impairment, like missing a limb.

Dissatisfied with the narrow extension of reductionist theories that appear to fail to
do justice to the fact that disability cannot be reduced to only one of its facets, theorists and policy-makers have expanded the list of criteria to create *mixed* models,

defining disability as a more complex phenomenon, such as an interaction between individual traits and the social environment (Shakespeare 2014, 74–75; World Health Organization 2002).

However, even multiplying criteria may fail to do justice to the complexity of disability. One philosophical strategy is to maintain hope that we can achieve a complex conception of disability by tinkering with the criteria until we get it right. An alternative solution is to retreat into a more abstract definition. Proponents of a more abstract understanding of disability make room for the fact that disability can refer to various phenomena (what I call *open-endedness of referents*) or be valued in positive, neutral, or negative ways (*open-endedness of value*). Instead of defining a list of determinate criteria, open-ended accounts develop procedures, mechanisms, or higher level ways of dealing with the polysemy of disability. Those procedures or more abstract commonalities still offer a unified account of disability, even if it is a "second-order" one. I call those accounts "second-order" accounts because they do not offer first-order rules to decide what counts as a disability, but instead second-order rules to decide what those first-order rules should be.

Finally, other philosophers find that there is no unifying (descriptive or normative) feature common to various phenomena called "disability." They talk of disability as a purely open-ended notion. The virtue of radically open-ended accounts lies in the possibilities opened by embracing polysemy.

One of the main tensions that my survey highlights relates to practical considerations regarding the tasks that disability models can accomplish. On one hand, defining disability precisely seems to allow us to efficiently respond to disability-related needs by setting up mechanisms that streamline disability claims and reasonably prioritize between them.[2] On the other, fixed definitions are likely to be set by a socially dominant group, to be ideologically tainted, or to be otherwise used as a tool of governance (Oliver 1990; 1999; Tremain 2001; 2015). If the latter, insisting on the indeterminacy of the concept rather than on its solid metaphysical or moral grounds would facilitate its counterhegemonic appropriation. We may call this the *dilemma of specificity*. Philosophers negotiate it when they answer the hard question: Can or should the concept of disability achieve consistency and stability? This chapter examines each of the five kinds of disability account listed earlier. The value of each depends on how it answers the dilemma of specificity and how it responds to a related, and similarly difficult, question: *Should we adopt a theory of disability which has oppressive effects on people with disabilities?*

DETERMINATE ACCOUNTS OF DISABILITY

Reductionist Models

If the letters "a, b, c, d…" each stand for a specific *definition* of disability, a reductionist way to handle the complexity of the notion of disability would be to opt for one single

definition at the exclusion of others. Disability would mean "a" *or* "b" *or* "c," and proponents of the "a" definition would deny the validity of "b" or "c" as accurate or helpful definitions of disability.

Prime examples of reductionist accounts are *medical* and *social* models, which define
"disability" *exclusively* in terms of biological dysfunctions or social oppression, respectively. Medical models of disability hold that disability is a private issue, exclusively or
primarily caused by biological impairments. By contrast, social models claim that
disability is socially created through a variety of obstacles that prevent people with
impairments from having equal opportunities, access to public spaces, and institutional
resources. Non-socially caused harms should be captured by other terms, like "impairments." The contrast between those models constitutes a seminal dichotomy in the sociology and philosophy of disability (Thomas 2004; Beaudry 2016).

These reductionist definitions of disability, however, can be difficult to defend, particularly because "conceptual definitions are neither true or false but are the . . . communications of the . . . person creating them. . . . [They] are either understandable or not, useful
or not" (Altman 2001, 101). The more exclusivist the account is, the easier it is to attack.
A definition that categorically excludes any biological, social, economic, legal, or experiential influences from the purview of "disability" is giving itself the almost insurmountable task of demonstrating that these other facets of "disability" are morally or
descriptively misguided or trivial and pointless.

Perhaps because of these issues, it is a challenge to find an explicit philosophical
defense of a *reductionist* medical model; that is, an argument to the effect that disability
ought to be understood as a purely medical condition in abstraction of all other dimensions.[3] Even medical sociologists who insist on the "causal relationship between illness,
changes in the body, and disability" (Bury 2000, 179) concede that disabilities are shaped
by social contexts. However, the medical model remains culturally influential, and its
lack of formal defense is not surprising; it reflects the ideological and invisible status
quo that fuels the popular ableist view that disabilities are private medical tragedies.
A related reductionist claim is that disability is a state of affairs which is inherently bad,
undesirable, or harmful. This view is mainstream among bioethicists and utilitarian
philosophers but is criticized for ignoring the subjective experience of disabled people
who do not judge their disabilities to be sources of discontent or harm.[4] While social
modelists have focused on discrediting their main competitor, the medical model, for
failing to recognize the primary importance of social factors in creating disability (e.g.,
Oliver 1990; UPIAS 1976), the social model itself has been criticized for its inattention to
impairment either as a medically manageable phenomenon or as subjectively experienced by PWD (e.g., Shakespeare 2014).

The best parry to an anti-reductionist attack is essentially to give in and narrow one's
claims down to specific dimensions of disability. For instance, one may claim that specific pathologies are highly likely to make one's life worse off without endorsing the
bolder, dubious claim that a person is necessarily made worse off by any disability. One
may speak about managing impairments medically or criticize the oppression or discrimination that particular groups of PWD suffer from without denying the positive
impact of "disability pride."

The main advantage of a reductionist view seems to be that it targets specific issues (e.g., medical care *or* social oppression) and draws policymakers' attention to them. Whether this can be done without a reductionist stance is questionable. For instance, Colin Barnes (2004, 22) sees the social model as a tool to help PWD gain political ground and criticizes the academic turn toward medical sociology for its failure to grasp "the enormity of the challenges facing disabled people and their organisations." In addition, Barnes, as well as Oliver (2009; 2013), take issue with the fact that disability scholars, perhaps like medical practitioners, usurp epistemological authority over the concept of disability, removing it from the control of the disability community struggling for recognition. Reciprocally, critics of the social model hold that its focus on oppression fails to attend to the body and impairments as subjectively experienced by PWD (Crow 1996; French 1993; Morris 1991) and is used in the constitution and control of the "disabled subject" (Hughes and Paterson 1997; Liggett 1988; Shildrick and Price 1996; Tremain 2015).

Even as we move into mixed theories of disability, readers may still detect how a reductionist drive influences nonreductionist disability theorists who conceive of disability as a Russian nesting doll. A disability model may well encompass both impairment and disability and both scientifically tested and socially constructed elements. However, theorists often place one of those two sets at the heart of the doll and suspect models that invert the doll's order of imbrication of being unrealistically politicized (e.g., Bury 2000) or overly medicalized (e.g., Oliver 1990).

Mixed Models

Mixed or multifactorial models of disability identify more than one cause of disability or incorporate distinct dimensions of disability within a single definition. Historically, mixed models were a response to the (reductionist) medical and social models of disability. Whereas reductionist models hold that disability means a *or* b *or* c, mixed models hold that disability means "a *and* b," or "a *and* c," or "a *and* b *and* c," etc., wherein a, b, c, etc. denote different dimensions or referents of disability. Mixed models typically define disability as the product of an interaction between physical or psychological facts and social ones. The overall gravity of a disability may then be measured by a contextual benchmark (e.g., functional limitations) although its treatment may be compartmentalized (e.g., physiotherapeutic treatment or reasonable accommodation in the workplace). Mixed models that reconcile individual and environmental causes of disability are mainstream in disability studies (e.g., Bickenbach 2012, 14–15, 79).

Theorists of mixed models also generally pay attention to a constellation of disability-connected notions (such as pathology, impairment, and handicap) as they typically situate disability among those notions or make them constitutive of disability. Reductionists, by contrast, generally assume that their understanding of disability rests on a distinct pillar.

Sociologist Saad Nagi's influential mixed model of disability was one of the first to address the confused multiplicity of concepts falling under the umbrella notion of "disability." His publications on disability span more than four decades, and his latest definition of disability loosens its connection with impairment while incorporating the insights of the social model. He defines disability as "an inability or limitation in performing socially defined roles and tasks expected of an individual within a sociocultural and physical environment" (Nagi 1965; 1991, 315). Another famous example of a mixed model is the WHO's (2002, 9–10) "biopsychosocial model" in which "disability and functioning are viewed as outcomes of interactions between health conditions (diseases, disorders and injuries) and contextual factors."

Whereas the WHO and Nagi models, as well as the social model, can be seen as responses to a reductionist *medical* model of disability, other multifactorial models of disability can be seen as a response to the *social* model's reductionism by emphasizing the significance of impairments in creating people's limitations. This is the case with Tom Shakespeare's (2014, 74) understanding of disability as "always an interaction between individual and structural factors." He conceives of "disability" as an interaction between intrinsic factors, such as impairments, and contextual factors, and he juxtaposes a realist ontology of the former with a constructionist understanding of the latter. Shakespeare calls this "critical realism" (73).[5]

Another strand of multifactorial accounts has suggested that disability is a scalar and universal condition in the sense that all human beings are at risk of some degree of disability over the course of their lives. This approach prevents conditions a, b, and c from acting as demarcations of a special category ("the disabled") by interpreting a, b, and c as universally possessed traits *in potentia* if not in actuality. "[W]ithout such a perspective," Irving Zola wrote in 1989, "we will further create and perpetuate a segregated, separate but unequal society—a society inappropriate to a larger and older 'changing needs' population" (401). Zola's influential model is a kind of mixed model since it recognizes that disability is a function of "the fit between any impairment and the larger social environment" (406).

Multifactorial models do justice to the complexity of disability-related issues. However, they have issues of their own. The main one also affects reductionist accounts: people must meet determinate criteria before being considered "disabled." As a result, certain claims for justice may be denied for reasons that appear formalistic, arbitrary, or substantially misguided. A striking illustration of the humiliation and attrition which PWD and their families are often put through as the result of such a stilted evaluative "grid" is Ken Loach's (2016) movie *I, Daniel Blake*, which depicts disability claimants tormented by Kafkaesque bureaucracy.

Analyzing legal successes and failures, Judith Mosoff (2009, 141) has noted that some disabilities rate lower on a "hierarchy of legitimacy." For instance, people claiming a disabled status due to chronic fatigue or pain, temporary or invisible disabilities, obesity, mental illness or addictions may be suspected to "fake" their condition. Under the Canada Pension Plan (CPP), a person must have "a severe and prolonged mental or physical disability" to be deemed disabled.[6] These criteria are further narrowed with reference to both contextual and biomedical factors, with "severe" defined as "incapable regularly of pursuing any substantially gainful occupation" and "prolonged" as "likely to be long continued and of indefinite duration or is likely to result in death."[7] Allan

Granovsky's temporary, intermittent disability prevented him from working sufficiently to access CPP. In *Granovsky v. Canada*, he challenged this definition of disability. The Supreme Court of Canada decided, however, that the legislation was not discriminatory as "drawing lines is an unavoidable feature of the CPP" and because Parliament was entitled to not provide benefits for "more fortunate people" who do not have a permanent disability.[8]

Problems resulting from fixed criteria can involve laws and policies but also daily interactions with people who often implicitly endorse a lay disability model of some kind. For example, a young man with an invisible disability that requires him to sit may be frowned at if he were to ask someone to give up his seat on a bus. Conversely, Anita Silvers (2003, 478) describes how offering wheelchair users the chance to cut in line at the post office assumes they are suffering when in fact they may be more comfortable waiting than those who are standing. Part of the issue is that *interpreters* of disability models are biased, but I am more interested in the fact that reductionist and mixed accounts of disability simply exclude new (or continuously ignored) but legitimate disability-based claims. They use a fixed[9] list of steady features (physiological or social) to determine if a condition is a disability or not.

Faced with such problems, proponents of mixed, determinate models suggest refinements in order to better capture those whose disability should be recognized and exclude those who should not benefit from that recognition (e.g., Bickenbach 2012). Critics of determinate models may agree that under- or overinclusiveness can be perpetually corrected, but they argue that a commitment to fixity of criteria, in spite of its pragmatic virtues (namely, that the law needs bright lines), is conceptually wrongheaded. In particular, the assumption that disability is a fixed, rather than evolving, concept invites the question: Why start with the goal of developing a determinate account at all? Descriptively, it may not do justice to the extraordinary variety and evolving cultural nature of "disability." Moreover, even though a determinate model may be more or less successful at enabling the identification of nearly all cases of disability, it is not clear we should endorse a framework that inevitably excludes those deemed "peripheral cases." Finally, determinate models might fail even on their own terms, as point-based policies construct disability instead of merely "capturing" it. According to critics, these models invite people to constitute themselves as disabled subjects, create disability and abnormality, and serve to control both able-bodied and disabled people (Shildrick and Price 1996; Tremain 2001). Determinate models' inherent lack of flexibility risks excluding some people and normalizing others, thus becoming tools at the service of ideologies rather than at the service of the likes of Daniel Blake and Allan Granovsky.

Mixed models can also produce conceptual issues, as the ambition to provide a unified understanding of disability can exacerbate the contradictions between a model's conceptual components. Many debates around disability would dissolve if competing sides recognized that they are concerned with different phenomena, problems, or values. In other words, mixed models include an assumption of commensurability, or at least of coherence between the constitutive elements of disability, which causes unnecessary clashes between theorists or practitioners who are expected to explain how their compartmentalized goal fits within this holistic outlook and coheres with other specific goals.

To sum up our conclusions so far:

Determinate models of disability (including both reductionist and mixed models) set up stable qualifying criteria that may lack flexibility to accommodate unusual, new, peripheral, or otherwise neglected disability-related claims that are nonetheless morally compelling. The virtue of determinate models is that they lead to a stable, uniform, predictable, and efficacious basis for disability claims.

Reductionist models of disability have generally fallen into disfavor amongst theorists and policy discourses because they tend to neglect the diversity of causes and experiences of disability, although many agree that the social model has been politically effective than its alternatives (Thomas 1999, 16). The medical model also remains *de facto* influential, if not an unspoken *status quo* tempered mostly by the increasing presence of disability rights in public discourses. (Legal, political, and medical actors may act in a way that suggests that disability is primarily a biological issue, while paying lip service to more progressive models. This reflects a clash between theory and political rhetorics, on the one hand, and longstanding cultural practices lagging behind, on the other.)

Mixed (typically medico-social) models are the most influential and mainstream models, probably because they are thought (correctly or not) to offer a compromise between medical expertise and activist critiques, a descriptively superior outlook compared to reductionist models, and potentially useful qualifying criteria.

Second-Order Accounts of Disability

"Open-ended" approaches employ more abstract criteria in identifying disability. These criteria are still determinate in the sense that they conceive of limits on what can count as disability. They are more open-ended, however, since they propose generalized content to delineate disability or focus on the process for determining disability rather than providing specific descriptors.

Open-Ended Referents

David Wasserman (2000, 158) pushed for an open-ended stance toward disability when he argued that the American with Disabilities Act (ADA) should be extended to provide protection "to all disfavored physical and mental differences." This proposal relies on the notion of stigma to give shape to disability. The ADA, he says, should "challenge discrimination based on physical or mental difference" rather than only "protect a vulnerable class of people bearing the most salient or substantial difference" (148).

Wasserman's argument would enable the ADA to consider kinds of unfair discrimination (e.g., those related to norms of beauty and sexual attraction) that currently elude discrimination law.

Content-based open-ended accounts have the virtue of allowing theorists, activists, and policymakers to ask whether and to what extent the notion of "disability" should be extended to capture those not-yet-theorized or politically recognized social ills. Consider the following cases: (1) someone who is disfigured by neurofibromatosis; (2) someone who is disfigured by a fire; (3) someone whose face is heavily tattooed and whose nose, ears, eyes, lips etc. are pierced with a great number of rings; and (4) someone who wakes up from a coma to discover they were involuntarily tattooed and pierced in the same way. Many criteria used to evaluate a discrimination claim (the presence or absence of choice, limitation, or impairment) would fail to detect the "lookism" that unifies all four cases.

On the other hand, consider Savulescu and Kahane's (2011, 45) "welfarist" account of disability as a biological or psychological state that "makes it more likely that a person's life will get worse, in terms of his or her own well-being, in a given set of social and environmental circumstances." Consider, also, Tom Koch's (2008) claim that Tom Shakespeare is not disabled by his achondroplasia but rather by his decreased influence within, or rejection from, parts of the disability community because of his controversial views. Koch defines disability as any state of affairs (including choices made by relatively socially privileged individuals) that undermines an individual's power or ascendency. Kahane and Savulescu's (2009) account captures "stable intrinsic properties" that are not typically thought of as disability even though they significantly diminish individual well-being in particular circumstances (such as being gay in a homophobic society). Koch's suggestion is even more radical, detaching the concept of disability from the notions of body, normality, or significant negative effect on well-being. While open-ended accounts of disability can expand the concept of disability in fruitful ways, others can be excessively broad in that they fail to even consider our ordinary intuitions about "disability" and to explain why they should be discarded.

One promising kind of open-ended account focuses on process, offering a mechanism to decide the rules according to which disability will be identified and/or dealt with. This sort of account provides rules about rules. It has the virtue of avoiding substantive disagreements by developing agreement on a way to handle such disputes.

An example of this kind of process-based, open-ended account is Elizabeth Barnes's (2016, 38) "moderate social constructionism," which posits disability as "rule-based solidarity." She argues that disability was shaped by "a form of group solidarity" where "[a]lthough they had a strikingly heterogenous range of physical conditions, they perceived a commonality in how those physical conditions were stigmatized" (46). Barnes does not think that a bodily feature should be a disability only because the disability community says it is and adds an important further procedural constraint on identifying "disability." This identification must rely on *rules*. The disability movement has the authority to make rules to identify disability rather than the authority to directly identify disability. Barnes thus makes room for the movement to be mistaken in applying its own rules, but not, *ex definitio*, in making the rules in the first place. This latter authority is exposed to diverse criticism, but Barnes would likely defend it as the best available way to counterbalance the testimonial injustice that paradigmatically "disabled people" suffer from.

According to Barnes (2016, 45), the "disability rights movement" tends to consider a person to be "disabled" if they possess a sufficient number of features it associates with disability. These are instances of first-order rules (R1) to identify disability. While R1 remain *open*, Barnes's (2016, 48) model includes *fixed* notions about how R1 are to be decided, which I refer to as second-order rules (R2). These include the requirement that R1 are to be decided by members of the "disability rights movement," that their content relies on "judgements of solidarity," and that their normative orientation relies on a theory of justice (Barnes 2016, 28).

Open-Ended Values

So far, I have discussed open-ended accounts that give constraints on, but do not offer definitive lists of, conditions that counts as disability. This open-endedness applies to *referents*. Theories can also be *axiologically* open-ended: they may allow for the same disability referent to be valued positively, neutrally, or negatively depending on the context. There is intuitive appeal to such a perspective, given that having a mild intellectual disability and being in a wheelchair have different repercussions in a preindustrial farming context compared to a society trading knowledge as valuable currency. Many in the disability movement have deplored the general assumption that PWD are necessarily made worse off by their disability and urged the development of a culture that sees disability in a more positive light (e.g., Morris 1991). Both Elizabeth Barnes (2016, chaps. 3, 6) and Anita Silvers (1998; 2003) have countered that assumption and argue that the value of disability should be left open-ended. Silvers also writes (2003, 475–476), conversely, that disability activists must refrain from insisting that all medical treatments or social measures to eliminate or cure disability are necessarily wrongheaded.

A worry one might have with these open-ended accounts is that they are still not inclusive enough. A more radical approach to "disability" renounces this universalizing goal as irreparably misguided, doomed to exclude human difference rather than welcome it, and to accidentally recreate and foster the conditions of exclusion, oppression, or marginalization which it sought to transcend. Such views are associated with postmodernism, which "fragment[s] the concept of identity" and "substitute[s] a fluid, shifting notion of a process of becoming that defines neither its own corporeal boundaries nor a fixed content" (Price and Shildrick 2002, 62). Such perspectives challenge the "ingrained tendency for disability activists and scholars to claim a clear set of identities *as* disabled people" (Price and Shildrick 2002, 62). While second-order accounts of disability avoid settling on a stable definition of disability and instead look for a stable method to get to that definition, radically open-ended accounts resist *any* notion of determinacy.

RADICALLY OPEN-ENDED
ACCOUNTS OF "DISABILITY"

What does it mean to take seriously the open-endedness of the concept of disability? What would a model embracing the fact that disability has many, evolving, referents look like? What would its strengths and weaknesses be? Radically open-ended understandings of disability do not necessarily abandon the concept of "disability" but instead encourage its adherents to (1) specify the particular meaning or referent they have in mind while (2) remaining aware that disability's pluralistic and fluctuating nature can encapsulate a variety of ethical problems and (3) consider whether different referents could be compatible instead of contradictory in the case at hand. They also (4) encourage disability theorists and practitioners to cultivate a critical distance from the concept of disability, even as they deploy it to achieve desirable ends. This critical distance requires awareness that the very use of "disability" risks reasserting the problematic ideologies, affects, and conceptual and psychosocial imaginaries upon which the concept (perhaps inevitably) rests.

The invitation to recognize the indeterminacy of one's own choice of referent(s) may be trivialized as an acknowledgment of fallibility or ridiculed as legitimizing any (e.g., a Nazi) model of disability. I believe it survives these criticisms as well as more serious objections, though it also has substantial limitations.

Radically open-ended approaches stem from dissatisfaction with determinate accounts that seek to define disability in a unitary or universalizing way. They challenge the assumption that the philosophy of disability fails us if it does not provide us with a unified concept. What is lost in stability, they say, is gained in critical capacity. This critical outlook answers the dilemma of specificity by prioritizing long-term over short-term emancipation.[10] Its proponents concede that medical, social, or civil rights models of disability can helpfully orchestrate the pursuit of specific goals to improve the well-being of PWD while insisting that these models will not challenge the issues at the heart of the problem. Those include the "fundamental binary of disabled/non-disabled," the "psycho-social imaginary that disavows morphological imperfections" (Shildrick 2009, 5–6), the powerful negative affective responses felt toward differences, and the "metahistorical narratives that exclude important dimensions of disabled people's lives and of their knowledge" (Corker and Shakespeare 2002, 15). Those powerful vectors undermining the well-being of PWD can only be challenged by radically "reconfigur[ing] the meaning of disability [in order to] disrupt the whole nature of the relationship between differently embodied subjects" (Shildrick 2009, 171).

Such approaches maintain a skeptical stance toward the possibility of a better unitary theory of disability because such a theory inevitably involves the exclusionary and reductionist tendencies they criticize. Even a more complex, multilayered theory of disability would "misleadingly fix what is fluid and reduce what is multidimensional to a few impoverished aspects" (Silvers 2003, 228). Margrit Shildrick (2009, 172) writes that she "refuses to flatten out the multiple layers of significance and meaning" and argues that what critical disability theory needs "is not to settle on a singular perspective...but rather to continue a process of intersectional exploration that is not afraid to utilize critique even in the absence of an alternative way forward." Proponents of a radically open-ended account of disability think that determinate value-neutral accounts of disability are compelling because of the plurality of evaluations they invite, not because of any unitary notion of disability they put forward.

Proponents of radically open-ended approaches aim at developing a more nuanced and holistic description of disability as a phenomenon that is not only collectively engineered but also subjectively experienced in a variety of ways, including as a constituent part of one's identity. They also problematize the boundaries of the concept of disability or the social structures within which it is used and do not shy away from testing its elasticity to the point of radically transforming its purpose.

Critics of an open-ended approach would say, however, that agreeing to disagree does not move a philosophical discussion very far, and conceptual breadth comes at the cost of a conversationally sterile incommensurability. As indicated by the dilemma of specificity mentioned before, there is also the risk that too fluid, broad, or thin a conception of disability will be politically inert.

The strongest criticism of radically open-ended approaches comes, as one would expect, from the reductionist end of the spectrum. In particular, "first wave" disability theorists (e.g., Barnes 2013, 9; Oliver 2013, 1026), have strongly criticized the political efficacy of "second wave" perspectives. They argue that the focus on subjective experiences and deconstructing categories has distracted from the all-important, concrete emancipatory goals advocated by disability rights movements. For instance, the hope that a critique of the cultural depreciation of the "disabled body" would correct economic inequality ignores the fact that markets "generate economic inequalities that are not mere expressions of identity hierarchies" (Fraser 2000, 112; Vehmas and Watson 2014, 647). However, one may reply that open-ended approaches can create avenues for new kinds of emancipatory self-understandings. The matter is therefore complicated, since, even if we agree with the position that disability research should be unabashedly partisan and "should be judged in terms of its capacity to facilitate the empowerment of disabled people" (Mercer 2002, 245), empowerment may be understood in conflicting ways.

An open-ended outlook on disability can also be criticized for squandering hard-earned political capital related to the term "disability." However, this claim is much narrower than a broad rejection of nonreductionist models and needs to be substantiated on a case-by-case basis. For instance, a pluralistic understanding of disability may become a distraction within a particular discourse (e.g., within the legal discourse and, more specifically, within a single judicial decision or a single statutory framework). However, in most cases where courts, policymakers, and legislators are criticized for not properly attending to disability issues, scholars attribute their failures to a paucity, not an excess, of conceptual options.

Postmodern and poststructuralist writers are well aware that disabled activists will struggle with radically open-ended models. They are complicated and difficult to comprehend without an understanding of their philosophical underpinnings (Corker and Shakespeare 2002; Pfeiffer 2001). Critical disability theorists must endeavor to remedy this practical issue. A more substantial problem, however, is that some accounts of disability can simply not be operationalized within existing legal and political frameworks, insofar as they challenge some basic liberal assumptions underlying them. Take, for instance, Foucault's (2003) notion of the "monstrous" as being partly defined by the fact that its existence is a challenge *to* the legal order, or Derrida's (2000) ethical call for absolute hospitality which precludes asking guests to identify themselves before agreeing to host them. Such ideas are powerful but clearly difficult, if not impossible, to operationalize *within* a liberal legal order. I am optimistic in thinking that disability theorists can nonetheless go a long way in making at least some of those radical solutions palatable within our liberal framework, even as we continue to criticize some fundamental tenets of said framework (Beaudry 2017). Besides, even an open-ended understanding of disability, which seems to be "virtually unusable" before courts, may have great impact on legal culture.[11]

Proponents of radically open-ended accounts therefore have different intuitions regarding the best way to solve the dilemma of specificity. They acknowledge that their "critics find intolerable . . . that the question of what comes next is deliberately left open" (Shildrick 2009, 171) but believe that alternative modes of struggle fail to address what disability truly is: a complex, never static, relational, discursive phenomenon, reproduced by "normals" and "abnormals" alike, and emancipatory only when used as an object of deconstruction.

Proponents of determinate accounts may answer that such cultural critiques take the romantic tone of revolutionary movements, the success of which seems less likely than piecemeal strategies. Yet they may at least come to terms with what radically open-ended accounts have to offer by using them to think about disability referents in novel ways, keeping our minds open to many complicated factors that we might not have otherwise noticed while resisting the view that disability is an undefinable concept or is nothing but a call for dialogue, expression, or resistance surrounding different human embodiments. In other words, they may use such ironic, critical postures as ethical constraints upon theorists of disability rather than as theories of disability. However, true reconciliation seems impossible. Taking a critical posture seriously requires theorists of determinate accounts to water them down to a vague unified definition (e.g., "different embodiment"). Those who advance determinate theories would not find this conceptually illuminating or politically useful. Those who develop critiques of culture and power would answer that nothing less will do: even if they try to make the best of current emancipatory tools, theorists of determinate accounts of disability are unwitting accomplices of apparatuses of power over "disabled subjects" (Tremain 2001; 2015).

CONCLUSION

In this chapter, I have argued that polysemy is a philosophically interesting feature of disability and that some theoretical disagreements about disability are productively articulated as disagreements about how to handle that polysemy. I have categorized and examined the main philosophical strategies—from reductionism to radical open-endedness—to manage the semantic breadth of the term "disability" in descriptively or normatively helpful ways. I presented some of the strengths and weaknesses of each view. I suggest that they may be deployed simultaneously if they do not pursue inevitably clashing goals. They may not clash as often as their apparently mutually exclusive theoretical commitments suggest, as they at least often converge in their ambition to improve the well-being of people who regard themselves or are regarded as PWDs, simply addressing different facets of this well-being and justifying different practices to improve it.

Negotiating the coexistence of a multiplicity of disability models does not imply the need to completely abandon the concept of disability in favor of more specific notions. "Disability" remains a term that at least denotes or connotes "abnormal, exceptional, or different embodiments," including phenomena entirely external to the bodies of "disabled persons" (such as prejudices directed at imagined embodiments or strictly cultural artifacts). It is a useful commonality between a constellation of discourses that relate to objects that are at least united by this family resemblance and may overlap or interact with each other, even though it is unlikely that a "master theory" would neatly choreograph all such interactions. This view does not require giving up on the various disability theories and models that exist. It only circumscribes their ambition to provide an all-encompassing framework to deal with a cluster of shifting dilemmas and moderates their "romantic optimism that all the values we cherish ultimately will fit into a single system, that no one of them has to be sacrificed or compromised to accommodate another" (Hart 1958, 620).

Acknowledgments

The author thanks his research assistants, Gabe Boothroyd, Ian Heckman, and Mark Iyengar, for their meticulous editorial support, as well as Professors Adam Cureton and David Wasserman for their insightful comments.

Notes

1. Such as preventing them from benefitting from certain disability benefits (Altman 2001).
2. The more clearly defined a goal is, the easier it is to monitor; and the more clearly defined the conditions of application of a rule are, the less controversial is its application to particular cases.
3. Wasserman et al. (2016) write that "[t]he medical model is rarely defended, but often adopted unreflectively by health care professionals, bioethicists, and philosophers who fail to appreciate the disabling effects of environmental and social factors." The closest I have found to an explicit defense of the medical model is Dominic Sisti's (2014, 1) argument that "a naturalist theory of function may serve as the core concept of disability." Sisti's position invites the question: a naturalist understanding of disability *may* be placed at the heart of the concept of disability, but why *should* it? His argument relies on a naturalist understanding of the ontology of impairment, most commonly associated with Christopher Boorse's (1977) biological and value-free understanding of health, disease, and pathologies. Sisti points to Boorse's naturalist understanding of *pathology* and Vehmas and Mäkelä's (2008)

partially naturalist understanding of *impairment*, but these authors explicitly do not extend their naturalist outlook to the concept of disability.

4. Consider, e.g., Kahane and Savulescu (2009), Harris (2001), Singer (2004), McMahan (2005), and Daniels (2007). Criticizing those views, see Morris (1991), Vehmas (1999), Silvers (1998; 2003), and Barnes (2016). Critics of the social model declare that it belongs to the past (Shakespeare and Watson 2001), while its defenders claim we need it for the future (C. Barnes 2013; Oliver 2013). I have argued elsewhere that this disagreement does not prevent philosophers from imagining tomorrow's vocabulary for disabled identities *and* reflecting on the propriety of postulating reductionist definitions when it is politically opportunistic (Beaudry, 2018).

5. Here, as in other disability discussions, it is not obvious whether those views would best be described as a combined, distinct metaphysical view ("critical realism") applied to a holistic concept of disability or, rather, as two ontological views, each suited to understanding different kinds of disability referents.

6. *Canada Pension Plan*, RSC, 1985, c C-8, s 42(2).

7. Ibid.

8. *Granovsky v. Canada (Minister of Employment and Immigration)*, 2000 SCC 28, [2000] 1 SCR 703 at para 79.

9. Those lists of atypical functions and social features are not definitively *closed*; most mixed models would consider amending them. However, both the lists and processes of amendments are rigid in a way that risks being harmful or unfairly burdensome on claimants.

10. Of course, disability theorists who disagree are not against long-term emancipation. Instead, they think that it will be brought about by using the traditional legal and political frameworks and liberal theories that postmodern and poststructuralists question.

11. Consider Wasserman (2000, 156), who notes how a more open-ended (stigma-based, legal) conception of disability would be much harder to successfully use in legal proceedings, but nonetheless advocates its adoption on the basis of its overall impact.

REFERENCES

Altman, Barbara M. 2001. "Disability Definitions, Models, Classification Schemes, and Applications." In *Handbook of Disability Studies*, edited by Gary L. Albrecht, Katherine D. Seelman, and Michael Bury, 97–122. London: Sage Publications.

Barnes, Colin. 2004. "Disability, Disability Studies and The Academy." In *Disabling Barriers, Enabling Environments*, edited by John Swain, Sally French, Colin Barnes, and Carol Thomas, 28–33.

Barnes, Colin. 2013. "Disability Studies and the Academy: Past, Present and Future." *Vivendi Journal* 4(March): 3–12.

Barnes, Elizabeth. 2016. *The Minority Body: A Theory of Disability*. New York: Oxford University Press.

Beaudry, Jonas-Sébastien. 2016. "Beyond (Models of) Disability?" *The Journal of Medicine and Philosophy* 41(2): 210–228.

Beaudry, Jonas-Sébastien. 2017. "Welcoming Monsters: Disability as a Liminal Legal Concept." *Yale Journal of Law and Humanities* 29(2): 291–338.

Beaudry, Jonas-Sébastien. 2018. "The Vanishing Body of Disability Law: Power and the Making of the Impaired Subject." *Canadian Journal of Family Law* 31(1): 7–56.

Bickenbach, Jerome E. 2012. "Disability Key Issues and Future Directions." In *Ethics, Law, and Policy* edited by Gary L. Albrecht (volume 6). Sage.

Boorse, Christopher. 1977. "Health as a Theoretical Concept." *Philosophy of Science* 44(4): 542–573.

Boorse, Christopher. 2009. "Disability and Medical Theory." In *Philosophical Reflections on Disability*, edited by D. Christopher Ralston and Justin H. Ho, 55–90. Dordrecht: Springer.

Bury, Michael. 2000. "On Chronic Illness and Disability." In *Handbook of Medical Sociology*, 5th ed., edited by Peter Conrad, Chloe Bird, and Allen Fremont, 173–183. New Jersey, PA: Prentice Hall.

Corker, Mairian, and Tom Shakespeare. 2002. "Mapping the Terrain." In *Disability/ Postmodernity: Embodying Disability Theory*, edited by Mairian Corker and Tom Shakespeare, 1–17. London: Continuum.

Crow, Liz. 1996. "Renewing the Social Model of Disability." In *Encounters with Strangers: Feminism and Disability*, edited Jenny Morris. London: Women's Press.

Daniels, Norman. 2007. *Just Health: Meeting Health Needs Fairly*. Cambridge: Cambridge University Press.

Derrida, Jacques. 2000. "Hostipitality." *Angelaki: Journal of Theoretical Humanities* 5(3): 3–18.

Fraser, Nancy. 2000. "Rethinking Recognition." *New Left Review* 3(May–June): 107–120.

French, Sally. 1993. Disability, impairment or something in between? In *Disabling barriers-enabling environments*, edited by John Swain, Vic Finkelstein, Salially French, and Michael Oliver, 17–25. London: Sage.

Foucault, Michel. 2003. *Abnormal*. Edited by V. Marchetti and A. Salomina. Translated by G. Burchell. London: Verso.

Harris, John. 2001. "One Principle and Three Fallacies of Disability Studies." *Journal of Medical Ethics* 27(6): 383–387.

Hart, Herbert L. A. 1958. "Positivism and the Separation of Law and Morals." *Harvard Law Review* 71(4/February): 593–629.

Hughes, Bill, and Paterson, Kevin. 1997. "The Social Model of Disability and the Disappearing Body: Towards a Sociology of Impairment." *Disability and Society* 12(3): 325–340.

Kahane, Guy, and Julian Savulescu. 2009. "The Welfarist Account of Disability." In *Disability and Disadvantage*, edited by Kimberley Brownlee and Adam Steven Cureton, 14–53. New York: Oxford University Press.

Koch, Tom. 2008. "Is Tom Shakespeare Disabled?" *Journal of Medical Ethics* 34(1): 18–20.

Liggett, Helen. 1988. "Stars Are Not Born: An Interpretive Approach to the Politics of Disability." *Disability, Handicap and Society* 3(3): 263–275.

Loach, Ken, director. 2016. *I, Daniel Blake*. Produced by Sixteen Films, Why Not Productions, and Wild Bunch.

Lysias. 1930. *Lysias*, translated by W. R. M. Lamb. Cambridge, MA: Harvard University Press.

McMahan, Jeff. 2005. "Causing Disabled People to Exist and Causing People to Be Disabled." *Ethics* 116(1): 77–99.

Mercer, Geof. 2002. "Emancipatory Disability Research." In *Disability Studies Today*, edited by Colin Barnes, Michael Oliver, and Barton Len, 228–249. Cambridge: Polity Press.

Morris, Jenny. 1991. *Pride Against Prejudice: A Personal Politics of Disability*. Ann Arbor, MI: Women's Press.

Mosoff, Judith. 2009. "Lost in Translation: The Disability Perspective in Honda V. Keays and Hydro-Quebec V. Syndicat." *McGill Journal of Law and Health* 3: 137.

Nagi, Saad Z. 1965. "Some Conceptual Issues in Disability and Rehabilitation." In *Sociology and Rehabilitation*, edited by Marvin B. Sussman, 100. Washington, DC: American Sociological Society.

Nagi, Saad Z. 1991. "Disability Concepts Revisited: Implications for Prevention." In *Disability in America: Toward a National Agenda For Prevention*, edited by Andrew M. Pope and Alvin R. Tarlov, 309–327. Washington, DC: National Academies Press.

Oliver, Michael. 1990. *The Politics of Disablement: A Sociological Approach*. New York: MacMillan.

Oliver, Michael. 1999. "Capitalism, Disability and Ideology: A Materialist Critique of the Normalization Principle." In *A Quarter-Century of Normalization and Social Role Valorization: Evolution and Impact*, edited by Robert J. Flynn and Raymond A. Lemay, 163–173. Ottawa: University of Ottawa Press.

Oliver, Michael. 2009. "The Social Model in Context." In *Rethinking Normalcy: A Disability Studies Reader*, edited by Rod Michalko and Tanya Titchkosky, 19–30. Toronto: Canadian Scholars' Press.

Oliver, Mike. 2013. "The Social Model of Disability: Thirty Years On." *Disability and Society* 28(7): 1024–1026.

Pfeiffer, David. 2001. "The Conceptualization of Disability." In *Exploring Theories and Expanding Methodologies: Where We Are and Where We Need To Go*, edited by Sharon N. Barnartt and Barbara M. Altman, 29–52. Amsterdam; New York: JAI Press.

Price, Janet, and Margrit Shildrick. 2002. "Bodies Together: Touch, Ethics and Disability." In *Disability/Postmodernity: Embodying Disability Theory*, edited by Mairian Corker and Tom Shakespeare, 62. London: Continuum.

Shildrick, Margrit, and Janet Price. 1996. "Breaking the Boundaries of the Broken Body." *Body & Society* 2(4): 93–113.

Savulescu, Julian, and Guy Kahane. 2011. "Disability: A Welfarist Approach." *Clinical Ethics* 6(1): 45–51.

Shakespeare, Tom. 1999. "What Is a Disabled Person." In *Disability, Divers-Ability and Legal Change*, edited by Melinda Jones and Lee Ann Basser Marks, 25–34. The Hague: Kluwer Law International.

Shakespeare, Tom. 2014. *Disability Rights and Wrongs Revisited*, 2nd ed. New York: Routledge.

Shakespeare, Tom, and Nicholas Watson. 2001. "The Social Model of Disability: An Outdated Ideology?" In *Exploring Theories and Expanding Methodologies: Where We Are and Where We Need To Go*, edited by Sharon N. Barnartt and Barbara M. Altman, 9–28. Amsterdam; New York: JAI Press.

Shildrick, Margrit. 2009. *Dangerous Discourses of Disability, Subjectivity and Sexuality*. New York: Palgrave Macmillan.

Silvers, Anita. 1998. "A Fatal Attraction to Normalizing: Treating Disabilities as Deviations From Species-Typical Functioning." In *Enhancing Human Traits: Ethical and Social Implications*, edited by Erik Parens, 95–123. Washington, DC: Georgetown University Press.

Silvers, Anita. 2003. "On the Possibility and Desirability of Constructing a Neutral Conception of Disability." *Theoretical Medicine and Bioethics* 24(6): 471.

Silvers, Anita, and Leslie Pickering Francis. 2005. "Justice Through Trust: Disability and the 'Outlier Problem' in Social Contract Theory." *Ethics* 116(1): 40.

Singer, Peter. 2004. "Ethics and Disability: A Response to Koch." *Journal of Disability Policy Studies* 16(2): 130.

Sisti, Dominic A. 2014. "Naturalism and the Social Model of Disability: Allied or Antithetical?" *Journal of Medical Ethics* 41: 553–556.

Thomas, Carol. 2004. "How Is Disability Understood? An Examination of Sociological Approaches." *Disability and Society* 19(6): 569.

Thomas, Carol. 1999. *Female Forms: Experiencing and Understanding Disability*. Buckingham: Open University Press.

Tremain, Shelley. 2001. "On the Government of Disability." *Social Theory and Practice* 27(4): 617.

Tremain, Shelley, ed. 2015. *Foucault and the Government of Disability*. Ann Arbor: University of Michigan Press.

Union of the Physically Impaired Against Segregation (UPIAS). 1976. *Fundamental Principles of Disability*. London: UPIAS.

Vehmas, Simo. 1999. "Discriminative Assumptions of Utilitarian Bioethics Regarding Individuals with Intellectual Disabilities." *Disability and Society* 14(1): 37.

Vehmas, Simo, and Pekka Mäkelä. 2008. "A Realist Account of the Ontology of Impairment." *Journal of Medical Ethics* 34(2): 93.

Vehmas, Simo, and Nick Watson. 2014. "Moral Wrongs, Disadvantages, and Disability: A Critique of Critical Disability Studies." *Disability and Society* 29(4): 638–650.

Wasserman, David. 2000. "Stigma Without Impairment: Demedicalizing Disability Discrimination." In *Americans with Disabilities: Exploring Implications of the Law for Individuals and Institutions*, edited by Leslie Francis and Anita Silvers, 146–162. New York: Routledge.

Wasserman, David, Adrienne Asch, Jeffrey Blustein, and Daniel Putnam. 2016. "Disability: Definitions, Models, Experience." In *The Stanford Encyclopedia of Philosophy*, edited by Edward N. Zalta. Available at https://plato.stanford.edu/archives/sum2016/entries/disability/.

World Health Organization (WHO). 2002. "Towards a Common Language for Functioning, Disability and Health." Available at http://www.who.int/classifications/icf/icfbeginners-guide.pdf?ua=1

Zola, Irving Kenneth. 1989. "Toward the Necessary Universalizing of a Disability Policy." *The Milbank Quarterly*: 67 (Supplement 2, part 2) 401–428.

CHAPTER 2

IN PURSUIT OF JUSTICE FOR DISABILITY: MODEL NEUTRALITY REVISITED

ANITA SILVERS

INTRODUCTION

THIS chapter's discussion is aimed at clearing away confusion about the uses of models of disability that contributes to ongoing conflicts about who is disabled and what ascribing disability means.[1] Understanding why modeling disability is undertaken and what modeling disability does will help to indicate whether the differentia that models of disability ascribe are mere differences or whether instead judging such differences as bad rather than neutral is integral to modeling disability.

I'll apply accounts of modeling to an ongoing debate: disagreement about whether generalized models of disability can or should be normative rather than neutral.[2] That disability is a normative concept could render it "essentially contested," (Gallie 1956, 167–198; MacIntyre 1973, 1–9; McKnight 2003, 261–262; Silvers 2003, 471–487) meaning that although generally accepted paradigm instances exist, models differ in regard to the relative importance of various elements, and ascription is open-ended, with modifications being neither predictable nor prescribed in advance. These are features of "essentially contested concepts," designated as such because they are subject to irresolvable dispute.[3]

Proper disability policy is sometimes presumed to be derivable from normative models that specify the distinguishing features and distinctive value of being disabled.[4] But neither theorists, nor policymakers, nor service providers, nor advocacy, nor affinity, nor other organized disability groups agree even amongst themselves as to which models are best adopted (Wasserman, Asch, Blustein, and Putnam 2016). Shaped by their own different experiences of living with a disability or of intimately assisting someone who lives this way, each disabled person or caregiver may endeavor to foreground personal perspectives and priorities by which they believe disability theory ought to be informed and inspired. Thus, seemingly ceaseless struggle about what disability is has proliferated, not least among individuals who have direct experience of living with disability.

Models of disability may be used to represent being disabled or (in fancier language) experiencing or living a disability-inflected life. We can begin understanding what modeling a notion like disability involves through discussions of two main functions of modeling: classifying and explaining. Subsequently, discussion will turn to a third function, appraising, which is pursued by proponents of designating disability as a "bad" kind of difference. (Kahane and Savulescu 2016, 774–788; Barnes 2016a, 295–309). Appraisive models invite rather than resolve contestation (McKnight 2003).

Modeling

The process and products of modeling disability serve at least two importantly different roles. One is that models may be used as standards or guides for identifying or classifying individuals. But models also may be used to prompt or convey explanations of how or why individuals acquire properties or characteristics on which their identification or categorization turns. These might be deemed empirical models, whose features are drawn from encounters with individuals or instances sorted into a class. Although distinguishable, these two modeling processes often are co-temporaneous and, moreover, they often interact.

Modeling for the former purpose is typically pursued to facilitate aggregation of individuals into categories based on important similarities or affinities they share. When in this classificatory mode, models serve as definitive instances or examples. They function as standards, patterns or prototypes or typical, definitive or canonical instances by illustrating the character that underwrites recognition or authorizes conferral of group or class membership.

A model may be a partial or full image or other sort of facsimile or imitation of what it represents. Rather than providing a typical or commonplace example, however, modeling in the classificatory mode may instead provide a perfected instance, paragon, or ideal that indicates or establishes what attributes an instance of the kind of thing in question should be expected to possess. Modeling in this aspirational mode usually manifests a full complement of attributes relevant to determining that an individual should be included or is eligible to participate as a member of the categorized group.

Objects functioning as near replicas with the same model need not possess all the properties that could be relevant to their purpose. Facsimiles or imitations sketch or otherwise simplify the object or token of interest in order to facilitate learning about its type, whether about common or exceptional instances. Thus, for example, we draw floor plans of differently configured condominiums in the same building. The floor plans are skeletonized renditions that may be taken in with one or a few glances. From them, prospective buyers can quickly find out such facts as the number of bedrooms and of baths and their proximity to each other, the path from the kitchen stove to the place where a dining table might go, and so on. They thus can identify the abodes most compatible with their needs and hence most suitable to inspect in person. Floor plans are models that guide our choices for week-end home-viewing so that this phase of home-buying may become manageable.

To take an example from another cognitive domain: Aristotle famously analyzed tragic theatrical pieces as imitations of events so horrendous when actually encountered that observers of a real world scene become frozen with fear and sorrow and incapable of action (Silvers 2000). Appraisal of the central figure of the plot is instrumental in determining whether the portrayal is of a tragic hero and thereby whether the dramatic imitation of events models a tragedy at all. For Aristotle, eligibility to be such a protagonist requires being eminently respectable but flawed by over-confidence or some other kind of over-reach (Aristotle 1961). By presenting an imitation of tragic events befalling that protagonist, the playwright and actors permit audience members to study the sad situation the play portrays and to reach a resolution without being overwhelmed by their own understandably tumultuous feelings. Tragedies thus enable us to theorize about such personally threatening circumstances in preparation for knowing how to act were we to encounter the real thing.

We can acknowledge that two objects with quite different properties are modeled after the same thing. Think, for example, of the vast differences between Man Ray's realistic photographed portrait of Dora Maar and Picasso's cubist paintings for which Dora Maar modeled. Yet both these very different configurations portray Dora Maar (Silvers 2000).

Models can fail their purposes in several ways. In regard to their classificatory function, they can be under-inclusive, usually by treating a component as necessary when it is only a contingency for some of the model's most obvious referents, or over-inclusive by treating a component as a sufficient condition for membership in the category when its occurrences commonly extend far beyond the model's least obvious references.

In regard to explanation, models can misdirect by imposing a fruitless depictive frame. An example from molecular biology, more precisely from molecular phylogenetics, illustrates. Until close to the end of the twentieth century, the evolutionary story of species was modeled on the form of a tree, with new kinds (species) developing at the ends, as extensions, of branches. Thus the presence or contributions of genes that characterized species and influenced what, on the molecular level, species members did and did not do, were explained in the branching-tree model's terms, as being alterations of growth at the end of the branch and therefore fully accounted for by lineal descent from a molecular forebear, that is, by a molecular lineage within the species. This was how, on the branching-tree model, life diversified.

But a different model was needed as molecular biology progressed amid increasing observations that some subsets of individuals within species (and sometimes the entire population of a species) can have genes more characteristic of other species than of those within their species' own boundary. In other words, improving technology reveals that humans have genes sourced not from our primate lineage and not found in other primates but apparently coming directly from nonprimate sources, a fact that some scientists who study biological systems consider to have impacted human identity (Quammen 2018). Such genes might be absent from most primates but show up, inexplicably on the lineal model of diversification, in some or all humans. They must have passed laterally, not lineally, sometimes even from other kingdoms of life. Moreover, the lineal descendant model had no place for a "transforming principle" to explain phenomena such as strains of bacteria suddenly changing from harmless to humans to deadly and virulent, as with pneumococcal pneumonia.

As medical science has encountered more and more such phenomena needing to be explained, horizontal gene transfer has become a more favored explanatory model, with the concomitant impact on modeling for classification. Linear and horizontal gene transfer are visualized representations of biological processes. They are not to be taken literally, of course. They help organize the phenomena we encounter, focusing our mind's eye on processes that can explain effects we observe.

Although models of disability rarely represent graphically, they do organize phenomena we encounter so as to facilitate a focus that assists us in fulfilling one or another cognitive function. In the next several sections, I will explore the two functions for which models of disability are mainly formulated and used: (1) categorizing individuals as being disabled or not, and (2) explaining why people experience limitations associated with disability and determining whether unnecessary limitations on functioning may be dissolved, disposed of, defeated or otherwise eliminated.

MODELING DISABILITY

In current applications of disability scholarship and policy formulation, what is conveyed by "disability" is often explicated by reference to models rather than to other ontological forms.[5] Often appeals to models of disability are meant to invoke a standard or paradigm for classifying people as disabled for a programmatic or policy purpose, such as to authorize eligibility for social insurance benefits, or for statutory protection against disability discrimination, or to determine ineligibility for social roles such as employment or responsibilities such as parenting. This is the understanding of what ascriptions of disability can do that informs an important 2012 US Census Bureau report about the 2010 census survey. In that survey, according to the 2012 report, one out of every five Americans self-reported as, or was reported by the head of their household to be, disabled (United States Census Bureau 2012b). That so much as 20 percent of the working-age US population is disabled might seem surprising, but the Census Bureau explains this datum in the following way:

> Because health professionals, advocates, and other individuals use the same term in
> different contexts, disability does not often refer to a single definition. Medical models

view disability as an extension of a physiological condition requiring treatment or therapy. In contrast, social models view disability as the result of societal forces on impairment, and suggest that changes to social norms and practices would reduce restrictions. As a demographic category, disability is an attribute with which individuals may broadly identify, similar to race or gender. In contrast, certain federal programs narrowly define disability as the impairment or limitation that leads to the need for the program's benefit—such as the Social Security Disability Insurance program's income support for individuals who are not able "to engage in any substantial gainful activity." The agencies and organizations that provide benefits to, advocate for, or study these populations, each refer to their targeted group as people with disabilities; but because of the differences in definitions, an individual may be considered to have a disability under one set of criteria but not by another.[6]

(Brault 2012)

Attributions of disability in programmatic contexts like those cited above by the US Census Bureau use such ascriptions as terms of art, with various subsets and overlapping or otherwise partially related criteria for delineating its precise usage in various programs.[7] A "term of art" is "a word or phrase that has a specific or precise meaning within a given discipline or field and might have a different meaning in common usage" (Dictionary.com). Elsewhere I have pointed out pitfalls of conflating these specialized meanings of "disability" with general common usage (Silvers 2016b, 843–863).

To illustrate, programs meant to distribute economic benefits to persons who are unable to support themselves due only or preponderantly to being disabled identify being disabled with proof of being unable to work. Advocacy programs concerned with making the lives of individuals suffering from a particular health deficit or injury go better identify disability using the criteria for diagnosing a given disease (United States Census Bureau 2012a). Given the diverse practices that the multiplicity of meanings of "disability" serve, there is no apparent necessity for all individuals legitimately categorized by one use of "is disabled" to be included in any or all of the others.

The high profile of the narrow Social Security Administration (SSA)'s definition of disability in the United States may result from its gatekeeping role, directing the distribution of income and other benefits for individuals based on their categorization as members of the disability group. Navigating the complicated, sometimes adversarial, Social Security Disability Insurance (SSDI) process, individuals learn that to be considered disabled and thereby eligible for substitute income support, they ordinarily must have either a medical condition considered so severe that it is specifically listed in the Social Security Administration's disability manual or one established as being of equal severity to a listed condition (Blake 2011, 885–889). For example, cystic fibrosis automatically qualifies an individual as too disabled to work, based on a physician's description of symptoms and the positive results of tests for the symptoms' cause. This is so even though some people with cystic fibrosis who are "suffering from low forced expiratory volume" and "enduring a designated number of respiratory incidents requiring specified physician interventions in a specified time period," and thus who meet the diagnostic criteria for being too ill to work, nevertheless are successfully employed and self-supporting (United States Social Security Administration 2018a).

The US Centers for Disease Control (CDC) also relates attribution of disability to diagnosis of disease, but because the CDC and the SAA differ in purpose, the standards for "being disabled" in these two programs are not the same. An important difference between the models for determining disability arises from a disparity in the deference afforded to a patient's displaying symptoms. The CDC is in the business of detecting threats to the population's health, and so must be responsive during various stages of the development of medical knowledge about how disabling dysfunction is connected to purported or proven causes. According to CDC protocol, symptomatic dysfunctions signify chronic fatigue syndrome (CFS) and are acknowledged as sufficing for a CFS diagnosis, even without a cause or mechanism that explains the disabling symptoms being identified.[8] For CDC purposes, disabling dysfunctions that members of the medical profession, and eventually the public, take to be evidence of a particular disease need not be discounted because a cause or mechanism has not been found.[9]

So for the CDC, but not the SSA, disability may be identified even absent having determined the dysfunction's cause. For the SSA process, some diagnoses can entail disability, but diagnostic symptoms without medicalized causes are insufficient to do so. But the CDC's diagnostic criteria for CFS, consisting as they do of symptoms (Centers for Disease Control and Prevention 2018), do not suffice for the SSA. In contrast, the SSA instructs clinicians as follows: "In evaluating disability for persons with CFS…statements merely recounting the symptoms of the applicant or providing only a diagnosis will not establish a medical impairment for purposes of Social Security benefits. We must have reports documenting your objective clinical and laboratory findings" (United States Social Security Administration 2018b).

The Census Bureau's approach to delineating disability also diverges from the Social Security Administration's. The Census Bureau has been collecting data about certain disabilities since 1830, when Congress added questions to the census regarding difficulty in hearing, seeing, and speaking. For the purposes of conducting the census, first-person testimony about the extent of one's own or one's dependents' dysfunctions prevails. (The one-fifth of working-age Americans living outside of institutions who the 2010 Census counts as being disabled either self-reported, or were reported by the head of their household, as being so (United States Census Bureau 2012b).

USING MODELS OF DISABILITY: MANY MINORITIES, MANY MODELS

Models of disability may be used to delineate disability identity and by doing so to determine who is eligible to assume this identity. In the classificatory case just described, models of disability present as contextualized paradigms or standards to which people can appeal in deciding who is disabled for a particular purpose. Appeals to models of disability are currently used, mainly but not always, to categorize people as disabled for a specialized beneficial programmatic purpose. This has not always been so; as recently as a quarter-century ago, and continuing to some degree even today, the main purpose of categorizing people as disabled was exclusionary or destructive.[10]

When they serve as theory-dependent components for constructing meanings for specialized programs, models of disability may differ from each other by proposing quite different properties as being the importantly qualifying ones and thus may diverge, and yet not compete. Also consonant with programs' specialized purposes, the construction of such models may be shaped in normative terms as, for example, the SSA model of disability which explains why disabled individuals are powerless to be gainfully employed and links this explanation to criteria for being eligible for income replacement. If not intended solely to play such a gate-keeping function, or even to do so at all, what are the nature and import of the claims that constitute the supposed models of disability and that may widely but mistakenly be believed to be in contention with each other?

Models of disability can also facilitate theorizing how disability comes about or explaining why disability is.[11] Modeling disability can be central to accounts of how people come to be disabled or, more explicitly, why they have limitations characterizing or associated with disability. Such explanatory usage is often embedded in conversations regarding how limitations attributed to or associated with disability may be individually or societally overcome.

Often, but not exclusively, characterizations of disability that are treated, or at least talked about, as being models have been formed for or from some (sort of) social scientific study. Or, at least, these models are constructed as tools for studies that utilize explanatory framework(s) drawn from the science of their respective eras to explain why some individuals manifest important functional insufficiencies—that is, are unable to execute personal or interpersonal activities important for humans in that time, and to propose countermeasures for the deficiencies. The most prominent, persistent, and pernicious of these is to assume that there must be a single substantive master blueprint that serves as a standard or paradigm for identifying who is disabled, explains the cause(s) that result in people's being so, and imputes a definitive valuation to being in this state or situation in life.

Models used in science are of many epistemic types. There are, to illustrate with just a few of the kinds, *idealized models, analogical models, computational models and phenomenological models, each of which represents its target in a different way and bears a different relationship to the phenomena of the target system.* Scientists often successfully use several incompatible models of *one and the same* target system to enhance explanatory power and predictive precision.

The same can be said of models of disability. Sometimes appeals to models of disability are meant to categorize people as disabled for a particular purpose while on other occasions models of disability help explain how and why disability comes about. In the former cases, "disability" operates as a term of art with different specialized meanings, typically developed for a particular policy or program. Identifying the attributes that categorize individuals as being "of a kind" is different from explaining how individuals come to have those properties or predicting what will befall particular individuals (or the preponderance of those) who possess those properties. Sometimes, however, identification and explanation coordinate to further context-relevant goals. Thus, for example, the SSA standard for being disabled identifies who is eligible for income replacement in terms that also explain how individuals have come to be in such a state.

Competing models of disability may be more or less plausible and powerful depending on whether their classificatory or their explanatory effectiveness is being assessed. Whether the "what" purpose or the "why" purpose of conceptualizing disability is more significant becomes crucial when, for instance, we want to judge the medical model of disability and decide whether it is superior or inferior to the social model of disability. Weighing the relative importance of the classificatory and explanatory roles requires a clearer notion of the circumstances in which people invoke the concept of disability. It might be argued, for example, that the medical and social models do not directly compete because the former is most prominently involved in describing functional classification while the latter is best invoked in explaining social location.[12]

A multiplicity of models all may contribute to different aspects of understanding disability, or the same model may be assumed or explicitly introduced to serve both classificatory and explanatory purposes. The latter interpretation is the most common approach to the familiar medical and social models, according to which they constitute competing explanations. As such, the former presumes that being dysfunctional in some crucial respect is correlated with or caused by being in pathological physical, psychological, or cognitive conditions or states, while the latter proposes that dysfunction results from being in a pathologically hostile or dismissive society.

These models offer different explanations for, and thus call for different courses of action to address, being disabled. On the medical model, disease or injury cause anomalous individuals to be damaged and therefore dysfunctional, and thereby disables them. On the medical model, freeing individuals from biological dysfunction is the recommended approach to alleviate the suffering that is a familiar consequence of disability. On the social model, social disregard or downright discrimination cause anomalous individuals to be disregarded and therefore dysfunctional, and thereby disables them. The social model proposes that freeing disabled people from stigmatization and exclusion offers the most effective relief from that same suffering.[13]

Many other explanatory models of disability also have been devised. The moral model represents being disabled as resulting from moral or religious failings of the dysfunctional or atypically functional individual or the individual's family. The tragedy model represents being disabled as the undeserved misfortune of individuals who, because they are destined to be unlucky victims who cannot manage their own affairs and require charitable governance as the price for charitable support. The relational model of disability represents the situation or state of being disabled as fundamentally a mismatch between the person and the natural or built environment. Shifting emphasis from the relational model's focus on environments, the functional limitation model focuses on the personal deficits that distance those with deficits in normal functioning from fully functional individual people; on this model, being disabled or not is importantly a matter of whether one's attributes favor or impede functional achievement.

The minority or diversity model posits that, like other minorities who diverge in major ways from the majority of the population, disabled people are excluded from the opportunities that majoritarian citizens, who have political power, typically enjoy. The positive identity or affirmation model, influenced by strategies that work for some other minorities (including the powerful DeafPride movement), urges disabled people to construct positive self-images and celebrate pan-disability pride (Darling and Heckert 2010, 131–143; Swain and French 2000, 569–582). Two other political representations of disability are the civil rights and human rights models. The former portrays individuals with disabilities as entitled to, although too often deprived of, equitable protection and full benefit of the law, while the latter adds entitlement to special support that, due to disabling deficits (both medical and social), may be needed to compensate for shortfalls in thriving or well-being.[14]

What Can Make a Model of Disability Bad?

As Roman Frigg and Stephan Hartmann (2018) observe in their entry "Models in Science" in *The Stanford Encyclopaedia of Philosophy*, we are confronted with a patchwork of types of models, most of which are more or less useful in their specific domains of applicability. So I turn now to explore the kinds of considerations that may be raised when the usefulness of models of disability is assessed. To do so, I will focus on a single example, the United Kingdom's Work Capability Assessment (WCA), which adopted a questionable model, the biopsychosocial (BPS) model of disability, to determine eligibility for a state-supported income supplement.

The BPS emerged from research on the common complaint of musculo-skeletal pain. Claims about health conditions precluding steady employment were tested in cases where individuals asserted that due to lower back pain, they could not work. Not inconsequently, during the period of this research, clinical practice for lower back pain shifted from bed rest to continued activity and gentle exercise, which suggested that if psychological deterrents could be overcome, then returning to work might even be considered therapeutic. Presuming that such pain does not prevent most work from being done, the original research then promoted policy that deployed the disincentive of shortening workers' time on sick leave. (The study's conclusion was rated as based on poor-quality evidence by the American College of Physicians/American Pain Society review of acute low back pain.) (Chou et al. 2007)

Unsurprisingly, the research that adopted the original biopsychosocial (BPS) model of disability concluded with a report of success in promoting conduct that brought employees back to work by emphasizing treatable psychological rather than stubborn physiological factors. When this model's application was extended to the United Kingdom's Work Capability Assessment (WCA) process, cardio-respiratory and mental health states were problematically treated as if these health issues were relevantly similar to lower back pain. Proponents of this biopsychological model of disability extrapolated from the lower back pain context to the cardio-respiratory insufficiencies and mental health contexts, and many other chronic health deficit contexts, theorizing that, similarly to the lower back pain context, remaining at or returning to work for those with other types of disabilities would be effective for them. There was, however, no attempt to establish the kinds of relevant similarities required for modeling informative representations.

Problematically, the original model then was misapplied to explain claims of disability for purposes of government policy for income replacement, where the standard for eligibility is aimed at determining total work incapacity—that is, who is too disabled to ever work again. Critics of use of BPS by the WCA, questioned its accuracy and impact in determining whether, due to disability, an applicant is eligible for income supplement benefits. In "Blaming the victim, all over again: Waddell and Aylward's biopsychosocial (BPS) model of disability" (2017), sociologists Tom Shakespeare and Nicholas Watson, and disability organization manager Ola Abu Alghaid (henceforth "SW&A") argue that, although the mistaken model was initially constructed as explanatory support for research that took work incapacity to be mainly temporary rather than ongoing, it was rolled out to play a role in a different context—a role it is not suited to: representing disability where the underlying illness or injury is chronic or irreversible. Unsurprisingly, in the new context, the response favored by the misapplied model —namely, shortening sick leave instead of replacing income—strikes many (disabled) people as punitive.

The similarities between the situation that the model initially represented and those of many disabled people who are unemployed are at best strained: back injury is more likely to occur and become chronic in people already in the workforce, so the model is not designed to contend with societal barriers such as employers' disinclination to offer entry-level positions to individuals with disabilities and stereotyping of disabled people as unproductive. Yet such prejudice is still an enormous deterrent to people in the disability category being offered employment.[15] Extrapolating the original model, which assigns individual psychological factors prominence over disabling socially created impediments such as physical and sensory worksite and work tool barriers and discriminatory employer and co-worker attitudes, misrepresents the extent to which access to the workforce is in disabled workers' personal control.

Suspicion about the model's accuracy in representing disability in the context of income replacement policy is raised by the high rate at which appeals from WCA eligibility denials are upheld – roughly 50%. Another sign of trouble, suggesting severe adverse impact of the model, is the precipitous increase in the rate of mental health problems (suicides, self-reported mental health problems and antidepressant prescriptions) among individuals who rely, or attempt to rely, on disability benefits.

SW&A criticize the BPS model of disability because it portrays the crucial factor in obtaining, retaining, and returning to employment as centering on disabled individuals' psychological strength. By depicting disabled individuals as driven from the workplace by inadequacies in psychological factors that are in their control rather than physical and social factors that are not, the model predicts that many who are not working could with greater personal effort be doing so. SW&A argue that the biopsychosocial (BPS) model's depiction of why disabled people do not work applies to only a comparatively few such individuals and is not generalizable. To suppose it explains all or most of unemployment among the disabled is, they concluded, a despicable example of blaming the victim. People who are not employed due to physical or social effects of disability are harmed by it because the psychological strategy the model recommends does not emerge from a generally accurate explanatory picture of why disabled people are unemployed.

SW&A's objections to the modeling of disability presupposed by the United Kingdom's Work Capability Assessment process remind us that models may be flawed explanations but yet may be embraced as policy tools, despite failing in explanatory power, depending on what the programmatic aims may be.

To summarize, the UK supplementary income disability policy is harmful and misguided, because it is supported by a model that sociologists expert in disability research have argued is severely flawed. Two different kinds of problems with the modeling process appeared. First, the model becomes an instrument of injustice by arbitrarily imposing a normatively biased, rather than an equitably neutral, notion of what kinds of disabilities deserve the income supplementing program's support. Second, the model fails to meet epistemic standards for representations: in this case, the research subjects—sick leave users with certain kinds of back pain problems—are insufficiently similar to the intended target population in relevant respects to represent, or be generalized or extrapolated to, the members of the target class.

The United Kingdom's Work Capability Assessment revised income replacement policy, to the extent it has been informed by and thereby has promoted a model of disability problematic for the purposes to which the theory informing the policy proposes it be put, places disabled persons with neither employment nor improved prospects for work, at enormously increased risk of being stripped of state-supported income and thus having no income at all. Based on little more than a shaky surmise, the WCA applied a misleading model of incapacity to work due to disability, an application that mistakenly and harmfully treated the preponderance of disabled people displaced from state-supported income supplement as capable of finding sufficiently remunerative employment to survive.

Modeling Badly: Modeling Disability as Bad?

Models of disability, whether they facilitate classification or explanation or both at the same time, profoundly influence how living with a disability is conceptualized and, consequently, what assessments—both minor and momentous—are made about individuals who live with disabilities. As being disabled can be modeled in many different ways that may or may not be compatible with each other, how are we to determine the appropriateness of models that assign negative normativity to disability? Of central importance in regard to whether resolution can be reached is whether, in addition to facilitating classification and explanation, disability modeling can be evaluative as well. In addition to categorizing and explaining, does modeling disability also have an apprai- sive aspect, purpose or use?

Suppose that being disabled categorically carries with it a future of irremediable dis- advantage. Accepting such a supposition makes it very hard for even highly optimistic persons to think about any disabled individual's future free of dismay. Adopting a nega- tively normative model of disability invites obsessing about the damage being disabled might do to the future lives of neonates at risk for morbidity associated with disability, as if enabling such patients to live makes one responsible for the patient's and the patient's family's future suffering. This usage, if accepted as guidance for conceptualizing disabil- ity, urges nondisabled individuals who hold the fates of actually or potentially disabled ones in their hands—for example, neonatal intensive care unit health-care professionals with power to decide which neonates should be supported to live and which allowed to die—to draw a line against individuals who are or are likely to be disabled.

If the context were a specialized one, a model of disability might be understood as doubly purposed, for example, both defining individuals to whom disability is ascribed as not being eligible for life-saving treatment (Silvers and Francis 2017, 37–39), and explaining why and how they have acquired this status. What is unclear, however, is whether given its substance such a usage can be passed off as being narrow in the mode of the specialized SSA definition of disability. What considerations might be marshaled in favor of a widely applicable model sufficiently general to discourage whoever might hope to give life to or save the life of a disabled child?

To investigate, we may turn to arguments deployed by Guy Kahane and Julian Savulescu (henceforth "K&S") in advancing such a negatively normative model for dis- ability. In their papers on disability, K&S repeatedly represent life as a member of the minority of the population with disabilities as being irremediably inferior to how well (at least some of) the nondisabled majority can live. Appealing to what they claim actually happens in practice in our world as it currently is, they mount an energetic effort against equating being disabled with merely being different from the majority of people.[16]

In a presentation of his view in "Disability or Difference?" (2016), Savulescu presumes that attributing disability is in part evaluative. In support, he adverts to observing that "we speak of people as *suffering* from a disability" and "we take a disability to be a misfortune to those who suffer it, something that makes their life worse, and thus some- thing that gives us reasons to try to avoid or correct it."[17] At least one concern that seems to prompt the attention he gives to this issue is the impropriety he perceives in the pref- erences of some people to give birth to disabled rather than nondisabled children.[18] Savulescu begins the PowerPoint presentation of the K&S "bad difference" welfarist account with cases called "The Famous Deaf Lesbians" and "Dwarfism," where pro- spective parents with these conditions desire to apply reproductive technology to create offspring who are deaf, or dwarfs, claiming they can best parent children like themselves (Savulescu 2016). They are mistaken, he urges, because in the world in which we actually reside, to choose to make disabled children is to choose lives comparatively lacking in well-being.

NOT INTRINSICALLY BUT NEVERTHELESS INVETERATELY BAD?

Instead of building badness into a definition of disability, K&S try to find an independent explanation of why being disabled is inescapably bad. They say: "To reject the Mere Difference View, one needn't claim that disability is intrinsically bad or necessarily a great harm. Nor must one hold that "disability is by itself something that makes you worse off" or always or even nearly always automatically leads to reduction in well-being, independently from one's contingent physical and social environment" (Kahane and Savulescu 2016).

K&S are adamant that attributing disability does not entail badness. But Savulescu's PowerPoint presentation shows him insisting that, at least in our actual world, attributing disability is a negatively normative act. Modeling disability on being (dys)functional would make the concept purely descriptive, he says, but "the concept is partly evaluative." But does advancing a figure of speech that ties disability to suffering—perhaps commonplace in Savulescu's circle but surely not ubiquitous—establish that to be disabled carries with it incorrigible disadvantage? That "disability" sometimes has a normative use—for example, to confer eligibility for programs that either impose suffering based on disability (e.g., eugenics policies, employment bans [United States Supreme Court 2002: see *Chevron USA Inc. v. Echazabal*]) or relieve suffering based on disability (e.g., SSDI and SSI benefits, Shriners Hospital, the ADA)—does not prove the concept must be used normatively. Adverting to casual figures of speech seems a precarious platform on which to rest the contention that commonplace attributions of disability include appraisals of their subject's life.

K&S offer not a definition of disability, nor an analysis that unpacks the idea, but instead an explanation of why disability cannot help but suppress well-being. All that one need predict, according to them, "is that most of the conditions commonly described as disabilities are significantly likely to considerably reduce an individual's level of well-being in the contingent physical and social environment that we actually inhabit and that this would remain so even if prejudice against disabled people were removed" (Savulescu and Kahane 2011, 45–51). As they insist that their conclusion is empirical rather than a definitive delineation of disability, the challenge is to offer at least moderately persuasive evidence that disability is highly likely to damage well-being in some enormous decisive way.[19]

Crucial to their conviction that to be disabled is to be inescapably globally disadvantaged is a theory of well-being that places an implausibly high value on accumulation of options: "Many believe that disabilities such as deafness, blindness, paraplegia, and severe intellectual impairment are harmful and have a significant overall negative impact on a person's life.... To lack certain basic sensory, physical, or cognitive capacities is, in the world we actually inhabit, to also lack a broad range of valuable options and opportunities, as well as to find many of the remaining options significantly harder to pursue, compared to a similar person who does have these capacities..." (Kahane and Savulescu 2016).

The representation of well-being embedded in K&S's account is at best unjustified by empirical evidence and appears unlikely to be uncontroversial, given the wide range of different ways of life in which humans have been found to thrive.[20] Moreover, in setting out this standard K&S favor what may be their personal experience and preferences over other people's by over-valuing having a multiplicity of options:

> "For the Mere Difference View to be viable, the positive effects have to balance the negative ones. This seems to us doubtful for most disabilities.... there is a straight-forward asymmetry between the disabled and abled. A deaf person cannot listen to classical music, but a hearing person can learn sign language. Moreover, a hearing person has the second-order option of removing her ability to hear, whether temporarily or permanently, and thereby gaining access to further options that perhaps require being deaf. But at present there is nothing that a completely deaf person can do to access the options available only to those who can hear."
>
> (Kahane and Savulescu 2016, 777)

Of course, like many other conditions and situations that influence how people live, being disabled can reduce an individual's life options. Surely, however, increases in well-being do not necessarily or even characteristically track increases in an individual's options, contrary to what the K&S model would contend. There is as much to be said (and how commonplace saying so is!) for the goodness of the simple, and even of a traditional single-option, life as there is in praise of the sophisticated, privileged lifestyle with multiple life choices on offer.[21]

Equally likely is that to facilitate and enjoy well-being all one needs is one good viable option. If such has been obtained, additional options may serve as distractions that can corrupt by creating confusion, cultivating discontent and an inconstant nature, and thereby detracting from well-being. The damage from having so many life options that one fails to be fully satisfied by any is a familiar religious and literary theme. Given the inaccessibility and exclusion prevailing in our actual world, in assigning such importance to the numerosity of individuals' options, K&S patently privilege nondisabled people's comparatively unfettered experiences of well-being. They prefer modeling well-being per se on the comparatively unfettered experiences of privileged nondisabled people of the prevailing social or economic class over well-being modeled on the strategies disabled people and others dealing with socially, economically or other straitened circumstances have devised in order to flourish.

Perhaps influenced by the potent blame-the-victim type of injustice currently widely practiced in our actual world, K&S are inclined to situate responsibility for injustice based on disability with the victim's being impaired rather than with societal disregard and oppression based on disability. Consider the account they give (in an endnote) of the death of deaf children in a 2003 fire at the Russian institution where the children had been placed by the state.[22] K&S seem to think the children's hearing deficit was responsible for their deaths, as apparently each had to be awakened individually and given instructions in sign language.[23]

Once their dormitory was fully ablaze, perhaps their deafness was disadvantageous, but their being in such a perilous place, where their welfare had been so profoundly ignored, was due to their deafness as well. The commonplace practice in Russia was to remove deaf children from their families and institutionalize them regardless of the families' desires to keep them at home. Due to such societal permission to disregard the children's interests, they had been placed in jeopardy in an understaffed, hazardous setting.

The simple provision of flashing lights used as fire alarms, plus fire drills, as is typically mandated in the United States, ought to have been in place. These children died not because their deafness destined their deaths (the ultimate reduction of well-being) but because, due to being deaf, their lives were so little valued as to sequester them from their families, as well as to excuse the absence of even the simplest, most inexpensive protective practices in the place to which they were removed.[24]

As in the income replacement model reviewed in section VI, K&S's negatively normative model of disability becomes an instrument of injustice by arbitrarily imposing a normatively biased, rather than an equitably neutral, notion of disability. Their model poses a problem for maintaining fairness, because they impose a personal preference for having many options, which is biased against all those minorities whose experience in our actual world, rife with depletions of welfare based on their powerlessness of various sorts, advises them to aspire to one good life option over seeking to assemble an array of life options from which to choose.

Throughout their writing on disability, K&S presume another questionable standard, namely that what is, ought to be. Limits on minorities' opportunities in the current non-ideal world, where injustices are replete, inhibit pursuing justice for the future as well as enjoying justice today. K&S insist that:

> The claim is only that, in the world we inhabit, disability tends to significantly reduce one's good options, even when we set aside the impact on these options of prejudice against the disabled, and that therefore disability tends to make a person overall worse off... What is ultimately at issue... is whether the overall loss of options and overall prospects associated with disability is entirely due to prejudice and, more generally, to injustice. We most certainly don't deny that some of this adverse effect on options is due to injustice and therefore that the prospects of disabled people could, and most certainly should, be better than they actually are.... But a great deal of this loss of options cannot, we believe, be traced to prejudice or other forms of injustice.   (Kahane and Savulescu 2016, 776–777)

K&S seem unmindful of the regrettable anti-aspirational effect the sentiment they express above can have. In deciding whether their approach is productive and fair, it may be helpful to recall that other historically disadvantaged minorities once were supposed to be pathologically different from the dominant group but now are accepted as being merely different. Surely, they are not (nor should they be) expected to absorb every social disadvantage imposed due to their differences just because not all such disadvantage can be readily remedied.

In this regard, K&S also seem to be unaware of their approach's impact on the perlocutionary force of ascriptions of disability. To complaints about disparate outcomes traceable to disparate access, such as poorer health or smaller educational gains or lower salaries or similar differences that make socially disadvantaged groups less well off, K&S's approach invites the response "well, what do you expect," given your group's low status in the world we inhabit. The force of issuing an anti-aspirational endorsement of an inequitably burdensome status quo is to place a further burden—a shift in the burden of proof—on a disadvantaged minority seeking a remedy to demonstrate that the source of the inequity is prejudice. In making this move, K&S appear indifferent to the importance of exposing prejudice, especially of the implicit sort.[25]

Note also the structure of the case they try to make, which depends on K&S's exaggeration of what those who seek justice for disability claim. In this vein they say:

> If it is within the means of a society to remove the overall disadvantage of disability, then, so long as that isn't done, that disadvantage must be due to prejudice and injustice and therefore the Mere Difference View is correct. Setting aside the question of the truth of the antecedent (which we in fact reject), it's important to see that this conditional is implausible. For lack of full social accommodation to imply such a conclusion, we have to add some further premise about justice. But few plausible theories of justice require that any given difference in prospects must be erased even if this can be achieved only at immense cost and would require radical leveling down.
>
> (Kahane and Savulescu 2016, 777–778)

In making this move, however, K&S seem to abandon the touchstone they themselves previously proposed: namely, that claims about disability should be rooted in the facts about the actual world we reside in. The UN Convention on the Rights of People with Disabilities (CRPD), and the Americans with Disabilities Act (ADA) that preceded it, are products of a participatory process that included many individuals with disabilities. Far from demanding radical leveling down, erasing all differences in prospects, and ignoring immense costs, the documents these processes produced express a standard for the pursuit of justice for disability in terms of reasonably achievable progress.

From where did the idea emerge that justice for disability is so rigidly demanding as to be deemed "implausible" compared to aims for justice adopted for other groups? Such inflationary distortion to ridicule values pertaining to minorities and marginalized groups facilitates ignoring their perspectives or discouraging giving serious attention to their views. Further, that K&S appear to construe the way disabled people live in our actual world in terms of social descent ("leveling down") suggests that implicit bias may have them in its grip.[26]

Conclusion

Thus, evidence of epistemic injustice marks K&S's strategy for pressing their dismally dismissive view of disability. Epistemic injustice subordinates people by categorizing them as deserving of inequitable treatment. Epistemic injustice wrongs victims by dismissing them from their deserved status as respected knowers, not even granting them the authoritative word about the lived quality of their own lives. Victims are wronged in regard to both their testimony about what experiences they have had and their apperception and estimation of those experiences.

While the majority of the population is accorded privileged acceptance of their reports by others when testifying to the directly experienced texture and valuation of their own lives, disabled people's personal testimony is regularly overridden by individuals whose acquaintance with being disabled is secondhand, skewed by their majoritarian societal roles or their self-interest, or worse. Whether or not well-being can be brought within disabled people's reach is a matter on which those of us who are disabled might be thought to merit respect as agents as well as knowers, and thus as interpreters of our situations.

Obtaining epistemic justice for disability has a long way to go. Societal aspirations to improve its influence should be encouraged to grow by bolstering respect for the judgments of prospective parents with disabilities—or at least, with whatever ways deafness and dwarfism may be disabling—as to the satisfactory lives they have achieved. K&S's strategy, by no means unique to them, not only practices epistemic injustice but is globally antithetical to justice's pursuit.[27]

Perhaps due to their focus on bioethical controversies and consequent concern with medically contextualized cases, K&S's ideas about being disabled may be saturated by over-exposure to specialized usages of "disability." Their presumption that to categorize individuals as disabled is to appraise them as lacking fits that context quite well. On their account of the usage of disability, which comports with medical practice, disability would be invoked due to the individual's exhibiting a characteristic disabling lack, to allot or deny access to treatment, such as the use of reproductive technology to determine whether one's offspring will inherit deafness or dwarfism.

As noted in earlier sections, the pragmatics of modeling disability calls for fitting the model to the programmatic purpose(s) for which the term is used. In most cases that purpose is best served by picking out a sub-group from the most generally constructed category whose members are construed in terms that suit them to be the proper targets of that purpose and thus as eligible to be served by the program(s) that serve that purpose. But disabled people who have an interest in cultivating justice for disability are not a subgroup of the members of the disability category, nor should being disabled be referred to solely or even mainly through the use of terms of art.

Nondisabled people have an interest in justice for disability as well. Justice is a good for all people—disabled and nondisabled alike—whether or not everyone is aware of or articulates aspirations to achieve it. Even if ideal justice is beyond our reach, surely there is value for all of us in better approximating (and thereby increasing) justice in the actual world we live in. If all of us have an interest in pursuing justice to improve it, appraising eligibility—approving some and denying others—makes little sense in pursuing generalized justice for disability. Everyone equally is owed equitable justice; some are not better suited than others to be treated so. And although appraisals of eligibility for at least some specialized disability programs may be essentially contentious to the point of being irresolvable, disabled people's access to justice should not be supposed to be similarly constrained.

Afterword

Commenting on my article "On the Possibility and Desirability of Constructing a Neutral Conception of Disability" (2003, 479–481) in their "The Welfarist Account of Disability," (2009) K&S suppose that

> there can be various pragmatic reasons for broadening or narrowing down a definition. But it is not as if the scientific community suddenly discovered that mild asthma is a more severe deviation from the species or statistical norm than was previously believed.   (Kahane and Savulescu, 2009, n. 42, 77)

To the contrary, I suggest, the discoveries may be very similar indeed, provided that certain conditions are met. These have to do with the state of disability theory. Nothing in principle prevents cogent critique of prevailing disability theory on either epistemological or appraisive grounds. Reasons for models that narrow possibilities for progress may be no more nor less pragmatic than those that commonly influence construction of models in scientific reasoning. Indeed, an aim that disability theories and scientific theories should value alike is to discover whether the facts of the actual world are bound by, or instead differ from, bonds and boundaries that stereotyping supposition has decreed.

Notes

1. Editors' note: Anita Silvers passed away before she could copyedit the draft of this chapter that she submitted to us. The draft contained typographical errors and raised minor editorial questions that almost certainly would have been resolved in the course of copyediting. The Handbook editors made some initial corrections themselves, with invaluable assistance from Maja Sidzinska, Prof. Silvers' research assistant. The manuscript was then reviewed by Leslie Francis, a friend and frequent collaborator of Prof. Silvers, and a contributor to the Handbook. In making these changes, we sought to conform as closely as possible to Prof. Silvers' style and approach, approximating the changes that she herself would have made had she been involved in the copyediting process.

2. It may be worth noting here that the "model neutrality" approach explored in this chapter is as inhospitable to the normative "disability pride" strategy Elizabeth Barnes (2016b) adopts to combat negative stereotyping of disability as it is to the negative stereotyping Julian Savulescu and Guy Kahane embrace in their effort to derail Barnes's delineation of disability as "mere difference."

3. Our discussion does not concern every model of being disabled that disability theorists, policymakers, service providers, and others may have proposed. The models we consider are those invoked to represent disabled people, not special subsets.

4. See, for example, Bickenbach (1993); Scotch and Schriner (1997), 148–159; Riddle (2017), 39–49.

5. See Silvers (2009), 19–36. See also Beaudry (2016), 210–228. Beaudry is unclear as to the relationships between modeling disability, defining disability, and doing ontology. This is a ground on which, thanks to Elizabeth Barnes's (2016b) *The Minority Body*, the study of philosophy and disability is just beginning to tread. For theories related to metaphysics as modeling see, for example, the work of Laurie Paul.

6. By summer 2018, this figure had risen to 25 percent, according to the CDC. See, Cone (2018). But also see, Schwartz (2018) for a summer 2018 report of an unprecedented plunge in new SSDI applications.

7. See dictionary definition of "term of art" (Dictionary.com). Also see Silvers (2016a), and Silvers (2016b), as well as Beaudry (2016); the term of art analysis easily resolves the problem he is concerned with.

8. This is true even of diagnoses based on discovery of alleles with 100 percent penetrance such as Huntington's Disease, as we cannot say whether in the presence of the allele the characteristic symptoms unexceptionably occur.

9. Possible CFS biomarkers, reduced diversity of gut bacteria and inflammatory molecules in the bloodstream have recently been identified. See Bakalar (2016).

10. For example, the medical and social models of disability facilitate understanding explanatory theories, the former identifying the cause of the main limitations associated with disability to physiological pathologies and the later identifying sociological and political processes as the cause.

11. Doing so mostly calls for more explanatory apparatus than is achieved by invoking biophysical deficits occasioned by trauma or disease. It's not unusual for individuals in similar biophysical states to enjoy very different levels of functionality or well-being, variations that apparently must be attributable to other kinds of circumstances.

12. See other chapters in this volume for discussions of the medical and social models.

13. Or at least the social model is often thought to recommend such solutions.

14. See Retief and Letšosa (2018). There are many such taxonomies of disability models. This is a recent and fair one. It is unclear when the first shift from "definition of disability" to "model of disability" occurred, but the early 1980s may be a reasonable guess. By that time, reference to models was embedded in the language of sociologists who aligned their discipline with science rather than humanistic studies; and equally important was that social scientific methodology was increasingly accepted by clinicians whose policies continued to ensnare disabled people by promoting public policy that classified them as chronic patients.

15. See Savulescu and Kahane (2011). Also see Shakespeare (2006), who rejects the social model whereas here he is (Shakespeare 2017) lead author in 2017 making social model-type objections.

16. And especially against Barnes's (2016b) "mere difference" view.

17. Until I saw Savulescu's claim about commonplace expressions in his PowerPoint presentation slides, I don't think I had ever encountered the expression "suffer from disability." "Suffer an injury," yes. "Suffer from berylliosis," yes. "Suffer from a chronic cough," yes. It is commonplace to mistakenly elide being subject to a diagnosis to being disabled, as participants did in an online Pea Soup (2014) discussion where they seemed to take diagnosing an individual with muscular dystrophy or epidermylosis bulosa as asserting that the individual is disabled. This can't be the case, as both medical conditions now are established on the basis of characteristic alleles, not on symptoms or experiences of suffering.

18. Although Savulescu (2016) focuses disapproval on prenatal decisions to have disabled children, Savulescu has a similar view about providing lifesaving resources to existing children with disabilities. See Wilkinson and Savulescu (2014).

19. See Kahane and Savulescu's dismissal of Barnes making a similar point (Kahane and Savulescu 2016, 774–788).

20. Parenthetically, a quarter century earlier Dan Brock deployed a similar strategy for dismissing "adaptive values" to support his preference for disregarding disabled people's own testimony that their lives can be good. The discussion in this chapter does not directly engage with the conceptualization of adaptive value. Those who deploy adaptive value dismissively presume it is irrational to prefer being ill or injured to being cured. But for disabled people with satisfying lives, it may be irrational to choose a risky and disruptive procedure with noticeable history of failure just to obtain a greater range of options. See Eyal (Forthcoming).

21. For a more detailed critique of the multi-option standard for well-being, see Silvers et al. (1999). The dangers of having too many options is a familiar theme in modern period literature from eighteenth century English novels to twentieth-century existentialist tracts.

22. Their text reads: "On the night of 10th of April, 2003, a school for deaf and mute children in Makhachkala in Russia caught fire. Twenty-eight children aged 7 to 14 died and more than 100 were injured. Rescuing the children was hampered because "each child had to be awakened individually and told in sign language what to do" (AFP 2003). A commentator suggested that Kahane and Savulescu would not dispute my account of this case as, for them, the children's well-being depended on their being kept safe; so, safety resources such as blinking lights and fire drills should have been distributed to them. But this is to miss my point by a wide mark, for Kahane and Savulescu name *impairment* as the fundamental cause of the children's dying, whereas I instead name *the stigma invoked* by their being impaired as that cause. For their causal claim to prevail, Kahane and Savulescu should demonstrate that in Russia at that time similar proportions of nondisabled children who enjoyed loving parenting also were removed from their families' homes to be stowed away in institutions. Russian removal of disabled children from their homes to institutions was condemned as a human rights violation at that time.

23. See Kahane and Savulescu (2009), 15.

24. Parenthetically, it is cases like this, where a disparate proportion of a minority group is disadvantaged due to societal disregard that should make us wary of supposing that a simple distributive issue is the sole consideration of justice in play. After all, however little expenditure by the state institutionalizing the deaf children in such deprived conditions took, it still would have been more than leaving them in their communities.

25. To dislodge the barriers to justice erected by "what now is what should be" fans, I introduced a thought experiment-type device called "historical counterfactualizing" in Silvers et al.

(1999) that reverses burden of proof expectations by hypothesizing what practices would be in place and what valuations embedded if disadvantaged minorities had been the prevailing populations.

26. Of course, social "leveling down" as a mechanism of justice is a radically democratic idea promoted by the seventeenth-century English levellers.

27. Little knowing in 1999 that I was protesting against testimonial injustice, I argued in Silvers et al. (1999) against the inequitable inflation of epistemic responsibility for burden of proof imposed on disabled people by writers who dismissed their reports of well-being as mere "adaptive" valuing: "The most familiar argument that goes to construing impairment as being necessarily bad is about the hardship of not being able to enjoy music or sunsets or skiing. For those who enjoy music, deafness seems an intolerable deprivation. For those who enjoy skiing, paraplegia seems the same. But many people who could enjoy these pleasures pass them up. Yet, unlike people who cannot hear or see or walk, people who can enjoy the pleasures of engaging in these performances are not expected to defend the quality of their lives when they choose not to pursue these pleasures.... it is odd to deem their absence disadvantageous to those who cannot enjoy them but indifferent to those who can but do not enjoy them. Only if, and to the degree, that others bereft of the pleasures of paintings or concerts or skiing are pitied should people with visual or hearing or mobility impairments be pitied for missing these pleasures.... although the experience of engaging in these activities can be (but is not always) intrinsically good, not engaging in them is not intrinsically bad... What contributes badness here is neither objective impairment nor any disability it occasions but rather the subjective enduring of disruption and loss. And, of course, it is these feelings that a social environment hostile to impairment exacerbates."

REFERENCES

AFP. 2003. "School Fire Kills 28." *Herald Sun*, April 11, 2017.

Aristotle. 1961. *Aristotle's Poetics*. New York: Hill and Wang.

Bakalar, Nicholas. 2016. "Gut Bacteria Are Different in People With Chronic Fatigue Syndrome." *New York Times*, July 7, 2016. https://well.blogs.nytimes.com/2016/07/07/gut-bacteria-are-different-in-people-with-chronic-fatigue-syndrome/.

Barnes, Elizabeth. 2016a. "Reply to Guy Kahane and Julian Savulescu." *Res Philosophica* 93, no. 1: 295–309.

Barnes, Elizabeth. 2016b. *The Minority Body: A Theory of Disability*. Oxford: Oxford University Press.

Beaudry, Jonas-Sébastien. 2016. "Beyond (Models of) Disability?" *Journal of Medicine and Philosophy* 41, no. 2: 210–228.

Bickenbach, Jerome. 1993. *Physical Disability and Social Policy*. Toronto and London: University of Toronto Press.

Blake, Valarie. 2011. "A Physician's Guide to Social Security Disability Determinations." *The American Medical Association Journal of Ethics: Virtual Mentor* 13, no. 12: 885–889. https://journalofethics.ama-assn.org/article/physicians-guide-social-security-disability-determinations/2011-12.

Brault, Matthew W. 2012. "Americans With Disabilities: 2010 (Report Number P70-131)." *United States Census Bureau*, July 2012. https://www.census.gov/library/publications/2012/demo/p70-131.html.

Centers for Disease Control and Prevention. 2018. "Myalgic Encephalomyelitis/Chronic Fatigue Syndrome." *Centers for Disease Control and Prevention*. Accessed January 28, 2019. https://www.cdc.gov/me-cfs/.

Chou R, Qaseem A, Snow V, et al. 2007. "Diagnosis and Treatment of Low Back Pain: A Joint Clinical Practice Guideline from the American College of Physicians and the American Pain Society." Ann Intern Med. 147:478–491. doi:10.7326/0003-4819-147-7-200710020-00006

Cone, Allen. 2018. "CDC: 1 in 4 Adults Have a Disability that Impacts Daily Life." *United Press International (Health News)*, August 16, 2018. https://www.upi.com/CDC-1-in-4-adults-have-a-disability-that-impacts-daily-life/8421534423136/.

Darling, Rosalyn B., and D. Alex Heckert. 2010. "Orientations Toward Disability: Differences over the Lifecourse." *International Journal of Disability, Development and Education* 57 no. 2: 131–143.

Eyal, Nir. Forthcoming. "On Health-State Utility, Ask Experienced Patients Who Were Cured!" In *Beyond Disadvantage: Disability, Law, and Bioethics*, edited by Glenn Cohen, Carmel Shachar, Anita Silvers, and Michael Stein. Cambridge, UK: Cambridge University Press.

Frigg, Roman and Hartmann, Stephan. 2018. "Models in Science." In *The Stanford Encyclopedia of Philosophy*, edited by Edward N. Zalta, https://plato.stanford.edu/archives/sum2018/entries/models-science/.

Gallie, W. B. 1956. "Essentially Contested Concepts." *Proceedings of the Aristotelian Society* 56: 167–198.

Kahane, Guy, and Julian Savulescu. 2009. "The Welfarist Account of Disability." In *Disability and Disadvantage*, edited by Kimberley Brownlee and Adam Cureton, 14–53. Oxford: Oxford University Press.

Kahane, Guy, and Julian Savulescu. 2016. "Disability and Mere Difference." *Ethics* 126, no. 3: 774–788.

MacIntyre, Alasdair. 1973. "The Essential Contestability of Some Social Concepts." *Ethics* 84, no. 1: 1–9.

McKnight, C. 2003. "Medicine as an Essentially Contested Concept." *Journal of Medical Ethics* 29, no. 4: 261–262.

Pea Soup: A Blog Dedicated to Philosophy, Ethics, and Academia. 2014. "Ethics Discussion at Pea Soup: Elizabeth Barnes' "Valuing Disability, Causing Disability, with Critical Précis by Tom Dougherty." *Pea Soup: A Blog Dedicated to Philosophy, Ethics, and Academia*. Accessed January 2, 2019. https://peasoup.typepad.com/peasoup/2014/11/ethics-discussion-at-pea-soup-elizabeth-barnes-valuing-disability-causing-disability-with-critical-p.html.

Quammen, David. 2018. *The Tangled Tree: A Radical New History of Life*. New York: Simon & Schuster.

Retief, Marno, and Rantoa Letšosa. 2018. "Models of Disability: A Brief Overview." *HTS Teologiese Studies/Theological Studies* 74, no. 1 (a4738): 1–8. http://www.scielo.org.za/pdf/hts/v74n1/06.pdf.

Riddle, Christopher A. 2017. "Grounding Disability and Human Rights With the Capabilities Approach." In *Human Rights and Disability: Interdisciplinary Perspectives*, edited by John Stewart-Gordon, Johann-Christian Põder, and Holger Burckhart, 39–49. New York: Routledge.

Savulescu, Julian. 2016. "Disability or Difference?" Powerpoint for paper presented at the 2016 Duke-Oxford Workshop in Practical Ethics: Medicine, Society, and Value, Trent Semans Center, Duke School of Medicine, Duke University, February 26. See Savulescu-Disability-or-Difference.pptx at https//sites.duke.edu.

Savulescu, Julian, and Guy Kahane. 2011. "Disability: A Welfarist Approach." *Clinical Ethics* 6, no. 1: 45–51.

Schwartz, Nelson. 2018. "Disability Applications Plunge as the Economy Strengthens." *New York Times*, June 19, 2018. https://www.nytimes.com/2018/06/19/business/economy/social-security-applications.html.

Scotch, Richard, and Kay Schriner. 1997. "Disability as Human Variation: Implications for Policy." *The Annals of the American Academy of Political and Social Science* 549, no. 1: 148–159.

Shakespeare, Tom. 2006. *Disability Rights and Wrongs*. London: Routledge.

Shakespeare, Tom. 2017. *Disability: The Basics*. London: Routledge.

Shakespeare, T., Watson, N., & Alghaib, O. A. 2017. "Blaming the victim, all over again: Waddell and Aylward's biopsychosocial (BPS) model of disability." *Critical Social Policy*: 37(1), 22–41. doi:10.1177/0261018316649120

Silvers, Anita. 2000. "From The Crooked Timber of Humanity, Beautiful Things Can Be Made." In *Beauty Matters*, edited by Peg Zeglin Brand. Bloomington: Indiana University Press.

Silvers, Anita. 2003. "On the Possibility and Desirability of Constructing a Neutral Conception of Disability." *Theoretical Medicine and Bioethics* 24, no. 6: 471–487.

Silvers, Anita. 2009. "The Social Model of Disability." In *Philosophical Reflections on Disability*, edited by Chris Ralston and Justin Ho, 19–36. Heidelberg: Springer Netherlands.

Silvers, Anita. 2016a. "Disability and Normality." In *The Routledge Companion to Philosophy of Medicine*, edited by Miriam Solomon, Jeremy R. Simon, and Harold Kincaid, 36–47. New York: Routledge.

Silvers, Anita. 2016b. "Philosophy and Disability: What Should Philosophy Do?" *Res Philosophica* 93, no. 4: 843–863.

Silvers, Anita, David Wasserman, Mary B. Mahowald, and Lawrence C. Becker. 1999. *Disability, Difference, Discrimination: Perspectives on Justice in Bioethics and Public Policy*. Lanham, MD: Rowman & Littlefield.

Silvers, Anita, and Leslie Pickering Francis. 2017. "Metaphors in the Management of Extremely Preterm Birth." *American Journal of Bioethics* 17, no. 8: 37–39.

Swain, John, and Sally French. 2000. "Towards an Affirmation Model of Disability." *Disability & Society* 15, no 4: 569–582.

United States Census Bureau (a). 2012a. "Americans with Disabilities: 2010." *United States Census Bureau*. Accessed February 7, 2019. https://www.census.gov/library/publications/2012/demo/p70-131.html.

United States Census Bureau (b). 2012b. "Nearly 1 in 5 People Have a Disability in the U.S., Census Bureau Reports." *United States Census Bureau*. Accessed February 7, 2019. https://www.census.gov/newsroom/releases/archives/miscellaneous/cb12-134.html.

United States Social Security Administration. 2018a. "3.04: Cystic Fibrosis." In *Disability Evaluation Under Social Security*, edited by the United States Social Security Administration. Accessed October 20, 2011. https://www.ssa.gov/disability/professionals/bluebook/3.00-Respiratory-Adult.htm#3_04.

United States Social Security Administration. 2018b. "Providing Medical Evidence for Individuals with Myalgic Encephalomyelitis/Chronic Fatigue Syndrome (ME/CFS)." *United States Social Security Administration* 64. Accessed January 28, 2019. https://www.ssa.gov/disability/professionals/documents/64-063.pdf.

United States Supreme Court. 2002. Chevron USA Inc. v. Echazabal. 536 U.S. 73. No. 00-1406. https://www.loc.gov/item/usrep536073/.

Wasserman, David, Adrienne Asch, Jeffrey Blustein, and Daniel Putnam. 2016. "Disability: Definitions, Models, Experience." *Stanford Encyclopedia of Philosophy*. Last modified May 23, 2016. https://plato.stanford.edu/entries/disability/.

Wilkinson, Dominic, and Julian Savulescu. 2014. "Disability, Discrimination and Death: Is It Justified to Ration Life Saving Treatment for Disabled Newborn Infants?" *Monash Bioethics Review* 32, no. 1–2: 43–62.

CHAPTER 3

DISABILITY, HEALTH, AND DIFFERENCE

JEROME BICKENBACH

INTRODUCTION

ALTHOUGH philosophers are generally unaware of it, for nearly 50 years—and across disciplines from the health sciences, rehabilitation, sociology, politics, and law—disability has been generally understood as conceptually rooted in physiological and psychological functioning and experienced in terms of simple and complex daily activities, relationships, and roles shaped by the physical, human-built, attitudinal, and social environment. There are various formulations of this (as it might be called) "interactional model" of disability, but the most developed and operationalized is found in the World Health Organization's (WHO) International Classification of Functioning, Disability and Health (ICF) (WHO 2001). It is also reflected in the characterization of disability in the United Nations' Convention on the Rights of Persons with Disabilities (CRPD): "...disability results from the interaction between persons with impairments and attitudinal and environmental barriers that hinders their full and effective participation in society on an equal basis with others" (UN 2007, Art 3).

Although the interactional approach is the modern consensus among health and social scientists, philosophers have tended to adopt either a purely medical approach, in which disability is identical to the underlying impairment, or have been seduced by various forms of "social constructivism" that focus on the—invariably disadvantageous—social status of persons with disabilities. Multidisciplinary—and considerably more politically engaged—academics working under the rubric of "disability studies" have for their part shaped their work primarily in the service of political activism and have offered up a bewilderingly diverse collection of theories and approaches, many of which incorporate some variant of identity politics.

Underpinning all of this academic and political activity, however, is a deeper ambiguity about disability that I will argue here has crystalized into two perspectives, one focusing on what it means to be a "person with disabilities" (or a "disabled person") and one focusing on what it means to "experience disability." One perspective links disability to a socially created, disvalued social status; the other to the outcome of suboptimal health states interacting with the physical and social environment.

The first of these perspectives has clear historical roots. The so-called *minority group analysis* of disability was the product of political activism in the 1960s and '70s in North America and Europe that eventually came to be called the "social model of disability." Advocates in the United States used the civil rights movement as their model (Anspach 1979; Scotch 1984), while in the United Kingdom the basis was the Marxist analysis of social oppression (Abberley 1987; Oliver 1990). Both relied on earlier, medical sociological accounts of the "sick role," deviance theory, and the dynamics of social marginalization (Becker 1963; Lemert 1962). This approach was often aligned with "identity politics" (Young 1990), which emphasized a rigid social dichotomy between those with and those without disability, while other scholars placed disability more fully within the context of political activism, underscoring the crucial role of political advocacy to secure equal rights. This latter work in particular paved the way to the passage of the Americans with Disabilities Act, 1991 (ADA), the preamble of which, using the phrase from *US v. Carolene Products Co.* 304 U.S. 144 (1938) identifying a class of people for which judicial "strict scrutiny" is appropriate, states: "Individuals with disabilities are a discrete and insular minority who have been faced with restrictions and limitations, subjected to a history of purposeful unequal treatment and relegated to a position of political powerlessness in our society" (for further historical details, see Bickenbach 2012).

To plausibly qualify as a discrete and insular minority, however, only individuals with long-term, serious, and severe impairments could count as "disabled." As the lives of people with severe impairments are more profoundly changed by the experience, the plausibility of being socially disadvantaged and adopting a disabled self-identity was greater for this group. Indeed, some disability advocates strongly objected to people with temporary or transitory health problems, however incapacitated (or discriminated against), or those whose impairments seen as self-created (the obese or substance abusers) as being viewed as bona fide persons with disabilities (Scotch 1984).

The other perspective on the experience of disability follows not from political activism, but from the brute fact that people are biological entities who experience diseases and injuries that directly affect the things they can do in their lives, from reading a book, going to school, performing a job, or being a parent, a neighbor, a community member, or a citizen. Human beings break down, fall apart, and eventually die. This is not social construction or the residue of prejudice. Importantly, too, impairments are intrinsically variable in severity. The basic body function of visual acuity ranges from unproblematic to mild and moderate impairment, to a serious degree of limitation, to total loss of visual acuity or blindness. All body functions (and structures) follow this pattern—they are experienced, and clinically assessed, on a continuum. Modern health science can prevent some health problems that lead to impairments or slow the progress of decline, but, in the end, impairments of some level of severity, like death itself, are simply unavoidable.

American sociologist and disability advocate Irving Zola captured the social consequences of this fact of life when he argued that the minority approach to disability, although a productive short-term political strategy, simply could not be sustainable for the long term (Zola 1989). It is a mistake, he argued, to think that disability is a dichotomous notion, applicable only to those with permanent and severe impairments. Instead, disability is a near universal phenomenon; it is, indeed, part of the human condition. Optimally, therefore, social policy should also be universal, applicable to everyone experiencing or at risk of experiencing disability of any level of severity. A just and universal policy would match the level of resource, service, or support requirement to the level of need, recognizing that impairments are dynamic over the life course and, in light of aging, tend to increase in both number and severity over time. As Zola put the point, "having a disability [is] not a fixed status, but rather a continually changing, evolving and interactive process" (Zola 1993).

Although quite different, both approaches can support the social justice argument for an enduring social obligation to provide resources and services for persons experiencing disabilities to secure equality. Both approaches are, for example, applicable to the robust argument for social justice found in Norman Daniels's book *Just Health* (Daniels 2008) or, similarly, Amartya Sen and Martha Nussbaum's vision of equality of capability (Nussbaum, 2006; Sen 1997). The minority group approach argues that social resources must be provided both in response to discrimination and other socially created disadvantages and for accessibility and accommodation to achieve full inclusion and social participation. The universalistic perspective, on the other hand, can make precisely the same case since social disadvantage is at least partially environmentally (and so to a large extent socially) created. The universalist perspective can, moreover, make the broader argument that social justice considerations apply to the entire population, all of whom are at risk of disability over the life course: in the fullness of time, everyone will acquire impairments that, in interaction with their environment, will be disabling to some degree or another.

On closer look, though, the minority group perspective is burdened by a bizarre claim that there is no essential, conceptual connection between disability and health, a claim that is empirically absurd, philosophically untenable, and politically counterproductive. For this reason, universalism is the far stronger stance, and the minority group approach should be rejected by philosophers and political activists alike.[1] I will try to make the case for preferring universalism, negatively leaving the more positive argument in favor of universalism—and in particular the case for mainstreaming disability in health—for another place. After some preliminaries to set the stage, I begin by more fully setting out and critiquing versions of the minority group approach. I then argue that the conceptual detachment of disability and health is an intellectual prejudice that is philosophically indefensible, but, more importantly, one that can only undermine efforts to achieve the stated aspirations of the Convention on the Rights of Persons with Disabilities.

DISABILITY, HEALTH, AND THE ICF

As mentioned, in the health sciences community, the consensus approach to disability is embodied in the WHO's ICF. At the heart of the ICF is the notion of "functioning" that denotes the sum total of all body functions and structures and the entire myriad of actions and intentional behaviors, simple to complex, basic and compound—including complex and culturally variable social roles that human beings engage in. Functioning is classified in terms of domains represented by classificatory "categories" or variables arranged in the standard Linnaean, genus-species fashion for ease of codification. Key to this arrangement is that each domain is continuous—that is, mathematically representable by an interval scale or metric—ranging from no level of functioning (or total absence of structure) to full or total level of functioning.

Functioning is interpreted in terms of two constructs: *Capacity* and *Performance* (for clarity, I will continue to capitalize these ICF technical terms). Capacity is wholly intrinsic to the person—it represents levels of physiological functioning in domains of body parts (and, since the brain is a body part, psychological functioning) and the resulting, emergent capacity of the person to execute actions, simple to complex. As a theoretical construct, Capacity represents the functioning of the body and the person wholly independently of the physical, human-built, attitudinal, and social environment. As this is a construct rather than an empirically observable phenomenon—for obvious reasons— capacity can only be inferred from observation and clinical or other tests and assessments. Performance constitutes the description of what the person actually does in her or his actual environment, taking full account of the impact of all aspects of the environment—both those features of the environment that enhance a person's Capacity to perform an action and those that hinder the full expression of that Capacity.[2]

Needless to say, "functioning" in the ICF sense is a multidimensional but universal feature of human beings as biological, psychological, and social entities (as arguably it is, *mutatas mutandis*, for all organisms). Functioning is a theoretical and descriptive concept, to be sure, but it is not an abstraction nor normative. Scientifically, it is a theoretical concept for description, assessment, and measurement—and, ultimately, explanation and prediction. In effect, the ICF offers a model of the lived experience of health—that is, a way of consistently and reliably describing, measuring, and ultimately explaining how one or more underlying health conditions play out in a person's life, affecting who they are, how they behave, and what they do (in interaction with their overall physical and social environment). A "health condition" is understood broadly to include, first, the obvious: diseases, injuries, syndromes, and related health "problems," and, second, the less obvious states of the human body that characteristically create problems in functioning: for example, pregnancy, stress, and aging. (Obviously, the ICF does not imply that pregnancy or aging are diseases, merely that, typically, these states create problems in body functions and structures that may impact on a person's Capacity to perform actions in daily life.)

Health conditions, by definition, are associated with decrements in body functions and structures—or *impairments*. In some instances the underlying health condition and the impairment are identical (the injury of losing a finger); sometimes the impairments associated with health conditions are so bound up in the complexities of comorbidities that they can be linked only statistically over a population (mild forms of speech apraxia arising from an interplay between arthritis and early-onset dementia). Impairments can be clinically described in terms of disease signs and symptoms, but the range and diversity of decrements in functioning extend far beyond these established clinical indicators. Impairments, finally, constitute a discernible decline in capacity in one or more domains of body function and structure.

Impairments may or may not have an impact on the actions, behaviors, or tasks that a person can perform. If they do, they may impact adversely on the Capacity to execute an action, simple or complex—for example, to listen and understand a radio program, handle stress, sustain a conversation with more than one person, grasp small objects, wash oneself, prepare meals, maintain a romantic relationship, hold down a job, or engage in community activities. For simple actions, the impact of Capacity is fairly easy to describe and measure; for complex actions, there may be far too many causal pathways from health condition to action to describe and measure the impact. This is an epistemic issue—and obviously a major clinical and practical problem—but it is not a conceptual problem. When people cannot, when they choose to, clean their house, there may be reasons associated with their Capacity that account for this; some may be observable or predictable, others less so.

At the same time, intuitively, when actions are complex—especially when culturally variant social roles are involved—the causes for being unable to perform the required actions will very likely be bound up in features of the person's physical, human-built, and social environment. The problems a person may have grasping a pencil might be easily traceable to impairments in finger joints—a Capacity problem. The problems a person has in keeping a job will not be so easily traceable to impairments, although impairments may indeed be the problem. The domain of human actions is vast and complicated. At bottom, though, Performance for any actions, tasks, behaviors, or social roles is conceptually the outcome of complex interactions between a person's Capacity to do the action and the environmental facilitators and barriers that contribute to some level and quality of Performance.

This, then, is the ICF conceptualization of disability: for any particular domain of action, simple or complex, disability is some decrement in Performance as an outcome of the interaction between a person's intrinsic Capacity in that domain and the hindering or enhancing effect of the overall environment in which the person lives—physical, human-built, attitudinal, social, and cultural. Disability, in short, is a decrement in functioning in a domain, as a result of the interplay between a limitation in Capacity and some feature of the person's environment.[3] Since a person's Capacity can be augmented by, for example, assistive devices so that she or he Performs better than Capacity alone would predict, in a fully accessible, accommodating, and nondiscriminatory world, Performance should outstrip Capacity, and, in this sense, disability will be radically reduced, if not vanish, even though the underlying impairment remains. For some impairments—blindness for example—even in this ideal and fully accessible world there might remain a residual disability (or risk of disability) associated with the Capacity problem alone.

Understanding Capacity and Performance as continuous, more or less, rather than dichotomous, yes or no, phenomena is essential to understanding the salient metric of Functioning. In health science generally, however, thinking in continuous rather than dichotomous terms is extremely common. Psychiatrists and mental health scientists, for example, tend to think that standard mental health conditions—depression, anxiety disorder, even psychosis—are not natural kinds but represent mental states that exist toward one end of a continuum, the bulk of which is "normal" behavior. Grief over the loss of a parent and depression are states of mind on a single continuum of the mood called "sadness," and where one segues into the other is a matter of practice, a clinical decision, or, more typically, a person's reason for seeking help. The ICF presumes that all health conditions are similar: their symptoms and signs are threshold points on continua of associated domains of functioning. But precisely where these threshold points are located on the continuum is a practical decision. More generally, for any functioning domain, the line between "normal" and "abnormal" is flexible (although surely not arbitrary) and can plausibly be different for different people at different ages in different cultures and times. We draw these lines for our purposes, and if the way we do so is fit for our purpose, then it stays; if it is not fit, then we revise it. As should be obvious, the claim of "universalism" in the space of disability flows directly from the fact that functioning is a continuous and not dichotomous phenomenon.

Despite its notorious 1948 definition of "health" found in its Constitution ("a state of complete physical, mental and social well-being and not merely the absence of disease or infirmity"), the operating definition of health in recent years has been further developed in terms of three "consensus points": "(1) that health is a separate concept from well-being, however much we value health, both intrinsically and instrumentally; (2) that health is comprised of states of functioning of the human body and mind, so that to measure health is essentially to measure body and mind functions; and (3) that health is an attribute of an individual person, although aggregatable to populations of individuals" (Salomon et al. 2003). The WHO thus now understands health as bodily and mental functioning at a threshold level determined independently for specified purposes. Philosophers will recognize here a version of the classic account by Christopher Boorse (Boorse 1975; 1977), stripped of its highly criticized threshold standard of "species-typicality" or reliance on some artificial notion of normality. For the WHO, health is a generalized or summative health state, which itself is a determined threshold level of optimal functioning. As impairments are by definition suboptimal functioning, impairments are decrements in health. In short, in the ICF, health and disability are conceptually linked and, although not "medicalized," in the ICF, disability is conceptualized as a decrement of health.

"DISABLED BUT COMPLETELY HEALTHY"

No one doubts that there is a strong empirical link between disability and health, in the sense that people with disabilities as a group tend to have more health problems and use more healthcare services than other groups. Nor would any thoughtful person doubt that many people with disabilities are denied access to adequate healthcare services because, as a group, they are poorer, are at greater risk of violence and unintentional injury, and health services are not always provided in locations that are accessible to them (Lollar 2002; WHO 2011, chap. 3). But these are very different claims from the conceptual point I want to pursue.

Wasserman et al. have framed the issues I want address in terms of two interconnected questions: "Do all disabilities result from, or in, a loss of health? Can a person with a disability be in good or even 'perfect' health?" (Wasserman et al. ND). Since I am very clear on how I would answer these two questions, I am perplexed when I read the kinds of remarks I recorded in an earlier paper (Bickenbach 2013): "many persons with disabilities are healthy and use wheelchairs" (Pfeiffer 1998); "deafness in and by itself does not make a person generally unhealthy" (Häyry 2009); or "the disadvantages experienced by people who are assessed as abnormal derive not from biology, but from implicit social judgments" (Amundson 2001); "having a disability does not mean a person is not healthy or that he or she cannot be healthy" (CDC ND).

As political rhetoric, I understand what is going on: any firm link between health and disability might turn disability into a medical problem, ignoring the impact of social barriers, lack of accessibility, and discrimination; moreover, the link might reinforce the prejudice that people with disabilities are abnormal, defective, inferior, or worse (Amundson 2001; Silvers 1994). As social commentary, both concerns are understandable, and, in any event, it would be politically näive to ignore the social impact of the reluctance to address environmental barriers or to confront common perceptions of inferiority.

Nonetheless, it is still an open question whether the social cost of detaching health and disability, even rhetorically, is too high. Epidemiologically, the estimated 14–18% of the world's population that lives with significant disabilities (WHO 2011) is overwhelmingly comprised of people with chronic health conditions and complex states of multimorbidity for which easy and continuous access to health resources, especially rehabilitation services, is essential. Even if decrements in health signal in some substantial portion of the population some form of biological inferiority, bad character, or cursed fate, might it not be more sensible to address these ridiculous prejudices than by denying the essential link between disability and health, thereby jeopardizing those whose health needs are directly related to or worsened by their impairments?

Recently, Tom Shakespeare in an as yet unpublished piece has argued that there are other negative consequences to drawing too close a link between health and disability. If a disabled person is, by definition, unhealthy, then what motivation would we—or indeed the individual her or himself—have to provide health services or avoid risky behaviors to improve their health? He worries: "If disabled people are inevitably unhealthy, it is possible that they could develop a sense of fatalism, in which they think 'I already have a decrement of health, so why do I need to bother living a healthy life?'"

But healthcare providers or individuals would only think this way if they believed health was a dichotomous and unidimensional state—that the only plausible health treatment was complete cure or that, if you have asthma, your health doesn't worsen if you receive a traumatic brain injury. I doubt if these are common views about health, nor that there is a plausible philosophical theory of health with such consequences.

Are there better conceptual arguments to support the "disabled but healthy" claim? A very weak and uninteresting interpretation is that a person can have one or more impairments but *otherwise be healthy*. Clearly, this is not what the fuss is about. Rather, as Wasserman et al. point out, the salient issue is the presumed philosophical account of health. They suggest these distinctions: an account of health either views health (1) as the mere absence of disease or something more, (2) as normative or value-neutral, or (3) if normative, then instrumentally valuable or intrinsically good.

So, what kind of plausible account of health would be consistent with the "disabled but completely healthy" proposition? I am persuaded by Wasserman et al. that the best candidate to support the "disabled but completely healthy" claim would be one in the tradition of Aaron Antonovsky's "salutogenic model" of health (Antonovsky 1987; 1997; Becker 2012). On this view there are both negative and positive aspects to the health experience. Whether it is a "sense of coherence," "symptoms of wellness" (Antonovsky), or "robustly active agency" (Becker), the positive aspect of health is something a person can cultivate and enjoy despite experiencing negative aspects of health. Shakespeare also makes this point, saying that if a person "does not have pressing symptoms, and feels able to meet their daily obligations, personal and occupational, he is likely to say that he feels healthy." Recently, a theory of health grounded in "self-management" pursues a similar line (Huber et al. 2011).

But clearly this won't do the job of rescuing "disabled but completely healthy" from self-contradiction, for two reasons. First, descriptions of the presumed positive aspect of health sound suspiciously like "subjective health" (Nordenfelt 1987), namely, how a person perceives, evaluates, or appraises his or her own state of health: Do I feel healthy, sick, or ill? Am I bothered by my state of health, or am I, generally speaking, satisfied with it? These are all perfectly legitimate questions, but they are not descriptions of my state of health. We do not believe that a person's ability to run a marathon is the same as a person's belief that she can run a marathon, so why should we think that a person's health state is the same as, or even depends on, her beliefs about her health state? Moreover, we have lots of evidence that people's level of satisfaction with their health is not a predictor of their state of health.

Second, a sense of coherence and locus of control, optimism, robust coping style, strong sense of self, and so on are all themselves domains of functioning—in this case brain functions. But then positive health is a matter of psychological domains of functioning that a person does not have decrements in, or indeed, may have higher levels of than you would normally expect. But this is merely a version of the trivial and uncontroversial claim that a person can have decrements in health, even very severe decrements, but *otherwise be perfectly healthy* (by virtue of his or her positive health traits).

But I don't want to let myself off too easily here. Surely, a person blind or deaf from birth has impairments, but is she or he on this basis alone unhealthy? This is where Shakespeare and others draw the line: even if it is not intrinsically insulting, it is at least nonsensical to say that a person congenitally blind is, for that reason alone, unhealthy.

To be precise, the putative nonsense here is not traceable to (1) the fact that blindness is not a disease or illness; (2) the fact that the person does not feel or believe he or she is unhealthy; (3) the fact that a person who is blind can cope perfectly well with that condition, live a full life, and be fully included in all social activities; or even (4) the fact that the person does not, because of congenital blindness, have medical or other healthcare needs. Obviously, blindness is not a disease, it is an impairment; people's beliefs about their health state do not depend on their health state; in an accommodating world people who are blind can participate fully; and, for some chronic health problems, there are no (currently available) healthcare interventions. Rather, the nonsense flows, as Shakespeare has implied, from the intuitive plausibility of there being "non-health functioning limitations" and the fact that the ICF rules this out.

But what precisely is a non-health domain of body function? Surely on no plausible theory of health is a person's state of health not, in some manner, linked to their body and how it functions. Since I am assuming that no one would deny that blindness is a feature of the human body, describable in part (even if inadequately and only partially) in physiological and biological terms, what we are asked to accept is that this biological phenomena is itself not an aspect of a person's state of health. Is this plausible?

To underscore the point, I would never deny that the *experience of being blind* might not be fully describable in purely biological terms. That experience is manifold and shaped by a myriad of personal, social, cultural, linguistic, and political factors. What I cannot accept is that, given that blindness is at least in part a matter of human physiology and biology, it could be a non-health phenomenon. In my previous attempt to make sense of this, the best I could do was turn to Aristotelian metaphysics and the notion of *ergon*, which is used by Aristotle and other early Greek philosophers to identify the intrinsically defining activity of a thing—what it essentially does and what it is meant to do: a knife cuts, a cup holds water, a human is rational (Aristotle 1980). One might argue with Aristotle that visual acuity—some level of seeing functioning—is an *ergon* for human beings, something that human beings, intrinsically, by their true nature, are meant to be able to do. But even for Aristotle, although seeing is metaphysically an intrinsic human capacity—or as Martha Nussbaum has claimed, a part of basic human capability (Nussbaum 2006)—it was also very much a part of a person's state of health.

In the end, I think non-health bodily functioning is conceptually incoherent and empirically meaningless. Of course, there remains the legitimate concern that linking disability too closely to health implicitly devalues people with disabilities. If so, then directly dealing with these attitudes seems the right tactic to take, rather than delinking disability and health. Recently, some philosophers have suggested that the true culprit here is any implicit evaluation of impairments, whether grounded in health or not. Impairments, it is claimed, are not bad-differences, they are value-neutral mere-differences.

DISABILITY AND MERE-DIFFERENCE

Any claim that disability is value-neutral needs to be anchored in a broader evaluative context, and usually that is subjective or objective well-being. Since we have an abundance of empirical evidence that there is, if anything, a reverse correlation between the severity of impairments and life satisfaction or happiness (Albrecht and Devlieger 1999; Amundson 2010; Bagenstos and Schlanger 2007; Goering 2008), it is the objective sense of what, in Parfit's phrase, "makes life go well" that is at issue (Parfit 1984). Steering close to the social model, the claim is that disability has no generally adverse impact on well-being once the socially created disadvantages of discrimination and exclusion are factored out. Disability, they argue, is a demographic characteristic like sex, race, or ethnicity.

It is important at the outset to pull apart two strands that have been merged in the proposition that disability is value-neutral: first, that disability does not necessarily adversely impact well-being; and, second, on analogy with sex, race, and ethnicity, that disability is a "mere difference," neither suboptimal nor intrinsically disadvantageous.

The relationship between disability and well-being is tangled up in many confounding considerations, the most prominent of which is temporal: Are we assessing well-being at some point of time, longitudinally over time, or overall (i.e., with respect to a completed life). Taking the last perspective first, the well-being of a life as a whole cannot plausibly be reduced to the sum total of all specific hardships and windfalls, good times and bad times, harms and benefits. The final judgment about how "a life went" must understand well-being as an emergent property—more than the sum of its parts. Here Aristotle was right: "one swallow does not make a summer, nor does one day; and so too one day, or a short time, does not make a man blessed and happy." There are far too many modulating factors in a life, whatever hardships one faces—resilience, adaptation, adjustment, exploration of new life options, to name only a few. Neither impairments nor, it seems to me, any positive or negative feature of living one's life will unambiguously determine the overall well-being of an entire life. It is just too complex.

On the other hand, it would frivolous to deny for philosophical purposes that episodes of experiencing extreme pain, discomfort and suffering, frustration and anxiety (all of which are associated with some impairments) do not, objectively, make life go badly when they occur. Because all these negative factors have characteristics that are unique to themselves, it is unlikely that they are statistically unidimensional, so that the experience of impairments cannot be plausibly mapped onto some metric of well-being (even assuming that there was such a metric). The point is that claims either to conceptually link impairments and well-being or to delink them are lacking in stable empirical evidence and tend to be somewhat contrived and rhetorical.

But the other strand of the argument for value-neutrality is far more problematic. Wasserman et al. have surveyed the range of reasons for rejecting any close analogy between impairments and sex, gender, race, or ethnicity, but recently Elizabeth Barnes has fleshed some of her earlier arguments (Barnes 2009a, 2009b) to strengthen her case for disability value-neutrality, a version of the mere-difference view (Barnes 2016).

It is difficult, however, to address her argument for value-neutrality without pointing out some suspicious methodological strategies she relies on. First of all, although she readily accepts the distinction between subjective well-being (the feeling of satisfaction or happiness) and objective well-being (life *really* going well or badly), much of her empirical evidence base for the conceptual argument about (objective) value neutrality is grounded in first-person testimony coupled with the claim that people without severe disabilities tend to overestimate how much unhappiness or dissatisfaction with life people with those disabilities actually experience (see Amundson 2010). Yet, at strategic points, she uses this evidence to create a fairly blunt *ad hominem*: "Since non-disabled folks are so wrong about how people with disabilities feel about their lives, we have no reason to think the non-disabled folks are right about whether disability is objectively bad *simplicitar* or not" (e.g., Barnes 2015 and 2016, 105).

Second, Barnes relies on an extremely idiosyncratic conceptualization of "disability." She claims that disability and impairment are the same thing, ignoring the obvious fact that two people with the same impairment can have very different problems in performing everyday actions in different environmental contexts. (Compare a person with a spinal cord injury who uses a wheelchair and one who does not, for example.) The conceptual reason for distinguishing impairments from disabilities is that impairments are not experienced outside of some environmental context. In addition, although she rejects the view that impairments are *decrements* of functioning, she accepts without comment the identical claim that impairments are *nonstandard* bodily differences. Finally, although she does not buy the full social model, she insists that disability is a minority social identity, which, of course, brings the environment back into the conceptualization of impairment, thus transforming her notion of impairment into something closer to the consensus view of disability.

This is not a harmless ambiguity; it is an obviously intentional argumentative ploy. By conceptually connecting this complex social-psychological phenomenon of "minority identity" to impairment as merely nonstandard bodily difference, she can employ this clearly positive feature of "impairment" to challenge the claim that impairments are intrinsically detrimental to well-being. But even if that were true, the argument depends on evidence that every person with a disability so identifies themselves. But that is very unlikely. The number of people with disabilities who embrace the disability minority identity is likely restricted to those who also self-identify as disability advocates. But among the roughly 1 billion people on earth with significant impairments (WHO 2011), the subset of these who self-identify as disability advocates is tiny. Although her argumentation depends on it and she spends an entire chapter arguing for the importance of first-person testimony, it is empirically fantastical to think that this very select group of advocates is in any way representative of the world's population of persons with significant impairments.

On the other hand, in order to challenge the claim that impairments are bad *simpliciter*, she strips away the social content of impairments and argues, on analogy with being a women or being a gay man, that the social and other disadvantages that arise from impairments are actually not intrinsic to impairment but contingent on background social phenomena of lack of accommodation, discrimination, and stigma. But she cannot have it both ways: if impairment is indeed value-neutral, it is not also a highly normative social identity; and, if it is conceptually a social identity, its linkage to well-being is intrinsic and not contingent. Truly value-neutral physical differences between people are indeed trivial and cannot support a social identity: nontrivial physical differences that are of such significance as to be the source of a social identity can hardly also be value-neutral.

And Barnes displays other argumentative flourishes that use this ambiguity to beg the question of value neutrality: (1) having posited without argument that impairment is analogous to sex, sexual orientation, and race, she responds to claims about the intrinsic negative impact of impairment on well-being by insisting that we would never say that about being a woman or a gay man, which would only be effective if the analogy was sound. (2) She repeatedly argues that the plausibility of intuitions about the negative impact of impairments reflect an overly medicalized view of disability, which, of course, would only be a concern if her idiosyncratic view about disability was itself defensible. And so on.

In the end, I do not believe Barnes has validly made her case, and that is a shame since some sensible version of value-neutrality is very plausible. On the consensus view, impairments are decrements in functioning in one or more domains. As mentioned, where the threshold on the continuum of degree of functioning "decrement" begins depends on the purpose we have for making the cutoff. We use the terms "suboptimal," "biostatistically abnormal," or "defective" if doing so is useful, but, at the end of the day, the threshold is determined by our preferences, needs, aspirations, values, and self-identification. We have found it important to define and operationalize impairments for the very pedestrian reason that some of these impairments are—as Barnes readily allows—"locally bad" in the sense that they lead to pain, discomfort, frustration, and premature death. We also find it important to identify impairments because they can interact with environmental contexts that make it harder or impossible to perform the actions, tasks, behaviors, and social roles we want to perform. And those things matter to most of us.

I have already granted that it is probably impossible to make the case for any normative feature of human existence—good, bad, or indifferent—to be "globally bad" in the sense of making an entire human life fundamentally lacking in well-being. So whether or not impairments are *globally bad simpliciter,* as defined by Barnes, is, I believe, a red herring. It is sufficient to say (what I believe is obvious) that some impairments are locally and for some individuals, some times and in some contexts locally bad (indeed very bad). That's why human beings are dependent creatures (Fineman 2008) who have non-negligible health and social services requirements. That is why impairments (and indeed our health states) matter to us; they affect how we live our lives. Mere-differences don't matter to us because they do not affect how we live our lives.

What Difference Does It Make?

I have looked at two subsidiary claims closely linked to the minority approach to disability—the view that disability is not conceptually linked to health and that disability (or rather impairment) is a mere, value-neutral difference. I have found some of the arguments used to support these view wanting in various ways. I began this chapter by describing what I take to be two general perspectives on disability, one that emphasizes the social characteristics of a purportedly discrete population of "persons with disabilities" and another that characterizes disability as a universal and continuous human phenomena that manifests as the interaction of intrinsic health and environmental determinants. At some level, the two perspectives are compatible; but, historically, in part because of the two subsidiary claims I have talked about, they are and have been generally viewed as being at odds. I want to end this chapter by asking: What difference do these differences in perspective and conceptualization really make in practice?

By "practice" I mean the overall social response to disability—shorthand for the sum total of formal laws and regulations, policy instruments, policies, and practices that define disability health and wider social policy (labor, education, transportation, communication, human rights, and so on), as well as individual and social beliefs, attitudes, and behaviors that can impact, positively or negatively, on the lives of persons with disabilities. To get a sense of the varieties and categories of what I mean by social response, one could do no better than review the provisions of the UN Convention on the Rights of Persons with Disabilities. Preserving and protecting these enumerated rights constitutes, arguably, the remit of a just society with respect to disability.

As I have argued more fully elsewhere (Bickenbach 2015), the minority group perspective on disability argues that the disadvantage of disability (its negative impact on well-being) is caused by society and social arrangements—either because of ignorance and benign neglect or by design and overt prejudice and discrimination. The appropriate social response must be to ensure social inclusion at the individual level by means of political advocacy that has both a negative focus—to prevent and compensate for discrimination and prejudice—and a positive focus—to provide accommodations and supports needed for enhanced participation. The universal perspective, for its part, entails that the disadvantages of disability are jointly determined by underlying health conditions and their resulting impairments as well as by environmental barriers (or the absence of environmental facilitators). As a result, this perspective advises a more nuanced and complex negative and positive social response, one that takes into account the role that health plays in the experience of disability.

Since underlying health conditions create decrements in functioning that can directly cause disadvantage, a just society must provide some form of health intervention to improve and optimize a person's Capacity or to prevent the onset of some other decrement in Capacity. This may involve medicine, but typically relies more on rehabilitation and social work and the support and services of other allied health and social professionals. Improving Capacity may not be enough (or may not be possible), in which case some form of environmental adjustment or modification will also be required. This can take the form of the provision of appropriate assistive devices (eye glasses, hearing aids, wheelchairs, and communication devices) or personal assistance, the removal of unnecessary environmental obstacles (providing ramps or widening doors for persons in wheelchairs), or both. As these services and supports are socially provided, inevitably facilitating laws and policies will also be required.

The end result—at least in a just society—may be the same, but the underlying rationale is subtly different. The minority group perspective insists that the social response to situations of injustice experienced by persons with disabilities is essentially compensatory or remedial, given that most environmental barriers (or failures to provide facilitators) are a result of social design. The universal perspective tends to focus on interventions that directly address health status while advocating for accommodating changes to the immediate and wider environments. Supports and services are provided, not as compensation for past discrimination, but as part of a general social obligation to ensure equal opportunity for all citizens. This social remit requires supports and services that (a) optimize functioning, (b) enhance Capacity where possible, and (c) increase Performance when necessary. While the minority perspective focuses on social change and downplays the need for health improvements, the universal perspective focuses on health improvements and downplays the importance of broader social change for inclusion.

Yet there was a reason that Irving Zola argued, more than 20 years ago, that although a highly effective political strategy, the minority approach is unsustainable. Impairment is a near-universal human phenomenon, very much part of what it means to be a human being. Recognizing that everyone is at risk of impairment, that impairments range for minor to serious and everywhere in between, and that aging is the accumulation of impairments, a sensible social response will be grounded in the epidemiological fact that more or less everyone is, or will be, disabled to one degree or another over time. From a long-term population perspective, therefore, it is essential for health and social services to scale up in order to address the current needs of people with mild or moderate impairments since these needs, with an aging population, will be experienced by a vastly larger population for whom prevention and rehabilitation efforts can have the greatest benefit (Chatterji et al. 2015). In short, a just society would tailor its response to epidemiological and demographic realities and respond to the universal phenomenon of disability by matching level of resource, service, and support to the level of actual need, rather than single-mindedly targeting a single group of persons with severe, chronic, and lifelong impairments.

Unfortunately, by latching onto implausible claims about the experience of disability—such as the two discussed here—advocates of the minority perspective have undermined the prospect of mainstreaming disability within broader health and social policy. By insisting that impairments are not really about decrements in health status or that impairments do not, intrinsically, create human needs that require social resources, the minority approach is, as Zola so clearly states, both unsustainable and ultimately counterproductive.

NOTES

1. What about the "social model of disability"? As I am constructing the two approaches, both are versions of the social model inasmuch as they take into account the fact that factors in the physical, human-built, attitudinal, and social environment are determinants of the experience of disability. The interactional approach, in ICF terminology, is described in the text but comes to this: the experience of disability is the outcome of the interaction of two sets of determinants—health and environmental. The problem about using the phrase "social model" in this context is twofold: (a) as mentioned in the text, it was created in opposition to the so-called medical model, which, as it happens, is a straw position that no one has ever actually held or defended; and (b) there are as many variations of the social model as authors who propose them.
2. The complex issue of intentionally—what, to speak simplistically, marks the difference between sleep-walking, walking involuntarily under duress, walking with the intention and purpose to walk, and so on—adds a layer of complexity to this simple Capacity–Performance distinction that is of philosophical significance. Unfortunately, branching off and discussing it here would take us too far afield.
3. Interestingly, the CRPD characterization of "persons with disability" is logically quite different: "Persons with disabilities include those who have long-term physical, mental, intellectual or sensory impairments which in interaction with various barriers *may* hinder their full and effective participation in society on an equal basis with others." The stressed word "may" suggests that a person with a disability may be someone with an impairment but with full and effective participation; that is, with no environmental hindrance. Logically, this entails that a person with a disability is defined by impairments alone (…who may or may not be hindered…), which sounds a bit like the so-called medical model. Presumably, this was not intended by the drafters.

REFERENCES

Abberley, Paul. 1987. "The Concept of Oppression and the Development of a Social Theory of Disability." *Disability and Society* 2: 5–12.

Albrecht, Gary L., and G. Devlieger. 1999. "The Disability Paradox: High Quality of Life Against the Odds." *Social Science and Medicine* 48(8): 977–988.

Amundson, Ron. 2001. "Against Normal Function." *Studies in the History and Philosophy of Biology and Biomedical Science* 31(1): 33–53.

Amundson, Ron. 2010. "Quality of Life, Disability, and Hedonic Psychology." *Journal of Theory and Social Behavior* 40(4): 374–392.

Anspach, R. R. 1979. "From Stigma to Identity Policies: Political Activism Among the Physically Disabled and Former Mental Patients." *Social Science and Medicine* 13A: 765–781.

Antonovsky, Aaron. 1987. *Unraveling the Mystery of Health. How People Manage Stress and Stay Well*. San Francisco: Jossey-Bass.

Antonovsky, Aaron. 1997. "The Salutogenic Model as a Theory to Guide Health Promotion." *Health Promotion International* 11(1): 11–18.

Aristotle. 1980. *Nicomachean Ethics*, trans. by W. D. Ross. Oxford: Oxford University Press, book 1, 1097b22–1098a20.

Bagenstos, Samual, and M. Schlanger. 2007. "Hedonic Damages, Hedonic Adaptation, and Disability." *Vanderbilt Law Review* 60(3): 745–797.

Barnes, Elizabeth. 2009a. "Disability, Minority, and Difference." *Journal of Applied Philosophy* 26(4): 337–355.

Barnes, Elizabeth. 2009b. "Disability and Adaptive Preference." *Philosophical Perspectives* 23(1): 1–22.

Barnes, Elizabeth. 2015. "Valuing Disability, Causing Disability." *Ethics* 125(1): 88–113.

Barnes, Elizabeth. 2016. *The Minority Body: A Theory of Disability*. Oxford: Oxford University Press.

Becker, H. S. 1963. *Outsiders: Studies in the Sociology of Deviance*. New York: Free Press.

Becker, Larry. 2012. *Habilitation, Health, and Agency: A Framework for Basic Justice*. New York: Oxford University Press.

Bickenbach, Jerome. 2012. *Ethics, Law, and Policy*. Volume 4 of the Sage Reference Series on Disability: Key Issues and Future Directions. Thousand Oaks, CA: Sage Publications.

Bickenbach, Jerome. 2013. "Disability, 'Being Unhealthy' and Rights to Health." *Journal of Law, Medicine and Ethics* 41(4): 821–828.

Bickenbach, Jerome. 2015. "WHO's Definition of Health: Philosophical Analysis." In *Handbook of the Philosophy of Medicine*, edited by Thomas Schramme and Steven Edwards, 1–15. New York: Springer Publications.

Boorse, Christopher. 1975. "On the Distinction Between Disease and Illness." *Philosophy and Public Affairs* 5(1): 49–68.

Boorse, Christopher. 1977. "Health as a Theoretical Concept." *Philosophy of Science* 44(4): 542–573.

Centers for Disease Control. ND. *Disability and Health: Health Living*. Available at http://www.cdc.gov/ncbddd/disabilityandhealth/healthyliving.html.

Chatterji, Somanth, Julie Byles, David Cutler, Teresa Seeman, and Emese Verdes. 2015. "Health, Functioning and Disability in Older Adults—Present Status and Future Implications." *Lancet* 385: 563–575.

Daniels, Norman. 2008. *Just Health: Meeting Health Needs Fairly*. New York: Cambridge University Press.

Fineman, Martha A. 2008. "The Vulnerable Subject: Anchoring Equality in the Human Condition." *Yale Journal of Law and Feminism* 20(1), Article 2.

Goering, Sara. 2008. " 'You Say You're Happy, but...': Contested Quality of Life Judgments in Bioethics and Disability Studies." *Journal of Bioethical Inquiry* 5: 125–135.

Häyry, Matti. 2009. "The Moral Contestedness of Selecting 'Deaf Embryos.'" In *Arguing About Disability: Philosophical Perspectives*, edited by Kristijana Kristjana, Simo Vehmas, and Tom Shakespeare, 154–168. London: Routledge.

Huber, Machteld, J. André Knottnerus, Lawrence Green, Henriette van der Horst, Alegandro R. Jadad, Daan Kromhout, et al. 2011. "How Should We Define Health?" *BMJ* 343: d4163–d4165.

Lemert, E. 1962. *Human Deviance: Social Problems and Social Control*. Englewood Cliffs, NJ: Prentice-Hall.

Lollar, Don J. 2002. "Public Health and Disability: Emerging Opportunities." *Public Health Report* 117(2): 131–136.

Nordenfelt, Lenord. 1987. *On the Nature of Health: An Action-Theoretical Approach.* Dordrecht: Reidel.

Nussbaum, Martha. 2006. *Frontiers of Justice: Disability, Nationality and Species Membership.* Cambridge: Harvard University Press.

Oliver, Michael. 1990. *The Politics of Disablement.* Basingstoke: Macmillan.

Parfit, Denis. 1984. *Reasons and Person.* Oxford: Clarendon Press.

Pfeiffer, David. 1998. "The ICIDH and the Need for Its Revision." *Disability and Society* 13(4): 503–523.

Salomon, Josh A., Colin D. Mathers, Somanth Chatterji, Ritu Sadana, T. B. Ustun, and Christopher J. L. Murray. 2003. "Quantifying Individual Levels of Health: Definitions, Concepts, and Measurement Issues." In *Health Systems Performance Assessment: Debates, Methods and Empiricism*, edited by C. J. L. Murray and D. B. Evans, 301–318. Geneva: World Health Organization.

Scotch, Richard K. 1984. *From Good Will to Civil Rights.* Philadelphia: Temple University Press.

Sen, Amartya. 1997. *Inequality Reexamined.* Oxford: Clarendon Press.

Silvers, Anita. 1994. "Defective Agents: Equality, Difference and the Tyranny of the Normal." *Journal of Social Philosophy* 25th Anniversary Special Issue: 154–175.

United Nations. 2007. Convention on the Rights of Persons with Disabilities, G. A. Res. 61/106; 2007. Available at http://www.un.org/esa/socdev/enable/rights/convtexte.htm.

Wasserman, David. 2001. Philosophical Issues in the Definition and Social Response to Disability. In *Handbook of Disability Studies*, edited by Gary Albrecht, Katherine D. Seelman, and Michael Bury, 219–251. Thousand Oaks, CA: Sage.

Wasserman, David, Adrienne Asch, John Blustein, and David Putnam. ND. Disability: Health, Well-Being, and Personal Relationships. *The Stanford Encyclopedia of Philosophy.* Available at https://plato.stanford.edu/entries/disability-health/.

World Health Organization. 2001. *International Classification of Functioning Disability and Health.* Geneva: WHO.

World Health Organization. 2011. *The World Report on Disability.* Geneva: WHO.

Young, Iris M. 1990. *Justice and the Politics of Difference.* Princeton: Princeton University Press.

Zola, Irving K. 1989. "Toward the Necessary Universalizing of a Disability Policy." *Milbank Quarterly* 67: 401–418.

Zola, Irving K. 1993. "Disability Statistics, What We Count and What It Tells Us: A Personal and Political Analysis." *Journal of Disability Policy Studies* 4: 9–23.

....

CHAPTER 4

HABILITATIVE HEALTH
AND DISABILITY

....

LAWRENCE C. BECKER

THE argument in this chapter is structured as follows. The first section outlines some common-sense connections between disability and related terms having to do with individual health and functioning—terms such as "inability," "disease," "disorder," "dysfunction," "deficit," "difference," and "difficulty." The second section connects this to a conception of "complete" good health and argues that all disabilities can be traced to an important form of ill health under that conception—namely, a lack of habilitative health—but not to ill health per se and not solely to ill health in the disabled person. The third and fourth sections lay out some practical connections between disabilities of various sorts and three aspects of habilitative health: self-habilitation, habilitation of others, and habilitation of the physical and social environments. It then sketches an argument for making the concept of habilitative health central to discussions of disability. A fifth section recasts that centrality argument into an elementary valid argument form and draws some conclusions. The sixth and final section adds some speculation about what all of this might mean for philosophical theories of disability.

COMMON SENSE ABOUT THE
CONCEPT OF DISABILITY

....

All inabilities can become disabilities when combined with other factors. Confusion arises when we begin the discussion of disability before the discussion of inability, moving too quickly to an account of the sources of human disabilities and what to do about them. When we do that, we immediately notice that many people who are officially labeled as physically disabled are in basically good physical health in most respects, and that many people with permanent physical, psychological, intellectual, and behavioral forms of ill health are not functionally disabled in the physical and social environments they arrange to inhabit. Once we notice those things, the discussion of disability can sometimes begin in an unproductive place. What follows is meant to avoid that unproductive place. It prepares the way for the argument (in the following sections) that all disabilities are instances of a lack of a fundamental kind of health: *habilitative health*— meaning the level of physiological, psychological, and behavioral health needed to perform various habilitative and rehabilitative tasks. Those tasks, as the term "habilitation" indicates, are all aimed at equipping people and things with functional abilities or capacities that they otherwise would lack.

Species-Characteristics and Associated Inabilities

Consider some common-sense remarks about human inabilities. We are all mortal, for instance. That is merely a characteristic of our species. So are various lethal physical limits traceable to being human: within minutes, we all die without air; within hours, we all die without shelter from extreme radiation. Injuries or diseases or choices or environments that push us near lethal limits are legion. But since human beings as a species are vulnerable to death, there is nothing in such vulnerabilities in themselves that leads us to think of them as disabilities. They are inabilities, to be sure. Limitations, to be sure. But not disabilities, unless we add something further. So it will be useful to begin with an overview of some primary types of human inabilities.

Mortality and the Meaning of Life

Some of us have very short lives and others very long ones. We are thus vulnerable, it seems, to having lives that are either *too* short or *too* long. These aspects of the human condition raise questions about the nature of a good life and a meaningful life. Most of us find effective ways of answering or avoiding such questions. But fear of death, our vulnerability to it, and pessimism about these aspects of the human condition can make us miserable at times and, at the extremes, can be disabling. Such fear or pessimism can become pathological, in an adjectival sense, if we can no longer act effectively to preserve our own health (or life), act decently toward others, or contribute effectively toward our rehabilitation.

That is a dangerous condition. But we probably need something more than that to justify the claim that it amounts to a disability. For one thing, if it is transient, we would probably want to call it a dark mood or depression, even a temporarily disabling one, rather than a disability (in a nominative sense) or even an inability. For another thing, if the fearful person is by all other measures in basically good physical and psychological health and not in any special danger of death in terms of age or environmental risk factors, it seems excessive to declare him or her disabled. At least it seems so unless the disabling fear or pessimism is persistent, all-consuming, and resistant to rehabilitation— in which case it seems sensible to say that the person's functional psychological health is *not* good overall. And for that kind of persistent and possibly permanent ill health, it also seems sensible to say that the person has a disability.

Typical, Functional but Problematic Individual Endowments

There are also developmental but species-typical characteristics of human anatomy and physiology. They emerge slowly in the process of gestation and continue to develop through growth, changes in function and strength, and in other respects during infancy (e.g., bone structure of the skull), early childhood (e.g., teeth), puberty (fertility), adolescence (e.g., frontal lobe brain structure), and early maturity. Some people may be unhappy with the species-typical characteristics they have been endowed with or have developed from their endowments. They may think they are too tall, too short, too thin, too fat, with eyes too close together, too far apart, and so forth—even though the characteristics they have are well within the range of normal or typical anatomy and physiology.

As is the case with human mortality and the dissatisfaction some people have with it, it does not seem commonsensical to apply the term "disability" to the dissatisfaction we may have with our typical anatomical and physiological endowments and developments—unless that dissatisfaction is the source of persistent and possibly permanent physical or psychological ill health. Then, as in the mortality case, it is the ill health that is the disability and not the species-typical characteristics themselves.

This has notorious consequences when that sort of disability is caused largely by social conventions about normality and subsequent discrimination. People of color are disabled in an adjectival sense by racism, but surely we would not want to say that *they* are by that fact alone the ones who have the disability in a nominative sense. Similarly for women and sexism. In both cases, it is sometimes more commonsensical to think that it is primarily the oppressors who have the ill health and disability (in the form of irrationality or sociopathy) that needs to change. This may, or may not, secondarily produce ill health and consequent disabilities in the people who are oppressed. (The obvious solution is to lift the oppression in a way that restores health, as necessary, to both oppressors and the oppressed.)

Atypical Anatomy and Physiology

Many people wind up with atypical anatomy during the developmental process. Even when this is dramatic, however, it does not always lead to inability, let alone disability. For example, in the congenital condition called *situs inversus totalis* all the thoracic and abdominal organs are reversed right to left. This is something that happens in an estimated 1 in 10,000 human beings. And, barring concurrent cardiac defects, the reversal of the typical arrangement of organs does not usually complicate health at all, though it may complicate emergency medical treatment if the medical personnel do not discover it. Similarly, congenitally missing parts or supernumerary ones may or may not be reflected in inabilities or disabilities. A missing kidney is a bit of a risk factor, but an additional kidney is sometimes not a risk at all. Congenitally missing limbs are another matter, as is a missing long bone, like a tibia. Such missing parts may require special surgery, prosthetic devices, and special habilitation in using them. Nonetheless, the result of such habilitation may reduce the individual's physical inabilities to the point that it is problematic to consider them disabilities.

Thus we have what will become a common refrain in this discussion: the question to ask in each case about any atypicality (deficit, surplus, or irregular placement in body part or function) is whether it amounts to a permanent form of physical or psychological ill health or the vulnerability to either—in a given range of environments of special importance to the individual involved. If not, the question of whether to treat it as a disability remains an open one.

Developmental Abilities

It is a species characteristic that our postnatal physical, intellectual, emotional, and agentic powers develop slowly from birth into maturity and then wane slowly as we age. Elderly people have declining powers of many sorts and, ultimately, of every sort. Age-appropriate inabilities are not *dis*abilities by that fact alone. Inabilities that everyone has—either throughout their lives or at various age-appropriate stages of their lives—do not need to be singled out with the additional (potent) label of disabilities. At most, they are the occasion for disabling pathologies in the individual or disabling treatment by other people.

It is important to notice, here, that strengths of agency and character are developmental abilities and inabilities. The extent to which an individual's development in those respects is functional or dysfunctional in a given physical or social environment is directly relevant to the assessment of whether that individual thereby has (or does not have) a disability. It turns out that the concept of habilitative health (as defined later) probably identifies all those disabilities successfully.

Individual, Nondevelopmental Diversity

Human beings also have inabilities that are the product of injury or disease. These inabilities are not necessarily disabilities either. Here again, the crucial factors are the connection to health, or to damaging treatment from the physical or social environment, or to neglectful or damaging treatment from others.

We are also variably vulnerable to life-threatening injury, disease, trauma, and illness throughout our lives. Some of us take this in stride. Others ignore it altogether. And still others become obsessively concerned with it. Deliberate ignorance of our vulnerability can become pathological. (Recklessness and foolhardiness are vices, and, to the extent that they resist correction toward some semblance of practical wisdom, they can be psychological and/or behavioral disorders.) Obsessive concern with human vulnerability—and perhaps especially with our own—can also generate phobias of various sorts, and phobias can become psychological and/or behavioral disorders. Once any of this reaches the level of a persisting, dysfunctional pathology in a given environment important to the individual and becomes resistant to rehabilitation, it can generate disabilities.

Common Sense About the Concept of Health

So far, this is much too vague. But some better focus can be gained in three steps. First, by a brief comment on the concept of "complete" health. Second, by outlining a conception of functional good health in a given range of environments. Third, by defining a conception of habilitative health. The first two steps will be taken in the succeeding paragraphs. They condense, rewrite, and repurpose material from Becker (2012, in chaps. 3.2, 4.3, 5.1). The third step will be taken in the section "Habilitative Health."

Complete Health

In medicine, public policy, and bioethics, there has long been a tendency in some quarters to define health in negative terms—as the absence of pathology—and then to deal first and foremost with pathological conditions that can be traced to a dysfunctional physiological source. That tends to leave out, or at least discount, the nature of positively good health—defined as the presence of functional strengths rather than the absence of dysfunctional strength levels. In medical practice, of course, the presence of functional strengths and the sort of good health they represent is certainly a prominent concern. But again the focus is predominantly on eliminating pathology: restoring physiological functioning through physical therapy, speech therapy, and occupational therapy as devoted to the physical activities of daily life. Psychotherapy and behavioral therapy are available but are also typically devoted to the elimination of pathology.

This runs counter to common sense about both disability and health. In both ordinary conversation and professional settings, people generally recognize that the absence of pathology is not equivalent to the presence of robust or even stable good health. And we certainly recognize that the presence of stable, good psychological and behavioral health is as important (in human affairs) as the presence of stable, good physiological health. Moreover, we recognize the importance of hospitable physical and social environments in sustaining good health of both sorts, as well as the importance of inhospitable environments in generating ill health. For debates in bioethics about these points, see Boorse (1997) and others in Humber and Almeder (1997) and in Nordenfelt (1995; 2001) as well, who explicitly connects health to the pursuit of vital goals.

So the first step to take is to notice that the discussion of health and disability must concern itself with what has been called "complete health": both good and bad health, both physical and psychological/intellectual/behavioral health, all of it relative to some specified range of physical and social environments. One can be in robustly good physical and psychological health in a peaceful, well-organized country village, but vulnerable to anxiety disorders in a well-organized but hectic city of millions; and not competent physically or psychologically to be an astronaut. So it is always wise to specify a range of physical and social environments in giving an assessment of an individual's good health: "The patient is in robustly good physical and psychological health and thriving in the challenges she faces here. But it is not clear how she will function in the large-scale urban environment she so much dreads, and will soon reluctantly move into."[1]

Furthermore, the discussion of complete health must concern itself with transient conditions (e.g., appendicitis) as well as stable traits (e.g., a missing kidney and a stable, well-functioning urological system with the remaining kidney). A common-sense health assessment should always be able to make the following sort of distinction: "The patient is a 35-year-old female with acute appendicitis requiring immediate surgery but is otherwise physically fit and in good psychological health as well."

What we need next, then, it is a more detailed conception of good health—one that is appropriate for our concerns about complete health in the sense described here. This conception of good health must be able to account for the variety of inabilities (short of disabilities) to which human beings are vulnerable. And, ideally, it will also point us toward an aspect of health that identifies the difference between inabilities and disabilities.

Good Health

Suppose we begin at the point where people have achieved health as defined in negative terms—as the absence of ill health—and ask what additional factors have to be in place for them to achieve health defined in positive terms—as the presence of good health.

A Health Scale

We can think of levels of health (both good and bad health) as arranged on a continuum from worst to best, with a dimensionless neutral point in the middle. Suppose we want each point on the continuum to refer to the same set of objectively measurable functional factors—factors that yield a functional assessment of underlying trait-health overlaid by transient health conditions and adjusted by reference to the physical and social environments of special concern. (Example: Your health is fine. Not astronaut material, maybe, but that doesn't matter. Don't worry about the ligament damage. It will heal.)

We want those factors to be broadly enough defined to cover physiological, psychological, and behavioral varieties of good and bad health of all sorts. And we also want those factors to be causally connected to each other so that health is improved or diminished in reciprocal ways: the lessening or absence of factors of bad health contributes to either stabilizing bad health or building it up toward the good side of the continuum, while the presence or strengthening of factors of good health contributes to either preventing a decline toward bad health or to building good health further up toward better health; and the reverse. For the moment, let us leave out purely subjective reports of illness, wellness, happiness, or life satisfaction that either are not, or cannot be correlated with, objectively measurable functioning.

Functional Good Health

Moreover, let us just stipulate for the moment that typical, age-appropriate human anatomy and physiology—as it functions in the absence of disease, deficit, or any other pathology—is at the dimensionless zero point between ill health and good health. Such nonpathological functioning obviously includes some strengths, of course, in the nominal functioning of the neurological system, immune system, digestive system, and so forth. It may be that typical human functioning at the zero point will itself provide some strength and momentum for moving beyond that point into the region of good health. But, as the emergency room's revolving door phenomenon shows, we cannot count on this alone to keep us stable at the zero point or at any point in good health above zero, rather than declining into ill health. We apparently need some additional strengths and momentum to keep us in, and improving in, good health.

Suppose we summarize these strengths as follows, noting that they all have both physiological and psychological components. (1) Resistance to declines toward ill health, in traits or conditions. (2) Resilience, via homeostatic mechanisms, in returning to a previous level of health from a lesser level. (3) Restorative capacities that can, under some conditions, reverse the declines toward ill health that occur despite an individual's resistance or resilience, or can repair damage to the mechanisms of resistance and resilience themselves. (4) Generation of agentic energy to avoid lethargy, helpless passivity, and paralyzing anxiety or fear. (5) Generation of momentum for development toward good health and along the typical developmental track for human beings. (6) Generation of the self-initiated agentic activity characteristic of good health along its typical developmental track over a complete life.[2]

Functional good health might then be understood as some stable combination of those six strengths above the zero point between ill health and good health.

Getting the Strengths of Good Health

The question now is about what is needed to increase those six strengths so that they are sufficient to bring people out of ill health, prevent declines back into it, raise people above its mere absence, and improve their level of good health.

For all these cases, the answer is the same. In order to survive and thrive, human beings need at least a minimally hospitable physical and social environment. And, as the next section will argue, that turns out to require a special kind of good health (to be called "habilitative health"). In everyone, its complete absence is an apocalyptic disaster. In anyone, its complete absence is a lethal disability. And the partial lack of it in anyone is a disability under some (and sometimes all) environmental conditions. Habilitative health of the right kinds, in the right amounts, at the right times is an existential necessity for human beings. That is a very good reason for thinking that habilitative ill health and disability are matters of fundamental philosophical importance.

Habilitative Health

All human beings face three fundamental habilitative and/or rehabilitative tasks throughout their lifetimes: receiving habilitation from others as necessary; habilitating themselves as necessary; and habilitating, as necessary, the physical and social environments they inhabit.[3] Effectively addressing those fundamental tasks is a survival necessity for humans, so we need to have the requisite abilities. These abilities amount to having a certain level of what can appropriately be called *habilitative health*. To the extent that we lack that form of good health, we have some particularly unhealthy inabilities and, by that fact, potential disabilities.

We thus need to develop, as far as possible, the physiological and psychological abilities necessary for successfully addressing these essential tasks. We need habilitative abilities that are reliable and effective across the whole range of physical and social environments that we inhabit or might inhabit. What we need, in short, is *habilitative health*—not only in ourselves, but in others, and in our environments. What we want to avoid is fundamental habilitative inability—and, more than that, habilitative disability.

To reach those conclusions, a modest amount of restatement and reorganization of material from earlier in the chapter is necessary. As follows.

Habilitative Health and Its Necessity

If we cannot effectively *receive* the habilitation we need from other people we may die, languish, or isolate ourselves to the point where our lives are solitary, poor, nasty, brutish, and short—even outside a Hobbesian state of nature. Think of infants who cannot take or digest food. Think of adults who cannot accept the help or company of others without being grudging, contemptuous, or belligerent.

We face a similar fate if we never *give* habilitative help (when we are able to do so) to others in need of it from us. That also has the effect of isolating us—either because we have to avoid all the opportunities to give such help or because people around us eventually exclude us from the compassionate community of people who will gladly (or at least not grudgingly) offer habilitative help to others when it is needed. Such exclusion can be damaging to our health, both physically and psychologically. Think of the difficulty of finding a subculture of sociopaths in which we could live happily without giving habilitative help to others. A subculture of grifters, for example, as in Frears (1990). Then think of living in it.

And, finally, things do not go well for us if we are unable or unwilling to make any effective effort at all to habilitate ourselves (by, say, learning how to make ourselves agreeable to others) or if we are similarly unable or unwilling even to try to habilitate a hostile social or physical environment. Think of the homesteaders in the challenging physical conditions on the plains of the Nebraska and Dakota Territories in the nineteenth century. They did not survive unless they were willing and able to cope inventively with harsh winters in sod houses, crop failures, and long periods of social isolation. Not all of them could do this (Rolvaag 1927/1999; Jones, 2014).

Human abilities to perform habilitative tasks are always limited, of course. And this will be true no matter how strong and wise and talented we become and how fortunate we are in our circumstances. Some things are not within our control, as the Stoics dryly remind us. We are mortal. And, that large fact aside, we are limited by the extent of our physical and psychological endowments, whether they are typically described as disabilities or not. We are limited by age and the details of our development. We are limited by the extent and duration of our overall good or ill health. We are limited by the extent to which our physical environment can be made genuinely hospitable—that is, conducive to human survival and flourishing. (Say, on Mars.) And we are limited by the extent to which our social environment is stable, multigenerational, and hospitable—that is, characterized by enough cooperation and coordination to sustain a productive and reproductive social system at every degree of magnification from personal to global.

Such limitations raise urgent questions of justice about the tolerable extent of possible human abilities and inabilities throughout a given population, as well as their actual distribution in various environments. Everyone has some specific range of abilities and inabilities, including the disabled. Thus, it is not true that disabilities are just a special case of inabilities, because some persons with disabilities may have special abilities as well. (Adults who are 3'5" tall may or may not require special medical treatment. They may or may not have some functional advantages in a given physical and social environment. They may or may not be subject to disabling discrimination and inequality of opportunity. And so forth.) So it is best to think of various kinds of disabilities mapped (as overlays) over both categories: over both abilities and inabilities. This is a revealing entry point for discussing habilitative health and disability. We will return to its consequences for justice later.

Habilitative Health and Its Agentic Development

In the typical course of healthy human development in a reasonably hospitable social and physical environment, an individual's ability to cope successfully with the three habilitative tasks develops along with every other aspect of good health—physiological and psychological. But, unlike good health generally, habilitative health is essentially a version of agentic health aimed at accomplishing habilitative tasks. Just as we assess health generally in age-appropriate ways, we assess agentic health in age-appropriate ways.

The newborn's agency is characterized by limited situational awareness and mostly instinctual goal-seeking, where the goals are mostly the immediate satisfaction of security needs (warmth, comfort, no sudden changes, etc.). The newborn may or may not instinctively seek nourishment or be able to nurse effectively. But newborns typically are able to effectively *receive* habilitative help from others, and, with such help, their overall good health, as well as the beginnings of their self-habilitative health, can be sustained. Similarly for the ability to be comforted, to develop a predictable sleep cycle, and so forth.

At that point, the infant's agency typically begins to become more complex—in increased situational awareness and associative expectations (being held in a certain way is associated with being secure or being fed) and in the infant's developing abilities to signal needs and desires to others and to make efforts to elicit (rather than merely receive) care from others. Furthermore, the infant typically develops various exploratory interests (watching human faces, making exploratory movements) and the beginnings of reciprocal responses, including mirroring responses.

And so it goes throughout the typical course of human development generally, through the various landmarks of the development of various age-appropriate characteristics of species-typical human agency: increased physical mobility and coordination, walking unassisted, the acquisition of language and other forms of communication, the ability to understand and mirror other people's intentions and affective states (comparing them to their own), along with the development of an effective use of rudimentary practical intelligence in the achievement of some goals, eventually up to the acquisition of various effective traits of self-command (courage, prudence, moderation, delayed gratification, strategic reasoning) and the transformation of practical intelligence into something resembling practical wisdom (e.g., about what goals are worth pursuing). At that point, the individual has something we can unproblematically call *rational agency*.

Prosocial and Eudaimonistic Traits

Moreover, in the typical course of human development, the rational agency developed by individuals includes various prosocial as well as self-interested traits (including benevolent concern for the health and well-being of others as well as oneself), together with an appreciation of the agent's own causal responsibility (or lack of it) for events. When it does include these things, we can unproblematically say that the individual has developed a form of *moral* agency as well. This is a lengthy process, sometimes abruptly terminated or reversed by ill health, overwhelming physical or social environments, or old age.

Furthermore, there is good reason to believe that the typical course of individual human development proceeds along the lines put forward in eudaimonistic accounts of the virtues—an account in which practical wisdom is engaged in subordinating our vices to our virtues, resolving conflicts between various virtues (e.g., justice and mercy), prioritizing the virtues, and expressing them coherently in our attitudes, decisions, and behavior. (For detailed accounts of such matters, see Becker, [2017 chaps. 5–6].) and Becker [2012, chaps. 7–8].)

The important point to notice for present purposes is that, *a fortiori* from the preceding, it is species-typical for human beings to develop some level of habilitative health— the version of good health that equips us to effectively address (within the limits of our agentic abilities) all three habilitative tasks mentioned at the beginning of this section. At least this is so for human beings with typical anatomy and physiology, functioning without ill health in a reasonably hospitable physical and social environment. (The term is "reasonably hospitable" rather than maximally or perfectly hospitable just because the development of the six factors of basic good health described earlier—strengths of various sorts—often seems to require physiological or psychological challenges that stimulate the development of those strengths. Think about the way vaccines stimulate the immune system or the way in which difficult environments stimulate problem-solving. What we need for agentic growth is not a utopian environment or an overwhelmingly inhospitable one, but rather one that is optimal for developing habilitative health.)

Habilitative Necessities, Duties, and Disabilities

The concept of habilitative health suggests a way of identifying the disabilities that are of special significance for theories of justice and for ethics generally. This is so because the three essential habilitative tasks outlined earlier are necessities—they *must* be accomplished successfully if human beings are to survive and thrive in hospitable physical and social environments. So a permanent inability to perform one or more of the three essential habilitative tasks surely counts as a disability coming from habilitative ill health. And, perhaps perversely, we should note that human beings bent on destroying such health in themselves and others also need to start on their project with a good deal of habilitative health. Nihilistic, apocalyptic, or psychopathic annihilators—on any scale from themselves alone to their families, neighbors, fellow citizens, governments, and human beings generally—need some aspects of habilitative health to work with and against. So, even for them, a permanent inability to accomplish a significant range of habilitative tasks qualifies as a disability.

Disabilities Are Presumptively Connected to Habilitative Health

Is there anything we would want to classify as a disability that we would miss if we simply focused on those connected to habilitative (ill) health? It seems not. But it is hopeless to try to prove the point *a priori*. Or by enumeration. Rather, we make the following observations.

It is hard to think of people as disabled if they are fully functional—in age-appropriate ways—in contributing to the accomplishment of all three of the necessary habilitative tasks for themselves and others, even when they have seriously compromised health in other respects. After all, they will be age-appropriately self-habilitating. Think of an electrician, or a law professor, or an actor—each with an artificial leg. Presumably, they can accomplish all the activities of daily living and are thus self-habilitating in that way. Presumably they can contribute to the habilitation of others and their families through their work and through their duties as citizens. And presumably they can contribute in some way to the habilitation of a given physical or social environment as necessary. Similarly for people with more serious physical or intellectual inabilities that limit their mobility and the range of physical and social environments in which they can accomplish one or more of the habilitative tasks.

But that just means (so far) that they will have habilitative *inabilities*. Under what conditions would we want to say they are thereby disabled? Surely we can make a good case for saying that they do not have disabilities in a nominative sense (on those grounds alone) if in fact they can manage to accomplish all three essential habilitative tasks in some set of hospitable environments that are accessible and important to them. And when we think about when we would reverse that judgment and classify them as having disabilities, it seems always to come down to cases in which their habilitative health is actually compromised—for example, by an inhospitable, discriminatory society that prevents them from having satisfying and rewarding lives and work, thus damaging both their physical and psychological abilities to be self-habilitating, among other things. Everyone, disabled or not, has limitations, difficulties, and unavailable options. That is just to say that they have inabilities. They do not, by that fact alone, have disabilities.

So it seems safe, as a first approximation, to identify disabilities with significant habilitative ill health that is permanent or something that the individual cannot simply work around without significant help from others. This amounts to a rebuttable presumption. It is open to revision if we can find cases of inabilities that amount to disabilities even though they are unconnected to habilitative ill health. (Chronic pain is an instructive test case, and I thank the editors for mentioning this. It can be either disabling or non-disabling, in terms of habilitative functioning. That does not mean that nondisabling chronic pain should not be taken seriously, however, and treated therapeutically. But it does, apparently, mean that some mild forms of chronic pain are not disabilities in terms of the analysis given here.)

Necessities, Practical Requirements, and Disabilities

Further discussion of the same matter can begin with a sketch of how to rate the extent of an individual's habilitative health status. This is followed by some obvious conclusions about what counts as a disability in habilitative terms. Finally, a compact recital of the human importance of habilitation makes plain the basis for constructing an account of human duties to provide such habilitation for oneself, others, and the environment. Each of these elements contributes to the conclusion that disabilities are best understood as a lack of habilitative health.

Habilitative Health Status

The measurement of habilitative health plausibly requires an assessment of at least the following six multipart elements:

- **First**. An assessment of the six strengths of good health generally. Note that such typical development into adulthood—at least in reasonably hospitable social environments—includes the development of prosocial psychological dispositions to provide habilitation for at least some others (and some environments) as well as oneself.

- **Second**. Assessment of the extent to which the physical and social environments inhabited by the individual create and sustain momentum away from ill health and toward improved good health generally, as well as momentum toward or along the typical developmental track for human beings.
- **Third**. Assessment of the extent to which the individual is blocked or inhibited— by either some aspect of limited good health, some aspect of ill health, or some aspects of accessible physical or social environments—from deploying his or her strengths of good health for habilitative purposes.
- **Fourth**. Assessment of the variety of open paths into better habilitative health (either in the existing physical and social environments or other possible ones) if others supply habilitation for the individual or for some environments.
- Fifth, assessment of the extent to which the habilitation from others necessary for achieving and/or sustaining habilitative health for the individual would be extraordinary (compared to what is typical for human beings generally).
- **Sixth**. Assessment of the extent to which the individual has developed strength in developmentally typical psychological and behavioral dispositions to engage in self-habilitation as necessary, providing habilitation for others as necessary, and working to habilitate physical and social environments as necessary.

Habilitative Disabilities

The rebuttable presumption is that people are not disabled if they have enough good health to accomplish all three habilitative tasks in ways that are age-appropriate over a complete life. People *are* disabled, however, if they lack enough good health to accomplish all three in the environments they *must* inhabit. (A trivial inability in a temperate climate on earth may be a lethal disability in Antarctica or on Mars. So if people with that trivial inability in Virginia *must* go permanently to Mars, their consequent disability is no longer trivial.) This is certainly consistent with refusing the label of disability to a wide range of inabilities that various people can work around in a given environment. Moreover, it is consistent with identifying people as disabled if they are unable (more or less permanently) to accomplish *some* of those habilitative tasks but are sometimes able to accomplish others.

There is, however, a fairly dramatic difference in the list of disabilities often now in use (for health insurance purposes) and the list that would be generated by a focus on habilitative health. This difference has to do with the healthy individual's level of psychological resilience in the form of adaptability, agentic energy, and species-typical psychological and behavioral development (as it occurs in hospitable social environments). Many things that we tend to identify as malingering, for example, might instead be identified as a lack of habilitative health and treated as such. This is also the case for people who have been pushed off the typical developmental track that generates prosocial dispositions and cooperative behavior and who end up with deeply rooted antagonistic or disruptive dispositions. These are also likely to be regarded as disabilities in terms of habilitative ill health.

This difference in the list of disabilities need not "medicalize" social responses to them, of course. But it should increase our interest in making sure (through educational interventions, for example, or rehabilitative ones) that the underdeveloped elements of good health that create the inability to be resilient and adaptable, or to be inclined (as a sort of default position) to engage in cooperative prosocial behavior, are appropriately addressed. Something like this conclusion, drawn from things other than habilitative health, can be found in Fisk (2016), who argues that ethics itself is fundamentally motivated by concern for social survival; in Pickett and Wilkinson (2009), who argue that "more equal societies always do better"; and in Nordenfelt (2001), who connects the goals of health enhancement to social welfare.

To sum up, then, fully functional habilitative health includes all three of its aspects: abilities related to self-habilitation, the habilitation of others, and the habilitation of the physical and social environment. Anyone who lacks one or more of the three elements of habilitative health completely—in an age-inappropriate or permanent way—obviously has a serious disability. And, as the following will make clear, if everyone lacks all three even for short periods, the results would be catastrophic for human beings generally. But most societies and the individuals in them can probably survive (and possibly even thrive) even if most people have even a modest amount of age-appropriate ability in each of the three aspects of habilitative health—especially in well-organized societies with a complex division of labor.

Habilitative Disabilities and Social Duties

To see this more clearly—and to see the places where a lack of habilitative health always clearly generates serious disabilities that arguably generate social duties to rehabilitate, care for, or compensate for people with those disabilities—it is helpful to lay out a sequence of practical necessities for habilitation in human life generally. The following outline reorganizes and retraces earlier material about the practical necessities for habilitative health during an individual life from infancy to old age. It begins with a series of descriptive propositions in an elementary valid argument form, then restates the argument in terms of prudential oughts, and finally suggests how to reach a corresponding normative judgment, all things considered.[4]

Recipient Health

The argument begins by affirming the practical necessity of recipient health:

A. All human beings must be able, as a matter of practical necessity, to elicit and receive effective habilitation from others as necessary for survival (and for thriving) throughout their lives and to be able to provide habilitation for others as necessary for receiving it themselves.

The practical necessity asserted in "A" requires (but is not guaranteed by) some closely related abilities in themselves and others—namely,

B. All successful recipients must have, even as infants and at every stage of life beyond that, at least a minimal level of (egoistically oriented) self-habilitative health themselves, which includes enough reciprocal response and activity from them to elicit habilitation from others as necessary, even if those others are themselves egoistically oriented. *That is, A only if B.*

Caregiver and Donor Health

B requires, but is not guaranteed by, something further—namely,

C. Each human being's receiving enough habilitation from caregivers and donors requires—throughout the species-typical developmental track from gestation, infancy, childhood, and adolescence—enough habilitation from enough others to achieve a mutually sustainable level of habilitative health in themselves (as recipients, caregivers, and donors) and in a sufficient number of others (as recipients, caregivers, and donors). *That is, B only if C.*

Note: Even a system of mutual advantage among egoists requires reciprocity. So it requires not only self-habilitative health, but also other-directed habilitative activity as well.

Multigenerational Health

C, in turn, requires but is not guaranteed by

D. the presence of a stable, self-sustaining, multigenerational social environment of a sufficient number of people who have at least minimal habilitative health in all three of its aspects and who are appropriately placed, able, and motivated to habilitate and/or rehabilitate others into a sustainable level of habilitative health when that is possible—either directly to given individuals (such as their children) or to habilitative social institutions engaged in cooperative activities aimed at creating and sustaining hospitable social environments. *That is, C only if D.*

Note: It is plausible to think that sustaining other-directed habilitative activity requires at least the minimal level of prosocial habilitative health, characteristic of species-typical psychological development beginning in childhood, in which caregivers and donors have genuine concern for the well-being of others, for the sake of those others.

Hospitable Environments

Finally, D requires but is not guaranteed by

E. the presence of a sufficiently stable and hospitable physical and social environment in which human beings generally can survive and thrive in habilitative health so as to accomplish, as necessary, age-appropriate habilitative tasks of self-habilitation, habilitation of others, and of the physical and social environment. *That is, D only if E.*

Conclusions

Thus it follows that because we have affirmed that *A* is a practical requirement insofar as it is possible to achieve, and because *A* can be achieved only if *B, C, D,* and *E* are achieved, they, too, are practical requirements to the extent that they can be achieved. *That is, A only if B & C & D & E. / And A. / Therefore B & C & D & E.*

It also follows that *if* we can affirm the corresponding prudential ought judgment—that we *ought* to achieve *A* to the extent that it is possible—then *A* is at least a *prudential normative* requirement. (Note: By the time we develop rational and moral agency as defined earlier, we have implicitly been affirming that *A* is both a practical and prudential normative requirement.)

The remaining question is whether *A*, and thus *B, C, D,* and *E* ought to be achieved *all things considered* and are thus moral requirements in that sense. Given the practical and prudential necessity for human beings of accomplishing their habilitative tasks, it is plausible to answer that question in the affirmative. These are paradigm cases of tasks that ought to be achieved, all things considered, and the burden of proof would surely be on skeptics and nihilists to show why these practical and prudential necessities are not requirements, all things considered.

DISABILITIES, GOOD LIVES, AND A HOSPITABLE WORLD

Habilitative health is only one aspect of good health, and, as defined here, it deals only with habilitative necessities—those abilities with respect to one's self, others, and the environments that are essential to survival and thriving. Such good health—indeed, good health of any sort—is not enough to guarantee much of anything about one's success in surviving or thriving, let alone having even a minimally good life in a minimally hospitable environment. Habilitative inabilities and disabilities further limit the prospects. But there are some reasons for optimism.

Good Health Is More Than Just Enough for Immediate Necessities

Think of a quadriplegic lawyer working as a highly specialized researcher in a large government agency, depending for his daily needs on a succession of groups of two or three live-in graduate students from a university near his spacious apartment. The graduate students are paid a small stipend and get free living accommodations, including the food they all eat. They have the run of the place. He confines himself mainly to his bedroom, bathroom, and a small den near his office. He is good at what he does at work, but not exceptionally good. And everything he does is dependent on every aspect of his life continuing to work in exactly the same way. The power wheelchair has to work. The graduate students have to be there, on time, when they have promised. Every reorganization of the government agency threatens the whole arrangement, either by threatening his job itself (his only source of income) or the special accommodations and assistance he needs on the job. In habilitative terms, under exactly the right conditions, he can succeed to some extent at all three habilitative tasks. He is self-habilitating in the sense that he lives a meticulously planned and scheduled existence, even though it requires a lot of equipment and assistance from others to carry out his plans. He contributes to the habilitation of others (by employing the graduate students). And he devotes some attention to sustaining and improving the larger physical and social environment (by his work in the government agency itself). But he continually skates right along the edge of his abilities to succeed at any of this. And he is pretty thoroughly miserable. But the misery doesn't come from his disability itself so much as from the relentless, daily difficulties of his life. Many people without disabilities have such relentless difficulties.

The moral is this. We do not have good habilitative health if we lack the strength to cope with the misery of relentless difficulties. If our pursuit of essential habilitative tasks consumes 100% of our energy and strength, we will not have an adequate level of habilitative health. Even for necessities, we need a reservoir of strength to draw upon from time to time. That reservoir also supplies energy and strength for both habilitative and nonhabilitative activities beyond essential or necessary ones. Such energy and strength can be put to use in pursuit of other aspects of a good life. This means we should be wary of disabilities that confine a person to exactly one way of thriving in exactly one environment. That, in turn, means we should *not* be willing to accept rehabilitation strategies that provide *only* this sort of confined life. The same thing applies to parenting, and education, and social policy (including the criminal justice system). Preparing children, students, workers, apprentices, job re-trainees, and convicted felons for exactly one confined and insecure path to habilitative health can generate crushing disabilities.

It Helps that Habilitative Health Is So Focused on Agentic Health

The quadriplegic lawyer's misery is not necessarily a product of his disability. As described, he is a relentlessly self-habilitating agent, living in a hospitable environment. It is a confining environment, but it is hard to believe that it needs to be crushing. Instead, he needs to cut himself some slack and presumably can do so because he has such good agentic health. If he needs to be less miserable (or wants to be), then he ought to spend some energy arranging a less demanding, less all-or-nothing way of life.

The same cannot be said for people who have serious agentic disabilities, with or without physical ones. Otherwise robustly healthy adults with localized brain injuries can have aphasia and related memory and behavioral problems that profoundly affect their agency. They may not be able to live on their own and be reliably self-habilitating, but, in a care center, they may be able to help others in kind and compassionate ways and help the staff with their work. Attention to habilitative health identifies the source of the problem accurately. And it also suggests where the rehabilitative focus should be placed. And that, in turn, identifies an important task for medical rehabilitation research.

NOTES

1. It is probably no accident that there seems to be a distinction between rural and urban conceptions of health itself. See Gessert et al. (2015). And for a gripping narrative account, see Arnow (1954/2009).
2. The elaboration of all of this into a genuine health scale that might be usable in practice may be found in Becker (2012, 82–94).
3. Many habilitative endeavors are not fundamental, of course, because they are not actually necessities. Some, like making an especially good meal, may just be optional improvements. Some may even be superfluous.
4. A more elaborate argument on the topic of agentic patients and healthcare, using some of the same materials, may be found in Becker (2016, 16–17).

REFERENCES

Arnow, Harriette Simpson. 1954/2009. *The Doll Maker*. New York: Scribner.

Becker, Lawrence C. 2012. *Habilitation, Health, and Agency: A Framework for Basic Justice*. New York: Oxford University Press.

Becker, Lawrence C. 2016. "Habilitation, Healthy Agency, and Patient-Participation." In *Promoting Patient Engagement and Participation for Effective Healthcare Reform*, edited by Guendalina Graffigna, 1–24. IGI Global Medical Information Science Reference.

Becker, Lawrence C. 2017 [1998]. *A New Stoicism: revised edition*. Princeton: Princeton University Press.

Boorse, C. 1997. "A Rebuttal on Health." In *What Is Disease?*, edited by J. Humber and R. Almeder, 1–134. Totowa, NJ: Humana Press.

Fisk, Milton. 2016. *Ethics as Social Survival*. New York: Routledge.

Frears, Stephen. 1990. *The Grifters*. Screenplay by Donald E. Westlake, based on a novel by Jim Thompson.

Gessert, Charles, et al. 2015. "Rural Definition of Health: A Systematic Literature Review." *BMC Public Health* 15(1): 1–14.

Humber, J., and R. Almeder (Eds.). 1997. *What Is Disease?* Totowa, NJ: Humana Press.

Jones, Tommy Lee. 2014. *The Homesman*. Screenplay by Jones, et al. and based on a novel by Glendon Swarthout.

Nordenfelt, L. 1995. *On the Nature of Health: An Action Theoretic Account*, 2nd ed. Dordrecht/ Boston: Kluwer Academic.

Nordenfelt, L. 2001. "On the Goals of Medicine, Health Enhancement and Social Welfare." *Health Care Analysis* 9(1): 15–23.

Pickett, K., and R. Wilkinson. 2009. *The Spirit Level: Why More Equal Societies Always Do Better*. New York: Allen Lane.

Rolvaag, O. E. 1927/1999. *Giants in the Earth*. New York: Harper Perennial Modern Classics.

FURTHER READING

Barnes, Elizabeth. 2016. *The Minority Body: A Theory of Disability*. Oxford: Oxford University Press.

Becker, Lawrence C. 2005. "Reciprocity, Justice, and Disability." Ethics 116(1/October): 9–39.

Becker, Lawrence C. 2018. "Disability, Basic Justice, and Habilitation into Basic Good Health." In *Disability in Practice*, edited by Thomas Hill and Adam Cureton. New York: Oxford University Press.

Bok, S. 2008. "Rethinking the WHO Definition of Health." In *International Encyclopedia of Public Health*, vol. 6, edited by K. Heggenhougen and S. Quah, 580–597. San Diego, CA: Academic Press.

Fogel, Sarah C., Leslie Calman, and D. Magrini. 2012. "Lesbians' and Bisexual Women's Definition of Health." *Journal of Homosexuality*. 59(6/July): 851–862.

Hofmann, Bjørn. 2016. "Obesity as a Socially Defined Disease: Philosophical Considerations." *Health Care Analysis* 24(1): 86–100.

Keyes, C. L. 2009. "Toward a Science of Mental Health." In *Oxford Handbook of Positive Psychology*, 2nd ed., edited by C. R. Snyder and S. J. Lopez, 89–96. New York: Oxford University Press.

Kittay, Eva Feder. 1999. *Love's Labor: Essays on Women, Equality and Dependency*. New York: Routledge.

Nussbaum, Martha. 2007. *Frontiers of Justice*. Cambridge, MA: Belknap Press of Harvard University Press.

Nussbaum, Martha. 2011. *Creating Capabilities: The Human Development Approach*. Cambridge, MA: Belknap Press of Harvard University Press.

Peterson, C., and M. Seligman. 2004. *Character Strengths and Virtues: A Handbook and Classification*. New York: Oxford University Press.

Richardson, Henry S. 2016. "Capabilities and the Definition of Health." *Bioethics* 30(1): 1–7.

Sen, Amartya. 1985. "Well-Being, Agency, and Freedom [The Dewey Lectures, 1984.]" *Journal of Philosophy* 82(4): 169–221.

Sen, Amartya. 2009. *The Idea of Justice*. Cambridge, MA: Belknap Press of Harvard University Press.

Sen, Amartya, and Martha Nussbaum (eds.). 1992. *Quality of Life*. Oxford: Clarendon Press.

Silvers, Anita, David Wasserman, and Mary B. Mahowald. 1999. *Disability, Difference, Discrimination: Perspectives on Justice in Bioethics and Public Policy*. New Jersey: Rowman & Littlefield.

Snyder, C. R., and S. J. Lopez. 2009. *Oxford Handbook of Positive Psychology*, 2nd ed. New York: Oxford University Press.

Zelazo, P. D. 2013. *The Oxford Handbook of Developmental Psychology*. Oxford: Oxford University Press.

CHAPTER 5

PHILOSOPHY AND THE APPARATUS OF DISABILITY

SHELLEY L. TREMAIN

A NATURALIZED NARRATIVE

THROUGHOUT the last decades of the twentieth century, discussions about disability became increasingly prevalent in mainstream philosophy, especially with the resurgence of work on social justice from the publication of John Rawls's *A Theory of Justice* (1971) forward and the emergence and expansion of the subfields of cognitive science and bioethics. Despite the apparent variety of the questions that mainstream philosophers have asked about disability, however, the cluster of motivational assumptions that underpins almost all their inquiries takes for granted the metaphysical status and epistemological character of the category of disability and designation itself, casting them as self-evident and thus philosophically uninteresting. On the terms of this cluster of assumptions, disability is a prediscursive, transcultural, and transhistorical disadvantage, an objective human defect or characteristic that ought to be prevented, corrected, eliminated, or cured. That these assumptions are contestable, that it might be the case that disability is a historically and culturally specific and contingent social phenomenon, a complex apparatus of power, rather than a natural attribute or property that certain people possess, is not considered, let alone seriously entertained. Indeed, many feminist philosophers uncritically accept the aforementioned assumptions about what disability is and what we know about it. Even some philosophers of disability do not rigorously question the metaphysical and epistemological status of disability, but rather advance ethical and political positions that largely assume the self-evidence of that status.[1]

The bias in philosophy that the inequalities that accrue to disabled people are self-evidently natural and inevitable has yielded the belief that these disadvantages are most appropriately addressed in the domains of medicine, the life sciences, and related fields rather than in philosophy departments. Thus, the assumption that critical analysis of the status of disability is not appropriate subject matter for philosophical inquiry has shaped philosophy departments, influencing hiring practices and decisions, course curricula, the composition of conference lineups, professional networks, and editorial boards, the contents of edited collections, and so on. In other words, the assumption that disability is a philosophically uninteresting human characteristic and the underrepresentation of disabled philosophers within the profession are inseparably embedded in the institutional infrastructure of the discipline, mutually constitutive and mutually reinforcing.

Insofar as philosophers have conceived the social inequalities that accrue to disabled people as the inevitable consequences of a self-evident physiological, or natural, human characteristic, they have presupposed certain assumptions about the relation between biology and society—that is, between nature and nurture—that I aim to undermine.

Dorothy E. Roberts (2016) has distinguished heuristically between two approaches to the question of the relation between biology and society: "the old biosocial science" and "the new biosocial science." As Roberts explains it, the old biosocial science posits that biological differences produce social inequality, whereas the new biosocial science posits that social inequality produces biological differences. The biological determinism of the old biosocial science, she notes, is achieved in several ways: first, the old biosocial science approach separates nature from nurture in order to locate the origins of social inequalities in inherent traits rather than imposed societal structures; second, the old biosocial science postulates that social inequalities are reproduced in the bodies, especially the wombs, of socially disadvantaged people rather than reinvented through unjust ideologies and institutions; third, the old bioscience identifies problems that stem from social inequality as derived from the threats that oppressed people's biology itself poses to society rather than from structural barriers and state violence imposed upon oppressed people; and fourth, the old bioscience endeavors to intervene and fix perceived biological deficits in the bodies of oppressed people rather than end the structural violence that dehumanizes them and maintains an unjust social order.

Roberts explains that, by contrast, the new biosocial science posits that every single biological element, every single biological process in the human body, every human cell, and everything that happens to a human cell is affected by society. All of life, Roberts remarks, is at once biological and social. There is, in short, no natural body. Genes do not determine anything. Moreover, our brains are plastic, with the ability to be modified by social experience. Both epigenetics and social neuroscience, Roberts points out, show that biology is not a separate entity that interacts with the environment; rather, biology is constituted by these interactions (2016; see also Roberts 1998, 2012; Prinz 2012; Gilman and Thomas 2016). With Roberts, various authors have argued, furthermore, that critical analyses of biosocial science must consider how claims about the social construction of biological phenomena are produced, in what contexts they are mobilized, and for what political purposes. Victoria Pitts-Taylor argues (2010, 635), for example, that if we are to take the plasticity of the brain seriously, we must think critically about the historicity of this ontology and the political and economic forces that have produced the historical and epistemological conditions of possibility for its uptake. As Andy Clark (1998) puts it, the plastic brain is a situated brain, culturally, biologically, and socially.

Michel Foucault's insights can be used to denaturalize and de-biologize disability. Many of Foucault's insights upon which I have drawn for this purpose were introduced and refined in his discussions of abnormality, madness, deviance, and other discursive objects that intellectuals and nonintellectuals alike commonly associate with disability. Indeed, my argument has extended these discussions and is most aptly characterized as a feminist philosophical inquiry into what Foucault referred to as the "problematization" of phenomena in the present. Foucault's studies of abnormality, madness, and deviance (among other things) were not intended to provide normative responses to these phenomena, but rather were designed to show how these phenomena emerged *as* problems to which solutions came to be sought. Likewise, my philosophy of disability does not offer an explicitly normative feminist proposal or response to the phenomena of disability, nor does it provide a (normative) feminist critique of a given normative response to the phenomena of disability. Such a given proposal, response, or critique would allege to show that there is a certain definitive solution to the "problem" of disability.

The feminist philosophical inquiry into the problematization of disability that I have developed was designed in large part to indicate how a certain historically and culturally specific regime of power has produced certain acts, practices, subjectivities, bodies, relations, and so on as a problem for the present, as well as to indicate the role that philosophy has played and continues to play in the elaboration of this problem. I followed Foucault's suggestion that inquiry into the problematization of a given state of affairs attempts to uncover how the different solutions to a problem have been constructed, as well as how these different solutions resulted from the problematization of that given state of affairs in the first place. Thus, I have aimed to show how a certain regime of power has produced impairment as both the prediscursive—that is, natural and universal—antecedent of culturally variant forms of disability and a problem for this regime of power to which the regime offers solutions. In other words, one of my aims has been to indicate how a certain apparatus of power has brought impairment—the naturally disadvantageous foundation of disability—into being as that kind of thing.

The Apparatus of Disability

Foucault's innovative conception of apparatus (*dispositif*), technique of genealogy, analyses of biopower, and prescient claims about liberalism and neoliberalism (among others) can be used to investigate the ways that the tradition, discipline, and profession of philosophy have contributed to both the problematization and apparatus of disability, as well as to the naturalization of the allegedly objective antecedent of disability—namely, impairment. In "The Confession of the Flesh," Foucault (1980, 194) defined an apparatus (*dispositif*) as a thoroughly heterogeneous and interconnected ensemble of discourses, institutions, architectural forms, regulatory decisions, laws, scientific statements, administrative measures, and philosophical, moral, and philanthropic propositions that responds to an "urgent need" in a certain historical moment. In other words, an apparatus is a historically specific and dispersed system of power that produces and configures practices toward certain strategic and political ends.

To understand disability as an apparatus is to conceive of it as a far-reaching and systemic matrix of power that contributes to, is inseparable from, and reinforces other apparatuses of historical force relations. On this understanding, disability is not a metaphysical substrate, a natural, biological category, or a characteristic that only certain individuals embody or possess, but rather is a historically contingent network of force relations in which everyone is implicated and entangled and in relation to which everyone occupies a position. That is, to be disabled or nondisabled is to occupy a certain subject position within the productive constraints of the apparatus of disability. In the terms of this understanding of disability, there are no "people with disabilities" and "able-bodied people," but rather there are "disabled people" and "nondisabled people." Just as people are variously racialized through strategies and mechanisms of the apparatus of race but do not "have" races and, furthermore, just as people are variously sexed through strategies and mechanisms of the apparatus of sex but no one "has" a sex, so, too, people are variously disabled or not disabled through the operations of the apparatus of disability but no one "has" a disability. In the terms of the feminist philosophy of disability that I have advanced, to refer to someone as "a person with a disability" is to commit a category mistake. That females and people of color (which are by no means mutually exclusive social groups) have been perceived in the recent histories of Western and Northern nations as the bearers of sex and race, respectively, does not mean that males are not also sexed in accordance with the apparatus of sex, nor that white people are not racialized in the terms of the apparatus of race. Equally, the fact that one is not subjected as a disabled person does not indicate that one occupies a space apart from the apparatus of disability.

Key classificatory schemes and distinctions made in disability theory—such as the distinctions between visible disabilities and invisible disabilities, mental disabilities versus psychological disabilities, physical disability versus cognitive disability, physical impairments as opposed to sensory impairments, severe disabilities versus moderate or mild disabilities, high functioning and low functioning—are, themselves, strategies of these relations of power; that is, these distinctions and designations are performative artifacts of the apparatus of disability that naturalize this state of affairs, reinstituting disability as a personal attribute or individual characteristic. That disabled people reify these (and other) historically contingent products of the apparatus of disability and incorporate them into their sets of beliefs, theories, values, and practices in a host of ways, interpreting them as the substratum or ground of putatively natural or even socially constructed identities, should be recognized as a strategic mechanism of the "polymorphism" (as Foucault referred to it) of (neo)liberalism; that is, the continuous capacity of a liberal regime of force relations to respond to critique by molding the subjectivities of individuals in particular ways. When disability is situated within the domain of force relations, that is, when disability is construed as an apparatus of power, its collaboration with other apparatuses of force relations—such as settler colonialism and heteronormativity—can be more readily identified and investigated.

The conception of disability as an apparatus is premised on an understanding of the relation between power and causation that runs counter to current and emerging work in philosophy of disability and disability studies. For this conception of disability does not rely on some variation of the assumption that impairment and disability could be taken up as politically neutral and value-neutral objects of inquiry were it not for disabling practices and policies of exclusion that the ideological requirements of power place on them. This assumption is fundamental to a dominant sociopolitical conception of disability—namely, the British social model of disability—according to which impairment is a politically neutral human characteristic on which disability (construed as social oppression) is imposed. With the conception of disability as an apparatus, by contrast, no domain of impairment or disability exists apart from relations of power. Impairment and disability can never be freed from power, nor, furthermore, can there be a phenomenology that articulates these supposedly prediscursive domains. Power relations are not external to impairment and disability and their nexus in the apparatus of disability, but rather are integral to this relationship, constituting the knowledge and objects that these historical artifacts affect, as well as the artifacts themselves. As Foucault explained,

> Relations of power are not in a position of exteriority with respect to other types of relationships (economic processes, knowledge relationships, sexual relations), but are immanent in the latter; they are the immediate effects of the divisions, inequalities, and disequilibriums which occur in the latter, and conversely they are the internal conditions of these differentiations; relations of power are not in superstructural positions, with a role of prohibition or accompaniment; they have a directly productive role, wherever they come into play. (1978, 94)

Since there is no exteriority between techniques of knowledge and strategies of power, and insofar as knowledge–power relations are constitutive of the objects that they affect, one of my aims is to identify and examine discussions within philosophy around which historically specific responses to disability, produced in accordance with the requirements of the apparatus of disability, have coalesced; that is, I aim to identify and examine "especially dense transfer point[s] for relations of power" (Foucault 1978, 98) within philosophy that the apparatus of disability has produced, thereby contributing to its expansion and to the constitution of its naturalized elements, of which impairment is only one. Within the discipline of philosophy, the subfields of bioethics and cognitive science are most easily recognizable as domains within which the constitutive effects of the apparatus of disability are produced; however, such sites of power can be identified across and throughout the discipline.

Philosophers of disability ought to ask: How has the combination of (1) philosophical discourses that reinforce the apparatus of disability and (2) discursive practices within professional philosophy that consistently ignore disability enabled (3) resistance to the apparatus of disability within the discipline and profession of philosophy themselves? That is, how has this combination of discourses made possible the formation of a "reverse" or "counter" discourse on disability—namely, philosophy of disability? As Foucault wrote, "Discourse can be both an instrument and an effect of power, but also a hindrance, a stumbling block, a point of resistance and a starting point for an opposing strategy. Discourse transmits and produces power; it reinforces it, but also undermines and exposes it, renders it fragile and makes it possible to thwart it" (1978, 101). Where there is power, there are resistances; yet these resistances, too, contribute to the elaboration of the very objects to which they are directed as resistance. Thus, the historical conditions of possibility for resistance to the apparatus of disability are also historical conditions of possibility for its expansion and consolidation.

HISTORICIZING AND RELATIVIZING THE APPARATUS OF DISABILITY

Given the nonfoundationalist conception of impairment and disability that I have elaborated and continue to hold, it should come as no surprise that the philosophy of disability that I advance is both relativist and historicist. I define *relativism* as the philosophical doctrine according to which different societies and cultures create different beliefs and values under different historical conditions. I define *historicism* as the philosophical doctrine according to which beliefs and values emerge as a consequence of historical events and circumstances (see Prinz 2007, 215, 234–235).

An interlocutor might point out that the aforementioned definition of relativism refers to a form of it—namely, descriptive relativism—that is uncontroversial among philosophers: most philosophers grant that different cultures have different beliefs and practices. Such an interlocutor might in turn argue that I need an additional argument if I wish to advance a stronger relativism whereby different cultures have different beliefs and practices that have equal claims epistemologically and ethically. Let me point out, therefore, that although philosophers generally agree that descriptive relativism is true with respect to science, religion, and values—that is, every culture has its own beliefs about these things—most of them implicitly presuppose a kind of universalism about certain categories taken to be fundamental, especially categories that they believe are based in biology, categories such as life and death, health and disability, and pleasure and pain. In short, not even descriptive relativism is an obvious thesis.

Nevertheless, the relativism of my position does not require the sort of epistemological or ethical appeal upon which the interlocutor insists. For the relativism of the philosophy of disability that I have advanced is established and substantiated by and through its historicism; that is, the historicism of my philosophy of disability should be conceived as both theoretically prior and antecedent in practice to its relativism, which is, therefore, a derivative of the historicism. Insofar as I argue for the historicist and artifactual character of disability, I establish its relativist character. Claims about the historical transformation of concepts and practices need not necessarily imply their improvement and progress. By both definition and design, the relativist and historicist feminist philosophy of disability that I elaborate offers a new approach to the questions and concerns about disability that philosophers of disability and disability theorists raise, an approach that is dynamic and historically and contextually sensitive to an extent that other philosophies of disability are not.

My choices of relativism and Foucault's historicism as vehicles through which to articulate a feminist philosophy of disability will be unpopular, if not dismissed, in many circles within philosophy. Indeed, Foucault himself explicitly denied that his work was relativist (see Foucault 1982, 212). Although he offered no explanation for this denial, the fact that, in the same context, Foucault also denied that his work relies on skepticism suggests that he may have assumed that a relativist approach required that he refuse even historicist claims to truth, a refusal that he did not make. Nevertheless, many philosophers trained in Anglo-American philosophy continue to refer to Foucault's work as relativist as means to discount its philosophical significance and complexity. As David Wong (2006), who has written extensively about relativism, points out, most philosophical discussions of relativism in Anglo-American philosophy are designed to make relativism an easy target for derision and condemnation, seldom revealing what motivates people who are attracted to it as a philosophical approach. Such discussions, Wong notes, usually come early in standard introductory textbooks in order "to get relativism out of the way so that the 'serious' philosophy can start" (xi). The strategy, he explains, is almost always negative or purports to show some incoherence in relativist argumentation. Rarely do philosophers who are critical of relativism attempt to formulate a version of it that is "nuanced and plausibly motivated" (xi). Despite Foucault's own denial that his claims were relativist, I nevertheless associate both his refusal to universalize and his historical approach with a form of relativism to develop a historicist and relativist feminist philosophy of disability that is nuanced and plausible, politically informed and provoked. In my view, the historicism at the heart of Foucault's claims establishes them as relativist or, at least, makes them amenable to a relativist approach.

That Foucault used historical approaches to the phenomena that he investigated, rather than purportedly ahistorical conceptual analysis, deductive reasoning, and logical argumentation, is another reason why many, if not most, mainstream "analytic" philosophers dismiss or at least disregard his work. Jesse Prinz (himself a relativist), who draws on the work of Friedrich Nietzsche to recommend a genealogical method for philosophical inquiry, is a notable exception to this rule in mainstream analytic philosophy. Prinz asserts that the important lessons to derive from Nietzsche's genealogical approach to morality are that each of the values that we currently cherish has a history, that these histories may not be favorable, and, furthermore, that these histories may not suggest our progression toward ideas that are truer or more beneficial. Our disregard for the historicity of our values, Prinz writes, gives us a "false sense of security" in them:

"We take our moral outlook to be unimpeachable" (2007, 217). In other contexts, Prinz has drawn on Nietzsche's genealogical method and the sentimentalism of David Hume to develop a historicist and relativist approach to morality that takes account of historical contingency and cultural variation in ways that, and to an extent that, normative ethical theories do not. Prinz's aim is to show that the genealogical method can be effectively used to inquire into the genesis of human values. A genealogical investigation of human values, Prinz explains, confirms that moral convictions are products of social history and accident, rather than derived from intuition, revelation, or deductive reasoning from normative principles. Philosophers who investigate where moral beliefs and values originate are usually said to commit the "genetic fallacy," according to which the origins of morality are irrelevant; however, Prinz (217, 235) argues that genealogy— as a method to investigate origins—can enable us to discern when a given value originated in circumstances that are ignoble and therefore is especially suitable for reassessment. Genealogy, he states, "is an under-utilized tool for moral critique" (243).

BIOPOWER AND NORMALIZATION

In his lecture of January 7, 1976, at the Collège de France, Foucault introduced an analysis of power that contrasted with accepted understandings of it that he referred to as "juridico-discursive" conceptions of power. In the terms of juridical conceptions, he pointed out, the individual possesses power (as one would possess a commodity) in the form of inherent, inalienable rights, the transfer or surrender of which (through a juridical act or a contract) constitutes a sovereign. Foucault argued to the contrary that power is not something that is exchanged, given, or taken back but rather is exercised and exists only in action. In addition, Foucault disputed the assumption of juridical conceptions according to which power is fundamentally repressive. Though consensus and violence are the instruments or results of power, he remarked, they do not amount to its essential nature (2003, 13). As he put it, "The exercise of power can produce as much acceptance as may be wished for: it can pile up the dead and shelter itself behind whatever threats it can imagine. In itself the exercise of power is not violence; nor is it a consent, which, implicitly, is renewable" (1982, 220). For Foucault, the question that political philosophy should ask about power is this: How—that is, by what means—is it exercised (217)? Indeed, one of the most original features of Foucault's analysis is the idea that power functions best when it is exercised through productive constraints. Furthermore, he argued that the continued preoccupation with juridical conceptions of power in modern political philosophy has obscured the productive capacity and subtle machinations of a form of power that began to coalesce at the end of the eighteenth century, namely, *biopower*. In the January 11 lecture of his 1977–78 course at the Collège de France (subsequently published in English as *Security, Territory, Population: Lectures at Collège de France, 1977–1978*), Foucault described biopower as "the set of mechanisms through which the basic biological features of the human species became the object of a political strategy, of a general strategy of power, or, in other words, how, starting from the eighteenth century, modern [W]estern societies took on board the fundamental biological fact that human beings are a species" (2007, 1). The apparatus of disability has been integral, indeed vital, to the strategies of this relatively recent form of power.

From the eighteenth century forward, biopower, by taking as its object "life itself," has worked toward increasingly efficient and economical management of the problems that variables of sex (and other phenomena) pose for the political economy of populations and individuals. Biopower, Foucault wrote, is "what brought life and its mechanisms into the realm of explicit calculations and made knowledge-power an agent of transformation of human life" (1978, 143). Life—its enhancement, amplification, quality, duration, continuance, and renewal—has become an urgent economic and political concern that government policy and practice address to wrest management and control of it. Biopower's management of life has entailed the inauguration of a novel set of strategic measurements, including the ratio of births to deaths, the rate of fertility in the population, and the rate of reproduction, as well as a body of statistical knowledge and administrative cataloging of states of health and perceived threats to it.

The consolidation of the modern concept of "normal" legitimized and occurred in tandem with the new statistical knowledge and other techniques of population management that stemmed from biopower. As François Ewald (1991, 138) explains, the norm enabled biopower, "which aims to produce, develop, and order social strength," to steadily do the work that juridical modes of governance, characterized by forcible seizure, abduction, or repression, had done in the past. The norm accomplished this expansion by enabling discipline to develop from a simple set of constraints into a mechanism and by transforming the negative restraints of the juridical into the more positive controls of normalization (141). From the eighteenth century on, the function of technologies of normalization has been to isolate so-called anomalies in the population, which can be normalized through the therapeutic and corrective strategies of other, associated technologies. Technologies of normalization are not merely benign or even benevolent responses to these anomalies in the social body. On the contrary, technologies of normalization are instrumental to the systematic creation, identification, classification, and control of such anomalies; that is, they systematically contribute to the constitution of the perception of anomalies (such as impairment) and operate as mechanisms through which some subjects can be divided from others. Foucault introduced the term *dividing practices* to refer to modes of manipulation that combine a scientific discourse with practices of segregation and social exclusion to categorize, classify, distribute, and manipulate subjects who are initially drawn from a rather undifferentiated mass of people. Through these practices, subjects become objectivized as (for instance) mad or sane, sick or healthy, criminal or law abiding (1982, 208). Through these practices of division, classification, and ordering, furthermore, subjects become tied to an identity and come to understand themselves scientifically.

In the final chapter of *The History of Sexuality*, volume 1, provocatively titled "The Right of Death and Power over Life," Foucault explained the historical shift away from the juridical exercise of power to regulatory control and the coercion of normalization:

> [A] consequence of this development of bio-power was the growing importance assumed by the action of the norm, at the expense of the juridical system of the law. Law cannot help but be armed, and its arm, par excellence, is death; to those who transgress it, it replies, at least as a last resort, with the absolute menace. The law always refers to the sword. But a power whose task is to take charge of life needs continuous regulatory and corrective mechanisms. It is no longer a matter of bringing death into play in the field of sovereignty, but of distributing the living in the domain of value and utility. Such a power has to qualify, measure, appraise, and hierarchize, rather than display itself in its murderous splendor; it does not have to draw the line that separate the enemies of the sovereign from his obedient subjects; it effects distributions around the norm. I do not mean to say that the law fades into the background or that the institutions of justice tend to disappear, but rather that the law operates more and more as a norm, and that the juridical institution is increasingly incorporated into a continuum of apparatuses (medical, administrative, and so on) whose functions are for the most part regulatory. A normalizing society is the historical outcome of a technology of power centered on life. (1978, 144)

Foucault regarded normalization as a central—if not the central—mechanism of biopower's management of life, the life of both the individual and the species. Biopower can thus be defined as a historically specific combination of normalization and population management conducted through vast networks of production and social control. Beginning in the eighteenth century, Foucault noted, the power of the normal has combined with other powers such as the law and tradition, imposing new limits on them. The normal, he explained, was established as a principle of coercion through the introduction of standardized education, the organization of national medical professions and hospital systems that could circulate general norms of health, and the standardization of industrial processes and products and manufacturing techniques. Normalization thus became one of the great instruments of power at the close of the classical age; that is, the power that the norm harnessed has been shaped through the disciplines that began to emerge at this historical moment (Foucault 1977, 184). For, from the end of the eighteenth century, the indicators of social status, privilege, and group affiliation have been increasingly supplemented, if not replaced, by a range of degrees of normality that simultaneously indicate membership in a homogeneous social body (a population) and serve to distinguish subjects from each other, to classify them, and to rank them in a host of hierarchies.

In *Discipline and Punish: The Birth of the Prison*, Foucault (1977) noted that normalization initially emerged in eighteenth-century military schools, orphanages, and boarding schools as an effective form of punishment, "a perpetual penalty," a persistent disciplining. In Foucault's terms, discipline is neither an institution nor an apparatus but rather a type of power and a modality for its exercise, comprising a whole set of instruments, techniques, procedures, levels of application, and targets. Discipline is an "anatomy" of power, a technology of power that may be assumed by (1) particular institutions—such as schools or hospitals—in order to achieve a certain end, or (2) authorities that use it as a means to reinforce and reorganize their established means of power, or (3) apparatuses that use it as their mode of functioning, or (4) state apparatuses whose primary function is to assure that discipline reigns over society in general, namely, the police (215–216). As a technology that has facilitated the expansion of bio-power, disciplinary normalization aims to make the body more efficient and calculated in its acts, movements, gestures, and expression, to produce a body that is "docile," that is, a body that can be subjected, used, transformed, and improved. Modern discipline can be summed up thus: it enables subjects to act in order to constrain them.

Disciplinary "punishment"—that is, normalization—has brought into play five distinct normalizing operations. First, individual actions are referred to a totality that is simultaneously a field of comparison, a space of differentiation, and a rule to be followed. Second, individuals are in turn differentiated from each other in relation to this rule that functions as a minimal threshold, as an average, or as an optimal outcome toward which individuals must move. Third, the natures, grades and levels, and abilities of individuals are hierarchized and quantified. Fourth, these quantifying and hierarchizing measures introduce the constraint of a conformity that must be achieved. Fifth, the limit of difference, the far side of "the abnormal" that will define difference per se in relation to all other specific differences, is codified and enforced by penalty (correction, segregation, and so on). The five elemental modes of normalization are thus comparison, differentiation, hierarchy, homogeneity, and exclusion. The punitive impulse that regulates normalization compares, differentiates, hierarchizes, and excludes individuals in order to homogenize a population that, by virtue of its homogeneity, can be more effectively utilized and modified. In short, the disciplinary power of the norm relies on coercion, rather than open repression or violence. Hence, Foucault pointed out, the centrality of normalization to a form of power (biopower) that aims to exert a more positive influence on life, undertaking to administer it, to multiply it, and to impose on it a system of regulations and precise inspection (1977, 182–184; see also Knobe 2017).

In his January 25, 1978, lecture at the Collège de France, Foucault described disciplinary power in this way:

> Discipline, of course, analyses and breaks down; it breaks down individuals, place, time, movements, actions, and operations. It breaks them down into components such that they can be seen, on the one hand, and modified, on the other. It is this famous interdisciplinary analytical-practical grid that tries to establish the minimal elements of perception and the elements sufficient for modification. Second, discipline classifies the components thus identified according to definite objectives. What are the best actions for achieving a particular result: What is the best movement for loading one's rifle, what is the best position to take? What workers are best suited for a particular task? What children are capable of obtaining a particular

result? Third, discipline establishes optimal sequences or co-ordinations: How can actions be linked together? How can soldiers be deployed for a maneuver? How can schoolchildren be distributed hierarchically within classifications? Fourth, discipline fixes the processes of progressive training (*dressage*) and permanent control, and finally, on the basis of this, it establishes the division between those considered unsuitable or incapable and the others. That is to say, on this basis it divides the normal from the abnormal. (2007, 56–57)

Foucault, in his writing on punishment and his subsequent writing on the history of sexuality, described how knowledges produced about the "normal" case become vehicles for the exercise of disciplinary force relations that target certain people. The etymology of the term *normal* offers clues to the relation between this form of power and the notion of normality. Ian Hacking (1990) notes that the first meaning of *normal* that current English dictionaries provide is something like "usual, regular, common, typical." This usage, according to the *Oxford English Dictionary*, became current after 1840, with the first citation of "normal, or typical" appearing in 1828. Hacking remarks that the modern sense of the word *normal* was not, however, furnished by education or cloistered study but rather by the study of life (1990, 161–162). In an illuminating discussion, Hacking explains that the word *normal* became indispensable because it provided a way to be objective about human beings, especially given the inseparability of the notion of normal from its opposite, namely, the pathological. The word *normal*, he writes, "uses a power as old as Aristotle to bridge the fact/value distinction, whispering in your ear that what is normal is also all right" (160). The word *normal* bears the stamp of the nineteenth century just as the concept of human nature is the hallmark of the Enlightenment, says Hacking. Whereas in the past we sought to discover what human nature is, we now concern ourselves with investigations that will tell us what is normal (161). He points out that although the normal stands "indifferently for what is typical, the unenthusiastic objective average, it also stands for what has been, good health, and what shall be, our chosen destiny." "That," he contends, "is why the benign and sterile-sounding word 'normal' has become one of the most powerful ideological tools of the twentieth century" (169). It is especially noteworthy for my argument that, as Hacking explains, the modern usage of the word *normal* evolved in a medical context (165).

In the late 1700s, there was a significant reconfiguration of the concept of the pathological and its relation to the normal. Disease came to be regarded as an attribute of individual organs, rather than as a characteristic of the entire body. Pathology, likewise, was reconfigured, becoming the study of unhealthy organs, rather than the study of sick or diseased bodies. Unhealthy organs could be investigated, in part, by the chemistry of fluids, such as urine or mucus, that actual living beings secreted. The concept of the normal came into being as the inverse of this concept of pathology: a given state of affairs or process of the body was normal if it was not associated with a pathological organ. In other words, the normal was secondary to, derivative of, and defined by the pathological.

F. J. V. Broussais's principle—that life is a matter of excitation of tissue and disease is "irritation" of the tissue of a given organ—inverted this relation of entailment between the pathological and the normal (Hacking 1990, 82). The pathological became defined as deviation from the normal, and all variation became characterized as variation from the normal state. Pathology was no longer conceived as different in kind from the normal but rather as continuous with it (164). This new understanding of the normal and the pathological that emerged in the late 1700s is one, but only one, component of what I refer to as "the diagnostic style of reasoning," a style of reasoning that has enabled the consolidation and expansion of biopower. Given the importance of statistical knowledge to the operations of biopower, it is not surprising that Broussais—to whom Auguste Comte, for one, attributes our modern understanding of the normal—was connected to the first use of statistical data to evaluate medical treatment (Hacking 1990, 81).

The category of normal is generally assumed to identify an objective, static, universal, and ahistorical internal disposition or character or state of a given human being. As I have indicated, Foucault endeavored to show that the notion of the normal is a historical artifact that emerged through and facilitates the operations of a historically specific regime of power—namely, biopower. Following Foucault, Hacking (1990) and other philosophers and theorists have worked to demonstrate how the coercive and contingent character of the normal operates, in specific contexts, in incremental and other ways (for example, McWhorter 1999). These discussions about the historical and cultural contingency of the concept of the normal and its embeddedness in apparatuses of power are vital to my argument about the historical specificity of disability; for once we recognize that the category of the normal is historically and culturally specific, rather than ahistorical and universal, it becomes easier to show that the idea of disability—and its antecedent, impairment—too is a historically and culturally specific invention of force relations. If the category of the normal is a historical artifact, then any phenomenon whose identity—including objects and practices that make up the identity—is established and distinguished on the basis of its departure from and relation to that category must also be a historical artifact.

Bioethics as a Local Center of the Apparatus

Mainstream bioethicists generally assume that their task is to apply the universalizing and ahistorical principles of deontology, utilitarianism, or virtue ethics to situations that arise in biomedical contexts; that is, they presuppose that medical encounters provide opportunities for the expression and application of extant values such as autonomy, well-being, and liberty (see Beauchamp and Childress, 2012). I have assumed Foucault's insight that power is productive in order to show that the very articulation and practice of these values through (for instance) the use of technologies and the decision-making procedures that surround them effectively generates and configures the values (see also

Hall 2015, 169; 2016). A neoliberal governmentality—in support of which the apparatus of disability and other apparatuses of (for instance) racialized and gendered force relations have coalesced—undergirds the academic field of bioethics and has motivated its emergence and expansion, including the incessant production within certain areas of the field of questions and concerns about impairment and the refinement of positions that rationalize its prevention and elimination.

Foucault (2008) argued that the phenomena that, from the eighteenth century onward, begin to appear as problems that require management emerged as such and developed their urgency within the framework of liberal governmentality. Foucault defined governmentalities—that is, rationalities of government—as systems of thinking about the practice of government that have the capacity to rationalize some form of this activity to both the people who practice it and the people upon whom it is practiced, where this capacity entails to render both thinkable and applicable or acceptable. Consider Foucault's remarks about the three major forms that technologies of government take in their development and history: first a given technology of government takes the form of a dream or utopia; then the dream of the technology of government develops into actual practices or rules to be used in real institutions; finally, the practices and rules of the technology of government become consolidated in the form of an academic discipline (Foucault 1988, 145–162; see also Hall 2015, 166–169; 2016).

My argument is that the academic discipline of bioethics is an institutionalized vehicle for the biopolitics of our time; that is, bioethics is a technology of government that provides intellectual resources designed to facilitate the "strengthening" (read: fitness) of a certain population and the elimination of others. I submit, furthermore, that the implicit and explicit governmental tenor of bioethical inquiries and discussions contributes substantially to the hostile environment that disabled philosophers confront in philosophy. As a product of biopower, bioethics, I contend, implicates the discipline and profession of philosophy in the apparatus of disability and the subordination of disabled people in ways that, and to a degree that, no other subfield of the discipline does, although cognitive science and cognate fields continue to gain considerable ground in this regard.

Bioethics is generally regarded as the most suitable (if not the only) domain in philosophy for critical considerations of disability. My argument is, however, that bioethics actually operates as an area of philosophy whose guiding assumptions and discursive practices are significant obstacles to (1) acknowledgment that the questions—metaphysical, epistemological, political, and ethical—that the apparatus of disability raises are genuinely philosophical and (2) recognition that disabled philosophers who investigate these questions are bona fide philosophers. Indeed, bioethicists serve as gatekeepers, guarding the discipline from the incursion of critical philosophical work on disability and shielding the profession from infiltration by disabled philosophers. Exceptions to this exclusion are of course admissible and even serve to legitimize both the subfield of bioethics and the discipline in general, typifying the polymorphism of the (neo)liberal governmentality from which the subfield of bioethics has emerged and enabling philosophy to proceed under the guise of political neutrality, objectivity, and disinterest. The charge according to which critics of genetic technologies, physician-assisted suicide, and euthanasia employ "slippery-slope reasoning" is a striking case in point. Many bioethicists, some of whom have substantial influence on public policy, argue that the philosophers and theorists of disability (and disabled activists) who criticize these practices engage in fallacious argumentation by using "slippery-slope reasoning" to advance their claims; thus, their positions ought not to be taken seriously (for instance, see Schüklenk et al. 2011).

Jocelyn Downie and Susan Sherwin (1996, 316) distinguish between two kinds of slippery-slope arguments that critics of assisted suicide and euthanasia make: logical slippery-slope arguments and psychological slippery-slope arguments. Downie and Sherwin explain logical slippery-slope arguments in this way,

> If we allow assisted suicide and euthanasia, we will not be able to draw any meaningful distinction between acceptable and unacceptable killings, and, hence, we will *inevitably* slide toward the bottom of the slope (i.e., toward allowing involuntary euthanasia and thus the killing of demented patients, mentally handicapped humans, indigent human, and any other group deemed to be "unfit" for continued existence). (emphasis in original)

Downie and Sherwin claim that there is a simple response to this sort of slippery-slope argument; namely, that if there is a morally significant difference between evaluation of life at the top of the slope and evaluation of life at the bottom of the slope, then the necessary materials to erect a barrier on the slope are available; or, if there are good reasons why practices at the top of the slope should be allowed that are not available at the bottom of the slope, then descent down the slope is not logically necessary (317). The second type of slippery-slope argument—psychological slippery slopes—poses more difficulty, Downie and Sherwin write. Psychological slippery slopes, they explain (quoting ethicist James Rachel), take this form: "Once certain practises are accepted, people *shall in fact* go on to accept other practices as well. This is simply a claim about what people will do, and not a claim about what they are logically committed to" (Rachels 1975, 65, in Downie and Sherwin 1996, 317; emphasis in Rachels). Downie and Sherwin write that the question of whether people will accept involuntary euthanasia if they previously accepted voluntary assisted suicide and euthanasia is an empirical one, requiring investigation that has not been conducted. They remark, furthermore, that "There are many reasons to doubt the validity of the Nazi experience as an appropriate test, since the death camps were created under a totalitarian regime with little concern for individual autonomy" (Downie and Sherwin 1996, 317).

My argument is that the critiques of assisted suicide, euthanasia, and prenatal and other genetic technologies that bioethicists associate with slippery-slope reasoning astutely identify the incremental normalization of modern force relations that operates through the inculcation and utilization of a relatively recent kind of subjectivity; that is, I contend that the charge of slippery-slope reasoning that (many) bioethicists direct at critics of genetic technologies and physician-assisted suicide results from the failure of these bioethicists to recognize that the critiques address the nature and operations of force relations under neoliberal governmentality, including the production of neoliberal subjects whose management and modification of biological life is taken as fundamental to self-hood and responsible citizenship (see Pitts-Taylor 2010).

Let me underscore and elaborate these assertions. I maintain that (1) these critiques cohere with a sophisticated and compelling account of the productive character of modern force relations; (2) these critiques cohere with the conception of disability as an apparatus of force relations that I have articulated throughout this chapter; and (3) the arguments with respect to autonomy, choice, and informed consent that mainstream and feminist bioethicists advance to undermine these critiques are themselves products of and implicated in this apparatus of disability, operating in the service of neoliberal governmentality (see also Koláŕová 2015; Hall 2016; Tremain 2006, 2008, 2010).

Note

1. Some of the material in this chapter is reproduced or adapted from my book, *Foucault and Feminist Philosophy of Disability* (Ann Arbor: University of Michigan Press, 2017) and is reprinted with permission.

References

Beauchamp, Tom, and James F. Childress. 2012. *Principles of Biomedical Ethics*. Oxford: Oxford University Press.

Clark, Andy. "Where Brain, Body, and World Collide." *Daedalus* 127 (2): 257–280.

Downie, Jocelyn, and Susan Sherwin. 1996. "A Feminist Exploration of Issues Around Assisted Death." *St. Louis University Public Law Review* 15(2): 303–330.

Ewald, Françoise. 1991. "Norms, Discipline, and the Law." In *Law and the Order of Culture*, edited by Robert Post, 138–161. Berkeley: University of California Press.

Foucault, Michel. 1977. *Discipline and Punish: The Birth of the Prison*. Translated by Alan Sheridan. New York: Vintage Books.

Foucault, Michel. 1978. *The History of Sexuality. Vol. 1, An Introduction*. Translated by Robert Hurley. New York: Vintage Books.

Foucault, Michel. 1980. "The Confession of the Flesh." In *Power/Knowledge: Selected Interviews and Other Writings, 1972–1977*, edited by Colin Gordon, 194–228. New York: Pantheon Books.

Foucault, Michel. 1982. "The Subject and Power." Appended to *Michel Foucault: Beyond Structuralism and Hermeneutics*, edited by Hubert L. Dreyfus and Paul Rabinow, 208–226. 2nd ed. Chicago: University of Chicago Press.

Foucault, Michel. 1988. *Technologies of the Self: A Seminar with Michel Foucault*. Edited by Luther H. Martin, Huck Gutman, and Patrick H. Hutton. Amherst: University of Massachusetts Press.

Foucault, Michel. 2003. *Society Must Be Defended: Lectures at the Collège de France, 1975–1976*. Edited by Mauro Bertani and Alessandro Fontana. Translated by David Macey. New York: Picador.

Foucault, Michel. 2007. *Security, Territory, Population: Lectures at Collège de France, 1977–1978*. Edited by Michel Senellart. Translated by Graham Burchell. New York: Palgrave Macmillan.

Foucault, Michel. 2008. *The Birth of Biopolitics: Lectures at the Collège de France, 1978–1979*. Edited by Michael Senellart. Translated by Graham Burchell. New York: Palgrave Macmillan.

Gilman, Sander, and James M. Thomas. 2016. *Are Racists Crazy? How Prejudice, Racism, and Antisemitism Became Markers of Insanity*. New York: New York University Press.

Hacking, Ian. 1990. *The Taming of Chance*. Cambridge: University of Cambridge Press.

Hall, Melinda. 2015. "Continental Approaches in Bioethics." *Philosophy Compass* 10 (3): 161–172. doi: 10.1111/phc3.12202.

Hall, Melinda. 2016. *The Bioethics of Enhancement: Transhumanism, Disability, Bioethics*. Lanham, MD: Rowman and Littlefield.

Knobe, Joshua. 2017. "Cognitive Science Suggests Trump Makes Us More Accepting of the Morally Outrageous." *Vox*. January 10. Available at http://www.vox.com/the-big-idea/2017/1/10/14220790/normalization-trump-psychology-cognitive-science

Kolářová, Kateřina. 2015. "Death by Choice, Life by Privilege: Biopolitical Circuits of Vitality and Debility in the Time of Empire." In *Foucault and the Government of Disability*, edited by Shelley Tremain, 396–423. Ann Arbor: University of Michigan Press.

McWhorter, Ladelle. 1999. *Bodies & Pleasures: Foucault and the Politics of Sexual Normalization*. Bloomington: Indiana University Press.

Pitts-Taylor, Victoria. 2010. "The Plastic Brain: Neoliberalism and the Neuronal Self." *Health* 14(6): 635–652.

Prinz, Jesse J. 2007. *The Emotional Construction of Morals*. Oxford: Oxford University Press.

Prinz, Jesse J. 2012. *Beyond Human Nature: How Culture and Experience Shape the Human Mind*. New York: W. W. Norton.

Rachels, James. 1975. "Medical Ethics and the Rule Against Killing: Comments on Professor Hare's Paper." In *Philosophical Medical Ethics: Its Nature and Significance*, edited by F. Spricker and H. Tristram Englehardt, Jr., 63–72. Proceedings of the Third Trans-Disciplinary Symposium on Philosophy and Medicine, Farmington, Connecticut. Dordrecht: D. Reidel.

Rawls, John. 1971. *A Theory of Justice*. Cambridge, MA: Belknap Press of Harvard University Press.

Roberts, Dorothy. 1998. *Killing the Black Body*. New York: Vintage Books.

Roberts, Dorothy E. 2012. *Fatal Invention: How Science, Politics, and Big Business Re-create Race in the Twenty-First Century*. New York: The New Press.

Roberts, Dorothy E. 2016. "The Ethics of the Biosocial: The Old Biosocial and the Legacy of Unethical Science." Tanner Lectures on Human Values. Mahindra Humanities Center, Harvard University. November 2.

Schüklenk, Udo, Johannes J. M. van Delden, Jocelyn Downie, Sheila McLean, Ross Upshur, and Daniel Weinstock. 2011. "End-of-Life Decision-Making in Canada: The Report by the Royal Society of Canada Expert Panel on End-of-Life Decision-Making." *Bioethics* 25(1): 1–4. doi: 10.1111/j.1467-8519.2011.01939.x.

Tremain, Shelley. 2006. "Reproductive Freedom, Self-Regulation, and the Government of Impairment In Utero." *Hypatia: A Journal of Feminist Philosophy* 21(1): 35–53.

Tremain, Shelley. 2008. "The Biopolitics of Bioethics and Disability." *Journal of Bioethical Inquiry* 5 (2,3): 101–106.

Tremain, Shelley. 2010. "Biopower, Styles of Reasoning, and What's Still Missing from the Stem Cell Debates." *Hypatia: A Journal of Feminist Philosophy* 25(3): 577–609.

Tremain, Shelley L. 2017. *Foucault and Feminist Philosophy of Disability*. Ann Arbor: University of Michigan Press.

Wong, David. 2006. *Natural Moralities: A Defense of Pluralistic Relativism*. Oxford: Oxford University Press.

CHAPTER 6

DISABILITY LIBERATION THEOLOGY

ROSEMARIE GARLAND-THOMSON

DISABILITY ETHICS AND THE CULTURAL WORK OF IMAGES

THE question "How should we live?" is one of the West's most enduring philosophical and moral questions. From Plato to Peter Singer, the normative challenge of "should" has kept philosophers and, more recently, bioethicists engaged with both the question and one another. My own recent work in bioethics has addressed a focused version of this question that goes something like this: "How should we live as people with disabilities, not just as disabled people trying to become nondisabled?"[1] One way to address such a question is to consider the deep narrative tradition that represents the human variations, experiences, and ideas that comprise what we now think of as disability. Our narrative archive of the human enterprise in the Western tradition is primarily either textual or imagistic. Therefore, our received stories of disability have come to us mainly by way of words and pictures whose meanings emerge through the material conditions of the production and reception of these representations across time and place. In other words, representation mediated through temporal and spatial context structures our realities.

I approach here the question of how we should live with our disabilities—or in a more contemporary sense, how we should live as people with disabilities—through a semiotic understanding of the cultural work of images. The long imagistic archive of human experience appears on stones, cave walls, in statuary, domestic, and public decorative art, religious iconography, formal artworks, and modern mechanical and iterative technologies such as photography and video graphic narrative.[2] Throughout human history, most of us have accessed the narratives of our cultural time and place through pictures rather than written words. This collective iconography of human being and endeavor is an accretion of didactic stories about how we have lived and how we should live. From the

mysterious pictures our earliest ancestors left for us up through the proliferation of commercial imagistic narratives in today's media, we have a continuous, conflicted story of
how we have lived. This story of what it means to be human is available to us in an inter-
textual pentimento in which shadows of older imagistic narratives haunt new images and
from which we can and do draw our stories about how we should live. What we think of
as modernization cleaves this human history into then and now. This narrative divides
human history into the old and new, the stable and dynamic, the agrarian and industrial,
the superstitious and rational, the religious and secular. In thinking about the didactic
cultural work of images to instruct us, I reach from now back to then to find traces of premodern iconography that appear to us now in both older and current forms to consider
our contemporary visual conversation about how we should live with our disabilities.

For us here and now in twenty-first-century wealthy liberal nations, the question of
how we should live as disabled people has a new urgency that even our recent ancestors
were not obliged or privileged to consider in the same way. Before the sweeping civil and
human liberation movements of the mid-twentieth century, such considerations about
how to live were significantly circumscribed for the majority of Americans, and people
in wealthy liberal nations in general, by structural and ideological limitations as much as
by one's available economic or personal capital. For instance, until the US civil rights
movement and the concurrent women's movement, barriers to participation in civic
culture and institutions through which a person could accrue capital, influence, or
autonomy kept almost all women and men of color from freely living as they may have
wanted, from acting on many of the "shoulds" of life making and world building.
With the expansion of rights and the removal of structural and legal exclusions that
came through these liberation movements, many people in the United States who
had been previously excluded from participation in public life and access to cultural,
economic, and structural opportunities could redefine themselves. To those who
could access these new benefits and inclusions came the conceptual as well as perhaps
the genuine capacity for self-determination required to be able to consider questions
such as "How should we live?"[3]

Modern Civil and Human Liberation Movements

The civil and human liberation movements of the mid-twentieth century arose at the
end of World War II with a post-war prosperity that supported a demographically
strong youth culture of what we now call the baby boom generation, and it followed
those members as they moved into young adulthood from the 1960s through the 1980s.
This enormous collective refusal of the status quo and envisaging of a just democracy
sprang from a combination of a strong economy, the restlessness of a huge young generation differentiating itself from its elders, and the idealism of extending human rights
and justice. Covenants such as the 1948 United Nations Declaration of Human Rights,

which arose in part from the collective exhaustion and disgust with the violence and violations of egalitarian principles by totalitarian regimes, codified the ethical impulses of this revolutionary movement. These civil and human liberation movements literally remade American culture by changing laws, removing barriers, and generating pictures, stories, and cultural products that opened access to opportunities for whole segments of the American population to reimagine how we should live. Whether the promise of those movements and what they made has been fulfilled, blocked, or squandered is the substance of much political and ethical conversation over the last decades. Indeed, the skeptical turn known as postmodernism in the academic world is a response, an impatience, to the intransigence of the socioeconomic order to be remade through the demanding implements of an expanded justice. The halting, convoluted course of this broad social and political liberation enterprise is often blocked with the barriers of complacency, resistance, and persistent socioeconomic inequality. Nonetheless, many occupants of wealthy liberal modern nations such as the United States gained new frameworks through which to consider the question "How should we live?" Even though many people still fall into the trench stretching between aspiration and realization, many others find in the ideological and material provisions of the human and civil rights liberation movements possibilities for imagining themselves. More of us now than then gain access to the resources we need for self-determination and living deliberately.

LIBERTY AND LIBERATION

We must, then, historicize the "we" in the classical philosophical question "How should we live?" by calling out the historical considerations about who might be included in our society as authors of our own lives, as having access to the opportunities and situations to live as we determine we should. This series of sociopolitical liberation movements in mid-twentieth century America revived the founding concept of liberty arising from the ideals of the egalitarian European Enlightenment as liberation from an oppressive governmental status quo. The spirit of these movements suggested that the way we should live, as the New Hampshire state motto asserts, is to "Live free or die." The new liberal egalitarian United States of the eighteenth century understood itself as liberated from both older monarchical and religious government, from the traditional European entanglement of King and God. This central premise of modern democratic sociopolitical orders is to exercise not only freedom to carry out one's life projects but also freedom from restraints in life enterprises. Liberty, in other words, by implication requires a liberation from some sort of constraining force or situation, or at the very least, a protection from such potential constraints. Liberty, then, is a fragile capacity in need of perpetual reestablishment. The mid-twentieth-century liberation movements rejuvenated this clarity about the struggle for freedom from oppressors and the more elusive struggle for the freedom to do something. In contrast to the revolution that liberated an emerging United States, the mid-twentieth-century liberation movements comprised contrasting and sometimes competing identity groups who had been collectively and individually blocked from liberty on the basis of membership in biologically defined subgroups within the whole of American society.[4] The liberty seekers of the American Revolution imagined themselves as united through political and geographical membership as colonists or patriots. In contrast, the liberty seekers of the civil and human rights movements imagined themselves as united through shared embodiments and the social positioning that an unjust social order forced them to occupy either because of or by way of these human embodied variations.

Consequently, one crucial difference between liberation movements of eighteenth-century Europe and North America and twentieth-century liberation movements in the United States is that the founding of the United States did not recognize what we might call pluralistic embodiment and its role in the achievement of the egalitarianism and self-determination that this new social order afforded citizens.[5] Twentieth-century liberation movements in the United States, however, were inherently pluralistic because of expanded enfranchisement and inclusion in citizen rights that developed in the nineteenth and twentieth centuries in the United States. This plural embodiment becomes, then, a central organizing principle of the aspiration toward egalitarian justice, which is the fundamental commitment of modern liberal social orders. Indeed, this commitment to justice as equality across human bodily variation is encoded in a wide range of declarations, covenants, laws, and policies. These justice implements emanate from government, public and private organizations, and citizens groups as diverse as the Women's Temperance Christian Union, the League of the Physically Handicapped, and the NAACP to international alliances such as the United Nations and traditionally influential nongovernmental organizations such as the Roman Catholic Church.

DISABILITY LIBERATION

The aspiration to equality across bodily variation emerges most fully in the concept of liberating people with disabilities through access to and exercise of human and civil rights and inclusion. A broad disability liberation movement could only emerge at a historical time and place when a liberal society had been compelled persistently to recognize categories of social identity secured by traditionally recognized and relatively uniform bodily signifiers such as those associated with racial and sex categories. We pretty much know as a culture what we think constitutes membership in the category "women" and "black people," no matter how blurry the edges of that group membership might be. Both the defining characteristics and experience of disability, in contrast, cross all kinship, social, economic, geographical, and physiological boundaries. Disabled people are an imagined community of people diverse in almost every way and usually quite different from their families and communities, united only by the unstable phenomenological situation of being mind-bodies considered "disabled," a way of being whose parameters shift significantly over time and place.

The covenants and policies of the civil and human rights movement of the mid-twentieth century constituted, or hailed, this community of disabled Americans into being as a broad sociopolitical rights-bearing group. Before the disability rights movement, always nascent in some form in American egalitarianism, people with disabilities had almost no way to imagine themselves outside available narratives of bodily deficiency, victims of fate, medical cases, abnormality, social stigma, objects of benevolence, or *memento mori*. Social or support organizations were most often disability specific and operated in charity, medical, or educational settings such as schools for the deaf or blind, asylums, or medical rehabilitation units. Moreover, such cultural scripts and the segregation they wrought advanced through structural, material, and attitudinal exclusions from public life and participation in democratic institutions such as education, employment, religious, and social organizations, political and social leadership, and the marketplace. Because cultural custom, social policy, and restrictions to economic resources segregated disabled people, they usually either never entered or quickly fell out of economically stable sociopolitical life soon after they became disabled. Those with a substantial amount of cultural and economic capital, such as Franklin Delano Roosevelt, could continue to participate in public and economic life by paying for their own accommodations in the form of private infrastructure and supportive technology, both human and mechanical, to maintain former status and position. Ordinary people with disabilities either returned to or never emerged from the home or the asylum, or they took up the traditional role of public beggar or vagrant.

The laws, policies, practices, and attitude changes that accrued in the wake of the civil and human rights movements re-scripted what it meant to be disabled by changing people with disabilities from medical subjects to political subjects. Starting in 1968, mandates to rebuild public and private spaces, antidiscrimination statutes, educational inclusion mandates, and provisions for accommodation meant that disabled people were no longer responsible for privately providing their own accommodations. Moreover, they had legal recourse if they were excluded or discriminated against. Wheelchair users could follow FDR's legacy and equip their private cars with hand controls that disability technology markets developed, but they could also access public transportation vehicles and transit spaces. Blind people could get orientation training from nongovernmental organizations such as the National Federation for the Blind, but they could also expect publicly provided tactile paving, brailled text, and auditory street crossing aids. While disparities between intention and achievement stubbornly persist, beginning in 1968, people with disabilities became a distinct, protected class of political subjects conceptualized as having access to the rights, privileges, and obligations of their nondisabled peers. This new status and set of supports for living with disabilities offered a material and conceptual situation from which one could be in a better position to exercise the agency and autonomy implied in carrying out the classic question "How should we live?"

This reimagining of subjectivity that constituted the politically identified group of people with disabilities was, I have suggested, part of a mid-twentieth-century distinctively pluralistic civil and human rights enterprise understood as a liberation movement. The concept of liberation rests on some kind of a binary understanding that one group, constituted by certain social and embodied distinctive characteristics, oppresses another group understood as lacking those distinctive bodily and social characteristics.

This is the logic of tribalism, a traditional form of social organization based on biological kinship. With the rise of national states, local tribalism expands into an imagined national community that extends far beyond the face-to-face relations of traditional tribal organization.[6] Opposing tribal groups based on relatively recognizable physical features constitutes much of the thinking about group belonging and who are the oppressors and the oppressed. We tend to recognize tribal or gender membership based on relatively predictable physical features. Disability, however, confounds this familiar pattern of social recognition. In other words, our collective and received thinking about liberation draws from our understandings of who oppresses whom and who is in need of liberation from whom or what.

Modern liberal democracies, then, understand liberation through the principle of self-determination by which one kind of recognizable people liberates themselves from another kind of recognizable people. Eighteenth-century egalitarianism gave us citizens seeking liberation from an aristocracy and workers seeking liberation from the owners of production. The nineteenth century and beyond saw women imagining liberation from men. The twentieth century and beyond saw black people and people of color struggling to liberate themselves from white people. After the mid-twentieth century, race and gender liberation movements have generally shed the assumption of inherent inferiority that justified subordination in the past.[7]

The concept of disability liberation confounds this relatively stable reasoning based on observable physical characteristics that grounds such freedom movements. What exactly is oppressing disabled people? From whom or from what do disabled people seek liberation? Although people familiar with the disability rights movement of the late twentieth century find a ready answer for this by invoking an oppressive built and attitudinal environment, the wider culture easily and generally understands that disabilities of the body itself are the source of oppression and from which disabled people need liberation. Not the master, monarch, dictator, tyrant, advantaged group, or political order but rather disabled bodies themselves seem to "confine" disabled people, to be what limits, restricts, binds, excludes, persecutes, and is the source of their suffering. The wider culture now accepts that black people do not need to become white to be liberated nor do women need to become men. In the public imagination and discourse, disabled people, in contrast, need to be liberated from their disabilities through healing or some kind of restoration to a nondisabled former self or altered into a normal or healthy form of human being. This deep and persistent iconography and narrative of healing as transformation, supported and largely carried out through medical science, has contributed to an enduring conviction that the source of restriction for disabled people lies in their own broken or deficient bodies or minds.

THE ICONOGRAPHY OF LIBERATION

This conviction that disability liberation comes through healing or cure emanates from two pervasive Western narrative and iconographic traditions, one theological and the other medical. Simply put, the former says that the enterprise of Jesus is to heal the soul while the latter holds that the enterprise of medicine is to heal the body. Both enterprises rely on narratives of transformation, sometimes restoration to a former state and sometimes conversion into an ideal state. Disability scholarship, advocacy, and activism have challenged both the theological and the medical traditions of framing disability. The disability rights movement and disability scholarship sought to break the hold of the older religious moral view of disability as a punishment for sin or vice. Along with this, they have also productively developed liberatory theological perspectives and practices for people with disabilities. Disability cultural and political work more definitively critiques the medical tradition on practice, policy, and conceptualization, first by challenging the attribution of disadvantage to biomedical impairment, then questioning the idea of blaming disabled people for their conditions, and most boldly by rejecting the very notion of biomedical impairment. The religious studies scholar Sharon V. Betcher terms these narratives of transformation the requirement "for differently abled persons to be redeemed by science and/or by Spirit" (2007: 4). Because religious redemption or conversion relies on transforming an internal state of the soul or psyche that is not easily legible or manifest, such a change can be effectively represented through an embodied metaphor such as healing, particularly through the iconic healing narratives in which the transformation is literally performed by the body. Raising the dead, stanching a hemorrhage, rendering the blind sighted and the deaf hearing, and making withered hands or lame legs newly enlivened are operatic opportunities that dramatize Jesus's miraculous power to convert and redeem. Betcher devotes much of her eloquent book, *Spirit and the Politics of Disablement*, to re-narrating what she calls the "rescue tactics" of healing stories as "metaphors of disablement" (2007: 6–7). She does this by proposing a postcolonial reading of disabled people as occupying subjugated identities, thus firmly locating oppression within social systems rather than the bodies of the subjugated. While such a move is satisfying to a modern secular sensibility, the dramatic emotional appeal that bodily transformation offers is lost.[8]

To counter the narrative of disability as a form of deficient existence implied in the healing narratives of religion and medicine, the twentieth-century disability liberation movement follows the iconography of the race and gender rights movements. Like the women's liberation or the black civil rights movements, the disability liberation movement presents individual, newly politicized subjects gathered in communal solidarity, asserting the right to occupy a public sphere that had previously excluded them. All these movements cleaved to some extent to a logic of nationalism that asserted the distinct particularities of their identities as an intentional contrast to the identities of the dominant group. So black nationalism developed the iconic "Afro" costuming of kente cloth fabric and full hairstyles that serve to differentiate them from the costuming of the European descended people who represented the group of oppressors. Women threw off their bras and skirts, claiming unisex or androgynous clothing as a form of physical liberation from femininity's constricting costuming. In solidarity with this movement, men of all races cultivated long hair as an emblem of protest against a restrictive establishment ethic of social and economic regulation. People with disabilities appeared in public in their wheelchairs and all manner of prosthetic equipment. Such political theater called upon the bold display of what had been stigmatized differences as proud emblems of identity group belonging. Taken together, this iconography was a cacophonous assault on public propriety and the established claim to superiority by the entitled majority whose ways, appearance, and general cultural capital had too long ruled American power relations. This casting of subjugated groups as minority groups became an uprising that sought to establish credibility for traits, practices, and cultures suppressed and excluded from many of the privileges and benefits of American citizenship.

This iconography of political and cultural liberation involved individual subjects signaling their differences through displaying their bodies. Revealing the truth of their

FIGURE 6.1 American sprinters Tommie Smith (center, gold medal) and John Carlos (right, bronze medal) both stand with heads bowed and black-gloved fists raised in the air during the men's 200-meter medal ceremony at the 1968 Summer Olympics in Mexico City. Both African-American athletes demonstrated the iconic Black Power salute while "The Star-Spangled Banner" played, in solidarity with the black nationalist liberation movement and human rights. Silver medalist Peter Norman (Australia) stands on the left. John Dominis. Courtesy of GDA Photo. © AP Photo.

embodiment enacted individual sociopolitical empowerment carried out in a context of community based on subjugated identity. The choreography of these liberation movements was most often the rally or march in which individual subjects gathered in group solidarity in public spaces and used gestures that claimed the right to occupy the spaces and what they represented. The iconography of the black nationalist liberation movement and the women's movement, or what was at the time referred to as "Women's Lib," adopted the protest gesture of the raised fist first introduced at the medal ceremony at the 1968 Summer Olympics in Mexico City, when African American athletes Tommie Smith and John Carlos each raised a black gloved fist during the playing of the US national anthem. Iconic images from the women's liberation movement in the late 1960s and early 1970s show protest marches in which banners displayed the raised clenched fist, suggesting both solidarity with and imitation of the Black Power movement. This iconic image of the Black Power salute continued to inform a range of liberation gestures as a universal human rights salute.

The iconography of multiple raised fists became a widespread symbol for individual disenfranchised citizens claiming their rightful positions in a social order founded on the premise of equality and equal access to public opportunities and benefits. The message of this choreography was fundamentally individualistic in its suggestion that liberation might be enacted in separate bodies collected together side-by-side in public space, even though two athletes stood together in this original gesture of defiance. The meaning-making function of this Black Power salute draws from the competitive sport model of human relations in which people function as atomistic units engaged in parallel performances and organized in groups whose performances are internally coordinated and cooperative with one another but oppositional in their competition against the other group of performers. This is a version of male-centered tribal kinship practices like war that operate through divisions of labor that are collaborative within the group and competitive with other groups. The multiply raised fists, individual and parallel but not touching, suggest that liberation is an embodied individual achievement by a member of a subjugated group struggling together with other individual members in a performance of liberation against an oppressive dominant group.

The iconography of political empowerment through the costuming of identity and assertion of presence dominated the disability rights movement of the mid-twentieth century as well. Images of disability liberation such as the many now iconic photographs by Tom Olin and Anthony Tusler of protests and marches show people with disabilities marching in wheelchairs; displaying prosthetics, crutches, canes, and guide dogs; chanting slogans; bearing banners; shaking fists; and getting around in public in unusual and unexpected ways.[9] Perhaps the most distinctive disability liberation images are of the famous "Capitol Crawl," the 1990 protest that took place just as the Americans With Disabilities Act was coming forward. At this demonstration, activists with disabilities deserted their crutches and wheelchairs at the base of the steps of the US Capitol and crawled up the steps to protest the inaccessibility of the US Capitol building and by extension all inaccessible buildings in the United States.

FIGURE 6.2 Tom Olin's iconic photograph of the "Capitol Crawl" protest features disability-rights activists drawing public attention to physically inaccessible buildings in support of the Americans With Disabilities Act. The photograph looks upward at the rotunda and dome of the U.S. Capitol building in Washington, DC, as two activists wearing jeans and t-shirts actively pull themselves up the concrete steps using their arms. Tom Olin. Capitol Protest for ADA, 1990. Courtesy of the Tom Olin Collection.

DISABILITY LIBERATION THEOLOGY

To append the word "theology" to the concept of "liberation" offers an opportunity to consider more capaciously the potential and promise of how we should live. The Capitol Crawl is a visual discourse of political liberation for people with disabilities that suggests a modern empowered version of disabled subjectivity to counter the passive recipient of healing and charity that is the inheritance of Christian iconography and that so grates against the logic of a rights-based claim to political and social inclusion for people with disabilities. For theologians of disability, the primary challenge has been to conceptualize how the Judeo-Christian representations of disability subjectivity comport with modern political empowerment models of how to live in a way that counters being the passive recipient of rescue tactics. In other words, what can disability liberation theology draw from the narrative and iconographic religious traditions that offers modern people with disabilities models for considering the question of "How should we live?" To take on the sociopolitical agency of entering into public space that the broad liberation movements of the mid-twentieth century granted requires a concomitant assumption of newly defined subjectivity that goes beyond being the object of "rescue tactics" that Betcher repudiates in the Christian healing stories.

The limitations of an asymmetrical model of liberation that structures the healing narratives persist in the Latin American tradition of Roman Catholic liberation theology based on "a preferential option for the poor" (Danforth 2005) who suffer from economic injustice in societies with extreme income disparities (Gutíerrez 1973). Such liberation theology marries the political to the religious by constituting a focused group in need of communal salvation who are disadvantaged and subjugated because of race or ethnicity. Although this tradition of Catholic Latin American liberation theology, Scot Danforth suggests, creates a relationship of existential solidarity between subjects from affluent societies and the destitute disabled of the Global South, the fundamentally asymmetrical relation between the affluent redeemer and the "poor" replicates the asymmetrical relationship between Jesus the healer and the to-be-healed. This Christian model of redeeming the least of these creates a dynamic of difference and distance between redeemers and redeemed characteristic of the healing stories in which Jesus's power to heal is the focal point. In such an asymmetrical relationship, the disabled sufferer is the passive recipient of Jesus's benevolence. In other words, redemption comes not through identification but through divine power.

We find a similar, albeit individual, model to this preference for the poor expressed in *Adam: God's Beloved*, which is Catholic theologian Henri Nouwen's 1997 account of his own renewal through the L'Arche community. Adam, a L'Arche resident with significant intellectual disabilities, becomes Jesus incarnate in Nouwen's story of his own rebirth into faith. Nouwen's anointing of Adam as Jesus positions disabled people, particularly those with intellectual disabilities, as a conduit to salvation and renewal for believers who have accrued doubts, lost faith, or become disaffected with the mission of Jesus. Such a projection across a vast social and existential chasm is a colonizing move that turns the disabled subject into a sacred version of the noble savage figure whose purpose is to renew and redeem the nondisabled believer. Spiritual redemption tolerates asymmetry between redeemers and redeemed; political liberation does not.

RESYMBOLIZATION AS LIBERATION

A modern disability liberation theology, then, must offer something empowering to people with disabilities, just as political liberation offers the political agency to march in and occupy public space to demand inclusion, rights, or citizen benefits. In her 1994 manifesto, *The Disabled God: Toward a Liberatory Theology of Disability*, the theologian and sociologist Nancy L. Eiesland proposes a promising model of liberation that counters both the rescue tactics inherent in a model of liberation as transformation and the Black Power salute mode of liberation as individual empowerment through public protest. Eiesland rehearses the prefatory laments of all modern theologians of disability by rejecting the Judeo-Christian traditional link between sin and disability, the exclusion of people with disabilities from religious communities, the traditional religious charity model, and the narrative of virtuous suffering. Drawing from the anthropology of Clifford Geertz, she invokes the "performative power" of symbols to create a transformative "cultural ethos" that can be liberatory for marginalized groups (Eiesland 1994: 91). What Eiesland proposes to transform is "the symbol of Christ" from "suffering servant, model of virtuous suffering, or conquering Lord toward a formulation of Jesus Christ as a disabled God" (1994: 94). Calling on the methods of narrative and the meaning making function of representation that are fundamental to humanities knowledge making, Eiesland proposes a "resymbolization" of the figure of Jesus on the cross. With wounded hands, feet, and side, Jesus is a figure of disability with whom people with disabilities can identify. What this offers to disabled people is a form of individual empowerment through identification with the sacred symbol of Christianity, the crucified body of Jesus, in a transaction in which their own disabled but not healed body becomes sacred. In other words, this representation of Jesus as wounded and woundable through the enfleshment that is the essence of Jesus on the cross creates a symmetrical relation between this version of Jesus and humans who, like him, are disabled. Furthermore, after the resurrection, Eiesland's disabled God offers neither healing nor rescue to people with disabilities, but rather a continued relationship of identification with disabled people through the revelatory gesture of presenting "his impaired hands and feet to his startled friends" (1994: 100). The message of such a gesture is one of solidarity with disabled people now and to come, an invitation to enter into redemption, not healed of disabilities, but rather "embodied as we are, incorporating the fullness of human contingency and ordinary life into God" (1994: 100). With this reading of Jesus as refusing healing redemption, Eiesland rewrites the biblical narrative of the crucifixion as injustice and suffering, offering instead a narrative of disability acceptance or even celebration.

With this resymbolization of Jesus as disabled, Eiesland invokes a representational strategy she calls "liberatory realism" to give us a God figure as "a survivor," a fellow disabled human being "who needs care and mutuality" (1994: 103). This Jesus is not a victim, but rather a humble enfleshed figure with whom people with disabilities are invited to identify. In Eiesland's narrative of Jesus's transformation from embodied life to death to spiritual enlivenment, disabled people can find a model of liberation through displaying disabled bodies. Redemption here comes not through healing disabilities but by incorporating the bodily particularities we think of as disabilities into a positive and politically charged image of self.

This narrative of a disabled God appropriates Christianity's central didactic pageant: the image of the wounded Jesus on the cross, endlessly iterated with unnerving realism in Catholic iconography from medieval to modern iconography. Such an image serves the sociopolitical liberation, the minority uprising, that the mid-twentieth-century civil and human rights movement demanded.

This iconography of embodied gestures presented to fellow humans to counter political inequality is parallel to the Black Power salute or the Capitol Crawl. In proposing the image of a crucified Jesus as a figure of disability who refuses healing, Eiesland crafts a strategy that brings together the modern sociopolitical aim of "liberation" with the didactic narratives of premodern religious iconography central to what we now think of as theology.[10] This long stretch from the image of the crucified Jesus to the image of the Black Power salute or the Capitol Crawl may give disabled people a liberating iconography of positive identity politics. Nevertheless, it does not adequately counter the arguments of the philosophical tradition that gives us liberal eugenics, a view that frames disability as a deficit state of dependency, a repudiation of human dignity, and a justifiable reason for exclusion or elimination. Liberal eugenics is a contemporary conversation among philosophers and bioethicists debating conflicting liberty interests that makes a moral argument asserting that reproductive autonomy should include both the obligation and right to select against bringing disabled children into the world. A concomitant argument supports voluntary euthanasia as a practical solution to reduced quality of late life due to disability. The liberal eugenics rationale finds support in utilitarian and trans-humanist positions and garners opposition from egalitarian and theological positions. An escalating market of reproductive technologies and disparities in access to resources contribute to strong social prejudices about the quality of life and social value of people with disabilities.[11] The remainder of this chapter lays out an iconography of disability liberation and justice drawn from the Christian theological tradition that may offer a counter argument to liberal eugenics.

THE IDEOLOGY OF ABILITY AND THE DENIGRATION OF CARE

Such liberty arguments include what liberal eugenics understands as rights and obligations such as access to death with dignity, physician-assisted suicide, reproductive choice, and procreative beneficence, the moral obligation to have the best child with the prospects of the best life. Whatever position one supports in relation to these logics and the practices they yield, all rely on what both John B. Kelly and Tobin Siebers call the *ideology of ability*, the conviction that living with disabilities produces dependency that reduces prospects for a good life for both disabled persons and those who care for them. Such an ideology of ability emanates from and persists in liberal conceptions of proper citizens as slightly varying versions of competing, masculinist rugged individuals independent of mutual support and care from one another.[12] This myth of autonomy and its denial of human interdependence and universal need for care in order to flourish underpins prevalent liberal beliefs that disabled lives are not worth living. Such a conviction within public conversations and legal debates often focuses specifically on the topic of incontinence. The development of secular liberal egalitarian societies places a high premium on independence as bodily control. Such overvaluing of continence as control over bodily functions has evolved the figure of the Cartesian subject for whom a transcendent mind undertakes mastery of a body perpetually threatening to overtake the individual will. The proper work of this Cartesian subject is to render tractable unruly flesh. This modern drama of mind over matter plays out in gender relations, which assign embodiment and body care to women and allocate the life of the mind, along with a concomitant dominion over nature and other humans, to men.[13]

Throughout modern history, the aspiration toward continence as mastery over bodily functions has been a moral imperative, predominantly in the temperance and anti-Onanism movements of the nineteenth century. This imperative has bestowed upon the liberal citizen a dread of incontinence as a threat to bodily integrity and a violation of human dignity.[14] As feminist theologians have asserted, the masculine duty to tame the natural world and the human body, drawn from the Judeo-Christian God's command and invitation in Genesis to take dominion over all that He created, has given modernity the colonization of tribal societies and the subjugation of women. It has also produced a strong prejudice against people understood as incontinent and a vivid fear of becoming what is understood as inappropriately incontinent. John B. Kelly points out that incontinence, as well as needing assistance in bodily care and cleaning, is "a natural feature of human variability: ubiquitous in childhood, not uncommon through adulthood, and increasing with age. The problem for incontinent people," Kelly goes on, "is that incontinence has been made into a life-disqualifying ideological marker."[15] This life disqualifying status is expressed as a life quality threshold in which people avow the common sentiment of "Kill me when I am in diapers!"

Such an ideology of ability figures in policy decisions and lawmaking as well as the personal exercise of autonomy. Losing control of bodily functions serves as a justification for over half of the assisted suicides under the Oregon Death with Dignity law. The iconography of adults in diapers metonymically represents the undignified and the ultimate test of patient autonomy, as Kelly shows in a quote from a Ninth Circuit Court Judge whose judgment reflected the cultural prejudice against the need for bodily care: "The right to die is a choice 'central to personal dignity and autonomy.' A competent terminally ill adult," the judge goes on, "has a strong liberty interest in choosing a dignified and humane death rather than being reduced at the end of his existence to a childlike state of helplessness, diapered, sedated, incontinent" (Kelly 2002; see also Kelly 2015).

Nonetheless, even the most ordinary stroll through any grocery or drug store's enormous adult diaper section confirms Kelly's point that human incontinence and the need for assistance in body management is a common fact of human life. Both this proliferation of adult diapers in our contemporary moment and the capacious work throughout human history of women as caretakers of all that is human confirm what the philosopher Miranda Fricker (2007) would call the "epistemic injustice" of denying the sacred and profoundly human work of human touch as care in the service of mutual body maintenance. Throughout the whole of human history, women have primarily carried out this care work, a history brought forward by largely feminist historians, philosophers, humanists, and social scientists.[16] This history and its logics has come to be known as the ethics of care.[17] Care ethics, often understood as a feminist ethics of care, asserts that there is moral significance in the fundamental elements of relationships and dependencies in human life.[18]

The denigration of disability, imagined as a state of deficit existence, draws from this classical tradition that elevates spirit over body, independence over dependence, man over woman, singularity over multiplicity, transcendence over immanence. Few representational traditions that emanate from these classical interpretations of the human can offer people with disabilities images or narratives that affirm that theirs are livable lives, that the human variations we have considered as disabilities over time and across place are compatible with human dignity and value.

A SACRED ICONOGRAPHY OF CARE

The iconography of the medieval and early modern Catholic Marian tradition offers a resymbolization of care relations as affirmations of human life and dignity through which people with disabilities might reimagine acts of body care as sacred rituals. The pervasive images of the Nursing Madonna, or Maria Lactans, in which the mother cradles the infant Jesus, feeding the child from her breast or expressing milk from her breast as a fountain of sacred nourishment, sacralizes the quotidian acts that support human embodied life. Whereas the Maria Lactans symbolizes the interdependence of human life at its beginnings, the parallel image of the Pieta, the Madonna cradling her dead child in adulthood, suggests that care for and of human bodies extends throughout the arc of human life.[19] The figure of Jesus occupying the fragile embodiments of infant and corpse, tenderly embraced at both the beginning and the end of life by the being from whom life has emanated, universalizes human dependency and the mutual reliance that upholds the sacred human duty of living and dying. The essence of sustaining human life, these images suggest, is feeding, cleaning, comforting, touching, holding, warming, and maintaining our enfleshed being.[20]

The iconography of care the Marian tradition sacralizes, whether Madonna Lactans or Pieta, is singular in the Abrahamic faiths, inflecting with the feminine principle of abundant vitality the broad representation of touching as a sacred interchange in the Christian imagistic archive.[21] In the Madonna Lactans and Pieta, the maternal figure is larger than the God figure but she enfolds rather than dominates the fragile Jesus. In contrast, both the textual and imagistic healing narratives show the adult Jesus's touch transforming disability, illness, and mortality. In the Marian tradition's iconography of care, however, the Madonna's touch sustains human enfleshment as it is. The Madonna comforts, while Jesus converts. Whereas the singular figure of the disabled Jesus on the cross that Eiesland offers is a symbol of liberation with whom disabled people can identify, the double figures of mother and child engaged in the work of body care provides a different story of human embodiment. This alternative version of Jesus tended by the hands of a loving caretaker in both life and death presents a cultural script that

FIGURE 6.3   Michelangelo's *Pietà*, housed in Saint Peter's Basilica in the Vatican City, features the large marble Madonna seated in draping robes, cradling the dead Jesus across her lap. She looks down at his limp body with an expression of maternal tenderness. Michelangelo's *Pietà*, Saint Peter's Basilica, Vatican City. Photograph by Wikimedia Commons user Jebulon. Creative Commons license CC 1.0. Image is in public domain.

affirms human interdependence rather than independence. In other words, the crucified Jesus tells a story of being alone whereas the Marion tradition tells a story of being in relationship.

Cultural images and rituals of care—whether religious or secular, traditional or contemporary—witness the inherent dignity of human embodied existence. We both make and look to cultural imagery and rituals as directives for world building and human community formation. From Eiesland's disabled God on the cross and the Madonna figures, to the Black Power salute, the Capitol Crawl, and images women post of their tattooed mastectomy scars, all are part of a pervasive cultural meaning-making tradition that shows us who we are and how we should live.

This chapter lays out an iconography of liberation for people with disabilities that reaches across the individualistic representation emblematized by Jesus on the cross, alone and abandoned on the edge of transformation, to representations of communal care giving and acceptance that resists transformation. The images from the Marian tradition offered here suggest conserving human enfleshment through mutuality and interdependence rather than transforming our being through transcendence. Care, in this sense, involves maintaining the world of, and meeting the needs of, ourselves and others. Dependency relations can and should guide public policy about human equality. Eva Feder Kittay has argued persuasively that the "perspective from a life lived with disability" should be primary evidence in bioethical decision-making (Kittay 2011: 615). Care ethics, then, gives us the theoretical armature to link intimate body care as affirmations rather than diminishments of dignity.

The answer to the question, "How should we live?" can come, then, from a care ethics liberation theology that frees people with disabilities from the rescue tactics of healing narratives. We should live, care ethics tells us, supported through mutual interdependence that sustains human embodied being.

NOTES

1. See Garland-Thomson (2016).
2. For definitions and explication of visual culture, see Berger (1990), Mitchell (1995), and Sturken and Cartwright (2017). In philosophy, theories of visual culture and visuality have grown primarily from phenomenological accounts of knowledge and experience from Maurice Merleau-Ponty and more recently from Michel Foucault on visuality as surveillance.
3. Much of the critical theory and social science research from the 1970s to the present rightly centers on explicating, analyzing, and documenting the failures of these human and civil rights promises that emerged during the second half of the twentieth century. Exposing this gap between aspiration and realization is perhaps the most important work of liberal societies. This critical work that we think of broadly as postmodernism is a correction, sometimes perhaps an overcorrection, to the narrow optimism of what history considers the progressive era, in which a narrow view of what counts as human and who counts as valuable dominated political, social, and economic life in the United States. Such a limited understanding of progress yielded a robust worldwide eugenics movement and tightened structural exclusions for a majority of the population. It was against this constricted and enforced understanding of social, moral, and political progress that the human and civil rights movements arose.
4. From 1776 up to 1968 and beyond in the United States there were, of course, a number of liberation movements in a broad sense mounted from and for groups of people excluded on the basis of biological markers such as sex, race, or ethnicity. These include racial and gender suffrage movements; temperance, eugenics, and other supposedly progressive movements; and a wide range of protests and resistances understood as reform, justice, tolerance, progress, health, morality, or alignment with divine will.
5. Human bodily variation was indeed salient in eighteenth- and nineteenth-century America, but that salience was not recognized as such because the embodied and status qualifications for citizenship—which were generally white, male, and property owning—were not explicit or explicitly challenged in the eighteenth-century American liberation movement that resulted in the founding of the United States.
6. Although social science theories of social constructivism and other postmodern understandings of identity and social organization have revealed that this understanding is mythological, it is still of course widely held as an understanding of the social organization

we think of as race, gender, and ethnicity. For the concept of imagined communities, see Anderson (1991).

7. Ascriptions of inherent inferiority for African Americans and women certainly persist in the twentieth and twenty-first centuries, but these ideas are contested strongly in a way that they were not in the eighteenth and nineteenth century in America. For an historical overview of theories of biological inferiority, see Gould (1981) and Tavris (1993).

8. Most work on disability and theology struggles to renarrate the healing narratives that frame disabilities as deficits to be corrected, either divinely or medically, and that inform a charity model of disability social relations in which a nondisabled majority rescues disabled people from subjugation and despair. Such rewriting of the healing narratives mobilizes what critical theory calls social constructivism to refocus the problem to disability in social relations instead of the disabled body. See, for example, Betcher (2007, 2013) and Creamer (2009). For an account of how subjugation builds oppositional consciousness, see Sandoval (2000).

9. For images of the "Capitol Crawl" and other disability rights protest and liberation demonstrations, see: http://mn.gov/mnddc/ada-legacy/ada-legacy-moment27.html, https://www.arts.gov/art-works/2015/ada25-disability-rights-through-tom-olins-lens, https://share.america.gov/crawling-up-steps-demand-their-rights/ Also see the exhibit of the 504 protest in 1973 called "Patient No More," curated by the Paul K. Longmore Institute at San Francisco State University, https://longmoreinstitute.sfsu.edu/patient-no-more.

10. For additional examples of this resymbolization that works against the rescue tactics of healing narratives, see Belser (2014) and Solevåg (2016, 2017).

11. There is a vast literature in philosophy and bioethics on the liberal eugenics debate; see, for example Nicholas Agar, whose position has shifted. Major supporters of liberal eugenics include Peter Singer, Julian Savulescu, John Harris, and Jeff McMahan; opposition to liberal eugenics comes from Eva Feder Kittay, Juergen Habermas, Michael J. Sandel, Nathaniel Comfort, Joel Michael Reynolds, and most religious bioethicists.

12. This critique of individualism and its harms to all is widely made; see, for example, Macpherson (2011), and Fox-Genovese (1992). An especially strong and convincing critique of individualism and its denial of mutual care relations as the basis of society comes from Kittay (1999), Fineman (2005), Faludi (1999), and Kimmel (2011).

13. This critique of the Cartesian subject is prevalent in twentieth- and twenty-first-century philosophy, political theory, and social science. For good examples from philosophy, see Beauvoir (1989) and Tuana (1993). For another excellent example of incontinence as a threat to bodily integrity, see Shildrick (1997).

14. For a history of taming the body, see Elias (2000).

15. John B. Kelly, "Capital Offense: Incontinence and the Ideology of Ability," paper presented at the University of Vermont, October 15, 2002.

16. Abel (2000), Held (2006), Hochschild (2003), Tronto (2015), and Walker and Snarey (2004).

17. Sarah Ruddick's term "maternal thinking" describes how practices of attention create mutual interdependence and confer mutual dignity as attention to body. Eva Feder Kittay's critique of autonomy and elaboration of dependency in her book Love's Labor (1999) and articles such as "Equality, Dignity, and Disability" also develop the centrality of care ethics that the Marian tradition represents as sacred.

18. Growing out of 1980s cultural feminism, care ethics develops in several academic disciplines, ranging from Gilligan (1982) in moral education to Chodorow (1978) in psychology. An account of feminist epistemology emerged as well in the 1980s often under the

rubric of women's ways of knowing. A distinctive feminine voice, perspective, mind, psychology, and social history asserting women's preference for interdependence, formed the broad and still-developing category of feminist care ethics (see Belenky et. al. 1986). For a current overview and discussion of care ethics, see Schaffer (2019) and chapters 18 and 43 of Garry et. al. (2017).

19. For cultural explication of the Marian tradition, see Warner (1976).

20. The recent development of vulnerability theory, particularly in regard to human rights and social policy, carries into secular liberal societies this care based understanding of human social organization and meaning. See Fineman (2008), Turner (2006), Butler (2006).

21. Another body care ritual represented in the Abrahamic tradition is ablution, ritual cleansing of the living and the dead found in Christian baptismal practice and other ritualized cleansing practices such as hand washing in Christian narrative. Abrahamic ablution rituals include baptismal, Eucharistic, cleansing, preparation of dead, and toileting. Ablution rituals in Christian iconography are generally carried out by men and between men rather than the body care represented in the Marian tradition.

References

Abel, Emily K. 2000. *Hearts of Wisdom: American Women Caring for Kin, 1850–1940.* Cambridge, MA: Harvard University Press.

Anderson, Benedict. 1991. *Imagined Communities: Reflections on the Origin and Spread of Nationalism.* New York: Verso.

Beauvoir, Simone de. 1989. *The Second Sex.* New York: Vintage Books.

Belenky, Mary Field, Blythe Mcvicker Clinchy, Nancy Rule Goldberger, and Jill Mattuck Tarule. 1986. *Women's Ways of Knowing: The Development of Self, Voice, and Mind.* New York: Basic Books.

Belser, Julia Watts. 2014. "God On Wheels: Disability And Jewish Feminist Theology." *Tikkun* 29, no. 4: 27–29.

Berger, John. 1990. *Ways of Seeing.* London: BBC and Penguin Books.

Betcher, Sharon V. 2007. *Spirit and the Politics of Disablement.* Minneapolis, MN: Fortress Press.

Betcher, Sharon V. 2013. *Spirit and the Obligation of Social Flesh.* New York: Fordham University Press.

Butler, Judith. 2006. *Precarious Life: The Powers of Mourning and Violence.* London: Verso.

Chodorow, Nancy. 1978. *The Reproduction of Mothering.* Oakland: University of California Press.

Creamer, Deborah Beth. 2009. *Disability and Christian Theology: Embodied Limits and Constructive Possibilities.* Oxford: Oxford University Press.

Danforth, Scot. 2005. "Liberation Theology of Disability and the Option for the Poor." *Disability Studies Quarterly* 25, no. 3. http://dsq-sds.org/article/view/572/749.

Eiesland, Nancy. 1994. *The Disabled God: Toward a Liberation Theology of Disability.* Nashville, TN: Abington Press.

Elias, Norbert. 2000. *The Civilizing Process: Sociogenetic and Psychogenetic Investigations.* Oxford: Blackwell.

Faludi, Susan. 1999. *Stiffed: The Betrayal of the American Man.* New York: William Morrow.

Fineman, Martha. 2005. *The Autonomy Myth: A Theory of Dependency*. New York: The New Press.

Fineman, Martha. 2008. "The Vulnerable Subject: Anchoring Equality in the Human Condition." *Yale Journal of Law and Feminism* 20, no. 1: 1–23.

Fox-Genovese, Elizabeth. 1992. *Feminism Without Illusions: A Critique of Individualism*. Chapel Hill, NC: University of North Carolina Press.

Fricker, Miranda. 2007. *Epistemic Injustice: Power and the Ethics of Knowing*. New York: Oxford University Press.

Garland-Thomson, Rosemarie. 2019. "Welcoming the Unexpected." In *Human Flourishing in an Age of Gene Editing*, edited by Erik Parens and Josephine Johnston. Oxford: Oxford University Press.

Garland-Thomson, Rosemarie. 2016. "Becoming Disabled." *New York Times*, August 19, 2016. https://www.nytimes.com/2016/08/21/opinion/sunday/becoming-disabled.html.

Garry, Ann, Serene J. Khader, and Alison Stone. 2017. *The Routledge Companion to Feminist Philosophy*. New York: Routledge.

Gilligan, Carol. 1982. *In a Different Voice: Psychological Theory and Women's Development*. Cambridge, MA: Harvard University Press.

Gould, Stephen Jay. 1981. *The Mismeasure of Man*. New York: W. W. Norton.

Gutiérrez, Gustavo. 1973. *A Theology of Liberation: History, Politics, and Salvation*. Maryknoll, NY: Orbis Books.

Held, Virginia. 2006. *The Ethics of Care: Personal, Political, and Global*. Oxford: Oxford University Press.

Hochschild, Arlie Russell. 2003. *The Commercialization of Intimate Life: Notes From Home and Work*. Oakland: University of California Press.

Kelly, John B. 2002. "Incontinence: Ragged Edge." *Ragged Edge*.

Kelly, John B. 2015. "John Kelly: A Social Policy of Assisted Suicide is Just as Dangerous as the Death Penalty: Testimony in Strong Opposition to AB2x 15." *Not Dead Yet*, September 3. Accessed June 14, 2016. http://notdeadyet.org/2015/09/john-kelly-a-social-policy-of-assisted-suicide-is-just-as-dangerous-as-the-death-penalty.html

Kimmel, Michael. 2011. *Manhood: A Cultural History*. Oxford: Oxford University Press.

Kittay, Eva Feder. 1999. *Love's Labor: Essays on Women, Equality, and Dependency*. New York: Routledge.

Kittay, Eva Feder. 2011. "Forever Small: The Strange Case of Ashley X." *Hypatia* 26, no. 3: 610–631.

Macpherson, C. B. 2011. *The Political Theory of Possessive Individualism: Hobbes to Locke*. Oxford: Oxford University Press.

Mitchell, W. J. T. 1995. *Picture Theory: Essays on Verbal and Visual Representation*. Chicago: University of Chicago Press.

Nouwen, Henri J. M. 1997. *Adam: God's Beloved*. Maryknoll, NY: Orbis Books.

Ruddick, Sara. 1989. *Maternal Thinking: Toward a Politics of Peace*. Boston: Beacon Press.

Sandoval, Chela. 2000. *Methodology of the Oppressed*. Minneapolis: University of Minnesota Press.

Schaffer, Talia C. 2019. "Care Communities: Ethics, Fictions, Temporalities." i *South Atlantic Quarterly*, 118 no. 3: 521–542.

Shildrick, Margrit. 1997. *Leaky Bodies and Boundaries*. New York: Routledge.

Siebers, Tobin. 2008. *Disability Theory*. Ann Arbor: University of Michigan Press.

Solevåg, Anna Rebecca. 2016. "No Nuts? No Problem! Disability, Stigma, and the Baptized Eunuch in Acts 8:26–40." *Biblical Interpretation* 24, no. 1: 81–99.

Solevåg, Anna Rebecca. 2017. "Listening for the Voices of Two Disabled Girls in Early Christian Literature." In *Children and Everyday Life in the Roman and Late Antique World*, edited by Christian Laes and Ville Vuolanto, 290–302. New York: Routledge.

Sturken, Marita, and Lisa Cartwright. 2017. *Practices of Looking: An Introduction to Visual Culture* (3rd ed.). Oxford: Oxford University Press.

Tavris, Carol. 1993. *Mismeasure of Woman*. New York: Touchstone.

Tronto, Joan. 2015. *Moral Boundaries: A Political Argument for an Ethic of Care*. New York: Routledge.

Tuana, Nancy. 1993. *The Less Noble Sex: Scientific, Religious, and Philosophical Conceptions of Woman's Nature*. Bloomington: Indiana University Press.

Turner, Bryan S. 2006. *Vulnerability and Human Rights*. State College, PA: Penn State University Press.

Walker, Vanessa Siddle, and John R. Snarey, John, eds. 2004. *Race-ing Moral Formation: African American Perspectives on Care and Justice*. New York: Teachers College Press.

Warner, Marina. 1976. *Alone of All Her Sex: The Myth and the Cult of the Virgin Mary*. New York: Alfred A. Knopf.

PART TWO

WELL-BEING, ADAPTATION, AND CAUSING DISABILITY

CHAPTER 7

....

DISABILITIES AND WELL-BEING

The Bad and the Neutral

....

JOSHUA SHEPHERD

INTRODUCTION

....

I maintain that, for a significant class of disabilities, possession of the disability itself does not make you significantly worse off overall, although social stigmatization, prejudice, and lack of proper care for the disability certainly may make you so. For this class, even if there are some negative effects connected to the disability itself, well-being is robust against the effects. I also maintain that, for a significant class of disabilities, even if we remove factors connected to social stigmatization, prejudice, or lack of proper care, possession of the disability itself makes you worse off overall. What explains the asymmetry? I maintain that a key part of the explanation revolves around the impact a disability has on those capacities that undergird and enable what I call *control over one's situation*.

First, after clarifying terms, I discuss recent arguments according to which possession of a disability is inherently neutral with respect to well-being. I note that, although these arguments are compelling, they are only intended to cover certain disabilities, and, in fact, there exists a broad class of disabilities regarding which they do not apply. In the section "Two Problem Cases," I discuss two such problem cases: locked-in syndrome (LIS) and the minimally conscious state (MCS). In the next section, I explain why these are cases in which possession of the disability makes one worse off overall. I do so by explicating the notion of control over one's situation. I argue that disabilities that significantly impair control over one's own situation—for example, LIS and the MCS—strongly tend to be inherently negative with respect to well-being, while disabilities that do not strongly tend to be inherently neutral. The upshot is that we must draw an important normative distinction between disabilities that undermine this kind of control and disabilities that do not.

Disability and Well-Being

Our question concerns the relationship between disability and well-being. Any answer is complicated by the fact that the nature of disability as well as the nature of well-being is contested. Before beginning, then, I offer explications of both notions, aiming for as much agnosticism regarding contested theoretical issues as possible.

Some explicate "disability" essentially in terms of detrimental effects on well-being (Harris 2000; Kahane and Savulescu 2009). To do so, however, rules out by definition the question I confront in this chapter. Since I take it that this question makes sense and is interesting, we need a different explication of disability. One option here is to opt for a more substantive account that is agnostic about the relationship between disability and well-being (e.g., that of Barnes 2016). But I do not wish to argue for a substantive account of disability here. I will understand disability in the medicalized sense Wasserman and Asch (2013) use to identify conditions generally regarded as disabilities. In this sense, a disability is an "impairment, injury, or disease that involves or results in the absence, loss, or reduction of normal or species-typical function" (140).[1] Note that this is consistent with social conditions contributing to the relevant impairments.

Well-being, as I understand it here, is a property that attaches to the lives of individuals and that qualifies how things are going for them in terms of some valenced assessment. So, things can go well or poorly for someone, they can go better for one person than for another, and they can go worse for me at one time than another. Furthermore, these assessments can apply to stretches of time that do not amount to a whole life, as well as to whole lives. Ultimately, of course, we need some sense of the kinds of things that ground or explain these assessments—the things in virtue of which one's life (or some stretch of it) goes well or poorly. As much as possible, I will try to appeal to shared territory here. For example, most views accept that positive experiences contribute positively and negative experiences contribute negatively. And most views accept that other factors are (at least instrumentally) relevant to one's level of well-being. I have in mind here factors such as the ability to satisfy one's desires and intentions, the ability to enter into meaningful relationships, and the ability to appreciate and/or achieve highly valued items (e.g., personal accomplishments, aesthetic beauty, moral virtue, or whatever).

How does disability affect well-being? The assumption that disability is obviously and often severely negative with respect to well-being is prevalent in most Western societies. But recently many theorists and disability rights advocates have argued that this assumption is indefensible—in fact, they claim, disability is neutral with respect to well-being. What might it mean to say this? Often proponents of a neutrality view offer analogies and comparisons that give a good sense of the spirit of their view. Elizabeth Barnes (2016) outlines several claims characteristic of neutrality proponents. Such proponents claim, for example, that in its neutrality "disability is analogous to features like sexuality, gender, ethnicity, and race," that "disability is a valuable part of human diversity that should be celebrated and preserved," and that much of the negativity associated with disability stems from "society's treatment of disabled people, rather than disability itself" (69–70).

But it is possible to be more precise regarding claims of neutrality. Barnes offers one useful explication. According to Barnes, neutrality should be understood as holding *overall*, or with respect to one's level of well-being considered at some distance from individual events or experiences. Barnes concedes that a disability could be negative with respect to some aspects of a person's life. But she notes that the same is true of a range of aspects of a person's life (e.g., one's race, gender, or sexuality). And most would find it difficult to defend the view that any of these are inherently negative with respect to well-being. With that said, Barnes explicates "neutrality" in terms of sameness of well-being levels across nearby possible worlds: "Φ has a *neutral effect* on x's well-being just in case the closest world(s) w in which x lacks Φ is a world in which x's level of well-being is the same as the level of well-being x has in the actual world" (80). While that is obviously a valid way to understand neutrality, in the present context it seems excessively precise. My own understanding of neutrality is one on which there exist differences in well-being levels small enough that it is not irrational to prefer one over the other. Spelling this out in full is beyond the scope of this chapter, but imagine being asked to care about or choose two very different life possibilities—a well-loved and very fulfilled fireman with seven interesting and healthy children living in twentieth-century Chicago, or a well-loved, very fulfilled, wealthy and famous actress living in nineteenth-century Paris. Say, also, that one of these was marginally better than the other on whatever scale of measuring well-being that you prefer. Given the number of factors that enter into the calculation, it seems rational to prefer either of these scenarios. (Well-being levels are not like monetary levels.) My view of neutrality, then, maintains that if two well-being levels fall within some such range, they meet a neutrality requirement.[2]

This gives us a sense of what it means to claim that disability is neutral—a mere difference—with respect to well-being. But this neutrality claim faces a difficult objection. My formulation of it follows that of Guy Kahane and Julian Savulescu (2016), who call it the Unacceptable Implications Objection.

> Unacceptable Implications Objection. If we accept the Mere Difference view of disability, then—in a society free of all the negative features associated with social stigmatization, lack of access to proper care, etc.—it would be morally permissible to intentionally cause a non-disabled person to become disabled (in a society free of all the negative features associated with social stigmatization, lack of access to proper care, etc.), and it would be morally permissible to intentionally omit to cause a disabled person to become non-disabled.

Many find these implications repugnant. As Kahane and Savulescu note, acceptance of these implications "would mean that prospective parents have no reason to prefer to create an able-bodied . . . child rather than a disabled one. And it would also mean that it is misguided to exert so much effort to develop ways of preventing or removing disability" (2016, 775).

In response to considerations like these, Barnes argues that our intuitions that causing disability is bad do not track the causing of disability in isolation, but rather track ancillary factors. Barnes names three: the absence of consent, high transition costs, and a general principle of noninterference. According to Barnes, causing disability may be impermissible if it proceeds without consent, generates high transition costs, or violates a principle of noninterference. But none of these reasons identifies causing disability in isolation as impermissible.

We can, however, ramp up the counterintuitive nature of Barnes's position. Kahane and Savulescu point out that all three ancillary factors Barnes identifies are entirely symmetrical: the proponent of the mere-difference view ought to apply the same reasoning to the causing of non-disability. So Barnes is committed to accepting that causing non-disability in the absence of consent is just as bad as causing disability in the absence of consent, that causing non-disability given transition costs is just as bad as causing disability given transition costs, and that, to quote Kahane and Savulescu, "removing disability from a fetus is as wrong as causing a male fetus to become female, or causing a fetus' hair color to change from red to brown, let alone causing an abled fetus to become disabled" (2016, 779).

These implications are highly counterintuitive. What can the defender of a mere-difference view say in response? One might double down on skepticism about intuitions here, claiming that our intuitions are stained by our participation in a society dominated by ableist thinking (Barnes 2016, 155–156). I think there is something to this skepticism, but it is not entirely satisfying in the present context for it leaves us without a positive defense of a mere-difference view.

I turn, then, to an argument Asch and Wasserman (2010) offer. The argument explicitly concerns what they call "static" disabilities—disabilities that involve "the simple absence of a sensory, motor or cognitive function, without the pain or progressive character of a disease" (2010, 202). Regarding at least these disabilities, Asch and Wasserman offer a package of related claims. First, a disability could qualify as neutral even if the disability represents the absence of an instrumental good for a subject. Second, a disability could qualify as neutral even if the disability is not compensated for in any direct way by a subject's existing capacities and functions. The reason is that no single capacity or function should be regarded as "an all-purpose good, essential for virtually any life plan" (208). Rather, the kinds of capacities and functions static disabilities concern should be understood as affording means to the realization of goods, values, achievements, positive experiences, and so on. And, according to Asch and Wasserman, "human beings enjoy a fortunate redundancy in many of the capacities that are instrumental for, or constitutive of, valuable human goods and activities" (208).

The broader picture here is that a complex means–end structure connects instrumental access to the constituents of well-being with the constituents themselves. If this is right—and I think it highly plausible that it is—then human beings will have available to them a wide range of ways to access the core constituents of well-being (whatever they turn out to be). This picture is behind Wasserman and Asch's (2013) proposal regarding the asymmetry problem discussed earlier. The main claim is that we can have reasons to prevent loss of a capacity or to restore a capacity even if the capacity itself is neither intrinsically bad or good. The reason is, of course, that in preventing its loss or restoring it, we would be giving the agent something valuable—access to more means to the constituents of well-being—even if we do not give her something that in itself will positively impact her well-being compared to the case in which we do nothing. In explaining this point, Wasserman and Asch compare static disabilities to the absence of a capacity like literacy.

> Like sight and hearing, literacy is a good thing to have. Indeed, it is often touted as opening up new worlds inaccessible to the unlettered... [But] despite the great value of literacy, lives can go as well without it as with it. There is little reason to doubt that the best lives of our illiterate forebears went just as well, or incommensurably well, on any plausible account of well-being, as the best lives of our literate contemporaries.   (Wasserman and Asch, 2013, 155)

I find this argument compelling, and I concur. There exists a significant class of disabilities—I think deafness, blindness, and some mobility impairments (e.g., loss of a limb or the ability to walk) clearly fall into this category—for which a mere-difference view states an important truth about the relation between disability and well-being. We are left, however, with the pressing fact that, as least as Asch and Wasserman have it, this argument only covers some disabilities. Is there an argument that all disabilities are a mere difference?

I think not, and I offer reasons to agree with me in the next section. In the next section, I consider a further pressing question: What explains the distinction between mere-difference and bad-difference disabilities?

Two Problem Cases

Locked-in Syndrome

LIS typically results from a brainstem lesion that fully preserves consciousness and cognitive functioning but results in almost complete paralysis—often, only eye movements are spared, and these are how patients communicate (although there are cases of total LIS that involve paralysis of eye motility).

Most people unfamiliar with LIS would, when given a brief description and asked, find the prospect of LIS horrifying—perhaps even worse than death. But this is not what many people with LIS say. A recent survey of LIS patients asked them to report on various aspects of their condition, including their perceived quality of life (Bruno et al. 2011a). Ninety-one out of 168 invited patients responded, a fact that the experimenters admit may have biased the sample toward higher quality of life ratings. Sixty-five of the surveys could be used for statistical purposes. The results are interesting.

The experimenters asked participants to rate their quality of life on a scale from −5 to +5, with −5 indicating their current level is "as bad as the worst period in my life," +5 indicating "as well as in the best period prior to LIS," 0 indicating "neither well nor bad," and other numbers indicating something in between these options. For reporting purposes, experimenters grouped participants into "happy" if they reported in the 0 to 5 range and "unhappy" if they reported in the −1 to −5 range. According to this grouping, 47 reported happy and 18 unhappy. Moreover, participants were significantly more likely to report happy than unhappy if they were in LIS for longer, had recovered some speech production, reported positively to the prompt "I move around my community as I feel necessary," reported positively to the prompt "I am able to participate in recreational activities (hobbies, crafts, sports, reading, television, games, computers, etc.) as I want to," responded positively to the prompt "I feel that I can deal with life events as they happen," responded positively to an absence of depression or anxiety, and responded to having a lower than average frequency of suicidal thoughts. Bruno et al. summarize these results as follows: "Although most chronic locked-in patients self-report severe restrictions in community reintegration, the majority profess good subjective well-being…" (1).

In my view, it is very important to take these kinds of reports seriously, and it is important to note that a majority reported that their quality of life was "neither well nor bad" or better. But it is equally important to note that this grouping into happy and unhappy is somewhat artificial. A plausible interpretation of the scale given to participants is that many reports below a +5 indicate a reduction in well-being due to the injury. Only five participants reported +5, and many of those grouped in the "happy" class reported 0 or +1 (16 by my count: the graph Bruno et al. offer is not clear). This should be coupled with the observation that 13% of participants reported depression, 67% reported moderate or extreme anxiety, 46% reported moderate or extreme pain, 58% did not want resuscitation in case of cardiac arrest (including 49% in the "happy" group), and 32% reported having suicidal thoughts occasionally or often.

These numbers are comparable to another recent study on LIS well-being (Rousseau et al. 2015). In that study, a cohort of 67 LIS patients was surveyed: 44% reported chronic pain, 55% reported anxiety or mood disorders, 27% reported suicidal thoughts, 67% wanted resuscitation if needed.

Minimally Conscious State

MCS exists on a spectrum of similar conditions, usually due to traumatic brain injury, all of which severely impair consciousness and cognitive functioning. A rough ordering can be imposed in terms of preserved elements of consciousness and cognitive function, with persistent vegetative state (PVS) at the low end of the scale, MCS in the middle (MCS is sometimes separated into MCS− and MCS+ (Bruno et al. 2011b), and emergence from MCS (eMCS). It must be noted that behavioral differences between these conditions are often very slight: misdiagnosis rates are high, with misdiagnosis of PVS instead of MCS often estimated at roughly 40%, and misdiagnosis of MCS instead of eMCS occurring frequently as well (although, given low sample sizes, it is hard to offer an accurate percentage; see Schnakers et al. 2009).

To give some indication of how the diagnosis of these conditions is made, consider the deployment of the Coma Recovery Scale-Revised (CRS-R, see Kalmar and Giacino 2005). Administration of the CRS-R involves presenting a patient with stimuli of various sorts. The CRS-R divides the stimuli into an Auditory Function Scale, a Visual Function Scale, a Motor Function Scale, a Verbal Function Scale, a Communication Scale, and an Arousal Scale. Although a patient will be given an overall score from 0 to 23 depending on his or her individual scores on the subscales, most of the subscales offer sufficient conditions for a diagnosis of MCS: given the distributed and unpredictable effects of traumatic brain injury, the scale incorporates significant redundancy. Failure of all of these will lead to a diagnosis of VS, which is considered permanent if a patient shows or has shown no improvement for 30 days following injury.

Consider, for example, the Auditory Function Scale. It is insufficient for a diagnosis of MCS that the subject orients head or eyes toward an auditory stimulus. It is sufficient if, on three-fourth of the trials, the patient displays "object-related eye or limb movement" to aurally delivered commands—that is, commands like "stick out your tongue," or "look at [some object]," or "look up at the ceiling." On the Visual Function Scale, it is insufficient for a diagnosis of MCS if the patient fixates on a visually presented target for more than 2 seconds. It is sufficient if the patient follows a moving mirror for 45 degrees without loss of fixation for 2 seconds, on 2 out of 4 trials.

The Communication Scale of the CRS-R offers a way to distinguish MCS from eMCS. A patient is diagnosed as in MCS if he or she offers clearly discernible and accurate yes/no answers to at least 2 out of 6 visually or aurally based questions (e.g., "Am I touching my ear right now?"). And a patient is diagnosed as eMCS if he or she clearly and discernibly answers 6 out of 6 such questions.

Both MCS and eMCS, then, preserve some elements of consciousness and cognitive functioning. But the amount preserved varies by case and is often extremely limited—a patient can be diagnosed as in MCS even if he or she scores 0 on many of the subscales. Neuroscientific studies including MCS and eMCS patients demonstrate that they lack many of the neurofunctional structures necessary for sophisticated information integration, such as the kind of connectivity between the thalamus and frontal cortex that could enable performance of "top-down" cognitive control tasks such as, for example, counting the number of times a target word is spoken over a 4-second period (Monti et al. 2015). In line with this, most MCS and eMCS patients lack the capacities required for legal competence (e.g., capacities for understanding their condition, appreciating its gravity, developing a view about how their own treatment should proceed, and communicating this view), a fact which often raises difficult questions that family members, doctors, surrogates, and, in some cases, the courts have to answer.

Most patients in MCS and eMCS, then, often cannot report on their quality of life because they do not retain the mental capacities necessary for such reports. Thus, one important way to measure a subject's quality of life is missing. Nonetheless, it is the working assumption of many doctors, scientists, and judges that there is something it is like to be in MCS and that things can therefore go subjectively better or worse for them. Whether it is overall subjectively good or bad to be in such a condition is generally unknown, although one can find empirically informed speculation in the literature (Shepherd 2016; Wilkinson and Savulescu 2013).

Implications for the Mere-Difference View

What are the implications of these disabilities for how we understand the relation between disability and well-being? Regarding LIS, one has to acknowledge that these well-being–relevant reports are much lower than what one would find in the general populace. Indeed, by Bruno et al.'s (2011a) own scale, it looks like a vast majority of patients rated their current quality of life as lower than it was before the injury. Some of the well-being reduction—or alternatively, some of the reduction in quality of life reports—can certainly be attributed to social conditions, access to adequate care, and so on. But it is not at all clear that the entirety of the reduction is due to social factors. LIS patients often suffer from chronic pain, anxiety and depression, and suicidal thoughts. A high percentage of LIS patients do not want resuscitation. LIS gives many indications of qualifying as a bad difference.[3]

The case is, in my view, even clearer regarding MCS. One might resist this verdict by pointing out that, since MCS patients do not explicitly report on their quality of life, it is possible that at least some MCS patients enjoy a good quality of life. Perhaps their lack of knowledge regarding their own condition prevents them from conceptualizing it as bad, as seems to happen in some cases of LIS.

Even if this is true, however, I doubt one can plausibly maintain that MCS patients in general maintain a quality of life as good as LIS patients. Some of these reasons have to do with injuries and complications associated with the severe brain injury that causes the condition. But the chief reason is the absence of many so-called higher psychological capacities in MCS patients. To be in MCS is to lack normal capacities of attention, reasoning, imagination, memory, and cognitive control; to lack access to the range of patterns of thought and streams of consciousness that were likely available before the injury; and to lack access to the full, rich range of emotional and social experiences available before the injury. With proper care, much of this is available to LIS patients. On most plausible theories of well-being—hedonist views, objective list views, desire satisfaction views—access to a range of rich emotional experiences and capacities to exercise sophisticated agency with respect to one's inner mental life and with respect to one's world-involving goals and desires will be critical for higher levels of well-being. Whatever one's theory of well-being, then, it seems to me that, in virtue of their disability, prima facie MCS patients are worse off overall than LIS patients.

Both LIS and MCS are bad-difference disabilities: independently of the effects of social stigmatization, they tend to make a person worse off overall. But they differ in important ways. Is there a unifying explanation regarding their relationship to well-being? And does it generalize to other disabilities? In the next section, I argue in the affirmative. The upshot is a general and tractable normative distinction between classes of disabilities.

CONTROL OVER ONE'S SITUATION

Here, I argue that a central factor in an explanation of the difference between mere-difference disabilities and bad-difference disabilities is that the latter significantly[4] undermine control over one's situation, while the former do not. Strictly speaking, I offer this control-based explanation as sufficient to explain the asymmetry in a wide range of cases. As features of complex biological beings, disabilities are diverse: we should not expect one factor to offer an exceptionless explanation of this difference. (Accordingly, I do not aim to explicate a necessary condition for some disability's qualifying as a mere or bad difference.) Furthermore, in many individual cases, there will be other factors relevant to a full explanation of some singular disability's relationship to well-being. To take one example, a disability that causes chronic pain may be negative with respect to well-being both because it undermines control over one's situation and because it causes chronic pain. To take another, a disability that significantly impairs one's memory may well undermine one's control (by impairing mid-range and long-term planning) while at the same time undermining the significant richness that a fully functioning memory adds to one's ongoing stream of consciousness. On views of well-being that give weight to the value within one's stream of consciousness, memory impairment will undermine one's well-being in two distinct, though intertwined, ways.

Those qualifications aside, in this section, I focus on *control over one's situation*. The terminology is my own. As such, I owe readers an explication of it. As an introduction, I note that the notion is similar to the more normatively loaded term *autonomy*.[5] I choose not to use that term because I do not want to commit to any particular view of autonomy. It is worth mentioning, however, that on most plausible views of autonomy, central to the possession of autonomy will be possession of psychological capacities that enable processes of effective practical reasoning and decision-making. These are processes that include not only inference-making, evidence-weighing, and intention formation, but general background capacities for knowledge acquisition, the integration of information with one's goals and values, and so on. Just which psychological capacities enable these kinds of processes will depend on how one decomposes the mind—plausibly some of the perceptual capacities, along with capacities for attention, memory, practical reasoning, imagination, cognitive control, emotional regulation, and perhaps metacognition will play important roles. When decomposed in terms of contributory mental capacities, then, autonomy is a wide-reaching condition. The same thing is true of control over one's situation.

Why do I refer to one's situation? I need a notion that is sufficiently general. While control of one's situation will include control over elements of one's stream of consciousness (e.g., one's imagination, one's ability to ruminate coherently and reason practically and theoretically), it is broader than this. Given the kinds of beings we are, control over one's situation for beings like us must include abilities to execute intentions, satisfy desires, and accomplish naturally arising goals in the world outside the mind. Roughly, then, possession of control over one's situation can be understood as possession of capacities—these capacities may not stop at the skull or body since assistive technology and caregivers may significantly enhance one's control—that enable one to enhance good experiences and inhibit negative experiences (via, e.g., attention, reappraisal, imagination, targeted planning for the future, inhibitory control), to find and seek beneficial experiences and avoid negative ones, to shape one's conscious mental life, and to shape one's broader patterns of action in the world.

I have said control comes in degrees (see Shepherd 2014). Humans are in many ways fragile, and no matter how healthy or how well placed in society, no human adult possesses total control over her situation. Items hijack our attention, motivational levels fluctuate, the body can be difficult to work with, the environment can be uncooperative, and our desires are often wayward or regrettable. But adults display a significant amount of control in many ways. We exhibit significant degrees of freedom and control over what we attend to, over our trains of thought, over a life of imagination, over our responsivity to positive and negative events, over the ways we satisfy intentions, desires, curiosities, and so on.

Allow me to apply the key claim of this section—that in virtue of the fact that they significantly undermine control over one's situation, some disabilities are inherently negative with respect to well-being—to both MCS and LIS. It is clear that the brain injury that results in MCS significantly impairs many of the capacities that enable such control. The same thing is true of LIS, although the impact of LIS is more indirect. And it is here that a contrast between LIS and MCS affords an important insight. For, when given access to proper care—and perhaps in societies that do not stigmatize such a condition—LIS patients can enjoy high levels of well-being. Notice, in this connection, that 5 out of 65 patients surveyed by Bruno et al. (2011a) reported that their well-being was as high as it had been in the best period prior to LIS. That's a low number, but that any LIS patient could report such a number is important. Notice, as well, that the elements that correlated with higher reports of quality of life were in the main those that indicated the LIS patient possessed greater control over her situation. As I discussed earlier, surveyed LIS patients were significantly more likely to rate their quality of life as higher if they had recovered some speech production, reported positively to the prompt "I move around my community as I feel necessary," reported positively to the prompt "I am able to participate in recreational activities (hobbies, crafts, sports, reading, television, games, computers, etc.) as I want to," reported positively to the prompt "I feel that I can deal with life events as they happen," reported an absence of depression or anxiety, and reported a lower than average frequency of suicidal thoughts. In addition, Rousseau et al. (2015) report that access to good electronic communication devices and to powered electric wheelchairs made a positive difference. This is some evidence for the view that retention of control is a central factor in enabling a level of well-being that is robust against even severe perturbation.

LIS illustrates two important aspects of control over one's situation. First, one cannot control one's situation very well without *some* degree of control over one's body. That said, the amount of control over one's body required for a robust level of well-being may seem, to many, surprisingly low. This is because, second, control with respect to one's inner mental life appears to be weighted more heavily with respect to well-being than control with respect to one's body.[6] The upshot is a graded spectrum on which control over one's situation can be impaired by bodily disability or psychological disability (however we wish to make that distinction). But bodily disabilities on their own rarely lead to significant impairments to control, while psychological disabilities more readily lead to such impairments given that many psychological disabilities target capacities central to the possession and exercise of this control.

The central claim of this section, then, enables an explanation of the difference between bad-difference disabilities like LIS and MCS and mere-difference disabilities like deafness and blindness. The resultant typology is similar to that set up by Asch and Wasserman's (2010) discussion of static disabilities. (And note, in this connection, that while Barnes's (2016) account of disability is only meant to apply to bodily disabilities, many disabilities in view in this chapter blend the bodily and the psychological in ways that suggest the distinction may not be helpful.)

There will be important differences. In particular, control over one's situation may be significantly impaired when one suffers from various static psychological disabilities. Hopefully, then, my appeal to control affords a more illuminative explanation of the relevant distinction. In this connection, consider the following list of potential disabilities.

- Impairments to limbs due to congenital conditions or injury
- Mobility impairments due to spinal cord injury or stroke
- Loss of perceptual function, leading to, for example, blindness, deafness, or deafferentation
- Congenital insensitivity to pain
- Language aphasias, e.g., global, anomic, Wernicke's, or Broca's aphasia
- Attention deficit hyperactivity disorder (ADHD)
- Depression
- Bipolar disorder
- Personality disorders (e.g., obsessive compulsive disorder, scrupulosity, narcissistic personality disorder)
- Learning disabilities (e.g., dyslexia, dyscalculia, or dysgraphia)
- So-called severe cognitive disabilities associated with, for example, traumatic brain injury, Down's syndrome, or dementia
- Impulse disorders (e.g., intermittent explosive disorder, kleptomania)
- Volitional disorders (e.g., abulia, or akinetic mutism)

It is possible to organize this list in a rough fashion according to the degree to which items on it undermine control over one's situation. As already claimed, given adequate care and a non-ableist society, loss of perceptual function and certain mobility impairments undermine this control very little, if at all. Other items are much worse, although, given the complex interaction of capacities that enable control, various items will undermine control in various ways. That said, however, the notion of control over one's situation is helpful in assisting reflection on the relation between the items on this list and well-being.

Some items on this list fall in something of a gray area. These items might, in very idealized conditions, qualify as mere-difference disabilities. Congenital insensitivity to pain is often a debilitating condition, and proper care is high-effort and difficult to find. The reason is that pain sensitivity is crucial for navigation of our world. But one could perhaps imagine circumstances in which this disability did not undermine well-being. Language aphasias are a very different kind of thing. Some are mild and undermine control very little, if at all. Some (e.g., Wernicke's aphasia, which renders an agent unable to understand written or spoken language) seem to leave control over one's inner life largely intact while undermining control over how one interacts with others in most imaginable human societies. Plausibly, this latter kind of aphasia is much worse with respect to well-being than the former kind.

Other items on this list seem clearly to be negative with respect to well-being, although there will be differences in degree. Intermittent explosive disorder undermines emotional regulation. It is possible to manage the condition such that its impact on well-being is minimal, but, in most cases, the condition's impact seems decidedly negative. Those with intermittent explosive disorder sometimes lose control of their behavior, engaging in violent bouts of rage and aggressive behavior. It is difficult to consider these episodes as merely different ways of behaving. The behavior and the consequences are often very negative.

To take a different kind of case, one condition on this list—abulia, which, in extreme form is classified as akinetic mutism—targets the ground floor of control over one's situation, namely, one's motivation to perform actions at all. Abulia in general is often classified as an absence of willpower, a lack of initiative, or the presence of apathy. With appropriate external prompting, some of those with akinetic mutism are capable of sophisticated actions, such as playing card games, going to and using the restroom, reading and remembering items read. But without external stimulation they tend to do nothing at all, lying unresponsive for hours on end. As Colin Klein comments, "The primary deficit in AM [akinetic mutism] patients seems to lie in forming intentions. AM patients present with a picture of profound apathy. It appears that they do not act because they do not want to act. That negation should be read with wide scope: the patients have no intentions whatsoever, rather than an intention not to act" (2017, 35). Such a disability may not lead to objectively negative experiences. But it seems clearly negative with respect to one's well-being insofar as it takes away all the normal patterns of thought and action that make one's life go well. Moreover, to reiterate, the way it does so is by undermining motivational capacities central to one's ability to control one's own situation.

At the extreme end we find conditions that target one's control to more significant degrees. Depression and bipolar disorder, for example, both in different ways target motivational, attentional, and volitional capacities, rendering stable patterns of thought and action difficult.

It appears, then, that a control-based explanation of the difference between negative and neutral disabilities can generalize to a diverse range of disabilities. Is significant control over one's situation sufficient to explain the difference in every case? I doubt it—as I said earlier, disabilities are multifaceted features of complex biological beings. I doubt that thinking in terms of necessary and sufficient conditions is fruitful in this context. But it is nonetheless worth noting how difficult it is to find cases that qualify as a bad difference in the presence of control (cases of long-standing chronic pain being the only obvious one) and cases that qualify as a mere difference in the absence of control.[7] I do not wish to deny that counterexamples to my proposed explanation could be found. But given that I do not wish to frame my explanation in terms of necessary and sufficient conditions, it is important that these counterexamples run against a general and strong trend. It is the general and strong trend linking control over one's situation and well-being that indicates the kind of control's explanatory significance.

I would not claim that control over one's situation can by itself regiment the relationships between the very diverse class of all disabilities and well-being. Clearly, control over one's situation is a high-level classificatory notion and unhelpful in explaining many of the details that render specific disabilities and conditions what they are. But, at a high level, the notion is fit for purpose. My aim here has been to render plausible and worthy of further consideration a view on which some disabilities are mere differences with respect to well-being and other disabilities are bad differences. In order to do that, I needed to develop some explanation of the distinction. The preceding discussion indicates that control over one's situation is critically important for maintenance of the type and level of well-being human adults typically enjoy. People with control over their situations possess a level of well-being that is robust against the kind of perturbations these disabilities create. Thus, the notion forms a key part of an explanation for why well-being is robust against some disabilities but not others.

Acknowledgments

Work for this chapter was supported by a Wellcome Trust Investigator Award [104347].

Notes

1. Notice that this makes the task of arguing that some disabilities are neutral with respect to well-being more difficult than if I adopted, for example, a social constructionist account of disability. One reason I do not do so is that it seems dubious to me that we could explain all disabilities in terms of processes of social construction, even if some are well-explained by such a model.
2. It would not be difficult to accommodate this point within Barnes's view. Campbell and Stramondo (2017) offer a different explication of neutrality on which it is those things that fall between what is prudentially good for a person and what is prudentially bad for a person.
3. As Adam Cureton points out in comments on this chapter, for all I say, LIS in an ideal society might qualify as a mere difference. This might be right—I confess I am not in an epistemic position that justifies dogmatism. If it is right, in my view, this would be for reasons I outline in the next section.

4. I say "significantly undermine" because control comes in degrees and because some disabilities undermine one's control only slightly. There will be a range of conditions for which it is unclear, and perhaps vague or indeterminate, whether they qualify as a mere difference or a bad difference. Those that clearly qualify as a bad difference will do so because the amount of control undermined passes a relevant threshold (the relevant threshold will likely differ depending on one's theory of well-being).

5. In other work (Shepherd 2016), I have argued that cases of MCS—and cases that are structurally similar in relevant ways, such as advanced dementia—raise difficult moral problems because of a moral conflict that arises in these cases. The conflict concerns how we ought to weight two morally important factors: on one side, the patient's well-being, and, on the other side, the patient's autonomy. In many cases, we let autonomy trump well-being: agents have the right to autonomously act in ways that diminish their well-being. What is difficult about cases of MCS is that the patient's autonomy has been compromised by their injury. So, when deciding whether to, for example, remove artificial nutrition and hydration, we not only have to determine what a patient's prior wishes might have been, we also have to decide how their prior wishes ought to be weighed in their current condition, which includes some level of well-being but no autonomy.

6. Of course, the body and the mind are closely intertwined, and bodily factors can influence the control one has with respect to one's inner life. LIS patients suffer from depression, suicidal thoughts, anxiety, and chronic pain. Many of these may stem in part from their bodily condition. But these are all features that may impair control over one's own situation—it is difficult to cultivate a rich inner life, to enhance positive experiences and inhibit the impact of negative experiences, if one is constantly beset by (e.g.) chronic pain or anxious thoughts. Some LIS patients do not recover speech production, cannot participate in recreational activities, and so on. In these cases, the bodily impairments associated with LIS seem to be overall negative with respect to well-being, even if much of the LIS person's mental capacity is preserved.

7. In comments on this chapter, David Wasserman offers an interesting proposal regarding this latter class. He asks us to imagine "a condition that filled most waking moments with ecstatic but uncontrollable reveries, or a psychosis that, unlike schizophrenia, was characterized by warm, friendly, supportive voices—a kind of internal cheerleading squad." Such conditions seem—on some views of well-being—to qualify as mere differences (or better) while undermining control over one's situation. But there are a few important observations we should make about such conditions. First, they only qualify as a mere difference on what I would regard as implausible views of well-being. It is a crude hedonism that cares about the tokening of ecstatic experiences to the exclusion of the wide range of rich, complex, positive experiences we typically undergo. If the ecstatic incidents were so frequent as to significantly undermine control, the subject would be blocked from many of these rich positive experiences. Second, in order to qualify as a bad difference, we only need a strong tendency of a disability to undermine well-being. This is consistent with some cases bucking the general trend. And it is plausible that any biologically plausible version of one of these conditions would, in many cases, present subjects with difficulties and problems precisely because these conditions take control away from the subject, rendering her at the mercy of her condition. Some individuals could get lucky and find a good match between positive symptoms of the condition and an environment that allowed these symptoms to flourish in the absence of side effects even as the disability on the whole qualifies as a bad difference.

REFERENCES

Asch, Adrienne, and David Wasserman. 2010. "Making Embryos Healthy or Making Healthy Embryos: Differences Between Prenatal Treatment and Selection." In *The Healthy Embryo*. Cambridge: Cambridge University Press.

Barnes, Elizabeth. 2016. *The Minority Body: A Theory of Disability*. New York: Oxford University Press.

Bruno, Marie-Aurélie, Jan L. Bernheim, Didier Ledoux, et al. 2011a. "A Survey on Self-Assessed Well-being in a Cohort of Chronic Locked-in Syndrome Patients: Happy Majority, Miserable Minority." *BMJ Open* 1(1): e000039.

Bruno, Marie-Aurèlie, Audrey Vanhaudenhuyse, Aurore Thibaut, et al. 2011b. "From Unresponsive Wakefulness to Minimally Conscious PLUS and Functional Locked-in Syndromes: Recent Advances in Our Understanding of Disorders of Consciousness." *Journal of Neurology* 258(7): 1373–1384.

Campbell, Stephen M., and Joseph A. Stramondo. 2017. "The Complicated Relationship of Disability and Well-Being." *Kennedy Institute of Ethics Journal* 27(7): 151–184.

Harris, John. 2000. "Is There a Coherent Social Conception of Disability?" *Journal of Medical Ethics* 26: 95–100.

Kalmar, Kathleen, and Joseph T. Giacino. 2005. "The JFK Coma Recovery Scale—Revised." *Neuropsychological Rehabilitation* 15(3–4): 454–460.

Kahane, Guy, and Julian Savulescu. 2009. "The Welfarist Account of Disability." In *Disability and Disadvantage*, edited by Kimberlee Brownlee and Adam Cureton, 14–53. Oxford: Oxford University Press.

Kahane, Guy, and Julian Savulescu. 2016. "Disability and Mere Difference." *Ethics* 126(3): 774–788.

Klein, Colin. 2017. "Consciousness, Intention, and Command-Following in the Vegetative State." *The British Journal for the Philosophy of Science* 68: 27–54.

Monti, Martin M., Rosenberg, Matthew, Finoia, Paola, Kamau, Evelyn, Pickard, John D., and Adrian M. Owen. 2015. "Thalamo-frontal connectivity mediates top-down cognitive functions in disorders of consciousness." *Neurology* 84(2): 167–173.

Rousseau, Marie-Christine, Karine Baumstarck, Marine Alessandrini, et al. 2015. "Quality of Life in Patients with Locked-in Syndrome: Evolution over a 6-Year Period." *Orphanet Journal of Rare Diseases* 10(1): 1.

Schnakers, Caroline, Audrey Vanhaudenhuyse, Joseph Giacino, et al. 2009. "Diagnostic Accuracy of the Vegetative and Minimally Conscious State: Clinical Consensus Versus Standardized Neurobehavioral Assessment." *BMC Neurology* 9(1): 1.

Shepherd, Joshua. 2014. "The Contours of Control." *Philosophical Studies* 170(3): 395–411.

Shepherd, Joshua. 2016. "Moral Conflict in the Minimally Conscious State." In *Finding Consciousness: The Neuroscience, Ethics, and Law of Severe Brain Damage*, edited by Walter Sinnott-Armstrong, 160–179. New York: Oxford University Press.

Wasserman, David, and Adrienne Asch. 2013. "Understanding the Relationship Between Disability and Well-Being." In *Disability and the Good Human Life*, edited by Jerome Bickenbach, Franziska Felder, and Barbara Schmitz, 139–167. Cambridge: Cambridge University Press.

Wilkinson, Dominic, and Julian Savulescu. 2013. "Is It Better to Be Minimally Conscious than Vegetative?" *Journal of Medical Ethics* 39(9): 557–558.

CHAPTER 8

CAUSING DISABILITY, CAUSING NON-DISABILITY: WHAT'S THE MORAL DIFFERENCE?

JOSEPH A. STRAMONDO AND
STEPHEN M. CAMPBELL

ON the face of it, there seems to be a significant moral difference between causing disability and causing non-disability.[1] For many of us, the idea of making a person disabled often raises moral alarms that the idea of preventing or removing disability does not. This may suggest that there is virtually always a strong moral reason to avoid causing disability that does not apply to causing non-disability. In this chapter, we want to examine this apparent moral asymmetry between causing disability and causing non-disability, most fundamentally asking: are there any differences between these two types of actions that could ground a general moral asymmetry of this kind?

One possibility that many find compelling, both in professional philosophy and in the social milieu writ large, is expressed by the *Standard View* about disability and well-being: the view that having a disability is always—or at least almost always—bad for a person in a way that non-disability is not.[2] The truth of the Standard View is often uncritically assumed and, with it, the plausibility of a moral asymmetry. After all, if the Standard View were true, then of course there would be an important moral asymmetry between causing disability and causing non-disability: the former diminishes human well-being, the latter does not. However, this widely accepted justification for a moral asymmetry is bankrupt because the Standard View is false. Or so we think. In a recent essay, we have offered a systematic critique of the Standard View, thereby joining a steadily growing chorus of philosophers who reject that view.[3]

Rather than accepting the moral asymmetry by appealing to the Standard View, some scholars have reversed this reasoning and tried to defend the Standard View by appealing to our intuitions about a moral asymmetry. The thinking goes something like this: the Standard View must be true since, if it were false, it would be permissible to cause disability in much the way that most people think it is permissible to remove or prevent disability; presumably that is not the case.[4] This argument appeals to most people's intuitive sense that, unlike causing non-disability, there is something morally problematic about causing a disability.

Elizabeth Barnes squarely confronts this defense of the Standard View in her 2014 paper "Valuing Disability, Causing Disability" and subsequent book *The Minority Body* (2016). Part of Barnes's strategy is to establish that even if the Standard View (or "Bad-Difference View" in her terminology) is false, there are other potential explanations of the wrongness of causing disability in certain cases. In particular, she identifies two independent factors that could explain this. First, causing disability in another person without their consent would constitute a form of unjustified interference in their life, even if it weren't bad for them. Second, even if *being* disabled is not in general a bad or harmful thing, *becoming* disabled usually involves the transition costs of having to adopt and adapt to a new lifestyle. However, when those factors are not present, Barnes seems willing to "bite the bullet" and say that causing disability is no more morally problematic than causing non-disability. In this way, she rejects the idea that there is a general moral asymmetry between causing disability and causing non-disability.[5]

While we sympathize with much of Barnes's discussion and will ultimately agree with her that we should reject the idea of a general moral asymmetry, there are other potentially promising explanations of a moral asymmetry between causing disability and non-disability that she doesn't address and that appear to be independent of the Standard View. These factors merit investigation, if only because the idea that there's something morally problematic about causing disability is a deep-rooted conviction for many people, including many of those who staunchly reject the Standard View and deny that disabilities need be bad for a person. What, if anything, might explain this belief? And more importantly for our purposes, are there any differences between causing disability and non-disability that actually do justify the apparent moral asymmetry? Our goal in this chapter is to answer this question.

THE SCOPE OF OUR INQUIRY

Before we launch into an analysis of these factors, it is worth putting a finer point on the scope of our inquiry. Foremost, we want to be clear about what we mean by the term "disability," given that there is a wide variety of competing models or definitions of the concept. Since our task is daunting enough without attempting to figure out the nature of disability, we'll help ourselves to the ordinary understanding of which conditions qualify as disabilities or impairments and not worry about whether there's a coherent and plausible metaphysical account underlying this grouping. Paradigmatic examples of conditions widely considered to be disabilities or impairments include blindness, deafness, Down syndrome, spina bifida, muscular dystrophy, achondroplasia, quadriplegia, and cerebral palsy. So, when we discuss causing disability and non-disability, we are merely referring to causing people to have, or not have, the kinds of embodiment commonly taken to be disabilities. We are not making any metaphysical claims about the nature of disability.

Next, our topic involves the concept of causation. For the purposes of this discussion, we'll understand "causing a feature X" in a fairly broad way: making an active, non-negligible contribution to either the creation or the continuance of X. Causing disability includes everything from selecting and implanting an embryo with achondroplasia to participating in a full-contact sport that is likely to result in a traumatic brain injury or other disabling injuries. Causing non-disability would include undergoing the procedure of phacoemulsification to replace an eye's lens that has a cataract on it, getting a polio inoculation, or embedding a cochlear implant in a child.

Since we are here concerned with a possible *moral* asymmetry between causing disability and causing non-disability, we are going to exclude cases only involving the *prudential* value of causing disability or non-disability. In other words, we will not focus on cases in which competent choosers are making a self-interested personal decision about whether to cause disability or non-disability in themselves. Instead, this chapter will investigate cases in which either (1) a competent chooser is acting as proxy to decide whether to cause disability or non-disability in another person who is not currently competent to choose for themselves, or (2) a medical professional or other third party must decide whether to assist in causing disability or non-disability when this has been requested by a competent chooser or their proxy.[6]

Putative Factors in the Explanation of a Moral Asymmetry

What considerations might explain the apparent moral asymmetry between causing disability and non-disability? As already noted, the Standard View probably helps to explain why many people find the moral asymmetry intuitively appealing. But since we reject the Standard View and have defended this rejection at length elsewhere (Campbell and Stramondo 2017), we will not consider it as a justification for the moral asymmetry. Likewise, we will not focus on the factors of unjustified interference and transition costs because these considerations have been adequately addressed in Barnes's work. Moreover, since these factors don't apply in every case of causing disability or non-disability, they could not justify a general moral asymmetry between causing disability and non-disability.[7] Instead, we will examine the following seven putative differences between causing disability and causing non-disability that might be thought to ground a general moral asymmetry.

- *Likelihood of lower well-being:* Being disabled is more likely to render a person worse off than being non-disabled.
- *Risk of very low or negative well-being:* A basic minimum of capacities is necessary to live a prudentially good life. Disability, unlike non-disability, entails having at least one diminished capacity, and thus involves a higher risk that, in the future, one will fall below that basic minimum and have a life with low or negative well-being.
- *Irreversibility:* Disability is irreversible, whereas non-disability is reversible.
- *Questionable preference in the individual:* The desire to be non-disabled is typical, whereas the desire to be disabled is atypical. This atypicality raises the question of whether a person lacks decision-making competence, has corrupted desires or false beliefs, or is not exercising good prudential judgment.
- *Questionable motivation in third party:* The desire or willingness to cause a disability springs from indifference to a person's well-being or even malicious intent, whereas this cannot be said of a desire or willingness to cause non-disability.
- *Vulnerability to stigma and discrimination:* Disability has a much higher chance of opening one up to discrimination or stigma than non-disability.
- *Social cost:* Disability generates more social burdens and costs than non-disability.

To be clear, we are not endorsing any of these supposed facts. Our aim in the remainder of this chapter is to analyze whether these claims are true and, if so, whether they thereby justify a general moral asymmetry that is independent of the Standard View.

Evaluating the Putative Factors

It is quite possible that some or all of the preceding factors help to explain why many people have asymmetrical intuitions about causing non-disability versus causing disability. But this empirical question about people's psychology will not be our focus here. Instead, our interest is in assessing whether these considerations are, in fact, compelling *reasons* for permitting the causing of non-disability and being leery of causing disability. In this section, we will assess each consideration with an eye to whether it identifies a genuine general difference between causing disability and causing non-disability and, if so, whether that difference represents a moral difference that can justify the asymmetry under consideration.

Likelihood of Lower Well-Being

According to the Standard View, being disabled always or almost always negatively impacts one's well-being. Even if this generalization is false, it might be argued that a different generalization about disability's impact on well-being gives us reason to accept a moral asymmetry between causing disability and causing non-disability: namely, that disability is *likely* to be worse for a person than non-disability. In other words, having a disability is likely to make a person worse off than she would be without that disability.[8] We will consider two distinct routes by which this claim of likelihood might be defended.

The first route appeals to population-wide trends. It might be claimed that, on average, disabled people are worse off than non-disabled people and, as a result, causing disability is likely to render someone worse off than causing non-disability.[9] We grant that this claim about likelihood is probably true, but it is noteworthy that the average well-being of disabled people as a group is brought down by three factors.

First, many disabilities are acquired and involve transition costs. As Elizabeth Barnes observes, "even if being disabled is not a harm, becoming disabled is still a difficult and painful process," and this is because when a person becomes disabled, "his lifestyle and perhaps even his self-conception will be radically, drastically interrupted. He will have to reshape his life around his new disability" (Barnes 2014, 96). To make an analogy, many people dislike moving, even if they know they will be equally happy in their new home once they settle in. This is due to the transition costs of moving. Relatedly, some "progressive" conditions involve something like transition costs since the nature and effects of the disability shift over time. Multiple sclerosis, for example, often involves the sudden appearance of new or relapsing symptoms that dissipate after a short time, only to return again after a remission. Of course, moving from disabled to non-disabled also involves transition costs, but presumably transition costs will tends to be greater when moving in the other direction—in large part due to society's favorable orientation toward the non-disabled. Second, there are some kinds of disabilities that, arguably, greatly diminish a person's well-being in a wide range of contexts.[10] Such disabilities are not offset by the existence of extremely beneficial disabilities that greatly enhance well-being in most contexts. Finally, as disability studies scholars and disability activists readily point out, inaccessible and otherwise hostile social institutions and practices diminish the well-being of many disabled people in significant ways. Given these three factors, it should not be surprising if, on average, disabled people are worse off than non-disabled people.

Yet, even if it is true that the average disabled person is worse off than the average non-disabled person, facts about population-wide patterns should not guide our behavior when making particular decisions about causing disability or non-disability. Unlike the statistician who drowned while trying to wade across a river with an average depth of four feet, we should appreciate that what is true on average may not hold in specific instances. What is true of the average disabled person does not necessarily hold for any particular disabled person. Decisions about causing disability or non-disability in specific instances should be judged on a much narrower, if not a case-by-case, basis. Factors like transition costs, particular disabilities that are typically very bad for a person, and hostile social environments should only influence our decisions in those cases where they are present. There are many instances in which causing disability is *not* likely to diminish a particular person's well-being partly because these factors are not present or are outweighed by other considerations. For a striking example, take the character Thomas from the television show *Downton Abbey* who, finding himself amidst the horrors of trench warfare, raises his hand into the line of fire to amputate it in order to be sent home. Contrary to what may be true on average for disabled people as a group, for this particular person becoming disabled likely *increased* his well-being. A less extreme, real-world example of a disabled person who, arguably, can trace much of her well-being to her disability is Temple Grandin. In her 2008 memoir *Thinking In Pictures*, Grandin describes how her enormous success as an animal scientist who designs livestock-handling facilities is not *in spite of* her autism but *because of* it.

The above examples illustrate why we need a fine-grained, context-dependent evaluation of the impact that causing disability or non-disability is likely to have on the well-being of a particular person in their particular context. We cannot justify a general moral asymmetry between causing disability and non-disability based on the notion that, on average, disabled people are more likely to be worse off. Judgments about particular cases should be based, as far as possible, on an assessment of the specific context.

Let us now consider a second route for defending the claim that having a disability is likely to make a person worse off than she would be without the disability. According to this line of thought, having a disability typically means there is something significant that you cannot do. For instance, a blind person cannot enjoy watching a fireworks show, and a dwarf cannot play as a center in the NBA. Hence, having a disability cuts one off from certain valuable things in life. It limits one's opportunities to secure a wider range of the goods of life, whereas non-disability allows for more opportunities.[11] This restricted opportunity to access the goods of life is likely to be bad for a person. So, the reasoning runs as follows:

1. Having a disability limits one's opportunity to access the goods of life (in a way that lacking that disability does not).
2. Something that limits one's opportunity to access the goods of life is likely to make them worse off than they otherwise would be.
3. Therefore, having a disability is likely to make a person worse off than they otherwise would be.

We think both premises in this line of reasoning are problematic.

The first premise states that disability restricts one's opportunity to access the goods of life. This claim is open to challenge on a few fronts. To begin, the features of a life that are most plausibly and widely regarded as "goods of life" (i.e., things that tend to contribute to well-being) have a general character. One often hears mention of such things as happiness, achievement, rewarding relationships, virtue, meaning, knowledge, aesthetic appreciation, and freedom. It is true, of course, that disabilities often render specific ways of realizing these goods inaccessible to a person, but these goods are *multiply realizable*. A blind person who cannot appreciate beauty through vision can do so through other senses. A person with quadriplegia cannot run marathons but might instead make achievements as a philosopher, poet, writer, or physicist. While specific avenues for securing the goods of life may be closed off as a result of disability, there are typically many other avenues available. Even in those cases where a given disability (or a social environment that is unwelcoming to that type of disability) cuts a person off entirely from a specific type of good, one can arguably still have an incredibly rich life if one has sufficient access to other types of goods.[12]

Furthermore, it is important to avoid an overly simplistic picture of the relationship between disability and opportunity. It just isn't the case that a decrease in the level of a particular function correspondingly decreases one's opportunities. Take, for example, someone who has extremely sensitive hearing such that they perceive *much* more of the auditory world around them than typical hearers. This could be a serious disadvantage to those aspiring to any number of careers that require intense concentration, such as computer programming, neurosurgery, or philosophy. There is some testimonial evidence from deaf individuals that an inability to hear is advantageous for some of these tasks and has opened up more opportunity for them in that context (Burke 2014, 96).

In addition, disabilities can open up opportunities in other ways. Disability narratives commonly attest to the beneficial ways in which having a disability can broaden one's perspective on life, generate a new sense of identity, and open up new social relationships. For all of these reasons, it is dubious that, as a general matter, having a disability restricts a person's opportunity to access to the goods of life. Causing disability will sometimes increase opportunity, just as causing non-disability will sometimes decrease it.

The second premise in the above reasoning asserts that one is likely to be made worse off by something that limits their access to the goods of life. There are three ways in which greater opportunity to access the goods of life might be thought to benefit a person: (1) it is likely to result in the person actually securing more goods and, as a result, having higher well-being; (2) it is likely to lead to a greater diversity of goods, which might be thought to be good for us; (3) the very opportunity to secure those goods of life might itself be good for us.

We are skeptical of all three claims. Regarding (1), more opportunity to access the goods of life does not necessarily result in a likelihood of higher well-being. Most of us have access to many more opportunities than we have the time, energy, or inclination to pursue. Consider various ways that one might bring aesthetic appreciation into one's life: listening to music, composing music, playing music, singing, painting, viewing others' paintings, sculpting, engaging with others' sculptures, photographing things, appreciating the photographs of others, designing buildings, appreciating architecture, appreciating natural beauty, dancing, attending others' dance performances, and so on. Most of us are only able to engage in a few of these activities, so it often makes little practical difference when some of them are made inaccessible to us (Asch and Wasserman 2010, 208). When there is a surplus of opportunities to achieve well-being, a diminishment of one's opportunity need not result in a likelihood of lower well-being.

This has a bearing on (2). Since more opportunity to access the goods of life does not always increase the odds that one will achieve more goods (of any type), more opportunity need not raise the odds that one will achieve a greater diversity of the goods of life. As noted above, a disability may not cut a person off from *any* of the widely recognized goods of life, even if it places some limits on the ways in which a person can access them. So there is no reason to associate disability in general with less diversity of goods. One might try to insist that diversity in particular forms of a good has value in itself, but we find this implausible. If a person derives much pleasure and meaning from, say, playing piano, she would not seem to be any worse off than a person who derives the same overall amount of pleasure and meaning from playing piano *and* chess. Thus, reflecting on the multiple realizability of the goods of life and the fact that most of us have more opportunity to access these goods than we are able to actualize suggests that we should not associate fewer opportunities to access the goods of life with less diversity in the goods one possesses.

Finally, we reject (3), the suggestion that opportunity itself is good for us. For this to be true, even unactualized opportunities would need to be of value. But this seems implausible. Consider a professor who prefers to bring her lunch to the office every day rather than buy lunch at one of the many eateries near her campus. If half of those restaurants shutter their doors next semester, is she made worse off merely because she no longer has the opportunity to eat lunch at these venues? We think not. It is the actualization of opportunity that is of benefit to a person, not the bare opportunity itself.[13]

In summary, we have argued that limitations on one's opportunity to pursue the goods of life is not always a bad thing and that disability's impact on such opportunity is not so simple. So, the assertion that disability is more likely to be worse for a person than non-disability cannot be defended by insisting that disabilities reduce opportunities to seek prudential goods.

Risk of Very Low or Negative Well-Being

A related but distinct way of trying to justify the alleged moral asymmetry between causing disability and causing non-disability appeals to the fact that having a disability raises a person's risk of having a prudentially impoverished life. One might defend this claim by appeal to the somewhat plausible suggestion that it would be difficult or impossible to secure the goods of life without a certain basic minimum of capacities. For instance, imagine a baby with congenital rubella that is born blind, deaf, and with a severe brain injury.[14] Lacking these sensory and cognitive capacities, it seems unlikely that such an individual would lead a flourishing life given the barriers that would separate her from other people, society, and human culture. One could reasonably predict that this condition of multiple disabilities would lead to low or even negative well-being. The worry is that having a disability, which typically involves the loss or diminishment of some capacity, involves a higher risk that at some future time one will fall below that basic minimum. So, even if a disabled person is actually living a full and happy life at a given time, they are still at a higher risk than a non-disabled person of being in a state of disability that would ensure low or negative well-being.

To illustrate this way of thinking about disability and well-being, imagine that an anvil is suspended above one's head by a number of cords. A certain number of cords is needed to keep it from falling, but there are currently more than enough cords in place. If someone severs a single cord, the anvil will not drop, but it won't be held in place as securely and the risk of it falling is increased. If instead one refastens a severed cord or introduces a new cord, the anvil will have greater stability. Intuitively, there is some moral reason to avoid severing a cord, whereas there is no such reason to avoid adding a cord. If anything, adding a cord might be morally good. In this analogy, the cords are one's capacities, and the dropping of the anvil represents a person's descent into a prudentially impoverished life due to a lack of capacities. Severing a cord represents causing a disability, and refastening or adding a cord represents causing non-disability. Drawing upon this analogy, it might be thought that it is morally better to cause non-disability (refasten or add a cord) than to cause disability (sever a cord). Causing non-disability decreases the risk of the person having a prudentially bad life due to lacking a basic minimum of capacities (the anvil dropping), whereas causing disability increases that risk. Even if a person's well-being can remain high with a disability, they have less "insurance" against a prudentially impoverished life than one who is not disabled and has a full complement of capacities.

However, this analogy is flawed in various ways. One shortcoming is that it presumes that causing disability always entails the loss of capacities. The distinction that is sometimes drawn between *mode* of function and *level* of function is informative here. The level of function refers to the efficacy or efficiency with which a function achieves a goal; the mode of function refers to how the goal is accomplished (Silvers 1998a, 101). So, one's level of function may be the speed at which one can mobilize down a sidewalk, whereas the mode concerns whether one does this using organic legs, a wheelchair, a unicycle, etc. As others have argued at length elsewhere, becoming disabled doesn't always occasion a *loss* of function but may only involve a *change* in one's *mode* of function (Silvers 1998a, 2002). A change in one's mode of function does not at all equate to a loss of capacity because the level of function may remain intact or even increase. For example, Hugh Herr was a rock-climbing child prodigy who had both of his legs amputated after an accident at the age of seventeen. Herr reports that, with less body mass and with prosthetics that he designed and built specifically for climbing, "I began ascending rock faces that I actually could not have ascended before the accident with biological legs."[15] In fact, sometimes gaining a disability means gaining an additional capacity. It is far too simplistic to treat causing disability as merely removing a capacity. The relationship between disability and capacity is more complicated.

There are at least two other important flaws in the anvil analogy. First, it does not obviously acknowledge the role that the social environment and a person's temperament play in determining disability's impact on well-being. On the face of it, the anvil analogy seems to embody a simple medical model in which the loss of capacities entails certain impacts on well-being irrespective of the social environment and features of the individual's psychology. One powerful challenge to this understanding can be found in cases where people with locked-in syndrome, who have lost most of their physical capacities, still manage to flourish in certain ways—largely thanks to their temperament and mindset and a supportive social environment.[16] Another shortcoming of the anvil analogy is that it treats all capacities alike, as so many cords supporting an anvil. But some capacities bear a trivial relationship to well-being and others may play a pivotal role—though, again, this is likely to depend on contextual factors.

All that said, we grant that sometimes causing a disability of a certain kind in a certain type of individual in a certain social context will increase the risk of that person ending up in a condition of multiple disabilities that would lead to low or negative well-being. Even so, it is questionable whether this fact can justify the moral asymmetry under consideration. After all, we make many choices for ourselves and our dependents that are not themselves harmful but do raise the risk of future harm or even death, and we often choose these things over less risky options. For example, taking an infant on an international trip to introduce her to extended family will sometimes expose the child to a myriad of risks, including serious health risks. Yet, many people would not find these risks, by themselves, compelling. An action that carries some risk of a very bad result can be the action that is likely to yield the greatest benefit, and people are frequently willing to take on such risks in the pursuit of higher expected benefit. Granted, there is probably some threshold of risk of ending up in a state of low or negative well-being that it would be morally problematic to cross. At some point, the likelihood of such diminished well-being is too great to justify any benefits that could be gained. However, we ought to be consistent with how we react to such risks and, in cases where causing disability doesn't incur a degree of risk that crosses this threshold, we ought to treat it as we would comparable risks that are routinely taken in other domains of life. Thus, the idea that disability increases one's risk of being in a state of very low or negative well-being is an unpromising candidate for justifying a general moral asymmetry.

Irreversibility

Another putative factor that might explain a moral asymmetry is that causing disability is irreversible, whereas causing non-disability is reversible. Colloquially, when some *thing*—like a ship—is said to be "disabled," this means that it has been damaged and is inoperable. We tend to think that something that is undamaged (whether repaired or never damaged in the first place) could always be damaged in the future but moving from a damaged to an undamaged state is not always so easy. In the case of fragile human bodies, repair is sometimes impossible. Thus, it is tempting to think that disability is irreversible in a way that non-disability is not.

However, it is overly simplistic to associate disability with irreversibility. Drawing again on the mode/level distinction, acquiring a given disability can mean that one irreversibly loses the capacity to achieve some function via a particular mode. But the outcome of the function is usually what matters most, and one's capacity to achieve a valued outcome may be preserved or even enhanced, even if one is unable to achieve it by a particular mode. So, it may be that concerns about the irreversibility of causing disability are actually about the irreversibility of removing one particular mode of function for achieving a valued goal. It is not clear that this kind of loss is always or even usually morally significant.

Furthermore, it's a mistake to associate non-disability with reversibility. Practically speaking, one typically can't find medical professionals who will "disable" them. Often it's just the opposite. Lasix surgery is commonplace now, but one will have enormous challenges finding someone who will surgically weaken their eyesight or blind them in some fashion.[17] In addition to deeply entrenched individual attitudes and professional codes of medical professionals that would make it difficult to find someone willing to cause disability, there are long-standing legal traditions and institutions that discourage or outright forbid causing disability but don't do the same for causing non-disability. Insofar as decisions to cause non-disability can also be, for all practical purposes, irreversible, this apparent difference in reversibility does not apply.

Even if we could distinguish causing disability and causing non-disability in terms of ir/reversibility, it is doubtful that this would ground a moral asymmetry between the two. We are not generally opposed to people making irreversible choices. In fact, it is common practice to celebrate certain choices that we believe, or at least hope, are permanent such as having a child, getting married, or graduating with a college degree. Perhaps there's a greater moral imperative to deliberate seriously about life-altering choices that are difficult or impossible to reverse, but it's not clear that there's any moral reason to actually avoid making an irreversible decision. Irreversibility, on its own, seems to have very little moral significance.

Irreversibility can become a morally salient feature of a choice when it is combined with an additional normative feature: the probable goodness or badness of the choice itself. Insofar as performing some action is deemed to be good or bad to begin with, it might be seen as even better or worse if it is irreversible. To illustrate this point, imagine a young person with socially conservative parents who warn him against getting a tattoo because of its permanence, while at the same time encouraging him to make a lifelong commitment of marriage to the girl next door. This seemingly inconsistent response to the feature of irreversibility is easily explained by the parents' drastically different judgments about the value of tattoos and marriages. For these conservative parents, and for everyone else, permanence is a bad thing when the choice will or might be a bad one, but a good feature of a choice when the choice itself is good. Thus, the irreversibility of causing disability is only a bad feature of a choice in those cases where disability is likely to make a person worse off. In sum, we think that the irreversibility justification for the moral asymmetry falls apart.

Questionable Preference in the Individual

One might argue that the justification for a moral asymmetry derives from the fact that the motivations of individuals who desire to be disabled are questionable or problematic in some way. This argument hinges on the perception that the desire to be or become disabled is highly atypical, whereas the desire to be or become non-disabled is commonplace. Just as it is atypical for a person to want to die, it is atypical for people to want to be or become disabled. This atypicality raises a question of whether a person lacks decision-making competence or has corrupted desires (perhaps as a result of illness), or has false beliefs, or is simply not exercising good prudential judgment. These would be reasons for proxies or third parties to exercise restraint in causing disability.

While the mere atypicality of certain desires is no reason, by itself, to dismiss them, we grant that the atypicality of a desire might sometimes signal a lack of competence. If so, this incompetence would need to be established on grounds that are independent of the bare fact that the person desires to be disabled. In such cases, people may not be competent to choose to cause disability in themselves, but they would not be competent to choose non-disability either.

That said, it is unclear that this applies generally to the desire to be disabled. While the desire to *become* disabled may be quite rare, many disabled people do desire to *remain* disabled. That desire is not so atypical. While the desire to be disabled may still seem somewhat foreign to non-disabled people, if we were to regard this desire as a reason to presume the holder of that desire is an incompetent chooser, we would need to radically rework the entire informed consent process. After all, a desire to remain disabled, for one reason or another, motivates many refusals of treatment that informed consent requires that we respect.

Nevertheless, some do call into question the rationality of disabled people who desire to be disabled. Specifically, they maintain that if a disabled person prefers to be disabled, it is because they have adapted their preferences to a narrowly constrained set of choices and would not have this preference if non-disability had been an option. Like the fox who tells itself that the grapes it cannot reach are sour, the disabled person who prefers disability over non-disability is thought to be merely settling for the lesser option because it is the only one available.

It seems clear that the temptation to see the desire to be disabled as adaptive or as signaling incompetence is rooted in the conviction that having a disability is bad for a person. This seems true whether the idea of an adaptive preference is understood in normative terms (e.g., a preference to be in a bad or suboptimal condition) or is given a purely procedural interpretation (e.g., a preference that one would not possess under conditions of full information and rationality). Thus, the assumption that a desire to be disabled is adaptive or indicates incompetence depends on something like the problematic Standard View.[18]

Once we abandon the faulty view that disability is almost always bad for a person, there is no reason to automatically assume that an individual's desire to have a disability is questionable. This consideration cannot justify a general moral asymmetry between causing disability and causing non-disability.

Questionable Motivation in Third Party

A related but distinct argument focuses on the motivations of any third party who either acts as proxy when deciding whether to cause disability or non-disability in another or assists another who has expressed a desire to cause disability or non-disability in themselves. This attempted justification of a moral asymmetry rests on the fact that the desire or willingness to take away or lessen another person's capacities in ways that would be regarded as disabling is more commonly associated with malicious intent than beneficence.

Whether and how the agent's psychology bears on the ethical status of an action is a complex and controversial issue in ethical theory. For present purposes, we will simply grant that *if* malicious motives can give one reason not to perform an action, this would clearly apply to cases where someone aims to cause disability (or non-disability) with malicious intent. That said, once we dismiss the view that disability is generally bad for a person, there is less reason to assume that a proxy decision maker's motivations for causing disability are suspect. If it is not inevitably irrational for someone to desire disability for themselves, why would it be so to desire it for someone else? A proxy who chooses disability for another need not be acting maliciously, but very well may be implementing the wishes of a formerly competent chooser or making a choice for a non-competent individual that shares significant contextual features with choices made by competent individuals who reasonably choose disability for themselves.

Likewise, there is little reason to be suspicious of the motivations of a third party who is not a proxy decision maker but has been asked by an individual for assistance to cause disability in themselves. The decision about whether or not to assist someone in causing disability or non-disability can rest squarely on whether that individual is a competent chooser who is not under duress of some sort. Implementing the wishes of an incompetent chooser (in the direction of either causing disability or causing non-disability) ought to be what is regarded with suspicion. Whenever a third party assists a chooser who is competent and free from coercion, it seems far more natural to suspect that this third party is committed to the autonomy of the chooser and a rejection of paternalism.

Vulnerability to Stigma and Discrimination

One might reject the view that disability generally decreases a person's well-being while still holding that the stigma and discrimination experienced by disabled people is an objectionable injustice. Perhaps a moral asymmetry is justified by the fact that causing disability has a much higher chance of opening a person up to harmful discrimination than causing non-disability would.[19]

The first point to make is that the relationship between disability and discrimination is a contingent one. The amount of stigma and discrimination surrounding disability can vary dramatically depending on such factors as the social context, the type of disability, the social status of the disabled individual, etc. Take the case of Magdiel Sanchez, who was shot and killed by police because he did not obey their commands to stop moving toward them while carrying a weapon. Sanchez was deaf and did not hear the commands being given and, according to witnesses in his low-income neighborhood, often carried some kind of stick to fend off the many stray dogs in the area

(Miller 2017).[20] Arguably, it was Sanchez's race and socioeconomic class in combination with his disability that exposed him to this sort of police violence. Yet, in other kinds of circumstances, having a certain type of disability will not increase, and could even lessen, the discrimination that a person faces. For example, in spaces where the social norms and expectations are set by disabled people, it is non-disabled people who may find themselves somewhat ostracized. It is commonly reported by average height siblings that they are socially isolated when accompanying a family member with dwarfism to a Little People of America meeting conference. Since an increased vulnerability to discrimination and stigma is not a static or essential feature of disability, this feature cannot ground a general moral asymmetry between causing disability and causing non-disability.

That said, disability-based oppression is a real phenomenon that often impacts the lives of disabled people and diminishes their well-being. In principle, we can imagine counterfactual scenarios in which ableist oppression was global in scale, impervious to change, and so harmful that it would justify a moral prohibition on causing disability that could be generalized to all or most cases. However, we suspect that, at least in a constitutional democracy like the present United States, the situation is not so dire and we ought to give moral priority to ending oppressive attitudes, practices, and institutional structures instead of reducing the number of people who have identities that are subject to this oppression. Our way of life gives us a good measure of control over the kinds and degree of social oppression that exist in our society, unlike citizens who are purely subject to the will of a dictator or a monarch. Thus, it would be deeply troubling to give so much ground to the social oppression that currently exists by using it as a justification for why more people with the oppressed identity ought not exist. Indeed, there seems to be something perverse about using this line of reasoning to serve as a justification for the moral asymmetry in a society in which there is the potential to change the widespread ableist oppression that is causing the harm to disabled people.

Social Cost

Finally, it might be thought that a moral asymmetry between causing disability and causing non-disability is grounded in the fact that disability has a higher social cost. It shouldn't be controversial to claim that disabled people require accommodations of various kinds in order to fully participate in social life. So, perhaps it follows that insofar as having a disability requires accommodations that will draw upon social resources that would not be needed for a non-disabled person, causing disability tends to generate greater social cost than causing non-disability.[21] While this line of thinking may seem to have a place in public policy debates rather than the ethics of individual action, presumably individuals have some responsibility to consider the collective impact of their private decisions on the common good. Just as one might reasonably take rising global temperatures into account when deciding whether to buy a full-sized SUV or a compact hybrid, one might consider social costs when deciding whether to cause disability or non-disability. In this way, social costs could be an ethical consideration even at the level of an individual proxy or clinician.

However, we don't believe that this consideration is ultimately compelling. Arguments have been made that the standard of equality of opportunity held by a liberal democracy like ours requires society to provide accommodations to disabled people as a matter of justice (Silvers 1998b).[22] The attempt to remedy inequality of opportunity for a marginalized group will typically generate a significant social cost for those in the advantaged social position. For example, ending chattel slavery in the American South incurred a tremendous cost for plantation owners and other white people benefitting from this brutally exploitative system. This is not at all to say that accommodating disabled people is the moral equivalent of emancipating slaves. Yet, someone always benefits from an unjust system and remedying the injustice typically harms those beneficiaries to some degree, even if such harms are ultimately outweighed by other beneficial consequences.[23] Thus, the bare fact that causing a disability that will later be accommodated might create social costs does not seem sufficient to justify a general moral asymmetry.

Further, it is important not to hold causing disability to a higher moral standard than we apply to other individual choices that result in serious social costs. People make major life-choices all of the time that are likely to generate significant social costs. Yet, society still leaves many of these choices up to the individual in the name of liberty. For example, there is evidence that the choice of whether to have one or multiple children has a much greater impact on the generation of greenhouse gasses than the kind of car one drives or whether they use solar energy in their homes (Wynes and Nicholas 2017). These and many other individual choices that generate social costs are typically regarded as falling within a protected sphere of personal liberty. It would be unreasonable to hold the choice of causing disability to a different moral standard than other choices that incur comparable social costs but enjoy strong protection. It may be that the choice to have children is common, while the choice to cause disability is less common. However, an essential feature of respecting personal liberty is that it protects uncommon choices to the same degree that it supports prevalent ones.[24]

Conclusion

Our goal in this chapter has been to assess whether there is a general moral asymmetry between causing disability and causing non-disability. To that end, we examined seven factors that might explain and justify such an asymmetry. Our findings are somewhat mixed. None of the factors can ground a *general* moral asymmetry between causing disability and causing non-disability, but each of them points in the direction of morally relevant considerations that generate at least *some* moral difference between causing disability and causing non-disability in *some* particular cases. These include:

- the likelihood that causing disability in a particular instance will render the person worse off than they would be otherwise

- a substantial risk that if a particular person becomes or remains disabled, they will end up in a state that ensures very low or negative well-being
- irreversibility of the choice to cause disability in those cases where the disability is likely to be bad for the person
- lack of decision-making competence in a person who wishes to become or remain disabled
- questionable motives for causing disability in another person (provided that motives are relevant to the ethical status of an action)
- a substantial risk that a person will experience harmful stigma and discrimination
- substantial social costs associated with the choice to cause disability

We think that each of these factors has some moral significance, though it is worth emphasizing that not all of these factors are present in all cases of causing disability. Further, many of them apply to some instances of causing non-disability. It is important not to hold disability to a double standard and give special weight to these factors in cases of causing disability when they are given little or no weight in other domains of life.

So, we have identified several factors that speak against causing disability in particular cases. This means that the falsity of the Standard View does not by any means entail that there's no moral difference between causing disability and causing non-disability. Often there is. At the same time, we join Barnes in rejecting the idea of a general moral asymmetry between causing disability and non-disability. Our analysis implies that we should avoid such crude generalizations about the ethics of causing disability and non-disability. Any intuitions we may have about an asymmetry, even if they apply in many particular cases, do not generalize enough to justify a broad moral principle that favors causing non-disability over causing disability. Such a principle would oversimplify the complex reality and would inevitably ignore morally relevant differences between particular cases. Whenever we encounter a choice about whether to cause disability or non-disability in another person, we should aim to base our decision, as far as possible, upon the nuanced details of that particular case and its context in order to judge whether or not it is a permissible or impermissible thing to do.

NOTES

1. We are very grateful to Adam Cureton, Daniel Singer, and David Wasserman for their insightful feedback on this chapter.
2. The label "Standard View" is drawn from Amundson (2005), 103.
3. Campbell and Stramondo (2017). Other philosophers who have challenged the Standard View or some variant of it include Amundson (2005); Wasserman and Asch (2013); Schramme (2013); Barnes (2016, ch. 3); Barker and Wilson (2019).
4. See Harris (2001), Singer (2004), McMahan (2005), Kahane (2009).
5. Barnes (2014) and (2016, ch. 5).
6. We also wish to set aside the complications in the so-called the non-identity problem (Parfit 1984, ch. 16). To that end, we will focus on cases where disability or non-disability

is caused in the same individual, rather than cases in reproductive medicine that involve causing disability or non-disability by opting to create one future person rather than another.

7. As it happens, the factor of unjustified interference doesn't even represent a *difference* between causing disability or non-disability. Causing non-disability in a person without their consent or against their will is as much of an unjustified interference as causing disability in this way. So, while Barnes is right to point out that unjustified interference helps to account for what's wrong with causing disability in certain cases, it is a non-starter as an explanation or justification for a moral asymmetry. (To be clear, the aim of Barnes's discussion is slightly different than our own. She sought to explain the apparent badness of causing disability whereas our focus is on the apparent moral asymmetry between causing disability and non-disability.)

8. In Campbell and Stramondo (2017), we refer to this as a "probabilistic variant of the Standard View."

9. The empirical literature on this matter is helpfully examined in Amundson (2010) and Barker and Wilson (2019).

10. While we hesitate to make claims about the value of particular disabilities, we expect that clinical depression is one example of a harmful disability that lowers the average well-being of disabled people.

11. Discussions of a child's "open future" are relevant here. See Feinberg (1980); Buchanan et al. (2000, 170–172); and Davis (1997, 2001).

12. Campbell and Stramondo (2017, 157–158). See also Campbell, Nyholm, and Walter (forthcoming).

13. Three qualifications about this point. First, a person's *perception* of having limited opportunity might be bothersome to her—but presumably the source of disvalue would be those negative mental states and not opportunity per se. Second, the fact that opportunity is not intrinsically good for a person does not mean that a person cannot be *wronged* when they are purposefully barred from opportunities by others (see Wasserman 1998, 198). Third, we grant that autonomy may have intrinsic prudential value and that some options may be needed in order to enable meaningful autonomous choices. However, it by no means follows that any restriction of options is bad for us.

14. This example is drawn from Savulescu and Kahane (2009).

15. https://www.businessinsider.com/bionics-researcher-hugh-herrs-mountaineering-accident-2014-8

16. See, for instance, Bauby (1998) and Tavalaro and Tayson (1998). We are certainly not suggesting that most people with locked-in syndrome do or could flourish. The point is only to emphasize that environment and individual temperament are extremely important. A highly restrictive disability can be compatible with flourishing under the right conditions, and a minimally restrictive disability can be devastating with the wrong environment or attitudes.

17. http://www.news.com.au/lifestyle/health/mind/woman-who-intentionally-blinded-herself-with-drain-cleaner-says-she-couldnt-be-happier-with-the-decision/news-story/e8b4764fad2407717fa504e04670ae7a

18. Granted, there is a sizable literature on adaptive preferences, and therefore much more to be said on the topic. For helpful discussions of adaptive preferences and disability, see Amundson (2005), Goering (2008), Barnes (2016, ch. 4), and the chapter in this volume by Jessica Begon, "Disability, Rationality, and Justice: Disambiguating Adaptive Preferences."

19. This point is related to the "likelihood of lower well-being" factor discussed earlier. However, it is a distinct factor provided that the moral relevance of being subjected to injustice and wrongs is not exhausted by its impact on a person's well-being.

20. Thank you to Teresa Blankmeyer Burke for highlighting this example of how ableism intersects with racism and classism in her talk "Grasping Power: Deaf Ethics and Signed Language Interpreting" given on October 17, 2017 at San Diego State University.

21. We are granting this assumption for the sake of argument. However, it is far from firmly established that causing disability is more costly than causing non-disability. Much of the health care industry can be understood as an apparatus for preventing disability or causing non-disability, and it is widely accepted that the societal costs of health care in the United States are escalating toward an unsustainable level.

22. Conversely, arguments have been made that there are limits to what non-disabled members of society owe disabled people because there are morally significant social costs generated by accommodations that must be recognized. See, for instance, Buchanan (1996).

23. These other beneficial consequences might include increasing virtue and decreasing vice, greater social cohesion and cooperation, an increase in happiness, etc.

24. Some of these points are addressed in Wasserman (2017) and Williams (2017), which raise further critical points about social cost arguments against causing or allowing disability.

REFERENCES

Amundson, Ron. 2005. "Disability, Ideology, and Quality of Life: A Bias in Biomedical Ethics." In *Quality of Life and Human Difference*, edited by David Wasserman, Jerome Bickenbach, and Robert Wachbroit, 101–124. Cambridge, UK: Cambridge University Press.

Amundson, Ron. 2010. "Quality of Life, Disability, and Hedonic Psychology." *Journal of the Theory of Social Behaviour* 40: 374–392.

Asch, Adrienne, and David Wasserman. 2010. "Making Embryos Healthy or Making Healthy Embryos: How Much of a Difference between Prenatal Treatment and Selection?" In *The "Healthy" Embryo: Social, Biomedical, Legal, and Philosophical Perspectives*, edited by Jeff Nisker, Françoise Baylis, Isabel Karpin, Carolyn McLeod, and Roxanne Mykitiuk, 201–219. Cambridge, UK: Cambridge University Press.

Barker, Matthew, and Robert Wilson. 2019. "Well-Being, Disability, and Choosing Children." *Mind* 128: 305–328.

Barnes, Elizabeth. 2014. "Valuing Disability, Causing Disability." *Ethics* 125: 88–113.

Barnes, Elizabeth. 2016. *The Minority Body*. Oxford: Oxford University Press.

Bauby, Jean-Dominque. 1998. *The Diving Bell and the Butterfly*. New York: Vintage.

Begon, Jessica. 2020. "Disability, Rationality, and Justice: Disambiguating Adaptive Preferences." In *Oxford Handbook of Philosophy and Disability*, edited by Adam Cureton and David Wasserman, 343–359. New York: Oxford University Press.

Buchanan, Allen. 1996. "Choosing Who Will Be Disabled: Genetic Intervention and the Morality of Inclusion." *Social Philosophy and Policy* 13, no. 2: 18–46.

Buchanan, Allen, Dan W. Brock, Norman Daniels, and Daniel Wikler. 2000. *From Chance to Choice: Genetics and Justice*. Cambridge, UK: Cambridge University Press.

Burke, Teresa Blankmeyer. 2014. "Armchairs and Stares: On the Privation of Deafness." In *Deaf Gain: Raising the Stakes for Human Diversity*. Edited by H-Dirksen L. Bauman and Joseph Murray, 3–22. Minneapolis: University of Minnesota Press.

Campbell, Stephen M., Sven Nyholm, and Jennifer K. Walter (forthcoming). "Disability and the Goods of Life." *Journal of Medicine and Philosophy*.

Campbell, Stephen M., and Joseph A. Stramondo. 2017. "The Complicated Relationship of Disability and Well-Being." *Kennedy Institute of Ethics Journal* 27: 151–184.

Davis, Dena. 1997. "Genetic Dilemmas and the Child's Right to an Open Future." *Hastings Center Report* 27: 7–15.

Davis, Dena. 2001. *Genetic Dilemmas: Reproductive Technology, Parental Choices, and Children's Futures*. New York: Routledge.

Feinberg, Joel. 1980. "The Child's Right to an Open Future." In *Whose Child?* Edited by W. Aiken and H. LaFollette, 124–153. Totowa, NJ: Rowman & Littlefield.

Goering, Sara. 2008. " 'You Say You're Happy, but': Contested Quality of Life Judgments in Bioethics and Disability Studies." *Journal of Bioethical Inquiry* 5: 125–135.

Grandin, Temple. 2008. *Thinking in Pictures*. New York: Vintage.

Harris, John. 2001. "One Principle and Three Fallacies of Disability Studies." *Journal of Medical Ethics* 27: 383–387.

Kahane, Guy. 2009. "Non-Identity, Self-Defeat, and Attitudes to Future Children." *Philosophical Studies* 145:193–214.

McMahan, Jeff. 2005. "Causing Disabled People to Exist and Causing People to Be Disabled." *Ethics* 116: 77–99.

Miller, Ken. 2017. "Witnesses Yell 'He Can't Hear You' as Cop Shoots Deaf Man." *Associated Press*, September 20, 2017. https://apnews.com/1ebeb1f11d694090bcc0d2e93df7f086.

Parfit, Derek. 1984. *Reasons and Persons*. Oxford: Oxford University Press.

Savulescu, Julian, and Guy Kahane. 2009. "The Moral Obligation to Create Children with the Best Chance of the Best Life." *Bioethics* 23: 274–290.

Schramme, Thomas. 2013. "Disability (Not) as a Harmful Condition: The Received View Challenged." In *Disability and the Good Human Life*, edited by Jerome Bickenbach, Franziska Felder, and Barbara Schmidtz, 72–92. Cambridge, UK: Cambridge University Press.

Silvers, Anita. 1998a. "A Fatal Attraction to Normalizing: Treating Disabilities as Deviations from 'Species Typical' Functioning." In *Enhancing Human Traits: Ethical and Social Implications*. Edited by Erik Parens, 95–123. Washington, DC: Georgetown University Press.

Silvers, Anita. 1998b. "Formal Justice." In *Disability, Difference, Discrimination: Perspectives on Justice in Bioethics and Public Policy*, edited by Anita Silvers, David Wasserman, and Mary Mahowald, 13–145. Lanham, MD: Rowman & Littlefield.

Silvers, Anita. 2002. "Bedside Justice and Disability: Personalizing Judgment, Preserving Impartiality." In *Medicine and Social Justice: Essays on the Distribution of Health Care*, edited by Rhodes, Battin, and Silvers. New York: Oxford University Press.

Singer, Peter. 2004. "Ethics and Disability: A Response to Koch." *Journal of Disability Policy Studies* 16: 130–133.

Tavalaro, Julia, and Richard Tayson. 1998. *Look Up for Yes*. London: Penguin.

Wasserman, David. 1998. "Distributive Justice." In *Disability, Difference, Discrimination: Perspectives on Justice in Bioethics and Public Policy*, edited by Anita Silvers, David Wasserman, and Mary Mahowald, 147–207. Lanham, MD: Rowman & Littlefield.

Wasserman, David. 2017. "Justice, Procreation, and the Costs of Having and Raising Disabled Children" In *Oxford Handbook of Reproductive Ethics*, edited by Leslie Francis, 464–477. Oxford: Oxford University Press.

Wasserman, David, and Adrienne Asch. 2013. "Understanding the Relationship Between Disability and Well-Being." In *Disability and the Good Human Life*, edited by Jerome Bickenbach, Franziska Felder, and Barbara Schmidtz, 139–167. Cambridge, UK: Cambridge University Press.

Williams, Nicola. 2017. "Harm to 'Others' and the Selection Against Disability View." *Journal of Medicine and Philosophy* 42: 154–183.

Wynes, Seth, and Kimberly A. Nicholas. 2017. "The Climate Mitigation Gap: Education and Government Recommendations Miss the Most Effective Individual Actions." *Environmental Research Letters* 12: 1–9.

CHAPTER 9

WHY INFLICTING DISABILITY IS WRONG: THE MERE-DIFFERENCE VIEW AND THE CAUSATION-BASED OBJECTION

JULIA MOSQUERA

THE VALUE OF DISABILITY AND THE MERE-DIFFERENCE VIEW (MDV)

RECENT philosophical discussion has focused on how disability, as a state of being, should be evaluated.[1] Is disability something bad for the disabled individual or is it only a neutral difference? How should disability be evaluated from the perspective of the individual who has it?

In her ground-breaking paper "Valuing Disability, Causing Disability" (2014) and her book *The Minority Body: A Theory of Disability* (2016), Elizabeth Barnes defends the view that disability is a mere difference (the Mere-Difference View, or MDV). Her paper is a response to critics who say that the MDV implies the permissibility of inflicting disability. Barnes defends the view that inflicting disability is nevertheless morally wrong because of (1) the transition costs of becoming disabled, and (2) the Principle of Non-Interference (PNI).

Barnes's MDV is the most recent and powerful defense of the view that disabilities are not bad states of being but rather only *different* states of being that do not, in themselves, negatively affect well-being. According to this view, disability alone does not put disabled people in a worse-off position compared with non-disabled people. MDV opposes views that ascribe *positive* or *negative* value to disability in itself. MDV says that disability is not a good or bad state of being but merely a different state of being. The value of being disabled within a particular society is partly dependent on, for example, social arrangements. If society makes the right provisions for integrating disabled people, then having a disability is not bad or an overall disadvantage, according to MDV. If society does not make the right provisions for integrating disabled people, disability often becomes a disadvantage for the disabled.

According to the MDV, a disability *can* in some cases have overall positive value for the person who has it even if it is disadvantageous due to other factors like social arrangements. Disabilities can be, as Barnes's refers to them, *local* bads. Local bads are, in Barnes's terminology, bads that do not compromise the overall wellbeing of an individual because (as opposed to *global* bads) local bads are detrimental in one area of one's life but can also bring about goods in other areas of someone's life that can be of high value for that person.[2]

Determining the value of disability matters in various ways. One of them is to decide which public policies aimed at addressing the impact of disabilities should be given priority. If the value of disability, positive or negative, is at least partly determined by social arrangements and *ableism*, there is a strong moral reason to arrange society so as to prevent disabilities from harming people by, for example, changing social structures and institutions.[3] But if disabilities have negative intrinsic value (i.e., if disabilities are bad for us regardless of the environment we live in), then it may well be that disabled individuals are owed special compensation because they are necessarily worse off than they would be if they did not have the disability. In addition, if disability has negative intrinsic value, this would give us strong egalitarian reasons to support medical research into preventing individuals from becoming disabled, as well as into eradicating or reducing the incidence of disabilities.

ARE DISABILITY INFLICTORS WRONGDOERS? THE CAUSATION-BASED OBJECTION

Barnes's view seems to be susceptible to what has been referred to as the causation-based objection (Barnes 2014, 89–95). This objection, attributed by Barnes to Jeff McMahan, John Harris, Guy Kahane, and Peter Singer, says that if disability were a mere difference rather than a bad difference, then causing disability would be permissible, and it would also be impermissible to remove disability.[4]

The Causation-Based Objection
(1) If disability were mere difference (rather than bad difference), it would be permissible to cause disability (and impermissible to remove it)

(2) It is (obviously) impermissible to cause disability

(C) Therefore, disability is not mere difference; disability is bad difference.

Barnes (2014) begins her response to this objection by questioning the view that disability is an overall bad, a view she later labels as the bad-difference view (Barnes 2016). The view that disability is an overall bad, she claims, is often assumed rather than argued for. She maintains that the burden of proof is on proponents of the bad-difference view to show how disability really is bad (Barnes 2014, 93–95).[5]

Barnes also rejects (1), the claim that if disability is a mere difference, then causing disability is not morally wrong. According to Barnes, this inference is illegitimate. Barnes agrees that causing a non-disabled person to become disabled is sometimes morally wrong. Nevertheless, she goes on to argue that this wrongness has different grounds than the ones her critics propose.

According to Barnes, commitment to the impermissibility of causing feature x does not itself entail (or even suggest) that x is somehow bad or suboptimal (Barnes 2014, 99). To put the point in the language of reasons, although we have reasons not to inflict disability, those reasons, the argument goes, are not grounded on disabilities being intrinsically bad states of being. The moral reasons against inflicting disability instead have to do with (1) the transition costs of becoming disabled and (2) the principle of non-interference (PNI). Barnes argues that (1) and (2) ground the moral reasons against making people disabled. If her arguments succeed, then one can both regard disabilities as not good or bad in themselves, and so subscribe to the MDV, and also hold that causing someone to become disabled is, in most cases, wrong.

The Transition Costs Argument

Becoming disabled can involve huge transition costs for the person in adjusting to her newly acquired disability. Barnes claims that the transition costs criterion makes it impermissible to inflict disability on a non-disabled person (Barnes 2014, 96–98). In Barnes's account, this cost is nevertheless independent of whether being disabled is itself a bad condition. On her view, the transition-costs-based impermissibility of inflicting disability implies nothing about the intrinsic value of being disabled.

The transition costs argument is vulnerable to at least two kinds of potential counterexamples: those in which disability can be inflicted on individuals but with easily avoidable transition costs, and those in which transition costs simply do not apply. In both kinds of cases, it seems nonetheless wrong to inflict a disability on someone. Barnes does not consider the first kind of potential counterexample. The following is an admittedly fanciful example of disability infliction with avoidable transition costs:

> *The Functionality Updating Pill.* Disability Inflictor goes to town once a week to cause disability by a painless method on every bystander that he finds. He does not

want to inflict harm on others. He believes disability is a valuable part of human diversity, but he recognises the problem of transition costs. There is a pill that eliminates transition costs. This pill instantly updates both our functionality and our attitudes to our new conditions if we were computers working under a new operating system. For example, this pill ensures that a person who has just lost her sight does not need to adapt to the new use of her other non-affected senses, which she immediately uses in a way that makes up for her lack of sight, as a well-adjusted non-sighted person would do after being non-sighted for a long period of time. The pill also updates the whole set of preferences of the person so that she does not have to see her old plans and projects disturbed; and her new preferences are aligned with her new state of functionality. Disability Inflictor administers this pill to every individual on whom he has previously inflicted a disability.[6]

If the only moral reason not to inflict disability on non-disabled individuals is the transition costs that they will have to experience, then it would be morally permissible to inflict disabilities in cases where, like in the Functionality Updating Pill, there are no transition costs involved. However, we seem to agree that inflicting disability on others is morally wrong even where there are no transition costs to becoming disabled.

There are other cases in which the infliction of disability does not result in transition costs, such as when disability is inflicted on infants. Barnes describes a case in which disability is inflicted on a six-month-old baby. Even when transition costs do not apply in the situation of the baby upon whom a disability has been inflicted, Barnes argues that there are reasons for why this would still be morally wrong. I discuss these reasons in the next section.

THE PRINCIPLE OF NON-INTERFERENCE AND THE "NATURAL PATH" BIAS

We have seen that the transition costs argument is insufficient to account for the impermissibility of all cases of disability infliction, since there are at least two types of cases where disability can be inflicted without producing transition costs. To cope with these types of cases, Barnes introduces the Principle of Non-Interference (PNI), which holds that it is pro tanto morally wrong (1) to interfere with people's lives without their consent and (2) to drastically alter someone's physical development (e.g., children's) (Barnes 2014, 95–98). Referring to (1), Barnes claims:

> You shouldn't go around making substantial changes to people's lives without their consent (even if those changes don't, on balance, make them worse off). We'd be inclined to say that Amy does something wrong if she carelessly (and permanently) turns Ben's hair from brown to blond, if she carelessly (and permanently) changes Ben's height by a few inches, and so forth. (…) We have a basic reaction that Amy

shouldn't alter Ben in any of these ways without his consent–regardless of the overall effect of such alterations on Ben's wellbeing.   (Barnes, 2016, 95)

To test the PNI, Barnes provides a case of a mother inflicting a disability on her
six-month-old baby. Barnes assumes that, in this case, there are no transition costs for
the child because presumably all the formative experiences of the baby will include her
disability (Barnes 2014, 97). Barnes argues that inflicting disability on this baby would
nevertheless be morally wrong, just as causing the baby to become homosexual or het-
erosexual would be wrong (Barnes 2016, 97–98).

The PNI is based upon a distinction between interferences in identity-determining
traits and interferences which do not substantially modify the identity of an individual (Barnes 2014, 100). According to Barnes, it is permissible to interfere in the development of a child only if the changes we inflict on him do not modify the child's
identity.

Unfortunately, the distinction between identity determining traits and non-identity
determining traits is not clear. Barnes mentions sexual orientation, and whether one
is disabled or not, as examples of identity determining traits; and as examples of interferences that do *not* alter a child's identity, she mentions whether a child goes to school
and what she eats (Barnes 2014, 98).[7] The only reference to her background conception of personal identity is a footnote in which she states her adherence to "a looser
sense of identity (self-conception)" as opposed to a "stricter one" (numerical identity)
(Barnes 2014, 98). Assuming that disability is an identity-determining trait is problematic, however, under the looser sense of identity (self-conception) that Barnes
adheres to.

The reading of personal identity that lies behind Barnes's PNI—the self-conception of
a person's identity—focuses on the features that are constitutive of who one is and that
make one different from others. Under this qualitative conception of self-identity, some
features seem more relevant than others for the constitution of one's self-identity. Barnes
places disability and sexual orientation in the category of features that contribute to the
qualitative conception of self-identity. And she contends that it is impermissible to
remove or alter these kinds of features from a person's qualitative identity without that
person's consent. But even under this conception of personal identity, Barnes's PNI is
problematic.

Firstly, Barnes frames the issue of the impermissibility of inflicting disability as having to do with the impermissibility of interferences with identity without permission. To
determine the substantiality of such changes in identity, Barnes seems to presuppose a
comparison between an individual's possible identities. This comparison can be historical or counterfactual, depending on which states are compared. If a disability is removed,
are we comparing the individual's non-disabled identity to her previous identity, or the
identity she would otherwise have had? Although Barnes does not acknowledge these
two possibilities, we might ask whether it matters whether this comparison is historical
or counterfactual.

The comparison is historical if it is a comparison between the individual before and after the infliction or removal of a disability. If this is the kind of comparison in play, then Barnes's contention that the person's identity is changed does not necessarily follow. Barnes contends that inflicting disability on a six-month-old baby is morally unacceptable because this would alter the identity of the baby without his consent, which conflicts with the PNI. But in order for a six-month-old baby's self-identity to be changed, the following must be true: first, the baby must have an identity in the relevant sense (a "self-identity"); and second, a six-month-old baby's identity must include being disabled among its constitutive features. Both of these claims are extremely implausible.

What is a six-month-old baby's self-conception? If it does somehow have one, its identity almost certainly does not involve disability, or for that matter, a particular sexual orientation. The effects of a great number of disabilities start showing up as the child develops. In cases like Down syndrome, children will not encounter much functional difficulty as a result of their disability until the age of two or three. Six-month-old babies with Down syndrome can be to some extent quite functionally similar to other babies.

Something similar would apply to the "good adjustment" criterion introduced by Barnes as a sub-criterion of the principle of non-interference (Barnes 2014, 100). According to Barnes's account, there is a potential risk for the baby on whom a disability is inflicted. The risk is that the baby can grow up to be poorly adjusted to her disability and may afterward resent her condition.[8]

It is not clear what the concept of "good adjustment" to disability means in this context. An example of someone not well adjusted to her disability could be someone who cannot manage to get used to living with a prosthetic leg, to the point where she ends up removing it and trying to function on one leg. Under this understanding, as with the PNI, the good-adjustment criterion is likely to be satisfied in the case of a very young child. If "good adjustment" is understood as non-problematic adaptation to functioning with a disability, a six-month-old baby on whom a particular disability is inflicted will likely not have to undergo any process of adjustment to this disability at any moment of her life. The baby will not have to adjust to any new functional state, since her current functional state just before the disability is inflicted is too undeveloped to require from him an adaptation to a different one. Thus, we should not assume that the historical identity of a six-month-old baby is modified by inflicting disability—or homosexuality or heterosexuality—on her.

Barnes seems to understand identity changes in counterfactual rather than historical terms. The counterfactual understanding of identity suggests that inflicting disability or removing it can make the individual become someone different from *whom she would have been had the interference not occurred.* This understanding of identity changes, is also problematic in various ways.

The first problem arises from Barnes's apparent assumption that disabled individuals always take their disability to be one of their identity determining features. In the picture Barnes paints, causing any disability to a six-month-old baby would alter the identity of the resulting future individual in that the individual would grow up to be someone who considers her disability a fundamental part of herself. However, some disabled individuals do not take their disability to be fundamental to their identity. Some disabled individuals think of their disability as ancillary in their conception of themselves and would not identify themselves primarily as disabled.[9] These individuals could perfectly envisage lacking their current disability without this changing their identity in the relevant sense.

Focusing on recent empirical studies, Darling (2013) has pointed out that for many disabled individuals, having a disability plays only a minor role in the way they view themselves.[10] In some cases, other devalued statuses overshadow disabilities in a person's self-conception. For example, studies suggest that for economically impoverished African Americans, race and class are more important than disability in determining their self-identity. It has also been shown that whether disability is perceived as a determining feature of self-identity will depend on different variables such as age, whether the disability is acquired or congenital, and if acquired, the age at which the disability was acquired (Darling 2013, 123–140). The idea is that whether disability matters for identity depends on the individual's other features; some other features can overshadow disability in determining self-identity.

Furthermore, Barnes's assumption that disability is an identity-determining trait seems to lead her argument into a potential internal conflict. She argues that although not all disabled individuals might like being disabled—even in an ableism-free society—disability is a feature that determines self-identity (Barnes 2014, 98). Moreover, the MDV maintains that an important source of that identity is the experience of facing stigma and social exclusion.

The phrase "fully accepting of the disabled" (Barnes 2014, 98–99) is ambiguous in this context, even when it is exemplified by a society that is not biased toward the able bodied. But let us imagine that the world becomes "fully accepting" of disabled individuals in the sense that it provides the adequate means to help disabled individuals flourish. In a world like this, would disability still be an identity-determining trait? And if so, what would be the features that would render it an identity-determining trait? More generally, what, on Barnes's view, makes disability an identity-determining feature? Is it having a functional biological limitation in, for example, seeing or hearing? Is it both having such functional limitation and being disadvantaged in society due to it? Or is it something else?

One striking implication of the second view is that, according to Barnes's PNI, bringing about an ideally just society—one in which no disabled person would be disadvantaged—would be impermissible because it would eliminate the "disadvantage" component of disability, thus changing people's identities in the sense Barnes's PNI objected against. But surely this is an unacceptable implication of any account of the value of disability.

Barnes could reply to the objection above saying that her account is not solely based on socially caused disadvantage but also on other common sources of identity. In describing what is perceived as part of the common identity of those who have conditions that count as disabilities, Barnes mentions not only stigma and other people's treatment but also how certain conditions make it difficult to access some public spaces, to complete everyday tasks, to get adequate health care, to get full-time employment and benefits, etc. (Barnes 2016, 46). She might claim that these latter sources of identity could exist even in societies that fully accommodate the disabled, but it is fair to ask to what extent these sources of identity would be equally salient in ableism-free societies, and salient enough so as not to erode the disability identity. One might also ask whether the presence of only one of those sources of identity would suffice to maintain disability identity, or whether they are all necessary sources of identity.

Barnes's classification of disability as an identity-determining trait rests on the fact that disabled individuals have bodies that function in a minority way together with the fact that people with disabilities experience exclusion due to society not being fully accommodating of their minority way of functioning (Barnes 2016). But if society becomes a full provider of the necessary means to accommodate and overcome disabilities (e.g., glasses to the nearsighted, wheelchairs and ramps to the physically impaired, school assistance for students with special needs, etc.), would disabilities go on being identity-determining features given that in those societies people with disabilities are no longer subject to exclusion due to their minority functioning? Would these conditions even remain as disabilities? If they would, then Barnes's account would need to provide a full specification of why under circumstances of full accommodation (and full inclusion), disability would still be an identity-determining trait. If disabilities stop being identity-determining traits once society fully accepts the disabled and the disabled can function well, then this internal conflict remains as an important problem for Barnes's account.

Let's turn now to the issue of consent, which is an important part of the PNI. Barnes's moral prohibition of interfering in the self-identity of others without their consent seems to go against our common intuitions. We would in different cases consent to interferences to our self-conceptions based on the positive value of the consequences that such interferences could have for us. In certain circumstances in which actual consent—both express or tacit—is not an option, such interferences could still be regarded as legitimate. The legitimacy of interfering in the self-identity of an individual could be grounded in the claim that any rational agent interested in making her life go as well as possible would, under normal circumstances, freely choose such interferences, given that they would secure a much greater benefit for the individual.

It might in turn be suggested that the consent constraint captures intuitions that we may have about the moral impermissibility of interfering with other people's self-identity in normal cases. We think it is normally impermissible to interfere with other people's self-identities without their consent. But that does not solve the problem for the PNI. Barnes's main examples apply to very young infants. The force of the consent constraint is much weaker in such cases. The PNI seems not to apply to cases involving the very young, or if does, it does so in a trivial way; it's trivially true that an infant has not consented to becoming disabled because an infant cannot give consent.

Children simply cannot consent to many of the ways parents and others interfere with their conception of themselves and the world. Nevertheless, that does not prevent parents, for example, from being morally allowed or even required in certain circumstances to interfere with their children's developing self-conceptions in different ways. Educating children consists in changing children's conception about the world and about themselves, by shaping their ideas about what is best for themselves and how they should treat others. Moral education is a clear example of these interventions, where children are often taught, for example, to think of themselves as one among equals. These interventions are performed for the sake of the children themselves, as well as for the sake of others. And parental education often involves getting one's own children to identify with their race and cultural heritage, which often become features of one's self-conception.

Barnes identifies schooling as an interference that does not determine identity (Barnes 2014, 98). She takes it to be an example of an interference that can permissibly be inflicted upon others without their permission. But taking schooling to be not determining of identity seems hard to reconcile with the idea that society is so powerful that it can render disabilities utterly irrelevant to people's well-being. One might believe that society is powerful enough to secure full inclusion and acceptance of disability but not to alter identity through education. This option seems rather implausible though.

Furthermore, we as adults are continuously exposed to information or situations that will predictably shape the conceptions that we have of ourselves, without having given our consent to them; and had we not been exposed to that information or those situations, we would have had different conceptions of ourselves. Suppose someone thinks of himself as having certain traits as a matter of choice, but then without his consent we expose him to compelling evidence that these traits are more likely the result of his biology. Couldn't this change his self-conception? Have we done something wrong here? Not necessarily.

The PNI has important similarities with the widely recognized status quo bias. The pattern of action that both recommend is non-interference in the current states of affairs. But the motivation behind these two patterns of action is different: while the status quo bias aims at promoting the current states of affairs, the bias behind the PNI aims at promoting the state of affairs that would obtain naturally without any intervention. The PNI is biased in favor of a non-interfered-with path of development of bodies and minds. Valuing this natural state of affairs puts Barnes in a dilemma with respect to the claimed impermissibility of interfering in self-identity.

Since the PNI seems to be based on a counterfactual comparison, such that it declares that it is wrong to alter someone's identity in such a way as to make it different from how it would otherwise have been, it contains an inherent bias toward one particular future identity—that which will obtain without interference. In other words, Barnes's account seems to imagine some "natural path" to a particular future identity, and that any departure from that path requires justification.

If interfering in the natural path of development of individuals is always impermissible, is trying to cure cancer or other illnesses impermissible? Furthermore, if the comparison is made with a "natural future identity," it would also be impermissible to inflict changes that would make the body develop differently from the way it would develop if we do not interfere. It would be impermissible to feed infants, which would lead them to an early death.

Barnes could respond to this objection by pointing to an equivocation concerning the notion of "natural-non-interfered-with path of development." She might say that destroying a living body is only natural for a virus but not for the victim of the destruction and that not feeding your infant is not a natural way of acting as a social animal. To reply along such lines would show that Barnes is working with a substantial notion of natural or "non-interfered," but her account does not specify this notion. If what she means by "natural/non-interfered" is "normatively significant," then her argument seems circular. And if the meaning is rather evolutionary—as in "what it is in our nature as human beings"—the notion would seem to be morally unappealing since evolution sometimes selects for, normatively speaking, the wrong dispositions. Furthermore, we might well have "natural inclinations" to eliminate differences that impair function.

Alternatively, Barnes could argue that departures from the natural path are justified when necessary to avoid harm, as in our examples above. And, as we know, she would deny that changes to or from disability are (necessarily) harmful to the person who becomes disabled. However, if the individual is pushed off the natural path (for reasons of harm avoidance) the individual will not end up having the self-identity to which the natural path would have led. Once the individual has been interfered with (in order to ensure survival) there appears to be no reason left to produce this rather than that future identity. Either way, they will not have the identity that they would have had further down the natural path.

Furthermore, the fact that the PNI is biased towards a "natural future identity" as the one that needs to be preserved makes it difficult for the PNI to tell us anything about the moral desirability of additional alternatives other than the ones that preserve the natural path of development.

Barnes's MDV argues that disabilities are not bad states of being but rather only *different* states of being that do not, in themselves, negatively affect the well-being of people who have them. According to this view, disability alone does not put somebody in a worse-off position compared with someone without disability. Adherence to the MDV seems to imply the permissibility of inflicting disability: if disability is not bad, then inflicting disability is not necessarily impermissible. This implication clashes directly with common intuition; we all agree that inflicting disability is simply wrong, and a view of disability that implies the permissibility of inflicting disability is not only counterintuitive but also implausible. Barnes attempts to defend her proposed MDV from this objection. For that, she tries to explain why inflicting disability is wrong without appealing to the idea that disability is a bad difference. According to Barnes, inflicting disability is wrong because of the transition costs of having to adjust to functioning as a disabled, and because inflicting disability is an impermissible interference in people's identity without their consent.

So far, I have raised a number of problems for both of these arguments, namely cases in which inflicting disability does not lead to transition costs and cases in which disability can be inflicted without affecting the individual's self-identity, or where the issue of consent simply does not apply. Thus, we are left with some cases in which inflicting a disability is intuitively wrong but that cannot be explained by Barnes's arguments. This would seem to suggest that the best explanation for why inflicting disability is wrong in these particular cases is the one provided by the view that claims that certain disabilities are bad.

Kahane's and Savulescu's Reply to the MDV

Barnes may offer another kind of defense against the causation-based objection by questioning the justification of its second premise (Barnes 2016b).

Recall the causation-based objection to the mere-difference view:

> *The Causation-Based Objection*
> (1) If disability were mere-difference (rather than bad difference), it would be permissible to cause disability (and impermissible to remove it)
> (2) It is (obviously) impermissible to cause disability
> (C) Therefore, disability is not mere difference; disability is bad difference.

According to Barnes, one may think that the justification of the second premise of the causation-based objection, namely that it is (obviously) impermissible to cause disability, is assumed in the conclusion of the objection, namely that disability is a bad difference. According to this defensive move, critics of the MDV would think inflicting a disability is impermissible because they already think that disability is a bad difference. The causation-based objection would thus seem to implicitly assume its own conclusion and would therefore seem not to inform us on whether disability is a mere difference or a bad difference.

Kahane and Savulescu (2016) responded to this defense by arguing that their objection is justified in appealing to an intuition shared by many people, the intuition that causing disability is wrong because disability is bad. When arguing against a view, the authors claim, appealing to intuitions that oppose the ones implied by that view is not begging the question, but it is rather a way of providing evidence against it, and this sort of evidence has independent traction (Kahane and Savulescu 2016, 782).

To illustrate their point, Kahane and Savulescu claim that many of the counterarguments commonly provided to refute certain ethical views also tend to appeal to intuitions that oppose the view that is being argued against, and this feature alone does not make these argumentative strategies question-begging:

> None of these objections [against other ethical views] is question-begging. The objection to moral nihilism, for example, doesn't appeal to any opposing metaethical view. Rather, since on reflection we find certain acts wrong [e.g., genital mutilation]—and

find them wrong even after we have considered the best arguments for moral nihilism—then we can justifiably conclude that some acts are genuinely wrong, and moral nihilism false.   (Kahane and Savulescu 2016, 784)

In reply to this point, Barnes denies that her original paper portrayed the causation-based objection as question-begging (Barnes 2016b, 295–296). She accepts that premise (2) of the causation-based objection argument (that it is obviously impermissible to cause disability) is a background assumption "that should be assumed by reasonable people", including disability advocates and defenders of the MDV (Barnes 2016b, 297). But she adds that advocates of the causation-based objection do not succeed in *showing* that it is obviously impermissible to cause disability. Advocates of the bad-difference view, Barnes says, support (2) only by explicit appeal to the claim that disability is bad, which is a claim that many disabled individuals deny.

The quote below shows the way in which Barnes originally framed her concern with regard to the bad-difference view:

> *The bad-difference view is often assumed rather than argued for: we are meant to have the intuition that it is correct, or simply take it as obvious.* But the bad-difference view is a characterization of disability which is *not* obvious to many disabled people. And relying on brute intuition can offer little in the way of dialogue for those who simply don't share the intuition and who might be skeptical that the intuitions of the majority offer particularly good insight into the well-being of the minority. The causation-based objections are an attempt to do better—to get some independent traction on the mere-difference/bad-difference debate. They try to show that the mere-difference view has implausible, impermissible consequences, even by the lights of its defenders.   (Barnes 2014, 94)[11]

Barnes's worry seems to be that the causation-based objection is not well supported. She considers the justification of premise (2)—the appeal to common intuition—insufficient to prove the MDV false. Advocates of the causation-based objection, she claims, do not succeed in showing that it is obviously impermissible to cause disability because they base their reasoning in an "epistemically precarious" assumption (Barnes 2016b, 301).

> It's just to say that you need very good reasons to say that the Disability Rights/Pride movement is systematically mistaken when they say that disability is not something sub-optimal. (…) Counterintuitiveness cannot be sufficient for dismissing the mere-difference view.   (Barnes 2016b, 300)

For Barnes, an appeal to intuition is an insufficient or "epistemically precarious" way of justifying the assumption in premise (2): "Such an assumption is unwarranted given the specific socio-political context in which we are discussing disability." (Barnes 2016b, 299)

She thinks the assumption is unwarranted in at least two respects. Firstly, advocates of the bad-difference view sustain premise (2) only by explicit appeal to the claim that disability is bad, which is a claim that many disabled people deny (Barnes 2016b, 298).

Secondly, she adds, the claim that disability is bad in itself clashes also with the prevalent conception in the academic community of sociology, humanities, psychology, or education, as well as in the general political discourse, and in popular television and film. (Barnes 2016b, 297).

Barnes's "epistemic precariousness" argument is itself precarious. It is safe to say that the fact that a view is prevalent in a number of fields (in this case, that disability is not bad in itself) can hardly be the best argument for the truth of this view. And even if a view is "a fringe position held only by a radical few" (Barnes 2016b, 297), this would not determine, either, the overall falsehood of such view.

Finally, in the quote above Barnes says that those who reject the MDV by appealing to the causation-based objection need very good reasons to reject the judgments of those who do not think of disabilities as suboptimal (like some disabled individuals themselves and some disability activists). Kahane and Savulescu provide at least two reasons for why anyone who supports the MDV—whether an activist, a philosopher, or an interested reader—may be wrong in their thinking that certain disabilities as a general phenomenon are not something sub-optimal. I will refer to these reasons as (1) the negative outweighs the positive argument, and (2) the asymmetry between the able and the unable.

The idea behind (1) is that although in many cases disabilities bring about positive features, as Barnes argues, for disabilities not to be bad differences, these positive features would need to outweigh the negative ones that they also bring about.

> Most of the conditions commonly described as disabilities are significantly likely to considerably reduce an individual's level of well-being *in the contingent physical and social environment that we actually inhabit* and this would remain *so even if prejudice against disabled people were removed.*[12]   (Kahane and Savulescu 2016, 776)

As for (2), even if some disabilities bring about certain positive features, it is also true that a hearing person, for example, has the second-order option of removing her ability to hear, thereby gaining access to further options that may require being deaf (such as communicating with sign language without being able to hear), while at present there is nothing that a completely deaf person can do to access the options available only to those who can hear (Kahane and Savulescu 2016, 777). The asymmetry between the options available to disabled people and the options available to non-disabled people stresses the idea that non-disabled people can usually access a greater number of options than disabled people, and this contributes to making the lives of non-disabled people generally better, other things being equal. Barnes focuses on arguing against (1).

For Barnes, although disabilities can reduce options in some areas, which can have a negative impact in the life of a disabled person, disabilities also can, at the same time, create more options in other areas of that person's life (Barnes 2016b, 303). To illustrate this point, think of blindness. One may think that blindness reduces the options of people who are blind in that it prevents them from experiencing the world through sight. But while it is true that blindness prevents people from seeing, it is also true that blindness increases the capacity of blind people to experience the world though other senses, such as hearing, touch, or smell, enabling them to do so in a more intense and sophisticated way than what sighted people can do. This, the argument would go, makes the lives of blind people simply different from the lives of sighted people, but not necessarily worse, since their lives contain goods that are also of value to them.

It may be obvious that some mild disabilities lead to the obtainment of certain goods, as in the case of disabilities whose negative impact is concentrated in a more or less isolated capacity (like audition in the case of deafness or sight in the case of blindness). Barnes's argument is less obvious though when applied to other, more severe disabilities (e.g., cerebral palsy), or disabilities that have a greater impact in the capacity to achieve a good life, especially those disabilities that affect a greater range of senses or capacities. The same could be said about intellectual disabilities, which have a broader and greater impact in people's abilities to interact with the world. And although Barnes restricts her focus to physical disabilities only, she does not elaborate on why physical and intellectual disabilities are so metaphysically different as to require different accounts of disability to explain them (Barnes 2016, 3–5). Absent this explanation, one may still want to press on what are the goods that intellectual disabilities bring about that make them only mere differences.

Clearly, more work needs to be done if we want to fully determine the value of disability as a general category. This work involves an empirical description of the features that are characteristic of each disability, and of the capacities that they enable and that they prevent individuals who have them from obtaining, as well as an evaluation of the role of each of these capacities for achieving a good life. In the meantime, there are reasons to think that Barnes and those like her who think that disability is only a mere difference must still show how disabilities (including severe ones) can be, only, mere differences.

CONCLUSION

Arguing that disability is only a mere-difference, not in itself bad, would seem to commit defenders of the Mere-Difference View (MDV) to the claim that inflicting disability is morally acceptable—if disability is not intrinsically bad, inflicting disability would be morally acceptable. Even of those who maintain that disability is a mere difference, few would accept that inflicting disability is morally acceptable. Thus, for Barnes's MDV to win acceptance, she needs to save the intuition that inflicting disability is morally wrong while remaining faithful to the original commitment of her view: namely, that disabilities are not intrinsically bad.

For this, Barnes argues that inflicting disability is wrong because and only because the person on whom the disability is inflicted (a) does not consent, (b) will have to endure significant transition costs, or (c) will have his or her identity changed by the infliction of disability. This chapter has argued that there are numerous cases where a disability could be inflicted without giving rise to issues of consent, transition costs, or identity change. This is the case of disability infliction on children. In such cases Barnes will have to say that inflicting disability is morally permissible. I take this to be a reductio ad absurdum of her position. Anyone would agree that inflicting disability in such cases is wrong. Barnes strongly agrees with this. But the reasons to support the moral prohibition of inflicting disability are subject to counterexamples. More remains to be said by defenders of the MDV if they want to both save the intuition that inflicting disability is morally wrong and maintain the belief that disability is only a mere-difference.

Notes

1. I would like to thank Adam Cureton, Alex Gregory, Brad Hooker, Patrick Tomlin, and David Wasserman for their insightful comments to this chapter, as well as the participants of the 2017 Value and Agency Conference on Philosophy of Disability at the University of Tennessee, Knoxville.
2. I take the *local* and *global* bads distinction to be parallel to the *pro tanto* bads and *overall* or *all-things considered* bads.
3. The term "ableism" is of common use in the literature on philosophy and disability. "Ableism" refers to the kind of discrimination performed on the basis of abilities. It most commonly refers to the discrimination performed toward those with fewer, lower, or different abilities from those possessed by the majority of the population, or from the average abilities of those who compose the *salient* group of reference.
4. The defenses of the bad-difference view that Barnes refers to belong to McMahan (2005); Harris (2001); Kahane (2009); and Singer (2001).
5. Defenders of the causation-based objection might disagree with this way of expressing their argument. They might instead claim that they are engaged in a sort of reflective equilibrium style of argument in which supposed implications of a theoretical claim (MDV) are tested against our considered moral judgments. Their argument is not, they may say, circular but rather *coherentist*. If MDV entails that it is permissible to cause disability and impermissible to cure disability, and if these implications conflict with deeply held considered judgments, then we have reasons either to abandon those judgments or abandon MDV. Thanks to Adam Cureton for suggesting this possibility.
6. One could argue that this example is circular because it seems to assume disabilities to be bad states since the individual ends up with a lower functionality level. But Barnes's account is not incompatible with disabilities implying lower functional states and lower levels of well-being. In Barnes's own words: "It is perfectly consistent with the mere-difference view that the actual well-being of disabled people is, on average, lower than that of nondisabled people, simply because of how society treats disabled people." (Barnes 2014, 90). Thus, a lower level of functionality becomes problematic for a person's well-being if society does not provide for the person with such level of functionality. This differs from saying that disabilities are in themselves bad differences.
7. But what a child eats can, undoubtedly, affect for example her height. Since height is used by Barnes as an example of identity-determining traits, it is not clear why what a child eats should not be also an identity-determining trait, under Barnes's account.
8. One may try to use this point of Barnes as a way of refuting Barnes's own argument. One could say that if disabled people face risks that non-disabled people do not face, this could be a bad-making feature of disability.

9. See, for example, the testimony of Audry Yap, in Shelley Tremain (2016). Although Yap blames ableism for her lack of identification as a disabled individual, the point is that sometimes disabled individuals do not in fact identify themselves as disabled.

10. For a detailed examination of the relationship between disability and other devalued group identities in the construction of self-identity, see Darling (2013, 49–66).

11. Emphasis added.

12. Emphasis added.

REFERENCES

Barnes, Elizabeth. 2014. "Valuing Disability, Causing Disability." *Ethics* 125, no. 1: 88–113.

Barnes, Elizabeth. 2016. *The Minority Body: A Theory of Disability*. Oxford: Oxford University Press.

Barnes, Elizabeth. 2016b. "Reply to Guy Kahane and Julian Savulescu." *Res Philosophica* 93, no. 1: 295–309.

Darling, Rosalyn B. 2013. *Disability and Identity: Negotiating Self in a Changing Society*. Boulder, CO: Lynne Rienner.

Harris, John. 2001. "One Principle and Three Fallacies of Disability Studies", *Journal of Medical Ethics* 27: 383–87.

Kahane, Guy. 2009. "Non-identity, Self-Defeat, and Attitudes to Future Children", *Philosophical Studies* 145: 193–214.

Kahane, Guy, and Julian Savulescu. 2016. "Disability and Mere Difference." *Ethics* 126: 774–788.

McMahan, Jeff. 2005. "Causing Disabled People to Exist and Causing People to Be Disabled", *Ethics* 116: 77–99.

Singer, Peter. 2001. "Ethics and Disability: A Response to Koch", *Journal of Disability Policy Studies* 16: 130–133.

Tremain, Shelley. 2016. "Ableism. Interview with Jesse Prinz, Tommy Curry, and Audrey Yap." In *Discrimination and Disadvantage: Dialogues on Disability*. [Blog post]. Retrieved from http://philosophycommons.typepad.com/disability_and_disadvanta/dialogues-on-disability/.

CHAPTER 10

··

EVALUATIVE DIVERSITY AND THE (IR)RELEVANCE OF WELL-BEING

··

SEAN AAS

DISABILITY scholars and activists have long argued against the widespread view that disability is a medical misfortune, wherein some individuals have the bad luck to be afflicted with conditions of body and/or mind that undermine their ability to live good lives unless treatable and treated by modern medicine (Wasserman et al. 2013).[1] They have argued that disability need not be a misfortune at all; and that when it is, any disadvantage due to disability comes not from the state of the body but rather from the state of the environment. Philosophers and bioethicists have recently taken up these claims about disability, health and happiness. Initially, the response from professional philosophy and bioethics was skeptical, as moral philosophers adduced arguments that the emerging pro-disability view carried implausible implications regarding the morality of causing and curing disability (McMahan 2005). More recently, another group of philosophers has begun to take the other side of this debate. A burgeoning literature explicates and defends the claim that being disabled is not, in itself, bad for a person at all. This literature focuses primarily on two *currencies* or metrics of value said to be possessed by disabled people no less than able-bodied people. The most prominent part of it argues that disabled people need be no less *happy* or generally well-off than non-disabled peopled; (Silvers 2003; Asch and Wasserman 2005; Goering 2008; Barnes 2009); a less prominent part, that disability need not entail any deficit in *health* (Amundson 2000; Kukla 2015; Aas 2016).

This chapter argues that this philosophical discussion, helpful has it has been, now risks losing sight of the original, *political*, concerns motivating the disability rights movements and its academic interpreters, putting excessive weight on a philosophical question that is not relevant to policy. I develop this notion by, first, explicating some reasons why pro-disability philosophers can and should reject welfarist arguments across a wide range of cases. Taking debates around *causing* disability in procreative ethics as an illustrative example, I argue that the best versions of pro-disability arguments in this area powerfully buttress long-standing liberal objections to utilitarianism and welfarism more generally—particularly concerns that decisions should not be publicly justified in terms of reasonably controversial conceptions of the good life.

The Well-Being Debate

Disability entered the agenda of analytic ethics largely by way of claims about the welfare effects of disabilities. Parfit's famous pregnant woman case, developed to test a much more abstract claim about the structure of moral theory, rests on the supposedly secure intuition that the badness of being disabled provides a powerful reason not to bring a disabled child into existence (Parfit 1984, Chapter 16). Separately, but around the same time, the disability rights movement began to argue that disability disadvantage is caused primarily by unjust responses to bodily difference (UPIAS 1976; Oliver 1990). A corollary of this *social model of disability* seems to be that the bodily conditions sometimes referred to as "disabilities" are not bad or harmful in and of themselves. Some philosophers then marshaled the intuition evoked by the Parfitian objection as an objection to this "mere difference" view of disability, arguing that *if* disability is not harmful in itself then it should be permissible to intentionally *cause* or *fail to cure* disability in cases like these (McMahan 2005).

Other philosophers responded, on roughly two fronts. First, disability-friendly philosophers argued that "causing" or at least "not preventing" disability is less objectionable then it might at first appear; indeed, that many objections to causing or failing to cure disability are themselves disrespectful to disabled people (Asch and Wasserman 2005). Second, relatedly, philosophers argued that one need not accept negative evaluative claims about disability to account for what is objectionable about causing disability, when that is indeed objectionable. (Both of these points are expressed powerfully in Barnes 2016, though others make them as well). Together these arguments constitute a defense of the claim, increasingly central in philosophical discussions of disability, that disabilities are mere differences; not intrinsically better or worse for those who manifest them than other bodily conditions.

My goal here is to provide a different sort of pro-disability argument. I argue that the debate over "causing" and "curing" disability need not, and should not, turn on claims about welfare, not even the claim that disability does not in general have positive or negative welfare effects. Recent twists and turns in this debate make it clear that the best arguments against policies and practices that require reducing the number of disabled people do not rest on general claims about the intrinsic evaluative neutrality of disability, but rather on minimizing the moral relevance of these sorts of welfare-based evaluative claims in the first place. For most of the purposes we are actually concerned with in discussing this issue, it does not matter what the truth is, about disability and well-being. What matters is what we can respectfully say to one another about these issues in a society of diverse people that disagree about fundamental matters like these. This, I argue, reflects a more general moral about disability and public reasoning: generally, both sides of debates regarding disability policy can and should avoid reasonably controversial claims about the impact of disability on well-being.

Causing and Curing

We can ask a number of questions about the moral status of decisions regarding causing or curing disability. Parfit's original case is pitched at one end of a spectrum, toward the question of *individual moral permissibility*: is it impermissible to bring a disabled child into existence when you can create an able-bodied child instead? In the applied ethics literature, questions about health care practice and policy have been more central: should practitioners *allow*, or even be legally *allowed to allow*, people to screen embryos for ability-relevant traits via pre-implantation genetic diagnosis (PGD), and to select on the basis of these screenings? (Asch and Wasserman 2010). Moral permissibility questions are also relevant here, of course—is it permissible to abort a fetus because it will develop into a severely disabled child and/or adult? Relatedly, is this a good or virtuous thing to do; or is it something someone should be blamed and/or censured for doing, by a properly pro-disability social morality, if not by the law?

Perhaps because of the influence of Parfit's original framing, and perhaps because the original disability-negative arguments in philosophy were made in the context of utilitarian moral theory, the stated topic of much philosophical discussion of these issues has been moral permissibility—whether and when it is right or wrong, choiceworthy or not, to act so as to either reduce or increase the number of disabled people in the world. Yet, I argue, much of the actual discussion of these issues has in fact focused instead on questions that are in some ways more important, questions concerning *the justice or injustice* of policies and practices, in light of their effect on the prevalence of disability in the population.

This is, perhaps, easiest to see when we consider pro-disability critiques of reproductive technology—particularly, critiques of PGD and subsequent selection of non-disabled embryos. A classic objection here holds that this and related practices *express disrespect* for disabled lives. How (or if) exactly this goes is open for debate (Asch and Wasserman 2010), but many such critiques seem to hold that deciding not to bring a child into the world *on grounds* that they would be disabled indicates a low valuation of the lives of people with disabilities; some sense that their lives are very bad, or at least worse than the lives of able-bodied people, such that the world is a better place without them.

As Asch and Wasserman point out, however, it is far from clear that any individual action need express any such attitude. So, they say: "the difficult, complex, often confused decisions of individuals and couples, [...] need not 'send a message' to others regarding the lives of disabled persons" (Asch and Wasserman 2015, 425). The idea here is that we cannot infer invidious attitudes towards disability from a choice not to have a disabled child, since many other factors might motivate such a choice. We might, to be sure, suspect that insulting assumptions about the value of disabled life enter into these motivations; but we can hardly be certain of that in most or every case.

To this sensible factual point I think we can add another, moral one: *even if* selecting against disability in PGD expressed disrespectful attitudes towards people with disabilities, it's hardly clear that this would be sufficient ground to render it morally impermissible, given all that is at stake for the decision-makers. Suppose, for instance, that choosing not to date or marry people with a given disability is indeed insulting to them. The importance of being able to make such personal choices, for one's own (possibly bad) reasons, suggests that this sort of choice is, though perhaps a sign of suboptimal moral character, at least minimally morally permissible in many cases.

Asch and Wasserman, however, also indicate some powerful reasons not to reject the expressive objection wholesale. They continue: "official policies and practices can indeed send a message of inferiority" (Asch and Wasserman 2015, 445). I would add: states have much different and potentially stronger reasons to express substantive respect for their citizens than perfect strangers have to express substantive respect for one another. Still, evaluating the expressive import of state policies, particularly permissive policies, remains a complex matter. Jeff McMahan's observations about the complex relations between our reasons for action and the expressive significant thereof (McMahan 2005, 84–90) suggest that we can no more infer state motivations from policy choices than individual motivations from personal choices. McMahan points out that diverse individuals could have diverse reasons to engage in selection, some insulting and some not; states as well might have reasons to select certain sorts of reproductive policy on grounds that are not intrinsically insulting—say, on efficiency considerations, focused on cost-savings achievable with a less functionally diverse population. Still, it is not entirely clear that state expression should be interpreted or evaluated in the same way as individual expression. The state may have a duty to act so as to preclude 'unintentional' insult as well as intentional ones, so that the mere fact that an innocuously motivated policy *could reasonably be viewed* as insulting might constitute an objection to it.

That said, given the force of individual interests at stake in particular PGD decisions, it seems difficult to prove that the goal of avoiding *possible* state insult to some provides sufficient reasons for the state to coerce others. Imagine, for instance, that the only good schools in a city are Catholic parochial schools. A bill is introduced to allow homeschooling, not previously countenanced; it is publicly justified on grounds that, despite the objective quality of these schools, much of the population (say, secular WASPs) find them ridiculous and archaic. Catholics are not wrong to be insulted by the bill, given that the rationale for it accedes to disrespectful prejudices. Still, it seems clear that their feelings about it do not and should not give them a veto power over the legislation, whatever other objections we might have to it. So in the end it is hard to show that "insult" considerations support legal prohibitions on disability-demoting uses of PGD—and indeed Asch and Wasserman, strong sympathizers with expressive concerns, strongly oppose any such ban.

Expressive concerns might well be more forceful, however, at a level between that of individual decision and state policy. Individual choices might be permissible in isolation; and there may be good reason not to bring the state into intimate reproductive decisions. But it might be bad if many people take an option, even if that option is and ought to be both morally and legally permissible. If sufficiently many individuals choose to do something, for a reason that they are willing to state and endorse, that very fact will tend to the production of a culture that recognizes this reason as a good reason to do that thing. In cases like these it makes sense to say that, whether or not every choice under a practice expresses an attitude, the *practice itself* does so. For instance, we might think that although the choice to undergo aesthetically "normalizing" cosmetic surgery could be motivated innocuously in any one case (say, by the desire to access better professional opportunities in a culture one personally recognizes as sexist and strenuously disapproves of), the effect of many people making this (relatively) innocuous choice is to buttress objectionable views about normality and beauty (Little 1998; Asch and Wasserman 2010). Many objections to PGD and/or selective abortion, I would argue, target this kind of informal social expression; whatever individuals can do, or are allowed to, do by the police, we should not as a society adopt practices that express negative valuations of our fellows.

Social practices in view, one might wonder why we should not go further: instead of objecting that some social practices (selective abortions, say) express objectionably negative attitudes about disability, why not say that these informal practices objectionably *fail* to express *disability-positive* attitudes? Compare debates about "acceptance" versus "toleration" of non-heterosexual orientations. Liberals once argued that the state should not take a stand on the relative value of different kinds of relationships between pairs of competent adults (Torcello 2008); at most, recognizing all such relationships via "civil union" contracts. Now, many would agree with United States Supreme Court (*Obergefell v. Hodges* 2015) that this does not go far enough: by extending civil marriage to all couples (i.e., same- or opposite-sex couples) the state fulfills a duty to *positively express* respect for everyone, a duty not fulfilled, say, by simply legalizing civil unions. The same could be said about non-state practices: what we owe to same-sex couples is not merely a sort of arm's-length 'live and let live' forbearing from blame and censure but a more robust kind of social integration and acceptance, recognizing the equal worth of various kinds of relationships and family structures that depart from hetero norms.

On reflection these kinds of state/societal expression are about something quite special: they concern respect for equal *status* as members of the community, capable of engaging in central forms of social relation, not just any kind of judgment about the prudential value of different kinds of lives (on this notion see Anderson 1999). There is good reason for society to actually positively express equal *respect* for everyone. But respect in the relevant *recognitional* sense is independent of judgments about well-being: I ought to respect you as a moral and social equal no matter how well I think your life is going or is likely to go. People who fare poorly are still deserving of this kind of respect; *ergo*, to suggest that people in a given class are likely (or even certain) to fare poorly, relatively or absolutely, is not in any way to suggest that they do not deserve the sort of respect that is the business of the state.

Drawing on the debate about disability and well-being itself, I propose that this sort of respect is not only consistent with but indeed requires reserving public judgment about well-being. Practices like those surrounding PGD should not express the view that it is in general bad to be disabled. But the reasons that this is true, as developed in recent philosophy of disability, are best understood as reasons for our justificatory discourses regarding policies and practices to reserve judgment altogether on the relevance of (dis)ability to well-being. Accepting disabled people as equals means *not* expressing our opinions about the quality of their lives, in justifying policies and practices *to them*—just as we, in general, do not go around judging the well-being of able-bodied people, in justification.[2] We can think and say what we want about how well someone else lives; but when we decide how we should act together, in constituting both formal and informal social institutions, respect requires us to leave these sorts of thoughts at the door, finding ways to agree in the face of disagreements we resolve to regard as intractable.

"You Don't Know What You're Talking About"

So, why not accept practices or policies that presuppose that disabled people have worse lives than able-bodied people? Some of the most influential recent arguments on this topic come from Elizabeth Barnes. In addition to rebutting numerous fallacious or insufficiently supported arguments for this "bad difference" view, she also collates and crystallizes a case against the bad difference claim, a case that comes from the experience of disabled people themselves. It is far from clear that disabled people, on the whole, report substantially lower levels of well-being or life satisfaction than non-disabled people (Gill 2000; though contrast Lucas 2007). Barnes argues that we have reason to accept this testimony, focusing in particular on the eloquent accounts several disabled writers have offered of how their disabilities make their life valuable. So for instance, Harriett McBryde Johnson writes:

> Are we [disabled people] 'worse off'? I don't think so. Not in any meaningful sense. There are too many variables. For those of us with congenital conditions, disability shapes all we are. Those disabled later in life adapt. We take constraints that no one would choose and build rich and satisfying lives within them. We enjoy pleasures other people enjoy, and pleasures peculiarly our own. We have something the world needs.   (quoted in Barnes 2016, 138)

Yet, on reflection, it is not clear that this testimony, *if accepted*, supports any general conclusions about disability and well-being. Certainly the testimony of individual authors like Johnson—Barnes's focus—does not suffice to establish general conclusions about the effect of disability on well-being. More would need to be done to argue that these disabled writers and activists—professionally successful by selection—are representative of all disabled people. Moreover, the content of this testimony as reported by Barnes consists largely in claims about how particular experiences and activities disabled people engage in contribute to their life satisfaction; little of it consists in reflective comparative evaluation of well-being overall, an activity few of us disabled or otherwise have much practice at (Marsh 2020). Moreover, there is reason to be suspicious of the judgments *anyone* comes to when they do report their own life satisfaction, as when surveys ask people about it. Whether well-being involves achieving certain objective goods, satisfying preferences, or having good experiences overall, it consists of an aggregate over time of values that are both difficult to "measure" in the moment, and difficult, over time, to remember and/or predict.

Steve Campbell and Joseph Stramondo offer further reasons to doubt that the testimony of disabled people can establish that disability is a "neutral" trait—as opposed to, providing reason *not* to accept it is a bad trait (Campbell and Stramondo 2017). These reasons are instances of general reasons to doubt that we can establish much of anything at all about how disability impacts well-being in general. Disabled people are a very internally diverse group; thus it is hard to see the testimony of any particular disabled person as representative, whether they are professionally successful or not. One might add: for similar reasons, it is hard to know whether you have a truly representative sample, in a quantitative survey of disabled people. The category itself is hard to define and operationalize. Moreover, as Campbell and Stramondo stress, one would not expect that, for any particular disabled person, their disability will be neutral in the sense of having made them neither better off nor worse off than they would have been its absence. Many disabilities make such a big difference to people's self-conceptions, social standing, and experience of the world that it is hard to imagine that many particular disabilities will have no effect one way or the other. Nor is there evidence that the positive and negative impacts of particular disabilities always average out to zero—*or above zero, or below it.*

The jury, it seems, remains out on disability and well-being: there is evidence that disability is a neutral, or at least not a bad, difference; there is also evidence to the contrary. This, perhaps, is the most pro-disability conclusion we can now confidently draw, from the testimonial arguments: those that maintain that disability is prudentially bad, on balance, are irrationally ignoring people who deny this, and who should know (Marsh 2020). This is not the same as an endorsement of the mere difference view, but it is enough, in itself, to powerfully undermine arguments in favor of policies and practices that presuppose the disability is bad. These arguments are, *at best*, on epistemically shaky ground.

"And Anyway Who Made You Boss"

Imagine, however, that in the end you conclude that we have good reason to accept a "bad-difference" view of disability. You should still worry about whether this view has the right *sort of justification* to make them reasonable premises for reasoning about which policies and practices we ought to have. The fact that I have a justified belief about what is better for someone does not always or in general give me the authority to put that belief into practice. Which sorts of authority relations we should recognize is a complex question; in many cases the answer depends on what practice of deference would result in better decisions overall. Relevant to the present context, Stramondo argues that our practice of deference to parents on questions concerning the well-being of their children ought to be extended to cover pre-natal and even pre-conception decisions; for example, that

> when it comes to making important health care decisions for minors, parents ought to be presumptive surrogates because they tend to 1) feel great concern toward a child's well being, 2) have the most accurate knowledge of what is required for a child's well being, and 3) hold an important stake in the consequences of such a decision.   (Stramondo 2017, 478)

On this view, neither the state nor the public more broadly should impose their conception of a child's goods on parents who are acting competently and with goodwill. It may be, of course, that sufficiently exotic conceptions of a child's good would themselves evidence incompetence or bad faith. Clear cases here include views that say female children are better off not being educated at all. But, as Stramondo argues, there is little reason to believe that any decision rooted in a rejection of a "bad difference" view of disability would be disqualifying in the relevant way. This is, not least, for the reasons cited by Barnes: these are hard issues, and reasonable people disagree. Moreover, as Stramondo points out, these disagreement are often rooted in differences of experience—so that, for instance, non-disabled people may not have easy access to knowledge about how hard (or not) life would be for a disabled child with disabled parents.

It seems especially important to recognize this sort of parental authority where the relevant prudential judgments reflect profound difference on central questions about what is important in life. Such differences exist regarding the prudential value or disvalue of a wide range of impairments. Some might think, for instance, that any parent acting in good faith will seek to prevent suffering in their child, so that parents certainly do not possess authority to select for (or even: not select against) conditions that involve suffering. As Barnes point out, however, there are a range of plausible views even on the prudential import of suffering (Barnes 2016, 115). We might deny that pain is intrinsically bad, in every single case; perhaps, for instance, pain is part and parcel of the value of certain sorts of achievement. Or, more modestly, we might notice that in many cases a painful condition is the cause of a greater pleasure. Barnes draws our attention to disability activist and scholar Nadina LaSpina, who says: "certainly the pain . . . of disability [is] not wonderful, yet that identity is who I am. And I am proud of it" (Barnes 2016, 115) As Barnes understands it, this is one case among many where a condition associated with pain produces pleasure (here, the pleasure of pride); in such cases, even someone who thinks that pain and pleasure are all that matter to well-being might think that a painful disability need not make a bad difference. For these reasons, it is far from obvious that caring parents will shield their children (actual or potential) from *all* pain: this sort of shielding could hamper or even prevent children from achieving important goods.

Again, the point here is not to endorse any such views about the evaluative import of impairment but rather to say that *within limits*, diversity with respect to them should be respected, both in policy and in public practices of discussing and evaluating parental decisions. The alternative is to adopt a practice which really does display disrespect for the worldview of people who are disabled and proud of it: a practice which says to them "you are more than wrong, about yourself; you are so wrong that you are outside the bounds of reasonable disagreement." That disrespect of actual, thoughtful people could only be warranted if we really were sure that their thinking had led them astray. But it seems clear that we are not, or should not be: there are powerful reasons on both sides of the "mere difference"/"bad difference" debate; powerful enough to render each side reasonable enough to deserve some substantial deference, as they use their view to shape their own lives and families. This debate, after all, is about the deepest and most difficult questions about the meaning and value of a human life; surely disagreement is reasonable in cases like this, if it ever is.

There are at least two strong arguments, then, that public reasoning about practices like those surrounding PGD should not rely on the assumption of a "bad-difference" view. First, these views are on shaky evidential ground, given the purely epistemic import of the testimony of disabled people. Second, recognition of the difficulty of determining how disability affects well-being should lead even those who still endorse "bad-difference" views as a philosophical matter to refrain from insisting on the relevance of those views in justifying public policies and practices to those who disagree.

Should we rely, instead, on a "Value Neutral" model, justifying policies and practices on grounds that disability is, as Barnes says, "not an intrinsic or automatic cost to well-being"? This proposal, notice, differs critically from *not* justifying policies in terms of the claim that disability *is* an "intrinsic or automatic cost to well-being." In general, being unable to rely on a proposition in public reasoning is not at all the same thing as being able to rely on its negation. So, for instance, state policy with respect to religion cannot presuppose that (say) Christianity is the only route to salvation. Even if true this proposition does not provide a reason to (for instance) establish a state church. But nor can the state presuppose that the Christianity is not only way to be saved, and promote some kind of syncretic or ecumenical faith instead. Accepting either proposition involves an *indulgence* in judgments where the state should be *abstinent* instead.

THE ADVISABILITY OF ABSTINENCE

I submit that pro-disability scholars and activists should take the more abstemious view about judgments regarding well-being and disability. This proposal is supported to some extent by intuitions about cases, like the foregoing but, I think, need not rely entirely on that justification. Even those who are more certain that disability is neutral should, on reflection, find good reason to refrain from appeals to claims about welfare in debates about disability policy.

The first sort of reason is broadly strategic, though not merely so. Above, I described two powerful lines of argument for pro-disability policies. The first appeals to the testimony of disabled people to undermine confidence in "bad-difference" views of disability. The second appeals to considerations of decisional authority to question the practical relevance of "bad- difference" views even if we could be confident in them as a philosophical matter. Neither argument relies, in premises or conclusions, on any assertion about the actual value or disvalue of disability; both can proceed, simply, by denying that any such assertion is relevant in a policy conversation. Both conclusions could also be reached, to be sure, on the basis of a more assertive "mere difference" view, since if any such view is well justified then the bad-difference view is not correct at all, much less obviously so. But resting the case for pro-disability policies on the logically stronger form of argument might hold public support for said policies hostage to skepticism about the "mere difference" view. This skepticism seems likely to remain resolute, even in the face of testimony to the contrary. This is partly for regrettable reasons, but partly for less regrettable ones. It is, after all, not a bad thing that people become attached to activities and capacities that figure importantly in their lives; difficulty accepting the possibility of a good life without these is understandable even if not ultimately justifiable.

I should emphasize that, though this concern about how far others can be expected to move from their own views is strategic, it is not entirely strategic. Abstinence evinces a kind of respect for the difficulty of coming to conclusions on these profound questions; the precise kind of respect, indeed, that disabled people themselves ask for when they ask that their own views about the good life be respected as reasonable, if not accepted outright. That is to say, the fact that others might reasonably disagree with the stronger view, but need not accept it, to draw the relevant practical conclusions, gives us a moral reason as well as a strategic one: it means that insisting on the stronger view is not just risky for their aims but also a morally problematic means to those aims, reflecting a failure to give the sort of respect disabled people demand for themselves (more on this broadly "liberal" idea, shortly).

A second reason to avoid assertions about well-being in public policy debates also concerns risks, particularly risks to the *privacy* and *dignity* of disabled people. Propounding positive assertions concerning the welfare of disabled lives invites scrutiny of those lives to check those assertions. Bad-difference views are deeply entrenched in the public consciousness and in "expert" policy discourses. Overcoming this inertia will likely require an overwhelmingly amount of evidence supporting the mere difference view. Even though these reasons will very often survive this scrutiny, many may prefer not to have the goodness or badness of their lives be up for public debate at all. Transgressing these boundaries fails to show what Adam Cureton calls "negative respect" for people with disabilities: "part of respecting someone […] is to keep ourselves at some distance from their inner-lives by allowing them to conceal certain aspects of themselves and by trying not to learn too much about their character, values, wellbeing, etc." (Cureton 2020, 388).

Finally, a strategy rooted in strong positive assertions about disability and well-being risks various harms to disabled people themselves. Some harms are mediated by group identity and representation; consider by comparison the reasonable offense taken by African Americans to discussions about a "culture of poverty", or rural "red-state" Americans to discussion about "what's the matter with Kansas?" These discourses involve a sort of scrutiny of certain subpopulations that is profoundly paternalistic, even patronizing. Discussions of "adaptive preference" and the like in disability also display these flaws. But some harms are more concrete and individualized. For reasons noted above, valid empirical studies on disability and well-being will need to sample not just activists ready and willing to describe their many opportunities and enjoyments but a broad spectrum of disabled people, including many who will be more reticent. Merely asking someone to participate in a study may not be a massive harm, but in many circumstances it might be a real one—particularly where, as here, it is likely that recruitments will require marking some people out in terms of a stigmatized identity that (rightly or wrongly) they may not be comfortable emb*racing. For all these reasons, it seems dangerous, maybe even disrespectful, for disability advocates to* pursue a political strategy that requires disabled people to try and change the deeply held beliefs of others by exposing themselves and their lives to intrusive public scrutiny.

Political Liberalism and the Scope of Public Reason

I mentioned earlier that the view developed here would have some affinities with what has come to be called "political" or "public reason" liberalism, a family of views, often attributed to Rawls, that demand that certain kinds of public policies be justified in terms acceptable to all reasonable people (Rawls 2005). Now, most of the arguments offered above do not *presuppose* any specific political liberal view, much less Rawls's. Rather, they are drawn from discussions of disability in bioethics that have been conducted largely in isolation from public reason theory. Still, they *could* be strengthened by appeal to Rawlsian or other forms of public reason liberalism. Thus, it will be worth a brief digression into public reason to further explicate and defend the kind of epistemic abstention proposed here. In particular, we should ask: regarding *which questions*, and on *which occasions for discussing those questions*, should we abstain from controversial claims about disability and well-being?

The first set of questions concerns what Jonathan Quong has called the "scope" of public reason: the set of policies or practices that must be justifiable to all reasonable points of view (Quong 2018). The traditional Rawlsian view holds that public reason applies to questions about "constitutional essentials" and more to our point, "matters of basic justice" (Rawls 2005, 445). "Basic justice" here refers to the "basic structure" of society (Rawls 1977). That structure, in turn, has been defined in various ways; roughly as either the main coercive institutions of the state, or those institutions, coercive or not, which have "profound and pervasive impact" on the lives of citizens. The latter view is more plausible, given Rawls's clarification that the family is part of the basic structure—and presumably, not just to the extent that some coercive laws (regarding child welfare, divorce, etc.) affect the family. And it seems clear that the choice of reproductive practice at least has "profound and pervasive" impacts on citizens; determining, at a very fundamental level, what sort of people we will have in society.[3] Even if we take the narrower, coercion-centric view, however, it seems likely that many of the issues in question here will fall within the scope of public reason. After all, as noted above, even where what is in question is how we publicly talk about reproductive decisions, rather than state policy, talk about these things has a way of hardening into norms of response that could amount to "social coercion" (Mill 1875).

A second set of issues concerns the "site" of public reason norms: roughly, the agents, and occasions, on which discussions about matters within the scope of public reason are restrained by norms regarding reasonable disagreement. These norms do not apply everywhere; political liberals do not mean, for instance, to put an end to the practice of discussing policy implications of religious or philosophical world views in the Madrasa or the philosophy seminar. There is some disagreement on where they actually do apply: somewhere in a space that excludes the seminar room, but includes the highest courts and the floor of the legislature. The underlying ideas of public reason, however, concerning public justification, suggest that the right view is close to the one Rawls ultimately takes: all citizens owe a "duty of civility" not to assert that tendentious arguments from their own worldview provide, all on their own, *sufficient* reason to impose policies that others reasonably disagree with. Rawls's "wide view," to be sure, allows people to express private reasons, so long as public reasons are forthcoming. Still, matters within the scope of public reason must ultimately be decided by *public reasons*. Recognizing this in all open public discussions of these issues is an important way of respecting one another and our differences.

To be sure: these ideas of public reasoning, already familiar in certain precincts of political philosophy, are themselves far from uncontroversial (Hampton 1989; Enoch 2015). Yet, as I have argued here, they are also powerfully motivated by points made in the disability movement and the philosophy of disability. Moreover, the disability critique of policy based on a bad-difference view enriches this "public reason" liberalism by clarifying that reasonable disagreement about the good concerns judgments about the import of various activities of daily life as well as more lofty matters like salvation and human perfection. And it provides further reason to think that public reason norms should extend beyond the sacred precincts of executive offices, legislative chambers, and the judicial bench: as cases like PGD show, respect requires reticence in public justification of informal practices as well as legally enshrined coercion.

DISABILITY, DISADVANTAGE, AND
REASONABLE DISAGREEMENT

It is, of course, not possible to avoid all judgments about individual advantage in evaluating policies and practices. It matters how policies and practices affect people. We need some measure of the benefits and burdens of social cooperation to evaluate existing institutions and decide how they should change. It can seem natural here to point to well-being, since this is what matters to us as individuals. However, the idea that well-being is what *ultimately* matters, often cited as a reason in favor of basing policy on a welfare metric, actually provides a reason to favor less evaluatively loaded methods for measuring advantage—say, measures of resources, opportunity, or capability. Ceteris paribus, the more significant a certain sort of information is to my conception of the value of my own life, the stronger are my reasons to want people to be careful discussing this information in public. Moreover, in pluralistic societies at least, disagreement about evaluative matters seems to expand and not contract, as we go "deeper," addressing matters more and more significant to the definition of a good life.

Fortunately, diverse populations can often agree about what to do, even if not, "all the way down," about *why*. Indeed, they can, often, even agree about *methods* for deciding what to do, forms of *public* justification, without agreeing on the deeper question of how these methods are justified. This requires what Rawls calls an "overlapping consensus" on one or more "political conceptions" of the good; *overlapping* because reasonable people disagree about many other things, *political* because as reasonable people they can agree on enough to make decisions together. These consensus conceptions of the good—whether specified in terms of *resources* (Rawls 1988; Pogge 2000) or *capabilities* (Anderson 2010)—take the place of controversial judgments about well-being in public policy. As I discuss in the concluding section, we can still judge policies for their consequences for what we can do and be in the public world, just not for consequences regarding evaluative matters over which there is profound disagreement. These judgments, I stress, might or might not favor the policies that pro-disability scholars and activists have historically preferred. The important point is that if they do have substantively unwelcome implications, these are drawn in a way that need not be procedurally problematic from the perspective of pluralism.

Objection: Pride and Pity

Pro-disability philosophers might object: an excessively broad injunction against welfare claims in public discourse may be advantageous, in some ways, for progress against ableist injustice; in other ways, however, such an injunction could slow or even prevent important forms of progress. Recall the comparison to "acceptance" versus "toleration" of non-hetero relationships and family structures; merely rejecting public claims regarding the disvalue of some people's lives can seem insufficient for the kind of acceptance a genuinely respectful society would require. This problem might seem particularly acute if our suspicion of positive (or negative) assertions about welfare extends beyond the traditional precincts of public reason (legislative debates; political campaigns; the courts) to more informal practices of praise and blame for (e.g.) reproductive choices. Yet, as I argued above, disagreement about the value of lives or life choices does not entail disrespect. Nor need such disagreement reduce our relationship to one of "mere," arms-length, toleration: there might be many local goods and interests we can share, much that we mutually value even if our judgment about the ultimate weight of values conflict. So for instance, a conservative Christian might admire the warmth and dedication a same-sex couple shows in raising their children, even if she thinks that this couple is missing something else of importance by departing from traditional gender norms or failing to follow the will of God, as she understands it.

Similarly, I suggest: able-bodied people who fear disability, and happy and proud disabled people, can share a great deal in terms of interests and values, even in the face of important disagreements about the good. Living with such diversity is not easy, of course. It does require a kind of reserve that we may reasonably regret, precluding a kind of community that can come with living and talking with people with whom we seek a more comprehensive sort of agreement. Yet, as the example of religious diversity shows, it does seem acceptable to live together this way—if we are a little careful in how we talk to each other about the things that divide us.

Still: the kind of carefulness required by public reason might seem especially, and unfairly, burdensome for disabled people. After all, they are harmed by a widespread perception that their lives are worse than the lives of able-bodied people. This perception promotes damaging attitudes of pity; and makes it difficult for anyone, including disabled people, to see a disability as a source of pride (Stramondo 2010). How, one might ask, are they to protect themselves against such harms, if they cannot directly and publicly rebut harmfully false presuppositions about the (dis-)value of disabled lives?

It is, however, not clear on reflection that the case against pity, or for pride, rests primarily on claims about well-being.[4] The proper response to disability disadvantage caused by injustice seems to be something less like pity, and more like solidarity (with the victims) and righteous outrage (against the perpetrators) (Stramondo 2010; Barnes 2016, Chapter 5). To argue that pity is unwarranted, then, we need not necessarily make or express judgments about the level of welfare disabled people experience, absolutely or relative to non-disabled people: we can rest our case, instead, on claims that concern how social institutions cause disadvantage for disabled people. It also seems far from obvious that pride in something is necessarily or even normally justified in terms of well-being (and thus justifiable only by rebutting claims of ill-being). Pride seems to be about aspects of the individual's "flourishing" or "perfection" that go beyond well-being: accomplishments, say, or talents and capacities relevant to producing them. People with hard lives often have much to be proud of; people with easy lives, often, ought to be ashamed of how little they've done with them. Pride in disability, like pride in anything, would seem to have less do with whether it makes one fare well, and more to do with what it allows us to do, to make the world a better, more kind, more interesting, more knowledgeable, or more beautiful place. Thus, it does not seem that assertions about well-being are required, either, to rebut disability-negative attitudes or to support disability-positive attitudes.

Moreover, it is not clear that the best or only response to the concrete harms pity does to disabled people is to convince pitiers that their attitudes are epistemically unjustified. An attitude in someone's head, offensive or not, arguably has no power to produce an experience of offense unless it is expressed, in word or in deed. A strong social norm precluding public judgment-making about the welfare of others might well obviate much of the harmful impact of pity, even if some private feelings of pity remain. Such a norm could be expected to grow from a culture precluding appeal to welfare claims in public justification, even if it is not strictly required by one. Nor need abstinence norms preclude the kind of self-assertions regarding welfare that some take to be central to disability pride. These assertions, even if made openly and in public, are about matters that are doubly private. They are private in the sense of *self-regarding*: about how disability does or does not affect one's own life, in all its intimate details. Moreover, they are, or can be, private in *import*: intended to justify attitudes or choices that are not the business of the state; offered in reasoning that does not fall within the scope of public reason, even on an expansive conception thereof.

Implications: Disability and the Public Value of Health

Pro-disability scholars and activists would thus do well to practice a kind of *prudential abstention* as they advance proposals for public policies and practices. Indeed, I have argued, many of the more compelling arguments in defense of pro-disability policies provide epistemic, strategic, and moral reasons to avoid positive assertions about the nature of well-being in pro-disability policy discourse. These arguments support, and are supported by, more general arguments advanced in the tradition of public reason liberalism, concerning reciprocity in justification in the face of reasonable pluralism in conceptions of the good.

In conclusion, I'd like to point out that these more general public reason constraints apply not just to *pro-disability* arguments in public reason but to *all* arguments in favor of or against public policies and practices. As discussed above, that includes many specific arguments regarding (e.g.) practices forbidding or discouraging the promotion of disability via various reproductive technologies. But it may also include more general bioethical paradigms often critiqued by disability scholars and activists. Claims that disability ought, in general, to be prevented are often explicated and defended using frameworks meant to measure the impact of various impairments or health-states on well-being. For instance, evaluating policies by reference to *quality adjusted life years* involves assigning "disability weights" to various impairments; weights best understood as attempts to say how much *worse* it is to live a year with that impairment than without it (Hausman 2015). The fire and fury of recent debates about the prudential import of disability amply demonstrates that these judgments are often profoundly controversial among reasonable people. If, as I have argued, this means that public justification should not take sides on such questions, then it looks as if standard metrics for measuring population health require radical revision—we will need to deploy some (potentially) consensus account of what Hausman calls the "public value of health," rather than (with most present practice here) simply taking an arithmetic average of dissenting views about private value (Haagsma et al. 2014).[5]

Part of that process will be to actually develop a fully fleshed-out political conception of the goods involved in health (be those resources, capabilities, both, or neither)—or perhaps, an account of the boundaries of a family of such conceptions, each acceptable in principle to all reasonable worldviews even if none is actually accepted by all.[6] This (these) metric(s) in hand, it may be possible to make progress on profoundly difficult questions about the appropriate political orientation to policies that seek to either increase or reduce the number of disabled people in the world. Constructing a non-welfarist metric of advantage remains a large task, which involves not only accounting for the public relevance of intrinsically disadvantaging states like pain, suffering, and early death but also, understanding just what sorts of claims we have to possess bodies that function well in our social world. Perhaps, indeed, the task of constructing consensus metrics is too large; perhaps ultimately public reason liberalism founders on it, requiring us to revert to comprehensive conceptions of the good in political justification. My hope for now is that illustrating the powerful interconnections between pro-disability arguments and public reason liberalism gives us some reason to be optimistic that we can do better: that many who are still convinced that disability is not mere difference might yet be convinced that their liberalism requires them to put that conviction aside for public purposes.

Notes

1. Thanks to the audience at the 2016 Tennessee Value and Agency Conference on the Philosophy of Disability; and particularly to Leslie Francis and Christie Hartley for extended discussion. For comments on drafts, and much else, thanks to David Wasserman and Adam Cureton

2. That is not to say that we cannot make these judgments in contexts that are not relevantly "justificatory"; say, in developing our philosophical theories of well-being or in telling stories about how we fare in our own lives. More on this in what follows.

3. Thanks to Christie Hartley for useful discussions of these issues.

4. For some other reasons to doubt this, see Howard (2018).

5. This suggestion is premised on the thought that it is *possible* (per Hausmann 2015) to construct a political conception of the value of health. (Mackay 2017) argues persuasively that, to the extent that this sort of deliberative overlapping consensus is *not* possible, existing methods of measuring the value of health may be an acceptable second-best option. Less persuasive, however, is his claim that existing methods for measuring QALYs would be appropriate if better methods were available, so long as these presently converge on the same results. Generally mechanisms for ensuing basic justice in a society need to be more modally robust than this; our methods for measuring the public value of health have to get it right *reliably*, not as a fortuitous matter.

6. I have in mind here Rawls's late thought that public reason is characterized by a "family of reasonable political conceptions," rather than a single consensus conception

(Rawls 2005, xlvii). The members of these political conceptions are reasonably controversial in one sense—reasonable people disagree about them, as they surely will on many contentious political issues—but not in another—one need not in principle adopt any particular set of deeper philosophical or religious worldviews in order to accept any one of them. Of course it remains an open question, for public reason liberalism, whether these particular patterns of actual and possible disagreement are compossible. My thanks to the editors of the volume for pressing this difficult issue in this context.

REFERENCES

Aas, Sean. 2016. "Disabled – Therefore, Unhealthy?" *Ethical Theory and Moral Practice* 19, no. 5: 1259–1274. doi:10.1007/s10677-016-9735-4.

Amundson, Ron. 2000. "Against Normal Function." *Studies in History and Philosophy of Biological and Biomedical Sciences* 31, no. 1: 33–53. doi:10.1016/S1369-8486(99)00033-3.

Anderson, Elizabeth. 1999. "What Is the Point of Equality?" *Ethics* 109, no. 2: 287–337. doi:10.1086/233897.

Anderson, Elizabeth. 2010. "Justifying the Capabilities Approach." In *Measuring Justice: Primary Goods and Capabilities*, edited by Harry Brighouse and Ingrid Robeyns, 81–100. Cambridge, UK: Cambridge University Press.

Asch, Adrienne, and David Wasserman. 2005. "Where Is the Sin in Synecdoche? Prenatal Testing and the Parent-Child Relationship." In *Quality of Life and Human Difference: Genetic Testing, Health Care, and Disability*, edited by David Wasserman, Jerome Bickenbach, and Robert Wachbroit, 172–216. New York: Cambridge University Press.

Asch, Adrienne, and David Wasserman. 2010. "'Healthy' Human Embryos and Reproduction Making Embryos Healthy or Making Healthy Embryos: How Much of a Difference Between Prenatal Treatment and Selection?" In *The "Healthy" Embryo: Social, Biomedical, Legal and Philosophical Perspectives*, edited by Jeff Nisker, Françoise Baylis, Isabel Karpin, Carolyn McLeod, and Roxanne Mykitiuk, 201–218. Cambridge, UK: Cambridge University Press.

Asch, Adrienne, and David Wasserman. 2015. "Reproductive Testing for Disability." In *The Routledge Companion to Bioethics*, edited by Jonathan Arras, Elizabeth Fenton, and Rebecca Kukla, 417–432. New York: Routledge.

Barnes, Elizabeth. 2009. "Disability, Minority, and Difference." *Journal of Applied Philosophy* 26, no. 4: 337–355.

Barnes, Elizabeth. 2016. *The Minority Body?: A Theory of Disability*. Oxford: Oxford University Press.

Campbell, Stephen M., and Joseph A Stramondo. 2017. "The Complicated Relationship of Disability and Well-Being." *Kennedy Institute of Ethics Journal* 27: 1–33. doi:10.1353/ken.2017.0014.

Cureton, Adam. 2020. "The Limiting Role of Respect." In *Oxford Handbook of Philosophy and Disability*, edited by Adam Cureton and David Wasserman, 380–398. New York: Oxford University Press.

Enoch, David. 2015. "Against Public Reason." *Oxford Studies in Political Philosophy 1*, edited by David Sobel, Peter Vallentyne, and Steven Wall, 112–142. Oxford University Press:. doi:10.1093/acprof:oso/9780199669530.003.0006.

Gill, C. J. 2000. "Health Professionals, Disability, and Assisted Suicide: An Examination of Relevant Empirical Evidence and Reply to Batavia." *Psychology, Public Policy, and Law: An*

Official Law Review of the University of Arizona College of Law and the University of Miami School of Law 6, no. 2: 526–545. doi:10.1037/1076-8971.6.2.526.

Goering, Sara. 2008. " 'You Say You're Happy, But...': Contested Quality of Life Judgments in Bioethics and Disability Studies." *Journal of Bioethical Inquiry* 5 (2–3): 123–135.

Haagsma, Juanita A, Suzanne Polinder, Alessandro Cassini, Edoardo Colzani, and Arie H Havelaar. 2014. "Review of Disability Weight Studies: Comparison of Methodological Choices and Values." *Population Health Metrics* 12, no. 1: 20. doi:10.1186/s12963-014-0020-2.

Hampton, Jean. 1989. "Should Political Philosophy Be Done Without Metaphysics??" *Ethics* 99, no. 4: 791–814.

Hausman, Daniel M. 2015. *Valuing Health?: Well-Being, Freedom, and Suffering.* Oxford: Oxford University Press.

Howard, Dana. 2018. "Disability, Well-Being, and (In)Apt Emotions." In *The Ethics of Ability and Enhancement*, edited by Jessica Flanagan and Terry L. Price, 57–78. New York: Palgrave Macmillan US. doi:10.1057/978-1-349-95303-5_5.

Kukla, Rebecca. 2015. "Medicalization, 'Normal Function', and the Definition of Health." In *The Routledge Companion to Bioethics*, edited by Jonathan Arras, Elizabeth Fenton, and Rebecca Kukla, 515–530. New York: Routledge.

Little, Margaret. 1998. "Cosmetic Surgery, Suspect Norms, and the Ethics of Complicity." In *Enhancing Human Traits: Ethical and Social Implications*, edited by E. Parens, 162–177. Washington, DC: Georgetown University Press.

Lucas, Richard E. 2007. "Long-Term Disability Is Associated with Lasting Changes in Subjective Well-Being: Evidence from Two Nationally Representative Longitudinal Studies." *Journal of Personality and Social Psychology* 92, no. 4: 717–730. doi:10.1037/0022-3514.92.4.717.

MacKay, Douglass. 2017. "Calculating QALYS: Liberalism and the Value of Health states. *Economics and Philosophy* 33, no. 2: 259-285. doi:10.1017/S0266267116000298

Marsh, Jason. 2020. "What's Wrong With 'You Say You're Happy, But...' Reasoning?" In *Oxford Handbook of Philosophy and Disability*, edited by Adam Cureton and David Wasserman, 310–325. New York: Oxford University Press.

McMahan, Jeff. 2005. "Causing Disabled People to Exist and Causing People to Be Disabled." *Ethics* 116, no. 1: 77–99. doi:10.1086/454367.

Mill, John Stuart. 1875. *On Liberty.* Longmans, Green, Reader, & Dyer.

Obergefell v. Hodges. 2015.

Oliver, Michael. 1990. *The Politics of Disablement: A Sociological Approach.* Basingstoke, UK: Palgrave Macmillan.

Parfit, Derek. 1984. *Reasons and Persons.* Oxford: Oxford University Press.

Pogge, Thomas. 2000. "Justice for People With Disabilities: The Semiconsequentialist Approach." In *Americans With Disabilities*, edited by Leslie Pickering Francis and Anita Silvers. New York: Routledge.

Quong, Jonathan. 2018. "Public Reason." In *The Stanford Encyclopedia of Philosophy*, edited by Edward N. Zalta. Stanford, CA: Stanford University Press.

Rawls, John. 1977. "The Basic Structure as Subject." *American Philosophical Quarterly* 14, no. 2: 159–165.

Rawls, John. 1988. "The Priority of Right and Ideas of the Good." *Philosophy and Public Affairs* 17, no. 4: 251–276.

Rawls, John. 2005. *Political Liberalism.* New York: Columbia University Press.

Silvers, Anita. 2003. "On the Possibility and Desirability of Constructing a Neutral Conception of Disability." *Theoretical Medicine and Bioethics* 24, no. 6: 471–487. doi:10.1023/B:META.0000006924.82156.5b.

Stramondo, Joseph A. 2010. "How an Ideology of Pity Is a Social Harm to People with Disabilities." *Social Philosophy Today* 26 (July): 121–134. doi:10.5840/socphiltoday20102610.

Stramondo, Joseph A. 2017. "Disabled by Design: Justifying and Limiting Parental Authority to Choose Future Children with Pre-Implantation Genetic Diagnosis." *Kennedy Institute of Ethics Journal* 27, no. 4: 475–500.

Torcello, Lawrence. 2008. "Is the State Endorsement of Any Marriage Justifiable? Same-Sex Marriage, Civil Unions, and the Marriage Privatization Model." *Public Affairs Quarterly* 22, no. 1: 43–61.

UPIAS. 1976. *Fundamental Principles of Disability*. London: Union of the Physically Impaired Against Segregation.

Wasserman, David, Adrienne Asch, Jeffrey Blustein, and Daniel Putnam. 2013. "Disability: Definitions, Models, Experience." In *Stanford Encyclopedia of Philosophy*, edited by Edward N. Zalta. Stanford, CA: Stanford University Press.

PART THREE

JUSTICE, EQUALITY, AND INCLUSION

CHAPTER 11

CONTRACTUALISM, DISABILITY, AND INCLUSION

CHRISTIE HARTLEY

INTRODUCTION

Social contract theory has enjoyed immense popularity in moral and political philosophy and has been put to various uses. Some employ the approach to account for the legitimacy of political authority, while others use it in the derivation of principles of justice. Central to any social contract theory is the idea that agreement among individuals in certain conditions has normative importance, although, overwhelmingly, social contract theorists focus on hypothetical, not actual, agreement when theorizing. As such, these theorists are concerned with the principles to which individuals would or could agree in idealized conditions. Also central to social contract accounts of justice is the idea that society is a cooperative venture for mutual advantage or, alternatively, reciprocal benefit.[1] Contemporary liberals concerned with justice for persons as free and equal citizens have found social contract theory especially appealing both for the idea of hypothetical justification and for the idea of society as a system of cooperation. Indeed, as Martha Nussbaum states, "The idea of basic political principles as the result of a social contract is one of the major contributions of liberal political philosophy in the Western tradition" (Nussbaum 2006, 10).

However, historically, proponents of social contract theories have not been inclusive of persons with some impairments or illnesses. In short, either individuals with certain impairments or illnesses were excluded from its scope or from membership in society *or* they were sidelined from consideration, as their moral status, needs and interests were not addressed. Consider some examples. John Locke claims that individuals with some mental impairments or illnesses fail to possess the requisite degree of reason needed for freedom. Such individuals, he thinks, lack the capacities necessary for consent to the social contract, and, so he says: "*Lunaticks* and *Ideots* are never set free from the Government of their Parents" (Locke 1988, chapt. 6, §60)[2]; they are excluded from membership in political society. And David Gauthier, a contemporary exponent of a social contract account of morality, unapologetically proclaims: "Animals, the unborn, the congenitally handicapped and defective, fall beyond the pale of a morality tied to mutuality" (Gauthier 1986, 268). Finally, consider the view of John Rawls, who developed the most influential theory of justice in the twentieth-century—justice as fairness. In his social contract theory, Rawls does not address in any detail what is owed to those with significant impairments or illnesses[3] in order to focus on the fundamental question of justice, which he describes as "what is the most appropriate conception of justice for specifying the terms of social cooperation between citizens regarded as free and equal, and as normal and fully cooperating members of society over a complete life?" (Rawls 2005, 20). Given these examples, it may not be surprising that contemporary political philosophers concerned with justice for persons with disabilities regard the most prominent statements of social contract theory unacceptable as they stand[4] and doubt the prospects for an appropriately inclusive social contract approach to justice.

In this chapter, I explain why social contract accounts may seem particularly ill-suited to address justice for all persons, and I discuss the possibility of a properly inclusive social contract approach to justice. To this end, I distinguish two variants of social contract theory, namely, contractarianism and contractualism. I argue that while contractarian theories may be able to address certain basic needs and interests of persons with impairments and illness, such theories are nonetheless unacceptable if one holds that (nearly all) human beings are owed justice because of their own value or intrinsic worth. However, I think contractualism can be a quite inclusive theory. Here, I discuss two ways of developing an inclusive contractualism, both of which focus on a capacity for cooperative contribution possessed by nearly all human beings and in which we can understand the intrinsic value of persons as inhering.

CONCEPTIONS OF DISABILITY
AND THEORIES OF JUSTICE

To begin, consider the relationship between conceptions of disability and theories of justice. In the 1970s and 1980s, disability rights activists and scholars demanded civil rights for persons with disabilities, and an important part of this movement was the development of the social model of disability as a tool for challenging the widespread view assumed in law, public policy, the medical community, and, generally, in public opinion that persons with disabilities were sick, unhealthy, in need of medical treatment, and/or dependent on others. These associations with disability resulted in what scholars and activists labeled as the medical model of disability according to which (1) an individual with a disability is not able to function at the level of the species norm in a given environment because of some persistent biological property of the individual, and (2) when it is possible, disablement should be corrected or prevented. By contrast, the social model of disability "locates the causes of disability squarely within society and social organization" (Oliver 1990, 11). According to the social model of disability, (1) an individual with a disability has an atypical persistent biological property that, due to discriminatory social practices or institutions, results in impaired functioning; and (2) when possible and reasonable, discriminatory social practices and institutions should be reformed and inclusive accommodations for persons with atypical properties should be constructed. Both the medical model and the social model are problematic for numerous reasons. The medical model, for example, fails to recognize the discriminatory social practices and institutions that disadvantage persons with impairments and infringe upon their civil rights. And the social model fails to acknowledge the way in which some impairments, in themselves, limit or preclude certain valuable functionings and disadvantage some persons. Of course, most scholars now reject extreme versions of these models and offer nuanced accounts of disability more sensitive to the incredible variations among persons and the relationship between impairments and discriminatory practices and institutions.

Models of disability play an important role in helping us understand the ways in which our laws, policies, institutions, practices, and attitudes fall short of what is required in a just society. And these models are important for helping those who develop theories of justice to make assessments about the inclusivity of their views, determine whether their views meet the needs and interests of persons with disabilities, and deliver theories that appropriately reconcile principles of justice with considered judgments. I think we can draw some crucial lessons from consideration of the medical model and social model and from the fact that most theorists now hold an integrated view. These lessons include that those theorizing about justice should consider (1) that the socially constructed world advantages or disadvantages persons with different abilities when it comes to matters of justice; (2) that any characterization of the interests (e.g., social primary goods) that are a matter of justice affects the assessment of which individuals have those interests (given that individuals have different abilities), and, relatedly, individuals with different abilities may have at least some interests that are different; and (3) that among the needs of persons with disabilities—as among the needs of all persons—is recognition that they have intrinsic value and have claims of justice like their fellow citizens.

Of course, how one understands the point of justice in one's theory determines how one thinks of unjust disadvantage, and this affects how one theorizes disability and how one understands the claims or interests of persons with disabilities (Barclay 2011). There are ways of thinking about the point of justice such that some human beings don't have claims of justice at all; on such views, no matter how such human beings are treated they do not endure *unjust* disadvantage. Those with such views may think that charity or benevolence for such individuals is appropriate or perhaps they may think some kind of duty (that doesn't concern justice) may demand certain treatment of them, such as duties of respect. Certainly, not all of morality is concerned with justice. The scope of justice delimits a particular area of moral concern. Although the notion of justice has not been static in recent debates, it typically concerns the rights and entitlements of persons as citizens, which they can claim from the state and which others must respect. In modern democratic states, having a disability does not affect one's citizenship status. Indeed, in the United States, for example, civil rights laws protect persons with disabilities from discrimination, and there are various laws and policies that protect the participation of persons with disabilities in education, the labor market, and the political sphere. With this in mind, we can now consider social contract theory and the exclusion of persons with disabilities.

CONTRACTARIANISM AND DISABILITY

There are two main variants of social contract theory. One is known as *contractarianism* and follows Hobbes's classic contract theory in key respects; the other is known as *contractualism* and is associated with the Kingdom of Ends formulation of Kant's Categorical Imperative (Cudd 2013; Darwall 2003). In this section, I argue that while contractarianism need not have the implication that certain basic needs and interests of some persons with disabilities go unaddressed or that such persons are, in Gauthier's words, beyond the pale of contractarian justice, this view cannot recognize that all individuals with disabilities are owed justice in virtue of features about them that give them intrinsic worth.

Contractarians hold that when individuals find themselves in certain conditions, it is to their advantage to cooperate (or to cultivate a disposition to do so) in order to promote their own interests. They view society as a cooperative venture for mutual advantage, and they call the conditions that make cooperation mutually advantageous the *circumstances of justice*. These include that individuals are among others who are "roughly similar in physical and mental powers," that there is a moderate scarcity of goods, and that individuals' interests are much alike but that a conflict of interests still exists.[5] Importantly, in most circumstances, there are multiple sets of terms for cooperation that are better for individuals than not cooperating, but each set affords each cooperator different benefits and burdens as individuals differ in their desires and aims, talents and skills, and their efforts in using them. The particular set of terms of cooperation that ought to govern society—the principles of justice—are those that would be selected by rational self-interested cooperators given the bargaining power of these individuals as determined by the value of their particular talents, skills, and efforts. On this view, one's bargaining power is limited by the Lockean Proviso, which, on Gauthier's view, "prohibits bettering one's situation through interaction that worsens the situation of another" (Gauthier 1986, 205). Still, given differences in the bargaining power of the cooperators, there may be significant inequalities in individuals' shares of the social product. In certain conditions, some human beings may not be able to secure, as a matter of justice, reliable access to enough goods to meet all their needs, and others may be excluded as parties from the contract altogether because what they have to offer others in cooperative projects will not make their inclusion advantageous for others. Indeed, the latter is why Gauthier states the "congenitally handicapped and defective" are outside the scope of justice; he simply doesn't think that cooperation with certain individuals is mutually advantageous due to their impairments. Of course, not all individuals with impairments will be excluded on this view. Those with moderate impairments such as blindness or deafness are, no doubt, capable of participation in schemes of mutually advantageous social cooperation. It is those individuals with certain severe impairments who are likely candidates for exclusion. This view provides an example of the point made in the previous section: there are ways of thinking about justice such that not all human beings have a claim to justice or can be unjustly disadvantaged. The view, too, illustrates the point that while in modern liberal democratic states, certain goods may be understood to be entitlements of citizenship, given certain theories of justice, this may not follow. Such observations may lead us to question the central ideas on which such theories are built and, on reflection, to reject such theories for failing to accurately or plausibly account for how we do or should understand the point of justice, the idea of cooperation, or important aspects of the social product.

It is worth noting, however, that some contractarians claim that, even though some human beings (or even nonhuman animals) may not be able to contribute to mutually advantageous cooperation, contractarianism can still recognize that such individuals have claims of justice. Some cooperators may care enough for otherwise excluded human beings that they make their participation in the cooperative enterprise dependent on the recognition that such individuals' have claims of justice. If these cooperators have enough bargaining power, those human beings who would have been excluded will be recognized to have equal moral standing to make claims of justice with others.[6] However, even if individuals are recognized as having equal moral standing with others, they may lack—or those who represent their interests may lack—the bargaining power to secure enough material goods to meet their needs or to secure important opportunities in education, employment, or those spheres important to their (view of the) good. Furthermore, their moral standing ultimately depends on the contingent feelings or judgments of others and not their own properties or capacities by virtue of which they possess the sort of value that gives them standing to make claims of justice.[7]

RAWLS, CONTRACTUALISM, AND DISABILITY

Can contractualists do better? Recall that, in his contractualist theory of justice as fairness, Rawls says that his focus is the fundamental problem of justice for a democratic society, which concerns fair social cooperation among normal and fully cooperating members of society over the course of a complete life; he thought that what is owed to those unable to engage in social cooperation in that way is a problem of extension. Rawls has been criticized for this approach (Kittay 1999; Nussbaum 2006). Such a view seems to suggest that those with disabilities who are not normal and fully cooperating members of society "in the usual sense" are second-class citizens, it leads to a conception of the goods of justice based only on the needs of some human beings, and it is based on an impoverished conception of the ways in which individuals can make essential cooperative contributions to society. Furthermore, this view offers a distorted picture of society. Any society includes numerous individuals who need care and who provide it for others; indeed, the work of caring for others is essential to any society. Those who provide this socially necessary work should be properly valued for their cooperative efforts and not disadvantaged relative to other members of society. Several commentators have discussed Rawls's postponement of what is owed to those with disabilities or considered the extent to which Rawls's view—suitably modified—can be properly inclusive of all individuals.[8] In this section, I outline Rawls's theory and the sources of its limitations, as it stands. In the next, I consider how contractualism might be developed to be more inclusive of those disabilities.

Of importance, Rawls's view is sometimes interpreted as a hybrid theory, combining important features from both the contractarian and contractualist social contract traditions (Barry 1989; Nussbaum 2006). However, I think this is a mistake and that his view is distinctively contractualist. To explore the inclusivity of contractualism, I present Rawls's view as squarely within the contractualist tradition. Recall that contractualism is a strand of social contract theory associated with the Kingdom of Ends formulation of the Categorical Imperative. Kant understands a Kingdom of Ends as a "systematic union of various rational beings through common laws" in which rational beings are always regarded as ends in themselves and in which rational beings are understood as both subject to and legislators of the laws (Kant 1996, AK: 433). Contractualists who aim to develop accounts of justice start with the idea of persons as ends and the idea of society as a fair system of cooperation over time. They claim that fair terms of social cooperation must be justifiable or reasonable to persons viewed as free and equal citizens, and they claim that fair cooperation is based on the idea of reciprocity.

With these ideas in mind, consider Rawls's view. He thinks that certain conditions make justice both possible and necessary. These "circumstances of justice" include that there is a moderate scarcity of goods, that individuals have similar yet conflicting interests, and that individuals are "roughly similar" in capacities (Rawls 1999, 109–110). Insofar as social cooperation is understood in the narrow sense of contributing to the production of those goods and services exchanged in the economy, these circumstances are the conditions under which cooperation can be mutually beneficial. However, unlike contractarians, Rawls doesn't think that justice is simply a matter of mutually advantageous social cooperation, even when such social cooperation is constrained by a Lockean proviso. Rather, Rawls is concerned with fair social cooperation among moral equals who, as free and equal citizens, engage in reciprocal exchange to live on terms of mutual respect with their fellows and enjoy equal freedom to pursue their idea of the good. Hence, Rawls starts with the idea that individuals are equal moral persons in virtue of possessing the two moral powers at a certain threshold level. These powers are a capacity for a sense of justice and a capacity to form, revise, and pursue a rational conception of the good (Rawls 2005, 19). Rawls says that cooperation based on reciprocity is distinct from cooperation motivated by either concern for the general good or expected advantage for oneself; he says it "is a relation between citizens expressed by principles of justice that regulate a social world in which everyone benefits judged with respect to an appropriate benchmark of equality defined with respect to that world" (Rawls 2005, 16–17). Fair terms for social cooperation must be justifiable to persons as free and equal citizens or, we might say, justifiable to a representative for these persons. The subject matter of the terms is the distribution of the social goods that meet persons' needs as citizens by the main institutions of society viewed as a system. These include basic rights and liberties, opportunities, income and wealth, and the social bases of self-respect.

Rawls claims that if we design a fair procedure for determining principles of justice, then the terms that are the output of that procedure will be fair. He proposes a hypothetical choice situation for the selection of terms of social cooperation, known as the *original position*. Rawls claims the original position is a fair procedure because the trustees for citizens who select the principles of justice are "symmetrically situated." They "do not know the social position, or the conception of the good... or the realized abilities and psychological propensities, and much else of the persons they represent" (Rawls 2005, 305). Although the trustees know the circumstances of justice hold, they do not know the more specific conditions of the society in which the person whose interests they represent will live; they just know "general facts about human society" (Rawls 2005, 119). Rawls thinks that those in the original position will select certain principles of justice over other alternative sets. To the extent that the interests of those who are not fully cooperating members of society are considered, it is simply a possible concern or interest of those represented, as certainly care for such an individual could be part of someone's conception of the good. And, arguably, while trustees for members of society will secure for those represented some means to pursue a conception of the good, many persons will not be entitled, as a matter of justice, to the resources needed for their specific conception.

Modifying Rawls's view to be inclusive of those with impairments is not an easy task. Two exclusionary and seemingly fundamental aspects of his view are important to highlight. First, Rawls has a narrow understanding of social cooperation as well as the social product. In the social product, he includes the goods and services that are part of the economy; he also understands the social product to include the labor of rearing children in the home, which is a matter of the reproduction of society over time (although Rawls says little about this) and the work of public officials in the political sphere. Not all human beings with disabilities, even given reasonable accommodations, can participate in the labor market, care for minor children, or work in political society. Hence, Rawls's notion of social cooperation is exclusionary of some human beings. Of course, from the mere fact that his view of social cooperation is exclusionary, it does not follow that his view is problematic. Indeed, there may be other ways of securing justice for people with significant disabilities. However, consideration of the fact that Rawls's notion of social cooperation is exclusionary may lead us to rethink our understanding of social cooperation and give us good reason to reject his narrow view of the idea. Second, Rawls also has a narrow conception of personhood. Recall that he posits that persons are those individuals who possess the two moral powers (a capacity to form, revise, and pursue a rational conception of the good and a capacity for a sense of justice) at a certain threshold level. Some individuals with certain cognitive impairments do not possess the two moral powers at the requisite threshold level and never will. Importantly, in *Theory*, Rawls stresses that the two moral powers are distinctive of personhood and a "sufficient condition for being entitled to equal justice"; but then he adds: "Whether moral personality is also a necessary condition [for being entitled to equal justice] I shall leave aside" (Rawls 1999, 442–443). Hence, while Rawls may not think that human beings who are nonpersons lack claims of justice, his notion of personhood is exclusionary and his view of the status of human nonpersons is not made clear. Again, his view of personhood may not be problematic merely because it is exclusionary as it doesn't follow either that human nonpersons lack claims of equal justice or that there isn't some good reason to understand the two moral powers as distinctive of personhood. However, the exclusion is serious and merits considered attention.

Inclusive Contractualism

There are a number of ways one might develop a more inclusive contractualism. One could, following Rawls's remarks, take what is owed to those who can't be fully cooperating members of society (in his sense) to be a problem of extension and try to develop a theory for extension. This would be no easy task. One would have to explain the nature of the claims for those who can't be fully cooperating members of society. Do they have a claim of justice or something else? And what is the ground for the claim, whichever type of claim it is? Furthermore, one would need an account of how to reconcile the claims of the fully cooperating with the claims of those who are not (and, too, one would need an account of the interests/needs of the less than fully cooperating as well as a theory of healthcare for everyone else). I will not pursue this approach as it can't deliver a truly inclusive contractualism. If those who are not fully cooperating members of society have a claim of justice, then the ground would not be understood in terms of contractualist justice (but some other additional conception of justice), and, if they don't have a claim to have their needs met on the basis of justice but due to obligations of some other sort, then, of course, the basis for their claim also does not have anything to do with contractualist justice either.

Perhaps we should start with a desideratum for an ideally inclusive contractualism. If a contractualist theory of justice can be properly inclusive of all or nearly all human beings, it should offer a plausible account of the concern of justice that captures what we think makes a claim of justice distinctive and that leads to all or nearly all human beings having claims of justice within contractualism. With respect to the latter, the thought is that the central features of contractualism must be such that when worked out it is clear why all or nearly all human beings have contractualist claims. This is to say that we don't want a theory in which the inclusion of some persons seems ad hoc. Furthermore, the theory should be such that all—and not just some—of the needs and interests of human beings that we think are part of justice are recognized and addressed. Arguably, among the needs and interests of human beings with profound impairments or illnesses is that they are regarded as moral equals and, more contentiously, that their claims of justice rest on the same ground as others.

However, one might think that while all or nearly all human beings have claims of justice and are moral equals, the claims of justice of human beings might rest on different grounds precisely because there are relevant differences among human beings. In particular, Cynthia Stark argues that some human beings have claims on the social product because they are cooperative contributors to the social product, and other human beings who cannot contribute have claims in virtue of having needs (Stark 2007, 135). She stresses that contribution to the cooperative enterprise that creates the social product is morally relevant; it gives one a claim on goods *because one helped create them*. Indeed, Stark contends: "the moral relevance of productive capabilities is linked to an aim central to social contract theory, which is to prohibit the exploitation of those participating in a scheme of social cooperation" (Stark 2009, 87). She holds that contribution matters for the kind of claim an individual has, to how an individual's claim should be assessed, and to what an individual is owed. And so Stark offers a revised statement of Rawls's view in which principles of justice for the *fully cooperating* members of society are determined first and then principles for addressing the basic needs of noncooperators are determined at a later stage of justice theorizing.

It is central to contractualism that society is viewed as a system of cooperation over time, and so, with Stark, we should hold that contributing to the cooperative enterprise that creates the social product is morally relevant for contractualists. But, how, then, is an inclusive contractualism possible? Not all individuals with disabilities can contribute to the social product as normally understood, and recognizing the moral relevance of cooperative contribution seems to pose an obstacle for constructing an inclusive contractualism if that means the claim of justice of all members of society should have the same ground. Reflections on the lives of persons with disabilities and insights from the disabilities rights movements and other social justice movements are helpful here. Historically, those with severe disabilities were viewed as noncontributing burdens on others and the proper object of pity, sympathy, or charity. Activists in disability rights movements demanded that the lives of persons with disabilities receive attention and demanded recognition of the important contributions to society that individuals with disabilities make—to the labor market, the family (an institution that Rawls has long counted as part of the basic structure), the political sphere, and civil society. Despite public perception, individuals with disabilities were not noncontributing members of society. Furthermore, activists called attention to the ways in which the social world excluded individuals with disabilities from further participation. For example, buildings with stairs are not accessible to persons in wheelchairs, and individuals with vision impairments need sound cues and other non–vision dependent communication to navigate the environment. If we constructed society differently, many of those with impairments could contribute and so activists demanded the redesign of society as well as reasonable accommodations when that was not possible or feasible. Finally, central to the civil rights movements for disability rights is the demand for social equality and inclusion of persons with impairments as equal citizens in the spheres of society central to citizenship. Elizabeth Anderson claims that when theorizing about justice we should consider the objectives of modern egalitarian political movements, which focus primarily on ending hierarchical social relations among members of society and on creating societies in which social cooperation fundamentally concerns the construction of a society based on relations of mutual respect among free and equal citizens (Anderson 1999, 312–313). With these remarks in mind, I will now offer two ways in which one might construct a more inclusive contractualism. Both involve recognizing, albeit in quite different ways, that most human beings with impairments or illnesses are cooperative contributors to society (or have the capacity for cooperative contribution) and thereby have a claim of justice.

First, one might develop an inclusive contractualism by building on Sean Aas's work on distributive egalitarianism (Aas 2019). Aas does not explicitly associate himself with contractualism. But he understands his view as a kind of cooperation theory, and, as such, his view is amendable to contractualist appropriation. Aas views society as a productive enterprise. People work together in basic social institutions to produce discrete, distributable goods. Importantly, though, he stresses the fact that the production of particular goods requires a "stable social background" or basic social institutions. Basic social institutions provide the conditions for particular productive endeavors as well as impart us with assurance that such endeavors can be completed. And so Aas says that the basic institutions in society create opportunities, opportunities for the production and acquisition of other things. Of importance, though, basic social institutions themselves are "cooperatively constituted" through the compliance of individuals with the particular norms and rules of institutions. Compliance, then, is a cooperative contribution to the basic social institutions; it helps to produce the opportunities that the basic social institutions provide. All those who comply have a claim to "something proportionately valuable" to those opportunities. When people contribute to particular institutions to produce specific things, they have additional claims, but this in no way diminishes the claims based on cooperative compliance.

Central to Aas's view is that nearly all human beings make a "relevantly equal contribution to basic social institutions" and that this "gives them a presumptively equal claim on the worth of the goods these institutions *themselves* produce" (Aas 2019). How can we understand nearly all individuals as making "relevantly equal contributions" to the basic social institutions in terms of cooperative compliance? Some individuals contribute more to the production of the basic institutions than others. Consider, first, that different sets of basic institutions produce different opportunities for production and acquisition. And institutional sets vary in advantaging or disadvantaging individuals as individuals differ with respect to factors such as their view of the good, abilities, and skills. To the extent that "those who contribute more are responsible for the fact that others contribute less" to a particular set of social institutions, we can understand individuals as having relevantly equal compliance-based claims to the value of the opportunities produced by the basic social institutions (Aas 2019). So, the fact that some individuals have impairments or illnesses such that they cannot comply with the basic institutions in society as they are does not mean that they do not have compliance-based cooperative claims. Aas says that those who could comply if the basic institutions were different (e.g., those "who could have understood and participated in simpler arrangements") also have a relevantly equal claim on the value that actual institutions produce since the producers of the actual institutions are responsible for other institutions not being in place. Those who are excluded on Aas's view are only those who could not comply with any possible basic institutions.

Building a contractualist theory based on Aas's work may seem appealing. He highlights an important cooperative contribution to society that is fundamental. This contribution is one that is quite inclusive of persons with disabilities since most people have the capability for compliance with some set of basic institutions for society, given the array of possibilities. However, Aas's view isn't as inclusive as we might hope. Some persons with cognitive impairments and mental illnesses will not be included because they do not possess the capacities necessary for compliance. Furthermore, Aas retains a picture of the social product in which the point of cooperation fundamentally concerns the production of something that is discrete and divisible (in his case, opportunities for the acquisition of specific items) and that gives individuals a claim to something that can be quantified—the worth of the opportunities created by the basic structure. This way of thinking about the social product and individuals' most basic entitlement is still too limited. It doesn't allow Aas to capture some of the most significant contributions to society, contributions which can be made by many of those who are, in fact, excluded from his view. And it does not make front and center the fundamental aim of egalitarian social movements: the creation of a society in which all persons stand in a relationship of mutual respect as free and equal citizens.

Consider a second way in which one might develop an inclusive contractualism, which I have developed in my work. Suppose we start by positing that the point of social cooperation is constructing a society based on mutual respect among persons viewed as free and equal citizens. The social product is not merely the aggregate of discrete and divisible goods; rather, the social product's fundamental good—a certain kind of relationship among members of society—is not discrete and divisible at all but is the social relation that holds among all members of society as free and equal citizens. Central to this relationship is that members of society recognize themselves and others as having the status or standing of an equal citizen and relate to others in recognition of this. For example, sexual harassment in education, employment, and the political sphere would be prohibited. Sexual harassment is a form of sex discrimination that subordinates women and undermines relations of mutual respect among persons as free and equal citizens. Being able to participate in all spheres of social life central to citizenship without such discrimination is crucial to the recognition of persons as free and equal citizens (Fraser 1997, 48). Distributable goods make this relationship possible (such as, e.g., certain rights, liberties, opportunities, and capabilities) as both means and as central to the constitution of the relationship itself (Anderson 1999, 314).

Given this view of social cooperation, the circumstances of justice are those conditions in which a society with this end is possible. This requires, among other things, that the natural resources required for this kind of society to exist are available, but it does not require that individuals are roughly equal in physical and mental powers. The point of social cooperation is not mutual advantage, which requires the acquisition of more resources or opportunities than available in the absence of cooperation. Rather, individuals cooperate to bring about a society in which persons stand as equal citizens and, in this position, can pursue their view of the good consistent with others doing the same. The possession of certain mental and physical abilities is necessary for some but not all members, and this bears on the inclusiveness of this approach, which I address shortly. Here, though, we should note that among the circumstances of justice are (1) that persons value living in a society so understood as an end and (2) that enough persons are motivated from a sense of reciprocity to make that kind of society possible.

There are different ways in which one might understand what reciprocal cooperation requires. One might think fair reciprocal cooperation requires that exchanges be fitting and proportional (Becker 1986). If it required this, then it may be the case that individuals would have to be roughly equal in abilities and—as a result—capable of roughly equal contributions *or* it may be the case that individuals must be able to contribute at a certain threshold level. However, the point of social cooperation bears on the norms that govern fair reciprocity (Hartley 2014). If the point of cooperation is not mutual advantage but living in a society based on relations of mutual respect among persons viewed as free and equal citizens, then, arguably, contributions to this project that promote, sustain, or partly constitute this end are sufficient. The capacity to make cooperative contributions to this project gives individuals intrinsic value, and the capacity for cooperative contribution is the criterion for personhood. The terms for fair reciprocal cooperation are just so long as the terms are justifiable to trustees for persons viewed as free and equal citizens.

This contractualist approach can be quite inclusive of all human beings. Again, all those who make cooperative contributions to living in a society based on relations of mutual respect among persons viewed as free and equal citizens are owed justice. There are numerous ways in which individuals can cooperatively contribute to a society so understood. Of course, individuals can contribute to the labor market and political sphere in the traditional ways. Many individuals with impairments so contribute, and, given that the capacity for cooperative contribution entitles individuals to justice, society should be structured so that those who are differently abled can participate insofar as this is reasonable. How a social environment is structured affects who is able to participate and different environments enable or preclude the participation of individuals with different capacities and abilities. Again, the ability to participate in all spheres of social life central to citizenship is part of equal citizenship; hence, when reasonable, accommodations for inclusion ought to be made.

As feminists have stressed, the family plays a crucial role in society. It is the primary site of caregiving for all dependents (children, the elderly, and any person who requires assistance—temporarily or permanently—in meeting her or his basic needs). It also is the primary site of care for nondependent adults who mutually support each other with care-related needs.[9] Those who help others meet their basic needs through caregiving make an essential contribution to society as all human beings need care at least for some part of their life. As Rawls also observed, the family is the first school of justice for children; from their caregivers and loved ones, children begin to learn the moral virtues crucial for citizenship. Historically, women have performed much of this work without compensation or recognition of their vital contribution to society, and, as a result, they have been disadvantaged in their ability to participate in other spheres of life central to citizenship. With this in mind, we can think of the family for purposes of theorizing about justice as a social institution in which individuals provide or receive intimate, personal care related to their basic needs as citizens and where children learn moral virtues important for civic education. Those who contribute to this essential institution should not be disadvantaged in their ability to participate in other spheres central to citizenship and must receive recognition for their contribution. This is especially important for sex equality. It is also important for the recognition of the valuable contributions of persons with disabilities, some of whom, while unable to participate in the labor market or political sphere, help care for others in the family or help with civic education.

Given the social product whose fundamental good is the relationship of mutual respect among persons as free and equal citizens, a key contribution that any person can make to society is with respect to how one relates to others. Individuals can only stand in a relationship of mutual respect with others if others recognize their standing and authority as co-citizens with the attendant rights of citizenship. Making a contribution to society through one's relationships with others is not limited to the relationship of mutual respect among co-citizens that is the aim of social cooperation but also includes—and, indeed, should help draw our attention to—all those relationships that make such a society possible. For example, children not only need help meeting their basic material needs but need intimate, caring relationships with personal caregivers for healthy psychological development. Most adults, too, need some intimate caring relationships as such relationships contribute to the development and ability to exercise the capacity for cooperative contribution. Brake argues that adult caring relations offer "psychological, emotional, and even health benefits," and she claims that such relations are among citizens' needs in the Rawlsian sense as they are "all purpose-means normally needed" for various views of the good (Brake 2012, 177).

The recognition of these relational goods as part of the social product is important for the inclusivity of this kind of contractualism. Nearly all individuals with impairments, including profound cognitive impairments, can contribute either to relations of mutual respect with others or (at least to some degree) to caring relationships with others. At the heart of the capacity for cooperative contribution is the capacity for engagement, which involves the capacity to see another as a responsive, animate being and to recognize the ability of the other to be responsive to something she interprets as a communication to herself. It involves the ability to communicate with another in some form, and we must keep in mind that communication can be verbal or nonverbal. Communication with another is itself a kind of cooperation, and it is the foundation of any cooperative enterprise. The ability to communicate allows persons to participate in the relationships that make possible a society in which members live on terms of mutual respect as free and equal citizens. Importantly, it is on the basis of individuals' capacity for cooperative contribution that they are included as members of society entitled to justice. On this view, then, those with impairments are not owed justice on the basis of need or as objects of pity, sympathy, or charity. Rather, those with impairments have a claim to justice—like all other members of society—on the basis of their capacity for cooperative contribution.

Of course, there are some human beings who do not count as persons on this view and are outside the scope of justice, namely, those who are wholly unable to communicate with others. This includes, for example, those infants with anencephaly and those with such profound cognitive impairments that they are merely responsive to stimuli in the environment such as light or sound. This set of human beings is extraordinarily small. Certainly, material care for such individuals is important. There are various ways this claim could be supported. And, even if we think that justice does not require such care, such care may be justifiable or required by us given considerations of sympathy or recognition of mere human need. Considerations of justice do not exhaust our moral obligations.

There are other strategies one might employ to develop an inclusive contractualism. While Rawls views society as a cooperative venture for reciprocal benefit, contractualists need not think of society in that way. There might be other, less exclusionary ways of thinking about how to understand society for purposes of theorizing about justice, which could be combined core contractualist ideas. In this effort, it might be fruitful to consider contractualist accounts of our moral duties. For example, Scanlon offers a contractualist account of the part of morality that concerns what we owe to each other. He says that "[a]ccording to contractualism, our concern with right and wrong is based on a concern that our actions be justifiable to others on grounds that they could not reasonably reject insofar as they share this concern" and so all those "to whom we have good reason to want our actions to be justifiable" are within the scope of this part of morality (Scanlon 1998, 202, 179). While Scanlon admits that there are different ways to think about the scope of those to whom we want our actions to be justifiable, he favors including within the scope all those capable of judgment-sensitive attitudes. This excludes only those with some severe cognitive impairments. And so, Scanlon says "[t]he mere fact that a being is 'of human born' provides a strong reason for according it the same status as other humans" as these individuals are born to those with the capability for judgment-sensitive attitudes. He proposes that trustees could consider what such individuals "could reasonably reject if they were able to understand such a question" (Scanlon 1998, 185). While Scanlon's view is not a view of justice, his approach to the scope of contractualism may inspire new directions for contractualist thinking about justice.[10]

Here, I have only sketched the foundation for some contractualist approaches to justice that are inclusive of persons with disabilities. Much work remains to be done. However, against those who doubt the inclusiveness of contractualism, we should not dismiss the theory as it can arguably provide a particularly inclusive and attractive way of grounding claims to justice for those with impairments.

Acknowledgments

I thank Adam Cureton and David Wasserman for comments on an earlier draft. This chapter reflects my most recent thoughts on contractualism and the inclusion of individuals with impairments, but I certainly draw from my previous work on this topic in the formulation of my ideas here.

Notes

1. Contractualists concerned with our moral duties do not make this claim. See, e.g., Scanlon (1998) and Hill (1992; 2000).
2. For discussion of Locke and disability, see Arneil (2009; 2016). See also Clifford (2014). Importantly, Arneil highlights that, on Locke's view, even if some individuals are not members of political society or outside the scope of justice, the principle of charity entitles all human beings to some goods.
3. Rawls briefly mentions how to address what is owed to those who "through some misfortune or accident…are unable to make decisions for their good" in his discussion of principles of paternalism (1999, 218–220). Thanks to Adam Cureton for reminding me of this passage.
4. See, e.g., Nussbaum (2006) and Kittay (1999).
5. Rawls offers and endorses such circumstances of justice in his *A Theory of Justice* (1999, 109–110).
6. See Cohen (2007) and Becker (2005).
7. For an extended discussion of the shortcomings of this kind of approach, see Tanner (2013).
8. See, e.g., Brighouse (2001), Cureton (2008), Freeman (2006), Hartley (2009a; 2009b), Richardson (2006), Stark (2007; 2009).
9. See Brake (2012).
10. Hill's moral contractualism, too, may be instructive. See Hill (1992, 2000).

References

Aas, Sean. 2019. "You Didn't Build That!: Equality and Productivity in a Complex Society." *Philosophical and Phenomenological Research* 98: 69–88.

Anderson, Elizabeth. 1999. "What Is the Point of Equality?" *Ethics* 109: 287–337.

Arneil, Barbara. 2009. "Disability, Self-Image, and Modern Political Theory." *Political Theory* 37: 218–242.

Arneil, Barbara. 2016. "Disability in Political Theory Versus International Practice: Redefining Equality and Freedom." In *Disability and Political Theory*, edited by Barbara Arneil and Nancy Hirschmann, 20–42. Cambridge: Cambridge University Press.

Barclay, Linda. 2011. "Justice and Disability: What Kind of Theorizing Is Needed?" *Journal of Social Philosophy* 42: 273–287.

Barry, Brian. 1989. *A Treatise on Social Justice, Volume 1: Theories of Justice*. Berkeley: University of California Press.

Becker, Lawrence C. 1986. *Reciprocity*. Chicago: University of Chicago Press.

Becker, Lawrence C. 2005. "Reciprocity, Justice, and Disability." *Ethics* 116: 9–39.

Brake, Elizabeth. 2012. *Minimizing Marriage: Marriage, Morality and the Law*. Oxford: Oxford University Press.

Brighouse, Harry. 2001. "Can Justice as Fairness Accommodate the Disabled?" *Social Theory and Practice* 27: 537–560.

Clifford, Stacy. 2014. "The Capacity Contract: Locke, Disability and the Political Exclusion of 'Idiots.'" *Politics, Groups and Identities*. doi: 10.1080/21565503.2013.876918.

Cohen, Andrew I. 2007. "Contractarianism, Other-regarding Attitudes, and the Moral Standing of Nonhuman Animals." *Journal of Applied Philosophy* 24: 188–201.

Cudd, Ann. 2013. "Contractarianism." *The Stanford Encyclopedia of Philosophy*, edited by Edward N. Zalta (Winter 2013 Edition). Available at http://plato.stanford.edu/archives/win2013/entries/contractarianism

Cureton, Adam. 2008. "A Rawlsian Perspective on Justice for the Disabled." *Essays in Philosophy* 9: 1–27.

Darwall, Stephen. 2003. *Contractarianism/Contractualism*, edited by Stephen Darwall. Malden, MA: Blackwell Publishing.

Fraser, Nancy. 1997. *Justice Interruptus: Critical Reflections on the "PostSocialist" Condition*. New York: Routledge.

Freeman, Samuel. 2006. "Frontiers of Justice: The Capabilities Approach vs. Contractarianism." *Texas Law Review* 85: 385–430.

Gauthier, David. 1986. *Morals by Agreement*. Oxford: Oxford University Press.

Hartley, Christie. 2009a. "An Inclusive Contractualism: Obligations to the Mentally Disabled." In *Disability and Disadvantage*, edited by Kimberley Brownlee and Adam Cureton, 138–162. Oxford: Oxford University Press.

Hartley, Christie. 2009b. "Justice for the Disabled: A Contractualist Approach." *Journal of Social Philosophy* 40: 17–36.

Hartley, Christie. 2014. "Two Conceptions of Justice as Reciprocity." *Social Theory and Practice* 40: 409–432.

Hill, Thomas E., Jr. 1992. "The Kingdom of Ends." In *Dignity and Practical Reason in Kant's Moral Theory*, 58–66. Ithaca: Cornell University Press.

Hill, Thomas E., Jr. 2000. "Must Respect Be Earned?" In *Respect, Pluralism and Justice: Kantian Perspectives*, 87–118. Oxford: Oxford University Press.

Kant, Immanuel. 1996. "Groundwork of the Metaphysics of Morals." In *Immanuel Kant: Practical Philosophy*, translated and edited by Mary J. Gregor, introduction by Allen Wood. Cambridge: Cambridge University Press.

Kittay, Eva Feder. 1999. *Love's Labor: Essays on Women, Equality and Dependency*. New York: Routledge.

Locke, John. 1988. *Two Treatises of Government*, edited Peter Laslett. Cambridge: Cambridge University Press.

Nussbaum, Martha. 2006. *Frontiers of Justice: Disability, Nationality, Species Membership*. Cambridge, MA: Harvard University Press.

Oliver, Michael. 1990. *The Politics of Disablement*. Basingstoke: MacMillan Press.

Rawls, John. 1999. *A Theory of Justice*, revised edition. Cambridge, MA: Harvard University Press.

Rawls, John. 2005. *Political Liberalism*, expanded edition. New York: Columbia University Press.

Richardson, Henry S. 2006. "Rawlsian Social-Contract Theory and the Severely Disabled." *The Journal of Ethics* 10: 419–462.

Scanlon, T. M. 1998. *What We Owe to Each Other*. Cambridge, MA: Harvard University Press.

Stark, Cynthia. 2007. "How to Include the Severely Disabled in a Contractarian Theory of Justice." *The Journal of Political Philosophy* 15: 127–145.

Stark, Cynthia. 2009. "Contractarianism and Cooperation." *Politics, Philosophy & Economics* 8: 73–99.

Tanner, Julia. 2013. "Contractarianism and Secondary Direct Moral Standing for Marginal Humans and Animals." *Res Publica* 19: 141–156.

CHAPTER 12

CIVIC REPUBLICAN DISABILITY JUSTICE

TOM O'SHEA

CIVIC republicans believe the most pressing problems of political justice should be understood in terms of social power: in particular, the domination that arises from relationships marked by arbitrary power over others. Classic examples of this domination are the power of masters over slaves, monarchs over their subjects, and colonial states over colonists—although civic republicans also identify others who are particularly susceptible to domination, such as undocumented migrants, wives under patriarchy, and workers in capitalist economies. This long preoccupation with dominating relationships has led civic republicans to fashion the tools needed to conceptualize many of the dynamics of personal and political subordination. This chapter asks both what civic republicanism can teach us about disability justice and what civic republicans themselves can learn from thinking through the experience of disability.

CIVIC REPUBLICANISM AGAINST NEGATIVE LIBERTY

Civic republicanism is a broad political tendency among thinkers who draw on the lessons of ancient Greek and Roman writing about self-governing republics (Honohan 2002). Among its major themes are an opposition to tyranny and the servility of the citizenry, a distinctive conception of liberty which informs how such servitude is understood, and an emphasis on the importance of civic virtue and political participation to maintaining this liberty. While some civic republicans have had affinities with elitist or oligarchic political formations (Ando 2010; McCormick 2003), others have pursued an egalitarian and solidaristic working-class politics (Gourevitch 2015). This chapter takes an ecumenical approach to the republican tradition and borrows liberally from several of its different currents.

At the heart of the recent revival of civic republican thought has been a conception of political liberty which opposes it to domination. Indeed, this account of liberty has overshadowed republican discussion of justice, which is now typically characterized in terms of the extent to which the domination of citizens is forestalled. Thus, for our purposes, we ought to have a strong grasp on contemporary republican accounts of liberty as nondomination.

Republican liberty can be helpfully contrasted with *negative liberty*, which has been the conception of freedom favored by many albeit not all liberal thinkers. Negative liberty is the absence of "interference by other persons" (Berlin 2002, 169). For instance, imagine that you are a patient on a mental health ward. If nobody else has locked the ward, restrained you, or otherwise impeded your activity, then you possess some degree of freedom; whereas if medical staff turn the key to the door or put you in a physical hold to stop you moving, then in these respects you are unfree. Defenders of negative liberty disagree about what constitutes interference—say, whether it is only physical coercion or if menacing threats also count. But the core idea remains the same: unfreedom is created by impediments to action introduced by others.

Negative liberty provides an economical, intuitive, and clear criterion for determining how free someone is: namely, the extent to which there is interference with their action. Why, then, do civic republicans think it is inadequate? Consider the following cases:

- The slave with a master who can assault them with impunity yet who presently chooses not to interfere with their actions.
- The wife under legal coverture who goes about her business unhindered but whose husband could at any point prevent her from doing so at his discretion.
- The undocumented migrant whose employer does not report them to the authorities yet nevertheless is able to do so if they were to organize to demand higher wages or better conditions.
- The colonists currently left alone by a colonizing state which nevertheless holds unaccountable coercive power over them and in which they have no political representation.

These are counterexamples to the claim that negative liberty captures our most important commitments about the nature of political liberty, insofar as the sheer vulnerability of these people to arbitrary interference makes it difficult to describe them as free. The slave, wife, migrant, or colonist acts only with the indulgence of the powerful, rather than in their own right, even when they are not subjected to actual interference. They cannot be secure in the knowledge that they will not be intruded upon in the future simply at the discretion of some influential individual or institution. We would expect this vulnerability to foster servile behavior because, in their state of fearful uncertainty, it will often make sense to flatter and be subservient toward those whose forbearance stands in the way of unwanted intrusion in their lives. Here we see what civic republicans have called the "tendency of the enslaved to act with slavishness" (Skinner 2008, 92).

The more sophisticated theorists of negative liberty have been sensitive to these concerns and claim that they have the resources to account for them. For example, Matthew Kramer defines liberty not as the absence of interference, but rather as the range of someone's conjunctively exercisable opportunities. He tells us:

> the overall freedom of a subordinate person *P* is significantly impaired when she has to resort to obsequiousness or unobtrusiveness in order to stave off a dominant person's punitive measures.... [I]f *P* acts in any manner that is insufficiently humble or furtive, she will not also be able to act in any manner precluded by the retaliation that will be undertaken against her as a response to her perceived audacity. (2008, 44)

Her liberty is said to be restricted because she cannot both eschew deference and act without reprisal. However, since the dominator can choose not to retaliate, then these opportunities *are* sometimes conjunctively exercisable. The republican concern is that they are not conjunctively exercisable on a sufficiently secure basis. When someone is actually able to avoid both deference and punishment as a favor of the powerful, then, by the lights of the revised negative liberty account, they should be deemed free. However, the civic republican believes we should reconsider, since this putative freedom is built on a foundation of sand. The leniency of the dominator can be withdrawn with ease—which leaves the dominated so vulnerable to the mercurial will or shifting designs of another that they can at best act freely in an attenuated sense.

DOMINATION AND DISABILITY

Civic republicans understand liberty primarily as nondomination. Frank Lovett provides a helpful definition of domination:

> persons or groups are subject to domination to the extent that they are dependent on a social relationship in which some other person or group wields arbitrary power over them. (2010, 100)

Of course, dependency, arbitrariness, and power can each be spelled out in different ways. For our purposes, we can provisionally characterize them as follows: *dependency* on a relationship is proportional to the cost, risk, and lack of feasibility of exit; *arbitrariness* is the degree to which an outcome is contingent on an uncontrolled or unaccountable will; *power* is the ability to interfere with the choices of another agent. Domination thereby becomes an uncontrolled or unaccountable ability to interfere with another's choices which arises within a relationship that is difficult for them to escape. There is no uniform way in which disability interacts with domination since disabilities are themselves so heterogeneous—being manifest in many different combinations of impairments with unaccommodating environments. Nevertheless, we can identify some characteristic tendencies by which certain disabilities (or the social response to them) can intensify dominating relationships or pull people within their ambit.

While not all disability deepens social dependence, the cost, risk, or impracticality of exiting certain relationships can sometimes be increased. For someone with mobility problems in an isolated rural area, then the cost of withdrawing from a relationship with a social worker or the volunteers at a local charity can be raised when they are reliant on these others to enable them to see their friends and relatives with any regularity. Likewise, if someone's chronic illness means they have to give up waged work, and it is not clear whether they will receive sufficient unemployment or disability benefits, then this can make it riskier to cut ties with a partner or a relative who makes a much-needed financial contribution to the household. So, too, the parent of a young adult with a developmental disability may be so entwined in their care that a life without the other strikes neither of them as a feasible proposition.

Disability can also make it easier for power over someone to be exercised arbitrarily. For instance, in the absence of adequate social support, then an expressive language disorder may hinder a person's ability to prevent others riding roughshod over them, whether that is due to finding it harder to push back against the influence of overbearing family members or to trigger a formal review of social care arrangements imposed on them by bureaucratic diktat. To take another example: an employer who is not yet convinced that a person with a disability is up to the job may agree to only employ them informally, where this leaves them exposed to summary dismissal. In neither case is the person insulated from powers which can be exercised over them with little robust control or accountability.

Some people with disabilities also face more extensive powers of interference. For example, cultural norms based on the assumption that people with syndromic intellectual disabilities will only have limited ability to shape their own lives may leave them with little *de facto* social power to resist the designs of domineering relatives and caregivers. Consider, too, the *de jure* authority claimed by the state to impose decisions about treatment, residence, sexual relationships, or finance that are granted under many mental health and decision-making capacity laws and which can apply exclusively or disproportionately to people with disabilities (see O'Shea 2018). Thus, in addition to deepened dependence and increased arbitrariness of power, the scope of the power to which some people with disabilities are subject can also be larger.

When disability leads to an increase in dependence, arbitrariness, or power, then it can generate or heighten domination so long as the other two features are also present. There is no need for all three features to be attributable to disability for the resulting domination to be of interest to a republican approach to disability. Other potential causes of disadvantage can contribute toward dependence on a relationship in which arbitrary power is held: the combination of disability with race-, gender-, sexuality-, or class-based inequalities can thereby result in intersectional domination. Conversely, the other contributors to domination might be otherwise benign background features, such as the bonds of dependence that arise among family, friends, or partners. When they coalesce into a dominating relationship, however, the civic republican identifies a threat to the free status of the dominated, as well as the attendant dangers of fueling a state of anxious vulnerability and subordination of those with disabilities to those holding arbitrary power over them.

Our discussion of domination has, so far, highlighted arbitrary powers to interfere with another's choices within relationships of dependence. Civic republicans understand this interference expansively, whereby not only coercion and manipulation but also deliberate omission or exploitation can also count as interfering in certain contexts. For example, the pharmacist who refuses to sell a medicine to someone in an emergency or who massively ramps up its price to capitalize on their needs thereby subjects them to interference (Pettit 1997, 53–54).

Other relationships resemble domination without involving a power of outright interference. Take someone managing a chronic physical illness who receives supplementary long-term treatment from a specialist healthcare team. If the team have the power to summarily withdraw this beneficial care should they conclude the patient is recalcitrant or occasionally misses an appointment, then this can have a disciplinary effect—which, like interference-centric domination, can produce compliance and obeisance whether or not the power is actually exercised. Some republicans can classify many such relationships as dominating by refusing to define domination in terms of powers of interference and instead grounding it in powers to change the benefits and costs of choices in either direction (Lovett 2010, 77). Whether or not the ability to arbitrarily withhold a benefit produces domination per se, we should recognize that it is a significant component of the power held in relation to people with disabilities and which can reproduce many of the same worrying social relationships as an arbitrary power to interfere (O'Shea 2017, 57–58).

It is also important to note that disability does not inevitably make people more vulnerable to domination. The experience and skills developed in living with a disability can help some individuals become more resilient than they would otherwise have been—better able to recognize and evade the arbitrary power of others or to extricate themselves from a dependent relationship that may turn toxic. This conclusion is consonant with feminist research in standpoint theory, which shows how "insider-outsiders"—"members of disadvantaged groups who need accurate knowledge of the worlds of the privileged to navigate them successfully"—sometimes gain an epistemic or practical advantage in solving certain problems (Anderson 2015, §9). In this way, disability is not only an occasion for domination but also for fostering the capacities to combat it.

DISABILITY JUSTICE AS NONDOMINATION

Civic republicanism gives us the conceptual tools to identify dominating relationships which threaten the liberty of people with disabilities. However, this is not yet a republican account of disability justice. Despite some initial discussions of disability and civic republicanism, there has been no sustained account of this kind, so we can begin to outline one here.

Two recent republican conceptions of justice can help provide orientation. The first is Frank Lovett's claim that justice consists in minimizing domination. He tells us:

> Societies are just to the extent that their basic structure is organized so as to minimize the expected sum total domination experienced by their members, counting the domination of each member equally. (2010, 159)

This captures the intuition that a society which enables domination to run rife will be unjust. We should note that this conception of justice focuses not on the actions or characters of individuals, but rather on the basic structure of society: its political constitution, economic order, legal system, and other major social institutions. Justice within this basic structure is most fully realized when expected aggregate nondomination is maximized. This is similar to how classical utilitarians hold an act to be morally right when it maximizes aggregate utility. However, this parallel suggests a problem.

Classical utilitarianism is vulnerable to a familiar objection: it fails to respect the separateness of persons (Rawls 1999, 164). It takes total utility to be the only relevant consideration in judgments of moral rectitude, rather than the distribution of this utility. The unpalatable implication is that there are no limits to the degradations to which any single person or group should be subjected if this increases aggregate utility overall. Likewise, the implication of Lovett's view is that justice is served by marginally reducing total domination at the expense of drastically increasing the domination of an individual or minority. This is particularly unattractive in the context of disability, where it can condone neglecting people who require the most resource-intensive armament against domination in order to help people who are already far less subject to dominating relationships. For example, this sum total minimization view would favor a basic social structure with slightly stronger protection from domination for citizens as a whole, even if the costs in terms of political capital and resources were borne by effectively writing off a minority with cognitive disabilities, should it turn out that their nondomination was far harder to secure. I take it that this is unattractive on egalitarian grounds; for, despite Lovett counting the domination of each member of society equally, this is very far from treating them as equal members of society with respect to their domination.

To avoid this objection, we could adopt Philip Pettit's alternative civic republican conception of social justice, which calls for each citizen to have a sufficient level of nondomination in the exercise of their basic liberties. This nondomination ranges over those choices promoting enjoyment and welfare that each person can exercise consistent with all others doing so, and it is to be achieved by means of public laws and norms (2012, 98). How much nondomination is sufficient? Pettit proposes what he calls "the eyeball test," which is passed when people are able to "look others in the eye without reason for the fear or deference that a power of interference might inspire; they can walk tall and assume the public status, objective and subjective, of being equal in this regard with the best" (2012, 84). This provides us with a vivid image intended to capture the lived experience of being a *liber* or free person.

Pettit's account of social justice is concerned with relationships between those citizens or settled residents "who, being adult and able-minded, can play an informed role at any time in conceptualizing shared concerns and in shaping how the state acts in furthering those concerns" (2012, 75). In contrast, special issues of justice and legitimacy are said to arise for those who are "not able-minded" (2012). If the relevant conceptualizing and shaping abilities are assumed to be available to all other adults—no matter the extent of their experience or concern with social and political life—then the standards Pettit is using must be rather weak, such that the vast majority of those of us with mental health problems or cognitive disabilities will meet them (perhaps more than Pettit anticipates). Nevertheless, the absence of an account of social justice for those who would struggle to meet Pettit's standards is a significant lacuna in a theory that aspires to completeness or a serious engagement with the politics of disability.

Further problems arise from the eyeball test. The metaphor itself is rather unfortunate for thinking through disability justice since it builds in forms of physical functioning, such as vision and confident mobility, which some people with disabilities lack. It will, therefore, fail to map onto what we might call the "phenomenology of justice" for a subset of people with disabilities: the lived experience of feeling and being treated as equal or unequal to others. To my mind, the language of walking tall and looking others in the eye also suggests a rather alienating and masculinist kind of "hail fellow, well met" sociality. The deeper problem with the test, however, is that it stands in for rather than supplements an account of the free and equal status of citizens. The eyeball test is intended as a heuristic, but the goal it aims to bring closer to our understanding remains impressionistic—in particular, with respect to the specific threshold levels of nondomination required for just social relations. Admittedly, some indeterminacy is an advantage insofar as it allows context-sensitivity, since different degrees of domination will foster more or less equality-inhibiting fear and deference depending on the social setting. Nevertheless, even factoring in this context, it remains unclear how much nondomination is sufficient to secure disability justice.

We might also be skeptical that domination is the only threat to social justice. Of course, in order to secure nondominating social relationships, then many other goods are necessary: without self-respect, economic security, or emotional satisfaction, we can be more vulnerable to arbitrary power within dependent relationships. Nondomination therefore indirectly presupposes that some other important human needs are met. But there is good reason to push back even against this more capacious view. Consider the kind of objection that Linda Barclay (2010) has made to accounts of disability justice that she claims are overly focused on combatting social oppression without addressing forms of disadvantage that arise predominantly from impairment. She believes that, even absent outright discriminatory treatment by others, some people with mental and physical impairments are owed additional support on the grounds of disability justice. Similar problems emerge for those republican theories of justice which focus only on social relationships of domination: they may neglect unfairness and disadvantage that do not have their origin in dominating social power. Excessive cuts to support services that result in hardship for people with disabilities will not count as unjust if they do not also increase dependency on relationships marked by arbitrary power. Someone disadvantaged by an impairment without this compounding their social domination would likewise have no claim to additional assistance on the grounds of justice. If these conclusions seem counterintuitive, then a single-minded identification of social justice with sufficient nondomination appears to be the problem.

Furthermore, the monism of this approach also implies that nondomination always takes precedence over other goods in matters of justice until the relevant thresholds are passed. Yet we may want to resist the claim that any small gain in nondomination below the relevant threshold should always be preferred on the grounds of justice to someone being more happy, wise, or loved. Consider a new system of oversight for support workers, one that marginally reduces their opportunities for autocratically imposing decisions on people with disabilities but that also involves extremely onerous reporting responsibilities that make them much less effective in helping people. It is far from obvious that social justice demands we achieve nondomination by any means necessary in such situations.

Our foregoing discussion has identified four main objections to extending existing republican conceptions of justice to disability. First, if justice is understood as minimizing total domination, then this can justify abandoning those people with disabilities whose nondomination is hardest to secure. Second, when an account of justice requires special measures to accommodate mental health and cognitive disability, then it will be at best incomplete until these are spelled out. Third, if justice is identified with sufficient nondomination, then we need a deeper understanding of the threshold for disability justice than has been supplied by heuristics like the eyeball test. Fourth, when justice is understood solely in terms of nondomination, then this can lead to an implausibly narrow understanding of disability justice. Can civic republicans accommodate these concerns while continuing to offer a lucid analysis of the ways in which the domination of those with disabilities constitutes an injustice?

A CIVIC APPROACH TO DISABILITY JUSTICE

We began with accounts of republican justice that accentuate domination. A more promising approach foregrounds the sociolegal status that republicans have often contrasted with domination and taken to be the political foundation of freedom: namely, citizenship. In Roman republican thought, "libertas is coterminous with civitas," such that "to be free means to be a member of a civic body" (Wirszubski 1950, 3). This was primarily a defensive understanding of citizenship, however, which took the sociolegal status it granted to be a collective protection against the arbitrary power of magistrates of the ruling class. Greek political thought presents us with a more substantive and active conception of citizenship, with Aristotle claiming that the citizen is "defined by nothing else so much as by his participation in judgment and office" (1998, 1275a). This participation presupposes that "the virtue of a citizen" consists in "the capacity to rule and be ruled" (1998, 1277a). Aristotle holds that "it is characteristic of a free man not to live in dependence on another" (2007, 1367a) and that living in such a condition—particularly economic dependency—inhibits the formation and exercise of the virtue of citizens. In short: freedom enables virtue, which enables political participation.

The gendered language in this account of the relationship between citizenship and freedom betrays its inegalitarian foundations, which not only exclude women but also presuppose widespread slavery (Gourevitch 2015, 25–26). Nevertheless, it is possible to frame these ideas in a more egalitarian mode. When a free person is understood as someone with the status of a citizen empowered to politically participate, then this suggests another possible conception of republican disability justice on which it requires equal citizenship. This allows us to reframe rather than displace concern with the domination of those with disabilities without claiming that social justice is no more than minimizing domination or achieving sufficient nondomination.

If we concentrate on what is needed for equal citizenship in late modern societies, then a compelling starting point is the democratic egalitarianism of Elizabeth Anderson (1999). Negatively, this requires eliminating oppressive relationships that inhibit equality—among which we can count domination. Positively, it involves ensuring that people have the capabilities necessary to relate to one another as politically equal citizens. This presupposes a series of capabilities of "special egalitarian concern" (1999, 316): to function "as a human being, as a participant in a system of cooperative production, and as a citizen of a democratic state" (1999, 317). Capabilities to function as a human being presuppose access to the means of biological subsistence (food, shelter, clothing, medical care) and human agency (deliberative capacities, confidence to think for oneself, freedom of thought and movement). The capability to participate in cooperative production calls for access to education, freedom of occupation, protection from exploitation, and social recognition of one's productive contribution. To be capable of functioning as a citizen requires access to infrastructure and to both public and private spaces, as well as the social conditions to be accepted and not shamed by others and the ability and opportunity for political participation. Domination constitutes not only a direct threat to relationships of equality but can also undermine many of these equality-supporting capabilities.

When republican disability justice is understood in these terms, we can avoid the four objections to attempts to extend existing accounts of republican justice to disability. First, this civic approach will not recommend abandoning individuals with disabilities whose domination may be particularly hard to tackle since it does not require maximizing total nondomination but rather seeks "effective access to levels of functioning sufficient to stand as an equal in society" (1999, 318). Nor will it recommend abandoning individuals with disabilities for whom this access is hard to secure, since injustice will persist when we fail to get as close as possible to it.

Second, there is a common criterion of justice for those with and without disabilities and so no missing special standard applies to those deemed "not able-minded." Of course, the means of achieving equal citizenship might have to be tailored to suit people's different initial capacities, and the possibility cannot be discounted *a priori* that some people may not be able to fully stand in the relevant equal relationships even after colossal efforts to enable them to possess sufficient capabilities of egalitarian concern. For instance, there is reason to be skeptical that even measures such as surrogate voting and jury service will be enough to secure sufficient levels of civic participation for equal citizenship among some of those with the most pronounced cognitive disabilities (see Wasserman and McMahan 2012 *contra* Nussbaum 2009). Nevertheless, this democratic egalitarian republicanism will resist the complacent and world-weary fatalism of those who suggest that people with disabilities ought to curb their ambitions. The desiderata of this civic understanding of justice remains substantially the same for all of us.

In light of this common standard of justice, critics could advance a converse objection to that leveled against Lovett, who appeared too ready to abandon people: that is, some people with disabilities may reach a point where an enormous investment of time and resources is needed for only minuscule additional gains in capabilities for equal citizenship. We might therefore pursue a "prioritarian" variant on which the capabilities of those who have not passed some threshold for equal citizenship would be weighted far more heavily than those who had not. This proposal seeks to avoid both the problem of outright abandonment (by weighting those below the threshold much more heavily) and the problem of minimal but excessively resource-intensive gains (by nontrivially weighting everyone else, albeit to a limited degree).

Third, citizenship is an idea which can help us come to a richer understanding of the freedoms presupposed by disability justice. While exclusion from relationships of civic equality is a broader harm than the deference and fear which the eyeball test tries to capture, it nevertheless points toward relatively determinate measures of injustice in terms of the absence of capabilities necessary for human life and agency, cooperative production, and participation in political self-governance, as well as relationships in which people are subject to oppressions, such as those leaving them subordinated to those with arbitrary power. The free and equal status of citizens is a particularly fitting way of articulating what we owe to other members of a civic association as a matter of political justice since it consists in provision of the conditions for robust standing within that self-same association, which we also have an interest in securing for ourselves in concert with them. The interpretation of such standing will require further democratic elaboration by those who guarantee it and to whom it is guaranteed, but I submit that it is an attractive egalitarian and solidaristic frame within which to pursue disability justice.

Fourth, democratic egalitarian republican justice is less monistic than the other republican approaches we have encountered since it seeks a wider range of goods: egalitarian relationships between citizens presuppose not only nondomination but also protection from other oppressive relationships in addition to the positive provision of egalitarian capabilities. Does monism recur in appealing to equal citizenship as a goal, even if such equality presupposes a broader set of other goods to be in place? We do not have to construe the account this way and can instead identify one specific injustice to which those with disability can be subjected: the kind of inequality that arises from being excluded from the social and political conditions for acting freely as an equal member of a civic association—rather than making the stronger claim that justice itself is to be identified with equal citizenship. This allows that other kinds of disability injustice are possible—for example, forms of substantive unfairness stemming from impairment but which are nevertheless compatible with the general condition of equal citizenship—but which do not consist in a failure to achieve these particular egalitarian relationships.

But does a republican appeal to citizenship exclude noncitizen residents and the stateless from disability justice? This result can seem perverse because these are populations of people with disabilities who are often in greater need, with less access to healthcare and social security systems, while being more vulnerable to exploitation, abuse, and coercion. It is true that republicans have sometimes noted both the bareness of rights which are not rooted in the membership of a civic association which can enforce them (Arendt 1973, 296–298) and the lack of precedent for free and equal relationships which are not "spatially limited" (Arendt 1963, 275).

This does not preclude the establishment of a "community of interest with the oppressed and exploited," however, which emerges "out of solidarity" and encompasses "not only the multitude of a class or a nation or a people, but eventually all mankind" (1963, 88). The republican approach to disability justice outlined here needs have no truck with nationalism—even a "civic nationalism" that claims to eschew xenophobia. Nor should it soft-pedal support and protection for resident noncitizens with disabilities in order to redirect resources to citizens. The commitment of democratic egalitarians as seen through the lens of a radical republicanism is to ensure that everyone can stand in free and equal relationships within civic associations, not to horde benefits for those who are already members.

Some Normative Recommendations

Specific normative recommendations have begun to emerge from republican thought about disability. Jürgen De Wispelaere and David Casassas have argued that dominating relationships in the context of disability can be fought by securing three broad republican rights: to social participation, civic contribution, and democratic contestation (2014, 402). We will pass over the rights to social participation and civic contribution since they support a relatively familiar set of disabilities policies—albeit on decidedly republican grounds—which center on antidiscrimination and deinstitutionalization, in addition to accommodations in the workplace, built environment, and within public life.

The right to democratic contestation is more distinctive—providing mechanisms outside of the usual electoral process to allow individuals with disabilities to challenge policies affecting them. In particular, Casassas and De Wispelaere believe the formulation and implementation of disability policy ought to be open to dispute, review, and revision, with legally enforceable results. This scrutiny could be directed at needs assessments, resource allocation, delivery of disability support, or the organizational structure of support services (De Wispelaere and Casassas 2014, 411). Both the grounds for upholding challenges to policy and the identity of those invested with the ultimate authority to adjudicate these challenges remain unclear. If Casassas and De Wispelaere follow the model of contestatory democracy developed by Pettit, which they invoke, then this would take the form of depoliticized judicial review, ombudsmen, and expert commissions seeking to strike down policies that mandated excessively arbitrary powers of interference over people with disabilities.

In support of democratic contestation, we are told:

> Contestation mechanisms importantly shift the balance of decision-making back to a state where disabled people are not mere recipients of policy, as in the social welfare model, but are instead regarded as genuine political partners in policy design and delivery. (2014)

But how true is this? While the ability to trigger contestation rests in the hands of citizens with disabilities, they are effectively supplicants in a juridical process controlled and enforced by others. It is too limited an interpretation of the civic republican tradition to take its championing of a fractious and upstart citizenry to be captured by permitting people to complain to a collection of depoliticized commissions or review boards staffed with unaccountable professionals.

In this vein, Hannah Arendt tells us that liberty "means the right 'to be a participator in government', or it means nothing" (1963, 218). The radical republican tradition went further still, advocating a "politics of solidarity, in which those who suffered from servitude were also expected to be the agents of emancipation," given that they possess the shared interests and insights to undertake effective collective political action (Gourevitch 2015, 183). In contrast, the danger of contestatory democracy as it has hitherto been propounded is that it reproduces rather than unsettles the unequal sociopolitical statuses that civic republicans oppose by entrenching institutions premised on acting for others rather than enabling them to act for themselves. This model would also do little to prevent the political deskilling of people with disabilities since, after someone raises a contestatory complaint, then action is not taken by them but only for them, with a concomitant lack of opportunities to hone their own political abilities (O'Shea 2015, 12–13).

What republican measures are more consonant with self-rule for people with disabilities? Two proposals especially relevant to disability are offered here—the first being self-education. We find radical republicans, in particular, stressing that thinking for oneself is a condition of breaking free of the wills of others. For example, the nineteenth-century labor republican William H. Sylvis recognized that while a "high degree of intelligence is necessary to enable us to discharge all the duties of citizens," we are "too apt to listen to the teachings of those whose interest it is to foster prejudices rather than cultivate intelligence" (1872, 113). This necessitated "an educational message that spoke directly to workers, through their own presses, which involved them writing their own speeches and pamphlets, and setting up their own libraries and reading rooms" (Gourevitch 2015, 160–161). Similar misinformation and ideological capture is rife in our ableist societies and stands in the way of free and equal citizenship for people with disabilities. The function of presses and pamphlets is now often performed by online communication—but there remains a need for a media of one's own in which to record, discuss, and reflect on individual and shared experiences of power as members of a subaltern group. This pedagogical role is one of the many contributions that can be made by a defiant and oppositional set of cultural institutions which those with disabilities have meaningful control over. The political self-consciousness that comes from individual and collective self-education can fuel a more refractory and militant culture of contestation among people with disabilities than one which proceeds from petitioning ombudsmen and the like.

The second proposal is the introduction of a universal basic income in service of achieving a civic minimum for all citizens. This is not a uniquely republican policy but is particularly well-suited to address some of the demands of republican disability justice we have encountered while remaining consistent with self-emancipation. Consider economic pressures in capitalist economies—with their often-unreliable welfare states, continuing discrimination in labor markets, and insufficient accommodation of disability in education and the workplace—which can underpin domination by making it too difficult to escape from familial, romantic, or employment relationships where financial support is provided but significant arbitrary power is also held. While a republican basic income is far from a panacea (Gourevitch 2013), it would make exiting these relationships easier by providing economic resources that are not contingent on the continuation of that relationship, thereby easing domination even when no exit takes place.

The risk is that basic income simply shifts the locus of domination from the relations between citizens (*dominium*) to the relations between citizens and the state (*imperium*). Hobbes tell us that the state is "an artificial man...of greater stature and strength than the natural" (1996, 7). In light of this, swapping dependence on an individual or small group for dependence on a much more powerful corporate individual appears to be jumping from the frying pan into the fire. However, when a basic income is unconditional, state support does not have to turn into state control. Guaranteed assistance that cannot be withdrawn from someone who displeases politicians or other officials is more difficult to transform into leverage over them. This stands in contrast to other republican proposals to make basic income conditional on assessing whether someone has been searching for paid work or performing some sort of public service (Dagger 2006, 166). Another advantage of breaking with this kind of welfare conditionality is that it partially insulates people with disabilities from often highly intrusive and partisan assessments of fitness to work (a policy so notorious that the slogan "ATOS Kills" became widespread in the United Kingdom in opposition to a company administering the assessments). Even after the introduction of an unconditional basic income, these tests might remain a *de facto* condition of supplementary disability-specific benefits, but their removal from at least part of the welfare system would itself be an important step in the right direction. Lending further support to universal basic income as a contribution to disability justice, there is evidence that universalist welfare policies are typically more effective and resilient than targeted support (Korpi and Palme 1998).

Dependence

An important objection to civic republican accounts of disability justice pushes back against republican hostility to dependency. We have seen that social dependence is a necessary condition of domination on Lovett's influential account, and other republicans also often associate or identify unfreedom with a condition of dependence (Skinner 1998, 84). This has prompted critics such as Marilyn Friedman to claim that civic republicans have an "inadequate grasp of the essential role of dependency relationships in human life" (2008, 254–255). She warns that relationships of dependence are so common that suppressing arbitrary power which arises within them would require a totalitarian state (2008, 266). Friedman draws on opposition to the denigration of dependency that emerges from the ethics of care approach to disability developed by Eva Feder Kittay, and this makes her critique especially apposite for our purposes. Kittay reminds us that dependency is "unexceptional" and "inescapable" (1999, 29). She worries that an "emphasis on independence extols an idealization that is a mere fiction, not only for people with disability, but for all of us," while also devaluing and marginalizing the work of caregivers (2011, 51).

It is true that civic republicans have extolled independence, but not without qualification: they only eschew dependence on those social relationships that enable arbitrary power to be wielded. This is compatible with roundly condemning "the ideal of uncompromising self-sufficiency and mastership" (Arendt 1958, 234) as well as recognizing that human life outside bonds of care is neither desirable nor feasible. Indeed, dependence on care is often the foundation of the independence from subjection to the arbitrary will of others that republicans seek. A "relational structure of independence" of this kind has been emphasized by republican feminists such as Mary Wollstonecraft (Coffee 2014, 911) and is not so far removed from Kittay's own considered position:

> We all are dependent—the fates of each of us hang on those of others. But, at any given historical moment, we know, nonetheless, what relative independence means, what it entitles us to, and what inclusion into the circle of equals signifies. (1999, 184)

Like Kittay, republicans are aiming for a relative rather than absolute independence and do not offer us "a critique of our interdependence but of how that interdependence is organized" (Gourevitch 2013, 605).

Nevertheless, could even the circumscribed forms of independence sought by civic republicans prove to be unattractive or unobtainable? Dominating relationships might be so entwined with our means of care and cooperation that it would prove too harmful or impractical to dispense with them. Friedman strikes a gloomy note in this respect:

> The capacity to clean someone's wound is also the capacity to infect it. The capacity to help someone climb the stairs is also the capacity to throw her down the stairs. (2008, 254)

However, civic republicans are not so perverse as to never allow relationships of dependence marked by arbitrary power, even if vulnerability to this power is seemingly unavoidable in delivering care. Recall that domination can itself be undermined by ensuring that someone is strong enough to combat it. So, the minor domination that arises from a certain caring relationship might be outweighed by the insulation from other domination that this care provides. Furthermore, the arbitrariness of power can be reduced in ways other than making its exercise an *ex ante* impossibility. It is one thing to be able to infect a wound with impunity because the victim dare not complain or no action will be taken if they do—but a robust system of *post hoc* review and redress that ensures such violations are swiftly stamped out may render such a power sufficiently nonarbitrary without simply eliminating it. Thus, Friedman's pessimism is not justified.

The civic republican riposte to Friedman and Kittay is that they recommend conceptual frameworks which tend to obfuscate the threat of unexercised arbitrary power in dependent care relationships. Kittay is alive to harms that a dependent care relationship may inflict, including both abuse that caregivers mete out and their own exploitation by those for whom they care. She even uses the language of "domination" to articulate these concerns. However, this domination is defined very differently as "the exercise of power over another against her best interests and for purposes that have no moral legitimacy" (1999, 34). An important contrast with recent republican accounts is that this precludes domination from arbitrary power which is held over another but not exercised. As we have seen, however, arbitrary power does not have to be actively wielded in order to produce fear, disquiet, or obedience. Our horizons are shaped by anticipating the possible actions of others as well as by what they actually do. For this reason, we need to be concerned not only with the exercise of arbitrary power but with its ability to distort a relationship even when presently held in reserve. It is a significant advantage of republicanism that it provides us with the resources to understand the precarity and marginalization of people with disabilities who know that their employer is able to summarily dismiss them, that the state could choke off support payments at will, and that their primary caregiver might well abuse them with impunity if antagonized.

CONCLUSION

The account of republican disability justice presented here began by contrasting republican accounts of liberty as nondomination with more familiar theories of negative liberty. We then saw how this domination can color the relationships of people with disabilities, especially when dependence or the arbitrariness or extent of power over them becomes particularly pronounced. This led to a consideration of whether disability justice could be defined in terms of maximizing or sufficient nondomination—neither of which were found to be acceptable definitions. In response, we developed a civic framework within which republican disability justice could be understood, one that encompassed both the absence of oppressive relationships and the presence of capabilities of special egalitarian concern. Then we looked at some of the more specific normative implications of a republican account of disability justice—doubting the suitability of contestatory democracy but pointing toward the merits of self-education and universal basic income. Finally, the objection that this republican approach to disability justice unreasonably denigrated dependence was rebutted. The resulting account of civic republican disability justice provides us with a compelling diagnosis of many of the political injustices imposed on those of us with disabilities while recommending tools to begin fixing these problems.

REFERENCES

Anderson, Elizabeth. 1999. "What Is the Point of Equality?" *Ethics* 109 (2): 287–337.

Anderson, Elizabeth. 2015. "Feminist Epistemology and Philosophy of Science." In *The Stanford Encyclopedia of Philosophy* edited by Edward Zalta. Stanford: The Metaphysics Research Lab.

Ando, Clifford. 2010. "'A Dwelling Beyond Violence': On the Uses and Disadvantages of History for Contemporary Republicans," *History of Political Thought* 31 (2): 183–220.

Arendt, Hannah. 1958. *The Human Condition*. Chicago: University of Chicago Press.

Arendt, Hannah. 1963. *On Revolution*. London: Penguin.

Arendt, Hannah. 1973. *The Origins of Totalitarianism*. San Diego: Harcourt Brace & Company.

Aristotle. 1998. *Politics*, translated by C. D. C. Reeve. Indianapolis: Hackett.

Aristotle. 2007. *On Rhetoric*, translated by George Kennedy. New York: Oxford University Press.

Barclay, Linda. 2010. "Disability, Respect and Justice." *Journal of Applied Philosophy* 27(2): 154–171.

Berlin, Isaiah. 2002. "Two Concepts of Liberty." Reprinted in *Liberty* edited by Henry Hardy, 166–217. Oxford: Oxford University Press.

Coffee, Alan. 2014. "Freedom as Independence: Mary Wollstonecraft and the Grand Blessing of Life." *Hypatia* 29(4): 908–924.

Dagger, Richard. 2006. "Neo-Republicanism and the Civic Economy." *Politics, Philosophy & Economics* 5(2): 151–173.

De Wispelaere, Jürgen, and David Casassas. 2014. "A Life of One's Own: Republican Freedom and Disability." *Disability & Society* 29(3): 402–416.

Friedman, Marilyn. 2008. "Pettit's Civic Republicanism and Male Domination." In *Republicanism and Political Theory* edited by Cécile Laborde and John Maynor, 246–268. Oxford: Blackwell.

Gourevitch, Alex. 2013. "Labor Republicanism and the Transformation of Work." *Political Theory* 41(4): 591–617.

Gourevitch, Alex. 2015. *From Slavery to the Cooperative Commonwealth: Labor and Republican Liberty in the Nineteenth Century*. Cambridge: Cambridge University Press.

Hobbes, Thomas. 1996. *Leviathan*, edited by J. C. A. Gaskin. Oxford: Oxford University Press.

Honohan, Iseult. 2002. *Civic Republicanism*. London: Routledge.

Kittay, Eva Feder. 1999. *Love's Labour: Essays on Women, Equality, and Dependence*. London: Routledge.

Kittay, Eva Feder. 2011. "The Ethics of Care, Dependence, and Disability." *Ratio Juris* 24(1): 49–58.

Korpi, Walter, and Joakim Palme. 1998. "The Paradox of Redistribution and Strategies of Equality: Welfare State Institutions, Inequality, and Poverty in the Western Countries." *American Sociological Review* 63(5): 661–687.

Kramer, Matthew. 2008. "Liberty and Domination." In *Republicanism and Political Theory* edited by Cécile Laborde and John Maynor, 31–57. Oxford: Blackwell.

Lovett, Frank. 2010. *A General Theory of Domination and Justice*. Oxford: Oxford University Press.

McCormick, John. 2003. "Machiavelli Against Republicanism: On the Cambridge School's 'Guicciardinian Moments.'" *Political Theory* 31(5): 615–643.

Nussbaum, Martha. 2009. "The Capabilities of People with Cognitive Disabilities." *Metaphilosophy* 40(3–4): 331–351.

O'Shea, Tom. 2015. "Disability and Domination." *Journal of Applied Philosophy*. doi: 10.1111/japp.12149: 1–16.

O'Shea, Tom. 2017. "Civic Republican Medical Ethics." *Journal of Medical Ethics* 43(2017): 56–59.

O'Shea, Tom. 2018. "A Civic Republican Analysis of Mental Capacity Law." *Legal Studies* 38(1).

Pettit, Philip. 1997. *Republicanism: A Theory of Freedom and Government*. Oxford: Clarendon Press.

Pettit, Phillip. 2012. *On the People's Terms: A Republican Theory and Model of Democracy*. Cambridge: Cambridge University Press.

Rawls, John. 1999. *A Theory of Justice: Revised Edition*. Cambridge, MA: Harvard University Press.

Skinner, Quentin. 1998. *Liberty Before Liberalism*. Cambridge: Cambridge University Press.

Skinner, Quentin. 2008. "Freedom as the Absence of Arbitrary Power." In *Republicanism and Political Theory* edited by Cécile Laborde and John Maynor, 83–101. Oxford: Blackwell.

Sylvis, William H. 1872. "Address Delivered at Chicago, January 9, 1865." *The Life, Speeches, Labors and Essays of William H. Sylvis* edited by James C. Sylvis, 127–171. Philadelphia: Claxton, Remsen & Haffelfinger.

Wasserman, David, and Jeff McMahan. 2012. "Cognitive Surrogacy, Assisted Participation, and Moral Status." In *Medicine and Social Justice*, second edition, edited by Rosamond Rhodes, Margaret Battin, and Anita Silvers, 325–340. Oxford: Oxford University Press.

Wirszubski, Chaim. 1950. *Libertas as a Political Idea at Rome During the Late Republic and Early Principate*. Cambridge: Cambridge University Press.

CHAPTER 13

DISABILITY AND DISADVANTAGE IN THE CAPABILITIES APPROACH

CHRISTOPHER A. RIDDLE

INTRODUCTION

THE World Health Organization (2011, xi) estimates that there are more than one billion people in the world living with a disability, or that approximately 13.5 percent of our population is disabled. Moreover, it reports that nearly 200 million of these people experience difficulty in functioning—disadvantage as a result of their disability (World Health Organization 2011, xi). I have previously observed how startling this number is, especially when we acknowledge that "this statistic fails to take into account the large number of people living with disabilities who refuse to disclose the presence of impairment out of fear of stigmatization or worse, blatant discrimination" (Riddle 2016, 1). Throughout the various international declarations, covenants, and measurement devices designed to promote the rights of people with disabilities, it is stressed that social disadvantage should feature centrally as a vital part of any descriptive framework (Chapireau and Colvez 1998, 65). The motivating factor behind this reasoning is, at least partially, that people with disabilities tend to be more likely than otherwise similarly situated able-bodied individuals to suffer from material disadvantage: "[T]hey earn less income than the non-disabled, and because of their special needs they need more income to achieve similar functionings" (Robeyns 2006, 366).

I propose that irrespective of how disability is conceptualized or defined, the aim of any model of disability, properly conceived, involves articulating the origin of disadvantage that may or may not emerge from disability. Thus, when one speaks of justice for people with disabilities or aims to promote principles that address injustice in the lives of the disabled, one does so with an aim at eliminating or minimizing disadvantage. If our goal within distributive justice discussions is to address disadvantage, then I suggest we acknowledge that disadvantage differs not only in degree but in kind as well (Riddle 2016, 31). More pointedly, while one might articulate a thorough and defensible objective list theory of the good (Parfit 1984, 493), and while all components of the good life might be required for a minimal conception of justice (Nussbaum 2000a, 167), this acknowledgment does not imply that we cannot and ought not prioritize some components of justice over others in an attempt to minimize disadvantage. In particular, the components of justice that are established prerequisites for other components of justice, or that are more foundational in nature, need to be prioritized.

In the context of the capabilities approach, an approach to justice I have endorsed elsewhere as the conception of justice most likely to promote well-being for people with disabilities, this observation implies that we ought to prioritize securing some capabilities over others.[1] Those capabilities that would result in disadvantage that is corrosive in nature if not secured—disadvantage that would adversely impact one's ability to secure other capabilities—ought to receive priority over the remaining capabilities that one would undoubtedly be disadvantaged to fail to hold, but where that disadvantage would not adversely impact other capabilities within one's set. I argue that, when one cannot secure other goods as a result of failing to secure something else of value, one suffers a disadvantage, and that that disadvantage is corrosive in kind. Most importantly, I have argued that not all goods or opportunities are the same—a failure to secure some goods results in *mere* disadvantage, while a failure to secure other goods results in corrosive disadvantage. More pointedly, one failure impacts other aspects of well-being, while another failure may only impact that aspect of well-being in isolation. I argue that *ceteris paribus*, when a failure to secure a capability would result in an individual suffering a corrosive disadvantage, priority ought to be given to assuring that capability over others.

I proceed to this end by dividing the argument into three sections. Section 1 highlights how attempts to define disability are rightly directed at identifying the source of disadvantage one might encounter as a result of being disabled. Section 2 suggests that as a result of this understanding of disability, distributive principles should be designed in a manner that address the disadvantages that matter most for purposes of justice. Finally, section 3 suggests that if our understanding of disability centers on the origin of disadvantage, and if the proper aim of a conception of justice is to address such disadvantage, then we ought to prioritize some components of justice over others.

Defining Disability Through Disadvantage

Definitions of disability have undergone significant transformation in the relatively short history of disability rights. Nonetheless, despite shifting definitions and contemporary debates surrounding how we should conceptualize disability, I suggest that the impetus for defining disability in whatever manner is chosen is a desire to best capture the experience of disadvantage, and that what differentiates these conceptions is where that disadvantage is said to reside.

Perhaps unsurprisingly, the first dominant view of disability emerged from medical professionals and the practice of medicine more generally. Disability was defined as a medical phenomenon—as a deviation from biomedical norms, attributed to trauma, disease, or any other variety of health-related concerns (Bickenbach et al. 1999, 1173; Bickenbach 1993, 12–15). The focus within a so-called medical model of disability was on functional limitations arising from the experience of disability. Disability was regarded as an individualistic consideration and was asocial in nature. In fact, I have previously highlighted how "this model is also sometimes referred to as an individual pathological model due to its focus on the inability of individuals" (Riddle 2013b, 378).

Under a medical model, one is disabled when an individual trait or impairment creates disadvantage in that individual's life. The means to address this disadvantage is, on this model, to treat it medically, or perhaps even to prevent it altogether through medical or technological means such as biomedical engineering or genetic screening. Nonetheless, the focus of medical professionals in understanding disability was on the way in which an individual's body deviated from biomedical norms, and thus created disadvantage for that individual. Any deviations from what was thought to be normal that were deemed to be minor and largely irrelevant to the well-being of a patient were deemed less important or not of immediate medical interest because those individuals were not *perceived* to be suffering from a disadvantage. The extent to which medical interventions were required or prioritized depended upon whether or not people could still function within a range of species-typical functioning, and minor deviations from this typical functioning were within an acceptable range of normal when little or no disadvantage was experienced.[2]

Conversely, proponents of a so-called "social model" of disability suggest that disability is not asocial or individualistic in nature. In fact, social model proponents advance a social pathological approach, suggesting that any ill-effects or disadvantage emerging from the experience of disability should be properly regarded as stemming from social (or attitudinal), geographical, political, or legal barriers (Riddle 2013c, 24).

The shift in thinking represented by the popularization of the social model of disability is rightly regarded as making a considerable improvement in the material lives of people with disabilities (Shakespeare 2006, 24). Propelling disability rights forward, the social model enabled people with disabilities to rightly blame society and ableist social attitudes for failing to offer an inclusive environment for the disabled. Despite such a significant shift in the conceptualizing of disability, disadvantage remained the proper target of concern for disability rights activists. In other words, the important conceptual change did not occur at the level of disadvantage, but rather, was the result of a reimagining of where that disadvantage resides. Disadvantage was still the problem, but by shifting the origin of that disadvantage, one was provided with the necessary push to begin to demand accommodations and changes in the structure of the environment people with disabilities found themselves attempting to navigate.

Still further refinements have been made to our understanding of disability. More recently, practitioners and theorists have suggested that disability is properly understood as a complex relationship between those traits inherent to an individual, and how those traits interact and manifest themselves in the environment (Shakespeare 2006, 24). A so-called interactional model of disability, largely modeling the World Health Organization's (2001) descriptive framework in the *International Classification of Functioning, Disability and Health*, suggests that "the experience [or disadvantage] of a disabled person results from the relationship between factors intrinsic to the individual, and the extrinsic factors arising from the wider context in which she finds herself" (Shakespeare 2006, 55).

In other words, interactional theorists have rejected a strict interpretation of a social model of disability, where *all* disadvantage is a result of social structures. Instead, they suggest that impairment is not necessarily a neutral condition—in fact, sometimes disadvantage can emerge from impairment. More often than not, however, the manner in which one's impairment interacts with its environment is the largest source of disadvantage for people with disabilities.

This push can chiefly be seen as one originating from the observation that for some people with disabilities, no amount of social accommodations can entirely remove disadvantage from their life. Instead, for some disabilities, despite accommodations and attitudinal adjustments, residual disadvantage could still remain.[3]

More recently, a shift has occurred to suggest that one is wrong to consider all disability as a bad difference. Instead, properly understood, disability does not always result in disadvantage, and it should be regarded as a mere-difference (Barnes 2016, 54–55). According to Elizabeth Barnes (2016, 55), "having a disability makes you physically nonstandard, but it doesn't (by itself or automatically) make you worse off."

Importantly, this "mere-difference" view of disability need not conclude that people with disabilities do not lose intrinsic goods or capabilities as a result of their disability (Barnes 2016, 56). Instead, the view claims that disability is "not intrinsically bad for you, or intrinsically something that makes you worse off" (Barnes 2016, 59). More specifically, the claim is that disability can often be composed of features that result in disadvantage or that are a bad-difference, but that something (disability) can be neutral, while having bad aspects or effects (Barnes 2016, 76).

Nonetheless, I contend that this is yet another instance of shifting the site of disadvantage, rather than an outright denial of the importance that disadvantage plays in relation to the experience of disability. Mere-difference views appear to be suggesting that disadvantage is present less often in disabled people than is typically attributed to the experience of disability. Minimizing the degree or frequency of disadvantage associated with disability does not undermine the suggestion that defining disability is about locating the origin of disadvantage that emerges as a result of such an experience. In other words, disability might become a matter of justice less often for mere-difference view proponents—disability might only be a matter of justice when it results in disadvantage.[4] But an understanding of disability nonetheless involves negotiating not only the origin of disadvantage but its extent and frequency.

JUSTICE, CAPABILITIES, AND DISADVANTAGE

I have maintained that disability matters for justice only when it results in disadvantage. But there are many types of disadvantage, and they do not matter equally. In order to understand the relevance of disability to justice, then, we must have a sense of the end of justice. For most contemporary theorists, that end is a basic equality among the members of a society, an equality threatened by certain types of disadvantage. Wolff and De-Shalit (2007, 10) suggest the relationship between equality and disadvantage in asserting that "a society of equals is a society [. . .] where there is no clear answer to the question of who is worst off."

Indeed, a society of equals is precisely the goal for most contemporary political theories. Will Kymlicka (2002, 4) picks up where Ronald Dworkin left off when he suggests, "[E]ach theory is attempting to define the social, economic, and political conditions under which the members of the community are treated as equals." Dworkin (1983, 25) suggests that the egalitarian thesis provides a plateau in political argument. This egalitarian plateau is the space that a whole host of contemporary political theories reside and it involves "a commitment to the idea that all members of the community should be treated as equals" (Kymlicka 2002, 377). All theories that share this goal are aiming, simply put, at articulating the proper currency of egalitarian justice.

John Rawls has been characterized as both the driving force to the egalitarian plateau as well as the prime candidate for a successful articulation of a currency capable of promoting justice and equality for all members of society. He is often considered to be largely responsible for the rejuvenation of interest in questions concerning distributive justice and egalitarian thought. The publication of his 1971 *A Theory of Justice*, is, I think, rightly viewed to be the starting point for all contemporary theorizing about justice. Indeed, one of the primary aims of *A Theory of Justice* was to push theorizing about justice away from consequentialist thought—a conception of justice far too reliant upon formal equality—toward a more robust understanding of the things owed equally to members of society (Rawls 1971, vii–viii). Rawls's (1971, 24) concern was that classical utilitarian theory was bound to under-value the importance of the distinction between persons. Instead, Rawls (1971, 54–117) suggests a contractarian model of justice focused on two principles of justice as fairness. The first focuses on liberty. Rawls (1971, 60) suggests that "each person is to have an equal right to the most extensive basic liberty compatible with a similar liberty for others." The second addresses matters of social and economic inequality. Rawls (1971, 60) argues that social and economic inequalities "are to be arranged so that they are both a) reasonably expected to be to everyone's advantage, and b) attached to positions and offices open to all."

However, Rawls was not without his critics. Foremost among them are those aiming to articulate a conception of justice for people with disabilities. Nussbaum (2006, 121) has suggested that Rawls's idealization of so-called "normal functioning" members of society was not merely a failure to articulate adequate principles of justice but that by asking people to imagine themselves as people with no needs for care or dependent relationships, much of what characterizes human life was, at best, ignored—and at worst, obliterated. Indeed, Nussbaum claims that the very distinction between persons Rawls aimed to defend was not being recognized in his own theory.

Eva Feder Kittay (1999, 88) shares Nussbaum's concern and thinks

> [Rawls'] idealization is seriously misleading…[Rawls puts] too much distance between the 'normal functioning individual' and the person with special needs and disabilities. Not a single citizen approaches the ideal of full functioning throughout a lifetime. The idealization, in contrast, suggests that those who are not fully functioning are relatively few, and that consequences of special needs is brokered only in monetary terms.

Because Rawls failed to articulate a conception of disability, it is no wonder that a Rawlsian conception of justice received somewhat hostile remarks from disability rights theorists for failing to include some aspects of the experience of disability.

Norman Daniels would explicitly take on Rawls's project and attempt to rescue a Rawlsian conception of justice from its critics by suggesting how it might be adapted with an eye on promoting health. Daniels (2008) prioritizes health and impairment within a conception of justice because according to him, adequate health and a life free from impairment are required for "normal functioning," or to function within what he calls a "normal opportunity range." In other words, health and the absence of impairment were required because of the opportunities one lacked due to ill health. Far from postponing the question of disability, as Rawls had done before him, Daniels tackles it head on but fails to adequately factor in the relationship between impairment and disability. In other words, despite an explicit effort to address disability and health, Daniels was also thought to have failed because of his over-reliance on a medicalized conception of disability.

Daniels (2008, 27) argues that the primary goal of health care was to promote normal functioning, and that, because normal functioning assured opportunity, we should regard health as having special moral importance. He suggests that Rawls's difference principle "significantly reduces allowable inequalities in income and wealth, and, more generally, in the index of primary social goods" (Daniels 2008, 96). Viewing health as being inseparable from other broader social justice issues, it is no wonder that he believed the difference principle was a suitable device to produce lesser disparity in health than we currently observe (Daniels 2008, 22–23). Nonetheless, his focus on the assuring of normal functioning smacks of a medicalized understanding of disability. Daniels views the experience of the disabled as being a deviation from a species-typical norm, and thought disability was a state of health to be addressed through medicine. Unsurprisingly, he also failed to account for the entire experience of disadvantage associated with disability.

Sen (1995) sets out to tackle this challenge by asking the simple question: equality of what? Sen eloquently addresses both utilitarian thought as well as resource-based conceptions of justice like Rawls's. Rawls proposes a set of primary goods, notably income and wealth, which would be valued across the diverse conceptions of the good pursued in a pluralistic society. Sen suggests that Rawls "tends to assume that primary goods in general are versatile enough to cater to the diverse human objectives that different persons may have" (Sen 2004a, 4) and that "there is evidence that the conversion of goods to capabilities varies from person to person substantially, and the equality of the former may still be far from the equality of the latter" (Sen 1995, 329). Sen (1995, 326) contends that Rawls's primary goods are guilty of being fetishistic insofar as they tend to take the value of goods to embody advantage or well-being, instead of understanding that it is the relationship between goods and individuals that produce advantage.[5] He contends that Rawls's emphasis is on "income rather than on what income does, on the 'social bases of self-respect' rather than on self-respect itself, and so on" (Sen 1995, 329). This view is somewhat reminiscent of Aristotle (1980, 7), who suggests, "[W]ealth is evidently not the good we are seeking; for it is...for the sake of something else."

To illustrate his claims, Sen asks us to consider the "cripple" with a utility disadvantage. Sen argues that Rawls's difference principle will give the disabled neither more nor less on grounds of being disabled. He argues that a utility disadvantage is irrelevant to the "difference principle," by which Rawls accords priority to the worst-off groups in society. (Sen 1995, 325).

Similarly, to address utilitarian based arguments, Sen (1973, 17) asks us to imagine two individuals, one of whom derives exactly twice as much utility as the other from any given resource or level of income. The argument unfolds by asserting that one individual's marginal utility is exactly twice that of the others, and should they be allotted the same income, this individual would derive twice as much utility from an additional dollar or resource. Subsequently, the egalitarian concern goes, the individual less capable of deriving benefits from resources (or the disabled or ill person), would be excluded from utilitarian distributive considerations by virtue of the fact that maximizing utility would call for the individual better able to benefit from the resources to receive them. Similarly to Rawlsian-based justice, this would understandably, compound, rather than rectify injustice.

As a result of these critiques, Sen proposed a new answer to his "equality of what?" question. He suggested that "the focus on basic capabilities can be seen as a natural extension of Rawls's concern with primary goods, shifting attention from goods to what goods do to human beings" (Sen 1995, 328–329). I concur and have argued previously that

> to treat *different* individuals *identically* with references to resources ignores the fact that different people have different costs associated with performing vital functions associated with a robust conception of justice. A focus solely on goods ignores the various conversation factors that impact what people are capable of becoming or doing.   (Riddle 2016, 48)

Instead, Sen suggests that disadvantage was best addressed through a focus on the various doings and beings a diverse set of individuals were able to accomplish, through what he called the capabilities approach. The capabilities approach provides a common understanding of disadvantage across cultures and people, as well as a means to compare and correct disadvantage (Vehmas and Watson 2014, 643). Indeed, the capabilities approach was first articulated by Sen as a means of measuring human development. For Sen, this approach consists of two primary components. First, "functionings" are things and/or activities that people have a choice between. In other words, functionings are various end-states or opportunities realized. Second, a "capability" is a set of functionings one has a choice between. If functionings can be viewed as various end-states, capabilities can be understood as the opportunities available to secure these outcomes. One's capability set, according to Sen, represents the freedom one has to choose between various alternative lives to lead. Perhaps naturally, a question arises concerning what various end-states or functionings are important as a matter of justice. Infamously, Sen (2004b, 77–80) has failed to articulate precisely what ought to be included within the capabilities approach to justice and instead has suggested that providing a list denies the relevance of the values people have come to hold and the value of democracy in arriving at these values.

Martha Nussbaum's version of the capabilities approach retains the core components of Sen's approach, while making an effort to articulate the capabilities to be assured (Nussbaum 2011) (Nussbaum 2006) (Nussbaum 2000a). For Nussbaum, properly understood, a capability is a freedom genuinely available to be pursued, and a functioning is a realized capability. Nussbaum (2006, 76–78) proposes the following ten central capabilities:

1. Life
2. Bodily Health
3. Bodily Integrity
4. Senses, Imagination, and Thought
5. Emotions
6. Practical Reason
7. Affiliation
8. Other Species
9. Play
10. Control over One's Environment

   a) Political
   b) Material

For a capability theorist, "[l]acking involuntarily any capability or central human functioning amounts to a disadvantage" (Nussbaum 2006, 644). A thorough articulation of the capabilities approach provides people with "the kind of measurement that should be used in comparing people's relative advantages and disadvantages" (Terzi 2005, 449).

The capabilities approach, at base, is a means of evaluating disadvantage that provides a more inclusive understanding of the origins and effects of disadvantage (Burchardt and Hick 2016, 25). Disadvantage, for the capability theorist, is viewed as a restriction in one's capability set—this notion includes resources as well as the goods or talents necessary to convert those resources into opportunities (Burchardt and Hick 2016, 31). Through an assessment of the capabilities set any given individual has securely available to them, one is able to take an inventory of disadvantage (Hopper 2007, 10). Importantly, the assessing of advantage or disadvantage associated with one's experiences is robust enough under such an approach to include both achieved well-being, as well as the freedom to achieve well-being (Robeyns 2017, 26).

The capabilities approach is thought to be more inclusive of the experience of disability because of its focus on actual opportunities for secure functionings. Sen and Nussbaum are concerned with not only the resources available at one's disposal but also with the various conversion factors that may influence one's ability to utilize those resources to reach valuable states of being. Through a recognition of the plurality of ways in which one might be limited in employing their available resources to reach a desired end, the capabilities approach assures that irrespective of the origins of disadvantage one might face—social or personal—that disadvantage ought not to limit the genuine opportunities one has available to pursue. More pointedly, unlike Rawlsian conceptions of justice, the capabilities approach is thought to be inclusive of the experience of disability. In other words still, the capabilities approach can be sensitive to both impairment as well as disabling social factors in the lives of people with disabilities. The capabilities approach, because of its focus on capabilities and functionings, moves beyond a medicalized understanding of disability to, instead, a more robust interpretation of the disabling factors in one's life. Understood properly, it finds itself necessarily in alignment with an interactional model of disability.

PRIORITY AND DISADVANTAGE

Nussbaum (2011, 98) states that "capabilities are seen not as isolated atoms but as a set of opportunities that interact and inform one another." She also stresses that "[i]t would be a grave error to single out any one of the ten to bear the weight of indexing relative social positions" (Nussbaum 2006, 84). Importantly for Nussbaum, despite the interconnectedness of capabilities, they are non-fungible.

However, any conception of justice aimed at assessing well-being and disadvantage must ask, at least minimally, what disadvantages exist in the lives of those living in unjust circumstances. A focus on disadvantage permits us to establish priority and sufficiency levels within our redistributive framework. I suggest that this goal flies in the face of Nussbaum's unwillingness to make comparative judgments about the disadvantages that result from a failure to secure the capabilities she articulates.

The first way in which an examination of disadvantage permits us to allocate resources within a conception of justice is to target those in greater need vis-à-vis interpersonal comparisons of well-being. With scarce resources often pulling our redistributive intuitions in opposing directions, it is important to be able to identify the least advantaged (or most disadvantaged). It may well be helpful or even necessary to be capable of approximating where members of society reside on a scale of relative advantage or disadvantage. Perhaps most importantly, it is of tremendous value to have the conceptual framework in place necessary to identify absolute disadvantage (Wolff and De-Shalit 2007, 21).

The second way in which a discussion of priority is important is in examining individual levels of disadvantage, irrespective of comparisons to others—intrapersonal considerations of well-being.[6] If disadvantage is best expressed by measuring one's capability set then it becomes important to ask what capabilities serve an instrumental purpose in securing other capabilities or valuable things.

As mentioned, Nussbaum (2000b, 138) herself concedes that "the capabilities are an interlocking set; they support one another, and an impediment to one impedes the other." Certainly some capabilities are more integral to securing her ten central capabilities than others however (Riddle 2015). In other words, some capabilities are in fact necessary for the enjoyment of other capabilities, while others may be an integral part of a conception of well-being because of their intrinsic worth, not because of their instrumental value.

Take, for example, the capability of "bodily health." As Daniels himself noted within a Rawlsian framework, health, properly understood, should be regarded as having special moral worth. Health, for Daniels, is best regarded as a condition or set of conditions that serve as building blocks for securing other valuable opportunities. In other words, a failure to live in reasonably good health, or in the absence of impairment or disabling barriers, results in disadvantage that is corrosive in kind—that adversely impacts one's ability to secure other valuable capabilities.

Within rights-based discourse, rights or freedoms of this nature are often referred to as *basic* in kind (Sangiovanni 2017, 235). I think Sangiovanni (2017, 246) is correct when she claims that we should understand a right as more or less fundamental (or important for the pursuit of well-being) "according to the degree to which its violation structurally undermines the pursuit of all or most of our interests, and most significantly, our interests in the most important goods."

Contrary to Nussbaum's assertions, Sen has echoed this sentiment through his claim that some capabilities should be regarded as more basic than others. He claims that "basic capabilities" are prerequisites for other, less basic capabilities (Sen 1993, 30–53).

While it may be the case that, as Nussbaum (2000a, 167) contends, capabilities are non-fungible—that "if people are below the threshold on any one of the capabilities, that is a failure of *basic justice*, no matter how high up they are on all the others"—by no means does that suggest we ought not prioritize those capabilities with a more basic, fundamental, or instrumental role in securing other capabilities. In other words, simply because all capabilities are needed for a minimal conception of justice, and simply because no amount of success in any one capability can make-up for a failure in another, it is not the case that, in order to minimize disadvantage, a distributional framework should not prioritize those capabilities more responsible for compounding disadvantage, or securing advantage.

Wolff and De-Shalit (2007, 10) have referred to capabilities that result in the insecurity of other capabilities as corrosive in nature. I suggest that while all injustices or failures to secure capabilities are disadvantageous, not all disadvantages are corrosive. The observation that sits at the heart of this distinction provides grounds to conclude that disadvantage differs not only in degree but also in kind. Thus, a minimal conception of justice is more likely to be promoted if foundational capabilities are secured to serve as intended—as the foundation for less basic capabilities to follow.

At the other end of the spectrum, the failure to secure a capability such as "other species" could result in disadvantage. But while it may be disadvantageous to lack adequate opportunities to interact with other species, that disadvantage is usually not corrosive in kind—it is disadvantageous with respect to the capability in question, but it does not usually reach into other capabilities and adversely impact one's ability to secure them to the same extent that poor health would. Of course, in particularly dire or unjust conditions, all the aspects of justice might be said to be capable of leading to corrosive disadvantage. Judgments of comparative disadvantage are predictive, however; they concern the probability of failing to secure any given capability (Riddle 2015). In this respect, a failure to secure a capability such as "other species" is far less likely to result in corrosive disadvantage than a failure to secure the capability of "health." It is less likely to adversely impact as many other capabilities as a failure to secure health, and less likely to adversely impact any one capability to the same extent as ill health.

To illustrate this claim, take the widely acknowledged parallel claim that "education, income, and a wide variety of other factors contribute to the overall bodily health of an individual. Certainly the connection between income and access to health care is an obvious example of how a whole host of factors contribute to health" (Riddle 2015, 113). In other words, the relationship between disability and other aspects of well-being is not unidirectional. Not only do social conditions influence health and disability, but health and disability affect social conditions. Like the World Health Organization, I suggest that health and the absence of disability is "a major resource for social, economic and personal development and an important dimension of quality of life" (World Health Organization, 1986).

Let us explore in greater detail the disadvantage that might emerge from the experience of disability by working through how a failure to secure the capability of "bodily health" might impact other capabilities. Perhaps obviously, some disabilities result in a decreased lifespan, thus impacting one's capability of "life." The lack of inclusive public transportation and buildings limits one's "bodily integrity" by restricting movement. Ableist conceptions of disability also often infantilize people with disabilities, leading to their being regarded as asexual; this further infringes their "bodily integrity" by limiting their opportunity for sexual satisfaction and meaningful romantic relationships. People with disabilities even face an affront to their securing of the capability of "senses, imagination, and thought" because of the often-inadequate forms of public education available for the disabled to receive basic education. Because of the unpredictability associated with living with a disability (Riddle 2010), people with disabilities can face difficulty in planning their lives and thus the capability of "practical reasoning" becomes insecure. Certainly, the stigmatization often associated with disability greatly impacts the capacity for the social basis of self-respect, which Nussbaum includes within her notion of the capability of "affiliation." Indeed, ableist conceptions of what it means to live with a disability restrict the opportunity of people with disabilities to engage in social interaction more generally. The often-covert, or even overt, forms of prejudice against people with disabilities in the workplace impact the ability to have "material control over one's environment." In short, if one lacks the capability of "bodily health," or if one experiences the disadvantage associated with living with a disability, that disadvantage is quite likely to be corrosive in nature.[7]

Of course, not all disabilities resemble health conditions, and not all disabilities result in corrosive disadvantage in the manner outlined above. Certainly, like able-bodied people, people with disabilities experience the world in a multitude of ways, resulting from complex interactions with people, places, and time (Riddle 2010). Nonetheless, I take the capabilities approach to offer a particularly vivid insight into the often-corrosive disadvantage introduced into the lives of people with disabilities as a result of both impairment and social oppression. Because Nussbaum departs from Sen's schematic presentation of the capabilities approach and enumerates the capabilities required by justice, the problem of corrosive disadvantage, the importance of good health, and the absence of disabling barriers have become more obvious.

Thus, bodily health and the absence of disabling barriers need to feature centrally within the capabilities approach because of the high likelihood that the failure to secure them will result in corrosive disadvantage. Other capabilities such as "other species," while important in their own right, would usually not result in such widespread, corrosive disadvantage. Properly conceived, I suggest that "bodily health" is a capability that ought to be prioritized as a matter of justice. Minimally, if interpreted broadly to include the experience of disability, "bodily health" should be seen as a paradigmatic example of a capability that ought to be prioritized because of the corrosive disadvantage introduced into the lives of those who fail to secure it. While the argument in this section has not yielded an exhaustive ordering or prioritizing of capabilities, I hope it has made a cogent general case for the need to prioritize some capabilities over others. I also hope that it has become clear that "bodily health" should be seen as an example of a capability requiring prioritization under this scheme.

While Nussbaum fails to acknowledge the need to prioritize some capabilities over others, this failing is hers alone and ought not to be attributed to the capabilities approach. As mentioned, Sen appears to be willing to concede that some capabilities are more fundamental than others through his recognition of more basic capabilities. The capabilities approach is best suited to address the disadvantage emerging from the experience of disability because of how it is situated to acknowledge all sources of disadvantage, whether they are social or personal. Moreover, notwithstanding Nussbaum's steadfast unwillingness to prioritize some capabilities over others, the capabilities approach has the ability to allow for the democratic prioritization of capabilities on the basis of the disadvantage emerging from a failure to secure them.

Those seeking to promote justice for people with disabilities ought to find this emphasis on corrosive disadvantage helpful, because unaddressed disabling barriers often result in disadvantage that not only exacerbate one's impairment, but more importantly, result in the experiencing of disadvantage in many other facets of one's life. Disability ought to be a priority within distributive justice discourse precisely because of how the disabling effects of society compound injustice against people living with impairments in multiple realms of life.

CONCLUSION

Because disability is understood in terms of the degree and source of disadvantage associated with particular bodily conditions, and because a primary function of justice and the capabilities approach is to address unjust disadvantage, it would compel those attempting to promote justice for people with disabilities to acknowledge that disadvantage differs in kind and not merely in degree. As such, even if we concede that all capabilities (however they are specified) are essential for a minimal conception of justice, priority ought to be given to those capabilities that serve a foundational role for securing the remainder of the capabilities.

A focus on priority is important in this context for at least two reasons. First, by prioritizing those capabilities whose failure to be secured would result in corrosive disadvantage, one increases the efficiency of corresponding efforts to promote justice. Without foundational capabilities secured, one expends valuable resources shoring up insecure capabilities that are only bound to become insecure yet again in the future. With basic capabilities secured, one can move forward with a foundation from which to promote all remaining capabilities.

Second, injustices are bound to be rectified more effectively if basic capabilities are promoted. Because the impact of basic capabilities on well-being is greater, injustices are more likely to be rectified sooner rather than later when priority is placed on their security.

Recognizing different kinds of disadvantage provides us not only with a means to understand the experience of disability and its relationship to broader environmental, legal, and attitudinal barriers but also with the normative framework to conceptualize a notion of justice designed to promote equality and to minimize injustices in the lives of people with disabilities.

NOTES

1. For more on this see Riddle (2010, 2011, 2012, 2013, 2014, 2015, 2016).
2. I borrow this phrase from Norman Daniels. For more on this see Daniels (1985, 1999,m 2001, 2008).
3. A wonderful example of this (albeit originally presented in a different context) can be found in Cohen (1989, 919).
4. This is a view I hold, albeit for different reasons than Barnes, in Riddle (2018).
5. Another example of this can be seen in Robeyns (2005, 99).

6. I explore this more thoroughly in Riddle (2010).

7. Of course, it is also possible that the presence of a disability might serve to enhance some other capabilities as well. While others, like Barnes (2016), have suggested this, the fertility of particular capabilities or states of being require further examination and thus will not be explored in adequate depth here.

References

Aristotle. 1980. *Nicomachean Ethics*. Translated by D. Ross. Oxford: Oxford University Press.

Barnes, Elizabeth. 2016. *The Minority Body: A Theory of Disability*. Oxford: Oxford University Press.

Bickenbach, Jerome. 1993. *Physical Disability and Social Policy*. Toronto: University of Toronto Press.

Bickenbach, Jerome, Somnath Chatterji, E. M. Badley, and T. B. Ustun. 1999. "Models of Disablement, Universalism, and the International Classification of Impairments, Disabilities and Handicaps." *Social Science and Medicine* 48 no. 1 (1999): 1173–1187.

Burchardt, Tania, and Rod Hick. 2016. "The Capability Approach to Advantage and Disadvantage." In *Social Advantage and Disadvantage*, edited by Hartley Dean and Lucinda Platt, 25–41. Oxford: Oxford University Press.

Chapireau, F., and A. Colvez. 1998. "Social Disadvantage in the International Classification of Impairments, Disabilities, and Handicap." *Social Science and Medicine* 47, no. 1 (1998): 59–66.

Cohen, G. A. 1989. "On the Currency of Egalitarian Justice." *Ethics* 99, no. 4: 906–944.

Daniels, Norman. 1985. *Just Health Care*. New York: Cambridge University Press.

Daniels, Norman. 1999. *Justice and Justification: Reflective Equilibrium in Theory and Practice*. New York: Cambridge University Press.

Daniels, Norman. 2001. "Justice, Health, and Health Care." *American Journal of Bioethics* 1, no. 2: 2–16.

Daniels, Norman. 2008. *Just Health: Meeting Health Needs Fairly*. New York: Cambridge University Press.

Dworkin, Ronald. 1983. "Comment on Narveson: In Defense of Equality." *Social Philosophy & Policy* 1, no. 1: 24–40.

Hopper, Kim. 2007. "Rethinking Social Recovery in Schizophrenia: What A Capabilities Approach Might Offer." *Social Science and Medicine* 65, no. 5: 868–879.

Kittay, Eva Feder. 1999. *Love's Labor: Essays on Women, Equality, and Dependency*. New York: Routledge.

Kymlicka, Will. 2002. *Contemporary Political Philosophy: An Introduction*. Oxford: Oxford University Press.

Nussbaum, Martha. 2000a. *Women and Human Development*. Cambridge, UK: Cambridge University Press.

Nussbaum, Martha. 2000b. "Aristotle, Politics, and Human Capabilities: A Response to Antony, Arneson, Charleswoth, and Mulgan." *Ethics* 111, no. 1: 102–140.

Nussbaum, Martha. 2006. *Frontiers of Justice: Disability, Nationality, Species Membership*. Cambridge, MA: The Belknap Press of Harvard University Press.

Nussbaum, Martha. 2011. *Creating Capabilities: The Human Development Approach*. Cambridge, MA: The Belknap Press of Harvard University Press.

Parfit, Derek. 1984. *Reasons and Persons*. Oxford: Oxford University Press.

Rawls, John. 1971. *A Theory of Justice*. Cambridge, MA: Harvard University Press.

Riddle, Christopher A. 2010. "Indexing, Capabilities, and Disability." *The Journal of Social Philosophy* 41, no. 4: 527–537.

Riddle, Christopher A. 2011. "Responsibility and Foundational Material Conditions." *The American Journal of Bioethics* 11, no. 7: 53–55.

Riddle, Christopher A. 2012. "Measuring Capabilities: The Case of Disability." In *The Capability Approach on Social Order*, edited by Niels Weidtmann, Yanti Martina Hölzchen, and Bilal Hawa, 49–62. Munster: LIT Verlag.

Riddle, Christopher A. 2013a. "Natural Diversity and Justice for People with Disabilities." In *Disability and the Good Human Life*, edited by Jerome Bickenbach, Franziska Felder, and Barbara Schmitz, 271–299. Cambridge. UK: Cambridge University Press.

Riddle, Christopher A. 2013b. "Defining Disability; Metaphysical Not Political." *Medicine, Health Care, and Philosophy* 16, no. 3: 377–384.

Riddle, Christopher A. 2013c. "The Ontology of Impairment: Rethinking How We Define Disability." In *Emerging Perspectives on Disability Studies*, edited by Matthew Wappett and Katrina Arndt, 23–39. New York: Palgrave Macmillan.

Riddle, Christopher A. 2014. *Disability and Justice: The Capabilities Approach in Practice*. Lexington: Lexington Books.

Riddle, Christopher A. 2015. "Ranking Capabilities." In *Discussing Capabilities, Emotions and Values: A Cross-Cultural Perspective*, edited by Koji Nakatogawa, Lydia de Tienda, Yousuke Mitsuke, and Yohei Fukayama, 111–118. Sapporo, Japan: Keyword.

Riddle, Christopher A. 2016. *Human Rights, Disability, and Capabilities*. New York: Palgrave Macmillan.

Riddle, Christopher A. 2018. "What We Owe: Disability & Non-Talent." In *From Disability Theory to Practice: Essays in Honor of Jerome E. Bickenbach*, edited by Christopher A. Riddle, 41–49. Lanham, MD: Rowman & Littlefield.

Robeyns, Ingrid. 2005. "The Capability Approach: A Theoretical Survey." *Journal of Human Development* 6, no: 1: 93–117.

Robeyns, Ingrid. 2006. "The Capability Approach in Practice." *The Journal of Political Philosophy* 14, no. 3: 351–376.

Robeyns, Ingrid. 2017. *Wellbeing, Freedom, and Social Justice: The Capability Approach Re-Examined*. Cambridge, UK: Open Book Publishers.

Sangiovanni, Andrea. 2017. *Humanity Without Dignity: Moral Equality, Respect, and Human Rights*. Cambridge, MA: Harvard University Press.

Sen, Amartya. 1973. *On Economic Inequality*. New York: Oxford University Press.

Sen, Amartya. 1993. "Capability and Well-Being." In *The Quality of Life*, edited by Martha Nussbaum and Amartya Sen, 30–53. Oxford: Oxford University Press.

Sen, Amartya. 1995. "Equality of What?" In *Equal Freedom: Selected Tanner Lectures on Human Values*, edited by S. Darwall, 307–330. Ann Arbor: University of Michigan Press.

Sen, Amartya. 2004a. "Disability and Justice." Paper presented at the International Disability Conference, Washington, DC, United States, November 30–December 1.

Sen, Amartya. 2004b. "Capabilities, Lists, and Public Reason: Continuing the Conversation." *Feminist Economics* 10, no. 3: 77–80.

Shakespeare, Tom. 2006. *Disability Rights and Wrongs*. New York: Routledge, 2006.

Terzi, Lorella. 2005. "Beyond the Dilemma of Difference: The Capability Approach to Disability and Special Educational Needs." *Journal of Philosophy of Education* 39, no. 3 (2005): 443–459.

Vehmas, Simo, and Nick Watson. 2014. "Moral Wrongs, Disadvantages, and Disability: A Critique of Disability Studies." *Disability and Society* 29, no. 4 (2014): 638–650.

Wolff, Jonathan, and Avner De-Shalit. 2007. *Disadvantage.* Oxford: Oxford University Press.

World Health Organization. 1986. *The Ottawa Charter for Health Promotion.* Geneva: World Health Organization.

World Health Organization. 2001. *International Classification of Functioning, Disability and Health.* Geneva: World Health Organization.

World Health Organization. 2011. *World Report on Disability.* Geneva: World Health Organization.

CHAPTER 14

....

DISABILITY AND PARTIAL COMPLIANCE THEORY

....

LESLIE FRANCIS

MUCH recent discussion in theorizing about justice attends to distinctions between ideal and non-ideal or partial compliance circumstances. These distinctions take many forms but can be put very roughly as whether the requirements of justice are different in circumstances of injustice than in circumstances where justice reigns, at least to a significant extent. Non-ideal theory answers questions such as these: Should social progress in addressing structural injustice be measured by the standards of an ideally just society? Or, should progress be assessed by improvements in inclusion in existing circumstances, or assessed in some other way? Do the obligations of individuals to act justly depend on the context in which they are acting, including the extent to which others are doing their part as justice requires?

Disability has been largely left aside in these discussions, which have primarily addressed structural injustice and poverty, racism and sexism, or widespread failures to act justly. Yet the failure to achieve disability civil rights across the globe suggests that disability raises partial compliance considerations at least as significant as these other forms of injustice such as racism or sexism. This chapter considers partial compliance theory from the perspective of achieving disability civil rights. I begin with a brief account of the non-ideal and partial compliance landscape. I then disavow the misleading assumption that the existence of disability might itself be non-ideal. I conclude with some thoughts about why disability has largely been left aside in partial compliance theory and how understanding disability civil rights can contribute importantly to our understanding of justice in non-ideal circumstances.

Non-Ideal or Partial Compliance?

The modern origins of the distinction between non-ideal and ideal theorizing about justice can be traced to John Rawls's *A Theory of Justice* (1971), which explicitly developed an account of justice under idealizing assumptions. To develop his theory of justice, Rawls famously postponed questions about what justice might look like under less than fully favorable conditions. Instead, Rawls began with a thought experiment designed to model assumptions of liberalism under idealizing conditions. The starting point of Rawlsian liberalism was to eschew dependence on an overarching comprehensive conception of the good and to assume that individuals might have very different conceptions of their own good. The thought experiment then asked what such individuals would choose as fundamental principles to govern distribution of the benefits and burdens of their social cooperation. Individuals participating in the thought experiment were themselves assumed to be fully cooperating citizens able to share in the production of the benefits and burdens of social cooperation (Stark 2007). They were placed in the circumstances of justice, including moderate scarcity sufficient to pose questions of distribution but not so great as to undermine the possibility of cooperation. They were assumed to want to flourish according to their own conception of the good, but not to know anything about themselves or their conceptions of the good that would allow them to tailor choices to their own advantage. And they were assumed to be choosing principles of justice for an ideal kind of society that exists under favorable conditions and that is fully governed by whatever principles of justice they choose. According to the Rawlsian thought experiment, principles of ideal justice then reflect the choice of such rational, impartial citizens.

Asked to choose the fundamental principles of justice to govern their lives together, Rawls thought, these hypothetical choosers would begin by protecting the worst off among them, requiring social structures to be arranged to work to the advantage of the least well-off representative social position among them. They would also recognize the importance of certain fundamental liberties for anyone, regardless of the conception of the good they hold. The result, Rawls contended, would be two basic principles: a principle of equal basic liberty and a principle requiring fair equality of opportunity and requiring inequalities to be arranged to benefit the worst off. These principles would be lexically ordered, with equal basic liberty taking priority. These principles would set out the basic framework of justice within which choosers could then fashion constitutions, legislation, and their application to the circumstances of their own societies. Ideal justice in the form of these two basic principles constrains all of these more specific institutional choices. For my purposes here, some of these choices would involve providing for the needs of those who are not capable of participating in the production of social goods, including people with severe intellectual disabilities.

Publication of *A Theory of Justice* in 1971 spawned extensive discussion and criticism of the thought experiment. One concern was the possibility that people with conceptions of the good inconsistent with liberalism would not find the reasoning justifiable to them, with instability a likely result. Objections in this vein led Rawls to limit the claims of his theory to the claims of *Political Liberalism*—that is, to provide an account of justice in the terms of liberal theory. For my purposes here, two additional lines of criticism of the Rawlsian thought experiment are more telling than the criticism that led Rawls to limit his claims to liberalism. First, the Rawlsian experiment marginalizes people with disabilities. Second, the experiment represents an idealization that misfires for the worlds in which people actually live.

Regarding the first criticism, disability theorists have objected to conceptualizing justice as a choice of principles by rational, impartial cooperators. Core to this objection is how people with disabilities, especially those with intellectual disabilities, are placed outside of the scope of the initial thought experiment because they are seen as incapable of participating in reciprocal arrangements for the production of goods. Martha Nussbaum (2006), for example, argued that the Rawlsian framework placed people with disabilities beyond the frontiers of justice, along with people from other nations and members of non-human species. More generally, disability theorists have been concerned that social contract theories modelled on bargaining cannot function for persons with disabilities (Hartley 2011, Silvers and Francis 2005). Nor can contractualist views such as Rawls's that consider justice as establishing the terms for fair cooperation among persons understood as free and equal (Hartley 2011).

Several responses have been offered to this objection that the Rawlsian thought experiment marginalizes disability. One response is that representatives or trustees should stand in for the interests of people who cannot speak for themselves. A threshold problem with this representational approach is that trustees may have built-in conflicts of interest, if they are to speak both as full cooperators and as representatives for the interests of those who cannot cooperate. Trusteeship, moreover, continues to see persons with disabilities as dependent rather than modelling them as full participators along the lines of the full legal personhood envisioned by the Convention on Rights of Persons with Disabilities (CRPD) (United Nations 2006). Trusteeship thus does not challenge the initial exclusion of persons with disabilities from the thought experiment model of justice as fair cooperation among free and equal persons.

Another response to the contention that the Rawlsian thought experiment marginalizes disability is to model the development of justice on interactions that do not involve bargaining, such as the development of relations of trust or inclusion (Silvers and Francis 2005). However, if conceived of as ideal theory, such other models may seem unable to yield conclusions about justice (Hartley 2011). In what follows, I take on this objection more directly, by describing how disability inclusive justice might function within non-ideal rather than ideal theory.

The second objection of concern here is that the Rawlsian thought experiment rests in the realm of ideal theory. Much recent discussion in political philosophy has attended to the possibility that Rawlsian ideal theory neither can nor should be applied to the real world of serious injustice. Rawlsian ideal theory postulated two assumptions: a compliance assumption and a favorable circumstances assumption.

The compliance assumption hypothesized that sufficient numbers of relevant agents comply with demands of justice. The favorable circumstances assumption postulated that natural and historical conditions are favorable to the realization of justice. The significance of each of these assumptions has come under scrutiny.

In a very helpful conceptual map of the non-ideal theory terrain (interestingly but not surprisingly, one that does not mention disability), Laura Valentini (2012) distinguishes three areas of theorizing that depart from the ideal: obligations of some when significant numbers of others are failing to fulfill their obligations, the extent to which feasibility of realization should constrain normative political philosophy, and requirements of justice in transitioning from the non-ideal to the ideal. The role of ideal justice in theorizing in each of these areas is controversial. Should individuals do what ideal justice would require them to do, even when others are not fulfilling their obligations under ideal justice? Should we continue to be guided by what is ideally just even when its feasibility is in question? Should our actions in non-ideal contexts aim toward ideal justice, should different moral considerations come into play, or should we somehow be trying to work between the ideal and the non-ideal? Some believe that ideal justice is relevant to answering questions about what to do in an imperfectly just world. Others believe that theorizing about justice in non-ideal contexts is simply different from theorizing in ideal contexts and should not be guided by images of ideal justice (e.g., Wolff 2017, Sen 2009).

DIFFERENCE OR BAD-DIFFERENCE?

An initial question about disability and non-ideal theory is whether disability itself is part of what might make circumstances non-ideal. If so, the very presence of disability would open the question of the relevance of ideal theories of justice. Rawls included some natural disadvantages in the stipulation that a context is non-ideal. Such natural disadvantages indicate failure of the favorable circumstances assumption. For example, persistent drought that significantly and unalterably limited food supplies in ways that affected some populations more than others would make circumstances non-ideal. So would high rates of naturally occurring diseases that significantly shortened life spans in a population or significantly narrowed functional capabilities of significant numbers of people to enjoy good lives.

Rawlsian ideal justice asks what justice would require under favorable circumstances, setting aside whether these idealized conclusions about justice would also dictate the requirements of justice under less favorable conditions. On this view, a society in which far greater numbers of people had significant disabilities might be judged non-ideal in comparison to a society in which far fewer people had disabilities. If ideal justice provides guidance for non-ideal circumstances, creating conditions in which disability did not occur would presumably be progress toward ideal justice, assuming this could be accomplished in ways that were otherwise morally acceptable. So, perhaps along these lines, Savulescu (2001) and others have argued that parents have duties to create the best children, or at least to avoid creating children with disabilities to the extent possible. On this view, practices such as selective abortion for certain kinds of disability or the use of in vitro fertilization to avoid conception of children with certain kinds of disabilities could represent progress toward justice. On other views, however, reducing disability in these ways might not represent progress towards ideal justice—or, indeed, might represent the reverse.

Analyzing the plausibility and implications of claims that policies aimed at reducing disability are justice-improving requires further discussion of what "disability" is, whether it is bad, and if so, what might be bad about it. On views such as Savulescu's (2001), disability is bad for the person who is disabled, but on other views the disadvantages of disability are located primarily in social conditions. On the first view, primary strategies for achieving justice might focus on the availability of opportunities for changing persons, or for adjusting the characteristics of persons who come into being, whereas on the second view, attention would primarily be devoted to how society is responding to persons with disabilities.

A long-standing distinction in disability studies lies between "the social model" and "the medical model" of disability (e.g., Shakespeare 2010). I have put these two terms in quotation marks because although they are usually referred to in this way, the terms mark out several different sets of distinctions. One set of distinctions is political, about how disabilities ought to be addressed as a matter of justice. Such political versions of the social model began with the observation that disability—the inability to do something—could and should be addressed by changes in the built or social world. By contrast, medical model approaches address disability through medical treatment or cure. On this political version of the medical model, the primary strategy for addressing disability should be interventions designed to alter the bodies or minds of people with disabilities: curing diseases, straightening crooked spines through surgery, or achieving some measure of auditory comprehension through cochlear implants.

A related but separate set of distinctions attends whether disabilities are socially or naturally caused. The causal origins of many disabilities rest largely in problematic social circumstances such as unsafe working conditions, water or air pollution, or toxic exposures. The origins of many others might be regarded as at least partially natural: deleterious genetic variations, novel infectious diseases, or processes of aging. Even these may be socially caused, however, as when toxic exposures are mutagenic or when infectious diseases become emergent due to human incursions into the landscape.

Whether causes of disability are relevant to how they should be addressed as matters of justice poses still further sets of questions about the extent to which justice is purely or primarily a matter of reforming social conditions. Some hold, for example, that social causes of disability should be addressed as matters of justice but that correcting naturally occurring circumstances is not a requirement of justice. Holders of this distinction between the social and the natural might, for example, argue that the United States has obligations to provide aid to those who are disabled by exposures to toxic waste left by extractive mining conducted by US industries but not to those whose disabilities are caused by mercury exposures subsequent to volcanic discharge of mercury into local fisheries. On this view, there might also be social obligations to intervene when lead exposures cause intellectual disabilities, but not when genetic differences cause similar disabilities. Put in more specific policy terms, an employer might be obligated to reduce lead exposure risks for employees but not to offer pre-implantation genetic testing and in vitro fertilization as part of employee health benefits. These causal claims are frequently transformed into conceptual claims, such as that disability just is social or medical. To the extent that these positions link disability politically, causally, or conceptually, to injustice, then presence of widespread disability, rather than simply impairment, would indicate or entail that circumstances are non-ideal by failing to satisfy the compliance condition.

More recent controversy attends whether disability is a "bad-difference" or a "mere-difference." On the view recently defended by Elizabeth Barnes (2016), physical disability is mere-difference of a kind that disability advocates seek justice for. On this view, arguably disability is non-ideal even though it is not bad-difference, because the presence of disability reveals injustice. Justice needs to be sought for people with disabilities and thus the continuing presence of widespread disability would be unjust.

Although Barnes holds that disability is not globally "bad," she also holds that "local bads" may be associated with disability. For example, certain disabilities may cause pain; others may involve atypical bodily functions that are damaging and that could be mitigated by medical intervention; and others may be associated with a wide variety of inconveniences many of which can be attributed to social practices and the built world. The ways in which a society addresses these local bads may also be non-ideal: people might be unable to access desired medical care, be forced or tricked to undergo medical care against their will, find their medical conditions created or aggravated by social conditions such as inadequate heat in their housing, or be refused reasonable accommodations for their disabilities. Thus even if disability is not globally bad, its presence may indicate non-ideal social circumstances that give rise to local bads. These circumstances may reveal multiple failures of the compliance assumption, such as healthcare systems not providing people with certain disabilities meaningful access to care, states refusing to pay Medicaid providers at rates sufficient to allow delivery of adequate services, landlords not complying with the requirements of the Fair Housing Act, employers refusing accommodations for people with disabilities, or restaurants failing to install accessible restrooms.

On views such as these just described, according to which any local or global bads associated with disability are social rather than individual, what is non-ideal about disability, as a matter of justice, is social. Differences—either physical or mental—are not non-ideal from the perspective of justice; what society makes of them, however, is non-ideal if it transforms difference into disability. The presence of relevant social bads indicates non-ideal circumstances, but the presence of differences among people does not. To be sure, if there were a radical change in human capacities—for example, if no one had language—justice would not be possible (Putnam 2000). But the presence of the range of human variation in bodies and minds by itself does not indicate the presence of significant injustice; injustice lies only in how the built and social world responds to these differences. This conclusion has significant implications for claims about issues such as so-called procreative beneficence, discussed in the section on eugenics below.

Non-Compliance

Failures to meet the requirements of justice—non-compliance—may be individual, structural, or (quite likely) both. For example, in the United States racial injustice is both individual and structural. Despite the Fair Housing Act, evidence continues that landlords continue to discriminate on the basis of race and religion. Evidence is also clear that practices such as interest rates, mortgage lending, and banking regulations have affected the ability of people of color to purchase homes and develop equity in them (Rothstein 2017). Disability, too, experiences both individual and structural injustice; these phenomena combine as significant explanations of the low employment and high poverty rates of people with disabilities in early twenty-first-century United States.

One important set of partial compliance questions attends the obligations of individuals to behave justly when many others are not doing their part to fulfill their obligations of justice. It may seem unfair to expect compliers to continue to behave justly, in the face of widespread bad behavior by others. Are they just "off the hook," too? Or, are they obligated to do what they would have been obligated to do in more ideal circumstances, or even obligated to try to make up for the failures of others? We might hold that obligations for full compliance continue to hold under imperfect compliance, whatever others are doing. Or, we might take a consequentialist view that these obligations continue only when the goals they further can be achieved at least to some limited extent. Otherwise, critics might ask, what is the point of fulfilling ideal obligations, if nothing can be achieved by doing so? Or, we might relieve people of ideal obligations on grounds of fairness, reasoning that people should not be expected to bear the burdens of obligations when others are not doing so. We might also hold that if the reasons underpinning the obligations are sufficiently strong, they justify expecting more of those who are willing to comply—at least up to limits that might be specified by fairness or in some other way.

With respect to disability, circumstances of non-compliance pose all of these questions about obligations. Take the Americans with Disabilities Act (ADA) obligation of non-discrimination in employment.[1] Employers are required to make reasonable accommodations for applicants or workers with disabilities who can perform essential job functions with or without these accommodations. A frequent concern expressed on behalf of employers is that they might be unreasonably disadvantaged by the costs of these accommodations. An undue hardship defense is available to employers, based on the costs of the accommodation and the employer's overall size, resources, structure, and type of business. This defense is especially likely to prevail when accommodations would impose burdens on other workers or raise questions about safety. High costs alone will not suffice, as Johns Hopkins found out when they contended that the costs of accommodating a nurse's need for ASL interpretation was too great in light of the unit's budget.[2] Although I have tried, I have been unable to find legal cases ruling on whether competitive disadvantage could ever be considered an undue hardship in light of the employer's type of operation. Such disadvantage might be claimed by employers who incur costs of non-discrimination when other employers are avoiding these costs through non-compliance.

In reply to concerns about accommodation costs, disability advocates have pointed out that they are often overestimated and based on stereotypes rather than evidence. What data there are suggest that accommodation costs are typically minor and may be offset by benefits such as increased productivity or lower worker turnover (JAN 2018; Hendricks, Batiste, and Hirsh 2005). Accommodation costs are somewhat greater for workers using personal assistance services (Solovieva et al. 2009) or some communication aids such as sign interpretation with skilled interpreters. Overall, evidence about the costs of these forms of disability accommodation remains limited (Padkapayeva et al. 2016), as does evidence about whether they create competitive disadvantages. In any event, these questions of competitive economic disadvantage in the marketplace are beside the point when accommodation costs are borne by public agencies, as they are in public education, public higher education, or public services such as Medicaid or Medicare.

In addition to fairness to compliers, another concern is whether compliance is required when it will fail to achieve its goals, at least to some significant extent, because of the non-compliance of many people. Where compliance requires non-discrimination, arguably it is still better for some not to discriminate even when others are discriminating. Suppose that disability bias is widespread and discrimination rampant. Individual acts of non-discrimination will avoid at least the harms associated with those discriminatory acts, even if they will not change the behavior of others. To be sure, they may not change the structural conditions that further disability discrimination, but it seems unlikely that they will make these conditions worse. Moreover, non-discrimination by some might contribute to the amelioration of circumstances that are generating non-compliance by others, either by providing examples or by enabling increasingly effective advocacy.

Consider employment. Employers who hire in a non-discriminatory way will not directly change problematic structural features of the economy under which employment takes place, such as failures to provide health insurance or paid family leave. But employment of people with disabilities might demonstrate the feasibility and even the advantages of hiring in a non-discriminatory way. It may also further the careers of people with disabilities who can then advocate for disability rights and contribute to achieving non-discrimination in other ways as well. The career in philosophy of the late Anita Silvers illustrates: she was able to become employed in philosophy because at the time San Francisco State University did not conduct in- person interviews and thus was unaware of her disability from polio. She became not only a well-known scholar in philosophy and bioethics but also a tireless advocate for disability rights in California higher education, in academia, and in healthcare. Or consider access to public accommodations. Investments in accessibility such as well-designed ramps or restrooms might demonstrate how people with disabilities can enjoy life with others out in the community.

In sum, that some are failing to meet obligations of non-discrimination with respect to disability arguably does not support the conclusion that others should be let off with respect to these obligations. Costs of compliance have been exaggerated. As under the ADA, employer claims of undue hardship should compare the costs of compliance to the employer's overall resources. Even if many other employers are failing to meet their obligations, it still enhances opportunities for people with disabilities if some employers continue to comply.

But what about the further possibility that when some are failing to comply, others must do more to take up the slack? Non-discrimination obligations as understood in the ADA do not extend to creating opportunities that would not otherwise have existed: for example, new jobs for those who cannot work at existing ones, different educational programs, or new services. What non-discrimination requires is reasonable accommodations that permit people who are otherwise qualified to function in existing jobs, succeed in existing programs, or access existing services in a meaningful way. Achieving such non-discrimination may require both accommodations designed to address individual differences and program modifications that augment access without fundamentally altering the program that is offered. These are not new obligations; they are obligations that already exist. Whether society should take steps to ensure more, bearing the costs socially, is a separate question I will return to at the end of this chapter.

The presence of structural injustice poses still further problems for people who are trying to do what is just under circumstances of injustice. Consider the situation of an employer who really wants to create opportunities for people with disabilities but who encounters structural barriers to her good intentions. Perhaps few disabled workers with the relevant skills are available in the local job market because the local schools have not been accessible. Or perhaps there is no accessible public transit that disabled workers can use to get to work. Remedying such forms of structural injustice is beyond what individual employers can be expected to achieve. However, in the next section, I consider why infeasibility claims should not be accepted too readily.

INFEASIBILITY

The second area of non-ideal theory delineated by Valentini is the extent to which feasibility constraints apply to normative political philosophy. In this domain, disability questions arise about whether it is feasible to modify the built or the social world to include people with disabilities. Southwood (2018) usefully distinguishes among several different feasibility questions, two of which are relevant for my purposes here: those involving costs and those involving probabilities of success.

Many objections to disability inclusion are cost-based. In the United States, for example, states contend that they cannot provide home care services or maintenance physical therapy for everyone who could benefit because widespread use of these services would be too expensive. Southwood contends that these claims involve normative choices about resource allocation rather than treating feasibility per se as a precondition for acceptable choices. Decisions about home care services for people with disabilities illustrate. Pennsylvania, for example, decided to provide home-based attendant care to people with physical disabilities who were also mentally alert, but not to provide such services for people with significant intellectual disabilities.[3] It justified this distinction in terms of what it claimed was the goal of the program to enable individuals to live independently and exercise control over their own lives, a goal that the state supposed could not be achieved for people with intellectual disabilities. Disability rights advocates brought two quite different objections to the state's claims. One objection was that the independent living justification was not the state's real reason but was a pretext put forth to justify the state's concerns about the costs if the program were extended to a far wider range of recipients. The other objection was to the state's asserted feasibility claim: that goals of independent living and self-direction could indeed be achieved through the use of supported or surrogate decision making with people with disabilities. If the goal of independence cannot be achieved, however, then the question is whether the state should be required to undertake a new program—for example, one with the goal of allowing people to live at home rather than in institutions. Whether to require the state to change its goals is not a feasibility question, but a question of what programs, beyond non-discrimination in existing programs, are required of a public entity in a given set of non-ideal circumstances. Southworth seems correct that costs and infeasibility should be distinguished, but they often are conflated in claims about disability policy where further normative choices are at stake.

Accounts of feasibility may also be based on claims about the likelihood of success in pursuing goals. These must account for an agent's disposition to undertake efforts to pursue the goals in question (Stemplowska 2016). When the action in question is political, likelihoods of success may depend on complex structural factors. For example, that a state is unlikely to expand its Medicaid program because of the political makeup of its legislature, does not show that it would be infeasible for it to attempt to do so in a morally relevant sense. But it might show that the society faces deeper structural problems that account for both the need to expand Medicaid and the difficulties in getting the legislature to act.

Another feasibility question arises when claims of justice are in conflict. Achieving justice for some may seem ineluctably in tension with achieving justice for others. For example, the presence of assistance animals may be necessary accommodations for some, while conflicting with the accommodation needs of others with allergies or phobias. Ideal theorists of justice might argue that we need a systematic account of complete justice in order to decide how to resolve these conflicts, perhaps imagining a world in which each can flourish in accord with his or her conceptions of the good and then working back from this world to the actual world. But this idealized situation is not the actual world in which accommodation decisions must be made. In that actual world, both structural injustice and histories of unjust treatment are part of the picture about why these conflicts exist and what might be done about them. Partial compliance theorists would consider whether there are methods to minimize the conflict or, if not, how incremental adjustments may be made to foster inclusion in a fair way. The imaginary perfect world does not provide guidance here. Consider this recent example from Americans with Disabilities Act (ADA) law. Two students both lived in a college sorority house. One student had applied, and been approved, for having her service animal live with her to help her manage anxiety and depression.[4] The other student contended that the service animal aggravated her allergies and Crohn's disease. The court determined that the ADA analysis favored the former, as the latter had not gone through the relevant procedures to establish the impact of the dog on her and her need for the accommodation of her allergy to dogs (although she had earlier requested and received other accommodations for her Crohn's disease). In the judgment of the court, use of these procedures would have established whether the presence of the dog actually did pose a direct threat to the student's health, as well as whether it might have been possible to work out a way for the dog to live with the one student without frequently encountering the other. If both accommodation needs were clear and conflicting, however, other strategies would have been necessary, such as considering which student had moved into the house first, what either student would lose by moving out of the house, or what opportunities were available to either student. This analysis will perforce refer to the students' own histories of unjust treatment, the university's obligations to offer inclusive housing options, and the roles of sorority housing at the university.

Non-Ideal Theory, Ideals, and Disability Civil Rights

A third question in non-ideal theory is the role of ideal justice in determining what ought to be done in non-ideal circumstances. Should we use ideals to guide what we ought to do in the here-and-now? A simplistic "yes" answer—that we should read off from the ideal what to do in the real—seems implausible on many grounds, including feasibility. A more plausible relationship between the ideal and actual circumstances is that ideals function as aspirational goals and that we should measure success in improving justice by assessing progress toward the ideal. This approach requires the ability to formulate ideals, separately from (some) actual circumstances, and to develop methods to measure progress at least in some rough way. Other theorists with whom I agree, such as Sen (2009), argue that such end-state theorizing is neither necessary nor sufficient for making judgments about what would be improvements in justice in the actual world.

Starting with ideal justice requires developing a picture of what ideal justice might require. The picture might be rough, but it must be at least a sketch. Civil rights perspectives, to the contrary, do not require an account of ideal justice. Rather, they require an account of current failures to realize rights, coupled with an account of how steps toward rights realization might be achieved. This approach does not require an ideal of a perfect world of rights-realization. It starts instead with problems in the here and now and how we might progress in addressing these problems. As with pragmatist accounts of moral progress, particular changes are assessed in terms of whether they solve an existing problem or create new ones—not on whether they proceed on a direction toward the best.

Consider street design as an example of civil rights in action. As aspects of the built world, streets are designed in light of existing social needs, technical capacities, and natural conditions. At given points in time, we are able to understand how street design interacts with bodily differences to affect the relative ease with which people can be in the world. We are also able to observe how social or legal structures may facilitate or hinder this access. Jacobus tenBroek (1966) made this point forcefully about tort liability over fifty years ago now. The right to live in the world, he observed, requires changing the basic assumption that loss should fall on the visually impaired person who falls into a hole in the sidewalk rather than the party responsible for failing to place an adequate protective barricade. tenBroek argued that this presumption violates a basic civil right: the right to access the world without facing barriers differentially imposed on people with disabilities without further compelling justification. Changing this presumption would further the civil rights of people who might otherwise fall into the unguarded hole.

Achievements of civil rights in this way is possible without an understanding of what an ideally built world would be like. For street design, all that is necessary is an understanding of particular barriers and how they may be altered, dismantled—or, if their removal is not feasible, addressed to the extent possible by individual accommodations for people with disabilities such as sound warnings or guides when particular dangers have been identified. There are many illustrations of such recognition and alteration of barriers in the built world: curb cuts, ramps, and widened doorways, to select but a few. As technology develops, more barriers may fall: the elevator, or the motorized wheelchair, or the kneeling bus, are but a few illustrations of how technology has removed barriers to moving about in the world. We may be only a few years away from a world in which vehicles are constructed that can safely drive people with severe mobility or even sensory impairments; the advent of these vehicles may change thinking about what count as reasonable accommodations in employment or accessible street design (Francis 2018).

Education is another example of civil rights in action. Historically, people with intellectual disabilities were considered unable to be educated (e.g., Rembis et al. 2018). Only recently has the idea of inclusive education taken hold. Even with such a paradigm shift, it has been difficult to understand what education as a civil right might mean. In a famous case in the United States Supreme Court in 1982, Amy Rowley sued her school district for failing to provide her with the statutory right to education granted by the Education of the Handicapped Act. (*Board of Education* 1982). Rowley, a hearing-impaired student, was receiving some extra tutorial services and speech therapy but not the sign interpretation she sought to enable her to understand more of what was happening in the classroom. She was a gifted lip-reader who was able to get along reasonably well, however, and the Court held that because she was achieving a "B" average in her fourth-grade classes, she had received the required "meaningful access" to an education. In the aftermath of the *Rowley* decision, some claimed that "meaningful access" meant only "some" educational benefit that is "more than *de minimus*" while others claimed that it meant education "reasonably calculated to enable a child to make progress appropriate in light of the child's circumstances." (*Endrew F* 2017) In the *Endrew F.* decision from which these quotations are drawn, the Court endorsed the latter standard: "meaningful access" to education means the services that allow a given child to make appropriate progress in light of her abilities. In reaching this conclusion, the Court was clear that, in its view, there is no ideal educational standard as a matter of justice, nor is such a standard what would be required. Rather, the Court said: "A substantive standard not focused on student progress would do little to remedy the pervasive and tragic academic stagnation that prompted Congress to act." (*Endrew F* 2017, 999). Indeed, the *Endrew F* decision may call into question whether *Rowley* had been rightly decided by its own standard. While Rowley was able to achieve decent grades, she was not able to comprehend a significant portion of what was occurring in the classroom and thus arguably did not have an opportunity to make the progress she could have with a more accessible education.

Importantly, this standard is not special privileging; rather, it is education that allows people to progress as appropriate for them. Moreover, as with street design, education may benefit from technology in ways that we could never have anticipated. The liberating effects of voice recognition software, screen readers, or personal assistive devices are by now familiar. Less familiar may be the use of virtual reality technologies for people with divergent ways of perceiving the world (e.g., Schroeder 2011). And there surely are possibilities for extended cognition that are as yet unimagined.

Street design and education are but a few illustrations of how a civil rights perspective can function. Each of these addresses an important aspect of living in the world: being able to get around and being able to learn. A civil rights perspective points out how persons with different bodies or minds are unable to access these aspects of life in ways that are meaningful. It identifies barriers and how they may be removed or addressed in ways that enhance inclusion.

Eugenics and the Perversion of the Ideal

An essay about non-ideal theory and disability would be remiss if it failed to mention how perversions of the ideal have damaged persons with disabilities through eugenics. The eugenics movement was premised on the idea that the science of breeding would eliminate human ills. By encouraging purity of the human stock, the American Eugenics Party (1964) thought, we could eventually attain a Eugenic Society. Scientists from Galton on believed that progress toward an ideal society could be achieved by encouraging the fit to reproduce and sterilizing the unfit (Goering 2014). These views culminated in a decision of the United States Supreme Court holding that it did not violate due process rights for states to require sterilization of those they believed were mentally deficient—a decision that to this day has yet to be overturned. In this decision, Justice Oliver Wendell Holmes Jr. opined that "three generations of imbeciles are enough" and that

> the public welfare may call upon the best citizens for their lives. It would be strange if it could not call upon those who already sap the strength of the State for these lesser sacrifices, often not felt to be such by those concerned, in order to prevent our being swamped with incompetence. It is better for all the world, if instead of waiting to execute degenerate offspring for crime, or to let them starve for their imbecility, society can prevent those who are manifestly unfit from continuing their kind.
>
> *(Buck vs. Bell* 1927, 207)

Developments in reproductive technology and genetic engineering are moving rapidly and have brought in their wake concerns about the revival of eugenics. For some, as mentioned earlier in this chapter, these technologies bring the possibility of an ideal world without the births of people with disabilities. Others argue that preimplantation genetic testing and embryo selection evoke the darkest side of eugenics. These issues have been extensively explored elsewhere (e.g. Francis, 2017) and I do not rehearse them here. Eugenics as the ideal of eliminating existing people in horrific ways, as the Nazis did, is surely a perversion of ideals. Whether efforts to formulate and pursue human idealization risk such perversion is not a claim I would make or even know how to assess empirically. What I can say is that justifications for improvements in the lives of people with disabilities, along with improvements in the lives of others who experience disadvantage, do not require forays into forms of ideal theory, whether or not they are perverse.

For my purposes here, it suffices to distinguish the bads of disability from consideration of whether disability itself is bad. Put in terms of the distinction between non-ideal theory and ideal theory, the distinction lies between ways in which a non-ideal world affects disabled lives deleteriously, and whether disability itself makes the world non-ideal. This is the distinction that the social model of disability draws so clearly: that there are bad features of a life with disabilities in a given social world does not entail that disability itself is bad. An approach to disability in non-ideal theory terms, such as the civil rights approach sketched above, can address the first problem successfully without trying to enter the uncharted—and, I would argue, unchartable—territory of the ideal.

Notes

1. 42 U.S.C. § 12112 (2018).
2. *Lauren Searls v. Johns Hopkins Hospital*, 158 F. Supp. 427 (D. Md. 2016). The hospital's overall budget was over $1.7 billion, but they contended that the hardship should be measured in terms of the limited budget of the unit that would have employed the nurse.

3. Easley by *Easley v. Snider*, 36 F.3d 297 (3d Cir. 1994).
4. *Entine v. Lissner*, 2017 WL 5507619 (S.D. Ohio 2017) (unreported).

References

American Eugenics Party. 1964. Party Platform. http://www.eugenicsarchive.org/eugenics/view_image.pl?id=762

Barnes, Elizabeth. 2016. *The Minority Body*. New York: Oxford University Press.

Board of Education of the Henry Hudson School District v. Rowley, 458 U.S.176 (1982).

Buck v. Bell, 274 U.S. 200 (1927).

Endrew F. ex rel. Joseph F. v. Douglas County School District RE-1, 137 S.Ct. 988 (2017).

Francis, Leslie P. 2017. *Oxford Handbook of Reproductive Ethics*. Oxford: Oxford University Press, 2017.

Francis, Leslie P. 2018. Disability and Automation: The Promise of Cars that Automate Driving Functions. *Journal of Health Care Law and Policy* 20: 229–252.

Goering, Sara. 2014. "Eugenics." In *The Stanford Encyclopedia of Philosophy*. Edited by Edward N. Zalta. https://plato.stanford.edu/archives/fall2014/entries/eugenics/.

Hartley, Christie. 2011. "Disability and Justice." *Philosophy Compass* 6, no. 2: 120–132.

Hendricks, D. J., Linda C. Batiste, Anne Hirsh. 2005. "Cost and Effectiveness of Accommodations in the Workplace: Preliminary Results of a Nationwide Study." *Disability Studies Quarterly* 25, no. 4. http://www.dsq-sds.org/article/view/623/800.

Job Accommodations Network (JAN). 2018. "Job Accommodation Network (Updated September 30/2018). Workplace Accommodations: Low Cost, High Impact." Retrieved January 21, 2019, from https://askjan.org/topics/costs.cfm.

Nussbaum, Martha. 2006. *Frontiers of Justice: Disability, Disadvantage, Species Membership*. Cambridge, MA: Harvard University Press.

Padkapayeva, Kathy, Andres Posen, Amin Yazdani, Alexis Buettgen, Quenby Mahood, Emile Tompa. 2016. "Workplace Accommodations for Persons with Physical Disabilities: Evidence Synthesis of the Peer-Reviewed Literature." *Disability and Rehabilitation* 39, no. 21: 2134–2147.

Putnam, Ruth Anna. 2000. "Neither a Beast Nor a God." *Social Theory and Practice* 26, no. 2: 177–200.

Rawls, John. 1971. *A Theory of Justice*. Cambridge, MA: Harvard University Press.

Rawls, John. 2005. *Political Liberalism*. New York: Columbia University Press.

Rembis, Michael A., Catherine Jean Kudlick, Kim E. Nielsen, eds. 2018. *Oxford Handbook of Disability History*. New York: Oxford University Press.

Rothstein, Richard. 2017. *The Color of Law*. New York: W.W. Norton.

Savulescu, Julian. 2001. "Procreative Beneficence: Why We Should Select the Best Children." *Bioethics* 15(5/6): 413–426.

Schroeder, Ralph. 2011. *Being There Together: Social Interaction in Virtual Environments*. New York: Oxford University Press.

Sen, Amartya. 2009. *The Idea of Justice*. Cambridge, MA: Harvard University Press.

Shakespeare, Tom. 2010. The Social Model of Disability. In *The Disability Studies Reader*, edited by Lennard J. Davis, 266–273. New York: Routledge.

Silvers, Anita, and Leslie P. Francis. 2005. "Justice Through Trust: Resolving the Outlier Problem in Social Contract Theory." *Ethics* 116: 40–77.

Solovieva, Tatiana I., Richard T. Walls, Deborah J. Hendricks, and Denetta L. Dowler. 2009. "Cost of Workplace Accommodations for Individuals with Disabilities: With or Without Personal Assistance Services." *Disability and Health Journal* 2, no. 4: 196–205.

Southwood, Nicholas. 2018. "The Feasibility Issue." *Philosophy Compass* 13, no. 8: e12509.

Stark, Cynthia. 2007. "How to Include the Severely Disabled in a Contractarian Theory of Justice." *Journal of Political Philosophy* 15, no. 2: 125–147.

Stemplowska, Zofia. 2016. "Feasibility: Individual and Collective." *Social Philosophy and Policy* 33(1–2): 273–291.

tenBroek, Jacobus. 1966. "The Right to Live in the World: The Disabled in the Law of Torts." *University of California Law Review* 54, no. 2: 841–919.

United Nations. 2006. Convention on the Rights of Persons with Disabilities. https://www.un.org/development/desa/disabilities/convention-on-the-rights-of-persons-with-disabilities/convention-on-the-rights-of-persons-with-disabilities-2.html. Last accessed May 3, 2019.

Valentini, Laura. 2012. "Ideal vs. Non-Ideal Theory: A Conceptual Map." *Philosophy Compass* 7, no. 9: 654–664.

Wolff, Jonathan. 2017. "Forms of Differential Social Inclusion." *Social Philosophy and Policy* 34, no. 1: 164–185.

CHAPTER 15

....

FAIR DIFFERENCE OF
OPPORTUNITY

....

ADAM CURETON AND ALEXANDER KAUFMAN

At least three kinds of contingencies tend to affect whether a person, over the course of her life, manages to develop the talents and earn the credentials that are needed to qualify for and obtain the offices and positions that exist in her society, such as elected political offices, civil service posts, occupations and careers (TJ 377).[1] Her *natural endowments*, such as her native intelligence, creativity, dexterity, and visual acuity can influence her chances of eventually winning offices and positions she seeks. Her chances can also be influenced by her *social circumstances*, such as her family and social class, any informal encouragement or adverse social pressure she felt as a member of a social, ethnic, religious, or gender group, any income, wealth, and other means she may have inherited or earned, as well as any education or training that helped her to develop her native capacities. And her chances can be influenced by her *motivations*, such as her choices, projects and ends, plan of life, and strength of will.

According to John Rawls, justice requires that the basic institutions of society ensure what he calls Fair Equality of Opportunity. This principle requires that people who have the same natural endowments and the same motivations must have the same chance of securing offices and positions in society, regardless of their social class of origin, family background, or other social circumstances.[2]

Our aims in this essay are, first, to raise some concerns about Fair Equality of Opportunity that arise from considering issues of disability; second, to propose an alternative to that principle; and, third, to argue that our principle is more faithful to Rawls's basic framework and more friendly to disabled people than Fair Equality of Opportunity.

Despite its name, Rawls's Fair Equality of Opportunity principle does not guarantee *equal opportunity for everyone* but instead only ensures equal chances at securing offices and positions for those with the same *natural endowments* and *motivations*. Rawls's principle allows these chances to be lower, in particular, for people with various kinds of physical and psychological impairments and diseases once the adverse influences of their social circumstances have been corrected for.[3] The parties in Rawls's Original

Position have good reasons to be concerned about this feature of Fair Equality of Opportunity. Behind the veil of ignorance, the parties must reckon with the possibility that they themselves may have impairments or other natural endowments of various kinds that tend to diminish significantly their chances to secure desirable positions in a society governed by Fair Equality of Opportunity. From their point of view, Fair Equality of Opportunity does not seem to go far enough in protecting their interests in securing opportunities for themselves, so they have reason to seek an alternative principle that protects more completely against the possibility that weak endowments of native assets and motivations might impair their ability to exploit opportunities to secure desirable positions.

This argument reflects the intuitive concern that if we have reason to correct for the arbitrary influence of *social circumstances* on a person's chances at securing positions in society, in the way required by Fair Equality of Opportunity, then we also have reasons to go beyond that principle and correct for the equally arbitrary influence of *natural endowments* and perhaps *motivations* on those chances as well.[4] Our alternative principle, which we call Fair Difference of Opportunity, does just that—it says that the default position should be true equality of opportunity in which everyone is assured the same chances for securing desirable positions, regardless of their natural endowments, motivations, or social circumstances; but if there are ways to improve the opportunities of everyone by allowing more and better opportunities to some people without violating the other principles of justice, then such arrangements would be justified.

Fair Difference of Opportunity is much more likely to ensure justice for disabled people than Rawls's Fair Equality of Opportunity principle. Fair Difference of Opportunity is especially sensitive to the multifaceted nature of disability as an interaction among natural and social factors that are often difficult or impossible to separate (Lippert-Rasmussen 2004, Lewens 2010, Nagel 1997). That principle aims to correct for all arbitrary factors, without needing to distinguish between natural and social ones, that diminish a person's opportunities; the principle also, in some cases, allows a society to use those factors to improve the opportunities of everyone.[5] Instituting Fair Difference of Opportunity would thus provide substantial improvements to the opportunities of disabled people over what they would have under Rawls's Fair Equality of Opportunity, which only focuses on correcting for social influences on opportunities. One of the main advantages of our alternative principle is that it does not depend on a distinction between "natural endowments" and "social circumstances" but instead incorporates the fact that many of our traits and abilities have complex and interconnected causes that are difficult or impossible to separate or classify.

Our plan is as follows. First, we describe Rawls's principles of Formal Equality of Opportunity and Fair Equality of Opportunity. We next describe Fair Difference of Opportunity as an alternative to the latter. Then we provide several reasons why the parties in the Original Position would accept Fair Difference of Opportunity instead of Fair Equality of Opportunity, with special emphasis on their interest in protecting the social bases of self-respect. Finally, although we are unsure whether Fair Difference of Opportunity is justifiable all things considered or whether Rawls would have accepted it, we provide some evidence that Rawls may have at one time endorsed a principle that is similar to Fair Difference of Opportunity.

FORMAL EQUALITY OF OPPORTUNITY

Opportunity principles, according to Rawls, must work in conjunction with other principles of justice. In particular, Rawls's Equal Liberty and Difference principles constrain and, in some cases, determine the sorts of offices and positions that may exist in a society. For example, a society needs various public offices in order to implement the principles of justice in a political framework; the Equal Liberty principle also limits the kinds of private positions that may exist; and the Difference Principle allows economic and social positions of associations and the private sector more generally to vary in their functions, authority, responsibilities, and advantages as long as these inequalities work as part of a scheme that improves the economic position of the worst off. Considerations of efficiency and the instrumental value of incentives provide one kind of reason why having offices and positions with unequal authority could benefit the worst off, by creating more wealth and transferring some of it to those who are least advantaged (TJ 58–62; 91–92). And having offices and positions that vary in degree of responsibility allows a broader and more diverse range of occupations and positions that are available to everyone, so such an arrangement helps the worst off members of society develop and employ their talents in ways that tend to reinforce their sense of their own worth (PL 181).

According to Rawls's conception of Justice as Fairness, a minimal formal requirement of equal access applies to the offices and positions that exist in the public and private sectors of a society—that is, all positions in society must be held *formally* open to all. This means that the qualifications for taking up those positions and the procedures for filling them must be reasonably related to their legitimate functions, as determined or constrained by the principles of justice, and no one may be prevented from applying for or seeking a position as long as she meets the requirements for holding it (TJ 59–63; 91; 245–246). Formal Equality of Opportunity prevents discriminatory formal restrictions on access to positions, ensures that selections for those positions are made on the basis of their legitimate functions, and prevents certain kinds of interference from others in seeking them.

Formal Equality of Opportunity for public and private positions treats natural and social contingencies in the same manner. Rather than singling out one or the other for special treatment, formal equality of opportunity guarantees that anyone, regardless of the nature of the person's natural endowments and social circumstances, has formal access to all public and private offices and positions, even if her chances at winning some of them are slim.

Why would parties in the Original Position require Formal Equality of Opportunity for public and private positions? We will examine the considerations that would persuade them to endorse Formal Equality of Opportunity. We will return to these considerations when we assess the relative merits of Rawls' principle of Fair Equality of Opportunity and our principle of Fair Difference of Opportunity, which both incorporate but go beyond Formal Equality of Opportunity.

(1) *The primary good of self-respect.* Concerns regarding the just distribution of shares of the primary goods of self-respect and the social bases of self-respect justify the choice in the Original Position to guarantee of Formal Equality of Opportunity for public and private positions.

Rawls assigns over-riding significance to self-respect as a primary good. Self-respect is, Rawls asserts, "perhaps the most important primary good" (TJ 386). Possession of an adequate share of the primary good of self-respect is an essential condition of the individual's pursuit of his or her own good, since "[w]ithout it nothing may seem worth doing, or if some things have value for us, we may lack the will to strive for them" (TJ 386). The adequacy of the shares of this primary good that are available to members of civil society is therefore a central concern of distributive justice.

Self-respect, Rawls notes, has three aspects. First, self-respect involves a sense of one's own value—a secure conviction that one's plan of life is worth carrying out (TJ 386). Second, self-respect requires confidence in one's ability to carry out one's intentions. Self-respect of this kind involves not merely a view of oneself as possessing worthwhile ends, but also a positive attitude about one's ability to pursue those ends. Finally, self-respect requires that the individual must be able to pursue their ends with a reasonable degree of skill: a person's "plan of life will lack a certain attraction for him if it fails to call upon his rational capacities in an interesting fashion" (TJ 386–87). Let's consider each of these aspects of self-respect in turn.

First, the parties in the Original Position, Rawls assumes, are motivated to secure adequate shares of the primary good of self-respect. Even behind the veil of ignorance, the parties know certain basic psychological facts about how human beings tend to develop and sustain a sense of their own worth.

The parties know, in particular, that the respect of others is a necessary element of the social bases of self-respect. A person's sense of his own worth tends to be strengthened when other people respect him, while public expressions of lack of respect tend to seriously undermine his sense of self-worth (TJ 155–158, 386, 437). The parties also reasonably assume that persons with a secure sense of their own worth tend to respect others as well, while people who lack such a sense tend to not respect others. And the parties know that lack of respect from others tends to undermine their self-respect and make them more contemptuous of themselves and others (TJ 155–156).

In view of these assumed features of human psychology, parties in the Original Position may reasonably suppose that if some group were formally and publicly denied access to certain public and private offices and positions, they would tend to have an inadequate share of the social bases of self-respect. Exclusion from the political process or from social and economic positions would convey the message that the excluded group lacks the publicly affirmed status of equal citizen (TJ 82, 91, 175, 326, 478). And the public nature of their exclusion and subordination would likely deal an even greater blow to their self-respect (TJ 158). Guaranteeing open access to the political process and to economic and social positions, on the other hand, provides a public way for citizens to express mutual respect for one another and so enhances each person's sense of her own worth.[6]

Second, Rawls assumes that it is a basic feature of human psychology that people—in order to sustain the sense that their projects and pursuits are worthwhile—require that others affirm the value of those projects and pursuits as well. In addition to the affirmation of others, a number of other factors tend to affirm a person's sense of the value of her pursuits. In particular, human beings tend to regard their ends and the ends of others as more worthwhile, the more they involve the intricate development and sophisticated exercise of natural talents and abilities. And our projects and aims, as well as those of others, tend to lose their appeal for us when they do not call upon the development and exercise of sophisticated and intricate abilities (TJ 374–376, 386). Moreover, when our plans and final ends complement those of other people in a group to which we belong, our successes in pursuing the final ends of the group are valued and appreciated as contributing to each member's own good, so that when others develop different natural abilities and employ them in pursuit of ends we share, we tend to value their goals and projects as ways of realizing our own nature as well (TJ 373–374, 459). A social union exists when members have shared final aims, when they engage in cooperative activities in support of them, and when these activities are publicly affirmed by the group. Membership in a social union provides a secure basis for each person's sense that his aims and projects in support of the group are worthwhile (TJ 458–463).

When the basic institutions of society are just, society itself is one kind of social union, in which members have shared final aims of realizing just institutions; members also engage in cooperative activities in support of those aims, such as by holding public office or voting; and these activities are publicly affirmed by the group (TJ 205, 458–463). Holding public office in a just society thus tends to lead others to value and appreciate our aims and ends in two respects: First, they tend to appreciate the sophisticated abilities and moral sensibilities we are called upon to develop and exercise as a public official, such as coming to have political opinions, explaining ourselves, to others, and finding mutually acceptable outcomes (TJ 463). And second, when we hold public office in a just society, we tend to be seen as furthering the shared ends of our common social union, by working to maintain and support just institutions that benefit everyone (TJ 463).

Holding various positions in the economic and social system also tends to secure admiration and appreciation from others, which reinforces our judgment that our own aims and projects are worth pursuing. First, many occupations and positions of authority are part of complicated and diverse activities that call upon us to develop and exercise our natural abilities and talents in various sophisticated ways. Second, the social union of wider society is likely to include many other kinds of social unions that have their own shared final ends and that engage in cooperative activities in which members openly appreciate and admire the realized talents and abilities of others (TJ 458–462).

Taking up positions of responsibility and authority in these groups is thus likely to meet with appreciation from our associates.

If a class of people were formally excluded from certain public or private positions, this exclusion would tend to undermine the kind of self-respect that involves valuing one's own ends, activities and pursuits. Formal exclusion would tend to send the message that their potential contributions, values and pursuits are less valued by others (TJ 157). The parties in the Original Position thus have reasons to require Formal Equality of Opportunity for all offices and positions as a way of protecting aspects of self-respect that depend on appreciation and admiration from others.

And, third, formal exclusion from positions that are essential to accomplishing our goals in life tends to make us feel impotent, powerless, and downcast (TJ 448, 469). Persons also tend to experience the public nature of these exclusions as humiliating to our self-respect (TJ 469, 472). This is a further reason for parties in the Original Position to choose Formal Equality of Opportunity as a way of avoiding the sense of resignation and humiliation that tends to come from being publicly excluded from positions that are essential to pursuing their own goals and projects.

(2) Moral development. A second class of considerations for endorsing Formal Equality of Opportunity concern moral development. Parties in the Original Position are eventually concerned with ensuring that a well-ordered society governed by the principles of justice is suitably stable. Rawls conjectures that there are various psychological laws that govern the moral development of a person born into such a society (TJ 429–434). These are all laws of reciprocity in which our sentiments of love, friendship, and justice develop when we find other people and institutions affirming our own good (TJ 433). Once a person in a just, well-ordered society has formed attachments and loyalties to his family and associates and has learned that the basic structures of society are publicly known to be just, he comes to recognize that he and those he cares about benefit from those arrangements, which strengthens his self-respect in all three senses and leads him to want to answer in kind by accepting and supporting those institutions himself (TJ 412, 417, 427). As he recognizes that other people and society as a whole affirm his own good, and as his sense of his own worth improves as a result, he also tends to develop bonds of civic friendship and affiliation with them (TJ 454).

If some people were formally excluded from the political process or denied access to certain economic and social positions, without receiving anything in return, these psychological laws would be much less effective. Those who are excluded would be less likely to see the basic structures of society as affirming their own good, and they would therefore feel less of a desire to reciprocate with those beyond their families or close associates, leaving them somewhat alienated and estranged from wider society. Those who were excluded would tend to see the political process or the economy and social system as simply forms of rivalry within which their interests are largely ignored. This view might in turn lead them to doubt the good faith and desire for justice of those in power (TJ 205). In both cases, if a group failed to develop a sense of justice and lacked ties of civic friendship with others in their society, justice would not be as congruent with their good, leaving the basic structure to some extent unstable and liable to collapse.

(3) *Envy.* Envy is a further potential cause of instability in a just, well-ordered society. The human propensity to envy motivates the tendency to deprive others of their greater goods, perhaps at some cost to ourselves, even though their greater advantages do not detract from our own (TJ 466–467). As we have seen, if some group were afforded fewer formal opportunities than others, they would tend to feel less confident in their own worth and plans as well as feel less sure in their ability to accomplish their goals. If they believe they have no other options to secure their self-respect, they may seek to alleviate their anguish and apathy by lashing out at those who have more formal opportunities than they do (TJ 448, 469, 472). Their envious behavior, though perhaps excusable, would tend to destabilize society by diminishing ties of civic friendship and encouraging destructive forms of rivalry and rancor (TJ 468). Giving everyone Formal Equality of Opportunity for positions thus tends to stabilize a just well-ordered society by eliminating one source of corrosive envy.

Fair Equality of Opportunity

Even when a society has justly established public offices and positions and ensured that everyone has the formal right to seek them and to be selected on their merits, many people may nonetheless lack the realized skills and credentials that are needed to qualify for positions or to succeed in open competitions for them. Poor natural endowments, including physical and psychological impairments of various kinds, as well as unfortunate social circumstances and bad luck, perhaps stretching back to early childhood, may have prevented persons from acquiring the skills needed to compete against those in more fortunate situations. A citizen may not have the requisite talents and skills for a position in the judiciary he seeks, for example, because he lacks the necessary combination of native ability and education. Someone who is qualified for holding a legislative office may be at a significant disadvantage in being elected because he has far less money and resources than his competitors. And a person may simply lack the desire to seek public office altogether because of her family circumstances, class background, and abuse she suffered as a child (Arneson 1999).

There are various ways a conception of justice might provide *fair*, and not just *formal*, opportunity to secure offices and positions in society.

One possibility is to establish a framework of Formal Equality of Opportunity for public and private positions without making any special provisions to help people secure them beyond what is required by the Difference Principle. The Difference Principle allows unequal distributions of economic goods such as income and wealth as long as those inequalities work as part of a scheme that benefits the worst off members of society in terms of their share of primary goods. Although a person's chances of possessing the realized talents and skills to secure various privileged positions in open competition against others will likely be affected by her natural endowments and social class, she is nonetheless compensated for these disparities with greater material resources.

Another possibility, which we call Strict Equality of Opportunity, is to eliminate the influence of natural and social contingency on one's chances of securing positions in society by implementing measures designed to ensure that everyone has an equal chance at holding every public and private office and position in society no matter one's motivations, social circumstances or natural endowments.[7] Formal Equality of Opportunity requires that positions are given to the best candidates, so under this restriction, Strict Equality of Opportunity cannot require simply filling positions by fair lottery. Nor would this principle be feasible if it could achieve equality of opportunity only by bringing everyone up to the same level of talent and ability. But Strict Equality of Opportunity could feasibly approximate affording equal chances for all offices and positions by, for example, using fair lotteries for distributing the educational resources that allow people to develop their talents and so secure positions that are awarded by merit. If everyone, for example, had equal chances of attending the best primary and secondary schools in their area then their chances of eventually securing desirable careers would come closer to equality with others than if their socio-economic status or realized talent determined which primary and secondary schools they attend.

Rawls's Justice as Fairness provides an intermediary interpretation of the idea that people should be afforded fair opportunity to secure offices and positions. Rawls's favored conception of justice requires, first, Formal Equality of Opportunity, so that qualifications are reasonably related to job-function and the best candidate wins. But, second, Justice as Fairness also requires Fair Equality of Opportunity, which says that those who have the same natural endowments and the same willingness to develop and use them must be guaranteed the same chances of securing public and private offices and positions (TJ 197).

Let's consider in more detail what Fair Equality of Opportunity means. Suppose a society guarantees equal basic liberties and satisfies Formal Equality of Opportunity and the Difference Principle. Consider person A at birth. His chances of securing any one of his society's positions over the course of his life, say becoming an orthopedic surgeon, depend on a number of factors. First, Formal Equality of Opportunity ensures free choice of public and private positions; absent special circumstances, then, A cannot be forced to take a position against his will or formally excluded from seeking it. Second, A's chances of eventually attaining the necessary credentials and developing the realized talents and skills to qualify as a surgeon and to win a surgical position in open competition in which candidates are judged on their merits will usually depend on various contingencies that may go back to his early childhood. These include: his natural aptitudes, such as his native intelligence, dexterity, and visual acuity; his social circumstances, including his early family life, the material means that were available to him, the education he received, and the informal support and adverse pressure he faced; his luck avoiding such things as accident and illness; his choices about what ends he aims to achieve and which natural talents and abilities he chose to develop; and the strength of his resolve to overcome obstacles and hardship in reaching his goals. Third, the process for identifying the best candidate for an open surgery position is often imprecise and ties may occur. There will often be an additional element of luck in a candidate's chances of being offered the position even if he is among the group of top candidates. Fourth, his chances of securing a surgery position can be affected by whether he knows about the position. And fifth, his chances of securing it also depend on how many open positions there are—the more orthopedic surgeons that are needed, the higher his chances of being selected, all else equal.

Fair Equality of Opportunity says that any two people who are born with the same native abilities, who have the same basic plans about preparing for and securing positions, and who have the same resolve to put those plans into effect must be afforded the same set of probabilities for attaining each position in society.[8]

Fair Equality of Opportunity, however, does not correct for the influence of all kinds of luck on a person's prospects for securing positions—a person's chances can still be affected by the natural endowments she was born with, on her motivation, on whether there are ties among the best candidates, on whether she knows about the available positions, and on the number of positions that are available. Fair Equality of Opportunity does not even correct for all influences of social circumstances on a person's chances for securing positions. This is because the ends that guide a person's choices about which abilities and talents to develop and what positions in society to pursue, as well as the strength of her will in carrying out her plans, can themselves be affected and shaped by her social background.[9] Fair Equality of Opportunity takes a person's native endowments, choices, and strength of will as given, and aims to ensure equal chances for those who are similarly situated by these measures, but it still allows those who have natural endowments that command large rewards in the market, and who were raised in more supportive environments that guided their choices and nurtured their determination, to have a better chance at securing positions than people in less fortunate circumstances. As a result, Fair Equality of Opportunity allows people with various kinds of impairments and disadvantageous natural endowments, which are just as arbitrary as one's social class of origin, to have fewer and worse opportunities than those with more advantageous natural abilities and talents. Many people with disabilities will thus tend to be relegated to inferior occupations, careers, and positions, or find themselves unable to secure any political or economic positions at all, under Rawls's principle of Fair Equality of Opportunity.

Fair Difference of Opportunity

As an alternative to Fair Equality of Opportunity that is more friendly to disabled people and others whose natural talents make it difficult to secure offices and positions in society, we propose a principle that we call Fair Difference of Opportunity. As its name indicates, this principle draws on ideas implicit in Rawls's Difference Principle.

The Difference Principle holds that the default distribution of income, wealth, and any other primary social goods besides rights, liberties, and opportunities is that of equality, but if those who are least advantaged with respect to the distribution of these primary social goods would enjoy more of them by allowing some people to have more of them than others, then those unequal distributive schemes would be permissible.[10] The various natural and social contingencies that can affect a person's income and wealth, for example, are treated on a par, without giving special consideration to one kind or the other, except insofar as allowing certain arbitrary differences of either kind to translate into greater income and wealth for some people results in greater income and wealth for those with less fortunate natural and social endowments.

If we abstract from the specific social goods that Rawls says are regulated by the Difference Principle, a similar line of reasoning could be applied to the social good of opportunity for position and, in particular, to the ways a society can or should prepare people to qualify for and win positions.

We can begin to explain Fair Difference of Opportunity by first defining a notion of what we call *real opportunity*, which is essentially a person's overall prospects of securing the various desirable and undesirable positions in society. Every person has a set of chances from birth of securing each economic and social position. Some positions, however, are more privileged, involve greater responsibility and authority, and are otherwise more desirable than others.[11] Each of us, according to Rawls, has a basic interest in not only having the option to take up many different positions in society but also in being able to take up more desirable positions (PL 181). A person's set of chances for securing offices and positions can thus be weighted by the quality of those positions in terms of the responsibility, authority, and privilege they involve. We can then combine a person's chances for securing each position in society, after weighting them by their respective desirability, to specify her overall real opportunity. One way of doing so is to say that a person's real opportunities have been improved if her weighted chances for one position in society are higher and none of her other weighted chances for other positions are lower. We could also simply add up a representation of the quality of each position discounted by her chances of securing it to produce an overall measure of a person's real opportunity.

The intuitive idea behind real opportunity is to specify a way of comparing the overall set of opportunities that different people have in their lives, by taking account of their chances of securing various positions in society as well as the quality of those positions. Each of us, according to Rawls, has an interest in maximizing our real opportunities, in ensuring that we have the highest chances to secure the best social positions we may seek. Someone born into the lower classes may have his pick of monotonous service jobs but lack the education and social status to favorably compete for more privileged positions that are nonetheless formally open to him. His overall opportunities in life are far worse than a person born into the upper classes who also has his choice of more desirable positions.

Fair Difference of Opportunity says that everyone must have the same level of real opportunity unless affording some people a higher level of real opportunity would improve the level of real opportunity for the group with the lowest level of real opportunity. The baseline, according to this principle, is Strict Equality of Opportunity, which we could implement to some extent by instituting measures designed to help people develop the necessary talents and skills so that their real opportunity is the same as that of everyone else.

Fair Difference of Opportunity allows variations in the level of real opportunity among people if this works as part of an arrangement that improves the real opportunity of the worst-off group. How might this happen? If real opportunity were equalized by giving everyone the same chance to develop the talents and skills needed to secure offices and positions in society then the result of this arrangement is likely to be economically inefficient. This is because those with the greatest potential may not have received sufficient educational resources to develop the talents that would have allowed them to secure certain privileged positions and to perform those job-functions better than the people who currently hold them. In such a situation, everyone's chances of securing social and economic positions they seek would tend to be quite low because there would be fewer available positions and more candidates for them. Instead of giving everyone an equal chance to secure educational resources, society could distribute those resources in ways that favor people who have the potential to achieve higher levels of realized talent and skill. Doing so would disproportionately improve the real opportunity of those people, but the economic efficiencies that would result from having more effective people in various offices and positions would tend to produce more resources that society could use to provide even better education and training to the worst off as well as create more and better positions that are available to them. The real opportunity of the least advantaged group would thus tend to be improved in such a scheme that allowed some people even greater levels of real opportunity than they would have had under Strict Equality of Opportunity. If, for example, everyone is given an equal chance to receive medical training then the medical profession is likely to be smaller and less effective than if such training is awarded to those who have demonstrated greater aptitude and ability for practicing medicine. Fair Difference of Opportunity says that if there are ways in which the real opportunity of the worst-off group could be improved by allowing inequalities in real opportunity then such arrangements are justified as long as they satisfy the other requirements of justice. Otherwise, Fair difference of Opportunity mandates Strict Equality of Opportunity in which educational resources are distributed by fair lottery.

Like Fair Equality of Opportunity, Fair Difference of Opportunity presupposes that everyone has equal formal access to all positions and that selections are made on the basis of realized merit, so it does not sanction formally excluding members of an ethnic group or social class from some occupations even if this would improve the prospects of the least advantaged. Also, like Fair Equality of Opportunity, Fair Difference of Opportunity forbids trade-offs between real opportunities and material means, so a society may not institute measures that diminish the real opportunity of some relative to others simply because this would increase their income and wealth or the income and wealth of others. Unlike Fair Equality of Opportunity, however, Fair Difference of

Opportunity permits real opportunity to be traded off for real opportunity but only in a specific way. It does not sanction merely maximizing the total level of real opportunity in society, whatever that might mean, but instead allows inequalities in real opportunity only if these differences improve the real opportunities of the least advantaged group.

ORIGINAL POSITION

Each party in the Original Position is motivated to secure her own real opportunity. How might they decide on a mutually acceptable principle for distributing real opportunity among them, assuming the principle they select will be conjoined to the other principles of Justice as Fairness? Behind the veil of ignorance, the parties do not know their natural endowments or social circumstances; they are concerned to maximize their own real opportunities; and they are disinterested in the real opportunity of one another. Under these assumptions, the default position is to agree that real opportunity should be, as far as possible, equal among them, no matter what a person's natural abilities or social background.

What reasons might they have for moving away from this default position, either in favor of Fair Equality of Opportunity, which allows one's real opportunity to vary with her native endowments and motivations but not her social circumstances, or in favor of Fair Difference of Opportunity, which allows a person's real opportunity to vary only as part of a system that improves the real opportunity of all?

On its face, there seem to be good reasons for them to reject Fair Equality of Opportunity because it allows unequal chances among those who are differently endowed and motivated. One of the parties might judge that, for all she knows, she may end up as someone who is disabled and whose early family life dissuaded her from trying for certain desirable positions and sapped her willingness to put much effort into pursuing them. Although the Difference Principle may nonetheless ensure her sufficient income and wealth, her real opportunity would tend to suffer under Fair Equality of Opportunity because that principle only ensures equal chances among those whose motivations and natural endowments are equal. Her interest in maximizing her level of real opportunity thus gives her reasons to object to a principle like Fair Equality of Opportunity that does not sufficiently protect her real opportunity if she turns out to have below-average natural abilities and motivations.

If, however, each party in the Original position is assured that her level of real opportunity could be improved by allowing some people to have greater real opportunity than others then each of them would be provided with the highest level of real opportunity possible if she were to end up in the least fortunate group. Some people have greater natural ability than others; the influences of some natural and social contingencies are more easily corrected for than others; and the incentives that would be created in such a system would result in more educational resources and open positions for all. The parties therefore have reasons to insist on equal real opportunity for everyone, no matter a person's natural and social endowments, *unless* these contingencies could be used to provide everyone with higher chances of securing better positions for themselves.

What other kinds of reasons could the parties in the Original Position appeal to when choosing between Fair Equality of Opportunity and Fair Difference of Opportunity? Let's briefly return to the considerations that led them to select Formal Equality of Opportunity.[12]

(1) *The primary good of self-respect.* Each of the three aspects of self-respect that Rawls discusses provides grounds for favoring Fair Difference of Opportunity over Fair Equality of Opportunity. First, the parties in the Original Position have an interest in protecting their sense of their own worth and securing that same kind of respect from others. If someone had lower chances of securing public and non-public positions because of his social class or early childhood then he would tend to feel that he was not fully respected in society (TJ 82, 91, 175, 326, 478). Fair Equality of Opportunity and Fair Difference of Opportunity both aim to mitigate these social influences on real opportunity and so affirm each person's sense of her own worth. But a person may also feel that he is not fully respected in society, and so come to doubt his own value, if his below-average native abilities and socially instilled lack of motivation diminish his chances at securing desirable positions in society. While Fair Equality of Opportunity would allow this person to receive a lower level of real opportunity, which would tend to undermine his sense of self-worth, Fair Difference of Opportunity aims to mitigate the influence of these factors on his chances of taking up desirable positions, which better protects his self-respect. His self-respect would be protected under Fair Difference of Opportunity because he is assured that any differences in real opportunity that exist work to his advantage by providing him with more and better opportunities for position than he would have if everyone had the same chances at securing desirable social positions. Thus, the parties may judge that Fair Difference of Opportunity is more effective than Fair Equality of Opportunity at securing each person's sense of his own worth, including those with less fortunate natural endowments and motivation.

Second, the parties also have an interest in ensuring that they are confident in their own values, aims, and projects as well as in securing appreciation and admiration from others (TJ 386). In particular, they are concerned with ensuring that their projects and aims involve intricate development and sophisticated exercise of natural talents and abilities; they are also concerned with actively participating in social unions whose members have shared ends and engage in activities in support of them (TJ 373–376, 386). The parties thus aim to ensure that they have a fair chance to hold public office as well as occupy various privileged positions in the economy and wider society. Fair Equality of Opportunity, however, allows the prospects of someone with less fortunate natural endowments and motivations to have lower chances at securing various positions that tend to garner admiration and approval from others. Fair Difference of Opportunity, by contrast, increases the chances of everyone to hold positions in mutually valued associations and as well as positions that call upon sophisticated uses of realized talents and skills.

And, third, the parties in the Original Position have an interest in ensuring that they feel confident in their ability to pursue their own aims and projects, which often requires them to take up positions of responsibility and authority. In order to protect themselves against feelings of powerlessness and impotence, they have reasons to ensure that everyone has a fair chance at securing those positions (TJ 448, 469). Those who have less advantageous natural abilities and socially infected motivations are particularly likely to feel ashamed of their diminished abilities, although Fair Equality of Opportunity provides no protection for them once they are assured equal chances with those who are just as unlucky in their natural endowments and motivations (TJ 389). Fair Difference of Opportunity, by contrast, provides everyone greater chances to secure public and private positions that tend to reinforce self-confidence and diminish feelings of resignation and apathy.

(2) Moral development. The laws of moral psychology that, according to Rawls, govern the moral development of people in a well-ordered society say that our sentiments of love, friendship, and justice tend to develop and prosper when we find other people and institutions affirming our own good (TJ 433). Someone who has less fortunate natural abilities and motivations, however, may be less likely to see society as working for his benefit because his diminished prospects for position are left uncompensated for, or they are only compensated by inferior values of income and wealth. A just, well-ordered society governed by Fair Difference of Opportunity, however, would be more stable because it ensures that any inequalities in real opportunity a person may suffer nonetheless improve his own real opportunities.

(3) Envy. Disparities in real opportunity can be destabilizing in certain circumstances by fostering envy among those who are less advantaged. Although Fair Equality of Opportunity more or less corrects for the influence of social contingencies on a person's real opportunity, it may still fail to discourage envious hostility among those with less advantageous natural endowments and motivations because they may have diminished real opportunities as compared to those with more advantageous natural abilities and motivations. Like the Difference Principle, Fair Difference of Opportunity is less likely to engender envy because it assures everyone that any inequalities in real opportunity that exist work to improve their own chances at securing better positions in society.

Fair Equality of Opportunity may have initially seemed to be the best way to ensure that everyone has a fair chance at securing offices and positions that are formally open to all. And a principle like Fair Difference of Opportunity that allows inequalities in opportunity might have at first seemed unjust. But when we take up the perspective of many people with disabilities or others who have below-average natural endowments and socially infected motivations in a society governed by Fair Equality of Opportunity, we find that they will likely have great difficulty maintaining their self-respect, accepting the institutions of society as affirming their own good, and avoiding feelings of destructive envy than in a society governed by Fair Difference of Opportunity. In light of these considerations, a more just way to ensure fair opportunity for all, including those with disabilities, is to ensure each person equal chances at securing desirable positions, regardless of their natural endowments, social circumstances, and motivations. But if the self-respect of everyone could be maintained or improved by allowing inequalities in real opportunity that increase the real opportunity of everyone then Fair Difference of Opportunity is a better way of fairly preparing people to compete for offices and positions in a just society.

CONCLUSION

When Rawls presents the "final statement" of his conception of Justice as Fairness in *A Theory of Justice*, he sets out the two principles of justice and—in addition—"Priority Rules" for specifying certain relations among those principles. What he calls the First Priority Rule not only asserts the lexical priority of the equal liberties principle over the other principles of justice, but it also says: ,

> The basic liberties can be restricted only for the sake of liberty. There are two cases:
> (a) a less extensive liberty must strengthen the total system of liberties shared by all;
> (b) a less than equal liberty must be acceptable to those with the lesser liberty. (TJ 266)

And, what Rawls calls the Second Priority Rule not only asserts the lexical priority of Fair Equality of Opportunity over the Difference Principle; but surprisingly, it lists a principle that is similar to Fair Difference of Opportunity as one of the relevant cases:

> (a) an inequality of opportunity must enhance the opportunities of those with the lesser opportunity (TJ 266).

What Justice as Fairness, in its final form, may give us is: (1) several types of goods that presumptively ought to be distributed equally (e.g., liberties, opportunities, income and wealth, etc.); (2) a lexical ordering of those types of goods that specifies their importance relative to one another and forbids any trade-offs among different types of them (e.g. liberties take absolute precedence over income and wealth and cannot be traded off for them); (3) and rules saying that each type of good can be traded off for a good *of that same type*, but only if this provides more good of that kind to those who have the least of it (e.g. the Difference Principle and Fair Difference of Opportunity).

In order to justify an unequal distribution of a type of primary good, on this interpretation, we must ensure that doing so does not undermine any primary goods that have a higher priority. The social bases of self-respect, according to Rawls, constitute the most important primary good, so justice requires that we adequately secure it (TJ 348, 386, 468). We have questioned whether Fair Equality of Opportunity is necessary to ensure the self-respect of everyone and suggested that it may actually undermine the self-respect of some people, especially some people with disabilities, by allowing them to suffer lower chances of securing social positions without compensating them for these inequalities. Under this principle, those who are born with less advantageous natural talents and abilities, or whose choices and resolve have been adversely influenced by social circumstance, may tend to doubt their self-worth and feel a sense of hopelessness because their prospects at securing various privileged positions in society are significantly worse than those with greater natural talent and fortitude. In order to secure the self-respect of everyone, the default distribution of real opportunity should not be to simply ensure equal chances for those who have the same motivations and natural endowments, as Fair Equality of Opportunity asserts, but instead to ensure everyone the same level of real opportunity to secure desirable positions, regardless of their native abilities, motivations or social background. We have also suggested some reasons why everyone's self-respect would be improved under an unequal distribution of real opportunity. Once we have checked to see that Fair Difference of Opportunity would not threaten, and perhaps would enhance, the self-respect of all, then Rawls's priority rules seem to allow inequalities in real opportunity that work to improve the real opportunity of the least advantaged—Fair Difference of Opportunity may surprisingly be a requirement of Rawls's Justice as Fairness itself.[13]

Finally, even if Justice as Fairness or a variant of it included Fair Difference of Opportunity, issues of self-respect will likely arise at further stages of application once the parties know more about the particular people to whom the principles apply and the history and culture of the society in which they live. We can only conjecture at what these facts might be in a particular society. But it could be that class barriers, discriminatory attitudes, social stigma, and other social obstacles to attaining public and non-public positions have a particularly strong and salient influence on the self-respect of certain historically disadvantaged groups in society, including those with disabilities. Fair Difference of Opportunity requires, however, that we not ignore those who are born with below-average natural abilities, including physical and mental impairments of various kinds, who, like all people, have interests of self-respect in improving their chances of securing desirable positions in society as well. If everyone's prospects of attaining privileged social positions would be improved by allowing some inequality in real opportunity, in a way that protects the self-respect of all, then Fair Difference of Opportunity would regard such an arrangement as fair and justified.

NOTES

1. See also Rawls (1999e, 1999c, 379). We will abbreviate three of Rawls's works as follows: TJ—Rawls (1999d); PL—Rawls (1993); R—Rawls (2001).
2. Many philosophers have attempted to apply Rawls's ideas about opportunity to social policy issues of various types, including Daniels (1985, 2008), Schopenhauer, Payne, and Cartwright (1995), and Buchanan et al. (2000). See also Roemer (1998) and Jacobs (2004) for discussions of equality of opportunity more generally.

3. Pogge (1989) notes this feature of Fair Equality of Opportunity as well.

4. Others have raised criticisms of Fair Equality of Opportunity that focus on whether it should have lexical priority over the Difference Principle, including Alexander (1985) and Arneson (1999).

5. Wasserman and Aas (2016) argue that society's obligation to assist the disabled should be determined by considerations of responsibility. We are concerned, however, that Wasserman and Aas insert concerns regarding responsibility where they do not belong, at least in a Rawlsian theory.

6. Arneson (1999) notes that this argument is stronger for Formal Equality of Opportunity than it is for Fair Equality of Opportunity.

7. See TJ 329 and Rawls (1999b, 127).

8. For related discussion, see Sachs (2012).

9. Rawls notes these possibilities at TJ 64, and especially with regard to the influences of early family life at TJ 447–448 and R 164–166. Arneson (1999) notes them as well.

10. Rawls focuses mostly on income and wealth but allows for the Difference Principle to apply to other primary social goods. See Daniels (1985) and Cohen (1989).

11. The desirability of a position, on Rawls's view, depends on factors such as whether it calls upon intricate and subtle abilities, whether it is part of a shared social union, whether those who take up the position are admired and appreciated, etc. Questions remain about how to interpret and combine these factors, but for our purposes we will simply assume that this can be done and, in the meantime, rely on intuitive understandings of the relative desirability of different positions.

12. Some of these considerations in favor of FEO are helpfully discussed by Taylor (2004).

13. See also Rawls (1999a, 133).

References

Alexander, Larry A. 1985. "Fair Equality of Opportunity." *Philosophy Research Archives* 11:197–208.

Arneson, Richard J. 1999. "Against Rawlsian Equality of Opportunity." *Philosophical Studies* 93, no.1:77–112.

Buchanan, Allen, Daniel W. Brock, Norman Daniels, and Daniel Wikler. 2000. *From Chance to Choice: Genetics & Justice*. Cambridge, UK: Cambridge University Press.

Cohen, Joshua. 1989. "The Economic Basis of Deliberative Democracy." *Social Philosophy and Policy* 6 (02):25–50.

Daniels, Norman. 1985. *Just Health Care*. Cambridge, UK: Cambridge University Press.

Daniels, Norman. 2008. *Just Health: Meeting Health Needs Fairly*. Cambridge, UK: Cambridge University Press.

Jacobs, Lesley A. 2004. *Pursuing Equal Opportunities: The Theory and Practice of Egalitarian Justice*. Cambridge, UK: Cambridge University Press.

Lewens, Tim. 2010. "What Are 'Natural Inequalities'?" *Philosophical Quarterly* 60 (239):264–285.

Lippert-Rasmussen, Kasper. 2004. "Are Some Inequalities More Unequal Than Others? Nature, Nurture and Equality." *Utilitas* 16, no. 2:193–219.

Nagel, Thomas. 1997. "Justice and Nature." *Oxford Journal of Legal Studies* 17, no. 2:303–322.

Pogge, Thomas. 1989. *Realizing Rawls*. Ithaca, NY: Cornell University Press.

Rawls, John. 1993. *Political Liberalism*. New York: Columbia University Press.

Rawls, John. 1999a. "Distributive Justice." In *Collected Papers*, edited by John Rawls and Samuel Freeman, 130–153. Cambridge, MA: Harvard University Press.

Rawls, John. 1999b. "Legal Obligation and the Duty of Fair Play." In *Collected Papers*, edited by John Rawls and Samuel Freeman, 117–129. Cambridge, MA: Harvard University Press.

Rawls, John. 1999c. "Social Unity and Primary Goods." In *Collected Papers*, edited by John Rawls and Samuel Freeman, 359–387. Cambridge, MA: Harvard University Press.

Rawls, John. 1999d. *A Theory of Justice*. Rev. ed. Cambridge, MA: Belknap Press of Harvard University Press.

Rawls, John. 1999e. "Two Concepts of Rules." In *Collected Papers*, edited by John Rawls and Samuel Freeman, 20–46. Cambridge, MA: Harvard University Press.

Rawls, John. 2001. *Justice as Fairness: A Restatement*. Edited by Erin Kelly. Cambridge, MA: Belknap Press of Harvard University Press.

Roemer, John E. 1998. *Equality of Opportunity*. Cambridge, MA: Harvard University Press.

Sachs, Benjamin. 2012. "The Limits of Fair Equality of Opportunity." *Philosophical Studies* 160, no. 2:323–343.

Schopenhauer, Arthur, E. F. J. Payne, and David E. Cartwright. 1995. *On the Basis of Morality*. Rev. ed. Providence, RI: Berghahn Books.

Taylor, Robert S. 2004. "Self-Realization and the Priority of Fair Equality of Opportunity." *Journal of Moral Philosophy* 1, no. 3:333–347.

Wasserman, David, and Sean Aas. 2016. "Natural and Social Inequality." *Journal of Moral Philosophy* 13, no. 5:576–601.

CHAPTER 16

··

THE DISABILITY CASE
AGAINST ASSISTED
DYING

··

DANNY SCOCCIA

THE term "assisted dying" in what follows will be used broadly to include not just assisted suicide and "active" euthanasia, but also the termination of life-sustaining care in cases where the patient did not or cannot request it. Should some forms of physician-assisted dying (PAD) be legal, and, if so, which ones and under what circumstances? The question here is not about the morality of isolated acts by individuals, but rather about whether we as a society ought to have public laws and norms that permit or even encourage some forms of assisted dying, especially by physicians within certain legally defined parameters. The aim of this chapter is to articulate and assess the reasons why disability rights (DR) advocates have urged a "no" answer to this question.

Several US states now permit physician-assisted suicide (PAS) for residents deemed to be "terminally ill" (likely to die of natural causes within 6 months), and some European countries now permit PAD for anyone with "unbearable suffering." The DR critique of assisted dying is meant to apply to both of these practices, but not to a legal right to refuse unwanted medical treatment (Not Dead Yet et al. 2004).[1] It doesn't apply to the latter because that right is perfectly general, had by both the able and disabled, whereas the PAD laws of the United States and Europe discriminate between the healthy/able and the sick/disabled. The DR critique alleges that those laws reflect and reinforce "ableist" prejudice about the disabled and chronically sick not having lives worth living and being "better off dead"—prejudices responsible for the marginalization, stigmatization, and rights violations of the disabled. The central contention of the DR movement is that the main disadvantages of disabilities like deafness, blindness, paraplegia, dwarfism, autism, Down's syndrome, and so on, are not a natural, inevitable consequence of the physical or cognitive impairments that disabled people have, but instead are due to social practices of marginalization and stigmatization.

Where efforts to legalize some form of PAD have been defeated, as they were recently in Great Britain (Gallagher and Roxby 2015), it has been through a political alliance of conservative religious groups committed to the "sanctity of human life," liberal religious groups committed to a "social gospel" of improving the lot of the poor and vulnerable, and DR advocates, many of whom are nonreligious. The first group is likely to oppose all abortion, while the latter two are likely to support gay rights, a woman's right to terminate pregnancy, affirmative action for racial minorities, and other progressive social causes. It is important to recognize that even though these groups agree in their opposition to legalizing PAD, their reasons for opposing it differ significantly. The socially conservative religious group's opposition is based on what Joel Feinberg called "pure legal moralism" or the idea that some practices are wrong and should be legally prohibited *even if they violate no one's rights and set back no one's interests*. According to the "sanctity of human life" ethic that is the basis of this group's position, intentionally taking the life of innocent human beings (oneself or others) is "playing God," which is morally forbidden *even if the person killed freely consents to it and is better off dead*. The DR critique of PAD has nothing to do with this "sanctity of life" ethic and is not a species of pure moralism.[2]

What, then, is it? The critique alleges that PAD wrongly discriminates against the disabled, but it has two strands: paternalistic and nonpaternalistic. According to the paternalistic strand, we should not legalize PAD for the good of the vast majority of those disabled and/or terminally ill people who would choose it. According to the nonpaternalistic strand, the reason for not legalizing it is to prevent harm to all disabled and/or terminally ill people, including those who might never choose it.

The Paternalistic DR Argument and Some Conceptions of Autonomy

The paternalistic argument proceeds roughly as follows:

> The choice of PAD is almost always a coerced, nonautonomous one. For those who are disabled, it is often due to despair at living in a society that marginalizes and stigmatizes the disabled. For the terminally ill, it is often due to fear of pain and suffering because hospice care is inadequate or unavailable. And, in both groups, it may be caused by shame at being or fear of becoming dependent on or a "burden" to others. Almost no one chooses the option of PAD autonomously, and it is in almost no one's interests to have it.[3] Society should deny people the legal option of PAD for their own good.

Joel Feinberg has distinguished a "hard" type of paternalism, which he claimed true (Millian) liberals must oppose, from a "soft" type, some of which he thought liberals may support (Feinberg 1984). Hard paternalism interferes with fully voluntary choices on the grounds that the ends or values of the person targeted are misguided (e.g., forcing a life-saving blood transfusion on an adult Jehovah's Witness who rejects transfusions as "contrary to God's law"), while soft paternalism interferes with choices that are substantially nonvoluntary.[4] The paternalistic DR argument is the soft type.

While it is possible to engage in wrongful discrimination in ways that have nothing to do with paternalism, it is also possible to fail to engage in paternalism in a wrongfully discriminatory way, and that is precisely what the paternalistic DR objection alleges. When the able try to kill themselves, it is usually assumed that they suffer from temporary but treatable depression, whereas when the disabled do so it is commonly assumed that they are competent and rational. If PAD is legalized, requests for it by the able will be closely scrutinized and often denied on soft paternalist grounds. Requests for it by the disabled will not be so closely scrutinized and will often be granted, despite being substantially nonvoluntary, because physicians, psychiatrists, and judges will assume that it is rational to want to die because of one's disability.

Our statement of the soft paternalist argument uses the term "autonomy," which may give rise to confusion because of its ambiguity. In what follows, we'll distinguish three senses of it. The first—call it "political" autonomy—refers to possessing the external resources needed for a good, self-directed life, such as minimal affluence, civil and political liberties, education, adequate healthcare, the "social bases of self-respect," and so on. Slaves, women living under the Taliban, those in extreme poverty struggling for subsistence, gay people forced to remain closeted in an intensely homophobic culture, and paraplegics in wheelchairs unable to navigate an urban environment due to the absence of simple ramps lack some or much "political" autonomy. Another more popular term for this kind of autonomy is "empowerment." Second, there is a more "formal" kind of autonomy—"moral" autonomy—that consists in choosing on the basis of reasons that one regards as good or justifying—or would, if one were factually well-informed about one's options and thinking clearly. Weakness of will, psychological compulsion, ignorance or mistaken beliefs about one's options, extreme fatigue, excitement, depression, the influence of drugs or alcohol, and mental illness can weaken or cancel one's moral autonomy. Because political and moral autonomy are separate but each seems important to autonomy, we should recognize a third sense of the term, where a choice is "fully" autonomous only if it is the product of both political *and* moral autonomy. It is in this sense—"full" autonomy—that the term is used in the DR argument. It alleges that the choice by most disabled or terminally ill people of PAD is not fully autonomous, because it is due to a lack of political autonomy, moral autonomy, or both.

There is another, supposedly "liberal" conception of autonomy that has been the target of much criticism from feminist and disability scholars and communitarian-minded political philosophers. While there is a "metaphysical" objection to it, the more important objection is ethical. The "liberal" conception supposes that the autonomous person's values are individualistic or egoistic in content; the autonomous man does not value the approval or respect of others or relationships based on love, care, or friendship.

He is (or so he *thinks*) a "self-made" man whose achievements are due entirely to his own talents and efforts, a "rugged individualist" with no weaknesses or needs that make him dependent on others. The ideal is objectionable because it is delusional, sexist, ableist, and selfish. It undergirds the Social Darwinist political philosophy extolled by the likes of Ayn Rand and extreme libertarians, which denies to the state any legitimate role in providing a "safety net" or redistributing the gains and losses from unfettered market competition. The prevalence of this "liberal" ideal of autonomy in the moral culture of capitalist societies is due to its role in promoting the interests of capital. That is, it functions as an "ideology" in Marx's sense.

We should grant the soundness of this critique of the "liberal" conception of autonomy but recognize that it does nothing to impugn "full" autonomy as a moral and political ideal. Indeed, that ideal inspires the DR movement's struggle for the increased empowerment of disabled people via the Americans with Disabilities Act and other legal reforms. Nothing in the "full autonomy" ideal implies that the autonomous person must be unemotional, strongly egoistic, or deluded about the extent to which she is dependent on others in society to meet her most basic needs. The conception of "full autonomy" sketched above does not entail the "liberal" ideal.[5]

If the "liberal" ideal is ideological, then doesn't it follow that any choices motivated by it *cannot* be fully autonomous? If a severely disabled or terminally ill man chooses PAD only because he accepts the "liberal" ideal and believes it would be "undignified" to become dependent on others for help to be fed or use the bathroom, shouldn't we think that such motivation renders his choice less than fully autonomous?

The correct answer to these questions is "no." The fact that some normative ideal is false or defective does not preclude its motivating autonomous choices, given the formal account of "full" autonomy just described. Some defenders of the paternalistic DR argument might reply that this only shows that the account is too formal. While that reply might have some merit, recall that we assumed that the argument is a species of *soft* paternalism. The distinction between soft and hard paternalism assumes that choices can be fully autonomous but motivated by ends or values that are foolish or normatively defective. If defenders of the DR argument say that *any* choice of PAD inspired by false, ableist ideology is not autonomous, they must give up the pretense that the paternalism they are defending is soft and admit that it is hard. Few seem willing to do that.

Assessing the Paternalistic DR Argument

Is the choice of PAD by sick or disabled people both lacking in autonomy (because it is coerced) and not in their best interests? There are really two separate questions here. In general, the mere fact that a choice is coerced, involuntary, or lacking in autonomy does not entail that it is contrary to one's best interests. Surrendering one's wallet to the armed robber who demands "your money or your life!" is certainly coerced but probably prudent. Consider a severely disabled man who asks for PAD only because his life is very bad due to disability discrimination; in a society without such discrimination, he would have a fulfilling life that's well worth living. It is quite possible that his choice to end his life is in his best interests despite its being coerced. Of course, even if it is, that does not mean that he should be given suicide assistance. Perhaps it should not be given because he has a moral duty to continue living and struggle against disability discrimination rather than surrender to it, if not for his own sake then for the sake of other disabled people. But that reason for denying his PAD request is not the paternalistic one that we're considering.

There also can be little doubt that at least *some* disabled people who request PAD are making a fully autonomous choice. One defender of the paternalistic DR argument, Jerome Bickenbach, concedes as much, citing the example of Sue Rodriguez, a Canadian woman with amyotrophic lateral sclerosis (ALS) who fought for a legal right to PAD after her illness made it impossible for her to take her own life without assistance. Bickenbach describes her (unsuccessful) attempt to win that right as "taking control over her own life" (Bickenbach 1998, 126). Doesn't the fact that the choice of PAD by severely disabled people is sometimes autonomous, prudent, or both refute the paternalistic argument?

It does not. The argument only claims that "almost" no choice of assisted dying is both autonomous and in one's best interests. As Bickenbach explains:

> the law must be written for everyone, not just the exceptional person. It is a commonplace in political theory that an institutional constraint on autonomy may well be justified if, in general and in the long run, it protects people who are vulnerable, though on occasion it produces undesirable, even right-infringing, results for the exceptional few.   (Bickenbach 1998, 126)

Bickenbach's "commonplace" is particularly relevant to the justification of "group paternalism." Paternalistic laws are group paternalism because they target everyone who satisfies some general description in the law—smokers, motorcyclists, anyone who wants to use crack or meth, and the like. Surely, in order for such laws to be *justified* soft paternalism, it is not necessary that the choice of *absolutely everyone* in the targeted group be both substantially nonvoluntary and harmful to the person making it. Consider laws that even states that permit PAD have, making it a crime for one private citizen to assist the suicide of another. (Thus, if A lends his gun to B, knowing that B intends to use it to commit suicide, A has broken the law.) Surely it is enough for this law to be justified soft paternalism that *only a large majority* of those who attempt suicide are acting from an emotional state that impairs moral autonomy, and ending their lives is not in their best interests. The same ought to be true of laws that forbid PAD for the terminally ill or seriously disabled: they can be justified as soft group paternalism even if the choice of assisted dying by some (but not many) terminally ill or seriously disabled people would be both fully autonomous and in their best interests.

Doctrinaire Nozickian libertarians, it should be noted, reject Bickenbach's "commonplace." They insist that rights impose "absolute side constraints" on morally permissible state action. Thus, a law that violates the rights of a single individual remains impermissible even if it is the only way to provide life-saving benefits to countless others. According to this libertarian view, so long as there are some terminally ill or disabled persons whose choice of assisted dying would be fully autonomous, a ban on assisted dying violates their *negative* right to liberty, making it impermissible even if it benefits thousands of other sick or disabled persons.

There are many possible replies to this libertarian view. One is simply to deny that rights are absolute side constraints on morally permissible action; the violation of any right is justified if necessary to prevent a large enough evil. Another is to deny that the case involves a conflict between respecting the rights of a small group versus "providing benefits" to a much larger one. Instead, many DR advocates will argue, the conflict is between respecting the rights of a smaller group versus the rights of a larger one. If the state legalizes assisted dying, it violates the *positive* right to full autonomy of those sick or terminally ill persons who choose to end their lives only because they suffer disability discrimination or are denied access to adequate hospice care. Of course, this second reply rejects the libertarian's assumption that the only natural rights we have are negative ones (not to be killed, assaulted, interfered with, etc.).

The paternalistic argument we're considering assumes that the case of Elizabeth Bouvia is typical of those in which a severely disabled person requests PAD.[6] Bouvia was a quadriplegic woman living independently when she suffered a number of personal setbacks (miscarriage, divorce) and incidents of disability discrimination from state agencies, educational institutions, and employers. At the age of 25, feeling defeated, she had herself admitted to a hospital where she tried to starve herself to death. The hospital tried to force-feed her, she resisted, and a legal battle ensued. In 1986, the California Court of Appeals overruled a lower court ruling that sided with the hospital, saying that court erred in neglecting to consider the low quality of life that her quadriplegic condition made inevitable. Bouvia later changed her mind and chose not to end her life. Her earlier choice of PAD was both substantially nonautonomous and not in her best interests. If her case was typical of those in which the seriously disabled ask for PAD, then the paternalistic DR argument against legalizing any PAD for which they are eligible would seem to be quite strong.

The force of the objection becomes more doubtful when we shift focus from PAD for disabled people like Elizabeth Bouvia to PAS for the terminally ill. Proponents of the objection contend that a number of factors, including the high economic cost of much end-of-life care, inevitably lead to strong social pressures on terminally ill people to choose it, thereby reducing the autonomy of their choice. But while it is true that many would choose it only because they've been manipulated or coerced, it surely is also true that many others would do so freely and autonomously. Which group would be larger? The "Philosopher's Brief" that was submitted in *Washington v. Glucksberg* (1997) admits that even if legalized PAS comes with "safeguards," they will sometimes fail and some nonautonomous requests for PAS by terminally ill people will mistakenly be granted. But it claimed that those cases will be far fewer in number than autonomously made requests that are denied under a ban on PAS (Dworkin et al. 1997, 46). Felicia Ackerman has objected that the Brief "gives no good reason to believe this far-from-obvious claim" (Ackerman 1998, 155).

Finally, DR advocates who wish to defend their opposition to legalized PAD via the paternalistic argument face an insurmountable problem. Consider severely disabled people who receive life-sustaining care, decide that they want their lives to end, and, rather than ask for PAD, opt to reject the care and "let nature take its course." Recall that the DR critique of PAD is not supposed to apply to a legal right of competent adults to reject unwanted medical care. But if the basis of the DR critique is the paternalistic argument, how can the critique avoid applying to the latter right too (Mayo and Gunderson 2002)? If society should not create a legal right PAD because there is no feasible way to prevent the incompetent, clinically depressed, subtly coerced, and so on, from exercising it, then shouldn't society either abolish or severely curtail the legal right to reject unwanted medical care, to protect the same vulnerable groups? Elizabeth Bouvia was rejecting medical treatment rather than asking for help to end her life, and the amicus brief of the DR groups in *Vacco v. Quill* maintains (plausibly) that she was not competent to exercise that right and so should not have been allowed to. But the existence of cases like hers does not lead the groups to demand the abolition of a legal right to reject unwanted care.

DR advocates who support the right to reject unwanted care must, to avoid inconsistency, admit that the paternalistic argument is not by itself sufficient to justify their opposition to legalized PAD. They have to appeal to another argument that does not threaten the legal right to reject treatment.

TWO NONPATERNALISTIC DR OBJECTIONS; THE NONEXPRESSIVIST OBJECTION

Let's turn now to the nonpaternalistic DR argument. We'll distinguish two forms of it: "nonexpressivist" and "expressivist." Both claim that legalized PAD is similar to Jim Crow laws, harming all disabled people just as those racist laws harmed all black people. Both appeal to a "prevention of wrongful harm to others" principle rather than pure moralism or soft or hard paternalism, claiming that a ban on PAD is needed to prevent the rights violations of many who do not want and would never ask for it. The difference between the two lies in the causal route through which the harm to all disabled people is thought to travel. According to the expressivist "harm to others" objection, the harm occurs because of the "meaning" or "message" conveyed by legalized PAD; namely, that the sick and disabled have less value than the healthy and able. If the objection is correct and limited-eligibility PAD really does express a message of disabled inferiority, then it harms disabled people directly by denying their equal dignity. That message affects the able as well, perhaps reinforcing their ableist prejudices and promoting behaviors by them that harm the disabled in more indirect ways.

We'll begin with the nonexpressivist version of the objection, which does not trace the harms suffered by the disabled to the meaning or message of legalized PAD. It proceeds as follows:

> Assisted dying may benefit the able (and perhaps some of those severely disabled people who would choose it), but it does so *at the expense of* the disabled as a group or class.[7] The able can autonomously choose to end their lives if they become terminally or seriously ill and find their condition unbearable, and having that option may well be in their best interests. But—and this large causal claim is the key contention in this version of the argument—giving them that legal option has the *effect* of sustaining disability discrimination. Since providing the disabled with PAD is much cheaper than providing them the social support and antidiscrimination protections that they need to have for minimally decent lives, legalized PAD encourages the able to support PAD *rather than* the elimination of disability discrimination. For that reason, PAD should not be legalized.

The objection is meant to apply not just to the limited-eligibility PAD laws of Europe and US states like Oregon, but also to the PAD law that extreme libertarians support (which would extend eligibility for PAD to all competent adults, whether or not they are disabled, sick, or suffering), for this law would (it alleges) have the same effect on the disabled as ones that limit eligibility to the disabled or terminally ill would. All of them encourage able people to support a cheaper PAD to more expensive accommodations, support, and legal protections for the disabled.

Is the large causal claim at the heart of this argument true? Certainly, it is at least plausible. The claim does not require that the able majority be motivated by animosity toward the disabled, a desire to see them suffering or stigmatized. Indeed, it presupposes that they have some minimal amount of compassionate concern for them, for why else would they prefer that the disabled have the option of PAD to a status quo in which they have neither that option nor the social support/legal protections that would give them real autonomy? But my sense is that many able people feel that our society already "bends over backward" to "accommodate" the disabled, that more accommodations would come at their expense, and that justice simply doesn't require that they make that sacrifice. Increased support for the disabled is the responsibility of relatives, churches, and charities.

Whether the causal claim in question is true may depend on which PAD practices are being considered. If it is true, it should be easiest to see that in the case of the very "liberal" PAD practices of Belgium and the Netherlands, which extend eligibility for PAD to the severely disabled. The Royal Dutch Medical Association has estimated that 650 infants are killed each year under its euthanasia law. Many psychiatric patients have also been killed or committed suicide, as has a 47-year-old woman who found her persistent tinnitus intolerable (Reid 2015).[8] Of course, the mere fact that many disabled but non–terminally ill people qualify for euthanasia and in fact die from it under this regime does not by itself show that the causal claim is true. Conversely, the fact that the Netherlands spends almost twice as much as the United States (as a percentage of gross domestic product) on disability pension benefits does not show that it is false (Ruffing 2015). What's needed is evidence that, after a society adopts PAD practices like those of the Netherlands, further empowerment for the disabled is slowed or reversed.

Whether legalizing PAS only for the terminally ill results in increased discrimination against disabled persons who are not terminally ill is even more disputed. If it does, then the interest of the able majority in having the option to end their lives if/when they become terminally ill is in conflict with the interest of the disabled minority in political autonomy and a minimally decent life. Even if PAS for the terminally ill does not immediately threaten the interests of the severely disabled who are not terminally ill, perhaps it is likely to lead (via a slippery slope) to the more "liberal" PAD laws of Europe, which are a direct threat to the interests of disabled people (Amundson 2002). Assuming this conflict of interests does exist, it raises the question of whose interests should prevail. DR advocates say that the interests of the disabled should because, even though the disabled are fewer in number, their interest in living a minimally decent life is much more urgent than the nondisabled majority's interest in controlling the circumstances of their death. The able who support Oregon-like PAS laws may not have any vicious desire to stigmatize the disabled, but they are being selfish if they prioritize their less urgent interest over the more urgent interest of the disabled. A defense of this view probably requires rejecting utilitarianism in favor of the prioritarian welfarist consequentialism proposed by Derek Parfit or theories of democratic equality of the sort championed by Elizabeth Anderson and Thomas Scanlon. But even these theories side with the DR critique of Oregon-type PAS laws only if the threat they pose to the interests of the disabled in having a minimally decent life is grave enough. Whether or not the threat is sufficiently grave is one of many issues on which DR advocates and the supporters of PAD continue to disagree.

We noted earlier that DR advocates face an inconsistency objection if they try to defend their position solely on the basis of the paternalistic argument. To avoid inconsistency they must argue that the case against legalized PAD rests partly on the paternalistic argument but partly on another argument that provides a reason against legalizing PAD but not a reason to curtail or abolish the legal right of competent adults to reject unwanted medical treatment. Can the nonexpressivist "harm to others" argument fill that role? That's doubtful, because the reason it gives for opposing a legal right to PAD seems to apply equally to the right to reject unwanted care. Surely many of the able support the latter right for reasons that are no less selfish and ableist—"it is much cheaper than increasing social support for the sick or disabled"—than their reasons for supporting a right to PAD.

Terry Schiavo and the Persistently Comatose

Disability rights advocates have been active in opposing not just the very permissive PAD practices of Belgium and the Netherlands or the PAS laws that are increasingly popular in the United States, but also the withdrawal of life-sustaining care from some patients in a persistent coma. Many DR advocates joined religious "sanctity of life" groups in opposing the legal efforts of Terry Schiavo's husband to remove the feeding tube that kept her alive but in a coma from 1990 to 2005. Both groups urged that the husband, her proxy decision-maker, did not have her best interests at heart and was not credible in his claim that she had earlier told him that she did not wish to be kept alive indefinitely should she ever become comatose. Both also denied that she had suffered higher brain death, claiming that she exhibited behaviors, such as tracking moving objects with her eyes, that proved that she retained some higher cognitive functioning. Despite this agreement, the position of the two groups seemed to differ in this regard: for the "sanctity of human life" groups, prior consent and strong evidence of higher brain death are immaterial; removal of the feeding tube that keeps those patients in a persistent coma alive is wrong even if those two conditions are satisfied. The position staked out by the more than a dozen DR groups (including ADA Watch and Not Dead Yet) in their public letter, dated October 27, 2003, seems to be that removal of her feeding tube was wrong, but only because those two conditions were not clearly satisfied (ADA Watch et al. 2003). It is wrong because it threatens the rights and interests of other disabled people—as the nonexpressivist "harm to others" argument alleges. After all, if Schiavo's care is suspended because she has "no hope of recovery" or because she needs a feeding tube to be kept alive, what's to prevent withdrawal of care from other disabled people who are not comatose but still need feeding tubes and have "no hope of recovery"? The DR groups in the aforementioned letter claim that if Schiavo's care is discontinued for these reasons, the denial of care to patients with advanced ALS is in the offing.[9]

The defenders of assisted dying are likely to reply that this objection misidentifies the reasons in favor of "pulling the plug" in cases like Schiavo's. The reason to do so is not that Schiavo had "no hope of recovery" and certainly not that she needed a "feeding tube" to be kept alive. The main reason for doing so was that she had suffered massive brain damage from a cardiac arrest that deprived her brain of oxygen for several minutes, and she had been in a coma for more than a decade. These facts, together with the expert opinion of several expert neurologists who had examined her, provided very strong evidence that she had suffered higher brain death resulting in a *permanent* loss of any capacity to *have or regain consciousness*. It was the loss of that capacity, not inability to move any parts of her body, that made it accurate (if indelicate) to describe her as a "living vegetable." While her body might legally have been alive, she, the person, simply no longer existed. The situation of most ALS patients is completely different, both because they clearly want their care to be continued and because they have a capacity for not just consciousness but higher cognitive functioning (indeed, in the case of the physicist Stephen Hawking, at a level higher than that of the vast majority of able persons).

The DR position on Schiavo claims that continuing her care did not violate her right to reject treatment since she did not leave behind a written advance directive to establish clearly that that was her wish. But the DR letter never explains why strong evidence of prior authorization should be needed in cases where the evidence of higher brain death is very strong. Why shouldn't terminating life-sustaining care be the *default option* in those cases, so that care continues only if the patient has left an advance directive stipulating that he or she, perhaps for religious reasons, wants it continued? Unless one accepts a "sanctity of human life" ethic, one is likely to believe that it is both "unnatural" and "undignified" to keep those who've sustained higher brain death alive indefinitely. Such a belief cannot be dismissed as reflecting the "liberal" ideal of autonomy or ableist prejudice toward disability. Since it is likely that a majority of citizens hold this view, a democratic society ought to make termination of care in cases of higher brain death the default option. It is hard to see how or why doing so would in any way imperil those severely disabled persons who have not suffered higher brain death.

THE EXPRESSIVIST OBJECTION

Jim Crow laws assaulted black people's sense of dignity or self-respect by expressing the white majority's judgment, "you are inferior to us." A few exceptional individuals may be able to sustain a strong sense of their equal moral worth despite the existence of many laws that proclaim their inferiority, but most of us cannot. Our sense of self-respect has "social bases," which an acceptable theory of social justice (such as John Rawls's) will recognize as a "primary social good" that societies can distribute justly or unjustly. Being denied this good is a separate harm from being denied one's fair share of other primary social goods, such as wealth, political liberties, educational opportunities, and so one; the stigmatizing harm that Jim Crow laws caused to black people was distinct from the harms of being denied opportunities for socioeconomic advancement in education, housing, or employment. The expressivist version of the DR objection alleges that legalized PAD conveys a message to disabled people ("you don't have lives worth living!") that inflicts on them a similar dignity-based harm. That message directly harms them. When the message is endorsed by the state, it is likely to reinforce ableist prejudice in the majority (just as Jim Crow laws validated white racism), and that is likely to harm disabled people in other, indirect ways.

The DR critique of assisted dying is directed primarily at a public legal norm rather than individual private acts. This is true, in particular, of the expressivist version of the critique. Thus, it has no application to the case in which all forms of assisted suicide are illegal, Joe decides to end his life because of his disability, and Jane secretly breaks the law by assisting him. Jane's assistance might be wrong (or it might not be), but if it is wrong, it is not so for any reason identified by the expressivist argument. The secret acts of private individuals cannot affect the social bases of self-respect in the way that the public acts of the state can.[10]

The expressivist objection to PAD assumes that laws express a collective moral judgment. Obviously, the criminalization of a type of act expresses society's collective moral disapproval of it. But it should be equally obvious that legally permitting a type of act need not mean that society approves of or means to encourage it. Smoking is legally permitted but still frowned upon in many ways. Supporters of legalizing PAD may claim that what's clearly true of smoking is true of PAD as well. The collective moral judgment expressed by PAD's legalization is not that terminally ill or severely disabled people should end their lives—and still less that they have a lower moral standing than the healthy and able—but rather that society has no business thwarting their wish to end their lives should they have that wish.

But defenders of the expressivist DR objection will note that the United States and Europe do not permit PAD for any competent adult who asks for it; they limit eligibility to either the terminally ill or anyone with "unbearable suffering." Isn't that rather like a law that allows only black women to have abortions? Such a law would, of course, harm both white and black women, but in different ways. It would deny to white women the material advantages of increased control over their reproductive lives. To black women, it would express a judgment like "there should be fewer black people," an insulting denial of their equal dignity. Isn't it reasonable for disabled people to perceive in PAD regimes that limit eligibility to the very sick or dying a similarly denigrating message?

Earlier we noted that the DR critique is limited to PAD and does not extend to the legal right to reject unwanted, life-sustaining medical treatment. The expressivist objection, unlike the paternalistic and nonexpressivist "harm to others" arguments, justifies that limit in the critique's scope. Since the right to refuse treatment is had by all, both able and disabled, the moral judgment that it expresses is that everyone is sovereign over his or her body. That doesn't stigmatize or discriminate against anyone.

Returning to our question whether limited-eligibility PAD is analogous to legalizing abortion only for black women, supporters of PAD might argue that it isn't because the latter policy depends on the racist assumption that black people have an inferior moral status, whereas the justification for legalizing PAD for the gravely suffering or terminally ill does not depend on the premise that the disabled and/or terminally ill have a lower moral standing than the able and healthy. Its justification does rest on the prudential value judgment that when suffering is severe and treatable only with powerful drugs that leave one semi-conscious, one may be "better off dead." But that prudential value judgment is different from and does not entail the objectionable moral status judgment that the interests of the healthy/able matter more than those of the sick/disabled—any more than the judgment that literacy is a prudential good implies that the illiterate have a lower moral status with fewer rights than the literate (Harris 1993).

Defenders of the expressivist objection can concede that there is a justification of legalized PAD that's consistent with the moral equality of all persons. But the existence of such a justification is, they might urge, simply irrelevant to whether the law has a denigrating social meaning. Consider again a law that permits abortions only for black women. Suppose there was some "neutral," innocent public health justification for it and that justification was what motivated its enactment. Many black people would still see it as carrying the denigrating "there should be fewer of your kind!" message, and they would be justified in feeling insulted by it, given the history of race relations in the United States. PAD laws can stigmatize the disabled, even if the able majority does not support them with the intent that they do so.

Even so, is it plausible to see limited-eligibility PAD laws as having a denigrating social message? Whether any law has such a message depends on what Deborah Hellman calls its "objective social meaning," which she admits is not always clear (Hellman 2018). Jim Crow laws clearly had such meaning, while the meaning of a law requiring retirement at age 70 for public employees is (Hellman surmises) less clear. (Should we think the latter shows solicitude to the plight of young jobseekers, or we should think it expresses the message that the aged are less valuable than the young?) The objective social meaning of limited eligibility PAD may be similarly unclear. Indeed, Anita Silvers worries that it is the *denial* of a legal right to PAD to the disabled that has a denigrating, infantilizing social meaning. Silvers claims that "characterizing people with disabilities as incompetent, easily coerced, and inclined to end their lives places them in the roles to which they have been confined by disability discrimination. Doing so emphasizes their supposed fragility, which becomes a reason to deny that they are capable, and therefore deserving, of full social participation" (Silvers 1998, 132). Whether Silvers is right seems to me moot. Maybe neither the legalization nor the criminalization of assisted dying has any objective social meaning regarding the moral status of the disabled and/or terminally ill at all. Or maybe the objective social meaning of limited-eligibility PAD depends on how the law is administered and other background facts. If states that legalize PAD erect administrative safeguards to ensure that PAD requests from the incompetent or coerced are denied, and if they make hospice care available for the terminally ill, enforce laws against disability discrimination, provide support networks for those with severe disabilities, and so on, then the message of laws probably isn't denigrating at all. If the states in question do not do any of this sufficiently, then perhaps the disabled are justified in viewing the laws as a slap in the face.

CONCLUSION

We've distinguished three different strands to the DR critique of legalizing PAD: to prevent harm to the sick/disabled persons who would nonautonomously choose it, to avoid encouraging the able to support PAD rather than more "expensive" measures to reduce disability discrimination, and to prevent the various harms suffered by all disabled people due to legalized PAD's expressing a moral judgment that denies the equal moral standing of the disabled. Our analysis of these arguments supports a couple of conclusions. First, if the paternalistic and the nonexpressivist "harm to others" arguments were strong enough (either each on its own or together) to support the DR position that PAD should not be legalized, then they would also support severely curtailing or abolishing the legal right to refuse medical treatment. So, to remain consistent in their opposition to a legal right to PAD but support for a legal right to reject unwanted care, DR advocates must appeal to another argument that provides a reason against the former but not the latter, and the expressivist version of the "harm to others" argument does that. Second, while some laws (Jim Crow, ban on abortion for black women only) do have a denigrating objective social meaning, it is not clear whether limited eligibility PAD is among them. For this reason it is unclear whether the DR position on legal rights to PAD and refusal of unwanted care is in the final analysis justified..

NOTES

1. I rely heavily on the amicus briefs authored by several DR groups (including Not Dead Yet, ADAPT, and the National Council on Independent Living) and submitted to the US Supreme Court in the cases of *Vacco v. Quill* (1997) and *Gonzales v. Oregon* (2006) as statements of the DR critique of PAD. The briefs concede that "certainly, people have a 'right to die' by removing their life supports, refusing life supports, and letting nature take its course."

2. Too many defenders of PAD assume that the religious, pure moralism argument is the only one they need to rebut. James Rachels (1986) is one. Ronald Dworkin (1993) also supposes that a ban on PAD for the terminally ill is defensible only via the religious argument.

3. Ron Amundson, as a representative of Not Dead Yet, in testimony before a Hawaii legislative committee considering a PAS bill similar to Oregon's, said: "Terminally ill or disabled people sometimes do have suicidal feelings when they feel a lack of support, or a shame for their own condition, or when they feel that they are a burden on their families. The desire for death under those conditions is not a free choice, but a forced choice" (Amundson 2002). Harriet McBryde-Johnson (2003) says "choice is illusory in a context of pervasive inequality. Choices are structured by oppression. We shouldn't offer assistance with suicide until we all have the assistance we need to get out of bed in the morning and live a good life. Common causes of suicidality—dependence, institutional confinement, being a burden— are entirely curable."

4. Note that on this usage a paternalism that uses noncoercive "nudges" is still "hard" if the choices it targets are fully voluntary.

5. For a defense of the view that liberal political philosophy as articulated by J. S. Mill, Joel Feinberg, Ronald Dworkin, John Rawls, and others is committed to "full" autonomy as an overriding value and *not* the *supposedly* "liberal" ideal of autonomy just described, see Kymlicka (1989).

6. For an account of Bouvia's travails, see Longmore (2003, chap. 8).

7. "The so-called free choice of assisted suicide is a forced choice, and it leads to the same kind of exploitation [as workers faced with the choice of accepting slave wages or starving]. The freedom it offers for a few people is paid for by the exploitation of many others" (Amundson 2002).

8. Skepticism about the tinnitus case may be warranted since it was reported by *The Daily News*, not the most reliable of news sources. It should be noted that right-wing "sanctity of life" groups often make outlandish claims about nightmarish abuses under the Netherlands

law. In 2012, Republican presidential candidate Rick Santorum made the outrageously false claim that 5% of all deaths in that country were from "forced" euthanasia.

9. "Consider David Jayne, a 42 year old man with ALS. Every five seconds, a ventilator on a cart next to his bed pumps air into his lungs. He is not able to move. Twelve years ago, Jayne would have dismissed this existence as a living hell. 'Yes, I am very passionate about the Terri Schindler-Schiavo issue, because I live it,' says Jayne" (ADA Watch 2003).

10. It might be claimed that her help expresses disrespect if motivated by ableist prejudice, whether or not the help and motivation remain secret. Even if that's right, it gives us a "moralistic" reason for judging her action wrong that's distinct from the harm-based reason of the expressivist objection being considered here.

REFERENCES

Ackerman, Felicia. 1998. "Assisted Suicide, Terminal Illness, Severe Disability, and the Double Standard." In *Physician Assisted Suicide: Expanding the Debate*, edited by Margaret P. Battin, Rosamond Rhodes, and Anita Silvers, 149–161. New York: Routledge.

ADA Watch et al. 2003. "Issues Surrounding Terri Schindler-Schiavo Are Disability Rights Issues, Say National Disability Organizations." *Ragged Edge Magazine* October 27, 2003. Available at http://www.raggededgemagazine.com/schiavostatement.html.

Amundson, Ron. 2002. "The Civil Rights Opposition to Assisted Suicide." Testimony presented to Hawaii State Senate on March 18, 2002. Available at https://hilo.hawaii.edu/~ronald/OpEd-suicide2.html.

Bickenbach, Jerome. 1998. "Disability and Life-Ending Decisions." In *Physician Assisted Suicide: Expanding the Debate*, edited by Margaret P. Battin, Rosamond Rhodes, and Anita Silvers, 123–132. New York: Routledge.

Dworkin, Ronald. 1993. *Life's Dominion: An Argument About Abortion, Euthanasia, and Individual Freedom*. New York: Alfred A. Knopf.

Dworkin, Ronald, Thomas Nagel, Robert Nozick, John Rawls, Thomas Scanlon, and Judith J. Thomson. 1997. "Assisted Suicide: The Philosopher's Brief." *New York Review of Books* 44(5): 41–47.

Feinberg, Joel. 1984. *Harm to Self*. Oxford: Oxford University Press.

Gallagher, James, and Philippa Roxby. 2015. "Assisted Dying Bill: MP's Reject 'Right to Die' Law." BBC, September 11, 2015. Available at http://www.bbc.com/news/health-34208624.

Harris, John. 1993. "Is Gene Therapy a Form of Eugenics?" *Bioethics* 7(2/3): 178–187.

Hellman, Deborah. 2018. "Discrimination and social meaning." In *The Routledge Handbook of the Ethics of Discrimination*, edited by Kasper Lippert-Rasmussen, 97–107. New York: Routledge.

Kymlicka, Will. 1989. *Liberalism, Community, and Culture*. Oxford: Oxford University Press.

Longmore, Paul. 2003. *Why I Burned My Book and Other Essays on Disability*. Philadelphia: Temple University Press.

Mayo, David, and Martin Gunderson. 2002. "Vitalism Revitalized: Vulnerable Populations, Prejudice, and Physician Assisted Death." *Hastings Center Report* 32(4): 14–21.

McBryde-Johnson, Harriet. 2003. "Unspeakable Conversations." *New York Times Magazine*, February 16, 2003.

Not Yet Dead et. al., 2004. "Amicus Brief to U.S. Supreme Court in case of *Gonzales v. Oregon*." Available at http://notdeadyet.org/wp-content/uploads/2013/09/gonzales.html.

Rachels, James. 1986. *The End of Life*. Oxford: Oxford University Press.

Reid, Sue. 2015. "The Country Where Death Is Now Just a Lifestyle Choice." *The Daily Mail*, January 1, 2015. Available at http://www.dailymail.co.uk/news/article-2893778/As-debate-assisted-suicide-dispatch-Holland-thousands-choose-die-year.html.

Ruffing, Kathy. 2015. "Netherlands Not a Model for U.S. Disability Reforms." *Center on Budget and Policy Priorities*, February 18, 2015. Available at https://www.cbpp.org/blog/netherlands-not-a-model-for-us-disability-reforms.

Silvers, Anita. 1998. "Protecting the Innocents from Physician-Assisted Suicide: Disability Discrimination and the Duty to Protect Otherwise Vulnerable Groups." In *Physician Assisted Suicide: Expanding the Debate*, edited by Margaret P. Battin, Rosamond Rhodes, and Anita Silvers, 133–148. New York: Routledge.

PART FOUR

KNOWLEDGE
AND
EMBODIMENT

CHAPTER 17

....

EPISTEMIC EXCLUSION, INJUSTICE, AND DISABILITY

....

JACKIE LEACH SCULLY

THE concept of epistemic injustice has infiltrated a wide variety of fields since the term was introduced by Miranda Fricker (2007) to denote several ways in which people are harmed by differential use of or access to the resources of knowledge. Epistemic injustice and a variety of associated concepts such as epistemic exclusion, epistemic oppression, and epistemic smothering, have been used to illuminate how status and position align with certain kinds of power over knowledge accumulation and dissemination and to point to the social injustices that follow.

This approach has only recently been applied to disability and the epistemic resources of disabled people (see, in particular, Barnes 2016). Yet, as we shall see, disabled people provide some powerful examples of epistemic exclusion and are uniquely placed to experience harm as a consequence. In this chapter, I first of all introduce some of the key concepts of feminist social epistemology, epistemic exclusion, and epistemic power and privilege. I then show how these concepts are applicable to and illuminate injustices within the lives of disabled people, examining how disability is distinct from other social categories in terms of the kinds of exclusion and injustice experienced by disabled people. Finally, I consider how the epistemology of disability could be improved.

FEMINIST SOCIAL EPISTEMOLOGY

In traditional epistemology, the epistemic agent—the person who knows something—is envisaged as an isolated figure for whom social status and position are irrelevant. A social epistemology, by contrast, acknowledges that people are socially situated and, by placing the "knower" within a social context, helps redirect attention toward marginalized groups and how their knowledge is controlled and excluded from the dominant epistemic resources of society. To feminist social epistemologists, knowing is both situated and relational (Grasswick and Webb 2002). We interpret the world and our lives with the help of background knowledge and understandings contained within the collective epistemic resources of the communities in which we grow up and live. These resources do things like indicate what it is necessary to take note of and what to ignore; provide the vocabulary for narrating and justifying our actions; identify the roles, processes, and institutions that organize various aspects of social life; instruct on common practices; and so on. Background understandings are *particular*: they are generated out of the concrete circumstances of groups and communities and the experiences and relationships of their members (Walker 1998, 111–113). While some experiences and relationships are widely shared by different groups of people, others are more specific, and, as a result, some epistemic resources are held in common while others are more confined. Hence a person's capacity both for knowing and for contributing to shared knowledge is informed and also constrained by her social position since social position plays a large part in shaping the kind of experiences a person has, and that, in turn, will determine the epistemic resources likely to be found salient to making sense of the world (Pohlhaus 2006). A corollary of this is that epistemological overconfidence often leads us to assume that we are already familiar enough with other situations and persons to fully understand their lives, and to predict what matters to them and what they think of as essential to a good life. That epistemological overconfidence goes hand in hand with the belief that people do not vary much in terms of the epistemic terrain they occupy. A theory of situated knowledge is sceptical of this.

Knowing is also *relational* because it is constructed in collaboration with others and (to an extent) shared with others (Code 1991). For a person to perceive, account for, describe, and evaluate experience, she needs a set of epistemic tools drawn from her community's shared epistemic resources. These "resources of the mind [include] language to formulate propositions, concepts to make sense of experience, procedures to approach the world, and standards to judge particular accounts of experience" (Pohlhaus 2012, 4).

POWER

Feminist thought, by its nature, is alert to both the obvious and the more obscure operations of social power—particularly, but not only, gendered power. Feminist epistemology in turn recognizes that the epistemic resources available to members of a society are generated and maintained within existing structures of power and domination. As a result, the extent and richness of epistemic resources tend to track alongside existing social and political structures. As Nancy Tuana wrote, "our theories of knowledge and knowledge practices are far from democratic, . . . [and] favour members of privileged groups" (2006, 13). They will therefore constrain everyone to varying degrees, but will be actively oppressive to some.

That power is differentially distributed in a community is epistemologically significant over and above the fact that it determines the kinds of experiences that someone can have. According to feminist standpoint epistemology, people in marginal or socially subordinated positions will possess knowledge that is not only different from that of the more socially dominant, but also (in some defined ways) more extensive. The classic example is that of the servants in a house: their dependence means that it is essential for them to know quite a bit about the lives and concerns of their master and family in order to be any good in their job. The master, on the other hand, has no such dependence, is not marginally situated, and hence has no immediate need to acquire the epistemic resources that would enable him to make sense of his servant's lives (Harding 1993). And finally, feminist critique has pointed out that the "generic knower" of traditional epistemology is socially disembedded in a way that is supposed to ensure it is universally applicable. But in reality, no epistemic agent can be decontextualized to that extent, and so the figure of the generic knower ensures that only the aspects of the world experienced from a dominant position make it to any prominence in the collective resources. More importantly, it also serves to hide the fact that this is going on.

Social and material power therefore equate to some people having more voice than others because they own the authority to establish and enforce epistemic practices. Through being able to decide which accounts to receive, from whom, in what form, whether they are legitimate and credible, the routes through which they are fed into public discourse or policy decisions, and so on, some people exert a disproportionate influence on the collectively available epistemic resources that enable people to make sense of their world and lives. Feminist and other forms of critical epistemology have recently started to pay a lot of attention to the mechanisms through which epistemic agency is exercised or suppressed, and epistemic resources are generated or excluded.

EPISTEMIC PRIVILEGE, EXCLUSION, AND INJUSTICE

Theories of epistemic agency, epistemic exclusion, and epistemic injustice were primarily developed within feminist philosophy and critical race studies. It is noticeable that the marginal knowledges invoked in this discussion are associated with social stratification by gender and race, and occasionally gender identity or sexual orientation. Although some attention has been paid to epistemic power processes in medicine and healthcare (e.g. Carel and Kidd 2014), overall this has rarely been extended to cover the experience of disability. Nevertheless, I want to argue here that epistemic exclusion and injustice are equally relevant to understanding the situation of disabled people in society today.

Epistemic agency is the ability to use "shared epistemic resources within a given community of knowers" in order to take part in knowledge production and in its revision when necessary (Dotson 2014, 115). People are *epistemically excluded* when they are unable to access epistemic resources and/or contribute to their generation (Langton 2000). Epistemic exclusion frequently (perhaps inevitably) follows from social and political oppression driven by existing and historical power relations. *Epistemic privilege* is enjoyed by dominant groups in society: their forms of knowledge are not excluded, but rather are preferentially absorbed into the epistemic resources that make up the background knowledge of a given community (Fricker 1999).

Several distinct though closely interlinked forms of epistemic injustice have been identified as following from the epistemic exclusion of marginalized social groups. All of them involve wronging another in her capacity as a knower, but they operate in different ways and cause different forms of harm. I'll discuss these and their relevance to disabled people's lives in the following sections.

Testimonial injustice is what happens when prejudice against a group results in its members being given less credibility than they would otherwise have. The injustice here is of giving "a deflated level of credibility to a speaker's word" (Fricker 2007, 158). Something about that group carries an epistemic load that means that whatever they say is afforded less credibility than if it were said by a member of a more trusted group. In the shape of having a person's own account of her life and experiences dismissed, testimonial injustice is commonplace in the interactions between disabled and nondisabled people. This kind of injustice can be mediated purely through individual responses and interactions. For example, I might be less inclined to take seriously my employee's request for a special computer screen to prevent her from getting headaches at work because my personal experience of my own sister's behavior leads me to suspect that people claiming this kind of accommodation will overstate their case in order to get sympathy and a cushier position.

Testimonial injustice is, however, even more toxic when it is systemic: not the result of an individual's personal prejudice but one that is broadly held across a range of social contexts. Such an identity prejudice is often an undifferentiated response to disabled people, irrespective of the nature of the impairment. One example of this systemic injustice is provided by the so-called *central disability paradox*. This refers to the compelling empirical evidence that assessments of quality of life after impairment (spinal cord injury, for example) differ markedly between disabled and nondisabled people. Asked about the "quality" (leaving open what that means) of their own lives, disabled people tend to report a level only slightly lower than that reported by nondisabled people. Significantly, the quality of life *reported* by people living with an impairment is much higher than that *imagined* by nondisabled people (Amundson 2005, 103). Even health-care and rehabilitation professionals, who might be expected to have more insight into the realities of disabled lives, evaluated their patients' quality of life as lower than the patients themselves did (Cushman and Dijkers 1990; Gerhart et al. 1994).

Of course, a critical and skeptical approach to statements that run flatly counter to our own intuitions is appropriate—at least up to a point. Nevertheless, these empirically observed discrepancies between reported and projected accounts of what it is like to live with an impairment highlight the limits to our ability to imagine the lives of others who have very different phenotypic (embodied) capacities from our own. When discrepancies like these occur, it is rare for the nondisabled observer to agree that disabled people might in fact be best placed to know how satisfactory their own lives are. This is classic testimonial epistemic injustice: because of their generally marginalized and subordinate social position, disabled people are subjects of deflated credibility. And, as Medina (2011, 20) notes, credibility is a comparative quality. If some people (such as health or social care professionals) are given *more* credibility, then others necessarily have less. The accounts of disabled people are dismissed because identity prejudice leads to the assumption that their claims are inherently untrustworthy and possibly self-serving in a way that those of nondisabled people are not.

The experience of the disability world is riven with similar stories of the denial of epistemic authority and its consequences, ranging from the tragic (Hardiker 1994, 262; Shakespeare et al. 1996, 135–145) to the merely infuriating. An example: people with hearing impairment who use a hearing aid can, in principle, make use of induction loops in public buildings such as theatres or cinemas. This technology couples sound from a microphone directly to the aid, cutting out background noise and improving the clarity of what the deaf person hears. Even when installed, however, induction loops are often poorly maintained and so stop working properly. Deaf people often have the experience of complaining about a nonfunctioning induction loop, only to be told that the loop is definitely installed, is definitely switched on, is definitely working (so the fault must lie in the person's own hearing aid: have you checked that it's switched on?), etc. There is overt skepticism that someone who may have been using induction loops for decades knows what they are talking about; there may even be suspicion that the complaint is being made for other reasons, perhaps with the aim of getting compensatory tickets from a cinema.

An explanation often offered for the central disability paradox is a version of "they would say that, wouldn't they?" aimed at both long-term and newly disabled people. The suggestion is that long-term disabled people necessarily evaluate their state as normal and therefore rank their quality of life highly because they have nothing better to compare it with, while newly disabled people are using psychological mechanisms of adaptation, coping, and accommodation to avoid distress over the tragic disruption of their lives. Many disability studies scholars have strongly rejected this explanation (Silvers 2005, 58), supported by some of the available empirical evidence. For instance, the participants in Jonathan Cole's study of men with spinal cord injury displayed a wide range of responses to their new lives as paraplegic or tetraplegic, including some who were very conscious that their prior expectations did not fit the new reality: "[Before the accident] I remember thinking clearly ... that if it ever happened to me I could not stand it. I would want to kill myself.... But once it did happen to me, all the things I thought I would think and feel, I never felt at all" (Cole 2004, 211).

Testimonial injustice results then from an unwarranted devaluation of credibility[1] resulting in a persisting epistemic exclusion that limits or blocks a person's ability to contribute to knowledge production. To be wronged specifically "in one's capacity as a knower," as Fricker points out, is to be wronged in a capacity that we consider essential to human value and personhood. Implicitly, people suffering testimonial injustice are being challenged in their status as human persons of equal value to others within the community. The consequences include injury to a person's sense of self and self-confidence, in such a way that their agential capacity, including their epistemic and moral agency, is compromised. The catch-22 here is that it is extremely difficult to break down any kind of epistemic exclusion because marginally situated knowers who develop epistemic resources that are better at making sense of more parts of the experienced world—and who thereby challenge identity prejudice—are precisely those suffering from credibility deficits and least likely to be believed (Townley 2003). The result is what Mills has described as an "epistemology of ignorance...that produces people who are in general unable to understand the world they themselves have made" (Mills 1997, 18; 2007).

A second type of epistemic injustice has been identified as *hermeneutical injustice*. This is defined as "having some significant area of one's social experience obscured from collective understanding owing to a structural prejudice in the collective hermeneutical resource" (Fricker 2006, 100). As we have seen, a social epistemology argues that the epistemic tools a person uses for the hermeneutical act of making sense of the world, both to herself and to others, are not a personalized interior resource maintained within her own head: they are a *collectively generated* set of concepts, vocabulary, and narratives. Our shared knowledge reflects the combination of perspectives of different social groups. Relations of unequal power generally skew the shared hermeneutical resources, and, as a result, members of the powerful groups are much more likely to have appropriate understandings of their experience easily to hand. In parallel, the marginalization of social groups such as disabled people causes the neglect or suppression of the concepts, vocabulary, and narratives that are particularly salient to the interpretation of *their* experience. Life as a wheelchair user, for example, generates a fund of knowledge that ranges from technical data about types of wheelchair, through social *nous* about how pedestrians and drivers respond to wheelchairs in public, to financial information about the relative costs of chairs and repairs, and about funding sources, embodied knowledge about handling the chair through space, and on and on. This kind of specialized experiential knowledge generally does not enter the collective stock in any substantial or accessible form. Of course, disabled bodies are not the only kind of embodiment whose knowledge is not widely shared—the embodied experiences of an elite sportsperson will be equally unfamiliar to most people. The important difference is that some of the knowledge created through the experience of being Venus Williams is readily incorporated into the collective resource because it is featured in books, memoirs, interviews and films. This is usually not what happens to the experiences and embodied knowledge of wheelchair users or other disabled people.

Having one's experiences rendered unintelligible to oneself is another factor that compromises epistemic agency because it also means experiences cannot be communicated to others in the larger epistemic community due to the deficiencies of dominant shared epistemic resources (Fricker 2007, 155). Those whose epistemic contributions are marginalized are prevented from understanding important areas of their personal and social experience; these people are *wronged* by being deprived of an important element of self-understanding. Like testimonial injustice, this is also a wrong to that person's capacity as a knower, but in a different way. That a wheelchair user's knowledge is not considered worth including in the corporate resource is testimonial injustice; but that other wheelchair users are thereby unable to access and use it is hermeneutical injustice. An epistemic wrong is done to the knower who has no access to meanings that help make sense (to herself) of her world.

And this is not a trivial wrong. A person who lacks the epistemic resources, including language and conceptual frameworks, to make sense of events and perceptions, to name her experiences accurately and well, and to account for them to others, also lacks a framework into which she can fit her choices and goals without distortion or which she can use to make judgments and name something, perhaps some treatment of herself, as just or unjust. In other words, this lack of epistemic capacity may also produce impoverished *moral* capacity as well and has a pernicious effect on important features of moral agency and self-determination.

What also needs to be emphasized is that epistemic exclusion involves damage to the larger epistemic community. Not having as complete information as possible of disabled experience *impoverishes* the collective epistemic resources. It also renders the collective hermeneutical resource *structurally distorted*, such that interpretations of disabled people's lives are biased because they are disproportionately shaped by the perceptions of a more hermeneutically powerful group (nondisabled people). The wider community's epistemic resources could be richer, more accurate, more comprehensive than they are, and the fact that they are not is a *harm*. Consider, for example, that any attempt to imaginatively project oneself into another person's shoes (Mackenzie and Scully 2007) requires at least some knowledge about an unfamiliar way of life. Not having that knowledge readily available weakens the capacity for imaginative projection and possibly also for empathy more generally. But it is not in itself an *injustice* because it does not disadvantage the collective in the same way as it disadvantages the individual disabled person; hermeneutical exclusion persists precisely because the resources as they are work perfectly well for the dominant community.

However, epistemic exclusion can also contribute to yet another form of injustice, which Dotson has called *contributory injustice* (Dotson 2012). Some years ago, I was at an academic conference that failed to provide the most basic disability access (despite what had previously been indicated in the conference information). At one point, participants were invited to send in written comments about the conference and its organization for discussion at a feedback session. Several disabled participants got together to compose a note detailing their complaints and asking for a guarantee from the conference organizers that these would be addressed in subsequent events. At the feedback session, the Chair revealingly introduced the point with the words, "And now there's a rather sad little note…." In fact, the wording of the note was clear, firm, and justifiably angry; it was certainly not sad. Yet the Chair, and in fact the rest of the panel, seemed literally unable to *read* what was written without *reading into* it their own understanding of disabled people as pitiable.

In this situation, the disabled person is well able to understand her experience and to articulate it to others. But the disabled person's claims "fail to gain appropriate uptake according to the biased hermeneutical resources utilized by the perceiver" (Dotson 2012, 32). The others are unable to respond appropriately, because—as we have seen— the limited epistemic resources they use are simply incapable of making disabled people's words intelligible.[2] Another example occurs with the use of the term "disablism" to describe systemic, unwarranted prejudice against disabled people. Given that the concept is not in general currency, many nondisabled listeners would struggle but fail to make sense of it, and hence pre-emptively dismiss what a disabled person is trying to convey by that term as nonsensical. Pohlhaus calls this *wilful hermeneutical ignorance*— wilful, because the listeners do have the option of recognizing, or suspecting, their epistemic limitations and acting accordingly (Pohlhaus 2012). And, as she points out, contributory injustice is distinct from the testimonial injustice of deflated credibility (not believing or not taking seriously what is being said), but it is also something more than just bad epistemic luck (i.e., the concept that would make sense of things simply does not yet exist). Instead, the dominant group *contributes* to the injustice by refusing to engage with marginalized groups' epistemic resources and insisting on comprehending them solely within their own terms.

Disability Is Distinctive

There are features of disability that distinguish it from the exemplar cases of sexism and racism most commonly used to characterize hermeneutic epistemic exclusion. These features significantly complicate how hermeneutic resources are distributed within and between different communities of disability.[3] For instance, some experiences that are familiar to people with one impairment (such as the use of mobility assistance by wheelchair users or the inaccessibility of aural public information to deaf people) won't be shared by those with other impairments: here, the knowledge is unevenly distributed across disabilities. But, in addition, there are more general kinds of knowledge (such as what it is like to live with an awareness of being physically anomalous, experiences of exclusion from the public sphere, how to navigate the bureaucracy of social care to obtain the support you or your family need) that the majority of disabled people will share, but the majority of nondisabled people will not.

Thanks to the social and political advances of the twentieth century, children and adults with impairments are far more likely to be living independently and not in residential schools or long-term adult care. Perhaps unexpectedly, this has had both positive and negative epistemic consequences. Mainstreaming in education, housing, and employment has been overwhelmingly beneficial to most disabled people, but it also means that it is becoming less common for disabled people to grow up or live together with others sharing the same impairment. Because of this, it is now harder for disabled people to form epistemic communities in which specialized knowledge about living with a particular impairment can be easily shared. (Concern about this outcome has been particularly well articulated by signing Deaf communities around the world, who note that fewer and fewer deaf children attend specialized schools and so no longer encounter Deaf culture and sign language, and the knowledge that goes along with them, at an early enough age for it to be useful.) This is unlike the situation for women or ethnic marginalities who will rarely be the only person with that identity in their family or neighborhood and who do not normally have to create their own understandings de novo.

A second feature arises from the fact that the form of epistemic exclusion depends on the site upon which knowledges encounter each other. Marginalized groups are denied epistemic credibility in general, everyday encounters through a variety of complex but relatively unstructured habits and practices. A person may realize that their epistemic behavior toward people from a marginalized category is wrong, understand that epistemic injustice is occurring, and take steps to improve the way they receive the claims of the marginalized knowers. But an individual's attempt to become a more "virtuous knower" may make no real difference to disabled people's experiences if wider policies, organizational practices, and epistemological structures remain unchanged. Disabled people are therefore potentially exposed to unique forms of lifelong epistemic exclusion because the highly specialized epistemological structures of health and social care expertise often dominate their everyday lives. Whether a one-to-one encounter with a healthcare professional or a confrontation with an aspect of policy, healthcare operates with implicit expectations about the forms of language, narrative construction, or evidence that will be used. For the providers of knowledge to be taken seriously in these contexts, they need to make use of the epistemic tools that are deemed appropriate in that setting. Many nonspecialist disabled people will be unable or unwilling to do so, in which case there is a risk that their testimony will be dismissed as lacking credibility, or as just incomprehensible, because of the structural epistemic privilege of professional healthcare.

Epistemic Exclusion Now

So epistemic exclusion may be experienced by many, perhaps all, disabled people although not necessarily in all social settings or at all times. The epistemic harms and injustices that follow disadvantage both disabled people themselves and the wider community through the impoverishment of collective epistemic resources. We have seen why this has important consequences for the agency of disabled people and social attitudes toward them. In this penultimate section, I want to suggest why the potential for epistemic injustice toward disabled people is of unprecedented significance at this particular historical moment in the early decades of the twenty-first century. It is for two main reasons.

One reason, ironically, derives from the greater visibility of disabled people in the modern world. Contemporary societies are highly regulated, and the more disabled people form part of the active citizenry, the more that regulatory frameworks of health-care, education, employment, and social care must take their needs into account. In order for, say, healthcare policy to be fair and work effectively for disabled people, there must be confidence that it is fair from their perspectives and responsive to their real needs, in accordance with the knowledge of disabled people themselves. The more such knowledge is excluded, the greater the potential for policy to be inadvertently insensitive or even unjust.

A second and perhaps less obvious reason is that contemporary biomedical develop-ments hold out the promise of increasingly powerful interventions into disability, and especially genetically associated impairment. Until very recently, methods to prevent the birth of infants with impairments have been restricted to termination of pregnancy following prenatal diagnosis or the use of preimplantation genetic diagnosis (PGD) to identify embryos with genetic anomalies in vitro (for a discussion of some ethical issues in prenatal selection see Wilkinson and Garrard 2013). On the horizon now are novel methods that may soon make possible direct, targeted "editing" of the genetic makeup of gametes, embryos, or perhaps early fetal tissues to ensure that the baby eventually born does not have a genetic anomaly associated with impairment (Nuffield Council on Bioethics 2016).

I have argued elsewhere (Scully 2008) that to make good ethical judgments about the responsible use of these technologies requires a fundamental shift in the epistemic resources that society in general, and ethicists in their more specialized work, draw on to comprehend disabled lives. The discipline that makes these judgments is bioethics, and we need a *disability bioethics* starting from the experience of disabled people at least as much as we need a *bioethics of disability*, which I define as a bioethical examination with a starting point outside the experience of disability. Bioethics is frequently called on to provide ethical grounds for a particular medical or public health intervention: to say whether an intervention is the right thing to do, in which cases it should be permit-ted, or whether public money should be used to support it. What this means in terms of disability is that bioethics is frequently making a judgment about *the quality of disabled life*: that is, to consider the impact (often just the *predicted* impact) of an impairment on a life and judge whether, according to that assessment, further steps (such as termina-tion of pregnancy, withdrawal of treatment, or surgery) are morally permissible or not. One of the major critiques leveled at bioethics, especially but not solely by feminist ethi-cists and epistemologists, has been the inadequacy of both the *content* and the *nature* of the epistemic resources that it brings to its deliberations on disability. There have been calls for a more "descriptive and empirical" bioethics supported by better information about the lives of the people about whom bioethical judgments are being made. As we have seen in the discussion of testimonial and hermeneutic epistemic injustice, it is sim-ply not ethically safe to assume commonality of epistemic resources in imagining the lives of others.

IMPROVING THE EPISTEMOLOGY
OF DISABILITY

To engage with disability as a concept and as a social phenomenon raises fundamental questions about the *kind of knowledge* that is needed to make policy or other decisions concerning people with embodiments that differ from the norm. Empirical information helps fill out our factual knowledge of situations where impairment is an issue. Effective engagement, though, requires something more than improvements in our empirical grounding.

The kind of critical moral epistemology I have described pays closer attention to the procedures and patterns of dominance that enable the perspectives of nondisabled people to take precedence over those of disabled people, or of particular types of impairment over other types. It encourages questions about how social and political structures give some people more voice than others, for instance, and asks whether and how the resulting allocation of epistemic authority is unjust.

Practically, what is needed are ways of subverting the social and historical power relations that prevent epistemic agency. In the case of disability, these would include ensuring the availability of education, communications, and assistive devices that enable people with different impairments to access information *and* the sites where information is exchanged, or making conscious efforts to have representation by disabled people on bodies that decide healthcare or social policy, acknowledging that the collective epistemic resources are inadequate and contain gaps because they exclude the knowledge of significant sectors of the community.

But repairing the inadequacies of the collective knowledge by incorporating the epistemic resources of more marginal others is difficult. For one thing, epistemological frameworks are highly resilient (Dotson 2014). Remember that these resources function very well for the dominant community (in this case, nondisabled people), which is why these are the forms of knowledge that are perpetuated along with social privilege and power. In other words, even obvious epistemic gaps will persist indefinitely unless there is conscious and concerted effort to reform the instituted social imaginaries (i.e., the social meanings, customs, and expectations about what constitutes norms of bodily form and function, communication, or mobility). This then involves not just taking the claims of disabled people seriously (i.e., affording them equal epistemic credibility), but also accepting the need to change your mind and modify the community's accepted wisdom as a result. There are psychic consequences to the recognition of one's own social and epistemic privilege. Realizing that you are benefiting from systemic, ingrained epistemic injustice can generate a sense of guilt and powerlessness that is counterproductive to improving the situation.

When (if) we notice that we don't have adequate language, concepts, or narratives to describe our own or others' disabled experience, then our epistemic resources have to be recalibrated or fresh ones created to provide new possibilities for organizing and making sense of experience. The reluctance to do so contributes to Pohlhaus's "wilful ignorance." Harding notes (1991; 272–295) that to get over epistemic inadequacy means being prepared to adopt a critical standpoint and this, in turn, demands a level of active interest in how the world is revealed from marginalized standpoints. Although there is always a cultural resistance to engaging with marginal identities, I suggest there is a particular difficulty in the case of disability because of the persistent and profound ambivalence, sometimes hostility, toward anomalous bodies. Disablement is normally regarded as an unfortunate state and one most people would rather not think about unless they absolutely have to; this reluctance does not foster the curiosity needed to explore new information and ways of knowing and incorporate them into the collective resources. To motivate ourselves to do it, we may need reminding that ignorance about disabled lives (including lives lived with impairments different from our own) is not an inevitability, but something we can and should choose to improve.

Notes

1. "Unwarranted" is an important qualifier. There are, of course, many situations in which it is entirely right not to confer full credibility. Someone may lack specialist or technical knowledge in circumstances where it is essential or give other evidence of not having relevant experience, deliberately lying, being mistaken or deluded, and so on.
2. There could also be an element of straightforward testimonial injustice here. "You have to take the complaints of those prickly, thin-skinned people with a grain of salt. They always make a mountain out of a molehill!" I thank the editors for drawing my attention to this.
3. This does not mean that other marginalized groups are homogeneous, only that, in this section, I focus on distinctive features of certain impairment and disability groups.

References

Amundson, R. 2005. "Disability, Ideology, and Quality of Life: A Bias in Biomedical Ethics." In *Quality of Life and Human Difference: Genetic Testing, Health Care, and Disability*, edited by D. Wasserman, J. Bickenbach, and R. Wachbroit, 101–124. New York: Cambridge University Press.

Barnes, E. 2016. *The Minority Body. A Theory of Disability*. Oxford: Oxford University Press.

Carel, H., and I. J. Kidd. 2014. "Epistemic Justice in Healthcare: A Philosophical Analysis." *Med Healthcare and Philos* 17: 529–540.

Code, L. 1991. *What Can She Know? Feminist Theory and Construction of Knowledge*. Ithaca: Cornell University Press.

Cole, J. 2004. *Still Lives: Narratives of Spinal Cord Injury*. Chester, NJ: Bradford Books.

Cushman, L. A., and M. P. Dijkers. 1990. "Depressed Mood in Spinal Cord Injured Persons: Staff Perceptions and Patient Realities." *Arch Physical Med Rehab* 71: 191–96.

Dotson, K. 2012. "A Cautionary Tale: On Limiting Epistemic Oppression." *Frontiers: A Journal of Women's Studies* 33: 24–47.

Dotson, K. 2014. "Conceptualizing Epistemic Oppression." *Social Epistemology* 28: 115–138.

Fricker, M. 1999. "Epistemic Oppression and Epistemic Privilege." *Canadian Journal of Philosophy* 29(Supp 25): 191–210.

Fricker, M. 2006. "Powerlessness and Social Interpretation." *Episteme: A Journal of Social Epistemology* 3: 96–108.

Fricker, M. 2007. *Epistemic Injustice: Power and the Ethics of Knowing.* Oxford: Oxford University Press.

Gerhart, K. A., J. Koziol-McLain, S. R. Lowenstein, and G. G. Whiteneck. 1994. "Quality of Life Following Spinal Cord Injury: Knowledge and Attitudes of Emergency Care Providers." *Annals Emergency Med* 23: 807–812.

Grasswick, H. E., and M. O. Webb. 2002. "Feminist Epistemology as Social Epistemology." *Social Epistemology* 16: 185–196.

Hardiker, P. 1994. "Thinking and Practising Otherwise: Disability and Child Abuse." *Disability and Society* 9: 257–263.

Harding, S. 1991. *Whose Science? Whose Knowledge?* Ithaca, NY: Cornell University Press.

Harding, S. 1993. "Rethinking Standpoint Epistemology: What Is Strong Objectivity?" In *Feminist Epistemologies*, edited by L. Alcoff and E. Potter. New York/London: Routledge.

Langton, R. 2000. "Feminism in Epistemology: Exclusion and Objectification." In *Cambridge Companion to Feminism in Philosophy*, edited by M. Fricker and J. Hornsby, 127–145. Cambridge: Cambridge University Press.

Mackenzie, C. and J. L. Scully. 2007. "Moral Imagination, Disability and Embodiment." *Journal of Applied Philosophy* 24: 335–351.

Medina, J. 2011. "The Relevance of Credibility Excess in a Proportional View of Epistemic Injustice: Differential Epistemic Authority and the Social Imaginary." *Social Epistemology* 25: 15–35.

Mills, C. 1997. *The Racial Contract.* Ithaca, NY: Cornell University Press.

Mills, C. 2007. "White Ignorance." In *Race and Epistemologies of Ignorance*, edited by S. Sullivan and N. Tuana, Philosophy and Race Series, 13–38. Albany, NY: SUNY Press.

Nuffield Council on Bioethics. 2016. *Genome Editing: an Ethical Review.* London: Nuffield Council on Bioethics.

Pohlhaus, G. 2006. "Knowing (With) Others." *Social Philosophy Today* 22: 187–198.

Pohlhaus, G. 2012. "Relational Knowing and Epistemic Injustice: Toward a Theory of Willful Hermeneutical Ignorance." *Hypatia* 27: 715–735.

Scully, J. L. 2008. *Disability Bioethics: Moral Bodies, Moral Difference.* Lanham: Rowman & Littlefield.

Shakespeare, T., K. Gillespie-Sells, and D. Davies. 1996. *The Sexual Politics of Disability.* London: Cassell.

Silvers, A. 2005. "Predicting Genetic Disability While Commodifying Health." In *Quality of Life and Human Difference: Genetic Testing, Health Care, and Disability*, edited by D. Wasserman, J. Bickenbach, and R. Wachbroit, 43–66. New York: Cambridge University Press.

Townley, C. 2003. "Truth and the Curse of Cassandra (an Exploration of the Value of Trust)." *Philosophy and the Contemporary World* 10: 105–111.

Tuana, N. 2006. "The Speculum of Ignorance: The Women's Health Movement and Epistemologies of Ignorance." *Hypatia* 11: 1–19.

Walker, M. U. 1998. *Moral Understandings: A Feminist Study in Ethics.* New York: Routledge.

Wilkinson, S., and E. Garrard. 2013. *Eugenics and the Ethics of Selective Reproduction.* Keele: Keele University Press.

CHAPTER 18

WHAT'S WRONG WITH "YOU SAY YOU'RE HAPPY, BUT . . . " REASONING?

JASON MARSH

DISABILITY-POSITIVE philosophers often note a troubling tendency to dismiss what disabled people say about their well-being.[1] Here is an example from Elizabeth Barnes:

> It's fair to say that most people today think it's 'common sense' that being disabled is less good than being non-disabled...But most people in the 1950's thought that it was 'common sense' that being gay was less good than being straight. And Europeans in the 1200's probably would have thought that it was 'common sense' that being female was less good than being male...In her groundbreaking book *Epistemic Injustice*, Miranda Fricker characterizes ways in which prejudice can cause uniquely epistemic types of harm. One of the main such forms of harm she highlights is testimonial injustice. In cases of testimonial injustice, a speaker is not believed or given due credence (where others would be) specifically because they are a member of a group that is the subject of stigma.   (Barnes 2016, 134–135)

In effect, Barnes argues that failing to believe physically[2] disabled persons when they make positive claims about their well-being often is to commit epistemic injustice. Similarly, Sara Goering notes a "troubling tendency in much mainstream bioethics to discount the views of disabled people" (Goering 2008, 126). According to both authors, then, there is something deeply wrong with common forms of "you say you're happy, but..." reasoning, particularly when this reasoning is more quick and instinctive than carefully thought out.[3]

I agree that a skeptical tendency in this context is often troubling. But what exactly is the problem with it? I argue that increasingly common epistemological answers, such as "it ignores lived experience," "it commits testimonial injustice," or "it rests on a view of adaptive preferences that overgeneralizes" are less convincing than is sometimes supposed. Or, put another way, these considerations, while they give us good reasons to trust people when they claim to value being disabled, do not go as far in supporting testimony according to which physical disabilities do not make people worse off. I then make the case for more openness to certain stronger forms of disability-positive testimony[4] by arguing that common varieties of disability-positive skepticism threaten everyone's well-being and are further challenged by an argument from moral risk.

"IT IGNORES LIVED EXPERIENCE"

We typically refrain from questioning claims and experiences that others are thought to have special access to. So, for instance, if someone tells me that I am mistaken to claim that I live in Minnesota, I am going to be puzzled. Or, if someone doesn't believe me when I say that I am physically attracted to a certain individual, I might become annoyed. Of course, my interlocutors are free to produce arguments for their skepticism. But I would be willing to bet on the basis of my experience that "you say you live in city X, but..." reasoning and "you say you're attracted to person X, but..." reasoning will rarely be persuasive once filled in.

It is tempting to think something similar about testimony concerning well-being. So, if someone doesn't believe me when I say that my life has been worth living so far, then, in the absence of very impressive and surprising information, I am going to be puzzled. My bewilderment will only increase, moreover, if the same person goes on to reject my testimony that I enjoyed my trip to Costa Rica last year. True, it's possible that I am mistaken about my memories and experiences (Haybron 2007), and global assessments of well-being are far from straightforward (Marsh 2014). But "you say you're happy, but..." reasoning is also fallible.

These observations lead me to think about disability and testimony. Perhaps what's wrong with skepticism about disability-positive testimony is that it downplays the authority of lived experience—an authority that traditionally marginalized groups often think about (Crasnow 2013, 417). So, if a deaf person—call her Anita—claims to be happy and to value being deaf, it seems wise to take her word for it, at least if we understand "happiness" in sufficiently subjective ways. Given her lived experience, after all, she seems better positioned than a hearing person to know whether *she* likes being deaf. Indeed, her lived experience, while fallible, seems a far better guide to the truth about what she values than, say, the intuitions of a stranger who imagines that her life must be a constant nightmare.

I fully concur with these ideas. If the question is whether someone is happy being disabled or whether she would wish her identity away, the argument from lived experience strikes me as quite powerful. But what about stronger forms of disability-positive testimony like the following?

Being blind is not subpar, overall. I would not have been better off (assuming it would still be *me*) if I had been born a seeing person. I am also not worse off than seeing persons in my socio-economic rank.

Being in a wheelchair makes me worse off than other people and worse off than I used to be, but only in virtue of the social prejudices and limitations I now encounter, and not in virtue of its intrinsic features.

Being deaf comes with costs, including intrinsic costs that have nothing to do with society or prejudice (I can't hear beautiful music or the voices of loved ones). But being deaf doesn't inherently make me worse off since it permits equally good things (I can feel music and enjoy deaf community that I wouldn't have otherwise accessed).

Stronger forms of testimony like these do get made.[5] And, in response to them, I want to argue not that they are false, only that appeals to an individual's lived experience by itself won't clearly justify them, let alone put notable epistemic pressure on hearers to believe them. And the reason is that an individual's experience is often too limited to ground comparative and counterfactual claims about their well-being.

I do not mean to be entirely skeptical about our comparative and counterfactual reasoning abilities. Perhaps one can reasonably believe and assert, on the basis of limited experience, that if one had been born into serious poverty then one would have been worse off. In addition, one needn't have experienced too much isolation to reasonably surmise that involuntary solitary confinement would likely lower one's emotional happiness. My point is just that counterfactual and comparative claims about well-being or happiness that are rooted in an individual's experience can easily go astray. For instance, suppose I tell my friend that I would have been less happy had I become a lawyer in Australia as opposed to a philosopher in Minnesota. I might—and in fact do—feel confident in my judgment given my current identity as a philosopher in North America. But I would also understand if my interlocutor didn't quite believe me or didn't think that this was the kind of thing I am in a position to know. Indeed, if I am fully honest with myself, I do probably lack knowledge about such matters. I am not even sure that I should have firm beliefs about them.[6] Maybe I would have liked being a lawyer more than I realize. This is not to say anything bad about philosophy or to express an interest in switching careers, only to highlight the limits of my imagination—limits that have taken me astray before.[7]

Similarly, if Anita testifies that, matters of prejudice aside, she wouldn't have preferred life as a hearing person, one might wonder how she knows this. Even if she is correct in her judgment, her lived experience, by itself, is arguably not what is getting her to the truth. In saying this, note that I am not assuming that hearing is objectively conducive to human flourishing such that, if you lack it, you are automatically worse off overall no matter how you feel about the matter. This Aristotelian claim, if true, would certainly undermine much deaf-positive testimony. But my claim is weaker. Even if we restrict ourselves to purely subjective well-being, lived experience remains fairly limited (on various theories of subjective well-being).[8] And the reason, again, is that lived experiences are limited to one's actual experiences, while comparative and counterfactual claims often go well beyond one's actual experiences.

Or, put another way, the problem, it might be thought, is that Anita doesn't have nearly *enough* experience to make the claims she wants to make. We could change the scenario so that Anita was once a hearing person and still claims that being deaf is not worse overall. In that case, her testimony will certainly make a much stronger claim on her hearers. Even this case is not entirely straightforward, however. For, as others have noted, it is possible that the transition costs involved in becoming deaf, even if deafness is itself neutral, could have a negative impact on global or overall well-being.[9]

Of course, if we discovered that those who become deaf in general fare as well as hearing persons, this would help. For then population level data could be used to extend Anita's experiential knowledge, justifying counterfactuals such as, "If I had always been a hearing person, I would not likely have been subjectively happier in any relevant sense." But notice that this largely empirically based strategy, even if sound,[10] would no longer be rooted in an *individual's* lived experience. And my point is just that many have not experienced hearing and do not know what it's like.[11] When such persons make counterfactual or comparative claims about their well-being, their testimony might not be fully authoritative.

These epistemic limitations, again, do not merely afflict disabled persons. This explains why those in the deaf community might be a bit skeptical when a hearing person confidently proclaims that (a) he would be less happy had he been born deaf, or (b) he is happier than the average deaf person now. Unless his testimony is supplemented with something beyond his limited experience, we might not find it persuasive.[12] We might even think he is a textbook example of how human beings in general overestimate their ability to do affective forecasting—a bit like those who, mistakenly, insist that they would be emotionally far happier for life if they won the lottery (Ott 2009).[13]

So, in short, while individual appeals to lived experience give us reasons to believe all sorts of interesting disability-positive testimony, there are important limits to what it can show even at the level of subjective well-being. I suspect that many philosophers, including some who hold a mere-difference view of disability, will agree with this claim. Since one often hears appeals to the epistemic value of lived experience in discussions about disability and well-being, however, it is worth getting clearer on its limits.

"It Commits Testimonial Injustice"

A second challenge to disability-positive skepticism makes appeal to testimonial injustice. As Miranda Fricker notes, testimonial injustice occurs "when prejudice causes a hearer to give a deflated level of credibility to a speaker's word" (Fricker 2007, 1). An example from Fricker is if the police do not believe you because you are black. Another example is if a female politician's arguments are taken less seriously merely because she is female. In these cases, we harm speakers not just socially but in their capacity as knowers and givers of knowledge.

In her book, *The Minority Body*, Elizabeth Barnes applies these ideas from social epistemology to disability-positive testimony (Barnes 2016, chap. 4). If we are generally disposed to believe what non-disabled people say about their well-being but regularly downgrade what disabled persons say about their well-being, then we may well commit epistemic injustice. Maybe we are failing to believe disabled persons, in a relevant sense, merely because they are disabled.

I find Barnes's discussion valuable in all sorts of ways. I especially like her argument that we have terrible track records when it comes to listening to and reasoning about what marginalized groups say about their well-being—including sexual minorities, racial minorities, and women—and agree that this should make us more open to hearing disabled voices now. Such an argument goes beyond the claim that non-disabled people have certain biases or lack certain relevant experiences. It is largely inductive. Despite my praise, however, I confess that I am still not fully clear about the scope of Barnes's testimonial injustice attribution or worry. Consider the following claims,

1. "I value being disabled and do not wish my disability away—I'm happy and not in spite of my disability."
2. "My disability does not make me worse off—or at least it wouldn't do so in a just society."
3. "Physically disabled people in general are not worse off than physically non-disabled people in general—or at least they wouldn't be in a just society."

Some passages from Barnes lead me to think she is restricting her focus to something like claim 1. She says, for instance: "I argue that skepticism about the testimony of disabled people who claim to value being disabled is a type of testimonial injustice" (Barnes 2016, 120). Other passages, however, lead me to think she might intend to include claims 2 and 3 in her argument. For instance, she cites the following testimony from Harriet McBryde Johnson:

> Are we "worse off"? I don't think so. Not in any meaningful sense. There are too many variables. For those of us with congenital conditions, disability shapes all we are. Those disabled later in life adapt. We take constraints that no one would choose and build rich and satisfying lives within them.

Barnes not only seems to endorse this testimony, which is directed at Peter Singer; she also seems to imply that others should as well so as to avoid committing epistemic injustice.[14] To clarify, even on this interpretation, Barnes is not saying that one automatically commits injustice by failing to believe testimony like McBryde Johnson's. I think she means only that common dismissals of claims 2 and 3 commit testimonial injustice, particularly when those dismissals are heavily guided by the bare intuition that disability is obviously bad.

In any case, whatever the nature and scope of Barnes's testimonial injustice worry, since forms of testimony like 1, 2, and 3 all get made, it is worth considering how easily failing to believe them would be epistemically irresponsible or otherwise commit epistemic injustice. Beginning with claim 1, I think Barnes's argument can do a lot of work here. We have already seen that lived experience can speak to what people value. If we have failed to appreciate this fact before, then Barnes's inductive argument gives us further reason to trust people who claim to value being disabled (at least if we bracket worries about adaptation that we explore in the next section). Indeed, when it comes to testimony like 1, merely failing to believe it, let alone disbelieving it, seems unjust.

As for claim 2, I think the force of this testimony, while real, is more defeasible and context-dependent. Sometimes it makes a strong claim on us. For instance, quick dismissals of dwarf-positive testimony made solely on the basis of an arguably mistaken intuition that there is an inherent connection between size and well-being seem unreasonable and unjust. Once again, our intuitions about the well-being of minorities have often taken us astray in the past. And, once again, we should be wary of relying on them now. To be fair, though, one can imagine other cases less reliant on intuition. For instance, someone might reason that their brother (who has been blind from birth) does not know what it's like to see and so isn't in a good position to assert that he is no worse off in virtue of being blind. It is not clear to me that such reasoning is uncommon or that it commits testimonial injustice. Much will naturally depend on the details of the testimonial exchange, however.

Turning to claim 3, this type of testimony strikes me as the least authoritative. In particular, I can imagine a skeptic arguing that testimony surrounding disability and well-being is notably less uniform than McBryde Johnson implies—and notably less uniform than testimony surrounding being female, for instance. More accurately, for all we know, goes the worry, a decent number of persons with diverse disabilities will report that their disability is a negative-difference. Call this the problem of mixed testimony. For instance, Eric Steinhart says,

> My disabilities are not goods in any sense. Even if all social stigma and shame were removed, my disabilities would not be goods in any sense. They are not moral evils for which I am responsible. But they are natural evils. And the intrinsic value of full human flourishing entails that we ought to strive to eliminate them.
>
> (Steinhart 2016)

Although Steinhart spends most of his time reflecting on depression, whereas Barnes is focused only on physical disability, he also includes his physical osteoarthritis in his negative testimony. In addition, some persons with osteogenesis claim to be happy overall but to "hate" their disability. For instance, Ellen Painter Dollar notes that disabilities are not "value-neutral manifestations of human diversity" (Dollar 2012). She goes on to say this:

> Bones are not supposed to crack under the weight of a laptop computer. They are not supposed to snap when a little girl is simply dancing in her living room. A routine fall from a scooter should not land a child in the emergency room with multiple fractures. Forty-something-year-old knees should not be completely stripped of their cartilage. No matter how much good (wisdom, love, understanding, compassion) comes out of living with this capricious disorder, the disorder itself is not good.

Turning to the empirical data—although much more work needs to be done[15]—this only seems to corroborate the worry. For instance, in one study, most persons with locked-in syndrome, 58%, declared they did not wish to be resuscitated in the case of cardiac arrest (Bruno et al. 2011).[16] In addition, some studies suggest that late-term disabilities not infrequently have a lasting negative impact on subjective well-being even following adaptation (Lucas 2007). When it comes to degenerative conditions, finally, some of their effects get worse over time, and many seem to be deeply frustrated about this nonsocial fact.[17]

Testimony like this is no doubt going to be as complex, multifaceted, and occasionally mixed with bad arguments as disability-positive testimony. What's more, it's often hard to tease apart the social from nonsocial causes of dissatisfaction.[18] But the testifiers in question often don't seem to be saying that their disability is merely a local harm or a social harm or a predominately extrinsic harm. And the point is that Barnes spends almost no time writing on actual cases of disability-negative testimony. To be sure, Barnes is very clear that being disabled, like being gay, can make life harder and isn't a "big, grand party" (Barnes 2016, 78).[19] She also notes that not every disabled person would say no to a "cure" even in a world without ableism. But that's not the same thing as reflecting on the problem of mixed testimony, its extent, or how it might impact her arguments.

I think that the problem could make it harder to heavily rely on testimony in defending a value-neutral model of disability.[20] But my point is different. If enough disabled people do, or would, more closely resemble Steinhart than McBride Johnson when testifying about their well-being, this could reveal that claim 3 is false—at least if voices like Steinhart's are deemed trustworthy.[21] It could do so by lowering the average well-being of physically disabled persons. In fact, even if it turns out that a small minority of disabled persons, say 5% or 10%, really dislike their disability in virtue of its physical features, this could still pull the *average* well-being of physically disabled persons down. Factoring in earlier worries about whether temporary transition costs are powerful enough to make a global impact on well-being only makes it harder to assert 3.

To clarify, the idea here is not that claim 3 is in fact false. I doubt that we have enough data to make decisive claims about 3 either way. The idea is that, for all we know, claim 3 is false. And this epistemic possibility seems sufficient to cast doubt on there being a *pro tanto* duty or even just a strong reason for informed persons to believe testimony like 3. Naturally, some might object to these claims. But we have seen enough to wonder if maybe some disability rights activists are too quick to speak for disabled people in general.

"It Rests on a View of Adaptive Preferences that Overgeneralizes"

A third challenge to disability-positive skepticism is that it frequently rests on a misguided psychological attempt to explain away people's testimony. The explanation I have in mind goes roughly as follows. Many disabled people claim to be happy and indeed claim to prefer being disabled. But it's not that they have good reasons for saying these things; it's rather that their minds gradually *cause* them to adapt to their circumstances, however limiting, and to change their beliefs and preferences after the fact. They're a lot like "happy slaves"[22] or "happy oppressed women" in this regard. If we factor in a status quo bias that makes people prefer what is familiar, then we have further psychological grounds for suspicion toward these predictably optimistic first-person reports.

In response to this challenge, Sara Goering thinks there are relevant differences between disabled persons and happy slaves or happy oppressed women. But she doesn't develop the point (Goering 2008, 131). Barnes notes that the strategy is notably more powerful than all other attempts to dismiss disability-positive testimony (Barnes 2016, 142). But she thinks that, aside from committing epistemic injustice, it overgeneralizes (Barnes 2009). I want to focus on the overgeneralization worry here. According to this worry, if the adaptive preference strategy could be used to explain away disability-positive testimony, it could be used to explain away all kinds of testimony in ways that seem implausible. For instance, consider:

> You say you're happy being gay and indeed prefer this identity, but that's just your adaptive preference talking—and keeping you from seeing the unfortunate truth about your life.
> You say you're happy being female and indeed prefer this identity, but that's just your adaptive preference talking—and keeping you from seeing the unfortunate truth about your life.

Clearly, many of us are going to think that there is something very wrong with these forms of reasoning. And Barnes thinks this shows that the adaptive preference strategy overgeneralizes. Since it could be used to explain away gay-positive testimony or female-positive testimony, it clearly can't be trusted.

Once again, I think Barnes's response is clever and interesting and advances the debate. But, once again, I think she overstates its force. In particular, I don't see why a disability-positive skeptic should endorse the claim that the strategy can be used to explain away these other forms of testimony. After all, she will think, let us suppose, that it is just false that being female or being gay is inherently subpar. She thus won't think the strategy legitimately overgeneralizes: she uses it only where it seems right to her. The fact that other people can mimic her strategy in ways that she deems illegitimate won't deter her from using her strategy in ways that she deems legitimate.

To be sure, many disabled persons will understandably not be impressed if told that *their* preferences and beliefs are merely adaptive. In fact, many might feel that the very decision to label their preferences adaptive "begs the question"[23] against them (Barnes 2009, 7). For, as Barnes notes, to invoke the adaptive preference strategy—under Martha Nussbaum's conception of adaptive preferences anyhow[24]—we already "need to assume that being disabled is somehow bad or suboptimal," which is "precisely what's up for debate" (Barnes 2016, 133). But there is a difference between what one can permissibly believe and what one can assert or philosophically demonstrate. There is also a difference between vocalizing one's skepticism and keeping it to oneself. The defender of the adaptive preference strategy needn't be arguing that everyone should affirm her claims, nor must she suppose that appeals to it would be dialectically effective in an exchange with someone who disagrees with her. The question (or at any rate one question) is whether she is reasonable in privately believing that much, even if not all, disability-positive testimony is problematically adaptive.

Perhaps it will be objected that the answer is "no." For Barnes's inductive strategy, recall, speaks against allowing a feeling of counterintuitiveness to heavily guide one's beliefs about the testimony of minorities—and places a burden on disability-positive skeptics to *justify* their stance with arguments. Unfortunately, however, even this inductive strategy is less persuasive now if Barnes's overgeneralization reasoning is endorsed. After all, many people (perhaps including Barnes)[25] think they reasonably resist the testimony of certain minorities, such as non–morally motivated hermits,[26] when they say that, lacking the capacity and desire to enjoy relationships with other people is just a way of being different. But it is hard to come up with a compelling argument for the intuitive judgment that a hermit's way of life really is suboptimal. Perhaps this can be done. But the attempts that I have heard do not make me confident.[27]

Relatedly, it would likely be very hard to give hermits an argument that *they* will find compelling for why they are deceived (especially if they really are). They will think we are the problem and that we make unfair assumptions about them. They might even call on Barnes's inductive strategy to support their claims: "You've been wrong before when it comes to reasoning about the well-being of minorities, so you should be very wary of rejecting our hermit-positive testimony now by way of a story of adaptive preference or something else that privileges your judgments over ours."

The worry here, to clarify, is not this: unless we are willing to accept *anyone's* testimony about their well-being, then Barnes's own inductive strategy itself overgeneralizes since it can be applied to *any* minority group. For Barnes can, and to some extent does, claim that we can reasonably downgrade the testimony of victims of Stockholm syndrome, who come to prefer having been kidnapped, if we can invoke independent and reasonable claims about how their psychological conditions make them unreliable testifiers. The worry is more specific: unless we are willing to accept *some* forms of testimony that many, perhaps including Barnes, want to resist, then, *if* overgeneralization is a problem for the adaptive preference strategy, it is also a problem for Barnes's original inductive argument. For both methods can generalize in ways that lead to unwanted conclusions. Or, put another way, there seems to be a conflict between Barnes's inductive arguments for trusting minority voices and her worries about overgeneralization.

What is needed, then, is an explanation for why overgeneralization with respect to adaptive preference arguments for skepticism about minority voices is problematic, whereas overgeneralization with respect to inductive arguments for trusting minority voices is not. Now, it may be that the answer is just that hermits are objectively mistaken about their well-being whereas disabled persons are not. This purely externalist explanation, if true, would certainly be relevant. But, if we are looking for our arguments (and epistemic injustice attributions) to have independent traction in contexts of disagreement, as Barnes to her credit seems to be, then we need something more.

Otherwise, the disability-positive skeptic will feel at liberty to make an exactly parallel move. She will claim that the externalist considerations favour her view and that the very decision to use induction to support disability, but not hermits, unjustifiably stacks the deck in favour of a mere-difference view of disability. She might add that she only accepts testimony from groups whom she deems reliable informants and that induction shouldn't be used against her view any more than it should be used to defend hermits.

"It Challenges Everyone's Well-Being—and Is Further Morally Risky"

So far, I have largely been playing the role of the skeptic or the devil's advocate. But I don't really want to side with the devil. My goal is to get clearer on what might be wrong with downgrading common forms of disability-positive testimony—particularly claims 1 and 2[28]—and to get clearer on our grounds for trust. I think the three explanations we have considered, though not without some merit, do less work than we might hope. So, I want to offer some fairly brief and tentative but hopefully worthwhile alternatives. These alternatives could stand on their own. But combining them with other explanations is likely the best way to improve the overall case for trust.

My first explanation is largely pragmatic. One thing that is wrong with (or at least undesirable about) the skeptical tendency we have been considering is that it is bad for everyone, including the skeptic. It's bad for disabled persons for obvious reasons. Being believed to have a notably worse life than other people is awful and, for many, might be the worst part about being disabled. But another far less commonly appreciated consideration is that disability-positive skepticism is bad for the skeptic. It's bad for the skeptic not just because they might one day become disabled. It is bad for the skeptic now.

Why? If disabled people are as systematically deceived as many assume, then we need an explanation for how such a large portion of our species could be so deceived about their well-being. But the main explanations on offer, recall, appeal to human psychology (Barnes 2009). Such appeals are extremely common. They pose a wider problem now, however. For if natural psychological processes are what lead disabled persons to adapt to (and even come to prefer) terrible and unchangeable truths about their life, this increases the likelihood that human beings in general have distorted pictures of their well-being. There are two main reasons for this. First, the same psychological factors and processes that lead disabled persons to adapt are also very much operative in the minds of others, including disability-positive skeptics. Second, there are many notable harms and benefits, given this kind of reasoning, that human beings in general fail to fully appreciate, in part, because of adaptation.

Beginning with the benefits, we human beings aren't clearly much subjectively happier now than we were 100 years ago, and this despite how many common markers of well-being (longevity, liberty, wealth, education, and valuable forms of technology) have increased—in some cases exponentially.[29] So we are not obviously sensitive to gradual increases in objective well-being, goes the worry. More than this, the tragic features of human lives often do not have a lasting impact on our feelings and judgments about life—at least not for the roughly 80% of us who have an optimism bias and who are fairly quick to adapt. As I have noted elsewhere,

> Life presents us with very bad things: we get depressed, we get cancer, we often fail to get what we want, and we must eventually lose everything, including those who brought us into existence. Given the severity of these things, it might be wondered how our quality of life assessments could be high in the absence of serious biases .... Serious harms aside, we perhaps especially fail to appreciate the mild and mundane minuses in life, something that Benatar nicely draws our attention to.... And yet these factors, when added up, may have significant impact on how our lives actually go. (If we were anywhere nearly as harsh as the average movie critic in assessing the narratives of our lives the results might be sobering.)
>
> (Marsh 2014, 444–445)

In this paper, I was partly responding to David Benatar's attempt to explain away people's basic optimism about their lives. I argued that Benatar overstates the psychologically based case for radical pessimism when he says that various distorting biases and adaptive processes keep us from seeing that all of our lives come out very bad on the standard theories of well-being. But the point remains. Our lives contain a lot of bad that we often don't fully appreciate. So, if we are highly comfortable with "you say you're happy, but..." reasoning toward disabled persons, we ought to turn this reasoning on ourselves. But, when we do that, it is not easy to see, given arguments I raised, how we can resist the conclusion that our lives may well be notably worse than we think or at any rate much harder to assess than we think.

True, some self-questioning is no doubt good for us. But the present argument is conditional. If we don't want to go too far down the road of well-being skepticism, and if we want to maintain our current degree of optimism about our lives, then we ought to be a little more trusting of disability-positive testimony. This pragmatic argument, like all pragmatic arguments, won't appeal to everyone. For instance, those who think that we should seek to follow the argument where it leads, even if the outcome is unfortunate, might resist the current strategy. I get their stance (Marsh 2017). But such persons should keep in mind a purely epistemic point that is often missed in these discussions. Seriously questioning the well-being of disabled persons without also questioning oneself or non-disabled people seems inconsistent and selectively skeptical. It does not follow the argument where it leads.

My final explanation of what's wrong with disability-positive skepticism takes the form of an argument from moral risk. As Dan Moller has noted, given a traditional Catholic view of ethics "the mere risk of making a deep moral mistake [in contexts of notable uncertainty] rules out certain acts" (Moller 2011b, 425). To see how such risk arguments work, consider the case of climate change skepticism. Even if you're not fully convinced by the empirical arguments that the environment is in serious danger, these matters are complicated, and there is a serious epistemic risk that you are wrong. If you're wrong, moreover, you might be very wrong. And your actions might cause serious harm—not least if lots of others are skeptical like you and behave like you. Of course, if you're extremely confident that you're right, then maybe you're fine (subjectively speaking) in living as you do. But matters as controversial and high-stakes as this rarely permit such confidence. So we might think that uncertainty in this context, assuming it is also believed that climate skepticism is our riskiest option, generates strong reasons for climate skeptics to change their ways.

Perhaps something similar can be said about acts of disability-positive skepticism. Barnes and others might be right about the nature and value of disability. And, if they are, then acts of disability-positive skepticism could be very painful and objectively disrespectful to disabled persons. The argument here, notice, is not inductive and does not rest on ideas about epistemic injustice. For, even if we had never been mistaken about minorities in the past, and even if there were no such thing as epistemic injustice, the present moral risks concerning pain and disrespect would still arise. Maybe the risk of serious moral wrongdoing under conditions of notable uncertainty by itself makes a strong claim on us.

Indeed, given what is at stake, and given how complicated well-being is (just read Barnes's claims about the ways in which local and global well-being can fail to interact), then, even if we set aside well-known ableist biases, we might question our distrusting tendencies a bit more. To be sure, we cannot simply decide what to believe about disability, however risky our skeptical attitudes might be. But the argument still has force since it can motivate actions or omissions that might indirectly influence people's beliefs. For instance, the argument might motivate more skeptics to listen harder to disabled voices or to read more work in the area. These actions might, in turn, soften people's skeptical stances.

I realize that arguments from moral risk are complex and don't always favour a single course of action.[30] Such arguments also can have implications that some won't like.[31] But, despite these considerations, many people find it natural to worry about the risk of wrongdoing in contexts of uncertainty about the objective status of one's actions. Of course, being too positive about the value of disability could be bad for disabled persons if it resulted in providing disabled persons with fewer resources or accommodations in the future. But few would disagree with this point (Amundson 2010, 376–377).

A more serious challenge, it seems to me, concerns how far risk-based arguments can extend. For it might be thought that we also risk harming hermits in failing to believe their words and that this very fact, on the present reasoning, gives us reason to trust hermit-positive testimony. This is a tricky matter that I cannot fully resolve here. But, whatever we say about it, there are far more disabled persons than non–morally motivated hermits. So, disability-positive skepticism is far riskier than hermit-positive skepticism.

Finally, even if no single argument is sufficient to require trust, which may be the case, the disjunction of various arguments—epistemic, pragmatic, and moral—might prove more powerful. I think the disjunction ought to be sufficiently powerful to motivate more people to at least try to trust disability-positive testimony more than they do.

ACKNOWLEDGMENTS

Thanks to Samantha Brennan, Stephen Campbell, Adam Cureton, Sara Goering, Sally Haslanger, Jennifer Hawkins, Dan Haybron, Richard Lucas, Jon Marsh, Laurie Paul, Lucia Schwarz, Joseph Stramondo, Valerie Tiberius, and David Wasserman for stimulating discussion. Thanks, also, to audiences in Toronto and Knoxville for their feedback.

NOTES

1. The terms "happiness" and "well-being" will be used interchangeably at various points when the distinction is less important. At other points, which the context should make clear, "happiness" will be used to denote subjective features of a life (e.g., positive states of mind, or life satisfaction) and "well-being" will be used to denote an objective condition (e.g., a flourishing life, or a life with certain objective goods). Naturally, how *much* trust we should have in people's prudential testimony could depend on our theory of well-being or happiness, but there may be quite a bit of agreement across theories.
2. Like Barnes, I am restricting my focus entirely to *physical* disability. And, like Barnes, I will not consider whether physically disabled people have equal value or inherent worth or moral status. I think they clearly do. But the value of persons and the value of their lives are distinct, and I am focused only on the latter, prudential, value here.
3. To clarify, neither Barnes—whose work I shall focus on here—nor Conly claim that disabled people are infallible testifiers. They just think that they are normally more trustworthy than skeptics who insist that disabled people are not happy at all, not as happy as other people, or not as happy as they think (or claim). These authors also worry about common forms of "you say you're happy but..." reasoning such as the following: "You say you're happy, but your testimony has an unreliable causal origin and so isn't to be trusted." Or: "You say you value your minority identity, but you only say this because it is personally and politically advantageous for you to do so. You don't really believe it."
4. I borrow the phrase "disability-positive testimony" from Barnes.
5. For instance, Deborah Kent remarks: "I will always believe that blindness is a neutral trait, neither to be prized nor shunned. Very few people, including those dearest to me share that conviction" (Johnson 2001).
6. I have neither been to Australia nor have I practiced law. And although philosophy fits my personality very well, being a lawyer might as well.
7. For instance, I have also often claimed that my life would have contained notably less happiness had I not taken up the guitar. But although losing my current ability to play the guitar would surely be bad for me now, given my actual interests, it's harder to assess my life in worlds in which I never develop these interests.
8. Maybe our lives would contain more pleasure, life satisfaction, affect balance, meaning, fulfilled desires, or be more enjoyable in a host of ways in other worlds that we don't currently inhabit. Our actual experience isn't a fully reliable guide to these matters.

9. On this view, painful transitions between states that are deemed inherently neutral might make a global (or all things considered) negative difference to someone's life even if she is glad about the end result and no longer suffers (Campbell and Stramondo 2017).

10. It is worth noting that the population-level argument, even if supported by data, wouldn't fully warrant the kinds of testimony that we have been considering, which are neither probabilistic nor made in light of the science of well-being, and which occasionally include claims about objective well-being.

11. See L. A. Paul's work for a related discussion about whether becoming disabled is a transformative experience (Paul 2014, 56–70).

12. True, fewer persons would be offended if a hearing person merely asserted (c) that he is as happy as the average deaf person. But it is not clear to me that this weaker testimony is warranted by the speaker's lived experience either.

13. Such individuals might have lots of practice imagining their winnings, to be sure, just as disabled persons might have often imagined their lives in different bodies. But their judgments aren't clearly reliable.

14. If Barnes meant to imply only that testimonial claims like 3 but not 1 and 2 can be fairly easily resisted, this would have been a good place to clarify this. Instead, she says, "McBryde Johnson's experiences reflect a common theme for those in the disability rights community. They make claims, repeatedly, about the value of disability and about the value of their own well-being. And yet those claims can't seem to get past the stereotypes and presuppositions that people have about disability. And this, I contend, is a classic example of testimonial injustice" (Barnes 2016, 138).

15. Physical disability is a very big and diverse tent, after all, and empirical work on its connection to well-being is still being done and replicated.

16. Some patients reported to be doing rather well, and many found this study surprising. But few patients claimed to be as happy as they were prior to their disability, and it seems reasonable to suppose that those who don't want to be resuscitated aren't flourishing.

17. I recall David Wasserman once making this point. Some might think that Duchenne muscular dystrophy (DMD) is a good example here (Yamaguchi and Suzuki 2013).

18. No doubt it can also be difficult to tease apart local versus global harms, but this very fact also makes it hard to assert claim 3.

19. Many mistakenly attribute to mere-difference views the idea that disability is harm-free. But Barnes notes that disabilities can be harmful, in a restricted sense, just like being gay or having a female body can be. In all three cases, however, the harms do not easily create a global or overall negative difference.

20. For even if it's logically consistent with *some* mere-difference views that there is mixed testimony (say because it's logically consistent with some mere-difference views that *some* disabilities are negative-differences), the more negative testimony there is, the less applicable the mere-difference label will become. Also, in light of testimony like McBryde Johnson's, Barnes is suspicious of attempts to say that any particular disability is bad. This constrains how she might reply to the problem.

21. Objection: Wouldn't trusting voices like Steinhart's also require trusting those who claim that being gay is bad for them and warrants conversion therapy? Response: Gay-negative testimony is almost always colored by the belief that living as a gay person is inherently immoral, whereas disability-negative testimony almost always lacks a moral component. Besides, if there were more gay-negative testimony than there seems to be (say enough people claimed that not being able to create a child with the person they love is a global

intrinsic harm), this additional testimony presumably would pose an evidential problem for comparably strong forms of gay-positive testimony.

22. As one author puts it, "Although happy slave examples are simplistic and fraught with hazards (not the least of which is that it they are completely imaginary), they do demonstrate the logical coherence of a claim that people can be mistaken about their QOL" (Amundson 2010, 374).

23. Barnes no longer seems to use this phrase but now focuses on worries about disagreement and independent traction.

24. Not all adaptive explanations assume that disability is bad, of course. Some take the form of an epistemic sensitivity challenge, such as the following: because of adaptation, a testifier would say x about her life whether or not x was true (Marsh 2014, 450)—which suggests that her testimony is not trustworthy.

25. Barnes doesn't discuss the hermit case to my recollection. But I recall her once noting that disability pride would be incoherent if the reasoning that grounds it could be applied to being a jerk. I think the hermit case is harder and more interesting.

26. We are not talking about hermits who value relationships with other people but sacrifice this interest in order to increase their relationship with the divine or to achieve something moral. We are talking about those who don't desire or value relationships with other people and who don't see this as a well-being deficit.

27. Some "Rawlsians" might focus on idealized conditions and relational goods. On this view, if only the hermit knew what it was like to have relationships, if only he took into account his current and future desires, if only he rationally weighed and balanced his various preferences into a coherent whole, it is likely that he would come to prefer a more social life despite his current preferences to be alone. Given full information and complete rationality, in other words, the hermit would choose not to be a hermit, which is comparatively bad for him. But, stated this way, this conditional response assumes that we know what people would choose under ideal circumstances and which ways of life are best, which are two of the very matters in question. To clarify, I personally think that relationships are objectively valuable and choice-worthy. But the challenge is how to argue for this claim on the ground without assuming too much. In my experience, arguments about what groups would prefer under ideal conditions are rarely subjectively persuasive to those who don't already agree with them. This explains why gay people, blind people, and females are rarely impressed by similarly structured arguments according to which they would never choose their identities under ideal conditions.

28. Until the problem of mixed testimony is resolved, I won't argue for trusting claim 3.

29. I recall hearing Paul Bloom once make a similar point. Also, Dan Moller has argued that some version of the Easterlin Paradox must obtain for beings like us (Moller 2011a).

30. Sometimes every course of action or inaction may be comparably risky.

31. For instance, Moller (2011b) notes that, in his experience, many people are more open to risk-based arguments against eating meat than risk-based arguments against having an abortion. For criticisms of risk-based arguments, see Weatherson 2014.

References

Amundson, Ron. 2010. "Quality of Life, Disability, and Hedonic Psychology." *Journal for the Theory of Social Behaviour* 40(4): 374–392.

Barnes, Elizabeth. 2009. "Disability and Adaptive Preference." *Philosophical Perspectives* 23: 1–22.

Barnes, Elizabeth. 2016. *The Minority Body: A Theory of Disability*. Oxford: Oxford University Press.

Bruno, Marie-Aurélie, Jan L. Bernheim, Didier Ledoux, et al. 2011. "A Survey on Self-Assessed Well-Being in a Cohort of Chronic Locked-in Syndrome Patients: Happy Majority, Miserable Minority." *BMJ Open* 1(1): e000039.

Campbell, Stephen M., and Joseph A. Stramondo. 2017. "The Complicated Relationship Between Disability and Well-being." *Kennedy Institute of Ethics Journal.* 27(2):151–184.

Crasnow, Sharon. 2013. "Feminist Philosophy of Science: Values and Objectivity." *Philosophy Compass* 8(4): 413–423.

Dollar, Ellen P. 2012. "Do I Hate My Life? No. But I Do Hate My Disability." *Patheos.com*. Available at http://www.patheos.com/blogs/ellenpainterdollar/2012/05/do-i-hate-my-life/

Fricker, Miranda. 2007. *Epistemic Injustice: Power and the Ethics of Knowing*, Oxford: Oxford University Press.

Goering, Sara. 2008. "'You Say You're Happy, But…': Contested Quality of Life Judgments in Bioethics and Disability Studies." *Journal of Bioethical Inquiry* 5(2–3): 125–135.

Haybron, Dan. 2007. "Do We Know How Happy We Are?" *Nous* 41(3): 394–428.

Johnson, Mary. 2001. "Airing the 'Disability Perspective' but Getting Few Converts." *raggededgemagazine.com*. Available at http://www.raggededgemagazine.com/0101/0101bkrev1.htm

Lucas, Richard E. 2007. "Long-Term Disability Is Associated with Lasting Changes in Subjective Well-Being: Evidence from Two Nationally Representative Longitudinal Studies." *Journal of Personality and Social Psychology* 92(4):717–730.

Marsh, Jason. 2014. "Quality of Life Assessments, Cognitive Reliability, and Procreative Responsibility." *Philosophy and Phenomenological Research* (89)2: 436–466.

Marsh, Jason. 2017. "On the Socratic Injunction to Follow the Argument Where It Leads." In *Renewing Philosophy of Religion: Exploratory Essays*, edited by Paul Draper and John L. Schellenberg, 187–207. Oxford: Oxford University Press.

Moller, Dan. 2011a. "Wealth, Disability, and Happiness." *Philosophy & Public Affairs* 39: 177–206.

Moller, Dan. 2011b. "Abortion and Moral Risk." *Philosophy* 86(3): 425–443.

Ott, Jan. 2009. "Our Imagination of Future Happiness and Its Shortcomings. Daniel Gilbert, Stumbling on Happiness." *Journal of Happiness Studies* 10: 253–255.

Paul, Laurie. 2014. *Transformative Experience*. Oxford: Oxford University Press.

Steinhart, Eric. 2016. "Eudaimonia and Disabilities as Mere Difference: A Response to Helen De Cruz." *philpercs.com*. Available at http://www.philpercs.com/2016/05/eudaimonia-against-the-mere-difference-account-of-disability-a-response-to-helen-de-cruz-guest-post-.html

Weatherson, Brian. 2014. "Running risks morally." *Philosophical Studies* 167(1):141–163.

Yamaguchi, Miku, and Machiko Suzuki. 2013. "Independent Living with Duchenne Muscular Dystrophy and Home Mechanical Ventilation in Areas of Japan with Insufficient National Welfare Services." *International Journal of Qualitative Studies on Health and Well-Being* 8: 20914.

CHAPTER 19

INTERACTIONS WITH DELUSIONAL OTHERS

Reflections on Epistemic Failures and Virtues

JOSH DOHMEN

My modest aim in this chapter is to consider some of the epistemic aspects of interactions with others who we believe to be delusional. While bracketing non-epistemic concerns is surely artificial, I will only gesture toward the ethical and political considerations that are tied up with our interactions as epistemic agents. Interactions with others who are delusional pose a special challenge since, in these cases, the nature of epistemic injustices may be less clear than in interactions with nondelusional people. If a person's beliefs are genuinely untrustworthy, for example, can they be subject to epistemic injustices? And if a person's delusions are maintained by constantly discounting the testimony of others, can they be held responsible for committing epistemic injustices?[1]

The chapter is divided into six sections. The first section provides background by summarizing some main trends in philosophical literature concerning disability and epistemic injustice. In the second section, I argue that, for the day-to-day purposes of most individuals, it is helpful to understand delusions as extreme epistemic failures, failures that all of us are guilty of to some degree. The third section offers a caution about attributing delusions to others because to call someone delusional can act to discredit them, and this can be especially dangerous when applied to groups that are already unfairly discredited. The fourth section considers two ways in which delusional individuals can be wronged by epistemic injustice. In the fifth section, I argue that responsibility for delusions needs to be extended beyond the individual holding delusional beliefs to the social and political conditions that shape those beliefs. Finally, the sixth section suggests that the virtue of epistemic humility, especially in the form of "radical listening," offers several important epistemic benefits in our interactions with others we believe to be delusional.

EPISTEMIC INJUSTICE
AND DISABILITY

Before moving on to my own suggestions, it will be helpful to review some of my starting points. Feminists, Marxists, critical race theorists, and disability scholars have long argued that there are epistemic components to oppression. For example, drawing on the work of Karl Marx, Jean-Paul Sartre, critical theorists, and other disability theorists, James I. Charlton (1998) argues (1) that many belief systems around the world construe disability as inherently harmful and ignore the social determinants of disability oppression and (2) that these beliefs can become internalized by disabled people such that it is difficult to understand their own oppression. In *The Rejected Body* (1996), Susan Wendell explains how people, especially medical professionals, problematically invalidate ill and disabled persons as epistemic agents. More recently, Licia Carlson (2010) has taken issue with the ways in which intellectually disabled persons are discussed in philosophical literature without sufficiently taking into account the experiences of those with such disabilities or the testimonies of those closest to them.

In her influential book, *Epistemic Injustice* (2007), Miranda Fricker synthesizes these analyses of epistemic oppression with developments in virtue epistemology. She discusses two forms of epistemic injustice: testimonial and hermeneutical injustice. A *testimonial injustice* occurs when a person's testimony is given a credibility deficit as a result of nonepistemic factors. Fricker is especially concerned with cases in which these credibility deficits are attributed based on oppressed social identities (like race and gender). *Hermeneutical injustice* occurs when a community's hermeneutical resources—that is, resources for interpreting the social world—obscure the experiences of members of a social group as a result of structural prejudices. A key example of hermeneutical injustice, for Fricker, is the development of the language of "sexual harassment." Prior to the development of such terms, attempts by women to articulate their discomfort at work and in other spaces were made difficult by the absence of apt language. Coworkers and bosses may have been considered "flirts," but language like this does not adequately capture the discomfort and fear that many women were experiencing. It took a change in the collective hermeneutical resources, such as the recognition and development of the term "sexual harassment," to make these experiences communicable.

Drawing on the work of Fricker and others concerned with epistemic justice, disability scholars and bioethicists have begun to analyze the ways in which disabled persons are wronged as knowers. One area of focus has been epistemic injustices within healthcare and service provision. Alistair Wardrope (2015) has argued that medicalization, or the application of medical terms and norms to various lived experiences, can constitute a form of hermeneutical injustice when alternatives for interpreting one's experiences are unjustly foreclosed. Wardrope cautions, however, that critiques of medicalization often commit testimonial injustices by failing to listen directly to those who are affected and by failing to consider the ways in which medical responses to illness and disability are often experienced as helpful by those who are suffering. Havi Carel and Ian James Kidd (2014; Kidd and Carel 2017) have argued that ill people, especially those who are navigating healthcare services, are subject to both testimonial and hermeneutical injustices that result from negative stereotypes about those who are ill (that they are, for example, too emotionally affected by their illnesses to be reliable) and from features of healthcare training and provision (such as the valuation of "objective" evidence over patients' perceptions). They have recommended a phenomenological "toolkit" to help address such injustices by focusing on the individual's experience of the illness (Carel and Kidd 2014, 538).

Some scholars (Ho 2011; Buchman, Ho, and Goldberg 2017) have analyzed the ways in which trusting medical experts can have negative epistemic consequences when that trust leads patients' experiences and interests to be ignored, when it undermines a patient's self-trust or self-esteem, and when it leads patients to lose trust in their practitioners or in medicine altogether. Anita Ho (2011) focuses on the ways in which these epistemic harms are of special concern for people with impairments since physicians may emphasize medical diagnoses and treatments rather than being attentive to social barriers. Buchman et al. (2017) focus on chronic pain since the subjectivity of pain often leads physicians to (consciously or not) deflate their credibility assessments of patients whose pain does not correspond to an objective symptom (like a lesion in a computed tomography [CAT] scan). Ho and Buchman suggest epistemic humility as a virtuous response to these injustices. Humility involves acknowledging the limits of the physician's knowledge, being attentive to the experiences and testimony of patients, and reflecting upon and seeking to address prejudices that may be leading to credibility deficits with regard to patients. Like Buchman et al. (2017), other scholars analyze epistemic injustices related to specific embodied experiences, such as chronic fatigue syndrome (Blease, Carel, and Geraghty 2017), pregnancy (Freeman 2015), and intersexuality (Merrick 2017).

Focusing on the experiences of disabled people in general, Jackie Leach Scully (2018) argues that not only are disabled people subject to a wide variety of epistemic injustices but also that these injustices have several distinctive features. First, the diversity of impairments and the degree to which disabled individuals are often isolated from people with similar disabilities make it especially difficult to formulate and disseminate alternative hermeneutical resources to express their experiences. Second, because disabled individuals are more likely to spend significant amounts of time interacting with healthcare and health service providers, they are especially likely to be affected by the epistemic hierarchies of medicine. Third, disabled people are likely to be attributed a "global epistemic incapacity" (Scully 2018, 116); that is, others are likely to assume that a specific impairment limits a person's epistemic capacities in general. Finally, because there is a widespread assumption that disabled lives lack value (i.e., that we should seek to cure or make disabled people as normal as possible), it is also assumed that the knowledge that arises from disabled lives lacks value.[2] Similarly, in *The Minority Body* (2016),

Elizabeth Barnes argues that skepticism about disability-positive testimony constitutes a testimonial injustice.[3]

Other authors have addressed epistemic injustices related to mental disabilities. Specifically *mental* disabilities, like mental illness, traumatic brain injury, and intellectual disability present unique challenges because these conditions may well lead to epistemic limitations. This does not mean, however, that mentally disabled persons are not subject to epistemic injustices. I have argued that mentally disabled persons are subject to a variety of epistemic injustices (Dohmen 2016). To respond to such injustices, we should be attentive to a person's attempts to communicate, whether such attempts take the form of shared language, gestures, or even simple expressions of preference or pain. I also argue, with certain cautions, that in cases where communication with an individual is difficult, we should be attentive to the advice of those who are close to or spend a lot of time with the individual. And I argue that we should foster the development of the individual's epistemic capacities rather than writing them off or assuming that they will not develop. Finally, I argue that there is a form of epistemic injustice, *intimate hermeneutical injustice*, that occurs when an individual's attempts at interpreting her own experiences in interpersonal interactions are blocked or ignored. Though intimate hermeneutical injustice is not specific to those with mental disabilities, this concept is especially helpful in understanding certain problems faced by those with mental disabilities. Focusing specifically on intellectually disabled interviewees in Sweden, Kalman et al. (2016) reveal three specific forms of epistemic injustice. The people they interviewed lacked adequate hermeneutical resources to describe their experiences within service-provision settings and, as a result, were subject to frequent testimonial injustices when attempting to articulate their experiences. A third problem is that the interviewees, especially the women,[4] were often kept isolated from their broader communities, causing them to lack important experiences that may help them develop more adequate epistemic resources.

Other authors have focused on mental illness. Writing with Paul Crichton, Carel and Kidd argue that psychiatric patients are often subject to epistemic injustices. They point to three "global" contributors to such injustices. First, those with mental illnesses are often held responsible for their own epistemic limitations. For example, a person who drops out of school as a result of a mental illness may be thought of as lacking the skills or intelligence to earn a degree (Crichton, Carel, and Kidd 2017, 67). Second, the valuation of hard (objective, quantifiable) evidence in the medical professions over soft evidence (like patient testimony) leads to patients' experiences being neglected in favor of biological causes and pharmaceutical treatments.[5] Third, negative stereotypes often lead to mentally ill persons being treated as violence-prone, as mentally weak, untrustworthy, or delusional regardless of the accuracy of these assessments. The authors suggest that responding to these epistemic injustices will require taking patients' experiences and beliefs into account throughout diagnosis and treatment, holding the media accountable for fostering unrealistic portrayals of mentally ill persons, and providing adequate resources for mental health care. Considering depression specifically, Jake Jackson (2017) analyzes several attitudes that wrong depressed persons as epistemic agents. One such attitude is disregarding the gravity of depressed person's experiences. If, for example, I assure a depressed friend that "you're just going through a hard time," I treat her concerns as if they are commonplace rather than acknowledging the unique difficulty of her depression. Instead of adopting such attitudes, Jackson suggests that we adopt empathy in interactions with depressed others. Empathy, for Jackson, seeks to understand the depressed person's experiences *from their point of view*, however incomplete this process will inevitably be.

Epistemic Failures and Delusions

Discussions of how to understand delusional beliefs are ongoing. No consensus has emerged. The American Psychological Association defines delusions as:

> A false belief based on incorrect inference about external reality that is firmly held despite what almost everyone else believes and despite what constitutes incontrovertible and obvious proof or evidence to the contrary. The belief is not ordinarily accepted by other members of the person's culture or subculture (i.e., it is not an article of religious faith). When a false belief involves a value judgment, it is regarded as a delusion only when the judgment is so extreme as to defy credibility.
> (American Psychiatric Association 2013, 819)[6]

Others argue that delusions should not be considered beliefs at all because, for example, they are not necessarily tied to action, as other beliefs are, and they are not necessarily influenced by or tied to other beliefs. Such arguments appear to rely on idealized conceptions of "normal" beliefs, however, as most people hold beliefs that they do not act upon, that do not cohere with other beliefs, or that are stubbornly resistant to change even in the face of contrary evidence (Bortolotti 2016a; Radden 2011, 44–46). Still others ask researchers to be specific about what type of belief delusions are being compared to because delusions often involve a level of subjective importance and affective investment that many strictly factual beliefs do not have (Mullen and Gillett 2014). Jennifer Radden's book-length treatment of delusions, however, notes that delusions consist of a variety of epistemic failures that are relative to the epistemic (and sometimes moral) norms of one's social and historical location (2011). So, for example, beliefs can be considered delusional for failures of (a) plausibility of content, (b) norms of acquisition or justification, (c) coherence with other beliefs, and (d) responsiveness to counter-evidence.

Rather than enter the debate about what counts as a delusion, I aim to focus instead on the epistemic failures that give rise to delusions. This is because, in our day-to-day interactions, most of us will probably only have guesses about whether or not another's beliefs are delusional in a clinical sense. If the literature on epistemic injustice is to be used to help everyone, not just practitioners and service providers, then the conclusions

I reach should be applicable to situations where we *believe* another person to be delusional with or without a clinical diagnosis.

Because the epistemic failures of delusions cannot be reduced to their falsity, I propose that they may be helpfully understood in terms of José Medina's "guiding principles." Both of these principles have to do with how we engage "cognitive forces," or motivations for and influences on our beliefs, understanding, and inquiry. The *principle of acknowledgment and engagement* states that "all cognitive forces we encounter must be acknowledged and, insofar as it becomes possible, they must be engaged in some way (even if in some cases only a negative mode of engagement is possible or epistemically beneficial)" (Medina 2013, 50). In other words, we should try to be aware of relevant cognitive forces and we should try not to ignore those cognitive forces that are influencing, or have had a tendency to influence, our beliefs. The *principle of epistemic equilibrium* states that we should seek "equilibrium in the interplay of cognitive forces, without some forces overpowering others, without some cognitive influences becoming unchecked and unbalanced" (Medina 2013, 50). This means that we should actively monitor and evaluate our reasons for holding beliefs without letting one influence or source become unquestioned (when they can be questioned). Understanding delusions as failures in these principles is helpful for a number of reasons. First, understanding delusions in this way does not require an absolute knowledge of what is true to determine that a belief is delusional. Take, for example, a person who believes that their water is contaminated without adequate evidence. This person is failing the principle of epistemic equilibrium if they allow their conviction that their water is tainted to overpower other cognitive forces, like awareness of the absence of material evidence or the testimony of neighbors who have had their water tested with no evidence of contamination. We do not need a "god's eye view" to know whether or not this belief is delusional. Second, understanding delusions as failures of these epistemic principles acknowledges the blurry distinction between delusions and other epistemic failures. Delusions on this account are on the extreme side of epistemic failures but are not categorically different from other kinds. For example, it is an unsettled question whether a person's idiosyncratic religious beliefs should be considered delusional or not. By focusing on these principles, I hope to draw attention to the failures and away from disputes about what is or is not a delusion.

To illustrate how these principles are helpful, consider the following examples. Richard McLean, whose autobiography offers a powerful description of his own experience of schizophrenia, explains many different paranoid delusions that he held. For example, he consistently heard the loudspeaker of a company adjacent to his workplace shouting vulgar things about him. At one point, he confronted several people about this. He told his own coworker, for example, about the conspiratorial messages and the coworker replied, "Why do you think you are that important?" (McLean 2003, 56). He then went to confront the manager of the company with the loudspeakers, and, in reply, the manager said, "I'm sorry. I have no idea what you're talking about" (McLean 2003, 58). In response, McLean felt on the one hand a temporary reassurance that he was just hearing things, but, on the other hand, he felt a sense of having been deceived by the others. In maintaining his belief about the broadcast vulgarities, he failed to engage with contrary evidence, like the absence of people's offended reactions at hearing vulgar things spoken over a loudspeaker or the testimony of those he confronted, and he gave his own aural hallucinations undue weight.

Second, consider a person who believes that vaccines cause autism (or that vaccines are generally more harmful than helpful for those who receive them). Research has suggested that even when presented with powerful evidence that vaccines do not in fact result in the harms they imagine, so-called vaccine denialists will not revise their beliefs (Nyhan et al. 2014; Nyhan and Reifler 2015). Here people are clearly failing to engage with and give due weight to relevant cognitive forces.

These examples suggest the broad epistemic failures of persons who hold delusional beliefs. In a later section, I will consider the extent to which those with delusions are responsible for their epistemic failures.

The Label of "Delusional" and Epistemic Injustice

In the previous section, I argued that delusions can be helpfully understood as extreme forms of more general epistemic failures. In this section, I discuss the way in which labeling people as "delusional" acts to discredit them. To be clear, discrediting a person in itself is not an injustice, but the label of "delusional" has historically been used in biased ways to discredit people unjustly. A person's social identities, like one's race or gender, may influence the ways in which others perceive them as delusional or not. Since the 1970s, for example, African Americans have been consistently overdiagnosed with schizophrenia and other psychotic disorders while underdiagnosed with affective disorders like depression, bipolar, or anxiety disorders (Baker and Bell 1999; Schwartz and Blankenship 2014). Schwartz and Blankenship also summarize findings that Latino Americans are more likely to be diagnosed with schizophrenia than are European Americans (2014). In his book, *The Protest Psychosis*, Jonathan Metzl (2009) shows how an (often unconscious) association between schizophrenia and black men was constructed and maintained by a complex web of social circumstances and historical events. These include the introduction of a new diagnostic category, "schizophrenia, paranoid type," applicable when an individual is "frequently hostile and aggressive, and *his* behavior tends to be consistent with *his* delusions" (Metzl 2009, 97, emphasis added); a trend in psychiatric literature claiming that black men were predisposed to psychosis; the spread of civil rights and anti-racist movements and language (and their perceived threat to the status quo); and the marketing of anti-psychotic medications using stereotyped images of black people. As a result of this history, the beliefs of black men in the United States, especially beliefs concerning racial discrimination and prejudice, are more likely to be perceived as delusional even by trained psychiatric professionals (Metzl 2009).

Black men are not the only social group affected by unjustified attributions of delusions. Consider the case of Kamilah Brock, a black woman who was forcibly institutionalized in New York in 2014. Brock accidentally went to the wrong precinct to recover her impounded BMW. As she was trying to leave, she was escorted to Harlem Hospital and then forcibly medicated and held for eight days. The city claims that Brock was "acting irrational, she spoke incoherently and inconsistently, and she ran into the middle of traffic on Eighth Ave" (S. R. Brown 2015)—a claim Brock and her attorney deny (Mathias 2016). According to Brock, officers at the precinct expressed disbelief that she owned a BMW. To counter this disbelief, she told them she worked as a banker and that President Obama's Twitter account followed hers. In the hospital, "Part of her treatment involved being forced to 'admit' that her career was a fabrication and that she had never interacted on Twitter with the President," even though these claims could easily be checked for accuracy and were in fact correct (The Law Offices of Michael S. Lamonsoff, PLLC 2015). In other words, Brock was considered to be delusional for stating beliefs that would likely not have been dismissed if she were white. Cases like these demonstrate how important it is to be cautious when labeling people as delusional, especially when a person is a member of a marginalized social group, and especially when the person doing the labeling is in a position of authority relative to the person being labeled.

EPISTEMIC INJUSTICE AND PERSONS WITH DELUSIONS

Of course, even taking the cautions from the previous section into account, there are cases in which we may well be justified in considering others to be delusional. Given that delusions are indeed epistemic failures, I turn in this section to consider if and how persons with delusions can be victims of epistemic injustices. My general conclusions are that they can be so victimized in two ways.

First, because delusional beliefs are often the result of bizarre experiences that call for explanations or interpretations, these beliefs should not be dismissed out of hand but instead understood for the explanatory roles they play in individuals' lives. Lisa Bortolotti (2016b) argues that some delusions qualify as "epistemically innocent," that is, they offer epistemic benefits that would not otherwise be available to the person. For example, rather than feeling overwhelmed by uncertainties or a flood of stimuli, a delusion may offer a condition from which to act in and investigate the world or to focus one's attention. To be clear, the claim is not that accepting a delusion is epistemically preferable to not having delusions, but that, given the experiences of some people with symptoms of psychosis, delusions may offer epistemic benefits when one's epistemic capacities are already undermined.

Indeed, I have previously argued for intimate hermeneutical justice: listening to others' interpretations of their own experiences in interpersonal settings, without feeling the need to fit those interpretations into mainstream or widely shared interpretations (Dohmen 2016). Practicing intimate hermeneutical justice with persons who are delusional would not be about trying to gain information from them, but about attempting to understand their experiences and how the delusion helps them interpret their experiences.

Second, following Scully's (2018) caution about "global epistemic incapacity," we should constantly guard against moving from awareness of a person's *delusional belief* or beliefs to a general disregard of *all of their beliefs* or dismissal of their credibility. McLean recounts an interaction with his psychiatrist in his autobiography that can serve to illustrate this point. Both before and after the onset of his symptoms, McLean was interested in understanding the nature of time. After his symptoms began to subside as a result of psychiatric treatment, he decided to ask his psychiatrist if he had ever considered the nature of time. In response, "The psychiatrist told me to double my meds. . . . So I began to monitor my own medication as I saw fit, only liaising with him on any questions I had to do with my illness" (McLean 2003, 153). One sees, here, the threat of dismissing as delusional any belief perceived as abnormal simply because the person does have some delusional beliefs. This interaction led McLean to distrust his doctor's advice about dosing and to restrict his interactions with his doctor to concerns about schizophrenia.[7] A consideration of metaphysical questions that are still unanswered to most of us was reduced to a symptom of a mental disorder.

RESPONSIBILITY AND THE POLITICAL AND SOCIAL CONTEXT OF DELUSIONS

In the previous section, I argued that delusional persons can be subject to epistemic injustices and suggested considerations for avoiding such injustices. In this section, I turn to the epistemic responsibility of delusional persons toward others. To what extent can persons be held responsible for their delusional beliefs, including those beliefs held in place through testimonial injustices? I will use what Medina (2013) calls (following Iris Marion Young) a "social connection model of responsibility" to argue that the extent to which one can hold individuals accountable for their delusional beliefs depends on a variety of internal and external factors. Individuals who have delusions as a result of schizophrenia or neurological damage may be held accountable for their delusional beliefs. For example, McLean and Pamela Spiro Wagner (2005), both of whom are diagnosed with schizophrenia, report that they value the ability to "reality check" their beliefs by consulting others. But this responsibility varies according to the extent that therapies (whether chemical, cognitive, or behavioral) are available to assist delusional persons in assessing and revising their delusional beliefs. Thus, what appears to be an issue for the individual is deeply social and political. Delusional beliefs must be understood in their social contexts, rather than treated as strictly personal deficiencies. This is true for epistemic failures in general. Take, for instance, Medina's example of the Vanderbilt student who left a pig's head on the doorstep of a center for Jewish life during the Jewish High Holy Days. Accepting for argument's sake the student's plea of ignorance about Jewish culture, Medina writes: "In an important sense, the ignorance that facilitated epistemically the pig-head dropper's unfortunate action is an *epistemic failure of all of us* who can be related to him; and, more specifically, those of us who had educational obligations to him" (2013, 148). To be clear, Medina is not saying that the student bears no responsibility for his own ignorance, but that it results from a "social division of cognitive laziness" (2013, 146). His community, especially his educators, contributed to his ignorance by paying little attention to Jewish symbols, customs, and holidays; by promoting self-segregation according to religion; and so on. In this way, many epistemic failures result from social and political circumstances.

Similar concerns are raised by widespread ignorance about traumatic brain injury, schizophrenia, and other conditions associated with delusions. McLean claims that he would have sought psychiatric help, and thus begun to address his own delusions, much sooner if he or others in his life had been more aware of the symptoms of schizophrenia (McLean 2003, 168–169). In this way, the degree to which McLean is responsible for his own epistemic failures would have been greater if he had had greater access to information about schizophrenia, if more people in his life were aware of mental illnesses and treatment options, or if social stigmas did not make it so difficult to discuss psychological issues or seek mental health treatment. But an important difference in the case of delusions is that social and political circumstances are not only of concern when it comes to distribution of epistemic resources (like exposure to different histories, ways of life, or educational resources), but also when it comes to nonepistemic resources, including access to therapy or prescription medications. In other words, our epistemic concerns in such cases will give rise to concerns for healthcare justice.

There are other ways in which nonepistemic factors play a role in individuals' epistemic failures. Research on conspiracy theories suggests that many people are inspired to hold epistemically weak beliefs not because of directly related evidence, but because of a disaffection with politics or general experience of lacking control. For example, a pair of studies led by Jan-Willem van Prooijen and Michele Acker conclude that "threats to control might increase belief in conspiracy theories" and that "affirmations of control might just as well decrease belief in conspiracy theories" (2015, 759). Analyzing data from the United States in 1999, for example, the researchers found that a perceived threat from Y2K glitches correlated with beliefs in UFO cover-ups.[8] My aim in discussing studies like these is not to conflate delusions with belief in conspiracy theories. Clearly not all delusions concern conspiracies, and not all beliefs about conspiracies are delusional. Instead, I am suggesting that experiencing a lack of control in one's life can make it easier to attribute control to external forces, especially, in cases like these, to conspiratorial plotters. And because conspiracy theories are often maintained despite a lack of evidence or in the face of positive evidence to the contrary, they are failures to take into account relevant epistemic forces in the same way that delusions are. In other words, a perceived lack of control over our lives may encourage us to ignore relevant cognitive forces. Taking this idea seriously, van Prooijen and Acker conclude that "whenever society is facing a substantial control threat, political leaders have an increased responsibility to install a sense of trust among the public, and to overtly display signs of moral behavior, particularly if they want to avoid increases in perceived threat and the virulent spread of conspiracy theories" (2015, 759).

Similarly, Mark Navin argues that while vaccine denialists manifest epistemic vices, such as confirmation bias and disregard for relevant expertise, they foster a "democratic allocation of epistemic authority" (2013, 254). He views this democratic allocation of credibility as an understandable response to epistemic practices within the medical community that often disregard, silence, or even mock the testimony of patients and their caregivers. To address the concerns of vaccine denialists, then, we need to consider not just their individual epistemic virtues and vices, but also the social factors that contribute to their suspicion. Those social factors are not limited to interactions between medical professionals and patients. As Crichton et al. (2017) emphasize, any adequate response would also need to take into account the uncritical reporting of purported scientific findings, such as Andrew Wakefield's discredited study that originally linked the MMR vaccine to autism.

As a final example, consider the group Life After Hate, which seeks to combat right-wing extremism not by engaging in ideological debates, but by addressing the underlying social and psychological issues that lead individuals to join hate groups and adopt racist and xenophobic beliefs. Summarizing their approach, Christian Picciolini has said,

> rather than argue ideologically with people, . . . we try to make the person more resilient, . . . by applying services, like mental health therapy or job training. . . . And when that person feels more confident, they tend to blame the other less. But I would follow that up with challenging their doctrine, not by telling them they're wrong, but by introducing them to the people that they think that they hate . . . because most people have never met the people that they hate. That helps them humanize these people.   (Picciolini 2017a)

Like the conspiracy theories and anti-vaccine attitudes discussed earlier, the racist and xenophobic beliefs of those in extremist groups tend to be resistant to change. They are also largely motivated, according to Picciolini, by nonepistemic concerns, like the need for identity, community, or a scapegoat, and kept in place through self-segregation and even violence. Life After Hate aims to address these nonepistemic foundations by helping people find identities, communities, and agency in ways that do not rely upon scapegoating or denigrating others.[9] Perhaps a key to addressing racist and xenophobic beliefs, then, is to empower people in their own lives, to create shared public spaces that encourage people of diverse identities to meet and interact, or even to ensure fair wages and ample paid time off to allow families to have more time together, leaving fewer young people feeling abandoned or isolated. Thus, we may well have epistemic motivations, not just political motivations, to make political processes inclusive, transparent, and just.

Epistemic Humility, Radical Listening, and Delusions

While we may struggle daily for a more transparent and just society, this does not answer how we can engage with delusional others in the opaque, unjust world we live in; nor does it explain how to act in a transparent and just society toward those who would still be delusional. In this section, I propose epistemic humility as an important virtue for interacting with delusional others. I have been inspired to emphasize epistemic humility in large part by Metzl's own recommendations to resist racist trends in schizophrenia diagnosis,[10] but also by disability scholars like Ho (2011) and Buchman et al. (2017). In the clinical setting, humility encourages practitioners to recognize that they, too, have unquestioned cultural starting points that they bring to clinical encounters and encourages them to listen patiently to those they serve rather than making unjustified assumptions about their beliefs and practices. Thus, the epistemic humility I am suggesting aligns with Jackson's (2017) call for empathy and Carel and Kidd's (2014) phenomenological toolkit. Humility in our interactions with delusional others would mean listening in a patient, nonjudgmental way. Lisa Heldke has called the type of listening I have in mind "radical listening," in which "one listens to understand, while suspending the matter of how this other set of beliefs will alter one's own" (2007, 29). Listening in this way, even to positions that we find abhorrent, offers a variety of benefits. To be clear, though, humility is only one relevant virtue, and, as I will specify below, Heldke is clear that we should neither ignore risks nor signs that it is not safe to listen radically in certain situations.[11]

The first benefit of radical listening is that it may help us learn about ourselves. This may not be obvious: What could we learn about ourselves from patiently listening to a person we believe to be delusional? If we find the belief to be frightening, or offensive, or incomprehensible, actually listening to and reflecting upon our own reactions may help us learn about ourselves. Such self-reflection may be especially important for those of us who feel exhausted at dealing with others who are delusional. Psychiatrists may ask themselves, for example, "Am I so overwhelmed with work or so tired of my patients that I can no longer empathize?" Or a friend may find that they cannot listen to their delusional friend anymore without rolling their eyes or failing to pay attention. To be clear, the point here is not to make moral judgments about the listener. Instead, the point is to learn something about oneself as a listener. Without taking the time to listen and pay attention to one's responses, one may never learn that one is too exhausted to patiently listen or care for delusional others. This is an epistemic benefit of radical listening without which it is difficult to make well-considered decisions about how to act.

A second benefit of radical listening is the ability to humanize and build trust with our interlocutor and, in turn, create the conditions for ongoing conversation. Spiro Wagner writes about years of seeing psychiatrists who held her responsible for "isolating" herself, misdiagnosed her, and then finally diagnosed her with schizophrenia only to tell her: "Schizophrenia is a serious condition. Incurable, deteriorating, and hard to treat.

While you may not be institutionalized, you will never fully recover" (Spiro Wagner and Spiro 2005, 192). None of these psychiatrists encouraged her to be open and honest with them, and when she was honest about her experiences, it was often because she felt threatened. Dr. Ginzer was the first psychiatrist to tell her that she was not hopeless and to recognize the difficulties she faced. Ginzer recognized, for example, that her auditory hallucinations, "must be pretty scary" (201). After her initial interaction with Ginzer, she reports feeling that "for the first time someone actually wants me to talk about things and doesn't seem prepared to discount or dismiss me as crazy" (201). Indeed, after flushing her medications in an attempt to be more "independent" and having a paranoid episode, she trusted Ginzer enough to call her for help even while believing that everyone else around her was involved in a conspiracy against her (217–223). Because of this trust, she was able to reach out for help when needed and, perhaps more importantly, truly felt comfortable sharing her experiences, thus releasing her, if only intermittently, from her epistemic isolation.

In some cases, building trust may have more profound and lasting impacts. Johnny Holmes was the head of security at a high school in Chicago and remembers a then-student, Christian Picciolini, saying "I live to see the day when a n***** will be hanging from every light pole in Blue Island" (T. B. Brown 2017). Remarkably, Holmes, who is a black man, reports thinking, "You were a 16-year-old kid. . . . I knew you had been brainwashed. . . . And so I wanted the opportunity to get through to you" (T. B. Brown 2017). Looking back on this and similar incidents, Picciolini says, "It was that compassion when I didn't deserve it that eventually stuck" leading him to leave his neo-Nazi organization and eventually help other members of far-right extremist groups to exit (T. B. Brown 2017). Being called a racist, irrational, or delusional is unlikely to have created the change in Picciolini's thinking that the compassion from Holmes and others did. Rather than confronting his beliefs aggressively or head-on (i.e., rather than being epistemically arrogant), Holmes sought to understand how Picciolini could feel such extreme hatred. This is a powerful instance of radical listening, and it speaks to the epistemic benefits of humility.

A third benefit of radical listening is gaining a more nuanced understanding of a person's beliefs, emotional investments, or experiences. One thing a listener may learn is that the experiences of those with delusions are not always completely negative. This is what McLean writes of his life before and after using anti-psychotic medications:

> Instead of feeling that I was always at the centre of something, albeit unpleasant, I found reality enveloped me in greyness and boredom. . . . Some of my "messages" . . . provided me with endless stimuli to ponder. In a way I missed it. All the same, I was much happier than I had been for a number of years.   (2003, 160–161)

The belief that messages were everywhere to be decoded gave McLean a sense of meaning and wonder. As he says explicitly, it is not that this would be choiceworthy for him over his current grey and boring life. But we can see an aspect of his experience that we might easily miss. In this way, radical listening shares the virtues of empathy as described by Jackson (2017) and the phenomenological toolkit suggested by Carel and

Kidd (2014) in that their aim is to understand the experiences of the other from the other's perspective, rather than from an objective perspective or through our own points of view.

The last benefit of radical listening I will discuss is learning about alternative points of view where we assumed a broad consensus. For an example of this benefit, consider Spiro Wagner's account of her experience in one hospital: "Doctors think agitated patients are so overstimulated they need solitude. Accordingly, patients... are routinely allowed no clothes except pajamas, no phone calls, visitors, or mail.... I find these restrictions useless and cruel since in the absence of distractions, the voices go haywire" (2005, 214). Listening to patients like Spiro Wagner could help doctors understand and reflect on their own epistemic limitations. Perhaps the received wisdom in the profession or in that hospital was that seclusion was the best treatment for overstimulated patients, but listening to Spiro Wagner would have revealed that there are patients who experience seclusion as cruel rather than comforting. To be clear, the danger here is not in forming theories or standards of practice, but in letting them ossify until it becomes too difficult to question them.

Before concluding, let me offer a few cautions. First, radical listening is only a partial solution. It offers some epistemic benefits, which I have sketched, but it does not remove one's responsibility to seek truth or to attempt to correct delusional beliefs. I have suggested radical listening as a provisional strategy, one that must be moved past in order to help people change their delusional beliefs, but also one that can be returned to for further reflection. Indeed, one lesson that one may learn from listening in this radical way is that, at least for now, it may be best to temporarily leave the conversation altogether or side-step the topic. For example, if, in the course of listening radically, one feels endangered physically or mentally, one experiences an urge to harm or ignore the other, or one feels compelled to listen to a person owing only to the relative power of the other, the conversation is clearly not productive and may be harmful. In cases like this, it is likely best to exit the conversation. On the other hand, radical listening may offer insights into the other's beliefs that are helpful in discussing, challenging, and hopefully revising them. I take this to be one of the lessons of the testimonies of McLean, Picciolini, and Spiro Wagner.

Second, seeking to understand the sources of another's beliefs does not justify explaining away their beliefs. Radical listening does not recommend saying to McLean, "You believe this because you like feeling important," but instead "I understand what it's like to have a change in your beliefs affect your sense of self." Nonepistemic cognitive forces influence all of our beliefs, and we must try to be aware of these influences in assessing others, even when their beliefs appear obviously delusional. Humility is not only a moral but an epistemic virtue.

Notes

1. To be clear, *any* person who is subject to epistemic injustices may also commit epistemic injustices in interactions with others. But here I aim to focus on the way in which delusional beliefs themselves may be maintained through epistemic injustices. In the case of those

with other mental disabilities who commit epistemic injustices, those injustices would be incidental to the disabilities.

2. For a powerful argument that disabled lives are valuable and do provide important insights, see Rosemarie Garland-Thomson (Garland-Thomson 2012).

3. For an extended discussion of Barnes's argument, see the chapter by Jason Marsh (2020) in this volume.

4. The authors discuss, for example, how many women with intellectual disabilities are sheltered for fear of assault or manipulation (Kalman, Lövgren, and Sauer 2016, 73–75).

5. The authors also gesture toward some interesting conclusions beyond the immediate consequences for patients. For example, they note that the entire field of psychiatry is itself made to feel inadequate relative to the other medical professions because of the reliance on "soft" evidence. Their analysis in this article is especially relevant to my claim later in the chapter that assessments of responsibility for delusional beliefs must take into account nonepistemic factors since they identify ways in which nonepistemic factors contribute to the epistemic injustices faced by psychiatric patients.

6. The Diagnostic and Statistical Manual of Mental Disorders (DSM-5) also notes, however, that "The distinction between a delusion and a strongly held idea is sometimes difficult to make and depends in part on the degree of conviction with which the belief is held despite clear or reasonable contradictory evidence regarding its veracity" (American Psychiatric Association 2013, 87).

7. Coming to distrust and limit interactions with medical professionals as a result of such disregard is a common concern among those who discuss the epistemic authority of medical professionals. Compare, for example, Blease et al. (2017), Buchman et al. (2017), Ho (2011), and Navin (2013).

8. Importantly, it was belief that they would suffer consequences of Y2K, and not a belief that Y2K was a conspiracy, that correlated with belief in other conspiracy theories (van Prooijen and Acker 2015, 756).

9. There is a worry, here, that the methods of Life After Hate actually constitute a testimonial injustice by attributing the individual's beliefs to her circumstances rather than her expressed justifications. After all, as the editors of this volume point out, we would find it disrespectful to attribute a woman's beliefs to her emotions. But there are two critical differences. First, Life After Hate does not aim to discredit racist beliefs, but to address the circumstances that motivate individuals to adopt and espouse them. Second, in addressing those circumstances, it seeks to enhance the agency, including the epistemic agency, of right-wing extremists rather than undermine it. In contrast, someone who attributes a woman's beliefs to her emotions is clearly seeking to undermine her epistemic agency.

10. Metzl, in turn, cites Linda M. Hunt (2001) and Sayantani DasGupta (2008) as influences.

11. Among these conditions are situations in which we feel endangered by the other, we risk being revictimized, we experience real urges to harm the other, we feel that such listening is being enforced or demanded by those in positions of relatively greater power, or we feel that there is no possibility of reciprocity or genuine conversation.

References

American Psychiatric Association. 2013. *Diagnostic and Statistical Manual of Mental Disorders, Fifth Edition*. Arlington, VA: American Psychiatric Association.

Baker, F. M., and Carl C. Bell. 1999. "Issues in the Psychiatric Treatment of African Americans." *Psychiatric Services* 50(3): 362–368.

Barnes, Elizabeth. 2016. *The Minority Body: A Theory of Disability*. New York: Oxford University Press.

Blease, Charlotte, Havi Carel, and Keith Geraghty. 2017. "Epistemic Injustice in Healthcare Encounters: Evidence from Chronic Fatigue Syndrome." *Journal of Medical Ethics* 43: 549–557.

Bortolotti, Lisa. 2016a. "Delusion." *The Stanford Encyclopedia of Philosophy*. Available at: https://plato.stanford.edu/entries/delusion/.

Bortolotti, Lisa. 2016b. "Epistemic Benefits of Elaborated and Systematized Delusions in Schizophrenia." *British Society for the Philosophy of Science* 67: 879–900.

Brown, Stephen Rex. 2015. "NYC Says Woman Suing for Being Put in Psych Ward after Saying Obama Follows Her on Twitter Tried To Run into Traffic." *New York Daily News*, July 9. Available at: http://www.nydailynews.com/new-york/city-woman-suing-psych-ward-stint-acting-crazy-article-1.2286229.

Brown, Tanya Ballard. 2017. *The Man Who Helped Change a Neo-Nazi's Mind*. October 6. Available at: http://wbgo.org/post/man-who-helped-change-neo-nazis-mind#stream/0.

Buchman, Daniel Z., Anita Ho, and Daniel S. Goldberg. 2017. "Investigating Trust, Expertise, and Epistemic Injustice in Chronic Pain." *Bioethical Inquiry* 14: 31–42.

Carel, Havi, and Ian James Kidd. 2014. "Epistemic Injustice in Healthcare: A Philosophical Analysis." *Medical Health Care and Philosophy* 17: 529–540.

Carlson, Licia. 2010. *The Faces of Intellectual Disability: Philosophical Reflections*. Bloomington: Indiana University Press.

Charlton, James I. 1998. *Nothing About Us Without Us: Disability Oppression and Empowerment*. Berkeley: University of California Press.

Crichton, Paul, Havi Carel, and Ian James Kidd. 2017. "Epistemic Injustice in Psychiatry." *BJPsych Bulletin* 41: 65–70.

DasGupta, Sayantani. 2008. "The Art of Medicine: Narrative Humility." *The Lancet* 371: 980–981.

Dohmen, Josh. 2016. "'A Little of Her Language': Epistemic Injustice and Mental Disability." *Res Philosophica* 93(4): 669–691.

Freeman, Lauren. 2015. "Confronting Diminished Epistemic Privilege and Epistemic Injustice in Pregnancy by Challenging a 'Panoptics of the Womb.'" *Journal of Medicine and Philosophy* 40: 44–68.

Fricker, Miranda. 2007. *Epistemic Injustice: Power and the Ethics of Knowing*. New York: Oxford University Press.

Garland-Thomson, Rosemarie. 2012. "The Case for Conserving Disability." *Journal of Bioethical Inquiry* 9(3): 339–355.

Heldke, Lisa. 2007. "The Radical Potential of Listening: A Preliminary Exploration." *Radical Philosophy Today* 5: 25–46.

Ho, Anita. 2011. "Trusting Experts and Epistemic Humility in Disability." *International Journal of Feminist Approaches to Bioethics* 4(2): 102–123.

Hunt, Linda M. 2001. "Beyond Cultural Competence: Applying Humility to Clinical Settings." *The Park Ridge Center Bulletin* 24: 3–4.

Jackson, Jake. 2017. "Patronizing Depression: Epistemic Injustice, Stigmatizing Attitudes, and the Need for Empathy." *Journal of Social Philosophy* 48(3): 359–376.

Kalman, Hildur, Veronica Lövgren, and Lennart Sauer. 2016. "Epistemic Injustice and Conditioned Experience: The Case of Intellectual Disability." *Wagadu* 15: 63–81.

Kidd, Ian James, and Havi Carel. 2017. "Epistemic Injustice and Illness." *Journal of Applied Philosophy* 34(2): 172–190.

The Law Offices of Michael S. Lamonsoff, PLLC. 2015. "Law Offices of Michael S. Lamonsoff Reports Woman Forcibly Committed to Mental Facility by the NYPD for Stating True Facts about Her Life." *Eworldwire*. March 24. Available at: http://www.eworldwire.com/pressreleases/213031.

Marsh, Jason. 2020. "What's Wrong With 'You Say You're Happy, But…' Reasoning?" In *Oxford Handbook of Philosophy and Disability*, edited by Adam Cureton and David Wasserman, 310–325. New York: Oxford University Press.

Mathias, Christopher. 2016. "Woman Says She Endured 8 Days in Psych Ward Because Cops Didn't Believe BMW Was Hers." *Huffington Post*, October 25. Available at: https://www.huffingtonpost.com/entry/kamilah-brock-nypd-bmw_us_55f2c9aae4b063ecbfa3e60d.

McLean, Richard. 2003. *Recovered, Not Cured: A Journey Through Schizophrenia*. Crows Nest: Allen and Unwin.

Medina, José. 2013. *The Epistemology of Resistance: Gender and Racial Oppression, Epistemic Injustice, and Resistant Imaginations*. New York: Oxford University Press.

Merrick, Teri. 2017. "From 'Intersex' to 'DSD': A Case of Epistemic Injustice." *Synthese* In press: 1–19. https://link.springer.com/article/10.1007/s11229-017-1327-x.

Metzl, Jonathan M. 2009. *The Protest Psychosis: How Schizophrenia Became a Black Disease*. Boston: Beacon Press.

Mullen, Richard, and Grant Gillett. 2014. "Delusions: A Different Kind of Belief?" *Philosophy, Psychiatry, and Psychology* 21(1): 27–37.

Navin, Mark. 2013. "Competing Epistemic Spaces: How Social Epistemology Helps Explain and Evaluate Vaccine Denialism." *Social Theory and Practice* 39(2): 241–264.

Nyhan, Brendan, and Jason Reifler. 2015. "Does Correcting Myths about the Flu Vaccine Work? An Experimental Evaluation of the Effects of Corrective Information." *Vaccine* 33: 459–464.

Nyhan, Brendan, Jason Reifler, Sean Richey, and Gary L. Freed. 2014. "Effective Messages in Vaccine Promotion: A Randomized Trial." *Pediatrics* 133(4): 1–8.

Picciolini, Christian, interview by Amy Goodman. 2017a. *Life After Hate: Full Interview with Nephew of Fascist Who Marched in Charlottesville and Former Neo-Nazi* (August 18). Available at: https://www.democracynow.org/2017/8/18/life_after_hate_full_intv_with.

Radden, Jennifer. 2011. *On Delusions*. New York: Routledge.

Schwartz, Robert C., and David M. Blankenship. 2014. "Racial Disparities in Psychotic Disorder Diagnosis: A Review of Empirical Literature." *World Journal of Psychiatry* 4(4): 133–140.

Scully, Jackie Leach. 2018. "From 'She Would Say That, Wouldn't She?' to 'Does She Take Sugar?' Epistemic Injustice and Disability." *International Journal of Feminist Approaches to Bioethics* 11(1): 106–124.

Spiro Wagner, Pamela, and Carolyn S. Spiro. 2005. *Divided Minds: Twin Sisters and Their Journey through Schizophrenia*. New York: St. Martin's.

van Prooijen, Jan-Willem, and Michele Acker. 2015. "The Influence of Control on Belief in Conspiracy Theories: Conceptual and Applied Extensions." *Applied Cognitive Psychology* 29: 753–761.

Wardrope, Alistair. 2015. "Medicalization and Epistemic Injustice." *Medicine, Health Care and Philosophy* 18: 341–352.

Wendell, Susan. 1996. *The Rejected Body: Feminist Philosophical Reflections on Disability*. New York: Routledge.

CHAPTER 20

DISABILITY, RATIONALITY, AND JUSTICE

Disambiguating Adaptive Preferences

JESSICA BEGON

A growing body of evidence suggests that the self-reported welfare levels of disabled individuals are no worse, and sometimes better, than those of nondisabled people.[1] This is so surprising to individuals without disabilities, many of whom consider the prospect of becoming disabled as one of the greatest possible misfortunes, that it has been called the 'disability paradox' (Albrecht and Devlieger 1999). Yet not only do disabled individuals rate their subjective quality of life highly, many also resist the suggestion that their conditions should be cured, and refuse cures when offered; many argue for the right to have disabled children, and against policies of prenatal screening for various disabilities; they march in Disability Pride parades, and insist that disabled lives are not inherently worse than nondisabled lives. Nonetheless, the idea of disability as tragic remains the common-sense view among most able-bodied (and, indeed, some disabled) people.

Faced with such a divergence of views, whom should we trust? On the one hand, it may seem that disabled people are best placed to understand the realities of living with their conditions and that, as such, their testimony should simply be relied upon. Yet, on the other, we may think that disabled individuals' experiences are exactly what give us reason to doubt their testimony. It is widely acknowledged that in conditions of great hardship or deprivation individuals may cope with their circumstances by claiming to prefer and, indeed, coming to prefer, their situation to any alternative. However, such 'adaptive preferences' (APs) need not constitute decisive evidence that these conditions are not, in fact, deplorable. We do not, then, consider women's support of patriarchal norms to justify them, or an abused partner's preference to remain in the relationship to mitigate this abuse. Along similar lines, it may be suggested that disabled individuals' apparent satisfaction with their lives is not reliable evidence against the claim that disability must be disadvantageous.

This might seem like a neat solution: if disabled individuals' preferences are simply hopelessly deformed by the terrible circumstances in which they were formed, then we can treat their positive claims about disability as suspect, and maintain our intuition that it is a tragedy after all.[2] However, we should be cautious. The unjustified silencing or mistrust of already underrepresented groups may constitute a serious epistemic injustice, quite apart from the possibility of being used to justify interference in their lives and choices. There has, on this basis, been considerable backlash against Western feminists' tendency to see women in the underdeveloped world as the "dupes of patri-archy", whose preferences can be ignored (Narayan 2002, 418).[3] Elizabeth Barnes, too, has argued against AP models of disabled individuals' preferences on the basis that when "misapplied... [they] can simply entrench pre-existing biases" (2009, 137).

However, worries about misapplication should not lead us to abandon the concept of APs. If we were to take individuals' claims to be satisfied with their lot at face value, this may mean that injustice and oppression would not be recognized or rectified. If those subject to oppression do not identify their own mistreatment, they may not be entitled to redress. Indeed, it may not be considered mistreatment at all since 'no one complains.' Thus, a balance must be struck between taking individuals' preferences and self-assessments as definitive, and ignoring them entirely.

A further problem with diagnosing APs, less frequently acknowledged, is the vagueness of the term and the breadth of phenomena it may cover. From the opening paragraph, we can see the various experiences that can be roughly grouped—and rejected—as APs despite not all being plausibly interpreted as preferences. Furthermore, we might reasonably think that if our concern is *adaptation*, then all preferences formed in response to our circumstances should also be included. It should be clarified from the outset, then, that 'adaptive preferences' as the term is used in the literature is both broader and narrower than an intuitive understanding of the concept. Broader because it includes not just preferences, but also something like 'evaluative states';[4] and narrower because it only includes adaptations that are, in some sense, unreliable. However, even accepting these restrictions, ambiguity remains, particularly concerning what constitutes *relevant* unreliability.

My goal is to respond to the problems of both misapplication and vagueness. By clari-fying the various phenomena loosely categorized as APs, I show that correctly diagnosing preferences as adaptive need not constitute epistemic injustice nor insultingly malign individuals' rational capacities. Further, an account of APs should be sensitive to our particular goals and context: no single account will be satisfactory for all the roles APs are expected to play. Our diagnosis of APs will depend both on the role these prefer-ences play (for example, being used to generate the contents of a theory of justice or an account of well-being) and on how information about preferences is extracted (from individuals' choices, expressed satisfaction, or expressed counterfactual preferences). Thus, individuals may, for example, be reliable guides to their well-being, but not to what they are owed as a matter of justice (and vice versa); they may be a reliable guide to the content of their distributive entitlements, but not to whether they possess them; and their choices and apparent satisfaction may be unreliable in all these regards, whilst their expressed counterfactual preferences are not. It would be a mistake, then, to distinguish individuals with APs from those without, and a mistake, too, to distinguish preferences that are adaptive (for all purposes, in all contexts) from those that are not.

In particular, I defend a distinction between 'well-being APs' (WBAPs), and 'justice APs' (JAPs). WBAPs are APs as classically understood: individuals adapt to constrained options in ways that render their resulting preferences procedurally irrational and non-autonomous, and so undermine their possessor's authority about their own well-being. In the context of social justice, however, this account is both over- and underinclusive: it includes preferences that do not warrant state interference, and excludes preferences that are a rational response to circumstances yet should not inform a theory of justice. Thus, I contend that we also need to identify JAPs: preferences that are a poor guide to individuals' entitlements. Some of these are rational (and so not also WBAPs), whereas others are both justice and well-being adaptive. JAPs and WBAPs, then, are overlapping but distinct categories. I elaborate my understanding of WBAPs (in the next section) and JAPs (in the subsequent section) and argue that both concepts are needed to understand the different ways in which preferences may be unreliably adaptive, and the different responses that may be appropriate.

Although I argue that not all APs are irrational, they *are* all nonautonomous. Thus, we may worry that the account remains vulnerable to the objection that diagnosing APs has the insulting implication that disabled individuals are defective agents or 'dupes.' However, this is not the case. First, APs may be a rational response to unjust circumstances. In these cases, autonomy is undermined by limitations of circumstance rather than defects in individuals' capacities. Second, all (or almost all) of us possess some WBAPs: preferences we hold for reasons that are necessarily opaque to us. That some of these are relevant to justice (JAPs)—and so justifiably ignored in formulating a theory of justice, and poten-tially legitimating state interference—is again, I argue, not the result of faulty individual capacities but of circumstances. Thus, in clarifying the concept of APs, I will also dem-onstrate that being diagnosed as having an AP need not have the insulting implications ordinarily supposed.

AUTONOMY, PROCEDURALISM, AND WELL-BEING ADAPTATION

Adaptation and the Political Project

Classic accounts of APs—developed by Jon Elster and his critics—are modeled on the "Fox and Grapes" parable (see Bovens 2002; Colburn 2011; Elster 1987). On realizing he cannot reach the grapes he desires, the fox insists "grapes are too sour for foxes" and he did not want them anyway. It is assumed that this response is irrational and not a reflection of his best interests. These accounts root this irrationality in *procedural* flaws in the process of preference formation. They focus on capturing the idea—central to our intuitions about the fable—that the fox's preference is unreliable because he is unconsciously 'fooling himself': he has failed to acknowledge his limitations or recognize that the *real* reason he no longer prefers grapes does not concern their sourness. If the fox, instead, responded to his desire being thwarted by consciously cultivating a preference for a sweeter, lower hanging fruit, this would not be an AP, but conscious, rational, and autonomous *character planning*.

When the problem of APs was raised in the context of social justice (notably development ethics) it might have been natural to assume that the APs referred to were of this procedurally flawed, 'sour grapes' form—especially given the lack of a clear alternative account. Yet examples used in the literature belie this: "the hopeless beggar...the dominated housewife, the hardened unemployed...[who] take pleasures in the small mercies and manage to suppress intense suffering for the necessity of continued survival" (Sen 1988, 45–46)[5] are not obviously 'fooling themselves.' Indeed, many seem well aware of their suffering, and make considerable conscious effort to suppress it. Moreover, there are cases where preferences *are* unconsidered yet do not seem to be a matter of injustice nor to warrant public mistrust or political interference. We may mistrust a woman's unconsidered preference to undergo female genital cutting (FGC) but not a similarly unconsidered preference *not* to undergo FGC. Indeed, we may mistrust a choice to undergo FGC that *is* procedurally autonomous and rational if it is made against unjust background conditions—for example, as a means to marriage, which in turn is necessary for economic security or social status.

We may, therefore, be tempted to conclude that, in the context of social justice, these procedural accounts of APs are useless. Indeed, this is the conclusion those writing in this context have come to. Serene Khader, for example, has argued against such accounts on the basis that they lead us to mistrust preferences that are not "worthy of public interrogation" (Khader 2011, 75), thus generating conclusions inconsistent with our intuitions (Khader 2009; Khader 2011, 74–106). Drawing on Khader's work, Rosa Terlazzo argues that an account of APs must meet a criterion of 'political efficacy,' "by explaining which preferences deserve social suspicion and why they do so. It must include paradigm cases of adaptive preference and exclude preferences that have nothing to do with the political project" (Terlazzo 2016, 210).[6]

It is true that traditional accounts will fail this test. This is unsurprising given that they were never designed to pass it, concerned as they are with procedural rationality rather than social justice. It is also true that we need an account of APs that is politically efficacious—for which reason I offer an account of JAPs. However, it does not follow that there is no value in maintaining an account of APs as procedurally nonautonomous and irrational, and so a poor guide to individuals' interests—that is, of WBAPs.

Well-Being Adaptive Preferences

How, then, might an account of procedurally nonautonomous preferences be cashed out? Elster saw the distinctiveness of APs in the fact that they are formed unconsciously, or 'behind our backs,' in light of diminished options (Elster 1987, 117–119). Nussbaum (among others) has argued convincingly that Elster's account is likely to be overinclusive, demanding conditions of procedural rationality few of our preferences meet. As she points out, we are not—and should not—be "suspicious of any desire that is formed through [unconscious] adjustment to reality" (Nussbaum 2001, 78). This is not simply the criticism that this account cannot pick out APs relevant to social justice, but the broader claim that it cannot distinguish unreliable preferences in any context because too many of our preferences are unconsciously formed. For example, abandoning our childhood career aspirations for reasons we are unconscious of is not usually thought to cast doubt on the rationality or reliability of our commitment to our adult occupation.

However, Elster's real concern with APs may not be that they are unconscious, but that they lack autonomy. If so, then the absence of a clear account of autonomy is a serious omission (and one that later authors have tried to fill; see Bovens 2002; Colburn 2011; 2010; Zimmerman 2003). I focus here on Ben Colburn's account, which seems to best capture the cases we have in mind. In brief, Colburn argues that APs are the result of 'covert influences': the reasons for our APs are necessarily hidden from us such that they could not explain our commitments if we were conscious of them—we would either adduce independent reasons for our preference or repudiate it. Thus, the fox's claim that grapes are sour could no longer explain his preference not to eat them if he were aware that the real (and covert) cause of this preference was their inaccessibility.

This does not imply that all unconsciously formed preferences are adaptive (as Elster's account seems to), nor that any influence on our preferences is suspect. Rather, we should be suspicious of APs because they result from influences their possessor would not reflectively endorse, given their current disposition and convictions. Insofar as they are acting for reasons they could not accept, someone who possesses an AP lacks procedural rationality. This also undermines an agent's independence, since someone cannot be "deciding *for herself*" when acting on reasons necessarily hidden from her (Colburn 2010, 26). If, for example, we discover that we revised our career aspirations because we lack the talent to pursue our original dream and possess the aptitude for our current path, this need not cause us to doubt our goals. Yet imagine if we realized we only abandoned our dream of being a scientist due to being subtly undermined by a sexist science teacher. We do not endorse his view (that "women are not cut out for science"), so this could not explain our preference. In this case, we may question the autonomy of our apparent preferences, and our well-being may improve if we revised them.[7]

We may worry that this account would be underinclusive when applied to the political task, since many paradigm APs seem to be consistent in this way. For example, a woman may internalize a complete set of sexist and patriarchal norms such that her acceptance of a lack of economic opportunities or rights to political participation is entirely consistent with her more general views about women's capacities and proper role within society. She would, then, endorse the reasons for her preferences: they could function as the explanation for her commitments even if no longer hidden from her. Disabled individuals' preferences, too, are often consistent in this way, so this approach cannot be used to discount them (Barnes 2016, 129) (though given that the reliability of disabled individuals' preferences is what is at issue, it is not clear whether this should count against an account of APs).

In response, we can point out, first, that our goal here is not political: we are attempting to identify procedurally nonautonomous and irrational preferences that are an unreliable guide to their possessor's interests. It is JAPs that warrant public suspicion, scrutiny, or even intervention. Thus, accepting that individuals who have internalized a complete set of oppressive norms may be rational and a reliable guide to their own interests does not imply that they are necessarily immune to scrutiny or intervention, as the next section will discuss.

In some cases, we can distinguish individuals' 'adaptive *choices*' from their counterfactual preferences. For example, a disabled individual may choose not to pursue higher education on the basis that the institutions in which it is offered are exclusive and unaccommodating. This may be consistent with their further preferences (not wishing to associate with those who exclude them), and being aware of their reasons need not lead them to change their mind. However, they may prefer a situation in which accessible higher education was available. In such a case, I contend, neither the choice nor the preference should be diagnosed as a WBAP (both are rational)—yet, as I will argue later, the choice (though not the preference) is *justice* adaptive.

In other cases, individuals' acquiescence in their mistreatment is more deep-rooted and not accompanied by counterfactual preferences for a more just alternative. For example, if the above individual internalized a conception of disabled people as 'not worthy' of higher education, they may not prefer it to be available in an accessible form since they simply think "it's not for people like me." Further, the internalization may be sufficiently complete that this view coheres with their other beliefs and preferences and would not change under conscious examination. It may be objected that this is psychologically implausible—experience of oneself and others as competent and intelligent will be incongruent with such a conception of disabled people. Nonetheless, it does seem possible that sustained oppression could lead to a consistent conception of oneself as worthless, at least with regards to certain opportunities (see Khader 2011, 13–17; 2012, 307).

This also should not be diagnosed as a WBAP. The individual is not necessarily unconscious of the reason for their commitment, and we have no reason to doubt their authority regarding their well-being *given their current preference set*.[8] However, as in the previous case, not being a WBAP need not mean this is not a JAP: though this preference may be *rational* and a good guide to their current interests, this does not mean it is fully *autonomous* or a reliable guide to their distributive entitlements. Thus, allowing that individuals may be rational even when their self-conception is seriously undermined does not mean that their acquiescence will be deemed autonomous, nor their underlying oppression legitimized.

Before finishing this section, it is worth considering how my account of WBAPs relates to Barnes's 'discordance view' since hers is one of the few accounts of APs developed directly in relation to disability. Barnes argues that preferences are unreliably adaptive if there is "a clear disconnect" with "the rest of the person's life," including "what produces things like anxiety, fear, and antipathy in their lives" (Barnes 2016, 140). Barnes does not flesh out this approach, so it is difficult to get a clear sense of how it would apply in practice, yet it seems unlikely to capture all the cases we would want. A battered woman might, as Barnes points out, experience anxiety, fear, and depression. However, women who have internalized more mundane forms of sexist oppression may not experience such cognitive dissonance, yet this surely would not give us reason to overlook it. Furthermore, situations and conditions we on the whole prefer can cause stress, anxiety, and fear, and such preferences are not obviously unreliable. Barnes's primary concern is the epistemic injustice entailed by unwarranted attributions of APs. Avoiding misdiagnosis is certainly important, but, as it stands, her positive proposal provides little guidance regarding when AP diagnoses *are* warranted.

Why Identify WBAPs?

To summarize, WBAPs lack procedural autonomy and rationality since they are the result of influences we are necessarily unconscious of.[9] Consequently, they are an unreliable guide to individuals' interests. In the context of social justice this concept is over- and underexclusive. First, it *excludes* preferences that are rational and so not WBAPs, but which are a poor guide to our distributive entitlements (see section entitled 'Justice Adaptive Preferences'). For example, the preferences of disabled individuals not to enter exclusionary educational institutions may be rational and a good guide to their interests in these unjust circumstances, but their satisfaction should not imply justice has been done.

Second, an account of WBAPs *includes* preferences that are irrelevant to justice. The fox, for example, has a WBAP, but this surely is not an injustice the state should rectify. As a more concrete case, consider preferences for particular aesthetic experiences. Deaf individuals, for example, may prefer a life without music as a result of influences they would not reflectively endorse.[10] I assume that whilst justice entitles individuals to certain opportunities—maybe even opportunities for aesthetic experiences—it does not entitle individuals to every possible opportunity in a domain, or even to the opportunities they would prefer (assuming scarcity of resources). Thus, if deaf individuals have access to other forms of aesthetic experience, their inability to hear music is not an injustice, so neither is it a concern of justice if their preference not to listen to music is a WBAP.

Given that an account of WBAPs fails to pick out cases of adaptation relevant to justice, it may seem that we should follow others working on APs in the context of social justice and abandon this account. I disagree. First, the arguments for doing so are often based on the assumption that diagnosing a WBAP will wrongly imply that its possessor is unusually irrational or unreflective or that their preferences warrant public concern or interference (see Khader 2011, 80). However, since WBAPs are not intended to meet the criteria of political efficacy, they need not capture only paradigm cases where interference seems justified. On the contrary, we can acknowledge that many people's preferences, much of the time, are WBAPs.[11] Adopting an account of WBAPs, then, does not require reaching the dubious conclusion that only oppressed and mistreated individuals have them, nor that they are less reflective or worse at reasoning, nor that possessing WBAPs justifies interference.

Furthermore, there are positive reasons to adopt such an account. Most obviously, to achieve conceptual clarity. If, as I contend, the term 'APs' is used to capture two distinct phenomena—wherein those discussing APs in the context of social justice have in mind something quite different from those discussing APs in the context of autonomy and rational choice—it is worth making this explicit. There are also more practical benefits to distinguishing WBAPs and JAPs. JAPs need not also be WBAPs, but the two categories do overlap and, as a later section considers, we should treat *rational* JAPs differently from JAPs that are also well-being adaptive.[12] Drawing this distinction also makes clear that having a JAP need not imply we are irrational, and that *not* having any JAPs does not necessarily mean we are fully rational and autonomous.

Furthermore, given that domains of justice might change, it is worth identifying WBAPs that are now irrelevant to justice since they may cease to be so. In the past, ensuring access to aesthetic experiences and leisure may have been considered to be beyond the scope of government activity—in future, other things might be included. Finally, whilst WBAPs may not warrant direct state action, acknowledging the irrationality of many of our preferences may guide individual behavior, encouraging us to critically reflect on our preferences, and, if we cannot find reasons for them that we would reflectively endorse, change them. Further, though state interference in individuals' WBAPs may be unjustifiably paternalist, if WBAPs are widely prevalent the state *may* legitimately attempt to reduce this prevalence—for example, with measures that promote individuals' capacity for reflection.[13]

PERFECTIONISM, SUBSTANTIVE ACCOUNTS, AND JUSTICE ADAPTATION

The Need for a Substantive Approach

If our goal is to combat injustice and ensure that preferences that endorse and perpetuate oppression are disregarded, then a more substantive account of APs is needed. At the far end of this spectrum is Nussbaum's account, according to which APs are simply those with the wrong content: preferences formed in light of diminished options for what we ought not to prefer (Nussbaum 2000, 122–142, 2001). Hence, for Nussbaum, identifying APs requires "a substantive theory of justice and central goods" (Nussbaum 2001, 79). Whether a preference is rational or 'considered' is not decisive in determining whether it is reliable. Thus, if an unconsidered preference is for a good way of life (say, economic empowerment) and a considered preference is not (physical abuse), it is the former that is reliable (for example, Nussbaum 2001, 84).[14]

Nussbaum's perfectionist approach will certainly allow us to identify paradigm cases and provide a tool for combatting oppression. However, we may worry that it is overly narrow, deeming reliable only preferences for what has been predetermined to be valuable. Thus, "persons whose conceptions of the good reject the items on the perfectionist list will not be shown the respect granted to those with 'proper' preferences" (Terlazzo 2014, 186). Particularly worrying in the current context, it may lead to the exclusion of disabled individuals' preferences if disability is taken to be suboptimal. Indeed, Barnes has argued that since "[p]hysical disability represents, according to the capabilities approach, an absence of one or more basic goods (bodily integrity, physical health etc.)," then it "*cannot* be as optimal as a relevantly similar non-disabled life" (Barnes 2009, 2, 6). Thus, disabled individuals' preferences for their life cannot be considered reliable. As I have argued elsewhere, the capability approach need not evaluate disability so negatively (Begon 2015).[15] Nonetheless, the general worry remains that Nussbaum's approach excludes those who dispute her conception of value and "counts a number of widely and sincerely-held conceptions of the good as necessarily non-autonomous" (Terlazzo 2016, 214).

In light of these problems, both Khader and Terlazzo offer substantive proceduralist accounts of APs: these set substantive conditions on preference formation but aim to avoid ruling out any preferences on the basis of their content alone. For Khader, "APs are preferences incompatible with an agent's basic wellbeing...formed under unjust conditions" (Khader 2012, 302). Khader, then, is more willing to focus on content, seeing APs as any "behavior or belief whereby an individual perpetuates her deprivation," though this must be "causally related to her deprivation" in the sense that it "would disappear upon exposure to superior conditions and/or information" (Khader 2013, 313). As such, we have special reason to worry about preferences with specific content—those that perpetuate deprivation, independently and substantively defined—but they are only APs if they arose in particular circumstances. Preferences formed in the same circumstances but with different content are not APs (an oppressed woman's preference for pineapple over mango), nor are preferences "nonconducive to basic flourishing" (Khader 2011, 17) formed in conditions conducive to flourishing (endangering one's life by engaging in extreme sports).

Terlazzo argues that individuals should engage in critical reflection on their preferences in the presence of valuable and 'live' alternatives: options that individuals can reasonably see themselves exercising, given their current values and ambitions (Terlazzo 2016, 215). The substantive conditions, then, concern the specification of these options. Furthermore, to meet the criteria of political efficacy, she restricts the category of APs to "*core* preferences...preferences that are centrally important to a person's broader plan of life or sense of self" (Terlazzo 2016, 216).

Both Khader and Terlazzo emphasize that having APs need not be irrational or imply that an agent lacks the capacity for autonomy. Khader allows for the existence of "paradigmatic APs" wherein someone "perpetuates injustice against herself because of a near-completely distorted worldview" (Khader 2013, 311). More often, though, individuals are mistaken in some domains but do not entirely lack the capacity for autonomous choice and critical reflection. For example: individuals may internalize some aspects of their oppression but question others; they may be mistaken about facts but not values; or they may engage in forced tradeoffs among well-being in different domains of their lives (Khader 2013, 317–320). Along similar lines, Terlazzo emphasizes the distinction between global and local autonomy: individuals can have the global capacity for autonomy despite occasional failures to exercise it locally (Terlazzo 2016, 217–220).

Yet though they delineate various ways preferences may be unreliable, these approaches still present a unified account, identifying a single central feature that typifies all APs.[16] They make a binary judgment between preferences that are adaptive and unreliable and those that are not, and this, I argue, obscures the different ways in which preferences may be adaptive.

Preferences in a Theory of Justice

On at least some welfarist accounts of distributive justice, no tenable distinction can be drawn between WBAPs and JAPs: if individuals' interests directly determine their entitlements, then if they are a reliable guide to their interests, they are also a reliable guide to their distributive entitlements (and vice versa). This distinction—and, indeed, any discussion of APs at all—will also have no relevance for objectivist theories that consider individuals' entitlements (and perhaps their well-being) to be entirely independent of their preferences. However, many theories of distributive justice do not fall into either of these camps: whereas individuals' entitlements are not reducible to what would make them happy or satisfied, entitlements are not determined wholly independently of the views and values of those they are provided to. In this group we might include Dworkin's equality of resources, Nussbaum's capability approach, Arneson's luck egalitarianism, Cohen's equal access to advantage, and Rawls's theory of justice (see Arneson 2000; Cohen 1989; Dworkin 2000; Nussbaum 2000; Rawls 1999). (This is not the place to defend a substantive theory of justice. For the sake of clarity I refer to Dworkin's approach, though the general claims apply to all.)

Preferences broadly play two roles in such theories of distributive justice. First, they play some role in determining the content of our distributive entitlements. For Dworkin, we are entitled to state assistance for those disadvantages we would consider significant enough to insure ourselves against. Thus, taxation rates are justified by reference to a hypothetical insurance market, the outcome of which depends on our particular tastes and ambitions (Dworkin 2000, 90–109). Further, state assistance should only be provided if individuals consider themselves to be disadvantaged: we should not compensate for circumstances individuals consider a matter of good fortune (Dworkin 2000, 294).[17] APs can limit the content of our entitlements and the realm of state assistance: if we no longer saw mental illness, for example, as something worth insuring against, we would not tax and redistribute to individuals who suffer from it. Furthermore, if an individual does not consider themselves disadvantaged by their condition, then they would not be entitled to payouts (though others with the same condition might be).[18]

Second, our preferences in a particular case determine whether we make use of opportunities or resources we are entitled to. Liberal approaches are unlikely to compel individuals to function, both because the intervention required would be illegitimately paternalist and because an individual's autonomous decision not to exercise an opportunity legitimates its absence. This is a central insight of the capability approach: that starving, but not fasting, individuals are the concern of justice. APs here may lead us to wrongly consider self-harm or self-sacrifice to be voluntary and hence not unjust. I will now consider the various ways preferences may be unreliable in either of these roles.

Justice Adaptive Preferences

WBAPs are procedurally nonautonomous and irrational since the causes of these preferences are necessarily opaque to their possessors. Some APs do not meet this criterion, yet, nonetheless, should not inform a theory of justice: they should neither determine our general entitlements nor justify self-sacrifice as voluntary. These are rational JAPs and can be divided into three further categories: nonautonomous character-planning (where individuals consciously downgrade opportunities they have been wrongly denied), justice-adaptive choices (where individuals' counterfactual preferences are autonomous and reliable, but their choices are rendered nonautonomous by the limitations of their circumstances), and the coherent internalization of oppressive norms (where individuals internalize a self-conception according to which they are not entitled to certain opportunities).

First, nonautonomous character-planning. When discussing traditional accounts of APs, I noted that they are usually defined in contrast to conscious, rational, and autonomous character-planning. Although the fox who could not accept that the reason he believes grapes are sour is their inaccessibility should not be trusted, this is not true of the fox who consciously cultivates a preference for sweeter, lower hanging fruit. However, this example is misleading. Consciously revising our preferences in light of diminished options *can* be autonomous, but it need not be, depending on the degree to which our options are constrained. For example, someone who has adapted to ableist biases in hiring practices and concluded that they do not really *need* opportunities for meaningful work may prioritize personal relationships and hobbies instead. Further, they may be aware of the reasons for this change of priorities, or would not repudiate them if they were. Such preferences are rational, and do not demonstrate a failure of their autonomous capacities. Indeed, these preferences may function as a reliable guide to their interests (in these unjust circumstances). Nonetheless, we surely should not use them to conclude *either* that the opportunity for meaningful employment is, in general, not a concern of justice *or* that this individual has voluntarily chosen to forgo this opportunity.

This preference is nonautonomous, then, not because the individual is a defective agent who lacks or has misused the capacity for autonomous choice. Rather, their circumstances prevent them from being autonomous: from deciding for themselves what is valuable, and being able to pursue it. Specifically, these circumstances undercut individuals' independence: they are subject to factors that undermine their ability to 'decide for themselves.'[19] Yet, in this case, their independence is not undermined by *covert* influences (as the discussion in 'Well-Being Adaptive Preferences' considered) but by a lack of acceptable alternatives that they may be well aware of.

The second set of rational JAPs can be called 'justice-adaptive choices.' When individuals engage in character-planning, their underlying preferences change. However, as discussed, there are also cases in which we can distinguish what people choose (given limited options) from what they counterfactually prefer. For example, in the earlier case, an individual chose not to partake in higher education while preferring that it were available in a more accessible form. Again, individuals' choices are rational and reflect a capacity for autonomous choice. Yet, again, their circumstances prevent them from being autonomous.

It may seem that, in these cases, individuals do not really have adaptive *preferences* at all since their counterfactual preferences are autonomous and reliable from the point of view of justice. This is true, and it is important to acknowledge that, when options are constrained, individuals' choices may only reflect their preferences in a very local sense. Furthermore, their counterfactual preferences *can* inform a theory of justice: we have no reason to doubt their testimony in determining an account of our general entitlements. Nonetheless, sometimes individuals' choices are the only guidance we have regarding their preferences, and when they are rendered nonautonomous in this way they should be deemed justice-adaptive: they should not be used to suggest that what individuals choose to forgo is generally unimportant or that they have voluntarily sacrificed it. For example, if someone with a mobility impairment is forced to choose between modifying their home so they can move around it more easily and pursuing leisure activities, the fact that they choose the former is not evidence that they dispute the value of leisure, nor that they have voluntarily chosen not to pursue it.

Third, and finally, are cases involving the coherent internalization of oppressive norms. These are preferences born out of mistreatment and manipulation so comprehensive that it does not conflict with individuals' other beliefs and preferences, and they would not repudiate the cause of their preference if they were aware of it. Consider, for example, if the sexist science teacher was sufficiently successful that, on being made aware of the reasons we gave up science, we say the teacher did the right thing since science, after all, is "not for women." As we considered earlier, these preferences might be a guide to our best interests given our wider preferences. Nonetheless, though this influence is not covert (we are not necessarily unconscious of it), it surely undermines the independence of our choice and so its autonomy. As such, these preferences should not determine individuals' distributive entitlements at either the general or individual level.

JAPs need not also be WBAPs, then, but of course they can be. The inaccessibility of grapes may not be a concern of justice, but many preferences that arise as the result of covert influences *are* relevant to justice. WBAPs are also JAPs when the diminished options to which individuals irrationally adapt occur in domains of their life over which they *ought*, as a matter of justice, to be able to exercise autonomy and pursue their own conception of the good. For example, a deaf individual's preferences not to listen to music and not to engage politically might both be WBAPs, but only the latter is also a JAP. Thus, it should be emphasized, that while we are all likely to have WBAPs, for those in unjust circumstances, these are more likely to be JAPs too.

Responding to JAPs

Different forms of intervention are called for depending on the sense in which individuals' preferences are adaptive. First, when only individuals' *choices* are adaptive (and their counterfactual preferences are reliable), our focus should be on providing the acceptable alternatives they lack. Moreover, we should engage in a process of deliberation with the affected individuals to determine what the content of these alternatives should be since we have no reason to discount their counterfactual preferences. Thus, the state should not intervene in individuals' adaptive choices (on the grounds that they are adaptive choices) but should provide the conditions so that they can choose in a way that reflects their underlying preferences.

However, in at least some cases of nonautonomous character-planning, the coherent internalization of oppressive norms, and irrational JAPs, the provision of further options will be insufficient. In these cases, individuals' adaptation to diminished options may have led to some degree of value distortion: those who have undergone nonautonomous character-planning have consciously devalued opportunities they have been deprived of; those who have undergone the coherent internalization of oppressive norms have internalized a conception of themselves as not entitled to various opportunities; and those who have irrational JAPs reject certain opportunities for reasons they could not, themselves, accept. I noted two roles that preferences might play in a theory of justice, and value distortions can occur that undermine both these roles: they may affect the content of our general entitlements, and they may cast doubt on whether an instance of self-deprivation is really voluntary.

First, then, an individual may repudiate the value of an opportunity or resource entirely. Such a preference would take the form: "I live well without *x*, so *x* cannot be essential to a decent life." For example, autistic individuals may question whether certain forms of social interaction are as essential as neurotypical individuals assume, deaf individuals may question whether hearing is essential, and paraplegic individuals may doubt the importance of being able to walk. In determining the content of our entitlements, we may not want to allow individuals who have not experienced some opportunity to veto its inclusion. For example, disabled individuals who reject the value of work, education, or relationships simply because they have been deprived of them as the result of ableist biases should not lead us to conclude that these opportunities are not a concern of justice. However, it is worth noting that if our entitlements are conceptualized at a relatively high level of abstraction (as I contend they should be [Begon 2017]), then individuals who repudiate, for example, the importance of being able to walk or hear do not threaten agreement on their content. The relevant opportunities here are for mobility and aesthetic experience, and these individuals have not been deprived of these capabilities, nor do they repudiate their value.

Moreover, individuals with APs do not tend to reject the importance of some opportunity in general; they merely repudiate its value in their life. Such preferences might take the form: "*x* might be good for others, but it's not for people like me—and I'm happy without it." For example, an individual with Down's syndrome might take the view that education is valuable but conclude that "it's not for them" if their educative environment is not inclusive. These individuals' preferences can be used to determine the opportunities that are relevant to justice but should not be used as evidence that an individual has what they are entitled to: the individual with Down's does not dispute the value of education, but their 'choice' not to engage in it should not lead us to conclude that justice has been done. A voluntary choice to reject an option requires not just that acceptable alternatives are available, but also that these choices are considered live options. Individuals need, in Nussbaum's terminology, the "internal capability," as well as the mere freedom, to exercise an opportunity (Nussbaum 2011, 20–23). Exactly how these meaningful opportunities can be provided is a complex question and will likely require deliberation with affected individuals, which involves consciousness-raising (such that they understand the significance and potential value of certain options) as well as the provision of opportunities.

Justice-adaptive choices, then, can be avoided by providing individuals with options that reflect their preferences, where they are entitled to these as a matter of justice. Other JAPs arise from value distortions, and avoiding these requires both that individuals have acceptable options open to them so their values are not distorted by a lack of exposure to reasonable alternatives *and* being taught to see why these options might be valuable and to see themselves as the kind of people who can exercise them.

Finally, it should be emphasized that, though APs are nonautonomous, diagnosing someone as having one need not be insulting.[20] First, having rational JAPs does not indicate any lack of the internal capacities for autonomy: the problem lies in circumstances. Second, having a value distortion on some particular issue does not imply an individual is wholly unreliable or lacks the capacity to make autonomous choices or form reliable preferences in any area of their life. Finally, though irrational JAPs do indicate flawed reasoning, it does not follow that their possessors are *unusually* irrational or incapable of formulating consistent preferences. We all adapt to restrictions in our options, and many of us do so in irrational ways (we have WBAPs). However, when these restrictions stem from oppression and mistreatment, the resulting adaptations are more likely to be a concern of justice (JAPs). The fault, though, lies in circumstances rather than individuals. The reason individuals in unjust circumstances are more prone to JAPs is not that they are more defective agents.

CONCLUSION

I began with a dilemma that discussions of APs raise: on the one hand, we do not want to disregard the preferences of oppressed groups and ignore their members as untrustworthy agents, yet, on the other, we do not want cases in which individuals have adapted to deprivation to no longer constitute injustices. I have argued that only JAPs should be considered unreliable in the context of social justice and that JAPs need not be irrational. When disabled individuals' preferences are JAPs, this is likely to be the result of their circumstances, which, as far as possible, should be changed. We have no reason to think that disabled individuals are unusually deficient in autonomy or more prone than others to adapting to their circumstances, and we should not dismiss the preferences of any individual or group out of hand. However, we are in danger of perpetuating injustice if we fail to acknowledge the ways in which restrictions of individuals' options can undermine their ability to form autonomous preferences in areas relevant to justice and prevent them from effectively pursuing those options they prefer and should be entitled to. Thus, when preferences are justice-adaptive, they should not determine the contents of our distributive entitlements nor determine whether a sacrifice is voluntary.

NOTES

1. For helpful comments and discussion on earlier drafts of this chapter, I would like to thank audiences at the CSSJ Seminar at the University of Oxford, the CELPA Seminar at the University of Warwick the Philosophy of Disability Conference at the University of Tennessee, and the Society of Applied Philosophy Conference at the University of Copenhagen, as well as Cécile Fabre, Carl Fox, Alex Geddes, and Katy Wells, and the editors of this volume, Adam Cureton and David Wasserman.
2. My focus is on cases where preferring life with an impairment is thought to undermine individuals' reliability and thus, with physical and cognitive impairments that do not, in themselves, undermine individuals' autonomous capacities. I do not consider severe cognitive impairment, nor take a view on which should be considered 'severe.'
3. Also, Khader 2011; 2012; 2013; Jaggar 2005.
4. As Terlazzo notes, the term incorporates both "comparative preferences proper" and "non-comparative states like desires, judgements of values, etc." (Terlazzo 2016, 206).
5. See Khader (2011, 8–10, 42–46) for discussion of the discrepancy between Sen's examples and Elster's account.
6. Also, Nussbaum 2000; 2001; Barnes 2009; 2016.
7. When we have pursued something for a sustained time, however, our well-being may not be improved by abandoning it, even if we originally engaged in it for reasons we do not endorse. If we can give independent reasons for our current preference, it ceases to be a WBAP (we now value philosophy more than science); if we cannot, it remains a WBAP that we would be better off for repudiating. I return to this case later.
8. For discussion of similar cases, see Baber (2007, 199–120).

9. What does it means to be unconscious of the reasons for our preferences? Imagine, for example, a disabled individual who learns, perhaps in therapy, that they have some preference due to being stigmatized. Yet, despite 'knowing' the primary cause of their preference they push it to the back of their mind and deceive themselves into thinking they have good reasons for it. There will always be borderline cases. However, insofar as someone deceives themselves about their reasons and fails to internalize the evidence they now have, they are not truly conscious of this influence. They are in some sense aware of the pernicious influence, yet continue to insist that the real reason for the preference is something else ("I didn't want to go to university anyway"). Thus, this remains a WBAP.

10. This is likely true of many individuals' tastes, and there is no reason to think individuals with impairments are particularly vulnerable to such covert influences.

11. However, while everyone has WBAPs, those subject to oppression are more likely to have JAPs *as well* (as discussed later).

12. Specifically, the former case may simply require the provision of additional options so individuals' choices can reflect their preferences, whereas the latter may also require deliberation, discussion, and consciousness-raising.

13. This seems to be required by Colburn's "autonomy-minded liberalism" (Colburn 2010, 94–98).

14. Given her appeal to a substantive account, it may seem that Nussbaum is not "relying" on preferences at all. Indeed, they primarily play a heuristic role in her account (Nussbaum 2004, 200; Begon 2015).

15. It is possible, though, that this is an implication of Nussbaum's account (Nussbaum 2006, 155–223).

16. This is also true of Barnes's account (see earlier discussion).

17. This is "the continuity test" (Williams 2002).

18. In practice, Dworkin may not endorse such an individuated approach, though he acknowledges it is theoretically justified (Dworkin 2002; Begon unpublished).

19. For a discussion of independence and its importance for autonomy, see Colburn (2011, 26–31).

20. I do not mean to downplay individuals' experiences or deny that (especially given currently unjust circumstances) this may be experienced as insulting.

References

Albrecht, Gary, and Patrick Devlieger. 1999. "The Disability Paradox: High Quality of Life Against All the Odds." *Social Science and Medicine* 48: 977–988.

Arneson, Richard. 2000. "Luck Egalitarianism and Prioritarianism." *Ethics* 110: 339–349.

Baber, H. E. 2007. "Adaptive Preferences." *Social Theory and Practice* 33: 105–126.

Barnes, Elizabeth. 2009. "Disability and Adaptive Preference." *Philosophical Perspectives* 23: 1–22.

Barnes, Elizabeth. 2016. *The Minority Body: A Theory of Disability*. Oxford: Oxford University Press.

Begon, Jessica. 2015. "What are Adaptive Preferences? Exclusion and Disability in the Capability Approach." *Journal of Applied Philosophy* 32: 241–257.

Begon, Jessica. 2017. "Capabilities for All? From Capabilities to Function, to Capabilities to Control." *Social Theory and Practice* 43: 154–179.

Begon, Jessica. Unpublished. "Disadvantage, Disagreement, and Disability: Re-evaluating the Continuity Test."

Bovens, Luc. 2002. "Sour Grapes and Character Planning." *The Journal of Philosophy* 86: 57–78.

Cohen, G. A. 1989. "On the Currency of Egalitarian Justice." *Ethics* 99: 906–944.

Colburn, Ben. 2010. *Autonomy and Liberalism*. New York: Routledge.

Colburn, Ben. 2011. "Autonomy and Adaptive Preferences." *Utilitas* 23: 52–71.

Dworkin, Ronald. 2000. *Sovereign Virtue*. Cambridge, MA: Harvard University Press.

Dworkin, Ronald. 2002. "*Sovereign Virtue* Revisited." *Ethics* 113: 106–143.

Elster, Jon. 1987. *Sour Grapes: Studies in the Subversion of Rationality*. Cambridge: Cambridge University Press.

Jaggar, Alison. 2005. "Saving Amina: Global Justice for Women and Intercultural Dialogue." *Ethics and International Affairs* 19: 55–75.

Khader, Serene. 2009. "Adaptive Preferences and Procedural Autonomy." *Journal of Human Development and Capabilities* 10: 169–187.

Khader, Serene. 2011. *Adaptive Preferences and Women's Empowerment*. Oxford: Oxford University Press.

Khader, Serene. 2012. "Must Theorising About Adaptive Preferences Deny Women's Agency?" *Journal of Applied Philosophy* 29: 302–317.

Khader, Serene. 2013. "Identifying Adaptive Preferences in Practice: Lessons from Postcolonial Feminisms." *Journal of Global Ethics* 9: 311–327.

Narayan, Uma. 2002. "Minds of Their Own: Choices, Autonomy, Cultural Practices, and Other Women." In *A Mind of One's Own*, edited by Louise Antony and Charlotte Witt, 418–433. Boulder, CO: Westview Press.

Nussbaum, Martha. 2000. *Women and Human Development: The Capabilities Approach*. Cambridge: Cambridge University Press.

Nussbaum, Martha. 2001. "Symposium on Amartya Sen's Philosophy: Adaptive Preferences and Women's Options." *Economics and Philosophy* 17: 67–88.

Nussbaum, Martha. 2004. "On Hearing Women's Voices: A Reply to Susan Okin." *Philosophy & Public Affairs* 32: 193–205.

Nussbaum, Martha. 2006. *Frontiers of Justice*. Cambridge, MA: Harvard University Press.

Nussbaum, Martha. 2011. *Creating Capabilities*. Cambridge, MA: Harvard University Press.

Rawls, John. 1999. *A Theory of Justice*. Cambridge, MA: Harvard University Press.

Sen, Amartya. 1988. *On Ethics and Economics*. Malden, MA: Blackwell.

Terlazzo, Rosa. 2014. "The Perfectionism of Nussbaum's Adaptive Preferences." *Journal of Global Ethics* 10: 183–198.

Terlazzo, Rosa. 2016. "Conceptualizing Adaptive Preferences Respectfully: An Indirectly Substantive Account." *Journal of Political Philosophy* 24: 206–226.

Williams, Andrew. 2002. "Dworkin on Capability." *Ethics* 113: 23–39.

Zimmerman, David. 2003. "Sour Grapes, Self-abnegation and Character Building." *The Monist* 86: 220–241.

PART FIVE

RESPECT, APPRECIATION, AND CARE

CHAPTER 21

IDEALS OF APPRECIATION AND EXPRESSIONS OF RESPECT

THOMAS E. HILL, JR.

OUR attitudes and not just our actions toward ourselves and other people, including those with disabilities, matter morally, but it is difficult to determine what the best attitudes are and why we should aspire to them.[1] Some philosophers tend to reduce them all to beneficence and negative respect. Adam Cureton, in his essay "The Limiting Role of Respect," highlights the negative side of respect and explains how it can come into conflict with beneficence.[2] I will focus attention, however, on two additional attitudes that are implicit in ordinary moral thought and practice, namely appreciation and positive respect. I will also consider how these attitudes can be justified from a broadly Kantian perspective as appropriate responses to human dignity in everyone, including ourselves. Finally, I will draw out some lessons about how we should aspire to regard, treat, and relate to disabled people in particular.

AIMS, METHOD, AND LARGER PROJECT

The primary aim here is to reach a clearer understanding of the shared ideals underlying the examples given and to draw out their implications for attitudes and relationships involving disabilities. The ideals of appreciation and positive expressions of respect considered here should be familiar from everyday experience, but they have been relatively neglected by contemporary moral philosophers. A secondary aim is to begin to show how these ideals have a natural home in conceptions of human dignity and, more specifically, in Kantian moral theory. The idea of human dignity has been increasingly recognized in law, theology, and philosophy, but its interpretation, implications, and value remain controversial.[3]

The way we can begin to pursue the primary aim here reflects a particular understanding of the methods, resources, and limits of moral theory. We face ethical questions in the first instance in real, particular cases. About these we have often conflicting gut-level "intuitions," many of which are notoriously rooted in ignorance, superstition, self-serving biases, and cultural norms uncritically inherited from earlier times. As conscientious responsible people, we have to try to filter and refine these initial reactions in critical reflection in order to form our considered judgments, and then in normative ethical theory we try to find or construct ways to unify them, squaring them with our more abstract and often vague values and working to eliminate inconsistences. We should always be ready to admit that the resulting theories remain revisable. These are lessons to take from the early work of John Rawls, who also reminded us of the need to be ready to learn from our predecessors in the history of moral thought.[4] The result, if we could achieve it, would be a more coherent critical understanding of the content and structure of our shared moral beliefs. In *metaethics* philosophers can raise further foundational questions, of course, and the more immediate task of *practical ethics* is to draw out the implications of our core values for the real problems in our daily lives. We begin with examples that are *not* concerned with disabilities because the same core values relevant to disabilities also underlie our considered judgments in cases having nothing in particular to do with disabilities. We return later to consider how these attitudes can be interpreted and applied for cases involving disabled people.

APPRECIATION

Consider the case of Distant Father, an old-school parent who has only recently learned that his son is gay and living with his partner in a loving relationship. The father is educated and liberal in his ideas but not yet in his sensibilities. He respects his son as a human being and sincerely believes that gay people should have equal rights under the law. A generally benevolent and generous man, he wants his son and partner to be happy. He does not hesitate to help them financially when they ask, and he is extraordinarily careful to respect their privacy and autonomy. The son acknowledges his father's respect for his privacy and is grateful for his father's generosity, but he feels sad that something is missing from their relationship. He is disappointed that his father shows little or no interest in the specifics of his life—his taste in music, his favorite TV shows, his friends, and the way he decorates his house. To be sure, the father hopes that his son will be happy in his own way, but he would rather not hear about many of the particular interests, attachments, feelings, and events in his son's life. The son feels that his father does not *appreciate* him or the things he cares about—and he is right.[5]

Contrast another family member. Let's name her Curious Sister. She, too, wants her brother to be happy and tries to respect his privacy, but she is interested to learn more about him and his life. She is busy with her own life, of course, and does not want to make him uncomfortable or to be a nosy sister always prying into her brother's personal affairs, but she listens to his stories, notices what he likes, and is eager to learn more about him. She has her own opinions about which things are especially interesting, pretty, and meaningful and which are boring, ugly, and trivial. She admires his persistence in exercising, for example, but not his utter contempt for couch potatoes. In short, unlike their father, she tries to *appreciate* the good things about him and his life, but without losing her sense of what is and is not good and worth attending to.

Now consider a third character—Grumpy Granddad—who is unwilling to see anything good about the grandson and his life. He sees his grandson's rock music as degenerate, his decorations effeminate, his hairstyle disgusting, and his politics beneath contempt. But Grumpy Granddad is equally dismissive about what may be good in other people and what they care about. In fact, he is even unwilling to see anything good about himself, and insists that his whole life is a waste, his interests trivial, and his offensive grumpiness unchangeable.

My examples are extreme, but I suspect that they are familiar types. They illustrate what could be called an *ideal* attitude of appreciation. An ideal attitude, as I understand it, is an attitude that it is good to aspire for, admirable to have, something we should try and cultivate but not necessarily a *duty* that makes one liable to punishment by others or by a stern conscience.[6] The ideal of appreciation is an openness to acknowledge, take in, and attend to the myriad good things about particular persons and the good things that they may experience in their lives. For practical reasons, this is an attitude applicable primarily to those individuals with whom we have personal relationships as family members, partners, friends, and caregivers. It is an attitude about good things that they can experience in the context of their lives, within their culture, and with the resources and opportunities that are available to them. The good things include not only their traits of character and personality but also the things that they can experience as valuable and worth attending to, whether this is deep or trivial, moving or funny, classy or just fun.[7] Obviously context matters: no one can be open to appreciate all that is good in any person or life, not even one's best friend or one's own life. But even without a precise definition of the ideal of appreciation (and its limits), we can hopefully see that the Grumpy Granddad in my story falls miserably short of the ideal, the Distant Father falls short with respect to his son and his new lifestyle, and the Curious Sister exemplifies the ideal at least in her relationship with her brother.

Appreciation, as I understand it, is not the same as *respect* or *beneficence*, or even *gratitude*. A *beneficent*, kind, or caring person is concerned with the happiness of others, their comforts, pleasures, and success in carrying out their projects. This is not the same as appreciating what is good about them and in their lives, though of course being appreciated by others tends to contribute to a person's happiness.[8] Distant Father, for example, sends his son money but does not try to appreciate him or his way of life.

A *respectful* person has due regard for the rights, autonomy, privacy, and status of a person, but respect is distinct from both appreciation and beneficence. One can *respect* someone *as a human being* with rights and an honorable status without particularly *caring* for the person's happiness or *aspiring to see the good* in their lives and the things they value. At least these things are conceptually distinct even if they are not entirely separable in actual cases. Also, one can have (what Darwall [1977] calls) *appraisal respect* for someone *as* a good doctor, tennis player, comedian, or whatever, but still without necessarily having a desire to make the person happy or attend to any other good things about the person or the person's life.

A *grateful* person has appreciation for the benefits that another person has voluntarily given him, but appreciation is a broader concept than gratitude. Genuine gratitude *presupposes* appreciation of the good that one has received and the good will that the benefactor has shown in giving it. Appreciation is also the broader concept because genuine gratitude usually implies a willingness to express thanks and reciprocate benefits to a benefactor in some way. Expressing thanks and bestowing reciprocal benefits, however, is not necessary or even relevant in most cases of appreciating the good in a person and the things that the person cares about.[9] Granted, people often say that they feel grateful to God, Nature, or their Lucky Stars for good things in their lives, but what they mean is rarely that they are disposed to return the favors by bestowing benefits on God, Nature, or their Lucky Stars. You do not have to be a theist, pantheist, or superstitious astrologer to appreciate the good things about other individuals and their lives, whether this is the person's character and distinctive personality, or the music, games, and stories that the person loves.

So, in short, my suggestion is that what is missing in Grumpy Granddad and Distant Father but is evident in Curious Sister is not just respect, concern for happiness, or gratitude but rather an openness to finding and paying attention to the good things in a person and in what the person values. The person with appreciation has the confident attitude, belief or faith, that there are really good things, actual and potential, in the people with whom they are closely connected and in their lives.[10] When the appreciative sister expresses this attitude, she is not just trying to make her brother happy; she is also demonstrating her recognition of the value in and of his life as an individual. She is not merely sharing or faking her personal *preferences*, saying "I happen to *like* that too!" The ideal of appreciation is to find genuine value in the particulars of a life and to able to express honest recognition of it as a shared value. What we want from others close to us is not just that they try to make us happy but that they recognize the good things in our lives and so recognize some of the reasons why we care about them. When others *seem* to recognize and share what we value, we are pleased because of this, but we hope that their appreciation is genuine and not merely a means to please us. We notice and dislike fake appreciation because, even if it is an attempt to make us happy, it is happiness of the wrong kind. When your mother says, "That was beautiful, dear" every time you play a piece of music, no matter how badly, you gradually realize that, though she is trying to please you, she does not (perhaps cannot) offer the appreciation that you really wanted and that, ideally, she should try to have.

Grumpy Granddad also illustrates an important point: that is, one can also succeed or fail to appreciate the good things, actual and potential, *in oneself and one's own life*. Genuine modesty and humility can be admirable, but refusal to see and value our own merits and potential, attending only to our failures and flaws, is itself a bad attitude. This unwillingness to find and value in oneself even limited talents, imperfect virtues, and latent capacities for improvement tends to be debilitating and depressing, an obstacle to both one's own happiness and the happiness of others. Beyond this predictable impact on happiness, the attitude exemplified by Grumpy Granddad is also an extreme and deplorable failure of *appreciation*, an implicit denial of all actual and potential good in a particular human being, who happens in this case to be the human being for and to whom he is most responsible. Intuitively and arguably, this is an attitude that we have reason to avoid and not just because it tends to diminish happiness.

Most human beings, unlike Grumpy Granddad, tend to be overly eager to promote their *own happiness*, even at the expense of others. Striving to make *themselves* happy is not usually thought to be a moral duty or even an ideal, unless, perhaps, a therapist prescribes it as a means to combat depression.[11] *Appreciation*, however, is an attitude that most of us, on reflection, will recognize as an ideal attitude regarding our own lives as well as those of others. What we admire and should aspire to in personal relationships is not just appreciation of a person's moral character and accomplishments but also openness to appreciate the myriad good things that a person may encounter in life. Disabilities can limit what is accessible to us but even those most severely restricted may find ways to realize in themselves the wonderful human capacity to find and attend to what is valuable and worthy in life. No one demonstrated an admirable attitude of appreciation better than Helen Keller. Here is her advice:

> Sometimes I have thought it would be an excellent rule to live each day as if we should die tomorrow. Such an attitude would emphasize sharply the values of life. We should live each day with a gentleness, a vigor, and a keenness of appreciation which are often lost when time stretches before us in the constant panorama of more days and months and years to come....
>
> Recently I was visited by a very good friend who had just returned from a long walk in the woods, and I asked her what she had observed. "Nothing in particular," she replied. I might have been incredulous had I not been accustomed to such responses, for long ago I became convinced that the seeing see little.... How was it possible, I asked myself, to walk for an hour through the woods and see nothing worthy of note? I who cannot see find hundreds of things to interest me through mere touch....
>
> I who am blind can give one hint to those who see—one admonition to those who would make full use of the gift of sight: Use your eyes as if tomorrow you would be stricken blind. And the same method can be applied to the other senses. Hear the music of voices, the song of a bird, the mighty strains of an orchestra, as if you would be stricken deaf tomorrow. Touch each object you want to touch as if tomorrow your tactile sense would fail. Smell the perfume of flowers, taste with relish each morsel, as if tomorrow you could never smell and taste again   (Keller 1933, 34–42).

Later we will consider how the ideal of *appreciation* coheres with a broadly Kantian idea of human dignity and what it means in relationships with those who have disabilities. But first we turn to another ideal attitude implicit in valuing human dignity, namely, a readiness to *express* respect for a person positively in ways appropriate to the context.[12]

POSITIVE EXPRESSIONS OF RESPECT

Some virtues become clearest in cases where they are conspicuously absent. Consider a case we might call the Unexpressive Uncle. He appears cold and distant because, although he appreciates and cares for his nephew and niece, he never expresses this in words or gestures. He would not think of mocking them, interfering with their privacy, or offending them by intrusively doing for them what they can and would rather do for themselves. He respects his nephew and niece as human beings, as individuals of admirable character, and as talented musicians, hard-working students, and committed volunteer workers. But the Unexpressive Uncle believes in keeping his feelings to himself. It is enough, he thinks, to *have* respect inwardly and to *behave* with respectful *restraint*. Words and gestures are unnecessary, he believes: to him, these are mere tokens that people use to fake their real attitudes. He hates the formalities of welcoming handshakes and hugs, having to say "please" and "thank you" and being expected to applaud at concerts and stand for the national anthem, no matter how he really feels. He conforms reluctantly to these conventions at times to avoid offending people and making them unhappy, but he thinks they should not need these external strokes to be happy and that they should not take offense because he chooses to keep his attitudes to himself.

The Unexpressive Uncle's attitude toward others, let us imagine, is an extension of how he treats himself. He tries not to care about whether others express respect for him in words or symbols, even when he thinks that he deserves their respect. He deflects all compliments and refuses to accept awards in his honor, though to avoid making others unhappy, he tries to avoid social occasions where his attitude would strike others as rude and offensive. He presents himself to others as slovenly, grumpy, and just as disdainful of symbolic gestures of respect for himself as he is for others. In fact, trying to follow the advice of the stoic philosopher Epictetus, when someone calls him stupid, he answers by saying (and showing), "I am more stupid than you think."

Contrast Unexpressive Uncle's more polite and expressive wife: I will call her Outgoing Auntie. Like Unexpressive Uncle, she inwardly appreciates the good things in family members' lives and outwardly restrains her impulses to interfere disrespectfully, but, unlike Uncle, she also expresses respect openly and readily in appropriate words, gestures, and body language. She also expresses respect formally, using the conventional tokens of politeness in her culture, except when these tokens reflect demeaning racial, class, or gender bias. She encourages others to speak and does not interrupt them, even though they often interrupt her. She politely expresses gratitude for gifts, even those she regards as ugly and useless. She asks others about their health and activities, and she listens, even when she is in pain herself and not really in the mood to admire them or share their pain or enthusiasm. She stands up and sits down appropriately at weddings and funerals, though she did refuse to shake the preacher's hand after an especially sexist sermon. Auntie expresses respect *for herself* as well, but not, of course, by addressing polite and self-congratulatory words to herself. Instead, her self-respect is expressed by maintaining her dignity in the midst of conflict, showing what she stands for, not allowing herself to be—or appear to be—less than she is, a *human being* with a fundamental standing equal to any and an *individual* with abilities and interests worthy of attention, especially by those with whom she has close relationships.[13]

Outgoing Auntie's positive expressions of respect to her niece and nephew are both direct and subtle ways of saying to them that *they matter*, not just as human beings but as the very individuals that they are. The ways in which respect is expressed are different in different cultures, of course. Sometimes respect is conveyed by silence and sometimes by loud cheers; in some places by wearing a covering on one's head; and in other places by taking it off. In some cultures one bows, and in others one offers a firm handshake. And *when* it is best to express respect is a matter of judgment. Obviously, context is important. There are times, for example, that it is better to withhold the tokens of respect in order to protest offenses and injustices—to refuse to laugh politely at racist jokes, for example, or to stand for a confederate flag ceremony at a white supremacist rally. There are also times when *fake* expressions of respect are called for. For example, victims in an utterly oppressive culture may need to pretend to be servile and obedient in order to survive.

The formalities of *good* manners are common ways of expressing respect, and they can send this important message of respect even when we do not feel particularly respectful. As Sarah Buss (1999) has argued, good systems of manners instruct us at least to *appear* respectful regardless of how we feel at the moment. Good manners call for a kind of conventional pretense in many cases, but this is generally understood and, as even Kant acknowledged, it does not always amount to lying, strictly speaking. Conventional expressions of respect through good manners serve an important purpose, Buss argues, by constantly reminding us that every human being has an intrinsic value, and we should add that tokens of respect are needed not only to remind us that each person has basic value and rights *as a human being*, but at least for those with whom we have close personal relations (for example, as family, friends, and caregivers), good manners provide ways to demonstrate respect for them as the distinctive individuals that they are.[14]

These ideals of appreciation and positive expression of respect are not unrelated: ideal *appreciation* calls for readiness to see the good things about our friends, family members, and those in our care, and the ideal of *positive expression of respect* calls for readiness to *show* respect for them as individuals in positive ways, among which is telling them what we appreciate and respect about them. Setting aside severe psychological disorders, the primary enemies of appreciation in close relationships are familiar weaknesses and vices—indifference and insensitivity, inattention and impatience, annoyance and anger, self-absorption and laziness. On reflection, we might notice too our tendencies to have *misplaced kindness* that is concerned only with others' pleasure and comfort and our *elitist conceit* that refuses to acknowledge the good in anything that we see as less than the best of its kind. The primary enemies of the ideal of positive expression of respect, I suspect, include also timidity, envy, and false pride. You know the problems: we respect someone but feel that it is not our place to say anything, or we worry enviously that other people are already getting too much respect, or we imagine that our superiority in social position, taste, and cognitive abilities mean that, although others should show respect for us, it is beneath our dignity to reciprocate with inferiors.

IDEALS INHERENT IN HUMAN DIGNITY

We turn now to consider how the ideals of appreciation and positive expression of respect can be grounded and unified in the idea of human dignity. Especially since World War II the idea of universal human dignity has gained recognition in many countries throughout the world. Though disparaged by some and disregarded by many, the idea has been given a central place in the UN Charter, in legal systems, and contemporary religious and philosophical discussions. As Rawls (1999b, 513) has suggested, *human dignity*, like other powerful ideas such as *freedom* and *equality*, are important but require interpretation within some theoretical framework. While interpretations vary and are yet to be fully developed, several general points seem to be widely agreed:

First, human dignity is a *universal* and *elevated* status or value. That is, *every* person has dignity and should *never be treated as anything less* than a human being. For example, people should not be treated as pieces of property, as mere commodities or expendable resources, as worthless trash, or as so-called "lower" animals. Accordingly, slavery is forbidden, husbands do not own their wives, workers must not be exploited, immigrants should not be rounded up and shipped off like cattle, and criminals should not be chained and caged like wild animals ("beasts").

Second, human dignity is commonly understood as an *equal* status or value that all persons have. So, for example, governments should not discriminate by race, religion, gender, or ethnicity, and corporations should not exploit impoverished people in third world countries.

Third, human dignity is supposed to *take precedence* over other concerns. For example, the UN charter implies that torture is "an offense to human dignity" that is never permissible even as a means to good ends. In this (and other) ways, respect for human dignity imposes a constraint on purely consequentialist policies that would sacrifice individuals for aggregate welfare. For example, even if it is, as some say, a by-product of economic efficiency, it is deplorable for people to have "to suffer the indignities" of gross poverty and homelessness, and security interests do not provide government agencies an unrestricted license to gather private information or give police unlimited authority to use violence.

Beyond these general points and their implications for law and justice, many of us believe that human dignity should be *honored* in the ways that we treat each other *on a personal level.* These include, first and most obviously, the several *negative* requirements mentioned earlier. For example, we regard it as an offense against human dignity *to mock* a person as utterly worthless, calling the person disgusting, a scumbag, a piece of excrement, and so on. We believe that a person fails to treat us with dignity if they do not respect our *autonomy*, our right to make our own choices so long as we are not harming or offending others. And, as Cureton (2016) has argued, dignity also *restricts beneficence*, placing limits even on our kind-hearted efforts to help other people. The flip side of our claim to respect from others is that to live with dignity, as a self-respecting person, we must *take responsibility* for our own affairs, insofar as we can. We should not, for example, make others take on the burdens of doing for us what we can easily do for ourselves because to do so is not only unkind to them but a failure of respect for ourselves. These are familiar points but, of course, they require further specification and wise judgment in applying them to particular cases.

An Analogy: Local and Global Dignity

The negative (limiting) aspects of human dignity seem to be increasingly recognized as a part of common morality, and our ideals of appreciation and expressing respect are at least a natural extension of our intuitive understanding of full respect for human dignity. This is suggested by *analogy* with the idea of dignity in the aristocratic, judicial, and church hierarchies from which the idea of human dignity evolved. Consider, for example, the dignity of judges. Their office or status is traditionally thought to come with special powers, rights, and prerogatives that others are supposed to respect. Judges, for example, can conduct criminal trials and pass sentence on those found guilty. Others must not violate their authoritative orders, and they often enjoy luxurious chambers and can access information that ordinary people cannot. Similarly, presidents, dukes, archbishops, generals, and samurai warriors have had special powers, rights, and prerogatives within their conventional structures. In each case the office or status carries conventionally defined duties and responsibilities to the office, to peers, and to those with higher and lower positions. What is important here is that to respect the dignity of their office or status, those in these elevated positions are also expected to meet standards regarding *how to present themselves* and to *demonstrate their respect for* others. Judges are supposed to wear their robes during a trial; even dukes must bow to the queen; American Presidents are expected to "act presidential;" and so on. Otherwise, they are considered less worthy, if not unfit, for their high positions. In short, those in elevated positions are expected to *express their respect* for others and for themselves *openly* and publicly, typically through conventional symbols as well as their demeanor.

Importantly, too, those in high positions are *ideally* supposed to *appreciate* at least the individuals who are their equals in the conventionally structured order. That is, especially when they have personal relationships with their peers, they are supposed to be *open to seeing the good* in them and in what they do. Judges, for example, may not *care for* each other or *think that overall their colleagues are very good* at their jobs, but we tend to admire them as judges for remaining open to finding (actual and potential) merits in their colleagues. The same probably holds for Presidents, dukes, archbishops, and samurai.

In modern times, with the help of philosophers such as Kant, we have come to see the dignity of officeholders and other conventional "dignitaries" as subordinate to human dignity, a fundamental, equal, and elevated position belonging to every human being. How is it an *elevated* position if everyone is equal? It is not just that human beings have awesome powers that "lower" animals lack or that we have traditionally chosen to accord rights only to human beings. Apart from this, everyone in a lower class or position (whether a serf, a servant, a clerk, commoner, or, in some cultures, a woman) is *elevated* from their previously low position by being counted as one among equals from a moral point of view. Even those privileged in local class structures are elevated from their dignity within their limited class to a dignity that should be respected globally, ideally in a moral community of all human beings. Here, by analogy, each person has rights, responsibilities, restrictions, and, I would add, an honorable status that calls for both positive expressions of respect and mutual appreciation in appropriate interpersonal contexts. Within particular cultures and jurisdictions, of course, some distinctions among positions of authority and honor remain justifiable, but human dignity takes precedence.

HUMAN DIGNITY FROM
A KANTIAN PERSPECTIVE

Now let consider the idea of human dignity and its role in a Kantian perspective. Our ideals of appreciation and positive expressions of respect are at least a natural extension of Kant's basic ideas.

From a Kantian perspective, dignity is a cluster concept that combines more specific norms and values concerning how we should regard and treat each other. These are *dimensions* or aspects of respecting human dignity—such as treating people justly and honestly, keeping our word, not interfering with their rights to autonomy and privacy, not mocking and demeaning them, and respectfully restraining our unwanted kindly (as well as cruel) impulses. Kantians rightly insist that the general requirement to respect human dignity is unconditional and without exception, but the more specific presumptions inherent in the idea of human dignity cannot all be fully satisfied in every particular case. They are presumptive claims, values, and ideals that say how we should treat every person *if we can*. They are, as Kant suggests, the *grounds* of particular judgments about what we should do, and the grounds can be in tension even though there can be no particular "conflicts of duty" in the strictest sense. That is, general principles may conflict but morality cannot rationally demand without qualification that on a particular occasion both "You *must* do this!" and "You *must* not do this!" In a perfect world, Kant suggests, human dignity can and would be universally recognized and fully respected. If, however, in our messy, imperfect world, we cannot find a way to *fully* satisfy the inherent standards in every case, they at least stand as strong *presumptions* about how we should treat each other. At times we must reluctantly and regretfully allow exceptions to some of these presumptions for the sake of what we reasonably judge is an aspect of dignity that has a higher priority in the circumstances. For example, the presumption that we should not kill fellow human beings may be over-ridden in cases of self-defense and a just war.

The inherent presumptions in the Kantian idea of human dignity include some version of the standards mentioned above, that is: (1) principles of justice concerning what ought to be established as human rights, (2) standards of honesty and integrity about being truthful and keeping one's word, (3) a principle of mutual aid concerning helping those in dire need, (4) a more general principle of beneficence that requires us to make it an end to promote the happiness of others, and (5) a negative principle of respect that requires us to respect autonomy and privacy. *In addition*, what we have suggested *here* is that human dignity also includes, at least for close relationships, (6) the ideal of *appreciating* the good in persons and their lives and (7) the ideal of *expressing* respect positively. Normative moral theory, in my view, should aim to refine and clarify these related standards, but, perhaps needless to say, we should not expect a precise codified set of rules that determine for each circumstance what is required or best to do.

The idea of human dignity does not refer to a mysterious metaphysical property but rather to a cluster or set of *related* norms that (arguably) express fundamental aspects of *what it means to take up a moral point of view*. In Kant's ethics, these are supposed to be articulated in three versions of the Categorical Imperative, which for Kant was the supreme principle of morality. All too briefly (and loosely), the *first* tells us to live only by principles (maxims) that we can, rationally, will for everyone; the *second* tells us to treat humanity, in any person, as an end in itself, never simply as a means, and the *third* puts the first two together to form an ideal of a more perfect moral world that we should *work toward, hope for, and live by* insofar as it is possible in our imperfect world. An aspiration of Kantian theory should be to clarify these ideas, to show how they are rooted in our moral thinking and practices, and to draw out their implications for real world problems.

The Kantian justification of our ideals, as well as our duties, starts from recognition of what it means to respect and properly value our own humanity. Arguably, even in Kant's texts, our humanity is not simply our freedom to fulfill our strict duties and set ourselves ends. Our humanity includes powers of mind and spirit that we employ in doing and appreciating science, nature, and art; constructing viable social orders; planning a good and moral life for ourselves; and even expressing our sense of belonging to an ideal community of human beings—that is, humanity across space and time. As reasonable and moral persons we cannot help but recognize our own humanity as worthy of protection, development, and expression in our own choices. Our choices, however, are constrained by the recognition that the principles that we use to shape our own lives (our fundamental *maxims*) must be suitable for any other reasonable and moral person to adopt in relevantly similar circumstances. And so, the argument goes, just as everyone must respect our humanity, so too we must respect theirs.

An alternative Kantian argument starts from the premise that our particular decisions should be guided and constrained by the mid-level principles that would be endorsed (or "legislated") by members of a possible "kingdom of ends." (This is a version of what earlier was described loosely as *working toward, hoping for, and living by* the ideal of a more perfect world *insofar as it is possible* in our imperfect world.) This premise, like the previous ones, is supposed to be implicit in a reasonable moral point of view. To flesh out this line of thought, we need, of course, to explain the ideal of legislating as members of a kingdom of ends that incorporates the decision-guiding values inherent in the ideal of human dignity.

This is not the time to try to develop and debate these arguments, so we will just leave them here as suggestions for how, from a broadly Kantian perspective, one might try to justify the several norms and values that we take to be dimensions of human dignity: that is, its inherent presumptions about how we should try to act and what we should aspire for. We will also leave for another time understandable objections, such as how Kantian theory can support *equal* respect for human beings with severe cognitive disabilities and decent treatment of "lower" animals.

APPLICATION TO DISABILITIES: APPRECIATION

How is the ideal of *appreciation* relevant when we are in relationships with a person who has disabilities? There is a general point and a special one. The first, more *general point* is obvious in theory though difficult in practice. That is, disabilities vary in kind and extent, but all of us with disabilities are human beings whose lives can and should be appreciated, especially by those closest to us. We all should be respected and valued as human beings who have rights and interests that matter and should be protected, by ourselves when we can and by representatives when we cannot. Although others have abilities that we lack, all of us have both common human capacities and individual personalities that can be appreciated. As friends, family, teachers, caregivers, and individuals with our own disabilities, we know not only that each life is to be valued but also that it is rich with actual and potential aspects that are good and worth appreciating—whether admirable, beautiful, enjoyable, or simply worth our attention apart from any further purpose.

So what follows? Most obviously we need to pay attention, to listen, to be open to observing good things in unexpected places and to acknowledge them. Less obviously, perhaps, we need to keep in mind that the person with disabilities has a life that can be enriched when they appreciate good things themselves, whether this is an Alzheimer's patient resonating with old familiar music, Stephen Hawking working out a new theory of black holes, or anyone's appreciation of a good joke. The point here is not necessarily that we are obliged to give them more (or "superior") pleasures or to demonstrate that we care for their happiness, but to give them what presumably they deserve and deeply want, especially from family, friends, and closest care-takers, namely recognition of the value in their lives. This is not just their existence as human beings, their welfare and comfort, but the good things, actual and potential, that they find worth attending to. Despite our efforts, *we* may not find value in the things that *they* appreciate, but even then we can, in a sense, "appreciate their appreciation." We may find too that, when we pay attention, we find more to appreciate than we imagined.

That was the general, more obvious application of the ideal of appreciation to disabilities, but the ideal also has a *special* relevance to disabilities. Context matters, and we have a long history of stereotyping, stigmatizing, and excluding people who appear different from what we are most accustomed to. Misunderstanding fuels dismissive thoughts, and unfamiliar looks and movements can prompt contemptuous attitudes and feelings of disgust. Even those of us who consider ourselves enlightened have been shown repeatedly to suffer from implicit bias. This is all familiar, but its *implications* regarding our ideals are worth highlighting. That is, in disability cases it is not enough to make the usual efforts to respect human rights and be appreciative, because history and society have poisoned attitudes and mined the road to proper treatment of people with severe disabilities. The analogy with race and gender relations should be clear. It is not enough just to try to straighten out one's own attitudes *by oneself* when laws, public policies, and social practices constantly reinforce biases. Politicians, as we know too well, both feed on and spread contemptuous attitudes regarding people with disabilities. Laws, policies, and social practices also protect and express these attitudes, but they can also be used to reform them. Ideal appreciation is a delicate flower that cannot flourish in a poisoned atmosphere. It cannot be mandated, but it can be nourished and its growth protected.

APPLICATION TO DISABILITIES: POSITIVE EXPRESSIONS OF RESPECT

We will turn, finally, to the ideal of *positive expressions of respect* in close friendships, families, and caregiving contexts when disabilities are involved. There is again a general point and a special point. The general point is a simply that each person with disabilities, like any person, is to be respected as a human being with fundamentally equal rights and as an individual with her or his own particular interests and abilities. Although respect for anyone is important, the positive *ways* in which we can express respect for people with disabilities are often special. For example, listening more carefully when we know that someone has a speech impediment, speaking more slowly and distinctly when we know that someone has limited hearing, removing slippery rugs and dangerous obstacles for those we know have difficulty walking, allowing extra exam time for those with learning disabilities, and asking rather than assuming to know when help is needed. This all is just common sense, of course, demonstrating the same respect that we would show others but in the special ways appropriate to the context. Similarly, we show respect to anyone within a close relationship by holding them responsible for fulfilling their obligations, which vary with their capacities. Respect calls for honest appraisals as well as acknowledgment of effort and success, but the appropriate tasks and what counts as admirable effort and success are different for someone, for example, with certain kinds of cognitive limitations than for a typical teenager or even an eight-year-old child. No one would pretend that the champions in a Special Olympics wheelchair basketball tournament could be successful in the NBA, but they can be just as honestly and respectfully encouraged, cheered, and congratulated.

All this should be obvious as simply an application of the ideal to relationships involving disabilities, but, again, there is a *special* point about positive expressions of respect in this context. The long history of failures to show respect for people with disabilities requires special attention and effort to counter the misunderstandings and biases that are still too much a part of our culture. There has been remarkable progress regarding some matters of justice and accessibility resources, and at least in classrooms and the mainstream media, the worst derogatory language is generally considered unacceptable. The attitudes involved in the *ideals* of *positive* expressions of respect cannot be mandated but at least the conventions of showing respect affirmatively (e.g., through common courtesy) can be encouraged and may eventually affect attitudes. Especially within family, friendship, and caregiving contexts, the ideal is not merely to avoid offenses but to *show* one's respect for others, as well as oneself, *affirmatively*.

Two final points about the special context of oppressive cultures that disparage and dismiss people with severe disabilities: First, as with matters of race and gender, victims of oppression tend to internalize the ideology of oppression. This makes it harder to secure one's *self*-respect and to express it positively. We especially admire those such as Frederick Douglass and Helen Keller, who manage to maintain their dignity, demonstrating their self-respect through their conduct despite the cultural forces pushing them toward shame and self-contempt.

Second, as stated before, context matters when applying the ideals to particular real-world cases. Sometimes, the ways that we affirm respect for some people is disrespectful of other people. For example, positively expressing respect for Nazi demonstrators can be disrespectful of the Jews, blacks, and immigrants that the Nazis are demeaning. When NFL players kneel during the national anthem, they mean to express respect for victims of racial profiling and police violence, but by the same act of kneeling they are (or are seen to be) refusing to give the conventional tokens of respect to other worthy people (e.g., those serving honorably in the military). Obviously, to express respect positively is not an absolute duty or even best in every situation. Judgment is needed. When someone is persistently threatening and showing contempt for others, then our withholding the conventional tokens of respect, and at times even responding rudely, can make sense from the point of view that aims to respect the dignity of every human being as best one can in our messy and often cruel world.

Notes

1. An earlier version of this essay was written for the conference Philosophy of Disability: Perspectives, Challenges, and Aspirations at the University of Tennessee, Knoxville, on October 27 and 28, 2017. I am grateful to all who organized and supported this conference, especially Adam Cureton. He and I coordinated our essays for this volume, and we share a common deliberative framework in which human dignity is a central value. He focused primarily on the *limiting* aspect of *respect* for persons, as a dimension of human dignity, and I will focus on two other, relatively neglected aspects—ideals of *appreciation* and *expressions of respect*.

2. Adam Cureton (2020), "The Limiting Role of Respect," chapter 22 of this volume.

3. See Rosen (2013, 2012). I reply to some of Rosen's objections in Hill (2013).

4. See Rawls (1999a) and discussions of "reflective equilibrium" in Rawls (1999b).

5. Appreciation, as will be explained, is not the same thing as love or caring, though it is in some respects like what David Velleman (1999) calls "love." What the ideal of appreciation recommends often coincides, of course, with what ideals of love and caring recommend, but this does not show that they are the same. Distinct values often overlap in what they give us reason to do. Appreciation, as we understand it, is essentially a matter of recognizing the non-instrumental value of or in something and this involves taking in and feeling that it gives us reason to have pro-attitudes in response (such as some degree of tendencies to admire, wish to continue, regret the loss, commend to others, or at least tolerate and "understand" others' attitudes of this sort). What we can imagine the gay son would miss in Distant Father is not just attention to the specifics of the son's life when attention is just *motivated by trying to please* the son. That attention could be given while never seeing anything good about the son's life except his feeling good, and being happy, and, though well-intended, this would strike the son who wanted appreciation as patronizing or at least disappointing. Of course, some may say that it is conceivable that a father who tried sincerely to find the value in the specifics of his son could not succeed, and so there is no guarantee that the father can give what the son wants. But, first, it would seem to take a closed mind or narrow view of value to be so pessimistic in real cases, especially if we take into account the good in a potential for good things in the son's life not yet realized, and, second, the ideal of appreciation that I have in mind is an openness, a readiness, a disposition to find good in and of a life, and this can be successful to various degrees.

6. *Ideals* are not necessarily *duties*, but extreme failures to live up to an ideal may be blameworthy and signs of a vice or character flaw. In an ordinary, loose sense we may say that we *should* seek to adopt and maintain ideal attitudes but *should* here is broader than *duty*.

7. It is a familiar idea that a wide variety of things can be regarded *good* in a broad sense (e.g., implying there being a reason to admire, commend, attend to, or have a favorable attitude toward the things) without implying that the things are good *as a means* to some further purpose, good *for a person*, good *of a certain kind*, or *good to produce as much as possible*. Philosophers may debate how to analyze these judgments, but one must assume here that such judgments are meant to be objective within their context but not about what is *unconditionally* good or *universally agreed* to be good.

8. Ideals, virtues, and moral requirements often overlap, calling for the same thing in particular contexts. When we ask why is it best (or virtuous or a duty) to do something, we should not always expect to get a simple one-dimensional answer. Sometimes it would be

disrespectful, ungrateful, unkind, and unfair to act in a certain way, but this does not mean that respect, gratitude, kindness, and fairness are indistinguishable.

9. See Velleman (1999). What Velleman calls love, rightly distinguishing it from the desire to make someone happy, incorporates what we can call "appreciation," but one could say that can we can appreciate someone without loving them.

10. "But we cannot be equally appreciative of everyone and honest too because, let's face it, some lives are more of mess than others and some are even nasty, mean, and vicious," we can imagine someone objecting. Yes, we would say in the end we cannot honestly claim to find equal good in each life, but we are not obliged to. The ideal is to be open to seeing the good, at least the potential good, in those with whom we are in close relationships of friendship, family, and as care-givers, being ready to acknowledge it as good in the appropriate ways. And what the ideal calls for is not a comparative judgment but an appreciation of the good that one finds. Contrast two museum visitors on a tour through various galleries. One looks at every art work with utter disinterest except the three most often photographed or praised by critics, and the other notices some good features in each even though she knows that they are not the best. The talent scout visiting a home may reasonably look for *only the very best* candidates and the electrician fixing wires in a home or an assisted living facility may have no reason to be looking for good in the lives of those who live there, but ideally care-takers, parents, and friends will be more like the appreciative observers at the museum. Their special relationships make appreciation more of an ideal for dealing with them than for dealing with strangers for whom they have no special role responsibilities.

11. Appreciation and positive expressions of respect, in my view, are *moral* ideals in a broad sense. That is, they are human excellences that we have reason to admire and aspire to, but they are not in general requirements the lack of which makes one *immoral* in a narrower sense, for example, implying the violation of other persons' rights.

12. There is a sense in which we may be said to "express respect" for a person *by refraining* from mocking, insulting, and humiliating the person but I will focus on overt "positive" words, gestures, and other acts that we use intentionally or conventionally to express recognition of a worthy status or something we consider valuable.

13. My focus here has been on "close relationships" such as friendships, family ties, and care-givers and those for whom they care for several reasons. First, the opportunities and need for appreciation and positive expressions of respect arise mainly when people interact personally on a regular basis. Public policies can no doubt take into account to some extent that individual lives have particular features worthy of appreciation and that it is good for people to express openly their respect for each other, but these concerns play out mostly in private interactions among people who know and care for each other. Second, although the ideals considered here have some broader applications, it is more evident intuitively and easier to explain why the attitudes of appreciation and readiness to express respect positively are ideals in the contents of friendships, family, and caretaking relationships. The ideals, arguably, are among the values built into the idea of these relationships in the cultures most familiar to us. The relationships are not *what make* the individual traits and interests *good and worthy of attention in appropriate contexts*, but they assign *the ideal (responsibility or best practice) of being open to appreciate and pay attention to* the good individual traits especially to friends, family, and caregivers. Similarly, what makes individual human beings worthy of positive expressions of respect is not that we have close relationships with them, but for good reasons the relationships have built-in norms

and values that include the ideal of expressing respect positively. The reasons for this are practical as well as theoretical but not solely utilitarian.

14. Both appreciation and respect for particular individuals ("as the distinctive individuals that they are") call for attention to particular aspects of a person's life, but these are not the same. We can appreciate (or "see and acknowledge the good in") all sorts of good things about a person and her life, for example, her looks, enjoyment of bridge, love of her dog, and naturally cheerful disposition, but one would not respect her for these; instead, we would respect her for her character, worthy commitments, and efforts, etc.

REFERENCES

Buss, Sarah. 1999. "Appearing Respectful: The Moral Significance of Manners." *Ethics* 109(4): 795–826.

Cureton, Adam. 2016. "Offensive Beneficence." *Journal of the American Philosophical Association* 2(1):74–90.

Cureton, Adam. 2020. "The Limiting Role of Respect." In *Oxford Handbook of Philosophy and Disability*, edited by Adam Cureton and David Wasserman, 380–398. New York: Oxford University Press.

Darwall, Stephen. 1977. "Two Kinds of Respect." *Ethics* 88(1):36–49.

Hill, Thomas E. 2013. "In Defense of Human Dignity: Comments on Kant and Rosen." In *Understanding Human Dignity*, edited by Christopher McCrudden, 313–326. Oxford: Oxford University Press.

Keller, Helen. 1933. "Three Days to See." *The Atlantic* 151(1):35–42.

Rawls, John. 1999a. "Outline of a Decision Procedure for Ethics." In *Collected Papers*, edited by Samuel Freeman, 1–19. Cambridge, MA: Harvard University Press.

Rawls, John. 1999b. *A Theory of Justice*. Rev. ed. Cambridge, MA: Belknap Press of Harvard University Press.

Rosen, Michael. 2012. *Dignity: Its History and Meaning*. Cambridge, MA: Harvard University Press.

Rosen, Michael. 2013. "Dignity: The Case Against." In *Understanding Human Dignity*, edited by Christopher McCrudden, 143–154. Oxford: Oxford University Press.

Velleman, J. David. 1999. "Love as a Moral Emotion." *Ethics* 109(2):338–374.

CHAPTER 22

THE LIMITING ROLE
OF RESPECT

ADAM CURETON

DESPITE a long and dark history of social exclusion, stigmatization, neglect, and outright abuse, people with disabilities often seem to elicit morally admirable reactions from people we encounter in our everyday lives.[1] When non-disabled people, for example, show heartfelt compassion and concern for those with disabilities, assist them with their conditions, make a concerted effort to include them in activities or groups, press for accommodations they are owed, or marvel at their perseverance, their attitudes and actions toward the disabled appear to be especially virtuous and praiseworthy.

Yet people with disabilities are sometimes offended by some of the ways that even well-meaning people tend to regard and treat them. When others are sympathetic, generous, community-minded, appreciative, and just toward disabled people, without any intention to harm, insult, or discriminate against them, many disabled people nonetheless bristle when others see them as "special," when they "single us out" for special treatment, when they "make excuses" or "make exceptions" for them because of their disabilities, or when they "put us on a pedestal" for how disabled people have responded to their impairments.

How should we explain these common concerns on the part of disabled people? Are they legitimate worries? And, if they are, what moral guidance can we glean for how we should aim to regard and treat them?

The approach I will take in addressing these questions is broadly Kantian.[2] The background idea is that our moral relations with ourselves and others are properly guided and constrained by a set of widely shared moral values, including welfare, community, justice, autonomy, appreciation, and respect. All of these values are arguably aspects of the fundamental moral value of human dignity because they would arguably be endorsed by all fully rational persons in light of our shared fundamental interests in protecting, developing, and exercising our powers of freedom and reason. Although this approach is "top-down" in terms of how moral ideals, values, and principles are ultimately justified, the justification of the theory as a whole depends on whether it coheres with the considered moral judgments of competent moral judges on due reflection. As we try to construct, interpret, and apply a moral theory that aspires to such a high standard of acceptability, we must also work from the "bottom up" by examining and evaluating our intuitions about particular cases.

In his contribution to this volume, Thomas E. Hill (2020) endorses this same basic approach to understanding various moral values as aspects of human dignity. Hill, in particular, explores the values of appreciation and "positive" respect as both part of properly responding to the dignity of persons. These values, according to Hill, are relevant to questions about how we should or should aspire to regard and treat all people, but he draws out some special implications for our attitudes and actions toward people with disabilities.

The main aim of this chapter is to highlight a different aspect of human dignity and to argue that this value competes with other aspects of human dignity, including the values of appreciation and positive respect that Hill discusses. Respect for something, as Hill argues, is often thought to involve understanding and acknowledging it, holding it in high regard, and engaging with it.[3] But many kinds of cases suggest that there is another aspect of our ordinary idea of respect, one that involves resistance, reluctance, and limitation.[4] This "negative" or "limiting" part of respect, I argue, is an underappreciated aspect of human dignity that has been missed, or misinterpreted, by those who tend to focus instead on other aspects of dignity, such as political justice, autonomy, beneficence, and thinner conceptions of respect. Negative respect presumptively requires us to recognize and acknowledge respectful limits on how we regard and treat others. Other aspects of human dignity, however, can provide competing presumptions about how to affirm the dignity of persons. Eventually, a comprehensive conception of human dignity should provide some guidance about how to adjudicate conflicts among these presumptive norms of dignity, including conflicts among the value of negative respect that this chapter discusses and the values of appreciation and positive respect that Hill discusses. In many cases, kindness, justice, appreciation, and positive respect might be more important than negative respect, while in other cases negative respect may defeat these other presumptions. The kinds of relationships we have with others, whether intimate ones of the sort that Hill highlights or more distant ones of the kind focused on here, will often influence how we should or should aspire to incorporate these values into how we regard and treat others. Appreciation and positive respect, for example, may be appropriate or demanded for loved ones but intrusive and presumptuous toward strangers. Nonetheless, we should take seriously a general theme that underlies many kinds of legitimate complaints that disabled and non-disabled people have, which is that even well-meaning people sometimes overstep bounds of respect in the otherwise good and virtuous ways that they regard and treat us.

The first two sections describe a variety of apparently virtuous attitudes that non-disabled people may have and express toward those with disabilities, with special emphasis on everyday contexts in which non-disabled people encounter people with disabilities who are more or less strangers to them. The third section draws on some examples that highlight a "negative" or "limiting" aspect of respect beyond its "positive" aspects of understanding, esteeming, and engaging with people or things. The fourth section gives some reasons why this "negative" or "limiting" aspect of respect is an attitude that we should have toward other people. The fifth section explains why the apparently virtuous attitudes and actions toward disabled people described here conflict with "negative" respect. And the final section provides some practical suggestions for how good, well-meaning people can observe respectful limits in their attitudes and actions toward disabled people.

DISABLED STRANGERS

The attitudes that non-disabled people have about those with disabilities, as well as the ways that non-disabled people express these attitudes in their treatment of disabled people, can vary depending on many factors, including social context, the sort of relationship (if any) that exists between the parties, the kind of disability the disabled person has, and other attitudes or features of the non-disabled person herself. For example, background institutions, systems of oppression, and social forces often influence our attitudes about disability. The ways that someone responds to her child's disability may be different from the ways she responds to the disability of one of her colleagues. A non-disabled person may tend to regard and treat physically disabled people differently than those who have cognitive disabilities. And, one person may be warm and kind to most everyone, regardless of disability, while others may be especially considerate to disabled people because they are disabled.

In order to more easily isolate some of the ways that non-disabled people regard and treat disabled people as such, let's initially limit our discussion to typical, everyday encounters between a disabled person and a non-disabled person who are more or less strangers to one another. More specifically, let's suppose the following: We are living in a modern, democratic society under reasonably favorable circumstances. Our society is reasonably though not fully just with regard to its treatment of disabled people, but it nonetheless stigmatizes and oppresses them to some limited but not insignificant extent. A disabled person and a non-disabled person, suppose, come across one another in the course of daily life, such as in a restaurant or store, at a social gathering, or on the street. They are basically unfamiliar or unknown to each other: They may have seen one another a few times or chatted briefly; perhaps they are distant acquaintances; but they are not friends, family members, or loved ones to one another. The non-disabled person in question is aware that the disabled person he encounters has a moderate disability, that she has been disabled for some time, and that she is not currently under duress or in need of emergency help. He is genuinely concerned to regard and treat her only in morally appropriately ways and, in particular, he lacks any intention to harm, discriminate against, or disrespect her on account of her disability.

Aspects of Human Dignity

Let's now examine some of the ways that people with disabilities are sometimes regarded and treated in everyday life on account of disabilities. Set aside the most apparent forms of discrimination, ridicule, mockery, malevolence, and injustice that disabled people often endure and focus instead on attitudes and actions toward disabled people that are commonly regarded as virtuous, meritorious, or even morally required. These attitudes and actions can be grouped into a few broad, and potentially overlapping, categories that are arguably each aspects of human dignity, although some of these ways of regarding and treating disabled people can also be offensive and disrespectful.

Welfare

A non-disabled person may be genuinely concerned about the welfare of a disabled person he encounters. His caring attitudes toward her may involve being especially sensitive to her disability, sympathetic to the challenges she faces, curious about the specifics of her condition, and intrigued by her ways of accommodating it. These attitudes may lead him to have a concerned look on his face, to use a warm, sympathetic tone of voice, and to keep a close eye on her in case she needs his assistance. He may also approach her and warmly say, for example: "I'm so sorry this has happened to you" or "Good for you for being out and about." He may offer her advice about, for instance, whether she should try an experimental treatment he recently learned about. And he may be pleased to give her direct material assistance, perhaps without prompting from her, in ways that actually make her better off, such as by helping her back on her feet or clearing a path for her.

Community

A non-disabled person may also have a sense of community and solidarity that influences how he regards and treats disabled people. He may feel a kind of kinship or camaraderie with a disabled stranger because of, for example, his own past medical conditions or his experiences with disabled family members or friends. He may try to develop social bonds with her by, for example, attempting to relate with her on the basis of shared experiences, values, and interests, salient features of her or her circumstances, or aspects of her that she cares about. For example, he may earnestly ask a disabled person certain questions, which are perhaps prefaced by phrases meant to convey that he is not trying to insult or offend her, even if he actually does so (e.g., "If you don't mind me asking"): "What exactly is your condition?" "What can you see, hear, feel, etc.?" or "How are you able to do this or that with your disability (e.g., read, shower or have sex)?" And, he may make a special effort to put her at ease in social settings, invite her to social events, include her in conversations, and otherwise get to know her better.

Justice

A non-disabled person's sense of justice may lead him to think that certain established rules, demands, and expectations do not apply to certain kinds of people, that various impairments count as legitimate excuses for not complying with them, or that those impairments are at least mitigating factors in assessments of blame and punishment. He may thus not ask a disabled stranger to perform tasks that are difficult or impossible for her and he may be more lenient or forgiving toward her when she fails to satisfy certain established rules or norms.

His sense of justice may also lead him to be angry or indignant at those who discriminate against a disabled person he meets on account of her disability or who fail to provide accommodations that she is owed. He may even take it upon himself to make demands, complaints, or requests on her behalf that are meant to secure her rightful claims. He may, for instance, demand the installation of a wheelchair ramp, complain that a speaker used handouts that are not accessible to her, or insist that dinner guests change seats to make it easier for her to hear the conversation.

Appreciation

A non-disabled person may be amazed and inspired by a disabled stranger for her courage, bravery, and fortitude—or for the ways she has overcome her disability or her resilience and cheerfulness under adverse circumstances. He may even be somewhat grateful or appreciative to her for setting an instructive example for him, leading him to rethink his own excuses, teaching him the power and importance of a positive outlook, enhancing his appreciation for his own fortunate circumstances, and inspiring him to redouble his moral efforts to fight injustice and discrimination (Holtman 2018). Appreciation, according to Hill, is "an openness to acknowledge, take in, and attend to the myriad good things about particular persons and the good things that they may experience in their lives" (Hill 2020, 365). A non-disabled person may express his appreciation of this kind for a disabled person with symbolic gestures, such as encouraging a philanthropic organization to give her a "perseverance" award, or simply by telling her how inspiring she is to him.[5]

Positive Respect

The respect that a non-disabled person has for a disabled person he meets may also influence how he regards and treats her. Out of respect for her, he may pay attention to her and notice if she is uncomfortable, unhappy, embarrassed, or in need of assistance. He may try to get to know her better in terms of her basic values, goals, convictions, aspirations, and character traits. And he may try and understand her specific rights, entitlements, and prerogatives as well as when these are being upheld, violated, or incorrectly enforced.

The respect someone has for a disabled stranger may also involve esteeming her as a person, which may dispose him to be around her, to engage her in conversation, to form a relationship with her, and to value and affirm her for who she is. His respect for her may also lead him to protect and enhance her sense of self-worth, to defend her against violations of her rights, and to encourage her not to subordinate or lower herself to others. He may, for example, attempt to improve a cognitively disabled person's sense of self-worth by allowing her to play in the final seconds of a one-sided basketball game or by bending the rules so that she appears to win some prize.

Our commonsense idea of respect seems to involve these two aspects, namely acknowledgment and high regard.

First, when we respect something, we tend to notice, pay attention to, understand, and give due consideration to it. For example, when we respect the Constitution, a religious ritual, or a professional code of conduct, we understand its structure, requirements, and aims. When we respect an opponent's backhand, we know how devastating it can be. When we respect a great composer, we are aware of her musical genius. When we respect a work of art, we want to view it and learn about its history. And when we respect someone as a person, we tend to notice and pay attention to her as well as give her proper consideration in our deliberations.[6]

And, second, respect seems to involve a kind of high regard and esteem. When we respect a set of traditions, rules, or practices, we venerate and cherish them; when we respect a person for her abilities or accomplishments, we admire, revere, and celebrate her. We pay our respects by welcoming or honoring someone, and we respect someone as a person by valuing her for her basic moral status. Respect for persons or things, as Hill and others argue, seems to involve feeling uplifted by them, being close to them, engaging with them, and expressing these attitudes to them.[7]

Some philosophers have even suggested that the ideal of respect for another person is acknowledging and revering many of her qualities, including her deepest aims and goals, her character traits, and her psychological makeup.[8] Although unachievable in most cases, these philosophers argue that respect requires us to aim for full familiarity with other people and to admire them for who they really are.

These two general aspects of respect can be interpreted in different ways, but together they emphasize the "positive" side of respect as familiarity and admiration. Respect of this kind, which underlies some of the ways that disabled people are regarded and treated, tends to bring us closer to people, to engage with them, to understand who they are, and to hold them in high esteem.[9]

NEGATIVE RESPECT

When reflecting on how people with disabilities are commonly regarded and treated by well-intentioned non-disabled people, it is clear that some of the attitudes and actions discussed in the previous section can, on occasion, be awkward or uncouth. But it may nonetheless seem that generally these ways of regarding and treating disabled people are quite virtuous, admirable, and praiseworthy. It is assumed, after all, that there is no intention to harm, embarrass, or offend anyone; disabled people usually benefit from these attitudes and actions; and many of them seem to be part of properly responding to the human dignity that all persons share.

And, yet, people with disabilities sometimes feel insulted by these apparently virtuous attitudes and actions. Disabled people can admit that many of the non-disabled strangers we encounter are well meaning, sincere, and concerned to regard and treat us with dignity; we can also admit that many of their attitudes and actions toward us would be morally appropriate or required in a variety of circumstances. But, to many of us, there seems to be an aspect of our human dignity that is often left out or underappreciated by non-disabled people in these contexts.

Earlier it was suggested that our ordinary idea of respect has a "positive" side that tends to bring us closer to people and things, to engage with them, to understand them, and to hold them in high esteem. There is another aspect of commonsense respect, however, that is not fully captured by and sometimes conflicts with these ideas of acknowledgment and reverence. The following examples suggest that respect, in general, also involves "negative" or "limiting" elements of reluctance, deference, resistance, aversion, limitation, and constraint.

When we respect a wild grizzly bear, we tend to leave it be. When we respect a deadly virus in the lab, we handle it with care. When we respect hurricanes, we are fearful of their fury. And when we respect an opponent's left hook, we tend to stay out of its way. Even respect for things that are not dangerous to us, such as certain works of art, pieces of music, and natural landscapes involve a tendency to resist them and to leave them as they are, perhaps because of the humbling effects they have on our own sense of self-worth. When we respect certain traditions or rituals, we are reluctant to change, violate, or mock them. Respecting someone's property often involves staying off of it. And respecting a person's wishes involves a tendency not to interfere with them or their satisfaction. We are respectful of a colleague's time by not wasting it. And we respect the dead by not disturbing their remains more than we need to.

This negative aspect of respect is also evident in the respect we have for other persons. We sometimes think about and express this kind of respect metaphorically, with phrases such as: "give me some space," "keep your distance," "don't get too close," "get off my case," "you're out of line," "mind your own business," and "good fences make good neighbors." Certain norms of etiquette and politeness seem to be aimed at keeping us apart from one another in various ways. Many of the recognized rules about personal space, eating, toileting, gift-giving, and conversing, for example, allow us to maintain our privacy as well as our physical and emotional distance from one another (Buss 1999a, Stohr 2018). And within families and close personal relationships, limiting norms of respect often allows us to maintain some privacy and independence from our loved ones. A teenager, for example, might appreciate the interest her father takes in her plans after graduation but eventually comes to regard his constant questioning as disrespectfully intrusive.

In general, our respect for something, it seems, includes broad tendencies not to interfere with, obstruct, meddle with, or concern ourselves unduly with someone or something. We are disposed to leave the people or things we respect as they are; to refrain from harassing, violating, challenging, or criticizing them; to uphold and sustain them as what they are; and to keep our distance from them by not becoming too familiar with them. It seems that someone who is respectful of other people tends to keep to herself, to maintain some emotional distance from others, to give them space, and to mind her own affairs. She tends not to intrude on others, put herself above them, violate their rights, judge their character, or moralize to them. And she tends to be reticent, self-possessed, private, and humble. Such a person respects herself, in part, by tending to resist those who overstep the boundaries that respect establishes, such as people who are forward, arrogant, pushy, or presumptuous toward her, those who attempt to pry into aspects of her personal life that she would rather not share, and those who try to interfere with or violate her prerogatives, responsibilities, and obligations.

We can try to be more specific about some of the negative or limiting presumptions that seem to be part of our ordinary idea of respect. We will focus on three presumptive boundaries of respect, which concern the assumptions we make about others, their privacy, and their prerogatives and responsibilities.

Making Assumptions About Others

Our ordinary idea of respect for persons seems to involve a reluctance to make assumptions about the character, values, convictions, emotions, abilities, and circumstances of others without sufficient evidence. It can be disrespectfully presumptuous for us to assume, for example, that our spouse always shares our opinions, values and preferences or that we know what she believes or wants without asking her. Relying on stereotypes can also be disrespectful when we, for example, assume that a student is good at something because of her race, assume that our neighbors are Republicans or Democrats from the way they dress and speak, or assume that a wealthy friend's many good works are actually motivated by greed, particularly when our purpose in making these assumptions is to offend, insult, or oppress these people. We can feel disrespected if others assuredly assume, without good reason, that we are envious, spiteful, or cruel, or even that we are generous, courageous, or wise. The assumptions that we make about others or that others make about us may sometimes be correct, but it seems that someone who is respectful of other people tends not assume that he knows people better than he does, tends not to pretend to great insights about them, and tends not to act as if he knows their true selves without sufficient evidence. When we lack such evidence about the characteristics of others, when we are biased in our assessments of that evidence, or when we are motivated by prejudicial attitudes, respect for them seems to presumptively require us to modestly withhold judgments about whether or not they have those features.

Privacy

If respect presumptively requires us to refrain from making unjustified assumptions about other people, then it may seem that we can avoid disrespecting them in this way by getting to know them better. Doing so, however, may involve a willingness to infringe on their privacy in ways that are incompatible with proper respect for them. It seems that part of respecting someone, in the negative sense, is to be disposed to keep some physical and emotional distance from them, which involves allowing them to conceal certain aspects of themselves and trying not to learn too much about them.

When we respect our neighbors, for example, we are reluctant to spy on or stare at them, to concern ourselves with their faults or their political and religious views, or to learn too much about their personal lives, which we might try to avoid by closing our windows during one of their loud arguments. We may have a respectful meeting with our dissertation director without noticing that his wedding band is missing or asking about a picture showing him on a small sailboat. Our respect for a mentor may make us reluctant to read a salacious biography of him that, perhaps accurately, exposes his alcoholism and adultery. Our respect for someone we love leads us to acknowledge and appreciate boundaries of privacy in our relationship by, for example, not reading her personal e-mails or inquiring about her previous relationships. And, our respect for the person beside us on an airplane may lead us to regard and treat him as the sort of person he presents himself to be rather than to look for disconfirming evidence about him.

Responsibilities and Prerogatives

A further aspect of negative respect for another person seems to be a tendency not to intrude on, challenge, or meddle with his or her various prerogatives and responsibilities. When we respect our subordinates, we tend to let them do their jobs without second-guessing their official decisions, micro-managing them, or assigning their responsibilities to others without good reason. We are also disposed to defer to our employees on some occasions and to hold them to the policies and expectations of our organization by, for example, sanctioning them for their infractions and rewarding them for their accomplishments. When we respect our military commander, we tend to acquiesce to her orders and directives and to refrain from challenging her authority, going over her head, or criticizing her leadership style. And respect for our neighbors may lead us to try not to irritate, inconvenience, or pressure them with, for example, too many late-night parties, requests to borrow sugar, unaccepted invitations to dinner, or suggestions about how they should care for their lawn or children.

Respect is a complicated notion, but these examples point to the general idea that our ordinary understanding of respect involves not just "positive" admiration and acknowledgement but also "negative" resistance, constraint, and limitation. The three more specific presumptions of respect described here are still somewhat vague and abstract, which makes it difficult to evaluate them or to interpret and apply them to actual circumstances. Attitudes and actions that may overstep the bounds of respect in one context may be quite respectful in another. Nonetheless, our love for other people draws us closer to them while the negative side of respect tends to keep us at a distance from them. Part of what is so difficult about having and showing proper respect to other people is not just that negative respect can conflict with other aspects of dignity but that respect itself seems to involve potentially competing reasons of esteem, engagement, and familiarity, on the one hand, and resistance and limitation on the other.

Negative Respect and Human Dignity

Before turning to consider, in more detail, how negative respect can conflict with and place limits on apparently virtuous attitudes and actions toward other people, this section will briefly consider why this aspect of respect is a morally appropriate attitude to have. This is a complex question that may have different answers for different kinds or aspects of negative respect, so the focus here will be on the negative side of respect for persons simply as persons.

The previous section gave some examples that suggest that negative respect is part of our ordinary moral idea of respect and that it figures in a variety of moral practices that we commonly endorse. Perhaps I can go further than this, however, by noting some connections that negative respect has to other moral ideas within one kind of broadly Kantian moral framework.

One of the distinctive features of Kantian moral philosophy is that persons are ends in themselves and so have an intrinsic, objective, and incomparable worth. What gives us this vaunted status is that we possess various rational capacities and abilities, such as to act freely, to deliberate, to think for ourselves, and to develop our own aims, projects and ideals. How we should regard and treat ourselves and others depends on interests we all have in developing, exercising, and preserving our rational capacities. And an (unachievable) ideal we should all aspire to is to fulfill these interests completely and so govern all aspects of our lives by reason. Virtually all human beings are rational persons in this sense and so have dignity, but broadly Kantian moral theories, in my view, must also ensure that the needs and interests of people with profound cognitive impairments are appropriately secured.

These basic ideas have inspired many people and led to ongoing debates about how to interpret and apply them to human conditions. But even at this abstract level, we find some reasons that apparently justify certain negative aspects of respect as ways of regarding people as the sort of beings they are.

Separateness of Persons

Persons, on Kantian ways of thinking, are, at our most fundamental level, connected by moral responsibilities, our human needs and dependencies, and our hopes for humanity over time, though we are also distinct and separate from one another as well. We have our own basic interests, which give rise to self-justifying moral claims on ourselves and others; competent persons have our own moral responsibilities that we must fulfill; and we have the capacity to think for ourselves and to freely develop, affirm, and pursue our own values, aims, and aspirations. We are not the kind of creatures who exist only as part of a larger whole, whose basic moral claims depend on others, who lack moral responsibility, or who cannot have our own opinions or values.

Respecting one another as the sorts of things we are seems to involve recognizing that we are separate persons and so not regarding one another as if we are "inseparable" or indistinct from one another. Much will depend on particular circumstances when applying this idea, but at this basic moral level, negative respect for others as distinct individuals seems to give us reasons not to interfere with or try to take over the moral responsibilities of others, not to pressure, meddle with or coerce others, not to assume that we can speak for or represent others without their consent, not to presume that we always know what is best for a person, and not to interfere with the permissible aims and projects of others. We must see one another as fundamentally separate persons, regardless of how close we are to others or how intertwined our projects and goals may be with theirs.

When this idea is interpreted and applied in light of natural human tendencies, we find additional presumptions that are involved in respecting others. If people tend to lose their conception of themselves as separate, or if others tend to lose it about them, when they are close to others in various kinds of relationships then the limiting role of respect for one another as separate persons is even more important so that each of us maintains an idea of ourselves as separate and distinct from others.

The three presumptive boundaries of respect described here, then, are partly ways for us to recognize and express the fact that we are separate persons, with our own interests, claims, responsibilities, values, and opinions. Respect for others imposes presumptive limits on assuming that we know other, distinct, people better than we do, on violating their privacy, and on interfering with their prerogatives and responsibilities.

Freedom

A second feature of persons, on Kantian views, is that we are free in the sense that we have the capacity to make our own choices, think for ourselves, and affirm our own values, aims, and aspirations without being caused or determined by anything. Respecting a person as free seems to require that we understand and acknowledge her as a free agent and not regard her as unfree.

As free persons, our desires, what causes us pain, and other aspects of our psychology may be predictable, but as imperfect human agents, the goals, aims and projects that we freely endorse, choose, or affirm are difficult, if not impossible, for anyone else to predict on the basis of empirical evidence because they are ones we, as imperfect human agents, choose for ourselves.[10] If we simply look at a person's external circumstances, empirical characteristics, and psychological makeup and conclude that we know what values, goals, or ends a person has, then we are not fully regarding her as a free person. As persons, we can freely adjust our values, convictions, and choices, replace them with different ones, give up some, and endorse new ones.

The three presumptive boundaries of respect previously described are ways for us to recognize and express the fact that we are free persons who can freely select, endorse, and affirm our own values, ideals, and opinions. Although we can make educated guesses about a person's values or choices, we can never know for sure what they were, are or will be, so if we assume we can or do know these things about someone then we are not regarding her as free. Regarding and treating someone as a free person thus seems to give us reasons for humility about how well we can really know another person. Respecting someone as free may also give us reasons not to try and get to know others too well, for this is impossible when the other person can freely adjust her values and opinions over time. And respecting a person as free involves acknowledging their ability to freely exercise or live up to their own moral responsibilities and prerogatives.

Conditions of Agency

In addition to having the capacity for free agency, we as rational agents also have a rational interest in exercising our agential capacities well by aspiring to the ideal of a fully reason-governed person. This ideal is in part to fully endorse, on reflection, our own values and commitments; to not accept them simply on authority or because they are traditional or commonly accepted; and to not be pressured into them by others. Other people can help us in this regard, by discussing our ideas with us, allowing us to try out our opinions on them, and providing us with opportunities to participate in joint activities and projects. But, for human beings, there is also a need for privacy and quiet reflection in order to mull over things in our own minds without various kinds of interference from others. A sphere of privacy is important for us to exercise our agential capacities well and to aspire toward the ideal of freely endorsing a set of values, norms, and convictions on due reflection.[11] Otherwise, we may be debilitated with shame if others knew our inner secrets, desires, or character; we may be subject to social pressures of various kinds; and we may be more likely to be distracted. Human persons often need privacy to aspire toward this rational ideal in order to try out ideas, think through them, and figure out what values and goals we truly affirm. And the flip side of this needed privacy is that we still have to be in the world, so we need some control about what aspects of ourselves we present to others and which we hold back. Others, then, have reasons not to overstep these bounds of privacy and also to refrain from making assumptions about us or interfering with our prerogatives and responsibilities when doing so is likely to unduly influence our rational deliberations about what is good and valuable in life.

Negative Respect for Disabled People

In any case, let's return to some apparently virtuous attitudes toward disabled strangers and examine why these attitudes and their expressions are sometimes incompatible with negative respect for people with disabilities. We will focus on the three presumptive requirements that negative respect includes.

Making Assumptions About Others

Many of the apparently virtuous attitudes and actions toward disabled people include, depend on, or presuppose assumptions about fundamental aspects of us, such as our character, values, well-being, convictions, and abilities. Non-disabled people sometimes presume to know, for example, that we are courageous, strong willed, or resilient; that we regard our disability as a something to be cured or corrected; that our disability substantially diminishes our well-being and self-esteem; that we want to form relationships and social ties with particular people; or that our disability makes it difficult or impossible for us to satisfy certain norms. All too often, people with disabilities are assumed to be dependent on others in ways that call for addressing their companions rather than the disabled person herself about, for example, her health or her restaurant order.

When a non-disabled person encounters someone with a disability, it can be disrespectfully presumptuous of him to make firm assumptions about these aspects of her, especially when he is more or less a stranger to her. "You don't know me," a person with cerebral palsy might think to herself, when a stranger on the street compliments her for her supposed bravery and fortitude. The non-disabled person might be right about her, of course, or he might be mistaking her survival instinct, deep desire for money and power, or fortunate circumstances for a good and strong will. She may be exceptionally perseverant and courageous. Or she may be handling her disability in much the same unremarkable way as anyone would in her circumstances. The problem is that the non-disabled person, if he were honest with himself, would admit that he does not know which it is. He oversteps the presumptive bounds of respect for the woman by assuming, without nearly enough evidence, that he has deep insights into her character.

The main presumptive failure of respect highlighted in this case is that of assuming we know people better than we actually do.[12] Respect may allow us in some situations to make educated guesses about a person's character, values, and other aspects of her inner life, perhaps after careful reflection on the basis of solid evidence. It can seem to many disabled people, however, that others act as if they are sure about certain aspects of our true selves. And disabilities, along with the personalities and circumstances of disabled people, vary so widely and the available information about people with disabilities is so scarce that it may not even be possible for many non-disabled people to form anything more than mere conjectures about the inner lives of disabled people. If we take a more respectful attitude toward disabled people by admitting that we do not know much about their character, values or other aspects of their inner-life then we are less likely to pity, feel sorry or embarrassed for, or admire disabled people we do not know or to act in ways that express these attitudes.

Privacy

It may seem as if we can avoid disrespecting a disabled person in these ways by getting to know her better, asking her questions, paying close attention to her and her circumstances, and engaging with her. Such actions and attitudes, however, may nonetheless involve a willingness to infringe on the privacy of disabled people in ways that are presumptively incompatible with negative respect for them. Part of respecting someone, in the negative sense, is to keep at some distance from their inner lives by allowing them to conceal certain aspects of themselves and by trying not to learn too much about their character, values, well-being, etc. "That's none of your business," a wheelchair user might think to herself if a passer-by asks if she is headed inside an inaccessible building or asks about the nature of her impairment.

Many of the apparently virtuous attitudes that people have about disabled people include tendencies to gather and pay attention to facts that those attitudes pick out as relevant. Respect, in its negative sense, seems to place limits on how curious we should be about private matters of others, how much we should acquire such information, and how much attention we should give information we do have. A disabled person, of course, may have no qualms about sharing certain information about herself, but negative respect also presumptively requires us not to presume we know what aspects of herself she prefers to keep private.

Responsibilities and Prerogatives

A third aspect of negative respect for someone, as has been suggested, is not to intrude on his or her various prerogatives and responsibilities. When a non-disabled conference attendant complains that a PowerPoint presentation is inaccessible to a blind participant, the blind person may think to himself: "I don't need you to fight my battles for me." The attendant's complaint may well be justified, but it may also be that those who are treated unjustly have a prerogative to complain or not and that others should take their cues from him. There may not be respectful ways to figure out what, if anything, he wants us to do on his behalf, which may mean that in many cases inaction is the most respectful option for the conference participant. Much depends, of course, on particular contexts and on who has standing to complain about injustice, but when a disabled person bears primary responsibility for doing so in his own case then it can be disrespectful to interfere with or supplant that prerogative.

Another prerogative that persons arguably have is to freely pursue their own goals, values, and ends without certain kinds of interference from others. If a disabled person prefers, for example, to open doors herself or to find her own way then assisting her in these ways, while potentially beneficial, may be disrespectfully intrusive. Again, many disabled people would welcome such help, but there are reasons of respect not presume to know whether we want assistance or not and also reasons of respect to maintain our privacy about such matters.

These three presumptions are especially important for how we regard and treat disabled people. This is because, as with gender and race, there is a history of cultural disregard for these concerns that, combined with ongoing implicit bias about disabled people, calls for heightened sensitivity and special attention to the limiting role of respect for people with disabilities.

Practical Suggestions

Let's conclude with a few practical suggestions about how to observe respectful limits in our treatment of disabled people.

Welfare

Genuine concern for the welfare of others is part of properly responding to their human dignity, but the respect we should have for others often places constraints on our caring attitudes and on the ways we express them. Although we may find ourselves feeling sorry for a disabled person or tempted to help her in various ways, our respect for her should also lead us to reflect on the assumptions we may be making about her quality of life or about whether she wants or needs our help. Relying on stereotypes, folk wisdom, and our own experiences may not, on reflection, justify our views about these matters, which gives us reasons to be more reticent about having and expressing sympathy, compassion, and pity toward disabled people. Perhaps our initial assumptions were correct, but perhaps not, so once we recognize how complicated it can be to determine someone else's level of wellbeing in her circumstances, we often have reason to withhold the kinds of judgments that would otherwise lead us to have and express especially caring attitudes toward them on account of their disability. When this happens, our care for the person can remain in place, but it presumptively should be tempered by our uncertainty about how well off she really is, whether she wants our help, and what we can do to assist her. Respect also gives us reasons to resist the temptation to gather more evidence about these matters so that we do not intrude on what can be very private and personal matters about, for example, the specifics of a person's condition, whether she regards it as a burden, and whether she prefers to exercise her prerogative to pursue her own goals and ends independently, without much beneficence or charity from others.

In some dire circumstances, it may be clear that a disabled person is in pain or needs our help, but even then we have reasons of respect to proceed with caution so as not to exaggerate her predicament in our own minds and not to intrude on her privacy and prerogatives that she may prefer to exercise herself. In most other situations, respect gives us reasons to let disabled people take the lead in whether we share aspects of our situation with others, communicate our openness to being assisted, or welcome their sympathy and compassion.

Community

A non-disabled person who has experience with disability in his own life may feel a kind of bond or kinship with a disabled person he meets because of what he supposes are their shared experiences, values, or circumstances. Some of these underlying assumptions about the disabled person may be correct, but others may be mistaken, so respect for her gives him reasons to scrutinize what he really knows about her and her situation, which may diminish his heightened sense of solidary toward her. Respect also gives him reasons to respect her privacy about some of the grounds that might provide a foundation for special social bonds between them as well as reasons not to force those bonds when they do not exist. A more respectful strategy, in many cases, is to avoid trying to form relationships with disabled people on the basis of our disabilities but instead to relate to us on the basis of the interests, values, and character traits that we have chosen to openly express.

Justice

Non-disabled people may come to recognize various ways in which social and political institutions are unjust in their treatment of disabled people, but it is sometimes difficult to know, in particular cases, what specific rights, entitlements, prerogatives, and duties a disabled person has, how well these are being upheld or fulfilled, and who is responsible for correcting any injustices that may exist. Respect gives us reasons not to make assumptions about such matters without good evidence, not to inquire about them in ways that risk violating the privacy of disabled people, and in some cases to let disabled people ourselves take the lead in how to respond to injustices that we, in particular, suffer. When we are unsure, for example, whether a disabled person has violated a legitimate rule, perhaps because we do not know whether the rule applies to her in light of her condition, respect for her gives us reasons to withhold judgment rather than to assume that the rule does not apply to her or to blame her for her supposed infraction.

Appreciation

Many of us are amazed and inspired by good or virtuous character traits that we think we detect in others, but while it is laudable for us to appreciate these traits in the abstract, it is often difficult to know whether particular people actually have them. Part of what can be frustrating about living as a disabled person is when others assume that our everyday forms of life are indicative of character traits that are especially worthy of appreciation even though we know that others have little idea about our underlying motives or what obstacles we have actually faced. Respect for a disabled people gives us reasons to be reticent about assuming we understand her underlying character and circumstances, even when these assumptions lead us to have and express admiration and appreciation for them. The challenges that a disabled person has faced, along with the ways she has coped with them, may be quite admirable, but they are also often deeply personal matters that she would prefer to keep private.

Positive Respect

Finally, the respect that a non-disabled person has for a disabled person may lead him to notice, understand, and think about her; to engage with and esteem her; and to work to reinforce her sense of self-worth. His respect for her, however, also gives him reasons to keep his distance from her and to mind his own business, to avoid getting to know her too well, and to not intrude on her prerogatives and responsibilities. Sometimes the most respectful action to take is to mostly ignore a disabled person who is, for example, simply shopping at the grocery store rather than to spend much time reflecting on and esteeming her for who she is. Navigating such conflicts within the idea of respect itself, as well adjudicating conflicts between respect and other aspects of dignity, is often very difficult, calling for significant moral sensitivity and wisdom, but many people with disabilities would be pleased by a broader recognition of the presumptive limits of respect on how others regard and treat us.

Notes

1. Thanks to Tom Hill, Teresa Blankmeyer Burke, David Wasserman, Julia Mosquera, Linda Barclay, Tom Shakespeare, Eva Feder Kittay, John Hardwig, Jessica Begon, Sam Kerstein, Steve Campbell, and audiences at the National Institutes of Health, University of South Florida-St. Petersburg, the 2017 Eastern APA, and the Philosophy of Disability Conference at the University of Tennessee for their feedback on this paper.
2. The broadly Kantian view sketched is influenced by Hill (1991, 1992a, 1992b, 2000a, 2000b) and developed in various ways in Cureton (2007, 2012, 2013b, 2013a, 2014, 2016).
3. This aspect of respect is interpreted in various ways in Velleman (1999), Anderson (1993), Feinberg (1973), Dillon (1992), Darwall (1977), Buss (1999b).

4. This "negative" aspect of respect figures in Feinberg (1973), Buss (1999a), Kant (1996, 449–450, 462–469), Carter (2011), Stohr (2018), Sensen (2018).
5. For further discussion of regarding disabled people as inspirational, see Barclay (2020).
6. See, for example, Darwall (1977), Buss (1999b), and Hill (1991).
7. See, for example, Raz (1999), Williams (1973), Velleman (1999), and Hill (2020).
8. See, for example, Williams (1973), Frankfurt (1999), and Vorhaus (2020).
9. There are important distinctions to draw among these various aspects of positive respect, but my aim here is primarily to highlight two general themes that underlie our ordinary idea of respect, namely familiarity and esteem.
10. That our choices are not empirically caused does not entail that our choices are not predictable—on some views, God is free, but his choices are also predictable because he is supremely rational. But, as free yet imperfect human agents who are not necessarily guided by reason, it is difficult to explain how the choices of others could be predicted on the basis of empirical evidence. In any case, the main point is that respect presumptively requires us to regard one another as free and, in particular, not to assume that we can know how a person will choose simply on the basis of empirical evidence.
11. For further discussions about the moral underpinnings of privacy, see Nagel (1998).
12. This idea has connections to what others have called "epistemic justice" although perhaps "epistemic respect" would in some cases be a better label.

References

Anderson, Elizabeth. 1993. *Value in Ethics and Economics*. Cambridge, MA: Harvard University Press.

Barclay, Linda. 2020. "A Dignitarian Approach to Disability: From Moral Status to Social Status." In *Oxford Handbook of Philosophy and Disability*, edited by Adam Cureton and David Wasserman, 432–447. New York: Oxford University Press.

Buss, Sarah. 1999a. "Appearing Respectful: The Moral Significance of Manners." *Ethics* 109(4): 795–826.

Buss, Sarah. 1999b. "Respect for Persons." *Canadian Journal of Philosophy* 29 (4):517–550.

Carter, Ian. 2011. "Respect and the Basis of Equality." *Ethics* 121(3): 538–571.

Cureton, Adam. 2007. "Respecting Disability." *Teaching Philosophy* 30(4): 383–402.

Cureton, Adam. 2012. "Solidarity and Social Moral Rules." *Ethical Theory and Moral Practice* 15(5): 691–706.

Cureton, Adam. 2013a. "A Contractualist Reading of Kant's Proof of the Formula of Humanity." *Kantian Review* 18(3): 363–386.

Cureton, Adam. 2013b. "From Self-Respect to Respect for Others." *Pacific Philosophical Quarterly* 93(4): 166–187.

Cureton, Adam. 2014. "Making Room for Rules." *Philosophical Studies* 172(3): 737–759.

Cureton, Adam. 2016. "Offensive Beneficence." *Journal of the American Philosophical Association* 2(1): 74–90.

Darwall, Stephen. 1977. "Two Kinds of Respect." *Ethics* 88(1): 36–49.

Dillon, Robin. 1992. "Respect and Care: Toward Moral Integration." *Canadian Journal of Philosophy* 22:105–132.

Feinberg, Joel. 1973. "Some Conjectures About the Concept of Respect." *Journal of Social Philosophy* 4: 1–3.

Frankfurt, Harry. 1999. "Equality and Respect." In *Necessity, Volition, and Love*, Harry G. Frankfurt, 146–155. Cambridge: Cambridge University Press.

Hill, Thomas E., Jr. 1991. "Servility and Self-Respect." In *Autonomy and Self-Respect*, Thomas E. Hill, Jr., 4–18. Cambridge, UK: Cambridge University Press.

Hill, Thomas E., Jr. 1992a. "Humanity as an End in Itself." In *Dignity and Practical Reason in Kant's Moral Theory*, Thomas E. Hill, Jr., 38–57. Ithaca, NY: Cornell University Press.

Hill, Thomas E., Jr. 1992b. "The Kingdom of Ends." In *Dignity and Practical Reason in Kant's Moral Theory*, Thomas E. Hill, Jr., 58–66. Ithaca, NY: Cornell University Press.

Hill, Thomas E., Jr. 2000a. "Basic Respect and Cultural Diversity." In *Respect, Pluralism, and Justice: Kantian Perspectives*, Thomas E. Hill, Jr., 59–86. Oxford: Oxford University Press.

Hill, Thomas E., Jr. 2000b. "Must Respect Be Earned?" In *Respect, Pluralism, and Justice: Kantian Perspectives*, Thomas E. Hill, Jr., 87–118. Oxford: Oxford University Press.

Hill, Thomas E., Jr. 2020. "Ideals of Appreciation and Expressions of Respect." In *Oxford Handbook of Philosophy and Disability*, Thomas E. Hill, Jr., Adam Cureton and David Wasserman, 363–379. New York: Oxford University Press.

Holtman, Sarah 2018. "Beneficence and Disability." In *Disability in Practice: Attitudes, Policies, and Relationships*, edited by Adam Cureton and Thomas E. Hill, Jr., 33–49. Oxford: Oxford University Press.

Kant, Immanuel. 1996. *The Metaphysics of Morals*, edited and translated by Mary J. Gregor. New York: Cambridge University Press.

Nagel, Thomas. 1998. "Concealment and Exposure." *Philosophy & Public Affairs* 27 (1): 3–30.

Raz, Joseph. 1999. *Engaging Reasons*. Oxford: Oxford University Press.

Sensen, Oliver. 2018. "Respect for Human Beings with Intellectual Disabilities." In *Disability in Practice: Attitudes, Policies, and Relationships*, edited by Adam Cureton and Thomas E. Hill Jr., 72–89. Oxford: Oxford University Press.

Stohr, Karen. 2018. "Pretending Not to Notice: Respect, Attention, and Disability." In *Disability in Practice: Attitudes, Policies, and Relationships*, edited by Adam Cureton and Thomas E. Hill Jr., 50–71. Oxford: Oxford University Press.

Velleman, J. David. 1999. "Love as a Moral Emotion." *Ethics* 109(2): 338–374.

Vorhaus, John. 2020. "Respect, Identification, and Profound Cognitive Impairment." In *Oxford Handbook of Philosophy and Disability*, edited by Adam Cureton and David Wasserman, 399–415. New York: Oxford University Press.

Williams, Bernard. 1973. "The Idea of Equality." In *Problems of the Self*, edited by Bernard Williams, 230–249. Cambridge, UK: Cambridge University Press.

CHAPTER 23

RESPECT, IDENTIFICATION, AND PROFOUND COGNITIVE IMPAIRMENT

JOHN VORHAUS

INTRODUCTION

IT is a familiar idea that showing respect for someone requires an effort to take account of how she sees the world. And there is more than one way we might do this. Williams suggests that each person is owed an effort at identification (Williams 1973), whereas Rawls remarks that "mutual respect is shown ... in our willingness to see the situation of others from their point of view" (Rawls 1972, 337). I explore these ideas as they apply to people with profound and multiple learning difficulties and disabilities (PMLD), whose condition raises special difficulties in the way of complying with the conduct described here. I examine the ideas of having a point of view and identifying with the person whose point of view it is, and I show how much—and also how little—shared points of view can contribute to a principle of respect that includes people with PMLD.

A word about profound and multiple learning difficulties and disabilities. I follow the latest edition of the *Diagnostic and Statistical Manual of Mental Disorder* (DSM –V; American Psychiatric Association [APA] 2013) in conceiving intellectual disability as impairments of mental abilities that have an impact on adaptive functioning in three domains: conceptual, social, and practical. Profound disability in the social domain is such that "the individual has very limited understanding of symbolic communication ... express[ing] ... desires and emotions largely through nonverbal, non-symbolic communication." And, in the practical domain, the "individual is dependent on others for all aspects of daily physical care, health and safety" (APA 2013, 58, 61). Although IQ is included in an assessment of the level of cognitive impairment—and for persons with a profound cognitive impairment this will be under 40, and for many it will be under 20 (Tassé 2013, 127, 129)—the emphasis is on the impact of impairment on an individual's functioning and her ability to adapt to and undertake everyday tasks.[1]

HAVING A POINT OF VIEW

How is having a point of view related to the idea of showing respect for someone? Dillon remarks:

> Barring certain cases of mental defectiveness, a person is…an individual and human "me": a being who is reflectively conscious of herself and her situation. She lives her life and has certain purposes in living it; and she has a certain understanding of what she does which informs and structures her living.…She has…a particular life of her own that she is interested in living, and she sees herself, and her situation, and the world from the point of view of living that life.
>
> (Dillon 1992, 126)[2]

We are conscious beings, with intentions and purposes, and we see what we are doing in a certain light. This is the reason why no one should be regarded merely as "the surface to which a certain label can be applied," and why we "should try to see the world (including the label) from [their] point of view" (Williams 1973, 236–237).

Some of the capacities referred to here do not apply to all human beings: anencephalic infants do not have minds and are therefore incapable of developing any point of view, and there are other human beings who will never become reflectively self-conscious, or develop a plan of life, or engage in efforts to interpret themselves or the world. However we specify the cognitive requirements for possession of these abilities, some persons with profound cognitive impairments will lack a capacity to form a sense of themselves that even loosely corresponds to Dillon's conception of an individual "me."

McMahan suggests that "respect for a person is closely connected with respect for the autonomous determination of that person's will; therefore, autonomy must be a significant element of the basis of the worth that demands respect" (McMahan 2002, 260). The higher psychological capacities characteristic of persons and necessary for autonomy distinguish us not only from most animals but also from some humans. This includes some people with PMLD who lack autonomy in the sense that they cannot direct their lives in accordance with values that they reflectively endorse; they do not have the "ability to form a picture of [their] whole life (or at least of significant chunks of it) and to act in terms of some overall conception of the life [they wish] to lead" (Nozick 1974, 50). McMahan concludes that the "congenitally severely retarded" fall below the threshold of respect (McMahan 2002, 260), and if autonomy is the basis of the worth that demands respect, then this conclusion looks unavoidable, at least as it applies to some people who fall within this category.[3]

In keeping with her distinctive conception of autonomy, Jaworska suggests that it is the capacity to care that we should concentrate on as a source of respect (Jaworska 2010). Caring in Jaworska's sense requires that some object can serve as a "steady focus of emotional attunement" for a person, such that her emotions and desires are "*about* the object, for example, a caring about Mom" (Jaworska 2010, 378). What is required is less than what is required for rational autonomy or the capacity to make evaluative judgments. It is not necessary that a person should weigh up her options, make rational decisions, or expressly evaluate her cares; rather, her emotional states will be responsive to an object or event in ways that reveal both their importance to her and some rational interconnectedness between the psychological elements that these states are composed of.

Many persons with profound learning difficulties have a capacity to care in the sense supplied here. But, then, so do some high functioning nonhuman animals. If a human and nonhuman being are alike in their capacities to function, including their capacity to care, then we may owe both respect in the sense that requires an effort at identification. This view may indeed warrant our endorsement, although it will be unwelcome to anyone who considers respect as owed exclusively to human beings. But if this latter view is right, we must find a basis for respect in characteristics that are intrinsic to all and only members of the human species.

The more demanding the cognitive elements included in having a point of view, the less likely it is that these will apply to nonhuman animals [4]; but, equally, it becomes less likely that they will apply to all persons with profound cognitive impairments. Even after allowing for underestimation of capacity, the "cases of mental defectiveness" that Dillon refers to will be few or many depending on where we set the cognitive bar, and some human beings will fall below it. It appears to follow either that they are not owed identification respect because there is no point of view to identify with, or, if they are owed respect, possessing a point of view is not a necessary condition of what is owed to them.

WARRANTING RESPECT

Some points of view do not warrant respect, either because they are abhorrent or because they themselves give evidence of lack of self-respect. As to the first, Cranor writes:

> We do not value, morally speaking, the mere fact of persons' having intentions, purposes, and their seeing the world in a certain light. Morally speaking, we value their having good intentions and purposes and their seeing the world from the moral point of view.   (Cranor 1975, 316)

Why respect someone whose point of view we find repugnant? We can appeal to a familiar distinction between appraisal respect and recognition respect: appraisal respect consists in a positive appraisal of persons, whereas recognition respect requires that we take someone seriously in the sense that we weigh appropriately the fact that she is a person when we deliberate about what to do (Darwall 1977, 183–184). The recognition referred to here will be included in any effort at identification, in so far as we are required to acknowledge as persons even those whose views we loathe, and this has implications for how we should act.

The question remains why any such acknowledgment is required, and, if it is, whether the explanation comes to rest on first-order moral principles which are implicitly presupposed by the demand for recognition. In this case, the work of a principle of recognition respect is confined to identifying the class of agents to whom these first-order moral principles apply (Cranor 1983, 108–109). As to the first question, the suggestion offered here is that recognition is owed in virtue of what almost all persons possess, a capacity to develop a point of view that takes the form of seeing the world in a certain light and attaching importance to what she sees there. Suppose that Cranor is right and that recognition respect is a second-order principle; still, as with a principle of identification respect, it serves to pick out the class of human beings to whom respect is owed. This is a valuable function: people with PMLD and other impairments are frequently ignored, rendered invisible, and treated as less than fully human. A requirement of identification directs us to not treat anyone like this, something which does not require a positive appraisal or even the least sympathy with any particular point of view.

Just as we can withhold respect from other people, some people fail to respect themselves; why should we make the effort to see another's point of view, if that view itself gives evidence of a lack of self-respect? It is a mark of oppression that the oppressed do not see their condition for what we take it be; rather, they take it as their oppressors do, or in terms that conform to the norms characteristic of the oppressive system they live under. Some disrespected disabled people remain unaware of their oppressive institutional environment under anything like this description; perhaps they adopt the adaptive and rationalizing strategies of people whose subordination stems from impairment and the institutional impositions to which impairment renders them vulnerable (Goffman 1991; Silvers 1995).

The suggestion is that respect for profoundly disabled people includes the idea of making an effort to see the world from their point of view. But in some cases we are quite uncertain what that view is, and, in others, we may believe it to be incompatible with what respect for its possessor requires. A common strategy at this point is to emphasize the value of autonomous choice, a strategy that extends to people who struggle to form and communicate preferences of their own. We know that, for people with PMLD, pedagogic and technological assistance can increase the scope for autonomous, self-respecting conduct in environments that encourage informed self-assertion over subordination and obedience (Dee et al. 2002). Alternatively, and for people not able to express their own preferences, there is the option of a surrogate or guardian (Silvers and Francis 2009; Nussbaum 2006). We can identify with someone who needs a surrogate to interpret and communicate her point of view to others so long as we first verify that it is *her* point of view, and not that of the surrogate, and not a view whose authorship it is impossible decisively to attribute to one or the other.

Perhaps we know very well what someone's point of view is, but we consider that it gives evidence of a lack of self-respect. We might then take account not only of her actual point of view, but also of a hypothetical point of view, where that is congruent with what we judge as best for her. The idea is that we act in accordance with what we assume she would want were she appraised of information she is now unaware of, or were she free of desires she is unable to resist and which are causing serious harm. There are familiar questions about how some hypothetical (rational/well-informed) point of view is related to how people actually see the world, and that relation should not be so tenuous as to raise a serious doubt as to whether any such attributed view is theirs (Miller and Wertheimer 2010).

Although someone's point of view may give evidence of a lack of self-respect, it does not follow that we cannot show respect for that person in virtue of the effort we make to understand how she experiences the world. And we can have good grounds for attributing a point of view to someone who is no longer capable of forming a view about anything, if we have reliable evidence of her previous beliefs and orientation. But the question remains whether there are some human beings who fall outside the ambit of identification respect because they have always lacked the capacities necessary to develop any views of their own. If the capacity to have, or previously to have had one's own point of view is a necessary condition of identification respect the answer must be, Yes. There is nothing for the act of identification to take as its object, and any attempt to rely on the imaginative efforts of others is not only delusive but carries the risk of exposing human beings to treatment at the hands of people whose imagination has nothing to do with benevolence.

Identifying with Others

The idea we are exploring is that each person is owed an effort at identification. The effort might be thought of as doomed to failure if success takes the form of knowing what it is like for you to experience the world as you do. I may know that you are in extreme pain, since I can see you writhing in agony, but that is not to say that I know what it is like for you to suffer like this. Nor do we always know that someone is suffering if they choose to conceal or disguise their pain: some people with PMLD may not give evidence of even significant discomfort after sitting for long periods in an uncomfortable chair or putting their hands in hot water. Perhaps what is required is not that I should know what it is like for you to have some experience but that I should know what it is like for me to have that experience. However, there may be some distance between these two alternatives. Whereas I might be sure of what it would be like for me to sit in a wheelchair for hours on end, any discrepancy between what I imagine and how it actually is for someone else sat in that chair may go uncorrected if her means of communicating are severely limited or her expressions are limited to the point that even those who know her best are left having to make a "best guess" at what she intends to communicate to them.

People with PMLD present special problems of interpretation, but these are not insuperable. They are related to a general problem, arising for all people with disabilities, that "our aversion to the very idea of being disabled forestalls our understanding the disabled from their perspective" (Silvers 1995, 37). Profoundly disabled people face the prospect of being overlooked or stigmatized, or they may be regarded as "defective" or subhuman. This is in stark contrast to how Eva Feder Kittay sees her daughter, Sesha, who has profound cognitive impairments:

> to be with Sesha is to enter her orbit, to gain a glimpse of the world as she constructs it...A slight upturn of the lip in a profoundly and multiply disabled individual when a favourite caregiver comes along, or a look of joy in response to the scent of a perfume—all these establish personhood.   (Kittay 2005, 568)

When Kittay sees Sesha's face as joyous she sees it in human terms: her facial movements are not regarded as a muscular spasm or something indecipherable, but as included in an expression of emotion, whereas a look in the eye is understood as indicating communicative intent in response to something that gives her pleasure. This is not always as straightforward as Margalit supposes:

> When we see a human face we do not first notice that the lips are curved downward, that the eyebrows are lowered...and then ask how to interpret this face. We see the face as sad just as we see the lip curved downward: not as a result of hypothesis testing and deduction from evidence, but directly.   (Margalit 1996, 94–95)

We do not always see human faces directly. It may have taken some time before Kittay learned to see a slight upturn of the lip as her daughter's expression of joy. Having limited or deteriorating muscular control, some people do not possess the range of facial gestures available to most of the rest of us and an alternative repertoire is developed, one which does not allow for the standard associations between physical expressions and the emotions and thoughts they serve to express. We must then learn to recognize new associations and, in some cases, as these apply to people who are not able to provide any explanatory narrative. Seeing a human face may then involve a protracted process comprising the very activities Margalit deems otiose: hypothesis testing and deduction from evidence (Vorhaus 2006, 320).

I am suggesting that, in order to gain some understanding of Sesha's point of view, it is necessary to learn how to interpret her bodily and communicative repertoire. These are examples of what an effort of identification requires on the part of people who care for profoundly disabled people.

The distinction I have referred to, as between imagining what it is like for you to be in your situation and what it is like for me to be in your situation, may look to be in danger of collapse: in order to imagine what it is like for me to be in your situation I need to grasp your situation, and that includes how you are likely to respond to that. Still, the two exercises are not identical. When I identify with you, in the sense I intend here, we need not suppose that I experience the world as you do. We can acknowledge that we are not in your situation and cannot experience the world exactly as you do, but we recognize that your situation includes your experience of the situation and our response includes an effort to take that seriously. And not as a sadist might, when seeking insight for a malevolent purpose, but as something owed to you, for your sake, not as something undertaken merely to further our own ends.

There is the objection that we do not need to know what it is like to lead your life in order to respect the fact that you have your own life to lead. A Head Teacher of a special school may succeed in creating an environment that encourages respect for children with PMLD, not because she makes much of an effort to identify with anyone, but owing to her knowledge that children with PMLD tend to thrive when offered a safe, nurturing, and affirming place in which to learn. A prison officer may learn to show respect to inmates following his observations of the effects of (dis)respectful behavior toward people locked up in prison, without making any special effort to get to know his charges.

Nevertheless, the effort at identification is not superfluous. Frankfurt writes of lack of respect as consisting in

> the circumstance that some important fact about the person is not properly attended to or is not taken appropriately into account.... The implications of significant features of his life are overlooked or denied. Pertinent aspects of how things are with him are treated as though they had no reality.   (Frankfurt, 1999, 152–153)[5]

It is one thing to treat someone as Petra, the loud and challenging pupil with PMLD, another to treat Petra as the pupil whose loud and challenging behavior is a sign of acute anxiety when the level of noise reaches a certain threshold. One thing to treat someone as an inmate who is aggressive and fractious, another to treat him as an inmate who has a name and whose aggression coincides with a time when he is struggling to come to terms with the fact that his partner has given birth while he remains locked away.[6]

Why should it matter if we fail to make the effort to identify with someone? Frankfurt writes that

> when a person is treated as though significant elements of his life count for nothing, it is natural for him to experience this as in a certain way an assault upon his reality. What is at stake for him, when people act as though he is not what he is, is a kind of self-preservation. It is not his biological survival that is challenged, of course, when his nature is denied. It is the reality of his existence for others, and hence the solidity of his own sense that he is real.   (Frankfurt 1999, 153)

This is a powerful statement of the connection between respect and identification. However, not everyone will respond to lack of respect in the ways Frankfurt suggests. Although for some people their sense of reality may seem under threat, others have a sufficiently robust sense of themselves to experience only the mildest resentment—if that—and certainly nothing approaching the existential crisis described here. The point that different people respond differently to lack of respect applies to profoundly disabled persons, not only because of their variable response to disrespectful behavior, but also because some remain largely unaware of what is withheld, and they will not recognize disrespectful behavior under that description. Of course, by means of their behavior and expressive repertoire, they may yet provide evidence of growing or failing self-belief and confidence according to how respectful or otherwise their environment and interactions generally are (Fitton 1994; Norris 1982; Vorhaus 2006). But for some human beings with profound cognitive impairments the effort at identification will have no impact on them, whether considered from the inside—how they experience their lives—or from the outside—what we observe of their welfare and development. In such cases as these we cannot claim that we are required to make an effort at identification for any reason that appeals to psychological benefit or harm. Once more, we reach the limit of any appeal to identification as a form of respect.[7]

SPECIAL RELATIONS

Not everyone has a point of view that demands identification nor, I will now suggest, is everyone required to make the effort. The requirement is agent-relative—sensitive to the presence and nature of interpersonal relations. Indeed, a skeptic might put the point more strongly than this: that only someone engaged in a close relationship is able to make the effort at identification I am concerned with

> pulling out all the stops for every individual one comes across is not only not humanly possible but may also be inappropriate for many individuals in many situations.... But the inappropriateness of always pulling out the stops for everyone does not mean that it would be either inappropriate or impossible to approach others generally with more constrained, context-sensitive expressions of care respect.
> (Dillon 1992, 130)

This underestimates the problem. It is not that we can pull out all the stops for some, and only some of the stops for others, but that we cannot pull out any stops for large numbers of persons who we either have no contact with or with whom contact does not admit of respectful attention in any sense that allows for identification. If the reply is that our behavior is always subject to constraints, no matter who we brush up against, then that is true in the sense that we can be expected to refrain from behavior that is offensive or contemptuous. And this is not a trivial aspect of respect—but it does not amount to making any effort at identification.[8] Acknowledging this, Dillon remarks:

> I may not care about an individual; I may be altogether unable to identify with her or to forge and sustain a relationship with her; I may never even encounter her in any non-metaphorical sense. But somebody might care for her: she is someone's daughter, friend, or sister; and so she constrains my actions.   (Dillon 1992, 130)

It is true that I may have reason to constrain my behavior toward you because you are someone's daughter, and I should show respect for that relation. But in this case it is not that I identify with you, or your mother, or that I have a reason to identify with either of you; it is the fact of the special tie between you both that acts as a constraint on how I should act.

Margalit draws a distinction between "thick" and "thin" human relations: "thick" relations—what I will call "special" relations—are grounded in such attributes as parent and caregiver, whereas "thin" relations are backed by the attribute of being human (Margalit 2002, 7). Although we have duties toward other human beings just because they are human beings—we should not subject anyone to torture or inhumane treatment—thick or special relations give rise to additional obligations, including a requirement to respect other people in the Frankfurtian sense of paying attention to their individuality.

This is too quick. The effort at identification is not required in virtue of the presence of *any* special relations between people: it does not apply to a prosecuting lawyer, in her cross-examination of the accused, or to a surgeon when performing a caesarean operation, or to the leader of a political party when confronting her opponent. In any case, not everyone has the ability to make the effort called for or to do it successfully: sociopaths are unable to; some people lack the insight, disposition, and fellow-feeling to do it well or often; whereas others manage it effortlessly. A variable capacity to succeed in doing something does not imply a variable capacity to make the effort to succeed. But the variability applies to the effort, too: it is just much harder for some people to make the effort to identify with others than it is for other people. If "ought" implies "can," then any insistence on a requirement to make the effort to identify with others must be seen to be consistent with the facts about the variable human capacity to comply.

Should we allow for a division of labor? If I am one of several people with a responsibility for Chrissie, a child with PMLD, it might be for the best that I, enjoying a close connection with her, should make the effort to identify with her while you attend to other business. But this does not yet show that I am *required* to make the effort nor that you are not. If someone is owed respect, then it is a requirement that it is shown to her; required, not only following an assessment that this is what is best or most convenient, but required—period.[9] And there remains the familiar problem: there may be no one who happens to find it easy to relate to Chrissie or no one to whom she is closely related. Any requirement that is contingent on the presence and details of special relations will leave her unprotected. And this is just one example of how the requirement of identification may lead to omissions on the one hand and bias and favoritism on the other. We might be tempted to give preferential treatment to someone we happen to get on with over someone else who is more in need; we might give more attention to someone who sheds tears over someone who remains stony-faced, although both equally warrant our attention; and we may be inclined to identify with those who look most like us and not with persons whose distinctive facial features and cognitive impairments are "foreign" to us.[10]

One response is that the morally untoward contingencies noted here are not a necessary consequence of any reliance on identification; they are the product of failures and deficiencies whose source lies elsewhere—in the bias and ignorance that stems from ideology, poor education, and social division. In a less divided society, with better education, and a culture that discourages any form of prejudice that has the effect of stigmatizing and dehumanizing other people, the requirement of identification would yield effects more aligned with the requirements of morality.

The measured reply will be that we are a long way from what is envisaged; the impatient reply, that what is envisaged is a fantasy. Neither response requires that we give up on identification. We are a long way from a just society, and global justice may never be realized, but that is not a reason to give up on justice as a social ideal. The requirement of identification is one element of what we ought to aim at in relations with other people that are marked by respect. We may often not do what we ought to do, or, when we do, the effects may not be uniformly good, but if we fail to make the effort, we should look at what is wrong with the world, and ourselves, before impugning the requirement.

This is to offer a defence of an ideal in an imperfect world. The question remains whether the imperfections apply only to the world and not to the ideal. We cannot identify with everyone. Our efforts are necessarily confined to a domain that includes a fraction of those to whom we are specially related and other persons we encounter, or have some knowledge of, who have a claim on our attention in a sense that requires us to attend to their individuality. Since any effort at identification is sensitive to the presence and details of our relations with others, we need to identify those among our relations that bring with them a requirement of identification and explain how they function so as to activate the requirement. And we still have to explain why the requirement belongs to the domain of morality and not only to the demands of personal life; that is, why it is not only a good thing to identify with someone, but something that is required of us and owed to other people.

IDENTIFYING WITH FELLOW
HUMAN BEINGS

The appeal to identification as an element of respect does not extend to all human beings. Some humans have no point of view to identify with, and they and others may register nothing when we fail to show the respect we owe people in virtue of their individuality. Perhaps McMahan is right to conclude that these people fall below the threshold of respect (McMahan 2002, 260). We should, of course, respect those to whom they are specially related, including how they choose to care for their dependent charges, who may be well loved and cared for irrespective of any threshold. In this case, the practical implications of McMahan's conclusion may prove to be slight. On the other hand, they might not, and anyway, is this the right conclusion?

To begin with the practical implications: there are consequentialist reasons for retaining the principle that we ought always to make the effort to treat people with respect even if they lack the capacities that provide the basis for the worth that warrants respect. Should we decide as a matter of policy not to grant the respect to these people that we owe to others, they may become vulnerable to forms of neglect or ill-treatment that fall foul of the requirements owed to people whether or not they have the capacity we deem them to lack. Or there may be less political urgency behind any effort to provide the assistance required to sustain or improve the prospects of their enjoying a good life. A decision in principle to regard a small number of people as falling below the threshold of respect may in practice yield consequences that the principle of itself would not admit, but which we are politically powerless to prevent (Nussbaum 2006, 190). This may yet be a decisive consideration, but it makes no special mention of identification, unless we can sustain the argument that requirements of respect are more likely to be met under a prevailing expectation that we ought always to make the effort to identify with others, even while we know there are some human beings in relation to whom the effort is unlikely or certain not to prove fruitful.

What about the principle itself: is there an interpretation of identification respect that applies to all human beings? Not if we insist on an interpretation under which respect is owed in virtue of having a point of view on the world. Not everyone has the requisite point of view, and not everyone is required to make the effort. If we are required to respect all human beings, in the sense of making an effort to identify with someone, then it is the fact that she is a human being that provides the source of the reason for respect, and what we are identifying with is her, in a sense that does not require that we look at the world as we assume she does. Mulhall writes of severely disabled people as "our fellow human beings, embodied creatures who will come to share, or have already shared, in our common life, or whose inability to do so is a result of the shocks and ills to which all human flesh and blood is heir—because there but for the grace of God go I" (Mulhall, 2002, 18). This is to suggest that we can identify with another human being in so far as we share a common human fate, and, in so far as her life includes shocks and ills that we have so far evaded, we identify with her by means of the thought that "her fate could have been mine." However, the coherence of this last thought is questionable (McMahan 2005, 361–369), and should it prove unavailable as a ground of respect we are left with the significance of the fact that someone is a human being, belonging to the same species as we do. These thoughts have received prominent endorsements (Nozick 1997, 308; Scanlon 2000, 185), although they come up against the charge of speciecism if used as a basis for asserting that human beings have a higher moral status than nonhuman animals irrespective of individual capability and levels of functioning (McMahan 2005; Singer and Kuhse 2001).

Williams writes of an ethical concept which includes the idea of a basic loyalty toward and identification with other human beings (Williams 2006, 150), and Wiggins refers to a disposition to "solidarity" among human beings, a disposition that lies, as he puts it, at the "root of the ethical" (Wiggins 2008). The idea is that we are disposed to identify with other human beings, not as a result of assessing each individual on her merits, but in virtue of recognizing someone as one of our own kind, and the disposition to identify with our own kind conditions our ethical orientation toward human and other creatures. A lot rests here on how we understand the idea of "our own kind." It might be taken to refer to those beings who are "one of us," but this same idea is used by racists when asserting of members of some group that they do not "belong" and their ways and lives are "foreign," usually meaning to imply that they are owed less—and usually a lot less—than are members of the "in" group. It therefore needs to be shown how we can appeal to the fact that someone is one of us, as a basis for respect, without leaving room for the same idea to function so as to legitimize prejudice. And there is, in any case, a residual question whether a human being is one of our own kind merely in virtue of belonging to the human species and irrespective of capacity and levels of functioning (McMahan 2005).

On a related view, we might deny that any human being falls below some threshold of respect, not because we deny that there are individuals who do not possess the capacities that provide the basis for respect, but because respect is owed to people in virtue of belonging to a human community, irrespective of their capacity to see the world from one point of view or another. Members of a school for children with PMLD may determine that all children are owed equal respect, regardless of the level of impairment, because that is what helps to define the school as the kind of community it aspires to be. This is the point that respect may be the product of a decision that characterizes the values and life of a community. Of course, in some communities, the decision might be rather different: to exclude or otherwise mistreat people with disabilities, and this is a serious objection.[11] In any case, there is no appeal to "identification"; rather, in appealing to some conception of "one of us," we are implicitly appealing to the importance of belonging to a human community. It is not clear whether any such appeal is defensible. If it is defensible, we should ask whether it is a consideration of this kind, after all, that is doing the explanatory work; that the fundamental reason why we should make an effort to identify with others is that they are our fellow human beings or that they belong to our community. The question then arises whether anything remains for the idea of identifying with someone's point of view as contributing to a principle of respect, and, if so, what the status of someone as having a point of view requires, in the way of respect, that is different from what is required in virtue of her status as an autonomous agent.

Perhaps, and after all, we should say that the effort at identification belongs to another subject: the subject of love (Gaita 1998, 17–28), or loving attention (Bagnoli 2003)—what Murdoch calls the "just and loving gaze," "seeing the other as she really is" (Murdoch 1970, 34, 40). Even supposing that love is included in an account of morality, we might be reluctant to think of it as any part of the subject of respect.[12] There is a connection, nevertheless: human beings are more likely to enter into loving relations in an environment in which respect is owed to everyone, without exception, as compared to environments in which some persons fall below a threshold of respect and are consequently vulnerable to indifference and worse. It remains another matter, however, whether this calls for any effort to identify with other people.

Extending the Argument

I have discussed a number of problems that remain to be solved in any account of identification as integral to respect for persons. Where does this leave us?

Among the possible solutions canvassed here is a response that appeals to the consequences of excluding persons with profound impairments from the demands of respect, leaving them vulnerable to treatment that we have a duty to prevent, a duty we are liable to conform to only if required to show respect to this group of people in just the same way as we are required to show respect to anyone else. The consequentialist argument has force, particularly once we take account of the heavy-handedness of policy and the vicissitudes of politics. But the argument also implicitly concedes that some people with profound cognitive impairments do not have the characteristics that would otherwise warrant respect, and we may not want to make any such concession. One alternative is suggested by Kant's view of autonomy of the will, as a capacity that may not be fully developed and realized, as with infants and young children, but which, nevertheless, suffices for dignity and the respect owed to any being who possesses it (Kant 2007, 127–128, 268–269, 328–330; Vigilantius 2001, 670–671). In keeping with an emphasis on the existence of a capacity, as distinct from its exercise, we might then advance the non-consequentialist claim that respect is owed to people who have the potential for developing a point of view but whose capacity remains latent or underdeveloped. A Kantian approach to respect for persons with PMLD warrants a long discussion in its own right.

There are people who lack any capacity for acquiring a view on the world, in the sense that they do not and never will have the level of cognitive functioning that would support the requisite levels of consciousness. If respect is owed to these people, too, we might consider the claim that it is owed to them because, as human beings, they are members of a species whose characteristic levels of functioning *will* support the requisite levels of consciousness or that we are warranted in treating such people as if they have the requisite capacity, although they do not, because that is what is entailed by other duties owed to all persons—treating people humanely and with dignity for example. These are examples of nonconsequentialist attempts to encompass people who lack any point of view on the world within the community of persons who possess a moral status that includes the requirements of respect.

It is by no means certain that the approaches mentioned here can succeed in conferring on all human beings without exception a moral status that demands respect. There are more alternatives, and I will end by mentioning two; these allow that identification is related to respect without supposing that this is accounted for by the capacity to form a point of view, at least in anything like the terms in which this capacity has been considered here.

The first alternative is consistent with the view that self-awareness is a ground of respect, but it denies that what matters for the moral status associated with personhood is *reflective* self-awareness; what matters, rather, is pre-reflective awareness. Reflective self-awareness treats awareness as something added to an act of experience, whereas pre-reflective awareness is built into the act of experience itself so that "in any conscious experience there is a pre-reflective awareness of the 'I' who has the experience" (Rowlands 2016, 15). This draws attention to the fact that there are conceptual as well as epistemic questions about how we should construe a point of view, and it raises the possibility that there is a state of being aware of oneself which does not entail having a point of view but which at the same time suffices to command an attitude of respect.

The second approach refuses to accept an assumption at work throughout much of this chapter and which is also characteristic of moral individualism: that we should look to any one or more of the capacities intrinsic to individuals as the basis of respect. Rather, in keeping with a Wittgensteinian tradition that includes Mulhall (2002) and Crary (2010), the recognition that a creature is a human being is thought of as having moral significance in its own right; at least, it does so in the context of a nonbiological understanding of "human being" and an ethical orientation internal to many ordinary modes of thought about the human species. The central claim is that when we bring human beings into focus in pursuit of an ethical understanding, this is *already* to see them as meriting certain attitudes and forms of treatment (Crary 2010, 23, 34).[13] On this approach we can concede that some human beings lack a point of view with which we identify, but we deny that this has any bearing on their fundamental moral status, including whether they are owed respect. This rather suggests that the whole approach adopted in this chapter is wrong-headed, and it might be. But, if it is, we would have to give up both one very ordinary mode of talking about respect for human beings, in the sense of making an effort to see the world from their point of view, and a long tradition of ethical enquiry that considers as fundamentally important the fact that human beings are creatures with their own understanding of the world and their place in it.[14]

NOTES

1. For a discussion of related conceptual and theoretical questions, see Vorhaus (2016).
2. Compare with Nozick (1981, 452–457), whose account Dillon refers to.
3. On some views respect is owed to people in virtue of possessing certain capacities, irrespective of whether these capacities are developed or exercised; see later discussion of this point.
4. Some animals may meet these more demanding conditions, as, perhaps, in the case of Koko, a gorilla who made fluent use of American Sign Language; see Jaworska (2010, 388–389).
5. Compare with Blum's emphasis on moral-perceptual capacities and our capacity to notice or ignore moral features of the persons and situations we confront (Blum 1991).
6. Adam Cureton (personal correspondence) makes the point that the effort at identification may not always be welcome, perhaps because it is thought to be intrusive or invasive of privacy. This is one of several considerations that place limits on how far any act of identification should extend, but it is another and stronger claim that any such consideration might render the effort of identification—however modestly enacted—as entirely inappropriate.

7. Unless, that is, respect is a basic moral requirement that does not require justification in terms of *any* effects, psychological or otherwise. I return to this view in the final section.

8. Adam Cureton suggests the possibility of a negative formulation of identification respect, namely: do not, in principle, exclude the prospect of identifying with anyone. This might allow for some discretion as to when and to what extent we identify with any one person. I am not convinced that there is any such coherent formulation of identification respect which, at the same time, helps to get round the objection leveled in the text.

9. This point holds if the requirement to respect someone is a perfect duty—something we are absolutely and always required to perform; but it may be an imperfect duty, in the sense that, although we are required to make it one of our goals that we should respect people, we have some discretion as to when and how we do this, so long as whatever we do is consistent with being a respectful person. Or respect may include both a perfect negative duty—some forms of conduct are absolutely ruled out—and an imperfect positive duty—there are some forms of conduct that we should try our best to achieve. I owe these points to Adam Cureton, and they require more discussion than I can provide here.

10. Identifying with someone is not the same as empathizing with her, but some of what I have said about identification applies equally to empathy (cf Coplan and Goldie 2011). The core idea of empathy is as a "kind of vicarious emotion…feeling what one takes another person to be feeling" (Prinz 2011, 212). Empathy has a role in caring relations: when caring for someone with PMLD, an ability to empathize with her will help us to "understand her and her world in her own terms" (Dillon 1992, 126), to pay "special regard for the particular person in a particular situation" (Noddings 2003, 24) and to show a "responsiveness to other persons in their wholeness and their particularity" (Friedman 1987, 105). However, there is evidence pointing to significant limitations with empathy as a basis of moral concern, and the summary charge sheet reads as follows: "It is not especially motivating, and it is so vulnerable to bias and selectivity that it fails to provide a broad umbrella of moral concern. A morality based on empathy would lead to preferential treatment and grotesque crimes of omission" (Prinz 2011, 227). For skepticism toward empathy and imaginative identification as a resource in ethics, see also Holton and Langton (1999, 209–232).

11. Including someone in our community may not be the optional decision I imply that it is, but, rather, something required or suggested by the norms characteristic of a moral orientation we consider as authoritative. This is related to the view that any assessment of the worth of human beings reflects both moral and empirical judgments and that the first are not simply a function of, but are in significant ways independent of the second. However, even were something like this view correct it would not show that we can dispense with empirical judgment altogether, nor, therefore, that we can exclude facts associated with profound impairment as having a bearing on the moral status of human beings, even if these facts do not alone provide the basis for determining that status.

12. But see Bagnoli (2003) for an alternative view.

13. Crary (2010); see also Diamond (1978) and Mulhall (2002).

14. I am grateful to Adam Cureton and David Wasserman for their many insightful comments on an earlier draft of this chapter.

REFERENCES

American Psychiatric Association. 2013. *Diagnostic and Statistical Manual of Mental Disorders.* Fifth Edition. Arlington, VA: American Psychiatric Association.

Bagnoli, Carla. 2003. "Respect and Loving Attention." *Canadian Journal of Philosophy* 33(4): 483–516.

Blum, Lawrence. 1991. "Moral Perception and Particularity." *Ethics* 101(4): 701–725.

Coplan, Amy, and Peter Goldie. 2011. *Empathy: Philosophical and Psychological Perspectives.* Oxford: Oxford University Press.

Cranor, Carl. 1975. "Toward a Theory of Respect for Persons." *American Philosophical Quarterly* 12(4): 309–319.

Cranor, Carl. 1983. "On Respecting Human Beings as Persons." *Journal of Value Inquiry* 17(2): 103–117.

Crary, Alice. 2010. "Minding What Already Matters: A Critique of Moral Individualism." *Philosophical Topics* 38(1): 17–49.

Darwall, Stephen. 1977. "Two Kinds of Respect." *Ethics* 88(1): 181–197.

Dee, Lesley, Richard Byers, Helen Hayhoe, and Liz Maudslay. 2002. *Enhancing Quality of Life: Facilitating Transitions for People with Profound and Complex Learning Difficulties: A Literature Review.* London/Cambridge: Skill/Cambridge University Press.

Diamond, Cora. 1978. "Eating Meat and Eating People." *Philosophy* 53(206): 465–479.

Dillon, Robin. 1992. "Respect and Care: Toward Moral Integration." *Canadian Journal of Philosophy* 22(1): 105–132.

Fitton, Pat. 1994. *Listen To Me.* London: Jessica Kingsley Publishers.

Frankfurt, Harry. 1999. "Equality and Respect." In *Necessity, Volition and Love*, edited by Harry Frankfurt, 146–154. Cambridge: Cambridge University Press.

Friedman, Marilyn. 1987. "Beyond Caring: The De-Moralization of Gender." *Canadian Journal of Philosophy* 17(supp.): 87–110.

Gaita, Raymond. 1998. *A Common Humanity.* London: Routledge.

Goffman, Erving. 1991. *Asylums*, Harmondsworth: Penguin Books.

Holton, Richard, and Rae Langton. 1999. "Empathy and Animal Ethics." In *Singer and His Critics*, edited by Dale Jamieson, 209–232. Oxford: Blackwell.

Jaworska, Agnieszka. 2010. "Caring and Full Moral Standing Redux." In *Cognitive Disability and Its Challenge to Moral Philosophy*, edited by Eva Feder Kittay and Licia Carlson, 369–392. Oxford: Wiley-Blackwell.

Kant, Immanuel. 2007. "Anthropology from a Pragmatic Point of View." In *Anthropology, History, and Education*, edited by Gunter Zöller and Robert B. Louden, 227–429. Cambridge: Cambridge University Press.

Kittay, Eva Feder. 2005. "At the Margins of Moral Personhood." *Ethics* 116(1): 100–131.

Margalit, Avishai. 1996. *The Decent Society.* Cambridge, MA: Harvard University Press.

Margalit, Avishai. 2002. *The Ethics of Memory.* Cambridge, MA: Harvard University Press.

McMahan, Jeff. 2002. *The Ethics of Killing.* Oxford: Oxford University Press.

McMahan, Jeff. 2005. "Our Fellow Creatures." *The Journal of Ethics* 9(3–4): 353–380.

Miller, Franklin, and Alan Wertheimer (eds.). 2010. *The Ethics of Consent.* New York: Oxford University Press.

Mulhall, Stephen. 2002. "Fearful Thoughts." *London Review of Books* 24(16): 16–18.

Murdoch, Iris. 1970. *The Sovereignty of Good.* London: Routledge and Kegan Paul.

Noddings, Nel. 2003. *Caring: A Feminine Approach to Ethics and Moral Education* (2nd ed.). Berkeley: University of California Press.

Norris, David. 1982. *Profound Mental Handicap.* Tunbridge Wells, UK: Ostello Educational.

Nozick, Robert. 1974. *Anarchy, State and Utopia.* New York: Basic Books.

Nozick, Robert. 1981. *Philosophical Explanations.* Oxford: Clarendon Press.

Nozick, Robert. 1997. "Do Animals Have Rights?" In *Socratic Puzzles*, 305–310, edited by Robert Nozick. Cambridge MA: Harvard University Press.

Nussbaum, Martha. 2006. *Frontiers of Justice: Disability, Nationality, Species Membership.* Cambridge, MA: Harvard University Press.

Prinz, Jesse. 2011. "Is Empathy Necessary for Morality?" In *Empathy: Philosophical and Psychological Perspectives,* edited by Amy Coplan and Peter Goldie, 211–229. Oxford: Oxford University Press.

Rawls, John. 1972. *A Theory of Justice.* Oxford: Oxford University Press.

Rowlands, Mark. 2016. "Are Animals Persons?" In *Animal Sentience* (10: 1): 1–18.

Scanlon, Tim. 2000. *What We Owe to Each Other.* Harvard: Harvard University Press.

Silvers, Anita. 1995. "Reconciling Equality to Difference: Caring (F)or Justice for People with Disabilities." *Hypatia* 10(1): 30–55.

Silvers, Anita, and Leslie Francis. 2009. "Thinking About the Good: Reconfiguring Liberal Metaphysics (or Not) for People with Cognitive Disabilities." *Metaphilosophy* 40(3–4): 475–498.

Singer, Peter, and Helga Kuhse. 2001. "Individuals, Humans and Persons: The Issue of Moral Status." In *Unsanctifying Human Life: Essays on Ethics,* edited by Helga Kuhse, 188–198. Oxford: Blackwell.

Tassé, Mark, Ruth Luckasson, and Margaret Nygren. 2013. "AAIDD Proposed Recommendations for *ICD-11* and the Condition Previously Known as Mental Retardation." *Intellectual and Developmental Disabilities* 51: 127–131.

Vigilantius, Johann Friedrich. 2001. "Kant on the Metaphysics of Morals: Vigilantius's Lecture Notes." In *Lectures on Ethics,* edited by Peter Heath and Jerome Schneewind, 249–452. Cambridge: Cambridge University Press.

Vorhaus, John. 2006. "Respecting Profoundly Disabled Learners." *Journal of Philosophy of Education* 40(3): 313–328.

Vorhaus, John. 2016. *Giving Voice to Profound Disability: Dignity, Dependence and Human Capabilities.* London: Routledge.

Wiggins, David. 2008. *Solidary and the Root of the Ethical.* Department of Philosophy. Lawrence: University of Kansas.

Williams, Bernard. 1973. "The Idea of Equality." In *Problems of the Self,* 230–249, edited by Bernard Williams. Cambridge: Cambridge University Press.

Williams, Bernard. 2006. "The Human Prejudice." In *Philosophy as a Humanistic Discipline,* edited by Bernard Williams, 135–154. Princeton, NJ: Princeton University Press.

CHAPTER 24

CARE AND DISABILITY: FRIENDS OR FOES

EVA FEDER KITTAY

THE QUARREL BETWEEN CARE ETHICS AND DISABILITY THEORISTS AND ACTIVISTS

PROPONENTS of constructivist conceptions of disability, especially when they espouse a strong version of the social model of disability, are committed to the claim that what is properly called disability is primarily a function of social and political conditions as these pertain to what Barnes (2016) has called "minority bodies." The minority body that Barnes designates has a minority status, not vis-à-vis a racial or ethnic category, but relative to the human race. The emancipatory thrust of this body of work has leaned heavily on rights: human rights, civil rights, and political rights. Disability theorists have attempted to decouple disability from inherent disadvantage and so remove the stigma of dependence and care. They have worked to allow disabled people to live "independently" and to counter the view of disabled people as incompetent, pitiful, and burdens on others. They have decried what they view as the "social construction" of dependency for people with disabilities. Writers such as Michael Oliver have maintained that dependency itself is central to the fact that disability is experienced "as a particular kind of social problem" (Oliver, 1989, 8).[1]

Positing the goal as the full integration of people with such minority bodies into the daily, social, and political lives of the majority, this critical theory primarily stands in contrast to medical approaches to disability, approaches that locate the "dis" of disability not in the sociopolitical domain but in the body itself. This disabled body requires fixing to restore normalcy or typicality—to whatever extent possible. To the extent that medicine falls short, the idea is to sustain the body, cause it less pain and suffering and for the rest, hand it over to caretakers.

Care then, appears to be the very antithesis to the emancipatory goal of full rights, participation and independence demanded of those who have dignity. On one view our dignity gives us each an equal claim to human rights. And in turn, our inherent dignity as beings who can fashion and pursue our own good is affirmed by the possession of these rights. The resort to care appears to erode that dignity.

Proponents of an ethic of care, on the other hand, have attempted to rehabilitate and revalue a concept that too often carries with it a saccharine sentimentality and a stigmatizing paternalism. They have insisted on the need to recognize and accept certain sorts of dependencies, claiming that all human life is steeped in dependency—some good, some bad, and some neither. They have attempted to unmask independence as a fiction and a myth that is overvalued to the detriment of the vulnerable and disenfranchised. Independence, for all its vaunted value, they have pointed out, can be a source of isolation; dependence, despite all the negativity associated with it, underscores our connectedness. They do not view care as diminishing dignity but as making dignity realizable for those who need care. They elevate care as a value equal to (if not still more fundamental) than rights.

Is the antipathy of disability activists and theorists to care warranted? Does an ethic of care take full account of the negative valence that disability theorists and activists assign to care? Is the conflict inherent? The claim in this essay is that care theory and disability theory need each other. Care theory needs disability theory to help it find a sense of care which is not merely descriptive but genuinely normative—care *as it should be*. Disability theory needs care theory because, properly construed, it can provide the basis for dignity for minority bodies—bodies that even with far better accommodations sometimes still will be functionally ill-fitted to the physical and social world we inhabit.

The theoretical perspectives we adopt often (and perhaps inevitably) are a function of the position we occupy. Those who are disabled scholars and activists can speak for themselves, and some of the most vocal have argued that what disabled people need is their full measure of civil rights. My perspective on disability comes from my location as a (temporarily) able-bodied mother of a disabled person: my daughter. I have written a great deal about Sesha, a beautiful woman, now forty-nine years old. Sesha is lovely—patient, sociable, incredibly sweet but strong willed in her own way. She loves her life. She takes great pleasure in the things that move her: the people she loves, her food, and above all her music. While disability scholars who can speak for themselves demand "nothing about us without us," my daughter cannot speak for herself because she cannot speak. Not only does she have no expressive language, but she also cannot walk or toilet herself (or really do any self-care) independently. Disability may be socially constructed in many ways. But Sesha's disability will not go away no matter how many supports and accommodations we put into place. She needs care—lots of it—merely to survive from day to day. From my perspective of a mother and carer of a person with such disabling conditions, care is central to my understanding of disability. As a philosopher interested in our moral lives, an ethic of care has been a theoretical perch from which to think about disability. It is from this same post that I have formulated the belief that working in unison, these two areas of inquiry and activism can help fashion an ethical theory that is truer to the human condition than traditional theories, which have rarely acknowledged the need for care or the presence of disabled lives.

The contestation over terms and values of disability theory and care ethics may be overstated. The rights discourse favored by disability scholars and advocates, especially when focused on negative rights of liberty from interference, generally presupposes agents who are independent, fully functioning, and rational: that is, those who can make rights claims on each other. But the rights included in lists of "human rights" need not be seen as the converse of care. Rights such as the right to food, shelter, and affinitive relations are often realized only through the caring work of others. Fully dependent human beings, such as my own daughter, realize their right to food only if there are caring others who provide food and assist with feeding. An adult quadriplegic can realize his rights to mobility, employment, and even participation in political life only if he is assisted with his personal care attendant. Since we all experience periods in our lives when we are dependent on the care of others, our ability to claim rights is similarly dependent on the care of others.

To the extent that the lives of people with disabilities are especially precarious with respect to social systems' and the body's shortcomings, they may be more dependent on care for more of their lives than those who are not disabled. But at the same time, whether or not we currently have a disability, none of us can avoid dependency, and all our lives are precarious; all of us need care at some point; and we all need to know that we can be cared for when we need care.

The Stigma of Dependence and the Illusion of Independence

While people with disability need to acknowledge the importance of care and the limits of independence, care ethicists need to acknowledge the possible damage and disadvantage in dependence and the ways in which care can be infantilizing. I propose that what we need is a clear-eyed view of dependence and independence alike, and we need an ethic of care that disability activists and scholars can embrace.

A Clear-Eyed View of Dependency

Seeing dependency writ large, through the extended and extreme dependency of my daughter, I have come to understand that while much dependency is socially constructed (Barton 1989; Davis 2007; Fraser and Gordon 1994b; Oliver 1989), independence is no less socially constructed (Fine and Glendinning 2005; Fineman

1995; Kittay 1996, 1999, 2015). Moreover, Sesha's dependency has not been merely a burden or a problem; it has been the occasion for a particular sort of interaction and a particular sort of closeness. This extreme dependency can shed light on the dependency we all experience at some time in our life.

If we step back, we well might ask why humans, who belong to a thoroughly social species, so despise dependence. Dependence on others allows for needed care, knowledge, culture, technology, and political, social and economic goods—the sine qua non of human life in any era. A reliance on government services (pejoratively called "welfare dependency" in the United States) (Fraser and Gordon 1994a; Marshall 1973) counts as a primary advantage of a modern, relatively well-ordered state. We might as well decry our dependence on air.

Senator Patrick Moynihan, a rather revered liberal, spoke of dependency as "an incomplete state in life: normal in the child, abnormal in the adult." He wrote: "In a world where completed men and women stand on their own feet, persons who are dependent—as the buried imagery of the word denotes—hang" (Moynihan 1973, 17). The sense of dangling on a thread, of being at another's mercy, of a noose about to tighten, is what frightens us so at the thought of dependence, and no matter how forcefully we argue that dependence is inevitable and universal, unless we can address these worries, we will fail to move beyond the stigma and the terror. What then are these concerns?

When one is dependent, one cannot meet important needs and wants oneself. We need others. But they then have the power to extend or withhold their assistance, and with this power comes the ability to dominate the dependent. Furthermore, a willing carer may find herself incapable of providing the needed care because the provisioner on whom she must depend has not discharged her responsibilities. A willing provisioner may fail to provide, because the others on whom she depends have failed her. What we see here is that dependencies can be (and usually are) nested in other dependent relations.

This nesting or linking of dependencies and interdependencies allow societies to function and be well ordered. But the failures also mean that the dependent may be left with needs, wants, and desires that are not addressed. In an asymmetrical relationship such as dependency relations, we are secure only as long as the other is able and chooses to provide for us and to care about what we care about, which we can call (somewhat bending common use) our cares. Moreover, the asymmetry leaves us with a debt of gratitude that we may be unable to repay, or resentful in having to repay. Not only do we remain vulnerable, but the sense that we cannot repay a debt of gratitude gnaws at our pride and sense of equal worth, and our distrust of the one who has power over us may fuel the resentful feelings of owing the other something.[2]

Another exceedingly difficult feature of dependency is that those things we most care about, which we most want or need, are the things that make us more vulnerable. We can avoid much of this vulnerability, but it comes at the cost of not caring about things—things that make life possible and worth living. The same can be said for the people we depend on. The thicker dependency relationships are, the more value they bring into our lives—value that goes well beyond the meeting of needs. But these relationships are also the most fraught because losing them is losing so much, and it is the person with the greater power in the inevitably asymmetric relationship of dependency who gets to decide whether the relationship remains intact. Again, the dependency makes us powerless in the face of something we really value. There is indeed much about dependency that is to be feared.

There are, moreover, historical, ideological, and structural reasons why we so often refuse to acknowledge our dependence. Contemporary philosophers Nancy Fraser and historian Linda Gordon (Fraser and Gordon 1994b) identify different "registers" of dependency and remind us that while independence was once a status reserved for elites who could command the services of others (310), it only later became a status assumed by the many. Today especially, dependency is considered a characterological flaw. Yet in their useful "genealogy" Fraser and Gordon bypass situations in which dependence on others is tied to inevitable biologically based constraints that reduce our ability to care for ourselves: those at the beginning and end of life, throughout life when we are injured, ill, or too frail, and whenever we are without important needed capacities. These are inevitable human dependences. While there are some sorts of inevitability we dread, such as death, most inevitable conditions we accept and meet with resilience. The need for food is inevitable, but we accept it as a condition of our lives. More interesting still, this inevitable need becomes the site of cultural identity, family warmth, artistry, and sociality. Dependence in this sense may not always be palatable. But neither must it always be undesirable. It is part of any human life lived intertwined with others.

The paradigm of the inevitable dependent is the child. Adults who are dependent are infantilized or viewed as incompetent, asexual, "cute," "in their second childhood," and presumed to be proper objects of scorn or paternalistic concern. We see adults in a dependent state and are reminded of our own infantile vulnerability. But beyond this emotional terror there is a conceptual error at play. The mistake is related to one in which we attribute to all members of a class the characteristics of the paradigm. Robins are paradigmatic birds, and penguins are also birds. Yet it would be a serious mistake to treat a penguin as if it were our red-breasted friend. Even features that the two species share can have different roles in the lives of the two birds. Both robins and penguins need their wings for mobility, but those of the robin are as useless in water as the penguin's wings are in air. Infants, people like my daughter, and more advanced Alzheimer's patients are dependent on others to be fed; however, what they eat, appropriate ways to feed them, and their response to being fed are as different as wings on robins and penguins.

Being treated with dignity, whatever else it is, is being treated in a way that we can remain recognizable to ourselves and those who love us. If we are to treat people with disabilities and people who are dependent in different ways with equal dignity then presuming an eighty-year-old woman is an infant offends against dignity because it fails to accord with both the woman's subjective sense of who she is and the objective facts of the life she has lived. We fail to recognize and respect her. We treat her as lesser and view her as undeserving of equal dignity. This is the danger that takes hold in our imaginings about being dependent. This conceptual error is comparable to gender or racial stereotyping.

A Clear-Eyed View of Independence

To contest the image of the disabled person as an infantilized object of paternalistic concern, disability scholars and activists have offered a counter-narrative (Lindemann 2001): With the appropriate accommodations and personal assistants who would be under their direction, disabled people could live independently. Judy Heumann, an early American champion of "independent living," promotes independence as "a mind process not contingent upon a normal body" (Heumann 1977). The counter-narrative depends on a shift from an understanding of independence as self-sufficiency to one of independence as self-determination (Young 2002, 45) and is exemplified in the "Independent Living Movement" (Heumann 1977, Zola 1988), the Americans with Disabilities Act (101st Congress 1990) and the Individuals with Disabilities Education Improvement Act (2004). Taking their cue from other civil rights movements, the British Council of Disabled People (BCODP) wrote:

> [H]owever good passivity and the creation of dependency may be for the careers of service providers, it is bad news for disabled people and the public purse. It is a viewpoint which meets with strong resistance in our organization
> (BCODP 1987, Sect 3.1, 5).

Sorting out the different senses of independence promoted by ILM has not always been easy, even for the disabled individual himself. Medical sociologist and disability rights activist Irving Zola writes that getting to some place under his "own steam" left him physically spent when he arrived, and so less able to perform the task that was important to him. Instead, he discovered, the independence to which he aspired was "the quality of life that [he]... could live *with help*." (Emphasis mine, De Jong (1983, 15), Zola (1988).

The counter-narrative redefined independence as including "the vast networks of assistance and provision that make modern life possible" (Davis 2007, 4). Then, as literary and disability scholar Lennard Davis, says "the seeming state of exception of disability turns out to be the unexceptional state of existence" (Davis 2007, 4). While Davis's attempt to normalize the assistance needed for "independence" is commendable, I believe that there is still more to be said for altogether unmasking the fiction of independence and self-reliance. As long as we maintain the fiction, those who are most disadvantaged when dependency needs go unmet will remain marginal members of society; public access to care and assistance will remain miserly; and the full participation and integration of people with disabilities will be hampered. Beyond this, the applicability of "independent living" may be limited. While the BCODP derides the idea that disabled people need to be "looked after," some people with disabilities and frailties do indeed require looking after. Surely, we should give all people as much self-determination and control over their lives as possible. But some impairments affect the capacity for self-determination, just as some impairments affect mobility or sensory perception.

Another problem with arguments for independence is that they trade on the belief that fewer public expenditures are needed when disabled people are independent: that independent living is less costly than residential placement, and that productive disabled people will replenish public coffers. The arguments strategically counter the image of disabled people as "burdens" on society. Unfortunately, they also feed the sentiment that the public should not have to be responsible for dependents who cannot pay their own way. Not only does this view disadvantage those least able to fend for themselves, shifting the cost and care to struggling families, but it also is liable to hurt those whose ability to be self-determining requires increased, not reduced, expenditures. Relatedly, arguments that bind independence to productivity are useful insofar as most people desire meaningful work. But for some this will not be possible, and for them meaningless tasks take the place of more fulfilling activity.[3] It is an especially punishing view for those whose capacities for productive labor diminish with age (Morris 2004, 2011).

Finally, the demand for independence for disabled people relies heavily on the availability and compliance of caregivers. But there is a danger that the "independence" of disabled people may render the assistant invisible and subordinate. Michael Oliver criticizes understandings of disability by "professionals" who, he writes: "tend to define independence in terms of self-care activities such as washing, dressing, toileting, cooking, and eating without assistance" (Oliver 1989, 14). Still, don't we have to ask: "What about those who do the washing, dressing, toileting?"

Although in fact, at least in the United States, family members most often fill the role of paid attendant, the preferences of many disabled adults, interestingly, do not favor this arrangement. The sense of independence to which disabled people aspire is, according to some, best served by a paid stranger with whom one has a thin relationship of employer to employee. In order to sustain a sense of independence—or, as I suggest, the illusion of independence—the personal attendant must become invisible. Lynn May Rivas speaks of the carer needing to turn over "the authorship" of her work to the disabled person (2002, 77). Drawing on interviews she had separately with carers, as well as the disabled people utilizing personal assistants, she notes, "Ironically, handing over the authorship of caring labor may itself be the most caring part of care" (2002, 79). But then again, she writes, "How could something unseen be completely valued" (80)? The consumers wanted a "businesslike relationship" but the attendants valued the work insofar as it was a labor of love. The logjam is, I believe, a feature of the over-valorization of independence and the stigma of dependence.

Beyond the Stigma of Dependency and the Over-Valorization of Independence

A consideration of dependency then forces a number of questions: can one still protect the benefits to be gained by disabled people's demands for independence without re-stigmatizing those who do not benefit? Can we accept the inevitability of dependence without denying the negative effects of an imposed dependency on the lives of many disabled people? And can we accept reliance on dependency workers without subordinating their interests to those of the disabled person? Can we accept the asymmetry of dependence as part of the human condition and not fear exploitation or abuse? Our powerlessness in the face of the forces over which we have little control, and our need to unite with others who are willing to work in concert or provide asymmetrical care when necessary, requires humans to develop relationships of trust, to create systems of entitlements that make assistance and access predictable, and to form affective bonds that motivate others to take our cares as their own and enjoins us to take another's cares as ours. While the vulnerabilities of the dependent in a relationship of dependency are multiple, unfortunate outcomes are not inevitable if the dependency is managed in the right ways, by the right individuals, with the right moral and emotional commitments, backed by appropriate institutional supports.

A care ethics opts for better ways to recognize and create conditions that foster relationships of dependency that are replete with affective bonds and a sense that each participant has received her due; relationships which can transform otherwise unpleasant intimate tasks into times of trust, and demonstrations of trustworthiness, gratifying and dignifying to both the caregiver and the recipient of care. A truly independent life, one in which we need no one and no one needs us, would be a very impoverished one, even if it were possible. The person with an impairment who requires the assistance of a caregiver is not the exception, but a person living out a possibility in any human life, our inevitable dependency. At best, life can be independent to the degree that it can be self-determining, and most of us, disabled or not, can be self-determining to *some* degree. But with self-determination comes a presumption of self-sufficiency and such self-sufficiency is always a lie, whether or not we are disabled. We are all better off when we refuse to live a lie.

An Ethics of Care—In Brief

An ethic of care takes care as a supreme value, and while the scope of care is restricted by contextual considerations in any one deliberation, it aims at a regulative ideal that everyone is cared about and receives the care they need. That is, everyone is enfolded into the circle of care. What does such a "care ethic" look like? It provides a tripartite conception of care as a labor, an attitude (or disposition) and a virtue. As a labor, caregiving requires attending to the needs of another, putting aside one's own needs for someone more vulnerable, and often becoming intimate with the body and the bodily functions of the cared-for (MacIntyre,1999; Gastmans, Dierckx de Casterle, and Schotsmans, 1998). The labor of care is, for the most part, carried out on the body of an individual and requires dignifying both our unique individuality in his or her embodied existence and respecting our material connectedness to one another (Miller 2005, 2012).

The custodial maintenance of the body is not yet care in the fully normative sense. Care in this sense requires an appropriate attitude, an open responsiveness essential to understanding what another person needs and wants. Care in a fully normative sense is also a virtue to be cultivated, a disposition to make the attitudinal shift as it is called for. Those in whom this virtue is present are able to respond to people in need of care even when the parties are not bound by intimacy. Carers not only care about and for those whom they encounter, they also care about *care* (Dalmiya, 2002; Kittay, 2019). That is, they place a supreme value on caring itself, caring, that is, in its fully normative sense.

Care as a Fully Normative Concept

What do I mean by care in its fully normative sense and why do we need such a notion for the purposes at hand? An ethic of care that disability activists and scholars can find acceptable will need to be one that is grounded in current practices but is based on the *best practices* of care. Answering needs in a way that diminishes those who need care is rightly disparaged, as when persons and institutions (including those that are state sponsored) address what *they* take to be needs but simultaneously run roughshod over the agency of dependent and disabled people. For the point of care is not only to address needs. That's the means to an end. The end itself is to promote the flourishing of the cared-for. Note that if we take that end as an ultimate value, then insofar as to flourish is a value for everyone, care is of value to all, for we all sometimes need care to flourish. The fully normative sense of care, which I designate orthographically CARE, is what we need to serve as our guiding virtue. Such an ethic is an *ethics of* CARE.

The moral virtues are already defined normatively. Consider that we never speak of a person as being "too just." We may speak of a person being too rigid or too lax in the application of laws or principles. Or we may say that a person serves up too stern a form of justice. What we do not say is that someone offers up bad or poor justice. If a decision which ought to be rendered justly is bad, it may be sheer revenge, or it may be heedless of the rule of law, but it is not just. For the outcome to be just, it must be something worthy of approval *as justice*—although a just act might not be sufficiently merciful.

The point of caring is to benefit the cared for, so when the person who is presumably being cared for says that the carer "cares too much," they are complaining that the benefit the carer assumes she is bestowing is not a benefit at all. That is, the person who "cares too much" fails to serve the point of care, which is to benefit another. Another way to see this is to consider Aristotle's view that a virtue is a mean between two vices. In the case of care, one extreme is over-solicitude; that is, the unwanted attention to another person and their needs. Alternatively, there is the paternalistic imposition of someone's idea of what is good for the cared-for, without consideration of what the cared-for regards as their own good. On the other extreme is a neglect borne either of indifference or a misplaced "respect for another's autonomy," that is, a failure (or unwillingness) to perceive and respond to the other's real need for assistance. In either case, the aim of benefitting the other goes unrealized. In the case of CARE, what is crucial is that the action of the putative carer needs to be taken up as care; needs, in other words, to have a beneficial effect on the person whose needs are under consideration. This means that however much the *intention* to care may be motivating the carer, caring *too much* is not CARE at all.

So what is CARE? We can provide the rudiments of an ethics of CARE with some definitions and principles. The definitions spell out the aim and the appropriate recipients of caring practices.

> Definition 1. The *telos* of caring practices is the flourishing of those who need care.
> Definition 2. Those who need care are those who will be harmed if care is not provided. Those most clearly in need of care are those who are *inevitably dependent*.

The principles articulate regulative ideals, that is, ideals that while never entirely realizable, are aspirations in the provision of CARE.

> Principle 1. The flourishing of those in need of care has to be a flourishing *as endorsed (implicitly or explicitly) by the one cared-for*. This means
>
> a. The carer needs to be guided by the regulative idea of *a transparent self*, that is, a self that attempts to bracket its own needs, desires, prejudices and preconceptions, and attends to what the flourishing of the cared for requires.
>
> b. That the activity of the carer has to be taken up as care by the cared for.
>
> Principle 2. The *regulative ideal* of care is to provide care by assisting those who require care in meeting needs and wants that are genuine and legitimate.
>
> a. *Genuine needs* have both an objective and subjective basis and if not attended to will impede the individual's flourishing and result in harming that individual.
>
> b. *Legitimate wants* are wants that can be satisfied without thwarting another's (including the carer's) possibility of receiving care from others. This requires that when we work to satisfy a particular want (which is less urgent than a need) that we consider whether doing so involves harming or doing some injustice to others.

These principles involve regulative ideals that may never be fully realized. To say that they are regulative ideals is to claim that they *ought* to guide our decisions and the ways in which we care. With regard to the first principle, no one can achieve total transparency. It is true that our self-interest, biases, and an opacity regarding the mind of another can only be partially overcome. Nonetheless, transparency is what we aim for when we CARE, for we need to *try* to set aside our own wants and prejudices, and work, as best we can, to gain access to what the other cares about. It is only when we are instrumental in the flourishing of the cared for, or assist the cared for's ability to gain an important benefit, that is, when they take up our caring as care, that we can say: we succeeded in caring for the other. Similarly, with respect to second principle, we sometimes cannot tell if something the other cares about is truly an urgent need, or sometimes we cannot determine correctly what the need is. And it is clear that we can never know for certain that satisfying another's want will not cause harm to another or exacerbate an injustice;

nonetheless, we should attempt to access the legitimacy of the want, especially when the care we are addressing is not an urgent need.

I believe that both people with disabilities and those who do caring labor can embrace an ethic founded on such a normative conception of care. With these definitions and regulative ideals, we can fill in some of the ways that an ethic of CARE differs from more characteristically liberal ethical theories in terms of the moral self, moral relationships, moral deliberation, and notions of harm.

Articulating an ETHICS OF CARE

Most ethical theories begin with an explicit or implicit understanding of the self, or *the moral agent*.[4] An ethic of care views the self not as an atomistic individual self, but as one that is both constituted by and is causally related to other relational selves. Most traditional liberal moral theories view *moral interactions* as being voluntaristic among equal moral agents. Within these relationships, we bind ourselves to moral principles. Care ethics recognizes that *moral relationships* are not always self-chosen, but often take place in relationships we find ourselves in. The conditions under which we enter or exit these relationships are sometimes highly constrained. And these relationships are generally asymmetric, that is between people who are not equally empowered or equally situated. This is not to say that the parties do not have moral parity—that is, are understood as having equal worth—only that they are not equally situated or empowered with respect to being able to realize their own good. These selves engage in moral deliberation using not only the resources of rationality—which most ethical theories (save sentimentalist ones) value most highly—but include empathy, and other emotional responses that allow us to gain *moral access* to another's situation.[5] They do not necessarily take an impartial stand (sometimes taken as the hallmark of morality). Instead in a care ethics we understand that the particular relationship one has to another gives a carer epistemic and moral access to which an impartial observer is not privy and imposes special obligations on carers by virtue of the relationship. We treat a friend differently than a stranger, and while there are some situations in which this is morally unjustifiable, in many situations such partialism is in fact morally required of us. Care ethics is not alone in understanding that certain special relations give rise to particular moral obligations to a particular other. These are obligations that are not agent neutral. But while such agent-relative obligations resulting from special relationships are recognized, in other theories they are exceptions to the more central agent neutral obligations resulting in judgments with a universal *scope*. By contrast, care ethics is a particularistic ethics where the judgments sought ought to consider the particularities of the situation and not the generalities that would yield universally applicable decisions. For example, an injunction as presumably universal as not lying gets complicated when we try applying it to the best standard of care for a person with Alzheimer's. Such judgments are particularized not simply because a caregiver has a special relationship to the person with the disability but because the carer needs to consider the extent of the disability, the sort of falsehood that may be employed, the reason for sidestepping truth telling, among others.

Perhaps the most fundamental difference between moral theories resides in how they conceive of the point and purpose of moral interactions and the notion of harm. An ETHICS OF CARE stresses, first of all, the concern for the wellbeing (or flourishing) of a person "for their own sake" (Darwall 2002, 1), and the moral importance of providing the care to that end.[6] Yet in care ethics, the relationship of care, and the valuable relations a person has, are themselves important. Our connectedness to others matters, and we see great harm when relationships are broken. Of course, some relationships should be broken—abusive or harmful ones. But even in the case of abuse, breaking off the harmful relationship may involve a significant loss if the faulty relationship also is laden with more positive connectedness. This is unfortunately the case when the abusive or neglectful person is a parent, a loved one, or a valued mentor.

An ETHICS OF CARE recognizes moral harm when the absence or severing of relationships leave genuine needs and legitimate wants (especially of vulnerable persons) unmet; when genuine needs and legitimate wants elicit only indifference; and when vulnerability elicits distain, abuse, or violence rather than care. When human connections are broken, whether through exploitation, domination, hurt, neglect, detachment or abandonment, we have harms that result from a failure of care.

Failures of Care

What are some of the ways in which the attempt to care can go wrong? The person who does care work poorly may give preference to her own interests and desires, even when detrimental to her charge. She may be inattentive, unmindful, or neglectful or might exert her dominance—abuse her relationship and power—over a vulnerable individual. It is not just negligent or abusive behavior that can sabotage care. Even good intentions can interfere with the care that is genuinely needed if the carer's desire to help is more about her desire to help than about the cared-for's need for assistance. Good intentions also do not produce good care if the carer is incompetent or badly trained, or if what the carer wants to impose on the cared-for is based *only* on the carer's conception the good, disregarding the cared-for's own response. What the carer presumes is good for the cared-for may be something that the cared-for rejects as a good, or as something that is good *for her*.

Central to these failures and abuses are the asymmetries in power between caregiver and cared-for. The asymmetries are not simply characterized by a powerless cared-for and a powerful carer. Carers themselves often have less socioeconomic status than those they care for. They are sometimes even physically less powerful than those they care for. But the essential dependence of the cared-for on the dependent remains even when other forms of power favor the cared-for. The way in which that dependence is handled by both parties will determine if the care can successfully be given and received or taken up as care. The concept of CARE allows us to see that the question for a care ethic is how to prevent power from turning into domination and instead make that power enriching primarily to the cared-for without effacing the carer.

The Taking Up of Care by the Cared For

An ETHICS OF CARE walks the line between the Scylla of paternalism and the Charybdis of neglect. To navigate this narrow pass is crucial if an ethics of care is to be useful for disabled people. Given that an ethic of care is a particularistic ethic, and we are not in possession of maxims that can readily be generalized, do we have some general criteria by which to determine if the actions carried out by the carer really are CARE? Yes. It depends on whether or not my action is taken up as care by the other. To bring the point home, consider the following scenario: I see a plant that is wilted. I pick up a pitcher next to it to water the plant. Now suppose that, unbeknownst to me, the pitcher is filled with vinegar, not water. I pour it into the plant. Predictably, the plant begins to wither instead of perk up. Have I cared for the plant? Most of us would answer, "No." I believe the example shows that we have a strong intuitive sense that a thing's or person's well-being must be positively affected by our actions if our actions are to be counted as care—at the very least, it ought not to be negatively affected. We can say that the action needs to be taken up as care by the cared-for. The plant cannot "say" whether we have cared for it, but it shows that it has when it responds positively to our actions. People generally can make it clear that what we have done is something that they do or do not welcome as care. Even people such as my daughter, who cannot speak, can communicate whether what we do is welcomed or not.

The important lesson here is that if the person we are trying to (or purporting to) care for doesn't accept that we are meeting their needs or ameliorating their situation, then, as much as we intend to care, we are not yet CARING. There are many complicated ways in which actions are taken up as care or are rejected. The taking up of an action as care can be deferred; it can be partial; it can be rejected even when it is answering a genuine need. But for an action to be care it must, as Noddings (1984) put it, "be completed in the other"—if it is to be care.

If what we do to promote the good of the cared-for is something that they, upon good reflection and information (were the cared-for able to reflect and process this information) would not want us to do, then we act paternalistically, not caringly. Thus, care has to be guided by the good as the person cared for determines it. In respecting what that person would want for herself is to provide care that also recognizes the dignity of an agentive self. We recognize the person herself as she recognizes herself. What I have suggested in insisting that care has to be taken up as care by the cared for is that care is congruent with the respect we give to those whose dignity we respect. In fact, if care is to be CARE, this sort of care *necessitates* respect for the cared-for. In this way CARE itself is a source of dignity, not something that diminishes us. If we think of care in this manner, then I believe we will address many of the objections that disability scholars and activists have voiced. And it is only care in this sense that is truly CARE.

Notes

1. A more recent trend, however, has urged pushing against this (Shakespeare 2001, 2006, 2014), (Weicht 2010).
2. See Kant (1996) on benevolence, especially 6:388, 6:448–454, 6:462–463; Also Cureton (2016).
3. Also see Sunny Taylor (2004) available at http://monthlyreview.org/2004/03/01/the-right-not-to-work-power-and-disability/.
4. For accounts of the notions of a relational self and moral interactions, see for example, Gilligan (1982), Friedman (2003), Noddings (1984), Meyers (1989, 1994), Brison (1997), (2002, 2017), Baier (1995), Held (2006). There are many versions and discussions of an ethic of care and criticisms from feminist philosophers. See Keller and Kittay (2017) for an extensive bibliography on the ethics of care.
5. For the notion of *moral access* see Kittay (2017).
6. For more political accounts of an ethic of care, for example, Bubeck (1995), Held (1995), Kittay (1995), Tronto (2013, 1994), Engster (2007), (Hamington and Miller 2006).

References

Baier, Annette C. 1995. "The Need for More than Justice." In *Justice and Care*, edited by Virginia Held, 47–58. Boulder, CO: Westview Press.

Barnes, Elizabeth. 2016. *The Minority Body: A Theory Of Disability: Studies in Feminist Philosophy*. Oxford: Oxford University Press.

Barton, Len, ed. 1989. *Disability and Dependency*. London: The Falmer Press.

British Council of Organisations of Disabled People. 1987. "Comment on the Report to the Audit Commission 'Making a Reality of Community Care'." http://disability-studies.leeds.ac.uk/files/library/BCODP-report-of-audit-comm.pdf.

Brison, Susan. 1997. "Outliving Oneself: Trauma, Memory and Personal Identity." In *Feminists Rethink the Self*, edited by Diana T. Meyers, 13–39. Boulder, CO: Westview Press.

Brison, Susan. 2017. "Personal Identity and Relational Selves." In *Routledge Companion to Feminist Philosophy*, edited by Serene Khader Ann Garry and Alison Stone, 218–230. New York: Routledge.

Brison, Susan J. 2002. *Aftermath: Violence and the Remaking of a Self*. Princeton, NJ: Princeton University Press.

Bubeck, Diemut. 1995. *Care, Gender, and Justice*. Oxford: Clarendon Press.

Cureton, Adam. 2016. "Offensive Beneficence." *Journal of the American Philosophical Association* 2, no. 1: 74–90.

Dalmiya, Vrinda. 2002. "Why Should a Knower Care?" *Hypatia* 17, no. 1: 34–52.

Darwall, Stephen. 2002. *Welfare and Rational Care*. Princeton, NJ: Princeton University Press.

Davis, Lennard J. 2007. "Dependency and Justice: A Review of Martha Nussbaum's Frontiers of Justice." *Journal of Literary Disability* 1, no. 2: 1–4.

De Jong, G. 1983. "Defining and Implementing the Independent, Living Concept." In *Independent Living for Physically Disabled People*, edited by Nancy Crew and Irving K. Zola, 4–27. San Francisco: Jossey-Bass.

Engster, Daniel. 2007. *The Heart of Justice*. Oxford: Oxford University Press.

Fine, Michael, and Caroline Glendinning. 2005. "Dependence, Independence or Interdependence? Revisiting the Concepts of 'Care' and 'Dependency.'" *Ageing and Society* 25, no. 4:601–621. doi: 10.1017/S0144686X05003600.

Fineman, Martha Albertson. 1995. *The Neutered Mother, the Sexual Family and Other Twentieth Century Tragedies*. New York: Routledge.

Fraser, Nancy, and Linda Gordon. 1994a. "Civil Citizenship Against Social Citizenship? On the Ideology of Contract vs. Charity." In *The Condition of Citizenship*, edited by Bart van Steenbergen, 90–107. Sage Publications.

Fraser, Nancy, and Linda Gordon. 1994b. "A Genealogy of Dependency: Tracing a Keyword of the U.S. Welfare State." *Signs* 19, no. 2:309–336.

Friedman, Marilyn. 2003. *Autonomy, Gender, Politics, Studies in Feminist Philosophy*. Oxford: Oxford University Press.

Gastmans, Chris, Bernadette Dierckx de Casterle, and Paul Schotsmans. 1998. "Nursing Considered as Moral Practice: A Philosophical-Ethical Interpretation of Nursing." *Kennedy Institute of Ethics Journal* 8, no. 1:43–69.

Gilligan, Carol. 1982. *In A Different Voice*. Cambridge, MA: Harvard University Press.

Hamington, Maurice, and Dorothy C. Miller. 2006. *Socializing Care: Feminist Ethics and Public Issues, Feminist Constructions*. Lanham, MD: Rowman & Littlefield.

Held, Virginia. 1995. "The Meshing of Care and Justice." *Hypatia* 10, no. 2:128–132.

Held, Virginia. 2006. *The Ethics of Care: Personal, Political, and Global*. Oxford: Oxford University Press.

Heumann, Judy. 1977. "Independent Living Movement." http://www.disabilityexchange.org/newsletter/article.php?n=15&a=134.

Kant, Immanuel. 1996. *The Metaphysics of Morals*. New York: Cambridge University Press.

Keller, Jean, and Eva Feder Kittay. 2017. "Feminist Ethics of Care." In *The Routledge Companion to Feminist Philosophy*, edited by Ann Garry, Serene J. Khader and Alison Stone, 540–555. London: Routledge.

Kittay, Eva Feder. 1995. "Taking Dependency Seriously: The Family and Medical Leave Act Considered in Light of the Social Organization of Dependency Work and Gender Equality." *Hypatia* 10, no. 1:8–29.

Kittay, Eva Feder. 1996. "Human Dependency and Rawlsian Equality." In *Feminists Rethink the Self*, edited by D. T. Meyers. Boulder, CO: Westview Press.

Kittay, Eva Feder. 1999. *Love's Labor: Essays in Women, Equality and Dependency*. New York: Routledge.

Kittay, Eva Feder. 2015. "Dependency." In *Keywords in Disability Studies*, edited by Rachael Adams and Benjamin Reiss. New York: NYU Press.

Kittay, Eva Feder. 2017. "The Moral Significance of Being Human." *Proceedings and Addresses of the APA* 91:22–42.

Kittay, Eva Feder. *Learning from My Daughter: The Care and Value of Disabled Minds*. Oxford; New York: Oxford University Press, 2019.

Lindemann, Hilde. *Damaged Identities: Narrative Repair*. Ithaca: Cornell University Press, 2001.

MacIntyre, Alasdair C. 1999. *Dependent rational animals: why human beings need the virtues, The Paul Carus lecture series*. Chicago, IL: Open Court.

Marshall, T. H. 1973. *Class, Citizenship, and Social Development: Essays*. Westport, CT: Greenwood Press.

Meyers, Diana T. 1989. *Self, Society, and Personal Choice*. New York: Columbia University Press.

Meyers, Diana T. 1994. *Subjection & Subjectivity: Psychoanalytic Feminism & Moral Philosophy, Thinking Gender*. New York: Routledge.

Miller, Sarah Clark. 2005. "Need, Care and Obligation." *Royal Institute of Philosophy Supplement* 57 (December):137–160. doi: 10.1017/S1358246105057073.

Miller, Sarah Clark. 2012. *The Ethics of Need: Agency, Dignity, and Obligation*. New York: Routledge.

Morris, Jenny. 2004. "Independent Living and Community Care: A Disempower- ing Framework." *Disability and Society* 19, no. 5:427–442.

Morris, Jenny. 2011. "Rethinking Disability Policy." https://www.youtube.com/watch?v=XHm4b2Y5j_U.

Moynihan, Daniel Patrick. 1973. *The Politics of a Guaranteed Income: The Nixon Administration and the Family Assistance Plan*. New York: Random House.

Noddings, Nel. 1984. *Caring: A Feminine Approach to Ethics and Moral Education*. Berkeley: University of California Press.

Oliver, Michael. 1989. "Disability and Dependency: A Creation of Industrial Societies." In *Disability and Dependency*, edited by Len Barton, 6–22. London: The Falmer Press.

Rivas, Lynn May. 2002a. *Global Women: Nannies, Maids and Sex Workers in the Global Economy*. Edited by Barbara Ehrenreich and Arlie Russell Hochschild. New York: Henry Holt and Company.

Rivas, Lynn May. 2002b. "Invisible Labors: Caring for the Independent Person." In *Global Women: Nannies, Maids and Sex Workers in the Global Economy*, edited by Barbara Ehrenreich and Arlie Russell Hochschild, 70–84. New York, New York: Henry Holt and Company.

Shakespeare, Thomas W. 2006. *Disability Rights and Wrongs*. London: Routledge.

Shakespeare, Thomas W. 2014. *Disability Rights and Wrongs Revisited*, 2nd ed. London, New York: Routledge.

Shakespeare, Thomas; Watson, Nicholas. 2001. "The Social Model: An Outdated Ideology?" In *Exploring Theories and Expanding Methodologies: Where We are and Where We Need to Go*, edited by Sharon N. Barnartt and Barbara M. Altman, 9–29. New York: JAI Press.

Taylor, Sunny. 2004. "The Right Not to Work." *Monthly Review* 55 (10).

Tronto, Joan. 1994. *Moral boundaries: A political argument for an ethic of care*. New York: Routledge.

Tronto, Joan. 2013. *Caring Democracy: Markets, Equality, and Justice*. New York: NYU Press.

Weicht, Bernhard. 2010. "Embracing Dependency: Rethinking (In)dependence in the Discourse of Care." *The Sociological Review* 58, no. s2:205–224. doi: 10.1111/j.1467-954X.2011.01970.x.

Young, Iris. 2002. "Autonomy, Welfare and Meaningful Work." In *The Subject of Care*, edited by Eva Feder Kittay and Ellen K. Feder, 40–60. Lanham, MD: Rowman and Littlefield.

Zola, Irving Kenneth. 1988. "The Independent Living Movement: Empowering People With Disabilities." *Australian Disability Review* 1, no. 3:23–27.

CHAPTER 25

A DIGNITARIAN APPROACH TO DISABILITY

From Moral Status to Social Status

LINDA BARCLAY

IT has been argued that dignity is a useless concept that adds nothing to existing moral vocabulary: it is just a slogan (Macklin 2003). In this chapter, I will argue that only a concept of dignity can adequately explain a serious moral wrong inflicted on people with disabilities; namely, their relegation to inferior social status. Far from being useless, it uniquely explains why fundamental changes to social relations are needed to secure justice. Moreover, dignity matters just as much for people with cognitive impairments as it does for everyone else. As such, fraught debates about their moral standing are largely irrelevant to explaining why they, too, should be treated as social equals.

WHAT IS DIGNITY?

I will develop a conception of dignity according to which dignity is conferred in social relations where we follow social norms for treating people as social equals. When we do so, we communicate to others that we consider them our social equals. To enjoy dignity is to reliably be treated in accordance with such norms. Conversely, people do not enjoy dignity when they are routinely treated in a way that relegates them to a lower social status. Such routine behavior communicates both to its victims (and to others) that they are believed to be of lower social status.

There have been a number of recent attempts to revive interest in the concept of "dignity" and to account for its moral importance. Many of these approaches aim to develop a single, unified conception of dignity (cf Killmister 2017). I have no such ambition. Given that dignity has historically meant many different things (Rosen 2012), I don't see any compelling reason to try to corral this diversity into a single conception. Instead, the conception I develop is just one among a number of possible conceptions of dignity, but one which is morally important.

On my conception, dignity is something conferred on people, rather than something inherent in them. It is by virtue of standing in particular kinds of social relationships that we can say a person has dignity. This is the kind of conception of dignity which falls under Jeremy Waldron's broad description of dignity as status (Waldron 2012). It is contrasted with dignity as worth, which conceives of a person's dignity as inherent in them, by virtue of their possession of a valuable nature or valuable capacities. It is the status conception that best seems to capture the idea that dignity is not (only) inherent in people "but is also at least partly constituted by distinctive forms of interpersonal interaction in which it is expressed" (Bird 2014, 160).

There are potentially numerous ways to expand on the idea of status dignity. Historically, dignity as status has been connected to social hierarchies. Michael Rosen suggests that dignity "originated as a concept that denoted high social status and the honors and respectful treatment that are due to someone who occupied that position" (2012, 11). The respectful treatment due to a social superior might have included tugging at the forelock, curtseying and bowing, and particular forms of deferential or obsequious address.

Waldron argues in favor of what Rosen dubs a more recent "expanding circle" narrative of status dignity that includes most human beings (2012). According to Waldron, the prevailing conception of status dignity for us is equal status, for the "modern notion of human dignity involves an upwards equalization of rank, so that we now try to accord every human being something of the dignity, rank, and expectation of respect that was formerly accorded to nobility" (Waldron 2012, 33).

Charles Beitz has questioned whether it is possible to distinguish worth and status conceptions of dignity. The challenge is whether status conceptions don't inevitably collapse into worth conceptions: we might think that we only have equal status because we are of equal worth (Beitz 2013). I will later argue that my conception of dignity is quite distinct from dignity as worth and, in particular, that the moral importance of dignity as the enjoyment of equal social status need not be derived from dignity as inherent worth. This, as we shall see, is of great moral importance for people with cognitive impairments.

What, then, might it mean to say that we confer dignity on one another? In particular, which forms of social relations confer dignity? It is intuitively clear that tugging at the forelock, bowing and scraping are at odds with equal status. It is more challenging to describe those positive social relations that constitute it and how they do so.

Let me narrow the focus of this enquiry by setting aside equal status in legal and institutional contexts. I have argued elsewhere that a range of legal rights protect us against being relegated to an inferior rank or to second-class status (Barclay 2016).

In this chapter, I am interested in our interpersonal interactions. When we listen to people with disability, we hear over and again that others with whom they routinely interact—shopkeepers, service providers, neighbors, colleagues, and strangers—fail to treat them as their social equals.

Here are some common examples:

Stella Young was an Australian comedian, journalist and disability activist who used a wheelchair. Despite her good education, evident high intelligence and substantial career success, she was routinely labelled an "inspiration" because she took an active part in public debate. Indeed, like many people with disability, Stella was labelled "inspirational" or "brave" for performing the most mundane activities, or, as Stella put it, for simply existing. A fellow commuter once patted her arm and said "I see you on the train every morning and I just wanted to say it's great. You're an inspiration to me." (Young 2012).

Christine is a young woman with both extensive physical disabilities and an intellectual impairment. She lives in supported accommodation and needs assistance with food preparation, toileting, and showering, as well as assistance with making decisions. Staff at the facility often engage in behavior that Christine and her parents object to. When staff claim they are busy, they sometimes leave her sitting on the toilet with the door open or fail to ensure she gets her daily shower, thus forcing her to wear soiled and disheveled clothing. They frequently speak to her as though she is a small child and typically enter her room without knocking on the door. They also make decisions about her medications, arrange medical appointments, and enrol her in social activities without consulting with her.

John is a person of small stature. Each and every day John is subject to staring, to extreme condescension, and to public ridicule. Whether he is catching the train to work, eating at a restaurant, or doing his shopping, each day is fraught with disrespectful exchange. John, too, is often spoken to as though he were a small child. Sometimes strangers yell out from across the street or ask all manner of questions about his sex life, his anatomy, and other deeply private matters.[1]

Stella, Christine, and John are routinely belittled: others regard them as incapable and pitiful, and those judgments are expressed in everyday social exchanges. They are routinely subject to condescension, rudeness, contempt, and a startling disregard for boundaries of privacy and other social norms of etiquette and decorum. Research in other domains reveals similar themes. Based on extensive interviews, Nora Jacobson documents how the day-to-day exchanges of the sick, homeless, and poor are characterized by rudeness, indifference, condescension, contempt, exclusion, and vilification. Her research participants had a vast range of phrases to describe how it felt to be subject to such social exchanges: "like a child," "like you are an inch high," "like an animal," "like a dog," "like a bum," "like a criminal," "like a second-class citizen," "like dirt," "like garbage," "like scum," "like a piece of shit," "like nothing." Jacobson says of her participants that "their language is replete with denotations of (lesser) size or position" (Jacobson 2012, 87).

People with disabilities, like the homeless, are clearly victims of stigma: they possess what others take to be a discrediting attribute, one at odds with our understanding of what a normal and worthy individual should be like (Goffman 1963). But my interest in this chapter is not so much with *why* we so often treat people with disabilities as though they are of lower status, but to account for *how* we do so and why such treatment is wrong.

Again, it has proved relatively easy to describe situations that fail to confer dignity on people with disabilities. But what forms of social exchange do treat people with equal status and thus confer dignity on everyone? I argue that dignity is secured when our exchanges with each other conform to whatever our social norms are for treating one another as social equals. Whether any given token of social exchange is dignity-conferring or not depends on the social norms in place. Just as social norms determine that tugging at the forelock and bowing and scraping are behaviors for treating royalty as social superiors, so too, our social norms determine that other forms of social exchange are ways to treat others as social equals.

Earlier defenders of dignity lauded obsequious behavior befitting social inferiority. There was dignity in knowing and accepting one's place in the social hierarchy and conducting oneself accordingly (Rosen 2012). The modern attachment to dignity as equal status largely rejects behavior connected to status hierarchies. We are often repelled by people who expect us to treat them as though they have higher status. We also pity those whose sense of identity and worth is bound to their lower status. The poignancy of Kazuo Ishiguro's *The Remains of the Day* is found in the depth to which the self-worth of Stevens the butler is contingent upon being treated, and conducting himself, in accordance with extensive and detailed norms that assign him to a lower social rank.

Cheshire Calhoun argues that behavior in accordance with social norms plays an important communicative role (Calhoun 2000). So too, I argue that dignity-conferring exchanges communicate to their recipients that they are considered social equals by those who engage with them. Successfully communicating this moral attitude is contingent on following shared social norms which express equal status. It is only because there are widely shared norms, which are "often codified, social rules" for what counts as treating one another as social equals, that we can successfully communicate an attitude of regard for others as our social equals.

Calhoun's specific interest is in civility, rather than equal status. To be civil is to follow social norms that communicate moral attitudes of respect, tolerance, and considerateness. She argues that civil behavior is not coextensive with behavior that is actually respectful, tolerant, and considerate according to critical morality. For example, opening doors for women and paying for their meals are socially conventional ways of displaying respect for women. But such behavior is not actually respectful, based, as it is, on sexist assumptions about women's weakness and need for male protection (Calhoun 2000, 263). So in our morally imperfect world, men have to choose between displaying or expressing respect and actually treating women respectfully, by, for example, taking it in turns to open doors and pay for meals. The central point, of course, is that social norms do not reliably track what is actually right and good.

While this may represent a real quandary with respect, tolerance, and considerateness, I am less convinced that the same quandary arises with norms of equal status.[2] It is in any case very hard to think of many concrete examples that would suggest it does. Norms of *equal* status are not compatible with morally imperfect worlds in the way that norms of respect can be. Norms of equal status challenge inequality rather than assume it. Calhoun's example trades on the fact that women do not enjoy equality, which is why treating them as weak can be considered a sign of respect. Conversely, norms that men should hold doors for women, or help them navigate stairs, or pay for their meals, or relieve them of the burden of employment or decision-making—and so on—are not norms for treating women as social equals. Of course, a woman might well object when men do not engage in these behaviors: she might object when a man merely takes it in turns holding the door, or wants to split the cost of the meal, or expects her to earn her own income or make major decisions. But she can't successfully argue that she is not being treated as someone with equal status. To the contrary, it seems to me that that is precisely what she does object to.

So I am skeptical that we are likely to confront the possibility that social norms which express equal status will be at odds with actually treating people with equal status. Importantly, this possibility is not established just by some people claiming that a set of obnoxious social norms communicate equal status. Social norms do not express and communicate whatever people say they do. Some people deny that making a group of people sit at the back of the bus communicates their lower status. Many people also argue that holding out a hand to help a perfectly fit woman navigate a set of stairs does not do so either. Such claims are false. Treating people in accordance with "separate but equal" norms usually has no other point than to establish and express status hierarchies. The woman who patted Stella's arm and congratulated her for taking the train might say that her behavior was in accordance with norms for expressing respect and consideration (and tolerance?). Whether that is true or not, she would certainly be wrong to claim her behavior expressed the attitude that Stella was her social equal. We have established norms for communicating a status that adults enjoy that children do not, and this woman's behavior failed to abide by them.

These claims are compatible with conceding that in specific circumstances it can be quite challenging to determine whether the way we interact with another person treats her as having equal status. First, there is undoubtedly cross-cultural variety with respect to norms that communicate equal status. Our norms might be different from those of some other group. Given such differences, an exchange might misfire if someone who does not share our norms understands such behavior differently to how we do. Even when staying within our own social environment, there can be uncertainty about how to apply our norms or use them well. Imagine that when lost in a strange city I deliberately ask directions from a person in a wheelchair because I am aware that people in wheelchairs are rarely called upon to provide this kind of assistance to others. There is no guarantee that the person in the wheelchair won't actually find my behavior condescending.[3]

Social norms are not like written law. There can be disagreement and uncertainty about what they express and communicate and what they demand of us, in certain circumstances. But these are different considerations from the possibility that established social norms for treating people with equal status might be at odds with actually treating them with equal status. I will put these complications aside for the rest of this chapter: I take it that the examples I focus on are all cases where we agree that people are not treated as having equal status.

One further clarification is particularly important. In no way do I intend to suggest that treating people with dignity always trumps other values. Consider Manuel Wackenheim, a man of short stature who chose employment in a "dwarf-throwing" competition. The local council prevented the competition from proceeding on the grounds that it was an assault on human dignity. Wackenheim steadily worked his way through every layer of the French court system and then the United Nations to argue that it was an egregious denial of his autonomy to prevent him from choosing such employment (Rosen 2012). This is plausibly described as a case of dignity clashing with autonomy. Being used as a laughable missile does not seem to belong to relations of equal status, but denial of their capacity for adult agency is also something which people with disabilities must routinely endure. It is at least not obvious that the value of dignity should trump the value of personal autonomy, although it did in this case. Indeed, in some contexts, treating people with unequal status seems quite defensible: consider legitimate ways of engaging with violent offenders or moral wrongdoers, or the requirement that we should stand when a judge enters court.

In the interpersonal realm, actually treating people with equal status amounts to just the same thing as following social norms that communicate equal status, notwithstanding the messy reality that there is sometimes confusion about what exactly our social norms demand of us. Equal status is largely constituted by nothing other than such norm-governed behavior. Whether or not a person has greater worth or value than the rest of us is independent of how we treat her. Her status, however, is not. We can readily appreciate that a judge is of no greater worth than you or I, but she still enjoys a different status, at least in the context of her professional role, by virtue of norms governing how we treat her: we stand up when she enters court, we refer to her as "Your Honor," and so on. Dignity as status is distinct from dignity as worth because status does not exist independently of the particular forms of norm-governed social relations that constitute it.

Is Dignity a Worthless Notion?

Ruth Macklin claims that dignity is a worthless concept (Macklin 2003). She argues that appeals to dignity are usually nothing more than vague restatements of existing, and clearer, moral notions such as respect for persons or for their autonomy. We are now in a position to see that Macklin is wrong. Respecting persons and respecting their autonomy are not coextensive with treating them with dignity.

While Macklin is not particularly forthcoming about what she means by respect for persons, she apparently has in mind something like the Kantian notion of treating persons always as ends: she refers to examples of discrimination and abuse and the need for voluntary, informed consent to medical treatment and research. This is one version of

Stephen Darwall's conception of recognition respect; namely, the respect due specifically to all persons because of their unique moral status (Darwall 1977).

I am happy to categorize my account of treating people as having equal status as a kind of recognition respect, but it is clearly distinct to the Kantian notion. A very broad range of interpersonal exchange can fail to treat people as social equals but have nothing to do with discrimination and abuse or more generally being treated as an end in the Kantian sense. People with disabilities could be treated with scrupulous care in regard to their legal entitlements, with respect to discrimination law, and with respect to their human rights; but when others shun and exclude, when they are rude, contemptuous, condescending, and hostile and when they ignore basic etiquette around privacy and norms of decorum, then people with disabilities do not enjoy dignity. They are relegated to an inferior social status. Moreover, as Calhoun's examples demonstrate, respecting people is sometimes at odds with treating them as social equals. In a wide range of contexts, we treat people with respect precisely by following norms that express their higher status, as when we defer to our elders or stand for a judge. So rather vague appeals to respect for persons fails to mark out the more specific concept of dignity conferred in social relations in which all enjoy equal status.

Similarly, failure to respect a person's autonomy can certainly be an effective way to lower his status. This is virtually an everyday experience for people with disabilities, especially when others interfere as though they are children. But there are many social exchanges that fail to confer dignity which have nothing to do with respect for autonomy. Being treated with contempt, condescension, rudeness, hostility, and vilification do not necessarily interfere with self-direction or the pursuit of one's freely chosen ends.

If there is any real substance to Macklin's accusation that dignity is a useless concept it must turn on the claim that dignity is not of genuine moral importance. What is the moral value in treating people as social equals? It might be argued that once dignity is distinguished from respect for persons or respect for their autonomy, it is something of at best only very minor significance. In the following sections, I will show that treating people as social equals is morally imperative.

The Importance of Being Treated with Dignity: "Psychic Harms"

One obvious way to establish the moral importance of status dignity is to derive it from dignity as worth. That is, an understanding of the equal moral worth of persons might itself be sufficient to generate the moral demand to treat people as having equal status.

While such arguments are quite familiar, I have flagged that I wish to defend the moral importance of status dignity without becoming entangled in vexed and intractable debate about the moral status of persons or human beings. In particular, I wish to show that we have powerful reasons to treat people with cognitive impairments with dignity, irrespective of our views about whether they share the same moral status as other human beings. To do this, we need to consider the harms that are done to people when they are routinely treated as having low status.

To begin with, and perhaps most obviously, social relations which confer dignity avoid humiliating people and inflicting blows to their self-esteem and self-worth. Indeed, it has been suggested that nonhumiliation is the paradigm meaning of dignity: Avishai Margalit boldly claims that "if there is no concept of human dignity, then there is no concept of humiliation either" (Margalit 1998, 149; see also Luban 2009; Statman 2000).

Human beings are highly attuned to the regard which others have for us (Statman 2000). It is therefore common to feel humiliated when treated as a social inferior. Furthermore, additional harms tend to follow from humiliation and the damaged self-worth and self-esteem it can cause: namely, diminished agency. Joel Anderson and Axel Honneth argue that being able to trust our own feelings and intuitions, to stand up for what we believe in, and to consider our projects and accomplishments worthwhile, are all central to autonomous agency. But such self-trust, self-esteem, and self-worth only develop within social relations that nurture and sustain them. Social relations characterized by disrespect and humiliation are at odds with emergent capacities for effective agency (Anderson and Honneth 2005).

Although I accept all of these claims, I am skeptical that the harms of low social status are exhausted by humiliation and diminished self-worth and agency. Many people who do not enjoy relations of equal status do not suffer from these "psychic harms." One of the profound achievements of the disability rights movement is that it helps insulate the disabled from feelings of humiliation and low self-worth. Stella found the behavior of others more irritating and contemptible than humiliating. This is not unique to disability: all social movements of this kind can play an important role in furnishing their beneficiaries with psychological resilience in the face of status-diminishing social exchanges. Of course it is still an injustice that people have to constantly guard against psychic harms (Anderson and Honneth 2005). But that people *can* ward off such harms gives us reason to question whether the importance of being treated with dignity is grounded solely in the avoidance of humiliation.[4]

There are further reasons to resist an exclusive emphasis on "psychic" harms. People with what are usually referred to as severe or profound cognitive impairments are often incapable of feeling humiliation, and questions of autonomous agency are sometimes otiose. It would nevertheless be wrong to conclude that it is morally irrelevant as to whether or not we treat such people in accordance with norms that express equal status. As I shall now argue, people with cognitive impairments are among those most harmed by social relations which constitute low status.

The Harm of Stigmatized
Cultural Schemas

I begin with Sally Haslanger's crucial insight:

> The harm of stigma...is not [only] private or [solely] psychic. It is a matter of public standing. Such social meanings are the threads in the fabric of culture. They matter. Social meanings have a significant effect on how we interact with each other and distribute power, opportunity, and prestige.   (Haslanger 2015, 6)

According to Haslanger, social relations are constituted by practices which consist of interdependent schemas and resources. The concept of schemas is especially important for our purposes. Schemas consist of "culturally shared concepts, beliefs and other attitudes that enable us to interpret and organize information and coordinate action, thought and affect" (Haslanger 2016, 126). Haslanger argues that it is a mistake to think of stigmatized schemas as consisting solely of false beliefs. Schemas are social meanings that shape perception, affect, and behavioral dispositions. While our schemas do consist partly of beliefs, beliefs are themselves also products of these psychological processes (Haslanger 2017b, 7). Schemas are like "shared tools that enable us to interpret and coordinate with each other" (Haslanger 2017a, 5). For example:

> White Supremacy teaches us to be selective in what we notice, what we respond to, what we value...the police academy trains the officer to ignore (or interpretively skew) certain behaviours, for example, all too often the cries of the Black person or the poor woman in labor.... They are not what matters; the local cultural techne [networks of schemas] produces "blinders" that filter and shape experience.
>
> (Haslanger 2017a, 12)

Practices in turn sustain social structures. Take the example of caring for infants. While both parents of the newborn infant may wish to parent equally, in most places only the mother is entitled to leave from work. Because the couple cannot afford for the father to quit his job, and given the lack of child care facilities, the mother takes leave. Based on her experience and routines, she continues to take long-term primary responsibility for the infant by returning to part-time work. The couple's decision-making is constrained in a number of ways. The public policy context (limited leave entitlements; lack of affordable child care) defines what options are available to each of them; their individual choices are also constrained by their relationship to each other, by the fact that infants can't care for themselves, and so on. The effect of this structure is that, over time, men typically acquire considerably more by way of salary and other resources which give them more power in the home and at work. We cannot ignore structures if we want to understand why men accumulate more power and resources than women.

Our culturally shared schemas partly explain the emergence of many of these constraints. That mothers rather than fathers should care for infants, that such care constitutes the best for the infant, and that mothers should prioritize such duties over career, are constituents of cultural schemas concerning the care of infants which, in turn, affect how we organize resources. Importantly, the organization of these resources reinforces the cultural schemas which shaped them. It looks to be just a natural fact about women and men that women are more suited to care for young infants while men are more suited to pursue career achievement. As Haslanger puts it, schemas shape resources that fit and reinforce those schemas. This false appearance of naturalness "is easily generated due to the 'loopiness' of social structures: we respond to the world that has been shaped to trigger those very responses without being conscious of the shaping, so our responses seem to be called for by the way the world is" (Haslanger 2012, 468).

Shared schemas around the disabled are heavily stigmatized. While the stigma of disability is complex, being seen as incapable, needy, and pitiful are at its core, as I have suggested. The stigmatized schemas that shape our practices and ultimately our social structures are central to producing the disadvantages of disability. Schemas that disabled people are naturally unfit to participate fully in society shapes our resources, such as the lack of accessible transport; the inaccessibility of many work, educational, and cultural institutions; and the unfair distribution of shared resources. The low participation and success of disabled people that predictably flows from the way our resources have been shaped reinforces those very schemas that produce a hostile and incommodious environment. It looks like a natural fact that people with disabilities are incapable of full and equal participation.

Our stigmatized schemas also shape the norms which govern our interpersonal exchanges. For example, suppose that adequate resources are provided for people who need assistance with personal care (preparing meals, showering). The way in which personal services are delivered will also conform to stigmatized schemas. People receiving care will have very little opportunity to make choices or exercise control over matters like what they eat and when they shower. The boundaries of privacy and intimacy will be ignored, and norms around etiquette and decorum will be violated. This is Christine's story: cultural schemas about her child-like incapability infect every aspect of her interaction with her caregivers, including her diminished agency and control, her loss of privacy, and her inability to maintain norms of decorum.

Just as incommodious environments reinforce stigmatized schemas about the natural inability to participate and succeed in social institutions, so too the way we engage with the disabled in more interpersonal contexts reinforces cultural schemas of incapability and social inferiority. When we observe disabled people in disheveled and soiled clothing, exposed for all to see during toileting and showering, spoken to with either extreme condescension or impatience and disregard, the schemas which shape these norms of interpersonal exchange are reinforced. Similarly, even though John and Stella participate fully and successfully in all aspects of society, schemas shape the way even well-intentioned people interact with them: what is routinely expressed is their lower status. That John and Stella are regularly subject to ridicule, condescension, and contempt reinforces those very stigmatized schemas that shape such behavior. We respond to people with disabilities according to how we perceive them, and such responses further bolster stigmatized schemas.

People with disabilities and others are right to be concerned about Wackenheim's employment choices. Only because we perceive such people in a certain way can we make sense of the desire to throw them about as missiles for fun. But so throwing them, to cheers and laughter, reinforces the very stigmatized schemas around short stature that make sense of the practice of "dwarf-throwing" in the first place. While I have reached no conclusion about what should be done in the case like this, given that Wackenheim's autonomous agency is on the line, it is wrong to dismiss out of hand the concerns that other disabled people have about such contests. They are right to be concerned, just as much as all women have at least something at stake in wet t-shirt competitions.

In sum, I have suggested that routine interactions in which people with disabilities are treated as social inferiors arise from, and reinforce, cultural schemas that profoundly affect their access to social institutions, to power, and to the ability to exercise control over their own lives. There are many constituents of stigmatized schemas around disability. The claim is certainly not that treating people as social inferiors is the only element that contributes to unjust social structures. But it is not trivial and certainly not irrelevant. Culture matters, as Haslanger says. It affects everything about the lives of people with disabilities: the lack of public transport, inaccessible work and educational institutions, the lack of adequate healthcare and decent housing, and everyday status-denying exchanges.

Finally, it is also plausible to suggest that our failure to treat people with disabilities as social equals, and the subsequent reinforcement of stigmatized cultural schemas, helps perpetuate even greater abuses. If we turn our attention to people with cognitive impairments in particular, we cannot ignore not only the long history, but also contemporary evidence of the violence, neglect, and maltreatment to which they are exposed. In numbers far exceeding the non-disabled population, people with cognitive impairments are killed, sexually abused, bullied, left to suffer and die from easily preventable and treatable disease, institutionalized in squalid and unsafe environments, and denied nurture and love (Baladerian 1991; Horner-Johnson and Drum 2006; Troller et al. 2017).

Dehumanizing stigma around cognitive impairment must play some explanatory role in such maltreatment. To routinely engage with people with disabilities as though they are helpless; to subject them to extreme condescension, rudeness, and contempt; to constantly force them into situations where they are unable to uphold social norms to do with privacy, decorum, and dignified bearing, is to sustain social meanings around disability that are a fertile breeding ground for maltreatment. We accept that the causes of violence against women cannot be isolated from a broader context of gender inequality (Jewkes 2002; WHO 2005). Essentially, the same claim is being made here about violence and disability, especially cognitive impairment.

To reiterate, the claim is not that failure to treat people with cognitive impairments as social equals is the sole or direct cause of abuse. We know of many factors that facilitate the abuse to which people with cognitive impairments are vulnerable: poor regulation of institutions, the relative isolation of people with cognitive impairments, and the inability or unwillingness to report abuse have all been identified as contributing causes. But routine behaviors that lower the status of people with disabilities also play a role. The failure to treat people with disabilities as our social equals in our everyday exchanges is part of a wider pattern of cultural, political, and legal maltreatment. It is harmful in ways that go beyond its contribution to humiliation and reduced agency.

While my main aim has been to show that dignity is morally important because the failure to treat people with equal status can be seriously harmful, my analysis raises the question of whether it is possible to rectify our harmful behavior. We are likely to be more confident in knowing how to tackle false beliefs than stigmatized schemas. For stigmatized schemas are not only a matter of false beliefs, but also influence affect, perception, and behavioral dispositions, including the social norms of interpersonal exchange. If our perceptive, affective, and behavioral responses to people with disabilities are shaped by stigmatized schemas, and those patterned responses make the stigma which produce them seem like a natural fact about disability, then "loopiness" looks like a trap. How do we stand outside schemas to critique and change them?

Haslanger herself stresses the role of broader social movements and experiments in living. I take it that the idea is that social movements can both challenge existing schemas and create new and better ones. These macro-scale enterprises are crucially important. The disability rights movement has already profoundly shaped the way we perceive, treat, and engage with people with disabilities. Virtually all of the positive changes for disabled people that have occurred were made possible by that social movement.

Nonetheless, I think Haslanger overlooks the potential for what I shall call micro-challenges to stigmatized schemas. We should also do what little we can in our day-to-day exchanges to challenge stigmatized schemas, notwithstanding my earlier concession that it can sometimes be difficult to know how to do so successfully. Just as women can change the car tyres and men can change the nappies, caregivers, neighbors, colleagues, and service-providers can respond to people with disabilities according to social norms that express equal status. They can refer to them as people, philosophical dispute notwithstanding. They can avoid condescension, rudeness, violations of privacy, and expressions of contempt. They can make it a habit to uphold social norms around etiquette, politeness, respect, and decorum in their interactions. Such behaviors make some contribution to challenging stigmatized schemas around disability. They contribute, along with changes to law, public policy, the distribution of resources, and social movements, to changing social meanings. The way we treat each other in our informal exchanges matters. We need to do much better with respect to our day-to-day exchanges with people with disabilities, and, as such, dignity also matters.

Is Equal Status Enough?

I assume that all of us agree that people with cognitive impairments should not be subject to the harms I have discussed. If we also accept that the failure to treat people as our social equals contributes to social meanings that help produce such harms, then we should also accept that treating people with disabilities as our social equals is morally important.

These arguments support the case that the status conception of dignity is not parasitic on the worth conception. We have good reasons to uphold the equal status of people with cognitive impairment, and those reasons are independent of any considerations about whether their moral standing is the same as that of people without cognitive impairment. At least when it comes to addressing the significant harms of violence, lack of access, discrimination, neglect, and other maltreatment, we can avoid fraught philosophical debate about whether people with cognitive impairments have the same inherent worth or capacities as people without such impairments. Irrespective of the inherent capacities of people with cognitive impairment, of how they might be different to the rest of us, whether or not they have rationality or autonomy or a conception of the good, we have powerful reasons to treat them as our social equals.

Many disability advocates will be skeptical of my suggestion that issues of moral standing are in some respects not as crucial as has been assumed. For example, dignity as equal worth or moral standing would seem to provide much more direct challenge to practices around preimplantation genetic diagnosis and selective abortion of so-called defective fetuses. This is true, but I doubt there will be any end to such practices in any case. Yet disability will always be with us. Many people do not have access to prenatal care or choose not to abort so-called defective fetuses. Accident, illness, and ageing aren't going away. So the importance of treating all people with disabilities as social equals, irrespective of their moral standing, is undiminished.

But isn't it plausible to suggest that such reproductive practices also contribute to stigmatized schemas around disability? After all, this seems to be one plausible way to understand what are known as "expressivist objections" to reproductive practices around disability (Asch 1999). Indeed, one might also argue that philosophical skepticism about the equal moral status of people with cognitive impairments also contributes to harmful stigma: certainly many disability activists see Peter Singer's work in this way. Although usually dismissed as failing to understand the sophistication of his philosophical views, I think that his disability critics are highly alert to the potential harm such talk might inflict on the living disabled, however much Singer denies his arguments apply to them (at least beyond a few weeks of age).

Whether or not reproductive practices and philosophical debate contribute to harmful social meanings about disability, it doesn't follow they should be banned. I have suggested that dignity will not always trump other values, so avoiding harmful stigma will not always take priority over reproductive choice and free academic debate. The boundaries shift all the time of course, and with respect to Singer, there is clear disagreement among us over whether what he says might contribute to harmful stigma and whether any such contribution is significant enough to justify suppressing academic discussion. Given that social meanings are only one contributing factor to the maltreatment of people with disabilities, it may be best to focus on other causes—such as poor legal protection, a lack of resources, and inaccessible environments—rather than sacrifice reproductive choice or stifle academic debate.

Finally, it should be acknowledged that there are some very limited situations where it may not be right or appropriate to treat people with very severe cognitive impairments in accordance with all of our equal status norms. For example, suppose that a doctor caring for a woman in a wheelchair addresses his questions to her husband instead of her. It seems uncontroversial to say that this woman is not treated with dignity. But now suppose that in addition to being a wheelchair user, the woman in question has very profound cognitive impairments. Should the doctor address his questions to her in any case, even when it is clear she cannot understand what he is saying? Would this be the right thing to do, given that this is the norm that usually governs these types of exchanges? Or would it be to treat her poorly, needlessly highlighting her impairment, and making something of a sham of social exchange?[5]

I think we should say that while the woman *is* treated as a social equal when the doctor addresses his questions to her, this case again demonstrates that dignity should sometimes give way to other values, like compassion and honesty. In contrast to this conclusion, I think some people will have the strong intuition that the doctor fails to treat this woman with dignity in addressing questions to her he knows she cannot understand. I share the intuition that he doesn't treat her well when doing so, but to characterize this as a lack of dignity is to use "dignity" in a different sense to that discussed in this chapter. I cannot see how the intuition that the doctor treats her badly can be fleshed out in terms of the doctor denying her equal status. He doesn't deny her equal status, but he may treat her badly nonetheless, and perhaps without dignity, according to some other meaning of the term. In terms of dignity as equal status, I think it is more accurate to simply concede that it does not always trump other concerns or values.

But these cases will be very limited. In the vast majority of circumstances, we can and should treat people with disabilities, including those with cognitive impairments, with dignity. Although not the only value, and not one that always trumps other considerations, dignity is of significant moral importance. It is not reducible to other values like autonomy or respect for persons. Rather, it identifies a value too often neglected in debates about our treatment of people who do not enjoy equality. To address persistent inequality, changes to the law, to institutions, and to the distribution of social resources are all important. But so are changes to our interpersonal interactions. The failure to treat people with disabilities as social equals harms them, both directly and by contributing to a culture that facilitates maltreatment and abuse. Changing such status-deny behavior should be a moral priority. Dignity matters.[6]

Notes

1. For many other examples, analyzed as violations of negative respect, see Adam Cureton (2020), "The Limiting Role of Respect," chapter 22 of this volume.
2. I am not entirely convinced Calhoun has established this case. Much probably hinges on what is meant by the term "respect." If we do not believe acting in accordance with sexist norms actually treats women with respect, as Calhoun suggests, then it seems as though the type of respect we have in mind is bound to some notion of equality. If so, then it is very doubtful that it is that notion of respect that Calhoun argues is successfully communicated

when men act on sexist norms. If she believes that men successfully communicate respect by acting on sexist norms, then there is a very different notion of respect at play, and perhaps it is also true then that, on that notion, they do actually treat women with respect as well.

3. I thank David Wasserman for pressing this point and for the example.

4. It is worth mentioning what is hopefully obvious; namely, that feelings of humiliation are certainly not a sufficient condition for having been treated as a social inferior. People often feel humiliated when others do treat them as social equals! A woman might feel humiliated if we expect her to take it in turns holding the door or paying for a shared meal, just as an older person might feel humiliated when a young colleague follows his example in addressing him by his first name. As we saw in our discussion of Calhoun, some social norms are deeply at odds with equal status, not least those which are often claimed to promote "separate but equal" or "different but equal" standards. As I have already argued, we do not enjoy dignity by virtue of social relations which conform to just any social standards.

5. I thank David Wasserman for this powerful example.

6. I wish to thank Adam Cureton, Suzy Killmister, and David Wasserman for their invaluable feedback on a draft of this chapter. I also wish to thank the audience at the Current Trends in Social and Political Philosophy Conference, Monash University, July 2017.

References

Anderson, Joel, and Axel Honneth. 2005. "Autonomy, Vulnerability, Recognition, and Justice." In *Autonomy and the Challenges to Liberalism. New Essays*, edited by John Christman and Joel Anderson. Cambridge: Cambridge University Press: 127–149.

Asch, Adrienne. 1999. "Prenatal Diagnosis and Selective Abortion: A Challenge to Practice and Policy." *American Journal of Public Health* 89(11):1649–1657.

Baladerian, Nora J. 1991. "Sexual Abuse of People with Developmental Disabilities." *Sexuality and Disability* 9(4):323–335.

Barclay, Linda. 2016. "The Importance of Equal Respect: What the Capabilities Approach Can and Should Learn from Human Rights Law." *Political Studies* 64(2):385–400.

Beitz, Charles R. 2013. "Human Dignity in the Theory of Human Rights: Nothing but a Phrase?" *Philosophy & Public Affairs* 41(3):259–290.

Bird, Colin. 2014. "Dignity as a Moral Concept." *Social Philosophy and Policy* 30(1–2):150–176.

Calhoun, Cheshire. 2000. "The Virtue of Civility." *Philosophy & Public Affairs* 29(3):251–275.

Cureton, Adam. 2020. "The Limiting Role of Respect." In *Oxford Handbook of Philosophy and Disability*, edited by Adam Cureton and David Wasserman, 381–398. New York: Oxford University Press.

Darwall, Stephen L. 1977. "Two Kinds of Respect." *Ethics* 80(1): 36–49.

Goffman, Erving. 1963. *Stigma. Notes on the Management of Spoiled Identity*. London: Penguin Books.

Haslanger, Sally. 2012. *Resisting Reality: Social Construction and Social Critique*. New York: Oxford University Press.

Haslanger, Sally. 2015. "Social Structure, Narrative, and Explanation." *Canadian Journal of Philosophy* 45(1):1–15.

Haslanger, Sally. 2016. "What Is a (Social) Structural Explanation." *Philosophical Studies* 173: 113–130.

Haslanger, Sally. 2017a. "Culture and Critique." *Proceedings of the Aristotelian Society Supplementary Volume* 91(4):149–173.

Haslanger, Sally. 2017b. "Racism, Ideology, and Social Movements." *Res Philosophica* 94(1):1–22.

Horner-Johnson, Willi, and Charles E. Drum. 2006. "Prevalence of Maltreatment of People with Intellectual Disabilities: A Review of Recently Published Research." *Developmental Disabilities Research Reviews* 12(1):57–69.

Jacobson, Nora. 2012. *Dignity and Health.* Nashville, TN: Vanderbilt University Press.

Jewkes, Rachel. 2002. "Intimate Partner Violence: Causes and Prevention." *The Lancet* 359(9315):1423–1429.

Killmister, Suzy. 2017. "Dignity: Personal, Social, Human." *Philosophical Studies* 174(8):2063–2082.

Luban, D. 2009. "Human Dignity, Humiliation, and Torture." *Kennedy Institute of Ethics Journal* 19(3):211–230.

Macklin, R. 2003. "Dignity Is a Useless Concept." *BMJ* 327(7429):1419–1420.

Margalit, Avishai. 1998. *The Decent Society.* Cambridge, MA: Harvard University Press.

Rosen, Michael. 2012. *Dignity. Its History and Meaning.* Cambridge, MA: Harvard University Press.

Statman, Daniel. 2000. "Humiliation, Dignity and Self-Respect." *Philosophical Psychology* 13(4):523–540.

Troller, Julian, Preeyaporn Srasuebkul, Han Xu, and Sophie Howlett. 2017. "Cause of Death and Potentially Avoidable Deaths in Australian Adults with Intellectual Disability Using Retrospective Linked Data." *BMJ Open* 7: e013489. doi:10.1136/bmjopen-2016-013489.

Waldron, Jeremy. 2012. *Dignity, Rank and Rights.* New York: Oxford University Press.

WHO. 2005. *WHO Multi-Country Study on Women's Health and Domestic Violence Against Women. Initial Results on Prevalence, Health Outcomes and Women's Responses.* Geneva: World Health Organization.

Young, Stella. 2012. "Title." *Ramp Up,* 2nd July 2012. http://www.abc.net.au/rampup/articles/2012/07/02/3537035.htm.

PART SIX

MORAL STATUS AND SIGNIFICANT MENTAL DISABILITIES

CHAPTER 26

....

COGNITIVE DISABILITY AND MORAL STATUS

....

ALICE CRARY

THERE is a straightforward respect in which questions about moral status and cognitive disability are important for ethics. "Moral status" is sometimes used as a technical term in moral philosophy, but suppose that we employ it in a relatively nontechnical sense, representing an individual as having moral status—or, alternately, moral standing—insofar as she herself merits consideration or solicitude of some kind (Warren 1997, 3). Adopting this parlance, we might say that *explicit* conversations about the moral standing of people with cognitive disabilities take place at the periphery of contemporary ethics. There are express discussions in bioethics, in which moral philosophers address, for instance, questions about the treatment of newborn and elderly human beings with serious cognitive disabilities, and there are also express discussions within the context of increasingly prominent debates about the moral standing of animals. Considered all together, these discussions at best demonstrate that cognitive disability is a modest preoccupation of moral philosophers. But the topic is in fact more central to ethics than a survey of explicit discussions would seem to suggest. When moral philosophers take an interest in the sorts of questions about human moral status that are at the heart of ethics—say, questions about forms of respect and attention that human beings typically merit—they not infrequently commit themselves to conclusions about the moral standing of people with cognitive disabilities. This is because they often at least tacitly accept or reject the idea that moral standing is a direct function of the possession of particular capacities of mind (e.g., self-consciousness or practical rationality) that some people with cognitive disabilities lack. To the extent that moral philosophers are inclined to accept this idea, they veer toward representing people with corresponding cognitive disabilities as having diminished moral standing. This means that core conversations in ethics supply an urgent motive for the activist endeavors of those moral thinkers and advocates who hope to show that people with cognitive disabilities are the equals, with regard to dignity as well as with regard to claims to respect and attention, of their cognitively better endowed human fellows. At the same time, it means that questions about cognitive disability and moral status are integral to some fundamental lines of ethical inquiry and that, far from being merely specialized concerns, these questions are capable of shedding light on organizing presuppositions of contemporary moral philosophy.

One thing that these initial observations bring into relief is that questions about cognitive disability come up, explicitly or implicitly, in a wide variety of contexts in ethics. This dispersion makes it difficult to perspicuously survey the pertinent philosophical terrain. A reasonable strategy for working toward an overview is to isolate and investigate some of the most basic assumptions that moral philosophers make about methods available to us for thinking about moral status both in general and in reference to cognitive disability in particular.

It will be helpful to have as a reference point a case in which questions about cognitive disability and moral standing arise. Consider a passage in a paper of Eva Feder Kittay's in which she describes an episode in the life of her daughter Sesha, who has cerebral palsy and who, as an adult, "cannot speak, walk on her own or care for herself in even minimal ways" (Kittay 2005b, 96). Kittay is concerned with an event that occurred soon after Sesha moved into a small group home for people with multiple disabilities run by an agency with high standards for care. Kittay writes:

> As [Sesha] is wheeled out of the bathroom, wrapped in only a towel, and brought back to her room, the director of the agency walks in and is dismayed by what she sees. Although [Sesha] is entirely draped in her towel, the fact that her room is so close to the public area of the house and that she had to be wheeled out through a corridor that was somewhat far from her room displeased the director. [The director] insisted that a room further back, one that afforded the resident more privacy, be transformed from an equipment room into one that was suitable for occupancy and that the room close to the public area serve instead for equipment storage. The agency head explained that having this young woman wheeled through a corridor where young male residents and staff could encounter her … was an offence to the resident's dignity.   (Kittay 2005b, 95–96)

Suppose that, faced with these remarks of Kittay's, we ponder questions about whether Sesha has the kind of moral standing in virtue of which she calls for various kinds of treatment. Does Sesha merit the care she receives in her group home—care that includes things like nourishing food, good healthcare, assistance with personal hygiene, a consistent and supportive social environment, and a schedule of engaging activities? And, taking for granted that Sesha is capable at least to some extent of appreciating *these* goods, does she—as Kittay suggests—also merit protection from some slights (such as, e.g., that of being wheeled through a corridor near a public room clad only in a towel) that she herself may well not experience as such? How strong is Sesha's claim to these different forms of treatment? Last, what resources do we have in ethics for answering such questions?

When moral philosophers defend views about cognitive disability and moral status, they at the same time at least tacitly supply answers to this last question (i.e., the question about available resources in ethics). To illustrate this, we can turn to what might, for the sake of convenience, be called *traditional approaches to ethics and cognitive disability.* This moniker can be used to bring together a loose set of views about cognitive disability and moral status that, although internally heterogeneous, are similar in operating with a metaphysical picture that belongs to the current Zeitgeist and that establishes the conceptual space in which today a great deal of research in ethics is undertaken. At issue is a picture on which the empirical or observable world is in itself bereft of moral values. It is possible to consistently accept a version of this metaphysical picture while also representing moral assessments as universally authoritative (i.e., while also allowing that these assessments may be such that *any* thinker should be able to recognize them as correct). What the metaphysic excludes is an account of moral assessments on which they are universally authoritative and on which their being so is essentially a function of fidelity to how things observably are. Notice that ethical outlooks that incorporate this metaphysic place distinctive constraints on the resources available to us for moral thought. Here it appears that we cannot require the use of moral capacities like moral imagination in order to get features of the observable world into focus in a fashion pertinent to ethics. It appears that it cannot be necessary to look at things from new cultural or historical perspectives, or to imaginatively project ourselves into the experience of individuals with very different backgrounds or life experiences, in order to do empirical justice to how things are. According to the conception of the observable world that we are helping ourselves to in ethics, this world is something that, instead of having aspects or features that are only revealed by such moral exertion, can be delivered to us entirely from disciplines like the natural sciences, where these are conceived as external to ethics. And, insofar as the conception of the observable world that we work with in ethics includes any conception we have of the observable lives of human beings, it appears to follow—against the backdrop of the influential metaphysic at play—that the project of doing empirical justice in ethics to the lives of human beings with or without cognitive disabilities is a project not for ethics itself but rather for disciplines rightly conceived as falling outside of it.

This metaphysical posture has consequences for how we approach the sorts of questions about moral standing that come up in reference to Kittay's daughter Sesha. It is an implication of the posture that the task of achieving the sort of worldly grasp of Sesha's life and circumstances that is relevant to ethics is one that should be outsourced to disciplines independent of ethics (say, perhaps, neurobiology and neurology) and that our task as moral philosophers lies elsewhere. Guided by these ideas, some moral philosophers who take an interest in cognitive disability suggest that it does not belong to their main enterprise to offer empirically faithful accounts of the lives of individuals with cognitive disabilities. They treat their operative accounts of cognitive disability as "stipulative" (Wasserman et al. 2013, section 1). Whereas, on the one hand, they maintain that there are good reasons to believe that the accounts faithfully describe some actual individuals, on the other, they treat the question of the accounts' bearing on particular cases as a secondary, applicative matter that can legitimately be postponed (e.g., McMahan 2009, 241–242; for a critique of this basic approach, see Carlson 2020, this volume).

Philosophers who adopt these very general methodological principles are effectively assuming that immersion in morally rich accounts of the experience of people with cognitive disabilities (even if it happens to shed light on notable empirical aspects of the lives of the cognitively disabled) cannot as such make a necessary contribution to an empirical grasp of their lives. Among the things that thus get excluded as essentially irrelevant for arriving at an empirical understanding of the circumstances of individuals with cognitive disabilities in ethics is engagement with contributions to the long history of—morally charged—exposés of the callous treatment of these individuals in public and private institutions. Consider, for instance, the investigative journalist Katherine Boo's 1999 article for the *Washington Post* about the coverup of fatal forms of abuse and medical neglect in a network of private group homes in the D.C. area (Boo 1999). One of the cases Boo discusses is that of Fred Brandenburg, a man with serious cognitive disabilities, who in 1991 was transferred to the private home in which he eventually died. Having failed for years to give him recommended medication for a heart condition, staff at his home tranquilized him without any medical indication one day in 1997, when he was 57. The effects on his health were dramatic and dire—within days he was sweating and shaking, unable to stand or eat without assistance—but no one called 911. When paramedics were finally summoned, he had already been dead for hours. That is how Brandenburg died, and, before offering a detailed account of the facts of his demise, Boo gives us a glimpse of his life. She writes:

> On the streets outside the city-funded group home where he had lived and died, kids sometimes called him Retard-O. Inside, he sweetened the hours by printing the name his mother gave him before she gave him up. Frederick Emory Brandenburg. He blanketed old telephone directories with that name, covered the *TV Guides* the home's staffers tossed aside. He glutted the flyleaves of his large-print *Living Bible*. The immensity of the effort made his hands shake, but the habit seemed as requisite as breath. In this way Brandenburg, whose thick-tongued words were mysteries to many, impressed the fact of his existence on his world.   (Boo 1999)

Boo offers this evocative account of Brandenburg's pursuits with an eye to countering what she describes as the official "erasure of [his] life." She reminds us that Brandenburg had a mother who named him because she—Boo—wants to give us an impression of him as an individual, as a person with a spark of life that could have been kindled with smiles, hugs, laughter, and talk. She hopes in this way to get us to look upon him as someone who, instead of being left to write his name obsessively on anything he can find, merited significant forms of attention he didn't receive, including among other things good healthcare, education, and consistent social contacts. Yet, however arresting or interesting we find Boo's efforts, if we accept a metaphysic on which the observable world is as such bereft of moral value, we will be compelled to reject any non-neutral perspectives that her words aim to cultivate as incapable of contributing internally to the kind of empirical understanding of Brandenburg's—or any other cognitively disabled person's—life that we want in ethics.

Versions of this sort of methodological gesture show up in many of the most well-known and widely discussed contributions to cognitive disability and ethics. Typically, the gesture is motivated by sympathy for the idea that the real weave of the observable world is free of moral values. This idea structures the writings of Peter Singer, one of the most high-profile moral philosophers and bioethicists who addresses questions about cognitive disability and moral status (see esp. Kuhse and Singer 1986; Singer 1993; 1994; 2010; 2015). Singer's point of departure in ethics for much of his career has been a type of preference utilitarianism, a position on which the right action in a particular context is the one that best fulfills the interests of all creatures concerned, where a being's "interests" are an expression of her capacity for pain or pleasure. Singer's work has had a big impact on debates about moral status—not only in reference to human beings with and without cognitive disabilities but also in reference to animals. What has left the biggest imprint, however, is not his utilitarian posture (which has varied in its details over the years) but one of its grounding presuppositions. It is an assumption of Singer's stance that any consideration a being merits is a reflection not of membership in any group (say, the group "human beings") but rather of individual capacities of mind. While it is possible to make an assumption along these lines without embracing an image of the observable world as morally neutral qua observable, Singer at many times signals his attachment to such an image (Crary 2016, 19–25), and the bioethicists and other moral philosophers who follow in his footsteps in connecting moral status with individual mental capacities overwhelmingly operate, at least implicitly, with the constraints of such an image as well. To be sure, members of this loose group of thinkers differ substantially in their views about which mental capacities are morally significant as well as in their views about whether the relevant capacities ground static levels of moral status once they reach a threshold, or whether instead they underwrite continuously varying degrees of moral status (Wasserman et al. 2013, sections 2.1 and 3). But the thinkers in question agree in at least implicitly taking it for granted that the identification of whatever individual capacities of mind they take to be morally significant is a job that is properly assigned, not to ethics itself, but to disciplines beyond it. In this respect, they resemble Singer in counting as advocates of traditional approaches to cognitive disability and ethics.

Advocates of these particular traditional approaches are sometimes described as fans of *moral individualism* (McMahan 2005; Rachels 1990). What speaks for this nomenclature is the fact that the thinkers in question ground their conclusions about moral standing in a certain kind of attention to individuals (viz., morally neutral attention to individuals' capacities of mind). However, as will emerge later, discussions about cognitive disability and ethics feature competing approaches to moral standing that likewise have claims to be grounding their conclusions in attention to individuals. So, with an eye to clarity, it makes sense to deny advocates of this first set of views the simple label "moral individualists" and to refer to them instead as *traditional moral individualists*.

Traditional moral individualists sometimes advance their main claims about the moral status of people with cognitive disabilities in the context of exploring the moral status of nonhuman animals. Starting from the thought that moral standing is a function of neutrally available individual capacities, traditional moral individualists sometimes stipulate that any capacities that are morally relevant in human beings are equally so in animals, and they sometimes follow up on this stipulation by taking an interest in the question of whether it is in fact the case that some human beings and some animals are equally well endowed with morally relevant capacities. It is against this backdrop that many of these thinkers turn their attention to human beings with cognitive disabilities. They present themselves as observing that some human beings who—as a result of illness, injury, age, or some congenital condition—are severely cognitively disabled are no better equipped than some animals with "morally significant capacities." Sometimes traditional moral individualists suggest that a person who is severely cognitively disabled—say, because she was born with a particular congenital condition—may be no better mentally endowed than, for instance, a dog or a pig or a chimpanzee (McMahan 2005, 364–366; 2009, 240–242; Singer 1994, 159–163; 2010, 322; 2015, 140). They then appeal to this suggestion not only to establish that some animals are morally significant beings who deserve far better treatment than they typically receive but also to fund the following conclusion about the moral standing of human beings with what they think of as serious or "radical" cognitive disabilities (McMahan 2009). They tell us that these people have lesser moral standing, and so merit less consideration, in virtue of their disabilities.

Advocates for the cognitively disabled have found the argument leading to this conclusion problematic in numerous interconnected ways. The argument is sometimes referred to as *the argument from marginal cases* (Dombrowski 1997), and, at the most fundamental level, advocates take issue with the idea that human beings with cognitive disabilities are "marginal" cases of humanity. Some traditional moral individualists have, admittedly, tried to avoid giving offence by redescribing themselves as fans of an *argument from species overlap* (Horta 2014). But this change in terminology doesn't eliminate the suggestion—the main target of the critique of advocates for the cognitively disabled—that human beings with "radical" cognitive disabilities have lesser moral status in virtue of their disabilities and are in this respect morally "marginal." Furthermore, in the eyes of many advocates for the cognitively disabled, traditional moral individualists compound the wrong of this suggestion by grounding it in comparisons between cognitively disabled human beings and animals. It's not that advocates for the cognitively disabled uniformly disagree with traditional moral individualists who are convinced that animals have moral standing and should be treated better. On the contrary, some insist that animals merit respect and solicitude (Carlson 2010, 146; 2020; Crary 2016, 150–160; Kittay 2005a, 125; 2009a, 132; Taylor, 2017). Their point is that in grounding the moral marginalization of cognitively disabled human beings in comparisons with animals, traditional moral individualists betray an insensitivity to, or at least lack of awareness of, the long and horrifying history of the use of such comparisons in rhetoric motivating the abusive treatment and killing of people with cognitive disabilities (Carlson 2010, 132–136; Kittay 2009b, 613; Gallagher 1989; Wolfensberger 1972, 17–19). To be sure, with reference to this history, some advocates for the cognitively disabled argue that it is appropriate to reject on principle any hint within discussions of cognitive disability of human–animal comparisons (e.g., Drake 2010; Price 2011, 133). This antagonism is to some extent the achievement of traditional moral individualists. To the extent that in comparing cognitively disabled people with animals they signal that they suspect that the former are often treated too well, they go beyond simple insensitivity and demonstrate a willingness to deny the annals of neglect of and violence toward people with cognitive disabilities (Bérubé and Ruth 2015, 46; Kittay 2000, 66–68; Taylor 2017).

These are substantial criticisms, and some traditional moral individualists register them and attempt to address them. Those who do so typically respond by insisting that they have simply followed rationally unobjectionable argumentative steps to conclusions that happen to conflict with received moral belief. They tell us that they don't merit censure for what we may regard as outrageous views, and that, if anything, they should be lauded for their willingness to unflinchingly stand behind the results of what in their eyes count as sound lines of reasoning. Their thought is that defending morally radical conclusions takes nerve and that they deserve respect for having the courage to break openly with established beliefs (e.g., Kuhse and Singer 1986; McMahan 2002; Singer 2013).

The basic argument that these traditional moral individualists are defending—the so-called argument from species overlap—counts among its premises that the mere fact of membership in the group "human being" (i.e., without regard to the level of one's individual capacities) is morally insignificant. Thinkers who run versions of the argument, and who thereby contest the tendency to treat being human as by itself morally important, sometimes attack this tendency under the heading of *speciesism* (Ryder 1989, 5–12). Speciesism is usually understood generically as unwarranted prejudice in favor of one's species, and what the thinkers in question are claiming is that we invariably express such prejudice if we suggest that the mere fact of being human matters morally. This interpretation of what speciesism amounts to is not, however, at home in the work of all fans of traditional approaches to cognitive disability and ethics.

There are a number of approaches to cognitive disability and ethics that qualify as "traditional" in the above sense (i.e., in that they take for granted that the empirical world is essentially morally neutral) and that nevertheless differ from the traditional moral individualisms surveyed thus far in maintaining that all human beings, no matter how well-endowed cognitively, have moral status. Many advocates of these further traditional approaches start from Kant's moral theory and demonstrate their "traditional" colors by at least implicitly taking Kant's core claims about ethics to be at home in the context of a conception of the world as—in Christine Korsgaard's argot—"hard" or bereft of moral and other values (Korsgaard 1996, 4). These thinkers follow Kant in basing their views about moral standing in a suggestion to the effect that, in acting, we can't help but place value on our own natures as rational beings and, further, that consistency therefore compels us to respect the rational natures of all rational beings. This suggestion might seem to speak for a familiar sort of traditional moral individualism. The idea might be that only human beings who, qua individuals, possess developed capacities of reason actually have moral status. While this idea is championed by some thinkers who present themselves as inheriting from Kant's moral philosophy (e.g., Regan 1984, 174–185), it is not uncommon for Kantian moral philosophers to move from observing that Kant himself represents all human beings as having basic moral status (for references, see Kain 2009, esp. 61 n.6) to searching for grounds, inside or outside Kant's writings, for saying that a Kantian orientation in ethics provides support for the conclusion that merely being human (i.e., without regard to the level of one's rational capacities) is morally important.

Some of the Kantian moral philosophers who make this move proceed by means of the following general strategy. They take as their point of departure a reflection about the peculiar logic of natural history; that is, a reflection about what's at issue when we discuss the truth of a claim about the natural history of a given life form (e.g., the truth of the claim that sunflowers produce one or more flower heads or the truth of the claim that human beings have 32 teeth). The point is that here truth is a matter not of statistical accuracy but of fidelity to a normatively loaded conception of how organisms of a particular kind ideally develop over time. Granted this point, it seems fair to represent "human beings are rational beings" as a true natural-historical claim that is consistent with the observation that many individual human beings lack sophisticated capacities of reason. Furthermore, granted this image of human rational nature, it seems plausible to make use of ideas from Kant's moral philosophy in arguing that every human being, irrespective of the level of her actual rational capacities, is a "rational being" and therefore endowed with full moral status. The conclusion of the resulting argument is that membership in the group "human being" by itself grounds moral status. The different Kantian or neo-Kantian approaches that run versions of this argument are sometimes referred to as *group-based approaches to cognitive disability and ethics* (Kumar 2006, 72–73; for an alternative Kantian group-based strategy, see Scanlon 1998, 185).

These sorts of group-based approaches have attracted criticism from advocates of other traditional approaches to cognitive disability and ethics. Like other traditional approaches, such group-based approaches presuppose that the real world is "hard" or bereft of moral and other values. So it may seem problematic that, at a central point in their ethical theorizing, fans of the approaches at issue advance a claim about how all human beings are rational beings—a claim that is supposed to have a necessary reference to a value-laden conception of human life. Starting from an observation along these lines, some traditional critics ask why we should accept this claim as licensing the spread of moral status from rational individuals to individuals with serious cognitive disabilities. The suggestion that moral status can be communicated in this manner appears, to these critics, to be a theoretically unmotivated effort at "moral alchemy" (McMahan 2008, 85). Admittedly, there is room to ask whether this criticism of the pertinent types of group-based approaches hits its mark. One of the most plausible lines of defense of the approaches centers on the idea that the perspective from which *all* humans show up for us as rational beings is not a theoretical but rather a practical one and that, as a result, any claims about the value of rational humanity it seems to sanction are metaphysically neutral and hence consistent with a hard metaphysic (for an extended treatment of relevant issues, see Korsgaard 2009).

At this point, we have before us a sketch of how a variety of different traditional approaches to cognitive disability and ethics cope with the sorts of questions about moral standing that we confront when we consider, say, the treatment of Kittay's daughter Sesha in her group home. Traditional moral individualisms ask us to deal with questions about Sesha's treatment by inquiring whether we are offering her respect equivalent to the respect we offer to others—nonhuman as well as human others—who in equal measure possess whichever mental capacities we take to be morally significant. Group-based views enjoin us to accord the same respect to all human beings, including those like Sesha who are severely cognitively disabled. It is not difficult to see that, in some cases, these approaches lead to different moral outcomes. Insofar as Sesha lacks the specific capacities that traditional moral individualisms identify as morally salient, these approaches invite us to regard her as meriting less solicitude than nondisabled human beings, and they are accordingly unlikely to embrace the idea—favored by Kittay—that Sesha is subject to slights she is incapable of registering. In contrast, insofar as group-based views invite us to regard Sesha as having undiminished moral standing, there is for them no problem about accommodating this idea.

Alongside this sort of difference among traditional approaches to cognitive disability and ethics, there is also a substantial commonality. Traditional approaches are united by the assumption that the sort of worldly understanding of human existence that is relevant to ethics needs to be pursued by means of the resources of disciplines that are external to ethics and, further, that there is no room for the use of moral capacities to contribute essentially to such understanding. This restriction on the methods of ethics is worth underlining because, although widely accepted within contemporary moral philosophy, it has forceful detractors. It is possible to identify a cluster of approaches to cognitive disability and ethics that reject the restriction, suggesting instead that we require moral resources of the sorts afforded by the employment of moral imagination in order to arrive in ethics at an adequate empirical understanding of many worldly things, such as human beings with and without cognitive disabilities. The unifying philosophical theme of these dissenting enterprises—namely, that entering into morally non-neutral perspectives is internal to efforts to bring the world empirically into focus in ethics—aligns them with prominent feminist, Black, and Marxist epistemologies, endeavors that have been grouped together under the heading of *alternative epistemologies* (Mills 1998). Suppose we refer to thinkers who are interested in the bearing of these ideas on reflection about individuals with cognitive disabilities as champions of *alternative approaches to cognitive disability and ethics*. These thinkers differ from many other champions of other alternative epistemologies in holding that the features of the world that are such that we require moral resources in order get them empirically into view include, in addition to features of rational human social life, also features of human life that don't rise to the level of full rationality.

The emergence of alternative approaches to cognitive disability and ethics takes place against the backdrop of a number of significant milestones in the political struggle for recognition for the cognitively disabled. After the early 1970s, which witnessed the first federal legislation in the United States to include language about the civil rights of people with disabilities (Fleischer and Zames 2011) and also the most highly publicized exposé—at the Willowbrook School—of the neglect and abuse of people with cognitive disabilities in a state institution (Kittay 2000, 65–77), efforts to agitate for rights and resources for the cognitively disabled gained steam. Among the main actors in this movement were not only parents of and caretakers for the cognitively disabled (e.g., Adams 2013; Bérubé 1996; 2016; Kittay 2000; 2009b) but also people with cognitive disabilities advocating for themselves (e.g., Debaggio 2002; Grandin 1986; 1995; Kinsley 2014; Kingsley and Levitz 2004; Schoultz and Williams 1984). One way in which the activism of the members of these two groups got taken up within moral philosophy was in a new interest in questions about the authority of non-neutral perspectives afforded by their experience; that is, the experience of people with cognitive disabilities and the experience of their caretakers (Carlson 2010, 120–122, 182–184; 2020; Taylor 2017). That is the political context in which alternative approaches to cognitive disability and ethics have been articulated and brought into conversation with traditional approaches. The resulting philosophical divide between traditional and alternative approaches arguably is not only the most basic within discussions of cognitive disability and moral status but also the most productive to investigate.

For a high-profile contribution on the "alternative" side of this dispute, we can turn to the work of Ian Hacking. Hacking has written at length about autism (Hacking 2009a; 2009b; 2010), and an organizing theme of his work is a conception of mind that is philosophically unorthodox in that it is at odds with the "traditional" assumption that the observable world is as such morally neutral. Hacking favors the view that aspects of mind are both observable in a straightforward sense and such that we need morally non-neutral resources in order to arrive at an empirical grasp of them. He develops this view by sounding themes from the research of psychologists Lev Vygotsky and Wolfgang Köhler. What Hacking takes from Vygotsky is the idea that early social interactions typically contribute to the internalization of psychological life in a manner that equips us to think and talk about things like intentions and emotions. Hacking combines this Vygotskean idea with a thought of Köhler's to the effect that the practical adjustments and responses that many of us thus develop in the course of early socialization contribute essentially to enabling us to noninferentially recognize the psychological states expressed in others' behavior. What emerges is a conception of mind on which psychological concepts are categories for picking out patterns of expressiveness and on which these categories are taken to be simultaneously metaphysically transparent and such that we require developed sensibilities in order to authoritatively project them. Hacking associates this conception—which appears heretical when considered against the backdrop of contemporary philosophy of mind—with Wittgenstein's later philosophy, and he sometimes glosses it, in Wittgensteinian terms, by saying that it is from within the weave of complicated human "forms of life" that we come into psychological focus for each other. Hacking takes the modes of practical responsiveness that, as he sees it, Wittgenstein represents as internal to psychological understanding to encode a sense of what is humanly important. Hacking thus champions a view on which it is only through the lens of an ethical conception of human life that we can get certain—psychological—aspects of human existence empirically into focus (see also Crary 2016; Gaita 2000).

Hacking explores this particular view because he thinks it sheds helpful light on challenges of doing justice in ethics to the worldly lives of people with autism. He describes the kinds of socialization-shaped responses and reactions that he thinks equip us to directly perceive states of mind as "Köhler's phenomena" (e.g., Hacking 2009a, 1471–1472), and he claims that autists to some extent lack these phenomena and, further, that this not only makes it difficult for them to understand nonautistic "neurotypicals" but also makes it difficult for neurotypicals to understand autists. Guided by this claim, Hacking turns to emerging bodies of literature about autism, including autobiography and a variety of fictional genres, that he takes to be in the business of engaging (autistic as well as neurotypical) readers in ways that are capable of developing our ethical conceptions of human life and of thereby internally contributing to our capacities for psychological understanding. He attempts to get us to see that the works of literature that interest him invite the kind of moral work that, in his view, we have to do to bring the worldly lives of people with autism into view in a manner relevant to ethics (Hacking 2009a; 2009b; 2010).

Abstracting from Hacking's specific concern with autism, we can say that, for him, it is only from perspectives afforded by an ethically charged conception of human life that it is possible to make sense of psychological aspects of the worldly existence of human beings and, further, that this is true without regard to the level or nature of the cognitive capacities of the individual human beings whom we are trying to understand. One consequence of Hacking's posture is that all human beings, however well-endowed cognitively, figure in moral thought as beings who, simply in virtue of being human, are morally important, meriting specific forms of respect and attention. So, for Hacking— and in this respect he is representative of advocates of alternative approaches to cognitive disability and ethics—there is no question of repudiating as "speciesist" the idea that the plain fact of being human is morally important.

It would be wrong to conclude that there are no substantial divergences between, on the one hand, Hacking and other champions of alternative approaches to cognitive disability and ethics and, on the other, those champions of traditional approaches— such as the advocates of Kant-inspired group-based approaches—who likewise treat the plain fact of being human as morally important. Hacking and others who favor alternative approaches agree in holding that the worldly lives of human beings only come into view for us in a manner relevant to ethics insofar as we look at these lives through the lens of ethical conceptions; that is, insofar as we avail ourselves of the sorts of non-neutral empirical methods that advocates of traditional approaches are committed to repudiating as essentially distorting. Against the backdrop of this alternative stance, it appears that modes of instruction that cultivate or enrich our ethical conceptions of human life may as such internally inform the sort of empirical grasp of human existence that we are after in ethics, and it is apposite in this connection that Hacking's writing on autism-oriented literary genres reflects a preoccupation with just such modes of instruction.

Alongside Hacking, there are a wide variety of projects that qualify as alternative approaches to cognitive disability and ethics (Bérubé 1996; 2016; Carlson 2010; Crary 2016; Diamond 1991; Gaita 2000; Kittay 2009a; 2009b; Lindemann 2014; Mulhall 2002). While differing in their accents, details, and sources of philosophical inspiration, these projects resemble each other in suggesting that the task of bringing the worldly lives of human beings into focus in ethics requires a type of moral exertion that involves not only cultivating a non-neutral conception of what matters in human life, but also surveying human beings in a manner informed by such a conception. Considered in reference to the case of Kittay's daughter Sesha, the point would be that, in order to bring her worldly circumstances clearly into focus, we need to see her in the light of a morally charged conception of human existence—for instance, the type of conception we might develop by immersing ourselves in works, such as the article of Katherine Boo's cited earlier, that aim deepen our sense of what matters in human life. There need be no question here of ingesting the nostrum that *every* attempt to shape our conception of what matters in human life will contribute internally to our ability to bring human beings empirically into focus in ethics. Any particular attempt—such as, for instance, Boo's in the article cited earlier or that of one of the autism-focused literary authors discussed by Hacking—may turn out to be sentimental or distorting in some other way. What champions of alternative approaches to cognitive disability and ethics are committed to holding is that, this caution notwithstanding, the exercise of exploring different conceptions of what matters in human life is integral to legitimate, world-guided moral thought about all human beings, without regard to the nature or level of their cognitive endowments. The idea is that we need to operate with relatively well-developed conceptions if, for instance, we are to be able to determine whether a given activity for an individual with specific cognitive disabilities is exploitative or engaging, or whether a given residential setting counts for her as schooling rather than as a form of confinement.

It's not difficult to see that, if we look upon Kittay's daughter Sesha in the relevant ethically inflected way, she will enter into our thought as someone who calls for respect and attention simply because she is human. Two points merit particular emphasis in this connection. The first is that the kinds of claims about Sesha's moral standing at issue here are claims grounded in attention to her as an individual. While the position at issue differs in fundamental ways from "traditional" moral individualisms, it would therefore not be unreasonable to speak of an *alternative moral individualism*. But, for all the appropriateness of talk of moral individualism, there is no obstacle—of the type confronted by traditional moral individualists—to sanctioning the possibility that Sesha may have suffered injuries that she herself lacks the capacity to register. It follows that—and this is the second point—within the framework of an alternative approach to cognitive disability and ethics, there is no problem about allowing that it may have been a slight to Sesha's dignity to wheel her through a hall near a public area in her group home with only a towel draped over her.

The conversation between traditional and alternative approaches to cognitive disability and ethics is, to date, a somewhat one-sided one. While alternative approaches are often explicitly presented as critical responses to traditional approaches, traditional approaches rarely engage substantially with their alternative critics, for the most part simply rejecting them as argumentatively loose or flawed. There is a respect in which this dismissive attitude on the part of advocates of traditional approaches is understandable. It is characteristic of advocates of alternative approaches to appeal to non-neutral perspectives in bringing the worldly lives of individuals with cognitive disabilities into view, and advocates of traditional approaches take it as a fundamental starting point that such perspectives are inherently distorting. That is, advocates of traditional approaches at least tacitly assume that the observable world is as such devoid of moral values and that the sorts of morally loaded perspectives to which advocates of alternatives approaches appeal incline necessarily toward blocking our view of how things are. This is what seems to enable those advocates of traditional approaches who do in fact discuss the work of their alternative interlocutors in some detail to dismiss its interest in good faith (see, e.g., McMahan 2005).

But we can credit advocates of traditional approaches with an understandable attitude vis-à-vis their alternative interlocutors without thinking that they have a decisive argument against alternative approaches. The philosophical position of advocates of traditional approaches seems insufficiently developed given that advocates of alternative approaches reject the metaphysical assumption it turns on; namely, the assumption that the empirical world is as such lacking in moral values. Advocates of alternative approaches favor a conception of observable reality on which it incorporates moral values, and, more specifically, they maintain that the worldly fabric of human life is suffused with such values. Granted this commitment, it appears that we require the use of morally loaded resources to achieve the sort of empirical understanding of the lives of human beings that we want in ethics. The result is that we need to revisit our view of what productive contributions to contemporary conversations about cognitive disability and moral status might be like. If we are to engage meaningfully with these conversations, we have to register that they are riven by a genuine, philosophically substantial disagreement about how to construe the worldly lives of human beings—including those with serious cognitive disabilities—and how to construe the demands of knowing these lives. This philosophical dispute is morally and politically consequential in that the side we take in it is likely to affect our answers to urgent questions about accommodations and social resources for individuals with cognitive disabilities. So it seems fair to insist that any decisive intervention in debates about cognitive disability and ethics should acknowledge and address it.

These debates are philosophically more nuanced than talk of a confrontation between traditional and alternative approaches may appear to indicate. In addition to traditional approaches, which presuppose that bringing the empirical world into view in ethics is the prerogative of morally neutral methods, and alternative approaches, which counter that we necessarily rely on the exercise of moral capacities such as moral imagination, there are also—to touch on but one other recognizable set of strategies—approaches inspired by *poststructuralism* (e.g., Campbell 2009). Poststructuralist approaches might seem similar to alternative approaches in that they typically maintain that the methods we use in ethics to illuminate the worldly lives of human beings cannot help but be morally non-neutral. But advocates of poststructuralist approaches typically give this methodological stance a skeptical inflection, suggesting that it follows from it that our theoretical modes of thought are invariably cut off from objective authority. So it turns out that there are additional categories of contributions to conversations about how to bring the worldly lives of cognitively disabled as well as nondisabled human beings into focus in ethics. The view of these methodological matters that we adopt has substantive implications, shaping the moral conclusions that appear defensible when we weigh in on questions about moral status in general and about the moral status of the cognitively disabled in particular. Any appropriately broad and thoughtful discussion of cognitive disability and moral status should for this reason assign a pivotal role to a critical examination of the range of different views at play here; that is, the range of different views about the resources available to us in ethics for arriving at an empirical understanding of our topic.

ACKNOWLEDGMENTS

I am grateful for helpful feedback on drafts of this chapter from audiences at a panel hosted by the Society for Philosophy and Disability at the Eastern Division Meeting of the American Philosophical Society; at the Philosophy Department at the University of Texas, Austin; and at the Wittgenstein Workshop at the University of Chicago. I would like to thank, for their constructive comments on these occasions, Mette Block, Caroline Christoff, David Finkelstein, Simone Gubler, Michael Kremer, Ben Laurence, Nethanel Lipshitz, David Miller, Ian Proops, Francey Russell, and Johannes Sudau. I owe significant debts for helpful discussion of these themes to Licia Carlson, Adam Cureton, Eva Feder Kittay, John Vorhaus, and David Wasserman.

REFERENCES

Adams, Rachel. 2013. *Raising Henry: A Memoir of Motherhood, Disability and Discovery*. New Haven, CT: Yale University Press.

Bérubé, Michael. 1996. *Life as We Know It: A Father, A Family and an Exceptional Child*. New York: Vintage Books.

Bérubé, Michael. 2016. *Life as Jamie Knows It: An Exceptional Child Grows Up*. Boston: Beacon Press.

Bérubé, Michael, and J. Ruth. 2015. *The Humanities, Higher Education and Academic Freedom: Three Necessary Arguments*. London: Palgrave MacMillan.

Boo, Katherine. 1999. "System Loses Lives and Trust." *The Washington Post*, December 5, 1999.

Campbell, Fiona Kumari. 2009. *Contours of Ableism: The Production of Disability and Ableism*. London: Palgrave MacMillan.

Carlson, Licia. 2010. *The Faces of Intellectual Disability: Philosophical Reflections*. Bloomington: Indiana University Press.

Carlson, Licia. 2020. "On Moral Status and Intellectual Disability: Challenging and Expanding the Debates." In *Oxford Handbook of Philosophy and Disability*, edited by Adam Cureton and David Wasserman, 482–497. New York: Oxford University Press.

Crary, Alice. 2016. *Inside Ethics: On the Demands of Moral Thought*. Cambridge, MA: Harvard University Press.

Debaggio, Thomas. 2002. *Losing My Mind: An Intimate Look at Life with Alzheimers*. New York: The Free Press.

Diamond, Cora. 1991. "The Importance of Being Human." In *Human Beings*, edited by David Cockburn, 35–62. Cambridge: Cambridge University Press.

Dombrowski, Daniel. 1997. *Babies and Beasts: The Argument from Marginal Cases*. Chicago: University of Illinois Press.

Drake, Stephen. 2010. "Connecting Disability Rights and Animal Rights—A Really Bad Idea." Available at http://notdeadyet.org/2010/10/connecting-disability-rights-and-animal.html.

Fleischer, Doris Zames, and Frieda Zames. 2011. *The Disability Rights Movement: From Charity to Confrontation*. Philadelphia, PA: Temple University Press.

Gaita, Raimond. 2000. *A Common Humanity: Thinking About Love and Truth and Justice*, 2nd edition. London: Routledge.

Gallagher, Hugh Gregory. 1989. *By Trust Betrayed: Patients, Physicians and the Right to Kill in the Third Reich*. New York: Henry Holt & Co.

Grandin, Temple. 1986. *Emergence: Labeled Autistic*. Novato, CA: Arena Press.

Grandin, Temple. 1995. *Thinking in Pictures: My Life with Autism*. New York: Vintage Books.

Hacking, Ian. 2009a. "Autistic Autobiography." *Philosophical Transactions of the Royal Society* 364: 1467–1473.

Hacking, Ian. 2009b. "Humans, Aliens and Autism," *Deadalus* 138(3): 44–59.

Hacking, Ian. 2010. "How We Have Been Learning to Talk about Autism: A Role for Stories." In *Cognitive Disability and Its Challenge to Moral Philosophy*, edited by Licia Carlson and Eva Feder Kittay, 261–278. Oxford: Blackwell Publishing.

Horta, Oscar. 2014. "The Scope of the Argument from Species Overlap." *Journal of Applied Philosophy* 31(2): 142–153.

Kain, Patrick. 2009. "Kant's Defense of Human Moral Status." *Journal of the History of Philosophy* 47(1): 59–102.

Kingsley, Jason, and Michael Levitz. 2004. *Count Us In: Growing Up with Down Syndrome*. Orlando, FL: Harcourt.

Kinsley, Michael. 2014. "Have You Lost Your Mind? More Bad News for Boomers." *The New Yorker*, April 28.

Kittay, Eva Feder. 2000. "At Home with My Daughter." In *Americans with Disabilities: Exploring Implications of the Law for Individuals and Institutions*, edited by Leslie Pickering Francis and Anita Silvers, 64–80. London: Routledge.

Kittay, Eva Feder. 2005a. "At the Margins of Moral Personhood." *Ethics* 116: 100–131.

Kittay, Eva Feder. 2005b. "Equality, Dignity and Disability." In *Perspectives on Equality: The Second Seamus Heaney Lectures*, edited by Mary Ann Lyons and Fionnuala Waldron, 93–119. Dublin: Liffey Press.

Kittay, Eva Feder. 2009a. "The Ethics of Philosophizing: Ideal Theory and the Exclusion of People with Severe Cognitive Disabilities." In *Feminist Ethics and Social and Political Philosophy: Theorizing the Non-Ideal*, edited by Lisa Tessman, 121–148. Binghamton, MA: Springer.

Kittay, Eva Feder. 2009b. "The Personal Is Philosophical Is Political: A Philosopher and Mother of a Cognitively Disabled Person Sends Notes from the Battlefield." *Metaphilosophy* 30(3–4): 606–627.

Korsgaard, Christine. 1996. *The Sources of Normativity*. Cambridge: Cambridge University Press.

Korsgaard, Christine. 2009. *Self-Constitution: Agency, Identity and Integrity*. Oxford: Oxford University Press.

Kuhse, Helga, and Peter Singer. 1986. *Should the Baby Live?* Oxford: Oxford University Press.

Kumar, Rahul. 2006. "Permissible Killing and the Irrelevance of Being Human." *The Journal of Ethics* 12: 57–80.

Lindemann, Hilde. 2014. *Holding and Letting Go: The Social Practice of Personal Identities*. Oxford: Oxford University Press.

McMahan, Jeff. 2002. *The Ethics of Killing: Problems at the Margins of Life*. Oxford: Oxford University Press.

McMahan, Jeff. 2005. "Our Fellow Creatures." *The Journal of Ethics* 9: 353–380.

McMahan, Jeff. 2008. "Challenges to Human Equality." *Journal of Ethics* 12: 81–104.

McMahan, Jeff. 2009. "Radical Cognitive Limitation." In *Disability and Disadvantage*, edited by Kimberly Brownlee and Adam Cureton, 240–259. Oxford: Oxford University Press.

Mills, Charles. 1998. "Alternative Epistemologies." In *Blackness Visible: Essays on Philosophy and Race*, 21–39. Ithaca: Cornell University Press.

Mulhall, Stephen. 2002. "Fearful Thoughts." *London Review of Books* 24: 18.

Price, Margaret. 2011. *Mad at School: Rhetorics of Mental Disability and Academic Life*. Ann Arbor: University of Michigan Press.

Rachels, James. 1990. *Created from Animals: The Moral Implications of Darwinism*. Oxford: Oxford University Press.

Regan, Tom. 1984. *The Case for Animal Rights*. London: Routledge & Kegan Paul.

Ryder, Richard. 1989. *Animal Revolution: Changing Attitudes toward Speciesism*. Bloomsbury: Bloomsbury Publishing.

Scanlon, Tim. 1998. *What We Owe to Each Other*. Cambridge, MA: Harvard University Press.

Schoultz, Bonnie, and Paul Williams. 1984. *We Can Speak for Ourselves: Self-Advocacy by Mentally Handicapped People*. Bloomington: Indiana University Press.

Singer, Peter. 1993. *Practical Ethics*. Cambridge: Cambridge University Press.

Singer, Peter. 1994. *Rethinking Life and Death: The Collapse of Our Traditional Ethics*. New York: St. Martin's Griffin.

Singer, Peter. 2010. "Speciesism and Moral Status." In *Cognitive Disability and Its Challenge to Moral Philosophy*, edited by Licia Carlson and Eva Feder Kittay, 331–344. Oxford: Wiley-Blackwell.

Singer, Peter. 2013. "Discussing Infanticide." *Journal of Medical Ethics* 39(5): 260.

Singer, Peter. 2015. *The Most Good You Can Do: How Effective Altruism is Changing Ideas about Living Ethically*. New Haven, CT: Yale University Press.

Taylor, Sunaura. 2017. *Beasts of Burden: Animal and Disability Liberation*. New York: The New Press.

Warren, Mary Anne. 1997. *Moral Status: Obligations to Persons and Other Living Beings*. Oxford: Oxford University Press.

Wasserman, Daniel, Adrienne Asch, Daniel Putnam, and Jeffrey Blustein. 2013. "Cognitive Disability and Moral Status." In *Stanford Encyclopedia of Philosophy*, edited by Edward N. Zalta. Available at https://plato.stanford.edu/archives/fall2013/entries/cognitive-disability/.

Wolfensberger, Wolf. 1972. *The Principle of Normalization in Human Services*. G. Allan Roeher Inst Kinsman.

CHAPTER 27

DIGNITY, RESPECT, AND COGNITIVE DISABILITY

SUZY KILLMISTER

INTRODUCTION

WITHIN disability studies, it is generally taken as given that individuals with severe cognitive disabilities have dignity and are thus owed certain forms of respect.[1] Within philosophy, that claim is much more contentious. Indeed, philosophers continue to debate whether or not severely cognitively disabled people even have full moral standing. My goal in this chapter is to put forward a philosophical justification for the dignity of those with severe cognitive disabilities and to show how it can vindicate claims to certain forms of respect.[2]

Here's how I'll proceed. First, I establish the goal posts by getting clear on which forms of respect I take to be at stake. I then turn to dignity, briefly surveying existent theories of the concept and highlighting their inability to vindicate severely cognitively disabled individuals' claims to the previously identified forms of respect. A fourth section makes the key argumentative move: I suggest we shift our focus from human as a *natural kind* to human as a *social kind*. That is, over and above the species *Homo sapiens*, we have constructed a social category "the human," members of which are imbued with a certain kind of value and are owed certain forms of treatment. The final section concludes by drawing out the implications of understanding dignity in this socially constructed way for people with cognitive disabilities.

I should stress at the outset that the view I develop here is offered as *a* justification, not as *the* justification for the dignity of severely cognitively disabled people. While I note general problems with competing theories of dignity, my intention is not to prove them definitively wrong, but rather to motivate exploration of an alternative—and underappreciated—way of thinking about human dignity, and demonstrate its applicability to issues around cognitive disability.[3] Nor do I suggest that the approach developed here is itself without problems. As will become increasingly clear, my position is far from uncontroversial, and it carries with it admittedly troubling implications, some of which will be examined in Section 5. Nonetheless, this approach has advantages that make it worthy of consideration. Two such advantages are worth stressing. First, it shifts the burden of proving eligibility for dignity off the shoulders of the most vulnerable: since dignity is not held in virtue of intrinsic features or capacities, the dignity of the severely cognitively disabled is no more inherently contestable than the dignity of anyone else.[4] Second, this approach illuminates what's at stake when philosophers *do* question the dignity (or moral status) of individuals with severe cognitive disabilities. If what it means to be human and the possession of dignity depend on how the social kind "human" is maintained and evolves, such claims have significant moral and political import: they function as nothing short of moves to expel those with cognitive disabilities from the human community.

RESPECT

To say that an individual has dignity is to say that she has a certain kind of moral status. More precisely, it is to say that she commands *respect*. In this chapter, I focus on forms of respect that are regularly denied to those with severe cognitive disabilities and whose denial plausibly involves either a violation of or an affront to their dignity. To be clear from the outset, the three forms of respect I will go on to sketch here are meant to be representative rather than exhaustive of what people are owed. The goal is simply to identify *some* forms of respect that it is plausible to claim are owed to people with severe cognitive disabilities and which seem to implicate their dignity. This will establish the goal posts going forward: the challenge will be to explain what dignity might be, such that it would be held by individuals with severe cognitive disabilities and command (at least) these forms of respect.

The first form of respect to consider is nonhumiliation. It is incompatible with respecting an individual in her dignity to humiliate her, especially in public. I take humiliation to involve treating an individual in ways that violate (or force her to violate) social mores, paradigmatically involving norms associated with the body. Unfortunately, public humiliation has been an all-too-familiar treatment meted out to those with cognitive disabilities. Eva Feder Kittay (2005*b*, 110) relates a poignant story involving her daughter, Sesha, and the agency director at Sesha's care home. The director was apparently horrified to find Sesha being wheeled through a public space wrapped just in a towel, describing it as an offense to her dignity. She then recalled how things used to be at the home she worked at in the 1960s, where "ten to twelve naked men were marched through the dormitory into a large room and unceremoniously hosed down." At least in the agency director's eyes, individuals such as Sesha have dignity, and that dignity commands respect in the form of upholding norms of bodily comportment.

The second form of respect is noncommodification. When, historically, those with cognitive disabilities have been experimented on without their consent or put on display for others' amusement, this constituted a distinct failure to treat them in accordance with the respect commanded by their dignity. In addition, noncommodification, as I understand it, involves a particular kind of interpersonal care: it demands that we interact with others *as* persons, rather than as mere objects to be managed. Consider, for instance, the way in which you might remove a cat that wanders across your laptop: without pausing from your work, you sweep him up and plunk him on the ground. So long as this interaction does not distress the cat, you do him no wrong—you certainly do not violate his dignity. To remove a person from your workspace in such a cavalier manner, by contrast, *is* to wrong her.[5] To interact appropriately with another human being requires a kind of caring attention, which functions as an affirmation of her standing *as* a human.

The final form of respect I am concerned with is "grievability."[6] When an individual with dignity dies, it *matters* in a way that goes beyond whatever personal affections her friends and relatives have for her. In particular, it calls for a very different kind of response than when other kinds of creature die. Imagine passing a dead pigeon on the side of the road: while the scene might illicit a twinge of pathos, or even sadness, the response it calls for is worlds apart from the response that would be called for if you passed by a dead human being, irrespective of their cognitive capacities. One of the ways in which we respect one another in our dignity is by marking one another's passing: deaths are to be *attended to*.[7] Whether this attending involves grief, somber reflection on the life led, or a celebratory send-off depends on both cultural context and facts about the particular individual—but whatever form it takes, it involves a recognition of the gravity of the event. This form of respect, in particular, is contested for those with cognitive disabilities, especially by philosophers. When Jeff McMahan (2002, 230) argues that "our traditional beliefs about the special sanctity of the lives of severely retarded human beings will have to yield," he is denying that individuals with cognitive disabilities command this form of respect.

As noted earlier, my goal here is not to suggest that these forms of respect exhaust what is owed to persons in virtue of their dignity. Rather, it is to provide concrete examples of the kinds of disrespectful treatment cognitively disabled people are routinely subject to and which seem (at least intuitively) to involve violations of such individuals' dignity. The challenge now is to see what dignity could be, such that it would command these forms of respect and be held by individuals with severe cognitive disabilities. I will first show that standard theories of dignity struggle to meet this challenge before turning to my positive account.

THEORIES OF DIGNITY

By far the most common way to define dignity is in terms of some inherent feature of human beings. Dignity is taken to be the special value human beings have in virtue of some inherent and universal quality we all possess. Construing dignity this way has both a religious and a secular expression.

Within the Christian tradition, to put it simply, human beings have dignity because we are created in God's image: in the words of Pope Benedict XVI (2009): "[the Church's social doctrine] is based on man's creation 'in the image of God' (Gen 1:27), a datum which gives rise to the inviolable dignity of the human person and the transcendent value of natural moral norms."[8] This way of thinking about dignity has some clear advantages, especially with respect to extending dignity to those with cognitive disabilities. Since dignity is typically taken to be held by *all* of God's children, irrespective of our personal qualities or capacities, there is no need to deny that people with cognitive disabilities have dignity. It would also be fairly straightforward to explain why those with dignity command the forms of respect sketched in the preceding section: it would be an insult to God's creation to fail to grieve for her, or to treat her as an object, or to humiliate her.

The key drawback with this approach is that it stands and falls with a belief in God. Since we cannot expect everyone to accept this justification of dignity, it cannot function as a basis for dignitarian claims in a pluralistic society. Nonetheless, it is worth noting one of the key benefits of construing dignity in this way: because dignity is not taken to depend on personal qualities or capacities, it places no demands on anyone to prove their dignity. As we will see, approaches which foreground particular qualities or capacities inevitably raise the question of whether a particular individual has that quality or capacity and hence whether she has dignity. As such, capacity-based approaches always stand ready to exclude some individuals from the realm of dignity.

This brings us to the secular tradition. Drawing inspiration from Kant, it is standard for dignity to be understood today in terms of a normatively salient human capacity. For Kant himself, we have dignity insofar as we have the capacity to give the moral law to ourselves (Kant 1976). Contemporary philosophers have argued in a Kantian vein that we have dignity insofar as we have the capacity to engage in the give-and-take of second-personal reasons (Darwall 2006) or insofar as we have the capacity for normative agency (Griffin 2008).[9] The problem with this way of approaching dignity is clear: if dignity is held in virtue of possessing a particular cognitive capacity, then those who lack that cognitive capacity will lack dignity. In turn, if respect is commanded in virtue of having dignity, as such approaches typically maintain, then those who lack dignity will not command the relevant forms of respect. Even those who support this approach concede this implication: for instance, James Griffin takes dignity to be held in virtue of the capacity for normative agency, and he takes dignity to command respect in the form of human rights. Since those with severe cognitive disabilities lack the capacity for normative agency, as he understands it, they lack dignity and thus do not have human rights.

There is a move that can be made in response here, which is often pressed by disability advocates. The move involves two parts: first, we are invited to broaden our understanding of the relevant capacity; and, second, we are reminded that there is a history of radically underestimating the capacities of people with cognitive disabilities. The central idea is that if we take a more permissive or pluralistic approach to the relevant capacities, coupled with more humility about our judgments of people's capacities, we will see that individuals with cognitive disability meet the criteria and thus have dignity. For instance, Jaworska and Tannenbaum (2014) suggest that high moral status is held in virtue of the capacity to participate in what they call "person-rearing relationships." If we apply this approach to dignity, it would follow that many individuals with cognitive disabilities would qualify as having dignity.

There are two key problems with this move. First, any capacities approach is going to face the challenge of explaining why possession of dignity (or moral status) commands the forms of respect sketched in the preceding section. While being rational, or having the capacity for normative agency, or even having the capacity to participate in person-rearing relationships may suffice to show that an individual is an object of moral concern, it is hard to see how any of these capacities could ground more specific claims like nonhumiliation or caring attention. The more inclusive a capacities approach tries to be, the thinner the qualities of the human it will need to pick out as sufficient for dignity. But the thinner these qualities are, the more difficult it will be to explain how they command respect in all but the most abstract sense.

Second, these modification leave the general shape of the capacities approach intact. Clearly, which capacities are privileged will have a profound effect on which human beings are taken to have dignity. Importantly, though, even purportedly inclusive theories have exclusionary implications. Tellingly, while Jaworska and Tannenbaum's approach would include many more people with cognitive disabilities in the realm of human dignity than would a normative agency approach, even they acknowledge that it will not include all: some human beings are not capable of the kinds of interactions Jaworska and Tannenbaum see as necessary for full moral status. As Michael Bérubé (2009, 355) aptly notes, "any performance criterion—independence, rationality, capacity for mutual cooperation, even capacity for mutual recognition—will leave some mother's child behind." Since species membership does not suffice for dignity, it is always an open question whether a given individual has dignity. Whether or not she does depends on whether or not she possesses the relevant capacity. On the capacities approach, the onus is thus on each individual to prove her dignity. The threat of exclusion is unavoidable.[10]

There is one final approach to dignity worth noting. Recently, Jeremy Waldron has defended an account of dignity as a conferred status, rather than an inherent feature of persons. Appealing to historical usage, Waldron invites us to see dignity as intimately connected to rank. To have dignity is to be a person of high stature, with special standing and possessed of a range of entitlements. On this view, then, dignity is a status that is constituted by a cluster of rights. Just as what it means to be a citizen can be unpacked in terms of the specific set of rights possessed by citizens, so too, Waldron claims, what it means to have dignity can be unpacked in terms of the cluster of rights held by the dignified. Historically, dignity was held exclusively by the nobility. Their standing was expressed through their legal entitlements, such as the fact that they were entitled to a trial by their peers and that it was forbidden for their bodies to be seized—entitlements that the lower ranks were distinctly lacking. While historically the only people who held the rights constitutive of dignity were the nobility, now dignity has an egalitarian flavor. We've all "leveled up," in the sense that we all now have a range of legal and social entitlements that were previously the preserve of the select few. As Waldron (2012, 34) puts it, "Every man a duke, every woman a queen, everyone entitled to the sort of deference and consideration, everyone's person and body sacrosanct, in the way that nobles were entitled to deference or in the way that an assault upon the body or the person of a king was regarded as a sacrilege."

Now Waldron does not say anything about cognitive disability in his work on dignity to date. Nonetheless, the idea that dignity is conferred rather than inherent has distinct promise insofar as it suggests an avenue via which dignity might come to be possessed by all humans, irrespective of their cognitive capacities. In the next section, I use Waldron's approach as a springboard for rethinking the grounds of dignity. Taking seriously the idea of dignity as a status, I take it one step further: once the status emerges, I claim, it generates a new social kind—the human—membership in which commands the forms of respect outlined earlier.[11]

From Natural to Social Kinds

We have seen that capacity accounts have difficulty justifying the dignity of individuals with cognitive disabilities. While there is much variation between these accounts, they all share one important feature in common: they presuppose that the relevant category— be it "the human" or the narrower category of "the person"—is a natural kind and seek to identify dignity with some feature that is relevant to membership in that natural kind. It is because these accounts are looking for a feature that is relevant to membership in a natural kind that we see appeals to capacities like rationality or agency, which inevitably excludes some humans.

The question I take up in this section is this: What happens to a theory of dignity if we shift our attention away from "the human" as a natural kind and start to consider "the human" as a social kind? The result, I propose, is an account of dignity that is distinctly well positioned to include those with cognitive disabilities and to vindicate their claims to the forms of respect outlined in the preceding section.

To begin, it will be useful to briefly outline the difference between natural and social kinds. With respect to natural kinds, I follow Bird and Tobin (2016), who say that a natural kind "corresponds to a grouping that reflects the structure of the natural world rather than the interests and actions of human beings." Social kinds, conversely, refer to groupings that exist in virtue of human activity. Common examples of social kinds include money, royalty, and nation-states. Only slightly more controversially, many have argued that categories such as race and gender are social kinds (see esp. (Haslanger 2012; Mills 1997). None of these categories reflects the structure of the natural world, and all owe their existence to human norms, institutions, and social practices.

If the human is thought of as a social rather than a natural kind, it opens up different ways of construing human dignity. Rather than look for some biological source of dignity—something about our "nature" in virtue of which we command respect—it suggests the possibility that dignity might be held in virtue of our membership in the socially constructed category "human." The basic idea is this: we've created a category "the human," membership in which entitles individuals to certain kinds of treatment. The human is thus a social kind in the way that royalty or race is: it is a social construct, but with concrete real-world effects.

Before examining how this category may have come about and what kinds of normative claims it may generate, it is important to say something about membership in social kinds. Recall that the whole point of considering the human as a social kind is because of its potential for vindicating the dignity of those with cognitive disabilities. If it turns out that cognitively disabled people are excluded from membership in the human community, understood as a social kind, it would follow that they lack dignity.

Here is how John Searle (1995, 33–34) famously described membership in some social kinds: "for social facts, the attitude that we take toward the phenomenon is partly constitutive of the phenomenon....Part of being a cocktail party is being thought to be a cocktail party; part of being a war is being thought to be a war." On this view, an individual is only a member of a social kind if it is recognized as such. For our purposes, this means that individuals with cognitive disabilities would only count as "human" if they were acknowledged as such by relevant others. Given the history of institutionalization and mistreatment of cognitively disabled people, leaving their membership in the human community entirely in the hands of those with whom they interact would place their dignity in a very precarious a position.

There is, however, a better way of construing membership in social kinds. On this alternative view, an individual is a member if she satisfies the socially constructed conditions of membership. For instance, we have conditions for a piece of paper to count as a $10 bill, conditions that refer primarily to its history. Likewise, we have conditions for an individual to count as a princess, conditions that refer primarily to her lineage. For both of these social kinds, membership does not depend on social recognition: a $10 can be a $10 bill even if everyone who interacts with it believes it to be a forgery, or if it is lost down the back of the couch and no one interacts with it at all (c.f. Searle 1995, 32). And where would Disney be without the tired trope of the young woman who discovers that, unbeknownst to those mean girls at school, she's actually a princess? Crucially, such a person doesn't *become* a princess when her lineage is uncovered; what's discovered is that she's been a princess all along.

When I claim that dignity is held in virtue of membership in the social kind "human," it is this latter sense of membership I have in mind. Everyone who meets the socially constructed conditions for membership in the human community counts as human and has dignity. What, then, are the conditions for membership in the human community? I posit that—at least at the present moment in history—membership in the social kind tracks membership in the natural kind. In other words, the one necessary and sufficient condition for membership in the social kind "the human" is that one is a human being. Treating a human being as if she weren't human—for instance, by failing to accord her the forms of respect outlined earlier—is to make a mistake. It's a mistake in just the same way that failing to accept legal tender is a mistake: each social kind involves rules for membership and rules for how members are to be treated, which hold irrespective of the personal attitudes of those interacting with them. (Over and above this category mistake, though, and as I'll say more about at the end of this chapter, to treat a human being as if she weren't human is to make a *moral* mistake.)

It is important to be clear about what follows from all of this. Just because the conditions for membership in the social kind reduce to the conditions for membership in the natural kind, it does not follow that the social kind is redundant. In particular, what it *means* to be human, *qua* social kind, does not reduce to the natural features that constitute us as members of the natural kind "human." The meaning of the human, *qua* social kind, is what we've made it, which extends well beyond what is given by our "human nature." Moreover, what we're *owed* qua members of the social kind does not reduce to what we're owed *qua* members of the natural kind. This means, importantly, that what we're entitled to doesn't have to be justified solely in terms of natural features such as susceptibility to pain or rational capacities. What we're entitled to will be tied up with the meaning we've given to the category "human." Just as, in some cultures, royalty must be curtseyed to, and this is in large part a product of what it means to be royal, so too humans must be treated in certain ways, such as not being humiliated, and this is in large part a product of the meaning we've given to the human.

On my account, then, dignity refers to the worth of being human, where that worth is an upshot of the meaning we've given to the social kind human. The kind of respect we command, in virtue of our humanity, is likewise an upshot of the meaning we've given to the human. As it stands, I claim, it is part of what it means to be human that we are not to be humiliated, that we are not to be commodified, and that our lives are grievable. The forms of respect surveyed earlier, then, are simply reflections of what it means to be human: this explains why it is so intuitive that failures to accord each of these forms of respect constitutes a violation of the victim's dignity. Since cognitively disabled people are members of the natural kind human, they are also members of the social kind human—they meet the sole entry condition—and hence they, too, are owed these forms of respect. They, too, have dignity.

Clearly, some story is owed here as to how the social kind "human" emerged and came to have the meaning I have attributed to it earlier. I cannot hope to do justice to that story here and will have to settle for a few suggestive words. This will involve temporarily stepping away from the issue of cognitive disability to look at the construction of the category of the human more generally.

To begin, it is worth noting that there has long been a category "the human" that has not carried with it the normative implications I am attributing to our current category. For brevity's sake, I'll leave aside the admittedly difficult question of how to distinguish the evolution of social kinds from the emergence of new social kinds. With that caveat in mind, my account draws attention to the emergence of the human rights regime, which takes as its subject all human beings. Importantly, human rights presuppose a politico-legal status of "the human," which applies to all members of the natural kind and for which no additional qualities or capacities are required. All of us (even those of us who lack the capacities to understand ourselves as human) are categorized as human by international institutions and are granted rights and powers in virtue of this. We have a standing now that was not held by people in earlier centuries. Along with institutionalizing this politico-legal status, the human rights regime also consolidates norms around the language available to describe ourselves (i.e., as rights-holders) and how we are to be treated (i.e., nonhumiliation).[12]

Of course, the human rights regime alone cannot take credit for the emergence of the human. What we've seen in the post World War II era is an interplay of international law, a globalized media, and human rights education (among other factors), each of which calls upon us to view distant others as members of a common human community.[13] For instance, children are taught that we all have human rights merely in virtue of being human. At the same time, newspapers report tragedies befalling people in far-flung lands, presupposing their suffering to be a matter of global concern, and international nongovernmental organizations issue reports on the degradations that states inflict upon their subjects. Each of these practices shapes understandings of who is a member in the human community and what kinds of treatment all of us are owed. As a result, we have largely come to understand ourselves *as* human. Even if this is not always the most salient category in our day-to-day lives, it is one that is readily available to most of us—especially if others fail to treat us as we think humans ought to be treated.[14]

This has admittedly been a very condensed and idealized story of how the social kind "human" emerged and came to have a certain kind of meaning. My goal here has not been to fully articulate and defend this idea but, more modestly, to sketch it in broad brush strokes so that I can draw out its general implications for thinking about the dignity of individuals with cognitive disabilities. To summarize: dignity refers to the worth of each and every human being, which incorporates the forms of treatment we are owed. Dignity is thus not a foundation in a strict sense: we cannot derive what we're owed from an understanding of what dignity is. Rather, dignity encapsulates the sense we have that all human lives matter and that we are all to be treated with care and respect. This "sense of the human" is not a mere superstition to be superseded by a naturalistic account of what humans are "really" like, but is in fact constitutive of the social kind. We are, in a very real sense, whatever we take ourselves to be.[15]

DIGNITY, RESPECT, AND COGNITIVE DISABILITY REDUX

On the account sketched here so far, dignity is held by every human being, irrespective of their capacities. It thus straightforwardly includes cognitively disabled people. In this final section, I consider two additional implications of this approach—one straightforwardly positive, the other more troubling—and then close with a clarification on the intended scope and normative import of the argument.

The first positive implication of this approach is that it avoids one of the key problems with capacities approaches, namely their intrusiveness. On a capacities approach, whether or not a given individual has dignity depends on whether she possesses the relevant capacity. *Whatever* that capacity is, it stands as an open question whether or not the individual in front of us has it, and hence whether she commands the relevant forms of respect. Those whose capacities are outside the normal range are thus called upon to prove their dignity. Even if practitioners adopt a policy of what Ian Carter (2011) calls "opacity respect"—assuming without question that those in their care are within the relevant range of capacities—this will still be done against the background assumption that *if* the individual lacked the relevant capacities, she wouldn't be deserving of the treatment she was being accorded. On my account, by contrast, there is nothing for an individual to prove beyond her species membership—and even the most strident critics of according moral status to those with cognitive disabilities don't deny *that* claim.

The second implication concerns precisely those theorists who do deny the dignity (or moral status) of individuals with cognitive disability and how we should understand the import of their claims. I noted earlier that membership in the human community does not depend on active recognition: even if a cognitively disabled person is surrounded by others who take her to fall outside the community, she nonetheless meets the membership conditions and thus deserves to be treated as human. This might lead us to think that there is no substantive damage done by these kinds of claims, aside from the emotional harm they inflict on concerned individuals. This would be too quick, however. While the membership conditions *now* track membership in the natural kind, this is not a given. The boundaries of the human were not always so, and they need not always remain so (c.f. Fernández-Armesto 2005; Stuurman 2017). If sufficient critical pressure is put on the membership conditions, they may alter. If such ideas get enough traction, they may bring about the moral boundaries they claim to describe. In the meantime, they work to position those targeted as marginal members, casting doubt over their entitlement to the forms of respect attributed to humans.

This implication connects back to the first. One of the important differences between the approach I advocate here and capacities approaches is where each places the burden of proving membership. As we've just seen, on a capacities approach, that burden falls primarily on individual with cognitive disabilities who must prove their possession of the relevant capacities to prove their worth. The social kinds approach shifts this burden. To claim someone is not a member of the human community is to make a move in a very important metaphysical game: it functions as a call to reconstitute the boundaries of the human so as to exclude certain others. On the social kinds approach, metaphysics alone cannot justify this move; there is no eternal truth concerning who is human, only the political reality of who we choose to *take* to be human, and so we bear responsibility for where we choose to draw that line.

Admittedly, this means that on the social kinds approach exclusion is always a possibility (and not just for those with cognitive disabilities, but for all the marginalized and abused), and this vulnerability is undoubtedly concerning. Nonetheless, the social kinds approach has the advantage of forcing us to confront precisely what's at stake in seemingly abstract philosophical arguments. It is not merely a matter of intellectual disagreement, but also has the potential to actually change what it means to be human. Defending the boundaries of the human can thus be recognized as political, and not merely philosophical, work.

That said, the elephant in the room of a social constructivist view like mine is its normative import. I noted earlier that those who treat someone with severe cognitive disabilities as if she weren't human aren't merely making a category mistake, but also a moral one. How might such a claim be vindicated?[16] The first move that needs to be made is to locate the moral justification for keeping the boundaries of the human such as to include all members of the species. That justification can't appeal to any independent moral entitlement humans have to be so included since this would inevitably lead back to a capacities approach (on what could such an entitlement be based other than some natural feature possessed by humans?). Instead, I propose that the boundaries of the human are to be justified with reference to their overall impact on the world.[17] In other words, the boundaries are not to be justified in terms of whether they track objective facts about who is entitled to membership, but rather in terms of whether the current boundaries produce more or less overall badness than would alternative boundaries.[18]

A comparison with nation-states is fruitful here. It is clear there is no "natural" answer to the question of who is a member of which nation-state. Nation-states are social constructs, and part of their construction involves determinations of membership conditions. That is not to say, though, that national membership conditions are above moral critique. We can consider the impact of various systems of membership and make moral arguments about which are impermissible.[19] Similarly, to say that those who would deny the humanity of individuals with cognitive disabilities make a moral mistake is, in the first instance, to say that they are proposing a redrawing of the boundaries of the human that would produce more overall badness than it prevents.

This still leaves open an important question, though: if the mistake is merely one of putting forward a morally problematic proposal, it does not seem to wrong those whose membership is being denied. To put it another way, is there a sense in which claims that cognitively disabled people are not fully human *wrong those very people*? I believe that there is. Assuming I'm correct that including individuals with cognitively disabled people within the category of the human is morally better than excluding them, then what we might call "the institution of the human" is, *ceteris paribus*, morally justified. When an institution is morally justified, and that institution confers entitlements on members, then we wrong those members by not treating them as they are entitled to be treated. Consider the following analogy: assume for argument's sake that a particular university is a morally justified institution. The university grants students a range of entitlements, including the right to have their work returned to them within a fortnight (clearly not a "natural right"!). If a professor refuses to return the work of a certain cohort of students within the allotted time, then he wrongs not only the institution whose rules he refuses to follow, but he wrongs *the individual students*. They are being denied goods to which they are entitled. This general principle can be applied back to the human, though in this case the moral stakes are much higher. To treat individuals in way that fails to accord with what they are owed, *qua* human, is to wrong them. Assuming one of the things we are owed *qua* human is simple recognition of our humanity, then to argue (in effect, even if not in words) that individuals with cognitive disabilities are less than human is to commit a grave moral wrong. The justification for recognizing the dignity of individuals with cognitive disability—as it does for everyone—thus operates on two distinct levels. On the first tier, the justification appeals directly to each of our status as human, which entitles us all to be treated with certain forms of respect. Moving up a tier, the justification for each of our status as human appeals to the broader moral import of maintaining the social kind human so as to include all human beings.

I recognize that the approach being presented here is a far cry from standard accounts of dignity and will be too radical for many people's tastes. In closing, I hope to temper some of this apparent radicalism by clarifying its intended scope.

I have argued for understanding dignity as possessed in virtue of membership in a social, rather than natural, kind. What we are owed as human, then, turns on how we choose to understand humanity and what kind of expectations we have for how humans are to be treated. This may seem like an exceedingly fragile basis on which to build moral claims. This worry would be appropriate if *all* we were owed were owed in virtue of humanity; this is not, however, the position I'm arguing for. I leave open that there are other grounds for moral claims: individuals may be owed certain things in virtue of their rationality, other things in virtue of their sentience, and yet more things in virtue of their susceptibility to pain. My claim is just that *in addition*, membership in the social kind human provides a further ground. Many moral claims, I suspect, will have multiple grounds. That is, an individual may be entitled not to be tortured because she's sentient, because she's rational, and because she's a member of the social kind human. What the appeal to the social kind does is provide an additional and supplementary ground to those provided by natural features, as well as enriching the content of those moral claims. It also provides an avenue to justify moral claims that are less easily grounded in natural features, such as the claim not to be humiliated or to be treated with caring attention. How much moral work is being done by natural features and how much by membership in the social kind is a question I leave for another time (though I suspect quite a lot will turn out to be done by the social kind). I hope simply to have shown that understanding dignity in terms of social kinds has underexplored resources for including those with cognitive disabilities and vindicating their claims to rich forms of respect.

Notes

1. Earlier version of this chapter were presented at the University of Melbourne, the Australian National University, the University of Sydney, and the University of Western Australia. Many thanks to audience at those talks for their very helpful contributions. I also benefited greatly from feedback at the Center for Ethics and Public Affairs at Tulane University.

2. A note on language is appropriate here. There is an ongoing debate within the disability community concerning how to refer to people with disabilities. Some push for a person-first approach (i.e., person with autism, child with Down syndrome); others push for a disability-first approach (i.e., autistic person; Down child). Since I see good reasons on both sides, I have opted to use person-first and disability-first language interchangeably.

3. I critique alternative theories at more length in Killmister (2017*a*).

4. This is not to say that there is no room for contestation. As will become clear, on my approach, dignity is only as secure as membership in the social kind, which in turn depends on norms that must continually be upheld. Insofar as powerful people and institutions press for the exclusion of those with cognitive disabilities, their dignity does become empirically contested and hence vulnerable. I will return to this issue and its implications for philosophical discussions of cognitive disability in the last section.

5. There may be an exception here for very young children. Consider the recent BBC interview with Professor Robert E. Kelly (available at https://www.youtube.com/watch?v=Mh4f9AYRCZY), which went viral after his two young children gate-crashed the room before being brusquely removed. While most commenters were sympathetic to Kelly's predicament, some nonetheless criticized him for "strong-arming" the toddler without breaking his gaze from the camera. The question of how and when young children become fully human is beyond the scope of this chapter, and so I set it to one side.

6. I borrow the term "grievability" from Judith Butler, who uses it in the context of the war on terror. As she puts it: "Some lives are grievable, and others are not; the differential allocation of grievability that decides what kind of subject is and must be grieved, and which kind of subject must not, operates to produce and maintain certain exclusionary conceptions of who is normatively human: what counts as a livable life and a grievable death?" (Butler 2006, xiv–xv).

7. Noticeably, this marking of death is something we also often do with our pets. To that extent, we are treating them as "honorary humans." Such marking is not sufficient in and of itself, however, to constitute membership in the human community. Most crucially, a critical mass of us would have to see pets *as* human.

8. Of course, different theological traditions will have different ways of cashing out the precise relationship between being human and having dignity, and not all will have the universal implications I point to here. My point is simply that religious accounts have important resources for positing an inclusive theory of human dignity, which it is worth attending to.

9. One of the key shifts in much contemporary work on dignity is the eschewal of any reliance on the realm of the noumenal, to which Kant was committed. In other words, those who today trace dignity to some inherent cognitive feature of person do so in a thoroughly naturalized way. This means that, technically, Kant's own account would not meet the definition I give later for natural kinds. Since my target here is a broad strand of contemporary thought on dignity and not the specifics of Kant scholarship, I leave that complication to one side.

10. Anne Phillips makes a similar point: "Whatever candidates we choose as our descriptors, they lead us into questions about who fits and who does not, and may tempt us into treating these as matters of empirical investigation" (Phillips 2015, 43).

11. One of the key ways in which my approach differs from Waldron's is in how it construes worth. For Waldron, dignity as status contrasts with dignity as worth. On my approach, the status of human *confers* dignity as worth.

12. I explore this idea in more depth in Killmister (2017*b*).

13. A fruitful comparison can be drawn here to the creation of nations and, with it, the category of co-national. While nationality involves formal political recognition, much of the meaning of being a co-national emerges from the ways in which the media and the education system call upon us to recognize specific others as co-nationals with whom we stand in special relationships (c.f. Anderson 1991).

14. For more on the role of self-understanding in shaping social kinds, see Ian Hacking's (1999) discussion of "interactive kinds."

15. There are similarities here with how Cora Diamond construes the human; see her (1991), especially the Appendix.

16. The following is an overly brief sketch of what needs to be a more fully worked out normative framework, which I hope to pursue in future work.

17. I deliberately leave open here just how such impact should be understood (i.e., what normative ethic provides the framework against which the impact should be measured). Space obviously precludes filling in and defending a full moral theory within this chapter.

18. This is an empirical claim that is likely to be contested, especially by animal rights activists. It rests on the assumption that excluding cognitively disabled people will further their suffering, without generating compensating improvements in the lives of nonhuman animals. For an argument to this effect, see Carlson (2009) and Kittay (2005*a*). Moreover, the claim that it is morally better to include individuals with cognitive disabilities is compatible with the claim that the boundaries should be extended to also include some nonhuman animals.

19. At the limit, we might even say that *no* system of membership is morally permissible, and hence the very category of the nation-state is not morally justifiable. Doing so would involve showing that all of the benefits the nation-state makes possible are either possible without the nation-state or are outweighed by the suffering that nation-state boundaries inflict. The same move could be made with respect to the human.

References

Anderson, Benedict. 1991. *Imagined Communities: Reflections on the Origin and Spread of Nationalism*. London/New York: Verso.

Benedict XVI. 2009. *Caritas In Veritate*. Vatican City: Vatican Publishing House.

Bérubé, Michael. 2009. "Equality, Freedom, and/or Justice for All: A Response to Martha Nussbaum." *Metaphilosophy* 40(3–4): 352–365.

Bird, Alexander, and Emma Tobin. 2016. "Natural Kinds." In *Stanford Encyclopedia of Philosophy*, edited by Edward N. Zalta. Available at: https://plato.stanford.edu/entries/natural-kinds/

Butler, Judith. 2006. *Precarious Life: The Powers of Mourning and Violence*. New York: Verso.

Carlson, Licia. 2009. *The Faces of Intellectual Disability: Philosophical Reflections*. Bloomington: Indiana University Press.

Carter, Ian. 2011. "Respect and the Basis of Equality." *Ethics* 121(3): 538–571.

Darwall, Stephen. 2006. *The Second-Person Standpoint: Morality, Respect, and Accountability*. Cambridge, MA: Harvard University Press.

Diamond, Cora. 1991. "The Importance of Being Human." *Royal Institute of Philosophy Supplements* 29: 35–62.

Fernández-Armesto, Felipe. 2005. *So You Think You're Human?: A Brief History of Humankind*. Oxford: Oxford University Press.

Griffin, James. 2008. *On Human Rights*. Oxford: Oxford University Press.

Hacking, Ian. 1999. *The Social Construction of What?* Cambridge, MA: Harvard University Press.

Haslanger, Sally. 2012. *Resisting Reality: Social Construction and Social Critique*. New York: Oxford University Press.

Jaworska, Agnieszka, and Julie Tannenbaum. 2014. "Person-Rearing Relationships as a Key to Higher Moral Status." *Ethics* 124(2): 242–271.

Kant, Immanuel. 1976. *Foundations of the Metaphysics of Morals*, translated by Lewis Beck. Indianapolis: Bobs-Merrill Educational Publishing.

Killmister, Suzy. 2017*a*. "Dignity: Personal, Social, Human." *Philosophical Studies* 174(8): 2063–2082.

Killmister, Suzy. 2017*b*. "Deriving Human Rights From Human Dignity: A Novel Political Approach." In *Political Approaches to Human Rights*, edited by Thomas Campbell and Kylie Bourne, 56–70. Routledge.

Kittay, Eva Feder. 2005*a*. "At the Margins of Moral Personhood." *Ethics* 116(1): 100–131.

Kittay, Eva Feder. 2005*b*. "Equality, Dignity, and Disability." In *Perspectives on Equality: The Second Seamus Heaney Lectures*, edited by Mary Ann Lyons and Fionnuala Waldron, 93–119. Dublin: The Liffey Press.

McMahan, Jeff. 2002. *The Ethics of Killing: Problems at the Margins of Life*. Oxford: Oxford University Press on Demand.

Mills, Charles. 1997. *The Racial Contract*. Ithaca: Cornell University Press.

Phillips, Anne. 2015. *The Politics of the Human*. Cambridge: Cambridge University Press.

Searle, John. 1995. *The Construction of Social Reality*. New York: The Free Press.

Stuurman, Siep. 2017. *The Invention of Humanity: Equality and Cultural Difference in World History*. Cambridge, MA: Harvard University Press.

Waldron, Jeremy. 2012. *Dignity, Rank, and Rights*. New York: Oxford University Press.

CHAPTER 28

ON MORAL STATUS AND INTELLECTUAL DISABILITY

Challenging and Expanding the Debates

LICIA CARLSON

THE treatment of intellectual disability (ID) at the hands of philosophers is not a new phenomenon. References to various kinds of disabilities, conditions, and states that designate some form of cognitive or intellectual impairment, deficit, or departure from a norm can be traced through the history of philosophy to the present day. References to a broad range of human kinds housed under this umbrella, with shifting terminology, appear in philosophical discussions of topics as varied as personhood, quality of life, justice, rights, autonomy, and dependency, and in subfields including bioethics, political and legal philosophy, philosophy of mind, philosophy of language, phenomenology, feminist philosophy, queer theory, and critical race theory. Not surprisingly, the assumptions, definitions, motivations, and methods behind these diverse treatments of ID vary; thus, there is not a univocal, single "philosophy of intellectual disability."

One of the themes that dominates philosophical discussions of ID is the question of moral status: How should the moral status of people with varying degrees and kinds of ID (or "cognitive impairments," more broadly) be defined, and what follows from these conclusions? Here again, answers fall along a broad philosophical spectrum, and these debates have inevitably engaged with issues regarding the definition and significance of disability; the value accorded to concepts like rationality, autonomy, dependency, relationships, and care; and the meaning and relevance of being human.

My aim is not to resolve the debate regarding the moral status of people with ID in this chapter; rather, I will tease apart some conceptual, methodological, and epistemological considerations that are relevant to philosophizing about ID. Two questions serve as a backdrop to these reflections: Why do "the intellectually disabled" matter to philosophy? And, conversely, (why) do philosophical claims about moral status matter to people with ID? I begin by calling for conceptual clarity and specificity with respect to certain categories, capacities, and aims that inform discussions of moral status. I then consider what is at stake in the continued associations between nonhuman animals and people with ID, a hallmark of many philosophical discussions of moral status. Finally, I point to a number of ways that philosophers are expanding our moral horizons in the face of ID, and I conclude with some thoughts on how philosophies of ID might be understood as critical, reparative, and generative.

CONCEPTUAL CLARITY AND SPECIFICITY

There are many challenges that attend philosophizing about ID. Though the question of moral status is focused on individuals ("the intellectually disabled" or, more often, the "severely" or "radically cognitively disabled"), the very definition of this group relies on some definition of *disability* itself. Given the critical scholarship and political activism that have emerged around definitions of disability, it is important to clarify what model of disability undergirds one's philosophical discussion (of course, in some cases, the focus may be on the definition and merits of the models themselves.) The terms of the discussion will be very different if one is treating ID as a fixed, pathological trait of the individual (as the medical model defines it) rather than as an interaction between the individual assumed to have certain cognitive features and her environment (as some social model proponents will maintain.) Yet this very question points to greater complexities within the category of *intellectual* or *cognitive* disability.

Intellectual or cognitive disability denotes a broad category that is both internally and externally heterogeneous (Carlson 2009). Internally, it can be subdivided according to various designations: severity, etiology, specific capacities or (dis)abilities, congenital or acquired. In some instances, the nature of the "impairment" is identifiable biologically or genetically (e.g., trisomy 21, fragile X mental retardation); in other instances, the cause may be less clear or unknown. "Intellectual disability" is also externally heterogeneous, insofar as it is defined by multiple disciplines and experts (e.g., in medicine, psychology, law, education) in a range of ways and with diverse criteria.[1] Within philosophical discussions, too, one finds a fairly broad range of definitions, though often the specifics are assumed rather than explicitly stated. Insofar as these designations are not self-evident natural kinds, specificity is crucial. Is one speaking about the "cognitively disabled" that might include individuals who have become so through a traumatic brain injury or dementia, or about congenital forms of ID? Does the category "intellectual disability" also encompass learning disabilities[2] and individuals on the autism spectrum? Autism, for example, is an increasingly complex, internally heterogeneous classification, and, depending on one's view, it may be considered an objective pathology, a social construction based on conceptions of what is neurotypical, and/or a form of "neurodiversity" that is cause for celebration. This underscores the importance of clarifying one's normative commitments at the outset and defining the nature and scope of the "disability" clearly.

Perhaps the most commonly specified group in discussions of moral status is some version of the "severely," "profoundly," or "radically intellectually disabled." Yet even if one is restricting the conversation to this group, conceptual clarifications are warranted. For example, if one is considering proxy or surrogate decision-making capacity, whether or not the person has been severely disabled as a result of a congenital disability, a traumatic injury later in life, or dementia is relevant to how the question is formulated. If one wishes to focus on a very specific condition like Down syndrome, for example, though the etiology and impairment are very clearly defined (trisomy 21), the question of severity is much less certain as there is a broad range of capacities within this group. Precision with respect to etiologic kind, then, does not always translate into specificity regarding severity.

As philosophers, however, we also claim the power to generate our own examples with as little or as much specificity as required. It is quite common, in discussions of moral status, to encounter stipulative definitions, thought experiments, or hypothetical cases that can be generated to suit and serve the philosophical question at hand. This may seem desirable in some instances insofar as it potentially avoids the messiness of *actual* embodied lives, yet it is precisely this "neatness" that some philosophers have challenged, on the grounds that there is no correspondence to actual existing individuals and that erroneous or attenuated portraits run the risk of perpetuating certain deleterious forms of oppression and marginalization (Carlson 2009; Kittay 2005; 2008; 2010). This is not to suggest that there is no room for such examples; rather, it is to acknowledge that there is much at stake, both epistemically and ethically, in how philosophical cases are constructed (a point to which I will return). It is crucial to employ precision with regard to the nature and definition of ID and the naming of the *individuals* (real or imagined) about whom one is making a philosophical argument and to be transparent about the underlying normative assumptions that inform our concepts and cases.

Finally, the impairments, conditions, and people to which "intellectual disability" refers have all had shifting definitions that reflect political and social norms and practices. One need only to look at the complex history of "intelligence" to see how porous and contested many of the concepts that lie at the heart of theories of ID are. There are countless historical examples where "the intellectually disabled" were defined according to racist and sexist doctrines associated with suspect political, social, and eugenic aims. This raises the question: Can philosophical discussions about the moral status of "the intellectually disabled" afford to disregard this history and ignore the social and political forces that shape the concepts and categories associated with ID?

Some might respond to this question with a definitive "yes." Insofar as attempts to define moral status are focused on specific capacities (or lack thereof) constitutive of ID as explicitly defined by philosophers, their theories are immune from external forces that might taint or distort these philosophical aims. Yet even if we assume that this is the case (and I would argue this is questionable), other challenges remain.

In order to grant or deny moral status to an individual with an ID based on a particular capacity or capability, that capacity must be definable and detectable. However, the issue of measurement and determining particular degrees of cognitive capacity or capabilities is not always straightforward (Vorhaus 2016). First, there are epistemic barriers that one may face in addressing individuals with varying degrees of ID. For example, in cases of individuals who are nonverbal, making such determinations can be particularly difficult depending on the capacity one hopes to identify (Kittay 2010; Vorhaus 2016; Wong, 2010). Of course, in cases of thought experiments restricted to philosophical discourse, these concrete difficulties are not a problem; however, insofar as philosophers hope their theories to have some practical import and impact, these difficulties must be addressed.

Another point of clarification that is necessary to address is whether the relevant capacities or capabilities (and lack thereof) are presumed to be static and fixed. There is a long history of defining people with ID as incapable of change, as hopeless cases who are uneducable, incurable, and locked in a permanent state of arrested development (think of the temporal nature of the term "mental *retardation*").[3] In a philosophical context, a number of questions must be addressed. First, is one speaking about *actual* cognitive capacities, and is one also including the *potential* for realizing these abilities? Second, how is it possible to detect or assess whether these (in)capacities are present in the group under discussion? While philosophers are clearly not expected to be diagnosticians, these questions are relevant and important to address insofar as arguments regarding moral status are based on the presence or absence of such characteristics. Moreover, there is ample evidence to suggest that there are complexities and difficulties that attend answering this second question. In his discussion of people with profound and multiple learning disabilities, John Vorhaus presents numerous examples of people with "spiky profiles," where the capacities and abilities of an individual vary greatly over time (Vorhaus 2016, 17–19). While one can consider the cognitive profile of an individual at a particular moment in time, there can be many unknowns regarding exactly what certain behaviors or actions signify about that person's capacities in a more global sense (particularly with respect to what they may be capable of at another point in time). There is good reason, then, to be wary of underestimating an individual's possession of or potential to develop certain capacities; at the very least, it is problematic to simply assume that there is a straightforward litmus test and to deny the epistemic challenges present, particularly in people with severe and profound disabilities. This is equally true of capacities that are relational in nature (e.g., social participation, reciprocity, care, expressions of affection). As Vorhaus argues, "What should be said is that, in view of the history of ignorance, error and under-estimation in respect of the capacities of people with disabilities, and in light of advances in pedagogy and technology, we are entitled to insist on stringent criteria for assessment before reaching a conclusion that someone has no potential to develop the capacity for responsiveness" (Vorhaus 2017, 70).

A final point when considering barriers to clarity and precision in philosophizing about ID is to acknowledge that there is not always a strict boundary between intellectual and physical disabilities. While there is good reason not to conflate physical and cognitive disabilities or ID (as may people with physical disabilities have been wrongly assumed to be intellectually disabled as well), many people with ID also have physical disabilities. Whether or not one chooses to limit the discussion to individuals who only have mental or cognitive disabilities, it is crucial to recognize the *embodied existence* and material lives of all people with ID. The perception and treatment of bodies, the experience of the lived body, and the corporeal dimensions of interactions between individuals all affect the meaning and significance of disability and cannot be understood as completely separate from conceptual definitions and moral arguments.[4]

IS DEHUMANIZING PHILOSOPHY DEHUMANIZING? THE PERSISTENCE OF ANIMAL COMPANIONS

One of the approaches to defining the moral status of people with ID that continues to dominate philosophical discussions is the invocation of nonhuman animals. These philosophical associations between nonhuman animals and people with ID have been challenged on a number of grounds: that they are offensive, epistemically unsound, and that they can have deleterious consequences. These critiques, in turn, have prompted a range of responses, from charges of speciesism and claims that there is no offense intended, to arguments that these are purely philosophical exercises and that they are not intended to justify mistreatment or harmful policies against this population.

My own critique of these associations has centered primarily on arguments that I called "indirect," cases where the "severely cognitively disabled" were marshalled to make the case *for* nonhuman animals. I argued that drawing these associations to make philosophical arguments regarding the moral status of nonhuman animals was neither necessary nor helpful and that, in addition to constituting a form of conceptual exploitation of this group, it could have harmful effects on a population that has been historically viewed as subhuman and animal-like (Carlson 2009). Yet these connections are also being drawn in philosophical discussions that *directly* focus on the moral status of people with ID. Comparisons to nonhuman animals are not only used to deny that people with severe ID should be accorded moral status; some use these comparisons to *affirm* that people with ID have a higher moral status than nonhuman animals. Discussions of people with ID and nonhuman animals can also be found in arguments that wish to *defend* a morally relevant notion of the human, not only in arguments against speciesism. After offering a brief sketch of these various positions, I consider whether this broader array of justifications for associating people with ID and nonhuman animals might allay the concerns that critics like myself and others have.

The arguments that have received the most critical attention have been those that argue for moral parity of humans and nonhumans with comparable capacities. These arguments challenge the claim that people with severe ID have a higher moral status than nonhuman animals and simultaneously affirm that species membership is not a morally justifiable criterion for moral status (McMahan 2003; 2010; Singer 2010). Some philosophers, however, have invoked particular cognitive capacities or relationships to argue that people with severe ID *do* occupy a higher moral status than nonhuman animals. For example, in "Person-Rearing Relationships as a Key to Higher Moral Status," Jaworska and Tannenbaum place the comparison between a mature dog, babies, and people with "severe cognitive impairments" at the center of their argument and conclude that a baby or a severely cognitively disabled person whose cognitive capacities "are otherwise on a par with a mature dog's capacities... nevertheless has a higher moral status" (Jaworska and Tannenbaum 2014, 244).[5]

There are other philosophers who wish to preserve a broader notion of the human or species-membership as the basis for moral status and who thus reject the notion that we can compare nonhuman animals and people with ID on the basis of certain capacities or features (Diamond 1991; Kittay 2005; 2010; Curtis and Vehmas 2016). Yet, just as comparisons with nonhuman animals based on particular morally relevant features can be used to argue that people with severe ID *do* have higher moral status than animals, arguments that defend species membership and the "importance of being human" can be compatible with arguments *for* the moral status of nonhuman animals. Contrary to what some critics would assume, it is not the case that preserving a morally relevant conception of the human necessitates the denial of the moral status of nonhuman animals. In Alice Crary's words, we do not have to "face a choice between affirming the status of nonhuman animals *or* people with disabilities" (Crary 2016, 123). In her book *Inside Ethics*, Crary argues that preserving a morally relevant concept of species membership can be the basis for affirming the moral status of *both* nonhuman animals and people with disabilities. Crary wants to offer "a philosophically provocative and practically important portrait of humans and animals as beings who merit solicitude simply as the creatures that they are and who are fellow travelers on a glorious and fraught mortal adventure" (Crary 2016, 273). Thus, she says, she is "setting out to show not only that the plain fact of being human is morally significant but that the plain fact of being an animal is so as well" (Crary 2016, 122).

The choice to bring people with disabilities and nonhuman animals together in discussions of moral status, then, can be done with very different aims: to investigate the moral status that various kinds of beings have, to argue for or against the moral relevance of being human, and to argue that people with ID possess capacities that either confer upon or deprive them of a certain moral status. In view of this array of arguments within this interspecies philosophical landscape, are there still reasons to be wary of these moves? Why resist these continued associations between animals and human beings with ID?

If one's philosophical project is explicitly aimed at discussing humans and nonhumans together (like Crary's and Martha Nussbaum's [2006]) and addressing the moral status of both groups (be it based on species membership, relationships, or certain capabilities), then obviously non-human animals must be present in the discussion. If the aim is to focus exclusively on the status of nonhuman animals (e.g., to argue for their moral status and/or to critique speciesism), I still maintain that the inclusion of people with severe ID, while rhetorically effective, may not be necessary (Carlson 2009). But what about discussions that are intended to be centered squarely on the moral status of people with ID? Does the continued invocation of nonhuman animals serve a purpose?

One reason given for perpetuating this connection is that the terms of the debate have already been established along these lines. Jaworska and Tannenbaum make this clear in a footnote: "Some readers may find the comparison of a human being to a dog offensive. Nonetheless, we want to take seriously and answer those who deny that human non-SSP's [self-standing persons] have higher moral status than, for example, dogs, on the ground that their cognitive capacities are comparable" (Jaworska and Tannenbaum 2014, 244). Thus, though they recognize that such comparisons may be offensive, they base their arguments on the comparison between babies, people with severe cognitive impairments, and mature dogs.

In "Sharing a Common Life: People with Profound and Multiple Learning Difficulties," John Vorhaus argues that it is participation in this common human life that serves as a basis for including people with "profound and multiple learning disabilities" within our moral purview (Vorhaus 2017). While he does not build his argument around a comparison with nonhuman animals, he does address the question of whether his account of participation must also include nonhuman animals with comparable capacities. He ultimately concludes that there is something distinctively human about the kind of participation (and potential for it) that lies at the basis of his account. Yet while he bases this on human culture, distinctly human practices, and human bodies, he argues that this position need not imply the exclusion of nonhuman animals from moral consideration. At the same time, however, he expresses some unease with the comparison, acknowledging the potential hazards and disturbing effects it may have (Vorhaus 2017).

There seems to be a way in which, insofar as the terms of the debate have already been set along these lines, philosophers wishing to define the moral status of people with ID (particularly profound or "radical" forms) feel compelled to respond to the animal question. Yet I believe that this expectation, and the continued associations between people with ID and nonhuman animals, remain problematic for a number of reasons. First, there is the (sometimes visceral) reaction that such comparisons are offensive and dehumanizing. When confronted with having to explain how her severely disabled daughter is different from a pig, Eva Feder Kittay powerfully captures why such questions take one's breath away as the parent of a child with ID, though I would add that such demands have similar effects on many of us who do not have any close relations to people with ID (Kittay 2010). In the face of such reactions, some philosophers have assured that no offense was intended and that arguments such as these do not denigrate any *particular* individual but are instead necessary for the philosophical task at hand.[6] Yet the devastating effects of such discourse cannot be ignored or dismissed.

Beyond causing personal offense, there are other reasons that these comparisons are troubling. First, consider the fact that these moves are typically centered upon the most severe cases. Given the complexities and difficulties involved in assessing the capacities (potential and actual) of people with severe ID, there are epistemic challenges to making such determinations in a way that would then allow one to draw meaningful comparisons to different species with "comparable capacities." Yet even if it *were* possible to do so, I believe there are still good reasons to decline the invitation.

The continued association with nonhuman animals and people with *severe* ID can perpetuate prototype effects, whereby a single kind becomes representative of a whole group. Despite the assurances that, in considering these extreme cases, the conclusions drawn only apply to the most "radically cognitively disabled," if only such cases are the topic of philosophical conversation, there is the possibility that they will become representative of "the intellectually disabled" more generally and fuel global, erroneous assumptions about this group as a whole (Carlson 2009). Moreover, can we be sure that the conclusions derived from these comparisons with nonhuman animals, reserved for the most "radical" cases, will always fall within the strict boundaries set up by philosophers? Even if it is only the most severe cases that are candidates for such comparisons, might animalizing people with severe ID spill over to other individuals and have deleterious effects for people with milder forms of ID as well? As I pointed out earlier, the very boundaries along lines of severity are not always clear and fixed, nor are disciplinary barriers always secured. In view of the fact that some of these arguments are being made in the context of concrete practices (e.g., considerations about biomedical practices and the "ethics of killing"), there is reason to take seriously the possibility that the effects of animalizing disability may reach beyond a philosophical audience.

Finally, tethering discussions of "the intellectually disabled" to nonhuman animals is not a recent development, and our contemporary philosophical arguments do not occur in a historical or social vacuum. Anyone familiar with the history of disability is well aware that it is replete with forms of dehumanization whereby race, gender, intellectual and physical disability, and moral inferiority coalesced in animalized portraits of certain individuals and kinds and justified horrific forms of treatment.[7] To be compared with or defined as animal-like, for certain groups, is neither historically neutral nor, as I have argued, politically benign (Carlson 2009). Though one might claim that such forms of dehumanization are in the past, the continued marginalization and abuses suffered by many in this community suggest that we must be attentive to what our arguments and examples express, even if the intended result is not to harm this group.

This leads to a final question. Can one challenge concrete, contemporary forms of dehumanization without a working concept of the "human?" In calls to dehumanize philosophy (i.e., remove the notion of the "human" from consideration in discussions of moral status), will other forms of dehumanization be perpetuated? In "Paradoxes of Dehumanization," David Livingstone Smith explores the meaning of dehumanization. Amid multiple meanings of the term, he fixes his own definition on a psychological one, where there is clear intent to cause harm: "Conflict precedes and motivates dehumanization: we dehumanize others because we want to kill, harm, or oppress them, rather than the other way around" (Smith 2016, 426). The paradox that Smith articulates is that perpetrators of dehumanization simultaneously view their subjects as human and less than human. There is certainly evidence of this paradox in the history of disability, where one often finds contradictory or competing notions of individuals with ID as both on the spectrum of humanity and completely alien from (and often positioned "below") any meaningful sense of human existence (Carlson 2009). We might consider whether there is a similar dynamic in philosophizing about ID. Though the motivation may be different (the comparisons, it is argued, are intended to yield philosophical clarity, not harm), people with severe ID are doubly dehumanized by stripping them of any meaningful, morally relevant attributes that would grant them moral status (thus deeming them as "less than" and, in some cases, suggesting that "we" might have more in common with or recognize ourselves more in some nonhuman alien being than in these human individuals) while simultaneously admitting that they are human but denying that species membership plays any role in our moral deliberations. Of course, viewing a subject as human, in its barest form, is no guarantee of being treated well. Kate Manne, in response to Smith's arguments, reminds us that acknowledging the humanity of another is no guarantee against violence and brutal treatment.[8] Yet she also acknowledges that "dehumanizing speech" in the form of likening someone or referring to them as an animal, functions as a form of degradation and humiliation because it "helps itself to certain powerful encoded meanings" (Manne 2016, 411). In a philosophical context, these comparisons are engaging in *philosophical* speech with the aim of reaching certain conclusions about the moral status of people with ID; yet is it worth risking the possibility of such arguments functioning, simultaneously, as dehumanizing speech, particularly if these moves are unnecessary to discuss the moral status of people with ID? Stacy Simplican puts it a bit differently and perhaps more bluntly: "You do not need to be a philosopher to know that comparisons with bugs is not the political answer people with disabilities have been searching for" (Simplican 2015, 70).

What follows, then, from these critiques of drawing human–animal comparisons in the context of cognitive disability? First, I am not suggesting that such comparisons should *never* be made. As I acknowledge earlier, exploring what humans and nonhuman animals share is a valid line of inquiry, and, even when doing so in the context of disability, it need not result in the kind of dehumanizing discourse and deleterious effects I have just outlined.[9] In fact, as Sunaura Taylor argues in her recent book *Beasts of Burden: Animal and Disability Liberation,* there is value in examining the intersections between animal oppression and disability oppression as it can yield liberatory results for both groups (Taylor 2017). In the case of Crary's and Taylor's work, the comparisons are necessary, rather than gratuitous or purely for rhetorical purposes, and, in drawing them, both authors acknowledge the oppressive and harmful history of animalizing disability. My point, then, is that there is too much at stake to continue to draw these associations without keeping certain critical questions in the foreground when speaking about moral status, nonhuman animals, and cognitive disability: Where and why are these comparisons made? Are they appropriate and necessary? And what are the effects of doing so, both theoretical and concrete, and by whom are they felt?

To argue that human–animal comparisons can be dehumanizing for people with cognitive disabilities does not, by itself, settle the question of what role the "human" can or should play in philosophical discussions of cognitive disability. Moreover, eliminating human–animal comparisons alone will not solve the problem of dehumanization as it is certainly possible to argue that people with "radical" cognitive disabilities have a diminished moral status and/or are inferior to other human beings without addressing nonhuman animals at all.[10] As Livingstone's and Manne's analyses of dehumanization underscore, the recognition of a being *as human* is not a guarantee against certain forms of abuse and violence. In my own view, these challenges only affirm the importance and necessity of working toward a philosophy of cognitive disability that is capacious and humane enough to grant moral consideration to and affirm the value of all human beings who bear this label.[11]

Moral Expansions

Whether the concept of moral status can provide a basis for establishing the moral worth of individuals with cognitive disabilities remains an open question.[12] As the burgeoning philosophical work in this area reveals, there are many rich and complex philosophical questions (guardianship and trusteeship, autonomy, empowerment, advocacy, flourishing, to name a few) that are worthy of exploration and analysis. In my article, "Philosophers of Intellectual Disability: A Taxonomy," I identified a number of positions or roles that philosophers might occupy in relation to ID (Carlson 2010). Continuing in this vein, I would like to conclude by considering how philosophies of ID are tracing new lines of inquiry that are critical, reparative, and generative.

As the foregoing examples have shown, some philosophical approaches to moral status are diagnostic, not in the medical sense, but insofar as they identify a group (commonly the "severely intellectually disabled") and offer an evaluation of moral status based on specified traits. Often, though not always, these philosophical diagnoses are accompanied by recommendations regarding the fate of these subjects: in some cases, they are only worthy of preferential treatment by virtue of their connections to others; in other cases, particularly in bioethical literature, the diagnosis of their moral status (or lack thereof) points to actions on the horizon that are aimed at amelioration, cure, and even at ending or preventing such lives from coming into existence.

Yet as philosophers of ID, we can also turn a critical, diagnostic lens on our own work. As I have argued earlier, it is important that we acknowledge both the history and materiality of disability. This involves recognizing the permeability and historical contingency of "intellectual disability" as a category and understanding how shifting modes of diagnosis and treatment have targeted certain populations unjustly. Though this history may not be directly relevant to particular contemporary discussions of moral status, it reminds us to ask critical questions regarding the presuppositions that shape our philosophical constructions and arguments and to consider the ultimate purpose they are intended to serve. This history also reminds us of the *materiality* of disability. People with ID, like all human beings, live embodied lives that are impacted and shaped by multiple dimensions of their identities (including race, gender, ethnicity, sexuality.) And there are social, economic, and cultural forces that continue to shape the contours of the categories themselves, as well as the fate of those who inhabit them (Erevelles 2011).

A second critical move is to problematize both the presence and absence of people with ID in philosophy and expose the ways that forms of ableism and cognitive privilege perpetuate these forms of erasure, marginalization, and exclusion. How can moral philosophy be inclusive of people with ID in ways that do not, paradoxically, establish their very exclusion from moral consideration? This effort requires rethinking epistemic authority and cognitive privilege and calls for a degree of humility when formulating our philosophical questions and acknowledging the epistemic barriers we face and our own forms of ignorance (Kittay 2005; 2010; Carlson 2009). The question of drawing moral boundaries with respect to personhood, citizenship, and other moral categories is inevitably shaped by those who are present and absent in this effort. Thus, an important part of recognizing cognitive privilege is acknowledging who is or is not included in our philosophical work and critically reflecting on exactly how and why ID is included in philosophical discourse: Is the purpose of its inclusion to present a marginal case whose exclusion is ultimately justified? To theorize about individual, embodied subjects as citizens, persons, and individuals who actively partake of human relationships in unique and morally significant ways? Is the point of departure that ID is a form of defect, lack, or undesirable, harmed state that is a problem to be solved? Or is the starting point one which assumes that disabled lives may be a critical source of philosophical insight?

More broadly, we might ask how the demands and values of our very professional lives shape the setting and ethos within which we philosophize and affect our assumptions about the moral value of people with ID. Literature professor Chris Gabbard, writing about his son in "A Life Beyond Reason," asks: "Especially in an academic environment that rewards being smart, how do I broach the idea that people with ID are fully equal? We academics advance in our careers by demonstrating how clever we can be, and because so much depends on flaunting intelligence, it is harder for us than for most people to steer clear of prejudice" (Gabbard 2010).

Beyond forms of prejudice, however, there may be more entrenched structural and philosophical forces at play that affect philosophies of ID. In her book *The Capacity Contract,* Stacy Simplican explores how "our allegiance to equality *and* an ideal cognitive subject reveals a deep tension in democratic theory" that constitutes "two sides of a *capacity contract* that pulls democracy to both embrace and expel vulnerability" (Simplican 2015, 4). She examines how the logic of "compulsory capacity," a naturalized, fictionalized threshold of cognitive capacity on which political membership is based, has functioned in both the history of philosophy (most notably in Locke and the development of contract theories) and in the scientific and social theories that dominated the history of ID (Simplican 2015, 4). This logic, she argues, continues to shape how people with a broad range of ID are defined and treated today, not only in philosophy but in disability studies and even in self-advocacy movements. The challenge, as she presents it, is to recognize the ways that "empowerment-as-compulsory capacity undermines the goal of empowering *all* people with intellectual disabilities" and to reconceptualize and foster a more capacious mode of empowerment (Simplican 2015, 95).

In a different context, Rosemarie Garland-Thomson argues against what she has called the "eugenic logic" that dominates bioethical discourse and biomedical practices. This logic "tells us that we can avoid disability and even eliminate it from the human condition. This understanding of disability as somehow detachable from human life rather than essential to it fosters the idea that disability does not have much to do with us unless we have the misfortune of having it descend upon us" (Garland-Thomson 2012, 342). Thomson counters this logic by making the provocative case for *conserving* disability based on its generative power as a narrative, ethical, and epistemic resource. In exposing how these various forms of logic work, Simplican's and Thomson's works raise critical questions for philosophers of ID: In what ways do discussions of the moral status of people with ID rely on normative judgments regarding the inherent undesirability of disability? And to what extent are they articulated with a logic that promotes the prevention and elimination of disability as its central aim or one that presents cognitive capacity as the sole criterion for empowerment and justice? To answer these questions, Simplican and Thomson, along with others, invite us to trace philosophical paths that are reparative and generative.

Whereas within medical models of disability, the person with the disability is the target of the "repair" or "fixing," some argue that it is philosophy that is in need of repair. From a methodological standpoint, there are calls to better integrate and draw upon the voices of people with ID into philosophical work about them. This can pose distinct challenges in cases of individuals who are nonverbal and who have more significant disabilities, yet there are a number of philosophers who are engaging in finding ways to "give voice to profound disability" and to find new models of trusteeship, surrogacy, citizenship, and solidarity in order to establish a more capacious concept of moral status and moral subjectivity.[13] Yet, as I have argued, it is important to expand moral considerations beyond just the most severe cases.

In her article, "Cognitive Diversity in the Global Academy: Why the Voices of Persons with Cognitive Disabilities Are Vital to Intellectual Diversity," Maeve O'Donnovan explores the ways that people with learning disabilities in particular are excluded, marginalized, and misrepresented in both philosophy of mind as well as in disability studies. In response, she calls for the valorization of the intellectual diversity of *persons*, not just ideas: "Calls for increased intellectual diversity in the academy regularly assume that such diversity is found only in ideas, not in the persons who generate them, and, ironically, serve as justifications for the return of enlightenment ideals of reason and disembodied knowers.... The unique value of cognitive diversity is its insistence on a radical shift in our conception of who can know and who can produce knowledge" (O'Donnovan 2010). Though O'Donnovan may not be speaking about the same group of individuals that philosophers who address the moral status of the "radically cognitively disabled" are, her point is an important one as it speaks to the extent to which our philosophical projects may be shaped, often in unanticipated ways, by the voices that are present and absent. Simplican, too, calls for finding creative ways to incorporate the voices of people with all forms of ID into the philosophical fold. Yet it is not merely as a way to foster inclusion that including the voices of people with ID is philosophically important; she writes that "[r]eflecting on the voices and actions of people with intellectual disabilities to guide theory is imperative for multiple reasons," including that it is inclusive, it "destabilizes a method of ideal theorizing that has promoted an exclusionary conception of being human," and it "suspends the epistemological authority of the researcher with the intent of allowing the experiences of those most marginalized to guide the development of theoretical claims" (Simplican 2015, 20). Though these philosophical attempts to redress forms of exclusion within philosophy do not necessarily resolve the debates regarding the moral status of people with ID, they are engaged in a reparative project insofar as they are expanding boundaries—both moral and institutional—that have kept many people with ID on the margins.

Finally, philosophies of ID can be generative in a number of ways that can inform and transform how we think about moral status and the moral community.[14] This can involve generating new metaphors and opening new spaces within which new forms of knowledge and discourse might emerge. Literary texts, including novels and memoir, can serve as a basis for expanding the moral imagination, presenting alternate portraits of ID, and facilitating critical reflection on our philosophical presuppositions (Bérubé 2016; Crary 2016). Moving away from conceptions of ID that are based on a deficit model or traditional measures of cognitive function can also allow different forms of individual and shared experience and well-being to emerge as morally relevant. There is increasing philosophical attention being paid to how alternate modes of cognition and expression, through music, the arts, theater, and humor, may bear upon discussions of moral status, subjectivity, and flourishing (Vorhaus 2016; 2017; Carlson 2013; 2015; Simplican 2015).

In this chapter, I have been concerned with how and why philosophers address the moral status of people with ID. While I have by no means resolved the debates, I have suggested that certain critical questions and clarifications should inform them. Conceptual specificity along multiple axes, including conceptions of disability and the nature, severity, and etiology of the particular ID in question, is paramount. It is also crucial to recognize that the philosophical terms and concepts that shape discussions of moral status do not appear in a historical, political, and social vacuum and that this is a population whose very humanity has been contested and denied in ways that have led to their abuse, dehumanization, and extinction. Finally, while they may grace the pages of our philosophical work as thought experiments and marginal cases, "the intellectually disabled" exist in the world as a diverse group of persons whose lived, embodied experiences are valuable and worthy of attention and care in their own right, an insight that lies at the heart of many critical, reparative, and generative philosophies of ID.

ACKNOWLEDGMENTS

I would like to thank Adam Cureton and David Wasserman for their helpful insights on earlier versions of this chapter.

NOTES

1. For example, the American Association on Intellectual and Developmental Disabilities currently defines *intellectual disability* as "a disability characterized by significant limitations in both intellectual functioning and in adaptive behavior, which covers many everyday social and practical skills, with onset before the age of 18" (www.aaidd.org).

2. In the United States, learning disabilities are understood as "intrinsic, perceptual processing problems due to impairment(s) in the central nervous system" (O'Donnovan 2010).

3. This assumption often justified and fueled the abusive treatments that these individuals received (Carlson 2010; Simplican 2015; Trent 1994).

4. Nirmala Erevelles, for example, has called for a materialist feminist disability theory (Erevelles 2012). This also becomes evident if we consider the nature of morally relevant encounters with people with intellectual disabilities as shaped by touch, movement, proximity, physical presence, and many other dimensions of embodied existence.

5. Martha Nussbaum's book, *Frontiers of Justice*, is another example that combines a discussion of nonhuman animals and people with disabilities and concludes that both are deserving of moral consideration based on her capabilities approach (Nussbaum 2006).

6. Kittay gives a number of arguments in response to these claims, some of which I touch upon here (Kittay 2005; 2008; 2010).

7. See Carey 2013; Carlson 2010; Simplican 2015; Trent 1994.

8. Manne writes, "I have argued that an agent's recognition of a human subject as such may be insufficient to dispose her strongly on balance—or, arguably, at all—to treat this subject humanely (i.e., with due consideration, respect, and care, in interpersonal contexts). This is not because I think the humanist is wrong that the recognition of someone's humanity will tend to motivate humane conduct, all else being equal. It is rather that all else is often not equal—indeed, is as unequal as can be" (Manne 2016, 407).

9. Alice Crary's book, *Inside Ethics* (2016) is an example of this.

10. I am grateful to David Wasserman for helping me clarify this point.

11. Though it is beyond the scope of this chapter to fully defend this position, I maintain (along with thinkers like Kittay, Crary, and Diamond) that there is a place for the *human* in philosophical discussions of people with cognitive disabilities. I believe that *being human* is morally salient and that this position neither entails a commitment to speciesism or the devaluation of nonhuman animals, nor does it foreclose the possibility of making meaningful distinctions when it comes to what certain human beings are owed and how they should be treated.

12. See Crary's (2020) chapter in this volume. For an argument for doing away with the very concept of moral status, see Anita Silvers, "Why Moral Status Is a Bad Idea" (2012).

13. Vorhaus (2016), Curtis and Vehmas (2017), Francis and Silvers (2010), Nussbaum (2010), Mietola, Miettinen, and Vehmas (2017). These proposals have also generated criticisms on various grounds. See Wasserman and McMahan (2012).

14. I am deeply indebted to Rosemarie Garland-Thomson's work for this notion of disability as generative.

References

Bérubé, Michael. 2016. *The Secret Life of Stories: From Don Quixote to Harry Potter, How Understanding Intellectual Disability Transforms the Way We Read*. New York: New York University Press.

Carey, Alison. 2013. "The Sociopolitical Contexts of Passing and Intellectual Disability." In *Disability and Passing: Blurring the Lines of Identity*, edited by Jeffrey Brune and Daniel Wislon, 142–166. Philadelphia: Temple University Press.

Carlson, Licia. 2009. *The Faces of Intellectual Disability: Philosophical Reflections*. Bloomington: Indiana University Press.

Carlson, Licia. 2010. "Philosophers of Intellectual Disability: A Taxonomy." In *Cognitive Disability and Its Challenge to Moral Philosophy*, edited by Eva Feder Kittay and Licia Carlson, 315–329. Malden, MA: Wiley-Blackwell.

Carlson, Licia. 2013. "Musical Becoming: Intellectual Disability and the Transformative Power of Music." In *Foundations of Disability Studies*, edited by Matthew Wappett and Katrina Arndt, 83–103. New York: Palgrave Macmillan.

Carlson, Licia. 2015. "Music, Intellectual Disability, and Human Flourishing." In *Oxford Handbook of Music and Disability Studies*, edited by Blake Howe, Stephanie Jensen-Moulton, Neil Lerner, and Joseph Straus, 37–53. Oxford: University Press.

Crary, Alice. 2016. *Inside Ethics: On the Demands of Moral Thought*. Cambridge, MA: Harvard University Press.

Crary, Alice. 2020. "Cognitive Disability and Moral Status." In *Oxford Handbook of Philosophy and Disability*, edited by Adam Cureton and David Wasserman, 451–466. New York: Oxford University Press.

Curtis, Benjamin, and Simo Vehmas. 2016. "A Moorean Argument for the Full Moral Status of Those with Profound Intellectual Disability." *Journal of Medical Ethics*, 42: 41-45.

Diamond, Cora. 1991. "The Importance of Being Human." In *Human Beings*, edited by David Cockburn, 35–62. Cambridge: Cambridge University Press.

Erevelles, Nirmala. 2011. *Disability and Difference in Global Contexts: Enabling a Transformative Body Politic*. New York: Palgrave Macmillan.

Francis, Leslie, and Anita Silvers. 2010. "Thinking About the Good: Reconfiguring Liberal Metaphysics (or Not) for People with Cognitive Disabilities." In *Cognitive Disability and Its Challenge to Moral Philosophy*, edited by Eva Feder Kittay and Licia Carlson, 237–259. Malden, MA: Wiley-Blackwell.

Gabbard, Chris. 2010. "A Life Beyond Reason." *The Chronicle of Higher Education*, November.

Garland-Thomson, Rosemarie. 2012. "The Case for Conserving Disability." *Journal of Bioethical Inquiry*, 9: 339–355.

Jaworska, Agnieszka, and Julie Tannenbaum. 2014. "Person-Rearing Relationships as a Key to Higher Moral Status." *Ethics*, 124(2): 242–271.

Kittay, Eva Feder. 2005. "On the Margins of Moral Personhood," *Ethics*, 116: 100–131.

Kittay, Eva Feder. 2008. "Ideal Theory Bioethics and the Exclusion of People with Severe Cognitive Disabilities." In *Naturalized Bioethics: Toward Responsible Knowing and Practice*, edited by Hilde Lindemann, Marian Verkerk, and Margaret Urban Walker, 218–237. Cambridge: Cambridge University Press.

Kittay, Eva Feder. 2010. "The Personal Is Philosophical Is Political." In *Cognitive Disability and Its Challenge to Moral Philosophy*, edited by Eva Feder Kittay and Licia Carlson, 393–413. Malden, MA: Wiley Blackwell.

Manne, Kate. 2016. "Humanism: A Critique." *Social Theory and Practice*, 42(2): 389–415.

McMahan, Jeff. 2003. *The Ethics of Killing: Problems at the Margins of Life*. Oxford: Oxford University Press.

McMahan, Jeff. 2010. "Cognitive Disability and Cognitive Enhancement." In *Cognitive Disability and Its Challenge to Moral Philosophy*, edited by Eva Feder Kittay and Licia Carlson, 345–367. Malden, MA: Wiley-Blackwell.

Mietola, Reetta, Sonja Miettinen, and Simo Vehmas. 2017. "Voiceless Subjects? Research Ethics and Persons with Profound Intellectual Disabilities." *International Journal of Social Research Methodology*. http://dx.doi.org/10.1080/13645579.2017.1287872

Nussbaum, Martha. 2006. *Frontiers of Justice: Disability, Nationality, Species Membership*. Cambridge, MA: Harvard University Press.

Nussbaum, Martha. 2010. "The Capabilities of People with Cognitive Disabilities." In *Cognitive Disability and Its Challenge to Moral Philosophy*, edited by Eva Feder Kittay and Licia Carlson, 75–95. Malden, MA: Wiley-Blackwell.

O'Donnovan, Maeve. 2010. "Cognitive Diversity in the Global Academy: Why the Voices of Persons with Cognitive Disabilities are Vital to Intellectual Diversity." *Journal of Academic Ethics*, 8: 171–185.

Silvers, Anita. 2012. "Moral Status: What a Bad Idea!" *Journal of Intellectual Disability Research*, 56(2): 1014–1025. doi: 10.1111/j.1365-2788.2012.01616.x

Simplican, Stacy Clifford. 2015. *The Capacity Contract: Intellectual Disability and the Question of Citizenship*. Minneapolis: University of Minnesota Press.

Singer, Pete. 2010. "Speciesism and Moral Status." In *Cognitive Disability and Its Challenge to Moral Philosophy*, edited by Eva Feder Kittay and Licia Carlson, 331–344. Malden, MA: Wiley-Blackwell.

Smith, David Livingstone. 2016. "The Paradoxes of Dehumanization." *Social Theory and Practice*, 42(2): 416–443.

Taylor, Sunaura. 2017. *Beasts of Burden: Animal and Disability Liberation*. New York: The New Press.

Trent, James W. Jr. 1994. *Inventing the Feeble Mind: A History of Mental Retardation in the United States*. Berkeley: University of California Press.

Vorhaus, John. 2016. *Giving Voice to Profound Disability*. London: Routledge.

Vorhaus, John. 2017. "Sharing a Common Life: People with Profound and Multiple Learning Difficulties." *Res Publica*, 23: 61–79. doi:10.1007/s11158-015-9306-x

Wasserman, David, and Jeff McMahan. 2012. Cognitive Surrogacy, Assisted Participation, and Moral Status.

Wong, Sophia. 2010. "Duties of Justice to Citizens with Cognitive Disabilities." In *Cognitive Disability and Its Challenge to Moral Philosophy*, edited by Eva Feder Kittay and Licia Carlson, 127–146. Malden, MA: Wiley-Blackwell.

PART SEVEN

INTELLECTUAL AND PSYCHIATRIC DISABILITY

CHAPTER 29

NEURODIVERSITY, AUTISM, AND PSYCHIATRIC DISABILITY

The Harmful Dysfunction Perspective

JEROME C. WAKEFIELD, DAVID WASSERMAN,
AND JORDAN A. CONRAD

INTRODUCTION: NEURODIVERSITY AND ITS ROOTS

"Neurodiversity" refers to a cluster of claims and an associated movement contending that a variety of conditions currently classified as psychiatric disorders are in fact normal-range differences in mental functioning caused by normal variations in brain wiring. Because the idea of neurodiversity was introduced by autistic people (Blume 1998; Meyerding 1998; Sinclair 1993; Singer 1999) and has been defended by autism scholars (e.g., Armstrong 2015; Chapman 2019; Jaarsma and Welin 2012; Ortega 2009), we will focus our discussion on autism, "on which the neurodiversity movement continues to be centrally focused" (Graby 2015, 233). However, the arguments we consider potentially have more general implications, and similar neurodiversity arguments have been applied to other psychiatric conditions, ranging from attention-deficit/hyperactivity disorder (ADHD) and dyslexia (Jaarsma and Welin 2012) to sociopathy (Anton 2013), bipolar disorder (Antonetta 2007), and schizophrenia (Chapman 2019).

The history of disability theory provides an illuminating guide here. Disability scholars have long distinguished "impairment"—a physical or mental deficit or dysfunction—from "disability," the personal and social limitations associated with that condition. According to the prevailing "social model," the primary sources of disabilities are not the impairments themselves but the exclusionary attitudes, practices, and structures favoring the unimpaired. Some disability scholars, though, have gone beyond the social model of disability to question the objectivity of the impairment classification itself. This more radical critique transforms what was essentially an argument about justice for the impaired into an argument about whether those individuals are in fact impaired in the usual medical sense. This critique, initially applied to physical impairments, has been extended to psychiatric impairments, overlapping with the critiques of psychiatric classification made by the neurodiversity movement. Thus, neurodiversity advocates claim that autism is a distinctive cognitive and perceptual style (or a range of such styles), not a mental impairment. They reject its classification as a psychiatric disorder, and they attribute the harms suffered by those so labeled to unjust social structures and practices rather than to internal dysfunction.

The neurodiversity movement has multiple roots and affinities beyond the social model. It also draws from, and frequently models itself after, the civil rights movement, demanding justice for what is claimed to be an oppressed minority. Moreover, the logic of its supporting arguments regarding disorder and normality appear directly modeled on the gay liberation movement that led to the depathologization of homosexuality in psychiatry.

In addition, neurodiversity has some obvious affinities to the antipsychiatry movement of the 1960s and 1970s, to the extent that it claims that psychiatry is being used to control socially undesirable but medically normal behaviors. (For a nuanced discussion of the relationship of neurodiversity to other movements challenging psychiatric orthodoxy, see Graby [2015].) However, unlike anti-psychiatrists, neurodiversity advocates typically do not challenge the entire psychiatric enterprise of diagnosis and treatment. Their critique is more differentiated and targeted, allowing that some of the traits and behaviors commonly associated with severe forms of autism are genuine disorders appropriately subject to medical or psychiatric intervention. Neurodiversity thus makes an understanding of the concept of disorder crucial to evaluating its claims.

However, it is important to acknowledge at the outset that neurodiversity is a social movement more than a theoretical position on psychiatric diagnosis. Its advocates have generally sought to shape public policy and public perceptions rather than enter into philosophical debates about the concepts of disorder and disability—even if the truth of their claims ultimately depends on the outcome of such debates. For purposes of philosophical analysis, neurodiversity's claims are thus undertheorized and often must be elaborated and disambiguated in order to evaluate them properly.

In this chapter, we reconstruct neurodiversity claims from the perspective of a prominent philosophical account of the concept of medical and psychiatric disorder, the harmful dysfunction analysis (HDA). We first sketch the HDA and use it to make a prima facie case that the conditions originally designated as "autism" are rightly classified as disorders. We then evaluate several of the most prominent neurodiversity objections to classifying those conditions, and other autistic conditions, as HDA disorders, finding some more persuasive than others. We conclude by considering the extent to which a social model of disability, attributing disadvantage to an unaccommodating environment, can be plausibly applied to autism.

THE CHALLENGE OF AUTISM'S
HETEROGENEITY

The neurodiversity movement's opposition to labeling autism as a disorder arose in parallel to—and, one might presume, in reaction to—a dramatic expansion of the number of individuals, as well as the types of conditions, labeled as autistic. The expansion occurred for numerous reasons ranging from theoretical developments in psychiatry to changes in special education laws, as well as the usual pathology "category creep" (Haslam 2016). The resulting heterogeneity of what is now in the broadest sense termed "autism" poses a challenge to interpreting and evaluating neurodiversity's claims.

The diagnosis of autism originally emerged from observations of children manifesting a now well-known triad of syndromally associated severe symptoms: impairment of social development, impairment of communication, and display of rigid and repetitive behavior (Kanner 1943). Kanner's original diagnosis of this severe condition, which we will refer to as "severe classic autism," covered a relatively narrow category of individuals and was immediately regarded as a disorder (*why* it was regarded as a disorder is considered later). Soon, a milder condition with similar social limitations was classified as "Asperger's disorder" (Asperger 1944).

The diagnostic criteria for autism and related conditions have varied over time and changed substantially from one DSM edition to another (Cushing 2018). In DSM-IV (1994), in addition to autistic disorder defined by the aforementioned triad of symptoms, milder conditions were added, including Asperger's disorder and "pervasive developmental disorder not otherwise specified." However, in 2013, in accordance with long-standing proposals (e.g., Narzisi et al. 2013; Ozonoff et al. 1991; Wing 1997), DSM-5 officially expanded severe classic "autistic disorder" into an "autism spectrum disorder" (ASD) of conditions varying along a dimension of severity, with the high-functioning domain engulfing most of the milder diagnosis of Asperger's disorder, which was eliminated as a stand-alone category (Barahona-Corrêa and Filipe 2016). Folding Asperger's disorder into ASD was controversial (Baron-Cohen 2018; Perry 2014) because some former Asperger's cases were excluded, diagnosable only as subthreshold cases (see p. 517). DSM-5 also reduced the classic triad of symptoms to a dyad of dimensions by combining impairment of social communication and impairment of social development into one overarching dimension of deficits in social communication and social interaction. But most important, the reconceptualization of autism as ASD officially extended the autism category to what has come to be called "high-functioning autism," in which, similar to Asperger's, certain basic functions such as intelligence, ability to communicate, and ability to live independently are not substantially impaired despite moderate to mild versions of other autistic cognitive and relational features.

Epidemiological studies indicate that increasing numbers of individuals are falling under ASD over time, with each new prevalence estimate yielding a seemingly relentless expansion of the category (Baio et al. 2018; Dave and Fernandez 2015). It appears that it is within the high-functioning subcategory that these increases are mostly occurring. The majority of the rise in prevalence has been among children with average or above-average intelligence (Baio et al. 2018; Lord and Bishop 2015), roughly half of all those now classified as autistic (Baio et al. 2018).

Beyond the DSM's low- to high-functioning ASD, the "autism" label now encompasses subthreshold cases, which do not satisfy ASD criteria but are still diagnosable under DSM-5's category of "other specified neurodevelopmental disorder" if they satisfy one of the ASD criteria or satisfy the criteria at a level of severity below the lower end of ASD (e.g., Christ et al. 2010; Dell'Osso et al. 2016, 2017; Kanne et al. 2012). Even more radically expansive, researchers have applied measures of the "broader autism phenotype" (BAP) and other autism-related personality trait measures to the general population. This approach uses various scales to identify individuals who possess one or more personality traits that are claimed to be milder, seemingly nonclinical versions of autistic-like symptoms. Yet such measures are widely used in research to identify those with presumed autistic conditions (e.g., Fitzgerald 2018; Hurley et al. 2007; Landry and Chouinard 2016; Nishiyama and Kanne 2014; Nishiyama et al. 2014; Ruzich et al. 2015; Skylark and Baron-Cohen 2017).

Autism's dramatic heterogeneity, combined with a problematic casualness about terminology and definitions, makes it difficult to keep track of precisely what is being claimed in various discussions in the autism and neurodiversity literature. Very often, in both scholarly articles and blog discussions, statements that appear to be about "autism" in general are in fact about high-functioning autism (e.g., Schriber et al. 2014). Many philosophers writing on autism have come to see that the same arguments do not always apply to different types of autism (e.g., Glover 2014; Robeyns 2016).

Much as autism forms a spectrum, neurodiversity itself can be understood as a spectrum of positions depending on where the line is drawn between disorder and normal variation. If one starts with the extended autism spectrum that includes all the various conditions mentioned earlier labeled "autism," one might arrive at three possible neurodiversity-inspired positions about the disorder status of autism. This "taxonomy" of neurodiversity claims is our own; neurodiversity advocates and their academic defenders fall into one group or another by virtue of the range of autistic conditions for which they reject the DSM-5 disorder classification.

What might be called *strong neurodiversity* is the claim that the entire autism category, including severe classic autism, consists of normal variations. At the opposite extreme, taking DSM's demarcation of the autistic spectrum as the standard view, one might define *weak neurodiversity* as a defense of the status quo, rejecting expansion of the spectrum to classify milder conditions as disorders.

Finally, between strong and weak neurodiversity there is what one might call *moderate neurodiversity*, which is implicit in a substantial number of neurodiversity discussions that omit severe classic autism in making the case for normal variation. Moderate neurodiversity accepts that severe classic autism is best understood as impairing and so as a legitimate disorder. However, rather than accepting the diagnostic status quo, it argues that DSM-5 has expanded the autism category beyond its valid pathological domain to encompass nondisordered normal variation, such as "high-functioning autism" and much of what was previously called Asperger's disorder.

We will argue that it is moderate neurodiversity—critical of psychiatric overreach but not anti-psychiatric in exiling the concept of disorder—that is the most plausible of the three forms based on what we know at present. We are well aware that a wide variety of syndromes fall between severe classic autism and Asperger's, in terms of symptom severity and functionality. We will make no attempt to adjudicate the disorder status of these conditions; our point is precisely that, given the heterogeneity within the autism category, we should expect disagreement and uncertainty in many cases.

THE HARMFUL DYSFUNCTION
ANALYSIS OF MENTAL DISORDER

Neurodiversity implicitly makes a theoretical claim that the kinds of neurological differences found in autistic individuals (or some subset thereof) are merely normal-range variations and not disorders. To evaluate this claim, we need some guidance in understanding what we mean beyond mere difference when we make disorder attributions. For such guidance, we rely on Jerome Wakefield's influential definition of "medical disorder," which he calls the "harmful dysfunction analysis" (HDA; Wakefield 1992a, 1992b 1993, 1999a, 1999b, 2000a, 2000b, 2001, 2007a, 2007b; Wakefield and First 2003). The HDA is a "hybrid" analysis that combines elements of the two traditional approaches, the normativist approach that sees disorder as simply a value concept and the biological approach that sees disorder as definable simply in scientific factual terms concerning the failure of biological functions. The HDA posits that "disorder" has two conceptual components that must both be present to justify attribution of a disorder. First, the condition must be caused by a "dysfunction," a factual concept that refers to a failure of some biological feature to perform a function for which it was biologically designed, where "biological design" can be cashed out in terms of evolution and natural selection. Second, the dysfunction must be harmful, as judged by social values.

Although Wakefield's analyses of disorder, dysfunction, and harm all remain disputed (Faucher and Forest in press), the HDA is the most widely cited account of disorder in the psychological and psychiatric literature and has been endorsed by several leading psychiatrists involved in shaping the DSM. It has proven to have considerable explanatory power when applied to the nuanced distinctions we make between problematic conditions that are disorders and those that are not (e.g., illiteracy versus dyslexia, grief versus major depression, delinquency versus conduct disorder). Most important, Wakefield's two-part definition is very helpful in clarifying issues concerning disorder categories, such as depression and personality disorders.

THE HARMFUL DYSFUNCTION ANALYSIS AND THE PRIMA FACIE CASE FOR SEVERE CLASSIC AUTISM BEING A DISORDER

It is not difficult to understand why clinicians and others assume that severe classic autism is a disorder, given its defining symptoms of impaired social development, impaired communication, and rigid, repetitive behavior. The HDA explains this common intuitive judgment. First, on the best available evidence, the condition is judged as likely to be caused by a dysfunction—a defect in biologically designed internal mechanisms, and second, the dysfunction's effects are harmful.

The harm is manifest in the reduced ability to communicate with others and to "read" social situations. The absence of these abilities often has powerfully negative effects, ranging from a solitary life and the inability to find work to dangerous interactions with the police and emergency responders and misjudgments that can lead to harm or even death. Even in specialized settings, such as schools that focus on the treatment of ASD, students with severe classic autism can have difficulty communicating the need for a bathroom break or that they are hungry.

The perplexing question raised by neurodiversity is not only whether the intuitive perception of severe classic autism as a disorder is justified, but whether that intuition has been legitimately extended to other domains in which the purported autistic symptoms are not as severe and impairing as in the severe classic case.

IS AUTISM A HARMFUL DYSFUNCTION?

In considering how neurodiversity advocates might challenge the application of the prima facie case for disorder to various parts of the autism spectrum, it is important to bear in mind that while dysfunction and harm are distinct components of HDA, the same evidence may be relevant to both. Evidence that a condition is harmful in current environments may suggest a defect in biological design; evidence that a condition represents a defect in biological design may suggest that it is harmful in current environments.

We will consider a variety of arguments presented by neurodiversity advocates against the disorder classification. While advocates rarely distinguish challenges to dysfunction and to harm, we will. Despite the evidentiary overlap, the claim that autism, or some kinds of autism, are "normal variations" is a denial of dysfunction, a denial that the condition in question displays the failure of an adaptive psychological process or mechanism rather than an adaptive variation. Normal variations can, as one of us has recognized (Wakefield and First 2003), become harmful in changed environments; such "mismatches" do not make them disorders. Conversely, many normal variations, like vicious personalities, can cause harm.

We begin by examining a strategy adopted by some of the most thoughtful neurodiversity advocates. This strategy deflects rather than denies that many features associated with severe classic and even milder forms of autism are dysfunctional and harmful. They argue that there is a core or essence of autism found across the functional spectrum—a distinctive but not disordered way of experiencing and interacting with the world.

Contingent Harms, Essential Benefits

The Essence of Autism—Autism Itself—Is a Normal Variation, Not a Dysfunction

Although autism is associated with a diverse symptomology and likely reflects a heterogenous etiology, some neurodiversity advocates suggest that there is one autistic essence, a normal variation found in all forms of autism and only contingently associated with harmful dysfunctions. These advocates identify the essence of autism in a way that excludes many disadvantageous features from autism "itself," while including, as integral to that condition, several advantageous features.

A striking illustration of the "autistic essence" approach is provided by Simon Baron-Cohen (2017), writing in defense of neurodiversity:

> Some will object that a child with autism who has epilepsy is not an example of neurodiversity but rather he or she has a disorder. And they are right. Epilepsy is a sign of brain dysfunction and causes disorder (fits) and should be medically treated. But epilepsy, while commonly co-occurring with autism, is not autism itself. Others may say that a child who has language delay or severe learning difficulties is not an example of neurodiversity but has a disorder, and I would support their demand for treatments to maximise the child's potential in both language and learning. But again, although commonly co-occurring these are not autism itself.   (744)

Advocates of an autistic essence resist the claims of irreducible heterogeneity made by some researchers. But to establish an underlying unity, more is required than a loose family resemblance uniting heterogeneous groups or individuals. For example, no support for an autistic essence is offered by Daniel Weiskopf's (2017) proposal to preserve autism as a scientific category in the face of its considerable heterogeneity as "a network category defined by a set of idealized exemplars linked by multiple levels of theoretically significant properties" (2017, 175). Such a loose unity lacks the cohesion necessary for an adaptive trait or a distinct perceptual and cognitive style.

The claim of a more cohesive core raises difficult empirical and conceptual issues. Without a clear basis for excluding undesirable features like seizures while including desirable ones like pattern recognition, this approach engages in nosological gerrymandering. The problem is that there is no systematic account of how one decides which of the many features that appear in various subgroups of autists are, or are part of, "the" core.

Our own view is that "autism" refers to whatever essential etiological feature explains the manifest (seemingly) pathological symptoms designated by the researchers like Kanner (1943) who "baptized" the severe classic condition. If one accepts that severe classic autism is a disorder, then according to the HDA, that essential feature must be whatever dysfunction (or dysfunctions) explains the observed pathological symptoms. According to this approach, the label "autism" may have been extended for research purposes to larger sets of individuals, such as those with Asperger's or on the BAP, who lack any such dysfunction. But then in one important sense—the original pathological sense—they are not "autistic." Even if one holds that a perceptual/cognitive style lies at the heart of autism, there can be pathological as well as normal variants of that cognitive style. "Autism" may have become ambiguous between the style and the pathology, much the way that other terms such as "depression" and "obsessive" have become ambiguous.

This approach reflects an understanding of mental disorder as what Wakefield (1999b) calls a "black-box essentialist concept." It is *essentialist* "because category membership is determined not by the observable properties that may have inspired us to define the concept in the first place, . . . but by an essential property that explains the observed features" (471). It is *black-box* essentialist because "it postulates a hidden essential nature and remains agnostic on its identity" (471). Of course, no such explanatory nature may be found; it may turn out that there is in fact no "thing called autism," as Verhoeff (2012) and others argue. The science is still young, but thus far, as Simon Cushing (2013) concludes, "[A]ttempts to locate the essence of autism at a deeper level than observable behavior have varied but unsatisfactory" (38). But if there is some perceptual/cognitive essence of the entire extended autism spectrum—from severe classic autism to BAP—it would have to be a different essence, and a different category, from the originally baptized pathology called "autism."

In the next two subsections, we turn to examine claims about the beneficial features of autism claimed to support its status as a normal variation that do not represent a failure of biological design nor cause significant harm in current environments. In each case, we argue that these claims are untenable as applied to the entire autism spectrum. They exaggerate the benefits of some autistic conditions and founder on the heterogeneity of the autism category.

Focus on Detail, Decontextualization, and "Weak Coherence" as an Evolutionary Trade-off

Is the decontextualized, detail-oriented cognition characteristic of many autistic individuals, sometimes called "weak coherence" (Frith 1989; Frith and Happé 1994), a benefit great enough for autism to be a biologically designed variation or a biologically normal-range trade-off for associated harms? In support of such a theory, it is often observed that under some circumstances this decontextualized focus on detail can yield interestingly divergent and creative insights that would not occur to someone subject to the usual contextual influences on judgment. In fact, it has been found that lack of sensitivity to context can yield more accurate judgments under some special circumstances, for example, the discovery that autistic individuals are not as subject to certain optical illusions (Happé 1999).

However, sensitivity to context is a sophisticated normal-range developmental achievement. Children, with their immature perceptual systems, are also more resistant to optical illusions than neurotypical adults (Doherty, Campbell, Tsuji, and Phillips 2010). Optical illusions seem to be a side effect of the way the normal-range biologically designed perceptual system develops.

It is not at all arbitrary that contextual understanding occurs as part of psychological development because, sadly, lack of contextual understanding in real life can be deadly, a far more relevant evolutionary influence than whether one is fooled by the Ebbinghouse or Müller-Lyer illusions. For example, a recent news article (McLaughlin and Sutton 2018) reports that an autistic young adult on a cruise with an autism organization jumped over the ship's railing into the water and drowned. It appears that this was neither a suicidal act nor accidental but that he purposefully jumped over the railing to go for a swim. Tragedies of this sort appear to result from an insensitivity to the contextual features that would override similar impulses in neurotypical individuals.

However, as one increases the level of autistic functioning, one can imagine a more modest lack of context sensitivity with perhaps a degree of flexibility in moving back and forth between contextually grounded and decontextualized understanding. Such decontextualization in conjunction with the normal functioning of other skills and abilities could conceivably confer, or have conferred, an overall advantage, and thus constitute a normal variation. There would then be empirical questions as to whether other skills and abilities needed to make mild context insensitivity advantageous (e.g., intellectual ability, gross and fine motor skills, impulse control) are present or absent; whether mild context insensitivity is sufficiently beneficial to have been biologically designed; and whether such selective context insensitivity occurs primarily among autistic individuals or is in fact a normal variant of most mature human cognition.

Savant Skills as an Evolutionary Trade-off

Another common argument in favor of strong neurodiversity is based on the fact that autism, unlike most other disorders, appears sometimes to carry with it a range of surprising and quite specific skills and talents known as "savant abilities." Whereas, for example, any additional atypical skills blind people acquire as a result of lacking vision (e.g., echolocation) are plausibly seen as compensating for their deficits, many autistic people not only lack skills that neurotypical people have but appear to come wired with skills that neurotypical people lack. These skills, like precise visualization, unusual calculating ability, or extraordinary memory for certain kinds of events, appear to develop not as compensation, but as part and parcel of the autistic condition. Neurodiversity advocates argue that given this complex mix of skills and deficiencies, autism should be seen as a different *manner* of thinking and perceiving that is a normal-range variant rather than a dysfunction.

In terms of the HDA, it is difficult to mount an argument that savant skills make autism harmless. For most autistic individuals, the benefits of any savant skills they possess do not nullify or even outweigh the negative effects of the condition. Even if they did in particular cases, that would not make the condition harmless for most autists. Many disorders provide *some* indirect benefit: cowpox prevents smallpox and Crohn's disease can reduce one's weight, and in some cases, those benefits may outweigh any harms. But those conditions still cause significant direct harm and are still disorders.

Neurodiversity advocates might instead direct their argument at the "dysfunction" component of the HDA, claiming that savant skills may have once conferred sufficiently great advantages to make the conditions of which they were part good candidates for selection despite their disadvantages. Their harms would then be seen as an evolutionary trade-off for their savant benefits, in the way that, say, morning sickness is a trade-off for the naturally selected process of pregnancy. This admittedly vague notion has been a feature of nosological thinking since the early work on the concept of medical disorder by Spitzer and Endicott (1978), who stated: "Conditions are not included [as disorders] if the associated distress, disability, or other disadvantage is apparently the necessary price associated with attaining some positive goal" (28).

For autism to qualify as such a trade-off, there would have to have been a close connection, as well as a favorable balance, between its advantageous and disadvantageous features. This connection could be present if some positive feature had a virtually inevitable negative effect, or if the development of some selected feature turned out to interfere with the development of other selected features.

We doubt that the social and behavioral limitations associated with autism can be seen as virtually inevitable negative side-effects of savant abilities that are highly beneficial on balance, analogous to morning sickness in pregnancy or grief at losing a loved one. Beyond the obvious point that the negative effects of severe classic autism appear far more substantial than the positive effects of savant skills, the case for an evolutionary trade-off is cast into doubt by three points. First, only a minority of autistic individuals have such savant talents, with the major studies placing the percentage between about 10% and 25% (Happé 2018, but see Meilleur, Jelenic, and Mottron 2014). Second, while savant talents might be productively exploited by the individual and society, such productive use would usually require a level of cooperation and communication precluded by severe autism. Third, such a trade-off is not necessary to explain this kind of advantageous talent. It is known that clear brain disorders, including frontotemporal dementia and traumatic brain injury, occasionally yield the same sorts of special talents as autism (Miller et al. 1998; Treffert 2009). This suggests, speculatively, that brain pathology can bring about disinhibition of certain other brain centers, yielding isolated skills. In such cases, no explanation in terms of a biologically designed trade-off is plausible. Even in cases of less severe autism, it seems more plausible that these talents emerge for reasons incidental to the occurrence of other autistic traits, no matter how integral they may become to the autist's experience of life.

We also doubt that the development of savant skills can be seen as interfering with the development of other positive traits. That process is exemplified by what has come to be called "Einstein syndrome" (Sowell 2001). It is sometimes claimed that Einstein's brain centers for spatial orientation were so enlarged that their growth may have impinged on the growth of language-learning centers, causing him to have delayed linguistic development. This conjecture, however, hardly provides a persuasive basis for understanding most varieties of autism as normal variations. Einstein's temporary speech delay was a minor setback compared to the enduring communication impairments found in autism. Moreover, so far as we know, Einstein manifested neither clear symptoms of ASD (e.g., stimming) nor serious inability to relate socially; even if he had some mild autistic traits, it is difficult to see what about his condition would suggest dysfunction or serious harm.

Our assessment of the so-called Einstein syndrome does yield an important positive conclusion. Tremendous normal-range neurodiversity exists, and there may be many types of trade-offs among strengths and weaknesses that do not imply dysfunction. Consequently, the higher reaches of the extended autistic spectrum may represent normal personality variants even if they show weakness in certain areas. But these cases would be "exceptions" fully consistent with the "rule" that severe classic autism, and other lower-functioning types of autism, are harmful dysfunctions.

Autism Is a Psychological and Social Identity, Not a Disorder

The preceding sections cast doubt on claims that there is an autistic core or essence with a sufficiently favorable balance of advantages to disadvantages to have been selected in the human environment of evolutionary adaptation (EEA) and to be beneficial or neutral overall in contemporary environments. Even if the skills found in many autists were as integral to the condition as some neurodiversity advocates maintain, they do not sufficiently outweigh deficits closely associated with them in severe classic autism to make a plausible case, on present evidence, that autism is, across the spectrum, a normal variation. We now turn to a different sort of essentialist claim: that even if the conditions labeled as autistic are too diverse to have a common core, they are a central part of the psychological or social identity of those living with them or of a nascent culture than imposes social unity on psychiatric heterogeneity.

Autism as Central to Personal Identity

Perhaps owing to the global effect autistic conditions have on mental functioning, they are generally experienced as being more integral to personal identity than most physical, and some mental, disabilities. For example, well-known autist and neurodiversity advocate Temple Grandin famously said: "If I could snap my fingers and be nonautistic, I would not—because then I wouldn't be me. Autism is part of what I am" (Grandin 2006, 180).

Similarly, Ari Ne'eman dismisses "the strange idea that there was or is a normal person somewhere inside me, hidden by autism and struggling to get out" (cited in Silberman 2010). But for other autists, such as poet Donna Williams (2002), autism is a contingent and unwelcome feature of the self.

A sense of identity as an autist does not imply the nondisorder status of autism, any more than the ego-syntonicity of a personality disorder implies no disorder. In fact, it is common in psychotherapy for treatment of recognized disorders to face resistance based on the individual's sense that if therapy succeeds and the condition is altered, the individual will no longer be the same person. Yet the reality is that change can occur and the pathology can be ameliorated, while the individual's overall sense of identity remains intact and proves quite robust in the face of significant change. But even if the individual's condition was integral to his or her identity, that would not make it less of a disorder, only a more challenging one to address if the individual so chooses.

Social Construction of the "Autism" Category and the Formation of an Autistic Community

An essentialist account of today's sprawling autism category is hard to reconcile with the category's evident heterogeneity, as well as the politics of DSM classification and the vagaries of legal definitions. This difficulty suggests that "autism," having started with severe classic autism, has been gradually enlarged into a socially constructed category encompassing a variety of types of individuals united through diverse social processes, rather than a natural kind with an autistic essence (Chapman 2016; Cushing 2018). What might be shared among them is an emerging community and culture, as well as some traits that result from the shared experience of and response to being labeled "autistic"— perhaps feeding back into the evolving definition of autism (Sarrett 2016; Verhoeff 2012). It might even be argued that the resultant community and culture provides a reason for respecting and preserving autism (Straus 2013).

However, neither the fact that social factors shaped the construction of autism nor the resulting emergence of an autism community has much relevance for the question of whether any type of autism is a disorder. The fact that the category was formed by social processes does not tell us whether some, all, or none of the heterogeneous subgroups it encompasses actually suffer from relevant dysfunctions; it says nothing about whether the traits of those placed in the category were adaptive or are now harmful.

Nor does community formation have any implications for disorder judgments. We are living in an era of social media in which virtually every disorder—let alone every political persuasion and lifestyle preference—has its own online community; people with disorders, even deadly ones, are perfectly capable of forming communities. Respecting such a community is not inconsistent with judging that the category uniting its members consists of or includes disorders.

Further, respect for a community or culture does not preclude offering its members treatment for the conditions on which their membership rests, even if such treatment might weaken the participation base. This is obvious in the case of disorder-based communities of individuals with serious illnesses, but not unique to them. Much valuable normal-range diversity, like monastic culture in Western Europe and Yiddish culture in the United States, has been lost as these groups assimilated to the larger culture. We may regret the loss of such cultures while respecting their members' decisions to embrace more mainstream options. A similar fate may await the vibrant Deaf culture and community, if measures to prevent deafness or confer hearing become more effective and less intrusive and are embraced by deaf individuals. Such a development would involve a significant social and cultural loss, but would not necessarily be an injustice.

Viewing autism as a community or culture has somewhat more relevance for judging whether an autistic trait is harmful in the present environment, as opposed to whether it is caused by a dysfunction. It does seem advantageous that a trait facilitates participation in a vibrant culture, and conceivably such participation can ameliorate much of the harm associated with the condition. However, avoiding harm from the larger culture by participating in a subculture is not the same as not being harmed. It does not undo the significant harm of lacking access to broader opportunity within that larger culture. To this extent, the formation of a protective subculture is in one respect analogous to a medical treatment continuously required to prevent symptoms; in both cases, the lack of apparent harm does not challenge the judgment of disorder because the potential for harm remains and is only mitigated by continuous intervention.

Even If Autism, or Some Autistic Conditions, Are Dysfunctional, They Are Not Harmful

None of the arguments considered thus far deny that there is harm in the impaired capacities associated with autism. A more radical approach, suggested by some neurodiversity advocates, does deny harm. It adopts an expansive conception of well-being under which most individuals with autism can be seen as living well, unharmed by their incapacities.

For example, one might argue that intense concentration on mundane details and patterns can be rewarding (Chapman 2016), and that an orientation to things can be as good as, or incommensurable with, an orientation to people. This approach might be taken so far as to insist that one could lead a good life even if, to take John Rawls's (1971) famous example, one's only desire was "to count blades of grass in various geometrically shaped areas such as park squares and well-trimmed lawns" (432). Such an approach is perhaps implicit in the suggestion that the measure of autists' well-being ought to start from the baseline of autistic capabilities (Robeyns 2016). If applied without qualification, this approach would, absurdly, relieve many afflicted groups of harm by recalibrating the baseline for harm to that group's nature and capabilities.

There is a clear commonsense limit to this approach, at least for severe classic autism. On any plausible understanding of human flourishing, a child would be doing badly if he or she could not speak or communicate in other ways, lacked the capacity to establish close relationships, and experienced sensory overload in most public spaces.

The Social Model of Autism: Attributing Harm to an Adverse Social Environment

Neurodiversity advocates argue that many of the most serious harms experienced by autists arise from hostile or exclusionary social attitudes and practices, not directly from the autistic condition. This approach applies the social model of disability to psychiatric conditions: autists are disadvantaged by the construction of the social environment by and for "neurotypicals," much as physically impaired people are disadvantaged by the construction of the social environment by and for people with typical physical functioning. In the case of autism and other psychiatric conditions, exclusion is at least as likely to result from prejudice as mere oversight; there is abundant evidence that mental disabilities are even more stigmatized than physical ones.

The claim that the social environment is the primary source of the harm suffered by autists finds precedent in the debate that led to the depathologization of homosexuality. It was argued that homosexuality is not intrinsically harmful but burdened by hostile social attitudes and practices (Jaarsma and Welin 2012).

The distinction between harms arising directly from a dysfunction and those resulting from society's reaction to a dysfunction tracks long-standing nosological criteria for drawing the disorder/nondisorder distinction. Robert Spitzer, the psychiatrist most responsible for eliminating homosexuality as a DSM disorder, made this distinction himself, writing with Paul Wilson in 1975 that to qualify as a "disorder" a condition must be "regularly and *intrinsically* associated with subjective distress" or "impairment," explaining that "the phrase 'intrinsically associated with' indicates that the source of the distress or impairment in functioning must be the condition itself and not with the manner in which society reacts to the condition" (Spitzer and Wilson 1975, 829, emphasis added; see also Spitzer and Endicott, 1978, 18).

The harms of autism are less clearly attributable to social environments than those of homosexuality. The latter are almost entirely due to prejudicial attitudes and practices; the individual's sexual orientation plays no role except in evoking that prejudice. Neurodiversity advocates emphasize that, similarly, *some* of the harm from autism results from such prejudice and a lack of accommodation (Dominus 2019). However, this use of the social model against the disorder attribution faces two problems. First, it appears to draw support from a misapplication of the direct/indirect and intrinsic/extrinsic distinctions. Harms from many disorders can be socially mediated but still fulfill the HDA's harm criterion. Humans are social animals, and many disorders are disorders of social interaction, so the social necessarily enters into the harm. For example, brain trauma-induced aphasia has as its only harm the inability to communicate with others, a social harm. But this harm suffices to justify labeling aphasia a disorder, because linguistic ability is a biologically designed capacity that is fundamental to social relationships, which, in turn, are central to human well-being. And because no changes in social attitudes or practices could significantly mitigate this harm, it cannot be attributed to a neglect or prejudice, however much they exacerbate it.

So the question becomes how to interpret the social mediation of harm from autism; is it more like the indirect social harm from homosexuality or the direct social harm from aphasia? On its face, it appears that the deficiencies claimed to be characteristic of autism—including the inability to understand what others may be thinking or feeling without explicit instruction ("mindblindness"; Baron-Cohen 1995), failure to appreciate the effects of one's behavior on others (Attwood 1998; Mercier et al. 2000), and limitations on empathic and emotional understanding (Burgoine and Wing 1983, cited in Attwood 1998)—are all presumptively biological dysfunctions with directly harmful effects on social interactions. Although these harms are properly regarded as social, they do not appear to be caused in a way that disqualifies the disorder attribution.

Yet the magnitude of these social harms depends on social attitudes and practices to a greater extent than in such disorders as aphasia. To the extent that accommodation at a relatively low social cost can substantially reduce these harms, we may attribute them to an unreasonable failure to accommodate. There are several dimensions on which the reasonableness of accommodations can be assessed in evaluating such an attribution (see Lim 2017): how costly they are in strictly financial terms; the extent to which they require other members of society to suppress or alter responses as hard-wired as the behaviors that elicit them; and the extent to which they would threaten core values or cherished practices. These dimensions of reasonableness have rarely been distinguished in applying the social model, perhaps because they rarely diverge in accommodating physical differences. In contrast, mental differences may compel their separate consideration.

In evaluating the attribution of harm, we must recognize that it would hardly be reasonable to modify our social practices to the extent that autism had a negligible impact on social interaction, for example, by relying as little as possible on context, spontaneity, emotional cues, and conversational implicature. Nor is it plausible to attribute the tragedy cited earlier in this chapter primarily to oppressive social arrangements; indeed, the restrictive measures in public spaces necessary to prevent such actions might themselves be oppressive—although on this sort of question there is always ample room for disagreement. Certainly, no neurodiversity advocate, to our knowledge, has proposed any such radical measures.

A second challenge for applying the social model to autism is its extreme heterogeneity with respect to the nature, severity, and malleability of its harms. As suggested earlier, it is often *high-functioning* autism and the higher reaches of the extended autism spectrum that are cited as falling under the social model. This reflects the reality, not always accepted by neurodiversity advocates who wish to keep a unified categorical approach, that the less severe types of autism are more likely to have their harms cost-efficiently remedied than the more severe forms.

In sum, many harms suffered by autists are no doubt socially caused. However, the argument that autism is not truly a disorder because its associated harms are not caused in a sufficiently direct way may work for only milder types of autism. Attributing all of the severe hardships experienced by autists across social contexts to unjust social attitudes and biased social practices is implausible on its face.

Concluding Comments

The category of autism has expanded dramatically in recent years to encompass many times the number of individuals classifiable as autistic just a few decades ago. This resulted from both the expansion of the psychiatrically diagnosable category of severe classic autism into ASD, and the further expansion of the entire extended autistic spectrum to include subthreshold cases, Asperger's cases excluded from the ASD, and the BAP, covering individuals with autistic-related personality traits. It was inevitable and appropriate that such rapid expansion of a diagnostic category, not based on any scientific breakthrough concerning etiology, would be viewed with skepticism about validity and suspicion about motivation. This resistance was especially predictable in the wake of the depathologization of homosexuality, in an era wary of "medicalization," when diagnostic labeling is taken quite seriously.

The neurodiversity movement arose as a response from within the autism community and has posed difficult questions for psychiatry about the diagnostic status of autism. These questions bring to the fore the most challenging issue for psychiatric nosology: how to distinguish normal variation from disorder. In claiming that autism is a normal variation made harmful by an intolerant society and its diagnostic system, neurodiversity highlights the difficulty psychiatry continues to have in distinguishing true disorders from socially disapproved normal variations.

Yet psychiatry has largely ignored these profound challenges, and philosophers of psychiatry have provided little systematic or critical analysis of the issues neurodiversity raises. We have offered a first pass at such an analysis from the perspective of the harmful dysfunction analysis. In so doing, we have given a qualified endorsement of some of the critiques made by neurodiversity advocates, while questioning their breadth and some of their assumptions, especially concerning the underlying unity of autism.

We have argued that, although much more scientific knowledge is needed, the current evidence suggests that the sort of nuanced, moderate view that neurodiversity takes toward disorder in general is likely true when applied to the heterogeneous extended autism category itself. Some autistic conditions—especially severe classic autism but also perhaps some conditions higher in functioning—are likely disorders, and some, as neurodiversity advocates claim, are likely not. Central to our analysis is the observation that the extended autism spectrum and even DSM-5's ASD encompass diverse groups that may well differ in diagnostic status and must be evaluated separately in accordance with their distinctive properties. Although this has been an initial exploration and our conclusions are tentative, our examination tends to support a moderate neurodiversity position, selectively critical of psychiatric expansionism but rejecting the stronger claim that the entire autism category is normal variation.

Although we have focused on neurodiversity as a set of claims about the diagnostic status of autism, it must be kept in mind that it is also a movement arguing for justice and respect for those classified as autistic. The relationship of these two central issues is easily misunderstood. In the original statement justifying the removal of homosexuality per se as a mental disorder in the DSM, Spitzer (1975) noted that "homosexuals have been denied civil rights in many areas of life on the ground that…they suffer from a 'mental illness'" (1216), and asserted that the depathologization of homosexuality "will be removing one of the justifications for the denial of civil rights" (1216). At the same time, he sought to make clear that a disorder classification did not justify rights curtailment. So, he added parenthetically: "By linking the removal of homosexuality from the diagnostic nomenclature with an affirmation of the civil rights of homosexuals, no implication is intended justifying the irrational denial of civil rights to individuals who do suffer from true psychiatric disorders" (1216).

This is a crucial point. Disorder status is often used as an excuse to curtail the rights of stigmatized groups. It is, however, a poor excuse; issues of justice and of diagnostic status are largely separable. It is risky for the neurodiversity movement to link depathologization with justice and respect too closely. If emerging etiological evidence supports a disorder attribution for some subset of autists, the implication might then be that continued injustice and inadequate respect are acceptable. That would be a terrible, utterly mistaken conclusion to draw from neurodiversity arguments. A vigorous movement has long fought to defend and expand the rights of people with recognized psychiatric disorders. Among its achievements are strong presumptions against institutionalization and enforced treatment, and a strong presumption of decision-making capacity for people with psychiatric disorders. To protect and advance this progress, claims about disorder and justice should be kept distinct.

A final point with regard to justice is that in our society certain kinds of valuable support tend to go with disorder diagnosis but not with problematic normal variation. Consequently, there is now a divergence in interests between those needing such support and those who can fare well without it. This divergence emerged in the DSM-5 process, when an initial attempt to narrow the range of ASD met with protests from parents and organizations concerned that children would lose needed benefits. Future discussion of justice in relation to diagnosis must consider the trade-off between two potential forms of injustice: the injustice of invalidly labeling someone disordered, and the injustice of invalidly refusing a diagnosis to an individual with a genuine disorder.

ACKNOWLEDGMENTS

The authors thank Marie Niccolini and Adam Cureton for helpful suggestions.

REFERENCES

Anton, Audrey L. 2013. "The Virtue of Sociopaths: How to Appreciate the Neurodiversity of Sociopathy Without Becoming a Victim." In *Ethics and Neurodiversity*, edited by C. D. Herrera and Alexandra Perry, 111–130. Newcastle upon Tyne, UK: Cambridge Scholars Publishing.

Antonetta, Susanne. 2007. *A Mind Apart: Travels in a Neurodiverse World*. New York: Penguin.

Armstrong, Thomas. 2015. "The Myth of the Normal Brain: Embracing Neurodiversity." *AMA Journal of Ethics* 17: 348–352.

Asperger, Hans. 1944. "Die 'Autistischen Psychopathen' im Kindesalter." *Archiv für Psychiatrie and Nervenkrankheiten* 117: 76–136.

Attwood, Tony. 1998. *Asperger's Syndrome: A Guide for Parents and Professionals*. London: Jessica Kingsley.

Baio, Jon, Lisa Wiggins, Deborah L. Christensen, Matthew J. Maenner, Julie Daniels, Zachary Warren, Margaret Kurzius-Spencer, et al. 2018. "Prevalence of Autism Spectrum Disorder Among Children Aged 8 Years—Autism and Developmental Disabilities Monitoring Network, 11 Sites, United States, 2014." *Morbidity and Mortality Weekly Report—Surveillance Summaries* 67(6): 1–23.

Barahona-Corrêa, J. B., and Carlos N. Filipe. 2016. "A Concise History of Asperger Syndrome: The Short Reign of a Troublesome Diagnosis." *Frontiers in Psychology* 6, 2024. doi:10.3389/fpsyg.2015.02024

Baron-Cohen, Simon. 1995. *Mindblindness: An Essay on Autism and Theory of Mind.* Cambridge, MA: MIT Press.

Baron-Cohen, Simon. 2017. "Editorial Perspective: Neurodiversity—A Revolutionary Concept for Autism and Psychiatry." *Journal of Child Psychology and Psychiatry* 58(6): 744–747.

Baron-Cohen, Simon. 2018. "Is It Time to Give Up on a Single Diagnostic Label for Autism?" *Scientific American* blog, May 4. Retrieved from https://blogs.scientificamerican.com/observations/is-it-time-to-give-up-on-a-single-diagnostic-label-for-autism/

Blume, Harold. "Neurodiversity." *The Atlantic*, September 1998. Retrieved from https://archive.is/20130105003900/http://www.theatlantic.com/doc/199809u/neurodiversity

Burgoine, Eyrena, and Lorna Wing. 1983. "Identical Triplets with Asperger's Syndrome." *British Journal of Psychiatry* 143: 261–265.

Chapman, Robert. 2016. "Autism Isn't Just a Medical Diagnosis—It's a Political Identity." *The Establishment*. Retrieved from https://theestablishment.co/autism-isnt-just-a-medicaldiagnosis-its-a-political-identity-178137688bd5

Chapman, Robert. 2019. "Neurodiversity Theory and Its Discontents: Autism, Schizophrenia, and the Social Model of Disability." In *The Bloomsbury Companion to Philosophy of Psychiatry*, edited by Serife Tekin and Robyn Bluhm, 371–389. London: Bloomsbury.

Christ, Shawn E., Stephen M. Kanne, and Angela M. Reiersen. 2010. "Executive Function in Individuals with Subthreshold Autism Traits." *Neuropsychology* 24(5): 590–598.

Cushing, Simon. 2013. "Autism: The Very Idea." In *The Philosophy of Autism*, edited by Jami L. Anderson and Simon Cushing, 17–45. Plymouth, UK: Rowman & Littlefield.

Cushing, Simon. 2018. "Has Autism Changed?" In *The Social Constructions and Experiences of Madness*, edited by Monika dos Santos and Jean-Francois Pelletier, 75–94. Leiden: Brill.

Dave, Dhaval M., and Jose M. Fernandez. 2015. "Rising Autism Prevalence: Real or Displacing Other Mental Disorders? Evidence from Demand for Auxiliary Healthcare Workers in California." *Economic Inquiry* 53(1): 448–468.

Dell'Osso, Liliana, Camilla Gesi, Enrico Massimetti, Ivan M. Cremone, Margherita Barbuti, Giuseppe Maccariello, Ilenia Moroni, et al. 2017. "Adult Autism Subthreshold Spectrum (AdAS Spectrum): Validation of a Questionnaire Investigating Subthreshold Autism Spectrum." *Comprehensive Psychiatry* 73: 61–83.

Dell'Osso, Liliana, Riccardo D. Luche, Camilla Gesi, Ilenia Moroni, Claudia Carmassi, and Mario Maj. 2016. "From Asperger's *Autistischen Psychopathen* to DSM-5 Autism Spectrum Disorder and Beyond: A Subthreshold Autism Spectrum Model." *Clinical Practice & Epidemiology in Mental Health* 3(12): 120–131.

Doherty, Martin J., Naomi M. Campbell, Hiromi Tsuji, and William A. Phillips. 2010. "The Ebbinghaus Illusion Deceives Adults but Not Young Children." *Developmental Science* 13(5): 714–721.

Dominus, Susan. 2019. "Open Office." *The New York Times Magazine*. Retrieved from https://www.nytimes.com/interactive/2019/02/21/magazine/autism-office-design.html

Faucher, Luc, and Denis Forest. In press. *Defining Mental Disorder: Jerome Wakefield and His Critics*. Cambridge, MA: MIT Press.

Fitzgerald, Michael. 2018. "The Broader Autism Phenotype: Expanding the Clinical Gestalt of Autism and Broadening DSM V Criteria of Autism Spectrum Disorder." *Journal of Psychology and Clinical Psychiatry* 9(3): 316-324.

Frith, Uta. 1989. *Autism: Explaining the Enigma*. Oxford, UK: Blackwell.

Frith, Uta, and Francesca Happé. 1994. "Autism: Beyond 'Theory of Mind.'" *Cognition* 50: 115–132.

Glover, Jonathan. 2014. *Alien Landscapes?: Interpreting Disordered Minds*. Cambridge, MA: Belknap Press.

Graby, S. 2015. "Neurodiversity: Bridging the Gap between the Disabled People's Movement and the Mental Health System Survivors' Movement?" In *Madness, Distress and the Politics of Disablement*, edited by H. Spandler, J. Anderson, and B. Sapey. Bristol: Policy Press.

Grandin, Temple. 2006. *Thinking in Pictures and Other Reports from My Life with Autism*. London: Bloomsbury.

Happé, Francesca. 1999. "Autism: Cognitive Deficit or Cognitive Style?" *Trends in Cognitive Science* 3(6): 216–222.

Happé, Francesca. 2018. "Why Are Savant Skills and Special Talents Associated with Autism?" *World Psychiatry* 17(3): 280–281.

Haslam, Nick. 2016. "Concept Creep: Psychology's Expanding Concepts of Harm and Pathology." *Psychological Inquiry* 27(1): 1–17.

Hurley, Robert S., Molly Losh, Morgan Parlier, J. Steven Reznick, and Joseph Piven. 2007. "The Broad Autism Phenotype Questionnaire." *Journal of Autism and Developmental Disorders* 37(9): 1679–1690.

Jaarsma, Pier, and Stelen Welin. 2012. "Autism as a Natural Human Variation: Reflections on the Claims of the Neurodiversity Movement." *Health Care Analysis* 20: 20–30.

Kanne, Stephen M., Jennifer Wang, and Shawn E. Christ. 2012. "The Subthreshold Autism Trait Questionnaire (SATQ): Development of a Brief Self-Report Measure of Subthreshold Autism Traits." *Journal of Autism and Developmental Disorders* 42(5): 769–780.

Kanner, L. 1943. "Autistic Disturbances of Affective Contact." *Nervous Child* 2: 217–250.

Landry, Oriane, and Philippe Chouinard. 2016. "Why We Should Study the Broader Autism Phenotype in Typically Developing Populations." *Journal of Cognition and Development* 17: 584–595.

Lim, Chong-Ming. 2017. "Reviewing Resistances to Reconceptualising Disability." *Proceedings of the Aristotelian Society* 117(3): 321–331.

Lord, Catherine, and Somer L. Bishop. 2015. "Recent Advances in Autism Research as Reflected in DSM-5 Criteria for Autism Spectrum Disorder." *Annual Review of Clinical Psychology* 11: 53–70.

McLaughlin, Eliott C., and Joe Sutton. 2018. "Autistic Man Who Went Overboard on Carnival Cruise Was Traveling with Special Needs Group." *CNN*, December 20. https://www.cnn.com/2018/12/20/us/autistic-man-overboard-carnival-cruise/index.html

Meilleur, Andree-Anne S., Patricia Jelenic, and Laurent Mottron. 2014. "Prevalence of Clinically and Empirically Defined Talents and Strengths in Autism." *Journal of Autism and Developmental Disorders* 45: 1354–1367.

Mercier, Céline, Laurent Mottron, and Sylvie Belleville. 2000. "A Psychosocial Study on Restricted Interests in High-Functioning Persons with Pervasive Developmental Disorders." *Autism* 4(4): 406–425.

Meyerding, Jane. 1998. "Thoughts on Finding Myself Differently Brained." *Autonomy, the Critical Journal of Interdisciplinary Autism Studies.* Retrieved from http://www.larry-arnold. net/Autonomy/index.php/autonomy/article/view/AR9/html#_ftnref8

Miller, B. L., J. Cummings, F. Mishkin, K. Boone, F. Prince, M. Ponton, and C. Cotman. 1998. "Emergence of Artistic Talent in Frontotemporal Dementia." *Neurology* 51: 978–982.

Narzisi, Antonio, Filippo Muratori, Sara Calderoni, Franco Fabbro, and Cosima Urgesi. 2013. "Neuropsychological Profile in High Functioning Autism Spectrum Disorders." *Journal of Autism and Developmental Disorders* 43: 1895–1909.

Nishiyama, Takeshi, and Stephen M. Kanne. 2014. "On the Misapplication of the BAPQ in a Study of Autism." *Journal of Autism and Developmental Disorders* 44: 2079–2080.

Nishiyama Takeshi, Masako Suzuki, Katsunori Adachi, Satoshi Sumi, Kensuke Okada, Hirohisa Kishino, Saeko Sakai, et al. 2014. "Comprehensive Comparison of Self-administered Questionnaires for Measuring Quantitative Autistic Traits in Adults. *Journal of Autism and Developmental Disorders* 44: 993–1007.

Ortega, Francisco. 2009. "The Cerebral Subject and the Challenge of Neurodiversity." *BioSocieties* 4: 425–445.

Ozonoff, Sally, Bruce F. Pennington, and Sally J. Rogers. 1991. "Executive Function Deficits in High-Functioning Autistic Individuals: Relationship to Theory of Mind." *Journal of Child Psychology and Psychiatry* 32: 1081–1105.

Perry, Richard. 2014. "Asperger's Disorder on Life Support." *Journal of Autism and Developmental Disorder* 44: 2072–2073.

Rawls, John. 1971. *A Theory of Justice*. Cambridge, MA: Harvard University Press.

Robeyns, Ingrid. 2016. "Conceptualising Well-being for Autistic Persons." *Journal of Medical Ethics* 42: 383–390.

Ruzich, Emily, Carrie Allison, Paula Smith, Peter Watson, Bonnie Auyeung, Howard Ring, and Simon Baron-Cohen. 2015. "Measuring Autistic Traits in the General Population: A Systematic Review of the Autism-Spectrum Quotient (AQ) in a Nonclinical Population Sample of 6,900 Typical Adult Males and Females." *Molecular Autism* 6: 2. doi:10.1186/ 2040-2392-6-2

Sarrett, Jennifer C. 2016. "Biocertification and Neurodiversity: The Role and Implications of Self Diagnosis in Autistic Communities." *Neuroethics* 9: 23–36.

Schriber, Roberta A., Richard W. Robins, and Marjorie Solomon. 2014. "Personality and Self-Insight in Individuals with Autism Spectrum Disorder." *Journal of Personality and Social Psychology* 106(1): 112–130.

Silberman, Steve. 2010. "Exclusive: First Autistic Presidential Appointee Speaks Out." *Wired*, October 6. https://www.wired.com/2010/10/exclusive-ari-neeman-qa/

Sinclair, Jim. 1993. "Don't Mourn for Us." *Autonomy: The Critical Journal for Interdisciplinary Autism Studies* 1: 1–4.

Singer, Jim. 1999. "Why Can't You Be Normal for Once in Your Life? From a 'Problem with No Name' to the Emergence of a New Category of Difference." In M. Corker and S. French (Eds.), *Disability Discourse*, 59–67. Buckingham, UK: Open University Press.

Skylark, William J., and Simon Baron-Cohen. 2017. "Initial Evidence that Non-clinical Autistic Traits Are Associated with Lower Income." *Molecular Autism* 8: 61. doi:10.1186/s13229-017-0179-z.

Sowell, Thomas. 2001. *The Einstein Syndrome*. New York: Basic Books.

Spitzer, Robert L., and Paul T. Wilson. 1975. "Nosology and the Official Psychiatric Nomenclature." *Comprehensive Textbook of Psychiatry* 2: 826–845.

Spitzer Robert L., and Jean Endicott. 1978. "Medical and Mental Disorder: Proposed Definition and Criteria." In *Critical Issues in Psychiatric Diagnosis*, edited by Robert L. Spitzer and Donald F. Klein, 15–40. New York: Raven Press.

Straus, Joseph N. 2013. "Autism as Culture." *The Disability Studies Reader* 4: 460–484.

Treffert, Darold A. 2009. "The Savant Syndrome: An Extraordinary Condition. A Synopsis: Past, Present, Future." *Philosophical Transactions of the Royal Society of London. Series B, Biological Sciences* 364(1522): 1351–1357.

Verhoeff, Berend. 2012. "What Is This Thing Called Autism? A Critical Analysis of the Tenacious Search for Autism's Essence." *BioSocieties* 7(4): 410–432.

Wakefield, Jerome C. 1992a. "The Concept of Mental Disorder: On the Boundary between Biological Facts and Social Values." *American Psychologist* 47: 373–388.

Wakefield, Jerome C. 1992b. "Disorder as Harmful Dysfunction: A Conceptual Critique of DSM-III-R's Definition of Mental Disorder." *Psychological Review* 99: 232–247.

Wakefield, Jerome C. 1993. "Limits of Operationalization: A Critique of Spitzer and Endicott's (1978) Proposed Operational Criteria of Mental Disorder." *Journal of Abnormal Psychology* 102: 160–172.

Wakefield, Jerome C. 1999a. "Evolutionary Versus Prototype Analyses of the Concept of Disorder." *Journal of Abnormal Psychology* 108: 374–399.

Wakefield, Jerome C. 1999b. "Mental Disorder as a Black Box Essentialist Concept." *Journal of Abnormal Psychology* 108: 465–472.

Wakefield, Jerome C. 2000a. "Aristotle as Sociobiologist: The 'Function of a Human Being' Argument, Black Box Essentialism, and the Concept of Mental Disorder." *Philosophy, Psychiatry, and Psychology* 7: 17–44.

Wakefield, Jerome C. 2000b. "Spandrels, Vestigial Organs, and Such: Reply to Murphy and Woolfolk's 'The Harmful Dysfunction Analysis of Mental Disorder.'" *Philosophy, Psychiatry, and Psychology* 7: 253–269.

Wakefield, Jerome C. 2001. "Evolutionary History Versus Current Causal Role in the Definition of Disorder: Reply to McNally." *Behaviour Research and Therapy* 39: 347–366.

Wakefield, Jerome C. 2007a. "The Concept of Mental Disorder: Diagnostic Implications of the Harmful Dysfunction Analysis." *World Psychiatry* 6: 149–156.

Wakefield, Jerome C. 2007b. "What Makes a Mental Disorder Mental?" *Philosophy, Psychiatry, and Psychology* 13: 123–131.

Wakefield, Jerome C., and Michael B. First. 2003. "Clarifying the Distinction Between Disorder and Nondisorder: Confronting the Overdiagnosis ("False Positives") Problem in DSM-V." In *Advancing DSM: Dilemmas in Psychiatric Diagnosis*, edited by Katherine A. Phillips and Michael B. First, 23–56. Washington, DC: American Psychiatric Press.

Weiskopf, Daniel A. 2017. "An Ideal Disorder? Autism as a Psychiatric Kind." *Philosophical Explorations* 20(2): 175–190.

Williams, Donna. 2002. *Exposure Anxiety—The Invisible Cage: An Exploration of Self-Protection Responses in the Autism Spectrum*. London: Jessica Kingsley.

Wing, Lorna. 1997. "The Autistic Spectrum." *Lancet* 350: 1761–1766.

CHAPTER 30

BEYOND INSTRUMENTAL VALUE: RESPECTING THE WILL OF OTHERS AND DECIDING ON THEIR BEHALF

DANA HOWARD AND DAVID WENDLER

THIS chapter explores the ethical responsibilities of those who make decisions on behalf of individuals who have intellectual and/or developmental disabilities that result in lifelong impaired consent capacity in certain domains. While the lessons aim to be generalizable, the focus will be on decision making in the medical realm, where the person with intellectual and/or developmental disabilities has impaired consent capacity with respect to an important clinical or research decision—such as whether to undergo surgery or whether to enroll in a clinical trial.

By impaired consent capacity we do not mean simply an individual whose capacity to make decisions is impaired in the sense of not being ideal or as good as it might be. That is true of most, if not all individuals who nonetheless are permitted to make their own decisions. Instead, we refer to individuals whose consent capacity is impaired to the point that it falls below the threshold on one or more of the capacities that are usually assumed necessary for legal standing to make one's own decisions: the capacity to understand, reason, make a voluntary decision, and communicate that decision.

Each of these necessary capacities is a function of a number of subcapacities. The capacity to understand, for example, requires that individuals understand the procedure or trial in question, as well as the risks, the potential benefits, and the alternatives. Individuals with impaired consent capacity include those who fall short on all of the necessary capacities for some decision, as well as individuals whose capacity falls short on some of the capacities but exceeds the thresholds on the others. The location of these thresholds is imprecise and debatable. How much does one have to understand to be allowed to decide for oneself whether to undergo surgery, or enroll in a clinical trial? How well does one have to be able to reason? The important thing to note is that wherever the thresholds are set, there will be people who fall short of them and some who have done so for their entire lives. We will describe this in terms of lifelong decisional incapacity, which is intended to cover individuals who were born with intellectual and/ or developmental disabilities as well as those who developed intellectual and/or developmental disabilities after birth but prior to gaining decisional capacity.

The question we focus on concerns the role of the person who is charged with making decisions on behalf of those who have impaired consent capacity with respect to a particular important decision.[1] We will call the individual with impaired consent capacity the *patient* and the individual making decisions on the patient's behalf, their *trustee*. How trustees should make decisions on behalf of patients with lifelong impaired consent capacity is an under-theorized question that fits awkwardly among the narratives of existing debates. First, as Michael Bérubé (2009) argues, thinking seriously about intellectual disability requires us to reconsider some of the founding premises of disability studies, which often take physical disabilities as the paradigm case. In particular, insofar as the social model of disability understands disability primarily as an effect of our built environment and stigmatizing relationships, it is difficult to fully capture the distinctive challenges that people with intellectual disabilities face. "It is easier... to speak of a barrier free environment when one is speaking of wheelchairs and ramps than when one is speaking of significant cognitive disabilities" (Bérubé 2009, 357). Moreover, Bérubé points out that proposals for self-representation and self-advocacy leave many ethical questions unanswered.

Second, while bioethics has long debated the ethics of surrogate decision making, it has paid little attention to those with congenital or early onset intellectual and/or developmental disabilities that result in lifelong impaired consent capacity regarding at least some important decisions. The focus in the literature has been on individuals whose impaired consent capacity is limited to a portion of their lives. Paradigm cases include competent adults who transiently lose decisional capacity (e.g., due to a car accident) and formerly competent adults (e.g., dementia patients). This literature asks how we can, and whether we should, respect the preferences and values the patient endorsed when competent: To what extent does respect for the patient align with strict adherence to their autonomously held past preferences? (Dresser 1995; Howard 2017) This debate, while important, is not relevant to persons with lifelong impaired consent capacity, since their past preferences are often no more indicative of their will than their occurrent preferences. Moreover, turning our attention to respectful decision-making on behalf of those with intellectual and/or developmental disabilities allows us to attend to the possibility that the experience of cognitive disability needn't be understood solely or even primarily as one of loss; the challenges that all people with impaired consent capacity face do not start or end with respecting their precedent autonomy.

Finally, when it comes to bioethical discussions regarding people with intellectual and/or developmental disabilities, much of the philosophical attention has been given to the moral status of individuals with profound intellectual disabilities—that is, the debate concerns whether such patients are persons or not (Singer 2010 [book]). When surrogate decision making is brought up in this discussion, it is primarily to ask whether surrogacy makes it possible for individuals with intellectual and/or developmental disabilities to be members of the moral community in full standing. This approach tends to mark out individuals with profound intellectual and/or developmental disabilities as constitutively different from people with mild to moderate intellectual and/or developmental disabilities who are uncontested members of the moral community.

The present chapter focuses on people with lifelong impaired consent capacity in order to highlight the potential for solidarity among members of the group given their common vulnerable social status. It starts from the assumption that all individuals with intellectual and/or developmental disabilities are owed respect and asks how decisions should be made that accord them appropriate respect. To this end, we focus on the entire range of decisional capacity that lies in between individuals who lack decisional capacity entirely (e.g., those in coma) and individuals who have decisional capacity in the sense that they pass the threshold on all the necessary capacities.

Standard analyses maintain, whether explicitly or implicitly, that respect for autonomy is irrelevant to patients with lifelong impaired consent capacity. It is thus appropriate for trustees to make decisions based solely on what best promotes the patient's interests. On this approach, the preferences, values, and decisions of those with impaired consent capacity are considered relevant to decision making only instrumentally, to the extent that they provide an indicator of the patient's interests. These preferences and values, and the patients' agential capacities more broadly, are not regarded as having independent and intrinsic normative significance. If a patient's expressed preference to avoid a proposed MRI is indicative of fear, that needs to be taken into account when determining which choice best promotes their interests. Similarly, if ignoring this expression and proceeding with the MRI would be upsetting to the patient, that needs to be taken into account as well. But, the mere fact that, following discussion and deliberation, the patient prefers to avoid the MRI is normatively silent. They are, after all, unable to make their own treatment decisions.

We argue that this approach is insufficiently respectful of patients with lifelong impaired consent capacity. Rather than emphasize the fact that they lack one or more of the capacities necessary for making one's own decisions, we emphasize the fact that they still possess agential capacities and life experiences that should be accorded due respect. Making decisions with the sole aim of promoting the patient's well-being fails to properly respect the existent agential capacities of these patients. We defend this claim by expanding the key ethical challenge of medical decision making: rather than emphasize the importance of respect for autonomy, we focus on decision making that does not insult the existent agential capacities of individuals.

When it comes to people who have decisional capacity, we insult their agential capacities by treating them as if they can't make their own decisions. Namely, we insult their agential capacities by disrespecting their autonomy. When it comes to people who have impaired consent capacity, it may not be insulting to treat them as if they can't make their own decisions. However, the potential for insult does not stop there. We argue that insofar as those with impaired consent capacity possess some elements of agency, they can be wronged by having those elements ignored or given insufficient consideration. This possibility arises with respect to individuals who have some capacities that exceed the threshold for being able to make one's own decisions, as well as individuals who have agential capacities all of which fall below the respective thresholds on consent capacity.

In brief, we argue that individuals with lifelong impaired consent capacity can still be disrespected if they are treated as though they lack all agential capacities. Trustees should not make decisions for these patients based solely on what promotes the patient's interests and regard the patient's choices and preferences as having only instrumental normative significance. Instead, trustees need to consider what decision is supported by appropriate respect for the patient's existing agential capacities, even if those capacities fall below the threshold for autonomous choice. Put very generally, trustees need to recognize that a patient's unique perspective and life experiences possess intrinsic normative significance.

A Common Vulnerability

The category of individuals with intellectual and/or developmental disabilities is not a homogenous group. It encompasses a constellation of different cognitive and communicative capacities and impairments, which themselves can be caused by a constellation of different congenital or degenerative conditions, such as Cerebral Palsy, Down syndrome, Autism, or untreated metabolic disorders (such as PKU).[2] This is a wide umbrella indeed. Some people with intellectual and/or developmental disabilities have consent capacity regarding all self-regarding decisions. Others may lack the capacity on specific occasions, when it comes to complex and high-stakes medical decisions for instance, even as they remain in charge of a good deal of their lives. And yet other patients may have impaired consent capacity with respect to most decisions that concern their livelihood; such patients may experience difficulty in language development, or may be nonverbal, and may require the comprehensive support of others in order to perform routine tasks such as dressing and eating.

Given the diversity of capacities correlated with intellectual and/or developmental disabilities, we may be tempted to conclude that there is nothing distinctive about how to make decisions on behalf of those with impaired consent capacity that is a result of their disability. In particular, we may be tempted to separate intellectual and developmental disabilities and analyze them independently. However, such a temptation neglects the common and precarious social status that all people with intellectual and/or developmental disabilities share: namely, people with these disabilities are vulnerable to being subjected to exclusion, exploitation, and/or disadvantage on the basis of their perceived lack of agential capacities (Howard and Aas 2018). This vulnerability is particularly pronounced in the medical setting and especially when members of this cohort have impaired consent capacity.

Having an intellectual and/or developmental disability makes a person vulnerable in two ways. First, it makes them easier targets of harmful abuse or neglect by healthcare practitioners, which negatively affects their welfare. While this vulnerability is most evident in notorious ethical failures of research—such as the Willowbrook hepatitis study—it has been shown more generally that people with intellectual and/or developmental disabilities are more vulnerable to avoidable deaths and health complications than those without such disabilities (Heslop et al. 2014).

This first kind of vulnerability extends to all people with intellectual and/or developmental disabilities, even those who do not have impaired consent capacity. People with developmental disabilities are often *perceived* as having intellectual ones as well that impair their decisional capacity and are treated accordingly. Consider the case of Henny Kupferstein, an autistic woman who, because of her use of regional offices to access resources and accommodations related to her developmental disability, was misidentified as having "mental retardation" during a hospital stay. This misperception led to the hospital staff second-guessing her reporting of symptoms and her explicit requests, and this ultimately worsened her overall health outcomes (Perry 2018). Because of the stigma, prejudice, and difficulties of communication that people with developmental disabilities often face, their developmental disability can lead others to question their decisional capacity, which can make them worse off as a result. It follows that *all* people with intellectual and/or developmental disabilities are vulnerable to maltreatment, including those who actually have impaired decisional capacity and those who are only perceived to have impaired decisional capacity (Iacono et al. 2019).[3] While it is only appropriate for trustees to make decisions on behalf of people who actually have impaired decisional capacity, these decisions are not made in a vacuum. The manner in which these decisions are made should be responsive to the shared vulnerability that all persons with intellectual and/or developmental disabilities share.

Second, and more controversially, the perception that an individual lacks agential capacity can itself be used as a rationale for disregarding their wishes and preferences in the medical setting. This marginalization can be unjust even when it doesn't lead to harmful health outcomes and even if the patients are wholly unaware of the disregard. For instance, the Federal Court of Appeals ruling, *Doe Tarlow v. District of Columbia*, argued that medical providers are not required to solicit the wishes and preferences of disabled people who have life-long impaired consent capacity before performing medical procedures on them, including elective surgery and abortion. The court ruled that because plaintiffs have "never been able to make informed choices regarding their medical treatment, their true wishes with respect to a recommended surgery 'are unknown and cannot be ascertained.' "[4] Moreover, the court argued that not only did the requirement of soliciting the wishes of such patients lack "logical sense," it also could lead to "erroneous medical decisions – with harmful or even deadly consequences to intellectually disabled persons" (*Doe ex rel. Tarlow v. D.C.* 2007). Consequently, the court ruled that medical decisions on behalf of people with intellectual and/or developmental disabilities who have lifelong impaired consent capacity should be based on the "best interest standard" rather than on the "known wishes standard."

This ruling denies the distinction between lacking consent capacity and lacking agential capacities altogether. It misses an important difference between having preferences regarding one's medical treatment and possessing the capacity to make one's own decisions in light of those preferences. On this ruling, if someone has been found to have lifelong impaired consent capacity, as a result of intellectual and/or developmental disabilities, then their preferences and wishes (past or present) need not be solicited in the process of making decisions on their behalf.[5] This case offers a clear example in which having an intellectual and/or developmental disability (and not just being unable to make a specific decision) is treated as making a normative difference in how it is permissible to be treated under the law. The preferences of people who have never had legal capacity to make independent medical decisions are understood as irrelevant and potentially detrimental to determining their appropriate medical care. Not only are people with impaired consent capacity judged to lack the legal standing to make medical decisions on their own behalf, they also are judged to lack the legal standing to have their wishes about medical treatment ascertained by whomever has the authority to make such decisions on their behalf.

Proponents of this ruling may claim that while we must take measures to guard against the first kind of vulnerability (i.e., to being made worse off as a result of one's impaired consent capacity), there is no moral requirement to guard against the second kind of vulnerability (i.e., to having one's preferences, reasoning, and values ignored on the basis of one's impaired consent capacity). They may argue that when it comes to people with impaired consent capacity, what solely matters is their welfare interests and not their interest in having their will respected. Call this the Welfare Only view. We argue against such a view next.

AGAINST THE WELFARE ONLY VIEW

It should be noted that those who hold the Welfare Only view of trustee decision making need not agree with the Tarlow ruling. They may concede that patients' preferences and wishes *should* still be solicited as a means to furthering these patients' interests—either by giving trustees a better sense of what is good for the patients or by making the patients feel better about their medical treatment and the process of selecting it. The Welfare Only view does not prohibit soliciting the views of patients, it just claims that patients' preferences have normative significance only instrumentally. On such a view, someone who lacks decisional capacity has a right to have their interests safeguarded, but they either have no active will that can be disrespected or their will falls below the relevant threshold that merits respect (Dworkin 1993, 229). As long as patients can have their interests safeguarded without their explicit preferences being solicited, there is no ethical demand to solicit their preferences.

One might try to defend the Welfare Only view based on a staunchly holistic understanding of agential capacities according to which a deficit in one or more of the necessary conditions on agential capacity undermines the validity of all one's agential capacities to the point of eliminating their normative significance. If one cannot weigh sufficiently the long-term risks of a particular treatment, for example, one's preferences regarding that procedure do not have any normative force at all. This view might be defended by pointing out that the expressed preferences of individuals with impaired consent capacity might simply be a result of their disabilities in the sense that if they did not have intellectual and/or developmental disabilities, they would have different preferences.

On this interpretation, the trustee has two options for how to make decisions on the patient's behalf. Trustees can either:

(Option A) Do what from the trustee's perspective is in the objective best interests of the patient, or

(Option B) Imagine what the patient would want were the patient capable of making their own decisions, perhaps by imagining what the patient's hypothetical self-regarding preferences would be, were it not for their underlying intellectual and/or developmental disabilities.

These two options are both ostensible methods for promoting the patient's welfare, each tracking a different conception of well-being. Were a trustee to decide on the basis of Option A, they would be attempting to promote the patient's welfare according to an Objective List theory of well-being. Objective List theories share a common understanding that "certain things are good or bad for people, whether or not these people would want to have the good things, or to avoid the bad things" (Parfit 1984, 499). Were a trustee to decide on the basis of Option B, they would be promoting the patient's welfare according to a variant of the Informed Desire Theory of well-being. Informed Desire Theories of well-being idealize the conditions in which the desire arises. This idealizing mechanism has taken on many different forms. Some Desire Theories claim that the only relevant desires are the ones that could have a grip on the agent were they fully rational and equipped with full information.[6] The idealization present in Option B does not require the trustee to imagine what the patient would decide were they to be fully rational and informed; rather the trustee idealizes away the patient's impaired consent capacity.

Both of these options for how to decide are insufficient. By focusing on the hypothetical preferences of the patient, Option B does not necessarily track the welfare interests of the actual patient standing before the trustee. The problem with determining the welfare interests of a particular person on the basis of what they would choose were they in a better epistemic or rational position is that it makes use of false subjunctive conditionals. Sometimes what we have reason to want is partly determined by the fact that *we are* less than fully rational or relevantly informed. The structural flaw of such reasoning is often called a "conditional fallacy" (Shope 1978). According to Option B, what a patient with Down syndrome has reason to want is determined by what that patient would want were she to not have an intellectual or developmental disability. But the patient has found her community and has developed her evaluative perspective partly in light of her intellectual and/or developmental disability. Were the trustee to make decisions on the basis of what the patient would want absent her intellectual and/or developmental disabilities, the trustee would risk making decisions that would advance the welfare of a very different person. Therefore, it is unclear how making decisions based on patients' hypothetical preferences advances their welfare interests.

More fundamentally, on either option, even if we were able to determine what the welfare interests of the patient are (with or without soliciting the patient's preferences), it is unclear why their welfare interests should always trump the patient's explicit preferences. It is often the case that individuals who have consent capacity and make a particular decision would have made a different decision had their agential capacities been better (e.g., had they understood more or been better able to evaluate long-term probabilistic risks). Barring extreme circumstances (such as a person mistakenly believing that the clear liquid in front of them is water instead of gasoline), the fact that they could have made a better decision does not imply that we should ignore the decision they actually make given the capacities and the information they have. Similarly, to recognize that an individual with an intellectual and/or developmental disability is incapable of autonomous decision making in a given circumstance does not justify our treatment of them as non-agents in every respect. Rather than treat them as a patient in coma, we should accord due respect to the agential capacities and the unique perspective they do possess (Jaworska 1999).

Consider a cancer patient with Down syndrome who falls below the thresholds for several of the capacities necessary for making a significant medical decision. This does not mean that she lacks the capacity to more generally direct the course of her own life. Even in the hospital setting, many of the decisions are still hers to make. She can decide what to have for lunch, whether to take walks or watch TV, whom to befriend on the floor, and so on. What she has been found to lack is the capacity to decide for herself whether to undergo surgery or to undergo surgery and radiation therapy. She may nonetheless still have preferences regarding this choice, and these preferences may be the result of significant deliberation and be consistent with the overall course of the life she has chosen for herself. Her preferences may be consistent with her values and self-identity that she can articulate: fidelity to one's family, curiosity about the world, or a commitment to combating the disease. The Welfare Only view directs trustees to take into account the patient's preferences and allow her to express her agential capacities regarding the surgery only to the extent that doing so is relevant to promoting her welfare interests. It may be good for the patient to ask questions about the procedure, to express her fears and hopes, to communicate what she understands and what she finds confusing, etc. Her agential capacities may thus be solicited and encouraged, but they are accorded no independent normative value.

We do not deny the instrumental importance of soliciting the preferences and decisions of individuals with impaired consent capacity in order to determine which option best promotes the patient's interests. Trustees should be motivated to promote their patient's interests, and these preferences and decisions can be informative. However, the preferences and decisions of individuals with impaired consent capacity should not be treated as being of solely instrumental normative significance. They also deserve respect in their own right as the manifestations of the perspective and life of a unique individual. While this view runs counter to standard analyses in the literature, we argue, in the next section, that it is implied by and implicitly supported by a number of these analyses.

Insulting the Agency of Another

Seana Shiffrin argues that what is objectionable about paternalistic treatment is that it conveys a special kind of insult to the agency of another: "It directly expresses insufficient respect for the underlying valuable capacities, powers, and entitlements of the autonomous agent" (Shiffrin 2000, 220). Being the target of this kind of paternalism differs from being disrespected in other ways. When the governor of Colorado offered executive clemency to prison inmates in exchange for their participation in a tuberculosis vaccine trial, he was disrespecting them by making such an offer, but wasn't acting paternalistically (Hornblum 1997, 1438). Such an offer insulted the moral status of these inmates as agents, but it arguably did not insult their capacity for agency itself. On Shiffrin's view, paternalism is distinctively insulting because it disrespects the person's agential capacities themselves, thereby insulting the individual.

We suggest that the Welfare Only view commits an analogous objectionable insult to the agential capacity of individuals with impaired consent capacity. It says of the person with Down syndrome who has impaired consent capacity, but who has largely been leading their own life: your deliberation and choices regarding the surgery, whether your life includes the radiation or not, have no normative significance of their own. Doing this fails to respect the person's distinctive evaluative perspective and their capacity to determine to the extent possible how their life goes.

Our suggestion can be understood as a modification or expansion on Shiffrin's account. Her focus is specifically on the way that paternalistic treatment disrespects the agency of *autonomous* others. Behavior is paternalistic only if it is "directed at matters that lie legitimately within" the authority of the paternalized agent (Shiffrin 2000, 218–219). It is insulting to one's agential capacities when other people, just because they take themselves to know better, insert their wills into realms over which one has ultimate decisional authority. On Shiffrin's explicit view, if the decision to be made does not lie in the legitimate control of a person who has impaired capacity, then they cannot be treated paternalistically. However, when Shiffrin is discussing the distinctive wrong of paternalism, it is the attitude of disrespect towards the agency of another, rather than the fact that the target of the attitude is autonomous, that, at its "most basic" level, makes such treatment problematic. Shiffrin writes:

> To a certain extent, one is wronged if one's self-regarding experience is dictated or imposed by another. Respecting another's decisions is not simply a way to promote another's welfare or to facilitate the valuable process of creating and expressing a distinctive character. In a more basic way, I believe it serves as an acknowledgment of the moral importance of the uniqueness and separateness of persons and the deep, irreducible fact that one's life is the only life one has.   (Shiffrin 2004, 203)

The fact that one's agential capacities fall below one or more of the thresholds on being able to make one's own decisions does not imply that one lacks a unique and irreducible perspective on the medical decisions at hand. Moreover, it is still the patient, not the trustees, who will intimately experience the consequences of the decision. So, it remains an open question to what extent patients without autonomy should retain some measure of "legitimate authority" over the decisions made on their behalf. While the patient may not be able to decide on their own, their evaluative perspective can play a guiding and normatively significant role in the decision making that is done on their behalf. The course of their lives should be guided by their views on how their lives should go, thereby integrating the individual's experiences, as well as their preferences and values. Being disposed to make decisions as a trustee in this way, even when doing so may end up being less beneficial for the patient's welfare interests, is a posture of respect toward the patient with impaired consent capacity.

WHAT DOES DUE RESPECT ENTAIL?

Put most broadly, trustees insult the marginal agency of persons with impaired consent capacity when they fail to give their subjective perspective the appropriate authoritative role in their deliberations. What this amounts to is, of course, going to be context sensitive. To begin to unpack this, consider the following case:

> Case 1: In 1969, a Court of Appeals was deciding whether to allow a kidney donation from a person with intellectual disabilities to his brother. The court documents describe Jerry Strunk as a 27-year-old with an "an I.Q. of approximately 35, which corresponds with the mental age of approximately six years. He is further handicapped by a speech defect, which makes it difficult for him to communicate with persons who are not well acquainted with him." The Department of Mental Health of Kentucky filed a brief in support of the transplant, arguing that while Jerry's intellectual impairments prevent him from being able to consent to the donation on his own behalf, he "has emotions and reactions on a scale comparable to that of normal person" that make the donation in his best interest. The brief states, "[Jerry] identifies with his brother Tom; Tom is his model, his tie with his family. Tom's life is vital

to the continuity of Jerry's improvement at Frankfort State Hospital and School. In light of these potential benefits and the relatively low risk of surgery, the court permitted the transplant." (*Strunk vs. Strunk* 1969)

The ruling does not disclose whether Jerry's views were or ought to have been solicited in the process of making a decision about his kidney donation. Rather, it articulated the justification for the procedure solely on the basis of Jerry's welfare considerations—the low risks of the surgery balanced against the devastation Tom's death would have on Jerry. It follows that even if Jerry's wishes were solicited and taken into consideration, they were not accorded any normative force in their own right. The extent to which they reflected Jerry's view of how his life should go didn't matter. By regarding Jerry's preferences as at best, only instrumentally valuable, we argue that this decision insults his agential capacities.

What would it look like to accord the wishes and preferences of individuals with life-long impaired consent capacity some normative force in their own right rather than treating them as merely instrumentally significant? Groll (2012) makes a distinction between two different ways in which a patient's wishes can make a difference in decisions made on their behalf. Using his terms, a patient's wishes can be *substantively decisive* or *structurally decisive*. According to Groll, we treat another person's will as *structurally decisive* when their say-so acts as an "authoritative demand" on our decision making. The expression of their will determines what we do "not because it outweighs other considerations but because it is meant to silence or exclude those other considerations" in our decision making (Groll 2012, 701). An expression of another person's will is only *substantively decisive* when we treat it as just one weighty reason among others, which when added to the balance of considerations, tips the scales in favor of acting in accordance with the person's wishes.

On Groll's account, it is possible to disrespect the agency of another even as we act in accordance with that person's wishes; in fact, it is possible to disrespect another's agency even as we treat that person's wishes as the decisive factor in our deliberation. When it comes to people who have decisional capacity, disrespect comes when one treats their wishes as only substantively decisive: they make the difference in the balance of reasons. When the wishes should be treated as structurally decisive, they make a difference by silencing other considerations. At the same time, Groll sees no such insult in treating the wishes of someone with impaired consent capacity as substantively decisive (Groll 2012, 710). On Groll's view, even if Jerry's wishes were solicited, it would be appropriate for them to play only a substantive and not a structural role in making decisions on his behalf.

Groll, in agreement with Shiffrin and others, argues that this difference between structural and substantive decisiveness is informative for how decisions should be made on behalf of those with impaired consent capacity. Insofar as a person lacks decisional capacity, as does Jerry, they do not have the sort of will that ought to be treated as structurally decisive. This is because they do not have the cognitive powers to make an authoritative demand on others, but they may have enough sense of their situation and of their life as a whole that acting according to their wishes would still turn out to be what is best for them. Recognition that we are acting against their wishes could be deeply distressing to them. It is thus both possible and appropriate for the court to decide in favor of the transplant and do so on the grounds that it was what Jerry endorsed (assuming he did). But it is important to note that such a ruling would treat Jerry's wishes as merely *substantively decisive*—as but one constituent consideration among others that can tip the scales regarding what is best for him. Imagine, for instance, if the court determined that, overall, Jerry's life prospects would not be greatly diminished if he lost his brother but that he would suffer great psychological harm knowing that he expressed his wish to save his brother and the court ignored him. Were the court to rule in favor of the transplant on this reasoning, Jerry's wishes would be substantively decisive without being structurally decisive. It is because of the psychological harm and not because of the authoritative force of the wishes themselves that the court would concede to Jerry.

While Groll's distinction between substantive and structural authoritative force is important, he moves too quickly to categorically deny that the preferences of individuals with impaired consent capacity have any structural significance with respect to decisions made on their behalf. Groll fails to consider the possibility that we can accord the decisions that one makes as having some structural significance without taking them as fully authoritative. This is because we can regard them as having structural force, even if they are not treated as structurally determinative. This possibility suggests that there are at least four possible stances on how the will of another can influence our decision-making on their behalf. We can, as Groll points out, treat their will as (a) structurally decisive or as (b) substantively decisive. But we can also treat their will as (c) structurally *forceful* or (d) substantively *forceful*.[7]

Groll's important conceptual innovation is the structural/substantive contrast and not the fact that we respect others *only* when we treat their will as decisive in our decision making. While we agree that Jerry's will should not be treated as (a) structurally *decisive*, there is still the possibility—and we will argue, a moral imperative—to treat his will as (c) structurally *forceful*. That is, for his will to make a structural difference in the way that the surrogate decision is justified.

Throughout the chapter so far, we have distinguished between instrumental and intrinsic value. Our conception of instrumental treatment of the patient's expressed preferences maps onto Groll's conceptual framework as conferring them with (d) substantive force in the trustee's decision making; a trustee who treats the patient's preferences as intrinsically valuable confers their wishes with (c) structural force. We argue that trustees should treat Jerry's preferences regarding the donation as having intrinsic or structural normative force. To pursue this possibility, consider the following decision-making on behalf of a person with mild intellectual disabilities:

Case 2: Williams syndrome is a genetic neurodevelopmental condition characterized by an extremely outgoing, empathetic personality, strong short-term verbal memory, along with a mild to moderate intellectual impairment. While people with Williams syndrome often appear outwardly happy, they are much more likely to suffer from generalized anxiety than a comparable population. By using EEG and fMRI, researchers propose to conduct a study to assess whether there are any neurological differences between how people with Williams syndrome respond to pictures of threatening facial expressions and how they respond to depictions of threatening scenes. The study allows for the enrollment of people who can make their own decisions as well as those who lack decisional capacity, provided a surrogate authorizes their enrollment. Samantha is a twenty-two-year-old with Williams syndrome and is interested in participating in the study. During the consent process, the researchers come to the conclusion that she does not have capacity to make an adequately informed decision about whether to participate. She can repeat verbatim the distinction between research and clinical interventions that the researchers laid out as they went over the consent form. However, upon further discussion, Samantha doesn't seem to appreciate or to be able to articulate how this difference relates to her own situation. When asked why she wants to participate in the study, she answers that she believes participating in the study will help her anxiety. When advised not to expect any therapeutic outcomes from participation, she responds that she wants her anxiety to go away and hopes this will help. The researchers believe that Samantha's ability to repeat the distinction between research and clinical interventions and her interest in participation is the result of her WS rather than evidence of adequate understanding. While they want to respect Samantha's wishes, they do not conceive of her preferences as sufficient for informed consent. The researchers turn to Samantha's sister, Amy, her next-of-kin surrogate, to make the decision on Samantha's behalf.   (Meyer-Lindenberg et al. 2006, 380)

Imagine that Amy thinks the study is a waste of time and agrees with the researchers that Samantha does not fully grasp the difference between therapeutic and experimental interventions. However, rather than see Samantha's wishes to join the study as based solely on confusion or as being a mere symptom of her genetic condition, she understands these preferences to be genuine expressions of Samantha's underlying values and character. From Amy's perspective, Samantha does not want to join simply because she thinks doing so will benefit her personally. Instead, this desire is a manifestation of Samantha's desire to help others, even if doing so is to her own detriment. Should Amy authorize participation in the study on her sister's behalf?

If we accept Groll's argument that Samantha's preference to enroll should not be treated as structurally decisive, this leaves Amy with the following three options:

1. *Accord Merely Substantive Force to Samantha's Will*: Even recognizing that Samantha wants to enroll, Amy may refuse to authorize participation because from Amy's perspective participation would not, all things considered, be in Samantha's best interest; or

2. *Accord Substantive Decisiveness to Samantha's Will*: Amy may authorize Samantha's participation in the study on the grounds that Samantha's expressed desire to enroll suggests, despite contrary factors, that enrollment is in Samantha's best interest.

3. *Accord Structural Force to Samantha's Will*: Amy may regard Samantha's expressed desire to enroll as providing a strong reason to enroll her, independent of the extent to which enrollment would be in her interests.[8]

On the face of it, choosing (2) or (3) could be understood as aligning with Samantha's stated preferences; however, that doesn't mean they are ethically on par. As we have seen, Groll's account implies that (2) is the more justifiable option. Given that Samantha's understanding of the nature of research participation falls below the threshold for informed consent, it would, on Groll's view, be inappropriate to accord her preference any structural significance. On our view, (2) expresses an insult to Samantha's existing agential capacities even if the decision ends up according with her preferences. This is because it is insulting for Amy, as Samantha's trustee, to focus solely on Samantha's well-being when it is clear that Samantha is articulating a choice, one that coheres with her overall commitments, albeit one that does not fully account for the distinction between research and therapy.

What it means to treat Samantha's will as structurally forceful but not structurally decisive requires further explanation. There are many ways in which a person's say-so can make a structural difference without it being decisive. Requests are like this. Take the difference between these two speech acts:

(A) Asking a friend to help one move out of one's apartment

(B) Intentionally saying things in front of one's friend which give them evidence that helping with the move would greatly benefit one's wellbeing (e.g., lamenting about the prospect of doing it alone, complaining about one's bad back, etc.)[9]

Both sorts of speech acts can lead one's friend to believe that they have most reason to help with the move. But they do so on different normative registers. The (B) types of speech acts are a form of epistemic reason giving; they give the friend *reasons to believe* that they should help their friend move. Requests, on the other hand, (i.e., A), are a form of practical reason giving. They don't merely inform others of what we hope they will do, they transform the relationship between speaker and audience and create a candidate reason for action. Our friends can choose to accept our request. And, if they do so, they can justify their actions directly by the fact that we asked them to do so rather than simply by treating our request as evidence for which option best promotes our welfare. Our requests, when they are heard and understood, thus often change the normative structure of our friend's deliberative position. The fact that I requested your assistance in moving often gives you a new reason to help. But notice that it does not necessarily obligate you to do so. In this way, requests are structurally forceful without being structurally decisive.

Other speech acts similarly work in structurally forceful but non-decisive ways, including, arguably, proposals, endorsements, among others. Expressing one's preferences and wishes, either verbally or otherwise, can similarly work in this structurally forceful way even if one has impaired consent capacity. The wishes and preferences can act as a default position for how to proceed on the patient's behalf. If the trustee wishes to veer from this default, she must be able to offer a specific justification in terms that would be acceptable to the patient, given the patient's own values, commitments, and lived experience. Deviating from the default position on the basis that doing so would be best for the patient's welfare would be an incomplete justification. Were the trustee to focus solely on the patient's well-being, they risk insulting the patient's capacity to share their unique and irreducible perspective. Now this risk of insult may still be excusable in situations where the risks to the patient are grave. However, to argue that welfare considerations may, in high-stakes situations, be used as an *excuse* for otherwise inappropriate disrespect is quite different from arguing that insofar as someone has impaired consent capacity, their welfare considerations offer the only *justification* for decisions made on their behalf in *any* situation. Just as in the case of insulting the agency of autonomous individuals, the high stakes of a situation may excuse a decision maker for overriding another person's expressed preferences for his or her own good.

These structurally forceful (and yet non-decisive) speech acts change the normative situation of one's interlocutor in two ways. First, they create a new candidate reason for action. I helped my friend to move because she asked me to do so. We are going out for a walk because you proposed the venture. Second, they change the interlocutor's standing. The requestee is put in a position where they may be called upon to justify the choice to decline the request. Now the person with intellectual and/or developmental disabilities may choose not to challenge her trustee and may not even be able to understand a challenge of this sort. This doesn't change whether one should be poised to justify one's decision. For instance, third parties can challenge the trustee on the patient's behalf. And perhaps, in some cases, trustees ought to challenge themselves.

How does this relate to Amy's obligations to her sister? Groll may be right that it is not disrespectful to refuse to treat the will of someone with impaired consent capacity as structurally *decisive*. However, option (2)—according substantive decisiveness to Samantha's will—still constitutes an insult to Samantha's agential capacities insofar as Amy treats Samantha's will as only substantively relevant when she should treat Samantha's will as having structural significance. Amy's justification for adhering to Samantha's preferences in option (2) would not be grounded in the fact that Samantha chose to participate herself; it would be grounded in the balance of her welfare interests. Amy would accordingly be making a determination on the balance of the risks of the study, against the level of Samantha's emotional investment in participating, along with the social injury that would befall her for being excluded from participation on the basis of her intellectual and/or developmental disabilities. Put differently, Amy would be treating Samantha as having moral status only to the extent that there are reasons to improve her experiences; any expressions of her agency are morally relevant to that extent only and have no independent moral significance.

We can thus see how this distinction between substantive and structural forcefulness is going to be important when we consider what it means to make decisions on behalf of another in a way that does not insult their agential capacities. One might argue that treating the wishes of those with impaired consent capacity as structurally forceful risks undermining their welfare interests to the extent that they endorse options that are worse for themselves. But this, of course, is just the test of whether individuals' decisions are treated as structurally decisive, and we allow them to be. Proper respect involves sometimes allowing competent individuals to make decisions contrary to their interests.

Likewise, due respect may mean that we are open to the possibility that treating the will of people with impaired consent capacity as structurally forceful (albeit non-decisively so) may undermine their welfare interests. They should be allowed to take risks and make sacrifices, if that is what they explicitly prefer. But, if respect for their agency would clearly and substantially undermine their interests, we may decide to prioritize their interests (whether this is a difference in kind or degree from how we treat autonomous individuals depends on whether there are cases in which an autonomous individual makes decisions that are so wildly contrary to their interests that they should be overridden).

So, Jerry and Samantha's cases illuminate the fact that insofar as a person has elements of valuable agential capacities and powers (albeit not fully formed or well integrated), these capacities can also be disrespected. The patients in the two cases exemplify a variety of different capacities and impairments: while they cannot make independent decisions regarding complex medical procedures, they do possess some constituent components of agency, which can be respected and supported. Second, one of the constituent components of their agency may be the capacity to express or indicate current preferences that are potentially at odds with their welfare interests. Third, these current preferences are not necessarily the result of capricious whims and urges; they could be tracking relatively stable values and commitments on the part of the patients (Jaworska 1999). Taken together, these features open up a space in which patients exhibit enough agency to be treated disrespectfully, even if they lack the autonomy necessary to be left fully in charge of their lives. It is at least possible that in ignoring the current preferences of such patients or in disregarding the components of their agential capacities, we end up treating them in an objectionable way.

Given this discussion, we suggest further questions for philosophical inquiry. Determining the appropriate normative force that the patient's wishes should have over the trustee's decisions is but one important consideration for respectful decisions on their behalf that requires further investigation. The trustee also needs to consider their level of certainty regarding the preferences of the patient, given the patient's own level of understanding of their situation. Moreover, the trustee must also gauge whether a specific utterance or gesture is in fact a communication of a preference. Regarding Samantha, Amy has good reason to believe both that Samantha is expressing her evaluative perspective and that her choice would not be different were Samantha able to discern the difference between therapeutic and clinical interventions. This information might be gleaned by discussing how Samantha would choose in cases where she could recognize that participation would not benefit her personally—such as blood donation or community service projects.[10] It is less clear from court documents whether Jerry could express his preferences in such a clear way.

Questions about interpretation and uncertainty over whether some behavior expresses communicative intent in cases such as Jerry's complicate the question of how to incorporate the patient's wishes and preferences into one's vicarious decision-making. These challenges are particularly pronounced in how we think about decision-making on behalf of people with profound cognitive impairment or with limited communication abilities. While it is beyond the scope of this chapter, we think that our shift in focus from taking measures required for respecting patient autonomy to taking measures to guard against insulting patients' distinctive evaluative perspective is an important one. It makes legible the question of whether we have moral reason to be open to the possibility that all people with intellectual and/or developmental disabilities, regardless of their cognitive impairment, retain to varying degrees some constituent components of agency and that many have a distinctive evaluative perspective from which to view the world. We believe that there are reasons of respect for the trustee to presume communicative intent, even if one cannot be assured that one is getting their interpretation right.

NOTES

1. This chapter starts with an assumption that even if people with intellectual and/or developmental disabilities are found to have impaired consent capacity for a particular decision, they still should be presumed to retain the capacity of self-determination more globally. There remains an important ethical question about whether someone who falls below the threshold should have a surrogate decision maker at all. We assume for this chapter that there is going to be some level of impaired consent capacity that falls sufficiently below the threshold of capacity that the appointment of a surrogate decision maker (either by the patients themselves or by a third party) is ethically permissible. Even if one rejects this assumption and contests the legitimacy of policies that appoint surrogate decision makers for those with intellectual and/or developmental disabilities at any level, there still remains the non-ideal ethical dilemma posed to those persons who are put, under the current system, in position to make decisions on behalf of such patients. Our chapter asks how such a trustee can make such decisions in a respectful manner.

2. Note that these genetic and congenital conditions are not synonymous with I/DDs. A person can have Cerebral palsy and still have consent capacity.

3. It should be noted that the question this chapter is concerned with is how to make respectful surrogate decisions on behalf of people with IDDs who actually lack consent capacity for a given decision. For those who do have capacity and are only perceived to have impaired capacity, the designated "trustee" may have other obligations—like advocate on behalf of the patient so that they can make their own decisions—or refuse to be their surrogate.

4. *Doe ex rel. Tarlow v. D.C.* (2007). This line suggests that the only way for a person's "true wishes" to be discerned is if the person was once fully autonomous decision maker.

5. "We agree with the District of Columbia that the 'best interests' standard, not the 'known wishes' standard-applies to medical decisions for intellectually disabled individuals who have always lacked the mental capacity to make those decisions for themselves" (*Doe ex rel. Tarlow v. D.C.* 2007).

6. Rather than talking about the sorts of conditions in which the desire could arise, some philosophers describe the conditions of scrutiny that the desires should be able to survive. See, for example, Brandt (1979), 113.

7. Throughout the chapter, we have distinguished between the patient's evaluative perspective enjoying instrumental verses intrinsic normative significance. Our view aligns with Groll's in that we believe there is an important difference in the kind of respect we accord another when we treat their will as structurally forceful: that is, as having intrinsic normative

significance in our decision making in comparison to the kind of respect we accord another when we treat their will as only substantively forceful (i.e., as only instrumentally valuable to our reasoning).

8. It should be noted that there is at least one other option available to Amy: (4) Refuse Proxy Decision-Making: out of respect for Samantha's will, she could refuse to act as Samantha's representative altogether and advocate that Samantha be allowed to make a decision about participation on her own behalf. This would likely lead to Samantha losing out on the opportunity to participate in the study, at least at present, though it could potentially lead to policy changes that would empower people like Samantha in future research. Consequently, choosing an option such as (4) may contradict Samantha's stated preferences to participate and yet may not constitute an insult to Samantha's agency. This is because Amy may refuse to act as Samantha's representative, not out of any suspicion as to Samantha's agential capacities but rather out of protest to the unjust conditions that are imposed on Samantha to require her to enlist a representative in order to allow her to participate in a research study that she finds meaningful and important. We say that option (4) *may* not constitute an insult to the agential capacities of Samantha because there is still room for such an insult. Insofar as Samantha expressly prefers that Amy just authorize the treatment and get on with it, while Amy thinks it would be better for Samantha if she were to refuse her role as surrogate, Amy may yet be making a disrespectful decision.

9. There are going to be situations where even the second sort of speech act could count as a request although it does not take the imperative form (e.g. a southern grandmother saying "it sure would be nice if one of my grandchildren would go collect the mail" or "we do not wear shoes in this house"). In such a context, these distinctions could collapse on each other, but they are important in other contexts. We thank Adam Cureton and Thomas Hill for supplying us with this sort of case.

10. Such an idealization would not bracket away Samantha's intellectual and/or developmental disability, it would merely consider Samantha's preferences to a cross-section of altruistic activities.

References

Brandt, Richard B. 1979. "A Theory of the Good and the Right". Prometheus Books.

Bérubé, Michael. 2009. "Equality, Freedom, And/Or Justice For All: A Response To Martha Nussbaum." Metaphilosophy, 40 (September): 352–365.

Cohen, Brenda, and R. B. Brandt. 1980. "A Theory of the Good and the Right." *The Philosophical Quarterly* 30, no. 120 (July): 271. doi:10.2307/2219262.

Doe ex rel. Tarlow v. D.C., 489 F.3d 376, 382 (D.C. Cir. 2007).

Dresser, Rebecca. 1995. "Dworkin on Dementia: Elegant Theory, Questionable Policy." The Hastings Center Report 25, no. 6 (November): 32. doi:10.2307/3527839.

Dresser, Rebecca. 1995. "Dworkin on Dementia: Elegant Theory, Questionable Policy." The Hastings Center Report, vol. 25, no. 6, (November): 32–38.

Dworkin, Ronald. 1993. *Life's Dominion: An Argument About Abortion and Euthanasia*. London: HarperCollins.

Groll, Daniel. 2012. "Paternalism, Respect, and the Will." Ethics 122, no. 4 (July): 692–720. doi:10.1086/666500.

Groll, Daniel. 2014. "Medical Paternalism—Part 1: Medical Paternalism—Part 1." *Philosophy Compass* 9, no. 3 (March): 186–193. doi:10.1111/phc3.12111.

Heslop, Pauline, Peter S. Blair, Peter Fleming, Matthew Hoghton, Anna Marriott, and Lesley Russ. 2014. "The Confidential Inquiry Into Premature Deaths of People With Intellectual Disabilities in the UK: A Population-Based Study." The Lancet 383, no. 9920 (March): 889–895. doi:10.1016/S0140-6736(13)62026-7.

Hornblum, A. M. 1997. "They Were Cheap and Available: Prisoners as Research Subjects in Twentieth Century America." BMJ 315, no. 7120 (November 29): 1437–1441. doi:10.1136/bmj.315.7120.1437.

Howard, Dana. 2017. "The Medical Surrogate as Fiduciary Agent." The Journal of Law, Medicine & Ethics 45, no. 3 (September): 402–420. doi:10.1177/1073110517737541.

Howard, Dana, and Sean Aas. 2018. "On Valuing Impairment." Philosophical Studies 175, no. 5 (May): 1113–1133. doi:10.1007/s11098-018-1074-y.

Iacono, Teresa. 2019. "An exploration of communication within active support for adults with high and low support needs." Journal of applied research in intellectual disabilities 32(1): 61.

Iacono, Teresa, Christine Bigby, Carolyn Unsworth, Jacinta Douglas, and Petya Fitzpatrick. 2014. "A Systematic Review of Hospital Experiences of People With Intellectual Disability." BMC Health Services Research 14, no. 1 (December): 505–513. doi:10.1186/s12913-014-0505-5.

Jaworska, Agnieszka. 1999. "Respecting the Margins of Agency: Alzheimer's Patients and the Capacity to Value." Philosophy and Public Affairs 28, no. 2 (April): 105–138. doi:10.1111/j.1088-4963.1999.00105.x.

Meyer-Lindenberg, Andreas, Carolyn B. Mervis, and Karen Faith Berman. 2006. "Neural Mechanisms in Williams Syndrome: A Unique Window to Genetic Influences on Cognition and Behaviour." Nature Reviews Neuroscience 7, no. 5 (May): 380–393. doi:10.1038/nrn1906.

Parfit, Derek. Reasons and Persons. Oxford University Press, 1984.

Parfit, Derek. Reasons and Persons. Oxford: Clarendon, 1992.

Perry, David M. 2018. "When Hospitals Mistreat Disabled Patients." Pacific Standard, June 29. Accessed April 9, 2019. https://psmag.com/social-justice/how-hospitals-mistreat-disabled-patients.

Shiffrin, Seana Valentine. 2000. "Paternalism, Unconscionability Doctrine, and Accommodation." Philosophy and Public Affairs 29, no. 3 (July): 205–250. doi:10.1111/j.1088-4963.2000.00205.x.

Shiffrin, Seana Valentine. 2004. "Autonomy, Beneficence, and the Demented." In Dworkin and His Critics: With Replies by Dworkin, edited by Ronald Dworkin and Justine Burley. Philosophers and Their Critics 11. Malden, MA: Blackwell.

Shope, Robert K. 1978. "The Conditional Fallacy in Contemporary Philosophy." The Journal of Philosophy 75, no. 8 (August): 397. doi:10.2307/2025564.

Silvers, Anita, and Leslie Pickering Francis. 2009. "Thinking About The Good: Reconfiguring Liberal Metaphysics (Or Not) For People With Cognitive Disabilities." Metaphilosophy 40, no. 3–4 (July): 475–498. doi:10.1111/j.1467-9973.2009.01602.x.

Singer, Peter. 2010. "Speciesism and Moral Status" in Cognitive Disability and its Challenge to Moral Philosophy, edited by Eva Feder Kittay and Licia Carlson. Wiley-Blackwell.

Strunk vs. Strunk. 1969. Court of Appeals of Kentucky, 445 S. W. 2d 145.

Wasserman, David, and Jeff McMahan. 2012. "Cognitive Surrogacy, Assisted Participation, and Moral Status." In Medicine and Social Justice: Essays on the Distribution of Health Care, edited by Rosamond Rhodes, Margaret Battin, and Anita Silvers. Medicine and Social Justice, 325–333. Oxford: Oxford University Press, 2012.

CHAPTER 31

EDUCATIONAL JUSTICE FOR STUDENTS WITH INTELLECTUAL DISABILITIES

LORELLA TERZI

INTRODUCTION

ALTHOUGH current legislation in almost all Western industrialized countries stipulates the equal entitlement to education for children and young people with intellectual disabilities, the specific meaning of such entitlement and its policy implications are highly debated. In practice, in all these countries children and young people with intellectual disabilities are among the most educationally disadvantaged. They experience deep inequality of access to schooling and, in most cases, they do not receive appropriate provision in terms of supports and services. Even when included on the school roll, many are still cognitively, emotionally, and practically excluded from learning opportunities (Rogers 2016). Identifying what educational justice might mean when considering the interests and needs of children with intellectual disabilities is therefore an important and urgent question, both theoretically and for practical implications.

The theoretical aspect of this question is, however, particularly complex given the variability of intellectual disabilities, which are broadly characterized by "significant limitations both in intellectual functioning and in adaptive behavior as expressed in conceptual, social and practical adaptive skills" (AAIDD 2018).[1] Children diagnosed as having intellectual disabilities, for example Down syndrome, or developmental delay, or autism, "encounter many obstacles in their lifetime because of limitations in their adaptive abilities" (Harris 2010, 56). They tend to develop at a different pace from other disabled and non-disabled peers, and their cognitive and communicative development depends on the severity of the impairment and the responsiveness of the environment. The extent to which these children make use of educational opportunities, and thus achieve valuable ways of functioning, varies also according to the availability of supports for each individual (Harris 2010). Moreover, much is still unknown about their potential for educational achievement, since children once deemed ineducable have, in recent years, proven to make significant progress given appropriate conditions (Wong 2010). Determining a just entitlement in education for these children requires therefore simultaneously addressing their atypical needs and strengths, while providing normative guidance on how to do so justly.

The notion of a just entitlement in education is broadly inscribed within liberal theories of justice in moral and political philosophy. Liberal perspectives on educational justice generally maintain that educational institutions should ensure that all have a fair share of educational goods and fair access to the benefits these yield, including socioeconomic advantages and more fulfilling and rewarding lives. Central to these perspectives is the principle of equal opportunity, understood "in the sense implying that no child's prospects for success in life are unfairly advanced over those of any other by the education he or she receives" (Deigh 2007, 593)[2]. This broad stipulation of the ideal is then differently specified in terms of different understandings of the fairness of the distribution and of the main purposes of education.[3] The latter are usually expressed in terms of educating children for equal citizenship (Anderson 1999; Gutmann 1987; Satz 2007), or in terms of equipping them to lead flourishing lives: that is, lives that go well for them overall (Brighouse 2006; Brighouse et al. 2018; White 2007).

Most of these formulations of educational justice are, however, challenged when considerations about the interests of children with disabilities, and intellectual disabilities in particular, are brought to the fore. Two main interrelated questions stand out as being of pressing concern. First is a question of distributive justice: how should opportunities for educational goods be distributed in order to respond to these children's interests? Although, on the one hand, the principle of equality of opportunity offers some initial guidance, its focus on equal prospects for success in life appears problematic in light of the characteristics of intellectual disabilities. On the other hand, a competing principle, namely the principle of adequacy and its related notions of thresholds of educational achievements, tends to rely on stringent criteria, some of which are insensitive to disabled children's real possibility of achieving the specified threshold (Ahlberg 2014; Terzi 2008, 2014, 2015).

A second, important challenge resides in determining whether a just educational provision for students with intellectual disabilities can be identified in relation to conceptions of equal citizenship, however broadly defined, or whether a more expansive and pluralistic educational aim, such as educating for flourishing, might best respond to their interests (Terzi 2008, 2014; Ahlberg 2014).[4] One question is whether the goal of equal citizenship is appropriate for students whose impairments might hinder any meaningful achievement of that aim; if not, the further question arises of how best to conceive of the educational goal of flourishing to include these students.

This chapter addresses these questions in light of the insights offered by a capability perspective on justice in education, based on Amartya Sen's capability approach

(Sen 1980, 1992, 1999, 2009). As I have argued elsewhere, adopting this approach provides a normative framework that is sensitive to the educational interests of students with disabilities (Terzi 2005, 2007, 2008, 2014). This chapter focuses specifically (and in much greater detail) on the case of children with intellectual disabilities.[5] It aims to show how the two questions above find a legitimate answer by adopting a principled framework for justice in education. In what follows, I articulate such a perspective to argue that a "threshold" approach, specified in terms of a threshold of capabilities for equal participation in society, is an appropriate principle for educational justice when equal participation is a condition for the well-being and the flourishing of the child, both as a child and future adult. This chapter also offers a rich and pluralistic account of citizenship, which, linked to a capability notion of well-being and flourishing, includes children with intellectual disabilities.

The first section of the chapter recapitulates my framework for educational justice in relation to the main concepts of the capability approach. The remaining two sections focus on providing answers to each of the two questions raised above, while expanding and deepening relevant aspects of the framework.

A Capability Approach to Justice in Education for Students with Disabilities

In developing the capability approach as a framework about well-being, freedom, and the justice of social and institutional arrangements, Amartya Sen (1980, 1992, 2009) and, albeit differently, Martha Nussbaum (2000, 2006, 2010) have drawn attention primarily to how well people can live with the resources they have.[6] According to the approach, the evaluation of well-being should be based on people's substantive opportunities (their capabilities) to choose, among different activities and states (functionings), those they have reason to value. People can choose among many different functionings, for example working as librarians, or becoming actors, or they can value engaging in political activism, or in sports, and so forth; the extent to which individuals have substantive opportunities to choose among different functionings, relative to their options, is a measure of their real freedoms and the well-being they can achieve. This provides the basis for the assessment of justice.

Three main concepts make the approach particularly suited to examining questions of justice for people with disabilities, and, as we shall see, questions of educational justice too: first is the evaluative space of relative advantage in terms of capabilities and functionings; second is a conception of well-being in terms of freedoms; and, third is the fundamental principle of each person as an end in herself, or the equal moral worth of each individual (Nussbaum 2006, 2010).[7] These concepts require some short elaboration, and I will start with the first.

Sen argues that the evaluation of people's capabilities is the relevant variable for considerations of advantage and therefore for assessing the justice of policy and institutional designs. He states, "A person's advantage in terms of opportunities is judged to be lower than that of another if she has less capability—less real opportunity—to achieve those things that she has reason to value." (Sen 2009, 231). Focusing on capability, Sen notes, importantly moves the comparative assessment of advantage from the means, such as resources and commodities, to the ends of good living (Sen 2009, 231).[8] Since justice is concerned with people's good living, any disadvantage resulting in lower levels of well-being should therefore be addressed. Moreover, focusing on capability captures a fundamental element for assessing advantage, namely people's different abilities to convert resources into valued functionings. These different "conversion factors" refer to individuals' physical and psychological constitutions, as well as the social, cultural, and physical environment they inhabit. As Sen reminds us, furthermore, conversion factors are particularly significant for evaluating the position of people with disabilities, whose use of resources might be affected by their impairment. The example of using a bicycle helps in illustrating these points. As Robeyns states

> An able-bodied person who was taught to ride a bicycle when he was a child has a high conversion factor enabling him to turn the bicycle into the ability to move around efficiently, whereas a person with a physical impairment or someone who never learnt to ride a bike has a very low conversion factor.   (Robeyns 2018, 45)

People's different conversion factors, therefore, together with their substantive opportunities, are essential elements for the evaluation of advantage. These concepts also provide a framework for reconsidering understandings of disability, and, as stated previously, the position of people with disabilities in relation to justice. More specifically, they support an interactional view of disability as resulting from the interaction of personal characteristics (impairments) with sociocultural and environmental conditions. Thus, impairments become disabilities, or limitations in functionings, when no alternative functioning can be achieved. This results in a limitation of substantive opportunities. A physical impairment, for example quadriplegia, might result in a disability if the only means of mobility are standard bicycles and no alternative mobility functionings can be achieved. Within a capability view, disability, unlike impairment, is therefore not only seen as inherently relational, but also as morally significant for considerations of justice, since it amounts to a deprivation of capability (Terzi 2005, 2008, 2010).

A second and important concept of the approach is the notion of well-being. Broadly speaking, most philosophical accounts of well-being are concerned with how well the life of a person is going, overall, for that person. The concept adopted in the capability approach is inscribed within an objective account of people's good life, since it is specified in terms of substantive opportunities for functionings and achieved functionings (Robeyns 2018). This relates to Sen's distinction between the freedom to achieve well-being and its actual achievement (Sen 2009, 282). A further element of well-being, moreover, consists in the exercise of agency in pursuit of valued personal goals.

Individual well-being, therefore, includes elements of opportunities both for freedom and for agency, and the related achievements (Sen 1980, 206).

Finally, the third important concept of the approach for considerations of disability resides in its notion of the equal moral worth of each person. Martha Nussbaum, in particular, insists on this moral principle in her specification of the approach. She provides a list of fundamental entitlements for good living, specified in ten Central Human Capabilities that governments should secure to all citizens (Nussbaum 2006, 70). According to Nussbaum, each of the capabilities identified as essential for the dignity of human life "should be pursued for each and every person, treating each as an end and none as a mere tool of the ends of others" (Nussbaum 2006, 70). Furthermore, in light of this principle, and in contrast to current liberal theories of justice entailing elements of reciprocity and mutual advantage, Nussbaum also cogently argues that people with disabilities, including intellectual disabilities, are owed equal respect and equal consideration, regardless of their ability to contribute to reciprocal advantage but uniquely in virtue of their humanity and dignity (Nussbaum 2009, 2010).[9]

This rich theoretical approach informs my perspective on educational justice for students with disabilities (Terzi 2007, 2008, 2014). Three points are worth considering. First, the assessment of advantage in terms of capability, as argued previously, entails both an understanding of learning disabilities and difficulties as inherently relational and as capability limitations. As noted about physical disabilities, learning disabilities and difficulties can also be identified as emerging from the interaction of individuals' personal features and schooling settings. A child with intellectual impairment, for instance an impairment in communicative functionings relating to forms of autism, might experience limitations in verbal and non-verbal language. The extent to which these limitations become disabilities depends on how the child interacts with the educational environment as well as the availability of alternative systems of communication and language developmental schemes, among other educational factors. This is important for understanding learning disabilities and difficulties in terms of limitations in opportunities, hence in capability, and consequently as morally significant for educational justice.

Second, it is important to highlight the role of education in developing and expanding capabilities, and therefore as essential to well-being and the enhancement of freedom. Formal schooling plays a crucial role in securing some fundamental functionings, for example literacy and numeracy, which are also foundational for the acquisition of more complex ones, such as reading literary texts or interpreting large sets of numerical data. These fundamental functionings are intrinsically valuable for living well and for exercising agency, as well as instrumentally necessary for accessing rewarding positions, thus ensuring good standards of living for the individual and for society. The development of these functionings, moreover, appears particularly important for children, since many functionings neglected in childhood are much more difficult to acquire in later life (Nussbaum 2000). In developing essential capabilities, the role of education is inherently linked to the achievement of well-being and the possibility of leading good lives.

Thirdly, although there are various and, at times, conflicting understandings of good living, it is widely recognized, philosophically and by the capability approach in particular, that significant components of living well include the possibility to participate on an equal standing in economic, cultural, social, and civic activities in one's dominant framework, while contextually pursuing one's valued ends (Anderson 1999). This notion of equal participation relates directly to the fundamental capability of "appearing in public without shame," which is at the core of Sen's account of justice (Sen 1992), as well as to Anderson's concept of democratic equality, which entails that citizens stand in relation of equality to one another (Anderson 1999).

In accordance with considerations of human variability and the equal moral worth of each person, both of which are central to the capability approach, equal participation does not require adherence to a predefined view. It can be seen instead as including the various ways in which individuals, free from limitations of capability inequality, can contribute to their framework. Economic productivity, for instance, can be diverse, from contributions through highly skilled jobs to less demanding but equally valuable activities. Similarly, cultural and social contributions allow for the significantly different ways in which citizens can engage in their environment. In short, the notion of equal participation in society is open to and includes the distinctive ways in which all people can contribute to their frameworks.

Consequently, in line with its role in expanding capabilities and contributing to well-being, education should aim at developing those functionings that form the enabling conditions for equal participation in one's dominant social frameworks. While being evidently and inescapably context dependent, such an education might well include foundational functionings such as literacy and numeracy, and forms of social and scientific understandings as well as important dispositions such as exercising effort and perseverance, and forms of reflection on means-ends relations (Terzi 2008). It might also require paying attention to the different ways in which children enjoy their childhood and therefore include forms of play and other activities that inherently enrich childhood.

An important consideration in relation to intellectual disability consists in determining whether this conception of equal participation requires forms of democratic deliberation, and therefore the development of deliberative functionings (Gutmann 1987). Although this point will be analyzed further on, it is perhaps worth mentioning here that participating as equals includes engagement in political democratic processes, without, however, stipulating it as an absolute requirement in terms of a civic threshold (more on this in the last section).

One further point is also worth addressing. It is widely acknowledged that Sen's approach is criticized by philosophers of disability for assuming that more opportunities (and more freedom) are always better. Several critics argue that this may not be the case; that "there can be too many as well as too few opportunities for choice, and that beyond some feasible and valued options with which to shape one's life and exercise meaningful agency, additional opportunities may have diminishing value."[10] This criticism, albeit important, does not seem sustained in relation to the view of education presented here. Recall that such an education entails the selection of those foundational and transformative functionings that will allow children to become participants in their dominant framework. This requires and legitimates focusing on specific functionings and related capabilities, rather than on all the possible functionings that educational institutions could develop, thus addressing the criticism at least in relation to education.

In light of the preceding discussion, the role of education is appropriately identified in the promotion of those functionings that are required for good living, expressed in terms of equal participation in dominant social frameworks, and whose unequal provision would create a significant disadvantage for individuals.

What, therefore, constitutes a just educational provision for all students, and in particular for students with intellectual disabilities? It seems reasonable to state that just educational institutions should provide equal, substantive opportunities (capabilities) for the development of those functionings that are necessary to participate in society as equals. This entails the projected achievement of a threshold level of functionings required for equal participation.[11] Since children with disabilities may experience limitations in functionings, and consequently limitations in their opportunities to be educated, they should receive additional resources that will ensure their functionings and, as far as reasonably possible, to the level necessary for their equal participation in society, as a matter of justice.[12]

A further, important consideration of justice relates to the principle of distribution beyond the threshold established for all, since further allocations of resources might well enhance the well-being of some and not of others, depending on the chosen principle. Here a recourse to a principle drawn from John Rawls's theory of justice (1971), and in particular his "Difference Principle" might be helpful. The Difference Principle broadly regulates permissible inequalities in income and wealth and stipulates that such inequalities are to be allowed only if they contribute to the benefits of the least advantaged members of society (Rawls 2001, 64). As I have suggested elsewhere, "applied to education, it seems plausible to argue that beyond the threshold level... those who can obtain the highest functionings in education should receive resources to that aim, provided that the benefits they gain from their education correspond to an equal long- term prospect of improvement and benefits for those least successful" (Terzi 2008, 163).

A principled framework of justice in education for students with disabilities consists therefore of two parts. The first stipulates that equal opportunities for fundamental educational functionings be distributed to all at the levels necessary for equal participation in society, including additional provision for children with learning disabilities. The second part states that resources should be distributed in ways that allow the higher achievement of some to benefit those achieving at a lower level (Terzi 2008, 163–164). These benefits are not limited to educational improvements but extend to all components of well-being.

While this framework does not constitute a complete theory of justice in education, it offers a legitimate answer to questions of justice for all children with disabilities. In order to be fully responsive to the interests of children with intellectual disabilities, however, two aspects of the framework necessitate more careful elaboration. These aspects correspond to the two initial questions concerning the appropriateness of, first, a threshold as a distributive principle for educational goods and, second, a conception of equal participation in society, albeit one inscribed in a notion of well-being, as the main purpose of education. I now turn to these questions.

Distributive Principles: Equality, Adequacy, and the Threshold of Capability Equality

The question of how best to distribute educational opportunities to meet the needs and expand the freedom of children with intellectual disabilities is usually inscribed within the assessment of principles of justice, and in particular two such principles: on the one hand, a principle of equality of opportunity, and on the other, a broad interpretation of the same in terms of "adequacy," whereby all should receive an adequate educational provision.[13] This section briefly considers one of the main understandings of the principle of equal opportunities in the current literature, with a view to highlighting some of its limitations in relation to the case of intellectual disabilities.[14] I then discuss how my perspective on a threshold for capability equality has a number of normative advantages over this view. First, on equality of opportunity.

Broadly speaking, the principle of equality of opportunity is "an ideal for the normative regulation of competitions that distribute valuable opportunities in society" (Jacobs 2016, 325). The case for equality of opportunity in education rests on the idea that competition for better careers and overall better life prospects should be fair. Since education is an important means to these ends, the distribution of educational opportunities should be fair as well. Although there are various interpretations of the ideal of equal educational opportunity (Jacobs 2016; Satz 2007), one of the most widely discussed draws from John Rawls' s principle of Fair Equality of Opportunity, as noted previously. Brighouse and Swift (2008) refer to such an understanding as the Meritocratic Conception, and define it as follows:

> An individual's prospects for educational achievement may be a function of that individual's talent and effort, but it should not be influenced by her social class background.   (Brighouse and Swift 2008, 447)

Although this meritocratic understanding might have immediate intuitive appeal since it is broadly based on an idea of merit and evokes considerations of desert, a closer examination reveals significant problems for education (Satz 2007, 629). First, there is a problem about notions of talent and effort, particularly as applied to children and within compulsory education. Brighouse and Swift acknowledge this point in observing that both talents and efforts are heavily influenced by the personal and cultural environment in which children are born and raised (Brighouse and Swift 2008). Furthermore, it is unclear whether the principle refers to some kind of "innate" talents and efforts or to developed ones. If the former, then it seems questionable to distribute resources on the basis of morally irrelevant factors such as innate abilities. If the latter, the distribution is still questionable, since talent is in itself dependent on the actual design of educational systems, whereby some abilities are developed over others, and also on prospective positions of office that are available for people to pursue (Scanlon 2018, 58).

A second problem concerns the fact that, in theory, the principle permits (albeit without requiring) significant inequalities both of distributions of resources and achievement, provided that these do not relate to social class (Brighouse and Swift 2008). As Brighouse and Swift note, the principle is consistent with concentrating resources on those with high levels of talent, which could then result in neglecting the position of those with lower levels of abilities, thus further disadvantaging them (Brighouse and Swift 2008). The principle is also consistent with concentrating resources on children with lower levels of abilities but with the possible consequence of limiting the achievement of those with higher levels, and, ultimately, potentially levelling down the overall level of achievement in society in the long term. These seem highly unappealing implications. In addition to that, the meritocratic principle is also silent on distributions across different levels of talent and effort (Ahlberg 2014), and therefore it precludes, in itself, considerations of different allocations of resources across levels of abilities as well (e.g., by prioritizing allocations for some children and establishing trade-offs). In short, the meritocratic principle remains overall normatively underspecified and does not seem to offer a response to our initial question concerning how to distribute educational goods justly for children with intellectual disabilities (Ahlberg, 2014; Satz, 2007).[15] In light of the foregoing discussion, it is perhaps worth considering other distributive ideals. And so now I turn my attention to the threshold level of capability equality, which is part of my principled framework.

I maintain that a threshold approach to capability equality, grounded in the principle of equal respect and consideration and the equal moral worth of each child, better responds to the interests of children with intellectual disabilities than other frameworks by establishing three important normative elements: a distributive principle aimed at the achievement of a high threshold of equality; a justification for additional resources for children with intellectual disabilities that avoids the problem of infinite demands of resources, and, finally, normative guidance on how to distribute resources beyond the threshold established for all. I now turn to consider these claims.

First, the threshold level. Recall here that a capability perspective on educational equality defines it in terms of equal and substantive opportunities to achieve levels of functionings that are necessary to participate in society as equals; this perspective also legitimates additional resources for children with intellectual disabilities. This already sets a high and demanding threshold, which, while requiring a substantive degree of equality, appears justified in light of the crucial role of education in expanding well-being and freedoms. It is also different from notions of sufficiency or adequacy in that it makes equality part of the idea of sufficiency (Nussbaum 2010), while withstanding the main critique leveled at notions of adequacy, namely that adequacy considers only some minimally required allocations of resources needed to achieve the stipulated outcome, and so permits significant inequalities (Satz 2007, 635). Furthermore, it is important to specify that what we are distributing are substantive opportunities, where opportunities are conceived in a broad sense to include educational resources, teachers' time and competence, and educational material and structures, whereas the established threshold level consists of projected achieved functionings (Terzi 2008).

Two critiques might be offered at this point. The first concerns the feasibility of concentrating on opportunities and projected achievements, rather than focusing uniquely on functionings. The question of whether to promote capabilities or functionings in relation to children, and children with intellectual disabilities in particular, is an ongoing debate and a few considerations are therefore in order. It is recognized that children in general, and some children with intellectual disabilities more specifically, do not have a fully developed ability to make autonomous choices, and therefore a limited paternalistic approach is needed to protect them. This is consistent with focusing on the promotion of functionings over capabilities. However, institutional considerations and broader insights about the nature of education support instead the promotion of capabilities for projected achieved functionings. As far as education is concerned, a focus on opportunities rather than achievements acknowledges the "value of students' evolving capacity for self-rule as childhood is left behind and access to the full right of adulthood draws near" (Callan 2016, 83). This point would seem to extend to many children with intellectual disabilities and may also apply to children with severe intellectual disabilities, provided that appropriate support is in place from educators who are able to enhance these children's agency. Furthermore, as Nussbaum argues, the principle of equal respect supports children's different levels and different pace of achievement and allows for different outcomes (Nussbaum 2010, 86). This seems to be consistent with a focus simultaneously on capabilities and on the projected achieved functionings of all students, including those with intellectual disabilities.

Another critique of the threshold of capability equality concerns the potentially very high cost associated with securing achievement for children with intellectual disabilities, and particularly those with severe disabilities. In response, on the one hand it may be worth re-stating the importance of each child's well-being and the high personal costs resulting from deep inequalities and exclusion. On the other hand, it is also worth noticing that existing legislation in the United States, for example the Individuals with Disabilities Education Act (IDEA, 1991), already acknowledges provision for children with intellectual disabilities that is both demanding and costly. IDEA ensures a "free and appropriate education" for these children in the "least restrictive environment," and it furthermore entails a highly personalized intervention to meet their needs. Thus, as Nussbaum states, the legislation, "if implemented well, will ensure that something like...equal concern has been shown, by the very fact of considering the child's educational needs individually, and designating a program to develop his or her human potential" (Nussbaum 2010, 85). Although this does not fully respond to the critique of excessive implementing costs for the threshold, it helps in defending measures that will support children with intellectual disabilities "so that they will have no education-related disadvantages as they prepare to enter society" (Nussbaum 2010, 85).

Finally, a further consideration in relation to the high cost associated with setting a threshold pertains to the possibility of stipulating an additional specification of the threshold, for example by adopting some versions of Pareto efficiency whereby additional distributions of resources to children with intellectual disabilities would be suspended when no further and significant improvement in their education can be promoted. This may also partially address the problem of ever-diminishing improvements (i.e., of continued allocation of resources to children below the threshold but with little prospect of reaching it). When improvements are overall minimal, and the cost is large and risks leveling down the potential achievement of other students, it may be permissible to stop the allocation. These are, however, difficult trade-offs, and may be best left to democratic deliberative processes, provided that equal representation from people with disabilities and their voices are consistently secured. This latter point leads to the next consideration about the threshold.

The second normative element provided by this threshold approach pertains to its justified response to the problem of "infinite demands". This problem arises, for instance, in relation to severe intellectual impairments, whereby some compensatory models would imply an infinite allocation of resources in order to equalize starting points, as compared to other individuals, thus ensuring fair chances over a lifetime. In setting a threshold level within educational capabilities and in specifying it at the level appropriate for functioning in society, we avoid the problem of infinite demand in two ways. 'First, the actual threshold sets a specific level of resources, which is the level required for individual's equal participation. Second, and more importantly, the demands of children with intellectual disabilities are considered within a framework of equality, which evaluates them in relation to the demands of other children. Thus, an infinite allocation of resources to a child with intellectual disabilities that would deplete others of resources necessary to achieve the specified threshold level would be contrary to the same principle upon which the distribution is based in the first instance' (Terzi 2008, 158). The problem of leveling down the overall level of education in society in the long term can be avoided by securing high levels of funding to education, thus not hindering the overall achievement of the threshold by all, and by ensuring a different distribution above the threshold. This leads to my final consideration.

The third and final normative element provided by my view relates to the distribution of resources beyond the threshold level established for all. Frameworks of adequacy are usually critiqued for lacking any concern about the distribution of resources beyond the level of adequacy adopted, thus allowing for significant inequalities. This principled framework for educational justice responds to this concern by stipulating that resources should be allocated by adopting a requirement based on Rawls's difference principle, as specified previously. This justifies the inequalities in distribution of resources beyond the threshold, while safeguarding the improvement in well-being for children with intellectual disabilities, thus withstanding the critique.

To sum-up: a principled framework for educational equality based on a threshold of capability equality provides some justified normative guidance on what might constitute a just educational provision for children with intellectual disabilities. Another major challenge, nonetheless, resides in determining what aims of education are more responsive to the specific characteristics of children with intellectual disabilities. The next section addresses this challenge.

Educational Aims: Equal Citizenship and Human Flourishing

As mentioned previously, the question of what aims of education are appropriately sensitive to the educational interest of children with intellectual disabilities focuses on the analysis of educational goals expressed in terms of democratic participation on the one hand, and in terms of flourishing, or leading a good life, on the other. Drawing from Ahlberg (2014) this section briefly analyzes some versions of the two perspectives, as well as some related critiques, and then argues in favor of the capability equality entitlement.

Perspectives on democratic education generally defend the view that education should develop those capacities that are required for full participation in a democratic society. This view reflects the liberal concern that governments should remain neutral on substantive conceptions of the good, and therefore compulsory education should prepare children for responsible citizenship based on broadly shared values and positions. Beyond this common baseline, however, there are various interpretations of what skills, knowledge, and functionings are required for democratic participation, and while some perspectives defend stringent requirements, other views are broader and more inclusive. This has obvious and immediate implications for the inclusion of children with intellectual disabilities within the scope of education for democratic citizenship, as discussed previously (Ahlberg 2014).

Among the proponents of these views, Amy Gutmann, for example, argues for a democratic standard threshold stipulating that education should equip children with the ability to participate in the democratic process (Gutmann 1987, 136).[16] She maintains that schooling should provide an adequate civic education, which primarily fosters skills and virtues of deliberative citizenship. In relation to students with disabilities, Gutmann advocates the need for a broad social intervention to achieve these goals and acknowledges that some American laws already incorporate a similar position when mandating a "free and appropriate education" for all.[17] This enacts her normative principle. While this stipulation is helpful since it includes children with disabilities in the democratic standard, it nevertheless leaves open the question of adjudicating whether this standard is relevant, at least in relation to children with severe intellectual disabilities (more on this later).

Other conceptions of democratic education, such as the position advanced by Satz (2007) face similar problems (Ahlberg 2014). Satz defends a democratic adequacy threshold in education that "requires that everyone with the potential have access to the skills needed for college" (Satz 2007, 638). Although Satz acknowledges the need to provide different avenues for those lacking this potential—and although some children with intellectual disabilities, given appropriate conditions, will certainly develop the skills required by her criterion—for many others (e.g., children with severe and multiple impairments), this may not be possible. As Ahlberg aptly notes, therefore, democratic educational aims generally do not seem sensitive to the case of children with severe impairments (Ahlberg 2014), and I should add, do not provide the required normative guidance on educational justice for *all* students with intellectual disabilities.

Perspectives based on conceptions of flourishing, according to Ahlberg, provide a more promising aim (Ahlberg 2014). Although, as for democratic education, there are various conceptions of human flourishing and different positions on how education can promote it, most views include forms of social, cultural, and economic participation as important for well-being and therefore maintain that education should promote related capacities and skills. Brighouse and colleagues, for example, provide a view of education aimed at developing a range of capacities considered foundational to flourishing (Brighouse at al. 2018, 20). These refer to the capacity for personal autonomy, economic productivity, democratic competence, and healthy personal relationships, as well as the capacity to treat others as equals, and the capacity for personal fulfilment (Brighouse et al. 2018, 23).[18] Ahlberg (2014) maintains that an expansive aim such as "creating the conditions for children's flourishing" constitutes a more suitable goal for the education of children with intellectual disabilities than views based on the goal of citizenship. Although it is easy to agree on this point, I maintain that in order to do so, such a goal needs to be more specific about the ways in which the well-being of these children is secured. After all, forms of economic productivity, democratic competence, and autonomous agency as elements of well-being seem to overlap significantly with the requirements of democratic accounts, albeit without the stipulation of threshold levels.

I argue that a capability equality framework in education goes some way in addressing the points raised above by incorporating important elements of democratic education within a view of wellbeing and flourishing clearly articulated (at least in principle). Recall that a fundamental educational entitlement stipulates that we owe to each child, including children with disabilities, equal substantive opportunities to achieve the educational functionings necessary to participate in society as equals. Some further considerations, however, are needed about the specified aim of equal participation in society, as well as about the expansion of children's capabilities and therefore of their well-being. I start by analyzing the first consideration.

As outlined in previous sections, my conception of equal participation in society includes the complex and multiple ways in which individuals interact within their social frameworks without requiring people to meet productivity standards or any related standard for mutual advantage. Rather, in accord with the equal moral worth of each individual, and with the view that "human beings are vulnerable temporal creatures, both capable and needy...and in need of a rich plurality of life activities" (Nussbaum 2010, 221), equal participation in society includes the different ways in which different people engage in their frameworks. Thus, many people with intellectual disabilities can meaningfully participate socially, economically, and relationally and are also able to perform political and civic duties, provided they have appropriate supports. People with severe and profound intellectual disabilities may participate in more personal and atypical ways, such as in affective and social interactions and expressions of enjoyment of various activities. On this view, education should promote those functionings that enable equal participation.

Two main questions, however, remain open to debate. The first concerns the role of civic engagement and preparation for civic duties, such as voting and jury service, as part of such an education, while the second pertains to the agency of children with intellectual disabilities. Let us analyze these more closely. As mentioned earlier, the capability equality threshold, although recognizing the importance of developing deliberative functionings, does not make it a necessary requirement for equal participation in society. Rather, it supports the view that while such functionings can and should be developed in all children who have the potential to achieve them, for other children this may not be appropriate or meaningful. The interests of children with severe intellectual disabilities, for instance, may be better fulfilled through the development of forms of expressions of personal preferences, as well as forms of interactions with peers and teachers. In supporting the development of these functionings for children with intellectual disabilities, education can also develop some forms of their autonomous agency. The latter can, in turn, lead to their future political representation via a surrogate, a position recently argued for by Nussbaum (2010). As Nussbaum notices, "the kind of sociability that is fully human includes symmetrical relations...but also relations of extreme asymmetry; we insist that non-symmetrical relations can still contain reciprocity and truly human functioning" (Nussbaum 2006, 160). Nussbaum further maintains that forms of surrogacy and guardianship are required for recognizing full citizenship status for individuals with intellectual disabilities.

Although the discussion of these important and delicate matters requires more careful elaboration than space permits here, the relationship established by many severely intellectually disabled children with their teachers, appropriately supported and monitored, may lead to ways in which the teacher understands and helps in the enactment of the preferences expressed by these children, thus broadening their agency, too. In other words, as Vorhaus argues, in treating children with profound intellectual disabilities as if they have the potential of agency, "We, and they, are liable to make more effort than otherwise to develop their capacities" (Vorhaus 2017, 74). This may constitute the basis for further relationships of surrogacy via a carer or a guardian in adulthood and their enactment of the civic duties of voting and jury service.

More careful analysis, however, is needed about this point, in particular about the questions of paternalism and possible substitution of agency by the surrogate.[19] A related consideration concerns the importance of developing functionings of democratic agency not uniquely or primarily, but as part of a broader development of functionings that include play, imagination, self-respect and enjoyment, all essential elements of childhood and of human well-being more broadly.

On the basis of these considerations, therefore, by adopting a threshold level of equal participation in society, my approach does not seem to preclude appropriate considerations for the educational interests of children with intellectual disabilities. This leads to our final point about providing the conditions for flourishing.

The fundamental educational entitlement I suggest is inscribed within a specific and rich view of well-being, assessed in the space of capabilities and functionings. Recall here that Sen insists on the importance of assessing social inequalities and public policy in the space of well-being (Sen 1992, 72). However, he also maintains that "the person's actual use of her well-being freedom" will allow well-being agency to be pursued. Thus, well-being freedom provides the conditions for effective freedom. An education that provides individuals with the conditions for their equal participation in society also provides the conditions for the possibility of exercising agency—and therefore with wide opportunities for freedom. Forms of agency and autonomous choice are all part of the functionings achieved by many people with intellectual disabilities, and therefore an education that fosters the achievement of these functionings provides them with the conditions for the expansion of their actual freedom (Terzi 2008). Beyond this normative point, it is also worth noticing that this conception of education aimed at creating the conditions for children's flourishing, both as children and the future adults they will be, is open to the different ways in which children with intellectual disabilities may flourish. While for some of these children the right conditions for flourishing may involve attending regular schools and achieving high levels in a broad range of cognitive and non-cognitive functionings, for other children they may entail being educated in more specialized environments and develop functionings of a relational nature or personal expression for the enjoyment of specific activities.

To conclude, this chapter has argued that the educational interests of children with intellectual disabilities find appropriate consideration within a fundamental educational entitlement specified by a threshold of capability equality for equal participation in society. On the bases of the arguments explored, such an entitlement provides the conditions for the expansion of the freedom of children with disabilities, and it is sensitive to the distinctive ways in which children with intellectual disabilities may flourish. Undoubtedly, however, a great deal remains to be done, both theoretically and more practically, in order fully to acknowledge the equal moral worth of children with intellectual disabilities in education and in society.

Acknowledgments

I am extremely grateful to the editors of this volume for their invaluable suggestions and kind support.

Notes

1. I have adopted the current definition provided by the American Association of Intellectual and Developmental Disability, 2018. Formerly defined in terms of "mental retardation," intellectual disabilities are also defined as learning disabilities. See, for example, Harris (2010, 58–59). Intellectual disabilities are specified in terms of the severity of impairment, including profound, severe, moderate, or mild. This distinction is usually correlated to some measurement of IQ, which is, however, a contested notion. Although some studies focus on the specific case of those with profound impairment, here we address the question of intellectual disabilities broadly considered.

2. This definition relates to the notion of equal protection under the law in the United States, but it is also widely used in the philosophical literature on educational justice.

3. Adequacy, equality, or some kind of priority are different specifications (Brighouse and Swift 2008).

4. These insights are drawn from Ahlberg (2014), who provides an interesting account of the two questions identified and highlights important points for the discussion.

5. Although my analysis so far has focused on disability in general, thus including intellectual disabilities, the latter case requires some further articulation of said approach.

6. This section draws on my extensive publications on the capability approach and justice for people with disabilities. These are referenced in detail throughout the chapter. The core concepts of the approach—capability, functionings, freedom and well-being—are endorsed by both scholars. Nussbaum provides a list of central capabilities that constitute the bases of a life well lived. These include "Life," "Bodily Health," "Bodily Integrity," "Senses, Imagination and Thought," "Emotions," "Practical Reason," "Affiliation," "Other Species," "Play," and "Control Over One's Environment" (Nussbaum 2000, 78-9-80).

7. These points have been extensively addressed in Terzi (2005, 2008, 2009 and 2014).

8. This moves beyond theories of justice based on assessing people's holdings of resources, such as John Rawls's primary goods (1971) or Ronald Dworkin's theory (2000).

9. Nussbaum refers mainly to John Rawls's theory and its requirement of reciprocal advantage and cooperation over a lifetime. This critique applies however to all theories adopting the idea of a social contract (contractarianism).

10. I am grateful to David Wasserman for raising this point (personal communication).

11. This view draws on Nussbaum's position, as outlined before. However, my framework is significantly more limited in scope and concerns only educational aspects.

12. Section 3 'Distributive Principles: Equality, Adequacy and the Threshold of Capability Equality' addresses the problem of justifying the threshold in relation to marginal improvements.

13. The principle of adequacy as a component of a theory of justice in education has recently been at the center of philosophical and policy debates, particularly in the United States. See Deigh (2007).

14. This section of my discussion draws from Ahlberg (2014).

15. It may be worth noting that the meritocratic understanding, although drawing from Rawlsian equality of opportunity, does not include considerations of the difference principle. Furthermore, it is not intended to address demands of justice for students with disabilities. See Ahlberg (2014, 168). Some scholars have suggested supplementing the meritocratic principle in order to include students with intellectual disabilities. Ahlberg argues that one such addition could consist in prioritizing the educational interests of the least advantaged (Ahlberg 2014).

16. Gutmann's perspective has influenced my threshold, alongside some of Anderson's views, as we shall see later.
17. See the discussion later on in this section and also Gutmann (1987, 156–157).
18. This brief account of Brighouse et al.'s position is not exhaustive of their nuanced view but aims at highlighting how the interests of children with intellectual disabilities are difficult to take account of within existing positions.
19. See Wasserman and McMahan (2012).

REFERENCES

Ahlberg, J. 2014. "Educational Justice for Students with Cognitive Disabilities." *Social Philosophy & Policy* 31, no. 1 (Fall): 150–175.

American Association of Intellectual and Developmental Disabilities (AAIDD). 2018. http://www.aaidd.org.

Anderson, E. 1999. "What Is the Point of Equality?" *Ethics* 109, no. 2: 287–337.

Brighouse, H. 2006. *On Education*. London and New York: Routledge.

Brighouse, H., Ladd, H., Loeb, S., and Swift, A. 2018. *Educational Goods: Values, Evidence, and Decision-Making*. Chicago and London: University of Chicago Press.

Brighouse, H. and Swift, A. 2008. "Putting Educational Equality in Its Place." *Education Policy and Finance* 4: 444–466.

Callan, E. 2016. "Democracy, Equal Citizenship, and Education." *Theory and Research in Education* 14, no. 1: 77–90.

Deigh, J. 2007. "Introduction. Symposium on Education and Equality." *Ethics* 117, no. 4 (July): 593–594.

Dworkin, R. 2000. *Sovereign Virtue: The Theory and Practice of Equality*. Cambridge, MA: Harvard University Press.

Gutmann, A. 1987. *Democratic Education*. Princeton, NJ: Princeton University Press.

Harris, J. C. 2010. "Developmental Perspectives on the Emergence of Moral Personhood." In *Cognitive Disability and Its Challenge to Moral Philosophy*, edited by E. Kittay and L. Carlson, 55–73. Malden, MA, and Oxford, UK: Wiley-Blackwell, 1987.

Jacobs, L. A. 2016. "Dealing Fairly with Winners and Losers in School: Reframing How to Think of Equality of Educational Opportunity 50 Years after the Coleman Report." *Theory and Research in Education* 14, no. 3: 313–332.

Nussbaum, M. 2000. *Women and Human Development: The Capabilities Approach*. Cambridge, MA: Cambridge University Press.

Nussbaum, M. 2006. *Frontiers of Justice*. Cambridge, MA: Cambridge University Press.

Nussbaum, M. "Human Dignity and Political Entitlements." In *Human Dignity and Bioethics: Essays Commissioned by the President's Council on Bioethics*, edited by Pellegrino, M. D., Edmund, D., Schulman, A., Merrill T. W. 351–379. Notre Dame, IN: Notre Dame Press, 2009.

Nussbaum, M. "The Capabilities of People with Cognitive Disabilities." In *Cognitive Disability and Its Challenge to Moral Philosophy*, edited by E. Kittay and L. Carlson, 74–95. Oxford: Wiley-Blackwell. 2010.

Rawls, J. 1971. *A Theory of Justice*. Cambridge, MA: Harvard University Press.

Rawls, J. 2001. *Justice as Fairness. A Restatement*. Cambridge, MA and London, UK: Harvard University Press.

Robeyns, I. 2018. *Wellbeing, Freedom and Social Justice. The Capability Approach Re-Examined*. Cambridge, UK: Open Book Publishers.

Rogers, C. 2016. *Intellectual Disabilities and Being Human: A Care Ethics Model*. Oxford and New York: Routledge.

Satz, D. 2007. "Equality, Adequacy, and Education for Citizenship." *Ethics* 117, no. 4 (July): 623–648.

Scanlon, T. M. 2018. *Why Does Inequality Matter?* Oxford: Oxford University Press.

Sen, A. 1980. *Equality of What? The Tanner Lectures on Human Values*. Salt Lake City: University of Utah Press.

Sen, A. 1992. *Inequality Re-Examined*. Oxford: Clarendon.

Sen, A. 1999. *Development as Freedom*. Oxford: Oxford University Press.

Sen, A. 2009. *The Idea of Justice*. London: Allen Lane.

Terzi, L. 2005. "A Capability Perspective on Impairment, Disability and Special Educational Needs: Towards Social Justice in Education." *Theory and Research in Education*, no. 3: 197–223.

Terzi, L. 2007. "Capability and Educational Equality." *Journal of Philosophy of Education* 41, no. 4: 757–773.

Terzi, L. 2008. *Justice and Equality in Education: A Capability Perspective on Disability and Special Educational Needs*. London and New York: Continuum.

Terzi, L. "Vagaries of the Natural Lottery? Human Diversity, Disability and Justice." In *Disability and Disadvantage*, edited by K. Brownlee and A. Cureton, 88–111. Oxford: Oxford University Press, 2009.

Terzi, L. "What Metric for Justice for Disabled People? Capability and Disability." In *Measuring Justice: Primary Goods Versus Capabilities*, edited by H. Brighouse and I. Robeyns, 150–173. Cambridge, UK: Cambridge University Press, 2010.

Terzi, L. 2014. "Reframing Inclusive Education: Educational Equality as Capability Equality." *Cambridge Journal of Education* 44, no. 4 (December): 479–493.

Terzi, L. "Cognitive Disabilities, Capability and Citizenship". In *Civil Disabilities. Citizenship, Membership, and Belonging. Philadelphia*, edited by N. Hirschmann and B. Linker, 186–203. Philadelphia: University of Pennsylvania Press, 2015.

US Senate. 1991. *The Individuals with Disabilities Education Act*, (IDEA) Pub Law 101- 476. US Senate.

Vorhaus, J. 2017. "Sharing in a Common Life: People with Profound and Multiple Learning Difficulties." *Res Publica* 23, no. 1: 61–79.

Wasserman, D., and J. McMahan. "Cognitive Surrogacy, Assisted Participation, and Moral Status". In *Medicine and Social Justice: Essays on the Distribution of Health Care*, edited by R. Rhodes, M. Battin, and A. Silvers, 325–334. Oxford: Oxford Scholarship, 2012.

White, J. 2007. *What schools are for and why*. Philosophy of Education Society of Great Britain IMPACT pamphlet No. 14.

Wong, S. "Duties of Justice to Citizens with Cognitive Disabilities". In *Cognitive Disability and Its Challenge to Moral Philosophy*, edited by E. Kittay and L. Carlson, 127–146. Malden, MA and Oxford, UK: Wiley-Blackwell, 2010.

PART EIGHT

TECHNOLOGY AND ENHANCEMENT

CHAPTER 32

A SYMMETRICAL VIEW OF DISABILITY AND ENHANCEMENT

STEPHEN M. CAMPBELL
AND DAVID WASSERMAN

DISABILITY and enhancement are commonly taken be in opposition in at least two respects.[1] First, they are thought to be *opposing concepts* that represent different ends of the same bipolar scale. To become disabled in some respect is to move away from those who are enhanced in that same respect; to become enhanced is to move away from the corresponding state of disability. Second, disability and enhancement are widely thought to call for *opposing attitudes*. Enthusiasm about the prospect of human enhancement is assumed to go hand in hand with disappointment or dread about the prevalence of disability in the world. Likewise, those who are appreciative and welcoming of the presence of disability in our world will likely be leery of the drive to develop enhancement technologies. In line with this idea, there has been some level of principled opposition between disability studies scholars and enhancement enthusiasts.

Our goal in this essay is to explore whether there is a viable way of seeing disability and enhancement as opposed in the first respect. By and large, we will assess different accounts of enhancement and disability by the following two criteria: (1) how well they capture our ordinary judgments about and ascriptions of disability and enhancement, and (2) the positive or negative consequences that might result from adopting these accounts. Based on these criteria, we ultimately conclude that a typical-functioning account is the most promising symmetrical understanding of disability and enhancement. This is not to say that we can or should exclusively think of disability and enhancement in this way. We expect that the terms "disability and "enhancement" are polysemic, having different but closely related senses or meaning in different contexts and for different purposes.[2] But since people commonly treat disability and enhancement as opposing concepts, it is worthwhile to carefully examine the best way to interpret this opposition. Examining the issue of how to understand disability and enhancement as symmetrical will set the stage for exploring whether these concepts call for opposing attitudes.

Narrowing the Search

How might we view disability and enhancement as different ends of the same spectrum? We begin our search for viable candidates by drawing upon Gyngell and Selgelid (2016) that helpfully catalogues the following accounts of enhancement:[3]

- *Non-Therapeutic Account*: enhancement = beneficial alteration to functioning that does not treat disease[4]
- *Beyond-Typical-Functioning Account*: enhancement = alteration that takes an individual's functioning beyond what is typical for the individual's species
- *Beyond-Maximal-Functioning Account*: enhancement = alteration that takes an individual's functioning beyond what is naturally possible for the individual's species
- *Welfarist Account*: enhancement = alteration to one's mental or bodily condition that improves well-being
- *Increased-Functioning Account*: enhancement = alteration that increases some type of functioning

The first thing to notice is that these are accounts of enhancing processes. This raises an important issue: we can distinguish between undergoing an enhancing/disabling *process* and having a *condition* that constitutes an enhancement/disability, and presumably one of these must be defined in terms of the other. Shall we take the former to be the fundamental notion and understand an enhancement/disability to be *a condition resulting from an enhancing/disabling process*? Or shall we take the latter as primary and define an enhancing/disabling process as *a process that causes a person to have an enhancement/ disability*? We favor this second approach. Many people are born disabled, and it seems a stretch of language (if not also of sensible metaphysics) to insist that they underwent a disabling process at birth or conception. At the same time, it would clearly fly in the face of our linguistic practices to insist that such people are not disabled. Moreover, we need not know anything about the processes involved to feel comfortable regarding a birth "atypicality" as a disability. Even if we were to discover the process, we would probably deem that process disabling precisely because of the condition it produced. Likewise, if in the future some person is genetically engineered to have superhuman strength or memory, it would be natural to describe her as enhanced in that respect even if she never existed in an un-enhanced state. For these reasons, we think it is best to give primacy to the condition concepts.[5]

This choice helps to limit our search for viable candidates. The Non-Therapeutic and Increased-Functioning accounts of enhancement are more naturally suited as process concepts since they are backward looking, making essential reference to one's pre-enhancement state. The former refers to one's previous (non-disease) state; the latter refers to one's earlier state of lower functioning.[6] The Beyond-Maximal-Functioning account of enhancement would need to be matched with a corresponding Below-Minimal-Functioning account of disability. While these accounts could be reinterpreted as condition concepts, they are uninteresting candidates in our view, in part because their applicability is so limited. Consider that on a Below-Minimal-Functioning understanding of disability, a process would only count as disabling in some respect if it is not naturally possible for a human to have lower functioning. Hence, on this view it would be impossible to have a visual disability since complete blindness is a natural possibility. We also think that these views attach unwarranted significance to whatever happens to be the naturally obtainable maximums and minimums for a given capacity in a species.

This leaves us with two potentially promising candidates: welfarist accounts and typical-functioning accounts. In the remainder of this paper, we will explore the prospects of these two ways of analyzing disability and enhancement.

Before proceeding, two qualifications about our discussion. First, we will focus on *individual* enhancements in two senses: we are not concerned with alterations that might improve the species, or a society, without modifying individuals, and we are only concerned with modifications that are at least in part "internal" improvements in a person. This leads us to the second qualification. In attempting to capture and refine the commonsense opposition between disability and enhancement, we will use "disability" to refer to a psychological or physical attribute of the individual. In doing so, we are hardly suggesting that this is the way "disability" should be generally understood; we are merely recognizing that the opposition we are examining is between individual attributes that count as disabilities and enhancements. Far from ignoring the role of the physical and social environment, we will be insisting that a variety of contextual variables determine whether an attribute counts as a disability, an enhancement, neither, or both. At the same time, we are not employing the sense of "disability" used in interactive and social models. If "disability" is understood as a kind of interaction between an individual attribute and a context, or as the exclusionary features of that context, it would not make sense to claim, as we do, that an attribute could be a disability in some contexts but not others. Under an interactive or social model, the individual attribute would never be the disability, but at most an aspect or component of it.

THE WELFARIST ACCOUNT

One way to achieve symmetry is to "go normative" with both concepts and view them as representing corresponding types of benefit and harm. Drawing upon Guy Kahane and Julian Savulescu's defense of a welfarist account of disability (2009; see also Savulescu, Sandberg, and Kahane 2011), we could understand enhancement and disability in the following way.

Welfarist Account

- Enhancement = a stable physical or psychological condition that positively impacts one's level of well-being
- Disability = a stable physical or psychological condition that negatively impacts one's level of well-being

On this account, the phrase "positively/negatively impacts one's level of well-being" is to be understood counterfactually. It effectively means: had the condition in question not been present, the person's well-being would have been lower or higher (2009, 23–24).

The Welfarist Account provides a coherent and symmetrical way of understanding disability and enhancement, and it accommodates the widespread tendency of associating "enhancement" with something positive and "disability" with something negative. Kahane and Savulescu are well aware that the Welfarist Account of disability deviates from our ordinary understanding of what disability is. In fact, a key part of their defense of this revisionist concept rests on a critique of our everyday concept of disability, which they contend is a "thick" normative concept—that is, a concept with both descriptive and normative elements. As they see it, on the ordinary understanding, disability is a stable physical or psychological condition that leads to a lack of or deficiency in some motor, sensory, or cognitive ability that most people possess (the descriptive element) *and* that is disadvantageous or a misfortune (the normative element). The problem, they claim, is that these two elements are not meaningfully related: there is no essential link between having a deficiency in functioning and being disadvantaged. The remedy to the problem is to revise our ordinary concept. Kahane and Savulescu think there is a danger in trying to revise this partly normative notion to be entirely descriptive. Better, they think, to fully embrace the normative dimension by understanding disability in terms of diminished well-being (2009, 17–20).

While we agree with Kahane and Savulescu that there is no essential link between diminished functioning and disadvantage, we believe there are good reasons to reject the Welfarist Account of disability. Since our task is to locate a viable symmetrical understanding of disability and enhancement, our rejection of the Welfarist Account of disability provides grounds for dismissing the corresponding welfarist view of enhancement.

First, it is by no means obvious that the dominant everyday concept of disability is partly normative, as opposed to being a descriptive concept of a family of conditions that happens to be highly stigmatized and widely believed to be harmful to people.[7] A common refrain among many disability advocates and disability studies scholars is that being disabled need not be a bad thing, and it seems unlikely that these individuals are all guilty of conceptual or semantic confusion, or that they are actively but covertly trying to revise our linguistic practices. If our ordinary concept of disability is not partly normative, it is difficult to see the Welfarist Account of disability as a revision of our preexisting concept.

However, setting that matter aside, suppose that our ordinary concept of disability is partly normative and is also a defective concept in the way that Kahane and Savulescu suggest. If we wish to revise this concept, shall we try to conceive of disability in purely descriptive terms or purely normative terms? Kahane and Savulescu think it can be dangerous to try to descriptivize a partly normative concept. They worry that if people attempt to understand "disability" in purely descriptive terms, the term may continue to carry pernicious normative associations for many people, even if they officially disavow those normative implications. We grant that this is a reasonable worry, though it would at least mark an improvement over the status quo. That is, it would be an advance if more people came to appreciate that conditions that we currently label "disabilities" need not be bad for a person and if all people at least paid lip service to the fact that the relationship between impairment and disadvantage is a contingent one.

We think the greater danger lies with the other strategy: attempting to normativize the term "disability." Currently, if you ask people on the street to name some disabilities, they will have no trouble providing a list of paradigmatic disabilities—blindness, Down syndrome, autism, paraplegia, dwarfism, and so on. If anything is well established in our discourse and practice surrounding disability, it is that conditions like these qualify as disabilities.[8] It is important to ask which of the following is stronger and more likely to be resistant to change: our tendency to think of conditions like blindness, autism, paraplegia, etc. as disabilities, or our tendency to see those conditions as bad for a person? We submit that the former tendency is stronger, even in an ableist society. The danger of trying to normativize "disability" in the way that Kahane and Savulescu suggest is that it will likely have the effect of exacerbating the already widespread assumption that certain conditions are harmful to those who have them. For instance, if the Welfarist Account took hold, we expect that many ordinary folk would continue to view Down syndrome as a disability but would also begin to think that, *by definition*, it is an unfortunate or harmful condition. This is a morally significant risk since the assumption that disability is harmful has real and often detrimental effects on the lives of disabled people—in interpersonal interactions, reproductive decision making, the allocation of healthcare funding, etc.[9] So, even if our ordinary concept of disability were partly normative (though we have our doubts), revising disability in purely normative terms seems to involve greater moral risk than revising in a more descriptive direction.

Our other main concern about the Welfarist Account is that it is too revisionist in various respects. First, it deviates rather drastically from our ordinary ascriptions of disability. The concept of a stable and harmful physical or psychological condition casts a wide net. Consider some physical or psychological traits that will sometimes count as disabilities on this approach: having a weak will, being excessively stubborn, being reckless, lacking confidence, being socially awkward, being a jerk, being excessively compassionate, having an awkward sense of humor, having deeply unpopular convictions, having an appearance that others regard as ugly or unattractive, being bald, having a disconcerting face tattoo, being un-athletic, etc.[10] None of these conditions are things that we would ordinarily consider disabilities, even if they have an adverse effect on people's well-being under many circumstances. So, the Welfarist Account overgenerates.

It also undergenerates insofar as it implies that some instances of blindness, paraplegia, Down syndrome, etc. (currently regarded as paradigmatic examples of disabilities) are not disabilities when they are not harmful to the individuals who have them. At best, it can be said that these conditions qualify as harmful stable conditions—and hence disabilities—for certain individuals in certain social contexts.[11] Thus, the Welfarist Account would require a radical departure from our current attributions of disability.

A second respect in which this account seems too revisionist is that it takes the *ability* out of "disability." On the Welfarist Account, disability bears no essential connection to the concepts of ability, capacity, or functioning. Having a socially disapproved face tattoo will count as a disability inasmuch as it is a stable physical condition that reduces your well-being—even if it does not limit or reduce your ability to function in any obvious sense. To be clear, we have no objection to devoting attention to the concept of a stable and harmful physical or psychological condition. We just question the value of adopting it as a revisionist analysis of disability.

A final worry about the revisionist nature of this account is that, as Kahane and Savulescu point out, it makes disability a ubiquitous condition: "It's a consequence of our account of disability that... all of us can be said to suffer from disabilities [in the welfarist sense]—conditions inherent to our nature which reduce our well-being and make it more difficult to realize a good life" (2009, 28). One potential advantage of this more inclusive approach is that it might lessen the stigmatization of disability (since we would all qualify as disabled) and contribute to greater support for those who are currently judged to be disabled (under a less inclusive understanding of the concept). But the inclusivity of Kahane and Savulescu's definition is a two-edged sword.

The downside of their hyper-inclusive understanding of disability is that it may trivialize the category and undermine a sense of group identity and solidarity (Wendell 1996, 66). This is not a danger, or is far less of a danger, with other forms of universalism. Most universalists on disability emphasize that all of us are likely to acquire traits commonly understood as disabilities and experience some of the same challenges as those who now have those traits. Some universalists suggest that it is both more accurate and less stigmatizing to see disabilities in terms of a spectrum, or spectra, of functioning rather than as distinctive traits. Neither approach invites spurious identification or undermines solidarity. The former cautions members of the "temporarily abled" majority to recognize that they could join "the unexpected minority" at any time (Gliedman and Roth 1980; Zola 2005). The latter insists that what appear to be differences in kind are in fact merely differences in degree; that stigma imposes a sharp dichotomy on a continuum of functioning.

In contrast, Kahane and Savulescu maintain that all of us, here and now, are disabled by virtue of possessing one or more welfare-reducing traits—a position that may threaten the potential of "disability" to serve as a basis for group identification or solidarity. People with conventionally defined disabilities are bound together by the experience of living in atypical bodies and facing social responses those bodies elicit. Although the experiences of people with different kinds of conventional disability are significantly different, they share far more than a general sense of human limitation or imperfection.

A proponent of the Welfarist Account might respond that the significance or magnitude of disabling traits, as they define them, could provide the basis for identification and solidarity with a social group, albeit one that only overlapped partially with the present social group of "people with disabilities." We are skeptical. While we could identify individuals with "severely" welfare-reducing traits (encompassing, among other things, recklessness, utterly obnoxious personalities, perceived ugliness, and debilitating empathy), individuals with these traits would hardly feel much affinity for each other. Some of the traits are stigmatized; others, celebrated or romanticized. All that their possessors share is traits that tend to lower welfare, and that is not a tie likely to bind. It is simply too broad and abstract. If there has ever been even a nascent movement toward the creation of a social group with these contours, we have found no evidence of it.

For all of these reasons, we find the Welfarist Account untenable as a basis for framing the opposition of disability and enhancement. We turn now to the other candidate for a symmetrical understanding of disability and enhancement.

The Typical-Functioning Account

An alternative way of seeing disability and enhancement as opposing concepts is to view them as measuring degree of capacity or functioning relative to some standard of typicality. As a first approximation, we can formulate this account as follows:

Typical-Functioning Account (First Approximation)

- Disability = a capacity to perform a type of action or function significantly *below* what is typical for one's kind.[12]
- Enhancement = a capacity to perform a type of action or function significantly *above* what is typical for one's kind.

This account seems to capture a popular symmetrical understanding of disability and enhancement. As we interpret it, a "capacity" can be for voluntary actions like running or talking, and non-voluntary bodily functions (over which we can sometimes exercise direct control) like hearing, seeing, circulation, and respiration—although the last two capacities are not usually thought of as "abilities." The "kind" in question will vary with context and purpose. It can be relativized to species, sex, age, or less biological variables. The question of the appropriate reference class is critical, but also very general since it arises in many areas where we seek to compare individuals' capacity or performance. We will address it only in passing.[13]

A crucial issue raised by this account is how to characterize an action. Actions can be described in terms of musculoskeletal movements (e.g. moving one's legs to the left and down), or with reference to external objects (getting out of bed) or to more or less proximate objectives (getting ready for work). They can also be serial and complex—getting out of bed typically involves some coordinated sequence of leg, arm, trunk, and head movements. On some theories, actions can be basic or non-basic. If action X is non-basic, then doing X requires doing some other action Y; if it is basic, we can do it without doing anything else.

Intuitively, most of us have a repertoire of things we can "just do" with our bodies, like swinging our arms or moving our tongue. We can increase the speed, force, or endurance with which we do these things. But most of the voluntary actions we do to survive and flourish are done with external objects in complex combinations or sequences, in order to achieve various proximate objectives in the environments we inhabit. Enhancing the speed, force, or endurance of our arm-swinging may be a very inefficient, or even counterproductive, way of achieving those objectives in those environments.

Commentators on enhancement rarely address these complexities in the characterization of actions because they often assume that there are capacities that have univalent effects on a wide range of actions and functions, however described. Thus, speaking of sight, Buchanan et al. 2000 claim:

> It can be thought of as a "natural primary good," analogous to what John Rawls . . . has called 'social primary goods'—in each case, 'general purpose' means useful or valuable for carrying out nearly any plan of life.   (167–168)

When it comes to enhancing sight, hearing, intelligence, strength, or agility, it is commonly assumed that we need not worry about the range of specific actions and functions the enhanced capacity extends to. Enhancing these "primary capacities" improves the performance of a wide range of actions or functions in almost all environments, with almost any stock of tools or equipment and for almost all objectives.

This assumption, however, is highly problematic. As a practical matter, enhancement processes are likely to involve piecemeal modifications of body and brain, whose direct effects will be far more local than those of enhanced intelligence, strength, agility, etc. Local enhancements will not always yield more global ones. Complex actions, functions, and skills are not necessarily improved by strengthening each or any of their component parts. Some athletic and gymnastic abilities, for example, require a balance between the strength or flexibility of the component body parts that might be impaired by enhancing only one or a proper subset of them. In part for this reason, training for one kind of athletic event may interfere with training for another. And, as anyone with the slightest familiarity with personal computers has learned, one must sometimes "disable" one feature to enhance the operation of another.

The assumption also ignores, or rejects, a central lesson of the social model of disability: the (dis)advantages associated with an individual's "internal" features largely arise from interactions with their environment. For this reason, those features rarely have uniform effects on complex, non-basic actions.[14] Interactions between intrinsic and environmental features can have a profound impact on hierarchies of capacity and function. In some cases, an environmental feature, tool, or technology will drastically alter the value of specific capacities to achieve important activities or functions.

Consider the North American Plains Indians living around 1600 (see Gwynne 2010). One outcome relevant to their survival and flourishing was traversing great distances across arid, rugged terrain. Prior to the introduction of the Spanish mustang, this outcome was accomplished on foot and was likely to be best achieved with a complex of traits and abilities that included long legs, balance and agility on foot, strong lungs, etc. The mustang's introduction did not result in an enhancement, as we use that term, since it did not itself improve individual capacities. But individuals in fact had widely variable capacities for horseback riding, and the features that probably contributed to enhanced capacity for foot travel—long legs, sturdy feet, etc.—may not have contributed to enhanced capacity for horse travel. Short, squat individuals were likely to have made better equestrians. Although general fitness was critical for these two modes of traversing long distances over harsh terrain, different kinds of strength, agility, balance, and endurance were likely to have been valuable for each.[15]

Similarly, people with disabilities often have capacities that enable them to achieve some outcome well above the norm, though in less familiar modes of acting or functioning.[16] For example, there are a range of different modes by which one can transport oneself from one place to another: walking, running, crawling, using a wheelchair, riding in a car, etc. Regular manual wheelchair users tend to be far better than the average person in getting around in that mode because of practice and acquired skill and strength. Some possess enhanced capacities, like upper-body strength or balance, that enable them to excel in wheelchair mobilization. One compelling reason to develop and promote "disabled sports" is to cultivate and highlight enhanced capacities that have been overlooked or underutilized in standard modes of athletic competition.

We do not deny that certain physical or psychological capacities may increase success or efficiency for many outcomes in many environments. But although characterized as single attributes, such general, primary, or all-purpose abilities may be best understood as ensembles of more specific abilities that do not contribute to the more general one in a simple additive way.[17] We suspect that the more general the characterization of an ability, the more plausible the case for its being a "primary ability," but the less likely it is to be susceptible to uniform enhancement. For the value of many abilities, especially at narrower levels of description, varies greatly with time and place. Moreover, the broader the description of the ability, the more likely it is to be a composite of sub-abilities, such that overall enhancement is better achieved by balance and coordination than by the enhancement of each component.

Take the example of sight. We need not deny that "the typical human's capacity for sight may be thought of as a general-purpose means—useful and valuable in carrying out nearly any plan of life or set of aims that humans typically have" (Buchanan et al. 2000, 167). This is, in fact, a fairly modest claim. Sight was highly useful in our evolutionary adaptive environments, and it remains so in environments built by and for the sighted. While we agree with many contributors to this volume that one can fare well without sight, examples of circumstances where the capacity to see is generally disadvantageous tend to be obscure or fanciful. What we deny is the implicit inference from the claim that a given capacity is a general-purpose means to the conclusion that increasing one major component of that capacity will yield a "general-purpose enhancement."

This inference appears to rely on a naïve additive assumption—that enhancing a part will enhance the whole. Because the visual system is highly complex, an increase in one component (say, visual acuity) might well result in a decrease in another (say, pattern recognition). Of course, this need not be the case; it might be that improving one component will improve the overall functioning of the system. Our point is merely that this cannot be assumed a priori and may well be false, especially for the most complex functions.

Consider recent findings from the even more complex domain of cognitive enhancement. A study on the effects of deep brain stimulation on mathematical ability raises doubts about the possibility of uniform enhancement. It finds that enhancing one component of mathematical ability impairs another component, and vice-versa:

> Notably, learning and automaticity represent critical abilities for potential cognitive enhancement in typical and atypical populations....Stimulation to the posterior parietal cortex facilitated numerical learning, whereas automaticity for the learned material was impaired. In contrast, stimulation to the dorsolateral prefrontal cortex impaired the learning process, whereas automaticity for the learned material was enhanced. The observed double dissociation indicates that cognitive enhancement through [transcranial electrical stimulation] can occur at the expense of other cognitive functions.   (Iuculano and Kadosh, 2013, 4482)

This study casts doubt on the prospects for enhancing mathematical ability as a whole by enhancing one component, or by enhancing two components that, at higher levels, interfere with each other. For specific purposes, we may want to enhance one of those components and be willing to impair the other by doing so. But in the face of such trade-offs, we can hardly claim to be enhancing a general-purpose means.

Thus, while we recognize that some traits, broadly described, may count as general-purpose means, we would urge caution or even skepticism about claims that those traits can be enhanced by specific biotechnological interventions. We would be even more cautious, or skeptical, about claims that impairments of specific components of a broadly described trait indicate a general disability in that trait. There is a powerful, damaging tendency to oversimplify and overgeneralize human capacities—to assume that a given trait or ability is disabling or enhancing for a wider range of outcomes, in a wider range of environments, than is warranted. Because of this tendency, individuals with a single local disability are all too often perceived as comprehensively disabled or incompetent.

We may avoid these pitfalls and better accommodate the complexities we have been discussing by adopting a more refined formulation of the Typical-Functioning Account:

Typical-Functioning Account (Refined)

- Disability = a capacity to achieve a given outcome through a given mode of action or function in a given environment at a level significantly *below* what is typical for one's kind.
- Enhancement = a capacity to achieve a given outcome through a given mode of action or function in a given environment at a level significantly *above* what is typical for one's kind.

In this refined account, "disability" and "enhancement" refer to capacities that are relativized to outcome, mode of action or function, environment, and kind. It is not meaningful to ask if an individual is enhanced or disabled, except with reference (which can be implicit) to each of these.[18]

The "mode of action or function" through which an individual achieves an outcome must involve (though not necessarily exclusively) the individual's own action or internal function. This requirement is critical in preserving the notion of an individual disability or enhancement. A person who lacks the latest labor-saving gadget, which requires little or no skill to employ, would be deprived, not disabled; a person who obtained that device would be better-provisioned, not enhanced.

This is certainly not to deny that an enhanced action may be done with the use of external devices or tools—hearing with cochlear implants, transporting oneself in a wheelchair, talking with a speech synthesizer, or pole-vaulting. But being carried by another person would not count as a mode of transporting oneself if one did not direct the other's actions closely, in a way that could be done adeptly or ineptly. Relatedly, an "outcome" in this account cannot be just any possible state of affairs. It must bear a close causal relation to its corresponding mode of action or function. Some action or function, or combination of actions and functions, must account for most of the variance in an outcome. Hence, we cannot plausibly speak of a capacity to achieve well-being, enduring fame, or enriching relationships, even though various individual capacities, actions, and functions undoubtedly contribute to those outcomes, since these outcomes depend to a much greater extent on factors external to the individual.[19]

On the Typical-Functioning Account, the fact that an individual has a disability tells us that she lacks the corresponding enhancement, and vice versa. For instance, someone with a diminished capacity to transport oneself by walking in a given type of environment cannot also have an enhanced capacity to move about by walking under those very same conditions. Beyond that, the bare fact that one is disabled or enhanced in one respect leaves open the overall impact of this capacity on a person's life. A capacity that is an enhancement or a disability in one respect (e.g. relative to one group of which one is a member, one outcome, one environment) could be neutral or disabling or enhancing in other respects. We can easily imagine "disabling" interventions that prove enhancing in other regards. For instance, it is possible that erasing certain memories could lead to improved functioning for people with post-traumatic stress disorder.[20] The intervention would give rise to a disability in one respect (decreased capacity to remember one's past), an enhancement in others (increased capacity for concentrating on current tasks, etc.). There is no way to deduce a priori what a given condition's overall impact will be. We simply have to examine individuals' particular circumstances and social context.

There are important advantages to adopting this more fine-grained approach. It defies the common oversimplifying tendency to generalize disability and assume that individuals with a single disability are comprehensively disabled (Silvers 1998b). On the Typical-Functioning Account, it is not perfectly accurate to label people as simply "disabled" or "enhanced," full stop. We have a staggeringly wide range of capacities and functions, and virtually no one is disabled, or enhanced, on every front.[21] Even so, people may still identify as disabled if they possess one or more disabilities that figure prominently in their experience. Although there has been far less public and scholarly attention to the relation between enhancement and identity, in principle a person could also identify as enhanced if they possess one or more enhancements.

This fine-grained version of the Typical-Functioning Account leaves room for the possibility that someone can identify as disabled *and* enhanced, though not in the same respect. This is a virtue of the account for at least two reasons. First, as more opportunities for enhancements become available, increasingly there will be these sorts of "mixed" cases where a person can be deemed enhanced along some dimensions and unenhanced or disabled along others. The late Stephen Hawking offered a prime example of this type of case since he could be reasonably deemed both intellectually enhanced and physically disabled. Second, this account allows us to make sense of the common opinion that a person who is disabled with respect to some capacity will sometimes have an enhanced capacity to achieve the relevant outcome with the aid of assistive technology while still qualifying as disabled. For instance, Oscar Pistorius (the first amputee to win a non-disabled world track medal) was disabled with respect to running "by foot" (which he had no capacity to do), but enhanced with respect to running with his prosthetic blades (which those with legs have no capacity to do).

Even with these revisions, the Typical-Functioning Account has important limitations. Like most of the other leading characterizations of disability, this account does not serve as a reliable marker for either stigmatization or self-identification. Imagine that we could clearly define and scale all of the capacities possessed by all people, so that a given individual's capacity profile would reveal the degree to which she falls near, above, or below the typical range with respect to each of her capacities. Many people would qualify as disabled in some respects and enhanced in various other respects. However, on the basis of such profiles, we could not predict who would be regarded, or regard themselves, as disabled. In terms of ascribed and self-identified disability, all capacities and functions are emphatically not equal. Some dysfunctions are more stigmatized or likely to be stigmatized than others. An individual who is slightly below the threshold on several basic functions might not be regarded, or regard herself, as disabled, in contrast to an individual with just one highly salient or stigmatized dysfunction. So, if we employ this account of disability, we must keep in mind that there is no essential connection between a condition's being a disability and its being subject to stigmatization or figuring prominently in individuals' self-identity. A corresponding lesson applies to enhancement. Capacities that qualify as enhancements may or may not be subject to public approbation (or disapprobation, for that matter) and may or may not loom large in any given person's sense of self.

The Typical-Functioning Account overgenerates in relation to our actual practices of attributing disability to others or ourselves. This tendency is partly rooted in the complexity of the account, which relativizes disability and enhancement to outcome, mode of action or function, environment, and kind. This complexity generates a proliferation of conditions that can be classified as enhancements or disabilities. Consider these examples:

- *Kind*: With respect to one's analytical reasoning abilities, a novice philosopher might qualify as enhanced *qua* member of the human species but disabled *qua* member of the philosophical community.
- *Outcome and Environment*: Compared to other humans, a person's deafness or hearing loss might qualify as an enhancement relative to some outcomes and environments (e.g. concentrating in noisy environments) but a disability relative to others (e.g. comprehending spoken conversations).
- *Mode*: With respect to the outcome of transporting oneself, a paraplegic may be enhanced relative to the mode of wheelchair use (having higher-than-average skills) but disabled relative to the mode of walking.

The Typical-Functioning Account gives no priority to any type of disabled or enhanced capacities. It merely provides a means of specifying the respects in which, and conditions under which, capacities qualify as disabilities or enhancements. Of course, we will have reasons to emphasize some rather than others, but we may have different reasons, and different emphases, in different contexts and for different purposes.

This complexity may (at best) limit or (at worse) undermine the usefulness of these categories in public discourse. We cannot say of a given condition (e.g. tallness, paraplegia, Down syndrome, increased memory capacity) that it is simply a disability, or an enhancement, or neither—end of story. It all depends on what particular outcome, mode, environment, and kind are picked out in a given context. Often, a single condition of an individual will qualify as a disability in some respects, an enhancement in other respects, *and* neither an enhancement nor a disability in still other respects. Even so, this account is better equipped to let us generalize about certain conditions than the Welfarist Account.

In spite of—or perhaps because of—its limitations, the Typical-Functioning Account appears to be the most promising way to conceive of disability and enhancement as opposing categories. Like the Welfarist Account, this account is revisionist. Many conditions that people do not intuitively regard as being disabilities or enhancements will merit the label. However, this account does better than the Welfarist Account in many respects. First, it does not seem to undergenerate with respect to our ordinary ascriptions of disability and enhancement. Most conditions that we today deem disabilities or enhancements will qualify as such on the Typical-Functioning Account. Second, the Typical-Functioning Account is unlikely to exacerbate the existing widespread tendency to associate disability with harm (which promotes various attitudes and practices that prove detrimental to persons with disabilities). It might even work to lessen existing biases and prejudices.

Lastly, the proposed account is less likely than the Welfarist Account to lead to a hyper-inclusive understanding of disability. While almost anyone can claim a disability under either account, the Typical-Functioning Account has the resources to recognize, and preserve, the group identification and solidarity of people with conventionally defined disabilities. In contrast to the Welfarist Account, it does not supersede but merely extends the existing understanding of disability and the social identities built around it. The Typical-Functioning Account indexes disability "significance" or severity not by general welfare deficit, but by functional limitation. It thereby conforms to the contours of disability group identity far more closely than the Welfarist Account. Disability groups are organized by functional atypicality or deficit; there are groups for people who are blind, deaf, paralyzed, etc. Eligibility for inclusion as a disabled participant has nothing whatsoever to do with general welfare. Indeed, some disability self-advocacy groups have been criticized for overrepresenting the "disability elite"—who can be presumed to have average or above-average levels of welfare. Rather, controversies over membership or inclusion arise over those with less substantial or severe limitations of the same kind, e.g., over the participation of those who are "merely" legally blind or hard-of-hearing. The question of who is "really" disabled on a typical-functioning account is thus more or less the same one confronting actual disability groups.

While it is probably true that all of us can claim to have at least one capacity that involves below-typical functioning with respect to some group of which we are a member (and, thus, are disabled in that regard), many of our disabilities are not particularly salient and can be reasonably dismissed as negligible.

LESSONS FROM A SYMMETRICAL UNDERSTANDING OF DISABILITY AND ENHANCEMENT

The Typical-Functioning Account provides us with a basis to talk about disability and enhancement as symmetrical and opposing categories. We will close with some important insights yielded by this symmetry.

First, disability and enhancement both stand in a very similar and complicated relationship to well-being. It is helpful to draw a distinction between low-impact versus high-impact conditions (Campbell and Stramondo 2017, 166–167). A low-impact condition has a minimal causal impact on how a person's life unfolds, whereas a high-impact condition has a significant causal influence. On the Typical-Functioning Account, some types of disabilities and enhancements will be low-impact traits.[22] To the extent that these traits are not, by themselves or in combination with other things, intrinsically good or bad for those who have them, it can be said as a general matter that they have a minimal effect on well-being. However, other disabilities and enhancements will be high-impact traits—including most of the conditions associated with the words "disability" and "enhancement." Here, the effect on well-being will be complex and varied, depending on a wide range of factors. There will be cases where a given type of disability or enhancement will be bad for people, cases where it will be neutral, and cases where it will be advantageous. On this approach, we must take care not to leap to generalizations that crudely associate disabilities with harm and enhancements with benefit (Wasserman and Asch 2014, Campbell and Stramondo 2017).[23]

On the Typical-Functioning Account, it is not possible to draw a single line between "disability" and "enhancement," and the multiple lines that can be drawn will shift in time and space. What constitutes a disability and an enhancement will vary by time period and by regions as what is typical for various kinds of being shifts, and as modes of function and environments disappear or become less common. Shifts in what counts as a disability will tend to go hand-in-hand with shifts in the corresponding enhancement. The interconnectedness of disability and enhancement also relates to their ineliminability. Of course, it is possible that specific conditions that often qualify as disabilities today may be eliminated from the population in the future. That is one sense in which it is true that disabilities could be eliminated. In another sense, however, it is deeply misguided to think that disability could ever be eliminated. Some people will always fall below typical functioning in various respects. Because disability is, in this important sense, practically ineliminable, it is crucial that we learn to "live with" disabilities—not stigmatizing or alienating those who have them and not adopting a (futile) oppositional stance toward disability. We should also be judicious in seeking to eliminate specific conditions or bring about others. As noted above, the relationship between disability, enhancement, and well-being is a complex one. In some cases, it makes little difference to a person's quality of life that they have more or less capacity in some regard. Even in cases where it makes a significant difference, it is unlikely to be a uniform one.

We are now in a position to say something about the idea that disability and enhancement call for opposing attitudes. Is it the case that a welcoming attitude toward disability and disabled people goes hand-in-hand with an aversion to the idea of human enhancement? Must enthusiasm about enhancement be attended by a corresponding aversion to disability? Given the complexity of the enhancement-disability relationship, as well as their complicated relationship to well-being, it is not surprising that we cannot make such simple, broad generalizations. Disability and enhancement are intermingled in important ways. A single capacity can constitute a disability in some respect (relative to a given outcome, mode, environment, and kind) and an enhancement in others. A medical intervention might be disabling in certain ways and enhancing in others. A single individual might self-identify as both disabled and enhanced. Furthermore, there is no simple story to be told as to the extent or prudential quality of the impact that disabilities and enhancements have on individuals' lives. Some disabilities and enhancements are low impact, others are high impact. Some have an overall positive influence on well-being, others have a negative effect.

In light of these facts, enhancements are neither a simple threat to people with disabilities, raising the mean further above them, nor a simple panacea, enabling them to match or even leapfrog over "merely" typical members of their societies. Enhancement technologies may reduce the stigma and adverse effects of disability by promoting ways of doing things for which people with specific disabilities are at no disadvantage. They may reduce the importance and salience of "normal" modes of functioning. On the other hand, the development and marketing of enhancement technologies may be driven by a relentless perfectionism that exacerbates the stigma of existing disabilities and creates new ones. The growth of those technologies may heighten intolerance for weakness and vulnerability of all sorts and increase disparities between the economically and socially better and worse off—with people who have familiar stigmatized disabilities disproportionately represented in the latter category (Hall 2020). All of us, including people with more severe, salient, or stigmatized disabilities, have reason to be profoundly ambivalent about the glorification of enhancement. Even if their grounds for ambivalence is sharper, people with disabilities should not be cast as the natural adversaries, or natural allies, of enhancement technology.

Notes

1. We wish to thank Adam Cureton, Guy Fletcher, Anita Silvers, and Joseph Stramondo for offering their feedback on this chapter.
2. See Beaudry (2016, 2020, this volume).
3. Some of these notions are also presented in Savulescu, Sandberg, and Kahane (2011).
4. Gyngell and Selgelid offer two versions of (what we are calling) the Non-Therapeutic Account, which differ in that one treats diseases as states disvalued by society while the other understands diseases in terms of negative deviations from normal functioning (2016, 112–114).
5. Admittedly, giving primacy to the notion of an enhanced condition undermines one prominent feature of our enhancement discourse. Typically, the notion of enhancement is essentially linked to some purposeful intervention. For instance, it would be natural to say that a person who was engineered to have a high IQ is enhanced, though we would not normally say that Einstein was enhanced. This is one way in which our choice has revisionist implications. However, if there is value in retaining that feature of our enhancement discourse, we can still distinguish between enhanced conditions with natural versus artificial origins.
6. Rejecting the Non-Therapeutic Account does not mean that we must sacrifice the benefits of a therapy/enhancement distinction. We can still distinguish between therapeutic and non-therapeutic processes that lead to enhancement.
7. In line with our earlier disclaimer, it is also worth questioning the assumption that there is a single "everyday concept" of disability.
8. Indeed, some conditions are so firmly established as paradigmatic instances of disability that it is reasonable to think that any plausible account or definition of disability needs to apply to such conditions (see Barnes 2016, 10–11).

9. This is not to deny that viewing disabilities as harmful could yield some benefits as well—e.g. increased motivation to provide social support and accommodations. We believe that the harms outweigh the benefits.

10. Some of these examples are explicitly acknowledged by Kahane and Savulescu 2009, 26.

11. A defender of the Welfarist Account might respond by claiming that the popular "Social Model" of disability undergenerates in the same way. If, say, blindness is not disadvantageous in certain contexts, both accounts will say that blind people in those contexts are not disabled. Therefore, the Welfarist Account might be thought to do no worse than the leading account championed by many disability studies scholars. However, there is a key difference. Insofar as the social account distinguishes between impairments and disabilities and implies that blindness always qualifies as an impairment, it arguably accommodates our common-sense categorizations (which do not draw fine distinctions between impairments and disabilities). The same cannot be said for the Welfarist Account.

12. We understand this account of disability to allow for cases where an individual has a zero-level capacity to perform an action or function. Admittedly, this phrasing is awkward since it is far more natural to speak of such people as simply lacking the capacity in question. For those who prefer it, a less awkward, and less elegant, formulation of this account might be the following: "a diminished capacity or lack of capacity such that one can only perform a type of action or function (if at all) at a level significantly below what is typical for one's kind."

13. We have opted to drop the term "stable," given that performance enhancements in sports can be short lived and there are some contexts where people are seen as disabled for limited periods. Still, discussions of disability are mostly focused on stable conditions.

14. The full range of such interactions has not been emphasized in disability contexts, perhaps because most of the salient interactions (e.g., those involving the use of wheelchairs, ramps, and canes) are seen as compensatory, merely reducing disparities in performance through accommodation and assistive technology.

15. Of course, what qualified as *enhanced* equestrian skill also depended greatly on the "kind" in question—a rider well above the mean for all humans might have been average for a Plains Indian and, perhaps, disabled for a Comanche.

16. For an introduction to the distinction between mode of function vs. level of function, see Silvers 1998a.

17. We thank Adam Cureton for raising the issue to which we respond here.

18. This account can be adapted to actions for which it is difficult to separate mode from outcome. For instance, it is not clear what counts as the mode and outcome in a musical performance on a single instrument. A pianist does not bring about the outcome of performing a piece by touching various keys and moving her fingers across the keyboard; those actions help constitute the performance. Nevertheless, we can talk about various modes of playing the piano. It may well be that we can enhance the performance by improving various modes of playing—different techniques or styles, even if improvements in some "modes," like playing with one's toes, are unlikely to yield enhanced performance. The point is that the refined account works, with a little tweaking, for actions in which mode and outcome do not have a cause-effect relationship, or in which there is no discrete outcome.

19. To take a limit case, one cannot have an enhanced capacity to achieve a winning outcome by tossing a fair die or spinning a fair roulette wheel. Whether we think individuals can

have enhanced traits to obtain other outcomes, like success in a given profession or happiness in love, depends on how much of a crapshoot (so to speak) we think it is to obtain that outcome.

20. http://news.mit.edu/2014/erasing-traumatic-memories-0116

21. Clearly, some capacities are necessary for the survival of the human organism, such as respiration and circulation. At present, the only alternative modes for achieving survival, like ventilators, are broadly disabling: their use requires a radical curtailment of a wide range of activities. But that, too, is a contingent fact. And the conditions that compel the use of such alternative modes of survival, or preclude survival altogether, are usually (aspects of) disease processes, as distinct from the disabled states with which this account is concerned (see Aas and Wasserman 2016).

22. This point is not in conflict with Campbell and Stramondo's assertion that disabilities tend to be high-impact traits, for they use "disability" to refer to conditions that are commonly labeled as such (2017, 152, 166). In contrast, the Typical-Functioning Account encompasses conditions that are normally considered too trivial to deserve the title of "disability."

23. The relationship of disabilities and enhancements to well-being is further complicated by the fact that people have many and varied preferences and goals, which can be described at varying levels of generality. Both disabilities and enhancements might be more or less beneficial or harmful depending on these factors.

References

Aas, Sean, and David Wasserman. 2016. "Disability, Disease, and Health Sufficiency." In *What is Enough? Sufficiency, Justice, and Health*, edited by C. Fourie and A. Rid, 164–184. Oxford: Oxford University Press.

Barnes, Elizabeth. 2016. *The Minority Body*. Oxford: Oxford University Press.

Beaudry, J. S. 2016. "Beyond (Models of) Disability?" *The Journal of Medicine and Philosophy* 41, no. 2: 210–228.

Beaudry, J. S. 2020. "Theoretical Strategies to Define Disability." In *Oxford Handbook of Philosophy and Disability*, edited by A. Cureton and D. Wasserman, 3–21. New York: Oxford University Press.

Buchanan, Allen, Dan W. Brock, Norman Daniels, and Daniel Wikler. 2000. *From Chance to Choice: Genetics and Justice*. Cambridge, UK: Cambridge University Press.

Campbell, Stephen M. and Joseph A. Stramondo. 2017. "The Complicated Relationship of Disability and Well-Being." *Kennedy Institute of Ethics Journal* 27: 151–184.

Gliedman, J., and W. Roth. 1980. *The Unexpected Minority: Handicapped Children in America*. New York: Harcourt Brace Jovanovich.

Gwynne, S. C. 2010. *Empire of the Summer Moon: Quanah Parker and the Rise and Fall of the Comanches, the Most Powerful Indian Tribe in American History*. New York: Scribner.

Gyngell, Chris, and Michael J. Selgelid. 2016. "Human Enhancement: Conceptual Clarity and Moral Significance." In *The Ethics of Human Enhancement*, edited by S. Clarke, J. Savulescu, T. Coady, A. Giubilini, and S. Sanyal, 111–126. Oxford: Oxford University Press.

Hall, Melinda. 2020. "Second Thoughts on Enhancement and Disability." In *Oxford Handbook of Philosophy and Disability*, edited by A. Cureton and D. Wasserman, 633–650. New York: Oxford University Press.

Iuculano, Teresa, and Roi Cohen Kadosh. 2013. "The Mental Cost of Cognitive Enhancement." *Journal of Neuroscience* 33, no. 10: 4482–4486.

Kahane, Guy, and Julian Savulescu. 2009. "The Welfarist Account of Disability." In *Disability and Disadvantage*, edited by K. Brownlee and A. Cureton, 14–53. Oxford: Oxford University Press.

Savulescu, Julian, Anders Sandberg, and Guy Kahane. 2011. "Enhancement and Well-Being." In *Enhancing Human Capacities*, edited by G. Kahane, J. Savulescu, and R. Meulen, 3–18. Malden, MA: Blackwell.

Silvers, Anita. 1998a. "A Fatal Attraction to Normalizing: Treating Disabilities as Deviations from 'Species Typical' Functioning." In *Enhancing Human Traits: Ethical and Social Implications*, edited by Erik Parens, 95–123. Washington, DC: Georgetown University Press,

Silvers, Anita. 1998b. "Formal Justice." In *Disability, Difference, Discrimination: Perspectives on Justice in Bioethics and Public Policy*, edited by A. Silvers, D. Wasserman, and M. Mahowald, 13–145. Lanham, MD: Rowman & Littlefield.

Wasserman, David, and Adrienne Asch. 2014. "Understanding the Relationship Between Disability and Well-Being." In *Disability and the Good Human Life*, edited by J. Bickenbach, F. Felder, and B. Schmidtz, 139–167. Cambridge, UK: Cambridge University Press.

Wendell, Susan. 1996. *The Rejected Body*. New York: Routledge.

Zola, Irving Kenneth. 2005. "Toward the Necessary Universalizing of a Disability Policy." *The Milbank Quarterly* 83, no. 4.

CHAPTER 33

COGNITIVE DISABILITY AND EMBODIED, EXTENDED MINDS

ZOE DRAYSON AND ANDY CLARK

INTRODUCTION

HUMAN beings are capable of impressive feats of intelligence and skill. Chess grandmasters can think fifteen moves ahead, for example, and baseball outfielders can anticipate exactly where a fly ball will land. It is often assumed that such feats are the result of the human capacity for rational thought: the way we can apply mental processes such as reasoning, calculating, and predicting to different task domains. Furthermore, these mental processes are assumed to be located in our brains. There are research programs in cognitive science, however, that challenge these assumptions by showing how our bodily interactions with the world can achieve the sort of cognitive success normally associated with neurally located thought. Proponents of these approaches to cognition allow that the brain plays a large role in generating our intellectual abilities, but they urge us to look beyond the brain to the way that our cognitive skills are *embodied* in our more basic capacities for sensing and moving and to the way that tools in the external environment can *extend* the cognitive abilities of our brains. This trend toward understanding cognition as embodied and extended has implications for how we think about both cognitive abilities and cognitive disabilities. If cognition is not solely the province of the brain, then cognitive impairment might occur without neural damage, and strategies for cognitive rehabilitation might be less reliant on neural intervention.

This article introduces the theory behind embodied cognition and extended cognition and suggests that they have implications for how we understand cognitive impairment and the rehabilitation strategies toward it. Furthermore, it proposes a new way to think about "cognitive reserve," the resilience that allows some people to function better than others with the same degree of neural damage. It concludes by suggesting that the ideas behind embodied and extended cognition can change the way we think about the distinction between medical and social models of cognitive disability.

Embodied and Extended Minds

Embodied and extended approaches to cognition reject or play down the role of neurally located high-level thought in explaining our capacity for flexible behavior. In this section we present the key features of these approaches and some of the arguments in their favor.

Brains, Bodies, and Beyond

What best explains our capacity for flexible, adaptive, intelligent behavior? The reasoning abilities of the human brain, of course, play a key role. But some cognitive scientists are concerned that if we focus solely on the thinking brain, we might lose sight of the contributions that our bodies and environments can make to our skilled behaviors. We focus here on two related approaches to cognition that challenge neurocentric assumptions in cognitive science: embodied cognition and extended cognition.

Embodied cognitive science shifts the focus away from thinking and reasoning as the explanation of our intelligent behavior, and toward our bodily abilities such as sensing and moving. Proponents of embodied cognition suggest that if our sensory and motor processes are coupled in the right way, they can allow us to perform complex tasks that we might previously have explained in terms of amodal thought and reason: the sort of mental processing that does not rely on specific modes of sensing or moving. And even when our abilities seem to require amodal thinking and reasoning, work on *extended* cognition suggests that such complex mental processes (e.g., calculating or remembering) need not be confined to the brain. Proponents of extended cognition suggest that mental processes can straddle the brain-world divide, manipulating and retrieving information that is stored in the environment as well as the information that is stored in the brain.

Embodied Cognition

Traditional approaches to cognitive science have often assumed that our sensory and motor skills are primarily just inputs to and outputs of genuine cognition: the reasoning processes that take information from the senses and issue motor instructions. Embodied approaches to cognitive science suggest that we should take more seriously the contributions of perception and action and the way they can combine directly with each other and the environment.

Consider a baseball outfielder successfully catching a fly ball. What explains their accuracy? On one approach, we might consider solely what is going on in their head. Their sensory systems, notably vision, process information about the speed and location of the ball, which allows the player to calculate (perhaps unconsciously) the trajectory of the ball and to predict where it will land. This gives the player the information they need to decide where and how fast to run in order to catch it.

Embodied approaches to cognitive science challenge this picture (McBeath et al., 1995). They demonstrate that if an outfielder simply moves in the right way with respect to the ball, there is no need for them to make any predictions about where the ball will land. If a fielder remains near the path of the ball and moves laterally so as to make the ball appear to trace a straight line, or if they align themselves with the path of the ball and run in a way that makes the ball appear to have a constant velocity, then they will end up at the same place as the ball when it lands.

The outfielder example demonstrates the ways that sensory input (e.g., the visual experience of the moving ball) couples with motor output (e.g., running in a certain direction at a certain speed) to solve a particular problem (e.g., how to catch a ball). The brain is still vital, but not for doing anything that looks like amodal thinking or reasoning: there is no need for complex cognitive processes such as calculation, prediction, or decision making. Instead, more basic sensory and motor capacities engage with an environmental problem to find a solution that bypasses the need for more complex cognition. The lesson from the outfielder example is that we should not necessarily assume that abstract reasoning processes do the main causal work in explaining our intelligent action. If we focus instead on the way that cognition is embodied, we can appreciate how the sensory and motor capabilities of our bodies can solve problems without being mediated by high-level thought.

Contemporary embodied cognitive science can trace its roots back to the work of J. J. Gibson in perceptual psychology (Gibson, 1967, 1979). Gibson challenged the view that visual processing builds up a detailed representation of the world for us to reflect upon before deciding how to act. Instead, he proposed that the visual stimulus is already far richer than we think, once we consider its relation to action: as we move around in the world, our sensory input changes in ways that provide information about our opportunities for action. Gibson claimed that once we understand how our sensory systems and motor systems interact, we can reject the need to posit detailed amodal representations of the world in order to explain intelligent action.

Some of the greatest subsequent advances in embodied cognitive science have been made in robotics. Traditional approaches to cognitive science focused largely on the complex information processing that took place *between* sensory inputs and motor outputs, so roboticists often tried to program their robots with complex computational systems that mediated between the sensory inputs and motor outputs. Rodney Brooks was one of the first to realize that other ways of designing a robot could yield intelligent behavior (Brooks, 1991). He rejected the assumption that robotic systems should feature a central reasoning component that bore the computational load, and peripheral systems for sensing and moving. Instead, he proposed that robots could be designed as systems of activity-producing layers, each of which solves a basic task by coupling a particular kind of sensory input to a certain motor output (e.g., light-directed motion). While each layer is little more than a reflex, Brooks showed that complex behavioral patterns emerge when the layers are stacked up. The robot has no equivalent of central reasoning processes, no overall perception of the world beyond each layer's specialized sensors, and no overall goals beyond the individual tasks performed by each layer. Communication between the layers is minimal: all they do is switch each other on and off.

To see how this might work, consider a robot based upon the abilities of rats to navigate mazes (Mataric, 1991). The robot rat investigates and maps its territory using a built-in compass and sonar sensors. Its first activity-producing layer generates boundary tracing or wall-following behavior. Whenever the robot comes across an obstacle, the second layer takes over and notes the obstacle as a landmark by registering it as a combination of the robot's sensory input and its motor output. A third layer generates a map of the landmarks, using this information. Notice that the map is not an objective description of the territory that the robot could use to direct another system, or to plot absolute distances: the robot registers the landmarks egocentrically, in terms of its own sensory inputs and motor outputs. To find its way back to a landmark, the robot does not have to first consult the map and then plan a route: the information about each landmark both describes where it is *and* how to get there, and can control the robot's movement back to a landmark without any further processing.

When it comes to explaining human behavior, embodied cognitive science has had most success at explaining the sorts of abilities that require environmental engagement and real-time skills, such as the outfielder example above. The extent to which these sensory-motor explanations scale up to account for offline intelligence (e.g., counterfactual thought, semantic memory, language comprehension) remains to be seen.

Extended Cognition

Both embodied and extended approaches to cognitive science challenge the centrality of brain-based explanations in accounting for our problem-solving abilities. We have shown how embodied cognitive science focuses on how the non-neural body might do some of the work traditionally attributed to complex thought processes. Extended cognitive science takes a different but complementary approach, by focusing on aspects of the environment beyond our bodies which might do some of the explanatory work normally attributed to the brain. Most proponents of extended cognition claim that there is no important difference between information that is stored in the biological brain and information that is stored in nonbiological structures: what matters in both cases is how the information is organized and accessed, rather than where the information is stored.

One of the most well-known arguments for extended cognition is Clark and Chalmers's (1998) thought experiment featuring Inga and Otto in New York. Inga and Otto each hear about an exhibition at the Museum of Modern Art (MoMA) and decide to visit. Inga thinks for a moment about the location of MoMA before recalling that it is on Fifty-Third Street and setting off. Otto suffers from a mild form of Alzheimer's disease, but he always carries a notebook and writes any useful new information in it. When Otto hears of the exhibition at MoMA, he retrieves the museum's address from his notebook (where he'd written it down previously) and sets off. The key step in Clark and Chalmers's argument is their claim that before he consulted the notebook, Otto had the dispositional belief that the museum is on Fifty-Third Street, and that this dispositional belief is the explanation of why Otto walks to that particular street when he wants to go to the museum. (We take it to be uncontroversial that after consulting the notebook, Otto has the occurrent belief that the museum is on Fifty-Third Street.) If we resist this move in Otto's case, then we have to say why we attribute the same dispositional belief to Inga before she retrieves it from her memory. Clark and Chalmers claim that the information stored in Otto's notebook plays a similar role to the information stored in Inga's brain: in both cases, we can explain why they headed to Fifty-Third Street by saying that they both wanted to go to MoMA and believed that MoMA was on Fifty-Third Street. There is, of course, a difference between the two cognitive processes for storing and retrieving long-term information: Inga's process is implemented entirely neurally, whereas Otto's process extends beyond his brain to include the notebook. But Clark and Chalmers argue that this locational difference ought not to make a difference as to whether we accept the processes as a cognitive process, and encourage us to endorse the Parity Principle:

> Parity Principle (PP): If, as we confront some task, a part of the world functions as a process which, were it to go on in the head, we would have no hesitation in accepting as part of the cognitive process, then that part of the world is (for that time) part of the cognitive process.   (Clark and Chalmers 1998, 8)

Clark and Chalmers are not claiming that *any* external information can mimic the resources of internal biological memory. Rather, they claim that there are certain circumstances in which external information can become so deeply integrated into cognitive systems that it would be arbitrary to draw a cognitive boundary at the metabolic boundary of the biological human. In the case of Otto and Inga, they argue, the functional poise of the stored information is sufficiently similar in both cases to warrant similar treatment. We should therefore attribute to Otto the same dispositional belief as Inga, that MoMA is on Fifty-Third Street, despite the fact that Otto's mental state is not confined to his brain or body.

These embodied and extended approaches to cognition, we propose, have implications for our understanding of cognitive impairment and its rehabilitation.

Cognitive Impairment and Rehabilitation

Cognitive impairment is often assumed to result solely from neural impairment, but extended and embodied approaches to cognition challenge this assumption.

This in turn places pressure on the standard distinction between types of cognitive rehabilitation techniques.

Cognitive Impairment

The World Health Organization's International Classification of Functioning, Disability, and Health (WHO-ICF) recognizes that bodily structures and functions can be impaired as a result of disease or injury, resulting in limitations to people's activities (Institute of Medicine 2011, 27). (We will return to the relationship between impairment and limitation when we consider in theories of disability in our final section, Cognitive Disability.) In the case of cognitive impairment, the limitations involved might include declining memory function, deficits in language comprehension, or problems with decision making and planning. Cognitive impairment is generally considered to be the result of neural impairment: disease or injury to the brain following stroke, traumatic brain injury, or degenerative diseases such as dementia.

We have already shown how embodied and extended approaches to cognition challenge the traditional assumption that our success at cognitive tasks is explained solely by the reasoning capacities of the human brain. Proponents of embodied and extended cognition encourage us to look to the way our brains rely on interactions with our non-neural bodies and aspects of the world beyond. In doing so, they suggest that some of our cognitive abilities might be best explained by sensory-motor couplings or external information storage. But notice that if this is the case, we cannot assume that a decline or deficit in our cognitive abilities is the direct result of neural impairment.

Consider a Scrabble player who, after a stroke, loses the ability to make long words on the Scrabble board. We might be tempted to assume that they are suffering from some neural deficit affecting linguistic processing in the brain. But what if the stroke has affected their movement, such that they no longer have the manual dexterity to shuffle the Scrabble tiles on the rack in front of them? Perhaps their previous Scrabble performance relied on their ability to physically rearrange the letter tiles, so now they are more reliant on their neural ability to mentally shuffle the letters in their head, and this works less well than the manual shuffling. In such a case, there need not be anything wrong with the areas of their brain associated with lexical capacities or mental imagery: their cognitive impairment is only a neural impairment to the extent that the motor impairment has a neural basis. Their previous skill at Scrabble was partly reliant on the incorporation of the external rack of letter tiles into their cognitive processes, just as Otto's ability to remember is reliant on his notebook. If cognitive function can be reliant on external factors, then impairment of that cognitive function need not involve neural impairment.

The Scrabble case may seem like a contrived example: someone watching the Scrabble player would immediately realize that that there was no impairment to their cognitive capacities more generally. But diagnosis of cognitive impairment often takes place in a clinical setting that neglects the normal environment of the patient.

Consider ideomotor apraxia, a dysfunction of gestures or skilled movements of the limbs. The common diagnostic test for ideomotor apraxia is the use of pantomime: subjects are asked to mime, just using their hands, how they would brush their teeth or use scissors for example. Apraxic patients are unable to pass this test, and it is tempting to think that a neural impairment is solely responsible for their inability. But this may not be the case: Andrew Sneddon points out that many patients who fail the mime test in the clinical setting have no problems brushing their teeth or using scissors when toothbrushes and scissors are provided in their normal home environment (Sneddon 2002). Their inability to pass the mime test is no doubt partly due to a neural impairment but also partly due to the test environment: their ability to perform the action seems to be context dependent. The assumption that the problem in question is entirely due to a brain deficit rules out the possibility "that such particular apraxias are problems of brain-world coordination" (Sneddon 2002, 306) rather than exclusively neural problems. Embodied and extended cognitive science suggests that some of our ability to perform such routine functions is a matter of brain-world coordination. If certain of our abilities are dependent on our external environments, then we cannot assume that loss of those abilities is due only to internal neural damage. The impairment in question might be an impairment of some part of the complex interactions between brain, body, and world that normally generate the cognitive capacity.

Cognitive Rehabilitation

Rehabilitation is the attempt to enhance human functioning and quality of life following some form of impairment. Rehabilitation takes two broad forms: *restorative* interventions aim to lessen the impairment by restoring it to its previous unimpaired state, and *compensatory* interventions leave the impairment as it is but aim to lessen the disabling impact of the impairment by compensatory strategies (Institute of Medicine 2011, 75–76).

This distinction between restorative and compensatory rehabilitation is found throughout the literature on both physical rehabilitation and cognitive rehabilitation. Cognitive rehabilitation aims to enhance functioning and quality of life (e.g., by increasing independence) following cognitive impairment. If we understand cognitive impairment as the result of neural damage or decline, then *restorative rehabilitation* will be focused on repairing circuitry: either through neurosurgery or by cognitive exercises designed to rewire the brain. Restorative techniques for memory loss, for example, might include training the patient to remember longer and longer lists in an attempt to build or strengthen neural connections. *Compensatory rehabilitation* strategies for cognitive impairment, on the other hand, leave the neural impairment as it is and focus on helping the patient adapt to it. Brain-focused training techniques such as the increased usage of mnemonics or associative imagery, for example, might be used to compensate for deficits in biological memory, alongside external aids and larger-scale environmental structuring. According to the neurocentric view that cognitive impairment results only from neural impairment, any rehabilitation technique which did not focus on the brain could only be a compensatory technique.

Restorative rehabilitation is often seen as the main goal of rehabilitation, with compensatory techniques understood as a fall-back when restoration of the impairment is impossible or unlikely. In the case of cognitive impairment, compensatory techniques such as those involving external aids are generally understood as a useful substitute when we lack either the knowledge or the technology to restore the damaged brain networks. Some neuroscientists think that as we learn more and more about the brain, compensatory strategies will be unnecessary because all rehabilitation will be restorative: Coltheart (1991), for example, suggests that models of neural functioning from cognitive neuropsychology are sufficient to plan cognitive rehabilitation.

Contrast this picture with the approach of embodied and extended cognitive science. If cognition is embodied or extended, then cognitive impairment does not necessarily arise from neural impairment. If cognitive functioning relies on the interactions between our brain, body, and the external world, then cognitive impairment can result from changes to those interactions. On this view, restoring a damaged cognitive function need not involve strengthening neural connections: restorative rehabilitation might involve intervention at other points in the web of brain-body-world interactions responsible for cognitive function. Some non-neural rehabilitation techniques which are currently dismissed as merely compensatory may actually be restorative, according to the implications of embodied and extended cognitive science.

Now reconsider the case of ideomotor apraxia described above. The neurocentric approach would class this as a case of cognitive impairment, where the patient lacks the ability to brush their teeth. Placing them in a certain environmental situation with toothbrush at hand would be considered compensatory rehabilitation, in the sense that it does not restore their cognitive ability to brush their teeth but merely allows them to function better. On the embodied and extended approach, however, we can say that whether the patient's neural impairment results in cognitive impairment will depend on the nature of the cognitive task. The patient's ability to mime certain actions can be impaired without their ability to perform those actions being impaired. Being in their home context with the appropriate tools does not just *compensate* for impairment: it *restores* the interactions between brain, body, and world that were previously responsible for their teeth-brushing ability.

Notice that this is not merely a theoretical re-description of the supposed impairment: work in embodied cognitive science has led to changes in how cognitive impairment is assessed and understood. The field of neuropsychological rehabilitation has increased the ecological validity of cognitive assessment techniques in response to the worry that traditional cognitive assessments in controlled environments are of limited use for assessing the real-world functioning of patients. Ecologically valid cognitive assessment, on the other hand, assesses people's impairments relative to their functioning on tests that represent everyday life contexts and predict behaviors outside the test environment (Dawson and Marcotte 2017). As a result, our idea of cognitive impairment and its rehabilitation is changing.

On the extended approach to cognition, the role of external aids takes on a new importance in cognitive rehabilitation. Andy Clark documents an encounter between himself and Carolyn Baum, then the head of occupational therapy at the Washington University School of Medicine in St Louis, Missouri (Clark 2003, 139–140). Baum felt that Clark's work on extended cognition was highly relevant to her own work with a sub-population of inner-city Alzheimer's sufferers in St. Louis. These patients performed poorly on standard tests such as the CERAD protocol, which suggested that they should have been unable to cope with the demands of unassisted living; but they still lived alone successfully in the city. On a sequence of visits to their home environments, Clark discovered that their homes were full of cognitive props, tools, and aids: message centers where they stored notes about what to do and when; photos of family and friends complete with indications of names and relationships; labels and pictures on doors; "memory books" to record new events, meetings and plans; and open-storage strategies in which crucial items (pots, pans, checkbooks) are always kept in plain view, rather than hidden in drawers. Clark suggests that their homes were carefully calibrated to scaffold their biological brains and invites us to view cases of potent non-biological scaffolding as implementing alternative but perfectly genuine forms of control and recall, rather than viewing them merely as compensatory props and patches enabling better performance. With increases in technology, the role of "intelligent assistive technology" (IAT) applications for people with cognitive impairment has changed. Ienca et al. (2017) observe that the number of IAT applications is doubling every five years, and they have evolved from safety-focused devices (e.g. GPS trackers, fall detectors) into more general cognitive support:

> the main focus of most current IATs is not simply monitoring older adults with dementia, but empowering them by promoting the autonomous and successful completion of daily activities and the support of their psychosocial dimension (e.g., entertainment, engagement, and communication).   (Ienca et al. 2017, 1336)

Not all external props are non-biological artifacts, however. In some cases, other human beings in our environment play an important role in our own cognitive abilities. When Clark and Chalmers (1998) first proposed the example of Otto and his extended mind, they considered whether our cognitive capacities could be *socially* extended:

> What about socially extended cognition? Could my mental states be partly constituted by the states of other thinkers? We see no reason why not, in principle. In an unusually interdependent couple, it is entirely possible that one partner's beliefs will play the same sort of role for the other as the notebook plays for Otto.
> (Clark and Chalmers 1998, 17)

The idea that other people can become part of our memory systems was suggested by Wegner (1987) in his "transactive" approach to autobiographical memory. Wegner argued that while individual people have physically separate neural memory stores, communication between two or more people can give rise to a transactive memory system: a socially coupled dynamical system of shared memories. Wegner suggested that these transactive systems arise because they allow individuals to encode, store, and retrieve information more efficiently than they can alone.

Drawing on Wegner's insights, memory researchers have explored the extent of socially distributed remembering by testing people's recall ability both individually and collaboratively (Sutton et al. 2010). In general, people in groups actually tend to remember less than individuals, probably because individual strategies for memory retrieval are disrupted by the strategies of other group members. The exception to this phenomenon of "collaborative inhibition" is found when the "group" in question consists of long-term friends or partners:

> Some couples remembered far better with their spouse, co-constructing rich autobiographical memories and overturning the usual finding of 'collaborative inhibition' for list recall [...] Indeed, collaborative recall has been proposed as a potential intervention to support memory abilities of older adults in care facilities.
> (Barnier et al. 2014, 261)

Collaborative recall research has practical implications for people with declining memories. Research suggests that "collaborative recall is a social activity that can be used to maintain or improve memory in the elderly, and point[s] to the development of interventions that involve collaboration" (Blumen, Rajaram, and Henkel 2013, 111). These authors point out that nursing homes and retirement communities provide shared daily experiences for residents, which could form the basis for group discussions as way of developing collaborative retrieval situations.

This shows that if we take the embodied and extended approaches to cognition seriously, it becomes increasingly difficult to draw distinctions between restorative and compensatory rehabilitation on the basis of a biological/environmental divide. Technological aids can be both external to and part of the mind, and other people's cognitive capacities can be deeply intertwined with our own.

Cognitive Reserve

Embodied and extended cognitive science raises questions for our understanding of cognitive impairment and rehabilitation, but it might also shed new light on the remarkable resilience that some people have in the face of neural generation and disease. For several decades, we have known that people with the same degree of apparent brain damage can show very different symptoms (Katzman et al. 1989; Esiri et al. 2001; Knopman et al. 2003). Some people seem to have a sort of "mental padding" or a "buffering" capacity, which protects them from showing the most serious effects of brain damage.

Archer and colleagues document the following case study of "John," a seventy-three-year-old man who visited the National Hospital for Neurology and Neurosurgery in London (Archer et al. 2005). John was concerned that his ability to play chess had declined over the past two years: he would previously plan his game seven moves in advance, but now he was only able to plan three or four moves in advance. His family were not aware of him showing any sign of cognitive impairment, there were no changes in personality or language, and he continued to look after the household finances. He scored normally on all the neuropsychological tests, and his condition had not changed by the time of his death three years later. But when the autopsy was carried out, John's brain was discovered to have all the signs associated with advanced Alzheimer's disease: severe neurofibrillary tangle pathology, cerebral amyloid angiopathy, and Lewy body pathology in the brainstem and limbic structures. This was unexpected, because most people with such severe brain degeneration would have lost many of their mental abilities and would not be able to function without lots of help and support. But John's only problem seemed to be that his chess game was not as good as it used to be.

John's case is surprising but not unique. Neuropsychologists have introduced the concept of "cognitive reserve" to refer to this capacity for resilience that people such as John exhibit (Baltes et al. 1992; Stern 2002; Stern 2003). The higher a person's level of cognitive reserve, the less likely they are to show the cognitive decline associated with age, head injury, stroke, HIV, Parkinson's disease, Alzheimer's disease, or poisoning with neurotoxins.

We know little, however, about the mechanisms that underlie the phenomenon of cognitive reserve and protect some people from the most devastating effects of neural degeneration. The standard theory behind cognitive reserve assumes that neural mechanisms are responsible, such as the formation of new nerve cells in the brain (neurogenesis) and the brain's capacity to reorganize itself (neural plasticity). Cognitive reserve seems to be correlated with high levels of educational and occupational attainment, high IQ and literacy, and a stimulating and social lifestyle, which prompts neuropsychologists to propose that "specific mental stimuli and challenges during both childhood and adulthood stimulate the formation of complex neuronal networks and promote cognitive reserve capacity" (Bosma et al. 2003), and that "neuronal plasticity permits cognitive reserve to be enhanced or maintained during the adult years" (Richards and Sacker 2003).

If proponents of embodied and extended cognition are correct, however, then we should be wary of assuming that our performance on cognitive tasks is to be explained solely by neural factors. Embodied and extended cognitive science suggests that cognitive impairment does not require neural impairment and that restoring cognitive function does not necessarily require neural intervention. If some people are able to perform cognitive tasks better than others with similar neural degeneration, perhaps it is precisely because they are not relying solely on neurally implemented reasoning. Perhaps such people are using embodied and extended cognitive processes to supplement their neural resources.

There are similarities between the case of John and the Alzheimer's patients in St. Louis, discussed previously. They both function better and more independently in everyday life than their degree of brain damage would suggest. In the St. Louis Alzheimer's patients, we explain their abilities in terms of the structure of their immediate environment, their support networks, and the way they rely on gadgets and tools. So why, in John's case, do we assume that the reason for his resilience must have a neural basis? Admittedly, there is no evidence that John was reliant on environmental scaffolding. But not all reliance on external props is obvious: even those of us with undamaged brains count on our fingers, write shopping lists, and use pen and paper for complex arithmetic. Perhaps John had always been someone who relied on such tools and props, and so found it easier to adapt to neural degeneration without his family noticing much difference.

Recall that high cognitive reserve is correlated with high educational and occupational achievement, stimulating hobbies and busy social lives. Instead of assuming that these factors increase cognitive reserve by supporting neurogenesis or neural plasticity, why not consider whether these factors increase people's reliance on non-neural forms of cognitive support? Perhaps people with more complex or demanding lives develop ways to offload some of the cognitive work on aspects of the environment and their bodily interactions with it. It is possible that people who rely heavily on such tools and props in everyday life could find it easier to adapt to some forms of brain damage, because they are already supplementing their brain's abilities with external aids. As neural functioning declines, these embodied and extended aspects of the mind might be relied upon more and more. The damage might only become functionally salient in artificial conditions, such as those enforced by the rules and practices of chess.

At least one mechanism for cognitive reserve might involve this "off-loading" of cognitive tasks. A compelling (although fictional) example of cognitive off-loading can be found in the film *Memento*, in which Leonard tries to solve his wife's murder (Nolan et al. 2001). Leonard has anterograde amnesia and cannot form new biological memories to store the information he accumulates: instead he offloads memory task onto external aids, including information tattooed on his own body. (See Clark 2010 for further discussion).

Cognitive Disability

There are different models for understanding disability more generally, which can be applied to cognitive disability. Cognitive disability also raises distinct concerns of its own, to the extent that it can reduce one's capacity for rational autonomy.

Models of Disability

We have thus far focused on cognitive impairment and its rehabilitation and said little about cognitive *disability*. Models of disability focus on the limitations that people face in their everyday lives. In physical disability those limitations might involve limited access (e.g., being unable to enter a building with stairs) or limited knowledge (e.g., being unable to read documents that are not available in Braille). In the disability litera-ture, different models are proposed to account for these limitations. We focus here on two of the most salient: the medical model of disability and the social model of disability (Wasserman et al. 2016).

The *medical model of disability* focuses on limitations that can be understood as the result of an objective, biologically grounded medical impairment or dysfunction: being paralyzed, for example, or being partially sighted. The *social model of disability*, by con-trast, focuses on how environmental (rather than medical) factors contribute to the limitations faced by people with disabilities. If buildings were step-free, for example, a paralyzed person in a wheelchair would not face limitations to their access; if docu-ments were available in Braille, a partially sighted person would not face limitations to their knowledge. According to the social model of disability, medical impairments only result in limitations if society does not cater to those impairments. On this view, disability should not be seen as an intrinsic property of people, but rather as a relational property that they possess only relative to certain environments.

How does this work for *cognitive* disability? We have seen that the neurocentric approach to cognitive impairment understands the impairment as a medical condition resulting from neural trauma or degeneration. People with cognitive impairments can face limitations: they might be unable to remember to feed themselves on a regular basis, for example. If we apply the medical model to a neurocentric view of cognitive disability, then a person who cannot remember to feed themselves would be considered to have a disability as a result of a neural impairment. If we apply the social model of dis-ability to the same neurocentric view of cognitive disability, then someone who forgets to feed themselves will be considered to have a disability if they live in a society where people tend to live alone and are expected to look after themselves. If we apply the same model to a society in which multigenerational families live together and eat together, however, it is less obvious that forgetting to feed oneself should be considered a form of disability.

The medical and social models of disability offer radically different ways of thinking about disability, focusing either on biologically grounded dysfunction or on con-straints in the disabled person's environment. But if we reject the idea that cognitive impairment is solely a neural matter, then something interesting happens to the relation between the medical and social models: it looks like embodied and extended approaches to cognition change the nature of the debate about models of cognitive disability. If cognitive impairment can be the result of changes to the interactions between the bio-logical brain and the environment, then cognitive impairment is not necessarily the sort of biologically grounded dysfunction that the medical model of disability requires. Instead, it can involve the sorts of environmental factors that social models of disability take to be key to the nature of disability. But the embodied and extended approaches do not entail that the medical model is entirely wrong: there is still objective cognitive impairment to cognitive processes, just cognitive processes that extend beyond the bio-logical brain. And the degree of disability will tend to map onto the degree of cognitive impairment, as the medical model would predict. But the degree of cognitive impairment will be partly a feature of the person's interactions with their environment, so the degree of disability will also be a matter of environmental context, as the social model would predict.

The tension between medical and social models of disability, when applied to cognitive disability, relies on being able to draw a clear line between the biological and environmental aspects of cognitive impairment. Our point is that once we understand cognition as environmentally scaffolded rather than wholly neural, we have lost any clear distinction between biologically caused cognitive limitations and environmentally caused cognitive limitations.

Can Extended Minds Enhance Rational Autonomy?

A liberal society allows autonomous adults the freedom to pursue their own ends. It takes a more paternalistic attitude, however, to non-autonomous adults and children: judgments about what is in their best interests are often made by other people. Cognitive disability, such as dementia, poses a problem for liberalism when it leads to a loss of rational autonomy. How should the liberal society address the interests of the dementia subject?

Nelson (2010) proposes that Clark and Chalmers' (1998) work on extended cognition can be brought to bear on answering this question. He compares the views of Dworkin (1993) and Jaworska (1999) on how we should approach the critical interests of the person with dementia. In Dworkin's view, the interests of the person with dementia are deemed to be what the person last competently endorsed before losing rational autonomy. Jaworska denies this conclusion, arguing that people with dementia can lack full rational autonomy but still be in a position to understand the relationship between their experiences, assessments, and achievements. In such a case, Jaworska proposes, the person with dementia should be allowed to pursue new values and goals that they develop. Nelson worries that where a person with dementia develops a new value that conflicts with one they have cherished and pursued for decades, Jaworska's account would have us simply reject the person's previous interest in favor of the new one. Nelson proposes that the framework of the extended mind can provide us with a way to endorse Jaworska's view while still respecting the previous values of the dementia subject.

Nelson suggests that if people use external resources as part of their minds, as Otto arguably does with his notebook, then this would allow for their previously held beliefs (including evaluative beliefs) to count as part of their mind even if have they have since developed new conflicting beliefs: "the demented person's previously formed, possibly inconsistent beliefs may well be as much a part of her mind as her recently formed views" (Nelson 2010, 234). While this is an intriguing idea, we do not think that the extended mind can play the role that Nelson requires. Clark and Chalmers (1998) argue that the contents of the notebook qualify as Otto's dispositional beliefs to the extent that they play the appropriate functional role: that Otto automatically endorses them when he retrieves them, for example, just as Inga automatically endorses the memories she retrieves. If the dementia subject retrieves and endorses a previously held evaluative belief from the notebook, then this becomes an occurrent (and presumably internal) evaluative belief and can thus contribute to the person's critical interests on Jaworska's view. (If it conflicts with another currently expressed belief, this is no different to the (notebook-less) dementia subject expressing an inconsistent belief set.) But if the dementia subject does not retrieve and endorse the previously held evaluative belief, then the notebook contents are no longer playing the functional role of dispositional belief: they are comparable to information that Inga stored in long-term biological memory but can no longer access. We thus fail to see how the case of the extended mind can play the role that Nelson seems to require of it, as creating a special kind of link between the dementia subject and their previously held values. Either the notebook contents are endorsed by Otto as occurrent beliefs, or they are simply a record of what he used to think and thus no different to a diary or letters expressing previously held views.

Francis and Silvers (2010) take a different approach to protecting the interests of people with cognitive disabilities but one that also has some parallels with the literature on cognitive extension. Francis and Silvers propose that we can protect the interests of a dementia subject in liberal society by assigning them a trustee: someone who collaborates with the subject "to build conceptions of their good that command considerability" (Francis and Silvers 2010, 247). Their theory of trusteeship doesn't explicitly draw on the extended mind literature, but there are clear parallels in their talk of trustees as "mental prostheses":

> In the collaboration we envision, the trustee does not step into the subject's role in shaping a personalized notion of the good. Instead, as a prosthetic arm or leg executes some of the functions of a missing fleshly one without being confused with or supplanting the usual fleshly limb, so, we propose, a trustee's reasoning and communicating can execute part or all of a subject's own thinking processes without substituting the trustee's own idea as if it were the subject's own.
>
> (Francis and Silvers 2010, 247)

We have nothing to say in opposition to the trusteeship approach, but it seems unlikely to gain support from the literature on extended minds. In all the paradigm cases of mental extension, the subject's internal cognitive processes extend beyond the boundaries of the human being, but the subject is still the locus of cognitive control and ownership. The contents of the notebook are the contents of Otto's own beliefs, for example, and Otto decides how to use his beliefs in order to fulfill his desires. If the notebook was not enmeshed in Otto's cognitive processes in this way, we would hesitate to refer to its contents as Otto's beliefs: we would be more inclined to see the notebook as an external tool that Otto uses to supplement his (internal) cognitive processes. In Francis and Silvers's case, the trustee is more like an external resource in this respect. The trustee is performing cognitive processes *on behalf of* the dementia subject, but these are still the trustee's cognitive processes and not those of the dementia subject.

The best example we have of someone using another person as a cognitive resource comes from the memory literature discussed already. The clearest cases of this sort of extended cognition came from a particular kind of intimate relationship where the cognitive processes of two or more people have become intertwined over time such that they share mental states like memories. Notice that this is not the kind of "mental prosthesis" that Francis and Silvers are looking for in their theory of trusteeship. For them, it is important that the trustee's cognitive systems are not enmeshed in this way with the dementia subject's cognitive systems: trustees and dementia subjects should not have intertwined mental states and processes, because the trustee should be an independent agent who can separate their own values and beliefs from the values and beliefs of the dementia subject. The trustee must "be able to abstract himself from the process and its product" (Francis and Silvers 2010, 254). We propose, therefore, that the relationship between the trustee and the subject is unlikely to constitute a case of genuine mental extension.

Conclusion

Embodied and extended approaches to cognitive science can be understood primarily as methodologies or research programs. They suggest that when thinking about cognition, we should be prepared to look beyond the brain. They can also be understood, however, as making a stronger and more metaphysical claim. Proponents of embodied or extended cognitive science can be interpreted as claiming that our minds are partly constituted by the non-neural stuff, such that Otto's notebook, for example, would literally be part of his mind.

On this stronger constitutional claim, ethical issues come to the fore. Consider the forceful relocation of an Alzheimer's patient from their own home into a hospital setting: this might not merely change their external environment but actually damage their cognitive processing further. And when an Alzheimer's patient such as Otto has their notebook stolen, are they merely the victim of theft. Or has some greater damage been done to them as a person or moral agent? As a society, we do not yet enjoy a structure of laws and social policies that recognizes the deep intimacy of agents and their cognitive scaffoldings: intimacy such that certain harms to the environment can simultaneously be harms to the person. And reflections on embodied and extended cognitive science alone do not seem to settle such questions. If anything, they highlight the complicated relationship between minds, persons, individuals, and agents. The question of morality arises with respect to mental interventions because having a mind generally denotes having other properties: consciousness, rationality, personhood, or agency, for example. But it is not clear that thinking of the mind as embodied or extended has direct implications for any or all of these features: it will depend on whether we identify the *individual* with the biological body, for example, while identifying the *agent* with the locus of causation and action. Whatever implications one takes extended and embodied cognitive science to have for ethics may be further mediated by one's views of personhood and agency in their various guises. Extended and embodied minds thus raise new ways of looking at the relationship between embodiment, individuality, and agency, while still leaving many important (and potentially morally salient) issues unresolved.

REFERENCES

Archer, H. A., J. M. Schott, Josephine. Barnes, et al. 2005 "Knight's Move Thinking? Mild Cognitive Impairment in a Chess Player." *Neurocase* 11(1):26–31.

Baltes M., Klaus-Peter Kühl, and D. Sowarka. 1992. "Testing for Limits of Cognitive Reserve Capacity: A Promising Strategy for Early Diagnosis of Dementia? *Journals of Gerontology* 47(3): 165–167.

Barnier, Amanda J., Alice C. Priddis, Jennifer M. Broekhuijse, et al. 2014. "Reaping What They Sow: Benefits of Remembering Together in Intimate Couples." *Journal of Applied Research in Memory and Cognition* 3(4): 261–265.

Blumen, Helena M., Suparna Rajaram, and Linda A. Henkel. 2013. "The Applied Value of Collaborative Memory Research in Aging: Behavioral and Neural Considerations. *Journal of Applied Research in Memory and Cognition* 2(2): 107–117

Bosma Hans, Martin P. J. van Boxtel, Rudolf Ponds, et al. 2003. "Mental Work Demands Protect Against Cognitive Impairment." MAAS Prospective Cohort Study. *Experimental Aging Research* 29(1): 33–45.

Brooks, Rodney. 1991. "Intelligence Without Representation." *Artificial Intelligence* 47: 139–159.

Clark, Andy. 2003. *Natural-Born Cyborgs: Minds, Technologies, and the Future of Human Intelligence*. Oxford: Oxford University Press.

Clark, Andy. 2010. "Memento's Revenge: The Extended Mind Extended." In *The Extended Mind*, edited by Richard Menary, 43–66. Cambridge, MA: MIT Press.

Clark, Andy, and David J. Chalmers. 1998. "The Extended Mind." *Analysis* 58(1): 7–19.

Coltheart Max. 1991. "Cognitive Psychology Applied to the Treatment of Acquired Language Disorders." *Handbook of Behavior Therapy and Psychological Science: An Integrative Approach*, 216–227. Oxford: Pergamon Press.

Dawson, Deirdre R. and Thomas D. Marcotte. 2017. "Special Issue on Ecological Validity and Cognitive Assessment." *Neuropsychological Rehabilitation* 27(5): 599–602.

Dworkin, Ronald. 1993. *Life's Dominion*. New York: Knopf.

Esiri Margaret M., Fiona Matthews, Carol Brayne, et al. 2001. "Pathological Correlates of Late-Onset Dementia in a Multicentre, Community-Based Population in England and Wales." *The Lancet* 357(9251): 169–175.

Francis, Leslie. P., and Anita Silvers. 2010. "Thinking About the Good: Reconfiguring Liberal Metaphysics (or Not) for People with Cognitive Disabilities." In *Cognitive Disability and Its Challenge to Moral Philosophy*, edited by E. F. Kittay and L. Carlson, 237–259. Oxford: Wiley-Blackwell.

Gibson, James J. 1967. "New Reasons for Realism." *Synthese* 17(1): 162–172.

Gibson, James J. 1979. *The Ecological Approach to Visual Perception*. New York: Houghton Mifflin.

Ienca, Marcello, Jotterand Fabrice, Bernice Elger, et al. 2017. "Intelligent Assistive Technology for Alzheimer's Disease and Other Dementias: A Systematic Review." *Journal of Alzheimer's Disease* 56(4): 1301–1340.

Institute of Medicine. 2011. *Cognitive Rehabilitation Therapy for Traumatic Brain Injury: Evaluating the Evidence.* Washington, DC: The National Academies Press. doi:10.17226/13220.

Jaworska, Agnieszka. 1999. "Respecting the Margins of Agency." *Philosophy and Public Affairs* 28(2):105–138.

Katzman, Robert, Miriam Aronson, P. A. Fuld, et al. 1989. "Development of Dementing Illnesses in an 80-Year-Old Volunteer Cohort. *Annals of Neurology* 25: 317–324.

Knopman, D. S., J. E. Parisi, Alessandro Salviati, et al. 2003. "Neuropathology of Cognitively Normal Elderly." *Journal of Neuropathology and Experimental Neurology* 62(11): 1087–1095.

Mataric, Maja J. 1991. "Navigating With a Rat Brain: A Neurobiologically-Inspired Model for Robot Spatial Representation." *From Animals to Animats: Proceedings of the Adaptive Behavior Conference '91,* edited by S. Wilson and J. Arcady-Meyer, 169–175. Cambridge, MA: MIT Press.

McBeath, Michael K., Dennis M. Shaffer, and Mary K. Kaiser. 1995. "How Baseball Outfielders Determine Where to Run to Catch Fly Balls." *Science, 268* (5210): 569–573.

Nelson, James Lindemann. 2010. "Alzheimer's Disease and Socially Extended Mentation." In *Cognitive Disability and Its Challenge to Moral Philosophy,* edited by E. F. Kittay and L. Carlson, 225–236. Oxford: Wiley-Blackwell.

Nolan, Christopher, dir. 2001. *Memento.* Culver City, CA: Columbia TriStar Home Entertainment.

Richards, Marcus, and Amanda Sacker. 2003. "Lifetime Antecedents of Cognitive Reserve." *Journal of Clinical and Experimental Neuropsychology* 25(5):614–624.

Sneddon, Andrew. 2002. Towards Externalist Psychopathology. *Philosophical Psychology* 15(3): 297–316.

Stern, Yaakov. 2002. "What is Cognitive Reserve? Theory and Research Application of the Reserve Concept." *Journal of the International Neuropsychological Society* 8(03): 448–460.

Stern, Yaakov. 2003. "The Concept of Cognitive Reserve: A Catalyst for Research." *Journal of Clinical and Experimental Neuropsychology* 25(5): 589–593.

Sutton, John, Celia B. Harris, Paul G. Keil, and Amanda J. Barnier. 2010. "The Psychology of Memory, Extended Cognition, and Socially Distributed Remembering." *Phenomenology and the Cognitive Sciences* 9(4): 521–560.

Wasserman, David, Adrienne Asch, Jeffrey Blustein, and Daniel Putnam. 2016. "Disability: Definitions, Models, Experience." In *The Stanford Encyclopedia of Philosophy.* Edited by Edward N. Zalta. Stanford, CA: Stanford University Press. https://plato.stanford.edu/archives/sum2016/entries/disability/.

Wegner, Daniel. M. 1987. "Transactive Memory: A Contemporary Analysis of the Group Mind. In *Theories of Group Behavior,* edited by B. Mullen B. and G. R. Goethals, 185–208. New York, NY: Springer-Verlag.

CHAPTER 34

··

THE VISIBLE AND THE INVISIBLE

Disability, Assistive Technology, and Stigma

··

COREEN McGUIRE AND HAVI CAREL

INTRODUCTION

THE heterogeneity of disability has presented a central challenge to philosophical and legal attempts to define it. The two cases we examine here, hearing loss and breathlessness (leading to reduced mobility), seem to have little in common. Yet both conditions are associated with aging and entail negative stereotypes that can be avoided by hiding or rejecting the ameliorating technology; namely, hearing aids and ambulatory oxygen.

Moreover, such assistive technology and the medical measurement of hearing loss and breathlessness often fail to take account of diverse and individual conditions and experiences.

Hearing loss can be affected by many variables, which makes its impact on people's lives difficult to measure.[1] Similarly, the subjective experiences and effects of breathlessness are notoriously difficult to correlate with objectively measured lung function and are significantly affected by the life experience and psychology of the person.[2] It also presents definitional difficulties, which we note but will not discuss further; here, we explore breathlessness as a pathological, impairing dysfunction.[3]

Both conditions are more common in adults, and prevalence increases with age.[4] This is especially important to our consideration of hearing loss. We focus primarily on the experience of those losing their hearing later in life because the use of hearing aids and the stigma associated with their use is far more prevalent among the "deafened" than it is within the Deaf community, who have their own cultural identity which often promotes sign language use and resists technological intervention.[5] While Deaf activists have chosen to reject or embrace auditory assistance in terms of a celebration of Deafness and Deaf identity, this chapter does not focus on this history, which has been thoroughly explored.[6] Rather, we are concerned with the experiences of the "deafened." That is, those who identify as hearing and experience their hearing loss as a loss.

Similarly, our consideration of ambulatory oxygen is mainly concerned with the experiences of those for whom the need for the technology represents a new and unwelcome hardship, often accompanied by a distressing diagnosis of a progressive respiratory disease. Respiratory diseases such as chronic obstructive pulmonary disease (COPD) affect mostly adults and are more prevalent with age because many are smoking and/or age induced.

The stigma attached to conditions associated with aging is complicated by the fact that, in addition, both conditions are potentially invisible and offer the potential to remain so for the sufferer who chooses not to accept assistive equipment. Thus, the temptation to hide the impairment is compounded by the invisible nature of these impairments. Hearing loss is only apparent if the person with hearing loss chooses to expose it. And there are good reasons why declaring an impairment is not always the best course of action for a disabled person, as Adam Cureton (2018) argues.

Breathlessness is largely invisible and its external manifestations can be masked by a respiratory patient motivated enough to conceal her condition. In addition, respiratory patients often have limited mobility, suffer from frequent respiratory infections, and struggle with weather extremes, so, when they are at their worst, they are usually confined to their house, bed, or hospital. This adds to the invisibility of respiratory conditions. Some respiratory patients are housebound because of their breathlessness and many hide their problem because they are afraid of being judged for making lifestyle choices such as smoking. This led Gysels and Higginson to term breathlessness an "invisible symptom" (Gysels and Higginson 2008; British Lung Foundation 2007).

Finally, both hearing loss and breathlessness are notable for a high incidence of user rejection and modification of prescribed technology. Stuart Blume has pointed out that

> [i]n designing medical, as any other, technologies, all kinds of assumptions regarding the intended users—their heights and weights, competences, preferences, behaviour and values—are made. But the user "inscribed" in a technology, imagined by its designers, may not correspond with real users in the real world.
> (Blume 2010)

This foregrounds the issue of the importance given to users' expertise. By exploring historical examples of users as experts, we add credence to Scully's recent claim that the specialist knowledge that the disabled have regarding how their bodies' needs are best met has been consistently undervalued, perpetuating a cycle of epistemic injustice specific to the disabled (Scully 2018). This argument can also be framed in terms of justice; as Goering and Klein have argued, the views of end users ought to be seriously considered at the start of the design process if the technology is intended to benefit the disabled (Goering and Klein 2020). Thus, the desire to avoid stigma extends to the epistemic domain, where visible signs of dysfunction, illness, or disability may unfairly compromise the credibility assigned to the disabled person *qua* knower and producer of knowledge, further damaging their agency (Carel and Kidd 2014; Kidd and Carel 2016).

In the following sections, we examine two historical case studies concerning auditory and respiratory assistive technology (AT). Following from these examples, we turn, in the next section, to phenomenology as a framework that can ameliorate the difficulties with adopting such technologies because of their stigmatizing costs, as well as combating the epistemic injustice just described. We use these ideas to explore how the use of technology affects disability, social relations, communication, and identity.

A final introductory comment is in order: in this chapter, we discuss both illness and disability but wish to retain a clear difference between the two categories. We think that retaining the difference between them is important because whether one identifies as ill or disabled may influence how one reacts to AT. The user's desire to mask the impairment or her willingness to trial AT is probably influenced, at least in part, by whether she identifies as ill or as disabled. In particular, people with adult-onset breathlessness or hearing loss are probably less likely to categorize themselves as disabled compared to people with a congenital hearing loss or those suffering from a childhood respiratory condition such as cystic fibrosis. So, their identity and interests may be quite different from that of some disabled people. In addition, the two literatures that have emerged— on illness and on disability—are distinct. We wish to appeal to both as well as to acknowledge the overlap between the interests and challenges facing members of both groups while retaining the distinctiveness of each.

Assistive Auditory Technology

Between 1912 and 1981, the British Post Office controlled a nationalized telephone system. Links between telephony and hearing loss have long been noted by both historians of sound and historians of science, and the Post Office's engineers had unparalleled expertise in both telecommunications and hearing assistive devices. Subsequent cross-fertilization between telephony and hearing AT embedded the connections between hearing loss and telephony in devices like electronic hearing aids and amplified telephones for "deaf subscribers."[7] The Post Office functioned as an arbitrator of both hearing loss and hearing aids. However, the Post Office's standardizations of "normal" hearing and devices to correct "abnormal" hearing did not always correlate with the needs and experiences of its users.

For example, with the advent of the British National Health Service (NHS), the Post Office decided to modify its amplified telephones so its "deaf subscribers" could use the telephone with their new NHS hearing aids. This case provides a microcosm of the issues at stake when designers produce prosthetics without consulting the users.

Plans for an NHS hearing aid were raised in 1947, after World War II, and this device became known as the Medresco, a contraction of "Medical Research Council."[8] Instead of designing a new amplified telephone alongside this, the Post Office engineers designed an adaptor to *link* the new hearing aids with telephone receivers. This, they believed, would have the advantage of allowing users to link into any telephone and not just their home sets.

The Engineering Department thus began to create an acoustic coupler to link the amplified telephone with the Medresco. Subscribers already using the amplified telephones were not consulted before the telephone was designed because "as far as likely users are concerned the subjective conditions likely to be met with will be extremely varied and cannot be satisfied equally."[9] Although there was recognition of the diverse needs of people with hearing loss, the design of the telephones was conducted entirely to the specifications of the engineers, with no input from relevant users. The Public Relations Department reiterated this conclusion and declared that "no useful purpose would be served by undertaking interviews with deaf persons as was originally proposed."[10]

However, it was the organization of user trials of the device that rang the death knell for this project.[11] When people actually used the adaptor, it became clear that the engineers had not considered the reality of hearing aid use from a female perspective. The stigma attached to hearing aids meant that most users concealed the devices under clothing. Men would easily conceal the aid in jacket or shirt pockets, but most women had to disguise the aid under skirts, making use of stockings and suspender belts to attach the device to their person. The failure of the engineers to envision practical use meant that the clip-on attachment for the phone was difficult for women concealing the aid to use without partially undressing. Moreover, the adapter had to be attached to the microphone of the hearing aid, which was usually embedded within garments.

The first tester to respond was female and she stated that "I consider the aid unsuitable for a girl who wears the aid concealed under clothing as I do."[12] The second respondent also emphasized the fact that, "if, like myself, the user wears the aid concealed, it means that one has to detach the microphone case from the inside of ones [*sic*] apparel each time it is used."[13] Similar objections were made by all the female correspondents, but perhaps the most succinct expression of the problem came from the Head Postmaster in Malton, Yorkshire, who had been using an amplified telephone for his work at the Post Office for years. He asked if he could test out the adaptor and responded to its trial with a detailed letter. While he felt the adaptor was useful for his purposes, he candidly pointed out that:

> Now, how a woman would manipulate the phone and where she would fit her aid is up to her, but she could hardly be expected to partly undress, and women are a bit keen to undisclose the aid outside, but to me—a man—I don't mind in the least as it is results I am concerned about. I must hear at all costs—regardless of sight of plastic bands etc.[14]

Essentially, the adaptor perfectly suited the needs of the engineers but not the needs of their so-called Deaf Subscribers. By choosing not to consult people with hearing loss who wore hearing aids and desired to use the telephone, the Post Office had engineered a device that was completely unsuitable for the everyday lived reality of hearing loss. In fact, they had designed an aid that was inconvenient for everyone except for a stereotypical man working in an office for the Post Office. Figure Figure 34.1 shows such idealized use of the telephone adaptor, with a man wearing work clothes and the microphone easily concealed in pockets.

This is a paradigmatic case of intersectionality, in which the hearing loss and female identity intersect to produce an outcome—rejection of AT—that is particularly pernicious to women with hearing loss. As can be seen from the postmaster's quote, there is an additional onus on women to "undisclose" the aid, more so than a man, so they are doubly affected. First, women experience a more powerful social requirement to hide their hearing loss, and, second, the device that can be concealed while being effectively used in a man's suit cannot be thus used by a woman wearing a dress.

The engineers' purely technical approach did not allow for the social aspects of deafness. There was no awareness of the stigma that surrounded hearing loss or the difference that gender made to the way people wanted to use such devices. In the case of the Head Postmaster in Yorkshire, he had to simply *hear* at all costs, whereas for the female correspondents, concealment was prioritized over efficiency. Due to the overwhelmingly negative feedback from users, the Post Office canceled the project. The decision not to consult end users at the start of the design process meant that the product was not acceptable to people with hearing loss who desired access to telephony.

ASSISTIVE RESPIRATORY TECHNOLOGY

The need to understand the lived experience of the user is also apparent in the early design of respiratory technology. This is particularly evident in the analysis of a "failed technology," The Bragg-Paul Pulsator. The Bragg-Paul Pulsator was an alternative to the iron lung respirators that encased the body of the patient in heavy, cabinet-type devices. These so-called iron lungs were designed by Phillip Drinker and Louis Shaw and were first used in the United Kingdom in 1930 (Science Museum London 2018). This early design was superseded by the iron lungs designed by E. T. Both, manufactured in the United Kingdom in William Morris's (the later Lord Nuffield) car factories in response to the large polio epidemics of 1947–1950. Lord Nuffield donated more than 5,000 of these devices (Hurley 2013). However, like the Drinker device, the Both Iron Lung meant that the patient was entirely encased in a cabinet with only her head protruding and with only the capacity to eat, drink, and sleep (Drinker 1931). The depth and rate of breathing was controlled by an attendant, not by the patient.[15]

In contrast, the Bragg-Paul Pulsator prioritized the mobility and freedom of the patient. It was designed for use in the home and for the patient's family to use easily (see Figure 34.2). The prioritization of patient freedom can be traced to the origins of its design, which was in collaboration with and prompted by the needs of a user. William Bragg, the Nobel Prize-winning physicist, had a neighbor who needed continual artificial

FIGURE 34.1 The Medresco Hearing Aid Telephone Adapter.

Special Apparatus Fitted on Telephone Exchange Lines Rented by Deaf Subscribers. BT Archives TCB_2_172.
McMillan, D., and W. West. 1951. "Post Office Engineering Department Research Report No. 12814:
A Hearing Aid Telephone Adapter." Plate 1.

respiration from nurses, meaning that his wife was unable to speak with him except in the presence of the nurses.[16] Bragg explained that:

> A neighbour of mine in the country has for some years been suffering from a terrible wasting of the muscles. He has long lost all power of moving his limbs and for the last 12 or 18 months has been unable to breathe without aid. For a long time two nurses were employed giving artificial respiration continually: the wife felt very much the disability of being unable to speak to him except in the presence of a nurse because her strength had considerably diminished due to the strain of her husband's illness, and she was unable therefore to give artificial respiration herself.
>
> I then had the idea that I could ease matters by a simple system of India rubber bladders, football bladders in fact. One of these was placed under a binder for the body, the other between two wooden boards on the ground: they are connected by a wide tube. The one on the ground was between a pair of hinged boards and a hand lever enabled anyone sitting in a chair to compress and release the air in this bladder. This has been entirely successful; it has been in use for many months and the wife can now give artificial respiration while she sits and reads to her husband; only one nurse is now required.[17]

This portable system offered the patient both more mobility and more control over their breathing. Moreover, it was much less intrusive, thus resulting in the potential for a better quality of life for the patient. Crucially, the Pulsator prioritized mobility and allowed patients to live outside of hospitals. This device was also cheaper than the cabinet-style iron lungs (Virdi 2016). However, the donation of iron lungs to hospitals throughout Britain allowed for free and easy institutional usage of the iron lungs. These

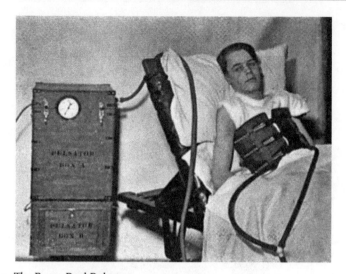

FIGURE 34.2 The Bragg Paul Pulsator.
Wellcome Collection Images, "Bragg Paul Pulsator." Available at https://wellcomecollection.org/works/hx4dtmc9

devices have become symbolic of polio and are still used by patients today, whereas the last of the Bragg Paul Pulsators were purchased by the Admiralty for use at sea during World War II (Woollam 1976). The pulsators were not patented because the developers wanted them to be freely available. However, a patent can allow for easier replication, so this may have backfired. (Arapostathis and Gooday 2013).[18] Whatever the reason for their failure, what can be seen in the preceding quotation is the engagement with the patient's needs and also those of his wife, including needs that go beyond the strictly medical need for respiration, such as the need for privacy.

Similar problems remain with us today. A 2002 study identified that many COPD patients do not use ambulatory oxygen due to many factors including lack of instruction, lack of confidence, inability to lift the device, lack of caregivers, and stigma. The study concluded by explaining that "this highlights the difficulties that patients face when asked to incorporate medical technology into their lives and illustrates the pitfalls associated with designing technologies without reference to the ultimate end users" (Arnold et al. 2011).

The problems of ambulatory oxygen technology arise from several characteristics of the equipment and engineering constraints. These are the equipment's size and weight, its limited portability, its prominent medical appearance, and the association of breathlessness with being lazy or unfit, leading to stigma. The equipment is also potentially hazardous (e.g., in case of a leak or fire) and requires training and confidence to use, which makes it unappealing to more frail or insecure patients.

In terms of weight and size, portability and usability are at a tradeoff. The more oxygen a user wishes to carry, the larger and heavier the canister. The less they carry, the shorter the duration away from a permanent source of oxygen (today in the form of an oxygen concentrating machine). For users with already compromised aerobic capacity and often limited strength and a relatively advanced age, the ambulatory oxygen can be too heavy to carry. Solutions in the form of a trolley or a caregiver further limit the independence of the user and may require staying on paved ground or having a caregiver with them at all times. Handling the equipment is also difficult, as refilling liquid oxygen flasks requires the strength of a typical adult and lifting canisters in and out of a car may also prove challenging to the respiratory patient.

Oxygen equipment also has a clear medical (and hence stigmatizing) appearance. Large oxygen canisters, nasal cannulas, and the noise created by the oxygen flow can be experienced as deeply stigmatizing and can interfere with some activities (e.g., in the cinema or at a concert, where the noise of the oxygen flow or the noise of a portable oxygen concentrator motor might be deemed unacceptable). The connotations of severe illness and the accompanying fear of contagion further exacerbate the user's sense that the equipment is stigmatizing. A further sense of shame may arise from the association between respiratory disease and smoking (possibly attributing to the user responsibility for her condition). The relative rareness of such equipment seen outside a hospital increases the interest of and thus questions and comments from strangers, so the user also suffers some loss of privacy and anonymity.

Thus the user may find herself trapped between the Scylla of attracting attention with cumbersome oxygen equipment and the Charybdis of appearing to suffer from excessive breathlessness upon performing routine actions. Such breathlessness is also a source of shame as it often gives rise to comments about the person's age or their being lazy or unfit. In short, there is no good way to deal with breathlessness without attracting some level of unwanted interest and condemnation, and these are particularly difficult for certain groups. For example, teenage cystic fibrosis patients are known to be particularly sensitive to their image, and this affects their willingness to take medication in public.[19]

How could these considerations be taken into account in designing home and ambulatory oxygen equipment for use outside the hospital? A recent example is Oxy-View—a product that delivers oxygen through tubes hidden inside glasses frames, thus making the oxygen delivery more "discreet" and offering "greater social acceptance" and "improved self-esteem."[20] As the website states: "when you're wearing Oxy-View eyeglasses, you'll feel better about getting out and doing the things you love. People will no longer see someone on oxygen, but rather the vibrant person you really are."[21]

There is no medical benefit to this product as compared to other devices. It is designed to conceal the fact that the person wearing the Oxy-View glasses uses oxygen. Literature for other products, such as portable oxygen concentrators, emphasize the "elegant" and "stylish" design of the machines, demonstrating awareness of user sensitivity to how they look and how they are perceived. This indicates that the stakes that are so obvious to users are increasingly acknowledged by assistive oxygen technology developers.

Such design connotes an implicit hierarchy of acceptable disability. It indicates that it is preferable to fake sight loss over revealing genuine respiratory illness. Related to this is the fact that people with respiratory illness (especially adult-onset illness) are unlikely to categorize themselves as disabled or link up with disability pride movements that might celebrate a prosthesis as an important and intrinsic part of their identity. Rather, they are more likely to experience loss of function *as a loss* that the AT might be able to augment. However, this augmentation may come at a high cost for those seeking to "pass" as non-disabled.

It is known that patients delay use of oxygen for several reasons, including fear of stigma, wanting to avoid the risk of "outing," and denial about the severity of their condition. There is a fundamental psychological difference between having a respiratory condition that requires oxygen and having one that does not. Oxygen indicates the advanced stage of the disease and the severe limitations on activity. Being told that one needs to use oxygen therapy can be a big psychological blow, especially for people who place a high premium on their appearance and what others know or think about them. Anecdotally, such responses seem to also conform to traditional conceptions of gender identity, so the need for oxygen equipment is perceived differently by men and women. Thus, for example, oxygen may pose a threat to strong traditional masculinity, while the focus on impact on appearance may be more of an issue for women.[22]

Without oxygen, many masking strategies are available. The advent of the Smartphone enables respiratory patients to mask their breathlessness by looking at their phone when they stop to catch their breath. Mobile phones have a myriad of social uses, and this is a good example of using the device to divert attention away from one's need to stop and make an awkward stop look natural. Other strategies include meeting people at a stationary meeting point, rather than walking there together, saying "I'll meet you there" or "I'll catch you up," and engineering social situations that involve little or no walking.[23]

A Phenomenological Framework for Assistive Technology Design

The previous sections demonstrate failures of technology development and lack of take-up that stem from a deep oversight—namely, the failure to engage users in the design of AT.[24] We claim that this oversight is conceptual as it stems from the view of such AT purely in terms of its function but does not consider users' needs and desires. That, we claim, arises from a narrow view of the AT as aiming to correct a physiological dysfunction, seen as divorced from its sociocultural context. As Carel argues, this narrow view constricts our understanding of illness and disability and restricts the ways in which we creatively respond to it, to the detriment of ill and disabled persons, as well as society at large (Carel 2013, 2016*b*; Kidd and Carel 2018). In the case of AT, failure to understand the subjective experiences of disabled people resulted in underuse and rejection of technologies aimed at ameliorating and supporting disabled people.

To briefly recap: in the late 1940s, the Post Office designed a link-up between telephones and hearing aids. A device was designed without asking potential users whether and how they would use it. As a result, only one man, himself a Post Office employee, could envisage using it in his day-to-day business. When women trialed the device after it was developed, it became apparent that the engineers had failed to imagine hearing aid use from a female perspective or to consider the way that stigma affected usage. This failure meant that the attempt was entirely discarded, to the long-term detriment of those with hearing loss wishing to use the telephone.

We also discussed the case of ambulatory oxygen, where cumbersome design, stigma, and difficulties using the devices led to the rejection of ambulatory oxygen. We touched on the objective engineering difficulties but also saw how those are coupled with a perception of ambulatory oxygen as a medical substance that is prescribed by health professionals, not one desired by users. From the user point of view, ambulatory oxygen is what enables some people with respiratory disease to be active, travel, and continue to participate in everyday activities and self-care. The primary medical goal of prolonging survival is some way off these more concrete and tangible aims that are the focal point of users.

In both cases, we see deep discrepancies between the AT design and users' identity, goals, and habits which impact on their acceptance of the technology. As in the historical case study, the origin of design—stemming from the user or the medical establishment—affects the extent to which lifestyle factors are considered as key to the design's remit.

Moreover, the use of AT in the cases we discussed serves to "out" the users as disabled and is thus rejected also because the technology forecloses the possibility of "passing," which is otherwise available to these invisible disabilities. "Passing" often involves foregoing medical technology to mitigate impairments, whereas adopting that technology often involves a rejection of "passing" since the AT can make invisible disabilities highly salient. This raises the possibility that consulting with users of AT might lead to more discreet, less salient devices since many of those users want to "pass." Users may want to "pass" for many reasons, including wanting to have control over their identity and personal information. But the effects of ableism are powerful enough to trump other needs so that "passing" may become more important than amelioration.[25]

We are not advocating prioritizing disguise over function. This is something that disabled people (especially the Deaf) have often railed against as being a result of prejudice that makes the devices less effective. What we are committed to is the fundamental phenomenological insight that people have different experiences of illness and disability and that this diversity of attitudes, needs, and goals needs to be captured by researchers prior to designing AT (Carel 2016b). Thus, if discreteness is of prime importance to certain users, they should at least be consulted so that can be an option. We are advocating for co-production because this process captures and gives salience to users' choices and their lifeworld. We reject disregard for the perspective and experience of people who are the intended users, whether they want to "pass" or not.

We end by suggesting that a phenomenological study, attuned to users' needs, goals, and capabilities, may shed light on such failures and pave the way to better co-productive AT design. Three phenomenological principles provide a framework for such design: understanding the lifeworld of the user, viewing the AT as something that needs to be incorporated into the body schema of the user, and considering the attentional focus of those who may come into contact with the designed technology.[26] We end the chapter by discussing each of these.

The first principle requires that we understand the lifeworld of the user: What are their goals? What material, social, environmental, physical, and psychological barriers need to be considered in order to ensure optimal design and uptake by users? How does the potential user perceive his or her place in the world, and how could that be modified by the AT? These are the kinds of questions that need to be asked prior to developing such technology. As noted in Carel's *Illness*: "being ill is not just an objective constraint imposed on a biological body part but a systematic shift in the way the body experiences, acts, and reacts as a whole. The change in illness is not local but global, not external but strikes at the heart of subjectivity" (Carel 2013).

In order to fully understand disability (or illness) one must see it as a particular form of life that may differ in important respects from that of other styles of embodiment. We need to understand that form of life so that amelioration will cohere and harmonize with the lifeworld of the disabled person. Without a close familiarity with the goals, desires, abilities, constraints, and ambitions of the disabled person, the AT design is unlikely to be maximally suited to those needs and abilities. This kind of information can be gleaned from qualitative interviews with disabled persons in which such questions are explicitly probed. It is also important to approach the issue not from a deficit approach which emphasizes the disability but from a strengths-based approach which focuses on what is possible and desirable for the person or community (Carel 2016*a*).

The second principle requires viewing the AT as needing to be incorporated into the body schema of the user. Such AT is not a machine that can be considered in terms of efficiency and function divorced from the body of the user. It cannot be conceived without seeing it in the context of embodied use. Designing ambulatory oxygen that can be carried by a healthy person but is too heavy for someone with impaired lungs is of little use to the user. Similarly, a hearing aid adaptor that does not allow for use when concealed under clothing was of little use to women in the 1940s. As Merleau-Ponty writes in his discussion of incorporation: "the blind man's stick has ceased to be an object for him, and is no longer perceived for itself; its point has become an area of sensitivity, extending the scope and active radius of touch, and providing a parallel to sight" (Merleau-Ponty 1962).

This paradigmatic example demonstrates how the stick becomes incorporated into the body schema of the blind person so it is truly part of the sensing of the blind man. The AT needs to be conceived of as an intimate part of the body schema and bodily habits of the user. Thus, understanding the body schema and bodily habits of users is crucial to such design efforts (Carel 2013). A prosthetic limb that remains foreign and obtrusive to its user is of little value, and different levels of incorporation could significantly impact our understanding of the AT as well as to our understanding of the body–environment boundary, as noted by Wasserman and Campbell (2017). As Wasserman and Campbell suggest, we need a more nuanced understanding of the relationship between body and environment, including challenging the dichotomy of individual–environment, which, in turn, challenges the social model of disability. We agree with Wasserman and Campbell that the "strong priority" the social model of disability gives to "changing the environment rather than the individual" unnecessarily limits thinking about AT (Wasserman and Campbell 2017).

The third principle is considering the attentional focus of those who may come into contact with the designed technology. Do users need or prefer for the devices to be completely or partially hidden? Can we give them control over when and whether to reveal the presence of the hearing aid or oxygen tank? Is the concealment an absolute requirement for potential users, such as the women in the case described earlier? Are there other needs, such as aesthetic properties or intelligibility, that are crucial to users? As we saw in the historical examples, there is a real need to cease thematizing such equipment purely in terms of its functional value.

In addition, the thematizing should include not only the perspective of the user but also that of others who may interact with and influence the user's sense of identity and agency. This is, of course, a most disparate group that ranges from health professionals and caregivers to complete strangers. How will the AT appear to each of these groups, and how will that impact on the user? Such thematization can help designers move away from function and engineering considerations to have a broader understanding of the social components of the experience of using a particular AT.

Last, it is crucial to remember that the AT may interact in complex ways with the user's understanding of his or her disability or illness. Thus, when a respiratory patient is told that they would benefit from ambulatory oxygen, part of the resistance may be linked to their denial of the progressive nature of their disease and a refusal to acknowledge their growing disability and possibly poor prognosis. Being breathless is one thing; requiring oxygen is another. Having a deeper phenomenological understanding of the relationship between the AT and the self-image and self-understanding, identity, and sense of agency of the patient or user is critical in this sense, too. We do not know how many potential users reject useful ameliorative technology because it clashes with their view of themselves as relatively well, only mildly affected, or as "coping well as it is." But anecdotal evidence suggests that this clash can be a major obstacle causing delays and sometimes complete rejection of the technology designed to assist.[27]

CONCLUSION

This chapter discussed some of the issues affecting invisible disabilities, such as loss of hearing and breathlessness, which are unique in being exposed through the AT intended to ameliorate them. The historical development of AT and the contemporary case of ambulatory oxygen devices were discussed in order to reveal the mismatch between design considerations and users' needs and values. We demonstrated that, in these two cases, users' need to "pass" and the salient appearance of the equipment made users ambivalent about—or even rejecting of—the AT.

We examined some of the tensions that characterize the encounter of invisible disabilities with visible and hypervisible (e.g., oxygen equipment) ATs, discussing the different features of this encounter. In the final section, we suggested a phenomenological framework that is attuned to users' needs, goals, and capabilities, which may pave the way to better co-productive AT design. Consulting users in this way can lead to the creation of distinctive knowledge, for example, about individuals' conditions and the attendant AT. This is the result of not only experience and familiarity through living with their condition, but also through their embodied knowledge about what works for them. People with hearing loss, for example, have long been highly involved in the creation of auditory prosthesis.[28] And yet assistive equipment has been designed without consulting users, often leading to technological "fixes" that do not fit with the desires of the intended users.

The real-life protagonist of the film *Breathe*, Robin Cavendish, was famed for being one of the longest surviving responauts in Britain, and his son Jonathan produced this film in 2017 partially to draw attention to current societal responses to disability.[29] At the start of the film, Cavendish and his new wife travel to Kenya, and, as they look out over the landscape spread before them, he points out the absolute silence that surrounds them. The attention drawn to the auditory landscape early in the film amplifies the artificial breathing of the mechanical respirator that breathes for Cavendish after he becomes paralysed by polio. The respirator plays a pivotal role in the film, and indeed in Cavendish's life, as it allowed him to leave the hospital bed that his doctor believed he ought to have remained in for the rest of his life.

Cavendish's "escape" from the hospital was only made possible because of his insight into his own condition and experience. He designed a wheelchair with a built-in respirator in collaboration with his friend, engineer and Oxford professor Teddy Hall. His invention allowed him to live independently of institutions and continue his global travels. Of course, Cavendish was in a uniquely privileged position in having the contacts and finances to enable this invention. However, the point is that it was his personal bodily knowledge that allowed for its initial design and eventual mass manufacture, which enabled more polio sufferers to live outside of institutions (Renton and Renton 1994). He was (eventually) acknowledged to be the expert on his own condition *and* on the attendant AT.

It is such bodily knowledge and insight that must be taken as a primary starting point, prioritized before the design of technological support for disability or illness. By treating users as experts on the equipment that they will be using we can advocate for co-production at a structural level and perhaps, in doing, can promote Cavendish's message of using technology not just to survive but to truly live.

Acknowledgments

This article was written with the generous support of a Wellcome Trust Senior Investigator Award (grant no. 103340; www.lifeofbreath.org). We are grateful to the Trust for supporting the Life of Breath project.

Notes

1. Such as the person's work, life, goals, priorities, onset of hearing loss, ability to lip-read, and visual acuity. For a summary of the problem of nonusage of hearing aids over the past 20 years, see Knudsen et al. (2010). For a discussion of the influence of stigma in hearing aid rejection, see Armitage et al. (2017).

2. See Jones et al. (2012); Jones (2001); Faull and Pattison (2017); Carel (2018); Macnaughton and Carel (2016).

3. Breathlessness is notoriously difficult to measure, and tools such as questionnaires and the MRC Dyspnoea Scale are used to try to ascertain the level of breathlessness that represents significant functional impairment. However, its etiology and affect on individuals spans a wide spectrum. For more on this, see our research project, *Life of Breath* (www.lifeofbreath.org).

4. Age-induced hearing loss and work-related hearing loss affects an older population. For detailed data on the older onset of respiratory illnesses, including breakdown by disease, prevalence, and groups effects, see British Lung Foundation (2016).

5. Deaf culture distinguishes between the culturally Deaf with a capital D and deafness in medical terms with a lowercase d. Throughout this chapter, we have reproduced the historically accurate phrasing which may not correspond with the modern distinction. For an overview of d/Deaf history and the history of hearing loss, see Gooday and Sayer (2017).

6. See Lane (1984); Sacks (1989); Baynton (1993); Branson and Miller (2002); Blume (2010); Padden and Humphries (2005).

7. For a fuller discussion of user involvement in the initial development of amplified telephones, see McGuire (2016).

8. The naming of this device has led to overemphasis of the MRC's role in its creation, with attendant erasure of the work of the Post Office.

9. Public Relations department memorandum to engineering department, July 27, 1946.

10. Ibid.

11. This trial was with members of the London League for the Hard of Hearing (who were also testing out the Medresco).

12. Letter from the National Institute for the Deaf to St Martin le Grande, October 16, 1950.

13. Letter from the National Institute for the Deaf to St Martin le Grande, December 13, 1950.

14. Letter from Head Post Office, Malton, to R. W. Clarke (Sales Division), April 26, 1951.

15. The attendant was also essential for enabling toilet function through bedpans and enemas (Drinker 1931).

16. Bragg-Paul Pulsator, March 15, 1938–August 15, 1938.

17. Letter from Bragg to Leonard Hill, January 4, 1934. Thanks to Jaipreet Virdi for originally locating this material.

18. The disappearance of the Pulsator may also be related to the 1938 death of one of its key promoters, Dr. Phyllis Kerridge. For more background on Kerridge's pivotal role in its design, see Virdi (2016); Virdi and McGuire (2018).

19. See Bregnballe et al. (2011).

20. See Oxy-View.

21. Ibid.

22. Dr. James Dodd, respiratory consultant (personal communication).

23. For more on the social architecture of breathlessness, see Carel (2013, 2016*b*).

24. Consultation with Dr. Sara Booth (personal communication) suggests that it is highly unlikely that ambulatory oxygen design was ever co-created with its intended users, although user responses have fed into the evolving designs in recent years.

25. See Brune and Wilson (2013); Cureton (2018).

26. For a full account of such a phenomenological framework, see Toombs (1999); Carel (2016*b*).

27. Dr. James Dodd, respiratory consultant (personal communication).

28. Such as the original amplified telephones, Edison's phonograph, Oliver Heaviside's work in long-distance telephony and radio signals. See Arapostathis and Gooday (2013); McGuire (2016).

29. A responaut is a person whose breathing is permanently dependent on an artificial respirator; see Sartin (2017).

References

Arapostathis, Stathis, and Graeme Gooday. 2013. *Patently Contestable: Electrical Technologies and Inventor Identities on Trial.* Cambridge, MA: MIT Press.

Armitage, Christopher, Deborah Lees, Kathryn Lewis, et al. 2017. "Preliminary Support for a Brief Psychological Intervention to Improve First-Time Hearing Aid Use Among Adults." *The British Journal of Health Psychology* 22(4): 687–700. doi: https://doi.org/10.1111/bjhp.12244

Arnold, Elizabeth, Anne Bruton, Maggie Donovan-Hall, et al. 2011. "Ambulatory Oxygen: Why Do COPD Patients Not Use Their Portable Systems as Prescribed? A Qualitative Study." *BMC Pulmonary Medicine* 11:9. doi: https://doi.org/10.1186/1471-2466-11-9

Bregnballe, Vibeke, Peter Oluf Schiøtz, Kirsten A. Boisen, Tacjana Pressler, and Mikael Thastum. 2011. "Barriers to Adherence in Adolescents and Young Adults with Cystic Fibrosis: A Questionnaire Study in Young Patients and Their Parents." *Patient Preference and Adherence* 5: 507–515. doi: 10.2147/PPA.S25308.

Baynton, Douglas C. 1993. "'Savages and Deaf-Mutes': Evolutionary Theory and the Campaign Against Sign Language in the Nineteenth Century." In *Deaf History Unveiled*, edited by John V. van Cleve, 92–112 Washington, DC: Gallaudet University Press.

Blume, Stuart. 2010. *The Artificial Ear: Cochlear Implants and the Culture of Deafness.* New Jersey: Rutgers University Press.

Branson, Jan, and Don Miller. 2002. *Damned for Their Difference: The Cultural Construction of Deaf People as Disabled.* Washington, DC: Gallaudet University Press.

British Lung Foundation. 2007. *Invisible Lives: Chronic Obstructive Pulmonary Disease (COPD)—Finding the Missing Millions.* London: British Lung Foundation.

British Lung Foundation. 2016. *The Battle for Breath.* Available at https://www.blf.org.uk/policy/the-battle-for-breath-2016

Brune, Jeffrey, and Daniel Wilson. 2013. *Disability and Passing: Blurring the Lines of Identity.* Philadelphia: Temple University Press

Carel, Havi. 2013. *Illness.* London: Routledge

Carel, Havi. 2016*a*. "Virtue Without Excellence, Excellence Without Health." *Aristotelian Society Supplementary Volume* 90(1): 237–253.

Carel, Havi. 2016*b*. *Phenomenology of Illness.* Oxford: Oxford University Press.

Carel, Havi. 2018. "Breathlessness: The Rift Between Objective Measurement and Subjective Experience." *Lancet Respiratory* 6(5): 332–333. doi: https://doi.org/10.1016/S2213-2600(18)30106-1

Carel, Havi, and Ian James Kidd. 2014. "Epistemic Injustice in Healthcare: A Philosophical Analysis." *Medicine, Healthcare and Philosophy* 17(4):529–540. doi: 10.1007/s11019-014-9560-2

Cureton, Adam. 2018. "Hiding a Disability and Passing as Non-Disabled." In *Disability in Practice: Attitudes, Policies and Relationships*, edited by Adam Cureton and Thomas E. Hill, Jr.,15–32. Oxford: Oxford University Press.

Drinker, Phillip. 1931. "Prolonged Administration of Artificial Respiration." *The Lancet* 217(5622): 1186–1188.

Faull, Olivia, Anja Hayen, and Kyle T.S. Pattinson. 2017. "Breathlessness and the Body: Neuroimaging Clues for the Inferential Leap." *Cortex* 95: 211–221. doi:10.1016/j.cortex.2017.07.019

Goering, Sara, and Eran Klein. 2020. "Neurotechnologies and Justice by, with, and for Disabled People." In *Oxford Handbook of Philosophy and Disability*, edited by A. Cureton and D. Wasserman, 616–632. New York: Oxford University Press.

Gooday, Graeme, and Karen Sayer. 2017. *Managing the Experience of Hearing Loss in Britain, 1830–1930*. London: Palgrave Macmillan.

Gysels, Marjolein, and Irene J. Higginson. 2008. "Access to Services for Patients with Chronic Obstructive Pulmonary Disease: The Invisibility of Breathlessness." *Journal of Pain and Symptom Management* 36(5): 451–460. doi: 10.1016/j.jpainsymman.2007.11.008

Hurley, Selina. 2013. "The Man Behind the Motor: William Morris and the Iron Lung." *Science Museum Blog*. Available at https://blog.sciencemuseum.org.uk/the-man-behind-the-motor-william-morris-and-the-iron-lung/

Jones, Paul, Marc Miravitlles, Thys van der Molen, and Karoly Kulich. 2012. "Beyond FEV1 in COPD: A Review of Patient-Reported Outcomes and Their Measurement." *International Journal of COPD* 7: 697–709.

Jones, Paul. 2001. "Health Status Measurement in Chronic Obstructive Pulmonary Disease." *Thorax* 56: 880–887.

Kidd, Ian, and Havi Carel. 2016. "Epistemic Injustice and Illness." *Journal of Applied Philosophy* 3(2): 172–190. doi: 10.1111/japp.12172.

Kidd, Ian, and Havi Carel. 2018. "Healthcare Practice, Epistemic Injustice, and Naturalism." in *Harms and Wrongs in Epistemic Practice*, edited by Simon Barker, Charlie Crerar, and Trystan Goetz (Cambridge: Cambridge University Press). *Philosophy* special issue (in press).

Knudsen, Line Vestergaard, Marie Öberg, Claus Nielsen et al. 2010. "Factors Influencing Help Seeking Hearing Aid Uptake, Hearing Aid Use and Satisfaction with Hearing Aids: A Review of the Literature." *Trends in Amplification* 14(3): 127–154.

Lane, Harlan. 1984. *When the Mind Hears: A History of the Deaf*. New York: Random House.

Life of Breath: Exploring Breathing and Breathlessness at the Interface Between Arts, Humanities and Medical Practice. A Wellcome Trust Investigator Award. Available at www.lifeofbreath.org

Macnaughton, Jane, and Havi Carel. 2016. "Breathing and Breathlessness in Clinic and Culture: Using Critical Medical Humanities to Bridge an Epistemic Gap." In *The Edinburgh Companion to the Critical Medical Humanities*, edited by Anne Whitehead and Angela Woods, 294–309. Edinburgh, Edinburgh University Press.

McGuire, Coreen. 2016. "Inventing Amplified Telephony: The Co-creation of Aural Technology and Disability." In *Rethinking Modern Prostheses in Anglo-American Commodity Cultures, 1820–1939*, edited by Claire Jones, 70–90. Manchester: Manchester University Press

Merleau-Ponty, Maurice. 1962. *Phenomenology of Perception*. London: Routledge.

Oxy-View. A Better Look and A Better Life. Available at http://www.oxyview.com/

Padden, Carol, and Tom Humphries. 2005. *Inside Deaf Culture*. Cambridge, MA: Harvard University Press.

Renton, Alice, and Tim Renton. 1994. "Obituary: Robin Cavendish." *The Independent*. Available at https://www.independent.co.uk/news/people/obituary-robin-cavendish-1382697.html

Sacks, Oliver. 1989. *Seeing Voices: A Journey into the World of the Deaf*. Berkeley: University of California Press.

Science Museum London. "Drinker-Type Iron Lung Respirator, London, England, 1930–1939." *Brought to Life* (blog). Available at http://broughttolife.sciencemuseum.org.uk/broughttolife/objects/display?id=10899

Sartin, Hank. 2017. "Movie Producer Jonathan Cavendish Tells the Story of His Parents in New Movie, Breathe." *Rotary*. Available at https://www.rotary.org/en/jonathan-cavendish-why-he-created-polio-movie-breathe

Scully, Jackie L. 2018. "From 'She Would Say That, Wouldn't She?' to 'Does She Take Sugar?' Epistemic Injustice and Disability." *IJFAB: International Journal of Feminist Approaches to Bioethics* 11(1): 106–124. doi: 10.3138/ijfab.11.1.106

Toombs, S. Kay. 1999. *The Meaning of Illness: A Phenomenological Account of the Different Perspectives of Physician and Patient*. New York: Springer.

Virdi, Jaipreet. 2016. "The Pulsator: How a Portable Artificial Respirator Saved the Lives of Children." *From the Hands of Quacks* (blog). Available at https://fromthehandsofquacks.com/2016/05/04/the-pulsator-how-a-portable-artificial-respirator-saved-the-lives-of-children/

Virdi, Jaipreet, and Coreen McGuire. 2018. "Phyllis M. Tookey Kerridge and the Science of Audiometric Standardisation in Britain." *British Journal for the History of Science* 51(1): 123–146. doi: 10.1017/S0007087417000929

Wasserman, David, and Stephen Campbell. 2017. "A More 'Inclusive' Approach to Enhancement and Disability." In *The Ethics of Ability and Enhancement*.edited by Flanigan, Jessica and Price, Terry. London: Palgrave Macmillan.

Wellcome Collection. Images of "Bragg Paul Pulsator." Available at https://wellcomecollection.org/works/hx4dtmc9?query=artificial+respirator

Woollam, Christopher H. M. 1976. "The Development of Apparatus for Intermittent Negative Pressure Respiration." Historical Note. *Anaesthesia* 31: 537–547.

Brown, Jennings. 2017. "The Last of the Iron Lungs." *Gizmodo*. Available at https://gizmodo.com/the-last-of-the-iron-lungs-1819079169

BT Archives. Public Relations Department Memorandum to Engineering Department, 27th July 1946. In *Special Apparatus Fitted on Telephone Exchange Lines Rented by Deaf Subscribers*. TCB_2_172.

BT Archives. Letter from the National Institute for the Deaf to St Martin le Grande, 16th October 1950. In *Special Apparatus Fitted on Telephone Exchange Lines Rented by Deaf Subscribers*. TCB_2_172.

BT Archives. Letter from the National Institute for the Deaf to St Matin le Grande, 13th December 1950. In *Special Apparatus Fitted on Telephone Exchange Lines Rented by Deaf Subscribers*. TCB_2_172.

BT Archives. Letter from Head Post Office, Wheelgate, Malton to R W Clarke (Sales Division) 26th April 1951. In *Special Apparatus Fitted on Telephone Exchange Lines Rented by Deaf Subscribers*. TCB_2_172.

BT Archives. *Special Apparatus Fitted on Telephone Exchange Lines Rented by Deaf Subscribers.* TCB_2_172.

The Papers of William Henry Bragg. William Henry Bragg Miscellaneous Correspondence, Bragg-Paul Pulsator 15 March–15 August 1938, Royal Institution, London. RI MS WHB/86.

The Papers of William Henry Bragg. William Henry Bragg Miscellaneous Correspondence, Letter from Bragg to Leonard Hill, 4 January 1934 27E/5 Bragg-Paul Pulsator 15th March –15th August 1938 Royal Institution, London. RI MS WHB/86.

CHAPTER 35

NEUROTECHNOLOGIES AND JUSTICE BY, WITH, AND FOR DISABLED PEOPLE

SARA GOERING AND ERAN KLEIN

INTRODUCTION

SPONSORS of the Brain Research through Advancing Innovative Neurotechnologies (BRAIN) initiative have great hopes that their efforts will lead to the clinical translation of neurotechnology. Some examples include exoskeletons, neuroprosthetics, neuroimaging, and recording/stimulating electrodes (one form of which is a brain–computer interface or BCI). Societal investment in the development of these technologies is often justified explicitly in terms of the near-term advantages that they will provide to disabled people—those with communication, mobility, sensory, or cognitive/psychiatric disabilities. The purported advantages to disabled people are offered as the first—if not the principle—reason for pursuing these technologies (Hochberg and Anderson 2012). As such, it would seem important to know what disabled people *want* from current and future iterations of these technologies and how they experience the functional barriers the technologies are meant to address.

The obvious way to find out what disabled people want is to *ask*. In practice, the perspectives of disabled people (i.e., "end users" in the engineering world) about technology are solicited and deemed valuable, though often late in the design process. The paradigmatic form of end user input in device design is determination of device *acceptability* and overlaps significantly with market research. Once a device is produced (or at least a prototype developed), feedback from prospective or actual users is gathered. A technology that is acceptable to an individual or group is more likely to be adopted and less likely to be "abandoned." While there may be different ways to determine acceptability, simply asking end users is an efficient way to determine who is likely to use (or not use, as the case may be) technology. This is valuable information to have in hand before large-scale investments are made to bring a device to market. But the economic viability of a device or concept for a device is not the only reason to gather end user input.

Seeking out and taking seriously the perspectives of disabled people (potential end users) is grounded at least in part by considerations of *justice*. Justice can be understood to have at least two dimensions[1]: distribution and recognition (see also Wasserman et al. 2015). Development of neurotechnologies involves significant investment in human and financial capital (and opportunity costs), risks to research subjects, and (hopefully) benefits to current and future users. As such, attention to distributive justice can help to ensure that these costs and benefits are shared fairly. Justice can also be understood in terms of recognition. The lived experience of disability often (though not always) shifts a person's perspective about the primary character of disadvantages associated with disability—less about the pain or suffering caused directly by the bodily condition and more about the sociopolitical constraints (institutional, environmental, attitudinal, etc.) put on people with atypical bodies (Barnes 2016). The disability rights movement has fought to ensure fair access to social participation and respect for different understandings of the meaning of disability (Charlton 1998). Thus, an important reason to gather end user input about neurotechnology is to recognize and *show respect* for people with atypical embodiment who have a diversity of ways of interacting physically, socially, economically, and politically through those bodies. As we will argue in this chapter, gathering prospective end user input—and the respect doing so shows for targeted groups—is a requirement of justice as well.

In this chapter, we will briefly explore how issues of justice—both distribution and recognition—come into play in the context of neurotechnology development and dissemination. We begin by illustrating some of the difficult issues of distribution and fairness that arise in the development of a particular kind of neurotechnology, the BCI.[2] We then argue that while such matters of distributive justice are important to address in an area like BCI, doing so still leaves to the side the dimension of justice as recognition. We make a case for attending to the recognition of disability perspectives on neurotechnology early in its development cycle. Finally, drawing on work we have done conducting focus groups about BCI with disabled individuals, we argue that there are likely to be a diversity of views within the disability community about neurotechnology that complicate discussions of justice but that this diversity is all the more reason to gather and take seriously the input of potential end users throughout the design process.

DISTRIBUTIVE JUSTICE AND NEUROTECHNOLOGY

BCI research ultimately aims to distribute tools that can help provide access to human goods—health and function. Although a paradigm good of biomedical research might be an intervention given to all, needed equally by all, and of similar benefit to all (e.g., a vaccine to prevent a life-threatening illness), the reality confronting public funding of science is quite different. Interventions—particularly unproved emerging technologies—come in different sizes at different costs with different benefits to different groups. Choices must be made among them, and these choices in turn determine which groups receive benefit from new drugs or devices and how much groups and individuals benefit. Decisions about which research and development is prioritized (i.e., gets public funding) are influenced by a complex mix of philosophical, economic, political, and interest group concerns (Resnik 2001). There is increasing attention to the need for these decisions to be made in accord with principles of justice (Schroeder and Ladikas 2015).

Persons with disabilities in motor, sensory, or communicative function or with mental health conditions are explicit targets of BCI research (Wolpaw and Wolpaw 2012). A common justification for pursuing a resource-intensive emerging technology like BCI research is that, eventually, such research could benefit individuals with disabilities (Hochberg and Anderson 2012). There are legitimate concerns about whether researchers adequately understand what these potential benefits are (in the absence of asking persons with disabilities about how *they* prioritize different functions) (Specker Sullivan et al. 2017). This is a matter to which we will return. But, putting this aside and assuming that there *are* benefits, important questions of distributive justice arise. Who will have access to commercialized BCI devices, and for whom will these be affordable? What, if anything, are BCI research participants owed at the completion of a failed (or successful) trial? These questions of distributive justice require careful attention.

Access to Devices

Downstream access to clinical and commercial products of BCI research raises an important set of distributive justice concerns. Will insurers pay for devices once they are produced? Which medical indications will qualify? Will BCI devices be subject to high or low insurance co-payments and deductibles? Will there be "hardship" programs, as currently exist for some expensive pharmaceuticals, for individuals who are uninsured or underinsured? Such questions are familiar enough from debates about distribution of expensive or scarce medical resources. But there are particularly difficult challenges in BCI. For instance, geographic proximity to an urban center (since device expertise is typically associated with medical centers and research institutes) determines access to (i.e., is a qualification for) devices like BCI. Individuals using BCI are likely to need to be in physical proximity to relevant BCI expertise.[3] This is particularly true of a BCI device that must be surgically implanted and regularly monitored and adjusted. An implantable system is critically different in this way from a medication that can be shipped to a home far from a medical center.[4] A slow or geographically skewed dissemination of BCI expertise will have implications for justice.

Access to devices requires that devices be developed in the first place for particular disabled groups or medical indications. So, which groups are targeted by research efforts has distributive justice implications as well. This can be evident when a potential neurotechnology can be put to multiple uses (or "dual use"). Consider that exoskeletons can be used for neurologic conditions like multiple sclerosis (MS) (Di Russo et al. 2013) but also for military uses (Tennison and Moreno 2012). Individuals with MS who have limb weakness can supplement their partial muscle strength with that afforded by an exoskeleton worn on paretic arms or legs. Similar technology could also help a soldier in the field engage in physical activity that requires above-average physical strength (e.g., pulling a heavy object off a fellow soldier) or that typically causes physical fatigue (e.g., picking up multiple heavy objects). In some ways, a dual-use technology seems to be a win–win. People with MS can benefit from advances in exoskeleton technology at the same time that soldiers can benefit. Examples are readily available. Think of the Defense Advanced Research Projects Agency's (DARPA) development of the Internet. So, what is the problem?

One problem is that people with disabilities may bear the burden of volunteering for research with BCI but with the benefits of research going predominantly to non-disabled populations. There are real risks to research participation. Consider implanted recording electrodes for a BCI-based system for essential tremor (Brown et al. 2016). Will implantation of electrodes cause permanent damage to cortical tissue? Will tissue reaction or induced changes in neural pathways due to these electrodes preclude use of a next-generation device (e.g., imagine that a new kind of electrode is discovered but won't work except in "naïve" brain tissue)? One of the challenges of working in an emerging scientific field is that, beyond basic safety assurances, there is a great deal unknown about long-term risks. When is it fair for those with disabilities to take on these risks—even with the highest current standards of informed consent? Should volunteering for early-stage research entitle people to be in the front of the queue for future devices? It seems that individuals who shoulder the burdens of research participation should be in a position to enjoy its benefits (Emanuel 2000).

Or consider the fact that currently implantable BCI research is considered to be too dangerous for "healthy" individuals.[5] As a consequence, implantable BCI research is conducted with individuals who are already undergoing brain surgery for diagnosis or treatment of a neurologic condition. For instance, individuals undergoing evaluation of epilepsy sometimes require temporary neurosurgical placement of electrocorticography (ECoG) leads to localize a seizure focus. While these individuals are being monitored for seizure activity, they can also participate in BCI experiments as this is considered minimal additional risk (Leuthardt et al. 2006). Thus, BCI experiments with a disabled group (e.g., persons with epilepsy) contributes to the development of BCI technology.

It is possible that contributions of disabled people to fundamental BCI research will lead to development of BCI devices used for military or commercial reasons long before (or to the exclusion of) devices that benefit the original research participant population. Whether a company chooses to develop a BCI device that will benefit a particular medical indication (e.g., stroke) depends on economic factors, such as the size of the market (number of people with stroke), likelihood of reimbursement, and other factors. It may be that the economics of developing a BCI device for particular groups (including those who may have participated in early BCI research) does not support investment in bringing a medical product to market.[6]

It can be argued that advancements in gaming or military technology will trickle down to disabled people. There is some evidence for this. Think about how the development of speak-to-text capability in cell phones was driven by the need to avert an unsafe practice of people finger texting while driving. This eventually benefited people with mobility impairments who wanted to communicate or control their environment through speech alone. Or consider how a global positioning system (GPS) developed by NASA to track satellites has ended up in cars and phones to help people navigate their routes. Such technology offers a significant improvement for many people, disabled and non-disabled.

Still, the trickle-down assumption may be problematic for two reasons. First, not all functions have such overlap, and people with disabilities may have confounding comorbidities. Think about exoskeletons in persons with MS who also experience muscle spasticity or cognitive slowing. While it is possible that these co-existing issues are mere additional obstacles that can be addressed later once the basics of an exoskeleton are worked out, it may also be that these "hiccups" are not minor challenges to go back and work around later but instead require a fundamental redesign. One can image that the economics of doing so may be prohibitive. Second, it is an open question whether devices specifically tailored to relatively small subgroups of disabilities will be financially worth the investment for companies. Some groups with disabilities may be too small in number to justify developing a device. For instance, some individuals with MS may have problems of coordination from cerebellar damage in addition to weakness due to spinal cord inflammation. It may be that this subgroup of individuals is too small to warrant the development of a separate system. So, the segmentation of groups based on neurological disabilities may create "orphaning" relative to developing devices. In short, the trickle-down assumption may be problematic in itself, and this highlights that accessibility to devices is more than just affording fully developed devices that are known to be useful or helpful (e.g., funding an exoskeleton vs. not doing so) but about whether devices are inaccessible because they were never developed for particular individuals or groups in the first place.

The delay that occurs in developing technology for people with mobility problems is a concrete and not insignificant harm. And, even in cases where there is minimal delay in technology transfer to assistive uses, it is worth giving serious thought to the message that this approach communicates about the value of disabled people. That is, their needs are only worth addressing if they happen to be coincident with addressing the needs of the non-disabled, but are not important in and of themselves. So, even if the goods of an emerging technology find their way to disadvantaged groups, this may happen in a way that fails to accord the respect owed to those disadvantaged groups. Showing such respect is part of a further requirement of justice, as we will argue later.

Post-Trial Access to Devices and Care

Disabled individuals who volunteer for BCI research trials, especially those that involve implanted devices, face the question of who is responsible for maintaining the device once the trial is completed, whether or not it is considered successful. Unlike pharmaceuticals that can be discontinued or replaced with alternatives relatively easily (or possibly continued through humanitarian exemptions to US Food and Drug Administration rules with coverage through insurance), implanted devices typically remain with the individual[7] and will require tuning, maintenance, and perhaps also updating (Hutchison and Sparrow 2016). Whose responsibility is it to provide and pay for those services? Typical research grants do not include options for long-term care for research participants beyond the period of the study. Industry-sponsored research likewise does not typically budget for follow-up beyond the study period, and even devices that work but are not deemed likely to be profitable may not be supported.

In a well-known case, the NeuroControl Freehand System—a neuroprosthetic that provided restored hand function to people with spinal cord injury—received premarket approval in 1997 but was only manufactured until 1998, given market concerns (Bowsher et al. 2016). Following the closure of NeuroControl, users of the device were left with a permanent implant but were unable to receive revisions to components that failed. Study-affiliated researchers at the Institute for Functional Restoration at Case Western Reserve University recognized the injustice and helped to develop an independent fund to provide some support for the roughly 250 users of the Freehand System. Still, their success may not be easily replicable, and it relies on researchers taking such responsibilities seriously. As Bowsher et al. (2016) report, "it is nevertheless clear that the developer's commercial viability has lasting effects on the user experience" (6).

Different theoretical approaches to distributive justice may suggest different solutions to these varied problems. Consider the problem of dual use. One area in which BCI technology may significantly improve function is in assisted communication for individuals with locked-in syndrome (LIS). LIS is a condition in which individuals are unable to communicate with speech and, in complete LIS, unable to communicate through any form of motor movement (e.g., changing eye gaze). LIS is a rare condition most often caused by amyotrophic lateral sclerosis or stroke. BCI devices could allow individuals with LIS to select letters or words on a computer screen using recorded neural signals (e.g., Oken et al. 2014). While assisted communication in LIS represents a small market for BCI, technology companies are interested in BCI for communication as well (e.g., Constine 2017; Winkler 2017), as there may be a wide applicability for such technology. BCI-based devices may allow enhanced gaming experiences or facilitate online interactions (interacting with social media, purchasing products).

The lack of assistive communication devices for persons with LIS is a problem that theories of distributive justice might approach in different ways. An approach that adopts a Rawlsian difference principle, in which distributive differences are allowed so long as the worst-off are made better off than they otherwise would be with the difference, might address this problem by directing research money to technology companies developing BCI devices for non-disabled populations on the presumption that doing so will lead to advances that will filter down and benefit persons with LIS. The taxing of commercial BCI devices might be used to address the "last mile" problem—to ensure that commercial devices are adapted to the particular needs of people with LIS. Such an approach would benefit a more disadvantaged group—persons with LIS—through predominantly market forces.

A more strictly egalitarian approach to distributive justice might focus on altering the funding of science to better meet the basic needs of all, including those with rare conditions like LIS. Such an approach might adopt an aggressive intervention in the organization of science. For instance, federal funding agencies might develop a scheme for distributing research grants for basic BCI based on which groups (indexed to their need) would likely benefit from a given technology. A grant allocation scheme could give priority to worse-off groups. Such an approach would carry the advantage of directly addressing disadvantage as well as explicitly acknowledging how science funding decisions can contribute to the advantaging and disadvantaging of groups. That said, such an approach could be disruptive to the culture and institutional mechanisms of scientific innovation without a guarantee of better outcomes for the worst-off.

JUSTICE AS RECOGNITION AND DISABLED PEOPLE

In addition to questions about fair distribution and access, justice involves a dimension of *recognition* (Fraser and Honneth 2003; Goering et al. 2008; Taylor 1994; Young 1990) to ensure that the individuals and groups for whom redistribution and access efforts are undertaken can voice their *own* needs and preferences and participate in decision-making about matters of justice. While distributive justice efforts often focus on material goods and fair access, recognition efforts are directed at social status and participation. As Nancy Fraser notes, the recognition element of justice "targets injustices it understands as cultural, which it presumes to be rooted in social patterns of representation, interpretation and communication. Examples include cultural domination... nonrecognition...and disrespect" (13). Some marginalized groups may be the *subjects* of distributive justice efforts but play little to no role in determining the content of what is just. In other words, distributive justice schemas may assume a "typical individual" as their recipient of distributed goods and, in so doing, wrongly characterize the aims or interests of individuals from marginalized groups (e.g., consider how discussions about the value of species-typical functioning for health may ignore the interests of deaf individuals in being Deaf; see Crouch 1997; Scully 2008). Ensuring justice for deaf people will require participation of deaf individuals. Justice as recognition requires *participatory parity* (36), such that groups have equal opportunities to enter dialogue regarding matters of justice, and to be heard (i.e., to have their views respected, but not necessarily privileged). Fraser clarifies: "When . . . institutionalized patterns of cultural value constitute some actors as inferior, excluded, wholly other, or simply invisible, hence as less than full partners in social interaction, then we should speak of *misrecognition* and *status subordination*" (29).

The problem of misrecognition has been applied widely to questions of gender, sexuality, and race or ethnicity in the philosophical justice literature but less so to disability (notable exceptions include Ikaheimo 2009; Knight 2015; Scully 2008; Wasserman et al. 2015). Yet disabled people surely qualify as a misrecognized group. Consider the ways in which disability rights activists and scholars have argued for revising the standard conception of what disability is and rethinking the sources of its disadvantages (e.g., Barnes 2016; Oliver 1996; Silvers 1998). They seek to change the structures (institutional, environmental, legal, architectural, etc.) that create barriers to participation and thus to alter the social status of disabled people (Ikaheimo 2009). The universal design movement—aimed at ensuring that access is universal without requiring individual accommodation (Hamraie 2017)—is easily understood as a demand for participatory parity, and it shows that achieving parity isn't simply about accommodating difference but also about transforming practices to be inclusive.

The misrecognition of disabled people is often tied to the fact that non-disabled people are unfamiliar with disabled life or assess it inaccurately. As Barnes notes, "a vast body of evidence . . . suggests that non-disabled people are extraordinarily bad at predicting the effects of disability on *perceived* well-being" (71). Yet few non-disabled people are aware of their deficits in understanding what disabled life can be, given prevailing norms, media, and the like. Relying on standard tropes of disability, they try to imagine themselves in an impaired body and make negative judgments based on what they expect their quality of life would be. Unfortunately, our imaginative capacities may be a limited resource for understanding someone whose body is different from our own (Mackenzie and Scully 2007). Or, listening to the positive testimony of disabled people, they judge it unreliable, or, alternatively, as philosophers say, the product of "adaptive preference" (for discussion of the problems with this approach, see Amundson 2005; Barnes 2016; Goering 2008). Either way, the negative presumption about living with a disability persists.

Emphasizing the different perspectives of non-disabled and disabled people need not presume any deep or essentialist divide between the groups. Disability is, after all, a fluid identity category into which most people will one day enter, if they are lucky to live long enough. Instead, we might think of the different perspectives as arising from experiences common to many disabled people, experiences that make apparent those features of the world that remain cloaked to those who, for instance, never realize the circuitous routes required to use accessible entrances to campus buildings until they require their use. Direct experience shapes our moral psychology, and individuals with shared experiences may develop an attunement to morally salient features of the world that otherwise go unnoticed (Stramondo 2016). Non-disabled people then can learn from their disabled peers and use those lessons in their own work.[8]

Given this state of affairs—disabled people's needs and well-being are often misunderstood by the non-disabled majority—claims of misrecognition can be understood as calls for participatory parity. Such participation is partly about gaining meaningful access to *all* broad civil rights (Nussbaum 2010) but, more pointedly, it is about ensuring active engagement with any disability-related policies or recommendations. "Nothing about us, without us" means demanding that disabled voices be part of every decision-making process that involves disability policy. In the context of research, this means a commitment to "prioritise the voices of disabled people. This is a very welcome move.... The ideal of emancipatory research suggests that the research agenda should be generated by disabled people, and that researchers—whether disabled or non-disabled—should be accountable to organisations of disabled people" (Shakespeare 2006, 186). Making space for the testimony of disabled people is a matter of epistemic justice that involves recognizing disabled people as credible knowers (Fricker 2007).

To be clear, the hard work of recognition has at least two parts: making sure that marginalized and oppressed groups have the opportunity to participate and be heard (*participation*) and then figuring out fair responses to what is learned (by all parties) in that process (*uptake*). The first part, participation, doesn't require that the disadvantaged or marginalized perspectives be taken as authoritative or necessarily true, but it does require engagement and opportunity to participate on equal footing. As Scully argues, "the *decision* to give serious attention to the embodied experiences of impairment is an ethical act in itself. It is a moral choice to respect (though not uncritically) a disabled person's accounting of her own life" (Scully 2008, 174). The second part, uptake, is likely to be challenging, at least in part given the great diversity contained under the single concept "disability." Which disabled perspectives are the most relevant or salient? What if disabled people within a particular category disagree? Even once participation of disabled people is ensured, a complicated issue of figuring out how to take up the disabled perspectives looms.

Soliciting disabled perspectives on any emerging technology is likely to elicit a wide variety of responses.[9] Some disability activists and scholars question the excessive focus on "cures" and medical technology, arguing that prioritizing low-tech supports and institutional or attitudinal change would be more effective at creating a fairer world for disabled people (Barnes 2016). Still, many disabled people are quite open to the idea of assistive technologies that can enhance their functioning or technologies that shift their impairment status entirely. The British Council of Disabled People notes that "only on the crudest reading of the social model could it be argued that this model is rejecting medical treatment or research. The medical model itself is not about medical intervention, but rather the medicalisation of disabled people. This is what we reject.... We are also not making a case against medical research, but rather one for a more equitable distribution of effort and resources in order that a real difference can be made now in the lives of disabled people" (cited in Shakespeare 2006, 104). Figuring out how to make a "real difference" surely involves understanding the complexity of the sources of the problems disabled people face, and doing *that* effectively recommends the inclusion of disabled people in the research process.

Recognition for Disabled People in Neurotechnology Research

Taking seriously the notion that incorporation of end user perspectives in neurotechnology device design is a matter of justice as recognition faces structural hurdles. Engineers designing neurotechnology often have relatively little exposure to or experience with the disabled people they are attempting to help through their work (Specker Sullivan et al. 2017). End user input that does occur typically happens late (or downstream) in the design process—in service to determining prototype acceptability and, relatedly, predicting market success. Thus, a reality of most technology research, even that aimed at disabled people, is that it does *not* include disabled people until the final stages of development. Presumably multiple explanations can be offered for this state of affairs: (1) non-disabled researchers may not think it is necessary to include disabled people at all, or (2) they simply may not know what to ask or whom to include.

Is It Necessary?

In the context of neurotechnology research aimed at creating technologies for disabled people, it is not uncommon to find researchers who have relatively little exposure to disabled people (Specker Sullivan et al. 2017). Given that one's experience as a disabled person can alter how one perceives the disadvantages of disability, understands notions of well-being, and evaluates the benefits of technology, inclusion of disabled people in the research process is a demand of justice. To ensure ample opportunity for input, this kind of inclusion would ideally happen quite early in the research development (i.e., in setting goals, establishing priorities, etc.) and continue throughout the research and development process.

We are part of a neural engineering research center that embeds ethicists in neural technology research labs. Through our work in this center, we have found that exposure to the perspectives of disabled people (e.g., through end user roundtables, access to focus group findings, etc.) helps to shift investigator perspectives on issues such as how to talk about their work (e.g., assistive vs. "fixing"), how to design their devices (e.g., levels of control given to participants), and how to recognize the salience of end user input. One investigator notes, "If the neural engineering community wants to address the highest priority needs of the population, I think we have to understand those needs much better than we do now," and another suggests that "It's important to consider the end user perspective because otherwise we'll build it twice. It's going to help people walk again, but what if they don't necessarily want to walk again, right? They want bladder function, they want hand function, but they don't have it. So those are things that we have to be...keenly aware of" (Specker Sullivan et al. 2017).

In focus groups that included people with spinal cord injury, we likewise heard some general concerns about disconnects between researchers and disabled people on priorities and needs.

> "[I]f you don't go into a community that is relevant, where people have the injuries, to find out what are their wants and their needs, their desires,...you're just going to keep spending and spending, not really knowing what the community wants.
>
> I wonder about whether it would be better to give us the money, and let us spend it on things we need now (e.g., personal assistance, or existing technology)?
>
> One worry is that you could end up in a worse place than you started; I have a tiny bit of function in my hands, but I could lose that.
>
> Engineers can get carried away with "how cool can we make this" vs. this is a person who is living and functions in a way ("it just makes me snort at this...")...they need to *think* like folks like us think, to get the most advantages.
>
> Sometimes designers focus on what the device can do, and they forget about the person.   (Goering and Klein, unpublished data)

Participants also expressed a desire to give early input into the research process, in order to avert at least some of the problems they refer to here. Importantly, these concerns were expressed against a background of participants thinking that the research was generally promising and worth pursuing.

Of course, it may also be the case that the perspectives of disabled individuals are not *devalued* so much as undervalued relative to other considerations. For instance, Grübler et al. (2014) interviewed 17 professionals working in the field of BCI. They note that some professionals "considered it problematic" that users might be asked to test BCIs at a stage too early in prototype development. They quote one respondent: "Immature prototypes might be used, leading to unnecessary stress for the patients and trivial feedback" (Grübler 2014, 35). While this reservation seems apt, working to obtain input from disabled people about their values and priorities—far earlier than the stages of early prototype development—could help to avoid the problem of "building it twice" mentioned earlier.

One might presume that this kind of stakeholder input gathering is already practiced. When any device company creates a product, surely they must check in with their target population to ensure interest and need. But, too often, this happens only very late in the development process. Consider what Patrick McGurrin, neuroscience researcher, notes about the consistently high rates of high-tech prosthetics abandonment: "Too often, it seems that device design lacks a 'human factors' approach, driven as it is by many scientists with relatively little input from patients. The people in need of prosthetics may get involved only when a product reaches testing, rather than at the initial stages of device design" (McGurrin 2016). Researchers are interested in high-tech devices that closely approximate typical biological functioning, but users may prefer a device that is easier to learn and to control, even if the design is more basic (Biddis and Chau 2008). McGurrin observes,

> In theory, designing a prosthetic device with full biological capability is a dream come true...a feat in engineering that would go down in history. But as a researcher in this field, I believe that too often, we overlook the potential for usability. Regardless of the technological advancement, it's important to consider whether this progress is also a step forward for designing a favorable device for the user. We assume that performing "at the [typical] human level" is the ultimate goal. But this may not always be the case from the user point of view, especially if mastering the technology that enables "[typical] human level" performance would render you incapable of concentrating on anything else. This dichotomy may explain why the prosthetic abandonment rate has not decreased even as technology has improved.   (2016)

Moving up the timeline for input from end user stakeholders would clearly help to avoid this problem. As Shah and Robinson (2007) note, "The involvement of users is important at each stage of the product development cycle....However, it is more meaningful and crucial for the nature and direction of the product if users are involved in the early stages, such as concept and idea generation...rather than only or mainly in the late stages of the product lifecycle" (132). Our claim is that this is not simply a point about efficiency; it would also serve as recognition of the values and interests of the targeted beneficiaries of the devices.

What to Ask and of Whom?

Even with a recognition of the importance of seeking out disabled perspectives and some funding to ensure that it happens, researchers are still faced with the difficult question of what they need to ask and of whom.

One of the worries may be that, before a technology even exists, potential users won't know how it will alter their lives. What is sometimes called "transformative technology" (e.g., the Internet, cell phones) can alter our experience radically in ways that few people could envision prior to the introduction of the technology. In such a case, researchers might think that asking about the relative benefits and costs of technologies still in development is not particularly helpful because people simply don't yet know how the technology may change them.[10]

Another hurdle may be figuring out how to present the technology projects in a way that balances their hopeful possibilities with the likely limitations and nuanced engineering challenges (Racine et al. 2007), all in language accessible to nonexperts. While simplification is always necessary for broader communication, researchers have an obligation to simplify carefully, so as not to give inaccurate impressions of what is possible. Furthermore, it is important to notice that a similar problem exists for the disabled people who are involved in the research project; they, too, need to figure out what parts of their experience are relevant to the technology at hand, how to simplify their complex experiences into digestible claims, and the like.

Conflicting Views of Technology within the Disability Community

A key question in respect to justice-oriented demands for recognition has to do with how the relevant group is identified. Under the broad category of disabled people, we find an incredibly diverse group of individuals with widely varying impairments, identities, and uses of technology.[11] Who should be included in research on neurotechnology? At the very least, when research projects are justified on the grounds that they will likely benefit a particular group (e.g., people with spinal cord injury), members of that group should be consulted as part of the research process.[12] But, even within that group, should it be people who are recently injured or those who are 5+ years out? People with complete or incomplete injuries, high or low lesions? People who have adjusted to their injury, or people who are eager for a "cure"?

The heterogeneity of disability can lead to different attitudes toward technology. Disappointment from promised "breakthroughs" can harden into skepticism of technology. Excitement of scientific advances can inspire optimism in the transformative potential of new technology. In focus groups and interviews with disabled individuals, we have encountered a range of attitudes toward technology, but these have tended to cluster into at least two broad groups: a highly skeptical attitude and a pro-technology attitude. This dichotomy presents a challenge for those who hope to incorporate the voices of disabled individuals into the development of neural devices. An overly skeptical attitude toward technology may lead scientists (and funders) to focus their efforts elsewhere, whereas an overly enthusiastic attitude may lead scientists to see technology as the only or preferred way to "fix" disabilities. Depending upon who speaks for the disabled community, scientists can be sent very different messages. What to do?

The first thing is to recognize that there are attitudes toward technology that lie at the extremes and to seek to understand why this is so. For some disabled individuals, neurotechnology is seen as a good to be promoted and secured. Devices carry the potential to benefit disabled individuals by improving function in ways that they desire. Given a history of disabled groups losing out on competition for societal resources, there is interest in fighting to secure the benefits of this technology against competing ways of distributing resources. On the other end of the spectrum, neurotechnology is viewed by some disabled people as implicated in a problematic worldview through which disabilities are inherently disvalued and that disabilities are necessarily the target of technological fixes (or patches). For those at this pole, the proper stance toward neurotechnology is somewhere between skepticism and resistance. This polarity—die-hard skeptics or eager adopters—represents a gross oversimplification but distills a central tension with regard to attitudes toward technology. For die-hard skeptics, the initial orientation to technology is a highly critical eye because embracing technological "solutions" carries with it the risk of undermining the status and disregarding the value of people with disabilities. For eager adopters, the initial orientation to technology is optimism because, whatever benefits technology may offer disabled people, these will only be realized by those open to using and willing to fight for the right to use technology. Not participating at all involves risking the opportunity to help direct the research pathways.

In our view, research projects need neither embrace nor ignore these poles, but rather contextualize their approaches, given varying aims. The inclusion of a broad range of disabled people (across the spectrum just described) enables a process that recognizes *differing* perspectives on disability (some likely at the poles, some in between). The result may be that the most die-hard skeptics can trust the process (and product) more because they know it involves disabled perspectives through and through, and the eager adopters may be moved to have some healthy skepticism about the promises of the technology and greater recognition of what it will not solve. Surely the diversity of disability perspectives should not result in the conclusion that no such input is needed (imagine a related scenario in which policy-makers focused on women's reproductive health decide not to include women's perspectives, given that they are so diverse).

In conclusion, neurotechnology researchers designing devices with the aim of benefiting disabled people must, as a matter of justice, pay close attention to what disabled people themselves say they need and desire through the inclusion of focus groups, interviews, and other methods to collect such input. Doing so is not simply a matter of economic efficiency or market research, but is also a demand of justice, given how widely disability standpoints are unrecognized or misunderstood. As neurotechnology research moves forward, attention must also be paid to ensure the fair distribution of the benefits and risks of neurotechnology.

Notes

1. In prior work, Goering et al. (2008) argued for three dimensions of justice, adding the dimension of *responsibility*, understood as a requirement to answer to the needs of marginalized others. In this chapter, we focus only on distribution and recognition.
2. We focus on BCI because it is the area with which we are most familiar.
3. Expertise needs here to be understood broadly. Not only are experts needed who deal directly with the device, secondary expertise is needed by clinicians to determine when an individual *could* be a candidate for a BCI device. If no clinician is available who knows the indications, costs, and benefits of BCI devices, people who could potentially benefit will not get referred for evaluation and thus will not benefit. See Hutchison and Sparrow (2016) for more on the variety of expertise that may be necessary for the maintenance of implanted devices.
4. The analogy with medications is, of course, an oversimplification. Someone who receives chemotherapeutic pills by mail, for instance, still must have ready access to the expertise to take the medication correctly, monitor for desired and adverse effects, and so on.

5. To the authors' knowledge, no Institutional Review Board in the US has approved a trial of an implantable BCI device without a related medical condition.

6. Distributive questions may arise not just between commercial and military uses and disabled people but *across* populations with diseases or disabilities. For instance, although the implantable BCI research field has benefited greatly from volunteers with spinal cord injury, the market for stroke rehabilitation would seem to be much greater.

7. Some trials recommend explantation of the device once the trial is over, especially if operating them requires significant technical expertise and assistance, but explantation requires another surgery with attendant risks.

8. One need not be disabled to have any insight into disability/impairment. Indeed, "the idea that having an impairment is vital to understanding impairment is dangerously essentialist. The skills and knowledge of an experienced and sensitive researcher, disabled or nondisabled, are required to develop an appropriate account" (Shakespeare 2006, 195). Women or minorities, for instance, may share insight into the experience of oppression.

9. The documentary film *Fixed: The Science/Fiction of Human Enhancement* does an excellent job of demonstrating this range through its interviews with a variety of disability activists and technologists.

10. This may be related to "transformative experiences"—experiences, such as becoming a parent, that can radically shift one's strongest preferences, making one's prior preferences and knowledge less than helpful in determining whether to take on a new possibility (Paul 2015).

11. It's important to keep in mind that not all disabled people have the same capacities for self-representation or communication (Fins 2015; Kittay 2011; Knight 2015).

12. We recognize that, in some cases, consultation may not be possible (e.g., research on infants or on people in persistent vegetative states) or necessary (e.g., research to find better computer algorithms to read magnetic resonance imaging [MRI] scans).

References

Amundson, Ron. 2005. "Disability, Ideology, and Quality of Life: A Bias in Biomedical Ethics." In *Quality of Life and Human Difference,* edited by David Wasserman, Jerome Bickenbach, and Robert Wachbroit, 101–124. Cambridge: Cambridge University Press.

Barnes, Elizabeth. 2016. *The Minority Body: A Theory of Disability.* Oxford: Oxford University Press.

Biddis, Elaine, and Tom Chau. 2008. "Upper-Limb Prosthetics: Critical Features in Device Abandonment." *American Journal of Physical Medicine and Rehabilitation* 86(12): 977–987.

Bowsher, Kristen, Eugene Civillico, James Coburn, et al. 2016. "Brain–Computer Interface Devices for Patients with Paralysis and Amputation: A Meeting Report." *Journal of Neural Engineering* 13 (2016): 023001.

Brown, Tim, Margaret C. Thompson, Jeffrey Herron, et al. 2016. "Controlling Our Brains: A Case Study on the Implications of Brain–Computer Interface-Triggered Deep Brain Stimulation for Essential Tremor." *Brain-Computer Interfaces* 3(4): 165–170. https://doi.org/10.1080/2326263X.2016.1207494

Charlton, James. 1998. *Nothing About Us Without Us: Disability Oppression and Empowerment.* Berkeley: University of California Press.

Constine, Josh. 2017. "Facebook Is Building Brain-Computer Interfaces for Typing and Skin Hearing." Available at https://techcrunch.com/2017/04/19/facebook-brain-interface/

Crouch, Robert. 1997. "Letting the deaf be Deaf: Reconsidering the Use of Cochlear Implants in Prelingually Deaf Children." *Hastings Center Report* 27(4): 14–21.

Di Russo, Francesco, Marika Berchicci, Rinalso Livio Perri, et al. 2013. "A Passive Exoskeleton Can Push Your Life Up: Application on Multiple Sclerosis Patients." *PLoS ONE* 8(10): e77348. doi.org/10.1371/journal.pone.0077348

Emanuel, Ezekiel, David Wendler, and Christine Grady. 2000. "What Makes Clinical Research Ethical?" *JAMA* 283(20): 2701–2711.

Fins, Joseph J. 2015. *Rights Come to Mind: Brain Injury, Ethics and the Struggle for Consciousness.* Cambridge: Cambridge University Press.

Fraser, Nancy, and Axel Honneth. 2003. *Redistribution or Recognition? A Political-Philosophical Exchange.* New York: Verso.

Fricker, Miranda. 2007. *Epistemic Injustice: Power and the Ethics of Knowing.* Oxford: Oxford University Press.

Goering, Sara. 2008. "'You Say You're Happy, But…': Contested Quality of Life Judgments in Bioethics and Disability Studies." *Journal of Bioethical Inquiry* 5: 125–135.

Goering, Sara, Suzanne Holland, and Kelly Edwards. 2008. "Transforming Genetic Research Practices with Marginalized Communities: A Case for Responsive Justice." *Hastings Center Report* 38(2): 43–53.

Grübler, Gerd, Abdul Al-Khodairy, Robert Leeb, et al. 2014. "Psychosocial and Ethical Aspects in Non-Invasive EEG-Based BCI Research – A Survey Among BCI Users and BCI Professionals." *Neuroethics* 7: 29–41.

Hamraie, Aimi. 2017. *Building Access: Universal Design and the Politics of Disability* Minneapolis: University of Minnesota Press.

Hochberg, Leigh, and Kim D. Anderson. 2012. "BCI Users and Their Needs." In *Brain–Computer Interfaces*, edited by Jonathan R. Wolpaw and Elizabeth W. Wolpaw, 317–323. New York: Oxford University Press.

Hutchison, Katrina, and Robert Sparrow. 2016. "What Pacemakers Can Teach Us About the Ethics of Maintaining Artificial Organs." *Hastings Center Report* 46(6): 14–24.

Ikaheimo, Heikki. 2009. "Personhood and the Social Inclusion of People with Disabilities: A Recognition-Theoretical Approach." In *Arguing About Disability: Philosophical Perspectives*, edited by Kristjana Kristiansen, Simo Vehmas, and Tom Shakespeare), 77–92, Oxon: Routledge.

Kittay, Eva Feder. 2011. "The Ethics of Care, Disability and Dependency." *Ratio Juris* 24(1): 49–58.

Knight, Amber. 2015. "Democratizing Disability: Achieving Inclusion (Without Assimilation) through 'Participatory Parity.'" *Hypatia* 30(1): 97–114.

Leuthardt, Eric C., Kai J. Miller, Gerwin Schalk, et al. 2006. "Electrocorticography-Based Brain Computer Interface: The Seattle Experience." *IEEE Transactions on Neural Systems and Rehabilitation Engineering* 14(2): 194–198.

Mackenzie, Catriona, and Jackie L. Scully. 2007. "Moral Imagination, Disability and Embodiment." *Journal of Applied Philosophy* 24(4): 335–351.

McGurrin, Patrick. 2016. "Why People Abandon High-Tech Prosthetics." Available at https://www.smithsonianmag.com/innovation/why-people-abandon-high-tech-prosthetics-180959598/

Nussbaum, Martha. 2010. "The Capabilities of People with Cognitive Disabilities." In *Cognitive Disability and Its Challenge to Moral Philosophy*, edited by Eva Feder Kittay and Licia Carlson, 75–96. New York: Wiley-Blackwell.

Oken, Barry S., Umut Orhan, Brian Roark, et al. 2014. "Brain-Computer Interface with Language Model EEG Fusion for Locked-In Syndrome." *Neurorehabilitation and Neural Repair* 28(4): 387–394.

Oliver, Michael. 1996. *Understanding Disability: From Theory to Practice*. New York: St. Martin's Press.

Paul, Laurie. 2015. *Transformative Experience*. Oxford: Oxford University Press.

Racine, Eric, Sarah Waldmann, Nicole Palmour, and Judy Illes. 2007. "Currents of Hope: Neurostimulation Techniques in U.S. and U.K. Print Media." *Cambridge Quarterly of Healthcare Ethics* 16: 312–316.

Resnik, David B. 2001. "Setting Biomedical Research Priorities: Justice, Science, and Public Participation." *Kennedy Institute of Ethics Journal* 11(2): 181–204.

Schroeder, Doris, and Miltos Ladikas. 2015. "Towards Principled Responsible Research and Innovation: Employing the Difference Principle in Funding Decisions." *Journal of Responsible Innovation* 2(2): 169–183.

Scully, Jackie. 2008. *Disability Bioethics: Moral Bodies, Moral Differences*. Lanham, MD: Rowman & Littlefield.

Shah, Syed G., and Ian Robinson. 2007. "Benefits and Barriers to Involving Users in Medical Technology Development and Evaluation." *International Journal of Technology Assessment in Health Care* 23(1): 131–137.

Shakespeare, Tom. 2006. *Disability Rights and Wrongs*. New York: Routledge.

Silvers, Anita. 1998. "A Fatal Attraction to Normalizing." In *Enhancing Human Traits*, edited by Erik Parens, 95–123. Washington DC: Georgetown University Press.

Specker Sullivan, Laura, Eran Klein, Tim Brown, et al. 2017. "Keeping Disability in Mind: A Case Study in Implantable Brain Computer Interfaces." *Science and Engineering Ethics*. doi: 10.1007/s11948-017-9928-9

Stramondo, Joseph. 2016. "Why Bioethics Needs a Disability Moral Psychology." *Hastings Center Report* 46(3): 22–30.

Taylor, Charles. 1994. "The Politics of Recognition." In *Multiculturalism: Examining the Politics of Recognition*, edited by Amy Gutmann, 25–74. Princeton, NJ: Princeton University Press.

Tennison, Michael N., and Jonathan D. Moreno. 2012. "Neuroscience, Ethics, and National Security: The State of the Art." *PLoS Biology* 10(3): e1001289.

Wasserman, David, Adrienne Asch, Jeffrey Blustein, and Daniel Putnam. 2015. "Disability and Justice." In *Stanford Encyclopedia of Philosophy*, edited by Edward N. Zalta. Available at https://plato.stanford.edu/archives/sum2015/entries/disability-justice/

Winkler, Rolfe. 2017. "Elon Musk Launches Neuralink to Connect Brains with Computers." Available at https://www.wsj.com/articles/elon-musk-launches-neuralink-to-connect-brains-with-computers-1490642652

Wolpaw, Jonathan R., and Elizabeth W. Wolpaw. 2012. *Brain–Computer Interfaces: Principles and Practice*. New York: Oxford University Press.

Young, Iris Marion. 1990. *Justice and the Politics of Difference*. Princeton, NJ: Princeton University Press.

....

CHAPTER 36

SECOND THOUGHTS ON ENHANCEMENT AND DISABILITY

....

MELINDA C. HALL

Let me repeat: there can be nothing more dangerous to a body than the social agreement that that body is dangerous.

—Ahmed (2017, 144)

INTRODUCTION

....

TRANSHUMANIST arguments in support of radical human enhancement are inimical to disability justice projects. Transhumanist thinkers, the strongest promoters of human enhancement, and fellow travelers who claim enhancement is a moral obligation, make arguments that rely on the denigration of disabled embodiment and lives. Indeed, as I will show, these arguments make assumptions and mistakes in reasoning that are ableist in origin and have ableist impacts. The promotion of human enhancement is therefore open to significant disability critique. There are several reasons to pursue such a critique. First, transhumanists claim they make natural allies with disability justice activists, especially given the integration of technology in the everyday lives of disabled people, and are engaged in a fight for disability justice because of their pursuit of human enhancement (Dvorsky 2003; *Fixed* 2013; Wasserman 2012). My account calls these claims seriously into question and serves as a warning about the ethical and political import of current enhancement thinking for disabled persons.

Some may claim that transhumanist argumentation exists on the extreme fringes of academic thought. For this reason, some may further contend that transhumanism ought not be taken seriously; if one means to analyze philosophical arguments for enhancement, one should consider the best and most careful arguments for enhancement, rather than the most enthusiastic, if ultimately dubious. On both counts, I disagree, and the various grounds for my disagreement provide a second reason to pursue a disability critique of transhumanism. With regard to the former claim, I argue that transhumanist thinking is consistent with fundamental assumptions within bioethics literature more generally. For example, both mainstream bioethics and transhumanists encourage conceiving of the self within a framework of choice and agency, and claim, explicitly or implicitly, that more choices and more capabilities obviously improve quality of life. Additionally, transhumanism is empirically not on the fringe as it is institutionally embedded in the academic and public-facing enterprise of bioethics, including Nick Bostrom's work at the Future of Humanity Institute and Julian Savulescu's work at the Uehiro Centre for Practical Ethics (Hall 2013*b*). Meanwhile, with regard to the latter claim, pursuing only the best arguments in philosophical debate counts as a sound policy but only if one assumes the best arguments are those with the most influence in social and political registers. Unfortunately, the most influential and ideologically extreme arguments are not necessarily the best arguments. I analyze arguments made by transhumanists Bostrom and Savulescu in this chapter. These arguments may be provocative—even specifically calibrated by their authors for a strong reaction—but they have undeniable purchase in academic circles, and enhancement literature routinely cites both thinkers. Therefore, I argue, one should take transhumanist claims seriously as key and telling expressions of the larger discipline of bioethics. There is yet another reason to pursue a disability critique of transhumanism: disability is significantly socially constructed—that is, disability is a product of power relationships, discourses, institutions, and contingent and historical circumstances—and, therefore, I argue that disability is enacted rather than discovered.[1] Bioethics literature, as a significant site of discussion, dissemination, and authority with regard to what counts as disability, is a site of that enactment. Taken together, these three elements of my overall perspective make critique of transhumanism, and its place in bioethics literature, urgent. On my view, transhumanism is not only a source of ableist and damaging argumentation but also a discourse in which meanings of disability take hold. These meanings are often damaging and even dangerous for already-existing persons. In this chapter, I lay out my disability critique of enhancement along these lines. To support my claims, I describe bioethics (and therefore transhumanism) as biopolitical, in the sense that Michel Foucault uses the term.[2]

Finally, I here further develop my earlier contention that an alternative vision of enhancement is possible and desirable (Hall 2016, 139). In posing an alternative vision of enhancement, one that imagines a disability-inclusive future, I present my "second thoughts" on enhancement and disability. Reclaiming the ground of debate over enhancement in the name of disability justice and disabled futures has radical critical potential. Given the failings in this regard of the current arguments promoting human enhancement, critical disability thinkers should develop a counterdiscourse of enhancement. This counterdiscourse would shift attention from the body to the social and the political, engaging intersectional argumentation strategies that support feminist, critical race, and queer perspectives. Such a counterdiscourse, I argue, is poised to meet future challenges, like climate change, while at the same time avoiding the negative eugenic implications of enhancement promotion from the transhumanist perspective.

BACKGROUND AND TERMINOLOGY

The terms I use here are contested and so require definition. In this section, I briefly describe my usage of the central concepts in my argument, including disability, enhancement, and transhumanism. Disability resists demarcation. Debates over chronic illness (Wendell 2001), the controversial conceptual divide between impairment and disability (Meekosha and Shuttleworth 2009, 50), and the desire among some theorists to avoid fixed definitions to better track pathologization and oppression (Kafer 2013, 11) complicate the issue. Recently, two influential arguments regarding what disability is have emerged. Elizabeth Barnes articulates and defends a view of disability that maintains that disability is mere-difference and not bad-difference, and she goes on to define disability as that status or identity for which disability justice movements promote justice (2016, 43). This definition relativizes and contextualizes the meaning of disability but unnecessarily limits the scope of the concept. Meanwhile, Shelley Tremain articulates and defends a historical-relativist account of disability that insists on viewing disability as an invention—that is, as a product of power relations. Tremain views impairment, too, as part of that apparatus (2017). Similarly, Rosemarie Garland-Thomson theorizes disability as a pervasive cultural concept, like gender, that is caught up in a disability–ability system of social organization and classification (2002, 4, 6). For Sami Schalk, one should see "*(dis)ability* as a system of social norms which categorizes, ranks, and values bodyminds[3] and *disability* as a historically and culturally variable category within this larger system" (2016). Along with Tremain and Garland-Thomson, I argue that disability is significantly socially constructed and therefore deeply contingent and, in a sense, unnatural, although it requires the appearance of a natural kind to function as an agent of pathologization.[4] In this way, disability becomes a way of marking bodies and an expression of power relations. Furthermore, I follow Tremain in preferring the use of theoretical resources in Michel Foucault's oeuvre to articulate how disability is produced. Dianne Pothier and Richard Devlin argue that "disability is not fundamentally a question of medicine or health, nor is it just an issue of sensitivity and compassion; rather, it is a question of politics and power(lessness), power over, and power to" (2006, 2). Given his unique and illuminating approaches to power, Foucault's work is exceptionally well suited to analyzing disability.

I turn now to enhancement. Many rely on a distinction between enhancement and therapy to describe enhancement as biomedical intervention that brings individuals to a level of capability that exceeds typical human functioning. Meanwhile, therapy is biomedical intervention that brings individuals to the level of typical human functioning. This species-typical functioning account is faulty for two reasons: first, it is extremely difficult to distinguish usefully between therapy and enhancement in specific cases of medical interventions (Parens 2009), and, second, the strongest promoters of enhancement do not distinguish between therapy and enhancement. For transhumanists, all humans are in need of enhancement, and so the traditional distinction between therapy and enhancement falls away (Bostrom 2003, 105). To gain clarity, I define enhancement in the same way transhumanists define it: as the improvement of existing capabilities or the addition of new capabilities through available intervention strategies. As Bostrom puts it, transhumanism, meanwhile, "is a loosely defined movement... [that] promotes an interdisciplinary approach to understanding and evaluating the opportunities for enhancing the human condition and the human organism opened up by the advancement of technology" (2003, 105).

Transhumanist Enhancement Strategies

In this section, I present two dominant transhumanist enhancement strategies. First, I consider Bostrom's strategy of the transcendence of embodiment. Second, I consider Savulescu's strategy of negative genetic selection, driven by his principle of procreative beneficence (PB; 2001a, 2001b). In selecting these two strategies for consideration, I mean to suggest that they are typical of underlying transhumanist reasoning, have deep import for disabled persons and arguments about the future, and that philosophers of disability should attend to them. I do not mean to suggest that they are the only enhancement strategies vulnerable to a disability critique.

Many desired capabilities enumerated by the promoters of enhancement are opposed to the strictures of embodiment. For example, the desire to eliminate aging and death is arguably incompatible with the fact of embodiment.[5] Bostrom's desire to transcend embodiment thereby becomes a central transhumanist strategy and expresses the transhumanist goal "to achieve a greater degree of control over our own lives" (Bostrom 2003, 105). Bostrom bemoans human complacency about our limitations; for instance, he argues that our embodiment limits our functionality, sensory modalities, special faculties and sensibilities, mood, energy, and self-control (2010). Human opportunity range is limited (2008). Our lifespan is limited (2005a). Finally, our cognition is limited; we cannot understand every book in the Library of Congress, and there may be a "cap on our ability to discover philosophical and scientific truths" (2010, 622).

For Bostrom, we cannot imagine what it would be like to be posthuman, with a greatly increased opportunity range, although the achievement of such a status is desirable: "Our everyday intuitions about values are constrained by the narrowness of our experience and the limitations of our powers of imagination. We should leave room in our thinking for the possibility that as we develop greater capacities, we shall come to discover values that will strike us as being of a far higher order than those we can realize as un-enhanced biological human beings" (2003, 106). With this in mind, Bostrom hopes to overcome the body's fragility to achieve posthuman status and save the intellect from the body (through, for example, mind-uploading strategies). For Bostrom, fleshly bodies are unworthy containers for human potential and are largely to blame for human constraint. Furthermore, the body is a vehicle of human suffering, especially the suffering of disease and death (2003; 2005a). In this way, Bostrom makes an enemy of vulnerability. The body is a target of innovation because it is unacceptably vulnerable. Of the body, he writes: "it is not well to live in a self-combusting paper hut!...one day you or your children should have a secure home. Research, build, redouble your effort!" (2010, 2, 5).

In this way, Bostrom discursively treats the human body as a trap or cage inhibiting the human intellect. He fantasizes that the intellect can exist even if released from embodiment and still experience desire, interest, and motivation in this separated state. His fundamental premise, that embodiment limits our capacities, can be easily reversed: our embodiment enables function, such as the senses, mood, energy, and self-control; our bodyminds enable cognition and provide the fundamental motivation and frame for the discovery of philosophical and scientific truths. Instead, regressively rather than progressively, Bostrom revivifies the old hierarchy and division between body and mind. His transhumanism focuses on "individual liberties" and suggests that fleshly dependence and human interdependence are barriers to happiness (2005b, 4). With Bostrom as a guide, radical human enhancement is not radical, after all. Overall, Bostrom paints embodiment as risky and eschews dependence where it appears. From the perspective of disability justice, these conceptions of human problems and solutions are both familiar and a locus of deep concern. Bostrom's devaluation of the body is articulated precisely in terms by which disability is pathologized, including functionality and vulnerability.

Furthermore, his separation of the body and mind—attended by the desire to release the mind from the body—implies that Bostrom may ally himself with physically disabled persons who wish to overcome their bodies but would not ally himself with cognitively disabled persons whose minds he would perceive as defective. Bostrom's primary concerns involve improvement of the intellect as a way to improve quality of life, indicating that the two are necessarily positively correlated. So, he would likely refuse any contention that cognitively disabled persons enjoy a high quality of life. He translates death in terms of intellect, likening the annual loss of human life (which he hopes to combat via life extension) to the loss of the library at Alexandria multiplied three times (2005c). He reckons each human life as worth a book. Finally, although he does not know what potential is involved in increased intellectual capacity, he marks it as desirable. This last point suggests that Bostrom's motivation or desire for improved intellect comes from rejection of what he associates with the lack of particular intellectual capacities, which, unlike enhanced intellect, is known (2010, 620, 622). These elements of his perspective speak against his potential allyship with cognitively disabled persons. Meanwhile, physically disabled persons who wish to revel in difference and explore the unique functionalities, modes, and desires of their bodies would not fit Bostrom's schema for exploration of human potential.

I turn now to highlight a second transhumanist strategy, proposed by Savulescu.[6] This strategy involves choosing to bear particular children using available reproductive technologies. Savulescu's principle of *procreative beneficence* issues a moral responsibility to apply evolving reproductive technologies to select the best child possible with the greatest overall well-being (2001b). He articulates PB as follows: "Couples should select the child, of the possible children they could have, who is expected to have the best life, or at least as good a life as others, based on the relevant, available information" (2001b, 415). Savulescu restricts this principle in two ways. First, he likens the level of moral responsibility involved in the "should" of procreative beneficence to the idea that one "should" stop smoking. This means that while one indeed should follow PB, and there are obvious good reasons to do so, there may be competing obligations that defeat it (2001b, 415). Relatedly, he also limits PB by arguing that those who want a child with diminished well-being can choose to do so if they have good reasons; this is due to the competing principle of respect for autonomy for the purposes of public policy (2001b, 424–425).

With currently available technology, PB involves the combination of in vitro fertilization and preimplantation genetic diagnosis. Another method, noted by Savulescu to be less acceptable because it may cause distress, is the combination of prenatal genetic diagnosis and selective termination (2001b, 416, 421). As an analogy, he suggests that the reasoning involved in reproductive decision-making that follows PB is similar to playing the Wheel of Fortune. Using partial information, parents should attempt to make the most reasonable available decision. This plays out, for Savulescu, as a good reason to select against embryos marked by positive tests for unwanted traits. Savulescu includes both disease and nondisease genes as sorting traits, as he argues that both have the potential to negatively impact well-being on any theory of well-being (2001a; 2001b, 419). He believes that medical professionals should inform and counsel parents with regard to these traits and that their role is to persuade parents to follow PB (425–426). He is careful to articulate this persuasion as falling short of coercion since he is dedicated to posing autonomy as a competing bioethical principle that may trump PB.

Similarly, the field of genetic counseling explicitly prizes the bioethical principle of client (parent) autonomy, upheld through a second principle: nondirective counseling (Davis 1997, 8). Yet, genetic counseling has governing force over clients. The logic of normality comprises this governing force; potential parents are expected to take action in response to medical, hereditary, and age-related statistics which are posed alongside the risks and costs of deviation (Waldschmidt 2005, 205). The discursive field of risk in which this counseling is embedded structures a form of agency for counseled individuals: within this milieu, subjects are expected to express autonomy by acting on genetic information in order to protect themselves from risk. As Anne Waldschmidt puts it, subjects in this position are described as autonomous insofar as they can choose against "misfortune" by utilizing the platform of "statistical calculation" (2005, 204–205, cf. Morrison 2008). Savulescu's principle of PB is open to the same concerns. He presumes that the discovery of genetic markers for disease and nondisease genes involves neutral information that can enhance individual liberty, even reproductive liberty, and that medical professionals can persuade parents to follow PB without being open to charges of coercion.[7] In the case of the former presumption, Savulescu does not appreciate the contingency of well-being, treating it as static. Again, he argues that any theory of well-being would encourage a potential parent to select against certain particular traits on behalf of their future child. In making this argument, Savulescu incorrectly implies that potential parents can usefully interpret genetic information and the meaning and impact of the traits in question from genetic profiles alone, without reference to a future child's particular goals or environment. Transhumanism here, as in the case of Bostrom, is therefore less progressive than it first appears—radical human enhancement should suggest open, expansive, and unpredictable forms of well-being. In the case of the latter presumption, Savulescu does not take into account the asymmetrical power relations of the clinic and the fundamental direction to parents to be responsive to statistical and genetic information. Indeed, there are merely two choices possible for those engaging in PB: a choice against a particular embryo or a choice for a particular embryo.

Given the foregoing, PB is the appropriate target of a disability critique. The principle will reliably pick out genetic markers presumed linked to disability as traits to avoid in reproduction. Furthermore, it presumes that the idea that disability and well-being are opposed to each other is a neutral, apolitical description that refers merely to facts about the body. To highlight the importance of this, consider that PB thereby naturalizes and depoliticizes disability by posing genetic profiles as informative with regard to a future child's ability status. Licia Carlson coins the phrase "prenatal prototypes" to refer to sets of information gained by screening technology, which are problematically "taken as representative of an entire class of future persons" (2002, 208). Furthermore, PB ultimately supports the pathologization of mere deviation as deviance. This is because evolving technology, such as chromosomal microarray (said to be more reliable than karyotyping in detecting fetal abnormality), directly compares fetal DNA to DNA from a presumptively "healthy person" to identify deviation (Fitzgerald 2012; Wapner et al. 2012). But, as Jackie Scully forcefully argues, constant variation in human genotype makes the idea of a canonical blueprint for human DNA meaningless. In this way, genetic "normalcy" is overvalued and genetic science cannot provide meaning for each form of deviation that screening technologies increasingly pick out (2008).[8]

For Savulescu, PB is preferable to other human enhancement strategies (Savulescu et al. 2006), although notice that no individual person is enhanced through PB. Rather, PB pursues population-level enhancement through negative selection. Savulescu, writing with Persson, urges the practice of human enhancement to avoid catastrophic effects such as species extinction (2012). Specifically, Savulescu and Persson argue that we will have a better, more moral, and more politically just future if we use enhancement strategies as we will be able to shed our parochial, kin-based morality and morally adjust to deal with large-scale problems like climate change and war (2012). Inherited from an early pack or herd setting, this parochial morality makes it difficult for us to be sympathetic to distant others, according to Persson and Savulescu. Without serious moral adjustments—which these authors believe are possible via radical enhancement technologies—they worry that we will never overcome the collective action problems that bar us from solving these issues. Again, Savulescu and Persson argue that our moral ineptitude will cause us to become extinct if moral enhancement—that is, an effort to make humans more altruistic—is not undertaken. So, to reiterate, prenatal testing and genetic selection are the technologies of choice for creating the best child, and creating the best child is a key human enhancement strategy. Meanwhile, enhancement is required to avoid species extinction. This means that Savulescu suggests, at root, that genetic abnormality is linked to existential risk. These arguments strongly suggest that justice requires that the future not include disabled people, or that disabled people do not belong in hopeful visions of the future.

A Foucauldian Critique of Transhumanism

Thus far, I laid out two dominant transhumanist enhancement strategies along with an evaluation of these strategies from the perspective of disability justice concerns and the desire for access to the future for disabled persons. I turn now to deepen my analysis using Foucault's notion of biopolitics, ultimately aiming to draw together a consistent disability critique of transhumanism. On my view, the discipline of bioethics and the practice of medicine are biopolitical. As Tremain argues, bioethics is a "predictable product and tangible outcome of" the movement of power in society as it classifies individuals, invests in the health of populations, and treats differences as pathological (Tremain 2008, 101–103). Bioethics is a patently political enterprise; bioethics experts are called on to judge who can speak (e.g., Goering 2008; Peace 2012; 2013), whose testimony counts (e.g., Hoffman and Tarzian 2001; Munch 2004), the flow of resources (e.g., Cohen 2013), and what decisions are permissible in the clinic and at home (e.g., Salem 1999). Bioethics thereby maintains and reproduces conceptions of abnormality and, at the same time, constructs a vision of the normal, healthy subject. Using a biopolitical frame reveals features of the discipline otherwise obscured from view, including the stakes of the political nature of bioethics.

Biopolitics (or biopower), as described by Foucault, is a governance strategy that attempts to mediate between the individual and the population in such a way that population-level phenomena are made predictable and thereby easier to control. This is a contemporary strategy of power that unites two superseded, historical forms of power in society: disciplinary power and regulatory power (Lemke 2011, 37). Briefly, disciplinary power focuses on individual bodies and minute levels of control; Foucault locates its appearance in the seventeenth century as surveillance and training, investigating the figure of the soldier of the *ancien régime* (1979, 180). Disciplinary power produces docile bodies through uninterrupted coercion; the prison, the school, and the hospital are, according to him, organized around this pattern (182). Meanwhile, regulatory power attempts to control life itself, focusing on the population rather than the individual (Foucault 2003, 249–250). In the nineteenth century, Foucault contends that interest in birth rate, death rate, the spread of disease, and other collective principles emerged along with this new strategy. Regulatory power "brings together the mass effects characteristic of a population" and seeks to control and predict "the series of random events that can occur in a living mass" (249). New forms of knowledge appeared as innovative fields of study, including statistics and epidemiology (250, cf. Lemke 2011, 5). Because it seeks homeostasis and balance, Foucault argues that regulatory power is distinguished from other forms by making the "security of the whole" in the face of "internal dangers" a priority (Foucault 2003, 249). These internal dangers are, in part, tied to the abnormal individual, which represents chance and risk for the population as a whole (244).

Again, biopower unites disciplinary and regulatory power; biopower links the two through the concept of the norm and produces a normalizing society centered on the body (Foucault 2003, 253). Consider, for instance, sex, which acts as a hinge between the individual and the population; in Foucauldian terminology, sex is an "apparatus" of power and a vehicle of normalization for the body (Lemke 2011, 38). Using the "relative logic of calculating, measuring, and comparing," sex as apparatus can produce, for example, the concept of problematic heredity (38–39). While problematic heredity refers to populations, past generations, and future generations, it applies on the level of sexual behavior to promote and discourage particular sexual partners for specific people. It should be obvious that the practice of medicine also behaves as a hinge between the individual and the population, norming the body (Foucault 2003, 253).

Biopower also maintains, at its heart, an even older form of power: sovereign power (Foucault 2003, 254). Sovereign power is the direct taking of life, or the right of the sword. Biopower maintains this older form by determining, for the sake controlling the living mass, a "break between what must live and what must die" and is "a way of fragmenting the field of the biological that power controls" (254–255). This is "racism against the abnormal," constituting what Foucault refers to as a "death drive" within biopower (254). For Foucault, the biopolitical logic of racism against the abnormal is captured in the following motto: "If you want to live, the other must die" (255). More elaborately, Foucault writes: "the more inferior species die out, the more abnormal individuals are eliminated, the fewer degenerates there will be in the species as a whole, and the more I—as species rather than individual—can live, the stronger I will be, the more vigorous I will be. I will be able to proliferate" (255).

Overall, according to Foucault, biopolitical governance attempts to calculate and manage risk—that is, quantify, evaluate, and mitigate it—ultimately picking out risky abnormality for death. On my view, this is a helpful and clarifying description of the forces undergirding bioethics literature. In much of bioethics discourse, the responsible medical subject is a responsible citizen who attempts to manage chance through individual decision-making on the level of the body rather than through collective social and political decision-making.[9] This is convenient for biopower as it seeks to understand and control populations as living masses subject to birth, death, and disease rather than cooperative action. In this larger discursive setting, the specific risk that transhumanists attempt to quantify, evaluate, and mitigate is, I argue, the risk of disability. I already partially indicate this claim in the previous section, insofar as Bostrom ties together embodiment and risk in his desire to transcend embodiment and Savulescu poses potential parents as risk managers via PB.

To clarify the connection further, however, I suggest that the two transhumanist strategies I cover in this chapter unite positive and negative eugenics. In other words, they closely follow Foucault's understanding of the biopolitical dictate: "the more inferior species die out … the more I—as species rather than individual—can live, the stronger I will be, the more vigorous I will be" (2003, 255). Transhumanists encourage individuals to discard embodiment (taking up a particular attitude toward the body) and to select particular prenatal prototypes as worthy of life (on behalf of the population, rather than one's particular potential child, who remains unenhanced regardless of one's decision). Foucault notes that, under biopower, death and, therefore, the death drive behind racism against the abnormal, takes multiple forms. He writes: "When I say 'killing,' I obviously do not mean simply murder as such, but also every form of indirect murder: the fact of exposing someone to death, increasing the risk of death for some people, or, quite simply, political death, expulsion, rejection, and so on" (2003, 256).

With a Foucauldian biopolitical analysis in mind, what does disability mean for the transhumanist? Transhumanist thinking *risks* disability, linking disability thoroughly to risk, even risk or danger to the entire species (Persson and Savulescu 2012). Indeed, bioethics literature on enhancement usually situates disability as risk that must be managed. Ironically, however, this treatment of disability *creates* and *directs* risk rather than identifying and mitigating it. As Sarah Ahmed suggests, "there can be nothing more dangerous to a body than the social agreement that that body is dangerous" (2017, 144). Consider: the transplant board that refuses a new organ to a patient with a disability (Cohen 2013); the difficulty Deaf persons have in attempting to secure medical care (Buck 2016); the adverse outcomes experienced by pregnant disabled women (Mitra et al. 2015); or, finally, the disabled persons whose testimony with regard to their quality of life is disregarded and disbelieved, thereby rendering them vulnerable to medical negligence and even death (Goering 2008; Peace 2012). These circumstances, in which disabled persons are at risk, could be radically otherwise. Transhumanist understandings of disability stigmatize already-existing disabled people, marking them out as inferior and unworthy of life and providing a backdrop and justification for their differential treatment. In this way, transhumanist thinking helps create and direct risk toward disabled people. One way that this situation could be otherwise is to incorporate intersectional, critical disability theory into the discussion about what counts as enhancement. This calls for a counterdiscourse of enhancement, to which I turn next. Again, the reality of transhumanist strategies and argumentation undermines the promises and rhetoric of transhumanism. Transhumanism does not enhance human life; instead, it enhances risk and vulnerability in ways that hold particular danger for disabled persons. For these reasons, I take transhumanist thinking to be fundamentally opposed to disability justice projects.

A COUNTERDISCOURSE OF ENHANCEMENT

The endorsement of transhumanist-style enhancement is also an endorsement of a particular vision for the future, one that explicitly excludes disabled people. Crip theorists have contested the fundamental assumption underlying transhumanism as I here describe it; that is, the assumption that disability attaches to lives "not worth living" and fundamentally involves a "future no one wants" (Fritsch 2016, 11; Kafer 2013, 1–3). Future-oriented thinking significantly governs the lives of already-existing people and so is immediately social and political. Kelly Fritsch writes: "The withering of some disabled lives and the capacitation of others result from neoliberal material and discursive processes that orient and imagine disability as a life without a future unless capacitated through such biocapitalist practices as cures or body/mind enhancement technologies and procedures" (2016, 11–12). In other words, as I argue, disability's meanings and implications are contingent and unnatural; disability is not a neutral description of the body with a settled meaning. Precisely the way we dream of the future impacts the materiality of disability and experiences of disability. This is a significant space to take up as a site of resistance (Kafer 2013, 153). Robert McRuer describes a version of this resistance as a "crip promise" that "we will always comprehend disability otherwise and that we will, collectively, somehow access other worlds and futures" (2006, 207–208).

It is with this desire in mind that I seek a counterdiscourse of enhancement, reclaiming the future from transhumanist visions and resisting the import of those visions. I argue that this counterdiscourse requires several conceptual shifts. First, enhancement should be understood as social and political, rather than biological or personal. Second, responsibility for risk should be taken on the level of the collective rather than by individuals. Yet, third, we must acknowledge that there is no such thing as a life without risk—even if one's body is made up entirely of inorganic materials, as transhumanists dream. Risk is not, however, antithetical to living well. Fourth, radical preparations for an uncertain future, including the uncertainty of climate change, requires radical openness and creativity in response to that very uncertainty. This openness should involve the acknowledgment that fitness for the future is unsettled. What capabilities, bodily modalities, and functionalities will serve us in the future? In planning for the future, transhumanists engage in unsupported speculation with regard to future conditions and what traits will be of value in those contexts.[10] A counterdiscourse of enhancement should avoid this mistake.

Understanding enhancement as social and political would denaturalize questions of well-being (rejecting biological and individual explanations) and has the potential to treat social and political problems through appropriate social and political means. Instead of asking what sort of people there should be, social and political enhancement focuses on making people better off and planning futures that can include all of us. This can involve the radical redistribution of resources, critical alliances among pathologized persons to critique oppressive circumstances, and calls for change that point back to political decision-making rather than inborn traits.

Undertaking enhancement as a social and political project does not require one to be a technological Luddite. Donna Haraway famously argues that, by taking a "slightly perverse shift in perspective," we can "use technology to challenge domination" rather than be dominated by it (1991, 613). Technology can indeed serve as a means of inclusion rather than a biopolitical tool. Appropriate political investment in assistive technologies, like wheelchairs, could lower prices and improve the quality of these devices while at the same time improving general access to them. Currently, such devices are overpriced and unavailable, even as reproductive technologies, like maternal serum screening, that seek to assist potential parents in determining what kind of people there should be, are taken as necessary investments. Furthermore, consider the use of virtual reality goggles in designing public spaces such as hospitals. Most imagine entertainment uses for virtual reality goggles, such as creating an overlay that improves the looks of our sex partners (Kurzweil and Grossman 2010, 96). But, instead, virtual reality goggles can be used by architects to simulate the experience of physical space from diverse embodied points of view, ultimately leading to inclusive changes in those spaces (Hess and Spiering 2017).

Collective responsibility for risk might look, for example, like recentering public health issues on the built environment and public policy rather than on individual behavior and traits. Areas of collective intervention in the arena of public health can include improving infrastructure for water in cities to combat lead levels in drinking water, cleaning toxic waste dumps linked to high cancer rates, building universal healthcare, and taking seriously the availability of nutritious food. Areas of collective intervention for public policy can include combatting bad environmental policy that drives up mosquito populations and viral illnesses, rather than warning individuals against mosquitos, and combatting economic policies (such as regressive taxation) that maintain inequality, rather than advising individuals in wealth accumulation. Taking up risk collectively should not devolve into attempts to eliminate risk, which would require the cessation of human projects and life.

Finally, radical planning for the future should involve better understandings of evolution than transhumanists have to offer and the support of greater, rather than less, diversity among modes of life. What counts as human life must be reconceptualized. The more sophisticated our understanding of epigenetic factors, the influence of the microbiomes in our guts, and the like becomes, the more we must grapple with an image of human life profoundly antithetical to the intellectualized and individual account found in transhumanism. We are many and porous, leaky and interactive. Again, trans-humanism is not as radical as it purports to be—its posthumanism is merely a revived humanism. Along these lines, Rayna Rapp and Faye Ginsburg see the potential to create a habitable future, one in which we "make disability count" for the future rather than "counting disability" (and attempting to eliminate it) in order to control the future (Ginsburg and Rapp 2015; see also Rapp and Ginsburg 2017). In other words, presuming the existence of disabled people in the future causes us to think creatively about and open ourselves up to a radically different future that supports radically different forms of life.

Overall, to pursue a counternarrative of enhancement, I argue that one should reject enhancement strategies that rely, for their desirability, on stoking the fear of death, injury, and disability or exploiting desires for the realization of disembodied autonomy and rationality. One should support, instead, enhancement strategies that emphasize collective responsibility, social and political change, and inclusive futures. This does not mean that one cannot seek care, including even genetic therapies. It seems possible to me to take up medicine and technology, including access and payment for these services, on behalf of and directed by those persons whose projects and desires would be served by them.

Conclusion

One may launch various objections against my claims in this chapter. For instance, some will claim that enhancement is obviously good, and some will claim that disability is obviously bad. John Harris claims that enhancements are always about making one better, and better is always good (2011). This suggests that "better" and "enhancement" are obvious or natural, resistant to history and context. But what counts as better and worse is changeable, political, and contingent. Enhancement, like disability, must be considered in and through material conditions and history. So, the former claim begs the normative question of enhancement and should be disregarded. Meanwhile, the latter claim begs the normative question of disability, which is also historically contextual and contingent, and so should be disregarded. Some will object that disability presents genuine risks in the form of medical conditions, needs, and vulnerabilities and that bioethics should take up these matters as fundamentally important to human life and medical decision-making. But the risks associated with disability are widely and wrongly understood to be merely or mostly biological, rather than, as I understand them, significantly social and political. A counterdiscursive shift to the social and political would help us reconsider the logic of the cure (Clare 2017) in favor of the demand for care in a variety of forms.[11]

Finally, some may object that many everyday activities are unproblematic enhancements without reference to disability. Examples include drinking coffee and practicing sports, or even more lasting interventions, such as gene therapy to boost one's immune system.[12] This objection does not challenge my account, however. I can refuse the linkage between these everyday activities and the enhancement strategies I target here. The enhancement strategies I target, unlike the everyday activities referenced in this objection, draw together positive and negative eugenics, refuse the body, or attempt to decide what sort of people there should be. Indeed, I contend elsewhere that transhumanist argumentation exploits the common-sense acceptability of everyday "enhancements" in order to push favored enhancement strategies of the sort that concern me (Hall 2016, 28–29).

The transhumanist strategies of the transcendence of the body and the selection of particular children involve assumptions that embodiment and disability are fundamentally risky and are barriers to happiness and justice. These assumptions, among others, oppose transhumanist discourse to a critical disability perspective and desires to include disabled persons in visions of a better future. Foucauldian biopolitical analysis further exposes the harmful norms and assumptions underlying the discourses of bioethics and transhumanist argumentation. By outlining these problems and using this Foucauldian method of analysis, I hope, minimally, to have shown that transhumanist enhancement strategies and thinking about the future are inimical to disability justice projects. Maximally, in these pages, I hope to have shown that the biopolitical logic of bioethics, and transhumanism within it, situates disability as risk that must be managed and that this treatment creates and directs risk rather than identifying and mitigating it, as both discourses appear to promise. In this way, I claim, transhumanist bioethical thinking as biopolitics produces risk and distributes it, unevenly, in the name of risk management, ultimately contributing to harm and stigma impacting disabled people and others caught up in pathologization.

Acknowledgments

I would like to acknowledge the Author Meets Critics panelists who responded generously and thoughtfully to my book, *The Bioethics of Enhancement: Transhumanism, Disability, and Biopolitics* (2016). Your commentaries assisted in the development of this chapter. For the panels held at the 2017 annual meeting of philoSOPHIA and the 2017 annual meeting of the Canadian Philosophical Association: thank you to Catherine Clune-Taylor, Jane Dryden, Ladelle McWhorter, and Shelley Tremain. For the panel held at the 2017 meeting of the Florida Philosophical Association: thank you to Jaime Ahlberg and Christine Wieseler.

Notes

1. Impairment, too, is significantly socially constructed, although it is taken as natural and plays the role of disability's referent (Tremain 2001; 2017, 93).
2. For a book-length treatment of these themes, see Hall, *The Bioethics of Enhancement: Transhumanism, Disability, and Biopolitics* (2016).
3. For Schalk, following Margaret Price (2015), "bodymind" is a term that refers to an intensive interweaving of body and mind, and its use is meant to refuse the tendency to treat them as separate entities.
4. This view is distinct from the social model and can be used to critique it. The social model assumes a distinction between disability and impairment, whereby disability refers to the lack or failure of social accommodation for impairment, and impairment in turn refers to potentially neutral differences presented by diverse bodies. The view that disability is socially constructed can question the divide between disability and impairment and does not require that the concept of disability is merely tragic or negative.
5. The risks and strictures of embodiment are not limited to the flesh. Even if one is made up entirely of inorganic materials, copper, silicon, and the like are also subject to degradation and the vicissitudes of time. Thank you to Ladelle McWhorter for this point.

6. Unlike Bostrom, Savulescu has not explicitly self-identified as a transhumanist. But the content of his published work on enhancement, upon analysis, tracks the definition of transhumanism I give here. Given this, and given the use of the transhumanist label in at least some of that work (e.g., Persson and Savulescu 2010), I claim it is fair to refer to him as such, rather than merely as a transhumanist fellow traveler.

7. For a full articulation of my argument that PB does not enhance reproductive liberty, see Hall (2013a).

8. By noting that stigmatization has increased beyond genetic meaning, I do not mean to suggest that medical professionals do not discriminate among various forms of variation. Indeed, they will communicate to potential parents what variations in human DNA they believe to be problematically deviant.

9. In offering this analysis of bioethics discourse, I do not intend to indict individual bioethicists as intentional agents of biopower. Rather, I mean to track contingent consequences of present and Western understandings of medicine, the role of technology in daily life, and the role of individual actions vis-à-vis large-scale problems. For Foucault, ideology hides from view; those forces we are aware of have less influence over our actions than those that appear natural or familiar. This means that, on my view, individual bioethicists should investigate what appears obvious to gain critical perspective.

10. Thank you to Catherine Clune-Taylor for this point.

11. Thank you to Jane Dryden for this point.

12. Thank you to Adam Cureton for this example.

BIBLIOGRAPHY

Ahmed, Sara. 2017. *Living a Feminist Life.* Durham, NC: Duke University Press.

Barnes, Elizabeth. 2016. *The Minority Body: A Theory of Disability.* New York: Oxford University Press.

Bostrom, Nick. 2003. "Human Genetic Enhancements: A Transhumanist Perspective." *The Journal of Value Inquiry* 37: 493–506.

Bostrom, Nick. 2005a. "The Fable of the Dragon-Tyrant." *Journal of Medical Ethics* 31(5): 273–277.

Bostrom, Nick. 2005b. "In Defense of Posthuman Dignity." *Bioethics* 19: 202–214.

Bostrom, Nick. 2005c. "Humanity's Biggest Problems Aren't What You Think They Are." *TED.* Available at: http://www.youtube.com/watch?v=Yd9cf_vLviI. Accessed December 1, 2012.

Bostrom, Nick. 2008. "Why I Want to Be a Posthuman When I Grow Up." In *Medical Enhancement and Humanity,* edited by Bert Gordijn and Ruth Chadwick, 107–136. New York: Springer.

Bostrom, Nick. 2010. "Transhumanist Values." In *Contemporary Bioethics: A Reader with Cases,* edited by Jessica Pierce and George Randels, 619–624. New York: Oxford University Press. Originally published in *Journal of Philosophical Research* 30 (Supplement): 3–14.

Bostrom, Nick. 2010. "Letter from Utopia." Available at: www.nickbostrom.com/utopia. Accessed June 15, 2012.

Buck, Claudia. 2016. "Deaf People Encounter Troubles with Medical Care." *The Sacramento Bee* July 11. Available at: http://www.sacbee.com/news/local/health-and-medicine/article88784482.html. Accessed July 26, 2016.

Carlson, Licia. 2002. "The Morality of Prenatal Testing and Selective Abortion: Clarifying the Expressivist Objection." In *Mutating Concepts, Evolving Disciplines: Genetics, Medicine and*

Society, edited by L. S. Parker and R. A. Ankeny, 191–213. Netherlands: Kluwer Academic Publishers.

Clare, Eli. 2017. *Brilliant Imperfection: Grappling with Cure*. Durham, NC: Duke University Press.

Cohen, Elizabeth. 2013. "Disabled Baby Denied Heart Transplant." *CNN.com*, November 30. Available at: http://www.cnn.com/2013/11/30/health/disabled-transplants/. Accessed July 26, 2016.

Davis, Dena. 1997. "Genetic Dilemmas and the Child's Right to an Open Future." *The Hastings Center Report* 27(2/Mar–Apr): 7–15.

Dvorsky, George. 2003. "And the Disabled Shall Inherit the Earth." *Sentient Developments: Science, Futurism, Life*. September 13.

Fitzgerald, Kelly. 2012. "New Genetic Testing Reveals More Prenatal Abnormalities." *Medical News Today*, December 7. Available at: www.medicalnewstoday.com/articles/253769.php. Accessed February 20, 2013.

Fixed: The Science/Fiction of Human Enhancement. 2013. Produced and Directed by Regan Brashear.

Foucault, Michel. 1979. *Discipline and Punish: The Birth of the Prison*. Translated by Alan Sheridan. New York: Random House.

Foucault, Michel. 2003. *"Society Must Be Defended": Lectures at the Collège de France, 1975–1976*. Edited by Mauro Bertani and Alessandro Fontana. Translated by David Macey. New York: Picador.

Fritsch, Kelly. 2016. "Cripping Neoliberal Futurity: Marking the Elsewhere and Elsewhen of Desiring Otherwise." *Feral Feminisms* 5(Spring): 11–26.

Garland-Thomson, Rosemarie. 2002. "Integrating Disability, Transforming Feminist Theory." *NWSA Journal* 14(3): 1–32.

Ginsburg, Faye, and Rayna Rapp. 2015. "Making Disability Count: Demography, Futurity and the Making of Disability Publics." *Somatosphere*, May 11. Available at: http://somatosphere.net/2015/05/making-disability-count-demography-futurity-and-the-making-of-disability-publics.html. Accessed December 21, 2018.

Goering, Sara. 2008. "'You Say You're Happy, but...' Contested Quality of Life Judgments in Bioethics and Disability Studies." *Bioethical Inquiry* 5: 125–135.

Hall, Melinda. 2013a. "Reconciling the Disability Critique and Reproductive Liberty: The Case of Negative Genetic Selection." *International Journal of Feminist Approaches to Bioethics* 6(1): 121–143.

Hall, Melinda. 2013b. "Vile Sovereigns in Bioethical Debate." *Disability Studies Quarterly* 33(4). Available at: http://dsq-sds.org/article/view/3870. Accessed December 21, 2018.

Hall, Melinda. 2016. *The Bioethics of Enhancement: Transhumanism, Biopolitics, and Disability*. Lanham, MD: Lexington Books.

Haraway, Donna. 1991. *Simians, Cyborgs, and Women: The Reinvention of Nature*. New York: Routledge.

Harris, John. 2011. "Enhancements Are a Moral Obligation." In *Human Enhancement,* edited by Julian Savulescu and Nick Bostrom. Oxford: Oxford University Press.

Hess, Michael, and Ryan Spiering. 2017. "Enhancing Healthcare Planning Through Virtual Reality." *Medical Construction and Design* September 20. Available at: https://mcdmag.com/2017/09/enhancing-healthcare-planning-through-virtual-reality/.W409MFuPLIU. Accessed August 31, 2018.

Hoffman, Diane E., and Anita J. Tarzian. 2001. "The Girl Who Cried Pain: A Bias Against Women in the Treatment of Pain." *Journal of Law, Medicine & Ethics* 29: 13–27.

Kafer, Alison. 2013. *Feminist, Queer, Crip*. Bloomington: Indiana University Press.

Kurzweil, Ray, and Terry Grossman. 2010. *Transcend: Nine Steps to Living Well Forever.* New York: Rodale.

Lemke, Thomas. 2011. *Bio-Politics: An Advanced Introduction.* New York: New York University Press.

McRuer, Robert. 2006. *Crip Theory: Cultural Signs of Queerness and Disability.* New York: New York University Press.

Meekosha, Helen, and Russell Shuttleworth. 2009. "What's So 'Critical' About Critical Disability Studies?" *Australian Journal of Human Rights* 15(1): 47–75.

Mitra, Monika, Karen Clements, Jianying Zhang, et al. 2015. "Maternal Characteristics, Pregnancy Complications, and Adverse Birth Outcomes Among Women with Disabilities." *Medical Care* 53(12): 1027–1032.

Morrison, Daniel R. 2008. "Making the Autonomous Client: How Genetic Counselors Construct Autonomous Subjects." In *Bioethical Issues, Sociological Perspectives*, edited by Barbara Katz Rothman, Elizabeth Mitchell Armstrong, and Rebecca Tiger, 179–198. Amsterdam/London: Elsevier.

Munch, Shari. 2004. "Gender-Biased Diagnosing of Women's Medical Complaints: Contributions of Feminist Thought, 1970–1995." *Women & Health* 40(1): 101–121.

Parens, Erik. 2009. "Toward a More Fruitful Debate About Enhancement." In *Human Enhancement*, edited by Julian Savulescu and Nick Bostrom, 181–197. Oxford: Oxford University Press.

Peace, William. 2012. "Comfort Care as Denial of Personhood." *Hastings Center Report* 42(4): 14–17.

Peace, William. 2013. "A Peaceful Death or a Risk to People with Disabilities?" *Bioethics Forum* March 19. Available at: http://www.thehastingscenter.org/Bioethicsforum/Post.aspx?id=6285&blogid=140. Accessed April 9, 2013.

Persson, Ingmar, and Julian Savulescu. 2010. "Moral Transhumanism." *Journal of Medicine and Philosophy* 35: 656–669.

Persson, Ingmar, and Julian Savulescu. 2012. *Unfit for the Future: The Need for Moral Enhancement.* Oxford: Oxford University Press.

Pothier, Dianne, and Richard Devlin, eds. 2006. *Critical Disability Theory: Essays in Philosophy, Politics, Policy, and Law.* London: UBC Press.

Price, Margaret. 2015. "The Bodymind Problem and the Possibilities of Pain." *Hypatia* 30(1): 268–284.

Rapp, Rayna, and Faye Ginsburg. 2017. "Cripping the future: Making disability count." In *Anthropologies and Futures*, edited by Juan Salazar, Sarah Pink, Andrew Irving, and Johannes Sjöberg, 43–60. London: Bloomsbury.

Salem, Tania. 1999. "Physician-Assisted Suicide: Promoting Autonomy—or Medicalizing Suicide?" *The Hastings Center Report* 29(3): 30–36.

Savulescu, Julian. 2001a. "In Defense of Selection for Non-Disease Genes." *The American Journal of Bioethics* 1(1/Winter): 16–19.

Savulescu, Julian. 2001b. "Procreative Beneficence: Why We Should Select the Best Children." *Bioethics* 15(5–6): 413–426.

Savulescu, Julian, Melanie Hemsley, Ainsley Newson, and Bennett Foddy. 2006. "Behavioural Genetics: Why Eugenic Selection Is Preferable to Enhancement." *Journal of Applied Philosophy* 23(2): 157–171.

Schalk, Sami. 2016. "Critical Disability Studies as Methodology." *Lateral* 6(1). Available at: http://csalateral.org/issue/6-1/forum-alt-humanities-critical-disability-studies-methodology-schalk/. Accessed December 21, 2018.

Scully, Jackie Leach. 2008. *Disability Bioethics: Moral Bodies, Moral Difference*. Lanham, MD: Rowman & Littlefield.

Tremain, Shelley. 2001. "On the Government of Disability." *Social Theory and Practice* 27(4): 617–636.

Tremain, Shelley. 2008. "The Biopolitics of Bioethics and Disability." *Bioethical Inquiry* 5: 101–106.

Tremain, Shelley. 2017. *Foucault and Feminist Philosophy of Disability*. Ann Arbor: University of Michigan Press.

Waldschmidt, Ann. 2005. "Who Is Normal? Who Is Deviant? 'Normality' and 'Risk' in Genetic Diagnostics and Counseling." In *Foucault and the Government of Disability*, edited by Shelley Tremain, 191–207. Ann Arbor: University of Michigan Press.

Wapner, Ronald J., Christa Lese Martin, Brynn Levy, et al. 2012. "Chromosomal Microarray Versus Karyotyping for Prenatal Diagnosis." *The New England Journal of Medicine* 367(23): 2175–2184.

Wasserman, David. 2012. "Ethics of Human Enhancement and Its Relevance to Disability justice." *eLS*. Chichester: John Wiley & Sons, Ltd. doi:10.1001/9780470015902a00241235

Wendell, Susan. 2001. "Unhealthy Disabled: Treating Chronic Illnesses as Disabilities." *Hypatia* 16(4): 17–33.

PART NINE

HEALTH-CARE ALLOCATION

CHAPTER 37

COST-EFFECTIVENESS ANALYSIS AND DISABILITY DISCRIMINATION

GREG BOGNAR

WHAT IS COST-EFFECTIVENESS ANALYSIS?

COST-EFFECTIVENESS analysis (CEA) is an analytical tool in health economics. It is one of the most important gadgets in the health economist's and the health-care policymaker's toolkit. It is used in health technology assessments, for making coverage decisions in health-care plans and insurance packages, and for setting priorities between different resource uses. It has a central role in the health-care systems of England and New Zealand. It is used for decisions about pharmaceuticals in Australia, Canada, and the Netherlands. In the United States, it is used widely by managed care organizations. More recently, international NGOs and charitable organizations have started using it in their funding decisions. With the growing costs of health care, CEA will inevitably play an increasingly important role in the future.

Cost-effectiveness analysis, however, is not without its critics. One of the most important objections to it is that its use leads to unjust discrimination against people with disabilities. This is potentially a very severe problem. It would undercut the moral basis of much health policy. It would entail that the National Institute for Health and Care Excellence (NICE) in the United Kingdom, the Pharmaceutical Benefits Advisory Committee (PBAC) in Australia, or managed care organizations in the United States engage in morally objectionable practices. Therefore, it is important to determine whether CEA can be defended from the disability discrimination objection. This is the task of this chapter.

First, a terminological note. The word "discrimination" is sometimes used in a descriptive sense. A sommelier discriminates among wines, preferring the best ones. An employer discriminates among job candidates, selecting the most qualified for the job. Other things being equal, there need not be anything wrong with discrimination in this sense. But it is a different matter if an employer refuses to give a job to the most qualified candidate merely because of her race or sex. In that case, the discrimination is morally wrong.

In what follows, I will use the word in the descriptive sense. When it is the normative sense that I have in mind, I will qualify it by saying *unjust* discrimination. Sometimes people talk of wrongful or unfair discrimination or ask what makes discrimination bad. For my purposes, these come down to the same thing, and so I use "unjust" for convenience. Thus, when people say that CEA discriminates against people with disabilities, they mean it discriminates unjustly.

I also take it for granted that the disability discrimination objection applies to real-life, paradigmatic uses of cost-effectiveness analysis. It claims that the use of CEA, *in practice*, leads to unjust discrimination against people with disabilities. For just about any institution or social policy can be used to unjustly discriminate against some group, if the people responsible for running or implementing it choose to use it that way. (Electoral systems, for instance, can be used to unjustly discriminate against some people by denying them the right or opportunity to participate in elections.) But the objection to CEA does not concern its deviant uses. It concerns how it is standardly used, and how it is intended to be used, in health policy. It is one thing to object to the use of CEA because it leads to unjust discrimination; it is another to object that the people using it act with the intention to unjustly discriminate against some group. I am unaware of anyone making the latter objection. It would not be, in any case, an objection to the use of cost-effectiveness analysis; it would be an objection to its *misuse*.

In anti-discrimination law, a distinction is commonly made between *direct* and *indirect* forms of unjust discrimination. In direct forms of unjust discrimination, the discriminator or policy or institution explicitly aims to exclude or disadvantage members of some group. The discrimination is intentional: the discriminator intends to act or design or implement institutions or policies in order to exclude or disadvantage. In indirect forms of unjust discrimination, there is no such intent. The act or policy or institution aims to be neutral, but it ends up having a disproportionate negative impact on members of some group.

It should be clear that the disability discrimination objection to CEA makes a claim about indirect unjust discrimination. It involves no claim about the intentions or mental states of health economists, health-care policymakers, or the staff at NICE or PBAC, for instance. Its claim is that unjust discrimination is an inevitable but unintended side effect of the use of cost-effectiveness analysis.

A final distinction needs to be introduced to clarify the nature of the disability discrimination objection. Some resource allocation choices in health care take place at the level of policy. Within the health-care budget, decision makers have to choose which treatments, pharmaceuticals, or health programs to fund, how to allocate human resources, plan health-care capacities, and so on. In short, these choices concern the allocation and delivery of all the goods and services provided in a health care system. (To save words, I will refer to all these goods and services as interventions.) These are *macroallocation* choices.

Other resource allocation choices take place at the clinical level. These are *microallocation* choices. They concern how particular hospitals or teams of physicians use the resources available to them: which patients they prioritize for organ transplants, whom they admit to the ICU, how they triage in an emergency, and so on. These choices concern the care of particular patients. They are made by hospital administrators, doctors and nurses, not policy makers or health economists.

The distinction between macroallocation and microallocation is important because choices are made differently on these two levels. Cost-effectiveness analysis is a case in point. It is relevant only to macroallocation. It deals with the ranking of interventions and not with the treatment of particular patients. CEA is not part of microallocation choices. This does not mean that costs and benefits—and their balance—are never relevant in clinical decisions. But doctors are not expected to make cost-effectiveness calculations at the bedside.[1]

Consequently, the moral demands for microallocation and macroallocation choices are likely to be different. But discussions of the disability discrimination objection often proceed by considering typical philosophers' problems of deciding whom to save from certain death. (You are in a lifeboat and have to decide whether you row the boat toward this person or that person when you can only reach one of them.) Such examples from microallocation, however, have little to do with cost-effectiveness analysis. At best, they might trigger irrelevant moral intuitions. At worst, they might lead to false conclusions. Hence it is worrisome that many philosophers take them to be representative of the problem.[2]

In order to evaluate the disability discrimination objection, I need to first describe how CEA is normally used in health policy. Here is a typical example.

Suppose there is a health problem and there is an intervention to prevent or treat it. The intervention could be a medicinal drug to treat a condition, a surgery to repair injury, a screening program to reduce the incidence of a disease, and so on. For intervention i, a *cost-effectiveness ratio* can be calculated by the formula:

$$\frac{cost\ of\ i}{expected\ benefits\ of\ i}$$

The costs of an intervention are expressed in monetary terms. The benefits can be expressed in just about any health outcome measure—number of cases averted, number of lives saved, the average number of years added to patients' lives, and so on. Normally, however, expected benefits are represented by some measure that combines the improvement in health-related quality of life with the duration of the improvement. One example is *quality-adjusted life years*, or QALYs.[3]

Before we go on, there is another point of clarification that needs to be added. Sometimes the objection to CEA is in fact an objection to what are considered inappropriate judgments of the quality of life of people with disabilities. It is well known that people with and without a disability may evaluate the quality of life with that disability differently. People with no familiarity with the disability, for instance, may think that living with it is worse than people who have experience of it.

However, I set this objection aside. I am going to assume that we have come to an agreement on the appropriate quality of life judgments (or QALY values) associated with a disability, whether they should be based on the judgments of those who have experience of the disability, or on survey results of the general public, or on the evaluations of experts. If the disability discrimination objection was just an issue of inappropriate quality of life judgments, there would be no further difficulty once the appropriate judgments are used. But the objection goes deeper than that.[4]

With these clarifications in mind, return now to the cost-effectiveness formula above. The smaller the cost-effectiveness ratio of an intervention, the more cost-effective it is. For instance, suppose intervention A costs $2 million and it saves 100 people. Its cost-effectiveness ratio is $20,000 per life saved. Another intervention, B, costs $1 million but it saves only 99 people. Its cost-effectiveness ratio is $10,101.01 per life saved. Thus, intervention B is more cost-effective even though it has a worse outcome— one fewer life saved.

In practice, decision makers do not directly maximize expected benefits subject to costs when setting health-care priorities. Rather, they set a *cost-effectiveness threshold*, below which an intervention is considered cost-effective and above which it is not. Any intervention whose cost-effectiveness ratio is under the threshold is considered to have a favorable cost-effectiveness ratio and to offer "good value for money." It then becomes part of a health-care plan or insurance package, or it is subsidized or provided free of charge to patients in a health-care system. In contrast, any intervention whose cost-effectiveness ratio is over the threshold is not considered good value for money. Either it is not provided in a health-care system or patients have to pay for it out of pocket.

For instance, if the cost-effectiveness threshold is set at $15,000 per life saved, then intervention B has a favorable cost-effectiveness ratio, but intervention A does not. Thus, while B might be provided by an insurer or the government, A might not.

It is important to recognize that cost-effectiveness analysis does not imply any particular cost-effectiveness threshold. Setting a threshold is a choice for policymakers. In reality, the threshold is usually more like a range, and it is often variable and implicit.[5] For instance, NICE uses a threshold between £20,000 and £30,000 per QALY. In Australia, PBAC does not endorse any explicit cost-effectiveness threshold, but researchers have estimated a threshold range roughly between A$45,000–75,000.[6] And the World Health Organization (WHO) once suggested a cost-effectiveness threshold of 1 to 3 times GDP per capita.[7] This would imply thresholds from approximately $400 to $400,000 per unit of health benefit around the world.

Note that these numbers are *incremental cost-effectiveness ratios* (ICER). They represent the difference between the cost-effectiveness of an intervention compared to some alternative (perhaps an intervention that is already provided). To return to my example above: compared to intervention B that costs $1 million and saves 99 people, intervention

A costs $2 million and saves 100 people. That A has a cost-effectiveness ratio of $20,000 per life saved and B has one around $10,101 per life saved is not ultimately relevant. What is important is that A provides an additional benefit of saving one life at a cost of $1 million. Its incremental cost-effectiveness ratio is $1 million per life saved. Compared to the alternative, this is not particularly impressive.

How Does CEA Discriminate Against People with Disabilities?

It has been argued that there are several ways in which the use of cost-effectiveness analysis for setting priorities in health care can lead to discrimination against people with disabilities. In this section, I examine the list that Dan Brock (2009) provides. Surprisingly, it turns out that none of the forms of discrimination on his list apply to cost-effectiveness analysis as it is used in practice. At the end of the section, I add a new item to the list—one that Brock ignores, even though in my view it is the only form of discrimination against people with disabilities that apply to CEA.

One item on Brock's list involves cases when a disability is not preexisting but the result of an intervention. Suppose two people are involved in an accident, and they need different treatments as a result. One of the treatments restores full health, while the other leaves people disabled. If the second treatment is not provided or receives low priority due to its poor effectiveness, patients in need of it end up being disadvantaged.

While this is possible, it is plainly not a case of discrimination against people with disabilities. At the time of the accident, no victim has a disability. The disability is the result of treatment. Thus, a patient who needs the treatment in question cannot be discriminated against *as a person with disabilities*. Normally, to discriminate against someone on some ground—their race, sex, or religious affiliation—the person must already have the characteristic that serves as the grounds of the discrimination. It must be preexisting. Therefore, while the patient may have a complaint, it cannot be that she is discriminated against as a person with disability.

Some other forms of discrimination may occur in the case of life-saving interventions. As Brock explains, "Since disabilities reduce an individual's health-related quality of life, life-saving interventions for a disabled patient . . . will produce fewer QALYs than with an otherwise similar non-disabled patient." Additionally, "when health interventions are life saving the QALYs produced will depend on the life expectancies of the patients who receive them" (2009, 30). In both of these cases, the problem is supposed to arise from the way QALYs are constructed; as I explained previously, they combine the health-related quality of life associated with a health outcome with the duration of that outcome. Hence if a life-saving intervention would extend the life of patients with and without a disability by the same amount of time, the health benefits would be smaller for people with disabilities on account of their lower resulting health-related quality of life.

Similarly, when people with disabilities have lower life expectancies because of their condition, they would be at a disadvantage in priority setting compared to those with normal life expectancies. This would be true on any measure that combines the value of health outcomes with the duration of those outcomes. Thus, these forms of discrimination do not apply only to QALYs, but more broadly.[8]

Now it is true that other things being equal it is a worse outcome if life-saving interventions can restore some patients to less than full health or prolong their lives only for a limited amount of time. But this in itself does not lead to discrimination against anyone. To claim otherwise is to misunderstand how cost-effectiveness analysis works in practice. When health technology assessment agencies consider the cost-effectiveness of an intervention, they do not proceed by calculating different cost-effectiveness ratios for different patient groups. They work with averages. When they consider the effectiveness of a new cancer drug, for example, they understand that it will extend the lives of some patients by many years, but it will make little difference to others. They calculate the benefits by what a typical patient can expect on average. Hence, they do not separate out cancer patients with disabilities from the general patient population. Their job is not to rank patients; it is to evaluate the average expected benefits of interventions. If the drug prolongs life by five years on average, and its cost-effectiveness ratio is below the threshold, it is provided to every patient regardless of their disability status. No patient is turned away at the point of care. As I already emphasized above, cost-effectiveness calculations are applied at the macro level for all patients who can potentially benefit from an intervention, and not for particular subgroups. Cost-effectiveness analysis has no role in microallocation.[9]

As a consequence, for paradigmatic uses of CEA, these forms of discrimination do not apply. They simply do not arise in practice. Of course, there might be a case for health-care analysts to consider, for instance, the cost-effectiveness of a cancer drug separately for early and late stages of a type of cancer. But this case applies to patients in different stages of the same condition, rather than patients with disabilities and patients without. In practice, cost-effectiveness analysis does not imply lower priority for life-saving interventions for people with disabilities just because they have lower health-related quality of life or worse life expectancy. So Brock's worries about these forms of discrimination are misplaced.

Similar considerations apply to other putative forms of discrimination on Brock's list. For instance: "when health interventions protect or improve health-related quality of life, a pre-existing disability in effect often acts as a co-morbidity that makes treatment less effective" (2009, 30). This may happen, as before, either because patients with disabilities cannot be returned to full health or because they have worse life expectancies than others. In either case, their treatment results in worse health outcomes. But just as before, there is an assumption in the background that different cost-effectiveness ratios are calculated for health interventions for different groups. This is not how CEA is normally done.

The remaining two items on Brock's list suffer from the same problem. He says, "persons with severe disabilities may usually, though certainly not always, be less productive of economic benefits as a result of their disabilities" (2009, 31). But non-health benefits, and people's contribution to economic welfare, are not part of the benefit calculations of standard CEA, and in any case this problem does not arise if, as I have argued, no separate cost-effectiveness calculations are carried out for people with disabilities. Finally, Brock worries that "the presence of a disability, or a more severe disability, can often make a treatment more complex or extended, and so more expensive" (2009, 30). Once again, while this may be true, it does not lead to discrimination, as CEA does not differentiate between patients.

Now as I have already noted, one might object that cost-effectiveness analysis *could* be used to differentiate between different patient groups by their capacity to benefit. There are two things to note in response. First, of course CEA *could* be used in all sorts of discriminatory ways. It could be used, for instance, to discriminate against the poor: after all, people in worse socioeconomic conditions tend to have lower life expectancies, more comorbidities, and lower quality of life. Yet no one objects to CEA on the grounds that it discriminates against the poor; it is understood that CEA is not intended, and normally is not, used in these ways.

Second, recall that the disability discrimination objection does not say that the use of CEA in priority setting is morally problematic because it could *possibly* be used in ways that lead to discrimination against people with disabilities. The objection says that it is morally problematic because its use *actually* leads to discrimination against people with disabilities. As I have already argued, these are very different objections. The former calls for vigilance and moral scrutiny of priority setting decisions; the latter entails that priority setting in health care needs radical reform.

There is another alleged form of discrimination that should be set aside, for it is rooted in a different kind of misunderstanding of cost-effectiveness analysis. It is sometimes pointed out that CEA is *aggregative*: permitting the combination or summation of individual benefits and therefore favoring those interventions that benefit a greater number of people. This is how, it is claimed, giving painkillers to a large number of patients with headaches can end up having greater priority than life-saving interventions, like appendectomies, that are needed by only a few people. And insofar as people with disabilities are a minority in society, their health care needs become less urgent than even the less important health care needs of the general population.[10]

A quick look back at the cost-effectiveness formula that I described in the previous section should suffice to reveal the fallacy in this argument. Cost-effectiveness ratios are insensitive to numbers. It does not matter whether an intervention benefits one person or one million. If you multiply both the numerator and the denominator by a million, you get the same result. Other things being equal, no patient is disadvantaged by CEA just because she has a condition that is relatively rare in the population. In cost-effectiveness analysis, the numbers do not count. This is another illustration of the fact that cost-effectiveness is only one factor to be considered in macroallocation: how many people in the population need an intervention should also be taken into account.[11]

Does this mean that standard CEA never disadvantages people with disabilities? No. There is another possibility that is absent from Brock's list. Consider an intervention *j* for the management or rehabilitation of a particular disability, k. Because of the nature of k, j may be expensive, complex, or extended; its outcome may be highly uncertain; or its expected benefits, in terms of improving health-related quality of life or extending life, may be modest. Because of one or more of these factors, suppose that the cost-effectiveness ratio of intervention j is over the cost-effectiveness threshold.

Suppose also that j is the *only* intervention available for disability k.[12] As a result, j, the only intervention available for the management or rehabilitation of disability k, is not provided in the health-care system or it is not part of available health insurance packages. Thus, no intervention is available for this disability.

People with this disability are put in a disadvantageous situation. The health-care system does not offer any intervention for the management or rehabilitation of their disabling condition. They are not disadvantaged, however, with respect to any other intervention. All the other interventions that are available to others are available to them too. But they do suffer a disadvantage that others do not. They suffer it because CEA is used to set priorities, and the balance of the costs and expected benefits of the intervention they need is unfavorable. Moreover, in this case CEA is used the way it was intended. People with the disability are not singled out for unequal treatment. It is just how the costs and benefits work out. Therefore, there is one kind of case where the disability discrimination objection applies. In this case, the use of cost-effectiveness analysis does lead to discrimination against people with disability.[13]

Is this form of discrimination unjust? One way to approach this question is to consider some general accounts of unjust discrimination. Is disability discrimination the kind of discrimination to which they apply?

What Makes Discrimination Unjust?

According to the disability discrimination objection, the use of CEA in health-care priority setting leads to unjust discrimination against people with disabilities. This discrimination is not unlike the kind that we are concerned with in anti-discrimination law. It is no different from unjust discrimination on grounds of race or sex in employment or housing, for instance.

I have argued, however, that most cases of the alleged discrimination do not apply to standard cost-effectiveness analysis. The only case in which the disability discrimination objection applies is when the cost-effectiveness ratio of an (only) intervention j for the management or rehabilitation of a disability k is over the cost-effectiveness threshold, and for this reason j is not provided or subsidized in a health-care system or insurance package. For conciseness, let us call this the *threshold case*. Is the threshold case a form of unjust discrimination?

One way to approach this question is to consider different accounts of the philosophical foundations of anti-discrimination law. These are theories that answer the question: what makes discrimination unjust when it is unjust? In this section, I look at some recently proposed accounts. What can they say about the threshold case?

On one view, discrimination is unjust, when it is unjust, because it violates people's right to equal *deliberative freedoms*. This account is proposed by Sophia Moreau (2010). Deliberative freedoms are "freedoms to deliberate about and decide how to live in a way that is insulated from pressures stemming from extraneous traits" (2010, 147). You lack deliberative freedoms when you have to take your race or sex into account in your choices about where to live or work, for instance. Your sex or skin color should not count as an additional cost in such decisions. They should not be used by others to deny opportunities from you. The purpose of anti-discrimination law is to protect deliberative freedoms and to provide them to everyone equally.

On this account, everyone is entitled to a set of deliberative freedoms, and everyone should have these freedoms equally. Unjust discrimination may occur when these freedoms are violated. The violation does not have to be intentional: it can be an unintended side effect. An institution, for instance, can lead to the violation of deliberative freedoms if it disproportionately disadvantages some group that possesses a relevant trait—for instance, being the member of a particular race or living with a disability. However, not all violations of deliberative freedoms are cases of unjust discrimination. In certain social contexts, other values may take precedence over deliberative freedoms. Thus, while anti-discrimination law applies in employment or housing, it does not apply in the personal sphere. In addition, deliberative freedoms must sometimes be weighed against other interests. In some cases, other interests are more important than their protection.

What can be said about the threshold case on this account? Is it a form of unjust discrimination if patients with a disability are not provided with the only intervention for the management or rehabilitation of their condition due to its unfavorable cost-effectiveness ratio?

On the one hand, health care may be considered a social context in which anti-discrimination law should apply. If people cannot deliberate about how to live without taking their health or disability status into account as a cost, then their deliberative freedoms are violated. Ill-health and disability are extraneous traits that can have this effect. The provision of health-care services should not disproportionally disadvantage people with disabilities this way. For example, if people with preexisting conditions are denied health insurance, then they are forced to take their condition into account as a cost.

On the other hand, health care provision is also a context in which different people's interests must be balanced. Priority setting aims to do just that by directing resources to their most beneficial uses. If no priorities are set between different interventions, more people's deliberative freedoms will be violated. Protecting deliberative freedoms must be balanced with other interests, including effectiveness and the opportunity costs of different resources uses. In this way, cost-effectiveness analysis can be considered a method for carrying out the balancing that's necessary for minimizing the loss of deliberative freedoms. Therefore, there is no unjust discrimination when it is used to set health care priorities. The threshold case is not accommodated by the deliberative freedoms account.

Another proposal is that discrimination is unjust, when it is unjust, because and only because it undermines equality of opportunity. This has been suggested by Shlomi Segall (2012). It is important to note that this account provides only a *necessary*, rather than a

sufficient condition for the injustice of discrimination. All instances of unjust discrimination involve a violation of equality of opportunity, but not all violations of equality of
opportunity are cases of unjust discrimination. For instance, they must also involve
unequal treatment for no justifiable reason.

In the absence of a fully developed theory of equality of opportunity, it is difficult to
determine whether specific cases of unequal treatment count as unjust discrimination
on this view. Furthermore, since inequality of opportunity is only a necessary condition,
this view must be augmented by other features of unequal treatment to provide a sufficient criterion for judging when unequal treatment is an instance of unjust discrimination. Nevertheless, it might be argued that the threshold case does violate equality of
opportunity: the health needs of people with a disability are not met by the health-care
system, restricting their opportunities in comparison to others.[14]

But this is not sufficient in itself. In the threshold case, there is a good reason for the
unequal treatment: health-care priorities must be set in a way that meets the greatest
number of health care needs, given their costs. Therefore, even if the threshold case leads
to less equality of opportunity, the unequal treatment is all things considered justified.
This view does not provide a reason to consider the threshold case an instance of unjust
discrimination.

The last account I discuss grounds the injustice of discrimination in the fact that it
harms its victims. Such a harm-based account is put forward by Kasper Lippert-
Rasmussen. Here is the definition of unjust discrimination that he provides:

X discriminates against Y in dimension W if:

(i) X treats Y differently from Z in dimension W;
(ii) the differential treatment is disadvantageous to Y;
(iii) the differential treatment is suitably explained by Y's and Z's being (members of)
      different, socially salient groups.[15]

Does this formula describe the threshold case? At first glance, it might seem so. For X
does not have to be a person or group of people. It can be an institution or practice or
social structure. Thus, you might say that X stands for the health-care system or the way
priorities are set within the health-care system; it can treat people with some disability,
Y, differently than others without the disability, Z, in the dimension of health care service provision, W, in a way that is disadvantageous to Y's. When an (only) intervention
for the management or rehabilitation of a particular disability is not provided to people
with that disability, and the resources are used to provide other cost-effective interventions to others, then people with the disability are treated differently, and they are treated
in a way that is disadvantageous to them.

The third condition, that the differential treatment is suitably explained by Ys and Zs
belonging to different socially salient groups, is not satisfied, however. For even though
Ys may be members of a socially salient group (namely, people with a particular disability), their treatment is *not* explained by their membership. The differential treatment is

explained by the costs and benefits of the intervention that *Y*s need, compared to the costs and benefits of other interventions. The disability itself plays no explanatory role. Priority setting decisions can result in treating some groups of patients differently, and the differential treatment may be disadvantageous, but this is not due to, nor explained by the group membership of these patients.

Where does that leave us? I have looked at three different accounts of unjust discrimination. I have found that none of them can accommodate the threshold case. On not one of them does discrimination against people with disabilities due to the use of CEA turn out to be unjust. Insofar as these accounts represent our best current thinking on unjust discrimination, the disability discrimination objection is unsuccessful.

There is, however, something else to be learned from the discussion in this section. On all of the accounts that I presented, the threshold case comes close to being an instance of unjust discrimination. It might result in the violation of the deliberative freedoms of people with disabilities. It might undermine equality of opportunity between people with disabilities and others. And it might involve disadvantageous treatment of people with disabilities. On all of these accounts, the threshold case meets a necessary condition of unjust discrimination. This, in turn, might explain why many people find the disability discrimination objection plausible. The threshold case resembles standard cases of unjust discrimination. But in each case, it falls short: it does not meet some sufficient condition of unjust discrimination. So it is natural to find the objection troubling, even if it does not succeed in the end.

INJUSTICE WITHOUT DISCRIMINATION?

Fine—you might say—but it nevertheless remains the case that the use of CEA can disadvantage people with disabilities, as it does in the threshold case. There is something wrong with that. Perhaps the wrongness cannot be identified by considering theories about the moral bases of anti-discrimination law. Perhaps it comes from somewhere else.

One way to proceed from here is to claim that the disability discrimination objection should be understood in a different way. The emphasis in unjust discrimination should not be on discrimination. Rather, it should be on *unjust*. Discrimination against people with disabilities due to the use of CEA is not analogous to discrimination on grounds of race or sex. It is more like the injustice suffered by people who are poor or disadvantaged. If the threshold case raises a moral problem, it is not of discrimination, but of injustice. To understand it, you must turn to theories of distributive justice.[16]

It is obviously beyond the scope of this chapter to provide a detailed discussion. I am going to discuss, very briefly, only two basic, general principles. They are:

> *The Principle of Equality*. It is in itself bad if some people are worse off than others.
>
> *The Principle of Priority*. Benefiting people matters more the worse off these people are.[17]

Which of these principles is more suitable for priority setting in health care? Which of them can help with the concern raised by the threshold case?

Consider the Principle of Equality first. Very few egalitarians accept *pure egalitarianism*—the view that only the Principle of Equality matters. Most egalitarians are pluralists: they complement the principle by some other consideration. For instance, they can also claim that it is in itself better if people are better off. Nevertheless, even pluralist egalitarian views are thought to be vulnerable to the *leveling down objection*. For, if equality is in itself better, then it does not seem to matter how it is achieved. Hence a more equal distribution that is achieved by making the better off worse off without making the worse off better off makes things better in one respect—namely, that they are more equal. But since there is no one for whom the new distribution is better and there are some for whom it is worse, it is incredible that it should be better in any respect: there is nothing good about achieving greater equality by leveling down. Even if pluralist egalitarians can argue that leveling down would not be better *all things considered*, they still seem committed to the claim that it is better *in one respect*. That's all the objection needs.

In the context of health care, the leveling down objection seems especially damaging. No one holds that there would be anything good about achieving greater equality in health by making the healthier less healthy. This cannot be better in any respect. And if that was not enough, there is a less familiar, but no less serious problem with egalitarianism in health care. It is the *bottomless pit objection*.

Suppose there are patients who are worse off than others but can benefit to a small extent from some intervention. However, the intervention has massive costs. If equality is your aim, you will think there is a reason for providing this intervention. However, should you do so, you would have to forgo providing greater benefits to those who are better off. The Principle of Equality leads you to ignore the opportunity costs of the intervention. It leads you to ignore the costs and benefits to others.

To be sure, pluralist egalitarians can argue that they can avoid the problem with the help of some other principle that they accept. But then they have already conceded that equality matters little in health-care priority setting. We might as well look for some alternative.

The Principle of Priority, I argue, is more promising. It underlies *prioritarianism*, a rival view of distributive justice. According to this view, benefiting a person matters more the worse off this person is. If you can benefit either a worse-off person or a better-off person, then benefiting the worse-off person has greater moral importance—and the worse off she is, the greater the importance—unless the benefit to the better-off person is sufficiently greater to become morally more important. But the benefit to the worse-off person matters more because of her bad situation regardless of how she fares compared to others. Since, on this view, equality has no value, there is nothing good about leveling down. And since the size of the benefits matters, prioritarianism can avoid the bottomless pit problem.

How can prioritarianism help with the threshold case? Prioritarians can argue that when it comes to setting priorities, you should give different moral weights to the health benefits of different patients, depending on how badly off they are with respect to health-related quality of life. For instance, rather than maximizing QALYs, you should maximize *weighted* QALYs, where the weights are greater the worse off patients are. In the threshold case, benefits (QALYs) to people with disability k would have a greater weight.

A practical application of this prioritarian idea in cost-effectiveness analysis may either be discounting the costs of an intervention in the numerator of the cost-effectiveness ratio or giving greater weight to the benefits of the intervention in the denominator. I think the latter is preferable. Cost-effectiveness analysis should not distort costs. But evaluating benefits is a different matter—how much moral weight we are willing to give to benefits is up to us in a way that counting the costs is not. Costs are given, but the moral evaluation of benefits is up to our consideration.

Needless to say, this discussion is too brief to be conclusive. At best, it just indicates the direction that future work for meeting the disability discrimination objection to CEA can take. And in any case, the proposal does not guarantee that threshold cases never arise. Sometimes the benefits to the worse off are too small to outbalance greater benefits to the better off, even with their greater moral weight. Sometimes the cost-effectiveness ratio of an intervention j to people with disability k may remain over the threshold due to its massive costs, meager benefits, or both. But at least applying prioritarianism to priority setting will reduce the frequency of threshold cases.[18]

CONCLUSION

In this chapter, I have examined whether the use of standard CEA in priority setting in health care leads to unjust discrimination against people with disabilities. I began by clarifying the nature of the disability discrimination objection. Then I considered a number of cases that have been presented as instances of unjust discrimination. I found that none of them applies to the way cost-effectiveness analysis is used in practice. But I did identify one kind of case that raises the possibility of discrimination: that when the cost-effectiveness ratio of an (only) intervention j for the management or rehabilitation of a disability k is over the chosen cost-effectiveness threshold. I called it the threshold case.

I then considered three accounts of unjust discrimination. I argued that the threshold case does not count as an instance of unjust discrimination on any one of them. However, on every one of them it meets some necessary, although not sufficient, condition. This might explain why the disability discrimination objection has seemed persuasive to many people. In the end, I argued that the objection should be considered as raising a problem of justice, rather than discrimination. It should be addressed as such. I proposed that prioritarianism might be the correct response to this problem of injustice and indicated how it might be introduced into cost-effectiveness calculations.

To be sure, some might want to insist that no clear line can be drawn between matters of injustice and matters of unjust discrimination. But this is not an objection to my analysis. There are two ways to think about the connection between injustice and unjust discrimination. Some might claim that unjust discrimination is not a distinct problem; it is part of distributive justice. If the demands of justice are satisfied, there is no unjust discrimination. The argument of this chapter does not conflict with this claim.

Others might contend that the problem of unjust discrimination is separate from distributive justice. It might occur even if the demands of distributive justice are met. But the argument of this chapter does not contradict this claim either. It concludes that disability discrimination due to the use of CEA is not a matter of unjust discrimination. It is a matter of distributive justice, which is separate. So, at the end of the day, I can remain agnostic on this issue.[19]

NOTES

1. In this volume, Dominic Wilkinson and Julian Savulescu (2020) survey the ethical issues in microallocation choices regarding ECMO treatment for newborns. See Wilkinson and Savulescu's chapter 38.
2. The list of authors whose discussions are susceptible to this worry include Beckstead and Ord (2013), Brock (2009), Harris (1987), John et al. (2017), Kamm (2013, 2015), McKie et al. (1998), Nord (1999), and myself (Bognar 2011).
3. QALYs are calculated by evaluating health states on a scale from 0 and 1, where 1 is full health and 0 is a health state that is at least as bad as death, and then multiplying these values with the time patients spend in those health states, expressed in numbers of years for convenience. For instance, if a patient after an intervention is expected to be in a health state with the value of 0.9 for one year and then in a health state with the value of 0.7 for three years, then the expected health benefit due to this intervention is three QALYs. For details, see Bognar and Hirose (2014).
4. It is also worth pointing out that the use of quality of life judgments does not imply that people with disabilities have less moral worth or dignity. Cost-effectiveness analysis is concerned with the health-related quality of people's lives. It does not deny that all people have equal worth or dignity. It is important to distinguish between the quality of people's lives and their worth or dignity. CEA makes no claims about the latter.
5. It is also important to remember that cost-effectiveness considerations are never the only criteria in priority setting. Thus, interventions with unfavorable cost-effectiveness ratios can and do get provided even in health-care systems that use CEA extensively.
6. More precisely, one study found that from drugs whose cost-effectiveness ratio was below A$45,000 per QALY, around half were recommended by PBAC; from those whose ratio was between A$45,000–75,000 per QALY, around a third was recommended; and from those whose cost-effectiveness ratio was over A$75,000 per QALY, only about 16 percent were recommended. See Mauskopf et al. (2013); see also Clement et al. (2009).
7. See, for instance, Woods et al. (2016).
8. I am assuming here that the costs of the intervention are the same for people with disabilities and for those without them.
9. In an earlier discussion (Bognar 2010), I called the separation of patients into different groups "partitioning." As I pointed out, it presupposes the intention to discriminate by patients' capacity to benefit. To my knowledge, no governmental health technology

assessment agency, like NICE or PBAC, engages in partitioning. If they did, it would be a *prima facie* case of unjust discrimination. It would then be a further question whether the discrimination may be justified all things considered because of the presence of other relevant moral considerations.

10. For this kind of objection, see, for instance, Kamm (2015).

11. In addition, it is possible that costs vary in a nonlinear fashion with the number of people who can benefit from an intervention. This is another factor policymakers should consider. Moreover, the numbers may make a difference in research priority setting: since the development of new interventions can be very costly, a condition from which many people suffer may get more attention from researchers—especially if the expected financial returns are greater due to its greater prevalence.

12. Or that the cost-effectiveness ratios of all available interventions for k are also over the threshold. For the sake of simplicity, I will suppose there is only one intervention.

13. A mixed case is also possible: intervention j might be needed not only by people with disability k but also by some people without k. In this case, a group of people, including some with disability k and some without, are equally disadvantaged.

14. Norman Daniels (2008) has argued that health has special moral importance because it protects people's opportunities.

15. Quoted, with some clauses omitted, from Lippert-Rasmussen (2006, 168). See also Lippert-Rasmussen (2014).

16. On this point, see also Wasserman (2013).

17. These formulations are quoted, with one minor change, from Parfit (1995, 4, 19). Parfit makes some further distinctions that can be set aside here.

18. We have proposed to apply prioritarianism to priority setting in health care in Bognar and Hirose (2014). Recently, John et al. (2017) made a similar proposal. In health economics, "equity weighting" to incorporate fairness concerns has been suggested from time to time; at least some of these proposals can be interpreted as applications of prioritarianism to priority setting.

19. I would like to thank audiences at the Stockholm Centre for Healthcare Ethics (CHE) at the Karolinska Institute in Stockholm, Sweden, the Chair Hoover d'Éthique Économique et Sociale, Université Catholique de Louvain, Louvain-la-Neuve, Belgium, and the 2017 Tennessee Value & Agency Conference on Philosophy of Disability in Knoxville, TN. I'm particularly grateful to Axel Gosseries, Niklas Juth, Refia Kadayifci, Samuel Kerstein, Anita Silvers, Dominic Wilkinson, Miklós Zala, and the editors of this volume for their comments.

REFERENCES

Beckstead, Nick, and Toby Ord. 2013. "Rationing and Rationality: The Cost of Avoiding Discrimination." In *Inequalities in Health: Concepts, Measures, and Ethics*, edited by Nir Eyal, Samia Hurst, Ole F. Norheim, and Daniel Wikler, 232–239. New York: Oxford University Press.

Bognar, Greg. 2010. "Does Cost Effectiveness Analysis Unfairly Discriminate against People with Disabilities?" *Journal of Applied Philosophy* 27, no. 4: 394–408.

Bognar, Greg. 2011. "Impartiality and Disability Discrimination." *Kennedy Institute of Ethics Journal* 21, no. 1: 1–23.

Bognar, Greg, and Iwao Hirose. *The Ethics of Health Care Rationing: An Introduction*. New York: Routledge.

Brock, Dan W. 2009. "Cost-Effectiveness and Disability Discrimination." *Economics and Philosophy* 25, no. 1: 27–47.

Clement, Fiona M., Anthony Harris, Jing Jing Li, Karen Yong, Karen M. Lee, and Braden J. Manns. 2009. "Using Effectiveness and Cost-Effectiveness to Make Drug Coverage Decisions: A Comparison of Britain, Australia, and Canada." *JAMA* 302, no. 13: 1437–1443.

Daniels, Norman. 2008. *Just Health: Meeting Health Needs Fairly*. Cambridge, UK: Cambridge University Press.

Harris, John. 1987. "QALYfying the Value of Life." *Journal of Medical Ethics* 13, no. 3: 117–123.

John, Tyler M., Joseph Millum, and David Wasserman. 2017. "How to Allocate Scarce Health Resources without Discriminating against People with Disabilities." *Economics and Philosophy* 33, no. 2: 161–186.

Kamm, Frances M. 2013. "Rationing and the Disabled: Several Proposals." In *Inequalities in Health: Concepts, Measures, and Ethics*, edited by Nir Eyal, Samia Hurst, Ole F. Norheim, and Daniel Wikler, 240–259. New York: Oxford University Press.

Kamm, Frances M. 2015. "Cost Effectiveness Analysis and Fairness." *Journal of Practical Ethics* 3, no. 1: 1–14.

Lippert-Rasmussen, Kasper. 2006. "The Badness of Discrimination." *Ethical Theory and Moral Practice* 9, no. 2: 167–185.

Lippert-Rasmussen, Kasper. 2014. *Born Free and Equal? A Philosophical Inquiry into the Nature of Discrimination*. Oxford: Oxford University Press.

Mauskopf, Josephine, Costel Chirila, Catherine Masaquel, Kristina S. Boye, Lee Bowman, Julie Burt, and David Grainger. 2013. "Relationship between Financial Impact and Coverage of Drugs in Australia." *International Journal of Technology Assessment in Health Care* 29, no. 1: 92–100.

McKie, John, Jeff Richardson, Peter Singer, and Helga Kuhse. 1998. *The Allocation of Health Care Resources: An Ethical Evaluation of the "QALY" Approach*. Aldershot, UK: Ashgate.

Moreau, Sophia. 2010. "What Is Discrimination?" *Philosophy and Public Affairs* 38, no.2: 143–179.

Nord, Erik. 1999. *Cost-Value Analysis in Health Care: Making Sense out of QALYs*. Cambridge, UK: Cambridge University Press.

Parfit, Derek. 1995. *Equality or Priority?* The Lindley Lecture, the University of Kansas, 1991, Department of Philosophy, University of Kansas.

Segall, Shlomi. 2012. "What's So Bad about Discrimination?" *Utilitas* 24, no. 1: 82–100.

Wasserman, David. 2013. "Is Disability Discrimination Different?" In *Philosophical Foundations of Discrimination Law*, edited by Deborah Hellman and Sophia Hellman, 269–277. Oxford: Oxford University Press.

Wilkinson, Dominic JC, and Julian Savulescu. 2020. "Prioritization and Parity. Which Disabled Newborn Infants Should be Candidates for Scarce Life-Saving Treatment?" In *Oxford Handbook of Philosophy and Disability*, edited by Adam Cureton and David Wasserman, 669–689. New York: Oxford University Press.

Woods, Beth, Paul Revill, Mark Sculpher, and Karl Caxton. 2016. "Country-Level Cost-Effectiveness Thresholds: Initial Estimates and the Need for Further Research." *Value in Health* 19, no. 8: 929–935.

CHAPTER 38

PRIORITIZATION AND PARITY

Which Disabled Newborn Infants Should be Candidates for Scarce Life-Saving Treatment?

DOMINIC JC WILKINSON
AND JULIAN SAVULESCU

INTRODUCTION

PUBLICLY funded healthcare systems (PHS) around the world face escalating demands and costs of medical treatment. Even in high-income countries with well-funded PHS there is a need to make difficult decisions about how to allocate healthcare resources. For low- and middle-income countries, agonizing choices arise from the wide gap between the need for healthcare and the system's ability to provide treatment. Which diseases will be prioritized, which treatments will be funded, which patients will be treated?

Resource allocation occurs at different levels (Kapiriri, Norheim, and Martin 2007). Higher level decisions (for example, national decisions about infrastructure, staffing, or budgets) can potentially avoid some of the most difficult ethical questions in allocation. However, decisions at the patient level are unavoidable (Ubel and Arnold 1995). Clinicians working within finite and fiscally constrained PHS must inevitably choose how to prioritize and allocate the limited resources available to them (Strech, Synofzik, and Marckmann 2008). This is a particular problem for those who work in intensive care. Expensive and intensive life-prolonging treatments simply cannot be provided to every patient who might benefit from them. Patients not provided with treatment have a high chance of dying.

Box 38.1 The Extracorporeal Membrane Oxygenation (ECMO) Disability Case

A newborn infant is gravely ill despite intensive medical treatment. Her lungs are failing, and she will almost certainly die unless she is urgently transferred to another hospital for a high-cost form of organ support (ECMO).

ECMO would normally be provided for newborn infants with this condition. However, testing has shown that this infant has a significant genetic disability.*

Should the infant be transferred and treated with ECMO?

* Variant 1. *Duration of treatment*: This genetic disability is associated with a more severe lung problem. She will require a significantly longer than average period of support with ECMO.

* Variant 2. *Probability of survival*: This genetic disability significantly reduces the chance that she will survive even if she receives the ECMO treatment.

* Variant 3. *Quality of life*: This genetic disability is associated with significant cognitive disability if she survives.

* Variant 4. *Duration of survival*: This genetic disability will significantly reduce her lifespan.

Decisions not to provide treatment are sometimes based on the presence of preexisting features in the patient. Box 38.1 contains a paradigm challenging case with a set of variants.

In an ideal situation, a decision not to provide a treatment like extracorporeal membrane oxygenation (ECMO) for a newborn infant would be based primarily on an assessment of the patient's best interests (Larcher et al. 2015). Treatment would not be provided if it offered no benefit or if the harms of treatment outweighed the benefits. A preexisting disability[1] might be directly relevant to this question, and such a decision would not necessarily be discriminatory (Wilkinson 2006). However, the ECMO disability case also potentially raises a more controversial issue. *In the setting of limited resources, is it ethically justified to prioritize beneficial treatment based on the presence or absence of a preexisting disability?* Some are likely to feel that this would be unfair discrimination and that disabled infants, children, or adults should have the same access to life-saving treatment as nondisabled infants, children, and adults. Yet, as the variants of the case also highlight, there are different ways in which preexisting disabilities might affect treatment (Wilkinson and Savulescu 2014). Some forms of prioritization may be more just than others. There are also different degrees. It may be important to give individuals with certain degrees of disability equal access to treatment, but justified to withhold treatment in other cases.

In this chapter, we will focus on scarce, life-saving treatment in the context of public health systems with a fixed budget.[2] We will use the example of ECMO, but similar analysis could be applied to solid organs, dialysis machines, or intensive care beds. We focus on newborn infants as this simplifies some elements of the analysis,[3] however, the core concepts we propose are relevant and applicable to older patients.

Should We Provide ECMO?

ECMO is one of the most burdensome and intensive of medical treatments. It developed initially as an extension of cardiopulmonary bypass for major heart surgery (Butt and Maclaren 2013). The patient is connected to an external machine via large tubes that have been placed in blood vessels in the neck, chest, or groin. Outside of cardiac surgery, ECMO is typically used in patients who would otherwise die because of overwhelming cardiac or respiratory failure. It is able to replace function of either or both of the patient's heart and lungs. Patients are usually heavily sedated to stop them dislodging their ECMO cannulas. Because of the severity of their underlying illness, many patients die despite attempted ECMO. Others are stabilized with ECMO but have irreversible lung or heart problems that mean they cannot be weaned off the machine. Unless they receive a heart and/or lung transplant they will die. There are multiple potential medical complications of ECMO (Butt and Maclaren 2013). For example, patients require high doses of anticoagulation, which carries a significant risk of internal bleeding, including in the brain.

When ECMO was first used in newborn infants, many doctors were uncertain whether this treatment would cause more harm than good (Kanto 1994). However, experience over time as well as data from trials have provided conclusive evidence. Infants with severe respiratory distress treated with ECMO in randomized trials had half the risk of death of infants treated without ECMO, while disability rates in survivors were similar (Mugford, Elbourne, and Field 2010). Indeed, for at least the past two decades, many clinicians in the United States and United Kingdom have regarded ECMO as so clearly beneficial that it would be unethical to conduct further randomized controlled trials of it (Lantos 1997).

Treatment-Level Prioritization of ECMO

ECMO is an expensive treatment. For patients requiring ECMO, daily costs in intensive care range from $4,000 to $20,000, while the average total per-patient hospital costs range from approximately $100,000 to $300,000 in the United States (Harvey, Gaies, and Prosser 2015). Each patient treated requires hours (and often days) of dedicated attention from highly skilled and specially trained clinical staff. This makes it crucial to assess whether ECMO represents a reasonable use of healthcare resources and how much priority to give it compared with other medical treatments.

In fact, health economic analysis has concluded that ECMO is often good value for money (Petrou et al. 2006). In the only large randomized controlled trial of ECMO in newborn infants, ECMO cost an additional £23,000 per disability-free life year gained. This fell within the notional willingness-to-pay threshold often used in the UK of £30,000 (~US$45,000) per quality-adjusted life year gain (Petrou et al. 2006). It is also comfortably within the cost range regarded as affordable in the United States.[4]

Cost-effectiveness analysis of medical treatments like ECMO is a form of *treatment-level prioritization* (T-prioritization).

> *Treatment-level prioritization (T-prioritization).* In the setting of limited resources, treatments or interventions are compared with other treatments. On the basis of that comparison, a decision is made by a health system to provide some treatments rather than others.

There are some challenging ethical questions about how to evaluate treatments and undertake T-prioritization (Bognar and Hirose 2014). For the sake of this chapter, though, we will set those aside. It is widely accepted that it is ethical for PHS to evaluate and selectively provide treatments that they are able to afford. We will assume that a given healthcare system has decided to provide ECMO for at least some newborns.

Patient-Level Prioritization of ECMO

However, if ECMO is a reasonable use of medical resources, there is a further question about *which* patients will be eligible for it. Even in wealthy countries there are a finite number of ECMO patients who can be supported (Kukora and Laventhal 2016). To help clinicians decide, international guidelines (Extracorporeal Life Support Organization, ELSO) list a set of absolute contraindications to ECMO (Table 38.1).

The ELSO guideline lists a further relative contraindication: "disease states with a high probability of a poor prognosis." It might be claimed that these criteria are based purely on the best interests of children potentially needing ECMO. However, in all of these cases, the judgment that ECMO is contraindicated is arguably based on an assessment that, given underlying disability (chromosomal abnormality, brain damage, or "poor prognosis"), the benefit is not high *enough* to justify providing treatment. Although it is unstated, one plausible justification of the ELSO criteria is that if one or more of these features is present, treatment would potentially benefit another patient *more*.

For now, we are going to set aside the question of choosing to provide ECMO or not based on an assessment of the infant's best interests. We will focus our attention on cases where treatment would at least potentially be in the interests of the child, and, if there

---

Table 38.1 Extracorporeal Life Support Organization Absolute Contraindications for Neonatal Extracorporeal Membrane Oxygenation (2013)

1. Lethal chromosomal disorder (includes trisomy 13 or 18, but not 21) or other lethal anomaly
2. Irreversible brain damage
3. Uncontrolled bleeding
4. Grade III or greater intraventricular hemorrhage

were unlimited resources, ECMO would be provided. The question is: Given limited capacity to provide ECMO, which patients should receive treatment? We could call this "patient-level prioritization" (P-prioritization) of ECMO.

> *Patient-level prioritization (P-prioritization):* In the setting of limited resources, patients are divided into sub-groups. A given treatment is provided to some patients but not others.[5]

While cost-effectiveness analysis per se and T-prioritization are not necessarily unjustly discriminatory (Bognar and Hirose 2014), P-prioritization appears to directly distinguish between patients on the basis of specific features. It is viewed by some as particularly ethically problematic (Bognar 2010). However, as noted earlier, for clinicians who provide treatments like ECMO, there is no way of avoiding the question. When they cannot treat everyone, how should they decide who to treat?

WHICH PATIENT SHOULD RECEIVE ECMO?

If we are contemplating P-prioritization for a treatment like ECMO, there are different ways in which it might occur.

Simultaneous Patients

One setting in which it may be impossible to aid all of the patients who could benefit from treatment is in an acute disaster setting with multiple casualties. The urgency of such situations, as well as the impossibility of aiding all equally, makes P-prioritization inevitable. The standard approach to emergency triage compares simultaneous patients and directs emergency attention to those patients who have the highest chance of dying or suffering serious harm without urgent treatment (Aacharya, Gastmans, and Denier 2011). Some patients receive a lower triage category—those who are sufficiently well that they can wait or so severely unwell that they may not benefit. These patients will receive treatment if there are no other patients with a higher priority, or once those other patients have received treatment. We could imagine a triage model being applied to ECMO referrals.

> An ECMO center has received two referrals for retrieval and ECMO. There are two critically ill newborn infants who will almost certainly die if they do not receive urgent ECMO. There are no other ECMO centers able to retrieve the patients.
>
> Infant A has severe pulmonary hypertension and respiratory distress due to a genetic disorder (congenital alveolar dysplasia). The chance of survival with ECMO is less than 3%.[6]

Infant B has severe pulmonary hypertension and respiratory distress due to a temporary disorder arising at birth (meconium aspiration syndrome). The chance of survival with ECMO may be as high as 94%.   (Short 2008)

Triage Case 1

In Triage Case 1, most people would choose to treat infant B rather than infant A (Arora et al. 2016).

However, most of the time in intensive care, clinicians do not face a stark choice between simultaneous patients. This means that a triage approach is harder to apply. If the ECMO center has a bed available and receives a single referral (for infant A), the triage approach would imply that treatment should be given. But that might mean that there are no machines, staff, or beds available for infant B tomorrow (Teres 1993). If the ECMO center decides *not* to provide treatment to patient A (because they are concerned about future patients who might need treatment), they risk foregoing treatment unnecessarily. Sometimes there will be no competing patient in need of ECMO in the short term, and infant A could have been treated.

Nonsimultaneous patients

When patients present for treatment at different points in time, clinicians cannot compare them directly.[7] Instead, they need to assess, for each individual patient, whether treatment would cross a *threshold* level of benefit that would make treatment worth providing. Is a 3% chance of survival too low to provide ECMO? Is 10% high enough?

P-prioritization using triage is simpler—it asks which patient has the better prospect from treatment.[8] Threshold approaches require us to answer a difficult and possibly even unanswerable question. When is the benefit of treatment *enough*?

BALANCING ETHICAL PRINCIPLES
IN P-PRIORITIZATION

Answering that question—about the level of benefit sufficient to provide treatment—depends on the principles that we think are important in allocation. There are several different ethical principles at stake, but here we will focus on two that potentially yield conflicting answers for prioritization. For example, we could aim to allocate treatment in a way that would yield the best *outcome* (benefit). Or we could be most concerned about allocating treatment *fairly*.

Fairness

There are different ways of understanding the concept of fairness in allocation. For example, we might focus on fair *chances* of receiving treatment, on distributing fair *amounts* of treatment, or a fair *process* for setting limits (e.g., one that is accountable and reasonable (Daniels 2001)). Here, we will follow Broome in suggesting that the central concept of fairness refers to the necessity of mediating between the claims of different people for treatment and of giving impartial weight to those different claims (Broome 1994).

If we place our main emphasis on fairness in allocation, we may be drawn to an approach that would give equally sick patients an equal chance of receiving a scarce treatment like ECMO. It would mean that no threshold would be used to decide when to start treatment. ECMO would potentially be commenced for any patient, no matter how low the chance of survival or how short their duration of survival might be. If patients presented simultaneously, as in Triage Case 1, doctors could toss a coin to choose. In practice, one way of applying a strict egalitarian approach is to provide treatment based on the time when patients first present for treatment. This "first come, first-served" approach to allocation of medical treatment has been used to allocate intensive care beds, ECMO machines, and some solid organs for transplant (Persad, Wertheimer, and Emanuel 2009). If treatment is available at the time when a patient requires it, he or she will receive it. However, if the ICU is full (or all the ECMO machines are in use), they will not.

Yet there are some counterintuitive implications of the strict egalitarian approach. In Triage Case 1, an egalitarian approach would mean tossing a coin. But if the two referrals had occurred in quick succession (only minutes apart, say), it would suggest that doctors should provide treatment for the first and not the second—even if the chance for infant A is vanishingly small. The egalitarian approach to allocation could see all ECMO beds being used for patients receiving very long runs of treatment with very low chance of survival, while other patients with a high chance of recovery die for want of treatment.

Benefit

The opposite approach would place great emphasis on benefit in allocation and none on fairness. One way of doing this would apply cost-effectiveness thresholds. For example, as noted earlier, in a number of publicly funded healthcare systems, treatment is usually provided if its incremental cost-effectiveness ratio (ICER) is less than a given value (the ICER threshold). Clinical trials suggest that ECMO is overall cost-effective for newborn infants. However, it may not be for subgroups of patients. For example, in the UK ECMO trial, treatment was not cost-effective for newborn infants with a severe malformation—congenital diaphragmatic hernia (Petrou et al. 2006).

Recall that, in Box 38.1, we identified a number of cases where a genetic disability might lead to a decision not to provide ECMO. Cost-effectiveness could be used to identify what prognosis would be sufficiently low that ECMO should not be provided—a benefit threshold.

> *Benefit threshold:* The worst predicted outcome that would still be consistent with treatment being cost-effective.

As an illustrative (hypothetical) example, Table 38.2 illustrates possible P-prioritization cutoffs for providing ECMO given a set of assumptions.

Based on a set of potentially plausible assumptions, Table 38.2 suggests that an infant should potentially not receive ECMO if the child has a less than 17% chance of survival, if the child would require more than 8 weeks of treatment, if the child's health utility/ quality of life is anticipated to be less than 0.2, or if the child would survive for less than 18 months.

The value of these limits are hypothetical. Different assumptions would yield different thresholds for treatment. Nevertheless, they show the potential implications in practice of P-prioritization focused purely on benefit. As already noted, if we were to use thresholds like these, patients' claims for treatment would not be treated equally. Infants with some genetic disabilities would be declined life-sustaining treatment. Such an approach to decision-making seems prima facie unfair (Broome 1994).

Compromise Combining Fairness and Benefit: Parity

The principles of fairness and benefit imply quite different ways of allocating ECMO. But there is merit in both approaches. Surveys of the general population suggest that people's intuitions sit somewhere in between these two extremes (Bognar 2010; Nord et al. 1999). Is there a way of balancing the two principles?

Imagine a variant of Triage Case 1 in which the two infants referred for treatment have identical prognoses. In that case, it would seem reasonable to toss a coin to decide which patient to treat. But we might also want to toss a coin in cases where there is a small difference in predicted outcome, for example, if infant A had a 48% chance of survival, while infant B had a 50% chance of survival. What if infant A had a 40% chance of survival? Would we still toss a coin? The more weight that we give to fairness, the greater the difference in predicted outcome that would be tolerated before we preferentially treat the infant with the better outcome. This is shown graphically in Figure 38.1.

If we place some value on fairness, this will imply that, within a range of different predicted outcomes, patients are treated equally. This overlaps with arguments in value theory that some alternatives are neither "better than" nor "worse than" the other, nor are they "equally good." Instead, they are evaluatively comparable, they are "on a par" (Chang 2002). We could employ the concept of *parity* in allocation:

> *Parity:* Patients with sufficiently similar features should be regarded as having a comparable claim. Accordingly, they should receive equal access to treatment.

Our concept of parity here is functional, rather than ontological. It is not dependent on the actual comparability of two options. In many of the cases discussed in this chapter, outcomes are not truly on a par. For example, if we faced a choice for an individual infant whether to choose treatment with a higher or lower predicted chance of survival,

Table 38.2 When Would Treatment Be Cost Effective in the Extracorporeal Membrane Oxygenation (ECMO) Disability Case (variants 1–4, Box 38.1)?

	Clinical question	Equation (based on cost-effectiveness)	Benefit threshold
Treatment duration threshold (D_T)	What predicted duration of ECMO treatment would be too long?	$D_T = \dfrac{(CET \times \bar{d}_s \times \bar{P}_{sur} \times \bar{q}) - C_f}{\bar{C}_d}$	DT ~10–46 days[1]
Probability of survival threshold (P_T)	What probability of survival would be too low to provide ECMO?	$P_T = \dfrac{\bar{C}}{CET \times \bar{d}_s \times \bar{q}}$	PT ~7–25%[2]
Quality threshold (Q_T)	What quality of life would be too low?	$Q_T = \dfrac{C}{CET \times \bar{P}_{sur} \times d_s}$	QT ~0.22–0.44[3] (Health-related quality of life)
Longevity threshold (L_T)	What predicted duration of survival would be too short?	$L_T = \dfrac{C}{CET \times \bar{P}_{sur} \times \bar{q}}$	LT ~1.7–5.4 years[4]

For this hypothetical model, we have imagined a public health system that uses a nominal cost-effectiveness threshold of £30,000 per QALY. We used costs and actual outcomes from the UK collaborative ECMO trial and published analysis of the cost-effectiveness of ECMO (Petrou et al. 2006), as well as an Australian pediatric ECMO cohort (Taylor, Cousins, and Butt 2007).

[1] Assuming 7-year survival, quality of life 0.57–0.87, probability of survival 0.33–0.66. Simple cost model based on costs in Petrou (approximately £13,000 for the average patient with a 5.7-day ECMO treatment and non-ECMO costs £17,000 on average).

[2] Assuming £30,270 average cost, 7-year survival, quality of life 0.57–0.87.

[3] Assuming £30,270 average cost, 7-year survival, probability of survival 0.33–0.66.

[4] Assuming £30,270 average cost, probability of survival 0.33–0.66, quality of life 0.57–0.87.

C, Cost of treatment; d_s, mean duration of survival; q, mean quality of life of survivors; C_f, fixed cost; C_d, mean daily cost of treatment; P_{sur} mean probability of survival.

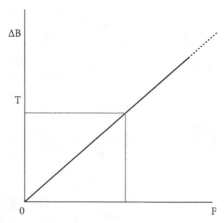

FIGURE 38.1 Balancing fairness. If two patients are in need of treatment (and only one can be treated), what is the greatest difference in outcome where it would be ethical to decide randomly which patient to treat? F, relative value placed on fairness; ΔB, the maximum difference in predicted outcome; T, parity threshold.

there is no question that the higher chance would be better (assuming that the infant has a life worth living) (Wilkinson and Savulescu 2014). However, if we faced a choice between two patients with close enough chances of survival, and we place some value on fairness in allocation, we may be drawn to treat the outcomes *as if* they are on a par.[9] As already noted, the greater the weight we give to fairness in allocation, the larger the number of cases when treatment would not be allocated to maximize benefit.

We have applied the concept of parity to simultaneous cases, but if we knew what maximum value of ΔB would be implied by giving an appropriate weight to fairness, we could apply this to nonsimultaneous cases. If the current patient's outcome is greater than ΔB worse than the median, we might decide not to commence ECMO. It is probable that the next patient requiring ECMO will have an outcome at or above the median level. This gives rise to what we could call a *parity threshold*:

> *Parity threshold:* The lowest predicted outcome that would be regarded as being comparable to the average and would warrant equal access to a scarce treatment.

The idea of the parity threshold is to treat patients within a range of outcomes as being on a par.

Applying this to decisions about ECMO: if we have concluded, for example, that the parity threshold lies at a 40% chance of survival, that would mean commencing ECMO for any patient with a predicted chance of survival of 40% or greater. If there were two simultaneous patients in need of treatment (whose chances of survival were both above the parity threshold), we should toss a coin to decide rather than automatically treat the patient with better chances. The parity threshold therefore represents a compromise between fairness and benefit in P-prioritization.

The Parity Threshold

How *much* weight, though, should we give to fairness? Should we give it some weight or considerable weight? Should we deviate from fairness only in the most extreme cases of poor predicted outcome, or should we aim to maximize benefits except in cases where it would be grossly unfair to do so? There has been considerable ethical debate about how to manage the conflicting priorities of fairness and benefit. It does not appear likely that this disagreement will be resolved, and we face the need to respect and tolerate diverging views and values. Given pluralism and uncertainty about how to proceed, we should potentially avoid a solution that favors one principle over the other, at least as a starting point.

One solution, which we will now explore, would be to give *equal weight* to fairness and benefit in P-prioritization.

Different-Number Cases (Duration, Cost)

Consider Triage Case 2:

> An ECMO center has received two referrals for retrieval and ECMO.
>
> Infant C is anticipated to require a period of ECMO support three times longer than average.
>
> Infant D has a similar prognosis to infant C but is anticipated to require a standard duration of ECMO

Triage Case 2

This hypothetical case imagines a tradeoff between two patients with different predicted requirements for treatment. We might feel that they are on a par and that fairness requires doctors to toss a coin between the two infants if they present simultaneously. There is, however, a necessary corollary of increased duration of treatment in a health system with scarce resources. If we provide ECMO treatment for infant C in situations where ECMO facilities are frequently at or exceeding maximum capacity, it could potentially lead to as many as three other infants (requiring average duration of treatment) missing out (infant D, but also E and F) (Arora et al. 2016).[10]

A decision to toss a coin in Triage Case 2 would seem to place significantly *more* weight on fairness than on benefit. As noted earlier, we are trying to avoid favoring one principle over the other. We have accepted that fairness requires us to give equal weight to the equal claims of different individuals (Broome 1994). If we toss a coin and then treat C (requiring prolonged duration of treatment) rather than D (and E and F), this appears to place greater weight on C's claim to treatment than on D's or E's or F's.

Indeed, it would appear to be *unfair* to treat C for a prolonged period. This would give C greater than his or her fair share of the available resource.[11]

Instead, it seems plausible that giving equal weight to the claims of C and D would imply that we should preferentially provide treatment to infant D because of his or her lower predicted duration of treatment.[12]

How would this apply to nonsimultaneous cases? It wouldn't necessarily rule out providing treatment for any patient requiring longer than average treatment (e.g., variant 1 in the ECMO Disability Case). Table 38.2 suggests that, based purely on benefit, it would be cost-effective to provide ECMO to infants for up to 46 days.[13] On the basis of the preceding argument, giving due weight to fairness would not change this threshold. It would be fair to provide treatment for any patient up to the maximum affordable duration within a PHS. However, if resources are limited, particularly if ECMO facilities are frequently at maximum capacity, it would be unfair to provide treatment for longer than 46 days since that would give greater weight to that patient's claim for treatment than to the claims of other patients.

Concentrating on the duration of ECMO treatment yields a parity threshold that is potentially equal or close to the benefit threshold. That is because it is what we might call a "different-number" P-prioritization case. In discussing the ethics of population, Derek Parfit famously distinguished between "same-number" and "different-number" cases (Parfit 1982). He argued that cases in which more or fewer people exist raised a set of ethical considerations distinct from cases where the same number of people exist. The context here is different. It is not whether different numbers of people exist; instead, it is whether different numbers of people will have their lives saved. However, we suggest that as in the population ethics cases (though for a separate reason) different-number and same-number P-prioritization cases need different treatment. We could summarize this conclusion:

> *Different-number P-prioritization:* It is fair to provide treatment selectively to a subgroup of patients if that will enable a greater number of equal patient claims to be fulfilled. (The parity threshold for different-number cases will be equal to the benefit threshold.)[14]

We have discussed so far cases of different *duration* of treatment. P-prioritization based on *cost* of treatment would also be a different-number case. In closed healthcare systems, costs of treatment potentially have an inverse correlation with the numbers of patients able to be treated. If a patient receives treatment that is twice the average cost, that potentially results in two other patients not being able to receive treatment.[15] We have argued elsewhere that fairness means that patients should have access to treatment that is equivalent in cost (even if it would be suboptimal) (Wilkinson and Savulescu 2017). However, it would be *unfair* to allow patients to demand excessively expensive treatment (beyond the cost-effectiveness threshold).

Probability of Survival

Although it is not as obvious, differences in the probability of survival (P_{Sur}) could arguably be regarded similarly. Recall Triage Case 1. In that case, clinicians were forced to choose between providing treatment to a patient with a high (94%) chance of survival or a patient with a low (<3%) chance of survival. This might seem at first glance as though it is a direct comparison between patients with an equal claim to treatment (i.e., a same-number case). Yet, consider the following extrapolation:

> ECMO Center 1 always tosses a coin when it receives simultaneous referrals for patients who only differ in chances of survival.

> ECMO center 2 always chooses patients with the higher chance when it receives simultaneous referrals for patients with different chances of survival.

Triage Policies 1

Imagine that, faced with iterated triage cases, each ECMO center applies its policy. Over a period of time, both centers have to choose between patients with high (>90%) and low (<10%) chances of survival on 10 occasions. At the end of that period, we would expect ECMO Center 1 to have 5 survivors, while ECMO Center 2 would have 9 survivors. The second center saves a greater number of infants. This might imply that policies for providing ECMO based on probability of survival can also represent "different-number" instances of P-prioritization.

Some may dispute this conclusion. After all, ECMO Center 1 and ECMO Center 2 treat the same number of patients. On one view though, ECMO Center 2 satisfies a greater number of *claims*. This is based on an assumption that claims to life-saving treatment actually reflect claims to have one's life saved. The benefit of receiving life-sustaining treatment is realized if a life is saved, but it is not for infants who die despite receiving treatment. If we think that it is fair for an ECMO center to choose a treatment policy (based on predicted cost or duration of treatment) because that will lead to a higher number of survivors, surely it would be fair for an ECMO center to choose a treatment policy based directly on chance of survival?

If decisions based on the probability of survival are regarded as different-number cases, it would arguably be fair if P-prioritization occurred at a probability of survival close to the cost-effectiveness–derived thresholds. Using our hypothetical model, it would appear reasonable to withhold treatment in Variant 2 of the ECMO disability case if the infant had a less than about a 17% chance of survival.[16]

Same-Number Cases (Duration of Survival, Quality of Life)

We have argued that in *different-number* cases fairness is compatible with (indeed, even requires) P-prioritization to benefit the greater number of infants. The parity threshold would be equal to thresholds derived from cost-effectiveness. We have suggested that this potentially applies to cases where a preexisting disability affects the duration of treatment, cost of treatment, or even the probability of survival.

If we now consider cases where infants differ in the duration of survival or in their quality of life with treatment, it appears that P-prioritization decisions will certainly benefit the *same number* of infants. Consider Triage Cases 3 and 4:

> An ECMO center has received two referrals for retrieval and ECMO.
>
> Infant G has a genetic disability and is anticipated to survive for a maximum of 3 years.
>
> Infant H is anticipated to survive for a normal lifespan.

Triage Case 3

> An ECMO center has received two referrals for retrieval and ECMO.
>
> Infant I has a genetic disability and is anticipated to have severe intellectual disability.
>
> Infant J is anticipated to survive without disability.

Triage Case 4

In these triage cases, the infants arguably have equal claims to treatment. Giving full weight to fairness might require clinicians to toss a coin to decide between infants; it might require this even if, for example, Infant G were predicted to survive for only a very short time (days or weeks) or infant I were predicted to survive in a persistent vegetative state. By analogy, a parity threshold in nonsimultaneous cases would also provide ECMO in cases of short survival or profound impairment.

But such a response appears to give no weight to benefit at all. We have been endeavoring to seek a compromise that steers a middle course between fairness and benefit.

> *Same-number P-Prioritization*: If treatment will benefit a similar number of patients with different characteristics, we should adjust our thresholds for treatment to balance fairness with benefit. The parity threshold for same-number cases will be lower than the benefit threshold.

Here are two possible approaches to such a compromise:

Split-the-Difference

Figure 38.2 identifies two different thresholds based on our competing principles. From Table 38.2, the longevity threshold based on benefit could be 1.7 years (20 months) if we use existing cost-effectiveness thresholds. In contrast, the longevity (fairness) threshold

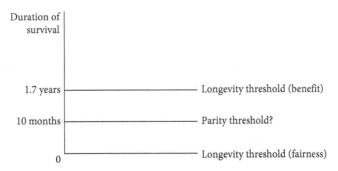

FIGURE 38.2   Split the difference. A parity threshold for longevity.

would appear to be close to zero. But perhaps we should aim for a midpoint between these extremes? That would allow P-prioritization for ECMO if predicted survival is less than approximately 10 months.

We could use the same approach for quality of life. If quality (benefit) thresholds based on cost-effectiveness yield a level of 0.22, while quality (fairness) thresholds are set at (close to) zero, the parity threshold might then be set at the halfway point between these at a quality of life/health utility of 0.1.

Probability of Benefit

Cost-effectiveness provides one reason not to provide ECMO to an infant who is predicted to survive (if treated) for only a matter of days or weeks. But there may be another reason. We earlier assumed that it was in the patient's best interests to receive ECMO. But perhaps that isn't so certain. Although it is possible that the infant would benefit from ECMO, many may feel that it would be wrong to put an infant through such an unpleasant and invasive procedure if the infant were only going to survive for a very short time. In a case where survival is very short, the burdens of treatment would arguably outweigh the benefits, and it would not be in the infant's interests to treat him or her with ECMO. As the longevity of an infant increases from days to weeks to months it becomes more likely that treatment would actually be in the infant's interests. We could express this uncertainty about whether or not treatment would be a net benefit in terms of the "probability of net benefit" (P_{Ben}).

> *Probability of net benefit*: The chance that overall a patient will benefit from receiving treatment.

We argued earlier that P_{Sur} cases were a form of different-number case. That is because a claim for treatment is actually a claim for the benefit of treatment. P_{Ben} might be treated similarly. If we compared ECMO centers with different triage policies, a center that directed treatment to patients with a higher chance of benefit would benefit more infants over time than a center that gave infants with low chance of benefit equal access to treatment. For example, consider Triage Policies 2:

> ECMO Center 1 always tosses a coin when faced with simultaneous patients who only differ in their expected duration of survival.
>
> ECMO Center 2 has a policy that if it has to choose between simultaneous patients with different length of survival *and* one of the patient's duration of survival is so low that it is unclear whether he or she will benefit, they will choose the patient with a longer duration of survival.

Triage Policies 2

The result of the triage policy in ECMO Center 2 is that a larger number of patients will have their claims to the benefit of treatment fulfilled. If that is correct, we might consider it a form of different-number case. We could apply a similar analysis to infants predicted to survive with very severe disability or illness. In cases where there is genuine uncertainty about whether or not the benefits of ECMO outweigh the burdens (because of the severity of the disability or illness), there is arguably a reduced probability of net benefit.

This argument, based on the probability of benefit, would have two implications for a parity threshold:

1. Patients who have a reduced duration of survival or a reduced quality of life, but for whom there is *no* uncertainty about whether or not treatment would be a net benefit, should receive the same access to treatment as other patients. Such patients, we argue, should generally receive equal access to treatment—even if it would not be cost-effective to do so. Fairness means that the parity threshold is below the benefit threshold (i.e., increasing patient access) for cases of reduced duration of survival or reduced quality of life.

2. Where resources are limited, it may be reasonable to decide not to treat patients whose future length or quality of survival is so diminished that it is uncertain whether they would benefit from treatment. The parity threshold is reduced to the point at which treatment is not clearly of overall benefit.

Where exactly would the same-number parity threshold lie? Cost-effectiveness analysis cannot readily answer this. It is difficult to see how we could quantify or even approximate the value of P_{Ben}. A more qualitative approach might be to ask those with relevant knowledge and experience to assess the benefit of treatment in cases of reduced duration of survival or quality of life. If the majority of those consulted believe that treatment would be overall of benefit to the patient, the patient should receive equal access to treatment.[17]

APPLYING PARITY

We have argued in this chapter that selection of patients (P-prioritization) for scarce medical treatment needs to balance both fairness and benefit. We have proposed one way to balance these competing principles. The result of balancing is different for the different ways in which disability affects outcome. In what we have called "different-number" cases, where a preexisting disability increases the costs or duration of treatment (or reduces the probability of an infant surviving), the parity threshold should be determined by the affordability limits of the healthcare system. For example, in those health systems that use it, this would be equivalent to the incremental cost-effectiveness threshold (Wilkinson and Savulescu 2017). It would not be just to provide treatment beyond these limits since that would give unequal weight to the claims of some patients. In contrast, in same-number cases, where a preexisting disability affects the length of survival or the quality of life for a child, the parity threshold should not be based purely on cost-effectiveness. Where it is probable that the child would benefit overall from treatment, we should try to ensure that the child has equal access to treatment.

What does this actually mean in practice? It is crucial that such judgments are made carefully and avoid bias. Imagine, for example, that the genetic condition in the ECMO disability case is trisomy 21 (Down's syndrome). Such infants have in the past been regarded as not eligible for ECMO (Southgate et al. 2001). On the basis of the preceding analysis it might be justifiable to exclude such infants if they would predictably require longer runs of ECMO or have lower chances of survival. However, recent international data on ECMO shows no increase in mortality (Cashen et al. 2015), nor any increase in the length of ECMO support compared with children without trisomy 21 (Gupta et al. 2014). While children and adults with trisomy 21 have significant cognitive impairment and a reduced lifespan, it is not likely that this would affect whether or not ECMO would be beneficial. Furthermore, the average lifespan and quality of life of adults with trisomy 21 is well above the compromise parity thresholds developed earlier. Accordingly, neonates and children with trisomy 21 should be eligible for ECMO on the same basis as other children.

How would parity thresholds affect different treatment decisions, or in different resource-settings? In the hypothetical model that we have used, the cost-effectiveness derived P-prioritization thresholds (Table 38.2) are fairly generous. ECMO appears to be cost-effective for newborn infants in a wide variety of cases. This means that the impact of parity thresholds may be small. On the other hand, for treatments that are on the borderline of affordability, benefit thresholds and parity thresholds may be significantly higher, meaning that some patients are not eligible for treatment.

In our analysis of parity thresholds, we have assumed equal value for fairness and benefit in allocation. What if we wanted to give more or less weight to fairness? On the basis of the preceding arguments, in different-number cases, parity thresholds would not change if we gave greater (or less) weight to fairness. It would appear unjust to give some patients access to longer treatment, more expensive treatment, or very low probability treatment than the limits affordable within a publicly funded healthcare system (Wilkinson and Savulescu 2017). However, for same-number cases, where preexisting disabilities affect the benefit of treatment through their effect on quality of life or longevity, if we place greater weight on fairness, the parity threshold may become lower and grant access to patients even where the magnitude of benefit is very low.

The model used in this chapter to allocate scarce life-saving treatment has distinct advantages over existing criteria for providing ECMO. Our account clearly identifies when and why disability might ground a decision not to provide ECMO. Our account also distinguishes clearly between withholding treatment on the basis of scarcity and withholding treatment on the basis of the interests of the infant. Where there are ample resources (for example, intensive care beds and ECMO circuits), the parity threshold for treatment will approach that of futility: where treatment would *possibly* be in the best interests of the infant, it should be made available. However, where resources are scarce, treatment should only be provided if it is *probably* beneficial and consistent with fair allocation of resources.

ACKNOWLEDGMENTS

Some of the ideas in this chapter were developed following helpful comments by David Wasserman on a previous paper. We have also benefited from generous comments on this chapter by David Wasserman, Adam Cureton, Greg Bognar, and Roger Crisp. D. W. was supported for this work by a grant from the Wellcome trust WT106587/Z/14/Z. J. S. was supported by a grant from the Wellcome Trust WT 104848Z/14/Z.

NOTES

1. We use the term "disability" in this chapter to refer to stable physical or psychological conditions that tend to reduce an individual's potential well-being in a given set of circumstances, even in the absence of prejudice or injustice (Kahane and Savulescu 2009).
2. Scarce: medical treatment of lower availability than demand, such that within the existing healthcare system it is not possible to satisfy all potential claims for treatment.
3. Critically ill newborn infants (who will die without treatment) have similar starting positions, thus removing questions of priority for the worst-off (Parfit 1997) or on the basis of clinical need.
4. While cost-effectiveness is not routinely used in the United States for healthcare funding decisions, treatments costing more than USD$100,000–$150,000 per QALY are often regarded as not offering reasonable value (Neumann, Cohen, and Weinstein 2014).
5. Patient-level prioritization is sometimes referred to as "partitioning" (Bognar 2010).
6. There have been more than 100 cases of congenital alveolar dysplasia (Bishop, Stankiewicz, and Steinhorn 2012). Those presenting early with respiratory symptoms have all died, even if ECMO has been attempted. Lung transplantation has not been reported, but would in theory be curative.

7. In a 1992 paper, Robert Truog suggested a modification of the triage approach specifically for decisions about provision of ECMO in intensive care (Truog 1992). The approach in this chapter could be seen as complementary to the approach described by Truog.

8. This is not to underestimate the complexities and uncertainties of real cases, which may make it epistemically challenging to determine which of two patients has a higher chance or magnitude of benefit.

9. Our view is compatible with there also being some cases that are genuinely "on a par," perhaps particularly where they differ in different respects (e.g., a choice between treating one patient with a lower probability of survival but higher quality of life versus another patient with a higher chance of survival but lower quality of life).

10. It is unclear how often this is the case in practice. If ECMO facilities are less frequently at maximum capacity, the impact of prolonged duration of treatment will be proportionately reduced but will still potentially mean that other patients are unable to access treatment.

11. As noted earlier, we have drawn on the idea of fairness as equal treatment of equal claims. Here, we employ a complementary notion of fairness, that of receiving a "fair share" of a limited resource.

12. An alternative solution, proposed by some philosophers but beyond the scope of this chapter, is to use a weighted lottery in cases like Triage Case 2.

13. If there is insufficient ECMO capacity to provide treatment for this duration, cost-effectiveness would appear to provide a case for more ECMO beds, staff, and the like.

14. A parallel view might hold that this would not be fair but that, in such cases, benefit trumps fairness. The problem of choices that involve saving different numbers of individuals is also referred to by philosophers as "The Numbers Problem" (Hsieh, Strudler, and Wasserman 2006).

15. In practice, excessive costs for ECMO treatment will not necessarily mean that other patients miss out on ECMO but may mean that other priorities within the health system are unable to be afforded. For health systems that use an incremental cost-effectiveness threshold or similar to decide on provision of treatment, patients most likely to miss out on treatment will be those who require treatment that will exceed this threshold. Accordingly, it would be unfair to provide treatment to one patient that exceeds the cost-effectiveness threshold.

16. If patients' claims are understood to be claims for treatment per se (rather than for the benefit of treatment), it may be unfair to give some patients priority because they have a higher chance of survival. In that case, reduced probability of survival would be regarded as a same-number case—see later discussion.

17. This would potentially yield a procedural approach to determining parity for allocation that has parallels to a process for assessing medical futility (Stewart 2011).

References

Aacharya, R. P., C. Gastmans, and Y. Denier. 2011. "Emergency Department Triage: An Ethical Analysis." *BMC Emerging Medicine* 11: 16. doi: 10.1186/1471-227X-11-16.

Arora, C., J. Savulescu, H. Maslen, M. Selgelid, and D. Wilkinson. 2016. "The Intensive Care Lifeboat: A Survey of Lay Attitudes to Rationing Dilemmas in Neonatal Intensive Care." *BMC Medical Ethics* 17(1): 69. doi: 10.1186/s12910-016-0152-y.

Bishop, Naomi B., Pawel Stankiewicz, and Robin H. Steinhorn. 2012. "Alveolar Capillary Dysplasia." *American Journal of Respiratory and Critical Care Medicine* 184(2): 172–179. doi: 10.1164/rccm.201010-1697CI.

Bognar, G. 2010. "Does Cost-Effectiveness Analysis Unfairly Discriminate Against People with Disabilities?" *Journal of Applied Philosophy* 27(4): 394–408.

Bognar, Greg, and Iwao Hirose. 2014. *The Ethics of Health Care Rationing: An Introduction.* London: Routledge.

Broome, J. 1994. "Fairness Versus Doing the Most Good." *The Hastings Center Report* 24(4): 36–39.

Butt, Warwick, and Graeme Maclaren. 2013. "Extracorporeal Membrane Oxygenation." *F1000prime reports* 5: 55. doi: 10.12703/P5-55.

Cashen, K., R. R. Thiagarajan, J. W. Collins, Jr., P. T. Rycus, C. L. Backer, M. Reynolds, and J. M. Costello. 2015. "Extracorporeal Membrane Oxygenation in Pediatric Trisomy 21: 30 Years of Experience from the Extracorporeal Life Support Organization Registry." *Journal of Pediatrics* 167(2): 403–408. doi: 10.1016/j.jpeds.2015.04.048.

Chang, Ruth. 2002. "The Possibility of Parity." *Ethics* 112: 659–688.

Daniels, N. 2001. "Justice, Health, and Healthcare." *American Journal of J Bioethics* 1(2): 2–16. doi: 10.1162/152651601300168834.

Extracorporeal Life Support Organization. 2013. "Guildelines for Neonatal Respiratory Failure. Version 1.3. December 2013." ELSO, accessed November 1, 2017. Available at https://www.elso.org/resources/guidelines.aspx.

Gupta, P., J. M. Gossett, P. T. Rycus, and P. Prodhan. 2014. "Extracorporeal Membrane Oxygenation in Children with Heart Disease and Down Syndrome: A Multicenter Analysis." *Pediatric Cardiology* 35(8): 1421–1428. doi: 10.1007/s00246-014-0945-z.

Harvey, Michael J., Michael G. Gaies, and Lisa A. Prosser. 2015. "US and International In-Hospital Costs of Extracorporeal Membrane Oxygenation: A Systematic Review." *Applied Health Economics and Health Policy* 1–17. doi: 10.1007/s40258-015-0170-9.

Hsieh, N. H., A. Strudler, and D. Wasserman. 2006. "The Numbers Problem." *Philosophy & Public Affairs* 34(4): 352–372. doi: 10.1111/j.1088-4963.2006.00074.x.

Kahane, G., and J. Savulescu. 2009. "The Welfarist Account of Disability." In *Disability and disadvantage*, edited by A. Cureton and K. Brownlee, 14–53. Oxford: Oxford University Press.

Kanto, W. P. 1994. "A Decade of Experience with Neonatal Extracorporeal Membrane Oxygenation." *The Journal of Pediatrics* 124(3): 335–347.

Kapiriri, L., O. F. Norheim, and D. K. Martin. 2007. "Priority Setting at the Micro-, Meso- and Macro-Levels in Canada, Norway and Uganda." *Health Policy* 82(1): 78–94. doi: 10.1016/j.healthpol.2006.09.001.

Kukora, S., and N. Laventhal. 2016. "Choosing Wisely: Should Past Medical Decisions Impact the Allocation of Scarce ECMO Resources?" *Acta Paediatrics* 105(8): 876–878. doi: 10.1111/apa.13457.

Lantos, J. D. 1997. "Was the UK Collaborative ECMO Trial Ethical?" *Paediatric and Perinatal Epidemiology* 11(3): 264–268.

Larcher, V., F. Craig, K. Bhogal, D. Wilkinson, and J. Brierley. 2015. "Making Decisions to Limit Treatment in Life-Limiting and Life-Threatening Conditions in Children: A Framework for Practice." *Archives of Disease of Childhood* 100(Suppl 2): s1–s23. doi: 10.1136/archdischild-2014-306666.

Mugford, Miranda, Diana Elbourne, and David Field. 2010. "Cochrane Review: Extracorporeal Membrane Oxygenation for Severe Respiratory Failure in Newborn Infants." *Evidence-Based Child Health: A Cochrane Review Journal* 5(1): 241–298. doi: 10.1002/ebch.522.

Neumann, P. J., J. T. Cohen, and M. C. Weinstein. 2014. "Updating Cost-Effectiveness—The Curious Resilience of the $50,000-per-QALY Threshold." *New England Journal of Medicine* 371(9): 796–797. doi: 10.1056/NEJMp1405158.

Nord, E., J. L. Pinto, J. Richardson, P. Menzel, and P. Ubel. 1999. "Incorporating Societal Concerns for Fairness in Numerical Valuations of Health Programmes." *Health Economics* 8(1): 25–39.

Parfit, D. 1982. "Future Generations: Further Problems." *Philosophy & Public Affairs* 11(2): 113–172.

Parfit, Derek. 1997. "Equality and Priority." *Ratio* 10(3): 202–221. doi: 10.1111/1467-9329.00041.

Persad, G., A. Wertheimer, and E. J. Emanuel. 2009. "Principles for Allocation of Scarce Medical Interventions." *Lancet* 373(9661): 423–431.

Petrou, S., M. Bischof, C. Bennett, D. Elbourne, D. Field, and H. McNally. 2006. "Cost-Effectiveness of Neonatal Extracorporeal Membrane Oxygenation Based on 7-Year Results from the United Kingdom Collaborative ECMO Trial." *Pediatrics* 117(5): 1640–1649. doi: 10.1542/peds.2005-1150.

Short, B. L. 2008. "Extracorporeal Membrane Oxygenation: Use in Meconium Aspiration Syndrome." *Journal of Perinatology* 28(Suppl 3): S79–83. doi: 10.1038/jp.2008.152.

Southgate, W. M., D. J. Annibale, T. C. Hulsey, and D. M. Purohit. 2001. "International Experience with Trisomy 21 Infants Placed on Extracorporeal Membrane Oxygenation." *Pediatrics* 107(3): 549–552.

Stewart, C. 2011. "Futility Determination as a Process: Problems with Medical Sovereignty, Legal Issues and the Strengths and Weakness of the Procedural Approach." *Journal of Bioethical Inquiry* 8(2): 155–163. doi: 10.1007/s11673-011-9297-z.

Strech, D., M. Synofzik, and G. Marckmann. 2008. "How Physicians Allocate Scarce Resources at the Bedside: A Systematic Review of Qualitative Studies." *Journal of Medical Philosophy* 33(1): 80–99. doi: 10.1093/jmp/jhm007.

Taylor, A. K., R. Cousins, and W. W. Butt. 2007. "The Long-Term Outcome of Children Managed with Extracorporeal Life Support: An Institutional Experience." *Critical Care and Resuscitation* 9(2): 172–177.

Teres, D. 1993. "Civilian Triage in the Intensive Care Unit: The Ritual of the Last Bed." *Critical Care Medicine* 21(4): 598–606.

Truog, R. D. 1992. "Triage in the ICU." *Hastings Center Reports* 22(3): 13–17.

Ubel, P. A., and R. M. Arnold. 1995. "The Unbearable Rightness of Bedside Rationing. Physician Duties in a Climate of Cost Containment." *Archives of Internal Medicine* 155(17): 1837–1842.

Wilkinson, D. 2006. "Is It in the Best Interests of an Intellectually Disabled Infant to Die?" *Journal of Medical Ethics* 32(8): 454–459.

Wilkinson, D., and J. Savulescu. 2014. "Disability, Discrimination and Death: Is It Justified to Ration Life Saving Treatment for Disabled Newborn Infants?" *Monash Bioethics Review* 32(1): 43–62. doi: 10.1007/s40592-014-0002-y.

Wilkinson, D., and J. Savulescu. 2017. "Cost-Equivalence and Pluralism in Publicly-Funded Health-Care Systems." *Health Care Analysis* doi: 10.1007/s10728-016-0337-z.

PART TEN

REPRODUCTION AND PARENTING

WHY PEOPLE WITH COGNITIVE DISABILITIES ARE JUSTIFIED IN FEELING DISQUIETED BY PRENATAL TESTING AND SELECTIVE TERMINATION

CHRIS KAPOSY

INTRODUCTION

IN recent years, a new generation of prenatal tests have made their way into clinical care. These noninvasive prenatal tests (NIPT) require only a maternal blood sample, through which pieces of fetal DNA can be detected (Norton et al. 2015; Nuffield Council on Bioethics 2017). The first such noninvasive tests on the market were used to detect Down syndrome (trisomy 21) and two other trisomies (13 and 18). NIPT has since been expanded to include other indications, such as genetic microdeletions (chromosomes that are missing small pieces) (Nuffield Council on Bioethics 2017). These tests are considered an improvement on previous prenatal screening tests. NIPT is not accurate enough for diagnostic purposes, and the tests for more common conditions like Down syndrome are more accurate than for rarer indications such as microdeletions (Lo et al. 2016). Consequently, for diagnostic purposes, NIPT results must be confirmed by tests, such as amniocentesis, that are more accurate.

Even prior to the introduction of this new generation of tests, there were high rates of termination after being given a prenatal fetal diagnosis of a cognitively disabling condition such as Down syndrome. Studies reveal a high "selective termination" rate in the range between 60% and 90% (Mansfield et al. 1999; Natoli et al. 2012). With the introduction of NIPT, some have reached the conclusion that the number of selective terminations will increase (Kaposy 2013; 2018; Nuffield Council on Bioethics 2017). Some people with cognitive disabilities, along with some of their advocates, have expressed concern about the use of prenatal testing and the high rates of selective termination. This chapter will argue that many such concerns are justified since the presence of bias against people with cognitive disabilities in our culture[1] is a motive in the uptake of prenatal tests such as NIPT and of selective termination.

To advance this argument, I outline three different ways that bioethicists try to reassure or rebut expressions of concern by people with cognitive disabilities about prenatal testing and selective termination. Bioethicists have claimed (1) that people with cognitive disabilities are not the target of prenatal testing—for instance, because they are not fetuses; (2) that prenatal decisions are not *necessarily* biased but are often innocent decisions about family and careers; and (3) that prenatal decisions are not *actually* motivated by bias. I outline why each form of reassurance is unlikely to be reassuring to people with cognitive disabilities. Furthermore, I give a positive argument showing that bias against people with disabilities must feature in the decision-making of prospective parents about prenatal testing when viewed from the perspective of the whole population of prospective parents. Many commentators on the ethics of prenatal testing and selective abortion direct their disability-positive critiques at healthcare professionals, institutions, policies, and practices, rather than at the decisions of prospective parents (Asch 1999; Shakespeare 2005). The analysis offered here differs from these critiques since it places the decision-making of prospective parents themselves (taken in aggregate) under scrutiny.

Expressions of Concern by People with Cognitive Disabilities and Their Advocates

Some people with cognitive disabilities and some of their nondisabled advocates and supporters feel disquieted by the use of prenatal genetic testing and selective abortion to avoid the birth of children with these cognitive disabilities. To give a few examples of this disquiet:

1. The Nuffield Council on Bioethics report in *Noninvasive Prenatal Testing: Ethical Issues* (2017) quotes a person with Down syndrome who says that prenatal screening programs for Down syndrome "makes me feel like I'm not wanted in society. And no one loves us" (Nuffield Council on Bioethics 2017, 59).

2. The Canadian self-advocacy group of people with Down syndrome, the Voices at the Table Advocacy Committee (VATTA), produced a YouTube video on how they feel about prenatal testing. In the video, while discussing the high rates of selective abortion for Down syndrome, one young man with Down syndrome asks, "has anyone ever wondered how that makes us feel?" (Canadian Down Syndrome Society 2014). The suggestion is, of course, that efforts to avoid the birth of people like him bring about unpleasant feelings for people with this condition.

3. An advocacy group in the UK calls itself Don't Screen Us Out (2017). This slogan is a statement of uneasiness. The slogan expresses alarm that prospective parents are refusing to bring children with cognitive disabilities into their families and their communities through the use of prenatal testing and selective abortion.

These examples show that some individuals with cognitive disabilities and groups representing people with such conditions are aware of the expansion of prenatal testing, and that many are opposed to this expansion and to high rates of selective termination.

First Form of Reassurance: "You Are Not the Target of Prenatal Testing"

Some bioethicists maintain that people with disabilities should have no reason to feel concerned about prenatal testing and selective abortion for their conditions. The elimination of fetuses does not mean that anyone who is already living with these conditions will be harmed. As Allen Buchanan says, there is "no existing individual who has rights that might be violated" by screening out fetuses with disabilities (Buchanan 1996, 31). This is the first form of reassurance: the claim "prenatal testing and selective abortion are directed at fetuses, not those who are already born." In the book *From Chance to Choice*, Buchanan and his colleagues point out that although they support the reduction of disabilities in the population through the use of prenatal genomics, they claim that, "We do not wish to reduce the number of people with disabilities by taking the life of any individual who has a disability" (Buchanan et al. 2000, 278).

This disavowal of eugenic murder is expected and unsurprising. Yet people with cognitive disabilities might not be entirely reassured by these claims. There are a range of different concerns about prenatal genomics, not all of which can be addressed by pointing out that a decision to end a pregnancy does not directly affect the rights or the lives of people with disabilities. Out of the range of possible concerns, I will focus on the prevalence of bias since reflecting on the nature of this bias shows why people with cognitive disabilities can justifiably be concerned about prenatal testing despite the fact that they are not involved in testing itself.

Though not stated explicitly, one can read the statements by people with cognitive disabilities about prenatal screening programs as concerns about bias directed at them. They might suspect that anti-disability bias is a motive behind the use of prenatal testing and widespread selective abortion. The message people with cognitive disabilities might take away from efforts to avoid having children like them is that the bias they experience in their daily lives is also manifested in prenatal decision-making and, by extension, in the screening programs set up by the medical profession and by governments that enable prospective parents to avoid having children like them. These organized screening programs might appear as further evidence that "I'm not wanted" or "no one loves us," as described by the interviewee quoted by the Nuffield Council (2017, 59). The majority of the discussion in the VATTA video is about the contributions people living with Down syndrome make to their communities and their value in the lives of the people around them (Canadian Down Syndrome Society 2014). This discussion can be seen as an implicit rebuttal of the problem of bias that they are addressing—the root problem that lies behind the technological pursuit of means for avoiding the birth of children with cognitive disabilities. While the use of these technologies might not be a direct violation of the rights of people with cognitive disabilities, living within an atmosphere of bias is surely a threat.

Second Form of Reassurance: "These Decisions Are Not Necessarily Biased"

Some bioethicists contest whether there is any close conceptual linkage between biased attitudes toward people with disabilities and the decision to undergo prenatal testing and selective termination. Buchanan and colleagues, for example, examine whether the use of genomics to prevent disabilities implies beliefs either that a life with a disability is not worth living or that "imperfect" people ought not to exist (Buchanan et al. 2000, 272–274). Their analysis is directed at the "expressivist" objection to prenatal testing and selective termination, which is the argument that these practices express negative messages about disabilities. According to these authors, a decision (e.g., to use prenatal testing or to selectively terminate) presupposes a judgment (e.g., that a life with a disability is not worth living)

> if and only if, as a matter of psychological fact, one could only be motivated to make this [decision] if the person ascribed to the judgment (i.e., that one could not psychologically make the decision if he or she did not believe to be true what the judgment affirms), or one cannot rationally make the decision without believing what the judgment affirms.   (Buchanan et al. 2000, 274)

According to this formulation, prenatal testing and selective termination decisions only express negative beliefs about disabilities if it is impossible to make these decisions without holding these beliefs. But, of course, it is possible to make a decision to undergo prenatal testing and selective termination for reasons other than biased ones. Suppose a couple wants to have a child but is in a precarious economic position and a child with a disability would have a greater likelihood of requiring greater expenses than they are able to manage than a child without a disability. One can imagine many such innocent reasons for making these decisions, so the standard of necessity evoked by Buchanan and colleagues is not met.

However, it is important to ask whether this standard of necessity is the correct one for providing reassurance. People with cognitive disabilities probably care whether prenatal decisions are *in fact* motivated by bias, not whether they are *necessarily* so motivated. Both Jamie Lindemann Nelson (1998) and Søren Holm (2008) make this point. Nelson, for instance, addresses an argument advanced by Buchanan like the preceding one. She points out that this argument precludes "the possibility that some or many acts of testing and abortion, if not *necessarily* expressing objectionable meanings, *may* do so. The question is whether in fact they do" (Nelson 1998, 175, emphasis in original). These decisions may not necessarily be biased, but if a large proportion of the population nonetheless makes these decisions as a result of bias, then this represents a continued manifestation of the negative attitudes toward cognitive disability under which these people must live. Some peoples' prenatal decisions might be motivated by bias while those of others might not be. But if enough prospective parents act on the basis of anti-disability bias, then people with cognitive disabilities are justified in feeling disquieted by the widespread uptake of prenatal testing and selective termination. The lack of a close conceptual linkage between biased attitudes toward people with disabilities and the decision to undergo prenatal testing and selective termination would not be reassuring to these people if it is contingently true that many prospective parents are motivated by bias.

Bias and discrimination can be harmful to people with cognitive disabilities even when they are not aware of the presence of this bias. These attitudes can affect prospects for employment or independent housing. Bias embedded in legislative or institutional priorities can affect access to healthcare, education, or social programs. On a more personal level, bias can affect social inclusion. Research into the lives of young people with Down syndrome in Canada, the United States, and the United Kingdom reveals troubling levels of loneliness and friendlessness (Cunningham 1996; Metzel 2004; Snowdon 2012). Even if people with cognitive disabilities report high levels of well-being, bias is a factor in the social environment that can create vulnerability and fragility in the determinants of well-being. Although people with cognitive disabilities are not directly affected by the decisions that prospective parents make about prenatal testing and selective abortion, if such decisions are motivated by bias, then the uptake of prenatal testing and selective abortion can be seen as a common symptom of a problem that affects people with cognitive disabilities as well. In such an environment, a feeling of being unnerved or "not wanted in society" would be reasonable.

Third Form of Reassurance:
"Prenatal Decisions Are Not
Motivated by Bias"

Philosophers and bioethicists who address prenatal testing often acknowledge the presence of bias against disabilities in our culture, but they tend to downplay its significance. For instance, Jonathan Glover, in his book *Choosing Children*, admits that "ugly attitudes" toward disability may play a role in efforts to avoid the birth of a child with a disability (2006, 33). Glover furthermore articulates a number of ideas about how to counteract these attitudes. The problem is, however, that his proposals tend to unjustifiably diminish the role that anti-disability bias likely plays in prenatal decision-making.

Glover has two recommendations to make about how to address the problem of ugly attitudes toward disability. The first idea is that "we" (presumably bioethicists, clinicians, and prospective parents) should communicate clearly to the disability community to avoid the misinterpretation of the motives behind prenatal testing and selective abortion. He says we should "send a clear signal that we do not have the ugly attitudes to disability" (Glover 2006, 35). However, these communications are likely to fail at reassuring people with disabilities. The first problem is that his assumption that we can "send a clear signal" presupposes that prospective parents tend not to be motivated by anti-disability bias. The truth of this presupposition is specifically what is at issue and specifically what might motivate the profound sense of disquiet that people with cognitive disabilities feel toward prenatal testing and selective abortion. Glover offers no evidence that such decisions tend to be innocent of bias in the way he presupposes.

Second, Glover's communication recommendation is likely to fail because of the content of the messages he thinks we should send to people with disabilities. The first message is that prenatal testing and selective abortion for disability are justified on the grounds of the diminished well-being of the child who would be born. He says, "To think that a particular disability makes someone's life less good is not one of the ugly attitudes" (Glover 2006, 35). I cannot imagine that a person with a cognitive disability would be reassured by the message that his or her life is "less good" or by the assertion that this message itself is not an expression of bias. I return to this issue in a later section.

The second message he recommends is that disabilities should be compared to cancer and HIV and our attempts to prevent and cure these illnesses in order to show that the concern supporting prenatal testing and selective abortion is with health and well-being, rather than with eugenics (Glover 2006, 35). Again, people with cognitive disabilities would not be won over by telling them that their disabilities are comparable to terminal illnesses or infectious diseases (though I think people with these conditions as well, in many cases, have grounds to contest Glover's assumption that their lives are "less good").

In addition to his recommendations about communicating clear messages, Glover also recommends that we address well-being in other ways to show that our paramount motivation is with maximizing the well-being of our children rather than anti-disability bias (Glover 2006, 35). He proposes that we engage in efforts to address poverty, the prevalence of abuse, and deficiencies in housing, for example. These measures would likely benefit people with cognitive disabilities themselves. Of course, these are causes we should continue to advance as matters of social justice, independent of attempts to demonstrate to people with disabilities that we are not biased, but are instead concerned about well-being. But again, Glover seems to presuppose that prospective parents and others involved in prenatal decision-making tend not to harbor biases against people with cognitive disabilities. We can only honestly demonstrate that we are not biased if we are in fact not biased. Insofar as Glover assumes that such social justice measures would be an honest demonstration of our innocence, he also assumes that bias does not play much of a role in prenatal decision-making. A person with cognitive disabilities might be unimpressed. In particular, there is a difference between, on the one hand, measures to improve well-being that help people who are vulnerable and, on the other hand, efforts to improve "well-being" that seek to eliminate types of people who are thought to have lives that are "less good."

Stephen Wilkinson is another author who gives faulty reassurance that prenatal decisions are not motivated by anti-disability bias. In his descriptions of such decision scenarios, he emphasizes motives that are innocent of bias. For instance, Wilkinson presents cases in which prospective parents make decisions motivated by innocuous concerns about health (Wilkinson 2010, 174) and about careers (Wilkinson 2010, 180). He acknowledges the possibility of "unduly negative attitudes" toward disabilities (Wilkinson 2010, 184). However, the impression that he gives is that we should not be concerned about these attitudes because we tend to be motivated by innocent reasons. In order to counteract the impression that unduly negative attitudes might be a motive, Wilkinson follows Glover's playbook. He says that, "we should make it clear to existing people with disabilities that it is this [concerns about the flourishing of people with disabilities] and not any hatred of them, or desire to eliminate them, that lies behind our actions" (Wilkinson 2010, 184). Of course, this strategy only works if it is true that our actions are not motivated by "any hatred of them." Wilkinson offers no evidence to suggest that this is true and appears confident that our motives are transparent to ourselves and are mostly innocent.

The problem with such assumptions of innocence has been pointed out by Nelson. She notes the possibility that

> women facing decisions to continue or to abort pregnancies may think of them-
> selves as perfectly accepting of people with disabilities, when in fact they may have
> feelings and beliefs of which they are not fully aware, which they would not reflec-
> tively endorse if they were fully aware of them, and which at the same time affect
> their behavior.   (Nelson 1998, 176)

Of course, Nelson here refers to pregnant women, but others involved in prenatal decisions might be just as subject to implicit biases. Glover and Wilkinson, in their discussion of anti-disability bias, do not take into account this problem of unconscious bias. Nelson, however, also downplays the significance of the possibility that bias might play a role in prenatal decision-making. She argues that the possibility of bias is not adequate justification to limit access to reproductive choice and that the social problem of bias is better addressed in other ways (Nelson 1998, 176). This may be true. However, the idea that prenatal testing should be left alone even though it is a practice potentially fraught with bias is hardly comforting to the people who suffer from this bias. To them, the expansion of prenatal testing and the high rates of selective termination would serve as reminders that people with cognitive disabilities should not feel so welcome in their communities.

An Argument that Bias Influences Prenatal Decisions

So far in this section I have been critical of writers who have assumed that anti-disability bias plays little role in prenatal decision-making. I have countered this assumption with an opposite supposition that such bias does play this role. At this point, I will now provide an argument that, from a population-perspective, anti-disability bias must influence decisions to undergo prenatal testing and selective abortion (see also Kaposy 2018).

My argument can be summarized in the following way:

1. Widespread bias against people with cognitive disabilities exists in our culture.
2. If widespread bias exists, it must affect prenatal decision-making on a population level.
3. Therefore, on a population level, anti-cognitive-disability bias must affect prenatal decision-making.

Of the two premises in the argument, both need further defence, though I regard 1 as more controversial than 2. This argument refers to the perspective of the "population level": I am making claims about the sum total of decisions about undergoing prenatal testing and choosing selective abortion in aggregate, rather than making claims about each individual choice. I am not claiming that since widespread bias exists, every single such decision is influenced by bias. I am not claiming that everyone harbors anti-disability bias. These biases are common, but not held by everyone. Instead, I am claiming that since such bias exists and is widespread, it must have an influence on many such decisions. I will defend premise 2 first and then move on to premise 1.

Premise 2 is an implication of the fact that prenatal decisions are decisions like any other and are likely to be subject to all of the same social influences that influence other decisions. Prenatal decision-making is not a special choice situation in which people suddenly become immune to their beliefs and typical motivations. Decisions made while pregnant and contemplating the birth of a child can be momentous. They are about the intimate details of our lives and have consequences for the constitution of our families. Because of the importance and intimacy of these decisions, our values and beliefs (which include negative attitudes and biases) are likely to play a crucial role in our choices. In fact, given the intimacy of the relationship between parents and children, the effect of biases on reproductive decisions is likely to be amplified in comparison to the effect of these biases on other, less momentous life decisions.

With regard to premise 1: Is there widespread bias against cognitive disability in our culture? There are various forms of evidence that this bias exists and that it is widespread. I will draw on two forms of evidence. The first is an argument drawing on observations about popular culture. While this argument is anecdotal, I believe it elucidates the phenomenon well. The second argument draws on empirical evidence from the social sciences and is meant to supplement any deficiencies to be found in the first.

The first argument: consider how commonly the term "retarded" is used pejoratively or as an insult in our culture, as well as the related term "retard." "Mental retardation" used to be a technical term applied to people with cognitive disabilities, but has long been taken out of currency in clinical and scientific terminology because it has devolved into an insult ("retarded") applied to people perceived to be unintelligent or to those who make poor decisions. The term "retard" is also used in this way and is a particularly graphic slur. The term "retarded" is also commonly used to refer to situations that exhibit disorganization or that cause the speaker frustration. It is always used when the speaker wants to make a point that something or someone is problematic, deficient, or incompetent. People with cognitive disabilities and their advocates have created a social movement intended to draw attention to the harm done by this slur and to ask people to reform their language. An example of this movement can found online (www.r-word. org), which asks us to "spread the word to end the word" (Special Olympics 2017).

In spite of the social movement to eliminate the "r-word," this insult is commonly used in popular culture. Hollywood films, in particular, provide many examples. To cite one example, the movie *Ted* (2012) features a foul-mouthed talking teddy bear and his buddy, played by Hollywood star Mark Wahlberg. At one point in the movie, the teddy bear pretends to have a speech impediment in an effort to trick the character played by Wahlberg into thinking he has a cognitive disability. The bear then ends the "joke" by explaining: "I'm just kidding you. I thought it would be funny if you thought I was fucking retarded" (IMDb 2012). There have been protests organized by disability rights organizations against movies that repeatedly use the term "retarded" or "retard": the protest against the film *Tropic Thunder* (2008), featuring star Ben Stiller, is an example (Associated Press 2008). What is notable about the *Ted* example is the total lack of protest against the use of the phrase "fucking retarded" while trying to get laughs. The absence of protest is probably due to the fact that this slur is so common in Hollywood films, and in popular culture is so widespread, that it is considered an acceptable term. In contrast, if a film similarly used racial epithets such as the "N-word" in order to get cheap laughs, or homophobic slurs, there would be justifiable outrage. *Ted* grossed a domestic total of about $219 million, and close to $550 million worldwide (Box Office Mojo 2017a). *Tropic Thunder* brought in $188 million worldwide, in spite of the protests (Box Office Mojo 2017b).[2]

For a further comparison, consider two examples from stand-up comedy. In 2006, the television star and comedian Michael Richards (Kramer from *Seinfeld*) performed in a stand-up comedy show in Los Angeles that ended in a tirade with him repeatedly using the "N-word" (TMZ.com 2006). Since that performance, Richards's career has been essentially over. Hollywood has ostracized him. In 2010, the comedian Sarah Silverman repeatedly used the term "retarded" in jokes about children with cognitive disabilities in an event organized by the TED (Technology, Entertainment, and Design) nonprofit group (Leo 2010). The jokes earned her disapproval from the organizer and a few attendees, but many people came to her defense when she was criticized. Silverman's career has thrived since then. Since 2010, she has won an Emmy and has given comedy specials on HBO and Netflix.

Anti–cognitive-disability bias is so widespread in our culture that high-profile and highly profitable products of our culture can routinely use derogatory language that makes fun of people with cognitive disabilities, that is hurtful to them, and that perpetuates stereotypes about them, and this causes little or no backlash.

My second argument draws on social science research. According to the emerging field of implicit bias research, participants in research studies tend to demonstrate "moderate to strong negative implicit attitudes towards individuals with [intellectual disabilities]" (Wilson and Scior 2014, 315). Insofar as groups of participants in implicit bias research are meant to be representative of the wider population, this research strongly suggests that implicit bias against people with cognitive disabilities is common. The methodology of this form of research contrasts with methods, such as surveys or qualitative interviews, which explore explicit attitudes. Implicit bias methodologies measure the strength of unconscious association between pairs of concepts such as "disabled" and positive terms like "pleasant" and negative terms like "terrible." Some studies also explore implicit positive and negative associations between concepts and visual images, such as pictures of people with Down syndrome (Enea-Drapeau et al. 2012). Inferences are drawn on the basis of differences between response times that participants exhibit when asked to pair different concepts or concepts with images. "Project Implicit," based at Harvard University, provides a number of online self-administered tests that demonstrate this methodology (Project Implicit 2011). Several studies show a common pattern of implicit bias toward people with cognitive disabilities among research partici-pants (Enea-Drapeau et al. 2012; Hein et al. 2011; Proctor 2012; Robey et al. 2006; Wilson and Scior 2014).

Interestingly, implicit bias findings often contrast with findings from studies of explicit attitudes toward people with cognitive disabilities (Ouellette-Kuntz et al. 2010; Wilson and Scior 2014). Explicit attitude studies suggest that people have much more positive attitudes toward people with such disabilities. However, such explicit attitude studies are complicated by the fact that respondents might have a motive to answer less than honestly when admitting to bias or when respondents themselves are unaware of their unconscious attitudes. The apparent implicit nature of the bias against people with cognitive disabilities is consistent with efforts to deny the existence of this bias or to rationalize it in various ways.

Objections to My Argument

There are a few possible responses to these arguments that I hope to anticipate and answer. First, against this depiction of bias that I am presenting with these arguments, one might point out the social improvements and the social progress we have seen in the lives of people with cognitive disabilities over the past few decades. These social improvements, such as the Americans with Disabilities Act (1990) and the Individuals with Disabilities Education Act (2004) and similar legislation in other countries, suggest that our culture does not harbor bias against people with disabilities. Undoubtedly, there has been such progress. Parents no longer commit their children to institutions where they will be warehoused, subjected to abuse and diminished life expectancy. The self-advocacy movement for people with cognitive disabilities is alive and well. However, the claim that I am advancing that bias against people with cognitive disabilities exists in our culture is consistent with the recognition that their lives have improved over the past few decades and are continuing to improve. But this progress does not indicate that bias is no longer a problem. There is still room for improvement in the circumstances of their lives.

A second possible response can be raised in defense of writers like Glover and Wilkinson who downplay the role of bias in prenatal decision-making. It might be said that these authors tend not to consider the implications of bias in such decisions because they are adhering to a version of the principle of charity in which we refrain from attributing unsavory beliefs to others when we can understand their decisions and reconstruct their reasoning with reference to less controversial beliefs. So instead of accusing prospective parents of bias against people with cognitive disabilities, we should see them as holding innocent beliefs about the health and well-being of their children and the effect of having a child with a disability on career and family.

To answer, I agree that Glover and Wilkinson may be engaging in this kind of charitable interpretation of prenatal decision-making. I also agree that, for any given decision made by prospective parents about prenatal testing or selective abortion, it is likely impossible to figure out who is motivated by biases against cognitive disabilities and who is not. Due to the nature of implicit bias, it is possible to be biased and not be aware of it. It is also possible in most cases to find a reason for engaging in prenatal testing and selective abortion that draws on concerns about health, well-being, family, or career and that stays clear of biased rationales. However, I do not find the principle of charity justified when there is good evidence at the population level that our culture exhibits this bias and that this bias often exerts an implicit influence of which people might not be aware. To be "charitable" in such circumstances is simply to be wilfully ignorant of an important feature in the debate about the ethics of prenatal testing as it applies to people with disabilities.[3]

A third response is to question whether allegations of bias are justified at all when the future child's well-being seems to be at issue. According to such an argument, people may have biases against those with cognitive disabilities, but if well-being is compromised by having such disabilities, decisions to undergo prenatal testing and selective abortion are warranted in spite of the existence of bias. This line of argument seems to be open to Glover and Wilkinson who tend to argue that disability negatively affects well-being. However, the issue of disability and well-being is highly contested, and I find Glover and Wilkinson's arguments unconvincing. For one thing, in empirical research, people with a range of disabilities tend to report levels of well-being that are comparable to those of nondisabled people—a phenomenon known as the "disability paradox" (Albrecht and Devlieger 1999; Amundson 2005).[4] People with Down syndrome, for example, tend to report high levels of subjective well-being and life satisfaction (Skotko et al. 2011). Philosophers such as Glover, Wilkinson, and the authors of *From Chance to Choice* attempt to contest these empirical findings by arguing that well-being has objective components or through the use of concepts like "flourishing" that appeal to definitions of well-being that are less reliant on subjective assessment (Buchanan et al. 2000, 278–279; Glover 2006, 15–23; Wilkinson 2010, 63–68).

Though I cannot recast this debate in its entirety here, I tend to side with accepting subjective reporting of well-being. Efforts by nondisabled philosophers to second-guess subjective reports and to reconstruct the concept of well-being so that people with cognitive disabilities end up having less of it show a lack of imagination about the lives of others. However, regardless of the merits of my position, there is a shorter answer to this objection. Since we are discussing the degree to which people with cognitive disabilities are justified in feeling disquieted by prenatal testing and selective abortion, what seems to matter most is how people with these disabilities perceive their own well-being.

People who perceive that their lives are going well will not be convinced by theories that imply their lives do not go well. If such theories are used to rebut the allegation that bias plays a role in prenatal decisions, these theories might be seen as themselves the product of bias. To recap the reasoning here: I have argued that anti–cognitive-disability bias plays a role in prenatal decision-making at a population level. In response, someone might claim that this bias does not matter because prenatal testing and selective abortion are justified by the low levels of well-being experienced by people with cognitive disabilities. Since this counterargument is predicated on the view that the lives of people with disabilities necessarily or objectively do not go as well as those of people without disabilities, then it is likely to reinforce the perception that prenatal decisions are motivated by bias. The view that people who live with cognitive disabilities have diminished well-being can easily be seen as itself a product of ableist bias, especially by people with cognitive disabilities themselves.

CONCLUSION

I have argued that three types of reassurance offered by bioethicists toward people with cognitive disabilities about why they need not worry about prenatal testing and selective abortion fail in the goal of reassurance. I have argued, furthermore, that the three forms of reassurance fail because prenatal decisions are influenced by pervasive cultural bias toward people with cognitive disabilities. To people with these disabilities, the widespread uptake of prenatal testing and selective abortion are reminders of this bias and evidence that bias is being further perpetuated in the name of healthcare.

It is important to be honest to ourselves and to people with cognitive disabilities about what we are doing when we try to avoid the birth of more people like them. We should admit that biased attitudes are common and that these attitudes inevitably influence prenatal decisions. However, despite this honesty, I do not believe that my arguments lead to a conclusion that prenatal testing or selective abortion should be banned. There is a strong requirement of respect for autonomy in prenatal decision-making. People should be able to make reproductive decisions based on whatever values they have, regardless of the social desirability of these values. Our culture justifiably endorses a strong right of autonomy in these decisions.

Nonetheless, there are other aspects in the development and expansion of new prenatal tests, in the formation of policy around the use of these tests, in the funding of research, and in resource allocation affecting access to these tests in which an honest recognition of the influence of anti-disability bias may be a relevant ethical consideration. Should further public funding be provided toward the development and perfection of new prenatal tests for cognitive disabilities like Down syndrome? Is it important that all pregnant women be offered NIPT as a part of prenatal care? Should these tests be covered by public funding or by private insurance plans? Which genetic conditions, if any, should be covered by publicly funded mass screening programs (Munthe 2015)? In answering these policy and funding questions, we should be mindful of the likelihood that improving access to prenatal testing and perfecting these technologies feed an ugly social attitude toward people with cognitive disabilities.

NOTES

1. I use this term loosely to refer to the social context of affluent Western countries, exemplified by English-speaking liberal democratic states such as the United States, the United Kingdom, and Canada, though not excluding other Western democratic states. My arguments have less applicability to cultural circumstances outside of this context: in the global South or to affluent and nonaffluent countries in Asia, for instance.
2. In other situations, the term "retarded" might be used in a script to contextualize a character—for instance, to make characters unsympathetic to the audience by putting crude or offensive language in their mouths. Season 1 of the show "Orange Is the New Black" appears to use the term "retarded" in this way. In this show, some of the characters who are meant to be cast as villains are shown telling a joke with a punch line involving the word. The usage comes off as less offensive. The term might also be used to create realism in the depiction of a character. Other offensive terms, such as racial epithets, could be used similarly. The realistic depiction of a bigot might require the use of bigoted language. However, the use of offensive terms in comedy, in order to get laughs from the audience by making fun of people who are weak, vulnerable, or stigmatized, is a different scenario altogether and less justifiable by such arguments.
3. If bias against people with cognitive disabilities did not exist, there would likely be very little grounds for objecting to prenatal testing for disabilities or to the termination of fetuses diagnosed with such conditions. In such a counterfactual scenario, such terminations

would be similar to terminations for other reasons, in which pregnant women just cannot deal with the repercussions of bringing any baby into the world. From a pro-choice perspective, there would be little reason to object absent the problem of bias. But this is not the world we inhabit. There is a case to be made that if people did not harbor biases against those with cognitive disabilities, prenatal testing for these conditions would not be as extensive, and there would not be such a concerted effort to perfect prenatal testing technologies. Anti-disability bias is a strong motivating force, and if people were not motivated to detect cognitively disabling conditions prenatally, the tests for detecting these conditions would not have been developed. Because of the importance of the problem of bias for the ethical discussion about prenatal testing in the kind of world that we inhabit, there is all the more reason to acknowledge the presence of bias in these decisions.

4. See also the chapter by Jason Marsh (2020) in this volume.

REFERENCES

Albrecht, Gary L., and Patrick J. Devlieger. 1999. "The Disability Paradox: High Quality of Life Against All Odds." *Social Science and Medicine* 48(8): 977–988.

Americans with Disabilities Act. 1990. 42 U.S.C. §12101.

Amundson, Ron. 2005. "Disability, Ideology, and Quality of Life: A Bias in Biomedical Ethics." In *Quality of Life and Human Difference: Genetic Testing, Health Care, and Disability*, edited by David Wasserman, Jerome Bickenbach, and Robert Wachbroit, 101–114. New York: Cambridge University Press.

Asch, Adrienne. 1999. "Prenatal Diagnosis and Selective Abortion: A Challenge to Practice and Policy." *American Journal of Public Health* 89(11): 1649–1657.

Associated Press. 2008. "Disability Groups Protest 'Tropic Thunder.'" *NBC News*. Available at http://www.today.com/id/26158247/ns/today-today_entertainment/t/disability-groups-protest-tropic-thunder/%20-%20.WZ25fUjnhaQ#.Wab1qojnhaQ

Box Office Mojo. 2017a. *Ted*. Available at http://www.boxofficemojo.com/movies/?id=ted.htm

Box Office Mojo. 2017b. *Tropic Thunder*. Available at http://www.boxofficemojo.com/movies/?id=tropicthunder.htm

Buchanan, Allen. 1996. "Choosing Who Will Be Disabled: Genetic Intervention and the Morality of Inclusion." *Social Philosophy and Policy* 13: 18–46.

Buchanan, Allen, Dan W. Brock, Norman Daniels, and Daniel Wikler. 2000. *From Chance to Choice*. New York: Cambridge University Press.

Canadian Down Syndrome Society. 2014. "What Prenatal Testing Means to Me by VATTA." Available at https://www.youtube.com/watch?v=VQp8OJN5Rjk

Cunningham, Cliff C. 1996. "Families of Children with Down Syndrome." *Down Syndrome Research and Practice* 4(3): 87–95.

Don't Screen Us Out. 2017. "Don't Screen Us Out." Available at http://dontscreenusout.org/

Enea-Drapeau, C., M. Carlier, and P. Huguet. 2012. "Tracing Subtle Stereotypes of Children with Trisomy21: From Facial-Feature-Based to Implicit Stereotyping." *PLoS One* 7(4): e34369.

Glover, Jonathan. 2006. *Choosing Children: Genes, Disability, and Design*. New York: Oxford University Press.

Hein, S., M. Grumm, and M. Fingerle. 2011. "Is Contact with People with Disabilities a Guarantee for Positive Implicit and Explicit Attitudes?" *European Journal of Special Needs Education* 26(4): 509–522.

Holm, Søren. 2008. "The Expressivist Objection to Prenatal Diagnosis: Can It Be Laid to Rest?" *Journal of Medical Ethics* 34: 24–25.

IMD*b*. 2012. "Ted (2012) Quotes." Available at http://www.imdb.com/title/tt1637725/quotes

Individuals with Disabilities Education Act. 2004. 20 U.S.C. § 1400.

Kaposy, Chris. 2013. "A Disability Critique of the New Prenatal Test for Down Syndrome." *Kennedy Institute of Ethics Journal* 23(4): 299–324.

Kaposy, Chris. 2018. *Choosing Down Syndrome: Ethics and New Prenatal Testing Technologies.* Cambridge, MA: MIT Press.

Leo, Alex. 2010. "Sarah Silverman in Twitter Fight with Chris Anderson & Steve Case Over 'Retard' Routine." *Huffington Post.* Available at http://www.huffingtonpost.ca/entry/sarah-silverman-in-twitte_n_462769

Lo, K. K., E. Karampetsou, C. Boustred et al. 2016. "Limited Clinical Utility of Non-Invasive Prenatal Testing for Subchromosomal Abnormalities." *American Journal of Human Genetics* 98: 34–44.

Mansfield, Caroline, Suellen Hopfer, and Theresa M. Marteau. 1999. "Termination Rates After Prenatal Diagnosis of Down Syndrome, Spina Bifida, Anencephaly, and Turner and Klinefelter Syndromes: A Systematic Literature Review." *Prenatal Diagnosis* 19: 808–813.

Marsh, Jason. 2020. "What's Wrong With 'You Say You're Happy, But…'Reasoning?" In *Oxford Handbook of Philosophy and Disability*, edited by Adam Cureton and David Wasserman, 310–325. New York: Oxford University Press.

Metzel, Deborah S. 2004. "Historical Social Geography." In *Mental Retardation in America: A Historical Reader*, edited by S. Noll and J. Trent, 420–444. New York: New York University Press.

Munthe, Christian. 2015. "A New Ethical Landscape of Prenatal Testing: Individualizing Choice to Serve Autonomy and Promote Public Health: A Radical Proposal." *Bioethics* 29(1): 36–45.

Natoli, Jaime L., Deborah L. Ackerman, Suzanne McDermott, and Janice G. Edwards. 2012. "Prenatal Diagnosis of Down Syndrome: A Systematic Review of Termination Rates (1995–2011)." *Prenatal Diagnosis* 32: 142–153.

Nelson, Jamie Lindemann. 1998. "The Meaning of the Act: Reflections on the Expressive Force of Reproductive Decision Making and Policies." *Kennedy Institute of Ethics Journal* 8(2): 165–182.

Norton, Mary E., Bo Jacobsson, Geeta K. Swamy et al. 2015. "Cell-free DNA Analysis for Noninvasive Examination of Trisomy." *New England Journal of Medicine* 372(17): 1589–1597.

Nuffield Council on Bioethics. 2017. *Non-invasive Prenatal Testing: Ethical Issues.* Available at https://www.gov.uk/government/news/safer-screening-test-for-pregnant-women.

Ouellette-Kuntz, Hélène, Philip Burge, Hilary K. Brown, and Elizabeth Arsenault. 2010. "Public Attitudes Towards Individuals with Intellectual Disabilities as Measured by the Concept of Social Distance." *Journal of Applied Research in Intellectual Disabilities* 23: 132–142.

Proctor, Stephon N. 2012. *Implicit Bias, Attributions, and Emotions in Decisions about Parents with Intellectual Disabilities by Child Protection Workers.* Pennsylvania State University, Unpublished doctoral dissertation.

Project Implicit. 2011. "Preliminary Information." Available at https://implicit.harvard.edu/implicit/takeatest.html

Robey, K. L., L. Beckley, and M. Kirschner. 2006. "Implicit Infantilizing Attitudes about Disability." *Journal of Developmental and Physical Disabilities* 18(4): 441–453.

Shakespeare, Tom. 2005. "The Social Context of Individual Choice." In *Quality of Life and Human Difference: Genetic Testing, Health Care, and Disability*, edited by David Wasserman, Jerome Bickenbach, and Robert Wachbroit, 217–236. New York: Cambridge University Press.

Skotko, Brian G., Susan P. Levine, Richard Goldstein. 2011. "Self-Perceptions from People with Down Syndrome." *American Journal of Medical Genetics Part A* 155: 2360–2369.

Snowdon, Anne. 2012. *The Sandbox Project: Strengthening Communities for Canadian Children with Disabilities*, report for Sandbox Project's 2nd Annual Conference, January 19. Available at http://sandboxproject.ca/wp-content/uploads/2012/01/SandboxProjectDiscussionDocument.pdf.

Special Olympics. 2017. "R-Word: Spread the Word to End the Word." Available at http://www.r-word.org/

TMZ.com. 2006. "'Kramer's' Racist Tirade Caught on Tape." *TMZ.com*. Available at http://www.tmz.com/2006/11/20/kramers-racist-tirade-caught-on-tape/

Wilkinson, Stephen. 2010. *Choosing Tomorrow's Children: The Ethics of Selective Reproduction*. New York: Oxford University Press.

Wilson, Michelle Clare, and Katrina Scior. 2014. "Attitudes Towards Individuals with Disabilities as Measured by the Implicit Association Test: A Literature Review." *Research in Developmental Disabilities* 35: 294–321.

Further Readings

Asch, Adrienne, and Wasserman, David. 2005. "Where Is the Sin in Synecdoche? Prenatal Testing and the Parent-Child Relationship." In *Quality of Life and Human Difference: Genetic Testing, Health Care, and Disability*, edited by David Wasserman, Jerome Bickenbach, and Robert Wachbroit, 172–216. New York: Cambridge University Press.

Murdoch, Blake, Vardit Ravitsky, Ubaka Ogbogu, et al. 2017. "Non-invasive Prenatal Testing and the Unveiling of an Impaired Translation Process." *Journal of Obstetrics and Gynaecology Canada* 39(1): 10–17.

Parens, Erik, and Adrienne Asch. 2000. *Prenatal Testing and Disability Rights*. Washington DC: Georgetown University Press.

CHAPTER 40

REPRODUCTIVE CHOICE, IN CONTEXT: AVOIDING EXCESS AND DEFICIENCY?

RICHARD HULL AND TOM SHAKESPEARE

INTRODUCTION

BERNARD Williams once said that "simple-mindedness consists in having too few thoughts and feelings to match the world as it really is" (Smart and Williams, 1973, 149). The world of prenatal screening and diagnosis is changing fast, and lay people may be more confused and troubled than ever about the new possibilities for testing and selecting among possible pregnancies. Some commentators point out that the social conditions and health systems for existing screening programs for Down syndrome and other trisomies, or spina bifida and other developmental conditions, are hardly perfect (Shakespeare 2006; Karpin and Savell 2012; Kaposy 2018). For example, there are too few genetic counselors or appropriately trained midwives. Appropriate and balanced information about the conditions being tested for is rarely available. Most societies fail adequately to support children and adults with disabilities and their families (Shakespeare 2006). Perhaps it is no wonder 90 percent of those women who seek knowledge about their fetus choose to terminate pregnancy if they learn that the fetus is affected by disability (Nuffield Council on Bioethics 2017).

With new genetic knowledge, and with safe and more accurate testing possibilities, a brave new world is on the horizon. The new cell-free fetal DNA (cffDNA) technologies mean that non-invasive tests can provide information about the fetus with a high degree of accuracy by the tenth week of pregnancy (Chitty et al. 2016; Taylor-Phillips et al 2016). Led by private providers, this approach is marketed as "Non Invasive Prenatal Testing" (NIPT), which sounds entirely beneficent and by ensuring no risk of iatrogenic miscarriage, seems to remove any reason not to test, at least for those couples who do not have concerns about abortion or selection.

Already, some American clinics are also offering whole genome sequencing. This implies a vast expansion in the detection possibilities: not just of trisomies such as Down syndrome, but potentially a "fishing expedition" to find any single gene condition, or indeed genetic difference, however trivial. For example, sex selection remains controversial but is a possibility that is actively promoted in this new world of reproductive choice (Scully et al. 2006).

These developments seem to have the potential to have a far greater impact than embryo selection, via pre-implantation genetic diagnosis (PGD), which is offered to couples undergoing in-vitro fertilization (IVF). PGD enables couples with a significant chance of a particular genetic condition to have a good chance of avoiding that outcome in their families. However, few people undergo PGD: in 2010, there were 100 babies born as a result of PGD in the UK (NHS Commissioning Board 2010). This has risen to 712 treatments in 2016, with a success rate of 30 percent—36 percent (HFEA 2018). However, it may be in future that more, most or even all IVF patients also engage in PGD, which would mark an expansion of this form of reproductive choice.

Within the context that we have sketched out, the loudest voices take strong and polarized positions in regard to prenatal testing (Shakespeare 1999). But in the current chapter, we will try and steer a course through both extremes of the "for" and "against" pregnancy testing dichotomy. We are suspicious of the linear rationalism that seems prevalent in current debate and that seems to miss so much that is hard to identify, even though many are trying to do so. Instead, we offer a more pragmatic, nuanced, and hopefully helpful approach to the issue. This may be of value both practically—to people struggling with decisions around testing in pregnancy—and conceptually, to ethicists and others engaging with these practices.

On one side of the dichotomy, advocates emphasize individual choice, access to information, and women's control over their bodies (Berer 2017). Some proponents argue for no restrictions on abortion, implying that women should be able to terminate pregnancy up until birth (WHO 2012). Information about the embryo or fetus is regarded as an unequivocal good. Those who propose Procreative Beneficence (Savulescu 2001) or the Impersonal Comparative Principle (McMahan 2005) consider that, certainly in embryo selection cases (and likely by inference in prenatal testing cases) women have a duty to have the best babies they can. However, as we have argued elsewhere, these approaches, supposedly maximizing welfare, are impossible to operationalize (Shakespeare and Hull 2018). Not only is it impossible to be certain about what genetic factors enable life to go well, but also all lives contain difficulties, traumas, complications, and indeed the chance of becoming disabled, which selection cannot avoid. Perfectionism becomes an unachievable and irresolvable quest, and the quest for perfection ends up so onerous and complex that it risks undermining the purpose and nature of parenting. Evidence demonstrates that many lay people reject this consumerist approach to reproduction, believing that children should be a "gift not commodity" (Scully et al. 2006). Rather than focusing on individuals and their genomes, it might be better to concentrate on improving society and promoting inclusive values (Kaposy 2018).

People on the other side of the dichotomy, who might oppose selection on the basis of fetal characteristics, would worry about incipient eugenics (Kitcher 1996, Iltis 2016) and might even regard any termination of pregnancy as akin to murder. The introduction of "NIPT" causes concern because it may lead to more fetuses with, for example, Down syndrome, being identified, with the consequence that the vast majority of those pregnancies will be terminated. This would raise the prospect of "an End to Down Syndrome" (Thomas and Rothman 2016; Van Schendel et al. 2017). Some have worries that the introduction of tests for disability implicitly suggests that testing and termination is the appropriate response to fetal impairment, and that the whole enterprise sends the message that disabled people are best prevented and society would be better off without them. This argument is often classed as "the expressivist objection" (Parens and Asch 2003), and it comes in a more concrete consequentialist form with concerns that selection may also lead to diminished societal provision for children and adults with disabilities.

Underlying this is the empirical evidence that families with disabled children almost always report themselves being happy and successful (Slotko et al. 2011; Slotko et al. 2016), that parenting a disabled child can bring unexpected benefits (Traustadottir 1991; Slotko et al. 2016), and that supportive social and educational settings can go a long way toward eliminating the difficulties associated with these differences. Above all, disabled people generally report that their quality of life is as good as (and sometimes better than) that of non-disabled people (Albrecht and Devlieger 1999; Amundson 2010; Slotko et al. 2011). This may be a surprise to those who espouse Utilitarian and Libertarian philosophies, but not to those who understand what makes life worth living.

However, we certainly do not want to flip over to the other side of the dichotomy and blame women (and men) for their choices around testing or termination. We support reproductive autonomy. We consider that it is a legitimate moral option to exercise the choice of testing pregnancies for significant health conditions and to choose to terminate pregnancy. It is also specifically permitted under UK law. We do not consider that denying women access to NIPT, solely on the grounds that it is a more accurate and safer test, could be acceptable in a liberal democracy where everyone has different values, expectations, and beliefs regarding parenting, disability, and abortion. Forcing women to continue with affected pregnancies and give birth to babies with disability, on grounds that they are likely to adapt to their different family and do well, surely cannot be defensible in a liberal secular society, whatever the practice in other countries.

Both hypothesized extremes—banning selective abortion or imposing a duty of procreative beneficence—are problematic. They would either impose unrealistic duties, or alternatively deny valid choices to women and men contemplating or going through pregnancy and parenthood. So we are left with the requirement either to sit with the complexity and responsibility of testing and possibly termination through those nine months of pregnancy; or alternatively, not testing and terminating, and then possibly supporting an individual with what could be significant lifelong disability. With Häyry (2010), we consider this to be a difficult decision, a personal balancing of moral harms, without any clear consensus as to the "correct" choice. The options are incommensurable, and the decision must finally rest with the woman (and partner) who will live with the outcome, whatever it is.

But this is not just a private decision; choices always depend on how society supports disabled children and their families, and the wider contexts of values and attitudes and inclusion, which surround the people directly affected. If society makes it hard to rear a disabled child, sends messages that disabled children are not welcome, or offers no choices or independence to disabled adults, then this will inevitably influence the choices of many conscientious parents. If almost everyone takes a particular course of action, the possibility that others will resist or take a different course is lessened (Kitcher 2006, Beck-Gernsheim 2011). Alternatively, if all children are welcomed, if medical interventions and inclusive education are available, if parents of disabled children are supported, then it becomes easier to choose to continue affected pregnancies.

Virtuous Parenting

How then, to approach the personal, ethical dilemma of whether to test and whether to terminate? We have argued that this is a private, highly individual decision, and that wider arguments about inclusion or procreative beneficence are not compelling. But does that mean there is no more to say about the morality of prenatal selection?

One set of arguments homes in on whether a baby is itself harmed by being born with a disability that could have been prevented. Derek Parfit's famous "non-identity problem" reminds us that the individual with a disability is not harmed, counter-intuitively, because they would not exist if the pregnancy had been terminated on grounds of disability. A different person would have been born at a later date, but they themselves only face the possibility of existence with disability, or non-existence. Unless the disability is so grievous that it would be better not to exist, then they are not harmed by being brought into the world with disability. At least for Down syndrome, spina bifida, achondroplasia, and many of the common conditions for which screening is offered, non-existence is usually not regarded as better than living with the condition.

Alternatively, it might be argued that a wrong is performed when disabled people are brought into the world, even if they themselves are not harmed. A world with more disability is worse, on this reading, than a world with less disability. On average, disability renders someone more likely to suffer, more likely to be dependent on others, and less likely to be economically productive, and thus, in utilitarian terms, disability reduces welfare overall. Note that this individualist reading of disability, in some of its forms, fails to see any value in the relationships disabled people have with family members and others, erases any social or cultural or indeed economic contribution that most disabled people do achieve, and reduces disability to dysfunction and misery. None of these assumptions are empirically accurate. But even if they were, how appropriate is it to claim that this would constitute an impersonal harm or wrong? Human beings have the moral freedom to commit many suboptimal acts, especially in such private domains, and disability is the outcome of many personal choices which we are free to make (over-eating, dangerous sports, over-indulgence in alcohol, etc.), not to mention social arrangements which are avoidable (working conditions, poverty, war, etc.).

However, we will bracket both these debates and avoid considering harms to the individual person, or even to society. Instead, we will explore the highly personal and contextual nature of reproductive choices, and utilize parts of Aristotelian ethical theory to consider how a prospective parent might navigate through such complex decisions, when faced, for example, with options around testing or not testing, terminating or not terminating.

Often, virtue ethicists discuss selection and abortion in terms of the moral character of the parents and which decisions are compatible with good parenting (Macintyre, 1999; Vehmas, 2002). Rather than discussing parental duties or fetal rights, virtue ethicists emphasize parental responsibility and the unconditional love of a parent for their child. For example, Macintyre argues that the virtuous parent is orientated toward the child's needs, not their own needs, whatever the child's needs may turn out to be:

> Good parental care is defined in part by reference to the possibility of the affliction of their children by serious disability. (1999, 91)

For him, many parents of disabled children are the paradigms of good parenthood, "who provide the model for and the key to the work of all parents" (1999, 91). Perhaps this approach to virtue ethics in parenting has more purchase after the birth of a disabled child than in pregnancy, when serious impairment is predicted (Wilkinson 2010, 21). Macintyre is arguably over-idealistic about the virtues of good parenting. Virtuous prospective parents surely do not have to accept all children and any children. A virtue is not the same as an obligation.

However, virtuous parents are perhaps still obligated to think hard about children, the good life, and the possibilities for their own family, as well as about termination of pregnancy. We might not think it was virtuous behavior if someone was entirely flippant or unconcerned about abortion. We would not consider the parent who treats their child in an instrumental way as virtuous or doing their duty—for example, if they manipulate the child's genome in order to serve their own ambitions or are pushy or controlling regarding their children. In the list of reasons for opting for prenatal selection, we would be more likely to respect authentic, thought-through moral reasons than trivial or selfish reasons. If prospective parents pause to think, rather than accepting unquestioningly the dominant antenatal screening process, they might wonder whether the harm of ending a life is justified by the potential restrictions or burdens that particular lives appear to entail. They might look at evidence about whether children with disabilities, and parents and siblings, thrive.

The arguments for and against testing and, potentially, termination of pregnancy are thus complex—ethically, psychologically, and socially. For this reason, the anthropologist Rayna Rapp has famously written of obstetric ultrasound that this technology turns every woman into a bioethicist (Rapp 1999). The empirical evidence suggests that, for many, choice is not an unreserved good. Prospective parents who test or terminate pregnancies may carry feelings of responsibility, guilt, and confusion (Bellieni and Buonocore 2013), although other evidence suggests no long-term negative outcomes (Biggs et al 2017). Others state that they are glad the technology did not exist when they were making reproductive decisions. On the other hand, prospective parents may think that they are saving their potential child from harm. The intuition to do one's best by one's children is strong and rests mainly on mothers. For example, from his ethnography of two UK antenatal services, Thomas concludes

> Screening for Down's syndrome, as such, is arguably viewed as an important type of care-work that is integral to assuming the role of a 'good mother'. Located in powerful cultural discourses related to good parenthood, screening instigates a process in which mothers-to-be become 'patients-in-waiting'.   (Thomas 2017, 154).

Thomas's research highlights how prenatal service personnel talk in terms of babies as they go through screening, unless termination becomes a relevant option, in which case the term fetus is used (Thomas 2017, 157). Cultural framing of pregnancy and testing thus becomes critical.

However, not only is there scant evidence of actual suffering, but also the non-identity problem reminds us that it is not this child who benefits, as a parent might imagine, but the future, presumably non-disabled replacement child who might be born after a subsequent pregnancy. Moreover, the potential "harm" of having a disabled child has to be balanced against any potential "harms" such as anxiety or negative psychological sequelae of testing and termination. Evidence is unclear, but overall it appears that psychological harms of termination are rarely reported.

Disability rights activists assume that abortion on the basis of impairment carries with it the implication that it would be better to be dead than disabled. However, as Anne Maclean and many others have argued, there is a distinction to be made between abortion implying that disabled people's lives are not worth living, and a case where an individual person cannot cope with a disabled child (Maclean, 1993). For example, parents may feel that having a disabled child will damage their partnership, or impact negatively on their other children. They may fear economic hardship, particularly if one parent has to give up working to care for the disabled child. They may be prepared to sacrifice freedoms to parent children for the first twenty years of their lives but not to continue in a parental role toward an adult disabled child who remains dependent. There are many extraordinary stories of the degree of selflessness and commitment that Macintyre calls for, and such people should certainly be welcomed and applauded. But not all prospective parents will be prepared to make the sacrifices and endure the difficulties that disabled families sometimes face, and it is their right to forgo this future, a decision that does not imply that they do not like, respect, and accept disabled people. Indeed, there are a number of complex contextual issues here, which we explore below.

The Contextual Nature of Reproductive Decision Making

There are a variety of considerations that legitimately factor in to (prospective) parental decision making, both singularly and in combination. One such consideration in the context of prenatal testing (more so than with PGD for most people who do not believe that life begins at conception) is a (prospective) parent's beliefs about termination of pregnancy. Views about termination of pregnancy tend to be deeply held and so, in turn, can play a critical role in (prospective) parental deliberations.

The recent Nuffield Council report on Non-Invasive Prenatal Testing, for example, cites research exploring the factors that influence women's decisions to continue with or terminate a pregnancy following a diagnosis of fetal anomaly. Reasons for continuing a pregnancy after a diagnosis include, among other things, "religious beliefs" and "not wanting to experience a termination" (Nuffield Council 2017, 11). Karpin and Savell also support the claim that what women are prepared to do to prevent the birth of a child who has an abnormality, genetic condition or disease is a crucial contextual matter (Karpin and Savell 2012, 283). They further observe that, as a pregnancy proceeds, the willingness to terminate that pregnancy can decrease, which is likely to be bound up with a correlation between gestational stage and parental attachment to the fetus. They also cite evidence that the stage of gestation correlates with clinicians' willingness to facilitate termination for certain disabilities (Karpin and Savell 2012, 283).[1] This, then, can be taken to illustrate how decisions may change as circumstances evolve.

The Nuffield Council report also expresses concern with the issue of gestational stage and increasing ethical and psychological concerns, given that offering NIPT only to women after they have had an initial combined test, may lead to a delay in diagnosis for some women.[2] The report states that such a delay (of a week or longer) "will be significant to some women, particularly those considering a termination" (Nuffield Council 2017, 42). The significance is said to lie in the fact that some research suggests that later terminations are associated with higher levels of stress and therefore increased harm to women, at least in the short term, which is clearly likely to be bound up with women's considered beliefs about the issue and procedure. The report thus recommends that "women are able to go straight to diagnostic testing after a high chance combined test result if they wish" (Nuffield Council 2017, 42).

It is obvious, then, that beliefs about the issue of termination of pregnancy can have a significant impact on decision making with regard to prenatal testing. Indeed, the decision to terminate a pregnancy following diagnosis of fetal anomaly "is frequently described by pregnant women and couples as shocking, painful and distressing, with some reporting feeling unprepared for making such a decision" (Nuffield Council 2017, 11), which further illustrates the gravity of the issue. The Nuffield report cites research from The Netherlands, which found that "a significant number of women experienced post-traumatic stress symptoms and depression in the 16 months following the termination, particularly among those who felt high levels of doubt during the decision-making period, lacked partner support, were religious, and were at more advanced stages of pregnancy" (Nuffield Council 2017, 11–12). This was the case even though, crucially, most women did not report regretting their decision to have a termination (Nuffield Council 2017, 12), which both illustrates the complexity and gravity of this issue for many and suggests that we should be deeply sympathetic to women's considered choices in such cases, in either direction.

Decisions to terminate pregnancy on the basis of a diagnosis of fetal anomaly are made on a number of grounds (Nuffield Council 2017, 11). We are going to focus on three loosely defined and interrelated sets of considerations that, along with beliefs about the issue of termination, legitimately factor into (prospective) parental decision making. First, we will look at concerns about potential suffering and lack of autonomy with respect to the life of the prospective child. Second, we will look at concerns about the impact of having a child with a diagnosed condition on the parent(s) and other family members. Third, we will look at the social, economic, and personal context in which a decision is being considered. While balancing such variables is no easy task and further illustrates the moral complexities described throughout, we want to suggest that any serious and sensitive evaluation will attempt to do so.

A diagnosed condition is likely to concern (prospective) parents because of the impact that it might have on a prospective child's life or, as Jonathan Glover puts it, their capacity to flourish (Glover 2006, 9). Judging the impact of a given condition on a potential child's capacity to flourish is problematic and controversial. As mentioned above, it is perhaps least controversial in what tend to be described as "wrongful life" or "sub-zero" cases.[3] These are cases where it is said that a prospective child's life will not be worth living or, put another way, that the life created will contain negative net utility. Wilkinson argues that wrongful life cases are extremely rare. "Most people with disabilities have a positive quality of life, even if their disabilities, or society's responses to them, cause them to have a lower quality of life than that of the average non-disabled person" (Wilkinson 2010, 71). Thus, unless we wanted to raise the threshold of wrongful life to include many or most of the types of conditions tested for via prenatal testing, which would be contentious, the concept of wrongful life has little to offer (prospective) parents when trying to balance concerns about the impact of a diagnosed condition.

Above the wrongful life threshold, it is hard to know what we can legitimately say about decisions made on the basis of an assessment of the likely impact of a diagnosed condition. As mentioned earlier, this is in no small measure due to the fact that such decisions are identity affecting, which brings in to play Parfit's famous non-identity problem (Parfit 1984). This is expertly articulated by Buchanan and colleagues where they point out that, in the case of disability, for example, when "a person's disability uncontroversially leaves him or her with a worthwhile life ... it would not be better for the person with the disability to have had it prevented, since that could only be done by preventing him or her from ever having existed at all" (Buchanan, Brock, Daniels, and Wikler 2000, 245). What this implies for the analysis here is that we cannot claim that it is a person-affecting wrong to continue with a pregnancy after most diagnoses of fetal anomaly, since it will likely result in a child with a worthwhile life who prefers to exist than to not exist.[4] However, for reasons already given, we do not want to claim that it is wrong to continue with a pregnancy after a positive diagnosis. Whether or not it could be said to exhibit a moral deficiency of some kind is a question to which we will turn later.

What discussion of the wrongful life threshold and the non-identity problem encourages, perhaps unexpectedly, is a more nuanced discussion of what might add to, detract from, or have a questionable impact in either direction on, our capacity to flourish. For it is fair to assume that no decent (prospective) parent would desire to have a child whose quality of life was just a little way above zero. Thus, while we do not wish to claim that it is wrong to have a child whose quality of life hovers just above the zero threshold, there are a myriad of serious moral considerations that legitimately apply above that threshold and that help us to form a view about whether or not to continue with a pregnancy in any specific circumstances.

While it is hard to claim that a child is harmed when it is brought into existence above the zero line, there are a number of ways of articulating worries about the impact of certain conditions. One is to question whether the level of suffering likely to be bound up with a given condition is reason enough to prevent it where that choice is available. These are cases where, as Herissone-Kelly puts it, "The possible child's life would be worth living but would contain what the prospective parent considers a greater load of suffering than she is prepared to allow her child to endure" (2006, 169). We consider this to be a sensible and humane approach. That is, a prospective parent might not want to become responsible herself, for bringing about a life with a capacity to flourish that is below a certain threshold. And, while we argue throughout that such a threshold is likely to be contextually influenced, a prospective parent's considered beliefs are highly morally relevant (even if they can be criticized in some cases). It is an approach that also illustrates at least two concerns that are articulated by the concepts of excess and deficiency that we explore later in the chapter. Firstly, we can argue that, although a possible child's life would be worth living, a (prospective) parent would show deficient concern for that child if s/he did not seriously consider the level of suffering that it might experience. In the same way that no decent (prospective) parent would choose to have a child whose quality of life was just a little way above the zero threshold, we can contend that the potential for deficient concern may extend far beyond that threshold.[5] Secondly, the focus on (prospective) parents and the character of their choices gives legitimate weight to their moral considerations, for example, concerning what they are prepared to take responsibility for bringing about. We can recognize (and sympathize with) a considered desire to refrain from bringing about a certain level of avoidable suffering in a way that can be said to avoid the non-identity problem, because the focus is on parental sense of responsibility as much as it is on the life of the potential child.[6]

There may be, then, defensible reasons to prevent suffering when we can (where, for example, it is considered to be both serious enough and highly likely to be experienced). Moreover, this need not entail raising the threshold of wrongful life. We are not claiming that such lives are wrongful: we are recognizing legitimate moral concerns about quality of life a good way above that threshold, which helps to determine what prospective parents are prepared to bring about. This will include serious and defensible concerns about the potential suffering of one's future child given the impact of certain conditions that, by implication, (prospective) parents may understandably rather avoid. While the concept of wrongful life matters a lot, so does a (prospective) parental sense of responsibility and, as we explore below, there are many more contextual factors to be considered when making honorable procreative choices. Moreover, the focus on (prospective) parental agency that we would argue is essential here gives their considerations more weight, as well as helping to explain why prenatal testing, including NIPT, exists.

Closely related to concerns about the potential suffering in a prospective child's life are concerns about a loss or lack of autonomy, particularly when it comes to adult life. (Prospective) parents tend to take for granted the idea that their children will grow up to lead autonomous lives, to live independently and to be able to act on their autonomous choices. Autonomy here is taken to be "a psychological property of persons and 'respect for autonomy' is a term for the moral constraints that a person's having this psychological property places on the way in which we should treat her" (Wilkinson 2010, 48).

Concerns about autonomy take two forms, according to Wilkinson, which he terms "the Failure to Respect Autonomy Worry and the Failure to Promote Autonomy Worry." The Failure to Promote Autonomy Worry is a worry about choosing to create future people whose autonomy will be limited (Wilkinson 2010, 51) (presumably, as a psychological property). The Failure to Respect Autonomy Worry is a worry about choosing to create future people with limitations that will, in adulthood, lead to the frustration of their autonomous desires and the failure of their autonomously formulated aims and projects (Wilkinson 2010, 53). While he argues that there are problems with the Failure to Respect Autonomy Worry, he concludes that, in as much as we value autonomy, "both 'worries' seem ultimately to count *in favour of* some forms of selection" (those that will increase autonomy) (Wilkinson 2010, 51, 54).

While this discussion takes place in the context of embryo selection prior to implantation, the reasons to favour some forms of selection would clearly be the very same reasons to worry about some diagnoses during pregnancy. Indeed, worries about potential suffering and lack of autonomy feature prominently in the practical concerns of healthcare providers. For example, the Royal College of Obstetricians and Gynaecologists 2010 guidance on termination for fetal anomaly states that doctors should weigh up the following factors when reaching a decision:

- the potential for effective treatment, either *in utero* or after birth;
- on the part of the child, the probable degree of self-awareness and of ability to communicate with others;
- the suffering that would be experienced;

- the probability of being able to live alone and to be self-supporting as an adult;
- on the part of society, the extent to which actions performed by individuals without disability that are essential for health would have to be provided by others (Nuffield Council 2017, 24–25).[7]

Concerns about suffering and lack of autonomy (especially later in life) are abundantly clear in the above guidelines. By implication, they need to be carefully balanced with considered views about termination of pregnancy in particular cases. They also need to be balanced with additional concerns about the impact of having a child with a diagnosed condition on the parent(s) and other family members.

An assessment of the impact of a particular diagnosed condition on the parent(s) and other family members is likely to play a significant role in (prospective) parental decision making. Moreover, that assessment will be bound up with a distinct-yet-related evaluation of just how serious a particular condition is; and both of these things are plausibly variable, depending on personal experience, the condition in question and context. For example, Karpin and Savell, drawing on the work of Wertz and Knoppers, suggest that there is little consensus about where to draw the line between serious and non-serious conditions; that there is a broad spectrum of opinions with greater agreement at the extremes (Karpin and Savell 2012, 273). They then follow Rosamund Scott's analysis, arguing that, between the extremes, disagreement is most prevalent with regard to what Scott describes as "mid-spectrum" conditions (Karpin and Savell 2012, 274).[8] In these types of cases (as well as others, in our view), perceptions of the impact on the parent(s) and other family members may be decisive. As Scott puts it, "The point of recognizing that parents will be the most important judges of the impact on them of a given fetal condition is to suggest that, given there is *room for doubt* about seriousness in the mid-spectrum area, parents' perceptions may legitimately *tip the balance*" (Scott 2003, 212; Karpin and Savell 2012, 275). For Karpin and Savell, this reinforces their point that "the question of what is serious may not be a purely clinical determination, as parents will have views about whether or not the disability being described to them is one with which they feel they can cope" (Karpin and Savell 2012, 275).[9] Indeed, given a serious and balanced engagement with all of the considerations hitherto discussed, we believe that (prospective) parental views will often "tip the balance." While we believe that any ignorance and bias should be challenged by provision of evidence-based information and counselling (e.g., Slotko et al. 2011; Slotko et al. 2016), we consider that for many people, there will remain valid reasons for concern about the impact of certain conditions.

Another reason (alluded to above) why the question of what is serious may not be a purely clinical determination is that (prospective) parental assessments will inevitably take place in different contexts. That is, what we consider to be acceptable might vary significantly given different circumstances and, by implication, different determinants of an authentic moral view. Different individuals bring varying personal and material resources to bear. As Rapp has argued, people's thinking about risks and chances will be different depending on the risks they already face in their daily lives, which will be much different for people who are poor or socially excluded than they are for people who are economically privileged. The consequences of having a disabled child depend greatly on the material resources an individual or family can draw on. For example, where a couple can afford to have one parent who does not do paid work, or who works part time, it may be easier to support a child who has additional needs in their life; similarly, it may also be easier to support a child if the parents can afford to pay privately for therapy, assistance, or transport. Along these lines, poorer individuals or couples may have a lower threshold of severity for conditions they feel that they could cope with, although this is by no means inevitable. In addition, the resources may not just be at the level of individual households, they might pertain to better and more supportive local networks or wider social environments being inclusive, via national policies on health-care, education, and accessibility. As barriers are removed and provision is improved, it may become easier to parent a child with additional needs, or to contemplate a good life for an adult with disability.

As well as these individual and structural resources—which include availability of services and networks, as well as funds—there are also individual resources at the psychological level. Some individuals and families are more resilient than others, or are part of more resilient or supportive communities, and/or have religious faith. They can cope with difficulties, and maybe even thrive and grow as a result (Traustadottir 1991; Slotko et al. 2016). Some individuals are more open to different experiences and indeed different forms of embodiment and others are more prejudiced against disability. People's values differ, and they may consequently place different weight on individual accomplishment, as opposed to other strengths such as sociability or inclusiveness. Individuals are all different in their responses to disability as are disabled people themselves.

Navigating Context-Sensitivity

The analysis above has shown how decisions around prenatal diagnosis are private, difficult, and highly contextual. In what follows, we suggest a way in which (prospective) parents navigate this complex ethical terrain, specifically, by avoiding excessive and deficient dispositions toward such choices. While we acknowledge that *what amounts to* excess and deficiency is highly debatable, we think it a suitable focus for debate in the light of current and future reproductive technologies.

The way of approaching reproductive decision-making that we consider to be worth exploring is via the loosely Aristotelian vision of striking a mean between excess and deficiency. We will argue that this is a useful approach because it effectively articulates what we ought to be doing: attempting to balance complex and sometimes competing considerations in an appropriate way given the particular situation faced.

Aristotle writes that "virtue must have the quality of aiming at the intermediate" (NE, 1106b, 15):

For instance, both fear and confidence and appetite and anger and pity and in general pleasure and pain may be felt both too much and too little, and in both cases not well; but to feel them at the right times, with reference to the right objects, towards the right people, with the right motive, and in the right way, is both what is intermediate and best, and this is characteristic of virtue.   (NE 1106b, 18–23)

This passage immediately makes clear that "too much" and "too little" are worth avoiding. As Aristotle puts it, "The vices respectively fall short of or exceed what is right in both passions and actions, while virtue both finds and chooses that which is intermediate" (Aristotle, 2009, 1107a, 3–5). The passage also suggests that no one kind of response is going to be right for all situations (Broadie 1991, 99). Virtue is concerned with choices lying in a mean "relative to us" (Aristotle, 2009, 1107a).

The idea that as moral agents we should be aiming at the intermediate has been described as a "substantively depressing doctrine in favour of moderation" (Williams 1985, 36). However, other writers suggest that this is rather a cheap shot (Broadie 1991; Urmson 1980, 1988). Urmson argues, for example, that if we take the doctrine of the mean as claiming that we should always feel and exhibit a moderate quantity of a given emotion, the doctrine is plainly absurd (Urmson 1980, 160). When some amount of a certain emotion is appropriate, the idea that the right amount is always a moderate amount is, as he puts it, "very stupid": "If you are trivially rude to me, should I be moderately angry with you, and also when you torture my wife? To be moderately angry would be absurd on both occasions" (Urmson 1980, 160–161).

A doctrine of the mean, then, does not amount to a doctrine of moderation or mediocrity. Urmson suggests that we can view a doctrine of moderation, sensibly interpreted, as a doctrine about where the mean lies while, at the same time, he forcefully asserts that moderation is "no part of the doctrine of the mean, nor is it a consequence of the doctrine of the mean, though it is perfectly compatible with it" (Urmson 1980, 162). Rather, what Aristotle is getting at is some sort of intermediacy belonging to the *disposition* that gives rise to the right responses (Broadie 1991, 101). On this account, what is primarily in a mean is a settled state of character: "Aristotle holds excellence of character to be a mean or intermediate disposition regarding emotions and actions, not that it is a disposition toward mean or intermediate emotions and actions" (Urmson 1980, 161). With respect to "too much" and "too little," Broadie adds that "virtue itself is a disposition such that whoever has it is protected from excesses and deficiencies of feeling and impulse that lead to faulty particular responses" (Broadie 1991, 101).

While the above analysis is of little use as a practical guide to moral decision making, it does tell us what we should be aiming at: a settled disposition of character that is protected from excesses and deficiencies and, by implication, less likely to make what we would ordinarily regard as faulty moral choices. Moreover, the emphasis on disposition suits the highly contextual nature of moral decision making that we have detailed above. As Broadie notes, no kind of natural response is either right or wrong in itself given the importance of the circumstances that will further determine the case: "With different determinants the same sort of response can be right and wrong, and wrong in different ways" (Broadie 1991, 102). Urmson similarly argues that Aristotle's claim is that we need to be present in the particular situation to judge and that "no general principle can be comprehensive enough to take account of the values of all the variables to be taken account of" (Urmson 1988, 36).

Urmson's claim is an important point at the level of ethical theory (Broadie 1991, 102).[10] It is also important with respect to the contextual and variable elements of reproductive decision-making hitherto described. As Van Zyl observes, "Virtue ethics allows for a range of actions that lie somewhere on the continuum between right (characteristic of the virtuous) and wrong (characteristic of the vicious)" (Van Zyl 2013, 178). Given the absence of universal principles, the complexity of most situations and thus the difficulty of finding the intermediate disposition, a lot of room is left for the practical wisdom or reasoning of the virtuous person (Swanton 2013, 330). And while it may be objected that the doctrine of the mean as described is not specific enough (Santas 1997, 275), we want to suggest that it is an approach that accurately captures the difficulties involved with making complex, real-life moral choices and decisions. It is not easy, linear, or formulaic.

The focus on a settled disposition of character that avoids excesses and deficiencies is also useful to our analysis here for a number of reasons. First, it justifies an emphasis on the experiences of (prospective) parents, the character of their choices and how the choices and decisions they make will affect *their* lives, not just the lives of their children. These are important considerations. Second, the idea of avoiding excess and deficiency translates well to ethical concerns about reproductive choices, which can worry us in both directions. Third, as already mentioned, the idea of avoiding excess and deficiency leaves a lot of legitimate moral space in which to find the mean "relative to us" when thinking about all contextual considerations. This is highly appropriate given the intensely personal nature of reproductive decisions. Altogether then, the loosely Aristotelian approach sketched above is both a sensible articulation of the complexities of moral decision-making and particularly suited to the subject at hand.

Our focus here is on the concepts of excess and deficiency rather than conjecture about the content and implications of specific virtues, as we think it most widely captures the difficulties bound up with particular moral choices. It is also worth stressing that we are not propounding an exclusively "virtue ethics" approach. We think that most moral approaches have something important to add to the debate. Instead, what we are suggesting is an approach to reproductive decision making that avoids both excessive and deficient attitudes to (prospective) parenting. Just as excessive and deficient behaviors in everyday life (as, for example, with road rage and negligence) comprise the things we tend to consider as bad or objectionable, we think them worth avoiding in the immensely important area of reproductive choices. Between those extremes, there will be a broad, contextually influenced mean "relative to us"; and we have suggested that this is likely to be a deeply personal matter encompassing many different values. As such, the mean could vary widely among individuals even though it can be characterized as falling between the extremes of perfectionism and indifference.

The analysis suggests that, with regard to prenatal testing, defensible beliefs about the issue of termination of pregnancy can be a crucial contextual matter that can outweigh other considerations. Given the importance of women's bodily autonomy, we strongly believe that such views cannot and should not be overridden. However, in some contexts and with respect to some serious genetic conditions, it could be said that the strength of a belief about termination of pregnancy may correspondingly imply a deficient concern for the projected suffering of a potential child, or the welfare of other family members. Indifference to the whole issue of potential suffering would also be absurd from the perspective developed here. And while we deny the claim that it is wrong not to terminate pregnancy in some circumstances, all things considered it may be far from a balanced view. As stated earlier, a (prospective) parent would show deficient concern for their (potential) child if he or she did not seriously consider the level of suffering that it might experience; and that may, in turn, recommend serious consideration of termination of pregnancy in some cases. Thus, while we would not prohibit their choices, some people may be deficient in their approach to screening on this account. The emphasis on women's autonomy with regard to the issue of termination of pregnancy may also help to explain why the Nuffield Council recommended in terms of public policy that NIPT be offered as an option, yet recommended that what they perceived to be excesses, such as sex-selection and whole genome/exome sequencing, be ruled out (Nuffield Council 2017).[11]

On the subject of perceived excesses, it might be said that some parental behavior can already be excessive enough *without* the choices afforded by current prenatal testing options and potential new technologies. Dan Brock points out, for example, that many parents "already carry the molding, shaping, scheduling and general controlling of their children's lives to excess in a manner that can verge on the tyrannical" (Brock 2005, 396). It is likely that it would be a disadvantage for a child to have a parent with such an attitude (Glover 2006, 64). As new technologies and possibilities emerge, we think that the language of excess is a useful way of criticizing the disposition of (prospective) parents where there may be no evidence of creating challenges for a future child and, indeed, where there may be evidence to the contrary. That is, even though future possible enhancements may be taken to improve life in some way, we might still worry about the excessive (prospective) parental attitudes that they could reflect. Eric Schmidt has argued, for example, that parental genetic trait selections that shift rather than expand the range of open futures are unacceptable because they amount to "an excessive form of parental determination regarding their children's futures" (Schmidt 2007, 197). On this type of account, deep moral objections can be leveled at an over-determining attitude to (prospective) parenting due to the human disposition that it expresses and promotes (Sandel 2007, 46).

If, then, post-natal parental behavior can worry us a lot, we might be rightly concerned with how such behavior will translate to pre-natal and pre-implantation deliberations. With whole genome and exome sequencing, for example, there is the worry that these technologies could in the future lead to termination of pregnancy on the grounds of possibly trivial genetic differences. They could, of course, be used for entirely honorable purposes, for example, where it would be beneficial given a family history of genetic conditions (Nuffield Council 2017). However, more widespread termination of pregnancy on the grounds of trivial genetic differences, with hitherto uncertain clinical implications, could be said to exhibit both a deficient attitude toward the morality of the procedure involved, and an excessive one about which genetic characteristics should be avoided. Where identified differences are not anywhere near any sensible threshold of seriousness, and other contextual issues do not apply, termination of pregnancy on the basis of those differences is likely to be excessive. It could also potentially exhibit an excessively over-determining attitude to (prospective) parenting, which is clearly not an intermediate disposition. We would argue that it is not a desirable one either. As Jonathan Glover suggests, we may lose something important if we unreflectively embrace the mindset of quality control (Glover 2006, 54).

NIPT is fast becoming the norm with regard to prenatal testing, hence the focus of our analysis. One relevant worry is that by removing the "ethical step" of possible iatrogenic miscarriage associated with invasive testing, it becomes routinized and hence prospective parents do not deliberate fully over its implications and possible termination of pregnancy.

We would argue that it is currently far-fetched to suggest that pre-implantation genetic diagnosis during IVF might or should become the procreative norm. However, it is worth pointing out that with technologies that eliminate concerns about the issue of termination of pregnancy, the mean or intermediate disposition could be different. PGD, for example, may lower the threshold of seriousness "partly because many women see embryonic deselection as less morally problematic than abortion" (Karpin and Savell 2012, 285).[12] Put another way, there may be fewer moral reasons to risk bringing about avoidable suffering or compromising the welfare of other family members because the moral weight bound up with the issue of termination of pregnancy is not part of the context. At the same time, worries about excessively determining or perfectionist behaviors may still apply or indeed increase.

It is also worth noting that the parameters of the mean could further change as technologies such as genome editing develop, although it could be argued that the reasons to think about meddling with a life should be equally strong as the reasons to think about ending it.[13] Having said that, there may be worries about the risks associated with genome editing and other forms of genetic modification that may lessen in the future, which may further change the moral landscape. Likewise, social and contextual changes could shift our future perceptions of the intermediate point. As mentioned above, for example, a heavier emphasis on social justice and inclusion may alter what we see to be challenging. What seems obvious is that further questions and issues are likely to arise; and some may not be currently anticipated.

In thinking about the future, we should not become estranged from the kind of richness and depth of character that will sense the subtleties and significance of reproductive choices. We would argue that that entails, at the very least, thinking seriously about all of the contextual issues explored above, along with how they are balanced in combination. This in turn may encourage that the decisions we make do not put at risk what may turn out to be cherished aspects of our humanity. We are dealing with complex, deeply held, and sometimes conflicting beliefs along with differing hopes and aspirations, in a variety of contexts. Nevertheless, the position we have developed does enable criticism of (prospective) parental choices and decisions on the grounds that they may exhibit both deficient attitudes to parenting and excessive ones. We have suggested that (prospective) parents can show deficient concern for the projected suffering of a potential child or the welfare of other family members. Likewise, termination of pregnancy is likely to be excessive where it is for reasons that do not involve any of the serious contextual issues that we have identified. And while questions about what amounts to excess and deficiency in particular situations are highly debatable, we think that attending to such questions is a fruitful focus of debate.

In trying not to be overly prescriptive, we recognize the difficult and personal nature of reproductive choices, along with the fact that, in the main, (prospective) parental decisions will be entirely honorable and well intentioned. Indeed, other than to suggest that (prospective) parents avoid deficient concern for themselves, their families, and the life they are creating—as well as avoid excessively determining, self-serving, or vain approaches to parenting—we think it shows worthy respect to (prospective) parents to encourage them to negotiate their path between the extremes, given their values and their circumstances. We have presented an analysis of some of the most important contextual considerations that we hope will assist with those deliberations, in the light of current and future reproductive technologies.

Notes

1. Karpin and Savell (2012, 283) further postulate that the interaction between severity and gestational age might work in reverse, "that is, that the threshold for seriousness might be lower early in pregnancy or before pregnancy."
2. Currently, UK prenatal screening takes the form of serum testing in the second trimester, which returns estimates of chance of having a fetus affected by trisomy, leading to the offer of diagnostic amniocentesis at fifteen to eighteen weeks. If NIPT is offered, as recommended, as a second tier screen, it would mean that serum testing is followed by NIPT, to be followed by the offer of amniocentesis to those at raised chance, all of which might mean that amniocentesis results are further delayed.
3. This is not to deny that some people's beliefs about termination of pregnancy may preclude that course of action, even in these types of case.
4. Of course, a child may not consider their life to be worthwhile, but this may be for reasons entirely independent of a diagnosed condition or for reasons that cannot be predicted or assumed. By implication, they cannot form the basis of a defensible reproductive decision.
5. This, of course, would have to be balanced with consideration of the strength and defensibility of a (prospective) parent's view about termination of pregnancy.
6. In this sense, *all* moral decisions could be said to be person affecting, whether or not they result in the birth of a different child or no child at all, as they are likely to deeply affect the person who makes them and, by implication, their capacity to flourish. Thus, while

deliberations about projected suffering may turn out to be non-person-affecting (for example, if one subsequently chooses to terminate pregnancy), we would maintain that they will be intensely personal and person-affecting for the (prospective) parents making the decisions.

7. Karpin and Savell observe further, that the RCOG guidance draws on the World Health Organization's definitions of Assisted and Dependent performance (Karpin and Savell 2012, 260).

8. These are conditions that are harder to classify. They may entail a good or reasonable quality of life yet have a significant impact on parents and other family members.

9. Karpin and Savell (2012, 275) suggest that there will be further complexities that inform the interpretive matrix. We explore some of these in the section on context.

10. Chappell similarly argues that "virtue ethics need not think of itself as a moral *theory*, in the sense of a systematizing enterprise, at all—and is well advised not to" (Chappell 2013, 168).

11. Our discussion is limited to the complexities contributing to individual decisions rather than the complexities involved in setting a public standard; The argument was that WGS information had limited clinical utility, that information would create anxiety, that it would lead to more confirmatory invasive testing, and that lay people generally lacked the information and support necessary to make an informed and ethical decision. However, the working group made an exception for situations where there is a family history of genetic conditions, or where NIPT is used diagnostically after an anomaly has been detected on ultrasound (Nuffield Council 2017).

12. Moreover, technologies like in vitro gametogenesis might further shift our perceptions of an appropriate threshold as well as raising additional moral questions.

13. Karpin and Savell argue, for example, that "the assumption that it is better to take the risks attendant on being born with an altered genome than to be born with a disability is highly questionable" (Karpin and Savell 2012, 326).

REFERENCES

Albrecht, G. A. and P. Devlieger, 1999. The Disability Paradox: High Quality of Life Against All Odds. *Social Science and Medicine* 48(8): 977–988.

Amundson, Ron. 2010. "Quality of Life, Disability, and Hedonic Psychology." *Journal for the Study of Social Behaviour* 40(4): 374–392.

Aristotle. 2009. *The Nicomachean Ethics*. Oxford: Oxford University Press.

Beck-Gernsheim, E. 2011. "The Post-Career Mom: Reproductive Technology and the Promise of Reproductive Choice." In *The Future of Motherhood in Western Societies: Late Fertility and its Consequences*, edited by Gijs Beets, Joop Schippers, Egbert R. te Velde, 149–158. Heidelberg, Germany: Springer.

Bellieni, C. V., and G. Buonocore. 2013. "Abortion and Subsequent Mental Health: Review of the Literature." *Psychiatry and Clinical Neurosciences* 67: 301–310.

Berer, M. 2017."Abortion Law and Policy Around the World: In Search of Decriminalization." *Health and Human Rights* 19(1): 13–27.

Biggs, M. A., U. D. Upadhyay, C. E. McCulloch, et al. 2017. "Women's Mental Health and Well-Being 5 Years after Receiving or Being Denied an Abortion." *JAMA Psychiatry* 74(2): 169–178.

Broadie, S. 1991. *Ethics with Aristotle*. Oxford: Oxford University Press.

Brock, D. 2005. "Shaping Future Children: Parental Rights and Societal Interests." *Journal of Political Philosophy* 13: 377–398.

Buchanan, A., D. Brock, N. Daniels, and D. Wikler. 2000. *From Chance to Choice*. Cambridge, UK: Cambridge University Press.

Chappell, T. 2013. "Virtue Ethics in the Twentieth Century." In *The Cambridge Companion to Virtue Ethics*, edited by D. C. Russell, 149–171. Cambridge, UK: Cambridge University Press.

Chitty, Lyn S., David Wright, Melissa Hill, et al. 2016. "Uptake, Outcomes and Costs of Implementing Non-Invasive Prenatal Testing for Down's Syndrome into NHS Maternity Care: Prospective Cohort Study in Eight Diverse Maternity Units." *BMJ* 354: i3426.

Glover, Jonathan. 2006. *Choosing Children*. Oxford: Clarendon Press.

Häyry, Matti. 2010. *Rationality and the Genetic Challenge: Making People Better?* Cambridge, UK: Cambridge University Press.

Herissone-Kelly, Peter. 2006. "Procreative Beneficence and the Prospective Parent." *Journal of Medical Ethics* 32: 166–169.

Human Fertilisation and Embryology Authority. 2018. *Fertility Treatment 2014–2016: Trends and Figures*, London: HFEA. https://www.hfea.gov.uk/media/2563/hfea-fertility-trends-and-figures-2017-v2.pdf (Consulted 1 December 2018).

Iltis, A. S. 2016. "Prenatal Screening and Prenatal Diagnosis: Contemporary Practices in Light of the Past." *Journal of Medical Ethics* 42(6): 334–339.

Kaposy, C. 2018. *Choosing Down Syndrome: Ethics and New Prenatal Testing Technologies*. Cambridge MA: MIT Press.

Karpin, I., and K. Savell. 2012. *Perfecting Pregnancy*. Cambridge, UK: Cambridge University Press.

Kitcher, P. 1996. *The Lives to Come: The Genetic Revolution and Human Possibilities*. London: Penguin Press.

Kitcher, P. 2006. *Lives to Come: The Genetic Revolution and Human Possibilities*. New York: Simon and Schuster.

Macintyre, A. 1999. *Dependent, Rational Animals: Why Human Beings Need the Virtues*. London: Bloomsbury.

Maclean, A. 1993. *The Elimination of Morality: Reflections on Utilitarianism and Bioethics*. London: Routledge.

McMahan, J. 2005. "Preventing the Existence of People with Disabilities," in *Quality of Life and Human Difference: Genetic Testing, Health Care and Disability*, edited by D. Wasserman, J. Bickenbach, and R. Wachbroit, 142–171. Cambridge, UK: Cambridge University Press.

NHS Commissioning Board. 2010. Clinical Commissioning Policy: Pre-Implantation Genetic Diagnosis, https://www.england.nhs.uk/wp-content/uploads/2013/04/e01-p-a.pdf

Nuffield Council on Bioethics. 2017. *Non-invasive prenatal testing: Ethical issues*. London: Nuffield Council on Bioethics.

Parens, E., and A. Asch. 2003. "Disability Rights Critique of Prenatal Genetic Testing: Reflections and Recommendations." *Mental Retardation and Developmental Disability Research Review*. 9(1): 40–47.

Parfit, Derek. 1984. *Reasons and Persons*. Oxford: Oxford University Press.

Rapp, Rayna. 1999. *Testing Women, Testing the Fetus: The Social Impact of Amniocentesis in America*. New York, NY: Routledge.

Rothman, Barbara Katz. 1993. *The Tentative Pregnancy: How Amniocentesis Changes the Experience of Motherhood*. New York: W.W. Norton.

Royal College of Obstetricians and Gynaecologists. 2010. *Termination of Pregnancy for Fetal Abnormality in England, Scotland and Wales.* London: Royal College of Obstetricians and Gynaecologists.

Sandel, M. 2007. *The Case Against Perfection.* Cambridge: The Belknap Press of Harvard University Press.

Santas, G. X. 1997. "Does Aristotle Have a Virtue Ethics?" In *Virtue Ethics: A Critical Reader,* edited by D. Statman, 260–285. Washington, DC: Georgetown University Press.

Savulescu, Julian. 2001. "Procreative Beneficence: Why We Should Select the Best Children." *Bioethics* 15 (5–6): 413–426.

Schmidt, E. 2007. "The Parental Obligation to Expand a Child's Range of Open Futures When Making Genetic Trait Selections for Their Child." *Bioethics* 21(4): 191–197.

Scott, Rosamund. 2003. "Prenatal Screening, Autonomy and Reasons: The Relationship between the Law of Abortion and Wrongful Birth." *Medical Law Review* 11: 265–325.

Scully, J. L., T. W. Shakespeare, and S. Banks. 2006. "Gift Not Commodity? Lay People Debating Social Sex Selection," *Sociology of Health and Illness* (28)6: 749–767.

Shakespeare, T., and R. Hull. 2018. "Termination of Pregnancy After Non-Invasive Prenatal Testing (NIPT): Ethical Considerations." *Journal of Practical Ethics,* 6(2): 32–54.

Shakespeare, Tom. 1999. "Losing the Plot? Medical and Activist Discourses of Contemporary Genetics and Disability." *Sociology of Health and Illness* (21)5: 669–688.

Shakespeare, Tom. 2006. *Disability Rights and Wrongs.* Abingdon, UK: Routledge.

Slotko, Brian G., Susan P. Levin Goldstein, Eric A. Macklin, Richard D. Goldstein. 2016. "Family Perspectives About Down Syndrome." *American Journal of Medical Genetics* Part A 170A: 930–941.

Slotko, Brian G., Susan P. Levin, and Richard Goldstein. 2011. "Self-Perceptions From People with Down Syndrome." *American Journal of Medical Genetics* Part A 155: 2360–2369.

Smart, J. J. C., and B. A. O. Williams. 1973. *Utilitarianism For and Against.* Cambridge, UK: Cambridge University Press.

Swanton, C. 2013. "The Definition of Virtue Ethics." In *The Cambridge Companion to Virtue Ethics,* edited by D. C. Russell, 315–337. Cambridge, UK: Cambridge University Press.

Taylor-Phillips, S., K. Freeman, J. Geppert, et al. 2016. "Accuracy of Non-Invasive Prenatal Testing Using Cellfree DNA for Detection of Down, Edwards and Patau Syndromes: A Systematic Review and Meta-Analysis." *BMJ Open* 6: e010002. doi:10.1136/bmjopen-2015-010002

Thomas, G. M. 2017. *Down's Syndrome Screening and Reproductive Politics.* Abingdon, UK: Routledge.

Thomas, G. M., and B. K. Rothman. 2016. "Keeping the Backdoor to Eugenics Ajar? Disability and the Future of Prenatal Testing." *AMA Journal of Ethics* 18(4):406–415. doi:10.1001/journalofethics.2016.18.4.stas1-1604.

Traustadottir, R. 1991. "Mothers Who Care: Gender, Disability, and Family Life." *Journal of Family Issues* 12(2): 211–228.

Urmson, J. O. 1980. "Aristotle's Doctrine of the Mean." In *Essays on Aristotle's Ethics,* edited by A. O. Rorty, 157–170. Berkeley: University of California Press.

Urmson, J. O. 1988. *Aristotle's Ethics.* Oxford: Basil Blackwell.

Van Schendel, R. V., A. Kater-Kuipers, E. H. Van Vliet-Lachotzki, W. J. Dondorp, M. C. Cornel, and L. Henneman. 2017. "What Do Parents of Children with Down Syndrome Think About Non-Invasive Prenatal Testing (NIPT)?" *Journal of Genetic Counseling* 26 (3):522.

Van Zyl, L. 2013. "Virtue Ethics and Right Action." In *The Cambridge Companion to Virtue Ethics*, edited by D. C. Russell, 172–196. Cambridge, UK: Cambridge University Press.

Vehmas, S. 2002. Parental Responsibility and the Morality of Selective Abortion. *Ethical Theory and Moral Practice* 5(4): 463–484.

Wilkinson, Stephen. 2010. *Choosing Tomorrow's Children*. Oxford: Oxford University Press.

Williams, B.A.O. 1985. *Ethics and the Limits of Philosophy*. London: Fontana Press.

World Health Organization. 2012. *Safe Abortion: Technical and Policy Guidance for Health Systems*. Geneva: World Health Organization.

CHAPTER 41

BIOETHICS, DISABILITY, AND SELECTIVE REPRODUCTIVE TECHNOLOGY

Taking Intersectionality Seriously

CHRISTIAN MUNTHE

INTRODUCTION

SELECTIVE reproductive technology (SRT) includes all kinds of elaborated human actions undertaken to have procreative attempts result in particular children with certain features rather than other children with other features, whether these features are described in biological, psychological, social, or economic terms. Such actions may involve sophisticated expertise and science but may also consist in combinations of actions that most would view as rather mundane. An example of the first is technologies like those applied in preimplantation genetic diagnosis (PGD) and prenatal testing (PNT) programs. The latter include, for example, reviewing easily observable features of potential partners or the prognosis for how a child born into one's life would be likely to fare when planning when to procreate. In between reside a wide variety of more or less sophisticated and complex practices, including paying attention to vague information about the more or less likely presence of biologically or socially hereditary conditions in families (skin colors, poverty, etc.) or buying commercial "preconception" genetic testing services for partner matching purposes. SRT may also vary in relation to different imagined timelines, one being the temporal order of significant events in a human biological reproductive process (conception, implantation, birth, etc.), another being the time of the procreating person's life across which the action is taken (e.g., within one in vitro fertilization [IVF] cycle; within a focused attempt to achieve a pregnancy across some weeks, months, or years; within the entire segment of someone's life when they plan to have children; and so on). SRT can be undertaken by individuals based on some idea of why it is desirable to attempt to control what children they have. But SRT can also be applied by a society to attempt to control the composition and size of its future population.

In bioethics, there has been particular concentration on those variants of SRT that target microbiological features and involve the use of genetic and assisted reproductive technologies. This also holds regarding what has become known as "the disability criticism" of technologies such as PNT and PGD (Asch and Barlevy 2012; Juth and Munthe 2012; Munthe 1996; 1999; 2015; Parens and Asch 2000; Silvers et al. 1998). This criticism has traditionally been delivered from a rather activist and decided disability rights standpoint. In the academic setting, this standpoint is usually linked to a critical disability studies perspective that explores how a continuous construal of the concept of disability and its role in normative practices claimed to disadvantage disabled people in turn grounds claims with regard to justice. The latter academic perspective belongs to a larger family of what we may call *(critical) social identity studies*, including also (critical) animal studies, gender studies, postcolonial studies, queer studies, race studies, sexuality studies, working class studies, and so on. The disability rights political activist movement in a similar fashion belongs to a larger group of movements employing what has become known as identity political strategies, using descriptions of how their respective types of social identities link to social practices in order to ground claims for justice and societal change. Over recent decades, both these broader areas of thought and political action have been increasingly influenced by the idea of *intersectionality*: the insight that there are many types of social identity that may underlie a position of social (dis)advantage that may ground a claim to injustice in a specific context and that such identity types may freely cluster together in a person or pull apart between persons, as well as within and across a population. While the importance of acknowledging this multitude of social identities has been increasingly recognized by disability study theorists (Ben-Moshe and Magaña 2014; Moodley and Graham 2015; Roulstone et al. 2012), it remains unclear what the outcome of taking an intersection turn at the level of theoretical analysis implies for specific normative ethical and political claims being wielded in the name of disability rights. Specifically, although some initial effort has been made to incorporate intersectionality into bioethical analyses (Hankivsky 2014), what this implies for arguments regarding specific practices is to a large extent left for further exploration.

This chapter explores the effect of applying an intersectional perspective to the traditional disability criticism of (some) SRT. I will argue that it may to some extent serve to strengthen this criticism but that the particularly *overarching* social perspective offered by the intersectional turn seems to partly undermine some of the most powerful themes in the traditional criticism. In particular, intersectionality serves to question any automatic linkage between being disabled and being unjustly disadvantaged, otherwise often assumed in the traditional critique of SRT. It also makes room for a public health perspective on SRT and reproductive policy often shunned or assumed to be unjustifiable by representatives of this criticism. At the same time, the intersectional perspective may serve to broaden the application range of the disability criticism to include all sorts of SRT, not only technologically sophisticated ones. This may or may not be seen as a problematic upshot of that kind of analysis from the standpoint of a more exclusive disability perspective.

INTERSECTIONALITY:
SOME MAIN STRANDS

While the very idea of an intersectional approach to (critical) social identity studies has been the subject of some critical conceptual appraisal (Nash 2008), its core idea seems to be the recognition that, to the extent that social identities are sources of unjust social disadvantage or privilege (in given but transformable societal and institutional contexts), there are a complex multitude of types of such sources. A person's identity-determined disadvantage may stem from this person's gender, looks, physical or mental functionality, wealth or income, cultural practices, sexuality, and so on, including virtually any sort of observable feature that may make social arrangements apply differently to a person due to a perceived difference of group classification based on such a feature. As long as social arrangements apply differently to different people based on such identity classifications, this implies a recognition of social identity as necessarily normative; classifying a person in such categories will activate perceived reasons to have this person treated or valued in one or the other way.

Within the critical social identity studies literature, this insight has been used to point out how, in many instances, social identity sources of social disadvantage cluster together to make the disadvantage worse. For instance, feminist theorists have long struggled to accommodate for the fact that gender-based disadvantage and privilege may come together with ones based on wealth, race, ethnicity, and colonial pasts to produce a variety of very different outcomes, experiences, and available political responses (Mohanty et al. 1991). In the area of disability, this type of claim has been brought forth with regard to, for example, gender, wealth, and race (Ben-Moshe and Magaña 2014; Moodley and Graham 2015; Shakespeare 2012). Already this step away from the focus on singular social identities seems to undermine the otherwise given notion in identity politics of having justice served by compensating or accommodating particular identities identified as disadvantaged. Rather, the idea becomes to first assess which people are *unjustly* disadvantaged (regardless of what social identities attach to them) and then attempt to understand how social identities may figure as sources of this disadvantage (e.g., by being a factor in openly oppressive policies, a structural barrier to constructive social change, an informal impediment due to prevailing normative assumptions, etc.).

Similarly, the more long-standing engagement with the intersectional turn within feminism and gender studies has uncovered how different social identity-based claims may generate incoherent positions. A case in point is the obvious tension between, on the one hand, feminism and LGBT-rights and, on the other, the idea of multicultural rights that allow cultural identities that entail violent oppression of women or other gender or sexual identities to practice their ways. The political theoretical ramifications of such conflicts and tensions have been to some extent addressed by philosophers (Kymlicka 1989, 1995; Wolff and De-Shalit 2007). However, it remains unsolved what to do with the very real possibility of stark conflict between the respective normative claims coming out of different "sections" of an intersectional social identity analysis *from a critical social identity studies and an identity political standpoint.* Therefore, just as taking on your intersectional spectacles may help you spot how worse examples of social disadvantage may link to much thicker and more complex layers of social identities than previously thought, it may also have you see a wider multitude of types of identities, each linked to particular disadvantages. Each such identity competes for social improvement with many others, and, from an identity political perspective, it is just as a priori worthy of winning that race as any of its competitors.

Therefore, a further possibility opened up by the intersectional perspective is that formerly firm identifications of some groups as particularly disadvantaged and unjustly so may crumble. This since, once the intersectional analysis is done and the gravity of different identity-based claims to injustice are assessed, it is an open questions what kind of groups will come out as most unjustly disadvantaged or privileged and what social actions would be recommended on that basis. Intersectionality thus comes with a potential for undermining identity political activist assumptions as they tend to appear in a number of movements, one of which is the disability movement. Holding out the identity of being disabled thus ceases to be an immediate ticket to having a justified priority in social policy, just as any other social identity does.

A unifying feature of these three implications of the intersectional turn is that it demonstrates a need for general normative ethical theory: to kick off the original identification of those who *are* the most unjustly disadvantaged or privileged, to determine the validity of different social identity–based claims when assessing policy suggestions, and to argue about what relative priority (if any) should be given to different social identities in such policies.[1] This has led some scholars to evade intersectionality, to avoid having identity political agendas muddled or the questioning of normative assumptions of particular identity political perspectives (Hindman 2011). But, on the whole, the recognition of the soundness of the intersectional insight seems to be prevailing within critical social identity studies.

At the same time, it is important not to overinterpret the theoretical implications of this general upshot of an intersectional turn for normative bioethics. Intersectionality as such does not a priori favor any particular philosophical standpoint or conclusion. Hankivsky (2014) is certainly right in noting that when care ethics applies a social identity perspective (in that case, as a rule, gender identity), an intersectional turn will open up many complexities and critical questions regarding the normative assumptions and implications for particular areas of care ethics itself. But this does not mean that a care ethical stance is thereby uniquely placed to fill the normative gap in critical social identity studies and identity political activism exposed by an intersectional perspective. Thus, Robinson's claim (2006, 321, my emphasis) that "*only* a care-centered perspective can provide the necessary moral orientation and policy framework through which to begin to solve problems of gender (as well as race and class) inequality related to both wage labour and paid and unpaid care work, as well as problems relating to the under-provision of care on a global scale," is to overstate the impact of intersectionality for bioethics. The lingering question of what underlying philosophical theory is the best one, all things considered, is left open for debate also in the wake of having accepted an intersectional turn of bioethics. At the same time, we may expect such a turn to reveal important aspects no matter what underlying philosophical assumptions guide bioethical analyses that make use of social identity perspectives.

In this brief chapter, therefore, I will not favor any particular philosophical standpoint within bioethics but merely use the disability criticism of SRT as an illustrative case in point for what effect the intersectional turn may have for bioethical argument in this area, applying some already established normative perspectives within bioethics that can each be grounded in many different underlying philosophical theories. These are the normative ethical assumptions that, other things being equal, people should not be negatively discriminated against due to any kind of social identity feature, that people should as a rule not be subjected to coercion or oppression, and that societal institutions have *pro tanto* obligations toward their members to provide public goods and basic resources to secure an overall (unspecified) level of health, security, and wealth.

The Disability Criticism of SRT

The disability-based criticism of SRT has to be distinguished clearly from other types of critical perspectives on PNT, PGD, and similar technologies (e.g., ones rooted in sanctity of life perspectives applied to embryos and fetuses or those emerging out of a general ethical opposition to human meddling in the reproductive process). The disability criticism of these technologies is not about them being morally wrong as such or necessarily involving actions that are morally wrong. Neither is it meant primarily as a moral critique of single individuals making use of PNT, PGD, and other SRTs. Rather, it is about the offer and organization of them in existing social contexts being somehow unjust; through discrimination, derogatory expression, actual oppression, or complicity in or contribution to oppressive and/or discriminatory political structures victimizing disabled people (Asch and Barlevy 2012; Juth and Munthe 2012, 33–42; Silvers et al., 1998).

Roughly, this criticism proceeds along two main strands: what is often called the *expressive argument* and what I will here refer to as a *structural argument*. At the same time, these two strands usually are deployed in support of each other: According to the criticism, what the societal deployment or sponsorship of these technologies is about is to prioritize helping people to avoid having disabled children and instead have other children who are not disabled. This occurs in a societal context heavily rigged against the prospect of welcoming a disabled child without substantial cost. Therefore, the technologies become contextually oppressive even if a standard of free individual choice is upheld. When society allows, offers, and/or promotes these technologies, it thus becomes complicit in this oppression, as well as in the ongoing discrimination against disabled people in terms of lack of inclusion, access to public goods, and prospects for a good life making up the context that makes the technologies oppressive. As society, by this prioritization, publicly expresses a commitment to rather avoid having disabled people existing in the first place than having the conditions of disabled people improved so that the prospect of having such children become less deterring for prospective parents, it communicates and promotes a disparaging message about the value of disabled people compared to people without disabilities. As such (unreflective) disparaging views are already part of the discriminating context making the technologies oppressive, society is thereby both promoting and proclaiming its support of that discrimination.

It should be noted that neither the expressive nor the structural strand of the criticism, or the mix of the two, claim to say something about the morality of the *conscious motives and decisions* of individual people who make use of SRT. A societal practice may be discriminatory and send a discriminatory and derogatory message without any single person at any time harboring any *thought* to such effects. Thus, a couple who make use of PNT or PGD will be participating in a wider social practice having these (communicative and distributional) features, regardless of to what extent they themselves hold the attitudes expressed by this practice and/or attempt to discriminate against disabled people. And even if they were to decide against using such technologies, they will be participating in a social practice perpetuating the false image of a system that promotes "free choice" (Juth and Munthe 2012). As I read it, the disability criticism of SRT is thus not a moral criticism of the intentions and decisions of individual people or of particular patterns of choice made by such people, but a *political* criticism of societal communications and priorities. True, these communications and priorities in turn frame individual reproductive decisions, but this means that people will be complicit regardless of what choices they make regarding SRT and what conscious motives they act on when making these choices. Although sometimes overlooked, this is a vital part of the criticism since Troy Duster's claim about "backdoor eugenics" (Duster 1990): It is *the SRT system* that oppresses, and while a sum of individual actions makes up and serves to uphold this oppression, each of these actions is conditioned by the system and therefore the object rather than the source of the oppression discharged by the societal employment and organization of SRT.

Likewise, although a lot of the bioethics debate around PNT and PGD that have addressed the disability criticism has been concentrating on the idea of selecting children based on purely genetic features, it is clear that the point of the criticism remains valid for whatever mechanism influencing the expected feature of possible children we consider. It does not matter from the point of view of justice if the source of the social identity (or target of discrimination) is transmitted through biological heredity, through biological environmental factors, through sociocultural mechanisms, or through some combination of these. The injustice held out by the disability criticism remains the same: these techniques are about accommodating to and thereby become complicit in existing discriminatory social structures. They offer people the opportunity to avoid having children who will otherwise be the victims of such discrimination rather than mobilizing social resources to stop the basic injustice.

Admittedly, there exist quite a bit of critical appraisal of various factual claims included in this criticism (Asch 2002; Buchanan et al., 2000; Chadwick 2006; Gillam 1999; Glover 2006; Juth and Munthe 2012; Parens and Asch 2000; Silvers et al. 1998; Wilkinson 2010). However, I will not question this aspect in the present context as it seems to be inconsequential to the issue of the impact of an intersectional appreciation of the critique. Rather, what is at stake is which normative conclusions are supported by the criticism, assuming that it is factually correct but viewed through an intersectional lens. So this is what the next section will be about.

Intersectionally Reframing the Disability Criticism of SRT

One immediately visible impact is this: to the extent that the social employment of PNT, PGD, and similar technologies do disparage, discriminate, oppress, or serve to socially exclude disabled people, those thereby *most* burdened and disadvantaged can be expected to be so through a multitude of social identity sources (and adjacent practices). That is, although the focus of the conception of reproductive control articulated in policy and practice related to SRT is on the presence or nonpresence of disabled persons in society, the alleged injustice of SRT may not stem from the presence of that particular type of social identity but mostly from other sources. For instance, the disadvantages in question may be assumed to hit those people worst who lack financial resources or live in cultural contexts with constraining norms and expectations linked to reproduction and parenting that would increase the discriminatory effect of having a disabled child, such as hostility toward people of particular sexual orientations, gender identities, or combinations of such becoming parents. In contrast, wealthy prospective parents in emancipated cultural contexts as regard reproduction and parenting, with a variety of gender and sexual identities widely recognized as fitting for having and caring for children, will face much less restriction of a real freedom of choice with regard to having a disabled child or not, partly since a disabled child in such a context will be far from as disadvantaged as one in a less privileged context. As long as brute state force is not used to enforce obligatory eugenic programs using SRTs, especially the wealth aspect would therefore seem to be much more important than the social identity of disability itself for determining the extent to which prospective parents would be oppressed, and their prospective disabled child discriminatorily disadvantaged, to an extent that could ground valid claims to injustice grave enough to warrant compensatory policy. If you only have the money, you can as a rule buy yourself and your child out of almost any social disadvantage burdening those less privileged.

Moreover, this intersectional image of the disadvantages suffered by disabled people that can be related to reproductive choices highlights how the traditional disability-based criticism of *high-technological variants* of SRT seems to be much more far-reaching in its implications. The core of the criticism is that it is the ability to control what children to have based on information about their expected features (in terms of the presence or nonpresence of allegedly disabling conditions) in light of prevailing social discrimination or disadvantaging of disabled people and their families that makes the practices of PNT, PGD, and the like unjust. However, the worst instances of this discrimination—thus the ones lending the strongest support to the claim about oppression and injustice—are now revealed by the intersectional turn to be not only *discrimination "due to disability"* but, just as well or to a greater extent, "due to" a number of other social identities, many of which seem to be more strongly linked to social disadvantage than disability, not least those relating to reproductive normative culture and wealth. This seems to mean that also socioeconomic, ethnic, or culturally normative (e.g., religious) considerations informed by some expectation of the features of a possible child would be as oppressive or unjust if used to control what children to have. That is, very nontechnological variants of SRT, such as choosing one's reproductive partner based on membership in some shared cultural community (e.g., religious faith), or a preferred physiological feature (such as skin, hair, or eye color), or socioeconomic status, also seem to be just as potentially unjust or oppressive as the much more debated PNT, PGT, and the like.[2]

Now, of course, it may still hold that disabled people themselves mostly hear from a system of SRT *a message* about the inferiority of disabled people. Moreover, they may (for good reason) take offence with this message, and it may plausibly be argued to constitute a bona fide "expressive harm" (Blackburn 2010). However, what is revealed by the intersectional analysis seems to be that a number of other social identities have just as good—if not better—reasons to take similar offence and claim similar expressive harm; it is just that they have not before had the social analysis available that makes these reasons and this harm visible. Simply put, when looking at programs of PNT and PGD, we see them as *being about* (avoiding) disabled people mostly because this is the social identity out of which our perception is framed. The intersectional turn, however, reveals this impression to be simplistic—the programs are just as much (or more) about structurally discriminating against people on the basis of poverty, culture, gender, or sexual identities, or other factors at work within societal structures that produce unjust outcomes. And it is not obvious that the reasons for disabled to take offence with PNT and PGD programs are more salient and strong than, for example, poor people's reasons to be offended by a system that keeps them in poverty.

But it does not end there. As recent works in population ethics have revealed, a number of very common reproductive choices not ordinarily thought of as selective in fact seem to involve selection between different possible future people. Due to the so-called nonidentity problem, famously characterized by Derek Parfit (1984, chap. 16), also "ordinary" family planning measures meant to adjust the timing of one's reproductive attempts across a life-span (using abortion, contraceptives, celibacy, etc.) amount to selecting between different potential future children. Such planning is typically made with socioeconomic considerations in mind, but may also be assumed to involve a non-negligible portion of being framed and influenced by normative-cultural ideals of parenthood and family formation (for instance, in relation to age, gender, social status, and other things), all affecting expected features of possible children under different conditions. For instance, being a young, financially deprived parent will affect the expected features of the child born as compared to if the parent would have been more mature and financially secure. Likewise, having children within an unstable relationship, with a partner one is not really interested in forming a family with, can also be expected to affect the features of children born under such conditions, as compared to more favorable relational conditions. On a more societal level, the design of policies around reproduction, parenthood, and family formation (e.g., parental social insurance, access to safe reproductive healthcare, day care services for returning to work, and so on) will likely affect what reproductive choices people can be expected to make, partly based on their perception of what the surrounding societal support system (or lack of such) will mean for the expected features of the child. Due to the nonidentity problem, most of these choices will be selective between different children, thus making the use of that information for reproductive planning just as much SRT as the use of PNT or PGD and making it potentially just as unjust and oppressive (as many of the factors we use to make these choices become relevant to us because of a surrounding discriminatory structure of a cultural and/or socioeconomic nature).

Both of these upshots of an intersectional perspective point to a challenge to the traditional, disability-based criticism of SRT having to do with its assumed identity political focus on disability. Even if SRT is unjust and oppressive in the way claimed by the critique of PNT and PGD, the intersectional turn reveals that this injustice should not necessarily be cashed out in terms of a *social identity of disability*. What the criticism is ultimately targeting (SRT) as a whole has only a minor portion of its variants openly addressing disability as a basis of selecting future children, and disability as such seems to have only a minor role in defining those in society who are most disadvantaged. SRT as a whole targets a large number of social identity types, with linked disadvantages mostly through broad cultural norms or socioeconomic circumstances independently of any disability, rather than discriminatory structures targeting disabled people or their families as such.

None of this needs to undermine the soundness of the critical social identity studies basis of the disability criticism of SRT. Rather, in line with Tom Shakespeare's observation with regard to the situation of disabled people in developing countries (Shakespeare 2012), the upshot is the discovery that an intersectional reading disentangles such an analysis from the identity political agenda otherwise associated with it: to improve the conditions of disabled people and to mitigate unjust discriminatory effects and disadvantages suffered by such people—that is, the very sort of structures making SRT unjust and oppressive according to the traditional disability criticism—we should focus not particularly on the social identity of disability or the type of SRT targeting it, but instead address broader factors mostly contributing to disadvantaging the people who are worst off (that is, culturally exclusionary reproductive norms and socioeconomic factors). Likewise, when addressing this worst-off group, we should accept that many of its members do not have "disability" as a primary social identity while realizing that a general "uplift" in terms of health, wealth, and individual emancipation will lift also those disabled people who are among the most disadvantaged in a society. In more orthodox terms, this could be reformulated as preferring a *general* social policy to mitigate basic disadvantaging conditions for all people, regardless of social identity, over selective policies targeting only some such identities to compensate these in particular for assumed injustices due to underlying disadvantaging and discriminatory factors that in fact seem to burden all who suffer them.

A particular upside of having the SRT criticism target the (most disadvantaging) underlying factors that may make all kinds of SRT unjust–rather than only *particular* SRT given the presence of such factors–is that disability political activism thereby can avoid the identity political trap of normative emptiness exposed by the intersectional turn. Faced with the challenge of why justice for disabled people should be prioritized before that of women, or gays, or poor people, the answer coming out of the intersectional analysis is that it should not necessarily be so prioritized. Instead, politics should target the most important discriminatory and disadvantaging factors for people who are worst off, regardless of their social identity. This may then benefit the worst-off of all social identities, who within an identity political setup would otherwise be forced to compete with each other for priority. Only two types of social identities seem to be excluded from this opportunity, namely, those linked to normative ideals that imply support for discrimination and disadvantage for the rest, such as members of cultural (e.g., religious) communities who want to retain a privilege of applying their norms to others while not similarly adapting themselves, or privileged people who want to hold on to affluence at the price of impeding the elevation of the conditions of the worst-off. It is, of course, open for broader debate to what extent a society should or should not grant such claims, but, in contrast to its identity political variant, an intersectionally interpreted critical social identity analysis of SRT will not provide any immediate reason to answer that question affirmatively.

However, taking a step back, it may actually do so *indirectly* due to pragmatic reasons, and this will be my last observation about the impact of applying an intersectional analysis to the disability criticism of SRT. Moving the focus to a more generalized scope of lifting all kinds of disadvantaged people in a society, I earlier mentioned general emancipation of individuals and general economic improvement. This may have relevant implications for how to view SRT in general and the more technological variants like PNT and PGD in particular that run contrary to the typical view advanced in the traditional disability criticism of these technologies.

One such implication arrives via the apparent fact that promoting population health through mitigating the general incidence of ill health in a society is usually an important element in policies aiming to lift disadvantaged people in society generally. But, of course, one way of trying to realize such a public health–oriented policy aim is to use SRT to attempt to prevent the birth of disabled people. Normally, that view of SRT is harshly dismissed from a disability rights standpoint, but such dismissal is not as obvious once the intersectional spectacles have been put on. As has been pointed out (Juth and Munthe 2012; Munthe 2015; Wilkinson 2015), to what extent a public health aim of, for instance, PNT or PGD, would be unjust toward disabled people and their (prospective) families may depend on to what extent policies pursued with such an aim would be needed to generally benefit the same group of people. So, if a society has limited means to emancipate and promote the situation of its worst-off members generally at the same time as the needs for assistance are drastic (e.g., due to poverty and lack of societal capacity), effecting a reduction in the volume in that very need may be a necessary means to be able to secure a general improvement of the conditions of the worst-off, including those in that group who are disabled.

Likewise, if a society is so structured that a sustainable emancipation and promotion of the health and wealth of society's most disadvantaged is dependent on dynamic factors of importance for growth, this may necessitate pragmatic adaption to special preferences of the more privileged (to have them keep their assets and resources in this society). Usually such preferences regard the freedom to dispose of one's assets as one pleases and to be able access various goods, among which may, of course, be various types of SRT. In parallel, if the uplift works, the conditions of disabled people and their families will at the same time improve with the rest, albeit disability will always imply a comparative downside (otherwise it is no disability). As more members of society are uplifted, more and more will have such special preferences, for instance to be able to use SRT to their liking (for whatever reason)—although they could manage all right without such technologies as society has now improved to make it possible to have a decent life also as a disabled person or as a family with a disabled child. One example of this is, of course, the current use in many developed and rich countries—not least the wealthier segments of such societies—of techniques such as PNT and PGD. Another example may instead be people who want to be able to continue to use SRTs of a more low-tech kind, such as selecting reproductive partners based on features influencing what people they are attracted to, such as hair or skin color, gender, sexual orientation or identity, cultural or religious group membership, or—indeed—visible disability and other things linked to expected features of their future children.

As already noted, none of this is to deny that someone who identifies as belonging to a social group targeted by such uses of SRT may rightfully experience derogatory or discriminatory messages and take offense with these. Such "expressive harm" may indeed be a price of the kind of social developments just described. However, pointing to a reason for taking offence or noting a particular harm is far from proving injustice. The intersectional reframing of the disability criticism of SRT has laid bare both that disabled people are far from alone in having good reasons to react against social disadvantage and discrimination in social systems where SRTs are used and that addressing the totality of these disadvantages to ease the injustice for all may require a pragmatic acceptance of a continuation of this use.

CONCLUSION

If you want to retain a narrow identity political focus of your activism, enhancing your underlying critical social identity analysis of society with an intersectional turn will often bring uncomfortable implications. So also when it comes to the traditional disability rights–based criticism of SRT in the form of PNT, PGD, and other technologically sophisticated means for selecting which children to have based on expectations of their features. Taking intersectionally seriously forces the critical disability analysis to embrace a larger view, both of the structure and roots of social disadvantage and injustice and of what social structures and practices are in fact included in the scope of the traditional criticism of SRT. It is far from obvious anymore that the specific social identity of disability provides the most important or obvious base for criticizing societies' attempts to control reproductive outcomes.

At the same time, as the intersectional reinterpretation of a critical social identity perspective on SRT is taken to its conclusion, it would appear that the outcome has some positive aspects from the point of view of disabled people. First, it serves to force disability rights politics out of an identity political competition where disadvantaged groups try to overtrump each other to justify compensation for alleged injustice without any access to a normative principle that could solve the issue. Second, it redirects the focus to social disadvantage as such, regardless of identity, and general policies aimed to lift disadvantaged people in terms of freedom, health, and wealth. At the same time, SRT may have an important role to play in such policies, both to facilitate them and as lingering side effects due to human preferences that remain when social conditions are much improved. In any case, if you start off from a disability rights standpoint and ask what an intersectional turn of critical disability studies means for what view to take on SRT, the answer seems to be: never mind SRT, mind whatever underlying social factors exist that may make SRT appear oppressive or unjust and attend to those factors to then see what SRT will be left at the other end of policy!

ACKNOWLEDGMENTS

I am grateful for the critical commentaries on a draft of this chapter provided by Dorna Behdadi, Leila El-Alti, John Eriksson, Robert Hartman, Thomas Hartvigsson, Benjamin Matheson, Per-Erik Milam, and Sofia Jeppsson. In addition, the editors of this collection provided a number of helpful suggestions for improvement. This work was supported by the Swedish Research Council for Health, Working Life and Welfare (FORTE), contract no. 2014-4024, for the project Addressing Ethical Obstacles to Person Centred Care; the Swedish Research Council (VR), contract no. 2014-40, for the project Lund-Gothenburg Responsibility Project; and the Dutch Research Council (NWO), project no. 236-20-009, for the project Practices of Responsibility in Change.

NOTES

1. Considerations like these have been addressed in discussions of the justification of civil disobedience activism in terms of a need for such a justified activist measure taken by some group to further its cause to be coordinated with other groups with potentially worthy (and possibly more important) causes (Rawls 1971; Raz 1979).
2. Again, what triggers the discriminatory effect of the system of having SRT available or on offer is independent of what the conscious beliefs and intentions are of those individuals who use (or choose not to use) SRT. A couple who uses SRT for the reason that most of their upper-middle-class friends do will nevertheless be complicit in the system of injustice created by the employment and organization of SRT in a society (or so the disability criticism alleges). Likewise, when people orientate their reproductive partner selection toward people of similar features, they will be complicit in a societal system making room for such segregative reproductive choices. The fact that people themselves do not think of or strive for this aspect is no argument against the structural function of the system.

REFERENCES

Asch, A. 2002. "Disability, Equality, and Prenatal Testing: Contradictory or Compatible?" *Florida State University Law Review* 30: 315–342.

Asch, A., and D. Barlevy. 2012. "Disability and Genetics: A Disability Critique of Pre-natal Testing and Pre-implantation Genetic Diagnosis (PGD)." In *eLS Encyclopedia of Life Science*. Chichester: Wiley. doi: 10.1002/9780470015902.a0005212.pub2

Ben-Moshe, L., and S. Magaña. 2014. "An Introduction to Race, Gender, and Disability: Intersectionality, Disability Studies, and Families of Color." *Women, Gender, and Families of Color* 2(2): 105–114.

Blackburn, S. 2010. "Group Minds and Expressive Harm." In *Practical Tortoise Raising: and Other Philosophical Essays*, edited by S. Blackburn, 64–89. Oxford: Oxford University Press.

Buchanan, A., D. W. Brock, N. Daniels, and D. Wikler. 2000. *From Chance to Choice—Genetics and Justice*. Cambridge: Cambridge University Press.

Chadwick, R. (ed.). 2006. *Ethics, Reproduction and Genetic Control*, Revised edition. London: Routledge.

Duster, T. 1990. *Backdoor to Eugenics*. New York: Routledge.

Gillam, L. 1999. "Prenatal Diagnosis and Discrimination Against the Disabled." *Journal of Medical Ethics* 25: 163–171.

Glover, J. 2006. *Choosing Children: Genes, Disability and Design*. Oxford: Clarendon Press.

Hankivsky, O. 2014. "Rethinking Care Ethics: On the Promise and Potential of an Intersectional Analysis." *American Political Science Review* 108(2): 252–264.

Hindman, M. D. 2011. "Rethinking Intersectionality: Towards an Understanding of Discursive Marginalization." *New Political Science* 33(2): 189–210.

Juth, N., and C. Munthe. 2012. *The Ethics of Screening in Health Care and Medicine: Serving Society or Serving the Patient?* Dordrecht: Springer.

Mohanty, C. T., A. Russo, and L. Torres (eds.). 1991. *Third World Women and the Politics of Feminism*. Bloomington: Indiana University Press.

Moodley, J., and L. Graham. 2015. "The Importance of Intersectionality in Disability and Gender Studies". *Agenda: Empowering Women for Gender Equity* 29(2): 24–33.

Munthe, C. 2015. "A New Ethical Landscape of Prenatal Testing: Individualizing Choice to Serve Autonomy and Promote Public Health: A Radical Proposal" *Bioethics*, 29(1): 36–45.

Munthe, C. 1999. *Pure Selection: The Ethics of Preimplantation Genetic Diagnosis and Choosing Children without Abortion*. Gothenburg: Acta Universitatis Gothoburgensis.

Munthe, C. 1996. *The Moral Roots of Prenatal Diagnosis*. Gothenburg: Royal Society of Arts and Sciences in Gothenburg.

Nash, J. C. 2008. "Re-Thinking Intersectionality." *Feminist Review* 89(1): 1–15.

Rawls, J. 1971. *A Theory of Justice*. Cambridge, MA: Harvard University Press.

Raz, J. 1979. *The Authority of Law: Essays on Law and Morality*. Oxford: Clarendon Press.

Parens, E., and A. Asch (eds.). 2000. *Prenatal Testing and Disability Rights*. Washington, DC: Georgetown University Press.

Parfit, D. 1984. *Reasons and Persons*. Oxford: Oxford University Press.

Robinson, F. 2006. "Beyond Labour Rights: The Ethics of Care and Women's Work in the Global Economy." *International Feminist Journal of Politics* 8(3): 321–342.

Roulstone, A., C. Thomas, and N. Watson. 2012. "The Changing Terrain of Disability Studies." In *Routledge Handbook of Disability Studies*, edited by N. Watson, A. Roulstone, and C. Thomas, 3–11. Abingdon, UK/New York: Routledge.

Shakespeare, T. 2012. "Disability in Developing Countries." In *Routledge Handbook of Disability Studies*, edited by N. Watson, A. Roulstone, and C. Thomas, 271–284. Abingdon, UK/New York: Routledge.

Silvers, A., D. Wasserman, and M. B. Mahowald. 1998. *Disability, Difference, Discrimination: Perspectives on Justice in Bioethics and Public Policy*. New York/Oxford: Rowman and Littlefield.

Wilkinson, S. 2010. *Choosing Tomorrow's Children: The Ethics of Selective Reproduction*. Oxford: Oxford University Press.

Wilkinson, S. 2015. "Prenatal Screening, Reproductive Choice, and Public Health. *Bioethics*" 29(1): 26–35.

Wolff, Jonathan, and Avner De-Shalit. 2007. *Disadvantage*. Oxford: Oxford University Press.

CHAPTER 42

PROCREATION AND INTELLECTUAL DISABILITY

A Kantian Approach

SAMUEL J. KERSTEIN

WHAT does Kantian ethics imply regarding procreative decisions involving offspring with intellectual disabilities? Kant's Formula of Humanity commands us to treat persons always as ends in themselves, never merely as means. Treating persons as ends in themselves requires respecting their dignity. In this chapter, I offer a partial reconstruction of the Formula of Humanity: a set of jointly necessary conditions for respecting the dignity of persons. I then argue that selecting against embryos or early fetuses that would develop intellectual disabilities (e.g., due to Down syndrome) does not typically fail to respect the dignity of persons according to these conditions.

I then turn to appeals to the Formula of Humanity bioethicists have recently made in efforts to defend positions in procreative ethics. According to Paul Hurley and Rivka Weinberg, in some "nonidentity" cases parents treat their child merely as a means and thereby wrong her (Hurley and Weinberg 2015). Suppose, for example, that despite knowledge of the risks posed by the Zika virus, a couple, in order to relieve parental pressure to produce grandchildren, reproduce in the midst of an outbreak. If the child they have suffers from Zika-induced intellectual disabilities, the couple treat her merely as a means and thus wrong her, Hurley and Weinberg imply. I try to demonstrate that their appeal to the Formula of Humanity is misguided, at least if we accept the Kantian dictum that "ought implies can."

David Wasserman claims inspiration from the Formula of Humanity in developing a necessary condition for morally permissible procreation (Benatar and Wasserman 2015). I urge rejecting this condition, partly because it does not take account of an idea I see as central to the Formula of Humanity: persons have a worth *in* themselves that is independent of how well their lives go *for* them. As a result of neglecting this idea,

Wasserman's condition sometimes implausibly implies that, in producing a child with intellectual disabilities, parents contravene the spirit of the Formula of Humanity, or so I attempt to show.

RESPECT FOR THE DIGNITY OF PERSONS

An agent treats a person as an end in herself only if she respects the person's worth or, equivalently, her dignity. Elsewhere, I have developed a Kant-inspired account of respect for the dignity of persons (Kerstein 2013). Before presenting this account, which I refer to as "KID," some preliminary remarks are in order. First, KID is intended to be a reconstruction, not an interpretation, of part of the Formula of Humanity. Some philosophers might judge that KID departs too much from Kant's doctrine to warrant the label "Kantian." I disagree, especially since I do not think that the label applies only to views that would have been endorsed by Kant, but that is a debate for another occasion. Second, KID does not specify jointly necessary and sufficient conditions for honoring persons' dignity; it is intended merely to shed light on much, but not all, behavior that fails to do so. Third, KID is not to be taken as a categorical imperative commanding us to refrain from all conduct that would fail to respect someone's dignity. Whereas Kant presumably holds that such conduct is always wrong, all things considered, KID specifies merely a *pro tanto* wrong. It is consistent with KID to hold, as I do, that we always have strong reasons to respect the dignity of persons but that these reasons might be outweighed by other reasons. An action might not respect the dignity of a person according to KID yet, in my view, be morally permissible, all things considered. For example, it might fail to respect the dignity of a person according to KID to refrain from saving his life and personhood in a tragic situation in which one had to choose between saving him and preventing quadriplegia in thousands of people (assuming, plausibly, that the quadriplegia would not truncate their existence as persons). But it is consistent with KID to hold, as I suspect many of us do, that failing to respect the person's dignity is morally permissible, all things considered.[1]

An abridged version of KID, which is sufficient for our purposes, is as follows[2]:

Dignity is a special status possessed by persons. This status is such that:

1. A person ought not to use another merely as a means. This first aspect of persons' special status is lexically prior to the following aspect:
2. If a person treats another in some way, then she ought to treat him as having unconditional, preeminent value.

An agent's treatment of a person respects the dignity of that person only if it accords with the special status just described.

KID requires clarification on several points. This is not the place to investigate in detail how to specify the notion of persons in KID. But here is a Kantian account, put forth as a proposal open to modification.[3] A being is a person only if it has the capacities to set and pursue ends, strive for coherence among its ends, be self-aware, conform its actions to practical rules that specify means to ends, and be motivated to act by some moral imperative. By a moral imperative, I mean a rule that someone sees as requiring her to do certain things even if she judges that refraining from doing them would better promote her immediate satisfaction or overall happiness. This account of a moral imperative leaves room for the possibility that a being is a person and yet never envisages her action to be morally constrained by, say, Kant's Formula of Universal Law. In addition, to count as a person, a being must not only possess but also have *exercised* the capacity Kant seems to associate most directly with humanity: the capacity to set and pursue ends. If a being possesses all of the capacities just described and has exercised the capacity to set and pursue ends, then it is a person.

The account incorporates a broad interpretation of what it means to possess a capacity. According to the account, for example, a typical toddler has the capacity to be motivated to action by a moral imperative given that, if her development proceeds as expected, she will be able to be motivated in this way. But a being who, practically speaking, cannot and will not be able to exercise one or more of the capacities fails to have them and so is not a person. In principle, a living being from another planet or a nonliving artifact such as a sophisticated computer might possess all of the capacities constitutive of personhood. A human being who has died or is alive but whose cerebrum can no longer function is not a person in the sense of the term employed here since, practically speaking, he neither can nor will be able to exercise the capacities.

I will not try here to answer the question of precisely when, in its development, a typical human being becomes a person. If human embryos and first-trimester fetuses do not engage in goal-directed activity, then they are not persons. If infants do engage in such activity, as appears to be the case (Woodward and Gerson 2014), then they presumably are persons. I will assume for the remainder of this chapter that human embryos and first-trimester fetuses are not persons, according to the Kantian criteria I have set out.

Personhood is here meant to be a threshold concept. If one has the features constitutive of it, one has personhood, no matter how well- or ill-developed those features may be. I have no expertise in assessing cognitive or psychological capacities. But, in my view, those who have Down syndrome would typically pass the threshold of personhood.[4] From what I can gather, it is likely that some children born with Zika-induced microcephaly would, but others would not, pass this threshold.

A few points are in order regarding the first plank in KID, namely, the constraint against treating others merely as means. First, "others" here refers to other persons. If, as we are assuming, embryos and first-trimester fetuses are not persons according to KID, then this constraint does not apply to them. Second, even if embryos were persons, parents would, in refraining from selecting them for procreation, typically not be treating them merely as means. To treat someone *merely as a means*, an agent must treat the person *as a means*: she must *use* that person. On my understanding, an agent uses another if and only if she intentionally does something to or with the other in order to realize her end, and she intends the presence or participation of the other to contribute to the end's realization.[5] But in refraining from selecting embryos parents would not typically be using them according to KID, for they would not intend the presence or participation of the embryos not selected to contribute to their end, say, of having a child.[6] Third, in selecting against an embryo with a certain genotype, for example, an embryo with trisomy-21 (Down syndrome) parents would not be treating existing persons with the same genotype, for example, existing persons with Down syndrome, merely as means. The reason for this is simple. The parents' action of selecting against an embryo with a particular feature would not itself involve using existing persons with this feature at all. In performing this action, the parents would not intend the presence or participation of these persons to make any contribution to their end (e.g., avoiding having a child with that trait). Finally, I have developed a detailed account of conditions under which someone treats another merely as a means (Kerstein 2013). Suppose a person uses another. She uses him merely as a means, I contend, roughly if the other can neither consent to her use of him nor share the proximate end(s) she is pursuing in using him. But there is no need here to elucidate or apply an account of such detail.

In its second plank, KID specifies that every person has a status such that if an agent treats him in some way, then she ought to treat him as having unconditional, preeminent value or, equivalently, worth. An agent treats another in some way, according to KID, just in case she intentionally does something to another to promote an end she is pursuing. Treating another in some way is a broader concept than using another: if a person uses another (i.e., treats him as a means), she treats him in some way, but if she treats another in some way, she does not necessarily use him. For example, suppose that a police officer who is running after a suspect intentionally pushes a bystander out of her path. She treats the bystander in some way, but does not use him, if, as is plausible to assume, she does not intend the bystander's presence or participation to contribute to her end of catching the suspect.

According to the concept invoked in KID, something has unconditional value only if there are no conditions, actual or possible, under which it exists but lacks value. Moreover, if a being possesses unconditional value, this value does not vary on the basis of its intelligence or talents, its instrumental value to others, or the magnitude of its health-related quality of life, personal satisfaction (i.e., happiness, in one sense of the term), or well-being. Its value also does not vary according to its impersonal value; that is, the value that an impartial rational spectator would assign to it.

To say that an unconditionally valuable being of a particular kind has preeminent value is to say that no amount of anything that is not a being of that kind can have a value equal to or greater than a being of that kind. Let us assume that persons have unconditional value. To say that they also have preeminent value is to imply that no amount of anything that is not a person can equal the value of a person. It is to imply that persons have a value that transcends that of nonpersons. Part of holding that an unconditionally valuable being has preeminent worth is, according to our concept of such worth, to hold that if one treats the being in some way, this treatment ought to reflect that the being has such worth.[7]

According to KID, respecting the dignity of persons requires that they be treated as having preeminent worth. But that fails to entail that nonpersons ought to be or even permissibly can be treated as mere things. Elsewhere I argue that it is consistent with

KID to treat some nonpersons (e.g., nonhuman animals) as having a value beyond price (Kerstein 2013). Kant himself sometimes suggests a division of the world into beings with dignity, who must be treated with respect, and all the rest, which may be treated as mere things (Kant 1996). But we need not follow that suggestion. There is room in Kantian ethics for the idea that beings (e.g., first-trimester fetuses or adults devoid of personhood) have a special value or status, albeit not equivalent to that of persons.

An agent treats another person as having unconditional, preeminent value, according to KID, if and only if, in the given context, the action she performs is among those that she might perform if she reasonably believed her action to be successfully and absolutely constrained by her holding the other to have this value (as the value is defined earlier). The notion of reasonableness at work here is nonmoral. What it is reasonable for an agent to believe is what the evidence available to the agent favors, given the information she has, her education, her upbringing, and so forth. An agent would not be treating another person as having unconditional, preeminent value if she kills him solely to prevent some third party from losing half of his inheritance (assuming, plausibly, that it is not reasonable for the agent to believe that money has unconditional worth). This action is not among those that she might perform if she reasonably believed what she did to be constrained by her holding persons to have unconditional, preeminent worth. The third party's balance sheet is obviously not the same thing as his personhood; a person who is poorer than he otherwise might be is still a person. But the one the agent kills is no longer a person.

Personhood or, equivalently, the capacity of rational choice, is something over and above a particular exercise of this capacity. To avoid failure to respect the worth of persons according to KID, agents typically need not promote, or even refrain from thwarting, a person's particular exercise of his capacity of rational choice. Among the ways of treating another that, an agent might reasonably hold, sometimes accord with the notion that persons have Kantian worth would be, for example, her denying the other's request for career guidance or defeating the other in an election. However, it would typically not be reasonable to believe that diminishing someone's overall capacity to exercise her rational nature (e.g., by luring her into heroin addiction) would harmonize with holding persons to have unconditional and preeminent worth.

Selecting Against Embryos and Respect for the Dignity of Persons with Intellectual Disability

Is the action of choosing not to implant an embryo on the grounds that it would develop into an individual with an intellectual disability disrespectful of the worth of persons according to KID? Suppose that through in vitro fertilization (IVF), parents have generated three embryos. Preimplantation genetic diagnosis has revealed that one of the embryos has trisomy-21 (Down syndrome), another has trisomy-13 (Patau syndrome, which results in severe mental and physical disability and death within one year for around 90% of patients), and the third has no known genetic disorder. Two of the embryos, if implanted, are expected to develop into persons, as defined earlier (i.e., the one with Down and the one with no known genetic disorder) and one embryo is not expected to develop into a person (i.e., the embryo with Patau syndrome). Previous to the IVF procedure, the parents decided that if it yielded any embryos, they would implant at most one. The parents implant the embryo with no known genetic disorder and discard the remaining embryos.

Do they thereby fail to respect the dignity of persons according to KID? KID would not imply that the parents fail to respect the dignity of any of the three embryos, including the ones they refrain from implanting. Since, as we are assuming, embryos are not persons according to KID, they do not have dignity to respect.

But are the parents failing to respect the dignity of any existing persons? To focus on what seems to be the possibility most worthy of consideration, are they failing to respect the dignity of people with Down syndrome? Regarding KID's first plank, the parents are not treating these people merely as means. In implanting one embryo and discarding the others they are not treating *these people* as means at all. The parents are not using them. They do not intend the presence or participation of people with Down syndrome to contribute to their ends in acting; for example, the end of having a nondisabled child.

But in implanting the one embryo and discarding the two others, including the one with trisomy-21, are the parents violating KID's second plank? Are the parents treating persons with Down syndrome in some way, but not as having unconditional, preeminent worth, and thereby failing to respect their dignity? No, for the simple reason that the parents are not treating persons with Down syndrome in any way at all. An agent treats another in some way, according to KID, only if she intentionally does something to another. But the parents are not intentionally doing anything at all to persons with Down syndrome.

Someone might object that the notion of a person treating another in some way employed in KID is too narrow. What if we employ a wider notion, according to which someone treats another in some way just in case she intentionally does something to another in order to promote an end she is pursuing *or* she does something that she foresees will have some effect on the other? That is a very wide notion of treatment. Someone taking a walk would, for example, presumably foresee that she would have some effect on all of those passers-by who so much as register her presence. If she does foresee this, she would count as treating all of those passers-by in some way even though, in an ordinary sense, she doesn't do anything to them. (Embedding this wide notion of treatment into KID might threaten KID's overall plausibility, but I will set this concern aside.)

Now let us return to our case of the parents and their embryo selection. Of course, even if we employ this wide notion of someone's treating another in some way, the parents are not treating existing persons with Down merely as means; they are not using them at all. But are they treating them as having unconditional, preeminent worth? Even our very broad notion of treatment would limit persons with Down syndrome the parents treat in some way to those the parents intentionally do something to in order to promote an end they are pursuing or those they foresee will be affected by their conduct. We can plausibly assume that in implanting the one embryo and discarding the two others they are not intentionally doing anything to persons with Down. In likely contexts, we can also plausibly assume that they would not foresee their conduct to have any effect on such persons. After all, their actions are presumably private, known only to themselves and fertility clinic professionals, including their doctors.

Suppose, however, that the couple do foresee that their conduct will impact someone with Down syndrome, namely, a person who learns what they have done. They foresee that, through family gossip, their cousin who has Down syndrome will eventually find out. He will, they believe, be upset by their embryo selection, taking it to imply that, in their view, it is better not to bring people like him into existence. Nevertheless, their embryo selection is presumably among the actions the couple might perform if they reasonably considered their conduct to be successfully and absolutely constrained by their holding their cousin to possess unconditional and preeminent worth. The conduct might result in the cousin suffering, for example, from a temporarily diminished sense of self-worth. But, they might reasonably hold, since it would not destroy his capacity of rational choice or overall undermine its effective exercise, their conduct would not fail to respect his dignity according to KID.

This example helps to illustrate the general point that parents' actions of selecting against embryos or aborting first-trimester fetuses that would develop into persons with intellectual disabilities typically do not run afoul of KID. However, I do not wish to imply that all choices regarding which embryos or fetuses to allow to develop (and become persons) would be free from dignity disrespecting implications. Consider a country in which there is state-funded universal health coverage, including coverage for genetic testing, in vitro fertilization, and preimplantation genetic diagnosis. Suppose that the head of state is contemplating forbidding by executive order use of state funds to implant embryos with Down syndrome and offering with such funds a financial incentive for aborting fetuses with Down syndrome. Let us further suppose, plausibly, that the head of state's action would amount to treating persons now living with Down syndrome in some way in the wide sense specified earlier; as she foresees, it would affect some of them. Is the action she is contemplating among those she might perform if she reasonably considered her conduct to be successfully and absolutely constrained by her holding persons with Down syndrome to possess unconditional and preeminent worth? Perhaps not. Such an order, which, we assume, would become public, might trigger in some persons with Down syndrome unrelenting feelings of unworthiness. And it might also encourage others to oppress these persons verbally and/or physically. These effects might undermine in some persons with Down syndrome their overall ability to exercise their capacity of rational choice, it might be reasonable for the head of state to believe. It might be that her signing the executive order would fail to respect the dignity of persons according to KID.

In contrast to this head of state, parents selecting against embryos or early fetuses that would develop into persons with intellectual disabilities would not typically disrespect the dignity of persons according to KID. But KID does not purport to contain jointly sufficient conditions for respecting the dignity of persons. Therefore, I stop short of concluding definitively that such selection honors Kantian dignity. In effect, I have derived a provisional conclusion regarding procreation from a partial reconstruction of the Formula of Humanity.

Treating Offspring Merely as Means in Nonidentity Cases?

Recently, philosophers have claimed that Kant's Formula of Humanity implies or at least suggests conditions regarding the moral permissibility of procreation. I now turn to their claims, discussing them in relation to children with intellectual disability.

Hurley and Weinberg associate the Formula of Humanity with a set of conditions under which procreation is wrong. They argue that in some "nonidentity" cases, a parent treats her child merely as a means and fails to treat him as an end in himself. Consider an example, based on one developed by Derek Parfit, of a 14-year-old girl who wants to have a baby. Instead of heeding advice to wait until she is an adult and prepared for motherhood, she decides that it is better for her to have a child now and gives birth to a son, Rick. Had she postponed having a child, she would have given birth to a different individual. Hurley and Weinberg claim that she wrongs Rick even if he approves in retrospect of her decision to have him on the basis of how well his life is going for him. Indeed, Hurley and Weinberg suggest that the mother treats Rick merely as a means (Hurley and Weinberg 2015). I remain agnostic here regarding whether, in her procreative actions, the mother wrongs Rick or in some other way acts wrongly. But I argue that if we embrace "ought implies can," we must deny that wrongness in the mother's treatment of Rick (if there is any) would stem from her treating him merely as a means.

The scope of the Kantian constraint on treating others merely as means extends only to persons. Unless a being is a person, the mother cannot be wronging it by treating it merely as a means. The mother's action of getting pregnant through sexual intercourse does not itself treat any person merely as a means—neither gametes nor zygotes are persons. Suppose the mother is in the first trimester of her pregnancy, gets advice to abort given her unpreparedness for child rearing, but continues her pregnancy because she believes having a child will make her happy. At the time she takes the action of continuing her pregnancy, she does not treat any person merely as a means, at least if we adopt the Kantian notion of a person sketched earlier, for a first-trimester fetus is not a person. The mother's procreative actions could, by definition, amount to treating another merely as a means only if and only when they have actually resulted in the existence of another person.

Hurley and Weinberg suggest that the teenage mother's actions treat the person she helps to produce, Rick, merely as a means. They say that nonidentity cases, like the one involving this mother, are "cases in which a perpetrator brings a victim into an interaction which violates the victim's second-personal claims, treating him as a mere means whose claims can be discounted in the satisfaction of her own ends. This wrongful interaction with the victim is also a 'but for' cause of the victim's existence" (Hurley and Weinberg 2015). Hurley and Weinberg follow Stephen Darwall (2006) in envisaging a second-personal claim as one that some particular individual addresses to another or to others. Such a claim typically gives those to whom it is addressed decisive reason to honor it. But the claim need not derive from consideration of the outcome that would be best for the person who has the claim or from consideration of the outcome that would be best overall. For example, a person might have a claim that a physician not force him to undergo some medical treatment even if his undergoing it would be best for him (e.g., maximize his well-being) and best overall (e.g., maximize overall well-being).

In effect, Hurley and Weinberg assert that the mother treats Rick merely as a means in the following way: in using him to attain her own end, she discounts second-personal claims he has on her.[8] The mother's end in having Rick is something like that of making herself happy, for example, by producing someone who, she believes, will always love her. But which of her son's second-personal claims does the mother discount to attain this end? Hurley and Weinberg do not specify, but they must be claims like that he have interaction with a parent conducive to his having an overall good life in terms of his well-being or that he have the love and attention from a parent to make it likely that he will flourish.[9] Given the scope of the Kantian principle, the mother actually treats Rick merely as a means only once he has passed the threshold of personhood.

Hurley and Weinberg are appealing to a Kantian principle forbidding the treatment of persons merely as means. Another principle Kant and Kantians typically endorse is "ought implies can": if someone is morally obligated to do something, then she can do it, or, equivalently, if someone cannot do something, then she is not morally obligated to do it.[10] This principle of "ought implies can" can be interpreted using various notions of what "can" amounts to. On one notion, which seems to me to be implied by Kant's own thinking, an action is possible for an agent only if she is able to perform it given the laws of nature and her particular context. So it is not possible for me right now to jump 10 feet vertically from a standing position.

Now we can see why Hurley and Weinberg's position is problematic. In their idiom, to say that Rick has a claim on his mother to do something is to say that she has a moral obligation to do it. So if we embrace "ought implies can," we hold that Rick has a claim on his mother to interact with him in a manner conducive to his well-being only if she *can* do so. Now it was in her power to put off pregnancy until she became an adult. If she had done that, then she perhaps could have interacted with her later-arriving child in this way. But this later-arriving child would not be Rick. Rick would not exist. The mother simply cannot interact with Rick in a way conducive to his well-being. It is built into the example that the mother does not have the maturity to do so. Whether because of brain development or circumstances, she is, in Hurley and Weinberg's words, "not competent to care for him" (16). In light of "ought implies can," that the mother cannot (and, we might add, could not, even if she had put off pregnancy) give Rick the care he needs entails the following: she does not have a moral obligation to provide it. In effect, Rick does not have a second-personal claim vis-à-vis his mother to do so. So, contrary to what Hurley and Weinberg assert, the young mother cannot be treating Rick merely as a means by subordinating his second-personal claim against her to the promotion of her own interests. If the mother's procreative actions are wrong, it is not because in performing them she is treating Rick merely as a means.

Let us turn to another case—one directly relevant to procreation and intellectual disability. A couple are considering having a child during a Zika virus outbreak. Their doctor advises them to wait until after the outbreak passes entirely or at least until winter, when it's far less likely that mosquitos will transmit Zika to them; if they do not wait and the fetus becomes infected during pregnancy, there is a significant chance that their child will be born with microcephaly. But since they want a child now, partly to dissipate unpleasant pressure from their parents, they have Karen, who is born with microcephaly. As a result, she is blind and has an intellectual disability that impacts her life significantly but leaves her above the threshold of Kantian personhood. Hurley and Weinberg would presumably say that the couple have treated Karen merely as a means. In using her to attain their end, they have discounted second-personal claims Karen has on them, such as the claim on them to give her a start in life conducive to her flourishing, and thereby wronged her. But it would be impossible for the couple to do this for Karen. Any child they did give such a start to would not be Karen, but rather someone else. In effect, if ought implies can, Karen does not have the second-personal claim at issue on her parents. Therefore, her parents are not treating her merely as a means by privileging their interests over the satisfaction of a second-personal claim she has on them. If the couple wronged Karen or in some other way acted wrongly in having her—and I am not here taking a position on whether they did—it is not because they treated her merely as a means.

Of course, Hurley and Weinberg might respond to this objection by rejecting "ought implies can." But note that versions of that principle have many adherents, not least among Kantians, including Darwall, to whom Hurley and Weinberg appeal for their account of second-personal reasons.

MOTIVES FOR PROCREATION AND RESPECT FOR THE VALUE IN PERSONS

Recently, David Wasserman has claimed inspiration from the Formula of Humanity in developing a necessary condition on morally permissible procreation. To be morally permissible, he says, procreation must be done for good reasons (Benatar and Wasserman 2015). By good reasons he means: first, the intention and expectation that the child have a life that is good for him, that is, one in which his well-being (e.g., pleasure, achievement) outweighs his ill-being (e.g., disease, disappointment); second, the intention and expectation that the child's parents have a mutually rewarding relationship with the child (Benatar and Wasserman 2015). Both of these reasons involve acting for the good of the child. If prospective parents fail to act on these reasons in procreating, then they act wrongly according to Wasserman.[11] A couple's procreating is morally permissible, he holds, only if they can justify it to their offspring. But a couple cannot do this, he suggests, if they do not act for good reasons as he specifies them (200–201).

Wasserman suggests that acting on these reasons "is the closest that prospective parents can come to treating a future child as an end but not a mere means" and that if parents fail to do so, they treat their future child with disrespect (205). Wasserman's main claim seems to be not that prospective parents literally violate the Formula of Humanity in undertaking procreation without doing so for the reasons he specifies, but rather that they violate the spirit of the principle.

Contrary to Wasserman, I argue that procreating without doing so for these reasons can accord with the spirit of the Formula of Humanity at least on my, admittedly incomplete, reconstruction of it. Reflection on this reconstruction will, moreover, shed light on why procreating might be morally permissible even if prospective parents do not act with the intentions he requires.

According to the Kantian account (KID) sketched earlier, the dignity of persons demands that they be treated, whether by themselves or by others, as having a special worth. This unconditional, preeminent worth does not vary based on persons' talents, instrumental value to others, health, personal satisfaction, or well-being. The dignity of persons demands that they be treated as having inherent worth (i.e., a worth *in them*), which is distinct from the value of their lives in terms of happiness (i.e., the value of their lives *for them*).

An example illustrates a challenge to Wasserman's views. Different parents procreate for different reasons, and some, perhaps even most, do so for more than one reason. With no claim to being exhaustive, one recent list (Lecce and Magnusson 2015) mentions eight different reasons, including to "experience the wonders of gestation and childbirth" and to "establish genetic connections with future generations." Suppose a couple procreate for these two reasons and, in addition, for a particularly Kantian one, namely, to bring into existence a very special being: one with dignity. To retain connection with everyday thinking, let us not take the parents to have precisely the notion of dignity embedded in KID. They envisage a being with dignity, let us assume, as one who has a special intrinsic worth: a being who, as long as it lives, has a worth in it that is constant, no matter how well its life goes for it and no matter what others' evaluation of it might be. They might think of this worth in human beings as stemming from features we share with God—as a kind of holiness. So this couple procreate for three distinct reasons. In addition, let us suppose they procreate against the background of a side constraint they have adopted. They would not have a child unless they believed that the good things in its life, such as friendship and delight, would outweigh the bad things, such as loneliness and suffering.

Wasserman is committed to the view that this couple act wrongly in procreating. Among their reasons for doing so we do not find the two he claims to be necessary for morally permissible procreation: the intention and expectation that the parents have a mutually rewarding relationship with him and that the child have a life that is overall good for him. Granted, the couple would not procreate if they did not believe that the good for their offspring would outweigh the bad. But, Wasserman suggests, that they procreate against the background of this side constraint does not entail that they do so to provide their offspring with a life that is good for him, as morally permissible procreation in his view requires (201).

The idea that the couple act wrongly in procreating strikes some of us as implausible, intuitively speaking. Perhaps the couple would act wrongly if they failed entirely to consider their child's interests. But they do take his interests into account. If they did not think that he would have a life that was overall good for him, they would not have had him.

Since the couple do not act on the reasons Wasserman specifies, they act contrary to the spirit of the Formula of Humanity, he believes. He even suggests that they treat their future child with disrespect. If we employ a very wide notion of treatment, then, in procreating, the couple do treat their child in some way, for they do something that they foresee will have some effect on him. Yet it seems far-fetched to claim that they treat him with disrespect. They bring him into existence in part because he will be the sort of being who is worthy of respect. In doing that, they obviously do not dishonor the worth that will exist in him. In a roughly analogous way, an artist might undertake a sculpture to bring into existence something of great aesthetic worth. In doing that, the artist would obviously not dishonor the worth that, she hopes, will inhere in her work. Perhaps Wasserman thinks it suffices to render the couple's procreation disrespectful that they do not produce their child to give him a life that is overall good for him. But why would that be disrespectful, given that they procreate on condition that they believe he will have a life that is overall good for him? Why does respect require more than that? Again, in a roughly analogous way, suppose that our artist does not produce a sculpture in order that it be well-cared for and well-displayed. It seems far-fetched to say that the artist's action is disrespectful of the sculpture if she creates it on condition that, in her view, it will be well-cared for and well-displayed.

Wasserman suggests that in acting on the reasons he specifies, the couple would be getting as close as possible to treating their future child as an end in himself (205). I do not wish to dispute that *one way* parents might approach treating their future child as an end in himself would be to act in order to bring about what is good for him. After all, what is good for him will at least in part be what promotes ends he sets and pursues through the exercise of his capacity of rational choice, ends such as finding a fulfilling way to support himself. But another way parents might get close to treating their future child as an end in himself would be to act to bring into existence special worth *in him*. It seems to me that either one of these two reasons for procreation would be in the spirit of the Formula of Humanity.

The example of the couple having a child has aimed to illustrate that, contrary to Wasserman, one can procreate for reasons that do not include the ones he specifies and yet both act rightly intuitively speaking and exhibit something like Kantian respect for one's progeny. That a couple have a child but not from the motive that he have a life that is overall good for him and that they and he have a mutually rewarding relationship fails to entail that they act wrongly or disrespectfully.

In response, Wasserman might point out that the discussion thus far has left out a key element of his view. According to him, that which makes it wrong to procreate for reasons that do not include the ones he specifies as good is that doing so renders parents unable to justify their having a child to the child herself. For procreation to be rightful, Wasserman holds, it must be justifiable to the individual it brings about (200). Human existence involves hardship: failure, pain, loneliness, and so forth. Imagine a teenager in the midst of such hardship telling her parents that she did not agree to be born and asking them what warrant they had to make her. It seems plausible to wonder whether her parents would be offering her sufficient justification if they said only that they had her to "experience the wonders of gestation and childbirth" and to "establish genetic connections with future generations." But suppose they also said, sincerely, to their teenage daughter that she has a special worth—one that does not vary depending on how well her life goes for her or what others think of her and that they reproduced in part to bring into existence a being of such special worth. And they point out that they would not have had her unless they believed that the good things in her life would outweigh the bad. Would they not then have provided a sufficient justification? That justification differs from the kind Wasserman takes to be legitimate, namely, a justification based on the parents' attempt to realize what is *good for* their offspring. But why can't an effort to realize what is *good in* one's child, independent of the grounds Wasserman endorses, constitute part of a sufficient justification for procreation?

Let us now return to disability. I am concerned that Wasserman's Kant-inspired conditions on morally permissible procreation would implausibly deem wrong some cases, or at least possible cases, of having an intellectually disabled child. Suppose that a woman in the first trimester of pregnancy learns that she is carrying a child who would in all likelihood develop into a person with autism. (Prenatal screening for autism has not been developed to date, but, for the sake of this example, we are supposing otherwise.) She has a brother with autism and has found it impossible to develop a loving relationship with him. It saddens her very much, but she does not expect to have a mutually rewarding relationship with the child she is carrying.[12] The woman has access to abortion, and she does not object to it in this case on moral grounds. She believes that, if brought to term, this child, like her brother, will have a life overall good for him. She intends to do her very best to make sure this happens. On this basis, as well as on the basis that the child will become a person, a being with a special intrinsic value, she continues her pregnancy and gives birth to him. In continuing her pregnancy, this mother seems to fail to fulfill one of the criteria Wasserman presents for morally permissible procreation. Granted, we may be convinced that in the end she *will* develop a mutually rewarding relationship with her autistic child. But that point is orthogonal to the criterion, which focuses on the mother's motivation. She fails to be motivated by the intention and expectation that she will have such a relationship because she thinks it impossible. And since she fails to act on this motive, she acts wrongly, according to the criterion. This conclusion does not strike me as very Kantian. Echoing the notion of respect for dignity embedded in KID, it seems to me that this mother can have a respectful attitude toward her future child even if her motive to have him did not include the prospect of a mutually rewarding relationship with her or another parent.

I have developed one Kantian perspective on ethical issues that arise in the context of having or choosing not to have children with intellectual disabilities. From this perspective, selecting against producing a child with intellectual disability does not typically fail to respect the dignity of persons. Moreover, contrary to what Hurley and Weinberg have recently implied, in nonidentity cases parents do not wrong their intellectually disabled child by treating her merely as a means. Finally, David Wasserman specifies what are surely good motives for procreation. But parents need not act on these motives to accord with the spirit of the Formula of Humanity, I have argued. Parents can act in harmony with this principle in producing an intellectually disabled child even if they produce him not to develop a mutually rewarding relationship with him, but rather for the sake of the special worth in him.

ACKNOWLEDGMENTS

Thanks to Greg Bognar, Adam Cureton, John Vorhaus, and David Wasserman for helpful comments.

NOTES

1. Elsewhere I defend KID's plausibility. See Kerstein (2013), especially chapters 3 and 5.
2. For a complete statement of KID, see Kerstein (2013, 127–128).
3. For a different account, see Kerstein (2013, 16–23).
4. It seems to me, for example, that individuals with Down syndrome discussed in detail by Andrew Solomon (2012, chap. 4) would clearly pass this threshold.
5. For defense of this account of an agent using another, see Kerstein (2013, 56–59).
6. Testing an embryo for genetic abnormalities would count as using it. If embryos were persons, testing them for such abnormalities would amount to using persons.
7. For a more thorough characterization of preeminent worth, see Kerstein (2017).
8. This assertion does not reflect my own notion of treating another merely as a means. But I accept for the sake of argument Hurely and Weinberg's idea that doing so involves subordinating the honoring of another's moral claims to the pursuit of one's own interests.
9. Let us assume, as seems to be implicit in the example, that Rick's father is totally unavailable to be a parent.
10. For a list of passages in which Kant affirms that "ought implies can" and makes closely related claims, see Stern (2004, 53–55).
11. Wasserman says that procreating "must be done for good reasons, or with good intentions. Those good reasons . . . concern the good of a particular kind of life for a future child, and the good for her and her prospective parents of the relationship she will enjoy with them" (Benatar and Wasserman 2015, 200; see also 188). But, in personal communication, he has indicated that, according to his considered view, procreation can be morally

permissible even if it is not motivated by the prospect of a mutually rewarding relationship with the child.

12. This example is not intended and should not be taken to imply that persons with autism spectrum disorder (ASD) are typically incapable of forming loving relationships. According to researchers, most children with ASD want to have friends and to interact socially (May and Reinhart 2012). The example would presumably be implausible if a lack of interest in close relationships were not a feature of *some* people with ASD. But evidence suggests that it is (Chevallier et al. 2012).

REFERENCES

Benatar, David, and David Wasserman. 2015. *Debating Procreation: Is It Wrong to Reproduce?* New York: Oxford University Press.

Chevallier, C. et al. 2012. "The Social Motivation Theory of Autism." *Trends in Cognitive Sciences* 16(4): 231–239.

Darwall, Stephen 2006. *The Second-Person Standpoint: Morality, Respect, and Accountability.* Cambridge, MA: Harvard University Press.

Hurley, Paul, and Rivka Weinberg. 2015. "Whose Problem Is Non-Identity?" *Journal of Moral Philosophy* 12(6): 699–730.

Kant, Immanuel. 1996. *Groundwork of the Metaphysics of Morals.* Translated by Mary Gregor. Cambridge: Cambridge University Press.

Kerstein, Samuel. 2013. *How to Treat Persons.* Oxford: Oxford University Press.

Kerstein, Samuel. 2017. "Dignity, Disability, and Lifespan." *Journal of Applied Philosophy* 34(5): 635–650.

Lecce, Steven, and Erik Magnusson. 2015. "Do Motives Matter?: On the Political Relevance of Procreative Reasons." In *Permissible Progeny?: The Morality of Procreation and Parenting,* edited by Sarah Hannan, Samantha Brennan, and Richard Vernon, 150–169. Oxford, UK: Oxford University Press.

May, Tamara, and Nicole Reinhart. 2012. "Five Myths About Autism." *The Conversation* March 19.

Solomon, Andrew. 2012. *Far from the Tree: Parents, Children and the Search for Identity.* New York: Scribner.

Stern, Robert. 2004. "Does 'Ought' Imply 'Can'? And Did Kant Think It Does?" *Utilitas* 16(1): 42–61.

Woodward, Amanda, and Sarah Gerson. 2014. "Mirroring and the Development of Action Understanding." *Philosophical Transactions of the Royal Society of London. Series B, Biological Sciences* 369(1644): 20130181.

CHAPTER 43

PARENTAL AUTONOMY, CHILDREN WITH DISABILITIES, AND HORIZONTAL IDENTITIES

MARY CROSSLEY

A child's marked difference from the rest of the family demands knowledge, competence, and actions that the typical mother and father are unqualified to supply, at least initially.... Whereas families tend to reinforce vertical identities from earliest childhood, many will oppose horizontal ones. Vertical identities are usually respected as identities; horizontal ones are often treated as flaws.

—Andrew Solomon, *Far from the Tree*

PARENTAL AUTONOMY

PARENTS enjoy a wide degree of latitude in raising their children. Notwithstanding copious advice on how to raise healthy, well-adjusted children, parents are typically the ultimate arbiters on the vast majority of questions entailed by raising a child. These questions range from the mundane to the profound. They comprise decisions about day care, schooling, extracurricular activities, social activities, media consumption, discipline, religious upbringing, and medical choices. While not unlimited, parents' broad authority to make decisions regarding their children's upbringing—or parental autonomy—is widely recognized in law, philosophy, and common understanding.

Indeed, because of the wide range of decisions parents must make in rearing children, we can think of parents as "constructing" their children's identity to some degree.

Notwithstanding findings from genetics and brain science that some aspects of a child's personality, interests, and physical endowments are innate or "hardwired," other research into the development of children and adolescents confirms the influence of parents (Beyers and Goossens 2008). Parents' own emotional investment and modeling of behavior can influence how children develop, and parents' choices about the external influences to which their child will be exposed also shape, though they rarely control, the environmental factors influencing child development. In short, parents' choices about how to raise their children may play a significant role in forming the person who emerges from childhood and adolescence.

Justifications for Parental Autonomy

What justifies giving one person (the parent) such substantial authority over decisions affecting the welfare and future identity of another person (the child)? Numerous justifications have been advanced for recognizing parental autonomy (Schneider 1995). One rationale is that respect for the pluralistic nature of our society precludes any one-size-fits-all set of rules for raising children. As the US Supreme Court put it nearly 100 years ago, our system of government "excludes any general power of the state to standardize its children" (*Pierce v. Society of Sisters*, 1925).

More fundamentally, however, deference to parental authority reflects an understanding that—since children are not equipped to care for and make decisions for themselves—parents ordinarily are best suited to fill the roles of caregivers and decision-makers. Imperfect though they may be, parents are superior to alternative decision-makers with respect to child-rearing, for a range of reasons.

One argument for parental superiority emphasizes that child welfare itself requires broad deference to parents' child-rearing decisions. The idea is that parents' daily proximity and involvement mean they are most likely to know and understand their child's needs. Moreover, parents are believed to harbor "natural affection" for their children, motivating them to make decisions that will advance the child's welfare.

A more parent-centered account for strong parental autonomy rights also exists. If parents must bear responsibility for providing and caring for their children, they must have a corresponding right to make the decisions entailed by those responsibilities. According to this account, parental satisfaction with and commitment to their roles as parents depends in part on their freedom to make parenting decisions consistent with their own values and priorities (Altman 2015). A related justification views parental autonomy from a social welfare perspective. Society depends on parents and families to produce well-adjusted, virtuous citizens and thus must permit parents to do that job without being subject to undue state intervention.

Though they may sometimes conflict with one another, these justifications for parental autonomy are often complementary and mutually reinforcing. Indeed, deference to parental authority has attained constitutional stature in the United States. As early as the 1920s, the Supreme Court recognized "the liberty of parents to direct the upbringing and education of children" (*Pierce v. Society of Sisters*, 1925). More recently, the Court reconfirmed that the Constitution "protects the fundamental right of parents to make decisions concerning the care, custody, and control of their children" (*Troxel v. Granville*, 2000).

Questioning Strong Deference to Parental Autonomy

Notwithstanding these rationales, some scholars have questioned the soundness of reflexively deferring to parents' authority regarding child-rearing. Barbara Bennett Woodhouse, for example, traces how the constitutional recognition of parental auton- omy grew out of a patriarchal view of the family, where parents (more particularly, fathers) effectively had a property right in children and their labor (Woodhouse 1992). Woodhouse cautions against a vision of parental autonomy that treats children as essen- tially a conduit for parental preferences. Similarly, some feminist scholars have criti- cized current approaches as treating children as objects of parental (and state) authority, rather than recognizing children as subjects whose own interests are entitled to respect (Rosenbury 2015). On a more practical level, a strong version of parental autonomy may leave children unprotected against choices that depart from their best interests and cause lasting harm. And evidence that the decisions of parents in culturally dominant groups, as compared to minority parents, receive greater deference from the state sug- gests that cultural biases infect the existing regime of deference to parental authority (Chiu 2008).

All that said, parental autonomy is not unbounded. Child welfare laws in each state define child abuse and neglect, thus establishing minimally acceptable levels for the care and control that parents must provide their children. If parents' conduct falls below these floors, the state is permitted to intervene to protect the child's safety and welfare (Schneider 1995). Thus, the child welfare system is the primary institutional limit on parents' ability to make decisions about their children.

Child abuse and neglect laws apply to parents' decisions about what medical care to provide—or withhold from—their child (Wadlington 1994). States may intervene to protect a child whose parents' medical decisions threaten her with death, serious harm, or a substantial risk of serious harm. For example, if parents refuse to consent to a life- saving blood transfusion for their child, the state may step in for the limited purpose of compelling that treatment over the parents' objections. State courts hearing these cases tend to view narrowly the circumstances when intervention is appropriate. If the harm a child faces as a consequence of his parents' medical decision is not truly severe, or if the chance of a harmful outcome from the decision is less than certain, courts typically default to deferring to parents' authority.

Parental Autonomy and Medical Choices for Children with Disabilities

How do these general principles apply to cases involving medical choices for children with disabilities? Medical decision-making for children with disabilities has been contentious for more than three decades. An early example of Congressional involvement in child welfare (typically the domain of state law) was in response to the widely publicized Baby Doe case in 1982. Baby Doe was born with Down syndrome, along with an esophageal blockage that could have been corrected with relatively routine surgery. Baby Doe's parents refused to consent to the surgery, and the infant died of starvation days after being born. Congress enacted the Child Abuse Amendments (CAA) in 1984, requiring states to define medical neglect to include parents' failure to provide life-saving medical treatment for infants with disabilities. This legislation limited parental authority to elect "selective nontreatment" for infants with disabling conditions.

Societal attitudes toward Down syndrome have shifted significantly since the early 1980s, but the CAA's incursion on parental autonomy remains controversial. Today, the controversial cases involve extremely premature infants whose long-term health and functional prospects are uncertain and for whom life-saving measures may be invasive, painful, and expensive (Conway 2009; Ouellette 2011). Decisions about whether to compel potentially life-saving treatment for severely compromised infants highlight the difficulty of drawing appropriate boundaries around parental autonomy.

This chapter focuses on a different type of case: *elective* medical interventions for children with disabilities. Here, the question is not whether the state should assume limited custody to compel treatment rejected by parents, but instead whether it may sometimes be appropriate to limit parents' authority to affirmatively pursue some types of interventions. This loosely defined category of elective interventions includes, among others, limb-lengthening surgery for children with dwarfism, facial surgery to diminish visible markers of Down syndrome, insertion of cochlear implants for deaf children, or sterilization of girls with developmental disabilities. Parents may decide to pursue such interventions for a variety of reasons. In some cases, parents may seek to normalize the child in some fashion in an effort to ease the stigma of difference for the child or to attempt typical (or near-typical) functioning. In other cases, the justification may be to make the child (and, later, adolescent and adult) easier for the parent to care for.

This chapter explores whether sometimes a child's disability may provide a basis for deviating from the standard presumption of parental autonomy to pursue these sorts of elective medical interventions. In short, should we be less sanguine about deferring to parents' judgments about elective interventions when the children involved are disabled? While many scholars and clinicians have analyzed ethical aspects of these judgments (Ouellette 2010; Parens 2006), this chapter's analysis is informed primarily by legal and constitutional thinking.

Similar Cases

Questions about parental autonomy to use medical, surgical, or psychological means to somehow alter a child are not limited to cases involving children with disabilities. Similar questions have arisen with respect to decisions to pursue sex-assignment surgery for intersex infants (Greenberg 2012), to subject children to conversion therapy designed to change their sexual orientation, and to follow cultural or religious traditions that involve cutting the genitals of girls. Movement has occurred in each of these areas to constrain parents' autonomy to alter their children. In the United States, the most severe limitation is found in federal legislation, passed in 1996, criminalizing the practice of female genital mutilation. A number of states prohibit mental health professionals from subjecting minors to "conversion therapy" that attempts to change their sexual orientation or gender identity. And, although no legislation in the United States to date addresses surgery for intersex infants, intersex advocates have pressed the issue in litigation and as a human rights issue. Rationales for limiting parental authority in these scenarios offer helpful points of comparison as we consider possible limits on parental autonomy regarding children with disabilities.

JUSTIFICATIONS FOR LIMITING DEFERENCE

What might justify limiting deference to parents' authority to pursue elective medical interventions for children with disabilities? This chapter considers five concerns about a strong version of parental autonomy in those cases (Koll 2010). The concerns fall into two broad categories: concerns based on potential harm to the child and concerns undermining justifications for parental autonomy. First, some of the elective interventions intrude significantly on the child's current or future interests in bodily integrity and reproductive capacity—interests that normally receive a high degree of legal protection against invasion. Second, in some cases, the elective interventions may seek to modify, or normalize, a trait that could be central to the child's identity. Third, because non-disabled parents do not share the impairments that are important to disabled children's identity, parents may be less able to appreciate what their child's welfare requires. Fourth, parents making decisions for their children with disabilities may have particularly strong conflicts of interest. And fifth, parents' decisions may be influenced by inaccurate but widely held stereotypes of disability—either their own or those of the health professionals treating the child. In a case where several points in this constellation of concerns co-exist, their cumulative effect may justify some constraints on parental decisions.

Invading Bodily Integrity and Reproductive Capacity:
The "Ashley Treatment"

The so-called Ashley treatment is an elective intervention that exemplifies many of the foregoing concerns but that illustrates particularly vividly concerns about invasions of bodily integrity and reproductive capacity. The moniker comes from the case of a young girl with severe physical and intellectual disabilities whose parents chose to subject her to hormone therapy to stunt her growth (thus ensuring her permanent short stature) and to surgically remove breast bud tissue and her uterus (thus preventing the development of breasts and sterilizing her). The parents sought this combination of interventions so that it would be more feasible for them to continue to care for Ashley at home as she (and they) aged. Reports at the time and more recently document that Ashley was not an isolated case, but that other parents in the United States and the United Kingdom have made similar choices (Field 2016).

Others have debated at length the ethical justifiability of parents' pursuit of such interventions, and my point here is not to rehash that debate (Wilfond et al. 2010). However sympathetically one views the parents' justifications, depriving a child of all reproductive capacity and the ability to develop into physical adulthood seriously invades interests that the law normally protects.

Indeed, sterilization of a minor is one of the few instances where the law regularly constrains parental autonomy regarding medical decisions (Tamar-Mattis 2006). Parents may seek sterilization of their developmentally disabled daughter (or son, but most often it is a daughter) in order to protect against possible pregnancy and motherhood. Today, consensus exists, though, that the permanent deprivation of reproductive capacity so seriously affects a disabled child's core interests that parents' authority must be checked. Parents typically must obtain prior court approval of the sterilization, with the court determining whether permanent sterilization advances the disabled offspring's best interests. This response recognizes that too much is at stake for the disabled child to permit parents to be the sole arbiters of a sterilization decision.

Thus, a medical decision may exceed the proper scope of parental autonomy if it infringes substantially and permanently on the reproductive capacity and interests of a disabled (or any) child. A principle requiring the protection of a child's core interests against severe and permanent infringement by parents' medical choices should be generalizable. Children—including those with profound disabilities—also have strong interests in maintaining their bodily integrity (Cantor 2004; Hill 2015). Although the existence and scope of a right to bodily integrity is the subject of philosophical debate (Viens 2014), from a legal perspective it is well recognized, at least in cases involving compelled invasion of the body. For that reason, disability advocates have argued that the medical interventions designed to stunt Ashley's growth and to prevent the development of her breasts also lay beyond the pale of parental authority (National Disability Rights Network 2012). Administering hormones and surgically excising Ashley's breast buds invaded her bodily integrity and diminished—both literally and figuratively—her ability to develop physically into an adult. While some question whether we should understand individuals with severe intellectual disabilities as having the same interests in physical integrity and developmental potential, these arguments disregard both the reality that we do not truly know what persons with severe intellectual disabilities experience (Kittay 2011) and key premises of the disability rights movement that people with disabilities are entitled to equal respect and dignity, including respect for bodily integrity.

Similar concerns also arise with respect to other interventions that parents may choose for children with disabilities. A prime example is limb-lengthening surgery for children with dwarfism. Parents who pursue this intervention commit their children to a series of painful surgeries that entail breaking bones and inserting metal screws (Solomon 2012). Other medical choices that parents make for their children—such as cancer treatment—may involve multiple surgeries and prolonged therapy, but these other interventions respond to a threat to the child's health. When physically invasive and painful treatments are not primarily therapeutic, but are instead pursued to accomplish a more normal appearance for the child or convenience for the parents, assertions of parental autonomy may require interrogation.

Affecting a Child's Identity

Thus, in the United States, a child's interests in reproductive capacity and physical integrity may sometimes limit the exercise of parental authority. Less well established in the law, but the subject of burgeoning scholarly consideration, is the idea that a child has an interest in maintaining core aspects of that child's identity (Ronen 2004). Parents' decisions to use medical means to somehow normalize a child with a disability or cure her impairment may, in some instances, threaten an important aspect of the child's identity.

Using the term "identity" risks complicating this discussion as the term may refer to either a person's self-conception (or "personal identity") or the person's identification with a larger group with whom the person shares an attribute (or "social identity," with its connection to identity politics) (Hahn and Belt 2004). Both meanings may be relevant for disabled children whose parents pursue interventions that may sometimes intrude on and shape the child's identity in ways that may be problematic. Neurodiversity advocates, for example, argue forcefully that the behavioral variations associated with autism are not defects to be cured but are instead integral to the autistic person's identity (Barry 2012).

Talking about disability as a positive aspect of a child's identity treads on contested terrain. People with disabilities have not historically shared a group identity across the range of diverse physical, mental, and cognitive impairments that produce disabilities. The concept of "disability pride" is relatively recent (Darling 2013). Indeed, as the disability rights movement gained steam in the late twentieth century, many advocates worked to persuade mainstream society to use "people first" language. Referring to someone first as a person, who also happens to have a disability ("a person with quadriplegia," rather than "a quadriplegic"), conveys that the person's disability is *not* identity-defining and stresses the common humanity that people with disabilities share with non-disabled people.

Nonetheless, people with disabilities have increasingly viewed disability as an important part of a shared social identity (Darling 2013; Hahn and Belt 2004), with some rejecting "people with disabilities" as a descriptor and instead favoring "disabled people" as a signal of collectivity and disability pride. More pertinent to this chapter's focus, a sense of shared identity has developed among people with some specific disabilities. Deaf culture is the most obvious example, but communities have also formed among other groups—people with blindness, dwarfism, spinal cord injuries, and autism, for example. These communities can provide both an antidote to the isolation that historically characterized the experience of being disabled and a richer sense of self and validation to members of the community.

In some instances, parents' efforts to mitigate their child's disabling impairment may threaten to diminish a potentially important aspect of their child's identity. Parents' decision to surgically insert cochlear implants in their deaf child likely prevents the child's becoming fluent in sign language and diminishes the child's opportunity to participate in Deaf culture. This decision affects both the child's opportunity to identify with a rich cultural tradition and persons with shared experiences, as well as the child's own sense of who she is and where she fits in the world (Engelman 2017). Although the communities and cultures surrounding other disabilities are less well developed, they may still offer a valuable sense of connectedness and identity.

One response is that a child's loss of potential connection to a disability community is outweighed by the benefits the child may enjoy if a normalizing intervention is pursued. Benefits could include parents' ability to relate better to their child or relief from some of the disadvantages associated with disability in a world where social and physical structures still assume ability, rather than disability (Wasserman 2017). In many cases, however, attempts to mitigate an impairment or to normalize a child's appearance or functioning do not completely "cure" the impairment. The risk is that they may damage the positive aspects of the child's disability identity (availability of a community and self-validation) without entirely eliminating the challenges associated with the impairment (Darling 2013). That tradeoff might be worth making, but, given its importance to the child's development, its gravity should be acknowledged. Moreover, the desirability of a "cure" for one's disability should not be assumed. Some persons with disabilities would *not* choose a cure for their own disabling impairment if one were available, and one study suggests that persons having a stronger positive sense of disability identity are less likely to desire a cure (Hahn and Belt 2004). To be sure, a decision *not* to pursue a normalizing intervention also affects how a child's identity develops, a point David Benatar suggests in the analogous context of decisions regarding separation of conjoined twins (Benatar 2006). The identity of any young child is to some degree malleable. My point is not that parents should refrain from making decisions that will shape their child's identity; that would be impossible. My point is simply that serious psychological integrity interests are at stake when parents choose elective medical interventions designed to normalize their child or mitigate her impairment (Miller 2006).

"Horizontal Identity": Discerning and Advancing Best Interests

Recognizing disability's potential role in constituting a child's identity also undermines one justification for strong deference to parental autonomy; namely, the assumption that parents are the persons both best positioned to understand their child's interests and most motivated to pursue those interests. A child's disability may sometimes throw that assumption into question.

In his 2012 book *Far From the Tree*, Andrew Solomon explores the concept of "horizontal identities." In contrast to most children whose identities are shaped largely by traits transmitted vertically from their parents (such as ethnicity or language), some children have traits that are foreign to their parents. Based on interviews with more than 300 families, Solomon explores how this concept plays out in families with children with deafness, autism, dwarfism, schizophrenia, and severe disability, as well as transgender children and prodigies. Solomon uses the phrase "horizontal identities" to describe how children with traits alien to their parents look to a peer group outside their family to develop their identity and find their way in the world.

To be clear, Solomon does not conclude that parents of children with horizontal identities love their children less than do other parents. But his work does suggest that dealing with a disabled child's "otherness" challenges parents' ability to understand and empathize with the child's interests; parents of children with horizontal conditions "must be constantly misapprehending their own children" (p. 4). Solomon heard this difficulty expressed with respect to parenting children with deafness, dwarfism, and autism, for example.

In addition, building non-family relationships with persons who share his disability may benefit a disabled child by helping him develop a positive sense of self and the adaptive skills needed to navigate society with a disability. A deaf child may develop nurturing, family-like relationships within the Deaf community. A child with dwarfism may find role models and easy social interaction at Little People of America gatherings. Parents who pursue medical means to "fix" a child's disability or to normalize the child's appearance or functioning, however, may be unlikely to foster those relationships and may undermine the child's ability to develop a positive self-concept. Making a related point about the decision-making process for "appearance-normalizing surgeries," Paul Steven Miller (2006) argued: "Even though the law presumes that a parent will act in the best interest of a child, this presumption may not always be true in the case of child, born to able-bodied parents, who is disabled and different from the norm" (p. 218). Miller concluded that traditional processes for obtaining parental consent do not sufficiently protect the interests of a child for whom appearance-normalizing surgery is being considered, at least not when the parent has not experienced the condition to be normalized.

An evolutionary biology perspective similarly questions parents' identification with children with disabilities. According to Margaret Brinig, evolutionary biology theories support the presumption of parental authority in most cases: The parents' "selfish gene" seeks to protect their offspring in order to ensure its own replication when those offspring reproduce. A disabled child, however, may appear less likely to succeed in passing along its parents' genes; therefore, parents may invest less in disabled children and treat them as scapegoats. Brinig supports this hypothesis by pointing to studies finding that children with disabilities are more likely to be abused or neglected than non-disabled children (Brinig 2012). Similarly, Solomon points out that at least half the children available for adoption in the United States have a disability (p. 19). This perspective reinforces the reluctance of disability advocates to presume that parents identify with a child who has a disability that is foreign to the parents' experience.

Elevated Conflicts of Interest

Another way the "horizontal identity" of a child with a disability could undermine the presumption of parental authority is when the child's disability (and its anticipated, perceived, or actual consequences) creates a conflict of interest between the disabled child and her parents with respect to a particular medical choice. If the alignment of the parent's interests with the child's justifies parental authority, evidence of a conflict of interest disrupts that justification. Even scholars generally supporting a strong version of parental rights acknowledge the need for closer monitoring of decisions when the parents' and the child's interests appear to diverge (Scott and Scott 1995).

Scholars considering parents' medical decisions for children also address potential conflicts of interest regarding a child's medical care (Ouellette 2010; Rosato 2000). Parents may have a financial interest in forgoing beneficial but expensive treatment if the family is uninsured or poorly insured (Wadlington 1994). Siblings' interests may also introduce conflicts. Cases where parents seek to use one child as an organ donor (exposing that child to risk without any medical benefit) for a sibling who requires a transplant to survive offer a stark example. Because of the conflict of interests, courts have concluded that parental consent is not sufficient to permit organ retrieval from the donor child.

With multiple interests arising in any family setting, the mere presence of some conflicting interests between children and their parents does not necessarily invalidate parental authority. Indeed, a desire to ease the burdens of parenting may be a legitimate concern of parents (Wasserman 2017). Jennifer Rosato (2000) proposes a framework for evaluating when conflicts of interest justify limiting parental authority to make medical decisions. Some of the recurring scenarios where Rosato would find that conflicts of interest abrogate parental authority include several that map onto particularly problematic medical decisions for children with disabilities. For example, situations involving extraordinary medical treatment (such as sterilization) or implicating a child's countervailing constitutional interests (such as commitment to an institution) would categorically require judicial oversight. Situational conflicts, by contrast, exist when the facts of a particular case show an impairment of parents' ability to decide in their child's best interests. Rosato recognizes as an example of situational conflict instances when parents' "bias against handicapped persons" impairs their judgment. Similarly, parents' interest in mitigating their own physical, financial, and emotional challenges in parenting a child with a severe disability could at times produce such conflicts, leading parents to pursue medical interventions that advance their interests without benefiting the child.

In discussing horizontal identities and a heightened potential for conflicts of interests, I am not saying that parents of children with disabilities typically feel disconnected from their children or disregard their interests. Historically, parents of disabled children (as a group) have been effective advocates for their children's interests with regard to funding for research and services, and many are deeply devoted to their children. The foregoing discussion does, however, suggest that the presumptions that parents are best situated to understand their children's interests and are best motivated to act in pursuit of those interests may be less robust in cases involving disabled children. Moreover, the possibility that cultural and medical biases regarding disability may influence parents' decisions magnifies that concern.

Influence of Cultural Biases

Any horizontal identity may challenge parents' ability to relate to their child and understand his best interests. Indeed, Solomon examines how prodigies and their parents face relationship challenges. When a child's horizontal identity is also the subject of long-standing and pervasive cultural biases, the wisdom of unquestioning deference to parents' choices is further weakened. Although public attitudes toward people with disabilities have grown somewhat more accepting and inclusive, biases against and misunderstandings of disability remain widespread. When children with disabilities have non-disabled parents, it is not farfetched to think that parents may share, perhaps unconsciously, cultural biases against their child's disability.

Compounding parents' potential biases, disability bias remains entrenched within the medical profession. The physicians whose advice often influences parents' choices for their disabled children may themselves devalue life with a disability. Several studies show that physicians' views of disability's negative impact on quality of life diverge from many disabled peoples' reporting a quality of life rivaling that of non-disabled people. These biased assessments may color the advice physicians provide when parents of disabled children are considering whether to pursue elective interventions (Asch 1998; Kittay 2011). Solomon's interviews reinforce this concern with ample anecdotal evidence.

Moreover, the dark history of involuntary institutionalization of and forced medical procedures on children with disabilities—often with physician and parental complicity—provides further reason to be cautious regarding unfettered parental choice. Willowbrook State School, the site of inhumane treatment of and experimentation on children with intellectual disabilities, now symbolizes broader patterns of physician mistreatment of disabled people. Baby Doe, the infant with Down syndrome permitted to die for lack of parental consent to routine surgery, was not an isolated case.

Surveys showed significant physician support for so-called selective nontreatment for disabled newborns, a practice one medical journal described as the "highest form of medical ethic."

Teasing out the respective roles of physicians' influence and parents' choices is difficult, both historically and today. But the two can combine to produce medical choices that fail to appreciate—if not outright ignore—disabled children's vital interests in physical integrity, freedom from pain, and personal and social identity. Moreover, the influence of culturally contingent bias on such choices seems clear when, for example, we consider the shift over recent decades in attitudes among both physicians and parents regarding the ethical (im)permissibility of permitting infants born with Down syndrome to perish for lack of treatment. These parental choices regarding medical nonintervention, once widely accepted (Goldstein 1977), are today discredited (Mercurio 2009; Ouellette 2011). Which choices that today are considered within the realm of parental autonomy might future generations condemn as reflecting a fundamental disrespect for people with disabilities?

(Un)acceptable Parental Discrimination?

The previous sections describe the constellation of factors that, together, give me serious pause about broadly deferring to parental autonomy when it comes to elective medical interventions to "cure" a disabling impairment, normalize a child's appearance, or make life easier for a parent. Significant interests of the child may be at stake. At the same time, implications of the child's horizontal identity and disability bias in society undermine the assumption that parents can be relied upon to identify with and advance their child's interests. Another way to understand some parents' choices, particularly those involving normalizing interventions, could be to view them as akin to discrimination. Might we understand parents who pursue normalizing interventions as attempting to change their disabled child into a non-disabled (or at least less disabled) child? Are those parents rejecting their child's disability in a way that may be objectionable?

At least as a legal matter, society generally tolerates discrimination in the private realm that would be prohibited in the public realm. For example, I can choose to date or marry only persons of my same race or religion if I wish (Emens 2009). It would be illegal for me, however, to choose not to hire someone based on the person's religion or to refuse to serve someone in my restaurant because of the person's race. Like the more particular concept of deference to parental autonomy, this broad public–private distinction reflects a rejection of state authority into private life based on the principle of respect for privacy and pluralism, as well as pragmatic concerns about enforceability.

But family privacy is a double-edged sword. It protects both the privacy that shelters the flourishing of intimate relationships and the privacy that shrouds abuses of power against vulnerable parties. Parental choices to commit physically or sexually abusive acts against their children are beyond the pale of what deference to parental authority requires. Might some parental decisions to pursue elective medical interventions for disabled children also exceed the bounds of justifiable deference?

A thought exercise involving cross-racial parenting suggests how the concerns about parental decisions regarding their disabled children are not exceptional but may also arise in other contexts. As when a child with a disability has a non-disabled parent, a black child who has a white parent may have, in Solomon's terms, a horizontal identity. To what extent would we deem it permissible—as an exercise of family privacy or parental autonomy—for a white parent to make choices to construct the race of their black child? In other words, might there be limits on what a parent can do to try to make her child white, rather than black?[1]

Prenatal decisions that construct the race of offspring include both decisions about whom to mate with or, if assisted reproduction is used, whose sperm to use. While not beyond debate (Fox 2017), these decisions are left to the would-be parent without state oversight. Similarly, although federal legislation prohibits federally funded adoption agencies from using race as a factor in denying or delaying a child's adoption, adoptive parents remain free to choose to adopt a child of their own race or a different race. Family privacy is generally believed to protect the choice of a white adoptive mother to adopt a white child rather than a black child.

When parents start trying to shape or construct their existing child's identity, however, the discussion becomes more fraught. Imagine a white parent who has a black child. What if that parent were to try to make the child white (or at least less black)? How would we respond? My sense is that the nature of the steps taken to promote whiteness (as well as other factors) would influence our reactions.

For example, one might view numerous parenting choices about a child's education, religious upbringing, and extracurricular activities as shaping the child's identity to be more white and less black. Providing examples admittedly risks reinforcing stereotypes, but it is not hard to imagine how a white parent—whether consciously or not—could steer the child's development toward a white identity via choices regarding the social, religious, academic, athletic, and artistic influences to which the black child is exposed. Such choices fall squarely within the traditional scope of parental autonomy. Some may find disturbing a parent's conscious efforts to shape her child's development to produce a white racial identity. But whether or not you judge such attempts to make a black child seem more like his white parent to be admirable or in the child's best interest, they are not plausible grounds for eliminating or legally constraining the parent's choices about these matters.

But what if the white parent went further? What if the parent sought to use surgical or medical procedures to make her black child appear more white? She might subject her child to skin lightening treatments. She might even have her child undergo cosmetic surgery to change facial features commonly viewed as racial markers.

At this point, more readers may be feeling uncomfortable about the white parent's choice to use medical interventions to try to change her child's race. But why?

The hypothetical medical interventions instantiate several factors setting them apart from other choices made by parents. They do something to a child that is physically invasive and risky, that is difficult or impossible to undo, that goes to a core aspect of the child's identity, that involve a child who has a horizontal identity with respect to the trait to be "fixed," and that responds to the parent's interest rather than the child's need.

This thought experiment about cross-racial parenting suggests parallels to the parental choices that are the subject of this chapter. The very factors that may make the white parent's pursuit of medical or surgical interventions troubling are the same factors developed earlier as bases for questioning broad deference to parental choices regarding elective, nontherapeutic medical interventions for disabled children. The presence of several of these factors justifies skepticism about deference to parental decisions to pursue such interventions. That skepticism does not necessarily warrant eliminating parental authority. Parental motivations and family circumstances in a particular case might well change our intuitions about the acceptability of an intervention.[2] However, the skepticism does justify constraining parental decisions in some instances and in some fashion. How, though, might we check parental autonomy in problematic cases without overly intruding on the parent–child relationship? The remainder of this chapter briefly considers that question.

Constraining Parental Autonomy

So far, this chapter has considered how concerns about non-disabled parents' decisions to pursue normalizing or otherwise elective medical interventions for their disabled child throw into question the legitimacy of broad deference to these decisions. Not all such decisions implicate all these concerns, but the combined presence of several of them erodes the conceptual foundations for unquestioning deference to parental autonomy. Finding that erosion in a particular case, though, does not mean that those parents are unfit or should lose their authority to make most decisions about their child's upbringing. The question is whether a way exists to somehow constrain the exercise of parental authority without overly intruding on that authority or the parent–child relationship? While fully considering that is a question for another day, I will offer a few preliminary thoughts about possible mechanisms.

Legal Constraints on Parental Decisions

One possible response would be to use legal means to limit some parental decisions. Legislatures or courts could conceivably erect legal limits that might either prohibit certain interventions or require some kind of third-party oversight. The Child Abuse Amendments (the federal legislation responding to the Baby Doe case) require state child welfare systems to define medical neglect as including parents' failure to provide life-saving medical treatment for infants with disabilities. The legislation effectively makes such treatment mandatory, categorically depriving parents of the legal authority to choose otherwise. Required judicial approval of parents' sterilization choices provides a contrasting example. Most states view parents' decision to sterilize as suspect—requiring judicial oversight—but not categorically contrary to the interests of a particular child with a disability.

Laws that apply directly to physicians or other providers could also limit parents' ability to choose specific interventions. For example, some states have enacted legislation prohibiting therapists from providing sexual orientation change therapy (aka conversion therapy) to minors. While not operating directly on parental authority, these laws reflect concerns about potential long-lasting harm to children's bodies and identities resulting from parents' choices. The federal ban on female genital mutilation takes a similar form, criminally prohibiting anyone from performing such a procedure.

Guiding Parental Decisions

An alternative approach would be to develop nonlegal mechanisms to guide parental decisions in this area. For example, a set of best practices or practice guidelines for providers might be developed for more frequently encountered interventions. Although not legally binding, practice guidelines could help shape the choices physicians offer parents and how they describe the benefits and risks of those choices.

The practice guidelines I envision would be informed not only by research and clinical findings, but also by input from persons living with the disability in question and persons who had been subjected to the particular intervention. These persons could offer both an informed perspective on the quality of life experienced by persons with the particular disability, as well as a personal assessment of the harms and benefits associated with the intervention. Practice guidelines of this sort could counteract prevailing biases in medical advice to parents.

Another possibility might be to find ways to more directly guide parents' decision-making. A guidance mechanism could seek to preserve and support parents' decisional authority, essentially by shoring up the justifications for deference. Thus, a guidance mechanism might seek to enhance parents' ability to value their child's identity as a disabled person and relate to the child's interests associated with that identity. For example, the National Association of the Deaf (NAD) in 2000 affirmed parents' authority to decide whether to seek cochlear implants for a deaf child, but emphasized the critical importance of fully educating parents on all the implications of the choice. As part of that education, NAD recommends that parents have an "opportunity to interact with successful deaf and hard of hearing adults, as well as with parents of disabled and hard of hearing children" (National Association of the Deaf 2000).

Paul Steven Miller also discussed the value of exposing parents to the perspectives of adults affected with the condition their child has. Unlike the child's non-disabled parents, those adults have a first-hand understanding of both the functional and psychosocial impacts of the disability at issue and a richer appreciation of how they weigh against the risks and burdens of the proposed intervention (Miller 2006). The point here is *not* that these adults would displace parents as decision-makers for a child with a disability, but instead to suggest the value of the guidance and insights they can provide, given the fragility of the presumption that parents naturally are best situated to identify with their disabled children's best interests. Solomon (2012) as well emphasizes the importance of sharing the "learned happiness" of parents who have learned to value their child's identity, even when they do not share it (p. 6).

Finally, a guidance mechanism might also provide parents with information about parenting a child with the relevant disability and the assistive technologies and resources available (National Disability Rights Network 2012). Legislation in the United States already calls for such guidance in the context of decisions by prospective parents. The federal Prenatally and Postnatally Diagnosed Conditions Awareness Act calls for government funding of projects to increase the information on a full range of outcomes and supports provided to prospective parents who receive test results diagnosing Down syndrome or other conditions. Laws in several states go further, requiring a professional conveying positive test results for Down syndrome to actually provide parents with both up-to-date information and contact information for support groups. Providing information to parents about the supportive resources available to people with disabilities and their families might diminish the conflict between the parents' interests in avoiding the anticipated burdens of raising and caring for a disabled child[3] and the child's interest in maintaining her identity and avoiding the pain and risks of physically invasive interventions.

CONCLUSION

Over the decades, many parents of children with disabilities have been among the fiercest advocates for the rights and interests of their children and have displayed deep and unreserved love for their offspring. At the same time, as this chapter explains, reasons exist why parents who contemplate nontherapeutic elective or normalizing interventions for their disabled children should not *always* be entitled to the normal, strong presumption of parental autonomy to make medical decisions. My point is not at all to suggest that these are somehow "bad" parents or that all the decisions they make in raising their disabled child are suspect. Acknowledging the concerns identified, however, should give us pause about uncritically presuming that parents of disabled children will always be the persons exclusively best positioned to appreciate their children's best interests. As a result, we should consider what "reasonable modifications" of the usual broad deference to parental autonomy may be justified—and, indeed, necessary—in order to protect the interests and identities of children with disabilities.

Notes

1. Some may find this example provocative and object to my failure here to plumb more fully the constructed nature of race in American society. My limited sketching of an analysis is not intended to suggest that these questions are straightforward. Considering in depth the interaction of race and parental autonomy is a different project, which other scholars have undertaken. My purpose is only to use examples involving race to provoke a fresh view of how we might think about the wisdom of potentially constraining parental autonomy regarding children with disabilities.

2. For example, some might find the pursuit of skin lightening treatments less problematic if a white parent is raising her black child in a community where oppression of dark-skinned persons is particularly severe and seeks for her child the benefits of a lighter complexion (Imadojemu and Fiester 2013).

3. Addressing the context of prenatal selection, Wasserman (2017) makes a related point about parenting disabled children, noting that "prospective parents are likely to underestimate their own adaptability, resourcefulness, and resilience" (p. 230).

References

Altman, Scott. 2015. "Parental Control Rights." USC Legal Studies Research Papers Series No. 15-24. https://ssrn.com/abstract=2636313

Asch, Adrienne. 1998. "Distracted by Disability: The 'Difference' of Disability in the Medical Setting." *Cambridge Quarterly of Healthcare Ethics* 7: 77–87.

Barry, Kevin. 2012. "Gray Matters: Autism, Impairment, and the End of Binaries." *San Diego Law Review* 49: 161–219.

Benatar, David. 2006. "Introduction: The Ethics of Contested Surgeries." In *Cutting to the Core: Exploring the Ethics of Contested Surgeries*, 11–29. Lanham, MD: Rowman & Littlefield.

Beyers, Wim, and Luc Goossens. 2008. "Dynamics of Perceived Parenting and Identity Formation in Late Adolescence." *Journal of Adolescence* 31: 165–184.

Brinig, Margaret F. 2012. "Abuse, Adoption & Attention Deficit Disorder." Notre Dame Legal Studies Paper No. 12-71. https://ssrn.com/abstract=2128575.

Cantor, Norman I. 2004. "The Relationship Between Autonomy-Based Rights and Profoundly Mentally Disabled Persons." *Annals of Health Law* 13: 37–80.

Chiu, Elaine M. 2008. "The Culture Differential in Parental Autonomy." *University of California Davis Law Review* 41: 1773–1828.

Conway, Craig A. 2009. "Baby Doe and Beyond: Examining the Practical and Philosophical Influences Impacting Medical Decision-Making on Behalf of Marginally-Viable Newborns." *Georgia State University Law Review* 25: 1097–1175.

Darling, Rosalyn Benjamin. 2013. *Disability and Identity: Negotiating Self in a Changing Society*. Boulder, CO: Lynne Rienner.

Emens, Elizabeth. 2009. "Intimate Discrimination: The State's Role in the Accidents of Sex and Love." *Harvard Law Review* 122: 1308–1402.

Engelman, Elizabeth. 2017. "My Deaf Son Fought Speech. Sign Language Let Him Bloom." *New York Times*. May 26.

Fox, Dov. 2017. "Reproducing Race." San Diego Legal Studies Paper No. 17-264. https://ssrn.com/abstract=2922826

Field, Genevieve. 2016. "Should Parents of Children with Severe Disabilities be Allowed to Stop Their Growth?" *New York Times*. March 22.

Goldstein, Joseph. 1977. "Medical Care for the Child at Risk: On State Supervention of Parental Autonomy." *Yale Law Journal* 86: 645–670.

Greenberg, Julie. 2012. "Health Care Issues Affecting People with an Intersex Condition or DSD: Sex or Disability Discrimination." *Loyola Los Angeles Law Review* 45: 849–907.

Hahn, Harlan D., and Todd L. Belt. 2004. "Disability Identity and Attitudes Toward Cure in a Sample of Disabled Activists." *Journal of Health and Social Behavior* 45: 453–464.

Hill, B. Jessie. 2015. "Constituting Children's Bodily Integrity." *Duke Law Journal* 64: 1295–1362.

Imadojemu, Sotonye, and Autumn Fiester. 2013. "Skin Bleaching as a Dermatologic Intervention: Complicity or Service?" *JAMA Dermatology* 149(8): 901–902.

Koll, Mary. 2010. "Growth, Interrupted: Nontherapeutic Growth Attenuation, Parental Medical Decision Making, and the Profoundly Developmentally Disabled Child's Right to Bodily Integrity." *University of Illinois Law Review* 2010: 225–263.

Kittay, Eva F. 2011. "Forever Small: The Strange Case of Ashley X." *Hypatia* 26 (3): 610–631.

Mercurio, Mark R. 2009. "The Aftermath of Baby Doe and the Evolution of Newborn Intensive Care." *Georgia State University Law Review* 25: 835–863.

Miller, Paul Steven. 2006. "Toward Truly Informed Decisions About Appearance Normalizing Surgeries." In *Surgically Shaping Children: Technology, Ethics, and the Pursuit of Normality*, edited by Erik Parens, 211–226. Baltimore: Johns Hopkins University Press.

National Association of the Deaf. 2000. *Position Statement on Cochlear Implants*. https://www. nad.org/about-us/position-statements/position-statement-on-cochlear-implants/.

National Disability Rights Network. 2012. *Devaluing People with Disabilities: Medical Procedures the Violate Civil Rights*. http://www.ndrn.org/images/Documents/Resources/ Publications/Reports/Devaluing_People_with_Disabilities.pdf

Ouellette, Alicia. 2010. "Shaping Parental Authority Over Children's Bodies." *Indiana Law Journal* 85(3): 955–1002.

Ouellette, Alicia. 2011. *Bioethics & Disability: Toward a Disability-Conscious Bioethics*.

Parens, Erik. 2006. "Thinking About Surgically Shaping Children." In *Surgically Shaping Children: Technology, Ethics, and the Pursuit of Normality*, edited by Erik Parens, xiii–xxx. Baltimore: Johns Hopkins University Press.

Ronen, Ya'ir. 2004. "Redefining the Child's Right to Identity." *International Journal of Law Policy & Family* 18: 147–177.

Rosato, Jennifer. 2000. "Using Bioethics Discourse to Determine when Parents Should Make Health Care Decisions for their Children: Is Deference Justified?" *Temple Law Review* 73: 1–68.

Rosenbury, Laura A. 2015. "A Feminist Perspective on Children and Law: From Objectification to Relational Subjectivities." In *International Perspectives and Empirical Findings on Child Participation: From Social Exclusion to Child-Inclusive Policies*, edited by Tali Gal and Benedetta Duramy, 17–33. Oxford: Oxford University Press.

Schneider, Carl. 1995. "On the Duties and Rights of Parents." *Virginia Law Review* 81: 2477–2491.

Scott, Elizabeth S., and Robert E. Scott. 1995. "Parents as Fiduciaries." *Virginia Law Review* 81: 2401–2476.

Solomon, Andrew. 2012. *Far from the Tree: Parents, Children, and the Search for Identity*. New York: Scribner.

Tamar-Mattis, Anne. 2006. "Exceptions to the Rule: Curing the Law's Failure to Protect Intersex Infants." *Berkeley Journal of Gender Law & Justice* 21: 59–110.

Viens, A. M., ed. 2014. *The Right to Bodily Integrity*. Farnham, UK: Ashgate.

Wadlington, Walter. 1994. "David C. Baum Memorial Lecture: Medical Decision Making for and by Children: Tensions between Parent, State, and Child." *University of Illinois Law Review* 1994: 311–336.

Wasserman, David. 2017. "Better Parenting Through Biomedical Modification: A Case for Pluralism, Deference, and Charity." *Kennedy Institute of Ethics Journal* 27(2): 217–247.

Wilfond, Benjamin S., et al. 2010. "Navigating Growth Attenuation in Children with Profound Disabilities: Children's Interests, Family Decision-Making, and Community Concerns." *Hastings Center Report* 40(6): 27–40.

Woodhouse, Barbara Bennett. 1992. "'Who Owns the Child?': Meyer and Pierce and the Child as Property." *William & Mary Law Review* 33: 995–1122.